W9-BMF-414

ASIMOV'S
CHRONOLOGY
OF THE
WORLD

Over 15,000,000,000 Years of History at a Glance

450,000,000 TO 370,000,000 YEARS AGO
The beginning of amphibia

370,000,000 TO 300,000,000 YEARS AGO
The land-based egg • the beginning of the reptiles

300,000,000 TO 220,000,000 YEARS AGO
The beginning of the mammals

220,000,000 TO 100,000,000 YEARS AGO
The beginning of the placental mammals

100,000,000 TO 70,000,000 YEARS AGO
The beginning of the primates

70,000,000 TO 65,000,000 YEARS AGO
The end of the dinosaurs

65,000,000 TO 40,000,000 YEARS AGO
The beginning of monkeys

40,000,000 TO 30,000,000 YEARS AGO
The beginning of apes

30,000,000 TO 17,000,000 YEARS AGO
The beginning of anthropoid apes

17,000,000 TO 5,000,000 YEARS AGO
The beginning of hominids

5,000,000 TO 4,000,000 YEARS AGO
The australopithecines • bipedality

4,000,000 TO 2,000,000 YEARS AGO
Genus *Homo* • stone tools

2,000,000 TO 1,600,000 YEARS AGO
Homo erectus

1,600,000 TO 1,000,000 YEARS AGO
The end of the australopithecines

1,000,000 TO 500,000 YEARS AGO
The use of fire • cooking

500,000 TO 300,000 YEARS AGO
Neanderthals

300,000 TO 200,000 YEARS AGO
Ice Age • burial

200,000 TO 50,000 YEARS AGO
The beginning of "modern humans"

50,000 TO 30,000 YEARS AGO
The end of the Neanderthals

30,000 TO 25,000 YEARS AGO
Modern humans reach Australia and the Americas

25,000 TO 20,000 YEARS AGO
Art • lamps

20,000 TO 14,000 YEARS AGO
The domestication of the dog

14,000 TO 12,000 YEARS AGO (12,000 TO 10,000 B.C.)
Herding

10,000 TO 8000 B.C.
End of the Ice Age • the beginning of agriculture • the beginning of warfare • cities and civilization

8000 TO 7000 B.C.
Rivers and irrigation • city-states

7000 TO 6000 B.C.
Baskets • pottery • textiles

6000 TO 5000 B.C.
Rise of Sumeria • priest-kings and religion • ships

5000 TO 4000 B.C.
Fermentation and alcoholic beverages • metallurgy

4000 TO 3500 B.C.
Bronze age • the wheel • oars • plows • rise of Egypt

3500 TO 3000 B.C.
Writing and history • nations • dyes

3000 TO 2500 B.C.
The calendar • the pyramids • the Sumerian flood • the epic of Gilgamesh • Crete

2500 TO 2000 B.C.
Sargon and the first Empire • feudalism • navies • Indus civilization • Indo-Europeans

2000 TO 1500 B.C.
The charioteers • Hammurabi of Babylon and law-codes • the rise of Assyria • volcanic explosion of Thera • end of the Indus civilization • China in the Bronze Age

1500 TO 1200 B.C.
Egyptian Empire at its peak • monotheism • Iron Age • Trojan War • Israelites enter Canaan

1200 TO 1000 B.C.
Peoples from the sea • the alphabet • the coming of the Dorians • feudalism in China

1000 TO 900 B.C.
David and Solomon • the beginning of Biblical writing • Phoenicians penetrate into the Atlantic Ocean • Caste system in India • Olmecs in Mexico

900 TO 800 B.C.
First Assyrian Empire • Yahwism in Israel • Homer's *Iliad* and *Odyssey* • Carthage founded • "Zero" invented in India • Israel splits into Israel and Judah

800 TO 700 B.C.
Second Assyrian Empire • end of Israel and survival of Judah • Olympic Games established in Greece • Greece colonizes the Mediterranean shores • rise of the Etruscans • Rome founded

700 TO 600 B.C.

Assyria reaches its height, and falls • rise of Chaldea and Media • Phoenicians circumnavigate Africa • Yahwism in the ascendant in Judah • rise of Lydia • militarization of Sparta • rise of tyrants in Greece • rise of Carthaginian Empire • first Emperor in Japan

600 TO 550 B.C.

Nebuchadnezzar and the Chaldean Empire • Jews in Babylonian captivity • coins used in Lydia • Cyrus and the rise of Persia • Thales and the rise of science in Ionia • the growth of democracy in Athens • the Etruscans at their peak

550 TO 500 B.C.

The Persian Empire at its peak • Zarathustra and Zoroastrianism • Jews return to Judah and the founding of Judaism • mystery religions in Greece • continued growth of Athenian democracy • Rome expels its king, and Roman Republic is founded • Jainism and Buddhism in India • Confucianism and Taoism in China • Pythagoreanism in Greece • rise of Nubia in Africa

500 TO 450 B.C.

Graeco–Persian war • Battles of Thermopylae, Marathon, Salamis, and Plataea • Syracuse versus Carthage in Sicily • decline of Persians and Etruscans

450 TO 400 B.C.

Pericles and Athens' Golden Age • Aeschylus, Sophocles, Euripides, Herodotus, Socrates • Peloponnesian War and Alcibiades • Xenophon and the Ten Thousand • fortification of Jerusalem • Rome at the head of the Latin League

400 TO 350 B.C.

Sparta at its peak • Agesilaus in Asia Minor • Epaminondas and the rise of Thebes • the fall of Sparta • Syracuse at its peak • Rome sacked by the Gauls

350 TO 300 B.C.

Philip II and the rise of Macedonia • Alexander the Great and the fall of Persia • Battles of Issus and Gaugamela • Plato and Aristotle in Athens • Rome develops the legion • Mayans appear in North America

300 TO 250 B.C.

Ptolemaic Egypt and the Museum and Library at Alexandria • Euclid • Hellenistic kingdoms • translation of the Bible into Greek • Achaean and Aetolian League in Greece • Archimedes in Syracuse • Rome defeats Pyrrhus and wars with Carthage • Maurya dynasty in India

250 TO 200 B.C.

Ptolemaic Egypt at its height • Eratosthenes and Apollonius • Antiochus III and Seleucid Empire at its height • Sparta tries to reform and fails • Hannibal and the Second Punic War with its Battles of Cannae and Zama • fall of Carthage and of Syracuse • China under the Chin dynasty

200 TO 150 B.C.

Rome defeats the Hellenistic kingdoms and is supreme in the Mediterranean region • decline of Macedonia and the Seleucid Empire • Judea under the Maccabees revolts against the Seleucid Empire • rise of Parthia • Hipparchus and Greek astronomy

150 TO 100 B.C.

End of Carthage • slave uprisings in Rome • the Gracchi try to reform Rome and fail • Marius destroys invasion of Cimbri and Teutones • Maccabean kingdom established in Judea • China under the Han dynasty

100 TO 50 B.C.

Pompey leads Roman armies to take over eastern region of the Mediterranean • end of the Seleucid Empire and the Maccabean kingdom • civil war in Rome • rise of Julius Caesar, who conquers Gaul • Parthia defeats Roman army in Mesopotamia

50 TO 1 B.C.

Caesar establishes dictatorship and is assassinated • Mark Antony and Octavian divide Empire • Mark Antony and Cleopatra • Octavian wins the final civil war and establishes the Roman Empire in place of the Republic • Herod rules over Judea and Jesus of Nazareth is born

1 TO 50

Germans defeat Romans in Teutoberg Forest • Jesus of Nazareth crucified amid messianic hopes of the Jews • St. Paul and the founding of Christianity • Rome conquers southern Britain • China is the world's most advanced nation

50 TO 100

Jews rebel against Rome and the Second Temple is destroyed • Britain rebels against Rome and is reconquered • kingdom of Aksum flourishes in east Africa

100 TO 150

Trajan conquers Dacia and Mesopotamia and the Roman Empire is at its peak • a second Jewish rebellion against Rome fails • paper invented in China

150 TO 200

Marcus Aurelius and the beginning of Roman decline • stirrup invented in India

200 TO 250

Rise of Christianity, of Mithraism, and of Manichaeism • Rome falls into anarchy • end of Parthia and the rise of Sassanid Persia

250 TO 300

Rise of the Goths • recovery in Rome under Claudius II and Aurelian • Diocletian reorganizes the Empire and there is a last persecution of Christians

300 TO 350

Constantine I and the Christianization of the Roman Empire • Council of Nicea and the rise of Arianism • the founding of Constantinople • Brahmanism regains ascendancy in India • the Huns begin to move westward

350 TO 400

Huns conquer the Ostrogoths and establish an empire in Europe • Visigoths defeat Romans at the Battle of Adrianople and the supremacy of the Roman legion comes to an end • Theodosius and the final split of the Empire into a western and eastern portion • Korean independence

400 TO 450

Visigoths sack Rome • establishment of German kingdoms in Gaul, Spain and north Africa • Britain returns to paganism • Attila brings the Hunnish Empire to its peak • rise of the Papacy • the walls of Constantinople are built • the Polynesians complete their spread over the Pacific Islands

450 TO 500

Aetius defeats Huns at the Battle of Chalons • end of the Hunnish Empire • "fall" of the West Roman Empire • Theodoric establishes the Ostrogothic kingdom in Italy • Clovis establishes the Frankish kingdom in Gaul • Anglo-Saxons invade Britain • Chichen Itza founded by Mayans

500 TO 550

Ostrogothic kingdom at its peak • Justinian I rules in Constantinople, puts an end to Plato's Academy, builds the cathedral of Hagia Sophia, codifies Roman law • his general Belisarius reconquers North Africa, Italy, and the Spanish coast • the rise of the Slavs, Bulgars, and Avars • Chosroes I and Sassanid Persia at its peak

550 TO 600

Lombards invade Italy • Pope Gregory I establishes the celibacy of the Catholic clergy • end of Arianism • St. Augustine and the conversion of England to Christianity • Ireland in its golden age • Avars at their peak • rise of the Khazars • birth of Mohammed

600 TO 650

Chosroes II of Persia nearly conquers the East Roman Empire, which recovers under Heraclius • Islam founded and the Arabs sweep out of Arabia to conquer Persia, Syria, and Egypt • end of the Avars • Khazar Empire established • T'ang dynasty established in China • Srivijaya established in Indonesia • Toltecs in Mexico

650 TO 700

Ommayad Caliphate has its capital at Damascus and is at its peak, ruling from India to the Atlantic • its attack on Constantinople fails when the Byzantines use Greek fire • end of Celtic Christianity in England • Venice has its first doge

700 TO 750

Muslims invade Spain and the Frankish kingdom but are stopped by Charles Martel at the Battle of Tours • Muslims fail again to take Constantinople • rise to power of the Carolingian "Mayors" in the Frankish kingdom • Khazars at their peak • T'ang China at its peak • Mayas in North America at their peak

750 TO 800

Pepin becomes king of Franks • foundation of the Papal States • Charlemagne crowned Emperor, and Frankish realm is at its peak • end of the Lombard kingdom • coming of the Vikings • Ommayad Caliphate taken over by Abbasids with a new capital at Baghdad • Harun ar-Rashid and the Abbasid Empire at its peak

800 TO 850

Decline of the Frankish realm • establishment of West and East Frankish kingdoms • Viking raids at their peak • growth of European feudalism • Bulgarians establish kingdom • Magyars begin raiding central Europe • Vikings penetrate Russia • Abbasid Empire and T'ang China begin to decline • first Mayan civilization collapses

850 TO 900

Alfred of England fights off the Danish invasion • Vikings discover and settle Iceland • Kievan Russia founded • Byzantine Empire regains vigor • Bulgarians converted to Christianity after the Byzantine fashion

900 TO 950

East Frankish line comes to an end • Otto I crowned Emperor and establishes "Holy Roman Empire" • he defeats Magyars at the Battle of Lechfeld and ends their threat • Viking raiders establish Norman dukedom • Moorish Spain at peak under Abd er-Rahman III • Papacy hits bottom • Bulgarian kingdom at peak • end of T'ang dynasty in China

950 TO 1000

End of West Frankish kingdom and founding of the Capetian line of French kings • horseshoes, horse collars, and moldboard plow come into use, increasing food supply of northern Europe • Moorish Spain begins to decline • kingdoms of Denmark, Sweden, and Norway established • Vikings discover and settle Greenland • Leif Ericsson lands in Vinland in North America • kingdoms of Hungary, Bohemia, and Poland established • Russia and Serbia converted to Byzantine version of Christianity • Fatimid Egypt at its peak • China under the Sung dynasty • Japan under the Shogunate

1000

Millenarianism

1000 TO 1050

Denmark conquers England and is under Canute • Macbeth in Scotland • Brian Boru drives Vikings out of Ireland • rise of Normandy • rise of Venice • Christian drive to retake Spain from the Moors increases in intensity • Kievan Russia at its peak • Basil II brings Byzantine Empire to a peak, destroying Bulgarian kingdom • rise of Seljuk Turks • *Tale of the Genji* written in Japan • Mayans enter final decline

1050 TO 1100

William of Normandy ("the Conqueror") invades and takes over England • Domesday book • final end of Celtic Christianity • conflict over investiture between Emperor Henry IV and the Popes • beginning of decline of the Holy Roman Empire • Normans take over southern Italy • Seljuk Turks defeat Byzantines at the Battle of Manzikert • Byzantine Empire begins slow decline • rise of the Assassins • the First Crusade takes Jerusalem • supernova in the constellation of Taurus observed in China, but not in Europe

1100 TO 1150

Civil war in England • German "Drang nach Osten" (push against the Slavs to the east) • Abelard and Heloise • Norman Sicily at its peak • city life revives in northern Italy • Gothic cathedrals built • Second Crusade is a fiasco • European scholars translating Arabic versions of Greek books of science • Cumans at the peak of their power • magnetic compass and gunpowder may have come into use in China

1150 TO 1200

Henry II founds the Angevin Empire • Richard the Lion-Heart and the Third Crusade • England begins to penetrate Ireland • end of the Norman kingdom in Italy • Moors in Spain driven farther south in Spain • Serbian kingdom established • Saladin of Egypt reconquers Jerusalem

• Khmer Empire in Cambodia • birth of Genghis Khan • Aztecs gain power in Mexico

1200 TO 1250

Genghis Khan founds the vast Mongol Empire, conquering northern China and Western Asia • under his sons, the Mongols invade Europe, taking over Russia and driving into Germany, but retire when the new Khan dies • end of the Angevin Empire • John of England forced to sign the Magna Carta • Sicily flourishes under Emperor Frederick II • Alexander Nevsky keeps Novgorod out of Mongol grip • Papacy at its peak under Innocent III • Fourth Crusade sacks Constantinople and Venice is at its peak • Albigensian crusade

1250 TO 1300

The Mongol Empire is at its peak under Kublai Khan • Marco Polo of Venice visits the Mongol dominions and writes an influential book that first acquaints medieval Europe with the far more advanced civilizations of the east • the beginning of the English Parliament • England conquers Wales and adopts the longbow • the Sicilian Vespers • Pope Boniface VIII attempts to establish supremacy of the Papacy • Thomas Aquinas • medieval France strong under Philip IV • independence of Switzerland established • Byzantine Empire feebly restored • the final crusades

1300 TO 1350

Scotland preserves its independence at the Battle of Bannockburn • beginning of the Hundred Years War between England and France, with English victories at Sluys, Crecy, and Poitiers • gunpowder comes into use at Crecy • the Black Death strikes Europe • fall of Boniface VIII and establishment of Papacy at Avignon • Dante, the *Divine Comedy*, and the beginning of the Renaissance • the rise of Swiss mercenaries • establishment of

(continued on next page)

Lithuania • rise of the Ottoman Turks
• Mali Empire in Africa is at its height
• Mongol Empire declines rapidly

1350 TO 1400

John Wyclif and the question of Church reform • Chaucer and *The Canterbury Tales* • the Great Schism of the Papacy • Scandinavia united under Margaret • Poland and Lithuania form dynastic union • Dmitri Donskoi of Muscovy defeats the Mongols • Murad I of Ottoman Empire establishes Janissaries and takes over much of the Balkans • Tamerlane establishes new Mongol Empire in Asia • China under the Ming dynasty • Majapahit Empire in Indonesia

1400 TO 1450

Henry V of England renews Hundred Years War, wins Battle of Agincourt, and brings France to the brink of defeat • Joan of Arc and the French recovery • artillery overcomes the longbow • Henry the Navigator of Portugal begins exploration down the coast of Africa • Great Schism healed and Papacy recovers • Florence at its peak under the Medicis • Jan Hus burned at the stake and the Hussite wars convulse Germany • Tamerlane dies and his empire declines • China explores Indian Ocean • Incas establish Empire in South America

1450 TO 1500

The Ottoman Sultan, Mehmed II, takes Constantinople • Portugal completes circumnavigation of Africa and reaches India • Castile and Aragon unite to form Spain, drive the Moors out of Granada, and subsidize Columbus's voyage of discovery of the American continents • Spain and Portugal drive Jews out of the country • Hundred Years War ends • Louis XI of France destroys Charles the Rash of Burgundy • War of the Roses in England • Papal luxury and Savonarola's puritanism • invention of printing and the start of modern times • Ivan III and the unification of Russia • Songhai Empire in Africa

1500 TO 1550

Ottoman Empire at its peak under Suleyman the Magnificent, who conquers Hungary and lays siege to Vienna • Emperor Charles V, ruling over both the Holy Roman Empire and Spain, is the most powerful Christian monarch in Europe • Martin Luther and the Protestant Reformation • France and Empire begin struggle in Italy, decline of the Italian Renaissance • Michelangelo and Raphael • Henry VIII and Anglicanism • Portugal establishes first world overseas Empire • Spanish conquistadors destroy the Aztec civilization of Mexico and the Inca civilization of Peru • Ferdinand Magellan leads expedition that first circumnavigates the Earth • Copernicus and Vesalius produce modern astronomy and anatomy, respectively, and begin the "Scientific Revolution" • Safavid Persia founded • Mogul Empire founded in India • Ming China declines

1550 TO 1600

Spain under Philip II at its peak • England destroys Philip's "Invincible Armada", however, and Spain enters decline • Netherlands revolts against Spain • Elizabeth of England rules over Golden Age of literature, including Shakespeare's plays • Mary, Queen of Scots, executed • Huguenots in France and the St. Bartholomew's Day Massacre • Henry IV becomes king of France • Counter-Reformation and the work of the Jesuits halts advance of Protestantism • Gregorian calendar established • Tycho Brahe and the best naked-eye astronomical observations • Ivan the Terrible defeats the Tatars and absorbs their territory, begins the advance into Siberia • Ottoman Turks defeated at the Battle of Lepanto • Safavid Persia at its peak under Abbas I • Mogul India at its peak under Akbar • Portuguese establish base at Macao in China • Japan under Hideyoshi invades Korea • Manila founded in the Philippine Islands • Songhai Empire destroyed at Timbuktu

1600 TO 1650

The Thirty Years War, the climax of the Wars of Religion, devastates Germany • Tilly sacks Magdeburg • Gustavus Adolphus of Sweden wins the Battles of Leipzig and Lutzen • war ended by Treaty of Westphalia, at which the Netherlands wins its independence • Dutch found New Netherlands on American coast • Miguel Cervantes writes *Don Quixote* • Richelieu of France struggles to centralize French power under the king and his successor, Jules Mazarin, does the same • Louis XIV becomes king of France • Quebec is founded and French North Africa (Canada) established • Galileo in Italy puts the Scientific Revolution in high gear, uses the telescope to study the heavens, overthrows Aristotelian physics, and is silenced by the Inquisition • England under the Stuarts rebels against Charles I, who is defeated and executed, leaving Oliver Cromwell in power • England establishes colonies in Virginia and New England • William Harvey establishes circulation of the blood, founds modern physiology • house of Romanov gains Tsardom of Russia • Taj Mahal built by Shah Jahan of India • Ming dynasty in China comes to an end and China is under Manchu rule • Dutch control East Indies • Portuguese and Spanish Empires in decline

1650 TO 1700

Louis XIV establishes absolutism in France, builds Versailles, racks Europe with wars, and dominates the continent • French literary golden age—Corneille, Racine, Moliere, La Fontaine • French explore Mississippi Valley and claim it ("Louisiana") for France • Charles II restored as English king • English colonies established in Carolinas, New Jersey, and Pennsylvania • Isaac Newton establishes laws of motion, the light spectrum, the reflecting telescope, the law of universal gravitation, and invents calculus • the "Age of Reason" is in high gear • James II of England driven out in favor of William and Mary, Protestant monarchs • New Netherlands conquered by England and becomes New York • Anton van Leeuwenhoek discovers microscopic life • Ottoman Empire lays siege to Vienna in last burst of aggression, but is then defeated and driven out of Hungary • Elector Frederick William militarizes Brandenburg • Peter I begins task of modernizing Russia, and conquest of Siberia is completed • Aurangzeb is last strong Mogul Emperor of India • Manchu China is at its peak under K'ang Hsi • Dutch establish settlements in South Africa

1700 TO 1725

War of the Spanish Succession • British general, Duke of Marlborough, defeats French at Battle of Blenheim and elsewhere • England deserts coalition and Louis XIV is saved • England and Scotland unite to form Great Britain • George I succeeds to British throne, leaves governments in the hands of Robert Walpole, so that Great Britain becomes limited Parliamentary monarchy with a modern party system • Defoe's *Robinson Crusoe* and Swift's *Gulliver's Travels* • Fahrenheit and the mercury thermometer • Elector Frederick III of Brandenburg becomes King Frederick I of Prussia • his son, Frederick William I, builds up magnificent Prussian army • Charles XII becomes King of Sweden and wins spectacular victories against Russia, Denmark, and Poland, but is in the end defeated by Peter I of Russia at the Battle of Poltava • rapid decline of the Mogul Empire

1725 TO 1750

Frederick II of Prussia uses his father's army to gain Silesia from Austria, but Maria Theresa manages to keep Austria from disintegrating • Great Britain defeats attempt of the "Young Pretender" (Bonnie Prince Charlie) to regain the throne • Russia explores and later settles Alaska • Nader Kuli of Persia is the last of the old-style Asian conquerors

1750 TO 1775

The Seven Years War (called the French and Indian War in North America) ends with Great Britain driving France out of Canada and India • British Empire becomes dominant political unit worldwide • Frederick II uses his military genius to save Prussia from onslaught of powerful coalition but is greatly helped by the sudden death of Elizabeth I of Russia • France is notable for reformers who try to improve French society—Voltaire, Rousseau, Montesquieu • George III rules in Great Britain • Britain adopts Gregorian calendar and faces unrest in North American colonies over taxation in view of the expense of the Seven Years War • Captain Cook explores the Pacific and crosses the Antarctic Circle • Watt invents a practical steam engine, beginning of the Industrial Revolution • Benjamin Franklin invents the lightning rod and the Franklin stove • Lisbon destroyed by gigantic earthquake and tidal wave • First Partition of Poland by Prussia, Austria, and Russia • Catherine II of Russia defeats Ottoman Turks and Russia gains its present-day European boundaries • British under Robert Clive slowly gain preponderance of power over India

1775 TO 1800

Louis XVI and Marie Antoinette rule France inefficiently and drive it into near-bankruptcy • France erupts in the "French Revolution," establishes a republic together with a "Reign of Terror," executes both king and queen, and must face the vengeful monarchs of Europe as a result • rise of Napoleon Bonaparte, who begins to win remarkable victories for France • Lavoisier founds modern chemistry • the British colonies in North America revolt against Great Britain and, under George Washington plus the help of France, win their independence • they work out a constitution that still forms the basis of American government • Gibbon writes *The*

Decline and Fall of the Roman Empire • Adam Smith and John Locke • William Herschel discovers the planet Uranus • Cavendish discovers hydrogen • factory system established • Mozart and Haydn • Goethe and Schiller • Poland wiped off the map by two more partitions • Captain Cook discovers the Hawaiian Islands • Great Britain begins to settle Australia

1800 TO 1820

Napoleon dominates Europe after his great victories at Austerlitz, Jena, and Friedland • but Great Britain remains an enemy and destroys a French–Spanish fleet at the Battle of Trafalgar, at which Admiral Nelson dies • Napoleon invades Russia and loses his army to the Russian soldiers and winter, slows and declines rapidly, is finally defeated at the Battle of Waterloo by the British general, the Duke of Wellington, and goes into exile at St. Helena • Louis XVIII restored as King of France • the United States buys Louisiana from France and doubles its territory • it fights Great Britain to a draw in the War of 1812 • Fulton builds the first practical steamboat • Romantic poets—Shelley, Keats, Byron, Scott • Spanish American nations revolt against Spain and eventually establish their independence • Manchu China in decline • Kamehameha unites the Hawaiian islands

1820 TO 1840

Great Britain begins to expand the franchise, increasing democracy, abolishes slavery in its possessions, and establishes modern postage system • Dickens writes his novels • French revolt evicts aristocratic monarchy of Charles X, establishes middle-class monarchy under Louis Philippe • France begins to build African Empire in Algeria • Daguerre invents photography • Victor Hugo and Honore Balzac • Austria's prime minister Metternich is the fount of European reaction after the fall of Napoleon • Hans Christian Anderson's fairy tales

• Greece gains its independence from the Ottoman Empire • increasing friction between American free states and slave states • United States advances rapidly in technology • Texas is overrun by Americans and declares itself independent of Mexico • Belgium becomes independent

1840 TO 1860

Louis Philippe is driven out of France as part of the Revolutions of 1848, which shake all of western Europe • a Second Republic is established, but Napoleon III becomes president, executes a coup and becomes Emperor • Dumas writes his historical novels • Italy, with the help of France, unites its parts and becomes the Kingdom of Italy • Metternich is driven out of Austria • an attempt to unify Germany fails • Great Britain wars on China, forces it to accept the opium trade, and founds Hong Kong • Darwin and Wallace advance the theory of evolution by natural selection • Crimean War pits Great Britain and France against Russia and prevents further Russian expansion • Charge of the Light Brigade • United States fights Mexico and gains the southwest and California, also the southern half of the Oregon Territory • gains its present 48-state boundary, and friction over slavery worsens • Mormons establish themselves in Utah • discovery of gold in California accelerates the settlement of the west • Sepoy Mutiny in India is crushed by Great Britain, putting an end to the Mogul Empire, and takes over all of India directly • France settles in Indo-China • T'ai Ping civil war in China weakens it and opens it to European exploitation • Commodore Perry forces Japan to open itself to trade with the rest of the world • British settling in New Zealand and war with the Maoris

1860 TO 1880

Otto von Bismarck in Prussia brings about German unification, forming German Empire under Prussian King William I • in the process he defeats Denmark, Austria, and France, so that Germany becomes the dominant land power in the world • Italy absorbs Venetia and Rome and gains its present boundaries • Napoleon III abdicates and the Third Republic is founded in France • Hungary breaks loose and Austria becomes a dual nation, Austria-Hungary • Alexander II of Russia liberates the serfs and seeks other forms of liberalization, then fights a war with the Ottoman Empire but a European coalition prevents him from gaining a victory • Turgenev, Tolstoy, and Dostoievsky • the United States fights a tremendous civil war, in which the northern free states win, preserve the Union, and liberate the black slaves • after the war President Lincoln is assassinated • the United States fights the Indians in the west, and Chicago burns down • Gilbert & Sullivan operettas begin to be written • Thomas Edison invents the phonograph and the electric light • European powers begin the partition of Africa and even Belgium builds a huge African Empire • Japan begins a successful policy of westernization • Canada becomes a dominion

1880 TO 1890

Bismarck forms alliances that successfully isolate France • Tsar Alexander II of Russia is assassinated • Tchaikovsky • Great Britain struggles with Irish home rule • the turbulent Balkan nations win freedom from the Ottoman Empire • Mark Twain writes *Huckleberry Finn* • in the Sudan, the Mahdi wins victories and destroys a British army • radio waves discovered

1890 TO 1900

The British Empire at its peak • Michelson–Morley experiment upsets the science of physics • William II becomes German Emperor and retires Bismarck • William's incapacity allows a French–Russian alliance to be formed, ending France's isolation

(continued on next page)

• Roentgen discovers x-rays • Becquerel discovers radioactivity • Thomson discovers the electron • Planck works out a quantum theory, founding modern physics • Zeppelin invents the airship • Freud founds psychoanalysis • the Zionist movement starts among Jews • Dreyfus Affair in France exposes French anti-Semitism • Marconi invents radio • Spanish–American War ends with the United States gaining the Philippine Islands and Puerto Rico • Hawaii becomes an American possession • British under Kitchener defeat Mahdists in Sudan • Italians defeated by Ethiopians • trouble between the British and the independent Boer Republics in South Africa • Japan defeats China and begins to compete with the European powers in exploiting that land • Boxer Rebellion in China is crushed by a European coalition • the United States insists on an Open Door policy in which all powers may trade equally with China • United States beats down Philippine rebellion • automobiles come into use

1900 TO 1910

Boer War—Great Britain wins and annexes the Boer Republics but grants Boers full liberty within South Africa • Queen Victoria dies after reign of 63 years • Great Britain makes alliances with Japan, France, and Russia • Europe divided into two antagonistic alliances • crises in the Balkans and in Morocco threaten war • Germany begins to build modern navy to the distress of Great Britain • Japan, in a surprise attack on the Russian far east fleet, starts the Russo–Japanese war • to the world's astonishment, Japan wins, absorbs Korea and drives Russia out of Manchuria • a revolution in Russia forces the Tsar to make some concessions and establish a kind of parliamentary government • the United States under Theodore Roosevelt forces Panamanian independence and builds the Panama Canal • Wright brothers invent the airplane, and Ford produces cheap

automobiles by mass production • Mt. Pelee erupts in Martinique • Peary reaches the North Pole

1910 TO 1914

Unrest becomes acute in the polyglot Austro–Hungarian Empire • Serbia is especially hostile • the heir to the Austro–Hungarian throne, Franz Ferdinand, is assassinated by Serbian terrorists • Germany supports Austria • Russia supports Serbia • no one wants war, but no one can stop it • Great Britain reduces power of House of Lords to a virtual zero • Rutherford proves the existence of the nuclear atom • Italy invades Libya and absorbs it into its Empire • Balkan wars evict Ottoman Empire almost entirely from Europe • China overthrows Manchus and endeavors to establish a republic, but is victimized by "warlords" • United States adopts direct election of the Senate • *Titanic* sinks on its maiden voyage • motion pictures become popular • Amundsen reaches South Pole

1914 TO 1920

World War I: Germany and Austria–Hungary fighting Great Britain, France, and Russia • Germany pushes westward invading Belgium, is stopped by the Allies at the Marne River, and a long stalemate follows • in the east, Russia wins victories over Austria–Hungary but loses to Germans • British attempts to attack Turkey at Gallipoli fail • German reliance on unrestricted submarine warfare brings in the United States on the Allied side • Russia dissolves in revolution • Tsar Nicholas II abdicates, is killed, and a Communist government is established • after one last push westward, Germany surrenders • President Wilson dominates peace talks and sets up League of Nations, which the United States refuses to join • Austria–Hungary broken up • Emperors Charles of Austria-Hungary and William II of Germany abdicate • Yugoslavia and Czechoslovakia appear as nations

1920 TO 1930

United States returns to isolation, establishes prohibition of alcohol, and suffers great growth of crime • Lindbergh crosses the Atlantic by plane • Kellogg–Briand pact • southern Ireland becomes dominion • Italy establishes Fascist government under Mussolini • Germany under Weimar Republic experiences inflation, humiliation, and the rise of Adolf Hitler • in Russia, now the Soviet Union, Lenin dies and Josef Stalin gains power • Turkey fights off Greek invaders, puts an end to Ottoman Sultanate, and reorganizes under Mustapha Kemal • Chinese Republic splits between Chiang Kai-shek, a conservative, and Mao Tse-tung, a Communist • stock market in New York crashes in 1929

1930 TO 1939

Great Depression envelopes world, stimulating unrest • Japan takes over Manchuria and invades other portions of China, paying no attention to world indignation and leaving the League of Nations • Italy attacks and absorbs Ethiopia into its Empire • Hitler becomes German Chancellor, initiating violent anti-Semitism • Germany is rearmed under repressive Nazi rule • Germany absorbs Austria and Czechoslovakia, with Great Britain and France responding only weakly • the Munich surrender • a Spanish civil war results in a Fascist Spain under Francisco Franco • United States fights depression with "New Deal" under Franklin D. Roosevelt • prohibition repealed • isolation continues • Stalin's repressive regime in the Soviet Union labors to advance economically under "Five Year Plans" • Edward VIII succeeds to throne and abdicates to marry a divorcée • most of Europe is Fascist • independence movement in India under Mohandas K. Gandhi

1939 TO 1945

World War II begins • Germany wins enormous initial victories, smashing Poland, occupying Norway and Low Countries, and defeating France, all in first year • Soviet Union, having signed a pact with Germany, defeats Finland and takes over Baltic States • Great Britain rescues army at Dunkirk and wins air-Battle of Britain • Germany takes over Balkans and invades the Soviet Union, which suffers great losses but fights back • Great Britain wins initial victories in North Africa but falls back before German general, Erwin Rommel • Japan strikes the United States successfully at Pearl Harbor • United States goes to war against Germany and Japan • Japan wins enormous victories for six months, taking over the Philippines, Malaya, and the Dutch East Indies • the United States wins the Battle of Midway and begins to island-hop toward Japan • Germany reaches Stalingrad, is defeated there, and begins a long forced retreat back across Russia • Allies land in North Africa and Great Britain wins the Battle of El Alamein • Italy is invaded and Mussolini is overthrown • in gathering defeat, Germany slaughters six million Jews in the Holocaust • Germany surrenders, Mussolini is executed, Hitler commits suicide • United States develops nuclear bomb, uses two over Japan, which surrenders, ending World War II

ASIMOV'S
CHRONOLOGY
OF THE
WORLD

Books by ISAAC ASIMOV published by HarperCollins

Measure of the Universe (1983)

Asimov's Chronology of Science and Discovery (1989)

Asimov's History of the World (1991)

ASIMOV'S
CHRONOLOGY
OF THE
WORLD

ISAAC ASIMOV

HarperCollins*Publishers*

ASIMOV'S CHRONOLOGY OF THE WORLD. Copyright © 1991 by Isaac Asimov.
All rights reserved. Printed in the United States of America. No part of this
book may be used or reproduced in any manner whatsoever without written
permission except in the case of brief quotations embodied in critical articles
and reviews. For information address HarperCollins Publishers, 10 East 53rd
Street, New York, N.Y. 10022.

FIRST EDITION

Designed by Alma Orenstein

Library of Congress Cataloging-in-Publication Data

Asimov, Isaac, 1920–
    Asimov's chronology of the world/Isaac Asimov.
        p. cm.
    Includes index.
    ISBN 0-06-270036-7
    1. Chronology, Historical.   I. Title.   II. Title: Chronology of the world.
D11.A76   1991
902'.02—dc20   91-55007

91 92 93 94 95 DT/RRD 10 9 8 7 6 5 4 3 2 1

DEDICATED TO

Human history: A dark and turbulent stream of folly,
illuminated now and then by flashes of genius.

ASIMOV'S
CHRONOLOGY
OF THE
WORLD

INTRODUCTION

The year 2000 is coming. In just a few years, it will be here, and people look forward to it with a mixture of elation and dread. Will it mark the beginning of a new and happier era, or will it mark a turning point that will lead us and the world downward to misery?

Why do we pick on the year 2000 as something to pin our hopes and fears on? Because it is "a round number."

A year that ends in a "0" is bound to seem significant; one that ends in "00," even more significant; and one that ends in "000" most significant of all. As usually conceived, a year ending in "0" begins a new decade; one ending in "00," a new century; and one ending in "000," a new millennium.

This is not exactly true, of course. If we begin counting with some year that we call "1," then the tenth year is "10" and the years 1 to 10 make up the first decade. It is the year "11," therefore, that marks the beginning of the second decade. By similar reasoning, it is the year 101 that marks the beginning of the second century, and "1001" that marks the beginning of the second millennium.

This means that the year 2000 will be the final year of the twentieth century and the second millennium, and it will be on January 1, 2001 that we begin the twenty-first century and the third millennium.

To persuade humanity to accept that bit of mathematical logic is, however, hopeless. On January 1, 2000, there will be the full clamor and noise that will mark the beginning of a new millennium and all the pedantic voices that will say, "No, no, we must wait another year," will be drowned out and ignored.

So we must make the best of it, for even I, who know better, accept the mythic value of 2000 and never think of 2001. Even when I was a teenager, caught up in the reading of science fiction, I realized that 2000 (not 2001) was *the* science fic-

tional year. Where would the world be in 2000? Where would *I* be in 2000?

That last question always made me nervous. Even when I was quite young, I was aware that in the year 2000 I would be 80 years old, and that that fact would never change. I also knew that 80 was a bit over the average life expectancy of human beings, so that there was a less than even chance I would be alive in 2000.

I have made it to 1989, however (as I write this), and I am in reasonable health for a person my age, so that, at the moment, the chances appear a bit better, than I had once thought, that I will still be alive in 2000. I hope so. Like everyone else, I am caught up in the mystique of the "000" and I would like to see its coming.

But what do we mean by the year 2000, anyway? The Earth is billions of years old, and the Universe is far older still. Why, then, has the number of the years still not reached 2000?

That is because we arbitrarily start the counting at a particular *recent* point in history that seems unique to us.

We could, after all, start counting in any year. The French Revolutionaries, about two centuries ago, were so elated over having established a new republic, in which they felt a new era of liberty, equality, and fraternity would begin, that they declared the year 1792 to be the year 1 of the Republic. That system only continued for about 14 years, but if it had taken hold and had been adopted by all the world, what we call 2000 would have turned out to be the year 208 of the Republic.

In the same way, in certain official documents, Americans not only give the year as it is ordinarily accepted, but also count the years from the Independence of the United States in 1776. The year we call 2000 would be the year 224 of U.S. independence.

The Moslems count from the moment when

their prophet, Mohammad (570–632), fled from the Arabian city of Mecca to Medina in the year we call 622. That is their year 1. What is more, they use a lunar calendar in which the year is only 354 days long and the year we call 2000 will be the year 1421 since the Hegira (i. e., 1421 A.H.).

The Greeks of Asia began to count the years from 312 B.C. (i.e., 312 years *before* the year we call "1"), for that was when their ruler, Seleucus I (358–281 B.C.), began his reign. This "Seleucid Era" became popular for a while and, if it had continued to this day, the year we call 2000 would be 2312 of the Seleucid Era. To put it another way, the year we call 1688 would have been the year 2000 of the Seleucid Era.

The Romans eventually counted the years from the founding of Rome, which they placed in the year we call 753 B.C. They called that year 1 A.U.C. (which stands for *Anno Urbis Conditae*, meaning, in Latin, "the year of the founding of the city"). That was used in Europe generally for centuries and, if it were still used today, the year we call 2000 would be 2753 A.U.C. The year we call 1247 would have been 2000 A.U.C.

Why not count the years from the beginning of the world, or of the Universe? For one thing, until quite recently, people didn't have the faintest notion as to when the world began. The Jewish rabbis, after studying the Bible thoroughly, decided that the world began in 3760 B.C. Thus, the year we call 2000 would be 5760 of the "Jewish Mundane Era" (where *mundane* is from the Latin word for "world"). The year 1760 B.C., was the year 2000 of the Jewish Mundane Era.

About 1650, James Ussher (1581–1656), a bishop of the Anglican church, also studied the Bible and came up with the year 4004 B.C. as the year of the creation of the world. This was long accepted by Protestants, and most Protestant Bibles give that date above the account of the creation at the very beginning of the Bible. In that case, the year 2000 would be the year 6004 of the Christian Mundane Era.

Nowadays, of course, scientists believe the Universe came into being billions of years ago, but it would be silly to try to number our years in the billions. It would be entirely inconvenient,

especially as we only know dates with reasonable accuracy for a few thousand years into the past.

So, where did the year-numbers that we use come from?

It began about the year 535, when a scholar named Dionysius Exiguus (500–560) studied the Bible and decided that Jesus had been born 535 years earlier, in 753 A.U.C.

About two and a half centuries later, the powerful monarch, Charlemagne, who ruled over much of western Europe, decided that it would be much more pious to count the years from the birth of Jesus than from the founding of the heathen city of Rome.

For that reason, 753 A.U.C. became A.D. 1 (where A.D. stands for *Anno Domini*, which is Latin for "in the year of the Lord"). Earlier dates are listed as "B.C." ("Before Christ"), so that Rome was founded in 753 B.C.

The use of this "Christian Era" spread throughout Europe, and then, after 1400, when European guns and ships increasingly dominated the world, this system of counting the years became worldwide and is now used everywhere (except for various religious ceremonies when other older eras are used.)

Unfortunately, Dionysius Exiguus was wrong in his calculations. The Bible does not give a clear statement of chronology anywhere in the usually accepted books it includes. It was therefore easy for Dionysius to make a mistake.

According to the Bible, Jesus was born when Herod I ruled over Judea, but Herod I, we are certain, from historical records of the time, died in 749 A.U.C. Jesus had to be born no later than that year, which is 4 B.C. of the Christian Era. He may have been born earlier still, perhaps even as early as 20 B.C. We don't really know.

Therefore, if we are *really* counting from the birth of Jesus, the year we call 2000 is really something between 2004 and 2020, and the real year A.D. 2000 may already have passed.

However, it is useless to worry about these things. The year we plan to call 2000 *is* 2000 to the whole world, and everyone is looking forward to it with excitement and trepidation.

It might be interesting, then, to cast our eyes

back to see how we got to where we are today by jumping from period to period, using round years to mark the boundaries of the gaps, those years that end with one or more zeros.

And I think it would be amusing to start at the very beginning, the time when the Universe began.

15,000,000,000 YEARS AGO

There is a temptation to say 15,000,000,000 B.C., but that would really be foolish. The difference between 15,000,000,000 years ago and 15,000,000,000 B.C. is not quite 2000 years, and what is 2000 years in 15 billion?

Besides, the year I'm discussing now is not certain. It is an approximation, and it may be as large as 20,000,000,000 years ago. Without worrying about that too much, let us say that about 15,000,000,000 years ago, the Universe came into being, and I will continue to use the phrase "years ago" until we reach times much nearer the present.

Naturally, we can't go back in time to see when this happened and how it happened. We can only study the Universe as it is today and try to deduce, from that, how it came into being.

By observation, we know that the Universe consists of clusters of galaxies, each cluster containing anywhere from a few dozen to a few thousand individual galaxies. Each galaxy is a cluster containing anywhere from a few billion to a few trillion stars.

All the clusters seemed to be receding from each other, judging by the nature of the light they send us. If we look backward in time (like running a motion picture film in reverse) the clusters of galaxies would be seen to be approaching each other and coming closer and closer together. At some time in the past they must have existed as an extremely tight ball of matter that exploded and gave rise to the expanding Universe that now exists.

This origin of the Universe, as a relatively small volume of matter that exploded, was first advanced in 1927 by a Belgian astronomer, Georges Edward Lemaitre (1894–1966). The explosion was called a "big bang" in 1948 by the Russian–American physicist, George Gamow (1904–1968).

Almost all astronomers accept the big bang in principle but the actual time is only known approximately. Scientists are also arguing the details of what happened in the instants immediately after the explosion, but that need not concern us here.

One question that everyone is bound to ask about the big bang is: Where did the original glob that exploded come from? Are we forced to say, at this point, that the only possible explanation is that it was created by some force, or entity, that lies outside what we consider the laws of nature and is, therefore, "supernatural"?

Not necessarily. In 1973, the American physicist, Edward P. Tryon, suggested that according to quantum theory (which is one of two basic, and so far entirely successful, theories for explaining the Universe), it is possible for the initial blob to have arisen out of nothing more than a "quantum fluctuation" in the vacuum.

Again, the details do not concern us. Let us simply say that the Universe seems to have come into being 15,000,000,000 years ago through the operation of natural law.

15,000,000,000 TO 4,600,000,000 YEARS AGO

By 10 billion years after it had come into existence, the Universe had become a mighty extent of galaxies, almost as large as we see about us today.

However, even after 10 billion years, our Sun and its family of planets did not yet exist. Other planets circling other stars undoubtedly existed, and some planets may conceivably have borne life, evolved intelligence, and developed technological civilizations. Some of these may still exist, and others may develop in the future. Yet we know nothing of them, at least so far, and we must concern ourselves with the only inhabited world we know—our own.

In the place of our Solar system—our Sun plus all the worlds and bits of matter that circle round it—there was once a vast cloud, or "nebula" (the Latin word for "cloud"), of dust and gas. This was first suggested by the German philosopher, Immanuel Kant (1724–1804), in 1755, and then, independently, by the French astronomer, Pierre Simon de Laplace (1749–1827), in 1798.

The process by which the nebula drew together to form the Sun and planets was described by Laplace, but his explanation was inadequate to account for all the facts. In 1944, this "nebular hypothesis" was modified by the German astronomer, Carl Friedrich von Weizsacker (b. 1912). Since then, and with further modifications, scientists are fairly assured that they have the mechanism essentially right.

The original nebula was slowly rotating about its axis (we are safe in saying this since all objects we have been able to observe in the Universe appear to rotate). The nebula also had a gravitational field, as do all objects containing mass. Under the pull of the gravitational field, the nebula slowly contracted. As it contracted, the speed of rotation increased in accordance with the "law of conservation of angular momentum," which has never been observed to be violated.

In addition, as the nebula contracted, the gravitational field (because of the increasing density of matter in the nebula) intensified, and this, in turn, hastened the further contraction. The kinetic energy of the matter falling inward was converted to heat, so that the center of the cloud became hotter and hotter and more and more compressed until the combination of heat and pressure brought about a process of "nuclear fusion," which converted hydrogen into helium.

Fusion produced enormous energies that turned the center of the contracting nebula into a glowing mass of extremely hot material. The Sun had been born.

On the outskirts of the cloud, turbulent eddies and subeddies brought together particles that built up bodies much smaller than the Sun, with centers that could not grow hot enough and compressed enough to ignite nuclear fusion. These bodies on the fringes remained cool on the surface, therefore, and became planets. Satellites, asteroids, comets, and all the other bodies of the Solar system also formed.

And, of course, among the bodies that formed was the Earth, third planet from the Sun.

One obvious question that arises from this quick description is: How do astronomers know that the Solar system assumed its present form 4.6 billion years ago, and not substantially before or after.

Beginning in 1896, with a discovery by a French physicist, Antoine Henri Becquerel (1852–1908), it was found that certain substances are radioactive and break down very slowly (in some cases) and with great regularity, to other substances. Thus, uranium breaks down to lead at such a rate that half of any uranium being studied breaks down to lead in 4.5 billion years. Other materials break down even more slowly, and, of course, some break down more quickly.

By studying the content of uranium and lead in rocks, one can estimate the length of time that particular samples of rock have remained solid and essentially undisturbed from the extent to which uranium has broken down. It is hard to find a rock on Earth that has been solid and untouched for much over 3 billion years, for the early history of the Earth must have been quite wild and volcanic. However, the Moon, a smaller and, therefore, more sedate body, has rocks that reveal an age of over 4 billion years, Meteorites which, presumably, have been left unchanged since they settled out of the original nebula, yield a date of 4.6 billion years. Astronomers feel confident, then, that the Solar system formed that long ago.

Another question is: Why did the Solar system form so late? Or so early? After all, if the nebula existed as a nebula for 10 billion years, why isn't it still a nebula today? What made it start to contract suddenly?

That is hard to answer. The Orion nebula, which still exists today, 15 billion years after the formation of the Universe, is only now beginning to contract and form stars. Other nebulas still remain nebulas.

One possibility is that a supernova—a huge star explosion—took place fairly close to our original nebula. The shock wave pressed the nebula together on the side toward the supernova and intensified the gravitational field there. That may have been enough to start the condensation going.

4,600,000,000 TO 3,500,000,000 YEARS AGO

For a little over a billion years, the young Earth may have circled the Sun without life on its surface.

That is not surprising. After all, we know for certain that the Moon has no vestige of indigenous life even today, although it is just as old as Earth is. Mars seems to be dead also, while Venus and Mercury can't possibly have life as we know it. The chances are small that any object in the Solar System, other than Earth, bears life.

We know, of course, that Earth possesses life now, but how can we be sure that Earth possessed life 3.5 billion years ago?

To begin with, people have been finding relics in the soil ever since ancient times, relics that seemed to be the remains of living things not quite like the living things we are accustomed to today. When most people took it for granted that the Earth was only a few thousand years old or so, some bizarre explanations were offered.

The remains might be of animals that died in the Flood described in the Bible. They might represent samples of life formed by God and discarded as insufficient. They might have been samples of life formed by Satan in a failed attempt to imitate God, and so on.

As early as 1570, however, a French scholar, Bernard Palissy (1510–1589), was suggesting that relics in the soil (*fossils*, from a Latin word meaning "to dig") represented early forms of life that were now extinct. This became more likely as the fact that the Earth was of great age became more apparent.

By 1859, the British biologist, Charles Robert Darwin (1809–1882), had worked out a complex description of the mechanism by which life slowly changed its form in a "biological evolution" under the driving force of natural selection.

Eventually, when rocks could be dated accurately, it could be seen that some fossils were hundreds of millions of years old.

Even the oldest fossils, however, were complex organisms, and they must have been preceded by simpler organisms. The fossils, after all, consist chiefly of the hard parts of organisms: shells, bones, and teeth. The simpler organisms, however, may not have possessed hard parts and might not, therefore, have left behind easily recognized fossils.

The simplest free-living organisms today are microscopic one-celled life-forms called "bacteria."

Bacteria are "prokaryotes," from Greek words meaning "before the nucleus." They are called this because in ordinary, much larger cells (such as those making up our own bodies), there are small nuclei containing the machinery that makes it possible for cells to multiply. In bacteria, the reproductive machinery is scattered throughout the tiny cell and there is no nucleus. Alternatively, the bacterium may be viewed as all nucleus.

Some prokaryotes contain "chlorophyll," a complex compound that makes it possible to gain energy from sunlight and, by this energy, to break down water to hydrogen and oxygen. The hydrogen combines with carbon dioxide to form cell components, and the oxygen is released into the air. These chlorophyll-containing prokaryotes are bluish in color and are called "cyanobacteria" (where *cyano* is from the Greek word for "blue").

Beginning in 1954, the American paleontologist, Elso Sterrenberg Barghoorn (1915–1984), managed to locate traces of what looked like prokaryote remains in very old rocks. He shaved thin slices of such rocks and studied them under the microscope. In them, he found circular structures that were about the size of prokaryote cells. What's more, there were signs of smaller structures within these objects that resembled the kind of structures that existed inside bacteria.

The oldest rocks in which these prokaryote traces have been found may be as much as 3.5 billion years old and that is what tells us that life must have existed that long ago—*at least*. It may even have existed at somewhat earlier periods.

The question arises, of course, as to how these prokaryotes were formed? When the Earth first came into existence, it must have had, or developed, an atmosphere and an ocean. These must have contained very simple molecules: nitrogen, carbon dioxide, methane, ammonia, water, and so on. In order for these very simple molecules to form the much more complex molecules that characterize even the simplest forms of life, energy must have had to be added.

That, in itself, is no problem. The early Earth must have been rich in energy—the internal heat of the Earth manifesting itself as volcanoes and hot springs, lightning in the atmosphere, ultraviolet light from the Sun, and so on.

Just exactly what the steps were, however, whereby simple molecules plus energy became the complex molecules of life, have, it must be confessed, not yet been worked out. But in any case, whatever the mechanism, life existed on Earth 3.5 billion years ago.

3,500,000,000 TO 1,400,000,000 YEARS AGO

For about 2 billion years after life formed on Earth, it remained prokaryote in nature. Nevertheless, the environment changed.

If only ordinary bacteria had existed (and, perhaps, to begin with, they were the only life-form of consequence), they would have had to obtain their energy from simpler, nonliving organic molecules that were built up from the small molecules of the air and ocean.

That would mean that bacteria could not grow beyond the mass that could be supported by the rate of formation of these organic molecules. Life concentration may have been thin, indeed.

Once cyanobacteria appeared, however, making use of chlorophyll systems that had slowly developed in some fashion, the energy of visible light became available. Visible light is more copious than ultraviolet light; it is also less energetic and, therefore, easier to handle. Organic molecules, formed by the use of chlorophyll, were stored within the cells, which thus gained their own food supply so that they could multiply to a much greater extent than if they had to depend upon the independent and random effects of ultraviolet light on the world outside their cells.

The cyanobacteria multiplied vastly, for that reason, and ordinary bacteria, unable to form their own food from visible light, made do by ingesting the cyanobacteria and making use of the food those other organisms had manufactured. Bacteria also multiplied for that reason.

In other words, life might still consist only of prokaryotes, but after 2 billion years of existence, prokaryote life on Earth was much denser and much more numerous than it had been in the earlier stages.

What's more, because of the activity of cyanobacteria in combining carbon dioxide with hydrogen from water, and expelling the excess oxygen, the atmosphere was changing. The carbon dioxide content was going down and the oxygen content was going up.

At the start, both bacteria and cyanobacteria got their energy for day-to-day living by splitting the food molecules (formed by the cyanobacteria through the use of the energy of the Sun) into smaller molecules. The energy thus obtained was comparatively small. Once oxygen existed in the atmosphere in substantial amounts, however, chemical mechanisms were developed to combine the food molecules with oxygen. This released up to 20 times as much energy as mere splitting released.

The prokaryotes not only became much more numerous, then, but they also had much more energy at their disposal—at least, those that specialized in oxygen-handling did.

With much more energy available, cells could afford to become larger, and still be able to support themselves.

This increase in size might come about in two ways: the cells might simply become larger without becoming notably more complex; or prokaryote cells might combine so that a given cell might contain some components that were specialized in one way, and other components that were specialized in another way.

This second development may have taken place, a view strongly supported in recent years by the American biologist, Lynn Margulis (b. 1938), and it resulted in the production of large, complex cells containing nuclei, which specialize in reproductive machinery; mitochrondria, which specialize in oxygen-handling; ribosomes, which specialize in protein manufacture; cilia, which specialize in movement; chloroplasts, which specialize in chlorophyll-content; and so on.

These more complex cells are called *eukaryotes* (from Greek words meaning "good nuclei," because separate nuclei are partitioned off inside the cell). The eukaryotes turned out to be more successful than prokaryotes or (which may not be the same thing) they at least turned out to be capable of further development. Thus, although prokaryotes still exist today, all cells, except for bacteria of various sorts, are eukaryotes, including the cells of our own body.

The earliest signs of eukaryotes have been located in rocks that are about 1.4 billion years old, so that eukaryotes have only existed during the last 30% of Earth's existence.

1,400,000,000 TO 800,000,000 YEARS AGO

For the first 600 million years of their existence, eukaryotes remained as single cells, so that life on Earth was unicellular, even 4 billion years after the planet had been formed. Some five sixths of Earth's existence had passed, and there was nothing more complex on the planet than something the equivalent of an amoeba.

However, just as different types of prokaryotes had combined to form a more complex eu-karyotic cell, eukaryotes, after cell division, began to cling together and form "multicellular organisms."

Again, we don't know the details, but in 1930, a German paleontologist, Georg J. E. Gurich, and, in 1947, an Australian paleontologist, R. C. Sprigg, found traces of multicellular life in rocks that were as old as 800 million years.

800,000,000 TO 600,000,000 YEARS AGO

For the first 200 million years of their existence, multicellular animals were more or less like modern jellyfish and worms, consisting of soft tissue only. This left little in the way of traces.

As the oxygen content of the atmosphere continued to climb, and as energy continued to become more available, it became possible for organisms to "invest" in hard parts that served as weapons, offensive and defensive.

About 600 million years ago, animals with shells and other hard parts proliferated and began to leave behind fossils that were large enough to be seen without a microscope and clear enough to show shapes that would allow deductions to be drawn about their functioning. From that point on, the course of evolution could be made out quite well.

By that time, though, evolution had produced a considerable complexity of multicellular life. Biologists could divide multicellular organisms into two "kingdoms," plants and animals. Each of these kingdoms could be divided into many broad divisions called "phyla" (singular "phylum," from a Greek word for "tribe"). Each phylum possesses a distinctively different body plan.

There are about a score or so of different animal phyla, and already, in the first tens of millions of years after the fossil record had become copious, examples could be found of every phylum but one. The one phylum that had not yet appeared—and that, therefore, was the last to appear—happened to be the one to which we belong.

600,000,000 TO 550,000,000 YEARS AGO

The phylum to which we belong is "Chordata," and we are "chordates."

The body plan of the chordates, which makes them distinct from all other phyla, includes three unique characteristics.

In the first place, chordates have a central nerve cord that is hollow, and that runs along the back. In all other phyla, the nerve cord, if it exists, is solid, and runs along the abdomen.

Secondly, all chordates have throats that are perforated by gill slits through which water can be passed. From that water, food can be filtered out, and oxygen can be absorbed. These are not present in other phyla. Even in land chordates, such as ourselves, which do not possess gills,

there are early embryonic stages in which gill slits begin to develop, but then wither away.

Thirdly, all chordates have, at some time during their embryonic development, an internal stiffening rod of a tough, light, flexible, gelatinous substance that runs down the back. This is a *notochord* (Greek for "back-string"), which gives the phylum its name.

These represent the minimum requirements for even very primitive chordates, the first of which, from which all others (including ourselves) have evolved, seems to have made its appearance about 550 million years ago. Chordates have existed on Earth, therefore, only during the last eighth of its existence.

550,000,000 TO 450,000,000 YEARS AGO

Even after Earth had endured for nine tenths of its present length of existence, all life upon it existed in water. The earth's land surface remained sterile for about 100 million years after the last of the phyla, the chordates, had appeared.

This is not so surprising, for the dry land is a much harsher environment than the sea. Water is essential to life, and, on land, the problem of getting and retaining water is a serious one. Life is adapted to obtaining oxygen from solution in water. On land, mechanisms have to be devised to dissolve atmospheric oxygen in water, without losing too much water in the process.

Then, too, in water, gravity is a minor force, since water buoyancy does much of the work. On land, gravity is a major force and motion is more difficult, requires greater energy expendi-

ture, and (except for those smaller organisms that can fly) is essentially two-dimensional.

The water environment is very stable. On land, there are variations that subject organisms to a temperature range far greater than exists in the sea. There are also wind and storms on dry land that offer more violence than almost anything that happens in the ocean.

Finally, life in water is protected from the more energetic radiation of the Sun, while life on land is exposed to it, particularly to the Sun's ultraviolet rays. It may be that it was not until enough oxygen had accumulated in the air to produce an ozone layer in the upper atmosphere (ozone is an energetic form of oxygen), which blocked most of the ultraviolet rays, that life became possible on land.

The result is that, even today, the world's

waters are substantially richer in life than is the world's land.

The question arises: With all the disadvantages of land life, why should any life ever have left the ocean and the waters generally? Why has the land not remained sterile to this day?

The answer is probably the result of population pressure. Life is so rich in the ocean that the eat-or-be-eaten competition is extraordinarily high. If some forms of life could manage to make it on land, they would find an empty environmental niche in which they could multiply securely. Of course, that would be only a short-term gain, for eventually the land population would increase to the point where competition would become high there as well. However, except for human beings, life-forms do not (and are not capable of) consider the long-range future. Short-range adventure is all that concerns them.

Then, too, the tides tend to move life-forms toward the shore, and any organism that could resist drying out during low tide had an advantage. With time, adaptations would make it possible to live out of water more or less permanently.

Plant life may have begun to cling to the land about 450 million years ago. The development of roots anchored them to the ground; the development of stems lifted them higher toward the Sun, which was the source of energy. Water could be absorbed from the ground and they would flourish in an environment which, harsh though it might be, would at least have the advantage of lacking predators.

450,000,000 TO 370,000,000 YEARS AGO

For 80 million years, perhaps, plant life on land flourished without serious problems with animal life. Plants would compete with each other, of course, each growing higher to gain a lion's share of sunlight. Each spread roots to get as much water as it could, leaving as little as possible for others.

The golden age could not last forever, just the same. Where plants existed, animals would eventually follow. By 370 million years ago, there was enough plant life on land surfaces to make it profitable for animals to seek them out as a new and as yet untouched food supply.

The first animal life to reach the land were various members of the phylum "Arthropoda" (Greek for "joint-footed"), such as spiders, scorpions, and primitive insects. Then larger animals followed, some to feed on plants, some on the arthropods.

By 370 million years ago, the chordates had developed as fish, which now dominated the seas. They had internal skeletons, made up of cartilage in the case of the sharks and their relatives, or bone in the case of the fish proper. Bone, a form of calcium hydroxyphosphate, is unique to chordates and doesn't occur in other phyla.

Fish developed two pairs of limbs that helped in propulsion. They also developed gas chambers or "swim bladders," which lowered their densities and helped them be buoyant.

In most fish, the two pairs of limbs were small and made up largely of thin, flexible plates called "fins." Some types of fish, however, had strong, if stubby, limbs, with the fins only present as fringes. Such fish could support themselves on their limbs if caught out of water and could, for instance, flop from one pool to another across land, if they had to. This was particularly useful if a pool was drying up and becoming brackish and a second, deeper and larger pool, which offered a better chance at life, was nearby.

Gradually, fish evolved into organisms that lived in water in the early part of their life but became acclimated to land life as adults. Their fins became legs; their swim bladders became lungs. They became "amphibians" (from Greek words meaning "double life"), which first appeared about 370 million years ago and whose modern descendants are frogs, toads, and salamanders.

Fish and amphibia belong to a branch of the chordates that make up almost all of the phylum. They belong to the subphylum "Vertebrata" and are, therefore, "vertebrates." They are so-called because they have backbones composed of a series of bones called "vertebrae" (from a Latin word meaning "to turn," because the human head turns on the topmost vertebrae.)

It is from the amphibia that all modern land vertebrates (plus some that were originally land vertebrates but had returned to the sea) have descended—including us.

This emergence on land was of the highest importance. Water is so viscous a medium that it tends to enforce streamlining on any organism that wishes to move quickly within it. Fast-moving sea organisms are smoothly "fish-shaped" in one way or another, and rarely have irregular shapes. In air, however, the medium is tenuous and an irregular shape does not interfere with fast movement.

That is why, for instance, human beings have hands with which to manipulate the Universe about them, while dolphins (whose ancestors were land animals that returned to the sea) have not. Dolphins have brains at least as large and as well-developed as our own, and must be highly intelligent, but their flippers simply cannot perform the manipulative tasks so easy for our hands.

Furthermore, the foundation of all technology is fire, and while fire can exist in an atmosphere rich in oxygen, it cannot exist in water. Hence, no technological civilization is conceivable, at least in our terms, except on land. That is why dolphins, although they and their ancestors have been brainy for longer than we and our ancestors, have never developed a technological civilization.

370,000,000 TO 300,000,000 YEARS AGO

The conquest of land by the amphibia was only partial. Amphibia had to lay their eggs in water, and spend their early life there. This continued for about 70 million years after amphibia first made their appearance.

About 300 million years ago, however, certain amphibia developed an egg that was surrounded by a protective shell of thin limestone. The shell was permeable to air, but not to water. Air could reach the developing embryo inside, but water could not leave it.

A small reservoir of water was present inside the egg, together with an elaborate system of mechanisms that allowed the embryo to tuck wastes into special membranes. Such eggs could be laid on land under dry conditions, and the organism that emerged could live on land from the start.

The organisms with such a land-based egg could finally be considered as totally adapted to land, requiring only enough water to replace what they unavoidably lost in getting rid of wastes. These first true land-vertebrates belonged to the class "Reptilia." They are "reptiles" (from the Latin word "to creep," since the most successful reptiles in existence today are the snakes).

300,000,000 TO 220,000,000 YEARS AGO

During the first 80 million years of reptilian existence, some developed certain characteristics that resembled organisms like ourselves. They were not particularly successful in the evolutionary scramble, but by about 220 million years ago, they had evolved into animals that had differentiated teeth, as we do; that had hair; that were warm-blooded; that laid eggs containing partially developed embryos (and eventually went on to develop mechanisms for giving birth to the embryos themselves); and that produced milk to feed their young.

Such hairy, warm-blooded organisms with advanced child-bearing mechanisms, belong to the class "Mammalia" and are "mammals." The word is from the Greek for "breasts," because mammals feed their young on milk developed in the mother's breasts.

The dominant land-animals in the world today are mammals, including ourselves, of course. However, at the time that mammals first made their appearance, they were small shrew-like organisms, which were not nearly as successful as the reptiles, and which developed into a wide variety of nonmammalian species, some of them extraordinarily large and powerful.

The only reason the mammals survived at all in the face of the great reptiles (the best-known of which are the "dinosaurs") is that they were small enough to hide and remain inconspicuous.

220,000,000 TO 100,000,000 YEARS AGO

For some 120 million years after mammals first came into existence, they either laid eggs, or gave birth to live, but immature, embryos. Their descendants today include the duck-bill platypus and various marsupials, such as kangaroos and opossums, which are found chiefly in Australia and, in a few cases, in the Americas.

About 100 million years ago, however, some mammals improved the child-bearing system and made it more complex. The embryo remained within the mother's body, nourished by a *placenta* (from Greek words meaning "flat cake" because of its shape). Food could diffuse from the mother's bloodstream into the embryo's bloodstream across the placenta, while wastes diffused in the opposite direction. (There was no *direct* connection between the blood of mother and embryo.) The embryo could develop within the body until it was in a comparatively advanced state.

Such organisms are "placental mammals." The dominant land organisms of today, including ourselves, are placental mammals. However, these, when they first appeared, were also small and of little account compared to the ruling dinosaurs.

100,000,000 TO 70,000,000 YEARS AGO

Some 30 million years after the placental mammals first made their appearance, a new subdivision or "order" evolved. These were the "primates" (from the Latin word for "first," since the order includes human beings).

The primates included a group of organisms that had better vision than other orders, more delicately manipulative hands, and, most important of all, larger brains for their body size.

However, the first primates that made their appearance continued to be small organisms whose survival depended on their ability to hide and to go unnoticed.

70,000,000 TO 65,000,000 YEARS AGO

Some five million years after the primates first made their appearance, a biological revolution took place. The dinosaurs all died out in a comparatively short period, about 65 million years ago, as did other giant reptiles and many other types of organisms.

Evidence has been accumulating since 1980 that there was a collision of a comet with the Earth. The collision, according to this theory, did not do much to harm the Earth itself, but it set off tidal waves and conflagrations and, in addition, threw so much dust into the upper atmosphere as to block the rays of the Sun for a considerable period. Most forms of life, especially small animals, survived.

Some mammals survived the catastrophe and found themselves in a world that was suddenly empty of important competitors.

Had the catastrophe not taken place, it seems likely that the mammals would have continued to be a group of small creatures of little importance. As it was, however, thanks to the catastrophe, mammals could expand into the niches left empty. They developed species that bulked huge (though never quite as huge as the largest dinosaurs) and could continue the development of primates in the direction of eyes, hands, and brains.

65,000,000 TO 40,000,000 YEARS AGO

The primates remained small creatures of little account for some 25 million years after the catastrophe. Those that existed resembled the lemurs that are now found in Madagascar, for instance.

About 40 million years ago, however, a suborder of primates developed, which are called the "Anthropoidea" (from Greek words meaning "man-like").

The anthropoidians could sit up easily so that they could use their forepaws for handling and manipulating objects with greater ease. Their fingers and toes had nails rather than claws, so that the softer, more sensitive parts of the digits could be exposed for the task of handling and manipulating.

What's more, their faces looked like those of little human beings, hence the name of the suborder. Their descendants today are "monkeys," a word which may possibly come from *homunculus*, which is Latin for "little man."

40,000,000 TO 30,000,000 YEARS AGO

About 10 million years after the monkeys appeared, one group developed into a super-family named "Hominoidea," from a Latin word for "manlike." These looked even more like human beings than monkeys did, for they lacked tails.

A tailless monkey that exists today is to be found in north Africa ("Barbary") and on the rock of Gibraltar and is called "Barbary ape." The Barbary ape is not a member of Hominoidea, but because of their taillessness, Hominoidea were also called "apes." To indicate that the Hominoidea more closely resemble human beings than the Barbary ape does, the former are called "anthropoid apes."

30,000,000 TO 17,000,000 YEARS AGO

The first anthropoid apes were rather small, like modern gibbons and stayed so for some 13 million years. About 17 million years ago, however, the subfamily "Ponginae" evolved. (The word is from a Congolese term for apes.)

This new subfamily produced species that were larger than other primates; therefore, they are termed the "great apes." Indeed, the largest primate that ever existed was one called "Gigantopithecus" (Greek for "giant ape"), which was about nine feet tall and may have tipped the scale at a thousand pounds. The largest living great ape is the gorilla, which is over five feet tall and may weigh 500 pounds.

The great apes were the most intelligent primates to have appeared up to that time, as is indicated by the size of their brains. The gorilla has a brain that weighs up to 19 ounces, the chimpanzee one of 13.5 ounces, and the orangutan one of 12 ounces. Dolphins, porpoises, and whales have larger brains, but they are sea organisms, which cannot develop a technology. Elephants have larger brains, too, but they also have much larger bodies. It is the ratio of the brain's mass to the body's mass that seems to count, so that the elephant is apparently not as intelligent as the great apes.

17,000,000 TO 5,000,000 YEARS AGO

The great apes may be called "pongids." Any pongid, however, that resembles modern human beings more than it resembles any ape, living or extinct, may be called a *hominid* (from the Latin word for "man").

The first hominid seems to have developed in eastern or southern Africa about 5 million years ago, so that hominids have existed on Earth only in the last one thousandth of the planet's existence.

The first hominids were comparatively small, perhaps four feet tall. They were no taller than the chimpanzees of today, and their brains may have been only 15 ounces in weight, not much more than that of a chimpanzee. Indeed, the first hominids probably split off the chimpanzee line.

The first hominids were more slightly built than chimpanzees, however, so that their ratio of brain mass to body mass may have been twice as great as that of a modern chimpanzee and four times that of a modern gorilla. These first hominids were, therefore, probably more intelligent than any of the pongids.

What most clearly made the first hominids resemble human beings more than they resembled any ape was that the first hominids could walk upright as easily and efficiently as we do.

5,000,000 TO 4,000,000 YEARS AGO

It used to be taken for granted that human beings were utterly different from all other animals. Human beings used reason, had big brains, could talk, didn't have tails, had very little hair, and so on. As human knowledge of the animal kingdom increased, many of the differences seemed less important. The anthropoid apes had no tails; elephants and dolphins had large brains and no hair, and so on.

Of all the separating characteristics, however, bipedality—the ability to walk on two legs—seems the most important. We are not the only bipedal animals, but most other bipedal animals are horizontal, with tails sticking out behind the legs and heads in front. We, on the other hand, are vertical.

Bears and chimpanzees can walk on their hind legs in a vertical position as we do, but they are clearly uncomfortable in doing so, and prefer the four-legged posture.

What makes it possible for human beings to walk *comfortably* and *permanently* on two legs is that the spinal column, just above the pelvis, bends backward. It assumes a shallow S-shape in us, and this allows us to remain generally vertical without trouble. This S-shaped spinal column adds a little spring and bounce to the human walk, too.

There is clearly some advantage to getting on your hind legs. It lifts your head and major sense organs higher so that you can spot food, or danger, at a greater distance. It also frees your forelimbs from the task of supporting the body; and they can be used, instead, for holding food, or a weapon, or a baby.

We know about these early hominids through the fossilized remains of their bones and teeth. Thus, a skull that was human-looking except for its extraordinarily small size was found in a South African quarry in 1924. It was brought to an anthropologist, Raymond Arthur Dart (1893–1988), who recognized it as belonging to a primitive hominid and, in 1925, suggested it be called "Australopithecus" from a Latin–Greek word combination, meaning "southern ape." It's a poor name because Australopithecus is a hominid and not a pongid, but you couldn't know that 60 years ago from a skull alone. It was only after fragments of thigh bones and pelvises were uncovered that the ability of Australopithecus to walk upright was understood.

Since 1924, other remains have been found of such hominids, and it is now believed that they existed as at least four different species, lumped together as "australopithecines."

The best remains of the earliest of these species was found in 1974, when a large fraction of the skeleton of an australopithecine was located in east-central Africa by an American anthropologist, Donald Johanson. It seemed to be the skeleton of a woman, so it was nicknamed "Lucy." It was at least 3 million, and possibly 4 million years old.

Lucy is an example of *Australopithecus afarensis*, so-called because Afars is the name of the region where the remains were found. Apparently, then, east-central Africa may have been the cradle of the hominids.

4,000,000 TO 2,000,000 YEARS AGO

For about 3 million years (60% of the full length of hominid existence), the only hominids that existed were the various species of australopithecines, who, as far as we know, were confined to eastern and southern Africa.

Very likely, they lived much as chimpanzees do today. They may have used tools, but not in any way markedly beyond what other animals could do. For example, sea otters routinely smash shellfish against a rock they keep for the purpose on their abdomens as they float belly-up. Chimpanzees have been observed to strip leaves from twigs and then use the bare twigs as devices with which to capture termites.

Undoubtedly, australopithecines could do anything that chimpanzees could do. We can be reasonably certain they used tree branches and long bones as clubs. They could surely throw rocks or use them as anvils, with another rock as hammer. And, if they happened upon a pebble that was pointed or sharp-edged, they could use that, too.

About 2 million years ago, however, one of the hominid varieties became rather closer to the modern human than to any of the other australopithecines. It was sufficiently similar to us to be placed into our genus. ("Genus," plural "genera," from a Latin word for "race," is a group of related species.) Our genus is *Homo* (Latin for "man"), and this hominid is the oldest member we know of genus Homo.

In the 1960s, the English anthropologist, Louis S. B. Leakey (1903–1972), his wife, Mary, and their son, Richard, located remains of this oldest member of genus *Homo* in the Olduvai Gorge, in east Africa, in what is now the nation of Tanzania.

The hominid thus uncovered was named *Homo habilis* (Latin for "able man"). *H. habilis* was smaller than some of the larger species of australopithecines. In fact, in the summer of 1986, a set of fossil remains of *H. habilis* was discovered that was some 1.8 million years old. It was the first time that both skull fragments and limb bones of the same individual of that species had been located, and they seemed to represent a small, light adult, about 3.5 feet tall, and with arms that were surprisingly long.

Nevertheless, *H. habilis*, though small, had a more rounded head than any of the australopithecines and a larger brain, one that was nearly half as large as that of a modern human being. The skull bones were thinner, the hands were more like modern hands, and the feet were completely modern. The jaw was less massive, making the face look less ape-like.

What's more, members of this species may have possessed the beginning of "Broca's convolution" in their brains, so that they might have been capable of making a larger variety of sounds than the australopithecines could.

But why *habilis*? Why "able?"

The reason is that *H. habilis* was the first species, as far as we know, with a brain sufficiently agile to conceive of *shaping* stone. *H. habilis* was not content with merely finding a rock that happened to suit his needs. He chipped away at one rock with another to make tools of various kinds for chopping, scraping, cutting, and so on. This was the birth of technology.

H. habilis was the first hominid to use its hands to their full potential. Perhaps the necessity of dealing with his hands in a deft way made it useful to have a still larger brain and led to its evolution.

H. habilis, with rock tools and a larger brain, was more formidable than the australopithecines. Indeed, *H. habilis* may have been the first hominid to have become a hunter rather than a scavenger. *H. habilis*, like the australopithecines, seems to have been confined to eastern and southern Africa.

2,000,000 TO 1,600,000 YEARS AGO

After 400,000 years, *H. habilis* evolved to the point where he could be given a new species name. About 1,600,000 years ago, *Homo erectus* existed.

H. erectus was the first hominid to be as large and as heavy as modern human beings. He could attain a height of as much as 6 feet, and could weigh over 150 pounds.

The brain was larger, too, with a weight of 30 to 40 ounces; up to three quarters the size of the modern human brain. It is not surprising, then, that *H. erectus* made much better stone tools than had been made before, and that he was an enormously successful hunter. A tribal hunting party of these hominids could take on the biggest animals they could find —even the mammoth.

H. erectus was the first hominid to expand its range beyond Africa. It made its way into Asia, undoubtedly in the course of pursuing the game herds. It eventually reached all the way to the Pacific and to some of the islands off southeastern Asia.

In fact, the first discoveries of the remains of *H. erectus* were made in Java, where the Dutch anthropologist, Eugene Dubois (1858–1940), discovered a skullcap, a femur, and two teeth in 1894. No hominid with so small a brain had as yet been discovered, and Dubois named it *Pithecanthropus erectus* (Greek for "erect ape-man.")

A similar find was made near Peking (now called Beijing), beginning in 1927, by a Canadian anthropologist, Davidson Black (1884–1934). He named his find *Sinanthropus pekinensis* (Greek for "China-man from Peking").

Eventually, it was recognized that both sets of remains, along with some others, were all of the same species and deserved to belong to genus *Homo*. Dubois's term, "erectus," was kept even though hominids had been walking erect for 3.5 million years by the time *H. erectus* had evolved. This, after all, had not been known in Dubois's time.

1,600,000 TO 1,000,000 YEARS AGO

By 1 million years ago, the australopithecines, which had lived on Earth for 4 million years, were extinct. All were gone.

It seems safe to guess that since the australopithecines shared their territory first with *H. habilis* and then *H. erectus*, and since they all probably ate the same food, there would be strong competition among them.

In that competition, the members of genus *Homo*, with their better stone tools and their higher intelligence (meaning they could work better in cooperation), had an enormous advantage. It seems very likely, then, that the australopithecines were killed off by genus *Homo*.

1,000,000 TO 500,000 YEARS AGO

About 600,000 years ago, the Earth entered the first of a series of "ice ages," which it had experienced in the most recent period of its existence. When the glaciers were at their peak, so much water was withdrawn from the sea that the sea-level dropped as much as 300 feet, exposing the continental shelves under the shallower sections along the coastlines. It was the formation of such land-bridges that made it easy for *H. erectus* to wander from Africa into Asia, and then from Asia into the Indonesian islands.

The cold weather enforced new habits. The chill in the air made it more important to do something to ameliorate the cold of the night particularly. In earlier times, hominids might well have fallen asleep wherever they happened to be, though they might have climbed into the branches of a tree for greater security, as the pongids do.

Now, however, they began to make shelters by building up stones to break the wind, or by suspending hides from a central pole. Or else, if they found a suitable cave, they may have found shelter within it, where rain or snow would not follow, and where the force of the wind was at least weakened.

The first traces of *H. erectus* in Asia were found in a filled-up cave near Beijing. That cave showed still another way in which *H. erectus* learned to fight cold. The cave near Beijing had traces of camp fires. This means that fire had been "discovered" by 500,000 years ago. (Recently, indications have been reported that make it seem possible that fire was in use a million years earlier still.)

The use of fire marks off genus *Homo* from all other organisms. Every human society in existence now, however primitive it might be, understands and makes use of fire. No living creature other than human beings or their immediate ancestors ever uses fire in even the most primitive fashion.

Fire was not really "discovered," of course, since its existence was obvious ever since Earth's atmosphere gained enough oxygen to sustain a fire, and Earth's land surface developed a forest-cover that could burn. This means that fire has existed for 400 million years.

Forest fires, if caused by nothing else, could be caused by lightning bolts. From such fires, then as now, any animal capable of fleeing would flee.

By the "discovery" of fire, then, we really mean its taming. At some time, *H. erectus* learned how to retrieve some burning object from the edge of a naturally caused fire, and how to keep it alive by feeding it fuel whenever the stolen fire showed signs of dying down.

Fire, after all, gave light when it was otherwise dark, and warmth when it was otherwise cold. This made it possible to extend activity into nighttime and winter, and for hominids to extend their range outside the tropics, for the first time.

Fire was also useful as protection against other animals, even the fiercest. A fire in a cave, or within a circle of stones would keep the predators away. If they weren't sufficiently intelligent to stay away in the first place, a close brush with a fire would teach them better at once, if they were at all teachable.

Then, too, fire made it possible to cook food. This is more important than it might appear. Meat was made more tender, and tastier, if roasted. What's more, roasting killed parasites and bacteria so that the meat was safer to eat. Fire also made some plant foods, otherwise too hard to eat, soft and edible.

At first, of course, fire could be obtained only after it had been started by natural means. Once one had a fire, it had to be kept burning continuously, and if it ever died out, then the search for another fire had to be instituted at once. If there were not a nearby tribe from which fire could be obtained (assuming they were friendly enough to grant it—and they probably would be, for it might be their turn next), then it would be necessary to wait for a natural fire again, and hope that conditions could be such that some could be taken home safely.

500,000 TO 300,000 YEARS AGO

By 300,000 years ago, hominids had developed who not only matched modern human beings in total weight but in brain-weight as well.

The first trace of such hominids was located in 1856 in the Neander Valley ("Neanderthal") in Germany. The hominids that left their fossilized bones there were called "Neanderthal men."

Their skulls were distinctly less human than our own. They had pronounced eyebrow ridges, large teeth, protruding jaws, a retreating forehead, and a smoothly receding chin—all rather resembling *H. erectus*. Neanderthals were shorter and stockier than we, and more muscular. Their brains were as large as ours, or even a little larger, but were differently proportioned, heavier in back and lighter in front.

They were at first termed *Homo neanderthalen-sis*, but they resembled us so closely, except for a few details of the skull, that they came to be considered members of our species, *Homo sapiens* (Latin for "wise man"). Nevertheless, they are thought of as a subspecies and are termed *Homo sapiens neanderthalensis*. It will be simpler to call them "Neanderthals."

300,000 TO 200,000 YEARS AGO

By now *H. erectus* was extinct, perhaps killed, in its turn, by the brainier and stronger Neanderthals. This meant that the Neanderthals were now the only hominids on Earth. They made their way into Europe, so that they were the first "Europeans."

The Neanderthals lived during glacial times and hunted the mammoth, the woolly rhinoceros, and the giant cave bear. Their stone tools were greater in variety, and more delicate and precise than had ever been seen before. They definitely knew how to start fires where no fire had existed before.

The Neanderthals were the first hominids to bury their dead. Earlier hominids, like animals generally, simply left their dead lying where they had fallen, so that they were scavenged by carrion-eaters and what was left over rotted.

The fact that Neanderthals buried their dead, thus preserving them from scavengers, if not from decay bacteria, tends to show that they valued life somehow, and felt affection and care for individuals even though they were dead. Sometimes, the dead were old and crippled and could only have lived on with the loving help of others of the tribe.

What's more, food and flowers were often buried with the corpse, which may mean that Neanderthals felt that, in some way, life continued on after death.

200,000 TO 50,000 YEARS AGO

Toward the end of this period, "modern man," whose formal species name is *Homo sapiens sapiens*, appeared on the scene. Exactly where he originated, we don't know. Modern men were taller, more slender, and less muscular than the Neanderthals. The brains of modern men were a little smaller than that of the Neanderthals, but were larger in the forepart. This, we are free to think (but don't really know), gave modern man an intellectual advantage and made him better able to indulge in abstract thought and elaborate speech.

50,000 TO 30,000 YEARS AGO

For 20,000 years, perhaps the two varieties of *Homo sapiens* coexisted. They may even, on occasion, have interbred. By about 30,000 years ago, however, the Neanderthals were gone. Once again, the less advanced was, presumably, wiped out by the more advanced.

From this time on, we will not speak of hominids, but of human beings or of people, for it will be understood that all people on Earth today, and for the last 30,000 years, are members of a single species, *Homo sapiens sapiens*, and can freely interbreed whatever the superficial differences in appearance and behavior might be.

30,000 TO 25,000 YEARS AGO

Until this time, hominids had been confined to what is called the "World Island"—Africa, Asia, and Europe, together with some offshore islands.

Sometime before 25,000 years ago, human beings took advantage of a low sea-level at the height of one of the periodic glaciations to cross over into North America and into Australia. In time, all the land was penetrated as far as Tierra del Fuego at the southern tip of South America; and Tasmania, the island off the southeastern coast of Australia.

Antarctica was the only continental mass to remain out of bounds of human penetration until contemporary times.

25,000 TO 20,000 YEARS AGO

Human beings, as hunters, developed rituals to improve their success. One way, apparently, was to draw pictures of animals being successfully hunted, in the conviction, perhaps, that life would imitate art, or that the spirits that animated animals would be mollified in this way and would cooperate.

In 1879, a Spanish archeologist, Marcellino de Sautuola (d. 1888), was excavating Altamira cave in northern Spain, when his 12-year-old daughter, who was with him, spied paintings on the dimly lit ceiling and cried out "Bulls! Bulls!" There were paintings of bison, deer, and other animals, in red and black, drawn perhaps as long as 20,000 years ago.

So excellent was the art that many people refused to believe it was truly ancient. Many felt it to be a fraud of some sort, and a modern hoax. It was only with the finding of other caves, and other examples, that the art was finally accepted as ancient.

By that time, people may also have invented the oil lamp, which provided a portable light that could be carried easily from place to place, and that allowed the cave paintings to be drawn. The bow and arrow may also have been invented. This allowed animals to be attacked from a greater distance and, hence, with greater security.

20,000 TO 14,000 YEARS AGO

Fossil remains of dogs have been found in human-occupied caves; the oldest date back some 14,000 years.

How dogs came to be domesticated is not known. My own guess is that children were responsible. A child could form a close bond with a puppy that had been abandoned, or that was picked up after the mother was killed, either in self-defense or as food. Once the bond was formed, the child would object to the use of the puppy as food, and parents might oblige.

It would quickly have turned out that dogs, being hunters and pack animals, would accept a human master as the pack leader. The dog would go hunting with his master, help in tracking and killing the game, and would then wait for the human being to take what he wanted and be satisfied with a minor share for himself.

In this way, human beings, for the first time, obtained the services of another species.

14,000 TO 12,000 YEARS AGO

The domestication of the dog may have led to the notion of other forms of domestication. By 12,000 years ago, goats may have been domesticated in the Middle East.

The goats would be cared for, fed, and encouraged to reproduce. They could supply milk, butter, and cheese. By dint of judicious culling, they could produce meat as well. What's more, since goats ate grass and other substances humans found inedible, the food supply was increased at no cost. (Dogs had to be given food that would otherwise fill human stomachs.)

In the 18,000 years since modern men had made their appearance (three fifths of their entire history), they had obtained their food by gathering plants and hunting animals, as hominids had done for millions of years, and as other predators had always done.

Now, for the first time, human beings had discovered a way of hoarding food (in the form of domesticated herds of animals) and of making it available for use without hunting. It meant a great increase in security and allowed an increase in population.

(We have now reached a point where we can switch to the usual method of marking the years. What I have called "12,000 years ago" is 10,000 B.C. From now on, then, we will count the years as "B.C." and, eventually, of course, as "A.D.")

10,000 TO 8,000 B.C.

During this period, the last period of glaciation that Earth has experienced (so far) was drawing to its close. The glaciers were receding, and Earth's climate was beginning to approach what it is today.

With the glaciers gone, great changes came about. The Sahara Desert, for instance, once a lush grassland, began to dry out and become a desert. The land-bridges joining Asia with North America in the north, and with Australia in the south, were drowned. The people, who had now occupied the Americas and Australia were separated from the main population on the World Island and would remain separated for over 9000 years.

The shores of the Arctic Ocean were gradually being cleared of a permanent ice-cover, and the people we now know as Inuits (Eskimos), Lapps, and Siberians were drifting northward.

The region we now know as the Middle East, the land that borders the eastern Mediterranean Sea, the Caspian Sea, and the Persian Gulf, was the most advanced technologically. Why that should be is not certain, but it is the people of that region who first domesticated the dog, and then the goat. And it is they who would make further advances.

The most important advance involved the domestication of plants. With the retreat of the glaciers and the changing of the climate, large stands of wild grain grew throughout the Middle East.

Somewhere about 8000 B.C., in what is now northern Iraq, people learned how to cultivate the grains which we now know as wheat and barley. They planted seeds deliberately, pulled up competing plants ("weeds"), frightened off animals that might want to eat it, did their best

to see that water was supplied when the plants needed it, and, finally, when the grain was ripe, harvested it and roasted it for food. The grains could also be ground into a flour that kept without spoiling for a long time if the outer layer was removed. The flour could then be baked into a nourishing, long-lasting, hard, flat bread.

In the process, naturally, enough grain would be saved and set aside for seed for the next growing season.

This period, in which herding and agriculture came into use, is called the "New Stone Age" or (in Latin) the "Neolithic Age." The advances in this period are sometimes referred to as the "Neolithic Revolution."

The invention of agriculture, like that of herding, supplied more food for the population engaged in it. Agriculture, however, was far superior to herding in this respect. Animals convert plant life into meat, but in doing so, they preserve only a small amount of the energy available in the plants. If human beings feed on plants directly, much more food energy is available to them than if they feed on animals that feed on plants.

Agricultural populations, therefore, increased markedly and, in fact, the invention of agriculture led to the first "population explosion" of mankind. The hominid population, which had been increasing very slowly through all the millions of years of their existence, quickly moved upward once agriculture was established. The population of the world reached about 5 million by this time.

There were disadvantages, of course. Farming was tedious and back-breaking work, which had none of the glamor and excitement of hunting; and it is easy to believe that farmers looked back on the tales of the hunting of their ancestors, and viewed the hunting of those neighbors of theirs who were not engaged in agriculture with a certain nostalgic envy. They must have viewed agriculture as a kind of slavery foisted upon them, which even the use of animal labor didn't do much to mitigate.

It is not surprising that so many agricultural communites told of a "Golden Age," when human beings hunted and gathered in freedom and comparative idleness, and wondered what had happened to evict them and force them to earn their bread by the sweat of their brow. The Hebrew tale of Eden and of the sin that caused God to curse man with agriculture is the best-known of these tales.

Then, too, Adam's first two sons are depicted as Cain, a farmer, and Abel, a herdsman. The farmers increased in population faster than the herdsmen did, since the farms supplied much more food than the herds did, so we can well imagine that areas devoted to farming spread, and steadily took up space that had earlier been freely used by herdsmen. (The same thing happened in the American west, when the farmers settled the land and fenced in their plots to the discomfiture of the cowboys.) No wonder the Bible pictures Cain as killing Abel.

Yet no matter how people might dislike farming and no matter how they might long for a happier, freer day, there was no way in which agriculture could be abandoned. The population of an agricultural region quickly reached a height that could not be supported in any other way. To abandon agriculture and to try to feed the population by herding or hunting meant mass starvation. Agriculture, with all its faults, gave people a reasonable chance of full stomachs.

Agriculture brought another change, too. Hominids had been wandering people ("nomads"), seeking out plants, or following game. Even when herding began, the herdsmen had to wander to find good pasture for their animals. In fact, the word *nomad* is from a Greek word for "pasture."

Herdsmen or hunters could not remain in one place, for the plant life would all be eaten, and the animal life would be killed or scared off.

There had to be an endless search for new ground, with a return to old grounds only after enough time had been given them to recover.

For nomads, there could be no possessions that were not portable; nothing that could not be abandoned at need; nothing that would correspond to "home," except for temporary sites.

Some such sites, to be sure, if particularly well-situated, might have gained a kind of semi-permanence, and it would be in those places where it would be easier to develop agriculture since the growing of plants would be useless if nomads did not remain where they were for at least a few months.

Once agriculture had been established, however, there was no question of "temporary" or even "semipermanent" sites. Now there were plots of land that had been cleared of weeds, that had been planted, that had to be tended, and that *could not be moved*. One might not even be able to abandon one plot for another because not all plots were equally desirable. You needed good soil and a ready supply of water, and if that was what you had, you held on to it. What's more, as the population grew, the whole fertile region was divided up into family plots. You had to hang on to yours.

Furthermore, because plots were, above all, immovable, farmers, unlike all preceding generations, had to adopt a completely sedentary life. They had to stay in one place. The notion of "property" arose for the first time.

In a way, this, too, added to security, since there was no need to find a new source of food periodically with, always, the chance of not finding a satisfactory one till half the tribe had starved. Now, there was the reliable plot that had supported you all your life, that had supported your father before you and your son after you.

Agriculture meant another change, too. In the days of nomadism, one roving band might meet another and there might be a quarrel as to which band had the right to exploit the area. The matter might degenerate to a mutual display of force. The force, however, could rarely be deadly, because it would quickly become apparent that one band was stronger than the other. The weaker, foreseeing inevitable defeat, would retreat, abandon the area, and search for another. There was nothing in any one area that was worth their lives.

Farmers, however, did not have the choice of retreating. They grew food and usually possessed stores to feed them over the winter, when plant life did not grow. Other farmers, whose harvest had for some reason failed, or nomads, who did not engage in agriculture, might well view the stores with greedy eyes and see no reason why they should not appropriate it if they could.

The farmers, defending their immovable farms, now had no choice but to stand and fight. They had to risk defeat, to be followed by death or enslavement, since the alternative was to abandon their farms and die of starvation or sell themselves into slavery in return for food.

Thus, the coming of agriculture also meant, eventually, the coming of organized warfare.

If farmers had to fight, and they learned soon enough they would have to, it was only prudent to take measures to make defeat less likely. It would have been most risky to remain scattered among their farms where they could easily be destroyed a family at a time.

Instead, the natural move was to collect together, setting up homes in a tightly packed fashion, homes from which they could move outward to their farms by day and return by night. It was to those homes they could fly at the first sign of a threatened attack and, fighting together, they might hold off the enemy.

The chances of doing so were increased if they set their home on an elevation so that the enemy would have to hurl their missiles upward, while the defenders hurled them downward. The homes should include a spring that would serve as a dependable water supply and there would have to be food-stores. And, of course, it would help if a wall were built about the homes.

In short, once agriculture was instituted, the "city" was sure to follow.

Prior to agriculture, human beings had grouped together in tribes (i.e., extended families) and had wandered. After agriculture, they grouped together in cities, and stayed put.

It meant less individual space, less freedom of movement, more complicated arrangements for bringing in food, disposing of wastes, providing for the common defense—but it all led to greater security. As in almost every case, people were willing to trade freedom for security.

The city, plus the surrounding farms that belonged to the city-dwellers, made up a community that came to be called a "city-state."

Once a city-state was a going proposition, and a reasonable security was established, it was usually possible to grow more food than could easily be consumed, if everyone worked at it. Therefore, it became possible for some people *not* to be farmers, but to do other kinds of useful work. Some people might be artisans, specializing in the manufacture of tools and ornaments; some might be soldiers or merchants or supervisors. They did their work in return for food, while farmers paid with food for the services of these specialists. In short, a differentiated society came into being.

All benefitted and the standard of living advanced. Thus, the invention of agriculture had initiated a drive toward "urbanization" by 8000 B.C., a trend that is still continuing at breakneck speed today all over the world.

In Latin, the word for a city-dweller is *civis*. The adjective derived from *civis* is *civilis*, and the noun derived from *civilis* is *civilization*. In other words, "civilization" is the way of life in a society that has advanced to the point of building cities.

It would seem then that after modern man made his appearance, four fifths of his history was spent in a precivilized state, and it was only as the final fifth dawned that he became civilized.

Nor did civilization spread at once to all men. It began in isolated spots here and there, and from those spots spread out wider. It was not till recent times that it has spread to virtually all the Earth.

The beginning came in the Middle East. In northern Iraq, for instance, there are the remains of a very ancient city, founded perhaps in 8000 B.C., at a site called Jarmo. It is a low mound into which, beginning in 1948, the American archeologist, Robert J. Braidwood, dug carefully. He found the remains of foundations of houses built up of thin walls of packed mud and divided into small rooms. It may have held no more than 100 to 300 people.

Another city that may date back to the earliest days of agriculture is Jericho, near the Jordan River.

8000 TO 7000 B.C.

Technological advances tend to diffuse outward. For instance, if a group of people begin engaging in agriculture and are seen to be better off as a result, other people, who have occasion to observe this, begin to adopt agriculture themselves.

A person who has occasion to travel may observe something in one place and carry the news of it to another.

Therefore, both herding and agriculture (and other technological advances that came later) spread outward from their original sites.

In the case of agriculture, the spread was toward river banks. This made sense. The original sites where agriculture would be invented might have been in the shadow of a mountain range. The incoming winds, forced upward, would cool, and its load of water vapor would drop as rain.

Reliable rains meant a good harvest, but rains could never be counted upon to be reliable year after year. There were bound to be dry years and, therefore, poor harvests and famine.

One way out was to cultivate the land near a large flowing river. The river was a dependable and perpetual fresh-water supply, and no one would have to depend on the fickle rain.

The nearest large river to the places in northern Iraq where early agriculture was practiced was the Euphrates River and its twin, the Tigris River. The nearest large river to Palestine, where early agriculture was also practiced, was the Nile River.

By 7000 B.C., then, city-states were beginning to be established along the course of the Euphrates and the Nile.

There is, of course, a catch. When it rains, it rains all over the fields in which crops are growing. The farmer doesn't have to do anything. If the farmer depends on the river, however, he can wait indefinitely and find that the water in the river is not likely to come to the crops of its own accord (except when the river floods, and then the coming of water is disastrous.)

It is necessary, then, for the farmer to dig irrigation ditches into which the river-water can flow to water the crops. He must labor to keep the ditches dredged so that they won't silt up and lose their function. He must also build levees to hold the river back at times when it shows a tendency to flood.

Once again, then, farmers must accept additional labor as payment for increased security.

Irrigating the land is clearly a community endeavor, and it must be carefully organized and supervised. The city, in such cases, becomes more necessary than ever.

The river cities were only beginning to be important in 7000 B.C. The older cities still held pride of place. Jericho, in particular, had grown. It extended over an area of 10 acres and had a population of about 2500.

7000 TO 6000 B.C.

Despite the fact that the pace of advance in the early millennia of civilization seems glacially slow to us, the rate of movement was much greater than it had been in precivilized times. Indeed, the rate of change, the rate of diffusion of old advances and the rate of invention of new advances has increased steadily with time from the earliest days of hominids down to the very present.

By 6000 B.C., then, the practice of agriculture had spread west and north into Asia Minor and Greece. Nor was it just a matter of diffusion. There was independent invention, too. Rice was beginning to be cultivated in southeastern Asia.

New cities were overtaking the old. There was, for instance, a city at a site known to us now as Catalhuyuk, in south central Asia Minor. It may first have been settled in 6700 B.C., but it was at its peak in 6000 B.C., when it may have been the largest city in the world. This was shown in the early 1960s when the site was excavated by the British archeologist, James Mellaart. It covered 32 acres.

Remains found at Catalhuyuk showed the prominence of pottery. Pottery is an outstanding sort of relic at these ancient sites of civilization. This is partly because pottery was important and partly because, unlike other objects that may have been equally important, pottery easily survives over long periods of time.

Pottery arose out of the need to carry things. The natural carry-alls are the hands and the arms. Both are limited in their scope. What is needed is something that is larger than hands or bent arms. Objects might be carried in hides, but hides are inconvenient and heavy. Gourds might do, but they had to be taken as they came. Eventually, human beings learned to weave twigs or reeds into baskets. These were light and could be made in any shape.

Baskets would, however, only be useful in carrying solid, dry objects made up of particles considerably larger than the interstices of the weave. Baskets could not be used to carry flour or olive oil, for instance, or, most important, water.

It might seem natural to daub baskets with clay, which, upon drying, would cake the holes and make the basket solid. The dried mud, however, would tend to fall away, especially if the basket were shaken or struck. If the basket were placed in the sunlight and allowed to heat there, the mud would harden further and the basket might then become fairly serviceable.

But, then, why need the basket? Why not simply begin with clay, mold a container out of it, and let it dry in the sun. You would then have a pot made of crude earthenware—but these would be soft and not durable.

As even stronger heat was required, the earthenware was placed in fire. Fired earthenware (especially after methods for building particularly hot fires were worked out) became hard pottery, and its production represents the first use of fire for something other than light, heat, or cooking.

By 6000 B.C., pottery was a well-established product. Pottery made it possible not only to carry liquids but to cook meat in boiling water. In this way, stews and casseroles came into existence to supplement roasts.

The notion behind the weaving of twigs into baskets could be applied to fibers that were much thinner, provided they were sufficiently strong. Flax produces a fiber suitable for the purpose and flax was being cultivated well before 6000 B.C. It may well have been the first plant cultivated for a purpose other than food.

Flax fibers could be woven together to form a long thread, which we call "linen." (The importance of a linen thread as an example of something long and straight, can be gathered from the fact that the word "line" comes from linen.)

By now, the use of farms along river banks was becoming much more important, and rivers became important in other ways, too. The first use of linen may have been to interweave them in such a way as to form nets for fishing.

Eventually, very fine nets were made—in other words "cloth" or "textiles" (from a Latin word for "weaving"). The formation of cloth from linen and, eventually, from other plant or animal fibers, such as cotton or wool, revolutionized clothing.

Textiles were light materials. They were flexible, porous, and could be easily cleaned. They have remained the preferred material for clothing ever since.

Life by a river meant that some means of tra- versing it had to be found. It must have been observed long, long before that wood floats. By 6000 B.C., people seemed to have learned to lash logs together to form rafts. This would keep them safely on the surface of quiet bodies of water and enable them to fish more efficiently than from the shore. By paddling, in fact, with their hands—if nothing else—they could even cross small stretches of water.

About this time, too, the wild ox had been tamed, and this was the ancestor of modern do- mestic cattle, which became perhaps the most important food animal in the world.

6000 TO 5000 B.C.

In the course of this period, a new group of peo- ple, the Sumerians, began to enter the Tigris– Euphrates valley. Civilization had existed there for some 3000 years by this time, but the Sumer- ians picked up the ball and carried it much fur- ther. They were the first to develop what we might refer to as a "high" civilization.

Where they came from, we don't know. Their language is not related to any other, so that we can't trace relationships. We can only be grateful to them.

For instance, they found the beginnings of ag- riculture along the river bank and took it over, and by 5000 B.C. had established working city- states along the lower course of the Euphrates river, beginning to make full use of irrigation. The southeasternmost portion of the valley is usually referred to as "Sumeria" at this time. (The Bible calls it "Shinar.")

To make sure that the cities were properly or- ganized and their complexities working effi- ciently, the rulers of the Sumerian city-states had to gain unquestioned authority. The logical way was to associate the ruler with the divine. He became a priest-king, capable of interceding with the gods on behalf of his people, in order to make sure that all the affairs of the city would remain prosperous.

A priestly hierarchy was established to serve as the bureaucracy of the city-state. Temples were built as homes for the gods and priests, as repositories for government records, storehouses for grain, and so on. Religion had become insti- tutionalized and made to support the state, which has been its usual function ever since.

The same advances in river agriculture and as- sociated religious institutions were now in full swing along the Nile River, too.

There were advances in other parts of the world as well. In the Andean region of north- western South America, the llama and alpaca (small American relatives of the camel of Asia and Africa) were domesticated. In Mexico, cotton and avocados were grown. Dates were grown in south Asia, and in the steppes north of the Black Sea, the horse was domesticated.

Along the Euphrates, too, people learned how to make use of the wind to power ships. By hoisting sails, wind was trapped against a large area and this tended to drive ships forward when there was no current, or even against a current.

5000 TO 4000 B.C.

James Ussher had calculated that the Creation had taken place in 4004 B.C., toward the end of this period. It was a ludicrously late date for the event. By 4004 B.C., civilization had been progressing for 4000 years; and human beings of the modern type had been in existence for at least 24,000 years.

About 4000 B.C., the Sumerians founded the city of Ur at the mouth of the Euphrates. (In those days, the Euphrates and the Tigris entered the Persian Gulf separately. In the 6000 years since, however, silt has filled in the gulf for about 150 miles, so that the remains of Ur are now that far from the sea. In those 150 miles of silt, the Tigris and Euphrates have flowed together and now the combined river flows 50 miles or so into the retreated coastline of the Gulf.)

For considerable periods of time, Ur was the most important city in Sumeria, and may have been the largest city in the world. (World population may have reached 85 million by 4000 B.C.) Our knowledge of Ur, and of Sumeria in general, arose in the 1920s, thanks to the work of the British archeologist, Charles Leonard Wooley (1880–1960).

By this time, people in the Middle East had learned about the fermentation of grape juice and of soaked barley (probably by accident to begin with), so that wine and beer were beginning to come into use. Undoubtedly, these drinks were popular because they induced intoxication and, in moderation, this felt good.

Such beverages were important in another way, although the early drinkers could scarcely be aware of it. Alcohol tended to kill microorganisms, so that drinking wine and beer was safer than drinking water which might be contaminated with human or animal wastes.

An important advance had its beginnings now. For some two million years, ever since *H. habilis* had come on the scene, the most advanced material for the manufacture of tools and weapons were stones of one sort or another, so

that the entire period of hominid history prior to 4000 B.C. might be termed the "Stone Age." This phrase was first used by the Roman poet, Titus Lucretius Carus (95–55 B.C.), about 60 B.C., and was then reintroduced in 1834 by the Danish archeologist, Christian Jurgenson Thomsen (1788–1865).

Occasionally, pebbles were found that were not like other pebbles. These unusual pebbles were shiny and were heavier than ordinary ones. What's more, if these shiny pebbles were struck with a stone hammer, they did not split or shatter as ordinary pebbles did, but underwent a simple distortion of shape. They were "malleable."

These unusual pebbles are examples of "metals." There are dozens of different metals known, but most of them remain in combination with nonmetallic substances and form the ordinary rocks and pebbles all about us. Only those metals that are inert and tend not to combine with other substances are likely to be found free. The three inert metals most likely to be found free are rare, even for metals. These are copper, silver, and gold. Their rareness is shown by the fact that the very word *metal* is from a Greek term meaning "to search for."

Metal nuggets, when found, were used almost exclusively for ornaments after being pounded into attractive shapes. (The lure of ornamentation must have preceded metals, too, and shaped wood, bone, and shells were probably also used for the purpose. Metals were more durable, however, were considered more attractive, and were —an important consideration—rare.)

It was only when human beings discovered that metals could be obtained from special rocks called "ores" that they became common enough for other purposes.

Copper is substantially more common than silver and gold, and it exists in certain ores to a far greater extent than silver and gold do. The most common copper ore is a kind of copper carbonate, which is blue and which contains (as the name indicates) carbon as well as copper.

Undoubtedly, the discovery of metal ores was accidental at first. A wood fire might have been built on a bed of rock that happened to contain copper ore. Under the heat of the fire, the carbon in the wood and in the ore would combine with oxygen in the ore and in the atmosphere to form the gas, carbon dioxide, which would escape, leaving metallic copper behind. Some observant person might notice the reddish globules among the ashes of the fire, and, eventually, the circumstances were understood. The ores were searched for and deliberately treated in such a way as to obtain metal.

Here was another use of fire. It made possible "metallurgy"—the obtaining of metals from their ores.

Like all such advances in early times, knowledge of the new technique diffused outward slowly. In this case, diffusion stopped at the edge of the ocean. Metallurgy never reached the people in the Americas or in Australia; nor did those people happen to discover the technique independently.

Meanwhile, civilization itself continued to spread outward. A third river valley was developing into a home for city-states. This was the Indus river, which flows through what we now call Pakistan. In 1921 and 1922, remains of such an early civilization were found along that river by the British archeologist, John Hubert Marshall (1876–1958).

From this point on, as known events multiply and as history unfolds in increasing detail, I shall consider progressively smaller intervals of time.

In addition, I will divide each interval into events taking place in particular geographic sections. I won't follow any fixed order in doing so, but will be guided roughly by the necessity of telling a connected story so that a region of central importance will be considered first. Naturally, I will have to be the judge as to what is of central importance, and I cannot help but attach particular importance to those historical events which have influenced Western culture, which is my culture and that of most of my readers—and which, in good truth, has more strongly influenced the world as a whole in the last several centuries than has any other.

4000 TO 3500 B.C.

SUMERIA

When copper was obtained from ore, it meant that there was a much greater supply for ornamentation, but it was not, at first, very useful as a material for tools.

This might well have seemed disappointing to early metallurgists. After all, if a sharp-edged piece of rock blunted its edge, that edge cannot be restored without laborious chipping. More likely, the rock tool has to be discarded and a new one must be shaped. If a sharp-edged piece of copper is blunted, however, it can simply and easily be beaten sharp again.

The difficulty was, however, that while stone was hard and might survive quite a long period of use (with care) without being blunted, copper was much softer and every minor use bent and blunted it.

Not all copper seemed to be the same, however. Copper obtained from some ores was harder than from others. The reason was that copper ore is not necessarily pure; it might be mixed with rocks that, on being heated, released another substance that would mix with copper to form an "alloy."

At first, such mixtures consisted of copper mixed with arsenic, but arsenic is poisonous and people who worked with it fell sick. Such mixed ores were abandoned, therefore (perhaps the first known case in which worker safety was a factor in technology).

Fortunately, another type of ore mixture was discovered that also resulted in the forming of hard copper. In this case, it was the use of tin ore that did the trick, and the hard copper was actually a copper-tin alloy. The alloy was called "bronze" (possibly from a Persian word for "copper").

Bronze was hard enough to compete with rock, could hold an edge better, and could be beaten back into shape if necessary.

The Sumerians began to use bronze tools and, about 3500 B.C., entered the "Bronze Age." To be sure, bronze was used sparingly at first, and stone continued to be the most common material for tools. As a result, the early centuries of the Bronze Age are sometimes called the "Chalcolithic Age" (which is Greek for "copper-stone age").

Another enormous advance introduced by the clever Sumerians was the wheel. Its first use may possibly have been as the "potter's wheel." In making pottery, clay was, to begin with, molded into shape by hand, with the result that the shape was not necessarily smooth or symmetrical. The pots were likely to be ugly and wobbly.

Someone in the Mideast, however, had the inspiration of setting the clay on a flat rock with a depression at the center of the lower surface that might pivot on a projection beneath and be set to turning rapidly. If a blob of clay is set on the flat rock, a touch of the hand would produce a smooth and symmetrical curve. Making use of a potter's wheel produced beautiful pottery in far less time than anything produced by hand.

The existence of the potter's wheel made it possible to see a way of simplifying transport.

It was always possible to pile objects on some sort of wooden sledge and then drag it along the ground. That meant that most of the work done was simply spent in overcoming the friction that resisted the drag. Even the use of oxen rather than men could not make it anything but a slow and arduous labor.

It could be made easier if crude rollers, such as wooden logs, were placed under the sledge. The rollers turned rather than dragged, and that cut down on friction considerably. However, rollers had to be picked up from the back and put down again in front and that quickly grew tiresome.

The use of wheels at the ends of two axles, one front and one back, suspended from leather straps that were attached to the sledge, might allow the sledge to roll while the wheels always remained attached. About 3500 B.C., animal-drawn wheeled carts were in use in Sumeria.

The Sumerians also began to use oars to propel ships against the Euphrates' current when the wind refused to cooperate.

Instead of simply digging little holes in the soil and dropping seeds into the ground, the Sumerians began to use plows dragged by donkeys or oxen. These had a sharp edge that scraped up the soil, loosening and aerating it. Seeds, which could be scattered through the loose soil, then grew more easily and rapidly.

EGYPT

Egypt was very fortunate in its possession of the Nile. Not only was it a source of water for a rainless land, but it flooded annually and fertilized the land in a kind of automatic irrigation.

In addition, its current was gentle and there were no storms, so that it was easy to float on it safely. What's more, the river flows almost due north, while the wind almost always blows due south. Therefore, a boat can be carried smoothly down river (northward) by the current, and returned up river (southward) by means of sails.

Egypt lacked forests, but it had luxuriant stands of reeds (called "papyrus") along the river in those days, and the reeds could be used in bundles to build a boat. (When Moses was set afloat in the Nile River, according to the Biblical account, he was placed in a little boat, or "ark," made of "bulrushes"—that is, of papyrus.)

This particularly easy form of communication served to unite the various city-states along the Nile, giving them a common language, a common culture, and a common world-outlook. The ease of trade enriched them all and the region had long periods of peace such as no other region ever experienced.

The city-states of the Nile delta, a triangular section in the north, formed a loose union called "Lower Egypt" (since it was down river), while the city-states of the narrow Nile south of the delta, which was upstream, was "Upper Egypt."

ELSEWHERE

Cities were beginning to make their first beginning in China, some 45 centuries after they had begun to appear in the Middle East. These cities appeared along the lower course of the Hwang-Ho River.

3500 TO 3000 B.C.

SUMERIA

In Sumeria, which was the most advanced and complex civilization in the world at this time, life had to be more complex, too. People had to keep track of the grain they produced, of how much they traded, of what other products they manufactured, and of what was contributed to the common fund ("taxes").

It became more and more difficult to keep it all in mind, and it was necessary to keep score. Almost anyone can think of making some sort of mark in the ground to stand for each basket full of fruit and, then, eventually, counting the marks in order to know how many baskets had been delivered.

As memory became strained, such marks were indeed made, and the Sumerians had begun this practice soon after 3500 B.C. Different marks might be made for numbers of different size, so that there wouldn't be too many unit-marks to count. The Sumerians worked out number systems based on 12, 60, and 360 eventually, because these numbers could be divided evenly in many ways and this lessened the chances of having to work with fractions. To this day, we have 12 units to the dozen, 60 minutes to the hour, and 360 degrees to the circle—all dating back to the Sumerians.

Aside from numbers, there might be special marks that meant "fruit," "grain," "man," and so on. By 3100 B.C., the Sumerians had a system of writing that could communicate anything they wanted to say. It was the first system of writing in the world.

The Sumerians made the marks of their writing by punching a stylus at an angle into soft clay, and then baking the clay to make the writing permanent. This made wedge-shaped marks, and it was later called *cuneiform*, from Greek words meaning "wedge-shaped."

The marks began as crude pictures of whatever was being talked about; however, as time went on, the symbols became more stylized and somewhat simpler and lost their pictorial representations. Nevertheless, each symbol stood for a word, more or less, so that there were always hundreds and even thousands of different symbols that someone had to memorize if one wanted to read and write.

This meant that the literates were always a small minority of the population, and a small and highly valued class of people arose, the "scribes," who undertook to read and write for the general population.

Writing made an enormous difference. It was a kind of frozen speech. Thoughts and records remained much more permanent when written than when transmitted by the spoken word. If carefully copied, now and then, writing persists indefinitely and remains more precise than the memory of the spoken word usually is.

This meant that each generation could learn, more precisely and more quickly, the accumulated experience and wisdom of the previous generation. The rate of advance quickened as a result.

Furthermore, the records kept in writing give us a reasonably exact version of events that took place in the past, complete with names, places, and details (provided we allow for self-serving lies). In order to understand what went on in a society without writing, we must try to interpret matters from the artifacts they left behind—from their art, their pottery, even their garbage.

Therefore, a society that possesses writing is "historic." One that does not is "prehistoric." In other words, human history begins with Sumeria not long before 3000 B.C. Thus, the first 5000 years of civilization were prehistoric and only the last 5000 have been historic.

Indeed, human beings could now be divided into two classes—the settled, literate, technologically advanced city-dwellers, and the tribal nomads who lacked agriculture and writing. Frequently, the tribal peoples attempted to invade and take over the far richer territories of the city-dwellers, but when they did, they also took over the culture, so that even when the city-dwellers lost, civilization usually won, even though a "dark age" might be temporarily experienced.

Beginning in 3000 B.C., for instance, a group of people called Akkadians drifted into the Tigris–Euphrates valley along the northern fringes of Sumeria. They spoke a language entirely unrelated to Sumerian, one of a group that we call "Semitic" today, because the people who speak it are described, by the Bible, as having been descended from Shem, the oldest son of Noah.

The Akkadians adopted aspects of Sumerian culture. They adopted the Sumerian system of writing, for instance, and modified it to make it suitable for their own language. The region, after 3000 B.C., is sometimes referred to as "Sumer-Akkad" for that reason.

EGYPT

Egypt quickly picked up the notion of writing from the Sumerians, but invented a different set of signs, as complicated, in its way, as the cunei-

form. The Egyptian writing is called *hieroglyphic* (from Greek words meaning "priestly writing"), because the Greeks later came into contact with it, mostly, in Egyptian temples. The Egyptian writing was brushed onto thin, flexible sheets of papyrus pith.

As in Sumeria, there was a multiplication and growth of city-states along the river. As city-states enlarged their boundaries and grew more populous, their territories were bound to run into each other and their interdependence grew.

As the occasion for antagonism increased with mutual crowding, the need for cooperation also increased. The irrigation system could not be controlled efficiently in bits and pieces. Different city-states had to act together.

The city-states of the triangular Nile delta, downstream, formed a loose union known as "lower Egypt," while those upstream to the south of the delta made up "upper Egypt." About 3100 B.C., the two regions were united under the rule of Narmer (known as Menes, to the Greeks). He was intelligent enough to found a new capital, Memphis, at the southern end of the delta, right on the border of Upper and Lower Egypt, so that neither region would seem to be dominating the other. It kept the two halves together long enough to establish a national identity.

Narmer was the first king of the "First Dynasty." (An Egyptian priest, Manetho, about 250 B.C., wrote a history of Egypt and divided its rulers into dynasties, each dynasty representing a family whose members ruled over Egypt for a period of time.)

The union was probably carried out by force, but, if so, it worked, for the Egyptian city-states shared a common language and culture. They melted together with less trouble than might have been expected and formed a "nation." It was the first nation the world had seen.

Partly, this worked because Egypt was bounded by a desert on the west, by the Red Sea on the east, by the Mediterranean Sea on the north, and by a more or less impenetrable jungle on the south. For a long time, the only route over which possible invaders might come was from Asia by way of the Sinai peninsula, and for a long time they didn't come. Egypt could, therefore, develop in peace, something other nations rarely had a chance to do.

CANAAN

Canaan is the land along the shore of the eastern end of the Mediterranean Sea. It was among the oldest centers of civilization for it was there that Jericho had existed. It was located between the civilizations of Egypt and of Sumer-Akkad, and its people served as middlemen in trade between these two sections. That always means prosperity, since middlemen can skim the profits in either direction.

An alternate name for Canaan, especially for cities along the shore, was "Phoenicia." This was used by the Greeks from their word for "purple," because in later centuries a purple dye was manufactured there. The northern portion of Canaan came to be called "Syria" in later times; this again being a Greek name, taken from that of a tribe that lived in the region.

ASIA MINOR

Asia Minor is the peninsula in western Asia that is now occupied by the nation of Turkey. It may also be called Anatolia. Catalhuyuk had flourished there, but that town had declined and disappeared, and other city-states now existed there. In the northwest corner, the first signs of a city began to appear that was eventually to be known as Troy.

ELSEWHERE

To the east of Sumeria, was Elam, with its capital at Susa, which was beginning to absorb Sumerian civilization. Still farther to the east, agriculture was beginning on the Indus River in what is now Pakistan. Farther east still, the city-states of the Hwang-Ho in China were growing.

Civilization was moving into Europe, too, for the island of Crete, which lies south of Greece, was beginning to be affected by civilization from Egypt.

3000 TO 2500 B.C.

EGYPT

Once union had been achieved, without undue bloodshed, Egypt became the most prosperous and most advanced nation in the world. As an example, the calendar, essentially the one we use today, was invented in Egypt, probably in this time period.

People have always been aware of the alternation of day and night, of the cycle of the Moon's phases, and of the cycle of the seasons (the day, the month, and the year, respectively).

In the days of hunting and gathering, attention had to be paid to the cycles because animals underwent seasonal migrations and it wouldn't do to be caught by surprise. In the days of agriculture, the cycles were even more important if

you wanted to be sure of planting and harvesting at the right times.

The phases of the Moon were particularly convenient. The month was neither too long nor too short, and the cycle of phases could be followed easily. It turned out that there were 12 new moons in the cycle of the season (12 months to the year), but this was not exact. Every once in a while a 13th month had to be added to the year to keep it even with the seasons. This began with the Sumerians, and eventually, a 19-year period was worked out in which certain years had 12 months and certain others had 13, and this kept reasonably exact pace with the seasons, but it was complicated. This calendar was passed on to the Greeks and to the Jews, and is still used today in Judaism.

The Egyptians, however, went by the flooding of the Nile, which took place once a year (because of the melting of ice in mountain ranges to the south, but the Egyptians didn't know that).

Close observation showed that the time from Nile flood to Nile flood averaged 365 days, so the Egyptians established a year of 365 days divided into 12 months of 30 days each (paying no attention to the phases of the Moon) plus five extra days that belonged to no month.

This "solar calendar" may have been worked out some time about 2800 B.C. With some modifications, it is still used today.

Thanks to the Nile, and to the unification of the nation, food production was efficient and copious and the Egyptian rulers could put the people to work on public projects designed to show the greatness of the ruler and, through him, of the nation and the people. They were also intended to serve as memorials to their power and to impress, suitably, both foreigners and future generations.

Thus, the Egyptian rulers built elaborate houses (or "palaces," as we now call them). Indeed, the ruler eventually came to be referred to as *pharaoh*, which is the Greek version of an Egyptian word meaning "big house."

The Egyptian rulers also built elaborate tombs for themselves in which their mummified bodies could be preserved. The feeling was that if the king's body were preserved so that it could live forever in the afterworld, the nation that he represented in god-like splendor would also flourish, and all Egyptians would benefit. For that reason, the pharaohs had oblong objects ("mastabas") built as secure tombs where they might lie, along with a sampling of their precious possessions that would be kept safe from the depredations of tomb robbers. (Nevertheless, the depredations always took place.)

In 2650 B.C., when Zoser, the first king of the Third Dynasty came to power, they decided to build a particularly elaborate tomb as a memorial to his greatness. His councillor, Imhotep, supervised the building of six mastabas of stone, one on top of the other, each smaller than the one below. Because these setbacks were like steps a giant might use in climbing to the top, the struc-

ture is called the "Step Pyramid." The base is an oblong about 400 by 350 feet, and the top is almost 200 feet high.

The Step Pyramid was the first large stone structure ever built and, since it still exists, it is the oldest large human-made structure in the world today.

The Step Pyramid set a fashion and, for a couple of centuries afterward, the pharaohs kept the people busy in their spare time building more and more elaborate pyramids. Far larger blocks were used than in the case of the Step Pyramid, and the structures were built with smooth receding sides from a square base, and then faced with slabs to make the sides smooth and bright. (The outer facing is long since gone, but the underlying blocks remain.)

The climax came when the pharaoh, Khufu (Cheops, to the Greeks), of the Fourth Dynasty, supervised the construction of the "Great Pyramid," the largest of all, in about 2530 B.C. When that pyramid was finished, its square base was 755 feet on each side, so that it covered an area of 13 acres. It was composed of 2,300,000 large blocks that weighed on the average of 2.5 tons apiece. The whole structure reached its uppermost point at a height of 481 feet.

This was Egypt at an early climax of its power and its population, which may have numbered about 2 million people.

Afterward, the fad for such large, vainglorious structures did not persist for long. They took too much time and too much work, even for Egypt; however, the pyramids still stand today as a remarkable testimony to what could be done with the simplest of tools, by sheer human muscle and ingenuity. It would be a hard job to pile up those rocks even today.

SUMERIA

In 3000 B.C., the Sumerian cities were prosperous. The city of Uruk (the Biblical "Erech"), about 75 miles upstream from Ur, was perhaps the leading Sumerian city of its time and was ruled by the legendary Gilgamesh. He is supposed to have built a brick wall about the city that was six miles in circumference.

Temples were then in the process of becoming "ziggurats." These were made of brick and were square or rectangular. Each had a smaller structure on it and a still smaller one on that. There might be five or more stages making it a kind of "step pyramid." Ziggurats had no internal chambers, but there were external stairs that the priests ascended and descended.

The Biblical tale of the Tower of Babel refers to the building of a tall ziggurat, and the tale of Jacob's dream of angels ascending and descending a ladder stretching from Earth to Heaven may also have been inspired by one.

However, the Sumerian cities received a rude shock from which they may never have completely recovered, and by 2500 B.C., Sumeria had definitely fallen behind Egypt in wealth and prosperity. What had happened was an unlooked-for natural disaster.

When Woolley was exploring the remains of the Sumerian cities, he came across a layer of silt, 11 feet thick, with no relics or artifacts anywhere in it. He decided that the silt must have been laid down by a huge flood.

After all, rivers do flood occasionally, and sometimes they flood to an unusual height, if rains are particularly heavy or winter snows in the mountains melt at an unusual rate. If this is combined with a neglected set of levees, the result can be unmitigated disaster. Woolley estimated that the silt he had found had been produced by a flood that was 25 feet deep and that covered a stretch of land 300 miles long by 100 miles wide. In short, virtually all of Sumeria may have been covered, and this may have taken place in 2800 B.C.

The death-rate must have been very high; and to the Sumerians, very few of whom knew much about the world outside of Sumeria, it must have seemed that the whole world was covered with water, and that the flood was a universal deluge.

A Sumerian legend of the Flood sprang up, and this turned out to be the world's first known epic. Our most complete version dates from a time more than 2000 years after the Flood, but older scraps also survive, from which much of the epic can be reconstructed.

The hero is Gilgamesh, who had been king of Uruk, to whose historic personality the fictional tale of the epic was added. A close friend of his had died, and he decided to try to find the secret of immortality. After a complicated search, he came upon Ut-Napishtim, who, at the time of the Flood, had built a large vessel in which he had saved himself and his family. Not only was Ut-Napishtim saved, but the gods also gave him the gift of eternal life. Ut-Napishtim directed Gilgamesh to the whereabouts of a certain magic plant. If Gilgamesh obtained the plant and ate it, he, too, would be immortal. He found the plant, but, before he could eat it, it was stolen by a serpent and Gilgamesh remained mortal.

It is clear that from that epic of Gilgamesh, which must have been popular throughout the Middle East, the Hebrews eventually got their tale of Noah, and part of their tale of Adam and Eve.

Sumeria's population may have been as high as 1.25 million before the Flood, and rather less than that afterward. As the various city-states tried to recover from the catastrophe, there was a tendency for each to try to grab as much territory as possible from a devastated neighbor.

So while Egypt was building its pyramids in peace, the Sumerian cities were beginning a series of wars among themselves, in which first one and then another would gain a brief advantage. As is always the case in such internecine struggles, however, the net result was to weaken all sides and lay the region open to easy conquest by an outsider.

CRETE

The island of Crete entered the Bronze Age about 2600 B.C., when the "Minoan" civilization (the first in Europe) was established. The name is derived from the legendary Minos, who was described as ruling over Crete in the Greek myths.

2500 TO 2000 B.C.

SUMERIA

In the period after 2500 B.C., warfare among the Sumerian cities continued to weaken them all. Three cities were chiefly involved—Lagash, Umma, and Kish. These cities formed a southeast-to-northwest line in the region between the Tigris and the Euphrates. The winner was Lugalzaggisi of Umma, who, after 2375 B.C., took over Kish and Lagash, as well as Ur and Uruk. By 2350 B.C., all of Sumeria was under his control.

Meanwhile, in Akkad, north of Sumeria, there was a ruler named Sargon of Agade (the leading city of Akkad). Legends grew about him in later generations, including one in which, as a baby, he was supposed to have been found in a small boat floating on the river. (The legend, famous in the Middle East, was taken over by the Biblical writers and applied to Moses.)

Sargon gained control of Kish and, about 2340 B.C., he easily defeated Lugalzaggisi and united all of Sumer and Akkad under his rule. He then went on to conquer Elam and the mountainous lands to the east, as well as the upper reaches of the Tigris–Euphrates, and Canaan to the west. His dominions spread from the Mediterranean Sea to the Caspian Sea in the north, and to the Persian Gulf in the south. It included all the civilized regions of western Asia.

Sargon's victories might well have been the result of novel military techniques. The Sumerians had used lances for thrusting, and had defended themselves with large shields, which made their armies slow-moving and only effective at close quarters. Sargon's armies used spears for throwing, and bows and arrows as well. He could attack at longer range, and with greater mobility and speed, and the Sumerians were helpless before him. (Military victory through the use of novel weapons and tactics has been a periodic feature of warfare ever since.)

Sargon of Agade was the first great conqueror of history. The people he ruled were not uniform in language and culture, but comprised a heterogeneous realm. This is called an "empire" (or *imperium* in Latin, from their word *imperator* for a military leader). Sargon of Agade was, therefore, the first "imperialist," the first empire-builder.

Sargon died in 2279 B.C., but the Akkadian Empire reached its zenith under Sargon's grandson, Naramsin, who reigned from 2254 to 2218 B.C.

Empires, however, tend to be unstable. One group of people (in this case, Akkadians) rules over others. Those who are ruled resent it, of course, and seek occasions to overthrow the rulers. Much of the strength of an empire, therefore, must be expended on suppressing revolts.

Furthermore, nomadic tribes along the borders of the empire are quite likely to invade in search of loot. Usually, the better organized and the more advanced technology of the empire can take care of such raids, but, all too often, the submerged nationalities make common cause with the tribal incursion, and the empire, trying to counter force from abroad and disaffection from within, may topple. In this way, the Akkadian Empire came to an end about 2180 B.C., less than 40 years after the death of Naramsin.

For thousands of years to follow, one of the themes in history has been the struggle of settled city-dwellers against nomadic tribesmen. Because histories are written by the city-dwellers, the tribesmen are usually described as "savages," from a Latin word meaning "people who live in woods" (i.e., rather than in cities). They are also called "barbarians," from a Greek word referring to anyone who does not speak Greek (i.e., of an alien culture). In this book, I shall refer to them simply as "tribesmen" or "nomads," terms which do not carry derogatory implications. After all, tribesmen are still people and can, at times, be decent and kindly; and it is well-known that civilized people can, for all their civilization, be incredibly brutal at times. So, there's no use in treating the struggle as a simple case of good versus evil.

The fall of the Akkadian Empire allowed the Sumerian cities to recover and to control their own destinies once more. Gudea of Lagash, who ruled from 2144 to 2124 B.C., was a prominent Sumerian leader in this period. He was a great patron of the arts, and a religious reformer as well.

Then, Ur took the leadership once again and, in 2000 B.C., reached a height of power. According to Hebrew legend, the patriarch Abram (later Abraham) was a native of Ur, and, about 2000 B.C., left the city to travel westward, ending in Canaan.

EGYPT

Egypt also experienced a period of decline after 2500 B.C., but not because of foreign conquest.

In any realm, there is a certain tension between the central ruling power (the king) and the various subsidiary officials (the nobility) that rule over different parts of the country.

When a weak king sits on the throne, the nobles are almost certain to take over power in their own districts and to ignore the dictates of the king. This further weakens the king, and the move toward a decentralization of power accelerates. A period in which the nobles are powerful and the central ruler is weak is sometimes referred to as a period of "feudalism" (from an Old German word for "property," because the power of the nobility depends on the land they control).

In general, history seems to show that a nation under a strong central power is better off economically, and stronger militarily, than it is when it is feudal. Under feudalism, endless struggles among the nobility sap the strength of the region.

It may seem to some that decentralization leads to greater freedom, and so it does—for the nobles. Replacing one central tyrant by dozens of petty tyrants does nothing for the people. In fact, the petty tyrants, being closer to home, are usually more unbearable, and history demonstrates that the usual tendency is for the middle classes

to support the king in the fight against the nobles.

In Egypt, about 2400 B.C., when the pyramid mania was passing, the central power began to weaken, and by the year 2000 B.C., Egypt was just beginning to recover from a period of feudalism in which both the economy and military power declined.

CRETE

The Cretans of this period were in the "early Minoan period." They did not yet have the wheel, and writing only began to appear toward the end of the period. Their forte, however, was shipping.

Ships were by now venturing into the Mediterranean Sea. Egyptian vessels, for instance, went as far as Lebanon, on the coast of Canaan, to collect wood from the fabled cedar forests of that land and to bring it back to Egypt. It was far easier to float the logs over water in ships, than to try to transport them overland in carts. The ships did not, however, venture into the open sea, where there were no landmarks to guide them and where storms might sink them. Instead, they hugged the coast of the eastern Mediterranean from Egypt to Lebanon and back again.

Crete, as the first island civilization, had the advantage in that the strong civilizations in Egypt and western Asia did not possess the kind of ships that could threaten it. For that reason, its city-states could unify in peace and remain unwalled. Crete's own ships could carry on trade with islands to the north—islands so thickly strewn over the sea that the ships were never out of sight of land for long.

Crete, by controlling the trade of the eastern Mediterranean, prospered and established the first *thalassocracy* (from Greek words meaning "rule of the seas"), in which power rested with a navy rather than an army.

INDIA

In this period, the Indus River civilization was at its peak. Two cities, in particular, have been excavated at the sites of Mohenjo-Daro on the lower Indus, and at Harappa, further upstream. Both cities were built in a checkerboard pattern, with brick houses, a central citadel on a hill, and surrounding farms with an extensive canal system.

HITTITES

Toward the end of this period, a group of people known to us as Hittites wandered into Asia Minor. Their language was not related to the Semitic one spoken by the Akkadians, for instance. Instead, the language was one of a group that we, today, call "Indo-European," and the Hit-

tites are the first Indo-European people to enter the stage of history.

Terms like "Indo-European" and "Semitic" refer only to languages, however, and do not necessarily refer to physical relationships. American Blacks speak an Indo-European language, but are of African descent just the same.

Historians in the past have been all too willing to give Indo-Europeans and Semites racial characteristics and, since the historians usually spoke Indo-European languages, they let the Indo-Europeans have all the best of it, making wars between them a combat of good Indo-Europeans versus evil Semites. That sort of racism is (or should be) quite passé by now, and there will be none of it in this book.

2000 TO 1500 B.C.

EGYPT

At the opening of this period, Egypt had established a centralized government once again. This was the "Middle Kingdom" under the rulers of the 12th Dynasty (as opposed to the "Old Kingdom" of the pyramid-builders).

Under the most powerful monarch of this Dynasty, Sesostris III, who ruled from 1878 to 1843 B.C., Egypt's government was reorganized into three parts, each with a governor. Sesostris also extended Egyptian power into Nubia, the region along the Nile River south of Egypt (which is now northern Sudan).

Some time after 2000 B.C., however, the Indo-European tribes east of the Caspian Sea put the horse to a new use. They had trained them to drag a light chariot with large wheels, consisting of nothing more than a platform on which two men could stand. One man held the reins and controlled the horse, while the other carried a spear or a bow and arrow.

This amounted to a new weapon. There would be a racing cloud of such charioteers bearing down on the foot-soldiers of the civilized re-

gions. The horses, with hoofs thundering and manes tossing, were fearsome sights. The foot-soldiers were sure to break and run, and the racing charioteers could overtake them, spear them, trample them, and wipe them out.

About 1720 B.C., such charioteers reached Egypt, whose people, till now, had not had occasion to fight an invading army. The charioteers, who were called "Hyksos" by the Egyptians (and who included not only the original Indo-Europeans but contingents of previously conquered tribes), came thundering in across the Sinai Peninsula, the one vulnerable chink in Egypt's armor.

The Hyksos had no difficulty. The appalled Egyptians were easily defeated. The Middle Kingdom came to an end and, for the first time, Egypt fell under foreign domination. The Hyksos did not try to hold the entire length of the Egyptian Nile. There were too few of them. They had won by their chariots, not by their numbers. Therefore, they established their capital in the northeast portion of the delta near the Sinai Peninsula, from which direction they had come. They quickly adopted Egyptian culture.

Two dynasties of Hyksos kings ruled over the Egyptians, the 15th and 16th dynasties. It may have been at this time that certain Canaanites entered Egypt and were treated kindly by Egypt's Asian rulers. This may have given rise to the Biblical tale of Joseph and his brothers.

Upriver, in the city of Thebes, however, the Egyptians retained a center of power, and its rulers reigned as the 17th Dynasty. Slowly, the Egyptians developed a charioteer contingent for their own armies, and when the 18th Dynasty came to power, with dynamic pharaohs, the Hyksos were defeated. By 1570 B.C., a century and a half after the Hyksos had made their appearance, the Egyptians, under Ahmose, who ruled from 1570 to 1546 B.C., drove them out of the land.

The Egyptians followed them across the Sinai Peninsula and annexed Canaan, hoping it would serve as a buffer against future invasions.

By 1500 B.C., then, the "New Kingdom" was established. This was also called the "Egyptian Empire," because it ruled over Asians as well as Egyptians.

BABYLONIA

After 2000 B.C., the Sumerians rapidly declined and passed out of history, although the language persisted for 2000 years and remained known to scholars (as Latin is today) before dying out altogether.

New invaders took over the Tigris–Euphrates valley, adopting Sumerian culture and adding some of their own. A tribe known as the "Amorites," speaking a Semitic language, took over a small Akkadian town named Bab-ilum (Akkadian for "gate of God") about 1800 B.C., and made it their capital. It then entered a 1500-year period of greatness. The later Greeks called it Babylon, and the region that had been thought of as Sumeria for 3000 years came to be called Babylonia.

In 1728 B.C., Hammurabi (d. 1686 B.C.) became king in Babylon and spread his rule over all of Babylonia. He is remembered, in history, chiefly because a stone pillar, dating back to his reign, still exists. It is inscribed with a law-code.

At first, the laws of a society are its customs and traditions; and people referred to the old men of the society for guidance as to what those customs and traditions might be. Dissatisfaction grew, however, along with the suspicion that those who ruled a land could "remember" the laws in such a way as to benefit themselves. The clamor grew, then, for a *written* law-code, and the "Code of Hammurabi" is one of the oldest known examples, and is certainly the oldest that we have in such detail.

ASSYRIA

Meanwhile, in the upper valley of the Tigris–Euphrates, the Amorites founded another kingdom with its capital at the Akkadian city of Ashur. The kingdom itself was also known as Ashur, and the later Greeks called it Assyria. It's most important early king was Shamshi-Adad I, who ruled from 1749 to 1717 B.C. After his time, Assyria fell under the domination of Hammurabi of Babylon.

However, about 1530 B.C., a century and a half after the death of Hammurabi, Babylonia and Assyria alike were conquered by charioteers from the north, a group called "Kassites" in the later histories.

MITANNI

At this time, certain charioteers called "Hurrians," whose language was neither Indo-European nor Semitic, settled down west of Assyria, founding the kingdom of Mitanni, in what is now northwestern Iraq.

HITTITES

Farther west still, in eastern Asia Minor, the Hittites had now founded a strong kingdom, Hatti, under Labarnas I, who ruled from 1680 to 1650 B.C.

CRETE

Crete reached the peak of its power in this period. It dominated the Aegean Sea and its coastlines.

By 1600 B.C., invading tribes from the north entered the land we now call Greece, and they were the people we call Greeks. (They themselves called the land Hellas, and themselves Hellenes. The name "Greece" was first used by the Romans.)

The early Greeks had as their chief city, Mycenae, in the northeast corner of the Peloponnesus (the southernmost peninsula of Greece) and are, therefore, referred to as Myceneans. At its height, however, Crete held the Myceneans in subjection. (Thus, there are well-known Greek legends of Minos of Crete demanding annual hostages from Athens until the Athenian legendary hero, Theseus, ended it.)

What really put an end to Cretan power, however, was a natural catastrophe.

About 80 miles north of Crete was the island of Thera. It was the center of a flourishing Minoan civilization, and was a busy trade center. The island, however, happened to be the top of a volcano sticking out of the sea, though it gave no signs of life, and no one suspected its nature.

Then, about 1500 B.C., it exploded with a thunderous roar, the most violent volcanic explosion that we know of in historic times. A rain of ashes fell on Crete, and tsunamis ("tidal waves") struck its shores, and also the shores of Greece, which may have given rise to Greek legends concerning a great flood. Where Thera had been, there was only a hole in the sea bottom; and it was this explosion that may have given rise to the Greek legend of Atlantis.

Crete was greatly weakened by this explosion and the Minoan civilization tottered to its end, thereafter.

INDIA

The charioteers invaded Asia by 1500 B.C., and put an end to the Indus civilization, which may have had a population of 1 million at its peak. The invaders of India called themselves "Aryans," from their word for "noble." They spoke an Indo-European language known as "Sanskrit." It is because they brought this language into India, while other charioteers spread related languages westward into Europe, that we call the language-family "Indo-European."

Occasionally, Indo-European languages are referred as "Aryan languages," and Indo-Europeans are spoken of as "Aryans." Events in modern times, however, have brought this term into total disrepute and it is no longer used.

CHINA

By 1500 B.C., China had entered the Bronze Age, and was ruled by the Shang dynasty, the first that can be considered historical. It was chiefly centered in what is now northern China. By now, China had its system of writing, as complex as that of Babylonia or Egypt. The Shang dynasty may have ruled over 5 million people, so that China was already more populous than any kingdom in the west, a situation that was to continue down to the present day.

PACIFIC ISLANDS

By 1500 B.C., the people of southeastern Asia were beginning to spread out to nearby Pacific islands, a process which was to continue for nearly 3000 years.

1500 TO 1200 B.C.

EGYPT

Egypt continued to be the world's leading power under the 18th Dynasty. Tuthmosis III, who reigned from 1504 to 1450 B.C., led Egyptian armies into Asia in 1483 B.C., and conquered Canaan. He then marched farther northward and defeated Mitanni. He also led his army far up the Nile, adding those regions to his dominions.

Tuthmosis III won his victories by the skillful use of charioteers. The conquered, as is often the case, had learned from the conquerors and gone them one better. He is called "Tuthmosis the Great" by some historians, who usually make use of "the Great" as a way of indicating successful military campaigns—though greatness in peace and humanity might seem a better excuse for the characterization.

By 1450 B.C., then, Egypt had reached its maximum expansion. It was at that time the strongest, wealthiest, and most advanced nation in the world, and its population may have reached 3 million.

His son and grandson, Amenophis II, who reigned from 1450 to 1425 B.C., and Amenophis III, who reigned from 1417 to 1379 B.C., maintained the empire and engaged in magnificent architectural achievements. Thebes, their capital, became the greatest city in the world.

Then came Amenophis IV, who reigned from 1379 to 1362 B.C. He found something that interested him far more than either war or architecture. He is the first person we know (as a historic figure and not as a legend) who was a "monotheist" and believed in a single God—in his case, the Sun-god, or "Aton." He renamed himself "Akhenaton" ("servant of Aton") and founded a new capital between Memphis and Thebes which he called Akhetaton ("place of power of Aton").

The priestly caste fought him bitterly, and so did the people, who wanted their old ways, and while this fight went on, Egypt's power was neglected and the Empire declined.

Akhenaton was succeeded by his son-in-law, Tutankhamen, who reigned from 1362 to 1352 B.C. Under him, the old religion was restored. He is best-known today because his tomb happened to be the only one that was *not* rifled by robbers. It was discovered, intact, in 1922, with all that had been buried with him, a find of the first importance for archaeologists.

A new and vigorous dynasty arose, the 19th, and Rameses II, who reigned for 67 years, from 1304 to 1237 B.C., strenuously defended the boundaries of the Empire. In 1298 B.C., he fought a violent and bloody battle in Syria against the Hittites. Both sides claimed victory, but the general feeling is that it was the Hittites who had won. (By tradition, Rameses II is the Pharaoh under whom the Israelites were enslaved and in whose court Moses grew to manhood. However, there is nothing outside the Bible to support this.)

In 1200 B.C., then, the Egyptian Empire was still a going concern, still the leading power on Earth apparently, although its very victories were destroying it.

This frequently happens. A nation is victorious and seems unstoppable, but, as it extends its boundaries, it has more and more land which it must guard. The people of the conquering nation grow war-weary, a large share of the seasoned soldiers have died in battle, and the defeated nations constantly rebel. The victorious nation becomes a mere shell—still imposing on the outside, but rotten and hollow inside. A puncture of that shell anywhere is likely to bring the whole structure down in collapse. That was the threatened case with Egypt in 1200 B.C., and with many other realms in later times.

ASSYRIA

Mitanni's defeat by Egypt made it possible for Assyria, to the east of Mitanni, to expand again. Two successive Assyrian kings, Shalmaneser I, who reigned from 1274 to 1245 B.C., and Tukulti-ninurta I, who reigned from 1245 to 1208 B.C., managed to conquer all the Tigris–Euphrates valley. (Tukulti-ninurta I may possibly have inspired the reference to "Nimrod" as a great hunter in the Bible. The Assyrian kings were devoted hunters, and much artwork was devoted to their pursuit of dangerous animals.)

By 1200 B.C., the Assyrian Empire seemed large and powerful and had begun its policy of waging war with deliberate frightfulness, sacking cities and killing their inhabitants indiscriminately, in order to sap the will of their enemies and to have them half-defeated even before the battle began. This sort of thing works for a time, but it breeds a fearful and never-ending hatred, which those who practice frightfulness often have to pay for in the end.

HITTITES

The Hittites had become a great power under Suppiluliumas I, who reigned from 1375 to 1334 B.C. Under his son, Mussilish II, who reigned from 1334 to 1306 B.C., the Hittites raided Babylon and were then at the peak of their power.

Under Muwatallish, who reigned from 1306 to 1282 B.C., the Hittites fought the Battle of Kadesh against Rameses II, and won, but the victory was a costly one. They recovered and continued to rule over most of Asia Minor, destroying and absorbing Mitanni, but they had been crucially weakened.

About 1200 B.C., as a result, when tribesmen called "Phrygians" invaded Asia Minor, the Hittites lacked the strength to fight them off and their empire came to an end, after over a century and a half of power. Before the Hittites passed out of history, however, they had accomplished an important feat.

For 1500 years, men had fought with bronze weapons, but there was something tougher and harder known. There were pieces of a gray-black metal occasionally found which, when beaten into plowshares, swords, knives or lance-heads, made for tools and weapons that were far superior to those made out of bronze. These lumps of metal were actually meteorites and were made up of an iron–nickel alloy that was unusually hard.

It was possible to form iron from rocky ores just as one could form copper and tin from ores. Iron ores, however, required considerably hotter temperatures in smelting, and charcoal rather than wood had to be used for the task. Even then, the iron that was formed (without nickel) wasn't hard enough for the tasks expected of it. Carbon had to be added to make "steel."

About 1300 B.C., the technique for smelting and carbonizing iron was developed in the Caucasian foothills. This was under the control of the Hittites, who picked up the technique. The Hittite kings carefully maintained a monopoly over the new technique for they recognized its importance in war weapons.

This marked the beginning of the "Iron Age" and, once the Hittite Empire was destroyed, their monopoly was broken and the use of iron, beginning in 1200 B.C., started to spread.

GREECE

With Crete shaken to its core by the catastrophe of the explosion of Thera, the Mycenean Greeks were able to take over the island and Crete was never again to play an important role in history.

The Myceneans attempted to spread eastward into Asia Minor as well, taking advantage of the havoc created by the Phrygian invasion. The commercial city of Troy in the northwest corner of Asia Minor was besieged and destroyed. This was eventually magnified into a great 10-year war, and the poetry of Homer made the incident world-famous. The siege took place about 1200 B.C.

ISRAEL

The Israelites laid the foundations for religions that are now the most important in the world. They also created the Bible, which contains their legends, history, poetry, and ethical teachings. It has proved to be the most important and influential book ever written.

Their legends describe a period of slavery in Egypt. There they may have picked up monotheist notions from Akhenaton. About 1200 B.C., when Egypt still had the appearance of strength, but was past its peak, groups of Israelites managed to escape from the land (the "Exodus") under the legendary leadership of Moses, and to join other tribes that were invading Canaan. Canaan was no longer being held by a weakening Egyptian Empire.

The Israelites were coming from the east.

From the west came the wave of invaders, Myceneans and Phrygians, that had struck Asia Minor, and now were landing on the Canaanite coast. They were the Philistines (who eventually gave the land its name of Palestine.) By 1200 B.C., Canaan was virtually in anarchy, and Jericho, which had existed for nearly seven thousand years, was temporarily destroyed.

1200 TO 1000 B.C.

EGYPT

Rameses III of the 20th Dynasty ruled Egypt from 1188 to 1156 B.C. He had to face the turbulent invaders who had wrecked Asia Minor and Canaan. They attacked from the sea, and the Egyptians called them "People from the Sea."

With a supreme effort, the Egyptians defeated the invaders, but the strain of doing so finally wore them out. By 1000 B.C., the Egyptian Empire was no more, and Egypt remained a minor power thereafter. The great days were gone, leaving behind only the imperishable monuments—the pyramids, the sphinx, the obelisks, and the colossal statues and temples—all of which served to impress later generations.

ASSYRIA

Assyria reeled back under the hammer blows of the Phrygians, but then, under Tiglath-Pileser I, who reigned from 1116 to 1078 B.C., it was resurgent and built up its empire again—for the third time.

After Tiglath-Pileser's death, however, a new wave of Semitic tribesmen, the Arameans, came flooding into the Tigris–Euphrates valley and into Syria. By 1000 B.C., the Assyrians had fallen back—for the third time.

ISRAEL

For two centuries, the invading Israelites from the east and the invading Philistines from the west tore at Canaan. For a while, the Philistines, who had iron weapons, dominated the Israelites and Canaanites alike; however, about 1000 B.C., the Israelites had gained iron weapons for themselves. David, of the southern tribe of Judah, managed to seize the Israelite throne and to defeat the Philistines, who effectively disappeared from history thereafter.

PHOENICIA

The Canaanites, having lost control of most of their land, maintained themselves only on the Lebanese coast, which the later Greeks called "Phoenicia." Their most important city was, at first, Sidon.

Since the Cretan thalassocracy had vanished, the sea was open to any seamen brave enough to venture forth, and this the Phoenicians did. They were, in fact, the first to venture out into the open sea far from the sight of land. This may be because they discovered how to tell direction on clear nights. It was obvious that the Sun rose in the east and set in the west and that, when it was high in the sky in the middle of the day, it was always to the south. What the Phoenicians may have noticed was that, by night, the Big Dipper was always to the north, and that gave you your directions.

By 1000 B.C., the Phoenicians were beginning to flourish through sea-trade.

The Phoenicians, located as they were between Babylonia (with its complicated cuneiform writing) and Egypt (with its equally complicated hieroglyphic writing), could not trade easily unless they could handle both languages. Life would have been far easier for them if they could have worked out a simpler writing code.

Attempts in this direction had been made as early as 1400 B.C., but without total success. By 1000 B.C., however, the Phoenicians had an alphabet, each letter representing a consonantal sound, and, using that alphabet, *any* language could be written down simply.

Writing was developed independently in a variety of places; in Sumeria, in China, and in southern Mexico, for instance. The alphabet, however, was developed only once, by the Phoenicians. All alphabets in use today, however different they may seem, are clearly descended from that of the Phoenicians.

PHRYGIA

By 1000 B.C., the Phrygians in Asia Minor had settled down and become civilized. Indeed, they flourished, as we can see from the later Greek legend of the Phrygian king, Midas, with his "golden touch." Obviously, the Greeks thought of him, enviously, as a wealthy king.

GREECE

The sack of Troy was the last important feat of the Mycenean Greeks. The turmoil of invasion struck Greece itself when new Greek-speaking tribes, the Dorians, invaded Greece. They had iron weapons, and the bronze-weaponed Myceneans could not stand before them. The Dorians took over the southern and eastern Peloponnesus (in particular, the old Mycenean city of Sparta, the legendary home of the beautiful Helen, over whom the Trojan War was supposed to have been fought).

A number of Greeks, now called Ionians, survived in eastern Greece, notably in Athens. Others fled the mainland and settled on the Aegean islands and on the coasts of Asia Minor. The central portion of that coast came to be known as "Ionia."

By 1000 B.C., the Aegean Sea was surrounded by Greek cities on all its shores and islands but, nevertheless, Greece went through a period in which civilization receded. It took a while for the new invaders to learn civilized ways, and so there followed a "dark age" for Greece.

ETRUSCANS

Just as the Greeks fled the mainland to escape the Dorians, so it may be that some people of Asia Minor fled by sea to escape the Phrygians. By 1000 B.C., such refugees had reached the western shores of Italy. They were later known as "Etruscans", and they represented the first civilization in Italy. Their language has never been deciphered, however, and we know little about them.

INDIA

In India, by 1000 B.C., the Indo-European tribes were spreading down the Ganges river, and were writing poetry. The oldest surviving poetry of this sort is the "Rib Veda," which contains over a thousand hymns to various gods.

CHINA

In China, by 1000 B.C., the Shang dynasty had been replaced by the Chou dynasty. At this time, the nobles grew to be important. China became feudalist, and that continued for centuries.

1000 TO 900 B.C.

ISRAEL

David, who reigned over Israel from 1000 to 960 B.C., extended Israelite territory from Egypt in the South to the upper Euphrates River in the north. The entire eastern coast of the Mediterranean Sea was Israelite, and this has always been remembered by the Jews as their "natural boundaries." This, in fact, is one of the miseries of history. Every nation remembers how things were at the time of its maximum extent and power, which is what it considers just and natural. Naturally, there are overlappings in every direction and the territorial quarrels never end.

David established the capital of Israel at Jerusalem, which has remained a holy city to important segments of the world's population ever since.

Solomon, David's son and successor, reigned from 962 to 922 B.C. He attempted no further conquests, but lived in luxury and, largely, in peace. He built a temple to the Israelite god; one that was unique in the ancient world because it contained no sculptured representations of any god-figure. On the whole, his reign was looked back upon as a golden age.

The people conquered by David, however, the Moabites, the Edomites, the Ammonites, and so on, were all restive. In fact, David and Solomon were Judeans—of the southern tribe of Judah— and the northern tribes resented the Judean domination.

In 922 B.C., after the death of Solomon, the Israelite kingdom (with the help of Egyptian intrigue) broke in two—Israel in the north and Judah in the south. The separated kingdoms could not hold on to the subject nations and, by 900 B.C., the brief period of Israelite glory was gone.

By 900 B.C., some Israelite writing had appeared that was later to be incorporated into the Bible. The Song of Deborah is an example of this.

EGYPT

Soon after the breakup of the Israelite kingdom, about 918 B.C., an Egyptian army, under Sheshonk ("Shishak" in the Bible) of the 22nd Dynasty, who reigned from 935 to 914 B.C., sacked Jerusalem and the Temple.

ASSYRIA

Assyria was going through a process of recovery. By 900 B.C., it was busy restoring its control over Babylonia and other regions that it had controlled before the Phrygian invasion.

GREECE

Greece had broken up into separate city-states. This was a natural consequence of the mountainous nature of the land, where each valley considered itself a separate political unit.

The city of Athens, however, managed to bring under its control the peninsula of Attica, so that it was large for a Greek city-state. Even so, it was only about 1000 square miles in area, about as large as the American state of Rhode Island.

Monarchy went out of fashion in Greece, with some exceptions at the fringes. In most of the city-states, the rule was held by a few important families. (These were *oligarchies*—Greek for "rule by the few.")

PHOENICIA

The Phoenicians were by now ranging the length of the Mediterranean Sea. It may have been the wonder-tales they brought back from the mysterious western portion of the Mediterranean that inspired Homer to write the tale of Odysseus' travels in the *Odyssey*.

The Phoenicians had established trading posts on the western shores and, by 900 B.C., may even have ventured past the Strait of Gibraltar out into the Atlantic Ocean. Tin ores were being exhausted in western Asia (the first case of a natural resource disappearing), and the Phoenicians may have gone to Cornwall ("the Tin Islands") to find new sources. They kept the location secret to preserve their monopoly.

INDIA

At about this period, the caste system was coming into existence in India. This divided the population into a hierarchy of positions, depending on birth, marriage, and occupation. This gave everyone a place (which has its comforts and se-

cuirties) but serves also to prevent anyone from moving out of it. This destroys ambition and enterprise, and prevents a society from making full use of gifted individuals. India's caste system acted to slow necessary change, and to enforce a certain stagnation.

NORTH AMERICA

The first important civilization to arise in North America was that of the Olmecs, who flourished in southern Mexico. It was at its peak in 900 B.C., and its most startling artifacts were colossal heads about nine feet high.

900 TO 800 B.C.

ASSYRIA

Assyria continued to grow stronger after 900 B.C. Under Ashurnasirpal II, who reigned from 883 to 859 B.C., the Assyrian army went out on annual campaigns and fought battles in which the killing of prisoners reached a sadistic peak. Ashurnasirpal's son, Shalmaneser III, who reigned from 859 to 824 B.C., continued the campaigns.

By now the Assyrians had learned the technique of making good iron in quantity, and their army was the first to be completely outfitted with iron weapons. In addition, the Assyrians had learned how to mount and control a horse. The chariot disappeared in warfare, since cavalry was faster and more maneuverable. It was these advances that were responsible for Assyrian victories.

However, Assyria grew war-weary and there were revolts that forced it, once again, to pause in its expansion. Toward 800 B.C., the Assyrian king was a minor, and his mother, Sammuramat, was the effective head of the government. Although she wasn't much of a warrior, it seemed so unusual to have a woman the head of a nation so devoted to war that the Greeks built their legend of Semiramis about her, describing

her as much more powerful than she really was.

ISRAEL

Israel, under its king Ahab, who ruled from 874 to 853 B.C., had to face Assyria, and it was done in combination with other nations of the west. These included Judah, which, in this century, was virtually an Israelite puppet, and Aram (better known as Syria). In 854 B.C., the coalition actually defeated Assyria in battle, and won some breathing room, but that just meant that Syria and Israel turned against each other, and Ahab died in battle against Syria. By 800 B.C., the situation looked quite dark. Assyria was, at the moment, quiet, but surely it would rise again.

Meanwhile, Israel and Judah were not truly monotheistic. The writers of the Bible tried to make monotheism the stern belief of Moses and David, but even if it were, the people did not follow them any more than the Egyptian people had followed Akhenaton. The Israelites, like the Egyptians, didn't want austere monotheism and preferred the colorful rites of gods involved with the realities of agriculture and daily life.

The Yahwists (those who believe in Yahweh as the single god of the Jews) were always a minority at this time, and were, in fact, persecuted by the kings—who found them rigid and extreme, and getting in the way of practical politics. The outstanding Yahwists of this century were Elijah and Elisha. The Bible, written in later times by Yahwists, present them as wonder-working prophets and their opponents as villains. Thus, Ahab, the king who actually stopped Assyria for a while, is painted in the darkest colors in the Bible, along with his wife, Jezebel. His victory over Assyria isn't even mentioned.

GREECE

By 800 B.C., Homer (concerning whom next to nothing is known—not even if he really existed) had written the *Iliad* and the *Odyssey*, two overwhelming masterpieces that are as alive and as popular now as they were when they were first written. The Greek language and these two epic poems were among those factors that held together the numerous city-states of Greece.

About the same time, Hesiod was writing *Theogony*, which was an important guide to Greek mythology and to the ancient aristocratic Olympian gods, led by Zeus, god of the sky and of storms.

PHOENICIA

Phoenicians continued to set up trading centers along the coasts of the Mediterranean Sea, all the way to Spain. In 814 B.C., the city of Carthage was founded near the site of modern Tunis.

INDIA

Some time before 800 B.C., Indian mathematicians began to use a symbol for "zero." Until that was done, there seemed no way of reasonably limiting number symbols to a very few. With the zero, we can easily distinguish between 1, 10, 100, and so on. Without the zero, separate symbols are needed for "one," "10," and "100." With the zero, we can easily distinguish between 23, 203, and 230. Without the zero, it is much more complicated.

The use of the zero symbol, and the concept of positional notation in numbers, spread outward from India, but (believe it or not) took 2000 years to come into use in Europe, although the idea was simple and the advantages were obvious and enormous.

URARTU

This (the Biblical "Ararat") was a kingdom established about 835 B.C. in the foothills of the Caucasus, north of Assyria. It had been where iron-smelting was first developed some four centuries earlier, and it was still rich in iron and copper mines.

800 TO 700 B.C.

ASSYRIA

After a 50-year period of comparative weakness, Assyria gained still another renewal of strength —its last and greatest—thanks to Tiglath-Pileser III, who reigned from 745 to 727 B.C. He began the process whereby the kingdoms along the Mediterranean shore were finally subdued. Aramaic Syria was conquered in 732 B.C., and vanished from history (although other people were to inhabit the land which would be called Syria down to the present day).

Tiglath-Pileser III was succeeded by Shalmaneser V, who reigned from 726 to 722 B.C., and then by the first king of a new dynasty, Sargon II, who reigned from 722 to 705 B.C. Sargon defeated Israel in 722 B.C. and Urartu in 714 B.C., and both nations vanished from history as well.

In 700 B.C., then, the Assyrian Empire included all the Tigris–Euphrates region and all the eastern shore of the Mediterranean. It was the most powerful political-military entity the world had yet seen.

ISRAEL AND JUDAH

During the period of Assyrian weakness, Israel gained strength and, under Jeroboam II, who reigned from 783 to 748 B.C., David's old empire was almost reconstituted. Even Judah was a vassal state of Israel. It was, however, an illusion. Once Assyria regained its strength and was on the march again, Israel could not stand. Israel was attacked and its capital, Samaria, was taken after a three-year siege in 722 B.C. Sargon had begun a new policy of deporting the aristocracy of a conquered nation, leaving the remnant leaderless and incapable of rebellion. This was cruel, but not as cruel as Assyrian massacres and mutilations had been in the past.

Israel's aristocracy was deported and the nation disappeared from history. There were legends for 2000 years afterward that the "ten lost tribes of Israel" had formed a mighty kingdom somewhere in the hidden depths of Asia, but the deportees had merely been moved a short distance, had intermarried with the surrounding population, and had lost their identity.

As 700 B.C. approached, Judah was still intact, but it was clearly next on the Assyrian timetable of conquest.

PHOENICIA

The Phoenician city-states were also conquered by Assyria and, under that nation's harsh rule, the Phoenician sea-trade withered. However, the Phoenician colonies in the west remained independent and, indeed, gained greater freedom of action as a result.

GREECE

The Greek city-states, with their population booming as they emerged from their dark-age period, took advantage of Phoenician subjection to Assyria, and became the new sea-traders and navigators of the period. In particular, they searched for colonies that might absorb their surplus population. Greek city-states sprang up along the shores of the Black Sea, in Sicily and in southern Italy, in North Africa, and so on. If they found competition it was not from the Phoenicians themselves, but from the expanding power of Carthage.

In the end, Greek colonies occupied most of the Mediterranean shores. The most notable colony, perhaps, was Syracuse, on the western shore of Sicily, which was founded in 735 B.C.

Within Greece itself, Sparta, in the south, fought a long war with Messenia to its west, defeating it and enslaving its people. In 700 B.C., Sparta had become the largest city-state in Greece, and it was on its way to becoming the dominating military force in the land.

The Greek Olympic Games were held in honor of Apollo every four years at Olympia in the western Peloponnesus. It developed into the most joyous festival in the Greek calendar, with athletic contests and cultural competitions. It lasted for days and was open to all Greek-speaking cities. Wars were suspended so that all might compete peacefully.

The first Olympic games were supposed to have been celebrated in 776 B.C., and eventually the Greeks counted the years by so many "Olympiads." Together with the Greek language and the Homeric poems, the Olympic games were the third factor holding the Greeks together.

CIMMERIANS

In the fertile plains north of the Black Sea (which we now call the "Ukraine"), various nomadic tribesmen appeared and impinged upon the settled kingdoms to the south.

About 750 B.C., for instance, the Cimmerians appeared and eventually occupied the peninsula of Crimea on the northern shore of the Black Sea.

("Crimea" may be a distortion of "Cimmeria.") They soon expanded into Asia Minor and helped the Assyrians defeat Urartu.

ETRUSCANS

In this period, Etruscan power expanded along the west-central coast of Italy. A loose union of city-states, each ruled by a king, was being formed. On the Tiber River, at the southern rim of Etruscan power, the city of Rome was founded. The traditional date was 753 B.C.

In later times, the history of Rome was traced back to Troy. When the city was taken by the Mycenean Greeks, the hero Aeneas, made his way out of the burning city, with his father, wife, and son. Aeneas was described as having traveled from Troy to the west coast of Italy by way of Carthage. In Carthage, he met Queen Dido, the legendary founder of the Phoenician colony. (The fact that Carthage was founded four centuries after the fall of Troy rather spoils the story.)

Needless to say, the story was pure fabrication, though it was taken as seriously by later generations as the tale of Adam and Eve was. Still, the story of Aeneas may have its faint kernel of truth in its reflection of the coming of the Etruscans from Asia Minor to western Italy. Rome was, at the start, a town that was either Etruscan or, at least, under Etruscan domination.

700 TO 600 B.C.

ASSYRIA

Under Sennacherib, who succeeded Sargon II, and who reigned from 705 to 681 B.C., the Assyrians attacked Judah, and, in 701 B.C., after having devastated the land, they laid siege to Jerusalem. Unlike Samaria, Jerusalem was not actually taken, and unlike Israel, Judah was not wiped out. The Bible describes this as the result of a miracle, but miracles are less common in real life than in religious legends. What happened was that Sennacherib was faced with threats from Egypt and revolts at home so that he was ready to accept a simple capitulation and a large tribute from the Judeans and leave them in peace as an Assyrian puppet nation.

Sennacherib's son and successor, Esarhaddon, who reigned from 680 to 669 B.C., attacked Egypt. For four centuries, Egypt had been a minor power, living on its past glories and barely able to hold its own against the Libyans to the west and the Nubians to the south.

In 671 B.C., it fell to Assyria, which occupied the northern portion of the nation, as once the Hyksos had done nearly nine centuries earlier.

Assyria now reached the greatest extent of its territory and power.

Under Esarhaddon's successor, Ashurbanipal, who reigned from 669 to 627 B.C., the city of Nineveh, which had been established by Sennacherib as Assyria's capital, was further beautified and enlarged. It was the largest city in the world at that time. Within it, Ashurbanipal established the largest library the world had yet seen, one that contained over 22,000 clay tablets.

However, the last century of endless Assyrian campaigning, even though victorious, had taken its toll. Ashurbanipal was forced to fight off rebellions in Babylonia, in Elam, and in Egypt, and the Assyrians, while again victorious, were brought to the edge of exhaustion.

Fifteen years after the death of Ashurbanipal, Assyria found itself fighting rebels again and this time, it could not gather the strength it needed. Nineveh fell in 612 B.C., and the strategy of frightfulness recoiled on Assyria terribly, for it was wiped out mercilessly by the people who fought against it. This time there would be no recovery ever. By 600 B.C., Assyria, which had seemed to be untouchable in its enormous power only a quarter century before, had been thoroughly wiped out, and vanished from the pages of history.

CHALDEA

The Chaldeans had dominated Babylonia for over two centuries but had lived in the shadow of Assyria. They had rebelled on several occasions but were beaten, and Babylon was temporarily destroyed by an angry and vengeful Sennacherib.

At the death of Ashurbanipal, however, the Chaldean governor, Nabopolassar, who was in power from 625 to 605 B.C., saw his chance and, in alliance with tribesmen to the north and east of Assyria, he attacked. The Assyrians, worn out, fell, and Assyria was wiped out.

When Nabopolassar died, his even more capable son, Nebuchadrezzar II (630–562 B.C.) succeeded. Nebuchadrezzar founded the Chaldean empire (also called the Neo-Babylonian Empire) and by 600 B.C., he ruled over much of the territory that Assyria had ruled over in 700 B.C.

MEDIA

The Medians (or Medes) were a group of tribes who lived in what is now northwestern Iran. They first made their appearance in history at about the time the Chaldeans did, but remained obscure for two centuries. They hung along the eastern rim of the Assyrian Empire, and were, for much of the time, a client kingdom of the Assyrians.

About 625 B.C., the Medes were united under a vigorous king, Cyaxares, who reigned from 625 to 585 B.C. (Cyaxares was the Greek version of his name. His Median name was more like "Uvakhshtra," but I will use the Greek versions of the various Mideasterners of the time since they are better known in this form to the western public.) Cyaxares reorganized the Median army and he, like Nabopolassar of Chaldea, took the opportunity of Ashurbanipal's death to rebel against Assyria. In alliance, the Medes and Chaldeans destroyed Assyria.

Cyaxares then ruled over the Median Empire, which included all the territory from eastern Asia Minor, where six centuries earlier the Hittites had ruled, stretching north of the Tigris–Euphrates and eastward into the dim stretches of central Asia. It bulked much larger on the map than the Chaldean Empire, but it was loosely organized and not very powerful militarily.

EGYPT

Egypt had remained under Assyrian rule for half a century, and Psamtik I, a native Egyptian, was governor of Egypt on behalf of Assyria from 664 B.C. As Assyria weakened, he declared Egypt independent and founded the 26th dynasty, ruling until 610 B.C.

He invited Greeks into the country. They set up trading posts on the coast, and their mercantile enterprise redounded to the benefit and prosperity of Egypt.

Psamtik I was succeeded by his son, Necho II, who reigned from 610 to 595 B.C. Necho II dreamed of reestablishing the Egyptian Empire and sought to take advantage of the death of Nabopolassar. He led an Egyptian army into Judah and Syria, but the new Chaldean king, Nebuchadrezzar, was more than a match for Necho. At the Battle of Carchemish in northern Syria, the Egyptians were badly defeated and fled back to Egypt.

Egypt was fortunate in that Nebuchadrezzar chose not to stretch his dominions unnecessarily and left Egypt to itself. In 600 B.C., therefore, Egypt was able to look forward to a period of peace.

Necho indulged in at least two large projects that we can admire today. First, he labored to build a canal that would connect the Nile River with the Red Sea, so that Egypt would have a river outlet to the east, as well as the north. He didn't succeed, but it was a noble try.

Second, he hired a Phoenician fleet to attempt the circumnavigation of Africa. The fleet succeeded in the task, taking three years to do so. The Greek historian, Herodotus (484–425 B.C.), writing a century and a half later, tells us that the

Phoenicians reported that when they rounded Africa in the south, the noonday sun was in the north. Since it was the experience of men in the civilized areas of the world (in the North Temperate Zone) that the noonday sun was always in the south, Herodotus considered this report to be against the laws of nature and disbelieved it.

We know, however, that the Earth, being spherical, would have the noonday sun always in the north when viewed from the South Temperate Zone. The Phoenicians would not have reported so apparently nonsensical a phenomenon if they had not actually observed it. It is because they did that we know they were successful at sailing around Africa.

JUDAH

After the siege of Jerusalem, Judah remained a loyal Assyrian puppet. Under the rule of Menassah, from 692 to 639 B.C., Judah paid its tribute and enjoyed a half century of peace. For this, and because Menassah further kept the peace by practicing religious toleration, he was vilified in the Bible.

As Assyria declined, however, Judah declared itself independent again, and, under Josiah, who reigned from 640 to 609 B.C., Yahwism won a temporary victory in Judah. Jerusalem was made the center of all worship, and all subsidiary cult centers were wiped out. A book of the law, our present biblical book of Deuteronomy, centered on Yahwism, was prepared and was "rediscovered" in the Temple with great publicity and attributed to the hand of Moses. Judah's territory expanded and, for a while, Judah dreamed of reestablishing David's Empire as Egypt was dreaming of reestablishing its own.

When Necho II marched northward through Judah, Josiah opposed him and died in battle. The Egyptian victory was short-lived, however, for waiting in the north was the powerful Nebuchadrezzar.

By 600 B.C., Judah, its brief dream of glory gone, found itself a puppet again. Now it was the Chaldean Empire that was master.

CIMMERIANS AND SCYTHIANS

The Cimmerians had not plunged southward into Asia Minor entirely of their own volition. They were pursued by another set of Indo-European nomads, the Scythians, who were skilled horsemen. The Scythians were the first of a long series of nomadic horsemen, in fact, who swept from Asia into the Ukraine to plague the settled regions to the south and (eventually) to the west. Undoubtedly, the Cimmerians and the Scythians inflicted enough damage on Assyria to contribute importantly to the decline and fall of that power.

In western Asia Minor, the Cimmerians were opposed by Lydia, a kingdom that was tributary to Assyria. The Cimmerians were defeated by the Lydians, and were also harried by the Scythians. After the defeat, the Cimmerians melted into the surrounding population and vanished from history. (Nomadic tribes, however impressive their military victories, are usually comparatively small in number. Once stopped, they intermarry with the people about them, accept the surrounding culture, and lose their identity.)

As for the Scythians, they were pushed back by Cyaxares of Media and retired northward to the Ukraine, where they remained a danger.

LYDIA

Once the Cimmerians had destroyed Urartu and Phrygia, and had themselves been defeated, Lydia was without a rival in western Asia Minor, especially after Assyria fell. The Lydian king, Gyges, had fallen in battle against the Cimmerians in 648 B.C., but by 600 B.C. Lydia was a strong kingdom under Alyattes, who had begun his reign in 619 B.C. By that time, the Lydians were dominating the Greek city-states on the Aegean coast of Asia Minor, but the Lydian rulers, like the Egyptian rulers of the time, admired Greek culture and treated the Greeks' cities leniently.

GREECE

Sparta. Sparta had to face the city of Argos to its north in a competition for control of southern

Greece. For a while, Argos, under its king, Phei-don, seemed to have the upper hand, but with Pheidon's death, about 650 B.C., Argos' power faded.

Sparta then had to face a revolt by the en-slaved Messenians to their west. The Messenians were finally defeated and reenslaved in 630 B.C. Sparta, which had had a bad fright, decided that the only way to maintain its supremacy was to establish a thoroughly militaristic state and to train its citizens for the sole task of fighting.

The Greeks had already developed the notion of the "hoplite" (from a Greek word for *armor*) as a result of their endless intercity fighting. The hoplite was a heavily armed foot-soldier, with a lance in his right hand for throwing, a shield on his left arm, a sword at his side, a helmet on his head, and armor encasing his body and legs. For some centuries, these hoplites were the best and most valued soldiers in the Mediterranean area, and were frequently used by non-Greek monar-chies as mercenaries.

What the Spartans did was to intensify hoplite training. The Spartan aristocracy was reserved for war. Boys were placed into barracks at the age of seven and made into complete soldiers. They were trained to fight in close order and to attack and defend in unison so that the line was a "phalanx" (a Greek word meaning *fist*). What's more, they were expected not to retreat but to fight to the death. The result was that Spartan soldiers almost invariably won their battles and Sparta became the military leader of Greece.

A second result was that Sparta was subjected to a merciless caste system, and Spartan society hardened into an unchanging mold that could not change with the times. Thus, Sparta, alone among the city-states of Greece, remained a monarchy—it had two kings, in fact, so that it was a "dyarchy." The kings, however, served primarily as army leaders, rather than as rulers.

A third result was that cultural activity, in which Sparta had, until then, been as active as the other Greek city-states, ceased entirely. Thereafter, Sparta had nothing to contribute to later generations in the way of literature, art, or philosophy.

By 600 B.C., Spartan militarism was in place,

but the Spartans later devised the legend that it had been instituted two centuries earlier by the legendary Lycurgus, just to give it greater au-thenticity.

Athens. In Athens, things moved in the oppo-site direction. The monarchy was abolished in 683 B.C., and Athens placed itself under an oli-garchy, from which an "archon" ("ruler") was chosen each year.

The trouble with an oligarchy is that they usu-ally slanted the social and economic milieu so as to benefit themselves, and the common folk out-side the oligarchy suffered. There was a clamor to have a written law-code, therefore, one that the oligarchy could not twist to its own service. Such a written code was worked out by Draco about 620 B.C. It was a harsh system of laws with heavy punishments for even trifling offenses (hence, the word "draconian" for severe treat-ment).

The peasantry continued to suffer and to sink further into debt. Furthermore, as Athens en-gaged in commerce more and more heavily, a middle class of traders and businessmen ap-peared who joined with the oppressed peasantry against the oligarchs.

Elsewhere. In general, when an oligarchy be-came too oppressive, some politician managed to put himself at the head of the downtrodden lower classes and made himself master of the city. The Greek word for master is *tyrannos*, and this becomes "tyrant" in English. A tyrant is not necessarily a vicious or unjust ruler, but it came to mean that because tyrants, however well-meaning, were not backed by hereditary "right" and therefore had to use force to remain in power. In addition, power corrupts. Although tyrants might begin their rule decently, they often used their power for their own aggrandize-ment and financial profit.

In this period, however, Corinth was an ex-ample of a city under a benevolent tyranny. Cyp-selus ruled the city from 657 to 627 B.C., and he was succeeded by his son, Periander, who ruled from 627 to 586 B.C. These tyrants ruled well, saw to it that the peasants were treated decently, patronized art and literature, and encouraged commerce, so that Corinth prospered and became Greece's major seaport.

On the Asia Minor coast, the Greek city-states squabbled with Lydia, and suffered some losses, but Lydian rule, in the end, proved light, and the cities led a flourishing cultural life.

In Sicily and Italy, Greek city-states were spreading along the shores. In Sicily, however, the Greek city-states in the east encountered Carthaginian power in the west; while in Italy, the Greek city-states in the south encountered Etruscan power in the north.

CARTHAGE

With Phoenicia first in the grip of Assyria and then of Chaldea, the western Phoenician colonies went their own way. By 650 B.C., Carthage had its own navy and, thanks to its flourishing commerce, could hire plenty of mercenary soldiers. It dominated and protected the other Phoenician colonies. It controlled virtually all the north African coast west of Egypt, together with western Sicily and the other western-Mediterranean islands: Sardinia, Corsica, and the Balearic islands. It had bases on the coast of Spain as well.

ETRUSCANS

The Etruscans continued to flourish in western Italy and were beginning to expand northward toward the Po River valley. The city of Rome continued to live under its (legendary) kings. The fifth of these kings was Tarquinius Priscus, who ruled from 616 to 578 B.C. He was an Etruscan, and this points to the fact that, even a century and a half after its foundation, Rome was still essentially Etruscan.

CHINA

China continued to be divided into feudal kingdoms but, by 600 B.C., it had entered the Iron Age.

JAPAN

No true historical writings can be found for Japan until several centuries later, but Japanese legends state that the first Emperor, Jimmu, began to rule in 660 B.C.

600 TO 550 B.C.

CHALDEAN EMPIRE

Under Nebuchadrezzar II, the Chaldean Empire was at its peak in this period. Babylon, his capital, which had been rebuilt since its destruction by Sennacherib a century before, was enlarged and beautified, so that it gained the height of its importance now, and became, for a time, the greatest city in the world.

Nebuchadrezzar completed a large ziggurat in Babylon. It had stood for a long time unfinished and had served as the inspiration for the Biblical story of the Tower of Babel. The ziggurat did not, however, aspire to reach heaven. When it was

completed, it was 300 feet tall, well below the height of the Great Pyramid.

Nebuchadrezzar also built an elaborate palace that rose in stages like a ziggurat. (Legend has it that he did it to simulate a mountain because a Median princess despised the flat plain of Babylonia and longed for the mountains of home.) On the terraces, he planted gardens. These were the famous "Hanging Gardens of Babylon," later considered one of the Seven Wonders of the ancient world, along with the pyramids of Egypt.

Nebuchadrezzar is sometimes, and rather deservedly, called "Nebuchadrezzar the Great," but appreciation of his feats is limited because of his relationship to Judah, where he had to fight repeated rebellions. Finally, in 586 B.C., he took Jerusalem and destroyed the Temple that Solomon had built nearly four centuries earlier. This meant that he was vilified in the Bible, and the appellation of "Great" has difficulty surviving that.

He also laid siege to the city of Tyre, the only portion of Phoenicia that had not submitted to him. The siege lasted from 585 to 573 B.C. and was not successful.

Nebuchadrezzar II died in 561 B.C., and there were no successors capable of maintaining the Empire. In 555 B.C., Nabonidus came to the throne. He was a capable archeologist, fascinated by Babylonian and Sumerian antiquities, but he was not much of a ruler, and disaster was on its way.

MEDIAN EMPIRE

The Median Empire had established its western border on the Halys River in the center of Asia Minor, and on the other side of the river was Lydia.

War broke out between Cyaxares of Media and Alyattes of Lydia, but it was a cautious one. After a couple of years, the two squared off for the deciding battle when, suddenly, a total eclipse of the Sun took place. So seriously did both armies take this to be a dire warning from the gods, that the battle was broken off at once and the two nations made peace.

The chief result is that the date of this aborted battle is the earliest event in human history that we can confidently say happened on a *particular* day, and no other. Modern astronomers, calculating the movements of the Sun and the Moon, have worked out the day of the eclipse and we know the incident took place on May 28, 585 B.C.

Earlier eclipses took place, and were recorded (notably in China), but we don't know of any significant human events that took place on those days, other than the sighting of the eclipse.

Shortly after the battle, Cyaxares died and was succeeded by his son, Astyages, who reigned from 584 to 550 B.C.

LYDIA

In this period, Lydia made a great advance in economic affairs. Metals, such as gold and silver, were commonly used as media of exchange. They were valuable, so that small quantities could be exchanged for large quantities of commodities, and those small quantities were easily portable.

The difficulty was that each piece of gold had to be weighed so that its value could be calculated. There was always the haunting fear, besides, that the gold or silver might be intermixed with less valuable metals.

The Lydian kingdom therefore issued "coins," pieces of gold, silver, or an alloy of the two, which were stamped with its weight and value, and had a picture of the king or some other design that indicated it to be official, and guaranteed its purity. The use of these coins greatly accelerated trade and added to the wealth of Lydia. The idea was quickly adopted by surrounding nations.

Alyattes of Lydia died in 560 B.C. and was succeeded by his son, Croesus, who reigned from 560 to 546 B.C. Under him, Lydia reached the peak of its prosperity. So fervently did the Greeks admire the wealth of Croesus (as two centuries before they had admired the wealth of Midas of Phrygia) that "rich as Croesus" is still a commonly used synonym.

Croesus admired the Greeks just as greatly. He poured wealth into the oracle at Delphi and made it a kind of religious center of the Greek world.

JUDAH

After the death of Josiah, in 609 B.C., Judah engaged in dynastic struggles and intrigued with Egypt against the Chaldean Empire. Nebuchadrezzar II lost patience and laid siege to Jerusalem. He carried it through to the bitter end, where Sennacherib, a little over a century before, had not. Nebuchadrezzar took Jerusalem and destroyed Solomon's Temple.

Nebuchadrezzar then deported the chief families of Judah into Babylonia as, a century and a half earlier, the chief families of Israel had been deported into Assyria. That should have been the end of Judah, as the earlier deportation had been the end of Israel.

A strange thing happened, though, for the Chaldean treatment of the Jews was benign and they prospered in Babylonia. What's more, the prophetic movement remained strong and preserved Jewish national feeling. The prophet Jeremiah had denounced non-Yahwistic practices bitterly in the time after Josiah, and the destruction of Jerusalem seemed to bear him out.

In Babylonia, therefore, the Jews finally adopted Yahwism and, with that, modern Judaism was born under the guidance of the prophet Ezekiel. The Bible began to be compiled and edited; and the early legendary books show many signs of Chaldean influence, and include many of the legends of creation and early history worked up by the Babylonians from the time of the Sumerians onward. (The Jews tried to connect themselves with Sumeria through Abraham, as the Romans tried to connect themselves with Troy through Aeneas.)

PERSIA

East of Babylonia was the land that had once been called Elam. It had often fought with Babylonia and had finally been destroyed by Ashurbanipal of Assyria, not long before Assyria itself was destroyed.

After the destruction of Assyria, Elam became part of the Median Empire and was called "Fars." To the Greeks, it became "Persis" and we call it "Persia." The city of Susa, once the Elamite capital, was now the capital of Persia. The people of the Persian province were very similar in language and culture to those of the main Median provinces, and they are often referred to together as "the Medes and the Persians."

The line of kings who ruled in Persia, under Median domination, were called the "Achaemenians," from a legendary ancestor, Achaemenius. About 558 B.C., Cyrus (585–529 B.C.), sometimes called "Cyrus the Great," became

ruler of Persia. He turned out to be an excellent and ambitious general. He rebelled against the Median central government and, in 550 B.C., took Ecbatana, the Median capital, and became ruler of Media himself.

The name "Median Empire" disappeared from the map, thereafter, and, in its place, there appeared the "Persian Empire" or, sometimes, to distinguish it from other Persian Empires later in history, the "Achaemenian Empire." Nothing much, however, had changed except the name. The Medes continued to occupy their provinces and to live much as they had always lived. Indeed, the Greeks often referred to the inhabitants of the Persian Empire as "Medes."

EGYPT

Egypt had a twilight glow of prosperity under its 26th dynasty. Under Ahmose ("Amasis" to the Greeks) Egypt was at peace. Ahmose was fascinated by Greek culture and made alliances with Lydia and with some of the Greek city-states in order to protect Egypt from the ambitious Persians.

GREECE

Ionia.   The Greek cities in Asia Minor were the intellectual leaders of Greece during this period.

In the cities of Miletus and Ephesus, in particular, there grew up a group of *philosophers* (Greek for "lovers of wisdom") who turned to the study of the physical universe on its own terms, without reference to the supernatural or to myths.

The first of these, by tradition, was Thales of Miletus (625–547 B.C.) who tried to reason out the fundamental structure of the universe, and who studied electricity and magnetism. He also apparently studied Babylonian astronomy and was able to predict the eclipse that stopped the war between Lydians and Medians in 585 B.C.

Anaximander of Miletus (610–547 B.C.) and Anaximenes of Miletus (fl. 545 B.C.) followed Thales, and began the practice of using logic carefully to back up their conclusions.

The Ionian cities shared in the Greek trend of

the period, in that oligarchies were displaced by tyrants.

This was also true of the Aegean islands, where Sappho of Lesbos (fl. 610–580 B.C.) was an outstanding poet of her times. Little of her work survives, but later Greeks compared her favorably with Homer.

Athens. In 600 B.C., Athens was in a state of deep economic turmoil and the oligarchic rule was so unpopular with the common people that a revolt was threatened.

Fortunately, the man of the hour was Solon (630–560 B.C.). He was elected archon in 594 B.C. and was a kindly liberal who arranged to ease the burden of debt on the ordinary people and set a limit on the amount of land that could be owned by the rich. He gave the poor a greater say in the government, reformed the currency to encourage trade, and set up a kinder and gentler law-code that guaranteed the right of every citizen to bring his case to court.

It was all a step in the direction of democracy ("rule of the people"). Many of the conservative nobility fought it viciously, however, so that there was no confidence among the people that Solon's reforms would long survive.

It wasn't surprising, then, that the people turned to Peisistratus, who became tyrant of Athens in 567 B.C.

Sparta. By 550 B.C., Sparta had formed a "Peloponnesian League" and dominated virtually all of Peloponnesus. Sparta was by this time fixed in its social structure as an unpleasantly mean-spirited oligarchy, with its particularly numerous and particularly ill-treated slaves ("helots"). What's more, Sparta interfered in other Greek city-states, wherever it could, in order to overthrow tyrants and reinstate oligarchies.

Elsewhere. The town of Sicyon in northern Peloponnesus was ruled by a capable tyrant named Cleisthenes from 600 to 570 B.C. He interested himself in the oracle at Delphi, just across the Gulf of Corinth, defeated those nearby towns that tried to control it, and set it up as an independent shrine. Thanks to this, and to gifts from Croesus of Lydia, Delphi became the most important oracle in Greece and the nearest thing to a religious center.

In Sicily, the first clash between Greeks and Carthaginians took place about 580 B.C.

ETRUSCANS

By 550 B.C., the Etruscans were approaching the peak of their power. Northward they had extended their sway throughout the Po River valley; and southward, they reached the Greek cities near Neapolis (known in modern times as Naples). The city of Rome was, in 550 B.C., ruled by their sixth king, Servius Tullius, who may also have been an Etruscan.

550 TO 500 B.C.

CHALDEAN EMPIRE

Nabonidus of Chaldea was more interested in archeology than in affairs of state—or, for that matter, the national religion. For this reason, the priests of Marduk were opposed to him, which meant that much of the populace was, too. Nabonidus went off hunting for his antiquarian relics and left his son, Belshazzar, in charge of his army, with the responsibility of defending a disaffected land.

When the Persians, under one of Cyrus's generals, attacked, Babylon could not mount an effective resistance. It fell in 539 B.C., and both Nabonidus and Belshazzar died soon after. The Chaldean Empire was destroyed only three-quarters of a century after its founding, and only a quarter of a century after the death of the great Nebuchadrezzar.

LYDIA

Croesus of Lydia noted the progress of Cyrus with alarm. He had formed an alliance with Nabonidus of Babylonia, and when Babylonia fell, he felt he would have to take strong action on his own. There is a tale to the effect that he sent a messenger to Delphi to inquire of the oracle what would happen if he attacked Cyrus. The oracle responded at once that if he attacked Cyrus "a great Empire would fall." Croesus assumed the Empire that would fall would be the Persian.

He attacked and was driven back. Cyrus then led his army into Lydia and, even though he was outnumbered by the Lydians, his handling of the battle won him a complete victory. He was the first general to make skillful use of mounted archers. He took Sardis, and Lydia disappeared from history. The great empire that fell had been Croesus' own.

Delphi's message has stood ever since as the typical "Delphic" or "oracular" utterance, which would come true no matter what happened.

EGYPT

Ahmose II died in 526 B.C., and his son succeeded him, reigning as Psamtik III. Almost at once, the Persian storm broke. Cyrus of Persia was, by then, dead, but his son, who reigned as Cambyses II from 529 to 522 B.C., invaded Egypt, won a battle at the borders and that was enough. Egypt was once again under foreign domination.

PERSIAN EMPIRE

Cyrus II, having founded the Persian Empire and taken over Chaldea and Lydia, died in 529 B.C. fighting the tribesmen in central Asia. His son, Cambyses, succeeded, and took Egypt.

Cambyses died in 522 B.C. and was succeeded by his brother-in-law, who reigned as Darius I

(550–486 B.C.) and is sometimes called "Darius the Great."

Under Darius I, the Persian Empire was at the peak of its power. It was by far the largest Empire that had been seen up to that time, since it included all of civilized Asia from the Aegean Sea to the borders of India, in addition to Egypt. Its east–west width was about 3000 miles, and it was the first realm that compared in area to modern nations, such as the United States. Its population may have been as high as 13 million— enormous for the times.

However, the primitive nature of transportation and communication in those days made this very size a weakness. It took a long time for the Persian monarch to find out what was happening at various places in his dominions, and a long time for him to be able to react appropriately.

Darius did his best to overcome this problem. He organized the Empire into 20 "satrapies," each under an administrator called a *satrap* (from a Persian word meaning a "protector"). He built an elaborate road system along which messengers could speed, with relay-stations for horses. He reorganized finances and built a new capital city, Persepolis, deep in the south–central section of the Empire.

In the days of the Median Empire, a religious reformer, Zarathrustra (628–551 B.C.) —known as Zoroaster to the Greeks—had been preaching in central Asia. In his view, the Universe was divided between two powers equal in strength. One was Ahura Mazda, who represented light and goodness; the other was Ahriman, who represented darkness and evil. The eternal cosmic war between the two produced no clear victory, but the struggle was so equal that the intervention of human beings on one side or the other might be all that was needed for a decision. Human beings should, therefore, be persuaded to be ethical and virtuous, thus helping to bring about the victory of the good.

Zoroastrianism flourished after the reformer's death, and, by 500 B.C., it was the predominant religion in the Persian Empire, replacing the older beliefs of Babylonia and Assyria (though the Egyptians, at this time, persisted more firmly in their religion).

JUDAH

After the fall of the Chaldean Empire, the Jews of Babylonia petitioned to be restored to Judea. The Persian government, which proved to be as lenient toward its heterogenous population (provided they accepted Persian overlordship and paid their tribute) as the Chaldeans had been, granted the wish and some Jews returned to Judah. Other Jews, however, remained in Babylonia and, ever since, there has always been a large percentage of the world's Jews outside the Jewish homeland. These outside Jews are the *Diaspora* (from a Greek word for "dispersion").

The Jews who returned to Judah managed to build a new temple in Jerusalem. This was completed about 515 B.C. and by 500 B.C., there was a new Judah (or "Judea," to use the Greek term —which I shall do from now on) that was but a shadow of the old one, but which gave the Jews a homeland again. This time, and forever after, the Jews were Yahwists, and Judaism was a going concern.

Indeed, as the Persian Empire was established, a nameless prophet, whose writings were attributed to Isaiah (who had actually lived nearly two centuries earlier) and who is therefore known as "second Isaiah" preached a new doctrine. Not only was Yahweh the only god of the Jews, he was the only god of all humanity. It was monotheism taken to its logical extreme, and it was from the second Isaiah that true monotheism descended to later Jews and, through them, to the Christians and Muslims.

GREECE

Ionia. When Persia defeated Lydia, it absorbed the Ionian cities into its Empire. It was less lenient than Lydia had been, and it made sure that only those tyrants ruled over the Ionian cities who were totally subservient to Persian wishes.

Intellectual life continued, however. Heraclitus of Ephesus (540–480 B.C.) emphasized the importance of change and thought fire was the fundamental substance of the universe. (If we substitute for "fire" the modern term "energy," he was not so far wrong.)

Xenophanes of Colophon (560–478 B.C.) was a skeptic. He denounced the immorality of the gods in the Greek myths, and objected to the way in which they were made humanlike. By 546 B.C., he found his views displeased those around him and he left Ionia and went to southern Italy, where the cities made up *Magna Graecia* (Latin words meaning "Great Greece").

Off the Ionian coast is the island of Samos, which remained free of Persia for a while. From 535 to 522 B.C., it was ruled by a tyrant, Polycrates, who built up a navy and, for a while, ruled the eastern Mediterranean. An important philosopher, Pythagoras of Samos (580–500 B.C.), who was the first to actually use the word "philosopher," found the atmosphere of Samos oppressive and also migrated to Magna Graecia.

The departure of Xenophanes and Pythagoras showed how the intellectual life of Ionia was declining under Persian rule.

Athens. At this time, Athens was under the tyrant Peisistratus, who ruled Athens from 567 to 521 B.C., with few breaks. He was one of the better tyrants, keeping Solon's reforms, protecting the peasantry, beautifying Athens, keeping the peace, editing the Homeric poems into the form in which they now exist, encouraging industry and trade, and, in general, ruling humanely.

He did encourage a change in religion, however. The old Olympian religion—the gods that appear in the works of Homer and Hesiod— tended to be rather sapless and bland. The people found much greater satisfaction in "mystery religions," which promised salvation and bliss in the afterworld for those who accepted their rituals. The rituals were kept secret (*mystery* is from the Greek word for "secret") and some remain secret to this day.

There were the Eleusinian mysteries, focused on Demeter, the goddess of agriculture; there were also mysteries involving Bacchus, the god of the vine; and others involving Orpheus, a semidivine musician. All involved ecstatic or orgiastic behavior and dealt with death and rebirth. Between the excitement of the rites and the promise of an afterlife, the mystery religions were very satisfying and fulfilling to the emotional needs of people.

Peisistratus encouraged this because it further broke down the power of the nobles who had reserved for themselves the priestly functions in the old religion.

After Peisistratus died in 527 B.C., Hippias and Hipparchus, his sons, succeeded as joint tyrants. They were less capable, and opposition to them grew. Hipparchus was assassinated and the frightened Hippias tightened his rule, which simply increased the opposition.

A liberal nobleman, Cleisthenes (570–505 B.C.), a grandson of Cleisthenes, the tyrant of Sicyon, headed the democratic opposition to the tyrant. He attained the help of Sparta, which was always ready to move against tyrants, and overthrew Hippias, driving him into exile.

Sparta expected the reestablishment of an oligarchy, but Cleisthenes went his own way, further reorganizing the Athenian government and spreading power to so many of the citizen population that we can call Athens a democracy, thereafter.

It was the first important democracy in the civilized world, but it was highly imperfect. It was a democracy only for its citizens, who had to be of native Athenian birth on both sides. Foreigners had only limited rights, and slaves (of whom there were many) remained slaves and without rights, however "free" Athens might be.

Cleisthenes also established "ostracism," a system whereby anyone thought to be dangerous to the state could be banished for 10 years without loss of citizenship or property. (The name was scratched on pieces of broken pottery, *ostrakon* in Greek; hence the name of the practice.)

Sparta. Cleomenes I, one of the two kings of Sparta, reigning from 521 to 490 B.C., helped drive Hippias out of Athens. Sparta then tried to prevent the establishment of a democracy in Athens, but failed at this.

By 500 B.C., the two most important powers in Greece were Athens and Sparta, with Athens comparatively free, democratic, and bursting with artistic energy; and Sparta, militaristic, enslaved, and intellectually empty.

Greek Italy. Pythagoras of Samos left the east and settled in Croton, a city located on the Italian toe. There he developed his rather semimystical view of life and founded what was almost a mystery religion. He was important in science and mathematics, discovering irrational numbers and the Pythagorean hypothesis. Either he or a pupil of his was the first to suggest that the Earth might move through space.

Croton meanwhile fought bitterly with Sybaris, another Greek city farther north, and in 510 B.C., Sybaris was defeated and destroyed.

By 500 B.C., the process of Greek colonization had come to an end. The available positions on shore in the east were now preempted by the powerful Persian Empire. In the west, it came to an end because of the enmity of Carthage.

CARTHAGE

In 535 B.C., the Carthaginian navy, in alliance with the Etruscans, defeated Greek ships off the island of Corsica at the Battle of Alalia. Greek expansion was blunted and further colonization ceased. This was the first decisive sea battle in history.

By 500 B.C., the stage was set for a struggle between Carthage and the Greek cities, just as in the east, the stage was set for a struggle between Persia and the Greek cities.

ETRUSCANS

The Etruscans were entering a period of decline after the brief triumph of the Battle of Alalia, because Celtic tribes from north of the Alps were drifting into Italy and placing pressure on the northern frontiers. The Etruscans were less able to keep watch on the south, where revolts broke out.

Rome, for instance, grew restive under its seventh and last king, Tarquinius Superbus (*Tarquin the Proud* in English.) He, too, was of Etruscan origin. Roman legends claim that the rape of a Roman noblewoman, Lucretia, by Sextus Tarquinius, the son of the king, was the spark that started the revolt. This is probably mere romance, but, in any case, something started it.

In 509 B.C., Tarquin was expelled and Rome became an oligarchy under the rule of two consuls, annually elected. The two consuls each checked the other from becoming too powerful, as in the case of the Spartan kings. Also, as in Sparta, the two consuls had, as their chief function, leading the army to war, while the actual government was in the hands of a Senate, consisting of the leading families (*patricians*, from a Latin word meaning "fathers").

CELTS

An Indo-European people, called Keltoi (Celts) by the Greeks and Gauls by the Romans had lived north of the Alps since before 1200 B.C. They had expanded westward into what is now France and Spain and northward into the British Isles. By 500 B.C., they were beginning to seep across the barrier of the Alps into Italy.

INDIA

Aryan tribes (the Sinhalese) had, by 500 B.C., reached the island of Ceylon (now known as Sri Lanka) off the southern tip of India. In doing so, however, they did not completely displace the pre-Aryan population.

There were revolts against the religion of Brahmanism that had been brought in by the Aryans, with its developing multiplicity of gods, its complicated ritual, and the caste system, that was now fully developed. New religions, therefore, appeared on the scene.

One new religion that developed was Jainism. It does not involve a Creator, but considers all life to be sacred and preaches asceticism. Jainism did not prove very successful. Even today, it is confined almost entirely to India and to those of Indian descent. Within India there are some 3 million Jains.

More successful was Buddhism, founded in northern India by Siddartha Gautama (563–483 B.C.) who came to be known as the Buddha ("enlightened one"). Buddhism also lacked a Creator, but stressed virtuous living, and preached the rebirth of a soul over and over until, through earned merit, the final reward of nirvana (peaceful nonexistence) was attained. By 500 B.C., Buddhism was spreading vigorously over India.

CHINA

In China during this period, schools of ethics appeared. One, supposedly founded by Lao-tzu (concerning whom nothing nonlegendary is known) started about 565 B.C. It is called Taoism, and eschewed all form, ritual, and ceremony. It taught that only right living was important.

Toward the end of the century, Kung Fu-tzu (551–479 B.C.), or "Confucius," in Latinized form, also taught morality and ethical behavior.

It is odd that in this century important religious reforms had arisen, apparently independently, across the entire width of civilization from China to Sicily.

There was Confucianism and Taoism in China; Jainism and Buddhism in India; Zoroastrianism in Persia; Judaism in Judea; Mystery religions in Greece; Pythagoreanism in Italy; and, for good measure, Rationalist Philosophy in Ionia.

AFRICA

South of Egypt, Nubia absorbed some of the culture of Egypt. At times when Egypt was particularly weak, Nubian raiders would make their way northward. About 750 B.C., Nubian rulers even set themselves up as Egyptian pharaohs, but were driven out by the Assyrian invaders.

About 500 B.C., Nubia had its capital at the city of Meroe, about 275 miles south of the present border of Egypt. Meroe had entered the Iron Age, and was the center of a prosperous region, concerning which little is now known.

500 TO 450 B.C.

GREECE

Athens. The Ionian cities rebelled against Persia in 499 B.C., and, for a while, did well. They appealed for help to other Greek cities, and Athens sent 20 ships, while five more arrived from the island of Euboea, north of Athens. The Ionians, under the leadership of the city of Miletus, dashed eastward and burned Sardis, the former capital of Lydia.

Persia's slow bulk, however, finally gathered its armies and struck back. The island of Cyprus was taken, the Ionian armies were defeated, their fleet sunk, Miletus was destroyed, and its surviving inhabitants deported. Ionian leadership in science and culture vanished.

Darius of Persia then planned to punish Athens for having helped the Ionians. In 492 B.C., Persian forces entered Europe for the first time and took over Thrace along the western shore of the Black Sea, where Bulgaria is now located. The Persians forced the kingdom of Macedonia, just to the south of Thrace, into puppethood.

In 490 B.C., a Persian force was sent across the Aegean Sea, compelling the submission of the Aegean islands, including Euboea. The expedition landed on Marathon in Athenian territory, but it lacked cavalry. The more heavily armored Athenians, under Miltiades (554–489 B.C.) attacked the Persian forces and beat them. It was the first clear indication that Greek infantry armor and tactics were superior to that of the Persians. A runner, Pheidippides, ran from Marathon to Athens to bring the good tidings to the Athenians, dying after he had delivered the message, according to the story. The distance from Marathon to Athens, a little over 26 miles, has ever since been that of the long-distance "marathon race."

The Persians withdrew. In 486 B.C., Darius died and was succeeded by his son, Xerxes, who had to deal with various rebellions within the Persian Empire. He was not ready to resume the attack on Greece until 480 B.C.

The interval from 490 to 480 B.C. was spent by the Athenians under the leadership of Themistocles (524–460 B.C.) in strengthening their navy. Those opposing him were ostracized so that Athens could continue on the path chosen without partisan bickering.

In 480 B.C., a large Persian army of about 100,000 (greatly exaggerated beyond that by Greek accounts) crossed into Thrace and marched southward through Greece. In August, 480 B.C., at Thermopylae, a narrow pass just south of Thessaly, they were held up by a band of Greeks. The Persians forced their way through at last, while a contingent of 300 Spartans, fighting under their king, Leonidas (half-brother and successor of Cleomenes I) resisted and died to the last man. That was Sparta's finest hour. The Persians then invaded Athenian territory and burned Athens, while the Athenians fled to the islands. The Persians were now at the peak of their power.

At Salamis, however, a small island just west of Athens, the Greek fleet met the Persian fleet in September, 480 B.C., and destroyed it. In the narrow strait, the clumsier Persian ships could not easily maneuver.

Xerxes returned to Persia, leaving the fighting to his generals. In 479 B.C., the Greeks under the Spartan general, Pausanias (d. 470 B.C.) smashed the Persians at the land battle of Plataea, just north of Athens. Once again, Greek military organization proved superior to that of the Persians, and the attempt to conquer Greece was abandoned by the Persian Empire.

Athens then formed an alliance with the Aegean islands and the Ionian cities, which, in 478 B.C., were freed of Persian domination. By 450 B.C., Athenian influence extended over all the coasts and islands of the Aegean Sea. Athens, between 460 and 457 B.C., also built stout walls about the city and about its port, Piraeus, and connected the two with a pair of long walls that extended the necessary five-mile distance. Behind these walls and with its navy controlling the eastern Mediterranean, Athens felt secure.

Athens continued to advance toward a complete democracy (for its citizens) with government offices filled by lot in many cases.

In 460 B.C., a liberal nobleman, Pericles (495–429 B.C.), became the virtual ruler of Athens, and under him, the city entered a period of great intellectual, literary, and artistic merit. The first of Athens' great tragedians, Aeschylus (525–456 B.C.) wrote his trilogy concerning Agamemnon (who had led the Greek army against Troy) in 458 B.C.

Outside Athens, Greek literature also flourished, of course. Great poets included Anacreon of Tos (570–488 B.C.), Simonides of Ceos (556–468 B.C.), and Pindar of Thebes (522–438 B.C.).

Sparta. Sparta had shared in the triumph over Persia, but somehow the victories of Athens at Marathon and Salamis seemed to outweigh the gallant Spartan defense at Thermopylae and its victory at Plataea. (The clever Athenians were much better at self-promotion than the stolid Spartans were.)

What's more, in 464 B.C., an earthquake wreaked destruction in the city of Sparta, and the helots of Messenia seized the opportunity to revolt. It took the Spartans three years to end the revolt. Cimon (510–451 B.C.), the son of Miltiades, who had won the battle of Marathon, was then influential in Athens. He believed Athens should maintain friendly relations with Sparta, and persuaded it to offer to help the Spartans to beat down their slaves. Sparta, out of suspicion and pride, rather churlishly refused the help, thus antagonizing Athens.

It took Sparta quite a while to recover from this disaster, which gave Athens a chance to build its walls without interference and to organize its Aegean influence.

By 450 B.C., Sparta was itself again, and it could be seen that Greece now had two masters: Athens by sea and Sparta by land. A contest between the two was inevitable.

Sicily. The Greek cities of Sicily and Italy did not participate in the war against Persia. To them it seemed far away, and there was a nearer enemy at hand—Carthage, which controlled the eastern third of the island of Sicily.

The Greek cities of Sicily fought among themselves, and Carthage was ready to take advantage of the situation. In 480 B.C., a Carthaginian army advanced eastward in Sicily. However, in a battle near Himera, on the northern shore of the island, the Greeks won a great victory. Tradition says that this battle took place on the same day as the Battle of Salamis, but that sounds too good to be true. In any case, Carthage was defeated in the west even as Persia was defeated in the east.

By 450 B.C., Syracuse emerged as the most important city in Sicily.

PERSIAN EMPIRE

The Persian Empire lost some coastal territory in the far west to the Greeks, but that seemed a small matter and, on the map, the Persian Empire looked as large and as formidable as ever. The total population of Greece at this time may have been 2.5 million, while that of the Persian Empire was 14 million.

Nevertheless, Persian self-confidence was smashed. In any battle with the Greeks, whether by land or sea, the Persians were half-defeated before the start. The Athenians, on the other hand, did not scruple to send troops to help regions rebelling against the Persians, or to attack the island of Cyprus, for instance. By 450 B.C., then, the Persian Empire, for all its size, was in decline.

ROME

In this period, Rome fought off all attempts to restore the monarchy, and battled endlessly with neighboring cities, usually with success. The common people, or "plebeians," struggled against the patrician rulers and, by threatening to secede and form a separate city, they managed to get certain reforms. "Tribunes" were appointed which would guard plebeian rights by crying *veto* ("I forbid") when the Senate passed laws they considered hurtful to the people.

By 450 B.C., Rome had a written law-code and

was establishing itself as a leader among the Latin cities to their south.

The Etruscans, however, were fading rapidly, chiefly because of the expanding presence of the Gauls in northern Italy.

450 TO 400 B.C.

GREECE

Athens, under Pericles (often referred to as "Periclean Athens") was at the peak of its golden age, the most brilliant seen up to that time and for a long time afterward. The great tragedians flourished. In addition to Aeschylus, there was Sophocles (496–406 B.C.), who wrote *Oedipus Rex*, and Euripides (484–406 B.C.), who wrote *Medea*. Herodotus (484–424 B.C.) wrote a world history, concentrating on the Persian Wars, and is known as "the father of history." Thucydides (d. 401 B.C.) wrote history less charmingly, perhaps, but was the first to make an effort to be objective.

Phidias (490–430 B.C.) was the greatest sculptor of the age. He carved the statue of Zeus that stood at the stadium where the Olympic Games took place, and which was considered one of the Seven Wonders of the Ancient World. He also supervised the construction of the great temples of the Acropolis. This included the Parthenon, dedicated to the patron goddess of the city, Athena, and widely considered one of the most beautiful buildings ever constructed.

Among its philosophers was Anaxagoras (500–428 B.C.), an Ionian who had emigrated to Athens, and who was accused of impiety for stating that the Sun was not Apollo's divine chariot, but was a blazing rock as large as the Peloponnesus. Hippocrates (460–377 B.C.) was the first physician of note and is often called the "father of medicine." Finally, there was Socrates (470–399 B.C.), perhaps the most influential philosopher who ever lived.

Athens grew in population, including 50,000 citizens, and also perhaps 100,000 slaves.

For all its freedom (for citizens) at home, however, Athens became increasingly tyrannical outside its borders. By 448 B.C., what had been an Aegean alliance had become an Athenian Empire. The money contributions from Athens' allies were used to help beautify Athens. When any ally objected to this and tried to leave the alliance, it was brutally beaten back into line. The result was that resentment against Athens grew steadily.

Then, too, Athens fell into the trap of overconfidence and engaged in unnecessary military adventures. A large force was sent to Egypt to help an Egyptian rebellion against Persia in 456 B.C., and that force was wiped out. Athens suffered land defeats at the hands of Sparta, Corinth, and Thebes, and though these did not shake their power at sea, they had a weakening effect.

Athens, by playing the role of master of Greece too openly and too undiplomatically, frightened and angered other cities, and caused them to turn to Sparta. In 431 B.C., war between Sparta and Athens broke out. It was called the "Peloponnesian War."

Athens did not attempt to fight the Spartans on land, since they were sure to be defeated in that case. Instead, the Athenians crowded inside the walls that encased Athens and Piraeus. There they huddled, and waited for their navy to harass the Spartans and wear them down.

Unfortunately, the ancient world knew very little about hygiene, and a plague struck Athens in 430 B.C., spreading rapidly and killing perhaps a third of the population, including Pericles himself in 429 B.C. Athens was badly weakened by this, and the war degenerated into a kind of stalemate, in which both sides won nondecisive victories—the Spartans under Brasidas (d. 422 B.C.), and the Athenians under Cleon (d. 422 B.C.).

A peace was established in 421 B.C. It was called "the Peace of Nicias," because the Athenian general, Nicias (d. 413 B.C.), negotiated it.

It didn't last, however, and the war broke out again. Athens was now under the influence of Alcibiades (450–404 B.C.), who was brilliant, but erratic. He suggested that a great expedition be sent against Syracuse so that the resources of the west could be turned against Sparta. It was a foolish idea, but Alcibiades might have carried it off. However, he was accused of impiety just before the expedition sailed. After it had sailed, in 415 B.C., he was called back to stand trial. Fearing conviction, Alcibiades defected to Sparta and taught the dull Spartans how to fight against the Athenians much more effectively.

Without Alcibiades, the Sicilian expedition went on, with Nicias in command. He was an uninspired general, who made all the wrong decisions, and the Athenian forces were eventually wiped out. This broke Athens' spirit, as Persia's had been by the battles of Salamis and Plataea.

Nevertheless, Athens fought on. Persia saw that it was to its advantage to help bring about the destruction of Athens as the most expansionist city in Greece. Therefore, Persia began a policy of paying subsidies to Sparta, and Sparta, in return, agreed to let Persia have the Greek cities on the Asia Minor coast.

As long as the Athenian navy remained intact, however, Athens could not be defeated. Fortunately, for itself, Sparta found an admiral, Lysander (d. 395 B.C.), who was capable of fighting at sea. In 404 B.C., Lysander defeated and destroyed the Athenian navy at Aegospotami, not very far from the ancient site of Troy.

Athens could fight no more. She was forced to accept defeat, pull down her walls, change her democracy into an oligarchy, and bow to Spartan domination.

By 400 B.C., Sparta was master of Greece;

however, all of Greece, including Sparta, was fatally weakened by the long war. The Athenian playwright, Aristophanes (450–388 B.C.) wrote political comedies (like the famous *Lysistrata*, produced in 411 B.C.), which bitterly portrayed the anguish of a senseless war raging on and on —with only victims and no true victors.

PERSIAN EMPIRE

The Persian Empire continued to look formidable on the map. It crushed revolts in Egypt, and it interfered skillfully in the Peloponnesian War, in such a way as to enfeeble Greece and reduce its danger to her.

Nevertheless, inner turmoil continued and there was the dynastic quarreling that destroys so many monarchies where no fixed system of succession is worked out. Every time a ruler dies, there is apt to be a civil war between different claimants for the throne.

Thus, when Darius II, who had ruled from 423 to 404 B.C., died, his older son began a reign that endured from 404 to 359 B.C., and his younger brother, Cyrus (called "Cyrus the Younger"), rebelled.

With the end of the Peloponnesian war, there were many Greek soldiers who suddenly had no employment, and they were willing to sign on as mercenaries to whomever would pay them. Cyrus hired 10,000 Greeks under a Spartan general and marched them eastward to make war.

The Greeks, along with Cyrus's Persian contingents, were led deep into the Empire, and there, not far north of Babylon, they fought the hosts of Artaxerxes II at the Battle of Cunaxa in 401 B.C. They fought well, but Cyrus was killed and that meant the revolt was over and that the 10,000 Greeks were stranded a thousand miles inside Persia. The Persians managed to kill the Spartan general by treachery, and felt that the Greeks could now be scattered and wiped out.

The Greeks, however, under an Athenian general, Xenophon (431–352 B.C.), held together, fought off all Persian attempts to destroy them, and made their way northward to the Black Sea in March 400 B.C.

By 400 B.C., the Greeks could see how far the

apparently imposing structure of the Persian Empire had decayed. They could see that if they could but unite, they might bring that Empire crashing down. But the catch was that they would have to unite, and could not.

JUDEA

The city of Jerusalem and its Jewish inhabitants lived quietly under the Persian Empire, but there was the constant danger that they would be wiped out by hostile neighbors, or, possibly, lose their identity by intermarrying with them.

In 445 B.C., however, Jerusalem came under the rule of Nehemiah, who had been a high official in the Persian government. By 439 B.C., he managed to obtain permission to rebuild the walls of Jerusalem.

About that time, or soon after, the scribe, Ezra, arrived. He brought with him the early books of the Bible and, in a series of revival meetings, persuaded the Jews to separate themselves from their non-Jewish wives and to live by the tenets of the Judaistic laws and rituals. That made it possible for Judaism to survive and, if it never became a world-religion, it did serve as the seed from which two world-religions were to sprout.

Just as the Jews had been influenced by the Chaldean legends of the Creation, the Flood, and early history, so they were now influenced by Zoroastrian ideas. They could not accept the existence of dual principles of good and evil in eternal and uncertain conflict. They did not wish to envisage evil as being as powerful as good. They did, however, accept Satan as a counterpart of God, and, though he was never pictured as equal to God, the vision of a good-versus-evil conflict did enter Judaism as a result.

ROME

Rome had become the head of the "Latin League," a combination of cities to its south. The Latin League now rivaled the Etruscan confederation of cities to the north.

By 400 B.C., Rome was rising rapidly and the Etruscans were declining even more rapidly, but the Celtic tribes of Gauls in the north were now advancing southward in force and were threatening to engulf them both.

400 TO 350 B.C.

GREECE

Sparta. Sparta was master of Greece after the battle of Aegospotami, but she proved to be as undiplomatic and tactless in emphasizing her leadership as Athens had been. All the Greek cities who had turned against Athens, now turned against Sparta; and Sparta was then compelled, as Athens had been, to use force constantly to keep the other Greeks in line.

Athens took advantage of Spartan involvement in the difficulties of mastery, to kick out the conservative nobility who had imposed a narrow and oppressive oligarchy on them, and restore the democracy. Athens rebuilt its walls in 393 B.C. as well as its alliances. A new Athenian-dominated naval league arose, although it was weaker than it had earlier been. Moreover, and what was far worse, the Athenians, ever-mindful of the Sicilian defeat, no longer had the courage to undertake risks, so that their foreign policy remained very cautious.

Culturally, however, Athens continued to shine. Socrates had been executed in 399 B.C. for his unpopular teachings, although his pupil, Plato, continued to teach and to describe his version of Socrates' views in a series of *Dialogs* that have been popular reading, among the scholarly, ever since, right down to the present day.

One of the Spartan kings was now Agesilaus

II (444–360 B.C.), who had come to the throne in 399 B.C. He was small and lame, and he epitomized all the Spartan virtues and shortcomings. He was brave and resolute to an extreme, but he was stubborn and short-sighted.

He led an army into Asia Minor in 395 B.C. and ravaged the territory at will. This further proved, if this was needed, that Persia was soft and ready to fall, but Agesilaus had to come back to Greece to deal with those cities that were trying to combine against Sparta, and lost the chance to win great victories.

Persia fell back on her best weapon—money. It could use the money to persuade Sparta to do things Persia's way. A Spartan negotiator, named Antalcidas, negotiated the "Peace of Antalcidas" in 386 B.C. (It was also called the "King's Peace," the king being Artaxerxes II, of course.)

By the Peace of Antalcidas, all Greek cities were supposed to be free. This meant that Sparta insisted on all alliances and leagues being dissolved (except for its own hold over the southern half of the Peloponnesus, of course). The intention of making all the cities free sounded good, but it was a device to weaken all of Greece to the benefit of Sparta (and, even more so, to the benefit of Persia).

In particular, Sparta, under the leadership of the aggressive and (as we would say today) hawkish Agesilaus II, forced its domination on Thebes.

Thebes. Thebes, a city about 35 miles northwest of Athens, was prominent in Greek legend. The famous Oedipus had been the king of Thebes, for instance. About 550 B.C., Thebes had formed a league of cities in its neighborhood ("Boeotia"), which it dominated. This had not been carried through peacefully, and Thebes had had to fight for 50 years before the Boeotian League was established.

By the Peace of Antalcidas, the Boeotian League would have to be broken up, but this the Thebans refused to do. In 382 B.C., a Spartan contingent, therefore, occupied the Theban citadel and dissolved the League by force. Thebes had been anti-Athenian and had fought on Spar-

ta's side in the Peloponnesian War, but now it turned anti-Spartan with a vengeance.

In 364 B.C., a Theban general, Pelopidas (d. 364 B.C.) managed to seize the citadel and expel the Spartan garrison. The Thebans then made an alliance with Athens against Sparta, and the Athenian fleet defeated the Spartan ships, so that Sparta no longer controlled the sea.

Sparta was willing to make a peace settlement with Thebes and Athens, for despite her victories and mastery, she was suffering the fate of all military powers who didn't know when to quit. Continual wars had been a serious drain on her soldiers, so that there were fewer skilled Spartan warriors than there had been, and those that still existed were war-weary. Sparta, however, would not give up the show of mastery.

When Epaminondas (410–362 B.C.), the Theban ambassador, showed up to sign the peace for the Boeotian League, Agesilaus II refused to allow it. Each Boeotian city would have to sign separately, and Epaminondas refused this demand.

Therefore, the Spartans sent an army under Agesilaus' co-king, Cleombrotus I (who had been reigning since 380 B.C.) to beat the Thebans and force their capitulation.

The Spartans encountered the Thebans at Leuctra, west of Thebes, and there Epaminondas planned a new type of battle. He did not line up his soldiers in a straight line three or four deep, the kind of phalanx the Greeks were accustomed to, and in the use of which the Spartans were perfect.

Instead, he built up his left wing till it was 50 soldiers deep. It was intended to have a massive weight that would crush the Spartan right wing where its best fighters would be massed. The center of the army was set back, and the right wing was set back still further. The center would strike the Spartans when they were already demoralized, and the right would do so in time to finish the havoc.

The Spartans were so used to winning by their usual tactics that they didn't try to adjust to the new set-up. In 371 B.C., the battle of Leuctra was fought and it went exactly as Epaminondas had hoped. The Spartans were crushed. A thousand Spartan soldiers (whom Sparta simply could not afford to lose) died, including King Cleombrotus himself.

That one defeat sufficed to put an end to Spartan mastery, as defeat is bound to do once a military power has been reduced to a shell. Never again were the Spartans to be conquerors. They lost their grip on everything but Sparta itself and a small bit of surrounding territory. They had trouble maintaining even that.

The Theban victory merely reduced Greece to chaos, however. None of the cities would accept Theban domination any more than they had accepted Athenian or Spartan domination. Fighting continued endlessly with no one city able to establish power over the others.

One Greek, Isocrates of Athens (436–338 B.C.), could see clearly what was happening. He knew that the cities were destroying themselves and that they must unite to prevent that destruction. He saw that the only hope for unification was to have them engage in some large common policy, and he suggested that they unite in a war against the Persian Empire. It was a matter of solving the problems of war by additional war, but nothing else seemed possible.

By 350 B.C., then, the Greek cities were in a virtual state of anarchy, and it was clear (though they could not see it for themselves) that they would all fall to some outside power.

Despite this endless fighting, the intellectual brilliance of Greek culture continued in this period. Democritus of Abdera (460–370 B.C.), for instance, put forward the notion of "atomism," claiming that all matter consisted of fundamental, irreducible particles. This was not accepted by the other philosophers of the time, but he was correct. Eudoxus of Cnidus (400–350 B.C.) made important advances both in mathematics and astronomy.

Thessaly. Thessaly was a plain in northeastern Greece that was important in Mycenean times. The legendary Jason, of Argonaut fame, and Achilles, greatest of the Greek heroes at Troy, were Thessalians. In later times, however, Thessaly was out of the current of Greek development and was not important in history. In 371 B.C., Jason of Pherae (a town in central Thessaly) succeeded in uniting Thessaly and, for a moment, as Sparta fell, it looked as though Jason might conceivably unite Greece under his leadership. In 370 B.C., however, Jason was assassinated, and the chance passed.

Syracuse. Syracuse was not involved in the internal battles in Greece. It had to fight the Carthaginians.

Soon after 400 B.C., Dionysius I (430–367 B.C.) became tyrant of Syracuse. He beat the Carthaginians and, by 383 B.C., he had seized control of five sixths of Sicily and had restricted Carthage to the western tip. He also seized control of many of the Greek cities in Italy and even extended his control over Epirus, a tribal area northwest of Greece that was slowly being penetrated by Greek culture.

At this moment, Syracuse was the strongest of the Greek city-states, and Dionysius was the most powerful man in Greece. It was at least conceivable that he might have been able to serve as the leader of a united Greece.

However, he was defeated by the Carthaginians in 381 B.C., and never fully recovered from that. He died in 367 B.C., and his son, Dionysius II, who reigned till 343 B.C., lacked his father's ability. By 350 B.C., Syracuse was clearly in decline.

EGYPT

Egypt did not rest quietly under Persian rule. After the Battle of Marathon and the death of Darius I, Egypt had rebelled but the rebellion had been crushed. After the "March of the Ten Thousand" had revealed the inner weakness of Persia, Egypt had rebelled again, with greater success.

One more native dynasty of pharaohs was established in 380 B.C., the 30th, and under three of these rulers it almost seemed as though Egypt was reborn. The last of these pharaohs was Nectanebo, who reigned from 360 to 343 B.C. He was the last native pharaoh in a line stretching back to Narmer 25 centuries earlier.

PERSIAN EMPIRE

The Persian Empire, even minus Egypt, still looked vast on the map. In 358 B.C., an energetic king, Artaxerxes III, came to the throne and reigned till 336 B.C. He managed to bring back under his control various rebellious provinces, and prepared an expedition to retake Egypt as well.

ROME

Rome, after a war of 10 years, had conquered and taken the Etruscan city of Veii, just to its north, which demonstrated the weakening of Etruscan power. Indeed, that power had come to an end,

for the Etruscan cities were falling to the Gauls.

Rome, too, fell to the Gauls in 390 B.C., and was sacked. The Gauls eventually withdrew after exacting tribute. (Roman tales of having defeated the Gauls may be taken as patriotic nonsense.) It took Rome considerable time to recover.

In 380 B.C., Rome began the construction of a wall about the city, and by 350 B.C. it was still laboring to revive its alliances and to regain what power it had possessed before the coming of the Gauls.

The sack of the city had, by the way, destroyed its archives. All tales about what went on before 390 B.C., are, therefore, strictly legendary, although, being romance, they are very interesting and are easy to remember.

350 TO 300 B.C.

MACEDONIA

Macedonia lay to the north of Greece. It spoke a Greek dialect and was absorbing Greek culture, even though the Greeks themselves considered the Macedonians as outsiders. They had remained a monarchy and did not take part in the war against Persia, but accepted Persian domination when Darius and Xerxes attacked Greece.

During the Peloponnesian War and thereafter, Macedonia, which remained at peace, grew prosperous. The great Greek tragedian, Euripides, spent his last years at Macedonia, as a haven of quiet.

While Thebes was briefly master of Greece, it interfered with the political infighting in the north and, to insure quiet in Macedonia, they brought back with them, as hostage, Philip (382–336 B.C.),the 13-year-old brother of the Macedonian king, Perdiccas III. In Thebes, the shrewd young Philip closely observed the manner in which the Thebans fought their wars. In particular, he studied the Theban phalanx.

When Philip returned to Macedonia, he found

that palace turmoil gave him his opportunity. In 359 B.C., Perdiccas III died in battle, leaving only a young son as heir. Philip served as regent and, in 356 B.C., he (as uncles sometimes did) took over the throne and began to reign as Philip II.

By then, he had conquered and quieted the tribal areas north of Greece, and all the area from the Black Sea to the Adriatic Sea was under his control. He reorganized his army, setting up a phalanx that was an enormous improvement over the Theban version. With long spears, held up or resting on the rank before, the new Macedonian phalanx resembled a giant hedgehog. It could maneuver (when thoroughly trained) and it was supported by cavalry. Philip also made use of the catapult and other newly invented forms of siege machinery. This made it possible to batter down walls and force entry, rather than having to sit down for a prolonged period waiting for the besieged city to starve to death.

Philip had married Olympias of Epirus, thus strengthening his hold on that Adriatic kingdom. In 356 B.C., Olympias gave birth to a son named Alexander (356–323 B.C.). According to the tale,

Alexander was born on the same day that some vandal had burned the Temple to Artemis in Ephesus (one of the Seven Wonders of the Ancient World). When asked why he had done this, the vandal said it was to make his name immortal. For that reason, his name was stricken from all records, but it was remembered just the same. It was Herostratus.

Philip II now turned southward, feeling he could gradually increase his strength as the Greek cities continued their endless and useless fighting. Gold mines had been discovered in Macedonia and that meant that Philip could bribe various Greek leaders to be on his side.

The Athenian orator, Demosthenes (384–322 B.C.) saw the danger of Philip and inveighed against him in masterly orations, called "Philippics" (a term still used to represent any vitriolic and eloquent oratorical attack on someone or something). The Athenians cheered while Demosthenes spoke, but they were no longer the dynamic people of the previous century. They did nothing, particularly since other orators, like Aeschines (389–314 B.C.) and Isocrates pointed to the Persian Empire as the greater foe.

It was only when Philip had taken over all of northern Greece that Athens stirred to the danger and made an alliance with Thebes against him. In 338 B.C., the Macedonians met the Theban-Athenian army at Chaeronea, west of Thebes. Philip II won a total victory, while his 18-year-old son, Alexander, led a cavalry charge that clinched matters. The Theban elite troops, like the Spartans at Thermopylae, died to a man, and 33 years after the battle of Leuctra, Thebes' mastery was as dead as Sparta's.

Philip II now forced himself on Greece as leader of a united league, which was to follow Isocrates' plan and conquer Persia. (Isocrates had died, according to the tale, on the day of the battle at Chaeronea, at the age of 98.) Where Pericles of Athens, Agesilaus of Sparta, Epaminondas of Thebes, Jason of Pherae, and Dionysius of Syracuse had all failed to unite Greece, Philip II aspired to succeed.

Of the Greek city-states, only Sparta refused to join the league. It was powerless but it clung to its past. It would not join any league in which it was not the leader. Philip II, honoring Sparta's past, left it to itself—but he never invaded Persia. He, too, failed, for in 336 B.C., he was assassinated.

The 20-year-old Alexander succeeded as Alexander III, and Philip's dominions rose in revolt at once against what was, presumably, a young and incapable king. Alexander quickly showed why he was eventually to be known universally as "Alexander the Great." With phenomenal speed and unerring design, he crushed all revolts, dashed southward, defeated Thebes, destroyed the city, and spared Athens the same fate, so he said, only for the sake of its services against the Persians.

Then, in 334 B.C., he crossed over into Persia. Artaxerxes had reconquered Egypt in 343 B.C., so that Persia was intact again, but he had died in 336 B.C., and was succeeded by the weak Darius III (d. 330 B.C.). There was no way in which Persia, no matter how large an army it brought against him, could hope to withstand the Macedonian phalanx and the creative tactics of Alexander.

In 333 B.C., Alexander defeated Persia at the Battle of Issus in the northeast corner of the Mediterranean coast. He then marched south to take over Syria, Phoenicia, and Judea, although the city of Tyre resisted a savage siege for seven months. Tyre was finally taken and destroyed, and that brought Phoenician history to an end. Only Carthage, far to the west, remained to remind the world of Phoenician greatness.

In 331 B.C., Alexander had conquered Egypt and established the town of Alexandria at the northwest corner of the Nile delta. That same year, he fought the battle of Gaugamela east of the Tigris River. Once again, the Persians were thoroughly smashed and they could resist no more. Alexander pursued the broken Persian army that, in despair, struck down Darius III and left him, dying, to be found by the pursuer. Alexander was merely the more enraged: when he caught up to the army, he savagely punished the assassins.

In 330 B.C., he allowed Persepolis to be burned as revenge for the burning of Athens by the Persians a century and a half earlier. In 326

B.C., he finally reached India at the extreme eastern boundary of the Persian Empire. He won a last big battle at the Hydaspes River over the Indian king, Porus. After that, his army rebelled and refused to follow him any further east.

Reluctantly, Alexander returned to Babylon, which he had chosen as his capital. He dreamed of a fusion of Greeks and Persians to rule the world. He established a common currency over the Empire, established Greek as the official language, founded many cities, and began to plan a campaign against Carthage.

However, Alexander was much given to wild feasts during which he ate and drank far too much. On June 13, 323 B.C., he died after one such feast. He was only 33 years old, but he had established the greatest Empire the world had yet seen. It was the old Persian Empire, plus Greece, and it had a population of about 20 million.

Alexander, however, left no heirs capable of carrying on his work, only a series of generals who had learned the art of war under him and his father, Philip. The generals naturally fought among themselves for the control of the Empire.

There followed 30 years of confused fighting, every bit of it as senseless as the wars between the Greek cities, but on a far larger scale and far bloodier. It came to an end with the battle of Ipsus in central Asia Minor in 301 B.C.

As a result of all the fighting, it turned out that *no* general was to control Alexander's Empire. Rather, the Empire fell apart into fragments making up what came to be known as "the Hellenistic kingdoms."

Most of the Asian dominions were held by the general Seleucus (358–281 B.C.), who established the "Seleucid Empire" in 312 B.C. and reigned as Seleucus I. Egypt was held by the general, Ptolemy (364–282 B.C.), who reigned as Ptolemy I. Macedonia and Asia Minor were fought over more strenuously, and these represented smaller fragments of the Empire.

In some ways, the spectacular conquest of the Persian Empire by a handful of Greeks and Macedonians further helped ruin Greece. Greek culture spread out over all the eastern Mediterranean and far into Asia, but Greece's own population and enterprise declined as Greeks went east and south, hoping to make their fortune in the new lands.

GREECE

While Alexander was off in Asia, the Greeks continued (in a much more subdued way) to fight each other. Sparta actually won some victories but was beaten by Macedonian forces under Antipater (397–319 B.C.), the old general left behind by Alexander to keep Greece in order. When Antipater sent messages to Alexander describing the outcome of the wars in detail, Alexander dismissed it impatiently as "a battle of mice."

In 322 B.C., the year after Alexander's death, the Macedonians, who had built a navy of their own, destroyed the Athenian fleet at Amorgos, one of the Aegean islands. That was an end, forever, of Athenian sea-power, a century and a half after the battle of Salamis.

By 300 B.C., it was clear that individual Greek city-states would never again be important powers in the world. Their day was done.

However, Greece remained an intellectual giant. Aristotle (384–322 B.C.), a pupil of Plato, had tutored the young Alexander, and was one of the greatest of the ancient philosophers. He produced a virtual encyclopedia covering all knowledge of the times, and he organized the laws of logic. He founded the "Lyceum," a school that concentrated more on what we would today call science than Plato's Academy did.

SYRACUSE

Syracuse was falling back before the increasing strength of Carthage, which now took over most of Sicily, except for Syracuse itself. It took a firmer grip on the island of Corsica and expanded its holdings on the Spanish coast, so that, by 300 B.C., it had reached the peak of its power.

In 317 B.C., however, Agathocles (361–289 B.C.) took control of Syracuse and called himself king of Sicily. (Monarchies were now the rage among the Hellenistic kingdoms.) He stopped the Carthaginians from destroying Syracuse by leading an army into North Africa and threatening Carthage itself. The Carthaginians, panicky, were willing to make peace in Sicily and that saved Syracuse.

Massilia, on the southern coast of what is now France, where Marseille is now located, was also being pressed by Carthage. It survived, however, and a Massilian named Pytheas, about 300 B.C., carried through the greatest of the Greek voyages of exploration. He ventured out into the Atlantic and brought back reports that made it clear that he had visited Britain and Scandinavia.

ROME

Rome finally recovered from the sack by the Gauls, and it was beginning to develop the Roman "legion," a very flexible fighting device that was much more adaptable to rough terrain than the Macedonian phalanx was. It could tighten itself into a phalanx, but it could also loosen itself into a formation that flowed about obstacles.

Rome was fighting, now, for mastery of central Italy against the tribes of the Samnites, long settled there, but by 300 B.C. it had not fully accomplished its goals.

INDIA

When Alexander the Great fought battles on the banks of the Indus, that was India's first major contact with Europeans. In 321 B.C., after Alexander's death, an Indian chieftain, Chandragupta, began the process of unifying India. Under him, a union of considerable portions of the peninsula took place for the first time.

In 305 B.C., he successfully held off an invading army sent into India by Seleucus I, the successor to Alexander in Asia. Chandragupta became a Jainist late in life, dying about 297 B.C.

The *Mahabharata*, the great Indian epic, which finally attained a length seven times that of the *Iliad* and *Odyssey* combined, was reaching something like its modern form by 300 B.C., though it continued to be developed and lengthened for additional centuries.

CHINA

China continued to be a collection of warring states. However, Taoist and Confucianist thought was being systematized, and Ch'u Yuan, the earliest of the great Chinese poets to be known by name, was writing his works.

NORTH AMERICA

By 3000 B.C., the earliest Mayan civilization was appearing in southern Mexico and in Central America.

---

300 TO 250 B.C.

EGYPT

Under Ptolemy I, and his son, Ptolemy II (308–246 B.C.), who came to the throne in 285 B.C., Egypt was prosperous and reasonably peaceful.

The two Ptolemies beautified Alexandria, their capital, and established a Museum (a temple dedicated to the Muses, who were thought of as the divine inspiration of art and science), which was the first real approach to a modern university. Through the Museum, Alexandria quickly became the intellectual center of the world.

Euclid (fl. 300 B.C.) systematized Greek geometry there, organizing it into a logical whole in a textbook that has been used, with various modifications, to this day—surely a record for longevity in textbooks. Aristarchus (320–250 B.C.) made his astronomic observations and suggested that the Earth moved about the Sun and not vice versa (though this notion was not accepted at the time). He also tried to determine the distance of the Sun and Moon from the Earth. Herophilus (355–280 B.C.) and Erasistratus (304–250 B.C.) studied anatomy sensibly, by the dissection of cadavers, until Egyptian religious susceptibilities put an end to this practice, and set back the study of human anatomy for over a thousand years.

The Ptolemies also founded a library in conjunction with the Museum, which eventually became the largest one the world was to see prior to the invention of printing. At its height, it contained several hundred thousand rolls of papyrus.

The Pharos, a lighthouse named for the peninsula on which it stood, was built in Alexandria harbor. It was about 440 feet high, and a fire was kept burning at its top to guide ships at night. It was considered one of the Seven Wonders of the Ancient World. (One that I haven't yet mentioned is the "Mausoleum," an elaborate monument erected in the Asia Minor town of Halicarnassus—the birthplace of Herodotus the historian—in honor of a ruler named Mausolus. It was raised by his widow, Artemisia, after her husband's death in 352 B.C.)

Alexandria was, for a time, the largest city in the world, and the most cosmopolitan. In addition to its Egyptian and Greek population, it also contained numerous Jews.

The first two Ptolemies controlled not only all of Egypt and eastern Libya, but also Judea, and much of the coastline of Syria and Asia Minor. It was the Egyptian Empire of a thousand years earlier reborn, except that its government was Greek and Macedonian, and *not* native Egyptian.

By 250 B.C., Ptolemaic Egypt was the most prosperous and the strongest nation in the world. It's population was approaching 4 million as compared with the 3 million at the height of the old Egyptian Empire.

SELEUCID EMPIRE

To begin with, the Seleucid Empire resembled the Persian Empire in its extent on the map—minus Egypt and Asia Minor.

The Seleucid Empire established the first chronology that counted the years steadily and without regard to the reign of any king or other type of ruler. It began with the year we call 312 B.C., which was the year in which Seleucus established himself in Babylon.

Actually, that was the last important event in Babylon's history. Seleucus began the building of a new capital, Seleucia, on the Tigris River, 40 miles north of Babylon, because he wanted one that was more Greek than Babylon was. As Seleucia grew, Babylon declined into ruins and, eventually, disappeared altogether.

A second capital was built in the far west of the Seleucid dominion, in Syria near the Mediterranean coast. It was called Antioch, in honor of Seleucus' father, Antiochus.

By 250 B.C., under a grandson of Seleucus I, who ascended the throne as Antiochus II (287–246 B.C.), in 261 B.C., the Seleucid Empire still seemed enormous, but its hold over the eastern territories was growing weak.

JUDEA

Judea passed without trouble from Persian control to Alexander's to that of the Ptolemies. Ptolemaic Egypt was tolerant of diverse views and Judea was left in peace. Indeed, many Jews moved on to Alexandria where opportunities for advancement were more numerous.

In Judea, Hebrew was no longer the language of everyday life. It had been supplanted by Aramaic, which, however, was close enough to Hebrew so that one language could be easily learned by those who spoke the other.

In Alexandria, however, the resident Jews learned Greek and, eventually, the Bible could not be understood by them. About 270 B.C., then, the project of translating the Bible into Greek began. Since 70 scholars were in charge of the project, the translation was called the *Septuagint*, from a Latin word for "seventy."

By 250 B.C., then, the Bible could be read by anyone speaking Greek, which meant that it had been opened to the most advanced civilization on Earth at the time. It was an important step in making Judaism known (through its daughter-religions) worldwide.

GREECE

Affairs in Greece and Macedon were particularly chaotic as various generals fought for control of Macedonia itself. Finally, in 276 B.C., nearly half a century after Alexander's death, the Macedonian rule was stabilized by Antigonus II (319–239 B.C.).

The Greek city-states still squabbled, but now leagues of cities were being formed. In northern Greece, the Aetolians, until then not a factor in Greek history, established the "Aetolian League." In the Peloponnesus, the "Achaean League" was established, led by Aratus of Sicyon (271–213 B.C.). Unfortunately, the two leagues fought each other, which played into the hands of Macedon.

The island of Rhodes, in the southeastern Aegean Sea, fought off Macedonian conquest and set up a giant statue of the Sun-god in celebration. This "Colossus of Rhodes" was still another of the Seven Wonders of the Ancient World, and Rhodes was for a while the leading trade-center in the east.

In 250 B.C., the existence of the two leagues and the prosperity of Rhodes gave Greece a faint shadow of its former eminence.

So did the continuing intellectual life. Important schools of philosophy were being established. Epicurus of Samos (342–270 B.C.) had founded a school in Athens in 306 B.C. His philosophy, Epicureanism, studied ways of maximizing pleasure by acting in moderation. Zeno of Citium (335–263 B.C.), established a school in Athens about 300 B.C. Since the school was on a porch (*stoa* in Greek), the philosophy was called "stoicism." It condemned emotion and called for a stern life of devotion to virtue and duty.

ASIA MINOR

The Gauls, who had ravaged northern and central Italy a century earlier, attacked Macedon in 279 B.C., and moved into Greece, where they were fought by the Aetolian League. They then moved into Asia Minor, where they established the kingdom of Galatia in the central region of the peninsula.

Other sections of the peninsula became more or less independent as the Seleucid forces proved insufficiently powerful to hold them. South of the Black Sea was the kingdom of Pontus. To the south of Pontus was Cappadocia, and to the east of both was Armenia. All, even including Galatia, were more or less Hellenized, with the upper classes, at least, speaking Greek.

EPIRUS

Epirus (located where Albania now stands) was the land from which Olympias, Alexander's mother, had come. In 195 B.C., Pyrrhus (319–272 B.C.), a second cousin of Alexander, began to rule over Epirus. He had military ability and, under him, Epirus, for a few years, became an important nation.

He fought in Italy and in Sicily with some success. In the end, however, he failed. In 272 B.C., he died in battle in the Greek city of Argos. By 250 B.C., Epirus was obscure again.

SYRACUSE

Hiero II (308–216 B.C.) became king of Syracuse in 270 B.C. and, under him, Syracuse had a last breath of prosperity. This twilight glow of Syracuse was brightened by the presence within it of Archimedes (287–212 B.C.), the greatest mathematician and scientist of the ancient world. He worked out the principles of the lever and of buoyancy, advanced a method for representing extremely large numbers, and introduced many mathematical innovations.

ROME

From 298 to 290 B.C., the Romans fought the Samnites for a third time, and this time, they won and became the masters of all central Italy. They also defeated the Gauls in the north and began to annex the Greek cities on the Italian coast.

The city of Tarentum, in the Italian heel, felt

they had good cause to fear that Rome's expansion would finally reach them. They called for help to Pyrrhus of Epirus, just across the narrow southern opening of the Adriatic Sea.

Pyrrhus, always eager for war, entered southern Italy with 25,000 men and 26 elephants. (Ever since Alexander's penetration into northwestern India, the Hellenistic monarchs had been using elephants in their battles, more for prestige than anything else. The elephants were rarely of any use. Unlike horses, elephants were far too intelligent to face the possibility of being wounded just because some man was urging it to do so. It was all to easy to panic elephants into hasty retreat to the ruin of their own army.)

Pyrrhus defeated the Romans in battles in 280 B.C. and again in 279 B.C., but at such a dreadful cost that, after the second, he said, "Another such victory and I will return without a man to Epirus." This gave rise to the phrase "Pyrrhic victory," for one that is bought at so great a cost as to amount to a defeat.

Pyrrhus then retired into Sicily where he fought the Carthaginians. Then, on returning to Italy, he was finally defeated by the Romans in 275 B.C., and had to go back to Epirus. Rome then took over the Greek cities in the south, including Tarentum.

This brought the Romans in Italy, and the Carthaginians in Sicily, face to face. War between them was inevitable. In 264 B.C., the "First Punic War" began. ("Punic" was Latin for "Phoenician.") The Carthaginians controlled the sea but the Romans, with help from the Greek cities in the south, began to build ships of their own, and with these they fought the Carthaginians on an equal basis.

In 250 B.C., the war was still continuing, but by now, five centuries after the city had been founded, it was clear that Rome was a world power. It had defeated one Hellenistic army, and if the Hellenistic kingdoms continued their suicidal warfare with each other, it was only Rome that would benefit.

INDIA

The Maurya dynasty, founded by Chandragupta, reached its peak under Asoka, who came to the throne in 265 B.C. He controlled all of India except for the extreme southern part, and could easily have conquered that. However, he was so sickened by the slaughter of battle early in his career that he refused to fight any more.

He was completely tolerant where religious matters were concerned, but he was a Buddhist himself, and an ardent one. He encouraged the sending of missionaries to Burma and to Ceylon and that began the process by which Buddhism ceased to be a local Indian cult and became a world religion. In fact, although Buddhism virtually disappeared within India, eventually, it remained popular outside its native land, throughout much of eastern and southeastern Asia.

In 250 B.C., India, under Asoka, was at peace and prosperous.

250 TO 200 B.C.

EGYPT

Under Ptolemy III, who reigned from 246 to 221 B.C., Ptolemaic Egypt reached the height of its power. He, however, was succeeded by Ptolemy IV, who reigned from 221 to 205 B.C., and who was a weak king. By 200 B.C., Egypt was beginning to decline.

Greek science continued, however. Eratosthenes of Cyrene (276–196 B.C.) was put in charge of the Library at Alexandria in 225 B.C. He made a map of the known world and calculated the size of the Earth's globe *correctly*, giving it a circumference of 25,000 miles. He was also the first to attempt to set up a consistent world-wide chronology for all nations, counting the years from the Trojan War. (It was about this time, also, that the Greeks began to number the years according to the Olympiads.)

Apollonius of Perga (262–190 B.C.) was the greatest mathematician of this period. He extended Euclid's work, dealing with the conic sections, curves that included the ellipse, the parabola, and the hyperbola.

SELEUCID EMPIRE

After 250 B.C., it seemed that the Seleucid Empire was breaking up. In 248 B.C., the eastern portions of the Seleucid Empire broke away. In what is now Iran, Arsaces I (who may have been of Scythian origin) set up the Parthian Empire, so-called because it was centered on the Persian province of Parthia.

To the east of Parthia, Diodotus (d. 239 B.C.) set up the kingdom of Bactria, about where Afghanistan is now located.

In Asia Minor, in 263 B.C., Eumenes I (d. 241 B.C.) made himself king of Pergamum, a land located where once the kingdom of Lydia had stood.

In 223 B.C., however, Antiochus III (242–187 B.C.) became the Seleucid king and, in a series of campaigns, he managed to force the various areas that had broken away to return to the Empire. By 200 B.C., the Seleucid Empire seemed to have returned to its former extent. In view of the decline of Egypt, it now seemed that the Seleucid Empire must be the strongest power on Earth and Antiochus III insisted on being called "Antiochus the Great" as a result. This was an illusion, however, for the effort Antiochus took to restore the Empire had merely weakened it further.

SPARTA

Macedonia was not particularly strong at this time and it could not keep the Greeks from fighting each other even at this date. The Achaean League was at the height of what power it had;

however, instead of opposing Macedonia, it saw its enemy as Sparta, which, a century and a quarter after the battle of Leuctra, was showing surprising signs of life.

In 245 B.C., Agis IV (263–241 B.C.) came to the Spartan throne. By that time, the Spartan system was moribund and Agis wished to reform it. He was a liberal who wanted to redistribute the land and revive the state. The few landowners who profited by Sparta's ruined economy howled objections and, in 241 B.C., Agis was put on trial and executed.

In 235 B.C., Cleomenes III came to the throne. He married Agis's widow and also embarked on a plan for reform. He did it by first leading out his army and defeating the Achaean League. Then, with the prestige gained, he forced reform on Sparta. He continued to win victories and, for one unbelievable moment, it seemed that Sparta was reestablishing its power over southern Greece.

The Achaean League betrayed Greece by calling in Macedonia. Antigonus III (263–221 B.C.), who had begun his reign in 227 B.C., brought his army south and defeated Sparta at the battle of Sellasia in 222 B.C. Cleomenes III fled to Egypt where he died in 219 B.C.

In 207 B.C., the Spartan liberal Nabis (d. 192 B.C.) deposed the last kings and took control of Sparta. He carried through to completion the reforms of Agis IV and Cleomenes III, abolishing debts, redividing the land, and even freeing the slaves. For this, of course, he was looked upon with horror as a villainous revolutionary by the surrounding cities.

ROME

Rome finally defeated Carthage in the First Punic War and, in 241 B.C., Carthage accepted a losing peace. Carthage had fought well, however, and the peace was not catastrophic for them. Rome took over Sicily—all except for Syracuse which remained independent under Hiero II.

In 238 B.C., Carthage fell into disarray when its mercenary soldiers remained unpaid and, therefore, revolted. The mercenaries were eventually crushed, but Rome took advantage of Carthage's preoccupation by taking over the islands of Sardinia and Corsica.

Carthage made up for its losses by expanding its holdings in Spain, where Hamilcar Barca (270–228 B.C.), who had fought particularly well in the closing years of the First Punic War, supervised the Carthaginian dominions. After Hamilcar Barca died in 228, his son-in-law, Hasdrubal, took his place. When Hasdrubal was assassinated in 221 B.C., Hamilcar's son, Hannibal (247–183 B.C.), only 25 years old at the time, took over. As it turned out, Hannibal was the most remarkable Carthaginian in history.

Rome, jealous of Carthaginian advances in Spain, demanded that Carthage remain south of the Ebro River and that it refrain from harming Saguntum, a Greek city south of that river.

Hannibal, however, destroyed Saguntum and then sent his army of 50,000 men, 9000 cavalry, and 37 elephants on a march through southern Gaul, and over the Alps into Italy. In 218 B.C., he defeated Roman armies in northern Italy in two battles and marched on southward.

The Romans opposed him at Cannae in southeastern Italy. Hannibal, with inferior numbers, carried through a perfectly planned battle, however, and simply wiped out the Romans, killing 50,000 out of 86,000. It was the greatest Roman catastrophe since the sack by the Gauls, and, for a while, it seemed as though Roman destruction was at hand.

However, the Romans held on grimly, and Hannibal lacked support from the home government, where the conservatives of Carthage disliked the Barca family even more than they feared Rome. Without being able to obtain reinforcements, Hannibal fought on in Italy for years. The Romans never dared to attack him directly.

Finally, a young Roman general, Publius Cornelius Scipio (236–184 B.C.) tried something daring. Like Agathocles, a century earlier, he led an army into north Africa and threatened Carthage itself. The Carthaginians, in a panic, sent for Hannibal, who loyally came back home.

There, with his best men long dead, and with some others bought off by Rome, Hannibal faced Scipio at Zama (the exact site of which is not

known) in 202 B.C., and lost a battle for the first time.

Carthage was defeated catastrophically, and a vengeful Rome enforced a ruinous peace on it. Carthage had to give up its navy and all its territory, except for that immediately around the city. Rome took over Spain, established a firm grip on those cities that had joined Hannibal after Cannae, and took over all of Italy to the Alps.

By 200 B.C., Rome was supreme in the western Mediterranean. The only comparable power remaining (at least in appearance) was the Seleucid Empire.

SYRACUSE

Hiero II of Syracuse had kept the peace with Rome throughout a long reign. In 215 B.C., soon after the Battle of Cannae, he died. His successor, Hieronymus, felt that Carthage was a sure winner and switched sides.

Rome, however, still had the strength to deal with Syracuse. In 214 B.C., a Roman fleet appeared to lay siege to the city. Syracuse fought back valiantly for three years, with a great deal of help from Archimedes, who is supposed to have invented war weapons for the Syracusians to use (including a large lens to set the Roman's wooden ships on fire).

In 211 B.C., however, Syracuse was taken and Archimedes was killed by a Roman soldier, even though the Roman general, Marcus Claudius Marcellus (268–208 B.C.), had particularly ordered that his life be spared.

INDIA

India under Asoka may have had a population of 30 million, considerably higher than that of any Hellenistic kingdom. In 236 B.C., however, Asoka died, and the Mauryan Empire disintegrated.

CHINA

In 221 B.C., China was finally unified under the Ch'in dynasty. The first emperor of the dynasty was Shih Huang Ti (259–210 B.C.). Like India at this time, China may have had a population of about 30 million.

Shih Huang Ti was anxious to wipe out the traces of the long feudal past and to begin history anew. For that reason, he ordered all books to be destroyed except for scientific works, and for those in the hands of official scholars. He also supervised the building of an earthen mound across the northern border. (This was something that eventually became the Great Wall of China.) It was meant as a barrier against the nomadic tribes to the north. The wall was not intended to keep people out, as much as to keep out their horses. Tribesmen without their horses were not terribly dangerous.

The Ch'in dynasty did not remain in power long. In 202 B.C., the Han dynasty replaced it, but China remained united.

200 TO 150 B.C.

ROME

Philip V of Macedon (238–179 B.C.) had become king in 221 B.C. He sided with Carthage after Hannibal's victory at Cannae, but a Roman fleet was sent across the Adriatic (the First Macedonian War) and that prevented Philip from doing anything much to help Hannibal.

Rome did not forget, and in 200 B.C., with Carthage disposed of, it found an excuse to turn on Macedon. Greece, anxious to be free of Macedonian domination joined Rome, which accepted the Aetolian League, the Achaean League, Athens and Rhodes as allies. In 197 B.C., Philip V was beaten at Cynoscephalae in Thessaly, and this Second Macedonian War ended with Macedon reduced to subservience to Rome.

The Roman general, Titus Quinctius Flamininus (227–174 B.C.), then declared all the Greek cities independent. This was, of course, a sham. They had come under the tight supervision of Rome. In fact, the first use the Greek cities made of their ''freedom'' was to beg Rome to destroy Nabis, the Spartan liberal who had freed the slaves. The Romans obliged, drove Nabis out of Sparta, and that city finally came to an end as an independent state.

The Achaean League was now under the rule of Philopoemen (253–184 B.C.), who is sometimes called the ''last of the Greeks'' because he was the last Greek general of ancient times to win victories. When he died in 184 B.C., it was in battle.

Antiochus III of the Seleucid Empire felt that it was up to him to take care of the upstart Romans. He felt no doubt that he could. In 192 B.C., he invaded Greece, but was defeated by the Romans in Thessaly. When Antiochus, chastened by this, returned to Asia, the Romans followed him, entering Asia for the first time.

There, the Romans defeated Antiochus decisively in 190 B.C. at the battle of Magnesia on the coast of Asia Minor. As a result, Antiochus III was forced to abandon all of Asia Minor, which was divided among various Greek kingdoms.

Hannibal, who had sought refuge in Asia Minor from the vengeance of the Romans, knew that the only way he could keep from falling into their hands was to commit suicide, which he did in 183 B.C.

In 178 B.C., Philip V of Macedon died and was succeeded by Perseus (212–165 B.C.), who prepared carefully for a war of vengeance against the Romans. The Third Macedonian War started in 171 B.C., and, for a while, Perseus did well. In 168 B.C., however, at the battle of Pydna on the Aegean coast of Macedonia, the Roman legion met the Macedonian phalanx for the last time. The Roman legion won. Macedonia was utterly defeated and was broken up into four republics. The Macedonian monarchy had come to an end two centuries after Philip II had made it great.

By 150 B.C., there was no question that Rome was the strongest power in the western world, and Greece found itself under a domination by Rome that was far tighter than the earlier one under Macedon.

While Rome never developed the level of culture Greece had displayed, the playwrights, Titus Maccius Plautus (254–184 B.C.), and Publius Terentius Afer (186–159 B.C.), better known in English as "Terence," were now writing dramas in Latin. (They are not forgotten. William Shakespeare's *A Comedy of Errors* and the Broadway musical *A Funny Thing Happened on the Way to the Forum* are both based on plays by Plautus.)

An important accomplishment of the Romans was that of road-building. They built straight, wide, well-paved roads, along which their armies could march swiftly. It meant that Rome could shift forces from one part of its realm to another with unprecedented speed, which gave it a great advantage over its enemies. There were also highways for commerce and ordinary travel, of course. Since the roads fanned out from Rome as the hub, we still have the saying, "All roads lead to Rome," when we are discussing an inevitable result.

Even more important, if insubstantial, was the Roman devotion to the law. The laws were worked out in great detail and were intended to apply to Romans and non-Romans alike. Legal opinions were binding and precedents were important. In short, Roman law has been the foundation of European law (and to some extent, now, even world law) ever since.

It was through Roman law that the Roman realm was so much more stable than earlier empires. The Romans rarely lived up to their ideals fully, but even an imperfect adherence to law, rather than to the arbitrary whims and dictates of a ruler, makes for a quieter and saner society. Those who lived under Rome found life better than it would be outside Rome and, on the whole, were content to remain Roman. For this reason, Rome held together for centuries and its memory remained, ghost-like, to animate later empires.

SELEUCID EMPIRE

Antiochus III died in 187 B.C., defeated and humiliated, and the Seleucid Empire, which he had restored, promptly fell apart. Parthia, Bactria, and Armenia were all independent again and Asia Minor had been lost in addition. The Seleucid dominions had been shrunk to the Tigris–Euphrates valley and Syria.

Antiochus IV (215–164 B.C.), a younger son of Antiochus III, came to the throne in 175 B.C. An energetic ruler, he didn't bother with the eastern holdings, which would always cost much more to regain than they were worth. It seemed to him that it made much more sense to invade Egypt, which had declined to an even further extent than the Seleucid Empire had.

Antiochus IV invaded Egypt in 171 B.C. and did well. In fact, he was about to take Alexandria in 168 B.C., when a Roman ambassador ordered him to return to Asia or face war with Rome. When Antiochus IV asked for time to consider the matter, the Roman ambassador drew a circle around Antiochus and ordered him to make up his mind before he stepped out of the circle.

The humiliation was complete. Antiochus gave in, abandoned Egypt, and undertook a futile campaign in the east after all. In the course of that campaign, he died in 163 B.C.

By 150 B.C., both Egypt and the Seleucid Empire were at the total mercy of Rome.

EGYPT

Egypt in this period was ruled by Ptolemy V (210–180 B.C.), who became king in 203 B.C., and by Ptolemy VI (d. 145 B.C.). It was a time when Egypt lost ground steadily to the Seleucid Empire, and might well have been absorbed altogether were it not for its subservience to Rome and for the protection it was afforded in return.

Alexandria continued to be intellectually important. Ctesibius, a Greek engineer, invented the water-clock in this period, and it was the most advanced timepiece of ancient times. (Dripping water, slowly and regularly, lifted a float that carried a marker that pointed out the hours.)

JUDEA

While Judea was under Ptolemaic Egyptian rule, it was peaceful. With Antiochus III, however, it passed from Egypt to the Seleucid Empire. The Seleucids were less tolerant and more anxious to have their realm Hellenized. There were Jews who were willing to Hellenize, and Judea was split between them and the old-fashioned fundamentalists.

Antiochus IV, after his humiliation by the Romans, needed a victory of some sort badly. Therefore, he turned on the Jews and decreed that the Temple in Jerusalem be made Greek, that a statue of Zeus be erected within it, and that sacrifices be made in the Greek fashion. Furthermore, copies of the Bible were to be destroyed, Jewish dietary regulations ended, the Sabbath abolished, and circumcision forbidden.

The Jews resisted, and the books of Daniel and Esther were written at this time to encourage such resistance to tyranny and persecution.

In 168 B.C., the resistance turned violent. The focus of that was an aged priest, Mattathias (d. 166 B.C.), and his five sons. They were supposed to be descended from a man named Hashmon, so they are sometimes called "Hasmoneans." One of the sons was Judah Makkabi (d. 160 B.C.) or, in Greek, Judas Maccabeus ("the Hammerer"), so they are also called the "Maccabeans."

Conservative Jews rallied round the Hasmoneans, and Judas Maccabeus showed himself to be a capable warrior. He beat the Seleucid forces in several battles and, in 165 B.C., managed to reenter Jerusalem and seize the Temple. The Temple was purified, and rededicated. Antiochus IV died in 163 B.C., and, thereafter, the Seleucid power was reduced to virtually nothing, and what little existed was wasted on dynastic struggles.

By 150 B.C., although the rebellion was still going on and Judas Maccabeus was dead, his brother Jonathan (d. 142 B.C.) was High Priest and what was left of the Seleucid Empire simply lacked the strength to force Judea back into submission.

PARTHIA

When Antiochus IV of the Seleucid Empire marched eastward on his last campaign, it was to move against Mithradates I of Parthia, who reigned from 171 to 138 B.C. Mithradates remained on the defensive until Antiochus IV died, and he then moved eastward into Bactria and westward into Media.

By 150 B.C., all of the old Persian Empire east of the Tigris–Euphrates valley was in Parthian hands, and we can speak of the "Parthian Empire." It was the eastern two thirds of the Persian empire, reconstituted one and three-quarter centuries after the death of Alexander the Great. It was Persian in language and culture and Zoroastrian in religion.

PERGAMUM

Pergamum gained territory as a result of the defeat of Antiochus III of the Seleucid Empire by the Romans. All of the western third of Asia Minor was theirs and they were a kind of rebirth of Lydia.

Pergamum prospered and was careful to maintain subservient relations with Rome. In 159 B.C., Pergamum came under the rule of Attalus II (220–138 B.C.), who established a library second only to that in Alexandria. Because the Egyptians would not let Pergamum have papyrus, they developed the use of stretched animal skins. These were far more permanent than papyrus, but much more expensive, too. The skins are called "parchment" (a distortion of "Pergamum").

GREECE

At this time, the only Greek region to retain a certain independence was the island of Rhodes. Since they were a little tactless in expressing this independence, openly defying Roman control, the Romans set up the island of Delos as a tax-free trading center, and the competition sent Rhodes into a decline.

Hipparchus of Nicaea (190–120 B.C.), who worked in Rhodes in this period, was the greatest astronomer of ancient times. He measured the distance of the Moon with surprising accuracy, made use of latitude and longitude in mapping the Earth and the sky, divided the stars into classes of brightness ("magnitudes"), prepared the first star map, and discovered the precession of the equinoxes. Most important of all, he worked out a mathematical system for predicting planetary motion on the assumption that all the heavenly bodies revolved about the Earth—as they certainly appeared to be doing.

150 TO 100 B.C.

ROME

By 150 B.C., Rome was becoming Hellenized thanks to the influence of Scipio (who had defeated Hannibal) and his friends. The Stoic philosopher, Panaetius of Rhodes (180–109 B.C.), taught in Rome. Polybius (200–118 B.C.), a Greek historian, was a friend of Scipio and wrote a history of Rome covering the period of the Second Punic War and thereafter. Even Romans were beginning to write in the Greek fashion. Gaius Lucilius (180–102 B.C.) wrote the first Latin satire.

There were people, of course, who objected to Hellenization and demanded that Rome cling to its old ways. The outstanding person on this side was a sour and cantankerous conservative, Marcus Porcius Cato (234–149 B.C.), usually known as "Cato the Censor."

Carthage, in 150 B.C., still existed and, within the narrow limits set by Rome's unforgiving desire for revenge, it was even prosperous. Rome harassed it endlessly (under the urging of Cato), and, in 149 B.C., they demanded that Carthaginians leave their city and settle inland. This the Carthaginians finally refused to do.

Rome sent an army against Carthage, which held out for three heroic years in the "Third Punic War." Finally, in 146 B.C., Rome beat them down. The city was burned to the ground, its surviving population was enslaved, and its territory was annexed to Rome. After six and a half centuries, the city of Carthage finally perished and, as a people, the Phoenicians were gone.

Meanwhile, the remnant of Macedonia was stirring across the Adriatic Sea. A Roman army was sent there and Macedonia was annexed to Rome. Because the Greeks had shown sympathy for Macedonia, the Romans sacked the city of Corinth in 146 B.C. It was then the most prosperous city in Greece, and, with that defeat, the last spark of Greek vitality was snuffed out. The Achaean League was dissolved, and Greece was annexed to Rome.

By 133 B.C., Rome had extended its dominions westward to include all of Spain except for the northwestern quarter. In the east, Attalus III of Pergamum (170–133 B.C.) died in 133 B.C. without heirs, after having reigned for five years. He realized that it was inevitable that Rome would take over the kingdom. Therefore, he left it to Rome in his will, hoping that the transition would at least be made peaceably. It was (more or less), and Roman dominion now extended into Asia.

Rome, however, was suffering from the rapid acquisition of territories. The overseas possessions were administered by Roman officials who, far from home, were not as subject to the severity of the law as they might have been under the eyes of the Senate and the populace. The provinces, therefore, were looted and money poured into Rome, corrupting (as money often does) all it touched.

Moreover, Roman victories were pouring slaves into Italy, and this invariably led to the loss of the dignity of labor. The small farmer, whose fields had been badly damaged by the long Second Punic War, found himself forced off the land, with his place taken by large estates run by slaves.

The impoverished farmers, unable to compete with slaves, flocked into Rome which developed a large and unruly population of poor people on what we would today call "welfare."

Nor were the slaves contented with their lot (and why should they be?). There was a slave rebellion in Sicily in 135 B.C., which took three years to put down. Some 200,000 slaves were in rebellion and, in the end, 20,000 of them were crucified—a very common Roman form of execution for those who rebelled against the state.

Parties were forming in Rome, which represented different economic interests as they had in Athens in Solon's time, four and a half centuries earlier. There were the upperclass "Optimates" (from a Latin word meaning the "best"—i.e., the most powerful) and the people's party or "Populares." They struggled with each other at elections when, increasingly, money was used to bribe voters, and violence was used to strike them with fear. In this period, the city of Rome began to dissolve into anarchy.

It was enormously clear that Roman government and society badly needed reforming (as Sparta had needed it, on a much smaller scale, the century before). Two brothers, Tiberius Sempronius Gracchus (163–133 B.C.) and Gaius Sempronius Gracchus (153–121 B.C.), attempted to put through land reform, to limit the size of estates, to smooth out the disparity of wealth, and so on. What happened (as with Agis III and Cleomenes IV of Sparta) was almost inevitable. The conservatives hired thugs, and first Tiberius and then Gaius were assassinated.

Rome rounded out its dominions along the northern coast of the Mediterranean by taking over the coastal regions that lay between Spain and Italy. This was the coast of Gaul (which took up the area of modern France) and which was populated by tribes related to those Gauls who invaded Italy nearly three centuries before.

On the southern shores of the Mediterranean, Rome wanted Numidia, that portion of the coast that lay west of dead Carthage. Here, however, they had to fight Jugurtha, a Numidian ruler who won battles by bribing Roman generals. (After all, if a society grows corrupt, all elements share in the poison, and it is not to be expected that generals will be more honest than anyone else.)

In the end, though, Jugurtha was taken out by a low-born Roman general, Gaius Marius (157–86 B.C.) and his aristocratic lieutenant, Lucius Cornelius Sulla (138–78 B.C.). This was done in 105 B.C. and Numidia was annexed.

But now a new danger threatened Rome. Germanic tribes, called the Cimbri and the Teutones, were ravaging Europe north of the Alps. Beginning in 113 B.C., these tribes were moving into the Roman sphere of influence. The two armies sent to stop them were defeated; and, by 105 B.C., they were beginning to threaten Italy, and had defeated a third force sent against them. The Romans had never forgotten the sack by the Gauls, three centuries earlier, and they were in a panic.

They turned to Marius, the conqueror of Jugurtha, and he raised a new kind of army. It was an army of the low-born, who found life much easier and better in the army than out of it, so that they were satisfied to become professional soldiers. Furthermore, since Marius made it plain that their good life was his responsibility, they were loyal to him rather than to the state. (Other generals learned to do this, too, and the armies became as dangerous to Rome's people and Rome's rulers as to Rome's enemies.)

Nevertheless, Marius' army did its job. In two separate battles, in 102 B.C. and in 101 B.C., he completely wiped out the invading tribes.

A second slave rebellion in Sicily, at this time, was also quelled, although with difficulty.

In 100 B.C., despite corruption within, and assault from outside, Rome was clearly master of the entire Mediterranean area from the Atlantic Ocean to the Euphrates River. Any portion of it that was not actually Roman was a servile puppet.

GERMANS

The German tribes seem to have existed in northern Germany and southern Scandinavia as early as 500 B.C. They tended to expand west and south at the expense of the Celts. They spilled over into Roman consciousness in 113 B.C.; and although the initial assault upon Rome was completely demolished, the Germans remained north of the Alps and west of the Rhine river. Rome would hear from them again.

PARTHIA

In 141 B.C., Mithradates I of Parthia captured the Tigris–Euphrates valley from the Seleucid Empire, and established a new capital at Ctesiphon, just across the river from Seleucia. The Seleucid Empire, with its capital at Antioch, was now confined to Syria. Even over that miserable remnant, dynastic quarrels clouded an increasingly worthless throne.

JUDEA

Such was the weakness of the Seleucids that, in 141 B.C., the last of the Maccabean brothers, Simon (d. 134 B.C.) could finally establish the independence of Judea. He and his descendants served as both king and high-priest.

The Judeans took over the petty regions on its borders under John Hyrcanus (175–104 B.C.), Simon's successor. By 100 B.C., when Alexander Jannaeus (d. 76 B.C.) was ruling over Judea, it was broader in its extent than modern Israel is.

EGYPT

Ptolemaic Egypt continued its decline in this period. Cyrenaica, the eastern portion of what is now Libya, was given to a younger Ptolemy, and the island of Cyprus to still another. Both portions eventually fell to Rome.

Ptolemies, all incapable, continued to rule over the Nile valley; and Egypt remained, thanks to the Nile, and to the unremitting labor of its peasantry, a rich land. However, it remained free only because of its equally unremitting devotion to Rome.

PONTUS

Pontus, in eastern Asia Minor, along the Black Sea coast, was still far enough from the Roman core to be independent. In 115 B.C., Mithradates VI (d. 63 B.C.), sometimes called "Mithradates the Great," came to the throne. He sent expeditions across the Black Sea to what is now the Crimea, and annexed the Greek cities there. They gladly agreed to this because they needed help against the Scythian tribesmen to the north.

His attempt to expand westward against Bithynia and southward against Cappadocia were stopped by Rome, since both lands were Roman puppets, and forced Mithradates back. By 100 B.C., then, Pontus was a considerable eastern power and Mithradates had developed a deadly hatred of Rome.

CHINA

Under the Han dynasty, in about 110 B.C., the Chinese, under the Emperor, Wu Ti, advanced south of the Yangtse River and annexed all of what is now southern China. In 108 B.C., Korea was conquered. Wherever Chinese armies established themselves, Chinese culture followed. Chinese culture was as attractive in the east as Greek culture was in the west.

A Chinese explorer, Chang Ch'ien (d. 114 B.C.), traveled to Bactria, at this time, to obtain help against the Hsiung-nu (Huns) north of the Great Wall. This was the first contact between China and the west—and thus began the western appetite for silk, for instance.

At about this time, the Chinese may have learned that magnetized needles point north and south. (As Greek science at this time was slowing, Chinese science was advancing. The time was approaching when China would be the technological leader of the world.)

100 TO 50 B.C.

PONTUS

In 88 B.C., Mithradates VI of Pontus, seeing that Rome was absolutely intent on limiting his power, decided to take the offensive. He swept westward in a surprise attack and drove the Romans out of Asia Minor, arranging to kill as many Roman civilians as possible. (He is supposed to have killed 80,000, but this may be a Roman atrocity story.)

The Greek cities, or at least some of them, including Athens, rallied to his aid, but the surprised Romans finally struck back. Sulla, who had helped beat Jugurtha of Numidia, defeated Mithradates in several battles in Greece. Sulla took Athens by storm and this, four centuries after the battle of Marathon, was the last military action in which Athens participated. Sulla drove him back into Asia.

As they had pursued Antiochus III a century before, so now the Romans followed Mithradates VI. The Pontine monarch had to give up his navy and pay an immense tribute. The Greek cities who had sided with him had to pay, too.

In his later years, Mithradates continued to fight Rome whenever he could, and he was repeatedly defeated.

ARMENIA

After Urartu had been destroyed by the Assyrians and the Cimmerians about 700 B.C., a group of people who came to be known as Armenians moved into the area about 600 B.C. They remained subject to the Persian Empire, then to Alexander, then to the Seleucid Empire.

Once the Seleucid Empire broke up, two Armenian kingdoms gained their independence. In 95 B.C., the two were united under the energetic rule of Tigranes I (140–55 B.C.), sometimes called "Tigranes the Great." He expanded his realm southward at the expense of Parthia, which was temporarily weakened by dynastic struggles, and

established Armenia as an important power for the only time in its history.

He married the daughter of Mithradates VI of Pontus. While Mithradates kept the Romans busy, Tigranes built a capital for himself, which he named Tigranocerta, and moved into Cappadocia in central Asia Minor. By 72 B.C., however, Mithradates' repeated defeats sent him fleeing for safety into Tigranes' dominions.

The Roman general, Lucius Licinius Lucullus (117–58 B.C.), followed Mithradates into Armenia and there he defeated Tigranes twice.

Then Gnaeus Pompeius (106–48 B.C.), usually known in English as "Pompey," replaced Lucullus and continued the push against Tigranes. Mithradates fled to the Crimea and died there in 63 B.C., at which time Tigranes surrendered.

Pontus was then annexed by Rome, but Tigranes was allowed to continue to rule over Armenia provided he remained a loyal puppet of Rome, which, for the rest of his life, he did.

SELEUCID EMPIRE

The Seleucid Empire by now was all but dead. For a time, it was held in the grip of Tigranes of Armenia, but after Tigranes was defeated, a Seleucid prince, Antiochus XIII, ruled from 69 to 64 B.C., but only over Antioch.

Pompey, advancing southward from his victories in Armenia, saw no point in continuing the charade. He annexed Syria to Rome and the Seleucid Empire, after two and a half centuries of existence, came to an end.

JUDEA

After the reign of Alexander Jannaeus, who died in 76 B.C., Judea entered a period of dynastic struggles. This continued until the approach of Pompey in 63 B.C. He had just annexed Syria, and it seemed to him that annexation was a sure cure for any kind of disorder. Therefore, Judea was annexed to Rome, and the Maccabean kingdom came to an end a century after the Maccabean revolt.

EGYPT

Egypt was the last of the Hellenistic kingdoms to remain under rulers of its own. To be sure, those rulers (the last Ptolemies) were utterly incompetent and ruled only because they were completely subservient to Rome.

In 51 B.C., Ptolemy XII (112–51 B.C.) died, and his daughter, Cleopatra VII (69–30 B.C.), along with her brother, Ptolemy XIII (63–47 B.C.), ascended the throne. It was totally unexpected for a woman to rule, but Cleopatra was to allow Egypt a last gasp of importance.

Hero of Alexandria, who may have done his work in this period, was perhaps the most ingenious of the ancient engineers. He built all kinds of clever mechanical devices, which were treated as amusing tricks in his time. He is best known for his invention of a very primitive steam engine. Water was placed in a closed vessel from which two bent pipes extended. The water was boiled, the steam whistled out, and the device turned just like a water-sprinkler. However, nothing came of any of his inventions. Society wasn't ready for them.

ROME

Rome continued to have internal troubles. Her Italian allies, disappointed that all attempts at reform had been defeated, rebelled in 91 B.C. That war went on for three years; and although the Italian allies were forced back into line in the end, the Romans felt it necessary in 88 B.C. to grant Roman citizenship to all Italians.

Continued attempts to bring about reforms, with continued conservative resistance, led to violence. Marius, of the lower classes, was on the side of the Populares. Sulla, the aristocrat, was an Optimate. Both had armies loyal to them rather than to Rome. When either dominated, there was a reign of terror against those of the other side.

The first civil war was won by Sulla, who returned from fighting against Mithradates to win a battle at the very gates of Rome in 79 B.C. He then established a conservative dictatorship that was supposed to grant the Roman Senate its old prerogatives.

Sulla, however, died in 78 B.C., and the civil war resumed. The reformers continued to lose and the conservatives to win. In 73 B.C., a third slave rebellion broke out, under the leadership of a gladiator from Thrace named Spartacus (d. 71 B.C.). It raged over Italy for two years before being put down by Pompey and by Marcus Licinius Crassus (115–53 B.C.). Crassus was Rome's richest man, who had gotten rich by business practices so questionable he would probably have felt right at home on Wall Street.

The two made themselves consuls, and Pompey cleared the Mediterranean Sea of pirates that were infesting it. Pompey then set out eastward to finish off Pontus and Armenia and to annex various eastern regions.

In Rome, in 64 B.C., another reformer, Lucius Sergius Catalina, attempted to force reform on Rome by, if necessary, rebellion. He was defeated by the orator, Marcus Tullius Cicero (106–43 B.C.), whose eloquence was so one-sided and effective that Catalina (like Nabis of Sparta) has gone down in history as an unprincipled villain.

Pompey and Crassus were now joined by Gaius Julius Caesar (100–44 B.C.), a charming and infinitely capable playboy, who was staked by Crassus and who finally made his money by looting Spain. The three formed a *triumvirate* (Latin for "three-man combination"). Caesar got himself assigned as governor of the Gallic areas in northern Italy and along the Mediterranean coast. It was his intention to conquer Gaul.

In 58 B.C., Caesar began his campaign. He was 44 years old and had no experience in warfare, but turned out, rather unexpectedly, to be a general of the first rank. Although it took him 7 years, by 51 B.C. all of Gaul—right up to the Rhine River—had become Roman, and, in the process, Caesar never lost a battle.

In the course of the campaign, in 54 B.C., he even crossed the English Channel and reconnoitered the island of Britain, though he didn't remain.

By 50 B.C., then, despite the battles with Pontus and Armenia in the east, despite insurrection and civil war at home, Rome was stronger than ever, and the only civilized nation on its borders that dared be independent was the Parthian Empire in the east.

The outstanding philosopher of the time was Poseidonius (135–51 B.C.), a friend of Cicero. He repeated Eratosthenes' observations and came out with a considerably smaller estimate of Earth's size—a circumference of 18,000 miles. This was altogether wrong, but it was accepted by other scholars and, in the end, had a powerful influence on history, since it played a role in the discovery of America.

The Roman scholar, Marcus Terentius Varro (116–27 B.C.), a friend of both Pompey and Caesar, wrote copiously, and initiated the manner of counting the years from the founding of Rome so that what we call 53 B.C., he called 700 A.U.C. This remained the most popular way of numbering the years for centuries.

Marcus Vitruvius Pollio (70–25 B.C.) wrote on architecture, one variety of technology in which the Romans outstripped the Greeks.

PARTHIA

Parthia, thanks to dynastic problems, lost ground to Tigranes of Armenia, but the loss was regained when Tigranes was defeated by the Romans.

King Phraates III, who ruled from 70 to 58 B.C., backed off from opposition to the Roman armies who were then in the east, but he knew they would come back, for Parthia was the only target left.

Sure enough, when the Triumvirate was formed and Caesar went off to find success and glory in Gaul, Crassus headed eastward to find the same in Parthia. Phraates III had by then died, and it seemed fair to count on the usual period of Parthian turbulence. However, in a surprisingly short time, one of Phraates' sons, Orodes (d. 36 B.C.), had established himself on the throne.

In 54 B.C., Crassus reached the upper Euphrates, which was the border between Syria and Parthia, and planned to follow the Euphrates downstream toward the center of Parthian power. He was persuaded by a guide (who was apparently in Parthian pay) to move farther east into the desert, however. There he came across the Parthian army waiting for him at Carrhae, 50 miles beyond the river. The Parthians, strong in cavalry, destroyed Crassus' army and killed Crassus.

It was a turning point for Rome. Until then, when they were defeated, whether by Pyrrhus, or by Hannibal, or by Mithradates, they did not accept defeat but continued to fight until the enemy was beaten and, eventually, its homeland was absorbed. This time, it was different. The Romans let it go. There were future wars against the Parthians, but never of the old, relentless fashion.

What it amounted to was that the Romans had, by 50 B.C., found a limit—in the east, at least.

50 TO 1 B.C.

ROME

Crassus was dead and Caesar was returning in triumph from Gaul. The city of Rome was in chaos with the kind of gang warfare that passed for elections at the time, and the conservatives feared that Caesar would throw his influence on the side of the people. They rallied desperately around Pompey, who was jealous enough of Caesar to let himself be used as a foil against him.

The Senate, therefore, ordered Caesar to return to Rome without his army.

Caesar knew that if he did that he would be tried on trumped-up charges and probably executed. When he reached the small Rubicon River in northern Italy, which was the boundary of his Gallic province, he had to make a decision. On the night of January 10, 49 B.C., he decided to cross *with* his army. "The die is cast," he said, meaning the gamble had been taken, and, ever since, "to cross the Rubicon" has meant to take an irrevocable step.

Pompey dared not face Caesar and his battle-hardened legions, and he fled to Greece, where he thought the legions in the east would support him. Most of the Senators, together with other conservatives, went with him.

Caesar followed him in 48 B.C., and the two Roman generals met at Pharsalia in southern Thessaly. There Caesar won, as he won all his battles, and Pompey fled to Egypt, which was not Roman territory and where he thought he would be safe. Egypt, however, did not want to fall afoul of Caesar and so, at the order of Ptolemy XII, Pompey was killed when he landed.

Caesar was continuing to follow Pompey and landed in Egypt where he found the Egyptian queen, Cleopatra. She was young and, apparently, beautiful. Caesar stayed there three months, fighting off the Egyptian army, and perhaps making Cleopatra his mistress for the while. During the fighting that went on in Alexandria between Roman and Greek forces, a fire broke out at the Library which destroyed many valuable books.

(There were periodic misadventures of this sort that ended by wiping out a large majority of the ancient books, so that our knowledge of the ancient world is distressingly sketchy. Until the invention of printing, books were always few, for copying them was an enormous task, and those few were subject to loss in the various disasters that have filled history.)

When Caesar left Egypt, it was to meet a son of Mithradates VI of Pontus. This son was Pharnaces, who reigned over Pontus from 63 to 47 B.C., and who now foolishly dared to challenge Rome. Caesar's army met him at Zela in western Pontus and, on August 2, 47 B.C., the Romans won so easy a victory that Caesar sent a message to Rome that said, simply, *Veni, vidi, vici* ("I came, saw, and won").

He then returned to Rome in 46 B.C. He spent a year defeating the conservatives, first in Africa, then in Spain, and in September, 45 B.C., he returned to Rome as absolute master. He then began the task of reform. He increased the number of Senators, instituted a distribution of land, and widened the Roman citizenship. He even reformed the calendar. With the help of a Greek astronomer from Egypt, Sosigenes, he set up the "Julian calendar," in which there were 365 days to the year divided into months of 30 or 31 days, with every fourth year a leap year containing 366 days.

The conservatives, however, though beaten, were not all dead. On March 15 (the "ides of March") 44 B.C., a group of conspirators, led by Marcus Junius Brutus (85–42 B.C.) and Gaius Cassius Longinus (d. 42 B.C.) assassinated Caesar.

The conspirators, however, were not ready to capitalize on the assassination. Caesar's lieutenant, Marcus Antonius (81–30 B.C.), better known to us as "Mark Antony," raised the people against the conspirators, who left Rome hurriedly.

Caesar's great-nephew, a 19-year-old youth named Gaius Octavius (27 B.C.–A.D. 14), arrived in Rome, too. He considered himself Caesar's adopted son, changed his name to Gaius Julius Caesar Octavianus, and was usually referred to as "Octavian."

Mark Anthony and Octavian joined with a Roman general, Marcus Aemilius Lepidus (d. 12 B.C.) to form the "Second Triumvirate" in November, 43 B.C. They followed the conspirators to Greece in 42 B.C., and, at Philippi in eastern Macedonia, Cassius was defeated and killed himself. Later, Brutus was tracked down, defeated, and he also killed himself.

The three victors then divided the Empire among themselves. Octavian took the west, including Rome, where the political power was. Mark Antony took the east where the money was. Lepidus took Africa, where nothing was.

Mark Antony encountered Cleopatra at Tarsus on the southern coast of Asia Minor in the summer of 41 B.C. He intended to force money out of her, but fell in love instead.

In the west, Sextus Pompeius (75–35 B.C.), the son of Pompey, had a fleet and managed to be a successful pirate, till Octavian's general, Marcus Vipsanius Agrippa (63–12 B.C.), defeated and destroyed him in 36 B.C. When Lepidus tried to extend his own power to Sicily, Octavian had him imprisoned and took over Africa himself. He was now supreme in the west.

Mark Antony's fortune was quite different. He was defeated by Parthia in 36 B.C. and had a hard job getting back to safety in Armenia. He then returned to Alexandria where he lived a life of ease and luxury with Cleopatra, even though he had married Octavian's sister as a way of insuring peace between the two leaders.

Octavian was easily able to turn Roman public opinion against Mark Antony by describing him as a slave of a foreign monarch and as planning to give half of the Roman realm to Egypt. War between them was inevitable and, on September 2, 31 B.C., the greatest naval battle of ancient times was fought at Actium off the west coast of Greece. Agrippa won it for Octavian. Antony and Cleopatra fled to Egypt and, when Octavian came for them with his army in 30 B.C., they killed themselves.

The Roman civil wars, which had begun with Marius and Sulla, 50 years before, were over. Octavian was the absolute ruler of Rome. He annexed Egypt as a personal possession, and three centuries after the death of Alexander the Great, the last remnant of his empire was gone.

Octavian, without altering the forms of the Republic, managed to modify them so that he was the supreme authority, holding all the important posts. On January 23, 27 B.C., Octavian was named Augustus Caesar. He was the "Imperator" (i.e., the generalissimo of the armies), meaning "Emperor" in English. In 27 B.C., then, the Roman Republic came to an end and the Roman Empire came into being, with Augustus as the first Emperor.

In 19 B.C., the Temple of Janus had been closed for the first time in over 200 years to indicate that the realm was at peace, but actually there was fighting going on at the borders, particularly east of the Rhine River in Germany.

About then, also, Augustus refounded Carthage, since the site was a supremely useful one for trade. Earlier, the Gracchi and Julius Caesar had attempted to do this, but it was Augustus who carried it through. It was not the old Phoenician Carthage, but a new Roman one. Before long it prospered and became one of the great cities of the Empire.

By 1 B.C., the Empire was at relative peace and had been for 30 years. This was the *Pax Romana* (the "Roman Peace") in which, for a while, the Mediterranean world was free of the endless torments of cities and nations fighting each other endlessly.

Despite the horrible confusion of the civil wars, this period was the golden age of Latin literature.

Cicero's public addresses and philosophical tracts were published in the most elegant Latin style ever written. Caesar wrote his *Commentaries* on the Gallic wars which, in prose style, was second only to Cicero.

Publius Vergilius Maro (70–19 B.C.), better known as "Vergil" to us, wrote the *Aeneid* in the last decade of his life. It was the supreme example of Latin poetry, for all that it was a rather pale imitation of Homer. Quintus Horatius Flaccus (65–8 B.C.), or "Horace," wrote satires and odes. Publius Ovidius Naso (43 B.C–A.D. 17), or "Ovid," wrote *Metamorphoses*, probably the most attractive of all the retellings of the Greek myths. Gaius Valerius Catullus (84–54 B.C.) wrote passionate love poems.

Titus Livius (59 B.C.–A.D. 17), or "Livy," wrote a long history of Rome of which only about a quarter survives. The first 10 books, dealing with the time before the Gallic sack of Rome in 390 B.C., survives, and comprise the source of all the romanticized and patriotic legends of the early city.

Titus Lucretius Carus (90–53 B.C.), or "Lucretius," wrote a long poem dealing with Epicurean philosophy and the atomism it espoused. Lucretius, more than anyone, was responsible for the survival of the concept of atomism into early modern times.

JUDEA

After Crassus' defeat by the Parthians, there were those in Judea who advocated a switch in allegiance to Parthia and rebellion against Rome. However, Antipater (d. 43 B.C.), a native of Idumea (the region south of Judea that had been conquered by the Maccabees and forcibly converted to Judaism), was high in the government and was pro-Roman, feeling that the Parthian victory was only temporary.

Once Julius Caesar was in control of Rome, he showed his gratitude to Antipater by making him governor of Judea.

Antipater was assassinated in 43 B.C., at a time when Caesar had been assassinated the previous year and all was still chaos in Rome. The Parthians seized their chance and marched westward, taking Syria and Judea, and reaching the Mediterranean.

Antipater's son, Herod (73–4 B.C.), sometimes called "Herod the Great," fled south to Egypt, and took measures to ingratiate himself with both Mark Antony and Octavian. Eventually, things quieted in Rome and the Parthians had moved out of the Roman provinces; thus, in 39 B.C., Herod was back in Judea as king. He remained king for the rest of his life and managed to keep the peace. He supported Mark Antony while Antony was strong, and, when matters began to shift toward Octavian, Herod prudently shifted in the same direction.

Herod kept Judea prosperous. A great builder, he enlarged and beautified the Temple. He was Jewish in religion and carefully held to Jewish ritual. However, he was an Idumaean and not a Judean, and the Judean nationalists hated him for that.

The more extreme Judean nationalists wanted to fight the Romans as once Judeans had fought the Seleucids—never noticing that Rome was enormously stronger than the declining Seleucid Empire had been a century and a half earlier. Herod kept those nationalists in check, for the sake of saving Judea from destruction, and he was hated for that, too. His unpopularity in Judea, and the clear memory of the assassination of his father, turned him tyrannical in his old age.

He died in 4 B.C. Some time before he died, Jesus of Nazareth was born.

PARTHIA

The Parthian drive to the Mediterranean in 40 B.C. had brought the Parthian Empire to the peak of its power, but it didn't stay there long. One of Mark Antony's generals, Publius Ventidius (91–37 B.C.) drove them out of the Roman provinces by 38 B.C.

Mark Antony wished to win a victory for himself and, in 36 B.C., invaded Parthia, but he was never quite as good a general as he thought he was, and he barely got out alive.

After that, Parthia lost itself in the usual morass of dynastic fighting. In 20 B.C., Augustus entered into negotiations with Phraates IV of Parthia (who reigned from 37 to 2 B.C.) and arranged to have the battle flags, which had been captured from Crassus 33 years earlier, returned to Rome. That seemed to wipe out the disgrace a little.

By 1 B.C., there seemed an unspoken agreement between Rome and Parthia to coexist, and about the only remaining source of friction was Armenia, which lay between the two and which both tried, periodically, to snatch.

[From this point on, all dates, given in simple numbers, may be taken as A.D. If dates before A.D. 1 must be mentioned, B.C. will be added.]

1 TO 50

ROMAN EMPIRE

Under Augustus and his immediate successors, the Empire was consolidated. Thrace and Moesia (located where one finds modern Bulgaria) were added to the Empire, so that the northern boundary ran along the Rhine and the Danube from the North Sea to the Black Sea. Those regions of Asia Minor which still had kings of their own, such as Cappadocia, were annexed to the Empire. On the southern shore of the Mediterranean Sea, Mauretania (where Algeria and Morocco are now located) was annexed.

In one place only was there a hitch. The province of Gaul, which had been Roman for only half a century, was, to some extent, insecure because the German tribesmen east of the Rhine could, and sometimes did, raid across the river. Roman forces, therefore, moved east of the Rhine with the intention of bringing Germany, conquered, into the Empire. They made their way slowly to the Elbe. However, in the Teutoberg Forest, the Germans, under Hermann (18 B.C.–19), or "Arminius", in Latin, ambushed three Roman legions under Publius Quintilius Varus (d. 9) in 9, and wiped them out.

Augustus, a cautious man, doubted that it would be worthwhile to scrape up the men and money to renew the attempt at conquest, so Germany was abandoned, and the Rhine remained the frontier, thereafter. Like the battle of Carrhae, 62 years before, the battle of the Teutoberg Forest set a limit to Imperial expansion.

In 14, Augustus was succeeded by his stepson, Tiberius (42 B.C.–37). Tiberius did attempt to punish the Germans, at least. His nephew, Germanicus (15 B.C.–19), was in Germany, and, beginning in 14, he carried out a raid that defeated Hermann and recovered the battleflags that had been lost by Varus.

Tiberius, as cautious as his stepfather, considered that to be enough, and pulled the army back west of the Rhine.

In 37, Tiberius was succeeded by his grandson, Caligula (12–41). He ruled only four years before being assassinated and, in 41, the throne went to his uncle, Claudius (10 B.C.–54), a younger brother of Germanicus. Under him, the southern portion of the island of Britain was annexed to the Empire.

Later Roman historians recorded the private lives of these early Emperors with the emphasis on seaminess of all kinds—intrigues, poisonings, sexual orgies, sadistic whims, and so on. Tales were told of the sexual enormities of the aged Tiberius and of Claudius's queen, Valeria Messalina (22–48), of the poisonous intrigues of Augustus' queen, Livia Drusilla (58 B.C.–29), of the lunatic behavior of Caligula, and so on.

How far these tales can be trusted is doubtful. Gossip-mongers then were no more reliable than they are now, and the historians who retold these stories were conservatives who resented the Empire and looked back to an idealized Republic that had never actually existed.

The stories were seized on by the later Christians to show how wicked the pagan Emperors were and, of course, they have appealed to the prurient in all ages. In modern times, they were popularized by Robert Ranke Graves (1895–1985) in his books *I, Claudius* and *Claudius the God*, which were then made into a popular television feature.

An outstanding writer of this period was Lucius Annaeus Seneca (4 B.C.–65), who, among other works, wrote a series of tragedies that specialized in blood and rant. (Shakespeare's *Titus Andronicus* is an example of what is called a "Senecan tragedy.")

Pomponius Mela (b. 5 B.C.) was the most important geographer of the period. He was the first to divide the Earth into five zones: North Frigid, North Temperate, Torrid, South Temperate, and South Frigid.

JUDEA

Philo of Alexandria (13 B.C.–48) was a Jew, living in Alexandria in this period. He did his best to reconcile Judaism with Greek thought, especially that of Plato, but, within Judea itself, the nationalists, who would have nothing to do with Greek and Roman ways, were gaining strength.

The Judeans were living with the constant mystical excitement of the expectation that a descendant of David (who had ruled the land a thousand years before) would arise. He would be the "Messiah" (meaning "the anointed one," a phrase frequently used for a king or high-priest, since they were anointed with oil as part of the ceremonies with which they began their office). The Messiah, once he came, would, more or less miraculously, make Judea free and independent, and would lead a world revival in which all men would turn to Judaism.

Many men were thought of, at one time or another, as the hoped-for Messiah, and Judea was in a constant state of semi-insurrection as a result. The ruling groups in the land rather desperately tried to suppress all would-be Messiahs lest Rome lose patience and crush the land.

One preacher of this period who was viewed as the Messiah by those who followed him was Jesus of Nazareth. He was actively preaching in 29, during the reign of Tiberius. When he entered Jerusalem, to the noisy acclaim of the nationalists, the high-priest and his party grew nervous indeed. They tried Jesus for heresy and abandoned him to the Romans, who considered him a rebel against the state because of his Messianic claims. Therefore, they punished him with crucifixion, which was the usual penalty for such rebellion.

That might have been the end for Jesus, as it had been for other suppressed Messiahs, but Jesus' followers eventually insisted he had returned to life after three days and had then been taken up to heaven. They continued to view him as the Messiah (or Christos in Greek, which became "Christ" in English). His followers eventually took to calling themselves Christians.

Herod Agrippa I (10 B.C.–44), a grandson of Herod I, was a friend of the Roman Emperor, Caligula. He received a high position in Judea in 37 and was eventually made king in 41. A tactful and capable man, he managed to placate both the Jews and the Romans. Had he lived a full life, he might have brought on an era of peace and saved Judea. However, he died, quite suddenly, in 44, and the chance passed.

About 46, a Jew named Saul (d. 65), who was a Roman citizen and took the Romanized name of Paulus or, in English, Paul, was converted to Christianity. Paul realized that it was important to make converts among the Gentiles, who far outnumbered the Jews, and that great obstacles to such an aim were the Jewish dietary laws and the insistence on circumcision. Therefore, Paul abandoned both, and asked the converts merely to follow the teachings of Jesus. In this way, by 50, Christians began to grow in numbers at the price of being so fundamentally different from Jews that they could no longer be considered merely a Jewish sect.

BRITAIN

The island of Britain was inhabited by Celtic tribes closely akin to those of Gaul. It first entered the purview of history when Caesar invaded the island in 55 B.C., and again in 54 B.C. Caesar did this to persuade the Britons not to help their Gallic kinsmen in their resistance to Rome. Caesar's demonstration worked in that respect and he made no attempt actually to occupy the land.

Britain thrived thereafter on trade with Roman Gaul. A Britonic chieftain in southern England who maintained friendly relations with Rome was Cunobelinus (d. 43), who was Shakespeare's *Cymbeline*.

The death of Cunobelinus was followed by tribal rivalries, and the Romans took advantage of that. Immediately after Cunobelinus' death, a Roman general, Aulus Plautius, and 40,000 men invaded the island. It was not an easy conquest, however. One of Cunobelinus' sons, Caratacus (also called Caractacus and Caradoc), fought on resolutely and was not defeated and captured till 51.

By that time, it was clear the Romans were in Britain to stay.

CHINA

In this period, China had reached a level of sophistication in which government officials were expected to take tests that indicated their qualifications for office.

In 9, Wang Mang, who had been serving as regent for some child Emperors of the Han dynasty, took the post of Emperor himself. He was an ardent reformer who labored to put through a redistribution of land, to abolish slavery, to put limits to usury, to establish a fair price policy, and so on.

Naturally, the merchants and businessmen who profited from the inequities of society provoked revolts, in one of which, in the year 25, Wang was killed. The Han dynasty was restored to the throne.

At about this time, Buddhism was introduced to China, where it spread rapidly.

50 TO 100

ROMAN EMPIRE

In 54, Claudius died, and was succeeded by his great-nephew, Nero (37–68), a spoiled young man who fancied himself an artist.

In 64, a great fire destroyed much of Rome. Nero hastened back from a vacation to supervise the fire-fighting, but, according to a story, he could not resist exercising his artistry by singing a song about the burning of Troy while accompanying himself on a lyre, as he watched the flames from his palace window. That gave rise to the story that "Nero fiddled while Rome burned."

The blame for the fire was placed on the new sect of Christians who seemed to the Romans to be atheists, since they denied the existence of all pagan gods. What's more, they were constantly predicting that the Earth would be destroyed by fire when Jesus returned in "the second coming." They might impatiently have started the job prematurely, the Romans thought, and a number of Christians were executed.

Palace intrigues made it clear to Nero that he was going to be murdered, so he committed suicide in 68. For the first time, there was no heir that could be traced back to Augustus, and different people tried to seize the post and failed.

Finally, the general, Titus Flavius Vespasianus (9–79), or "Vespasian," became Emperor in 69 and held on to power. He was followed by his sons, Titus (39–81), who reigned from 79 to 81, and then Domitian (51–96), who reigned from 81 to 96.

In 79, during the brief reign of Titus, Vesuvius, which had not been active in the memory of man, and was not even thought of as a volcano, suddenly erupted. Its lava and ashes buried the town of Pompeii and Herculaneum. (Many centuries later the excavation of Pompeii gave people notions as to the daily life in the early Roman empire and served as a strong push toward the creation of the science of archeology.)

Domitian was assassinated in 96, and an elderly senator, Marcus Cocceius Nerva (30–98) was chosen to become Emperor. He was the first of the five "good Emperors," who tried to rule humanely and avoid arbitrary behavior. Nerva lived only a short time after being made Emperor, but he lived long enough to adopt Marcus Ulpius Traianus (53–117), or "Trajan," who became Emperor in 98. This started a fashion of having the Emperor adopt some worthy young man and groom him for succession.

In 100 A.D., the Empire was still at peace and,

despite the occasional confusion in Rome, prosperous. Further imperial expansion had not taken place since the conquest of Britain half a century before.

In this period, Cornelius Tacitus (56–120) was the most important of the Roman writers. He wrote a history of Rome from the death of Nero to the death of Domitian. He also wrote a book about the German tribes, praising them highly, not so much that they deserved the praise, but because he wanted to contrast them with a Rome he felt was falling into moral decay.

The Greek writer, Plutarch (46–120), born in Chaeronea where, nearly four centuries earlier, Philip of Macedon had destroyed Theban power, wrote a series of biographies of important Greeks and Romans. He did them in pairs, comparing and contrasting them. Plutarch's pleasant anecdotal way of writing biography kept his *Parallel Lives* widely read right down to the present.

Another widely read writer of this period was Gaius Plinius Secundus (23–79), or "Pliny." He wrote an encyclopedic *Natural History* in which he inserted, indiscriminately, everything he had ever read. He was overcredulous and gave much information, but he was so interesting that he continued to be read avidly for many centuries. He died during the eruption of Vesuvius, which he was observing, overcuriously, from too close a distance.

Marcus Valerius Martialis (40–103), or "Martial," wrote biting, satirical, and sometimes obscene epigrams, while Marcus Fabius Quintilianus (35–100), or "Quintilian," wrote on educational techniques.

The greatest engineer of the time was Sextus Julius Frontinus (30–104), who wrote two volumes on Roman aqueducts and summarized Greek and Roman engineering techniques.

JUDEA

In 66, Judea finally exploded. The nationalists, still waiting for the Messiah, seized the Temple and then drove the Roman garrison out of Jerusalem. The Judeans won the first couple of battles over the unprepared Romans, and were convinced that miracles were on the way.

In 67, however, Nero sent Vespasian to Judea. He went about the job methodically, but met furious Judean resistance. He was further hindered by the fact that Nero killed himself in 68. Vespasian left Judea in order to claim the Emperorship for himself, but his son, Titus, remained in charge of the army.

In May, 70, Titus placed Jerusalem under siege, and on August 28, after Jerusalem had been weakened by famine, it was taken and the Second Temple was destroyed after six centuries of existence, and a thousand years after Solomon had constructed the first. There was never to be a third.

Other parts of the city held out for another month and some fortresses in Judea held out still longer. The last stand was the town of Masada on the western shores of the Dead Sea, 35 miles southeast of Jerusalem. It was not until 73 that the Romans could take it, and the last defenders —960 men, women, and children—killed themselves rather than surrender.

Because of the rebellion, the largest Jewish temple in Alexandria was destroyed and many Jews were killed there, too.

It was an utter disaster for the Jews, although in the quiet that followed, the Old Testament finally reached its present form as the result of the labors of pious Jews such as Johanan ben Zakkai, who were allowed to continue their work at Jamniah in the ruined land. The New Testament also reached its present form by 100.

Those Judeans who had become Christians were expecting Judea to be destroyed as part of the preliminaries to the Second Coming and they did not fight, but withdrew. As a result, they were execrated as traitors by those Judeans who had fought and survived, and Jewish conversions to Christianity stopped.

On the other hand, Paul was traveling through Macedonia and Greece, even on to Rome, preaching and converting Gentiles everywhere he went.

Thus, Christianity became a Gentile religion, albeit with Judaistic roots: and, by 100, the groundwork was laid for Christianity to become a world religion, while Judaism remained a small, nationalist cult.

BRITAIN

As was the case with Judea, Britain did not take kindly to Roman rule.

In 60, the ruler of the tribe of the Iceni (in what is now Norfolk) died, and left part of his possessions to the Emperor Nero, in the hope that the Romans, in return, would protect his wife, Boudicca, and his two daughters.

No such thing! The land was appropriated entirely, the daughters were raped, and when Boudicca objected, she was whipped. As a result, she roused her people to revolt, and the rebels burned Colchester, destroyed London, and killed every Roman they could find.

It took a while for the Romans to gather their army and defeat Boudicca, who killed herself. The entire structure of the Roman occupation was shaken and matters had to begin all over.

The confusion in Rome after Nero's death made things worse, and it was not till 77 that a Roman army under Gnaeus Julius Agricola (40–93, who was father-in-law of the Roman historian, Tacitus), could land in Britain and subdue the island as far north as what is now mid-Scotland. After that, the southern two thirds of Britain was again Romanized, a process that was well along by 100.

PARTHIA

In 51, Volegases I succeeded to the Parthian throne and reigned until 78. There had been peace between Rome and Parthia for nearly half a century, but Volegases thought it was now a good time to make an attempt to seize Armenia, which had been in contention between Parthia and Rome for two centuries. For the purpose, he placed his brother, Tiridates (d. 73), on the Armenian throne.

The Roman emperor, Nero, reacted by send-ing a military force under Gnaeus Domitius Corbulo (d. 67) to Armenia. Corbulo invaded Armenia in 58. After 5 years, Parthia accepted a compromise that Corbulo had offered at the very start. Tiridates might remain as king of Armenia, but he was to agree to swear allegiance to Rome.

By 100, that compromise was still holding, but it was interesting that Rome was willing to compromise. Earlier in its history, it routinely aimed for complete victory.

INDIA

About 78, Kanishka, a member of a nomad tribe, the Kushans, established his rule over the northern part of India and over Bactria, which now lost all traces of Hellenization. Kanishka was a patron of Buddhism, but was tolerant of other religions. He had contacts with China and encouraged the penetration of that land by Buddhism.

CHINA

Pan Ch'ao was Chinese Emperor from 74 to 94. He extended Chinese control far into what is now Sinkiang and into Central Asia. China, at this time, was extended to the boundaries of Kushan India and of Parthia. There was now, for the first time, a solid belt of civilization from the Atlantic to the Pacific across Eurasia: The Roman Empire; Parthia; Kushan India; and Han China. This encouraged trade across the entire 6000-mile expanse—particularly, the silk trade.

AFRICA

By 100, the kingdom of Aksum (or Axum), in what is now northern Ethiopia, had been established, probably through the influx of Sabseans from southwestern Arabia (the modern Yemen.)

100 TO 150

ROMAN EMPIRE

Trajan, the second of the "good Emperors," was the first Emperor not to have been born in Italy; he was born in Spain.

Under Trajan, the Roman Empire had a last spasm of expansion. Trajan crossed the lower Danube and, after two campaigns, annexed Dacia to the Empire in 107.

Dacia was located in what is now Romania (or Rumania). The very name, Romania, testifies to the fact that it was once part of the Roman Empire, and the Romanian language is even today related to Latin and is considered one of the "Romance languages."

Meanwhile, Parthia had another long period of disorder, until, finally, in 109, Osroes I became king of Parthia and decided to break the Armenian compromise that had been set up by Corbulo. He installed a new king of Armenia, who swore allegiance to Parthia.

Trajan led an army into Armenia and annexed it to the Roman Empire in 114. He then turned southward and marched through the Tigris–Euphrates valley, annexing that oldest of all civilized areas to the Empire. It became the provinces of Mesopotamia and Assyria. In 117, he reached the Persian Gulf and, looking out to sea, muttered, "If only I were younger!"

At that moment, the Roman Empire was at its maximum extent, having grown from a single, sacked city 500 years before. The Empire stretched out over an east-west length of 3200 miles. Its population was about 40 million, and China had a population of about 60 million. Add another 35 million in India, and perhaps 4 million in Parthia, and it would appear that more than three quarters of the world's population was in the civilized band across Eurasia. Those portions of the world not yet civilized contained perhaps 40 million people all told, so that the total world population of the time was 180 million.

Trajan died in 117 and was succeeded by his adopted son, Publius Aelius Hadrianus (76–138), or "Hadrian."

Hadrian did not by any means follow the expansionism of Trajan. In his reign, the Roman Empire went over, definitely, to the defensive. Hadrian voluntarily withdrew from areas in which he felt Rome was overextended. He abandoned the Tigris–Euphrates valley, for instance, and let it return to Parthian rule.

He also built a 72-mile wall ("Hadrian's Wall") across the narrowest part of Britain between 122 and 127. This was to keep the northern Picts out of Britain, but it also indicated that the Romans would make no serious effort to advance farther north.

In 138, Antoninus Pius (86–161) became Emperor and his 23-year reign was almost without incident, so smoothly did the Empire seem to tick along.

In 150, the Roman Empire was at the height of the "Pax Romana" and, 16 centuries later, the British historian, Edward Gibbon (1737–1794), whose *Decline and Fall of the Roman Empire* may be the greatest history ever written, judged it to be the time when humankind was happiest.

In this period, Gaius Suetonius Tranquillus (69–122), known to us as "Suetonius,'" wrote biographies of the early Emperors that were filled with sensation and sex and that have remained popular ever since. Decimus Junius Juvenalis (57–127), or "Juvenal," wrote savage satires on Roman life.

Epictetus (55–135) had been a Greek slave, but was freed by his master and became the outstanding exponent of Stoicism in this period.

Christianity had its interpreters who tried to place it in accord with Greek philosophy. Justin (100–165) was an important Christian Platonist of the period. He opened the first Christian school to operate in Rome, and because he eventually died for his cause, he is usually referred to as "Justin Martyr."

Some Christians moved in the direction of the

more mystical philosophies and tended to abandon the Judaistic roots altogether. Gnosticism was a kind of meld of Christianity with Zoroastrianism, which gained a certain temporary importance in this period.

JUDEA

In 116, the Jews in Cyrene rebelled, excited perhaps by some messianic hope. It was another disaster. Cyrene was a city in northeastern Libya that was the one remaining place in the Empire where Jews lived in considerable numbers in peace and prosperity. The rebellion, which was completely beyond sense, resulted in the eradication of that Jewish community.

The rebellion came in the last year of Trajan's life, and his successor, Hadrian, may have had the rebellion in mind when he passed through Judea in 130. Jerusalem lay in ruins still, but the Jews treated even those ruins with veneration. Therefore, Hadrian decided to build a new city on the site, one that was completely Roman and pagan.

When this news reached the Judeans, they broke into revolt again. The spiritual leader was Akiba ben Joseph (40–135), who was an ancient

who could still remember the Temple as it was before it was destroyed. The military leader called himself Simeon Bar-Kokhba ("son of a star"), perhaps indicating messianic status.

The rebellion started in 131, and it continued as fiercely and as stubbornly as the first rebellion had; however, by 134, the Romans had won again.

Judea was completely emptied of Jews, and the new Roman town was built. Nevertheless, Jews still lived in Galilee, and (in small numbers) in various cities of the Empire. Quite a few lived in the Tigris–Euphrates valley, which was now Parthian again, and was outside the Empire.

CHINA

About 105, a Chinese eunuch, Tsai Lun (50–118), invented a technique for using such substances as tree bark, hemp, and rags to make a thin, flexible, white sheet upon which one could write. Slowly, the process spread westward; and, in Europe, because of the similarity of the new material to Egyptian papyrus, the Europeans gave it that name, which became "paper" in English.

It is impossible to overestimate the importance of paper to a literate society.

150 TO 200

ROMAN EMPIRE

Marcus Aurelius (121–180) became Emperor in 161, along with a co-Emperor, Lucius Aurelius Verus (130–169). Marcus Aurelius was a convinced Stoic, who viewed duty as an ultimate good. He worked hard at being a rational and benevolent Emperor, and Verus was perfectly willing to leave all the hard work to him.

Marcus Aurelius could not, unfortunately, reign in peace. He was compelled, in 162, to send an army eastward because the Parthians were

again attempting to take over Armenia. The Romans did well in the field, but the soldiers returned afflicted with plague. Sickness spread over the Empire, weakening it, as a plague had weakened Athens during the Peloponnesian War six centuries earlier.

Then, in 167, Germanic tribesmen poured across the Roman borders for the first such invasion since the Cimbri and Teutones over two and a half centuries earlier. Marcus Aurelius managed to drive them back but only with the greatest of difficulty.

Marcus Aurelius was the last of the "good Emperors." When he died in 180, he broke the rule of succession by adoption, which had worked so well in the 80 years since Nerva. Instead, Marcus Aurelius' son, Commodus (161–192), succeeded. He neglected his duties and grew unpopular. He was assassinated in 192 and, after a year of turmoil, a provincial general, Lucius Septimius Severus (146–211), became Emperor.

By now, the Pax Romana was about over, and life was becoming increasingly severe.

In this period, Lucius Apuleius (124–174) wrote popular romances and fantasies of men being turned into animals, and of visits to the Moon.

GREECE

Greece was no longer a political power of any kind. Indeed, it was only a dream of the past. An Emperor, such as Hadrian, looked back to Greek times nostalgically, and showered gifts on Athens.

Nevertheless, what science still existed in the Empire was Greek. Claudius Ptolemaeus ("Ptolemy"), a Greek in Alexandria, summarized Greek astronomy about 150, and his writings survived into modern times. Galen (129–199) was the last great physician of ancient times.

By 200, though, Greek learning was fading, and was being replaced by mystic philosophies, by irrationalities such as astrology, and by Eastern religions. Nevertheless, it never *quite* died, and it remained to inspire later generations and, eventually, to help give rise to a new and still greater burst of science and learning.

GERMANS

The Germans had defeated and destroyed Roman legions in 9 and had since been benefiting by the nearness of the Empire. By the time of Marcus Aurelius, there were the Franks, who lived east of the lowermost Rhine. South of them were the Burgundians, and still farther south, the Alemanni.

The Germans found trade with the Empire useful, but when Rome seemed weak, there was the natural temptation to increase benefits by looting. In 167, when the plague was raging through the Empire, the Marcomanni (one of the Alemanni group, apparently) assailed the Roman borders. Though Marcus Aurelius beat them off, that effort, too, helped weaken the Empire, and paved the way for further attempts.

PARTHIA

In 161, Vologases III (who reigned over Parthia from 148 to 192) felt that with two emperors reigning in Rome, there was bound to be dissension and paralysis. Therefore, he seized Armenia.

He had guessed wrong. Marcus Aurelius sent a capable general, Avidius Cassius (d. 175) eastward. Cassius followed Trajan's route of half a century before.

In 165, he took Seleucia. It had been founded nearly four and a half centuries before as a Greek city, and it was still a Greek city, large and prosperous. It had a population of about 400,000 and was the largest Greek city outside the Roman Empire. Cassius saw it only as a Parthian city and had it burned. That put an end to Seleucia and to Hellenism in the east.

He also took Ctesiphon, and it is possible that the Romans might again have tried to annex the Tigris–Euphrates valley, but Cassius' soldiers were falling sick in large numbers of an epidemic (possibly of smallpox), which was raging in Parthia. He had to retreat and take the army and the smallpox back to the Empire. The whole Empire was devastated by the plague, and that plague (combined with the Marcomanni invasions) weakened the Roman Empire past the recovery point. Its population declined and never quite regained its pre-plague peak.

The next Parthian king, Vologases IV (who reigned from 192 to 208), tried to take advantage of the disarray that followed the assassination of Commodus and invaded Roman territory. Septimius Severus hurried eastward, and, for the third time, a Roman army took Ctesiphon, and sacked it thoroughly.

INDIA

In India, about this time, a very primitive stirrup had been invented, one of leather into which the big toe could be placed to help a rider keep himself steady on the horse.

CHINA

A serious rebellion by the "Yellow Turbans," aimed at the corrupt rule of court eunuchs, weakened the Han Empire; and, by 200, it was clearly winding down to its end.

200 TO 250

ROMAN EMPIRE

After the death of Septimius Severus in 211, a period of near-anarchy prevailed in the Roman Empire, as emperors followed each other rapidly. Few of them died in bed, and succession was usually by military coup.

In 212, Septimius Severus' son, Caracalla (188–217), reigning from 211 to 217, extended Roman citizenship to all inhabitants of the Empire who were not slaves. By this time, though, the citizenship didn't mean much beyond the privilege of saying "I am a Roman citizen." Citizens no longer participated in the government in any way, and their chief function was to pay an inheritance tax (which Caracalla might have had in mind).

In 248, Rome had existed 1000 years (it was 1000 A.U.C), and the anniversary was celebrated with great pomp. Marcus Julius Philippus was Emperor then, reigning from 244 to 249. He is termed "Philip the Arabian" by historians because his father was from a Roman province, just south of what had been Judea, a province that was at the northwest corner of the Arabian peninsula.

As emperors found themselves facing only the certainty of Germanic invasions from abroad and conspiracies at home, and seemed sure to die either in battle or at the hand of an assassin, they demanded more security and encouraged emperor-worship. Perhaps they felt safer as gods; however, as it happened, it did them no good.

Under these circumstances the growing sect of Christianity seemed dangerous, since Christians refused to grant any worship to the emperor. This made them seem rebellious, and under Decius (201–251), who reigned as Emperor from 249 to 251, there was the first general persecution of Christians.

In addition to Christianity, Mithraism was growing stronger in the Roman dominions. It was of Persian origin and included worship of a sun-god, with great celebrations of the "Day of the Sun" on December 25, marking the winter solstice, when the Sun began to rise in the sky again. (The Christians finally adopted the day as Christmas, since the celebration was too popular to fight.) Mithraism was very popular with the troops and had many of the emotional values of Christianity, but it had a fatal flaw. It was closed to women. This meant that Mithraist husbands were apt to have Christian wives and, therefore, Christian children.

There was also Manichaeism, propounded in this period by the Persian preacher, Mani (216–276). This had some of the elements of Christianity in it, but it accepted the Zoroastrian view of the existence of principles of good and evil of equal strength.

One last school of non-Christian philosophy was advanced by Plotinus (205–270), who added various mystical notions to Platonic thought to produce "Neoplatonism."

On the brighter side, there appeared one last major work of original mathematical importance to be written by a Greek. The mathematician was Diophantus (210–290, possibly), whose book dealt with what we now call algebra. It was the first significant work to be published on that subject.

By 250, the combination of anarchy at the top, of increasing tribal invasions, and of the coming of eastern religions, made it seem as though the Roman Empire was rapidly approaching its end.

PERSIA

If the Roman Empire seemed threatened with collapse, the Parthian Empire *did* collapse.

Persis, the old province from which Cyrus had arisen eight centuries earlier, rested uneasily under the Parthian monarchy. It wanted old Persian values and resented Parthian tendencies toward Hellenization.

By 211, the most influential leader in Persis was Ardashir (d. 241), a grandson of a local ruler named Sassan, so that Ardashir and his descendants can be called "Sassanids." In 224, Ardashir rose in rebellion and by 228, he had defeated and killed Artabanus V, who reigned from 213 to 224 as the last Parthian ruler. Ardashir occupied Ctesiphon and declared himself king.

The region remained as it had been. Language, religion, and culture generally did not change. It was only a change in dynasty, actually, as had been true eight centuries earlier when the Median Empire had changed to the Persian Empire. However, the new dynasty received a new national name. In place of Parthia, people speak of the "Sassanid Empire," or the "New Persian Empire" or the "Neo-Persian Empire." Actually, it would be simplest to call it Persia.

In 241, Ardashir was succeeded by his son, who ruled as Shapur I from 241 to 272. It was clear, by then, that the change was for the worse as far as the Roman Empire was concerned. The new Sassanid line was more capable than the old Arsacid line of Parthia had been, and that made Persia the more dangerous enemy.

JAPAN

The Emperor, Sujin, came to the throne in 230 and records began to be kept, though much of what was written about the period continued to be legendary.

AFRICA

By 250, Axum had become a major trading center, and was particularly active in the ivory traffic.

SOUTHEAST ASIA

Funan was located in what is now Cambodia. It was subject to the influence of both India and China and, by 245, was important enough to warrant a visit by a Chinese mission.

250 TO 300

GOTHS

The German tribes north of the Danube were now more restless than ever. Increasing population may have been driving them south, or pressure from the westward movement of the tribesmen of central Asia, or both.

The most important of the Germanic tribes at this time were the Goths. They may have originally dwelt in what we now call Sweden in the time of Augustus. With time, they drifted southward until, by 300, they formed a rather large, loosely bound realm in what is now Poland and the Ukraine. In Poland, they lorded over the primitive Slavs, who were a peaceful folk who were easily enslaved. (Some people think the word "slave" comes from "Slav.") In the Ukraine, they dominated the Sarmatians, Asian tribesmen who, over the centuries, had slowly displaced and absorbed the Scythians.

The Goths split up into two groups: the "Ostrogoths" to the east, and the "Visigoths" to the west. About 250, the Goths flooded into Dacia, crossed the Danube, and visited destruction on the Balkan peninsula. In 267, they sacked Athens, Sparta, and Corinth.

Other German tribes invaded other portions of the Empire, and Roman cities began to build walls about themselves since the frontiers seemed to have become porous.

PERSIA

Persia found the disarray in Rome, and the desperation with which the Roman Emperors were fighting off the Goths and other Germanic tribes, an opportunity too good to ignore. They attacked Armenia, the perennial bone of contention between Parthia and Rome and, by 251, were in control there. They even penetrated and took Syria.

The Roman Emperor at the time was Valerian, who reigned from 253 to 260. In 258, he marched east after having spent some years fighting the Germanic invaders.

He managed to retake Antioch and drove the Persians out of Syria, but at Edessa in northeastern Syria, he lost a battle to the Persians (this was fairly close to Carrhae, where, three centuries earlier, the Romans had lost to the Parthians). In the course of the battle, Valerian was taken alive, but died in captivity.

When that happened, Shapur I of Persia felt the Roman east was open to him and led his army into Asia Minor. However, he was stopped at this point by the action of an Arab chieftain, Septimius Odenathus (d. 267), who ruled over eastern Syria. Odenathus was left in peace by a weakened and distracted Rome, but a strong Persian rule over the region would have been dangerous to him. Therefore, he raided eastward into the Tigris–Euphrates valley, taking advantage of the fact that the Persian army was in Asia Minor.

Shapur was forced to leave Asia Minor to meet this new menace. In 267, Odenathus was assassinated, but his widow, Zenobia (d. 275), as capable as he, declared herself independent and seized the eastern Roman provinces. Meanwhile, the western provinces of Britain, Gaul, and Spain also broke away, declaring a new emperor over those regions.

ROMAN EMPIRE

In 268, the Roman Empire was at a low point and seemed to have fallen into fragments. In that year, however, Claudius II (214–270) became Roman Emperor, the first really capable one since the death of Septimius Severus, half a century before.

In 269, and again in 270, Claudius II won tremendous victories over the Goths, slaughtering them and driving the remnants beyond the frontiers. (Some Goths became Romanized and settled within the Empire.) The Emperor was called "Claudius Gothicus" because of his victories.

Claudius II died in his bed (unusual for the period) in 270, and succeeding him was the equally capable Aurelian (215–275). When detachments of Goths thought that, with Claudius II gone, it was safe to raid the Empire once more, Aurelian defeated them just as handily as Claudius had.

He then strengthened the northern border by abandoning Dacia (a century and a half after it had been taken by Trajan). Dacia, north of the Danube, was in an exposed position, and the Empire, it was thought, would be better off if it maintained the Danube itself as the northern border.

In 271, Aurelian began the task of building a wall about Rome—a city that had had no need of one for five centuries.

Only then did he feel it safe to leave for the east to deal with Zenobia. By 273, he had retaken Asia Minor, destroyed Palmyra, Zenobia's capital, and captured Zenobia herself.

He then moved westward and, in 274, brought the western provinces back into line. Aurelian was then hailed as *Restitutor Orbis*— that is, "the restorer of the world." Certainly, he had restored the Roman Empire, leaving it weakened, but intact, by the time it was his turn to be assassinated in 275.

In 284, the period of near-anarchy and frequent changes of Emperor came, at least temporarily, to an end. A general named Diocletian (248–316) became Emperor, and he was the first, since Marcus Aurelius a century before, to have both a long reign and a quiet death.

Diocletian totally reorganized the Roman Empire. He wiped out the last vestiges of the old Republican rule, converting the Empire into the type of monarchy common in the east, where the king is absolute. He abandoned Rome and set up his capital in Nicomedia in northwestern Asia Minor. In order to make the Empire easier to rule, he divided it into a western and eastern half. He chose a co-Emperor to rule the west, while he himself ruled the east. (He made sure, however, that the co-Emperor was subservient to him.) What's more, each Emperor chose a "Caesar" who would assist him and serve as his successor—a kind of Vice-Emperor. (This system looked good, but it never worked.)

As a result of all the disorders of the last century, the Roman economy was in ruins and the Empire was badly wounded. However, by 300, with Diocletian still on the throne, it looked as though Rome had weathered all its difficulties and was again strong and united, having lost only Dacia.

JAPAN

Confucianism reached Japan about 285.

NORTH AMERICA

The Mayan civilization was, by 300, arising in central America, and pre-Aztec civilizations were to be found in Mexico.

PACIFIC OCEAN

About 300, the Polynesians, based originally in islands fairly close to Asia and Indonesia, were beginning the series of long voyages that would take them to all the scattered islands in the Pacific Ocean.

300 TO 350

CHRISTIANITY

By the time of Diocletian, perhaps 10% of the population of the Roman Empire was Christian. It was an important 10%, for the Christians tended to be fervent in their beliefs, while the non-Christian majority tended to be lukewarm, or even indifferent.

The causes of Christian growth were several. For one thing, the imminent disintegration of the Empire, which had seemed likely and even almost inevitable after the death of Septimius Severus, made it appear that the things of the world were indeed coming to an end and that the predicted second coming of Christ (the new form of messianism) was soon to take place.

Then, too, the decay of society and the increasing hardships suffered by humanity made this world less alluring and the promise of the next world more desirable. And again, the Church, which was strengthening its organization and efficiency, even as the Empire was losing its own, seemed increasingly to be a rock of security in a troubled, miserable world.

Most of the Christians were concentrated in the east, near where the religion had been born, and where the people were more sophisticated and more used to philosophy and to theology. There were many bishops and theological teachers and disputants in the east.

In the west, there was a smaller percentage of Christians in the population, and only one important bishop, the one in Rome. He, by tradition, was a successor of St. Peter, who was supposed to have been the first bishop of Rome. This was important for, in the time to come, when disputations and argument rocked the east, the west remained firm in the doctrines advanced by the bishop of Rome (who eventually came to be called the "Pope" in English, from the Italian word for "father").

The increasing number of Christians inspired successive waves of repression. The firmest and most drastic of these was launched by Diocletian in 303. However, repression never succeeded in repressing. Instead, if anything, it accelerated the rise of Christianity. It was so with Diocletian's repression as well. Christianity grew still stronger.

ROMAN EMPIRE

In 305, Diocletian abdicated, and remained in peaceful and happy retirement till he died a natural death in 313. His system of two Emperors and two Caesars broke down at once, however. His abdication was the signal for various generals to fight for the throne. This boiled down to a fight between one general, Constantine (d. 337, sometimes called "Constantine the Great") in the west, and another, Maxentius (d. 312) in the east.

In 312, Constantine invaded Italy, defeated Maxentius, and marched on Rome. Maxentius opposed him again at the Milvian Bridge that spanned the Tiber River. It occurred to Constantine that since even Diocletian had failed to suppress the Christians, it might be good politics to get those enthusiasts on his side. Therefore, he spread the news that he had seen a glowing cross in the heaven and placed Christian insignia on his soldiers' shields. He won the battle (which he might have done anyway), and with the Edict of Milan in 313, he allowed Christians free exercise of their religion. After that, the Christians rallied to his side, and he was unstoppable.

By that time, Armenia had already, in 303, made Christianity its official religion so that it became the first Christian nation. The Roman Empire under Constantine followed as the second, although Constantine did not allow himself to be actually baptized a Christian until he lay on his death bed.

Constantine continued the reforms of Diocletian and labored to strengthen the Empire. There was legal reform. The treatment of prisoners and slaves became more humane, in line with Christian views, and he put an end to gladiatorial contests. However, offenders against sexual morality were treated more severely—again in line with Christian views. (However, the land did not become more moral as a result, for repression of immorality did as little long-term good as repression of Christianity.)

Constantine continued to make use of German tribesmen who were willing to accept Romanization, and inducted them into the army, which thus became less and less Roman and more and more German—a bad thing in the long run.

Constantine also demonstrated that a strong Emperor could overpower the Church. As long as Christianity was a more or less outlawed religion, the bishops could fight among themselves on points of doctrine and establish what came to be called "heresies" (from a Greek word for "to choose," meaning "to choose your own point of view"). There were endless quarrels and polemics as a result.

Once the Christian religion was under a more or less Christian Emperor, however, the Emperor could say which point of view was indeed a heresy, and which point of view was "orthodox" (from Greek words meaning "true opinion"). The heresies might continue, but the power of the state would then be behind what had been declared orthodox.

The coming of Christianity to power did not mean an end to persecution. Not only did the Christians instantly begin to persecute the pagans, denying to them what they had demanded for themselves (the usual way of the world), but one group of Christians would cheerfully and efficiently persecute another group.

In 325, for instance, a council of bishops was held at Nicaea in northwestern Asia Minor. Under Constantine's strong direction, the views of an Alexandrian deacon, Athanasius (293–373), sometimes called "Athanasius the Great", were declared orthodox, and those of another Alexandrian deacon, Arius (250–336), were declared heretical. The former view, "Catholicism", was thus given an advantage over "Arianism." (The two disagreed over the nature of the Trinity.)

There were occasions, however, where Arianism had the power of the state behind it, to say nothing of the fact that other heresies developed. There was, assuredly, far less religious peace after Rome became Christian than before.

Constantine, like Diocletian, preferred to keep his capital in the east. However, he wanted a new capital. He chose the site of the city of Byzantium, on the European side of a narrow strait, the Bosporus, which separated Europe from Asia, because it had an excellent harbor and a position that could be made very strong, if a good wall was built, and if there was a strong navy to control the sea.

He rebuilt it, beautified it by appropriating artwork from Rome and from other parts of the Empire, and renamed it after himself—so that in English it became Constantinople, although it was also called, sentimentally, New Rome. It became the capital of the Roman Empire on May 11, 330.

Constantine died in 337 after a reign of 31 years, the longest since Augustus, over three centuries earlier. He had three sons, who divided the Empire among themselves. They were the first Emperors who were brought up with a Christian education, but they behaved just as badly as the earlier pagan Emperors.

They fought each other and, by 351, the second son, reigning as Constantius II (317–361) was in firm, solitary control. The Empire was still united, and seemed still strong.

Technology continued to advance, which it often does when all else seems to be falling apart. Water mills were coming into greater use so that power existed, at least potentially, wherever running water was to be found. Glass was being manufactured with greater proficiency, and looms for weaving cloth with patterns had finally reached Europe from China where this had been invented perhaps four centuries before. Soap, too, was coming into use, and this may have been a Celtic invention.

Alchemy, a very primitive and often mystical prelude to chemistry, was making itself felt. The first important alchemist, a Greek named Zosimus, had perhaps completed his work during this period.

PERSIA

In 309, Shapur II (d. 379) of Persia was born. His father had died just before his birth, and the Persians recognized the unborn infant as king at once, which he remained for all of his life. He was 17 when Constantine died and, anticipating that there would follow confusion, he began his first war against Rome. He won some successes, but even though the sons of Constantine were fighting each other, their fortified positions on the borders held against Shapur and, by 350, that first war had ended in a virtual draw.

GOTHS

In 350, the Ostrogothic kingdom, in what is now Poland and the Ukraine, had reached its fullest extent of size and power under a king named Ermanaric (d. 376). The Visigoths, for their part, now occupied what had been the Roman province of Dacia.

HUNS

A central Asian nomadic people, the Hsiung-nu, had been raiding Chinese territory for many centuries. The Great Wall of China was built to keep them out, and the Chinese were increasingly effective at fighting them off. By 350, the Hsiung-nu, either through population growth or through the realization that they weren't getting anywhere against the Chinese, began to drift westward instead. To the Europeans, once they arrived there, the nomads were known as "Huns."

AFRICA

About 350, the increasingly prosperous Axum invaded Meroe to the north and destroyed it. Axum was now the sole civilized power south of Egypt. Christianity was penetrating it, and that forged a link between it and Egypt.

INDIA

About 320, the Gupta Dynasty united northern India and dominated neighboring portions of the region. The first ruler of the dynasty was Chandragupta I, who reigned from 320 to 330. Under his son, Samudragupta, who reigned from 330 to 380, the dynasty was at its height. At this time, the ancient Hindu religion of Brahmanism began to regain ascendancy, for Samudragupta was a devout Brahman.

350 TO 400

HUNS

The Huns, on their shaggy Asian ponies, crossed the Ostrogothic frontier and entered Europe in 374. They virtually lived on their horses, and could maneuver with a speed that left their foes helpless. What was important was that they had adopted and greatly improved the Indian notion of the stirrup. The Huns had metal stirrups into which the whole foot could be thrust. This fixed them firmly to their horses so that they could not easily be thrown off. Without stirrups, a horseman could only cast a spear, or shoot an arrow. With stirrups, a horseman could *thrust* with a spear and the full weight of man *and* horse would be behind it.

The Ostrogoths could not stand against the Huns. Ermanaric, who had ruled over their large territory, was (according to legend) forced to kill himself in despair at seeing his kingdom vanish under the thundering hooves of the Hunnish horsemen.

The Huns spread over the plain that stretched from the Caspian Sea to what is now Hungary (that name is no accident); and the Visigoths, who lived just across the Danube from the Romans, clamored in terror to be allowed across the river. The Romans allowed the Goths to enter, but it was not entirely an act of mercy, for the Roman officials plundered the Goths and profited in this manner.

ROMAN EMPIRE

Constantius II died in 361 and a cousin, Julian (331–363), became Emperor. Julian was a capable general who, even as a young man, defeated the German tribe of Franks who had crossed the Rhine River and invaded Gaul. Julian staged three raids east of the Rhine to make sure that the Franks would not return quickly.

Once he became Emperor, Julian did what he had longed to do all along. He abandoned the Christian religion in which he had been raised and returned to paganism. He dreamed of recreating the glorious days of Plato and Aristotle, now six centuries in the past. As a result, he is known in history as "Julian the Apostate," from a Greek word meaning "defection."

Julian's dream was unattainable, of course, since paganism in Roman society was just about a corpse and could not be resurrected. Nor was his secular rule successful. He fought Persia and invaded the Tigris–Euphrates once again, hoping to take Ctesiphon for Rome a fourth time, but he died in battle in 363 (perhaps being killed by a Roman soldier who happened to be a Christian). His successor was Jovian (331–364), a Christian, and the issue was never again in doubt. Christianity spread steadily through the Empire, and Julian's last words are supposed to have been, "Thou hast conquered, O Galilean."

Jovian agreed to an unfavorable peace in order to rescue his army and bring it back to the Empire, then died in 364.

Valentinian I (321–375) succeeded Jovian and appointed his brother, Valens (328–378) as co-Emperor. When Valentinian I died in 375, he was succeeded by his two sons: Gratian (359–383) and Valentinian II (371–392).

It was Valens who ruled in the east, and it was he who had to face the crisis created by the Visigoths who had entered the Empire to escape from the Huns.

The Visigoths, angered by mistreatment by Romans, had gathered arms and had begun to raid farming areas for the food that Roman officials were willing to sell them only at impossible prices. Valens rushed his army to Adrianople, about 150 miles west of Constantinople. (Adrianople had been founded by Hadrian—hence, its name.)

There, in 378, the Romans and Goths fought. Valens, overconfident, did not wait for reinforcements to reach him. He didn't even wait to rest his soldiers. He attacked at once. The Goths, moreover, were, for the most part, on horses, and they had stirrups (so much they had learned from the Huns).

The result was that the Romans were slaughtered and Valens himself was killed. The Battle of Adrianople put an end to the Roman legion. It had been the strongest fighting force in the west since the battles with Pyrrhus six and a half centuries before, but now there followed a long period in which the key to victory lay in the cavalry.

The situation was like that in the days when the Hyksos took Egypt 2000 years earlier, only then, soldiers were dragged behind the horse in chariots, whereas now they bestrode the horse with stirrups.

The Goths could not follow up their victory properly. They could not take the fortified towns of the Empire. In addition, Theodosius I (347–395), sometimes called "Theodosius the Great," became Emperor in 379, and he shrewdly encouraged the Goths to quarrel among themselves, soothed them with honeyed words, gave them land to settle on, and encouraged them to enroll in the Roman army. The result was that he managed to control the Empire and keep it quiet during his reign.

Theodosius was an ardent Christian and, with him, there began an active persecution of pagans. He put an end to the Olympic games in 394, after they had been part of the Greek tradition for nearly 12 centuries.

Theodosius died in 395, but before his death he had arranged to have the Empire divided between his two sons. The elder, Arcadius (377–408), ruled the east from Constantinople. The younger, Honorius (384–423), ruled the west,

not from Rome itself, but from Milan in northwestern Italy.

This was not unprecedented. Ever since the time of Marcus Aurelius, two centuries earlier, multiple Emperors had become more and more common. Nevertheless, until this time, when there was more than one Emperor, at least one of them was a capable man, and there were always times when one man might, like Theodosius, take over the entire job. The two sons of Theodosius, however, were both incompetent, and the Empire was never to be united again—although, of course, no one would have guessed this at the time. In any case, from this point on, we must speak of the "West Roman Empire" and the "East Roman Empire."

Despite this, a superficial observer in 400 would have noted that the Empire, despite all the civil wars, all the tribal invasions, and all the Persian attacks, was still intact and seemingly as strong as ever. This, however, was all facade. As so frequently happens, the outside looks good long after the inside has shriveled.

One leading Christian of the period was Eusebius Hieronymus (347–420), known to us as "St. Jerome." His greatest achievement was to translate the Bible into Latin, a task he completed in 405. The Latin version is called the *Vulgate* (from a Latin word for "the common people"). Until then, the Bible used by Christians was the Greek Septuagint, which had been prepared six and a half centuries earlier. Jerome went back to the Hebrew and prepared a version available to the people in the west, where Christianity was weakest, and that greatly helped growth there.

Another was Ambrosius (339–397), known to us as "St. Ambrose," who was bishop of Milan from 374, and who was the most powerful prelate of his time. He was a strong force for intolerance and set the standard in that respect. When the Emperor Theodosius punished a bishop for burning a Jewish synagogue, Ambrose rebuked him. Nor would he allow any moves for a reasonable attitude toward pagans or Arians. He did order Theodosius to do penance for angrily ordering a massacre of the people of Thessalonica in Greece, who had revolted, but that was only because the slaughtered people were orthodox.

PERSIA

Shapur II, having been king from birth to death, reigned for 70 years, a record only a few monarchs have surpassed. His long reign was filled with periodic wars against the Romans. Only the one in which Julian was killed was truly successful. Jovian, to extricate his army, had given up all recent Roman conquests in the east and had agreed that Armenia was to be under Persian influence, and not Roman, thus reversing a situation that had existed for four centuries.

Nevertheless, when Shapur II died in 379, Persia had not scored a really decisive victory, and the monarchs who succeeded him were weak.

INDIA

The Gupta dynasty continued with Chandragupta II, who reigned from 380 to 415. Brahman philosophy was developing notably at the time, and that aided the recovery of Brahmanism.

KOREA

Korea, which had been under Chinese influence, was able to shake it off, as China had been composed of competing states at war among themselves since the end of the Han Empire a century and a half before. It may be at this time that Japan attempted to secure footholds in Korea, under an Empress, semilegendary at best, whose name was Jingo.

400 TO 450

VISIGOTHS

The Visigoths, after their victory at Adrianople, were under a leader named Alaric (370–410), and were living in what had once been Epirus, the land of Pyrrhus nearly seven centuries earlier. It was a time when various leaders of Germanic tribes were given high posts at Constantinople, but Alaric had been passed over. Angered, he led his men into raids toward Constantinople. The city was secure behind its walls, so Alaric turned southward into Greece.

Alaric was a Christian, although of the Arian variety (as most of the Germanic tribes within the Empire were, at the time), and he put an end to the Eleusinian mysteries. In this way, another remnant of paganism was destroyed.

The two halves of the Roman Empire were at such enmity with each other that each was content to see the tribesmen destroy the other. The East Roman Empire got rid of Alaric and his Visigoths by encouraging him to turn westward.

Alaric invaded Italy in 400, but he was met by Stilicho (365–408), who was the power behind the feeble Honorius. (Stilicho was one of the Vandals, who were another set of Germanic tribesmen.) In the war of German against German, Stilicho beat Alaric in northern Italy, and Alaric was forced to withdraw.

It was clear, however, that Italy was not safe, and Honorius moved his capital to Ravenna, near the Adriatic coast. It was surrounded by marshlands and was easily defensible.

Since the fight against Alaric was diverting the limited resources of the West Roman Empire, other tribesmen took advantage of the situation. A group of Sueves and Vandals, who were north of Italy, crossed the Alps and invaded Italy. Stilicho defeated them, too, and drove them out, which just about exhausted the Romans.

On December 31, 406, other Sueves and Vandals crossed the Rhine River and moved into Gaul. This was nothing new. Germanic invaders had been punching through the Roman boundary lines ever since Marcus Aurelius nearly two and a half centuries before. To this point, however, the Romans had managed to fight them off and drive them back.

Now it was different. This time the Germanic tribesmen who entered the West Roman Empire were never driven out. The tribesmen took the land, made the laws, dominated the native Romans, and turned them into peasants and serfs.

It might be noticed that there was little or no popular resistance to the Germanic invasions. The Germans were opposed by Roman forces (often also German). If those forces failed, there were no guerrilla bands, no people's insurrections. The common people were so cowed by a century and a half of tribal incursions and civil wars that it seemed to make no difference to them any longer exactly who oppressed them.

The Sueves and Vandals crossed Gaul with scarcely any opposition and, by 409 B.C., were settling down in Spain. (The region of "Andalusia" in southern Spain is a reminder, with the *V* missing, of a time of Vandal domination.)

This successful invasion was blamed on Stilicho, who had done everything he could to protect Italy at least. In August 408, he was executed. The German tribesmen, who made up much of the "Roman" army, deserted in indignation, and Alaric, still waiting not far outside Italy, seized his chance. He marched into Italy again and, in 410, his soldiers actually took Rome.

For the first time since the sack by the Gauls, exactly eight centuries before, Rome was in foreign hands. Alaric remained only six days, then marched into southern Italy where he died of fever. The taking of Rome, however, was news that shook the Empire. Rome had for so long been unassailable—and now it was taken without even the ability to put up a respectable fight.

The Visigoths then trekked into Spain where they fought successfully against the German tribes that were already there. Afterward, they moved into southwestern Gaul, and there settled down and made it into a land of their own. They established their capital in 418 at the Gallic city of Toulouse, so that their realm is sometimes referred to as the "Kingdom of Toulouse." Reigning over them from 418 to 451, was Theodoric I, a son of Alaric.

The Kingdom of Toulouse was the first of the Germanic kingdoms to be established. It was friendly to the Romans and was allied with the Empire, and even fought battles at its side. However, within the Kingdom of Toulouse, it was the Visigoths who were the land-owning aristocrats and the native Romans who were the peasantry.

This was only 40 years after the Visigoths had crossed the Danube River as suppliants, seeking Roman help and protection.

VANDALS

The Vandals in Spain had been roughly handled by the invading Visigoths, and had been badly weakened. In 428, however, a new leader, Gaiseric (d. 477), sometimes called Genseric, proved to be the most capable of all the German tribal leaders of his time.

The West Roman Empire was under the rule of another nonentity at the time. This was Valentinian III (419–455), who had come to the throne as a 6-year-old in 425. The real power was in the hands of two generals, Flavius Aetius (d. 454) and Bonifacius (d. 432), who hated each other. Bonifacius lost out and was put in charge of the African province with Carthage as its capital. It kept him away from Italy and the center of what power existed there, and he was furious.

Bonifacius decided to seek help among the German tribesmen, and the Vandals, unhappy in Spain, were ready to supply that help in their own way.

In 428, Gaiseric and some 80,000 Vandals were carried in Roman ships to Africa. There, Gaiseric quickly showed that his idea of helping Bonifacius was to take over the African province for himself.

In 431, he took Hippo, where Aurelius Augustinus (354–430), known to us as "St. Augustine," was bishop. Augustine had been baptized a Christian in 387 by Ambrose of Milan. He was the most influential Christian writer and thinker since St. Paul, four centuries earlier, and few Christians have equaled his importance since. He was an able writer, the first to write an important autobiography. He skillfully expounded Christian theology and explained why it was that the Christian Empire was so weak when the Pagan

Empire had been so strong. He died in 430, just before the Vandals took the city.

Gaiseric took Carthage in 439 and established what was, under him, the strongest of the Germanic kingdoms. In 450, he was still on the throne, having lost none of his vigor in his old age, and he had developed a navy of his own. The Vandals of Carthage were the only Germanic kingdom to be strong at sea.

BRITAIN

Britain was the last province to be added to the Roman Empire and to stay Roman for centuries —for over three and a half, in fact. It was also the only portion of the Roman Empire to be entirely separated from the rest of the realm by the sea.

When Italy was being plagued by the Visigoths, the Sueves, and the Vandals, Stilicho was forced to draw on whatever troops were available, and he called upon the legions stationed in Britain to come to Italy. They left Britain, beginning in 407. The withdrawal was undoubtedly thought to be temporary at first, but it turned out to be permanent.

Britain had not been very Christian under Rome—it was farthest removed from the Christian centers, and, without the legions, it quickly lost its Roman veneer. Britain reverted to its Celtic culture.

They were not allowed to remain in peace, however. The Picts in the north of Britain, who had never been under Roman rule, seized the opportunity to raid southward and to spread devastation. By 450 B.C., the British ruler, Vortigern, was looking abroad for help, as Bonifacius had, and with the same results.

HUNS

In 433, two brothers, Attila (406–453) and Bleda (d. 445), began to rule over the Huns. The Huns were still expanding in all directions. Most important was their expansion into Germany, which drove some of the German tribes across the Rhine and led to the establishment of the Germanic kingdoms.

By 450, Attila, now sole ruler, was ready to attack the West Roman Empire itself.

WEST ROMAN EMPIRE

The West Roman Empire had no history of its own in this period. For 50 years, it kept trying to fight off German invaders, usually by making use of German commanders and soldiers itself. The Empire usually failed, under a line of singularly incompetent Emperors, so that the territory it controlled grew less and less.

By 450, the only general it had who might be considered Roman was Aetius. He was the last to win victories in the west and has sometimes been called "the last of the Romans" for that reason.

PAPACY

After the time of Theodosius, the Emperors in the west were feeble indeed, and usually were hidden away in Ravenna. That left the Bishop of Rome, the Pope, as the only prestige-filled figure to be present in Rome, a city which still had the mystique of Empire about it, though it had long lost its glory.

EAST ROMAN EMPIRE

The very fact that the West Roman Empire was so weak at this time protected the East Roman Empire. The Germanic tribesmen found the western provinces such easy targets that there seemed no sense in picking a fight in the east.

The East Roman Empire was now rich and urbanized. Constantinople was now the largest and wealthiest city in the western world.

Theodosius II (401–450), who came to the throne in 408 as a 7-year-old, was not a strong ruler, although he had a very intelligent sister, Pulcheria (399–453), who served as co-Empress. Under him, a written code of laws was prepared in 438.

Beginning in 413, and taking 34 years to complete, a triple set of walls was built across the landward approaches to Constantinople. Between those walls and the Roman navy, it was felt that Constantinople would be impregnable by land and sea and, as long as Constantinople existed, that enemy victories elsewhere could always be reversed.

In 450, while the West Roman Empire was crumbling, the East Roman Empire remained intact.

PERSIA

Persia lacked strong kings in this interval. Christianity was making itself felt in Persia, but Christians were bound to feel sympathetic to Rome, a traditional enemy for four centuries now. As a result, the Persian monarch introduced periods of persecution for Christians. This was more or less successful, for Persia never turned Christian.

KOREA

Korea was divided into three kingdoms at this time, of which the northernmost, Koguru, under Changsu, was now at the height of its power. It moved its capital from the Yalu River at the northern boundary of the peninsula to Pyongyang in the center. Buddhism was introduced into Korea at this time.

PACIFIC

About this time, the Polynesians reached Hawaii, their northernmost outpost.

450 TO 500

HUNS

In 451, Attila led his Huns westward across the Rhine River and into Gaul. It was the first time (and the last) that central Asian tribesmen penetrated west of the Rhine. To be sure, most of his forces were Ostrogoths, for the Huns had ruled over the Ostrogoths for 80 years now.

Aetius of Rome, in alliance with Theodoric I, the aged king of the Visigoths, and with some other Germanic groups, marched north to oppose Attila. The armies met on the Catalaunian Plain, about 100 miles east of Paris.

Aetius, maneuvering cleverly, won the battle —the last great victory of West Roman arms. Theodoric died in the fight.

Attila was forced to leave Gaul as the result of his defeat, but he was by no means wiped out. He turned toward Italy, where his looting was so terrible that he was called "the Scourge of God," the whip with which God was punishing the sins of Italy.

In 452, he laid siege to Aquileia, a city at the northern tip of the Adriatic Sea. He took and de-

stroyed it. Some of the inhabitants, fleeing from the devastation, took refuge among the swampy lagoons to the west, and there they made the first settlements of what became the city of Venice.

Attila then moved southward toward Rome and there was no resistance worth mentioning.

In Rome was Pope Leo I (400–461), sometimes called "Leo the Great," who had attained the Papacy in 440. He left Rome and came to meet Attila in full papal regalia, asking that Rome be left unharmed. Attila turned back (according to the story) because of the superstitious awe he felt at the Pope's majesty. That is, however, so unlike Attila, that it is much easier to believe that the Pope brought with him a sizable gift of gold for the Hunnish leader. Nevertheless, the story of Leo's facing down of Attila did much to raise papal prestige further.

Attila left Italy and, in 453, married again, celebrated overenthusiastically, and died that night in his tent. As soon as he was gone, the German tribesmen who made up the bulk of his army revolted. The Huns could not withstand that, and they simply disappeared from history (i.e., those who weren't killed intermarried with the surrounding peoples).

VANDALS

In the aftermath of the Hunnish invasion of Italy, Gaiseric, the leader of the Vandals in North Africa, mounted an expedition of his own against Italy. In June 455, his ships reached the mouth of the Tiber. There was no opposition and, for two weeks, the Vandals efficiently removed all that was movable and valuable for carting off to Carthage. There was no useless destruction, no sadisitic carnage, but the bitter Romans, writing about the event have so distorted it that the word "vandal" is now applied to anyone who indulges in senseless or malicious destruction.

In this way, Carthage (a different Carthage, of course) finally had its revenge on Rome for the destruction that had been visited on it six centuries earlier. Carthage remained strong until the death of Gaiseric, in his eighties, in 477.

VISIGOTHS

After the Battle of the Catalaunian Plains, Theodoric I was succeeded by his eldest son, Thorismond, who, in 453, was killed by one of his brothers, who then reigned as Theodoric II (426–466). Theodoric II expanded his dominion southward into Spain.

In 466, Theodoric II was, in turn, killed by one of *his* brothers, who reigned as Euric I (d. 484). Under him, the Visigothic kingdom reached its peak. It controlled almost all of Spain as well as southern Gaul. He had a written code of laws prepared and, under him, some Roman values continued.

In 500, even with Euric gone, the Visigothic kingdom seemed strong.

WEST ROMAN EMPIRE

The West Roman Empire was in fragments. The West Roman Emperor at Ravenna scarcely ruled any land outside of Italy, and even the home peninsula was shaky. Valentinian III, afraid that Aetius, after his victory over the Huns, might

gain too much power, had him killed in 454, and was himself killed by Aetius's soldiers in 455.

After that, the West Roman Emperors were only a series of do-nothings who had the name of Emperor but none of the power, while various generals fought for control of Italy.

The Germans in Italy wanted land and power, as their kinsmen in Gaul, Spain, and North Africa had. When the Romans refused to grant this, the Germans simply took it. Their leader, Odoacer (433–493), forced the Emperor, Romulus Augustulus, a boy who had come to the throne in 475, to abdicate on September 4, 476. Nor did Odoacer bother to name another puppet Emperor. He simply allowed the title to lapse, so that there was no Emperor at all in the west, five centuries after Augustus had become Rome's first Emperor.

For this reason, 476 is usually given as the date of "the fall of the Roman Empire." This is wrong in two ways. In the first place, the West Roman Empire had been disintegrating for seven decades and 476 was just one more step in that disintegration. In the second place, there was still an Emperor in Constantinople (his name was Zeno and he reigned from 474 to 491); and, if there was no Emperor in Italy, then Zeno became the ruler of the entire Empire—in theory, at least.

Certainly in 476, no one thought that the Empire had fallen. The empire was still there. It was just being ruled differently.

Nevertheless, looking back on it, it is clear that the West Roman Empire, which was intact in 400, had vanished by 500.

Roman technology worsened, too, as roads and aqueducts decayed and were not repaired, and as industries declined.

OSTROGOTHS

The Ostrogoths had been under Hunnish control for 80 years and had formed the bulk of the Hunnish army at the Battle of the Catalaunian Plains. After Attila's death, they rebelled and regained their freedom. They settled down in the East Roman Empire, south of the Danube River, where, a century earlier, the Visigoths had hidden from the Huns.

The Ostrogoths were converted to Arian Christianity. The Vandals and the Visigoths were also Arians, and this created a gulf between them and the Roman natives over whom they ruled, who were Catholic.

As Odoacer grew more powerful in Italy, the East Roman Emperor, Zeno, sought ways of weakening him, and it seemed to him that the easiest thing to do would be to send the Ostrogoths westward. In this way, they would get rid of them and would start a war in Italy that might weaken the German tribesmen all around.

However, the Ostrogoths were under the leadership of a particularly capable leader, Theodoric (454–526)—sometimes called "Theodoric the Great" and, by the Germans, "Dietrich."

Theodoric led his Ostrogoths into Italy. There he fought Odoacer in two battles and won both. Odoacer was forced to retreat into Ravenna. In 493, however, Theodoric enticed Odoacer into emerging from his lair and had him killed.

In this way, Italy became an Ostrogothic kingdom.

FRANKS

The Franks were a Germanic tribe just east of the Rhine who, even in the time of Julian, had carried through serious raids into Gaul. When the Huns took over Germany, many Franks fled into Gaul and fought with Aetius against the Huns.

The rulers of the Franks were descended from a leader named Merovech, so that they were called the "Merovingians." In 481, a 15-year-old Merovingian named Clovis (466–511) succeeded to the leadership of the Frankish tribes. Though young, Clovis was intent on war and aggrandizement.

In northern Gaul, there remained a region that was ruled, still, by Romans. Its capital was at Soissons, and its ruler was Syagrius (430–486). In 486, Clovis beat Syagrius in one quick battle and took over Soissons. The last bit of land in the west that might be considered Roman was gone.

Clovis then spent 10 years consolidating his power. The Franks were less civilized than the

Visigoths, the Ostrogoths, or the Vandals, and where the Franks ruled, Roman civilization was not preserved even to the extent that it was in the other German kindoms.

Clovis, himself, was pagan, but his wife, Clotilda (470–545), a princess of the Burgundians (another Germanic tribe) was Christian. Apparently, Clovis was an affectionate enough husband (or a weak enough one, despite his ferocity in war) to give in to her nagging. In 493, he turned Christian, and forced his tribesmen to follow suit.

What was particularly important was that Clotilda was Catholic, and so Clovis was converted to Catholicism. The Franks were the only Catholic Germanic tribe at this time. All the others in the west were Arian. This meant that the submerged Romans supported Clovis in his quarrels with the other Germanic tribes—and that was of infinite use to him.

BRITAIN

In 456, a party of Jutes from what is now Denmark (the Danish peninsula is still called Jutland in English to this day) landed in Kent, in the southeasternmost portion of Britain. They had been summoned by Vortigern to protect the land against the Picts. They promptly protected it by taking over Kent. By 477, other Germanic tribesmen, the Saxons, were also coming to Britain.

In 500, the situation was this: the Saxons and Jutes were entrenched in southeastern Britain; the Franks were in northern Gaul; the Visigoths were in southern Gaul and Spain; the Ostrogoths were in Italy; and the Vandals were in North Africa. Nowhere was there an inch of territory under Roman rule.

EAST ROMAN EMPIRE

The East Roman Empire, at this time, was no great model of success. It could not keep the West Roman Empire from falling to the Germanic tribes. If anything, the East Roman Empire helped the Germans in order to remove imperial competition in Italy. This worked but it did them no good.

In 468, the East Roman Emperor, Leo I (400–474), who had become Emperor in 457, sent a naval expedition against Gaiseric, but that was useless. Gaiseric defeated them easily.

However, in 500, the East Roman Empire was still entirely intact.

PERSIA

The East Roman Empire was helped by the fact that Persia was under a series of comparatively weak rulers. It was preoccupied with internal religious questions involving the conflict between Zoroastrians and Christians and in fighting on its eastern and northern frontiers against the Hephtalites, who were Asian tribesmen, probably related to the Huns.

INDIA

By 500, the Gupta dynasty had petered out, and India began to go through another period of small and competing states.

NORTH AMERICA

About 500, the city of Chichén Itzá was founded by the Mayans in Yucatan.

500 To 550

OSTROGOTHS

Theodoric did his best to run the Ostrogothic kingdom in Italy in a fair way. The Ostrogoths owned a third of the land, but the Romans owned the other two thirds, and were treated decently. Although Theodoric was an Arian, he tolerated Catholics and (the acid test) he even kept the Jews from being mistreated. He let the Romans run the civil service and treated his own people as though they were military allies of Rome. He remained friendly with the East Roman Emperor and did not try to infringe on his power. He kept Italy under Roman law and did his best to preserve Roman civilization.

Italy was, in fact, better off under Theodoric than it had been since the time of Marcus Aurelius three and a half centuries earlier. Unfortunately, Theodoric grew old and, in his old age, turned suspicious and cruel. In 526, he died, and his successors (as so often happens) were far less capable than he. Thus, the Ostrogothic kingdom began to decline.

The last spark of classical learning in Italy was represented by Anicius Boethius (480–524), who served Theodoric in Italy. He understood Greek (a rare accomplishment by then) and prepared commentaries on Aristotle and other philosophers, which survived in the west during a period when the classical works themselves were lost. In the end, he was executed by Theodoric in one of his tyrannical moods.

FRANKS

Clovis, with a firm base in northern Gaul, continued to expand his kingdom. About 500, he defeated the Burgundians, his wife's kinsmen, who had earlier seized eastern Gaul, and, in 507, he defeated the Visigoths and drove them out of Gaul. By the time of his death in 511, Clovis was master of virtually all of Gaul, founding the Frankish kingdom. He made his capital at Paris in 508.

Such was the power of the Frankish kingdom now, and in centuries to come, that Gaul was the one province in the west that lost its name. It was Gaul no more, but eventually became "France," from the word "Frank." In German, the land is called "Frankreich" ("realm of the Franks").

The Franks at this time, however, had the custom of dividing property among their sons, instead of leaving it intact to one of them. Thus, on Clovis's death, his four sons each inherited a portion of the Frankish kingdom and, as was inevitable, they fought each other. This happened over and over and kept the Franks from becoming stronger than they were.

EAST ROMAN EMPIRE

In 518, the East Roman Empire finally got a strong Emperor, Justin I (450–527). He was an old, illiterate peasant, possibly of Gothic ancestry, but he associated his clever nephew with himself. When he died, in 527, his nephew became Emperor as Justinian I (483–565), sometimes called "Justinian the Great." He was forceful and intelligent, and his wife, Theodora (500–548), of lowly origin, was even more forceful and intelligent.

The two were convinced Catholics and, in 529, they closed down Plato's Academy, which still taught pre-Christian philosophy to the few who would listen. It had been in existence for over nine centuries. With its closing, the last voice of paganism was silenced. Justinian also put an end to the annual appointment of consuls.

He put scholars to work preparing a new law-code. In 529, they came up with 12 volumes of a well-organized legal system. This was the "Code of Justinian," and was followed by a 50-volume collection of legal opinions. It has remained one of the bases of European law generally in all the centuries since. The Code of Justinian was written in Latin, but it was the last production of the East Roman Empire that was in this language. Increasingly, the language of the East was Greek, so that some people called it the "Greek Empire," which, however, should not be allowed to obscure the fact that to the very end of its existence, the realm considered itself the *Roman* Empire and spoke of its people as "Romans."

In 532, there were bloody riots in Constantinople over horse races, of all things, though the different factions disagreed in politics as well. Justinian would have fled, but Theodora would not allow him to. They used a general, Belisarius (505–565), who had distinguished himself against the Persians, to put an end to the riots, which he did. Some 30,000 people were killed, and Constantinople was virtually in ashes.

Justinian set about rebuilding the city, and a new cathedral called *Hagia Sophia* ("Holy Wisdom") was completed in 537. It had a magnificent dome, so cleverly designed and so skillfully pierced with windows that all the interior was bathed in sunlight. It gave the impression that it had no support, but was suspended invisibly from heaven.

The East Roman Empire was also raising the technique of mosaic art to new heights at this time, using new kinds of ceramic tiles in a greater variety of colors.

Then, too, Justinian bribed two Persian monks who had lived in China to return there and then come back with silkworm eggs secreted in hollow bamboo canes. About 550, Constantinople began its own silk production, and from those smuggled eggs descended all the silkworm caterpillars supporting the European silk industry ever since.

Constantinople may have had a population as large as 600,000 people at this time, while Rome had decreased to an impoverished population of less than a tenth that number.

Meanwhile, Justinian was involved in plans for a great offensive westward to win back the western provinces and restore the Empire.

In 535, Belisarius was placed in command of a fleet of some 500 ships that carried soldiers and horses toward Carthage. The Vandal power had greatly declined since the death of Gaiseric a half-century before. Belisarius had no trouble, in 534, defeating Gelimer, who was then the Vandal king. With that, the Vandal kingdom in North Africa disappeared after a little over a century of existence. Arianism was wiped out and Carthage became Roman again.

When Belisarius returned, a victor, to Constantinople, Justinian sent him out to Italy. In 535, he took Sicily, marched into Italy and moved all the way up to Rome, while the Ostrogoths (without the firm hand of Theodoric, who had died nine years before) seemed helpless. Belisarius took Rome, held off a counterattack by the Ostrogoths and then marched to Ravenna, placed it under siege, and took it in 539.

Justinian didn't want Belisarius to be *too* successful, lest he harbor dreams of succeeding the throne. He recalled him in 540, therefore, to fight off the Persians in the east. In 544, Belisarius was sent back to Italy where the Ostrogoths were doing better in his absence, but Justinian withheld reinforcements and Belisarius could not achieve much. The Ostrogoths retook a virtually ruined and depopulated Rome in 546, and Belisarius was recalled once again in 548.

One last offensive in 554 retrieved the southern third of Spain and placed it in East Roman hands.

By 550, it almost looked as though the Roman Empire would be restored, but the strain of war and conquest stretched Justinian's realm to the limit.

BRITAIN

The Germanic invaders of Britain, usually referred to as the "Saxons," continued to flood into the land. They were stopped for a while when they were defeated in a battle at Mount Badon (the place and the time are not exactly known), so that the Britons won a half-century respite. By 550, however, the Saxons were pressing westward again.

Nevertheless, that momentary flash of light for the Britons gave rise to the immortal (but entirely fictional) romance of King Arthur and his Knights of the Round Table.

SLAVS AND BULGARS

Even while the East Roman Empire was returning to the west, there were new incursions of tribesmen closer to home. The Slavs of eastern Europe had been dominated first by the Ostrogoths and then by the Huns. Now new Asian tribesmen were appearing, and some Slavs fled southward across the Danube to avoid them. They were peasants, rather than warriors, but where they went, they settled down and stayed, so that today the nations of Bulgaria and Yugoslavia speak Slavic languages and not the Greek that was spoken there in Justinian's time.

Mingled with the Slavs were some Asian tribesmen who had come westward. They had earlier lived along the Volga, and the words "Volga" and "Bulgar" may be of the same origin.

The Bulgars intermarried with the more numerous Slavs, whose society completely asssimilated them. The Bulgars were more aggressive than the Slavs, however, and in Justinian's time began raiding southward.

AVARS

Behind the Bulgars came the Avars, another set of Asian tribesmen who were very much like the Huns, and who, by 550, had set up an empire similar to the one the Huns had built a century earlier. It was their coming that served as the driving force that pushed the Slavs and Bulgars into the East Roman Empire.

PERSIA

After 500, war between the East Roman Empire and the Persians seemed endemic. The Persians won some victories, but, in 528, Belisarius defeated them in the first of the victories that revealed his military genius.

In 531, Chosroes I (d. 579) became the Persian monarch. He was the most capable of all the Sassanids, and to the Persians he was known as "Khosrow Anushirvan" ("Chosroes, the Immortal Soul").

He attempted to achieve peace with the East Roman Empire since the periodic wars solved nothing and weakened both. Such a peace was signed in 533, but it was of no use. Justinian took advantage of the quiet in the east to start his offensive in the west, and the success of that offensive raised fears that he might grow strong enough to overwhelm Persia. Therefore, another war began in 540.

The Persians reached the Mediterranean, as the Parthians had done six centuries before, and sacked Antioch. Belisarius, who was between his two stays in Italy, pushed the Persians back. At this point, a plague struck both sides indiscriminately in 542, and the war seemed more senseless than ever. In 545, Justinian bought peace in return for something like a ton of gold.

Chosroes I was civilized enough to accept the pagan Greek philosophers who had left Athens, sorrowing, after Justinian had closed the Academy. When they grew homesick for Greece, Chosroes allowed them to return, but only after he had extorted a promise from the reluctant Justinian to do them no harm.

CHINA

Through almost this entire period, Liang Wu-Ti ruled in South China. He was a devout Buddhist, and under him, Buddhism continued to spread through southern China.

JAPAN

In 538, Buddhism made its appearance in Japan, having been brought there by Korean missionaries.

AFRICA

Axum expanded further, and took control of Yemen in southwestern Arabia.

550 TO 600

ITALY

After Belisarius was recalled, Narses (480–574) was sent to Italy in 551 to continue the fight against the Ostrogoths. Narses was a eunuch and was already 71 years old at the time. He was the only eunuch in western history to shine as a military leader. In fact, he accomplished what Belisarius had failed to do, although, to be sure, Justinian supported him more than he did Belisarius. After all, a eunuch could not compete for the throne.

In 552, Narses finally defeated the Ostrogoths in the last pitched battle in a bitter war that had lasted over a quarter of a century. By 554, the last Ostrogoths were driven out of Italy. They vanished from history only 28 years after the death of the great Theodoric.

It was this war that finally ruined ancient Italy. Until then, Roman civilization had continued in diluted form, but now the "Dark Age" clamped down on Italy, as it had already fixed itself on Spain, Gaul, and Britain.

Even so, Narses ruled Italy well for well over a decade. In 567, two years after the death of Justinian, his successor, Justin II (d. 578), recalled Narses, who was, by then, 87 years old.

Without Narses at the helm, Italy was virtually helpless and the next year, a new wave of Germanic tribesmen poured over the Alps. These

were the Lombards. There was no resistance worth mentioning, but the Lombards were not numerous and they could only absorb the interior of northern Italy and the interior of southern Italy. The East Roman Empire retained central Italy (including Rome), plus the toe and the heel of the Italian boot.

By 600, Italy was divided into three parts. There were Lombards, with their capital at Pavia in northern Italy, which they had taken in 572. There were the East Romans with their capital at Ravenna (their portion of central Italy was called the "Exarchate of Ravenna"). And there was the Pope in Rome.

PAPACY

In 590, Gregory I (540–604), sometimes called "Gregory the Great," became Pope. He was a stern reformer, devoted to the eradication of graft and dishonesty, and to the promotion of social justice. He encouraged missions abroad to convert pagans, he supported the celibacy of the clergy, and under him the "Gregorian chant" entered church music.

Gregory was the most powerful personality in the Italy of his time and he was the real leader of the resistance to the Lombards. The Lombards were Arian Christians, but, by 600, had been converted to Catholicism, thanks to Gregory's labors in that direction.

SPAIN

In 568, Leuvigild (d. 586) became the Visigothic king of Spain and with that a certain recovery was made, after the defeats in the north by Clovis and in the south by the East Roman Empire. He expanded his realm by conquering the Sueves, who had held northwestern Spain for over a century and a half. Southward, he also forced the East Romans back till they held only the immediate shore.

In 586, Recared I succeeded to the throne and he turned Catholic, forcing all the Visigoths to do the same.

By 600, Arianism had just about been wiped out everywhere, nearly three centuries after it had been condemned at the Council of Nicaea.

BRITAIN/ENGLAND

By now, there were seven Germanic kingdoms in western Britain. The Jutes were established in Kent. To the west of Kent were three Saxon kingdoms: Essex, Wessex, and Sussex. To the north of Kent were three kingdoms of the Angles (Germanic invaders related to the Saxons and Jutes): East Anglia, Mercia, and Northumbria. It was the Angles who gave a new name to Britain. It became "Angle-land" or "England."

In 600, Kent in the southeast, longest settled, and closest to Europe, was the strongest of the new realms. It was under Ethelbert (d. 616).

Meanwhile, the story goes, Pope Gregory, in Rome, came across three children who had been captured and enslaved. He thought them exceptionally handsome and asked of what people they were. He was told they were Angles and said, "Not Angles but angels." (He said it in Latin, where the pun also works.)

He sent a missionary, Augustine (d. 604), to convert them. Augustine arrived in Kent in 596, and began the process, eventually successful, of converting England. He became the first Archbishop of Canterbury (the capital of Kent).

IRELAND

Ireland had never been part of the Roman Empire, but it had been converted to Christianity, beginning about 432, as the result of the labors of Patricius ("Saint Patrick"), a missionary from Britain. What developed was called the "Celtic Church," one that differed in some respects from orthodox Catholic doctrine.

In this period, Ireland was experiencing a kind of golden age in which learning flourished and missionaries such as Columba (521–597) and Columban (543–615) spread Celtic Church doctrines through England and the Frankish territories.

By 600, Ireland was at its height. It was the only place in the west where Greek was understood, and it seemed for a while that Celtic Christianity might prove a possibly successful competitor against orthodox Catholicism.

FRANKS

In the Frankish kingdom, the sons, and then the grandsons, of Clovis fought each other constantly, but in the shifting of boundaries, two chief areas came to exist.

On the east was Austrasia ("eastland"), from which the Franks had come and which was largely Frankish in culture. On the west was "Neustria" ("new land"), which Clovis had conquered and which still bore the faint twilight of Roman culture. Austrasia was to be the nucleus of the future Germany; Neustria of the future France.

AVARS

The Avars struck westward at this time, as the Huns had a century and a half before. The Avars, however, struck at the Franks, who were a much hardier foe than the Romans had been in the time of Attila. They won some territory, but had such a hard time of it that they attempted no further adventures in that direction. Still, they reached the Baltic Sea and, by 600, their realm was the peak of its expansion.

KHAZARS

To the north of Persia, there were Turkish tribes, related to the Huns and Avars. The westernmost of these, dwelling on the shores of the Caspian Sea, were the Khazars. They had been pressing against the Persians, but had been driven back. In 600, nevertheless, they remained a menace, as the Avars were.

EAST ROMAN EMPIRE

In this period, the Balkans continued to suffer invasions by the Bulgars and the Avars. In 558, the Bulgars penetrated to the walls of Constantinople and were defeated by Belisarius in his last victory. In 591, it was the Avars who reached those impenetrable walls and were then driven back.

By 600, the East Roman Empire still looked formidable on the map. It still held North Africa, parts of Italy, the Spanish coast, and the islands of the western Mediterranean, but it had been exhausted past the possibility of any new expansive adventures.

PERSIA

Just as the East Roman Empire was plagued by invasions of Bulgars and Avars, so Persia was plagued by invasions of Turks and Khazars. The Persians beat them back, but they, too, were seriously weakened. The war with Rome continued sporadically, both contestants being increasingly winded and staggering.

Chosroes II (d. 628) came to the Persian throne in 590 with the help of the Emperor Maurice (539–602) of the East Roman Empire, who had himself gained the throne in 582. The two remained friends and that seemed a chance of establishing peace.

ARABIA

Arabia did not play much of a role in history prior to this period. The northernmost section, Nabatea, was controlled by the old Persian Empire, then by Alexander, then by the Seleucid Empire, and then by Rome. Occasionally, its trading cities made their mark—Petra and Palmyra. It was a Nabatean, Philip the Arabian, who was the Roman Emperor when the thousandth anniversary of the founding of Rome was celebrated.

In southwestern Arabia, there was the Sabaean kingdom. (The Biblical Queen of Sheba may have ruled there.) It was from Sabaea that the kingdom of Axum was founded and Sabaea was, in turn, dominated by Axum for a period of time.

Mecca, located at an oasis in west central Arabia near the Red Sea, lying midway between Nabatea and Sabaea, was a holy city to the Arabs. It contained the Ka'bah ("cube"), with a black stone in the wall, undoubtedly a meteorite, and that was the holiest shrine in Arabia.

About 570, Muhammad (570–632) was born in Mecca. By 595, he married a rich widow, and this gave him the leisure to meditate. By 600, he was devising a new religion based on his understanding (rather imperfect) of Judaism and Christianity.

600   TO   650

PERSIA

Emperor Maurice in Constantinople, the friend of Chosroes II of Persia, was assassinated in 602.

Chosroes II, furious at this, soon declared war on the assassin, a minor military officer, Phocas (d. 610), who had made himself Emperor. (Undoubtedly, Chosroes II didn't want to miss the chance of using this as a good excuse to defeat and shatter the East Roman Empire since it was now falling to pieces under the inept rule of Phocas.)

This task was made easier by the fact that the people of Syria and Egypt were largely Monophysites, who believed that Jesus was wholly divine. The official Catholic view, as held in Constantinople, was that Jesus was both human and divine, and that he suffered as a human. People might have agreed to disagree on this point, but the times were against it. The Monophysites were persecuted relentlessly by the Catholic Emperors at Constantinople, and the hatred of the Monophysites in return was such that they would not fight and die for the sake of the Emperor. They would as soon be ruled by Ctesiphon as by Constantinople.

Consequently, when the war began in 603, the Persians found it easy going at first. By 608, the Persians had reached Antioch and most of Syria was in their hands. The Persians began to call their monarch Khosrow Parvez ("Chosroes the Victorious.")

In 613, Chosroes II took Damascus, and in 614, he took Jerusalem. In Jerusalem, he seized the "True Cross," the one on which Christians believed that Jesus was crucified. In 615, he invaded Asia Minor, and in 616 he took Egypt. By 617, he stood across the narrow strait from Constantinople, and the Empire of Darius I (of 11 centuries before) was finally restored, nine and a half centuries after Alexander the Great had destroyed it.

It looked as though it were now the turn of the East Roman Empire to follow the path to oblivion that the West Roman Empire had taken a century and a half earlier.

EAST ROMAN EMPIRE

The initial advances of Chosroes II panicked the people of Constantinople and, in 610, Phocas was killed by them. There still remained one substantial (and strongly Catholic) province of the Empire and that was North Africa, with its capital at Carthage, which, fortunately for Constan-

tinople, had been retaken for the Empire by Belisarius 80 years before.

It was governed by a capable general named Heraclius (575–641), and his ships carried him to Constantinople in 610. He was declared Emperor in place of the lynched Phocas.

It took Heraclius a dozen years to reorganize the army and to rebuild what was left of the Empire. Then, in 622, he readied his counterstroke. He did not attempt to attack Chosroes II head on. Instead, he made use of the Empire's control of the sea. His ships carried his army to Issus at the junction of Asia Minor and Syria, where Alexander had defeated the Persians nine centuries before. Hastily, Persian forces on the spot rallied to meet the East Roman forces, but Heraclius won in January 623, then marched toward Armenia. Chosroes, afraid his army would be trapped, evacuated Asia Minor.

Even as he did so, Chosroes called on the aid of the Avars, who were anxious, in any case, to share in the loot. They poured south into the Balkans and, in 626, were at the walls of Constantinople. Chosroes II had to seize the opportunity. He raced back into Asia Minor, returning to his position across the strait from Constantinople. Heraclius, he hoped, would be forced by the danger to his capital to march out of Persia.

In July 626, the Avars attacked, but Heraclius did not return to protect the city. He trusted in its walls, and continued his own campaign, in which he steadily defeated the Persians. When the Avars found they could not breach the walls, they retreated, and Chosroes II was forced to leave Asia Minor a second time. In December 627, Chosroes II and Heraclius met in battle and, for one last time, Greek-speaking soldiers fought Persian-speaking soldiers. The Greek-speakers won this last battle as they had won the first at Marathon, 11 centuries earlier.

The war was over. Heraclius recovered the True Cross and restored it to Jerusalem in 629. That same year, Chosroes II was killed by his own soldiers.

ARABIA

While the grand drama of the last Roman–Persian war was going on, Muhammad in Arabia was having an exciting time of it, too, although on a much smaller scale.

He was preaching the new religion of "Islam" ("submission"—i.e., to the will of God) but was not having much success with his fellow townsmen in Mecca. On June 15, 622, he was forced to flee to Medina, 220 miles north of Mecca. This is the *Hegira* ("flight").

In Medina, he gathered a following of "Muslims" ("those who submitted") and, ever since, the Muslim calendar counts its beginning from the date of the Hegira—but on a strictly lunar basis, 354 days to the year.

War began between the Muslims of Medina and the nonbelievers in Mecca; on November 1, 630, Mecca submitted and became Muslim. By the time Muhammad died in 632, he was in control of all of Arabia.

Muhammad had sent messages to both Heraclius and Chosroes II ordering them to become Muslims or be destroyed. Naturally, there was no answer from either.

Abu Bakr (573–634) became the first Caliph ("successor") on Muhammad's death, and with him, expansion began at once. Arab forces, a very mobile light cavalry, fighting with fanatical belief in their new religion, invaded both the East Roman Empire and Persia.

Heraclius sent an army against them, an army of heavy cavalry that was completely outmaneuvered by the Arabs and was totally destroyed at the battle of Yarmuk (in what had once been Judea) in 636. The Syrians, who were still Monophysites and who still hated Constantinople, did not resist and all of it was taken. Jerusalem fell a second time in 638, and the True Cross, restored only nine years before, was taken a second time and was never to reappear again.

The East Roman Empire, which had expended its last ounce of strength fighting off the Persians, simply lacked the ability to fend off this new conquest which came so closely on the heels of the first. This time, it was a permanent loss.

Meanwhile, the Arabs, now under Omar

(586–644), the second Caliph, were also invading Persia, which the exertions of the war just completed had reduced to a staggering wreck. The last Sassanid king, Yezdigird III, could not find the means to defeat the Arabs. By 642, all of Persia had fallen to the Arab hosts.

Also in 642, Omar's general, Amr-ibn-al-As (d. 663), completed the conquest of Egypt. (Heraclius had died in 641; his great reconquest gone for naught.)

There is a story that Omar ordered the library at Alexandria destroyed on the grounds that if the books agreed with the Koran (a collection of Muhammad's sayings, and the holy book of the Muslims), they were superfluous; if they disagreed, they were pernicious. In either case, the books ought to be destroyed. This may not be true. It is not likely there was much left of the library after three centuries of Christian control, when so many Christian leaders were utterly hostile to pagan learning.

By 650, then, Sassanid Persia was gone, after four centuries of existence, while the East Roman Empire was reduced to Asia Minor, the Balkans, and the western provinces in North Africa and in Italy. Since the lost provinces were never to be regained, it is not customary to speak of what was left as the East Roman Empire any longer. It became the "Byzantine Empire" to western historians, the name being taken from Byzantium, the city on whose site Constantine I had founded Constantinople over three centuries before. To the inhabitants of Constantinople, however, the land remained "the Roman Empire," no matter how small and weak it was to become.

The Arab advance was not all destructive, however. The Arabs introduced the windmill to Europe at about this time. It was a very useful power source that had been known for centuries in Persia.

AVARS

After their failure at Constantinople, the Avars declined rapidly. Like the Huns before them, they were only a small military clique that depended on the peasantry they dominated. Once defeat lessened their military prestige, the underlings rebelled, and the power of the aristocracy faded quickly.

To the east, however, the other Asian tribesmen, the Bulgars, Khazars and Turks, either held their power or were gaining it.

FRANKS

In 629, Dagobert (605–639), a great-great grandson of Clovis, came to the Frankish throne. He was the last vigorous Merovingian, and the last to rule, for a time at least, over a united Frankish realm. When he died, however, the kingdom was divided between his two sons. In 650, both those sons were still on their respective thrones —one of Austrasia, the other of Neustria. They and their descendants were all weak and are referred in the French language as "rois faineant" ("do-nothing kings"). There were, however, strong advisers who were the true rulers of the Franks.

Dagobert, for instance, had an adviser, Pepin of Landon (d. 640), who was "Mayor of the Palace" (or, as we would say today, "Prime Minister"). He was a capable man who kept the Franks strong.

PAPACY

In an attempt to win back the loyalty of the people of Syria and Egypt during the Persian war, Heraclius and the Patriarch of Constantinople, Sergius (who served in the post from 610 to 638), had worked out a compromise with Monophysitism. The compromise was called Monothelitism, and might have worked in a more reasonable age. The Monophysites would not accept it, however.

The Roman Pope, Honorius I, who held the position from 625 to 638, was tempted to be reasonable, but he couldn't carry the establishment with him. Theological disputes between Rome and Constantinople continued, and worsened.

SPAIN

The Visigothic kings of this period were as incompetent as their Merovingian contemporaries among the Franks.

At this time, there lived a cleric named Isidore of Seville (560–636), who published a diluted version of Pliny's encyclopedia. Almost worthless as science, it nevertheless was highly popular and encouraged the spirit of inquiry. Isidore strongly approved of astrology, however.

ENGLAND

The seven Anglo-Saxon kingdoms in England (the "Heptarchy") kept fighting each other, with power shifting between Northumberland and Mercia. Under Northumberland's lead, the Celtic Church reached its peak in England.

KHAZARS

As the Avars declined, and Persia weakened, the Khazars expanded and began to develop their power north of the Caucasus. They now governed the Ukraine, which had in the last 13 centuries seen the power of the Cimmerians, the Scythians, the Sarmatians, the Ostrogoths, the Huns, and the Avars successively come and go.

INDIA

Through most of this period, the important ruler in India was Harsha (590–647), who began his rule in 606. Once again, he unified the northern sections and even spread his influence southward. He was a convinced Buddhist, in an India that was returning more and more to Brahmanism. For the first time, firm diplomatic ties were established between India and China.

When Harsha died in 647, his realm splintered, and by 650, India was again a chaotic mixture of smaller states.

At this time, an Indian scientist, Brahmagupta (598–665), was the most important mathematician in the world, applying algebraic methods to astronomical problems, to follow the paths of the planets across the sky.

CHINA

In 618, the Sui Dynasty was replaced by the still more successful T'ang Dynasty. The second of the T'ang Emperors, T'ai Tsung (d. 649), came to power in 627 and reestablished the unity of China, which had been threatening to fail as the Sui dynasty had declined. Chinese unity has more or less been maintained ever since.

He put an end to the disintegrating nature of aristocratic rivalry for power, and restored the custom of requiring officials to pass public examinations that qualified them for their posts (which opened government service to wider sections of the populace). He defeated the Turks in the west, established relations with Tibet and India, and, in general, has been considered the best and most successful of all the Chinese emperors.

In his reign, Nestorian Christians reached China. These followed the teachings of Nestorius, who believed in two natures of Jesus, human and divine, but considered them more weakly linked than the Catholics did. Nestorianism lost out to Monophysitism in Syria and in Egypt, but it spread eastward into Persia where it retained importance even after Persia had fallen to the Arabs. They even managed to establish themselves, to some small extent, in India and China.

Science flourished, too. Ch'ao Yuan-fang wrote on the causes and symptoms of disease in 610, and this was far ahead of anything in the west at the time.

SOUTHEAST ASIA

At this time, what is now the Vietnamese coast was occupied by Champa and, to its west, was Chenia. Both managed to remain outside Chinese political control, although they could not help but absorb Chinese culture.

INDONESIA

At about this time, a realm called Srivijaya was established in Sumatra, and this soon extended itself to Java. It engaged in sea trade with both India and China, and it accepted Buddhism.

TIBET

Tibet, the huge plateau north of the Himalayan mountain range, had now coalesced into a kingdom. It had become important enough for a Chinese princess to be given as wife to the first king of Tibet.

NORTH AMERICA

The Toltec people may have been spreading over southern Mexico at this time.

650 TO 700

OMMAYAD CALIPHATE

Othman, the third Caliph, ruled from 644 to 656. He established the official version of the Koran, but was killed during a rebellion and was succeeded by Ali (600–661), who was Muhammad's son-in-law, and who reigned from 656 to 661.

Ali's succession was disputed, and it quickly developed that Muslims, just like Christians, fought each other relentlessly over power and over doctrinal issues—with the same result: it weakened all concerned.

In 661, Ali was killed in the course of the quarreling and Muawiya (602–680) became Caliph. He was a second cousin of Muhammad and, among his ancestors, was one named Ommaya. Muawiya and his family are, therefore, called the "Ommayads," and the government they headed is the "Ommayad Caliphate."

Ali's death split the Muslim world in two, and

that split has never been healed. Those who accepted Muawiya and all who followed him are the Sunnites (from an Arabic word meaning "the orthodox way"). Those who clung to Ali and considered everyone since to have been usurpers are the "Shiites" (from an Arabic word meaning "sect").

Muawiya moved the seat of government out of Arabia and established it at Damascus in Syria. It was more centrally located there and nearer the centers of civilization.

The internal quarrels did not prevent the Muslims from continuing to expand their sway. They penetrated eastward to the extreme borders of the Empires of Darius I and Alexander the Great. They took Kabul in 664 and Samarkand in 676. They reached the Indus River and stood at the western border of Tibet.

They also advanced westward in Africa into regions that neither the Persians nor the Macedonians had ever trod. The Muslims swept over northern Africa to the Atlantic Ocean; Carthage, the last holdout, fell in 698. Once again, Carthage was destroyed, as it had been by the Romans eight and a half centuries earlier. This time it never revived.

The Muslims had, in 670, established Kairowan, 85 miles south of Carthage, as their North African capital. Later on, Tunis, which had been a suburb of Carthage, became the most important city of the region.

In 700, then, the Ommayad Caliphate stretched from Tibet to the Atlantic Ocean. It was the most extensive Empire that the world had yet seen, although the T'ang Empire in China exceeded it in population.

The Ommayad Caliphate differed from the other Empires of Western Asia in the fervor of its faith. The nations it had conquered lost part of their identity. Zoroastrianism in Persia vanished (though some Zoroastrians fled to India where they still exist today as "Parsees," a distortion of "Persians").

In the same way, Christianity disappeared from Syria, Egypt, and North Africa (though some exist today as "Copts," this being a distortion of "Egypt"). All accepted Islam, and although Persia clung to the Persian language (or

"Farsi"), the rest of the Caliphate learned to read and write Arabic, since a Muslim had to be able to read the Koran, and it was forbidden to translate it from Arabic into any other language.

BYZANTINE EMPIRE

The Byzantine Empire was shaken by the progressive loss of Syria, Egypt, and North Africa. All that was left was Asia Minor (which was constantly being raided by the Moslems), the Balkan peninsula (which was constantly being raided by the Bulgars), Sicily, and parts of Italy.

Nevertheless, it held on grimly. In 673, the Muslims placed Constantinople under siege and maintained it for nearly half a year before leaving. They returned in subsequent years; however, by 677, the Byzantines had developed a chemical mixture with a naphtha base that burned on contact with water. (It was supposedly developed by an alchemist of Greek or Syrian origin named Callinicus, concerning whom nothing else is known.) In that year, the Byzantines used the "Greek fire," spurting it out of wooden tubes into the water, and burning any ships with which it then made contact. Their fleet destroyed, the Muslims made peace, and here at last their advance was stopped.

BULGARS

The Bulgars had been striking into the Byzantine Empire since the time of Justinian, a century and a half before. With the Moslems at the gates of Constantinople, the Bulgars raided more steadily than ever. Finally, in 680, they defeated a Byzantine army and settled in the region south of the Danube, which is now Bulgaria.

FRANKS

The Merovingian kings of the Frankish realm continued on their do-nothing way, and the realm might well have fallen apart but for the strong leadership of Pepin of Heristal (d. 714), who was the grandson of Pepin of Landen, and who was Mayor of the Palace from 687.

SPAIN

The only Visigothic king in Spain who was of any account at all in this period was Wamba, who reigned from 672 to 680, keeping the kingdom in order.

ENGLAND

In 654, Penda of Mercia, the last important pagan king in England, was killed in battle. His son, who succeeded, was Christian; and with that, paganism disappeared in England.

What's more, in 664, Oswiu of Northumberland (d. 670), whose armies had killed Penda, and who was now the strongest ruler in England, called the "Synod of Whitby," a gathering of churchmen at a town 40 miles northeast of York. There, the Celtic and Roman priests stated their respective cases, and Oswiu decided in favor of Roman Catholicism. With that, Celtic Christianity began to vanish from England, too, though it remained significant for a time in Ireland and Scotland.

ITALY

Venice, which had first been founded by refugees from the Hunnish invasion three centuries earlier, and had added more refugees when the Lombards had entered a century earlier, was now beginning to thrive as a seaport. Its first "doge" ("duke") was chosen in 697. It acknowledged the overlordship of the Emperor at Constantinople, and was thus part of the Exarchate of Ravenna.

KOREA

During this period, Korea was under the rule of the southern kingdom of Silla, which forced Japanese invaders out of the peninsula.

700 TO 750

OMMAYAD CALIPHATE

Under Walid I, who ruled from 705 to 715, the Ommayad Caliphate flourished. Non-Muslim subject peoples were becoming Muslims at a great rate, for the Caliphate had a good way of bringing that about. They used neither force nor persuasion; they merely taxed non-Muslims and not Muslims, and the people followed their pocket books.

Also, under Walid I, Muslims moved into Europe. In 711, the Muslims of North Africa, under Tariq ibn Ziyad (d. 720), crossed the narrow strait of Gibraltar and entered Spain (thus, reversing the trek of the Vandals from Spain to North Africa nearly three centuries before). It was at this time that Gibraltar (Jebel al-Tariq, or "the Mount of Tariq") got its name.

At the time of this invasion, Roderick (d. 711) was the Visigothic king of Spain, but the land had been mostly under weak rule for some two centuries and was no match for the fervent Muslims. In July 711, the Muslims won a total victory, and Roderick fled the battlefield into oblivion. He is sometimes called "the last of the Goths," for the Goths now disappeared from history, three centuries after Alaric had taken Rome, and following the disappearance of the Ostrogoths a century and a half earlier.

By 715, all of Spain except for the mountains on the northern coast was in Muslim hands. In that year, Sulayman (674–717) became the Ommayad Caliph and, under him, the caliphate was at its height, stretching 4500 miles from east to west.

It seemed appropriate then to make another attempt to take Constantinople. Since the last attack 40 years earlier, seven Emperors had ruled in Constantinople and there had been constant infighting. However, just as the Muslims advanced for their second offensive, a strong Emperor, Leo III (680–741), sometimes called "Leo the Isaurian," came to the throne. He reorganized the Empire and launched a strong defense, complete with Greek fire. In a year, the Muslims were driven off.

However, if the front door had been slammed shut, there was still the back door to Europe. The Muslims stood at the Pyrenees in Spain, and across the Pyrenees were the Franks. In 732, a Muslim general, Abd-er-Rahman (d. 732), led his forces into the Frankish kingdom, and what is now southern France quickly fell to him.

Ruling the Franks as Mayor of the Palace since 714 was Charles Martel (688–741)—that is, "Charles the Hammer"—who was the son of Pepin of Heristal. Whereas the Muslims had their usual light cavalry, Charles Martel gathered his heavy cavalry: large horses bearing armor over their bodies, who carried knights in armor with stirrups that held them tightly to their horses. (It was this sort of heavy cavalry that has given us our picture of King Arthur's knights—but that was two centuries earlier and there was no such cavalry then.)

The two armies met between Tours and Poitiers in what is now west central France. It was the most important battle in that region since that of the Catalaunian Plain nearly two centuries before. Again, the defenders won and the invaders were stopped. The Muslim horsemen dashed vainly against the immovable wall of Frankish knights. That night, feeling their attacks were costing them soldiers to no purpose, the Muslims retreated. The back door had been slammed shut also.

Back in Damascus, the Ommayad dynasty had increasing problems after the double failure at Constantinople and at Tours. For one thing, as conversions to Islam took place, the tax base narrowed, and it became necessary to tax Muslims, something which wasn't popular. Non-Arabs demanded equal treatment with Arabs; there were rebellions and civil wars. In 750, the Ommayad army was defeated by one under Abu-l-Abbas, a descendant of Abbas, an uncle of Muhammad. The Ommayad family was almost all wiped out, after less than a century of rule, and Abu-l-Abbas

became the caliph. This founded a new dynasty and began the "Abbasid Caliphate."

BYZANTINE EMPIRE

After the Muslims had been driven from Constantinople, Leo III reformed the religious life of the Empire. He objected to the superstition and miracle-mongering that filled Byzantine Christianity at the time, and also to the vast number of monks who were immune to military service and taxation.

Therefore, Leo forbade the statues and paintings that served as the core of the miracles, and demanded adherence to the Biblical injunction against idolatry. He took up an "iconoclastic" ("image-breaking") position. His son, Constantine V Copronymus (718–775), or "dung-name" because, as a baby, he had defecated during baptism, became Emperor in 741. Constantine continued the iconoclastic policy. It created a great deal of controversy, and even rebellion, but he held firm.

PAPACY

When the iconoclast movement began in Constantinople, Gregory II (669–731) was Pope, having gained the post in 715. He condemned iconoclasm and turned toward the Lombards for help. The Lombards were ruled by Liutprand (d. 744), under whom the Lombard kingdom reached its peak of power. He had brought the Lombards in southern Italy under his rule, and he was content to join with the Pope and use that as an excuse to subdue the Exarchate of Ravenna, which lay between the northern and southern Lombard areas. In 728, he took Ravenna itself, temporarily.

Gregory III (d. 741), who succeeded to the papacy in 731, was even more firmly anti-iconoclast than his predecessor had been. He excommunicated all the iconoclasts, including Emperor Leo III, and he considered himself independent of the Emperor after that. In 741, when Gregory III died, his successor, Zacharias (d. 752), accepted the Papacy without any reference to the Emperor —four centuries after the Roman Emperor, Constantine I, had placed Christianity in power in the Empire.

By now, though, the Popes were rather nervous about the Lombards. They had asked for Lombard help against the Byzantines, but the Lombards seemed just as dangerous. Occasionally, therefore, the Popes asked the more distant (and, therefore, safer) Franks for help, but Charles Martel had his hands full with the Muslims and with other problems, so that he refused to get himself into an Italian quagmire.

Liutprand died in 744, but his successor, Aistulf (d. 756), took Ravenna again; and this time, the Exarchate came to an end. The Byzantine hold on central Italy was lost forever, two centuries after Belisarius had taken Rome. Except for the extreme southern areas, Italy was now entirely Lombard, and the Pope needed help more than ever before.

FRANKS

After the Battle of Tours, Charles Martel spent the rest of his life harrying the Muslims and trying to force them completely back beyond the Pyrenees.

He died in 741. However, before he did, just as though he were a monarch, he divided the Frankish kingdom between his sons who were, of course, only to serve as Mayors of the Palace, for Merovingian nonentities still held the throne. Austrasia went to his son, Carloman (715–754), and Neustria to his son Pepin the Short (714–768). The king, at the time, was Childeric III the Stupid (d. 754).

In 747, Carloman abdicated and became a monk, and Pepin became sole Mayor of the palace in the Frankish realm.

Pepin, however, wanted to be king. For over a century, his ancestors had been the real rulers of the Franks and he was tired of having the fact of power, but not the title. The one person who could give him the title was the Pope—and the Pope needed help against the Lombards.

It was clear that a deal could be made.

In this period, the most important cleric was an English missionary, Wynfrid (675–754). He

became a monk, took the name of Boniface, and spent his life in spreading Christianity successfully among several of the pagan German tribes east of the Frankish realm. He also helped persuade Carloman to become a monk, and served as an intermediary between Pepin and the Pope in the former's plan to become a king.

KHAZARS

The Khazars were now at the peak of their power, their realm stretching from the Caspian Sea to the Danube, and well to the north of Moscow.

About 750, the Khazar aristocracy accepted Judaism as their religion, partly because they feared they would be hounded by Rome or Constantinople if they turned Christian—or by Baghdad, if they turned Muslim.

CHINA

The T'ang Empire reached its peak under Hsuan Tsung, the sixth Emperor of the dynasty, who reigned from 712 to 756. Under him, China was prosperous and peaceful. He encouraged education, while poetry and art flourished. True porcelain was developed, the first clock escapement was designed, and printing on paper came into use.

China was, in this period, clearly the most technologically advanced nation in the world, and was to remain so for centuries. Ch'ang An (the modern Sian) may have been the largest city in the world at the time, with Constantinople second.

JAPAN

In Japan, Shomu, the 45th Emperor, by the traditional count, ruled from 724 to 749. It was a period of great cultural activity. Shomu and his Empress were ardent Buddhists and, under him, Buddhism became almost a state religon. His capital city was Nara, and in it he built a temple that is, to this day, the largest wooden building in the world. In it, he built a 530-foot seated figure of Buddha out of bronze, one of the two largest bronze figures in the world.

NORTH AMERICA

The Mayas in Yucatan were at their peak at this time. Very little is known of their history.

750 TO 800

FRANKISH EMPIRE

The deal between Pepin and the Pope was struck in 752. Pepin, with Papal permission, was elected King Pepin I by the Frankish nobles, and Childeric III was forced to abdicate. That was the end of the Merovingian monarchy, two and three-quarter centuries after Clovis had become king.

That year a new Pope had begun to reign, Stephen II (d. 757). He actually came to the Frankish realm and anointed Pepin king. This was the start of the "Carolingian dynasty" from Carolus (the Latin version of Charles), who was Pepin's father.

In return, Pepin sent an army into Italy to defeat the Lombards in 754 and, again, in 756. In 756, Pepin gave the Pope the land that had made up the Exarchate of Ravenna. (He had no legal right to do this, but, then, the Pope had no legal right to make a king.) From this point on, what was the Exarchate of Ravenna became the "Papal States," and the Pope was a secular ruler as well as a religious leader.

Pepin completed the task of driving the Muslims behind the Pyrenees.

When Pepin I died, in 768, the kingdom was divided between his two sons, Carloman (d. 771) and Charles (742–814). After Carloman's death, Charles ruled alone. Charles is usually called "Charlemagne" (French for "Charles the Great").

In 773, Charlemagne invaded Italy again. Desiderius (d. 774) had become King of Lombardy in 757, and now Charlemagne defeated him and carried him off into imprisonment. Desiderius was the last king of the Lombards, two centuries after they had entered Italy. Charlemagne's

"Frankish Empire," as we may now call it, thus absorbed northern and central Italy.

South of the Papal States, the Duchy of Benevento still existed, independent of the Franks, and continued a faint twilight of Lombard rule.

In the next quarter-century, Charlemagne subdued the still-pagan Saxons to the east, forcing Christianity on them. He also invaded Spain and annexed a strip ("the Spanish March") south of the Pyrenees.

As the 700s came to a close, it was clear that Charlemagne's Frankish Empire was by far the strongest Christian power that Europe had seen since the time of Theodosius four centuries earlier. It included all the western lands that recognized the religious headship of the Pope, except for the British Isles and the Duchy of Benevento.

Pope Leo III (d. 816), who had gained the throne in 795, had troubles. He was driven from his position by riots and conspiracies, and he was accused of various crimes. He escaped to the Frankish realm and, in 800, Charlemagne brought him back to Rome and restored him to his Papal position.

As it happened, there was no Emperor in Constantinople at the time, but only an Empress, and it might be maintained that the Imperial throne was really vacant. Besides, even if there were an Emperor in the east, there ought to be one in the west as well, in line with the custom established on the death of Theodosius.

On December 25, 800, Pope Leo III crowned Charlemagne the Emperor of Rome, and once again there was an Emperor in the west—except that the east did not recognize Charlemagne's promotion.

Charlemagne ruled over his Empire with a

tight fist, and over the Pope as well. He encouraged the revival of learning and, for a time, one could speak of a "Carolingian Renaissance."

The leading light of the Carolingian Renaissance was an English scholar, Alcuin (732–804), who established a school in Charlemagne's capital at Aachen, and who reformed educational procedures in the Empire. He developed a way of writing letters compactly and neatly, which gave rise to "Carolingian minuscule," or what we now called "small letters" as opposed to capitals. He taught Charlemagne to read, as an adult, but the poor Emperor could not manage to persuade his aged fingers to form the letters properly so as to write.

SPAIN

When the Abbasids took over the Caliphate in 750 and slaughtered the Ommayads, one Ommayad prince, Abd ar-Rahman (731–788), escaped and made his way to Spain. There he established an Ommayad dynasty that did not acknowledge the sovereignty of the Abbasids.

Abd ar-Rahman made his capital at Cordova and ruled well. He tolerated Christians to a greater extent by far than Muslims would have been tolerated in any Christian land. What's more, he treated the Jews kindly. The Jews, who had been bitterly persecuted by the Visigoths, remained pro-Muslim in Spain, therefore, and many served in high political posts.

Abd ar-Rahman had to withstand attacks by Charlemagne and, while he was driven back a bit, he was never defeated in the sense that the Lombards and Saxons were defeated.

In northern Spain, Christian fighters established small states and chose kings.

SCANDINAVIA

Scandinavia played little or no part in civilized history until about this time, although the Goths, and possibly other Germanic tribes, may have originated there and traveled southward by land. In the late 700s, however, Scandinavian raiding parties began to radiate outward *by sea* in all directions.

This may have been partly due to population pressure, or to internal feuds that resulted in exile for those defeated. Or it may have simply been the discovery that raiding foreign coasts was an easier life than trying to live off a harsh countryside.

By 800, the rest of Europe was beginning to learn what "Viking" raids were like.

ENGLAND

In this period, Mercia was the strongest power in England under its king, Offa, who reigned from 757 to 796. He was one Christian king who was not subject to Charlemagne, and who could (and did) correspond with him on equal terms.

Hard times were coming, however, for, in 787, the first Scandinavian raiders (Danes—from Denmark) reached the southeastern tip of Kent. In 794, they first struck areas of Britain that lay north of the Saxon kingdoms, in what is now Scotland.

The leading English scholar of the time was Bede (673–735). He wrote a history of Anglo-Saxon England, pointed out the inadequacies of the Julian calendar, held the Earth to be a sphere, and (an original suggestion) maintained that the tides were influenced by the phases of the Moon.

IRELAND

The Irish were the first Europeans to explore the northern Atlantic since the time of Pytheas of Massilia, a thousand years earlier. About 790, Irish monks may even have reached Iceland, about 600 miles northwest of Ireland. It was uninhabited and (to be honest) not very habitable.

The Irish might have made a better go of it, however, if Ireland's golden age had continued; however, in 795, the Vikings attacked its coasts and, soon enough, Ireland was at their mercy. Its golden age came to an end.

BYZANTINE EMPIRE

Under Constantine V and his son, Leo IV (749–780), who became Emperor in 775, the Byzantine Empire advanced. It took back the island of Cyprus from the Muslims, and it fought successfully against the Bulgars. It lost the Exarchate of Ravenna, however, first to the Lombards, and then, by way of the Franks, to the Pope.

Leo IV's son, Constantine VI (770–797), was a child and under the influence of his mother, Irene (752–803). She was a vicious woman, who had one thing in her favor with much of the populace. She was against iconoclasm. She unseated her weak son in 797, took over the throne herself, and brought back the icons and paintings that had been outlawed some 80 years before.

She was still on the throne in 800 when Charlemagne was crowned Emperor in the west, and, of course, she absolutely refused to recognize the Pope's right to make an Emperor. In the course of her weak and intrigue-filled reign, the Bulgars grew strong again.

ABBASID CALIPHATE

Once the Abbasids gained control, the Muslim world strengthened again. It was not fully united (in fact, it would never be fully united again), for the Caliphate did not control Spain or Morocco. Still, the rest of the vast Empire remained firm and there was reasonable internal peace.

Since Damascus was associated too closely with the deposed Ommayads, the second Abbasid Caliph, Al-Mansur (710–775), who ascended the throne in 754, began the building of a new capital on the Tigris River in 762. This was Baghdad. It was near Ctesiphon, which dwindled and died as a result, as a thousand years earlier, Babylon had dwindled and died when Seleucia was built.

In 786, Harun ar-Rashid (765–809), became the fifth Abbasid Caliph. He achieved immortal fame, long after his death, because he figures in a number of tales that were eventually collected in what is popularly known as *The Arabian Nights*.

The Muslims were, at this time, picking up the use of paper from the Chinese, so that both papyrus and parchment disappeared from the Middle East.

The Muslims were beginning to take over the scientific lead in the west. An Arabian alchemist, Abu Musa Jabir (721–815), known in the west as "Geber," was the best of his time. He described ammonium chloride, prepared strong acetic acid and weak nitric acid. He worked with dyes and varnishes, and dealt with methods of refining metals. Most of all, he described his experiments clearly and carefully. Later alchemists usually did not follow Jabir's good example.

CHINA

The T'ang Empire was now past its best days. China was attacked and raided by Tibetans from the west and by various Turkish tribes from the north. About 800, a group of Turkish people, known as the Uighurs, established a large realm in the regions north of China, in what is now Mongolia and southern Siberia, but they remained fairly friendly with the Chinese.

JAPAN

The Japanese Emperor, Kammu, who reigned from 781 to 806, conducted campaigns in northern Japan against the Ainu. These were a non-Mongolian people who may conceivably have inhabited the islands before the Japanese arrived. They have more pronounced beards than the Japanese have, and consequently are sometimes called the "hairy Ainu.'" The Japanese north was brought under Imperial sway by these campaigns.

PACIFIC

At about this time, the Polynesians reached Easter Island, and the Maoris reached New Zealand. This represents the farthest expansion of prehistoric people in the Pacific islands.

800 TO 850

FRANKISH EMPIRE

The Frankish Empire did not remain powerful for long after Charlemagne's death in 814. It remained intact under his successor, Louis I the Pious (778–840), because he happened to be Charlemagne's only son. Louis I was, however, a weak king who spent much of his reign trying to divide up his realm among four sons, three of whom survived him.

The Carolingians, apparently, hadn't learned a thing from the Merovingian experience, since the result was merely a series of wars of the sons against their father and against each other, each son being convinced that he was being cheated.

In the course of these wars, all the Imperial administration set up by Charles weakened and was perverted, and all his attempts at reviving learning withered.

Even after Louis I died, the fighting continued until a settlement was reached at the Treaty of Verdun in 843.

By this settlement, the second son, Louis II the German (804–876), ruled over the eastern third of the Empire. The youngest son, Charles II the Bald (823–877), ruled over the western third. Lothair I (795–855), the eldest son, ruled over the middle third, and had the title of Emperor which, after Charlemagne, was meaningless.

The oaths taken by the opposing armies were in two languages: East Frankish, from which German was to descend; and West Frankish, from which French was to descend. Lothair's portion in the middle was called Lotharingia ("Lothringen" in German; "Lorraine" in French), and it remained more or less in contention between the two outer halves in later ages.

For a while, we will speak of the "West Franks" and the "East Franks."

SPAIN

During this period. Abd ar-Rahaman II (788–852) ruled over Muslim Spain, coming to the throne in 822. He pushed the Franks out of the Spanish March and fought off the Christians in the small northern kingdoms. He also put down Christian rebellions within his own dominions.

ENGLAND

The kingdom of Wessex, along England's south shore, had not loomed large in the land till now. In 802, however, Egbert (d. 839) became king of Wessex. He had been forced into exile earlier by Offa of Mercia. He returned after Offa's death, and defeated, conquered, and absorbed Mercia, which, in this way, disappeared from the map. He made Wessex the strongest of the Saxon nations, and it remained so after his death in 839. By 850, however, Wessex was bracing itself to meet the increasingly fearsome Danish raids and invasions.

SCANDINAVIA

In the 840s, the Viking raids were in full swing. The Vikings controlled the Atlantic Ocean and could sail wherever they wished and move up any river without fear of opposition. While the Danes ravaged the eastern coast of England, the Norse took over much of Scotland and Ireland. In Ireland, they founded Dublin in 841.

The long coastline of the Frankish Empire lay open to them. In 845, one group of ships sailed up the Elbe River to Hamburg, which they destroyed, while another group sailed up the Seine River to lay siege to Paris. Some of the Viking ships even found their way into the Mediterranean.

The Viking raids further disorganized the Frankish Empire, which was rapidly sinking under the weight of internal wars. The central governments were helpless to stop the raids, and the stronger local nobility had to take on the duty of fighting off the Vikings and withstanding sieges.

As a result, people grew used to turning to local magnates for safety and security, and the magnates grew accustomed to disregarding a distant and helpless king or emperor. This helped establish feudalism in western Europe, so that the lands that Charlemagne had strongly controlled became a crazy-quilt of a turbulent nobility endlessly fighting among themselves, when they weren't fending off raids or brutalizing the peasantry. The darkness of the Dark Ages continued, and in 850, the helpless people of western Europe could only pray: "From the fury of the Norsemen, good Lord, deliver us."

BYZANTINE EMPIRE

The Byzantine Empire continued to waste its strength on theological quarrels. During the 830s, iconoclasm was restored; then, in 843, it was beaten down again. There were no particularly strong Emperors in this period, and the Empire had all it could do to fight off the Muslims on the east and south, and the Bulgarians on the north.

BULGARIA

In 802, the Bulgarians gained a strong monarch in the person of Krum (d. 814). Krum was able to extend his rule north of the Danube River and set up an empire over the region now occupied by Bulgaria, Rumania, and Hungary.

In 811, Krum fought the Byzantines and defeated them in a great battle in which the Byzantine Emperor, Nicephorus I (who had become Emperor in 802), lost his life. Krum then fought his way to the outskirts of Constantinople and laid siege to it in 813 and again in 814; however, he died in the course of the second siege.

His son and, afterward, his grandson succeeded him. They made peace with the Byzantines, but continued to expand westward into what is now Yugoslavia. Bulgaria was strengthening even as the Frankish Empire was weakening.

MAGYARS

East of the Bulgars were the Magyars, another Asian nomadic tribe who were now crowding the Khazars eastward toward the Caspian Sea. They were also called Ugrians, and this has been distorted to "Hungarians," perhaps because, at their height, they frightened the west Europeans as much as the Huns had several centuries earlier. Another indication of their frightfulness is seen in the fact that "Ogre" is also derived from "Ugrian." In 850, however, they were still occupying the Ukraine in relative peace.

RUSSIA

The Slavs in what is now western Russia had been under the heel of the Ostrogoths, the Huns, the Avars, the Bulgars, the Magyars, and others. Now it was the turn of the Vikings to dominate. These Vikings, who by 850 were beginning to penetrate the deep land-mass of Russia, were Swedes, whose land faced the Baltic Sea (as opposed to the Danish Vikings, who faced the Atlantic Ocean). The stolid Slavs were used to these periodic changes of masters, and merely worked and bred patiently, in time outlasting and outnumbering all their conquerors.

ABBASID CALIPHATE

Haroun ar-Rashid was succeeded by his two sons, of whom the second was al-Mamun (786–833), sometimes called "Mamun the Great." He came to the Caliphate in Baghdad in 813. Under him, the Abbasid Caliphate reached its height. He established a "House of Knowledge" in Baghdad. There scholars translated into Arabic the great scientific works of the Greeks, including those of Aristotle, Galen, Euclid, Ptolemy, and so on. Most of these were now completely unknown to the western Europeans. It was the Arabs who preserved the ancient learning until the west Europeans were ready to receive it.

Even under Mamun, however, the Caliphate was beginning to fall apart. The North African lands west of Egypt were too far away to control, and they became independent Muslim nations. It was these Muslims, rather than the essentially peaceful Mamun, who continued the Muslim expansion in the Mediterranean Sea. Muslim refugees from Ommayad Spain conquered Crete in 825, and North African Muslims invaded Sicily in 827 and advanced steadily against stiff Byzantine resistance. By 850, the Byzantines were clinging only to Syracuse and a few other spots on the eastern coast.

Other islands were taken, too: Sardinia, Corsica, and the Balearic islands. The Mediterranean Sea was now completely dominated by the Muslims, who raided the Italian coast freely. In 846, they raided Rome itself.

After the death of Mamun, his brother, al-Mutasim (794–842), became Caliph in 833. He, in order to protect himself against conspiracies and military coups, set up a personal bodyguard consisting of Turks whom he could count on to be faithful only to him. By 850, the Abbasid Caliphate was entering its decline.

CHINA

The T'ang Empire was also in decline at this time and, by 850, the influence of Zen Buddhism had risen. It encouraged introspection and contemplation, a kind of escape from an increasingly difficult external world. Conditions might have been worse had not the Uighur Empire to the north been destroyed at this time by inflowing Turkish tribes. The Tibetan Empire also disintegrated, and the chaos across the borders prevented a concerted attack on China.

JAPAN

The decline of the T'ang Empire was noted in Japan, which sent a twelfth and last embassy to China in 838. They judged that China was no longer in a position to teach Japan, and the period of eager adoption of Chinese culture came to an end.

NORTH AMERICA

The collapse of the first period of Mayan civilization in Guatemala took place at about this time. The Mayan civilization underwent a second growth farther north in Yucatan.

850 TO 900

WEST FRANKS

The Carolingian rulers of the West Franks were by now every bit as incompetent as the later Merovingian rulers had been.

In 879, Charles the Fat (839–888), a great-grandson of Charlemagne, became king of the East Franks. He was crowned Emperor in 881, and was made king of the West Franks in 884. For three years Charlemagne's Empire seemed unified again. That, however, was only appearance. Charles the Fat was weak and the real power rested in the hands of the great nobles.

This was shown in 885, when the Vikings made the greatest of all their raids, coming up the Seine as they had come 40 years before, but in greater strength. They laid siege to Paris and Charles the Fat did absolutely nothing. Paris was defended by Eudes (860–898), the Count of Paris. For a whole year, he organized the defense and the Vikings were held off.

Count Eudes became the hero of the nation, and when, much too late, Charles the Fat appeared on the scene, it was not to fight, but to bribe the Vikings with money and to offer them a province to plunder.

The contrast was too great. Charles the Fat was deposed in 887 and the Frankish Empire broke up finally and forever.

In 893, a cousin of Charles the Fat came to the throne. He was Charles the Simple (879–929), and that was even worse than being fat.

EAST FRANKS

The East Franks were ruled by monarchs as incapable as those who were in power over the West Franks. They had problems not only with the Vikings, but with Moravian invaders from the east.

PAPACY

The Papacy was at a low point when the Muslims were raiding and looting Rome in 846. However, in 858, Nicholas I (820–867), sometimes called "Nicholas the Great," became Pope. Under him there was a recovery.

Nicholas was a strong supporter of the idea that Popes were supreme over all of Christendom, not only over other ecclesiastical officials, but over secular rulers as well.

He supported the "False Decretals" that were supposed to be a list of rulings issued by the early Bishops of Rome. These established a College of Cardinals to assist the Papal executive. This helped centralize the Church, and make it a kind of absolute monarchy under the Pope. (It was later discovered that these decretals were forgeries produced not long before Nicholas' time; hence, they were called "false." However, the College of Cardinals remained in existence.)

Nicholas also supported the so-called "Donation of Constantine." According to this, Constantine I had been cured of leprosy by Pope Sylvester I (who reigned from 314 to 335) and, in gratitude, he had given the Pope the whole of the West Roman Empire—another invention, of course.

After the death of Nicholas I in 867, however, the Papacy declined again; and, by 900, it seemed drowning in insignificance and corruption.

ENGLAND

England was, in a way, the first line of defense against the Vikings. The Danes sacked Canterbury and London in 851, Winchester in 860, and York in 866. The eastern half of England was completely under Danish domination. In 871, however, Alfred (849–899), sometimes called "Alfred the Great," became king of Wessex, the one Saxon kingdom that kept up a desperate defense against the Danes.

In 878, even Alfred was on the point of giving up after suffering a severe defeat. He clung to hope, however, gathered another army, won a victory over the Danes, and began to press them back. He even built a navy to attack them at sea —the first English navy. In 866, Alfred regained London.

Rather than keep on fighting to the ruin of the kingdom, Alfred agreed that, if the Danes accepted Christianity (which they did), he would divide the kingdom with them. They would take the northeast and he the southwest.

During his troubled reign, Alfred, like Charlemagne a century before, tried to stimulate learning. He encouraged the translation of useful Latin works into Old English (the term now used for the Anglo-Saxon language). He even did some of the translations himself. He reorganized the legal system as well.

SCOTLAND

The impact of Viking raids on the northern portion of Britain forced the scattered tribes there to unite in their own defense. The Picts combined with the Scots (a tribe who had originally come from northern Ireland), about 850, to form the nation we now call Scotland.

By 900, it was a going concern although it was small and weak, hemmed in by the Vikings to the north and the Danes and English to the south.

SCANDINAVIA

While the Viking sea-rovers were fighting in the British Isles and along the shores of the Frankish kingdoms, and were even beginning to penetrate Russia, they were also making their way across the sea to a new land.

A Norse chieftain, Ingolfur Arnarson, set sail in 874, and landed in Iceland. By that time, the Irish monks who had once dwelt in the island had died out or left. The Norse colonization that followed the discovery was, however, permanent, and Iceland became a new Scandinavian land.

MORAVIA

Moravia (located where Czechoslovakia is now) was the first Slavic state of note. It had been part of Charlemagne's Empire, but had become independent after Charlemagne's death.

The prince of Moravia, Rastislav, made a treaty with the Byzantine Empire in 862, and the next year two Greek monks were sent to Moravia. These were two brothers, Cyril (827–869) and Methodius (825–884). In order to translate the Bible into the Slavic tongue, the brothers invented an alphabet, based on that of Greek. This is the "Cyrillic alphabet" and is still used today by several Slavic nations, notably Russia.

By 900, Moravia was Christian and was taking advantage of the weakness of the East Frankish realm to mount raids deep into it.

RUSSIA

The Slavs of northern Russia dealt in furs, and hunters and trappers fanned out over the Arctic wastes in search of fur-bearing animals. A Viking band, under Rurik (d. 879), founded the town of Novgorod ("new town") in the area and ruled over it. (There is a legend that the Slavs themselves, despairing of not being able to rule themselves, *asked* to be dominated by the Vikings, but that sounds very unlikely.) The Viking bands were called "Varangians," though an alternate name was "Rus" from which "Russia" is supposed to have obtained its name.

On Rurik's death, a kinsman named Oleg (d. 912) succeeded to the throne. He ruled not only over Novgorod, but over Kiev, nearly 600 miles to the south. From the start, then, the Russian

realm spread out widely over the east-European plain. Kiev eventually became the capital of the Russian state under the Varangian princes, so that, in this period, one can speak of "Kievan Russia."

MAGYARS

The Magyars were moving westward at this time, squeezing the Bulgars outward, and establishing themselves in what is now Hungary.

BYZANTINE EMPIRE

At this time, the religious conflict between Rome and Constantinople—that is, between the Pope and Patriarch—sharpened. A particularly strong Patriarch, Photius (820–894), held office from 858 to 867 and again from 877 to 886. (The reason for this on-and-off business was that the Patriarch could always be deposed by an Emperor and then reseated by the next; whereas, since Charlemagne, the Pope had no Emperor with any power over him.)

Photius and Pope Nicholas I excommunicated each other and, for a while, the western and eastern halves of Christianity were split apart in what is called a "schism" (from a Greek word meaning "to split").

In 865, a Russian raid under Viking leadership attacked Constantinople for the first time. It was repulsed.

In 867, Basil I the Macedonian (812–886) became Emperor, founding the "Macedonian Dynasty," under which the Byzantine Empire had a new burst of energy. Basil I rebuilt the army and navy, reorganized the legal system and, in general, put the Empire on its feet.

The Byzantines drove back the Arabs in eastern Asia Minor and extended Byzantine holdings in southern Italy. The new Byzantine navy also fought successfully against Muslim pirates in the Mediterranean. However, Syracuse fell to the Muslims in 865, though the Byzantines still clung desperately to a few strong points on the eastern coast of Sicily.

Basil I was succeeded by his son Leo VI the Wise (866–912) in 886. Leo VI fired Photius and put an end to the schism with Rome. By 900, the Byzantine Empire seemed in better shape than at any time since the Muslim conquests of three and a half centuries earlier.

BULGARIA

In 852, Boris I (d. 907) became king of Bulgaria. In 865, he was converted to Christianity. For a while, he hesitated as to whether to adopt the Roman or Constantinopolitan rites, but in the end, he chose the latter.

The Byzantine Empire also managed to see to it that the Slavs living in the Balkans adopted Christianity according to the Constantinopolitan rites. The thought was that by making them Christians of this sort, they would be tamed. A feeling of awe for the holiness of Constantinople would keep them from attacking. By and large, this didn't work.

In 893, Boris's son, Symeon I (d. 927), sometimes called "Symeon the Great," became ruler of Bulgaria. He was the first Bulgarian ruler to adopt the title of "Tsar" (the Slavic version of "Caesar"). This meant there were two monarchs calling themselves Emperors in the east. A third was in the west—Arnulf (850–899), a nephew of Charles the Fat.

Symeon's religion, and the fact that he was a great admirer of Greek culture, did not prevent him from making war on the Byzantine Empire, however.

ABBASID CALIPHATE

The Abbasid Caliphate was in fragments now and the Caliph himself was more and more a figurehead. As often happens to monarchs who depend on mercenaries for protection, the Caliph had come to be at the mercy of his Turkish bodyguards. It was this which helped make it possible for the Byzantine Empire to stage a recovery at this time. The Muslims had some victories, however. There was not only the conquest of Syracuse, as, in addition, they acquired Malta in 869.

They also continued to shine in science. Muhammad ibn Al-Khwarizmi (780–850) wrote a book entitled *ilm al-jabr wa'l muqabalah*, meaning "the science of transposition and cancellations." This gave us "al-jabr" or, in English, "algebra," as the name of that branch of mathematics. Al-Khwarizmi's own name was distorted to "algorithm," which came to mean "a method of calculating." Al-Khwarizmi picked up the Hindu notion of zero and used it for writing numbers with positional notation. For this reason, such numbers came to be known later on as "Arabic numerals" in the west.

Al-Battani (858–929), known to the west as "Albategnius," was the best of the Arabian astronomers. He improved on Ptolemy in several ways, got the most accurate value yet for the length of the year and for the tilting of Earth's axis, and perfected spherical trigonometry.

CHINA

The T'ang dynasty was now in its last years.

JAPAN

The Japanese in this period devised a simpler form of writing than the Chinese had, writing by symbols that stood for syllables rather than for whole words.

900 TO 950

EAST FRANKS

The king of the East Franks, as the century opened, was Louis III the Child (893–911). He was only six years of age in 899 when he became king, and was still only 18 when he died in 911. He left no heirs and he was the last Carolingian to rule over the East Franks, a century after the death of Charlemagne. (However, members of the Carolingian line continued to rule the West Franks and some continued to receive the empty title of "Emperor.")

The East Frankish nobility nominated Conrad of Franconia to rule the nation as Conrad I (d. 918), but he wasn't much good at it, especially as he had to face Magyar raids from the east.

He died in 918, and Henry I the Fowler (876–936) was elected. He received his nickname from the fact that when the news of the election reached him, he was hunting birds (fowls) with a hawk. He was the strongest East Frankish king in 40 years and, in 933, was the first to defeat the Magyars in battle. It did not stop the Magyar raids, but it did cause them to call a temporary halt.

Henry I saw to it that the kingship remained in his family. He arranged to have the nobility choose his oldest son, by his second wife, as his successor. When Henry died in 936, that son succeeded him as Otto I (912–973), sometimes called "Otto the Great."

Otto proved even stronger than his father, and was indeed the strongest monarch in western Europe since the death of Charlemagne a century and a quarter earlier. He beat down all opposition to him within the East Frankish realm and brought the nobility to heel. He was still on the throne in 950, and he had his eye on the Imperial title that so far had graced only Carolingians.

WEST FRANKS

Over the West Franks, Charles the Simple, a great-great-grandson of Charlemagne, was ruler, and he had to face the last great raid of the Vikings in 911. The leader was one Hrolf the Ganger (i.e., "walker") because, according to the story, he was so tall and heavy no horse could carry him. His name in the West Frankish language was Rollo.

Charles the Simple was not in much of a position to withstand these Vikings, or Norsemen, particularly since he wanted to gain the kingship of the East Franks once his distant cousin, Louis the Child, had died. He needed all his attention

for that, so he determined to make peace, rather as Alfred of England had done with the Danes.

Provided the Norsemen turned Christian, and swore allegiance to him, he offered to give them the land about the mouth of the Seine, which, in any case, they occupied, and from which they could not be driven out.

Rollo agreed and the region about the mouth of the Seine, some 50 miles northwest of Paris, became known as "Normandy."

Charles the Simple did not gain the kingship of the East Franks, and his reign continued to be a weak and futile one. In 950, his son was reigning as Louis IV (921–954)—one more weak and incompetent Carolingian.

Despite the fragmentation and misery in the West Frankish realm in this period, there was a monastic revival at the Abbey of Cluny in the east central portion of the land. There was a strict observance of monastic discipline, and this Cluniac movement spread and produced prelates who greatly strengthened the Church.

MAGYARS

In 906, the Magyars conquered and destroyed the Moravian kingdom, and, in its place, they formed a strong state where once the Avars had ruled three centuries before. They spent the next 50 years raiding the East Frankish realm, spreading destruction, so that they are still remembered as "ogres" in western legends. They were defeated by Henry the Fowler in 933, but that stopped them only temporarily. In 950, they were still a terrible threat to the Franks to their west and the Bulgarians to their south.

SPAIN

The Muslims in Spain had largely come from Mauretania, that portion of North Africa south of Spain (whose name lingers on in "Morocco"). For this reason, the Spanish Christians called the Muslims "Moros," or, in English, "Moors."

Moorish Spain reached its peak under Abd er-Rahman III (891–961), its eighth ruler. He became king in 912 and was still king in 950. He pacified the country, kept it strong, advanced its agriculture and industry, and encouraged learning. His capital, Cordova, had about half a million population and was the strongest and largest city in Europe except for Constantinople itself. Cordova was the center of European learning, for there the old books of the Greeks and Romans were preserved and translated.

In the interests of peace, Abd er-Rahman III recognized the existence of the Christian nation of Leon in the northwest. It had expanded in size and power, but its eastern portion, centered about the city of Burgos, broke away and became independent after 930. The county of Burgos eventually became the kingdom of Castile. Abd er-Rahman III helped both nations, since he felt, shrewdly, that if there were more than one Christian nation in the north, they would fight each other rather than the Moors. He was right, but that only worked well, as a strategy, as long as the Moors themselves remained united.

ENGLAND

In the decades following the death of Alfred the Great, the English slowly absorbed the Danish sections peacefully. The Danes were not very different from the Saxons in language and culture, and once the Danes had accepted Christianity, the two peoples fused rather easily.

In 950, Edred (d. 955), a grandson of Alfred, was on the throne, and England was clearly on the way to being a united kingdom for the first time since the Saxon invasions began five centuries before.

The English kings held a vague rule over Scotland as well, and Scotland was slowly becoming Anglicized in language and culture.

PAPACY

In this period, the Papacy struck bottom. It was the plaything of the Roman nobility, and its influence dwindled almost to nothing. There were 14 Popes between 900 and 950. Agapetus II, who was in office from 946 to 955, was somewhat better than some of those who preceded and followed him.

BULGARIA

Symeon of Bulgaria had dreams of winning Constantinople and, from 913 to 924, he raided southward on a number of occasions, penetrating to the walls of the city. The walls were, as usual, unbreachable, and Symeon had no navy.

The Byzantine Empire fought back by encouraging the Patzinaks (or Pechenegs), a new wave of Asian tribesmen moving into Europe, to attack Bulgaria from the east. The Serbs, a Slavic people who were in control of the Adriatic hinterland (the Byzantines themselves still occupied the coasts), also fought the Bulgarians in the west.

In 926, however, the Bulgarians defeated the Serbs decisively, and, in 927, when Symeon died, his son, Peter, made peace with the Byzantines in order that he might deal more effectively with raids by the Magyars from the north and the Patzinaks from the east.

RUSSIA

Kievan Russia was interested in trade with the more advanced nations to the south, particularly with the Byzantines. In 941, a huge flotilla of Russian ships crossed the Black Sea to attack Constantinople and force favorable trade terms on the Byzantines. The Byzantines, however, totally destroyed the Russian ships by making use of Greek Fire for the purpose. It was its last use.

BYZANTINE EMPIRE

Despite attacks from the Bulgarians and Russians, the Byzantine Empire in this period remained strong. They fought well in eastern Asia Minor against the Muslims, and they strengthened their position in southern Italy. They defeated the Muslims in 916 at the Garigliano River, and forced them out of Italy forever.

CHINA

The T'ang dynasty came to an end in 907, and China fell into disunity again. It was some time in this period, however, that the Chinese discovered gunpowder—perhaps as early as 919.

MONGOLS

The Asian nomads north of China and Persia were Turkish to the west and Mongol to the east. The Asian invaders of Europe were largely Turkish, though the Huns may have been Mongol.

The Mongols enter history definitely, however, in 907, when the fall of the T'ang dynasty made it possible for a tribe known as the Khitan Mongols to surge southward to conquer what is now Inner Mongolia, plus the northern provinces of China itself. In 938, the Khitan Mongols chose Peking (now called "Beijing") as their capital.

JAPAN

In this period, the Fujiwara clan was dominating political life in Japan. Fujiwara Tadahira was dictator until his death in 949.

950 TO 1000

HOLY ROMAN EMPIRE

Otto I, king of the East Franks, responded to a Magyar invasion in 954; and, in August 955, he defeated the Magyars totally in the battle of Lechfeld in what is now Bavaria. That put an end to Magyar raids forever and greatly increased Otto's prestige. He also defeated the Slavs and advanced his eastern frontier from the Elbe River to the Oder River.

But Otto was dreaming of the Imperial crown. In 951, he had led an expedition into Italy and made himself king of the Lombards, but Pope Agapetus II refused to crown him Emperor.

In 955, however, a new Pope, John XII (937–964) was elected. He was having trouble with a minor Carolingian, Berengar II (900–966), and he called on Otto for help. That was exactly what Otto wanted. He led a strong second expedition into Italy in 961 and the Pope, in return for his help, crowned him Emperor on February 2, 962.

Otto confirmed the rule of the Pope over the Papal States, but claimed the right to ratify Papal elections and, indeed, Otto freely deposed some Popes and named others. In a third expedition to Italy that began in 966, he penetrated into the Byzantine south and obtained a Byzantine princess as the wife of his son. (This had its importance, too, for it meant that Byzantine refinement entered into the cruder Germanic world. The Byzantine princess introduced the use of forks when dining, for instance.)

The Empire, as refounded by Otto, was viewed as the reestablishment of the Roman Empire in the west, even more so than in the case of Charlemagne over a century and a half before. Because it was created by the Pope, it was distinguished from the old Empire, which had been founded by pagans, and was spoken of as the "Holy Roman Empire." It is usually referred to by that name in history books.

Otto's successes in Italy inspired future Holy Roman Emperors to consider Italy as part of their dominions and, because this distracted them from the German core of the state, this had a deleterious effect on the Empire.

Thus, Otto's son, who came to the throne as Otto II (955–983) in 973, campaigned in southern Italy, and Otto's grandson, Otto III (980–1002), who came to the throne as a child in 983 (and was the son of the Byzantine princess) actually settled in Rome and tried, unsuccessfully, to revive its past glories.

FRANCE

The West Franks were still ruled by Carolingians after the Carolingian line had come to an end among the East Franks in 911. The West Frank

Carolingians had no power, and the last of them, Louis V the Do-Nothing, died in 987 at the age of 20, with no direct heir. The Carolingian line, which had come into prominence with Pepin of Landon three and a half centuries earlier, and had reached its peak with Charlemagne, would never rule again.

During the reigns of the last of the Carolingians, the most powerful nobleman among the West Franks was Hugh the Great (d. 956), who was Count of Paris, and who overshadowed the kings who were nominally his superior, just as the Carolingian Mayors of the Palace overshadowed the last Merovingian kings.

Hugh the Great died in 956, but his son Hugh Capet (938–996), so-called because of a cape he liked to wear, inherited his title and his power. After Louis V died, the French nobility gathered and elected Hugh Capet as king.

With Hugh Capet's election, we need no longer refer to the land as the West Frankish realm. We can call it "France."

The Emperor Otto III recognized Hugh Capet's title and, in return, Hugh surrendered Lorraine to the Emperor. (Lorraine was the remnant of the middle kingdom inherited by Charlemagne's oldest son, a kingdom which had been fought over and disputed by the East and West Franks ever since.)

Hugh Capet died in 996 and was succeeded by his son, Robert II the Pious (970–1031).

Somewhere in this period, horsecollars came into use. This allowed a horse to be hitched to a plow in such a way that the pressure of the strap was against its shoulders and not its windpipe. This meant that the horse could pull with all its strength and the heavy moldboard plow could be pulled through the damp, dense soil of northwestern Europe with much greater efficiency than before. This, combined with iron horseshoes (which also came into use at this time) to protect horse's hooves, greatly increased the food supply in northern Europe. This, in turn, increased the northern population and led to the centers of European power moving northward.

PAPACY

During this period, the Popes were weak and were under the complete domination of the Holy Roman Emperors.

In 996, Gregory V (972–999) became Pope. He was a cousin of Emperor Otto III, and was the first German pope. He was succeeded in 999 by Sylvester II (945–1003), the first French pope, who had been a tutor of Otto III, and who was a learned mathematician and scientist.

He understood Arabic, which was necessary, since the ancient Greek books existed only in Arabic translations at this time.

SPAIN

Abd ar-Rahman III died in 961, and while his successors maintained Moorish domination of the land, under Hisham II (965–1013), who began his reign in 976, Muslim Spain was beginning to decline.

ENGLAND

In England, Edgar (944–975), a great-grandson of Alfred the Great, became king in 959, and was the first Saxon ruler to be recognized as the king of all England.

Edgar died in 975, and, after the short reign of his older son, his younger son, Ethelred II the Redeless (968–1016), became king in 978. "Redeless" means "unadvised" but the sobriquet is usually given as "Ethelred the Unready," which is not a good translation of "Redeless" but which conveys something just the same, for Ethelred was also unready to meet the emergencies of the time. In his reign, a fresh Danish invasion took place and he was unable to do much about it.

DENMARK

Harold II Bluetooth (910–985) was the first ruler of Denmark to make his mark on history. He was converted to Christianity in 960. His son, Sven I Forked-Beard (985–1014) ascended the throne in 985, and it was he who directed new raids against England.

NORWAY

Olaf I Trygvasson (964–1000) became king of Norway in 995. He tried, without much success, to ward off the strong Denmark of Sven I. He began the process of the conversion of Norway to Christianity.

A notable Norwegian of the time was Eric Thorvaldsson, usually called "Eric the Red" from the color of his hair. In 982, he was exiled from Norway for some offense and he decided to take the opportunity of sailing westward from Iceland. He came upon a huge ice-covered land. He sailed about it and found that the southwestern shore was not completely bleak. He called the place "Greenland" (to make it sound more attractive), and by 985 was collecting colonists in Iceland. In 986, a colony was founded on that southwest shore.

From Greenland, Eric's son, Leif Ericsson, sailed westward and, in 1000, reached a land he called "Vinland," by which, perhaps, he referred to the island we now know as Newfoundland. In this way, the American continents were first reached by Europeans. It was only a temporary attainment, however, and did not gain the attention of Europe's civilized centers.

SWEDEN

Olof Skutkonung (d. 1022) became king of Sweden, and began the Christianization of the country.

BOHEMIA

Bohemia is the westernmost part of what is now Czechoslovakia, and is the westernmost Slavic region of Europe. Under Boleslav II, who reigned from 967 to 999, the processes of Christianization of Bohemia proceeded.

POLAND

Poland became an important power under Boleslaw I the Brave (967–1025), who became king in 992.

RUSSIA

In 957, a Russian princess named Olga (890–969) visited Constantinople and was converted to Christianity. Her son, Sviatoslav (d. 972) became ruler of Kievan Russia in 964. He defeated the Khazars and put an end to their realm. He also defeated the Bulgarians, so that his power briefly extended to the Danube; however, he was then defeated by the Byzantines, and was killed in warfare against the Patzinaks.

His three sons ruled in rapid succession, his youngest becoming king in 980. He was Vladimir I the Saint (956–1015), who supervised the conversion of Russians en masse to the Constantinopolitan version of Christianity.

HUNGARY

After the battle of Lechfeld, and their defeat, the Magyars settled down in what is now Hungary. In 997, Stephen I (977–1038) became king and encouraged the Christianization of Hungary, choosing the Roman version over that of Constantinople.

SERBIA

The Serbians at this time adopted the Constantinopolitan version of Christianity.

BULGARIA

Most of this period was spent by Bulgaria in fighting off raids by Magyars, Patzinaks, and Russians. In 976, however, Samuel (d. 1014) became Tsar of Bulgaria and began the process of rebuilding the nation. He supervised its restoration to power.

GHAZNI

In western Asia, Arabic dynamism had burnt to a low ebb, and it was the Turks who were becoming the cutting edge of Islam. Thus, in 977, a Turkish slave, Subuktigin, founded a kingdom in Ghazni, which spread out over what is now Afghanistan. In 994, he was succeeded by Mahmud the Idol-Breaker (970–1030), who conquered Khorasan (in what is now northeastern Iran) and invaded northern India.

EGYPT

Egypt had broken away from the Abbasid Caliphate after the time of Mamun the Great, and, in 968, it came under the control of the Fatimid Dynasty. These were Shiites, who claimed to be descended from Ali, the fourth Caliph, who had married Muhammad's daughter, Fatima (hence, the name of the dynasty).

Under the Fatimids, Egypt experienced a period of power for the first time since the early Ptolemies, 12 centuries before. Little by little, they gained ground in North Africa, and took over Sicily from its earlier Moslem conquerors.

In 996, al-Hakim (985–1021) became the Fatimid ruler of Egypt. Because he claimed to be a god and because his temperament was erratic, he was called al-Hakim the Mad—although to some Muslim sectaries ever since he has been considered divine. Under him, Fatimid Egypt was at its height, for he controlled all of North Africa and Syria in addition to Egypt.

The greatest scientist in his realm was Alhazen (965–1039), who studied optics with greater precision than anyone before him. He explained the working of lenses and the nature of the rainbow. Unfortunately, he also vaingloriously claimed he could devise a machine that would regulate the flooding of the Nile. Al-Hakim ordered him to build such a machine on pain of execution and Alhazen had to pretend to go mad and to keep that up till al-Hakim was safely dead.

BYZANTINE EMPIRE

The Byzantine Empire continued to be strong. It reconquered Crete in 961. In 963, a five-year-old boy became Emperor as Basil II (958–1025). His position was respected and, during his minority, strong and loyal generals continued to lead the Empire on to victory. The Byzantines took Cyprus and beat the Muslims in eastern Asia Minor and in Syria.

In January 965, however, the last Byzantine fortress in Sicily was taken by the Muslims and, four centuries after Belisarius had retaken the island, imperial rule ended there forever.

In 976, Basil II was old enough to rule in his own name, and he spent years putting down the great magnates who had gained power during his minority.

CHINA

In 960, that portion of China south of the domain of the Khitan Mongols came under the rule of the Sung dynasty. Sung T'ai Tsung, who reigned from 960 to 997, unified all of China south of the Mongol domain but could not take back what had been lost in the north. His son, Sung Chen Tsung, accepted the inevitable and made peace with the Mongols, giving up the north.

Under the Sung dynasty, that part of China it controlled did well. Books were printed, paper money was used, art flourished, and the government instituted a humane welfare system. Trade and commerce expanded and the population of China, at 60 million, reached what had been its maximum in the days of the Han Empire, eight centuries before.

JAPAN

Fujiwara Michinaga became Shogun (Regent) in 995 and under him, the Fujiwara clan was at its most powerful. In his time, the Emperors were complete nonentities. It was a time of a literary flowering, but the warrior families were growing more powerful again.

AFRICA

Arabs controlled the western shores of the Red Sea and traded in gold, ivory, and slaves. In western Africa, north of the Gulf of Guinea, there was the flourishing kingdom of Ghana. It had iron weapons and it produced gold, which was its most important export. It was at its peak at about 1000.

INTERLUDE—1000

The year 1000 had a certain significance. To those who were alive as 1000 approached, it was clear that that year would mark the thousandth anniversary of the traditional year of the birth of Jesus, and that anniversary had the potentiality of being particularly significant.

It came about this way. In the early civilizations, 1000 was usually the highest number given a specific name, since there was little occasion in early times to count anything that was more than a few thousand.

Consequently, when the Biblical writers wanted to make use of a large number, the word "thousand" was what was often used. Thus, Psalms 90:4 reads: "For a thousand years in thy sight are but as yesterday when it is past, and as a watch in the night."

What that means is that God is eternal and is not limited by time. Any period of time, however large, means nothing to God, but the largest number word the psalmist had was "thousand," so that's what was used. It is natural, therefore, that readers of the Bible would attach more importance to that particular number than it deserves.

The number "thousand" eventually showed up in messianic thought, the feeling among the Jews that a king of the line of David would someday return and rule the whole world. Naturally, such a messiah never showed up, and the Jews are still waiting.

The Christians believed that it was Jesus who was the messiah, but since his coming did not result in the kind of world they expected, they began to assume there would be a "Second Coming," something for which they are also still waiting.

The Book of Revelation, the last book of the New Testament, in a confusing statement (Chapter 20:1–3), says that Satan has been bound for a thousand years and will then be loosed, after which there will be a final battle in which good will finally overcome evil and the world will then come to an end, to give way to a perfect and eternal new heaven and new earth.

The account is so confusing that there is really no hope of making sense out of the Book of Revelation as a whole. Still, one might interpret the term "thousand years" to mean an indefinitely long time. Others, however, accepted the phrase literally and felt that the old world would end and the new one would begin a thousand years after the birth of Jesus. For them, the coming of 1000 was a time of hope and fear.

However, the year 1000 passed as any other year did, and life and the world continued to move right along. Nevertheless, in every generation, there have been those who have expected an imminent end to the world, in the Biblical sense, and, on a number of occasions, specific dates have been predicted. None of these predictions have come true, however.

1000 TO 1050

ENGLAND

In 1002, Ethelred II (the Unready) married Emma (d. 1052), who was the daughter of Richard I the Fearless (922–996), the Duke of Normandy from 942. That same year, Ethelred consented to the slaughter of Danes in England by the Saxons, intending by this act of terrorism to frighten off the Danes of Denmark, who had once again been raiding England.

It was entirely counterproductive. Sven Fork-beard of Denmark, who had just conquered Nor-way, had had a sister killed in the slaughter and was furious. Therefore, Sven took a fleet to En-gland and ravaged to his heart's content. Eth-elred eventually fled to Normandy, and Sven was accepted by the English as their king in 1013.

Sven died almost immediately afterward, but his son, Canute (d. 1035), often known as "Can-ute the Great," stepped into his shoes. He was acknowledged king of England in 1017; and, since Ethelred had died the year before, Canute married his widow, Emma, as a way of strength-ening his legitimacy on the throne.

Canute was a good king against whom the English had no complaints. He completed the Christianization of Denmark, and ruled over a northern empire that included England, Den-mark, and Norway.

He died in 1035. His two sons, who succeeded in turn, were incompetent, and, in 1042, the son of Ethelred and Emma returned to England from Normandy and reigned as Edward III (1003–1066). He was gentle and religious (he was called "Edward the Confessor") but he was also incom-petent, and he relied a great deal on Norman advisers, since his mother was Norman and he had spent his youth in Normandy.

This alienated the Saxon nobility, the strong-est of whom was Godwin, earl of Wessex (d. 1053).

SCOTLAND

Scotland was still fighting off Viking raiders at this time. Malcolm II MacKenneth (953–1034) began to reign in 1005, and went through the formality of accepting Canute as his overlord.

His grandson, Duncan I (d. 1040), succeeded him, but he was not a strong king and there was a blood feud between him and the wife of his general, Macbeth (d. 1057). Macbeth rose against him and, in 1040, Duncan was killed in battle and Macbeth was accepted as king. He was, on the whole, a capable one, and Shakespeare's play, "Macbeth," gives a very distorted account of this period of history.

IRELAND

Brian Boru of Munster (941–1014), who had been high king of Ireland since 1002, led the Irish re-sistance to the Vikings, who had dominated the Irish coastline for two centuries. In 1014, at the battle of Clontorf, on the outskirts of Dublin, the Vikings were defeated, and their position in Ire-land declined rapidly thereafter. However, Brian was killed as the battle ended and there followed a period of anarchy in Ireland.

NORWAY

After the death of Canute of Denmark, Norway broke away from Danish domination and, in 1046, was ruled by Harold III Haardraade (1015–1066), meaning "severe ruler." He had fled Nor-way when it had been defeated and he served for a while in Kievan Russia, and then in Constanti-nople. He was nearly seven feet tall, and very handsome, and in both places he got in trouble over his success with royal women. He came back to independent Norway finally, with a Rus-sian princess as wife, and with considerable wealth. In 1050, he founded Oslo.

FRANCE

The early Capetian kings (Hugh Capet and his immediate descendants) had a rough time of it. France was broken up into provinces, each of which was governed by a nobleman who ac-knowledged the king in only a very offhand and limited way. In the time of Henry I (1008–1060), Hugh Capet's grandson, who came to the throne in 1031, the Capetian power was at a low ebb. There was several of the French nobility who were stronger than the king.

The population of France by 1000 had been restored to what it had been in Gaul in the time of Hadrian (nine centuries earlier), and in En-gland, it was now twice what it had been in Roman Britain.

NORMANDY

Normandy was a province of France, and its duke acknowledged the overlordship of the King of France, but that was just a legalistic form. Normandy was well and tightly run by its dukes, who usually had considerably more power than the contemporary French kings.

Duke Richard II the Good (d. 1027) kept Normandy strong and prosperous. Emma, who had married, first, Ethelred the Unready, and then, later, Canute of Denmark, was his sister. Richard II died in 1027 and was succeeded by his son, Robert I the Devil (d. 1035), who received his cognomen because of his cruelty and unscrupulousness. He kept his nobles in line, however. In 1034, Robert undertook the task of a pilgrimage to Jerusalem. On his way back, in 1035, he died, leaving only an eight-year-old illegitimate son, William (1028–1087) as heir.

Robert had made the nobility swear allegiance to the young William, but after he was dead, there was a strong temptation to forget the oath. After all, Duke William II the Bastard was young and illegimate. However, Henry I of France protected him (feeling it might be a good idea to have a Duke of Normandy who would be grateful to him).

As William grew older, however, he turned out to be strong, capable, and quite ruthless. When he was old enough, he ground down the nobles mercilessly and made himself feared and obeyed. He was a first cousin, once removed, of Edward the Confessor, and since Edward had no children, William felt that he ought to inherit the crown of England, on Edward's death.

HOLY ROMAN EMPIRE

Otto III died without direct heirs in 1002, and his second cousin was chosen to succeed him (not without trouble) and reigned as Henry II the Saint (973–1024). He was eventually made a saint because he had been interested in monastic reform and because he founded new monasteries. He also fought against Poland, but with only limited success.

On his death in 1024, another cousin was chosen and he reigned as Conrad II (990–1039). Conrad II and his son and successor, Henry III the Black (1017–1056), lifted the Holy Roman Empire to its most strongly centralized position. They kept the nobility under control, and continually insisted on Church reform. In this way, however, they managed to rouse increasing resentment among the nobles and the bishops.

PAPACY

The Popes, during this period, were weak and, sometimes, corrupt. There was, however, an increasingly strong movement toward church reform. There was a push toward ending "simony" (the purchase of ecclesiastical office), toward the abolition of "lay investiture" (where kings and other rulers appointed bishops for political reasons or in return for payment), and toward the enforcement of the celibacy of the clergy (so that high church officials not use their offices to enrich and promote their children).

The Church reformers also tried to suppress the continual fighting among the nobility, which impoverished all the land and endlessly increased human misery. In 1049, a new Pope, Leo IX (1002–1054), supported by Emperor Henry III, who was a relative, and took up the cause of reform. With him, the Papacy began to climb out of the pit into which it had fallen.

VENICE

Since Belisarius' wars, five centuries earlier, Venice had been friendly toward the Byzantine Empire and had more or less acknowledged its overlordship, provided it was left pretty much to itself. By 1000, Venice's trade had made it rich and strong and it dominated the Adriatic Sea and the northern part of its eastern coast (Dalmatia).

This meant that it was, in actual fact, independent, though it remained culturally bound to the east. Thus, when the Venetians began to construct their greatest church, St. Mark, in 1043, they did so in the tradition of Byzantine architecture. And, of course, the city's past connection gave it special trading privileges in Constantinople that served to enrich it further.

Italy, as a whole, was beginning to develop flourishing city life, particularly in the northern half. Italy had been the last of the west European provinces of the Roman Empire to experience the coming of darkness, and it was the first province (if Moorish Spain is excepted) where the darkness was now beginning to lift.

MOORISH SPAIN

By 1031, only 70 years after the end of the great reign of Abd er-Rhaman III, the Ummayad Caliphate collapsed in Spain when the last Caliph, Hisham III (975–1036), died. Moorish Spain broke up into competing fragments, which had to call on African tribes for help against the increasing power of the Christians to the north. The Africans were good fighters, but they did nothing for Moorish Spain's intellectual and cultural life, so Moorish civilization declined.

CASTILE

Ferdinand I of Castile (1017–1065), sometimes called "Ferdinand the Great," became king in 1035. He conquered Leon to the west, and extended his overlordship over Navarre in the east, so that all northern Spain was under his rule. He took advantage of the disarray among the Moors to reconquer territory in the south. He began the Christian reconquest of Spain, and it was against him that the African tribes were called in.

BOHEMIA AND POLAND

At this time, these two new Slavic powers competed vigorously for domination. Bretislav I of Bohemia (1005–1055), who became king in 1034, made inroads on Poland, while Casimir I of Poland (1016–1058) reversed the situation. For that reason, Bretislav I and Casimir I were each called "the Restorer" by their respective nations.

In actual fact, it was Emperor Henry III who kept them embroiled, and who prevented either side from getting too strong. Weak and competing Slavic powers to the east of the Empire were exactly what Henry III wanted.

RUSSIA

The power of Kievan Russia reached a peak under the rule of Yaroslav I the Wise (980–1054), who mounted the throne in 1019. He built a cathedral, produced the earliest known written Russian law code, and extended his sway over all the Russian lands from the Black Sea to the Baltic Sea. He used his daughters as a way of cementing relations with western states. One married into the Hungarian royal family, one married Harold Haardraade of Norway, and one even married Henry I of France.

HUNGARY

After the death of Stephen I in 1038, there was a period of dynastic rivalry that greatly weakened the nation.

BYZANTINE EMPIRE

Basil II brought the Byzantine Empire to a new peak of power. It was far smaller than it had been under Justinian, but that had its bright side, too. It meant there were no outlying provinces that were disaffected and that had to be held onto at great cost.

Asia Minor was secure, for the Muslims could not match the Byzantine armies at this time. On the Balkan peninsula, however, the Bulgarian kingdom under Samuel was a great danger, and it was against him that Basil II turned his arms.

For a while, the struggle swayed this way and that, but in 1014, at the battle of Balathista, in what is now southwestern Bulgaria, Basil II managed to send troops around the flank of the Bulgarian army and, at a crucial moment, attacked its rear. The Bulgarians collapsed and Basil II took 15,000 prisoners. In a horribly atrocious act, Basil II blinded 99 out of every 100 of their eyes, leaving 150 single-eyed men to guide the rest back to Samuel. The Bulgarian ruler had a stroke at the sight and died two days later.

The Bulgarians were completely beaten. All the Balkans to the Danube River was annexed to the Byzantine Empire, and the Bulgarians began to melt into the general population. Basil II came to be known as "Bulgaroktonos" ("slayer of the Bulgarians.")

Then, in 1018, the Byzantines defeated the Lombards at Cannae, where, nearly twelve and a half centuries before, Hannibal had inflicted a great defeat on Rome. As a result, the Byzantine hold on southern Italy was strengthened.

On December 15, 1025, the old Bulgar-Killer died, and there was no one quite like him to replace him.

Constantine VIII (960–1028), the younger brother of Basil II, survived him and, in 1028, when he died, he was succeeded by his daughter Zoe (980–1050), and by three husbands she married successively. She died in 1050 and up to that time, Basil's work in training the army and in developing good generals kept the Byzantine Empire doing well despite internal revolts, and despite attacks by Patzinak raiders on land and Muslim pirates at sea. One of the factors in Byzantine victories at sea was the leadership of Harold Haardraade, who was eventually to become the Norwegian king.

SELJUK TURKS

Another tribe of Turks came south from Turkistan, the region north of the civilized Middle East. They were the Seljuk Turks, so-called after the grandfather of their leaders, who were Toghril Beg (990–1063) and Chagar Beg, two brothers. From 1037, they defeated the Ghaznavid monarch and developed a realm of their own in what is now Afghanistan and northern Iran.

In 1010, the Persian poet, Firdawsi (935–1020), wrote a long epic poem dealing with the legendary and historical tales of the Persian kings up to the Islamic conquest. It is the great Persian national epic and contains the legends of Rustam, the Persian Hercules. He dedicated the book to Mahmud of Ghazni.

Another important Persian of the period was

Ibn Sina (980–1037), known to the west as "Avicenna." He was the most important of all the Muslim physicians. His works, based on the theories of Hippocrates and Galen, were the most important medical textbooks for centuries.

At about this time, the Muslims were learning how to prepare and concentrate sugar from sugarcane.

WEST AFRICA

The Almoravids were a confederation of North African tribes who, at this time, spread their power over what is now Morocco and Algeria. It was they who were called into Spain by the collapsing Moors to fight off the resurgent Christains.

BURMA

In 1044, a kingdom was founded east of India that developed into Burma.

KOREA

To guard against tribal invaders from Manchuria, Korea borrowed the notion from China of building a great wall across the narrowest part of the peninsula.

JAPAN

In 1015, a Japanese noblewoman, Shikibu Murasaki, wrote a long novel *The Tale of the Genji*, which long preceded any novels in the west. It can still be (and is) read today.

NORTH AMERICA

The Mayan civilization began a second, and this time final, decline in this period.

1050–1100

ENGLAND

Edward the Confessor, who had no heirs and expected none, favored his first cousin, once removed, Duke William II of Normandy, as his successor. The Saxon nobles, however, pointed out that William was of illegitimate birth, and that they didn't want a Norman to be king over them in any case.

When Godwin of Wessex, the most powerful of the Saxon nobles, died in 1053, his son, Harold (1022–1066) succeeded him and he, too, dominated the weak Edward. About 1064, Harold was going by ship through the English Channel and was driven ashore in Normandy by a storm. William took him prisoner and forced him to swear an oath to help William get the throne, but Harold later claimed the oath was void since it was wrung from him by force.

Edward died in January 1066, and Harold was voted King Harold II of England. His younger brother, Tostig (d. 1066), who ruled Northumbria, had rebelled and had been driven into exile. Now he returned with Harold Haardraade of Norway to take advantage of the confusion of the succession. Haardraade was leading one last Viking invasion three centuries after the sea-rovers had become the scourge of northwestern Europe. Harold Haardraade might be called "the last of the Vikings."

Harold II of England was forced to lead his army to the north where he beat and killed Tostig and Harold Haardraade after a very hard battle at Stamford Bridge. Word reached Harold II, however, that even as the battle was being fought, Duke William II was landing a force in southern England.

Harold hastened southward, driving his army to utter weariness and then, without giving them a chance to rest, hurled them at the Normans on October 14, 1066, at the Battle of Hastings.

Weary as they were, the Saxons gave a good account of themselves and it was only after Har-

old was killed that they broke. William became King William I of England, and was forever after known as "William the Conqueror." He spent the next six years subduing the Saxons in the west and north.

William then set up a firm, centralized government, making sure that all landholders owed allegiance to him, directly and absolutely. Moreover, he refused to yield any power over the English church to the Pope.

In 1085, he made a detailed survey of all the property in England ("the Domesday Book") in order that he might be able, more efficiently, to tax and administer the kingdom.

After his death, his oldest son became Duke of Normandy. He was Robert II Curthose (1054–1134) or "short pants," so-called because he had short legs. William's second son became William II Rufus (1056–1100) or "red" because of the color of his hair, king of England. The third son, Henry Beauclerc (1068–1135), meaning "good scholar," got money.

William II ruled England as firmly as his father had, but his cruelty made him unpopular and, in 1100, he was killed by an arrow in a hunting accident. It may well have been an assassination.

SCOTLAND

Macbeth, who had won his crown by defeating Duncan in battle, was, in turn, defeated and killed by Duncan's son in 1057. That son reigned over Scotland as Malcolm III Canmore (1031–1083). He was married to a niece of Edward the Confessor, and she was a strong influence for the continued Anglicization of Scotland and the abandonment of the Celtic rites of Christianity in favor of the Roman.

Malcolm had to go through a form of acknowledgment of the overlordship of William I and William II after the Norman conquest of England, but managed to maintain Scotland's political independence.

He died in 1093 and was succeeded by his younger brother, Donalbane (Donald the Fair), under whom Celtic Christianity made its last stand nearly six centuries after it had been introduced by the Irish monks. Donalbane died in 1098, and Malcolm's oldest son, Edgar (1075–1107), then succeeded.

HOLY ROMAN EMPIRE

After Conrad II and Henry III had succeeded in centralizing the government and establishing the Imperial dignity, there seemed a chance that the Empire might develop into a strong nation, as England and France were in the slow process of doing.

Unfortunately, however, when Henry III died in 1056, his son and heir, who reigned as Henry IV (1050–1106), was only six years old, and it was 10 years before he could wield the royal power on his own. By that time, however, the great nobles, both secular and clerical, had taken over, and the Imperial power would never again be what it was under Henry III.

Because much of the royal revenue had been appropriated by the nobility, Henry IV tried to use the Church as a source of money. By selling Church offices, he could get the resources he needed. The Church, however, was against this; it would not allow "lay investiture." It did not want laymen (and even the Emperor was a layman in the eyes of the Church) to appoint Church officials. They wanted that left entirely to the Church hierarchy—meaning, in the last analysis, the Pope.

Beginning in 1075, therefore, there was a strong conflict between Emperor and Pope over this matter of lay investiture, for the Emperor felt he could not rule without the money he could abstract from candidates for clerical posts. This further distracted the Emperor's attention from German affairs and prevented the coalescence of Germany into a nation. What was worse, Henry IV ran into the opposition of unusually strong Popes, which made the controversy even more severe.

Henry IV was aware that earlier strong Emperors had had no hesitation in forcing Popes out of office, and of engineering the election of one who would prove an Imperial puppet. Henry IV tried to do this.

The Pope, however, knew that he could excommunicate the Emperor and absolve the nobility from any allegiance to him. The Pope tried to do that.

Henry IV's move didn't work, while the Pope's did, for Henry's nobility were only too anxious to rise against him. Henry IV, in danger being overthrown by his nobles, dashed over the Alps into Italy in mid-winter to where the Pope was staying at a castle in Canossa in northern Italy. On January 21, 1077, the Emperor presented himself to the Pope as a penitent in the snow. He waited three days, and the Pope had no choice but to accept the penitence and declare the nobility to be on their allegiance again. Although it looked as though Henry IV had been humiliated, he had actually succeeded in outmaneuvering the Pope.

Henry IV continued to fight his nobles and the Pope, however; and, in 1100, the war was still continuing, to the great harm of the Holy Roman Empire.

PAPACY

At the beginning of this period, the Papacy was still weak, and the most important event was the final break between Rome and Constantinople. The two branches of the Church had been quarreling with each other periodically since the Lombard conquest of five centuries before, when the Pope had to seek help from the Franks rather than from the East Romans.

The enmity arose out of the fact that the two branches spoke different languages (Latin in the west and Greek in the east), that there was a political struggle for domination between the Latin Pope and the Greek patriarch, and that there were certain doctrinal differences that would seem tiny to most people but that loomed very large to the ideologues on both sides.

Always the continuing differences had been patched up in the name of necessary unity in the face of the overriding Muslim threat. In 1054, however, the quarrel gained so much in intensity that it seemed to each side that the Muslims were preferable to the other form of Christianity. The result was the "Great Schism." Christianity divided into the Roman Catholics (whose influence spread over all of western Europe from Spain to Poland) and the Greek Orthodox (whose influence spread over the Byzantine Empire and Russia). The division has never been healed to this day.

In 1056, there was a turning point. Henry III died, and the Imperial power decreased. And in Rome, a dynamic monk named Hildebrand (1020–1085), became the power behind the throne for several of the Popes of the period. He took advantage of a child Emperor and of the growing Imperial weakness to increase the power of the Papacy.

By 1061, Pope Alexander II (d. 1075) was elected without Henry IV having been given any role to play (he was still only 11 years of age at the time). Alexander II was a friend of William of Normandy and blessed his enterprise of conquering England.

In 1073, Hildebrand himself was elected to the Papacy, taking the name of Gregory VII. It was his notion that the Pope was the final court in Christendom; that the Pope could not err; that all secular princes, including the Emperor, owed the Pope allegiance; and that the Pope could depose kings and emperors at will.

No Emperor could endure such claims, and the Emperor Henry IV and Pope Gregory VII fought each other until Gregory's death in 1085. The war continued under Gregory VII's successors.

SOUTHERN ITALY

During this period, southern Italy was divided between the Duchy of Benevento, which was a last remnant of the Lombards, who had invaded Italy five centuries before, and the lands still farther south that were controlled by the Byzantine Empire. The Lombards and Byzantines fought each other, and there was enough confusion to make it possible for adventurers to rise to the heights.

The sons of Tancred of Hauteville, a Norman knight, made their way to southern Italy and proved excellent leaders of mercenary forces. The best of them was the fourth son, Robert (1015–1085), who has been known in history as Robert Guiscard ("Robert, the Clever").

Robert's feats paralleled those of his contemporary, William of Normandy, and the two were the most capable of the Normans. In some ways, Robert was even more remarkable, in fact. Where William was the leader of the best-organized land in western Europe, Roger was merely the leader of a rag-tag mercenary band. Nevertheless, Roger defeated both the Lombards and the Byzantines.

The last of the Lombard power was wiped out by him, and when he took Bari in the Italian heel in April 1071, the Byzantines lost their last foothold in Italy, five and a third centuries after Belisarius had invaded the land. This meant that all of southern Italy transferred its religious allegiance from Constantinople to Rome. This further exacerbated Constantinople's anger with Rome and made it more nearly impossible to heal the Great Schism.

Robert made friends with the Papacy, and allied himself with Pope Gregory VII against the Emperor Henry IV. In 1084, in fact, Robert Guiscard drove the Emperor out of Rome and sacked the city. This created so much anti-Papal feeling in Rome that Robert had to rush Gregory out of the city and keep him in his own capital of Salerno till Gregory died.

Robert Guiscard spent the last part of his life campaigning across the Adriatic in the Balkan peninsula, but died in 1085 before he could completely destroy the Byzantine Empire.

Robert's youngest brother, Roger (1031–1101), was sent to Sicily to see if he could take it from the Muslims. It took 30 years, but by 1091, the Muslims were totally evicted from Sicily, two and three-quarter centuries after they had first entered it. In 1090, Roger also took Malta from the Muslims.

By 1100, Roger was recognized as Roger I, king of Sicily, and all of Sicily and southern Italy were under Norman domination. The region then came to be as efficiently ruled as was England under the other conqueror, William.

The island of Sardinia represented another loss for the Muslims, for it was taken by the Italian city-state of Pisa in 1052, after having been in the hands of the Muslims for three centuries.

Some time in this period, crossbows came into use and gave the bow and arrow a greater range and penetration than it had ever had before. It fired slowly, however, as the stiff bow had to be cranked into a state of required tension.

FRANCE

During this period, France was ruled by Philip I (1052–1108), who came to the throne in 1060. He increased the strength of the central government against the resistance of the great feudal barons, but throughout his reign, he was overshadowed by Normandy, which was, in theory, part of his kingdom, but which was, in fact, independent and usually at war with him.

MOORISH SPAIN

The Almoravids from Africa won a victory over the Christians in 1086, but that was of little real use to the Moors for the Almoravids used their victory to make Moorish Spain part of their African empire.

CASTILE

Alfonso VI the Valiant (1040–1109) had come to the Castilian throne in 1072. In the early part of his reign, he advanced into Moorish territory. When he took Toledo in central Spain, the Moors called in the Almoravids. That stopped the Christian expansion for a time. Helping Alfonso VI at times was Rodrigo Diaz de Vivar (1043–1099), known as "El Cid" ("the lord"). He helped only at times, for he consulted his own interests and sometimes fought on the side of the Moors. Even so, he became the national hero of Christian Spain.

PORTUGAL

In west-central Spain, the city of Coimbra was captured from the Moors in 1064 by Ferdinand I of Castile (1018–1065), sometimes called "Ferdinand the Great," and it was organized as a county. By 1100, it had formed the nucleus of the present nation of Portugal.

POLAND

Under Boleslaw II the Bold (1039–1081), who began his reign in 1058, Poland had some spectacular successes. Boleslaw's army penetrated into Russia as far as Kiev, and a relative was placed on the Russian throne. The turbulent Polish nobility drove Boleslaw from the throne in 1079, however, and his younger brother Vladislav I chose the quiet life. By 1100, Poland was back within its borders.

RUSSIA

After the death of Yaroslav the Wise, Russia went through a period of disintegration, during which it was all it could do to fight off the Patzinaks and Cumans on the east and the Poles and Hungarians on the west.

HUNGARY

After a long period of weakness following the death of Stephen I, Laszlo I (1040–1095) came to the Hungarian throne in 1077. He initiated a push southwestward which, by 1100, had carried Hungarian control to the Adriatic seacoast, taking over what are now called Croatia and Bosnia. He also expanded into Transylvania in the east and found it to his interest to support Pope Gregory VII against the Emperor Henry IV.

SELJUK TURKS

Tughril Beg, who headed what had become a Seljuk Turkish empire, entered Baghdad in 1055 and was given the title of Sultan ("ruler") by the Caliph, who still held his state in that city although he was utterly powerless.

In 1063, Tughril Beg died and was succeeded by his nephew, Alp Arslan (1030–1072). Alp Arslan inherited one of the aims of Tughril Beg, which was to crush Fatimid Egypt and bring it back into the Sunnite fold. Fatimid Egypt had weakened greatly since the death of al-Hakim, and the conquest seemed a feasible project.

Alp Arslan cleared his rear by taking over Georgia and Armenia south of the Caucasus and then prepared to march against Egypt in 1071. However, a Byzantine army was moving to retake Armenia, and in August, 1071, Alp Arslan met that army at Manzikart in eastern Asia Minor. He smashed the Byzantines in what was a catastrophic defeat for them, and overran most of the interior of the peninsula which was, for a time, called "Rum" (that is, "Rome").

Alp Arslan died in a minor skirmish in 1073 and was succeeded by his son, Malik Shah (1055–1092), who was the greatest of the Seljuk Turks. His Persian vizier, Nizam al-Mulk (1019–1093), whom he had inherited from Alp Arslan, was an administrator of genius.

Malik Shah was not interested in war, but expanded his realm by diplomacy, eventually controlling virtually all the Muslim territories in Asia. He was the strongest Muslim ruler since Mamun two and a half centuries earlier.

Malik Shah was interested in literature and science, built mosques in his capital of Isfahan, and patronized Omar Khayyam, who wrote poetry and (being a mathematician as well as a poet) reformed the calendar. Under his rule, there was peace and religious toleration.

In 1090, however, a Shiite fanatic, Hasan Sabbah (d. 1124), founded a terrorist group dedicated to the murder of enemy leaders. It was hard to fight them for those entrusted with the task of murder were fanatical enough to believe they would enter heaven as a result and were not the least concerned with whether they would be caught and slaughtered in their turn. It was thought that they were fed hashish to increase their disregard of death and were therefore called "hashishim" ("hashish eaters"). This was distorted to "assassin" and political murderers have been called assassins ever since, while the murder itself is an assassination. The Assassins took over a mountain stronghold and the leader was, therefore, known as the "Old Man of the Mountain."

From then on, there began a reign of terror against Sunnites. Nizam al-Mulk was assassinated in 1091 and Malik Shah died a natural death in 1092. As happened so often after the death of a strong leader, Malik Shah's four sons fought each other for the throne and, in the process, the Seljuk Empire fell apart.

BYZANTINE EMPIRE

In 1056, the last of the Macedonian line died. She was Theodora (980–1056), a niece of Basil II, and it was in her reign that the final break came between Rome and Constantinople.

In the decades that followed, nothing but disasters struck the Byzantines. The Normans in southern Italy put an end to Byzantine dominion there. The Seljuk Turks took Armenia. The Cumans poured into the Balkans and were driven back only with difficulty.

In 1068, Romanus IV Diogenes (d. 1071) became the Byzantine Emperor. He had to face the hostility of the Byzantine nobility who hated the new Emperor more than they did any of the enemies outside the realm.

When Romanus IV marched eastward to recapture Armenia, he had a demoralized and divided army under him. At the Battle of Manzikert against the Seljuk Turks, which the Byzantines ought to have won, a number of Byzantine officers deserted and the Byzantine army was defeated with great slaughter. It was the worst military defeat suffered by the Byzantines, or their Roman predecessors, since the Battle of Adrianople seven centuries before.

The interior of Asia Minor was permanently lost; and, since this was the source of the best fighting men in the Byzantine Empire, it ceased being a world power. From that moment on, it could exist only by appealing for help to the nations of the west.

Even this might not have helped, considering that the much-weakened Empire continued to involve itself in intrigues and internal disorders. Not until 1081 did a strong and determined Emperor come to the throne. This was Alexius I Comnenus (1048–1118), who began a process of reform and conciliation. Even he had all he could do to hold off complete defeat.

Robert Guiscard was in what had once been Epirus and had defeated the Byzantines there. The Byzantines were defeated also by the Cumans, who (like so many before them) reached the walls of Constantinople but could not pass them.

The deaths of Robert Guiscard and Malik Shah helped the Byzantines, but even so Alexius was forced to ask for help from the west.

CRUSADES

West Europeans had long made pilgrimages to Palestine, even when it was under Muslim rule. The Muslims, more tolerant than the Christians of the day would have been had the position been reversed, allowed it. However, when the Seljuk Turks took over Palestine with a new Muslim fanaticism, conditions worsened, and atrocity stories abounded. These stories were spread by Peter of Amiens (1050–1115), usually called "Peter the Hermit," and sentiment began to build for the rescue of Palestine.

Urban II (1035–1099) had been trained at Cluny and had become Pope in 1088. He continued Gregory VII's policy of diehard opposition to the Emperor and the insistence on the independence and the supremacy of the Pope. He could see that the Papacy's moral force would be greatly increased, and its pretensions would more nearly be accepted, if it got behind a popular movement such as war against the Muslims.

What's more, it was clear that the endless fighting among the feudal barons in western Europe was ruinous, and often resulted even in the destruction of churches and monasteries. It seemed a practical endeavor, too, for Sicily and Sardinia had recently been freed from the Muslims and the Christian power in Spain was advancing against the Moors there. Why not, then, channel this surplus fighting energy into a war to defeat the Muslims in Asia?

When Urban II received Alexius I's appeal for help, he held a meeting at Clermont in south central France on November 26, 1095, and called for a war against the Muslims in the east. This came to be called a *crusade*, from the Latin word for "cross" (by way of Spanish), because those who promised to go east pinned crosses to their garments to show the religious nature of their determination.

What followed was the "First Crusade." It included masses of peasantry led by Peter the Hermit. They were totally ignorant of what they were doing, attacking inoffensive Jews, pillaging the lands they crossed, and being attacked in self-defense by those living there. A number of them finally flooded into Constantinople, and the horrified Byzantines quickly ferried them into Asia Minor where the waiting Turks promptly annihilated them.

In 1096, however, more organized armies made their way eastward. They were not led by monarchs (who happened to be excommunicated by the Pope at this time) but by lesser nobles. Among the leaders was Robert Curthose, son of William the Conquerer, and Bohemund of Tarentum (1058–1111), son of Robert Guiscard.

When they reached Constantinople, Alexius was dismayed. He had wanted a select corps of mercenaries, who would fight under his banner and at his direction. Instead, he got an unruly flood of some 30,000 westerners who despised the Byzantines as effeminate heretics.

Alexius I tried to force the armies to swear allegiance to him, which they eventually did, though they had no intention of honoring it. Alexius then ferried them into Asia Minor and waited to see what would happen.

The Crusaders could not possibly have lasted long against a united Seljuk realm, but it was their good fortune that the Seljuk Empire had disintegrated, that the Fatimid Egyptians had taken Jerusalem in 1098, and that the Muslims were too busy fighting among themselves to pay much attention to the Crusaders. Even as splinters, the Muslims could take care of a peasant rabble, and they almost took care of the Crusaders, too, who, in some ways, were a bit of a noble rabble.

The crusaders worked their way south through Syria and into Palestine and finally took

Jerusalem on July 15, 1099, after a five-week siege, under the leadership of Godfrey of Bouillon (1060–1100). They subjected the inhabitants of Jerusalem to a barbarous massacre and set up a feudal kingdom.

WEST AFRICA

The Almoravids attacked Ghana in 1076 and sacked its capital city. Ghana declined thereafter. Other states in the area were converted to Islam. One, notably, was Mali at the bend of the Niger River.

CHINA

During this period, Sung China was under the influence of a great reformer and idealist, Wang An-Shih (1021–1086), who was also a great writer. He cut the budget, and, at the same time, raised the salaries of officials to promote honesty. He fostered government loans to farmers at reasonable rates of interest so that they would not be compelled to go to loan sharks. He improved and made milder the collection of taxes. He cut

the size of the army and saw that those who remained were better trained. Prices were controlled and state banks were established.

As is almost always the case, the reforms were opposed by conservatives who had profited by the injustices the reforms were attempting to correct. Inertia and tradition were on the side of these conservatives. In 1076, Wang An-Shih retired in frustration and by 1100, the reforms, though not dead, had been much weakened.

The Sung Empire was, by this time, by far the most populous nation in the world, with 150 million people.

An interesting event indicates the scientific superiority of China over the West at this time. On July 4, 1054, the light from an exploding star in the constellation *Taurus* reached the Earth. The star brightened to where it was two or three times as bright as the planet Venus at its brightest. For three weeks, it was bright enough to cast a shadow and to be visible in daylight. Chinese and Japanese astronomers reported the event (which we now call a "supernova") in detail, but, so low was the state of Western astronomy, no report of the phenomenon appeared in Europe.

1100 TO 1150

ENGLAND

After the death of William II, who had no children, his younger brother seized the throne, reigning as Henry I. It should have gone to William's older brother, Robert Curthose of Normandy, but Robert was not on the scene. He was returning from the First Crusade and, by the time he got back, the deed had been done.

Naturally, there was war between the two brothers, but Henry was by far the abler man and, at the Battle of Tinchebray in Normandy on September 28, 1106, he won. Robert was imprisoned for the rest of his long life and Henry I ruled over both England and Normandy.

Henry I built a strong, though repressive, gov-

ernment, but all was ruined when his only son died at sea in 1120. Henry I had a daughter, Matilda (1102–1167), and he forced his barons to swear allegiance to her. After Henry I died in 1135, however, the barons would not allow a woman sovereign and rallied to Stephen (1097–1154), who was Henry I's nephew. There followed a prolonged civil war that reduced England to chaos. Stephen was a good-natured but weak king, and the barons grew in power, to the accelerating misery of the people.

A leading English scholar of the time was Adelard of Bath (1090–1150). He translated Euclid and al-Khwarizmi from Arabic into Latin, and made use of Arabic numerals.

SCOTLAND

In this period, David I (1082–1153), the youngest son of Malcolm Canmore, became king of Scotland in 1124, and the Anglicization of the county continued. David I had spent his youth in the court of Henry I, and throughout the civil war that followed, he fought on the side of Matilda against Stephen.

HOLY ROMAN EMPIRE

Henry IV died in 1106 and was succeeded by his son, who reigned as Henry V (1081–1125), and who had married Matilda of England. Henry V continued the policies of his father and kept up the fight with the Pope. Henry V was more fortunate in this respect than his father had been, for he faced weaker Popes. In 1122, the long quarrel was finally settled in a complicated compromise that would clearly not be long-lasting, for the Emperor and Pope were bound to continue to quarrel over who was the overlord of western Christianity.

Henry V died in 1125 without direct heirs. Lothair, Duke of Saxony (1075–1137) was elected as Emperor and reigned as Lothair II. He was much more subservient to the clergy than the two Henrys had been. Since he had no son, he planned to have, as his successor, his son-in-law, Henry X the Proud of Bavaria (1100–1139), who was a member of the House of Welf. Opposed were, of course, the members (by marriage) of the house to which the Henrys had belonged. They were Swabians, or Waiblingen.

There turned out to be, therefore, a continuing feud between the Welfs (on the side of Papal power) and the Waiblingen (on the side of Imperial power). This made itself felt in Italy, too, where the two sides were known as the Guelphs and the Ghibellines.

When Lothair II died in 1138, the throne went to Conrad III (1093–1152), who was a nephew of Henry V and, therefore, a Swabian. One of his castles in Swabia was known as Staufen, so Conrad III was the first Emperor of the house of Hohenstaufen, all of whom were to be tightly wedded to the notion of Imperial domination.

Conrad III was not a very successful monarch, as it happened. He had to fight with the Welfs, which meant confusion, and he went off crusading, which left the Empire to even further chaos.

In this period, however, the Germans were expanding eastward. (This was the "Drang Nach Osten"; or "the push to the east.") It was led by such men as Albert I the Bear (1100–1170), who carried out raids against the Wends, a Slavic people who lived east of the Elbe River. Albert established the city of Brandenburg east of the Elbe and became the first Margrave of Brandenburg.

PAPACY

The Popes, in this period, were not strong. Indeed, the strongest religious leader of the time was a monk named Bernard (1090–1153), who, in 1115, had become the abbot of Clairvaux, a monastery about 60 miles north of Dijon.

Bernard of Clairvaux was a reformer, whose force and eloquence made it possible for him to admonish kings and popes and to be listened to when he did. He might easily have been Pope himself, but he preferred to remain an abbott.

Bernard was a mystic, and was opposed, as a theologian, by Peter Abelard (1079–1144), who was a charismatic teacher at the University of Paris. Abelard was an unrelenting logician and insisted that theological matters be solved by reason.

Abelard had a famous love affair with Heloise (1098–1164), a pupil of his. He married her but kept the fact secret to avoid hampering his clerical career. Heloise's uncle had Abelard castrated in reprisal.

Bernard was far more powerful than Abelard and continued to denounce him. If Abelard had not died in 1142, Bernard would undoubtedly have seen that a trial which was in progress would have ended with the condemnation and execution of Abelard.

NORMAN ITALY

Roger II (1095–1154), a son of Roger I who had conquered Sicily, became Count of Sicily in 1105 and gained the title of King in 1130. Through shrewdness and ability, he made Sicily more prosperous than it had been since Roman times a thousand years before. He extended his rule over parts of southern Italy, and even captured the island of Corfu and established his power over much of what is now Tunisia. He had a Central Mediterranean Empire, which he ruled with toleration, for most of his subjects were Muslims and Greek Orthodox Christians.

Intellectual life was vibrant. The presence of Muslim scholars helped in the translation of many Greek classics from Arabic to Latin. Alchemists in southern Italy, working in the Arabic tradition, learned how to distil alcohol and how to form weak nitric acid. A medical school was founded in Salerno, the first of its kind since the disintegration of the West Roman Empire six centuries earlier.

NORTHERN ITALY

Northern Italy was developing a system of city-states of a type not seen since the days of ancient Greece, 15 centuries earlier. The city of Pisa on Italy's west coast was, at this time, rather impressive as a trading center and for the fact that it had seized control of the islands of Corsica and Sardinia.

Florence, in the interior, about 50 miles east of Pisa, had been recognized as a city-state in 1138, and farther north there were prosperous cities such as Genoa, Modena, Mantua, Parma, Padua, Bologna, and, especially, Milan. The merchants formed a middle class in these cities such as was not to be found as powerful elsewhere in western Europe just yet.

Venice, particularly, grew rich and powerful in these times, because its control of the Adriatic Sea made it essential in carrying crusaders (and goods) eastward and then westward. It also succeeded in establishing trading bases throughout the eastern Mediterranean, making it commercially powerful almost in the modern sense.

Important schools were springing up in northern Italy, including, notably, a law school at Bologna.

FRANCE

Louis VI (1081–1137) was the son of Philip I, and came to the throne in 1108. He was called both Louis the Fat from his appearance, and Louis the Wide-Awake from his behavior. He indulged in no far-flung adventures, but concentrated on consolidating his power over his own lands, weakening and limiting the feudal rulers, and supporting the growing middle class, the townspeople and merchants. He felt that they would, in turn, support a central monarchy as a way of opposing the oppression of the local nobility.

Louis also picked his advisers from the lower nobility, from the clergy, and from the townsmen, avoiding the great nobles who had strength of their own, for he wanted those who helped him to depend on him alone for safety and power.

His most important minister was an abbot named Suger (1081–1151), who strongly encouraged Louis VI in the path he had chosen and who lived long enough to serve as an adviser to Louis VI's successor as well. Suger also encouraged the development of a new type of cathedral structure, which concentrated the weight of the building on certain outside buttresses of masonry, thus allowing the wall itself, which did not have to support the weight, to be pierced by numerous windows. In this way, the cathedral could be built very tall and the interior could be filled with light.

Those who clung to the old ways called these new-style structures "Gothic" in derision (meaning they were barbaric), but these same Gothic cathedrals became the glory of their times and have not lost their luster since.

Louis VI died in 1137, and his son, Louis VII the Young (1120–1180), succeeded. He was only 16 at the time, but he had Suger to advise him. He married Eleanor of Aquitaine (1121–1204), who was then only 15, and it seemed a marriage made in heaven. Aquitaine was the southwestern portion of France, the most cultured part, with a mild climate. It was the haunt of troubadours who sang of love and chivalry. Aquitaine had picked up the notion of tales of love and romance from the Arabs and the troubadours introduced it to Europe.

All might have been well if Louis VII had not been pushed into the crusading movement by Bernard of Clairvaux (over Suger's strong objections), and if Queen Eleanor had not thought that Crusades would be romantic. By 1150, when he had returned from the Crusade, which had been a disaster, Louis VII found his life and his marriage darkened.

MOORISH SPAIN

The Almoravids, who had saved Moorish Spain from the advancing Christian states, had become soft. Another Berber tribe, the Almohades, had taken over their North African empire and had been invited into Spain in 1145. Once again, resistance to the Christians in the north stiffened.

CASTILE

Alfonso VII (1104–1157) succeeded to the throne of Castile in 1126 and, for a while in the 1140s, he actively resumed the southern drive, but that only succeeded in bringing in the Almohades, and Alfonso VII was stopped.

In Spain, as in Sicily, there were Moslem scholars who made it possible for the great Greek classics to be translated from Arabic to Latin. Gerard of Cremona (1114–1187) worked in Toledo and translated Aristotle, Ptolemy, Hippocrates, Galen, and Euclid. He and other translators finally brought as much of Greek science and culture as had survived to the attention of western Europe, and this began an intellectual recovery after six centuries of darkness.

PORTUGAL

Portugal was under Afonso Henrique (1109–1185) at this time. He managed to establish the independence of the country from Castile. He called himself king in 1143, and both Castile and the Pope were forced to recognize his royal title. By 1147, he had taken Lisbon, which eventually became the capital of Portugal.

ARAGON

Aragon, a region east of Castile, was ruled by Alfonso I the Battler (1073–1134) at this time. He managed to unite his kingdom with the neighboring regions of Navarre and Catalonia; and, by 1150, the Christian nations of Spain were three in number: Portugal on the west, Aragon on the east, and Castile, the largest, in the center.

POLAND

Boleslaw III Wry-Mouth (1085–1138) became king of Poland in 1102. Under him, Poland had another period of expansion. Boleslaw struck northward against the Pomeranians (a Slavic tribe) and forced them to accept Christianity. Poland, by annexing much of Pomerania, reached the Baltic Sea. Boleslaw died in 1138, however, and by 1150, his weaker successors were pushed eastward by the German "drang nach Osten."

RUSSIA

Vladimir II (1053–1125) became ruler of Russia in 1113, and spent most of his reign in fighting the Cumans, who were now at the peak of their strength, with their realm stretching from the Aral Sea to the borders of Hungary.

BYZANTINE EMPIRE

Under Alexius I Comnenus; under his son, John II Comnenus (1088–1143), who became Emperor on Alexius' death in 1118; and under John's son, Manuel I Comnenus (1122–1180), the Byzantine Empire had a last pale period of grandeur.

It remained weak and had to ask for help from the West now and then. Nevertheless, John II destroyed the Patzinaks, who were, however, merely replaced by the Cumans. The Comneni, in general, thanks to the disruptions inflicted on the Muslims by the crusaders, were able to regain about half of Asia Minor. The interior of the peninsula remained Turkish.

Manuel I, in particular, was enamored with the west. He married a Western princess, the sister-in-law of the Holy Roman Emperor, affected adherence to the Western chivalric ideal, and even considered the possibility of religious re-union with Rome (something his subjects would never have accepted). In 1150, Constantinople was still a large and wealthy city, and the most cultured in Europe.

CRUSADES

The establishment of the "Crusader States" along the eastern shore of the Mediterranean, in Palestine and Syria, was intolerable to the Muslim world. It was only a matter of time before some strong leaders would emerge to unify the Muslims (to a degree, at least) and begin a counterattack. In 1144, Zangi of Mosul (1084–1146) captured Edessa, the northernmost of the Crusader States.

The news of this shook western Europe, and Bernard of Clairvaux took the lead in preaching the necessity of another Crusade. Louis VII was attracted to the idea, and his wife, Eleanor of Aquitaine, was even more attracted, seeing it as a chance for romance and for the troubadour ideals of adventure and chivalry. She insisted on going along with all the court.

The Emperor Conrad III also decided to go crusading and, in 1147, two armies, a French and a German, marched eastward by separate routes. Unlike the First Crusade, this Second Crusade was led by monarchs.

Both armies reached Constantinople. The German army moved directly into the interior of Asia Minor, where it was destroyed by the Turks, although Conrad III got back to the Empire safely. The French army marched along the Asia Minor sea-coast, which was still Byzantine, but, in the process, Louis VII lost all his zeal for fighting. He visited Jerusalem but made no move to reconquer Edessa and, in 1149, went back to France.

If the First Crusade had been high drama, the Second was farce.

CHINA

In 1114, the Khitan Mongols in northern China were overthrown by another group of tribal people, who took over the northern provinces and came to be known as the Chin Dynasty. The Sung Dynasty continued in the south.

About this time, the magnetic compass came into use in sea-voyages, and, by 1150, gunpowder may have actually been used in battle (to frighten horses by the noise of the explosion). Neither discovery was reasonably nor properly exploited.

1150 TO 1200

ENGLAND

The civil war between Matilda and Stephen ended in 1153. Stephen was weary and near death, and his only son had just died. He asked only that he be allowed to remain on the throne till his death. This was granted him and he died the next year.

Matilda did not assume the throne. After the death of her first husband, the Emperor Henry V, she had married Count Geoffrey of Anjou (1113–1151), a French province to the south of Normandy. By him, she had a son, who assumed the throne in England, Normandy, and Anjou as Henry II (1133–1189) on Stephen's death.

Eleanor of Aquitaine, who now despised Louis VII, thanks to his failure in the crusade, had divorced him. He was glad to see her go even if it meant losing Aquitaine, since she had given him only daughters and he was sick of her sharp tongue. Eleanor, as though to do maximum harm to Louis, married Henry II of England at once. (She was 30 and he 19.) This meant that Henry II added Aquitaine to his dominions. He claimed Brittany, too, so that in addition to England, he ruled over three fifths of France. For the French provinces, to be sure, he accepted the overlordship of the King of France but he didn't take that too seriously. His dominions made up the "Angevin Empire" (from "Anjou").

Eleanor did for him what she had not been able to do for Louis. She gave Henry sons, two of whom survived their father. However, Henry II couldn't abide her sharp tongue any more than Louis could, but he had a better trick than divorce. He kept her in prison from 1173 to 1185.

Henry II's father, Geoffrey, was sometimes known as Geoffrey Plantagenet, because he is supposed to have worn a broom plant ("planta genet") in his bonnet when he went on a pilgrimage. The nickname was eventually supplied to those who were in direct male descent from him so that Henry II might be considered the first Plantagenet monarch of England.

Henry II put a quick end to the anarchy that prevailed in Stephen's time, bringing the nobility to heel. He had less success in asserting supremacy over the clergy. In this, he was opposed by his old friend, Thomas Becket (1118–1170), who turned into an enemy once Henry had seen to it that he was made Archbishop of Canterbury in 1162. Henry had expected a compliant tool and, instead, he got a firm upholder of the Church.

Even so, Henry II might have won out but, in a fit of rage over Becket's intransigence, he cried out hasty words that four of his knights assumed to be orders. They assassinated Becket in 1170 and Henry, suspected of having a hand in the deed, had to do penance and back down in his attempt to dominate the English Church.

Henry II revised England's law courts, its treasury, its tax system, and did what he could to encourage trade. What he couldn't do was to control his obstreperous wife and his rather unpleasant children. The last 16 years of his reign were filled with family wars.

Henry II died in 1189 and was succeeded by his oldest son, Richard I (1157–1199). He was known as Richard Coeur de Lion ("Lionheart") and he was indeed a large, magnificent fighter, and a good general—but he was a poor king. He spent his reign in fighting and neglected his kingdom except when it was necessary to gouge money out of it. He died at last as a result of a

festering wound received in a minor battle in 1199. He was succeeded by his younger brother, John I Lackland (1167–1216).

WALES

Wales had maintained its Celtic language and culture despite seven centuries of invasions by Saxons, Danes, and Normans. It remained secure in its mountain fastnesses. Henry II made the first serious expeditions into Wales and forced its princes to accept English overlordship, but this was largely a matter of form. Wales remained Welsh.

SCOTLAND

William the Lion (1143–1214), son of David I, became king of Scotland in 1165. He was captured by the English in one of the raids that Scottish forces mounted against the English north, and was forced to accept English overlordship, but this, too, was little more than a formality. Scotland remained Scottish.

IRELAND

Ireland had remained in tribal anarchy since the Vikings had been driven away a century and a half before. Some of England's Norman barons, trying to find greater freedom than Henry II's strong rule allowed them, went to Ireland in 1169 to make their fortune (as Robert Guiscard had done a century before in southern Italy).

Henry II, not wanting an independent Norman Ireland, followed in 1171 and made sure that those sections of Ireland that were subdued remained subject to the English crown. This was done under Papal authority for, some years earlier, in 1154, Pope Adrian IV (1100–1159), who had just become Pope, and who was the only Englishman ever to achieve that post, had awarded Ireland to Henry II.

The English established themselves at first only about the area of Dublin. Other parts of Ireland remained outside the English orbit for a long time. Indeed, eventually, the Dublin area was fenced in with palings to keep out the unsubdued Irish. It is from this that the expression arose "beyond the pale," meaning "outside the accepted limits of polite society."

DENMARK

Under Valdemar I (1131–1182), sometimes called "Valdemar the Great," who became king in 1157, Denmark expanded eastward after a war with the Wends. As a result, the city of Copenhagen in eastern Denmark became more centrally located and became steadily more important.

Valdemar's successor, Canute VI (1163–1202) continued to make conquests against the Wends.

SWEDEN

Under Erik IX the Saint (d. 1160), who became king of Sweden in 1150, Sweden also expanded eastward. Raiders crossed the Baltic Sea and established Swedish dominion over what is now southwestern Finland. Erik began the process of bringing about the Christianization of the area, for which deed he was eventually made a saint.

In 1194, Scandinavian voyagers discovered Spitzbergen. This was the farthest northward point at sea yet reached by explorers.

HOLY ROMAN EMPIRE

Frederick I Barbarossa (1123–1190), or "Redbeard," was the nephew of Conrad III and succeeded him in 1152. He was the first to refer to his realm, officially, as the "Holy Roman Empire." Frederick was a capable Emperor and might have achieved much if he had concentrated on Germany. The trouble was that he inherited the quarrel of the Emperors with the Popes and he spent much of his abundant energies on expedition after expedition into Italy in an attempt to establish a domination over the Papacy.

However, not only was the Papacy hostile, and not only did the nobility inside the Empire continue to oppose the Emperor so that their own importance would grow, but, in addition, the cities of northern Italy had grown strong and

preferred a weak Emperor to a powerful one. The cities formed "the Lombard League" under the leadership of Milan, and resisted Frederick resolutely.

At Legnano, northwest of Milan, Frederick's knights met the Italian pikemen in 1176. The pikemen were foot-soldiers with long spears, a kind of throwback to the Macedonian phalanx. They stood firm and the Imperial horsemen suffered losses. The Italian cavalry then circled the Imperial forces on either flank and won the battle. It was the first time that foot-soldiers had stood up to cavalry since the Battle of Adrianople, eight centuries earlier.

Frederick I went crusading in his old age and died in Asia Minor in 1190. He was succeeded by his son who reigned as Henry VI (1165–1197). When Henry died, his son and heir, Frederick, was only three years old. A period of confusion and civil war followed, with several claimants to the Imperial throne fighting it out.

Meanwhile, though, the "drang nach Osten" was continuing. Henry the Lion of Saxony (1130–1195) founded the port city of Lubeck on the Baltic Sea, east of the Elbe River in 1159.

PAPACY

The Popes in this period were caught between the Emperor in the north and the Norman kingdom in the south, to say nothing of a partially recovered Byzantine Empire in the east. Alexander III (1105–1181), who became Pope in 1159, managed best. He organized opposition to Frederick Barbarossa, encouraged the Lombard League, and was the beneficiary of the Imperial defeat at Legnano. He also forced Henry II of England to back down from his attempted control of the English clergy by skillfully exploiting the mistake of the assassination of Becket.

The civil war in Germany gave the Papacy its best chance. With the quarreling candidates for the Imperial office unable to pay any attention to Italy, a particularly strong Pope gained that office in 1198. This was Innocent III (1160–1216), who intended to maintain the supremacy of the Pope with all the vigor at his command.

SOUTHERN ITALY

William I the Bad (1120-1166), who became king in 1154, lost the Norman possessions in Africa between 1158 and 1160 and was succeeded by his son, William II the Good (1154–1189). He in turn was succeeded by his first cousin, Tancred of Lecce (d. 1194), who was, however, of illegitimate birth. Emperor Henry VI had married Constance of Sicily (1154–1198), the sister of William I, so that Henry's son (still a baby) was also the first cousin of William I—and legitimate.

Tancred and Emperor Henry VI fought it out and, when Tancred died in 1194, Henry saw to it that his little son was crowned King of Sicily. That was the end of the independent Norman kingdom after the existence of a century, during which, thanks to efficient Norman rule, it was probably the richest kingdom in Europe.

VENICE

Venice had enriched itself from the crusades and had become a complete commercial oligarchy, with the doge elected from among the leading families. It was *not* a hereditary title.

FRANCE

Louis VII, during the second half of his reign, was completely overshadowed by Henry II of England, who controlled more of France than Louis himself did. Louis did what he could, therefore, to aid the enemies of Henry. He sided with Archbishop Becket and, even more important, he encouraged Henry's sons to rebel against him.

Louis VII died in 1180, and was succeeded by his son who reigned as Philip II (1165–1223). He was the shrewdest of the Capetian line yet to ascend the throne and the most successful monarch of his time, so that he came to be called "Philip Augustus."

He continued his father's policy of encouraging Henry's sons to rebel against him, and did it so effectively that, when Henry died in 1189, he did so in despair. Henry's successor, however, till then a friend and co-conspirator of Philip, turned enemy even as he turned king. The enmity grew more marked when both went crusading.

SPAIN

Alfonso VIII (1155–1214) became king of Castile in 1158, when he was but a child of three. Once grown, he attacked the Spanish Muslims vigorously. However, the Almohades, who were then at the peak of their strength, defeated him in 1195, so that southern Spain remained in Muslim hands as the century closed.

BYZANTINE EMPIRE

Manuel I Comnenus continued to instill some strength into the Byzantine Empire. It was his hope to reconquer the interior of Asia Minor and reverse the decision of Manzikert a century earlier.

In 1176, therefore, Manuel I led an army eastward. While his army was strung out, passing through a defile near a place called Myriocephalon, Muslims, who were waiting in ambush on the heights on either side, swooped down and destroyed it. The chance to regain Asia Minor was forever lost.

Manuel I died in 1180 and, after him, there were dynastic problems and the strength of the Empire rapidly declined. In 1195, Alexius III (d. 1211), a great-grandson of Alexius I, gained the throne by deposing and blinding his older brother, who had reigned as Isaac II (1135–1204). The hatred between opposing members of the family was stronger by far than their fears of either the Westerners or the Turks.

BULGARIA

Bulgaria, which had been subdued by Basil II nearly two centuries before, seized the opportunity that followed the death of Manuel. Two brothers, Ivan Asen (d. 1196) and Peter Asen (d. 1197), gathered forces and rose in rebellion. They called in the Cumans for help and, by 1200, there was once more an independent Bulgaria south of the lower reaches of the Danube River.

SERBIA

The Serbians were Slavs who lived west of Bulgaria along the Adriatic Sea.

In 1168, they came under the rule of Stephen Nemanya I (d. 1200), who encouraged the adoption of the Constantinopolitan form of Christianity. Thus, the Serbians became Greek Orthodox in religion, while the closely related Croats and Slovenes to their northwest became Roman Catholics.

The Byzantines had controlled Serbia since the time of Basil II, but once Manuel I died, and Byzantine power plummeted, Serbia established its independence and competed with Bulgaria for control of the northern Balkans.

Stephen Nemanya I abdicated and entered a monastery in 1196. His son reigned as Stephen Nemanya II (d. 1228) and obtained the title of king.

EGYPT

The Fatimid dynasty in Egypt came to an end in 1171, after it had been in existence for two centuries. A Kurdish Sunnite took over power. His name was Salah ad-Din Yusuf ibn Ayyub (1138–1193), commonly known in western countries as Saladin.

Very carefully, Saladin managed to unify various Muslim factions and to extend his government over Syria and northern Iraq. What he was doing was to reach the point where he could present the Crusader States with something that they had not hitherto had to face—a united Muslim region under a resolute leader.

In 1187, he was ready, and he attacked. The crusaders advanced to meet him, but forethought was never their strong point, and they managed to get themselves into a waterless area at Hattin, just west of the Sea of Galilee. Their water supply ran out and Saladin placed his troops in such a way that the crusaders could not make their way to any water source. Then, when they were suf-

fering from thirst and were exhausted, Saladin's army attacked and wiped them out.

The Crusaders were left without an army, and Saladin simply rolled up the Crusader States. He took Jerusalem itself on October 2, 1187. (Despite the Christian behavior when they took Jerusalem nearly a century before, the civilized Saladin allowed no sack.) Before long, the crusaders held only the cities of Antioch, Tyre, and Tripoli.

Saladin then fought new crusaders from the west and died in 1193, after which there were the usual dynastic struggles so that Egypt was soon weakening again.

CRUSADER STATES

Saladin's capture of Jerusalem sent a shock wave through western Europe. A new crusade, the "Third Crusade," was led by the three most powerful kings of western Europe: Frederick Barbarossa of the Holy Roman Empire; Philip Augustus of France; and Richard the Lion-Heart of England.

Frederick Barbarossa marched by land through Hungary. He reached Constantinople, where Isaac II was reigning, and crossed into Asia Minor. There Frederick, now about 67 years old, drowned in a small stream, while bathing, and his army broke up.

Philip of France and Richard of England went by sea, but they had been quarreling at home and they continued to quarrel even more bitterly while they were both engaged against the common Muslim foe.

When they arrived in Palestine, they found a crusader force laying a lackadaisical siege to Muslim-held Acre. Richard, who loved a good fight, pressed the siege with vigor and Acre fell on July 12, 1191. The flamboyant English king was joyful and arrogant over the matter, treating Leopold V of Austria (1165–1197) with great contempt. Philip of France, in a fit of overwhelming jealousy, abandoned the Crusade and returned to France.

Richard then marched southward toward Jerusalem, maintaining strict discipline, and defeated Saladin in battle. By 1192, he was within sight of Jerusalem, but Saladin had been retiring slowly and was destroying all provisions en route. Richard realized that if he laid siege to Jerusalem, with no water for the soldiers and no fodder for the horses, and with discipline becoming an increasing problem, he would be wiped out. Therefore, Richard made peace and returned to England.

At least, he tried to return. Near Vienna, he was captured by forces of Leopold of Austria, whom he had most offended at Acre. Emperor Henry VI (1165–1197), son and successor of Frederick Barbarossa, forced Leopold to disgorge Richard into Imperial custody, and then set a high ransom for his release—a ransom that had to be paid by Richard's subjects.

The Third Crusade, though it failed to recapture Jerusalem, did restore a coastal strip to the crusaders.

INDIA

Mu'izz-ud-Din Muhammad (d. 1206) ruled in Ghur (which is in what is now Afghanistan), so that he is often called Muhammad of Ghur. In 1175, he began the conquest of northern India, taking Delhi in 1193. He was the first to establish a Muslim empire in India, and this led to the spreading of Islam into northwestern India, the region now known as Pakistan.

CHINA

The Chin dynasty in the north and the Sung dynasty in the south were at war. In 1161, the Sung forces defeated the Chin by making use of gunpowder, still using it only to scare the enemy horses.

CAMBODIA

The Cambodian Empire, with its capital at Angkor, was known as the "Khmer Empire" in ancient times. Under Jayavarman VII (1120–1215), who came to the throne in 1181 and rebuilt Angkor, Cambodia reached its greatest extent and power, ruling over what is now Cambodia, Laos, and parts of Burma and Malaya. He built temples, hospitals, and highways, and stimulated the spread of Buddhism in the land.

JAPAN

Civil war raged in Japan in this period and, by 1185, the land was in the grip of military feudalism once more. At this time, Zen Buddhism was entering Japan from China.

MONGOLS

In this period, a child named Temujin (1162–1227) was born in Mongolia. From lowly beginnings, he slowly began to gather forces about himself. There was no way of telling during his youth that he was the most remarkable military leader the world would ever see. Other great conquerors, such as Alexander, Hannibal, and Caesar, had inherited armies and a long military tradition. Temujin had to create his own army and develop his own strategies, which far surpassed anything that had gone before.

NORTH AMERICA

About 1200, the Aztecs were beginning to attain power in Mexico, displacing the Toltecs.

1200 TO 1250

MONGOLS

By 1206, Temujin had united the Mongolian tribes and formed a large empire just north of China. He established his capital at Karakorum in the very center of what is now the "Mongolian People's Republic" (also known as "Outer Mongolia"). He adopted the name of Genghis Khan ("Supreme Emperor").

In 1211, Genghis Khan went to war with the

Chin Empire in northern China. He had taught himself and his generals how to move speedily and decisively in battle, how to attack the flanks and rear, and how to obstruct all escape routes. That sufficed for open battle in the fields, but there was the Great Wall, which was a formidable obstacle, and the Chinese cities themselves had strong walls. Genghis Khan had to learn from the Chinese how to develop and improve methods for laying siege to cities and for battering down walls.

By 1215, he had taken Beijing and had forced the Chin Empire to accept his overlordship. The systematic way in which the Mongolian armies destroyed cities and killed people indiscriminately frightened potential adversaries so badly that they were half-defeated before they were attacked. Cities began to give up at once when the Mongols approached. This saved lives in the long run, which may have been Genghis Khan's intention.

In 1218, Genghis Khan sent ambassadors into Persia to deal with Ala-ad-Din Muhammad, who had set up a "Khwarezmian Empire" in 1200 over Persia and stretches of central Asia to the north. Genghis Khan's purpose was to set up trade relations, but Muhammad injudiciously had the ambassadors mistreated. This was, in fact, more than injudicious, for Genghis Khan did not accept insults.

Genghis Khan had developed a system of espionage that let him know exactly what was going on in any land on his borders, where its armies were located, and what their state of readiness was. When he sent his own army into one of these lands, his troops moved on their hardy desert ponies with the accent on speed. His army moved in separate contingents over ground that had been thoroughly reconnoitered. Communication among the contingents was maintained by riders dashing to and fro between them, and they all came together at the site of battle. Nothing so speedy was seen in war before the twentieth century.

The result was that the enemies of Genghis Khan were usually attacked long before they were ready and, generally, from an unexpected direction. They tended to dissolve in panic even before they were struck.

This happened to Muhammad. News kept reaching him of rapid advances, of the spreading of unparalleled devastation, and, finally, he heard that the Mongols had *passed* him and were advancing from his rear. In a panic, he fled—and fled—and fled, as once Darius III had fled from Alexander fifteen and a half centuries before. The Mongol armies followed remorselessly, as the Macedonian armies had followed Darius. By February 1221, Muhammad had been cornered and had no choice but to kill himself. The entire Khwarezmian Empire became Mongol.

Genghis Khan then sent forces to reconnoiter the land to the west. The Mongol general, Sabutai (1172–1245), led his army west of the Caspian Sea and, in 1223, the Mongols faced a combined force of Russians and Cumans. The Mongols sent envoys to arrange peace. The envoys were killed, whereupon the Mongols attacked and wiped out the opposing army, then returned to the main Mongol concentration in Asia.

Genghis Khan spent the next few years fighting in northern China. He died in 1227. In the space of 20 years, after putting himself at the head of a united Mongolia, Genghis Khan had built an empire stretching the full width of Asia, from the Pacific Ocean to the Caspian Sea.

The conquests did not stop with the death of Genghis Khan, however. Under the reign of his son, Ogodai Khan (1185–1241), the conquest of northern China and Korea was completed by 1234, and the Mongols then attacked Sung China. This was the hardest campaign the Mongols undertook and, though they won many brilliant battles, the Sung Chinese were still doggedly resisting in 1250.

Meanwhile, however, the Mongols struck westward under Sabutai and, in December 1237, they were back in Russia. Their espionage service had given them full information concerning the land, and they had no trouble. They crossed the frozen rivers and, in a matter of months, they had hurtled through Moscow and taken over the northern part of the land.

Carefully, they consolidated their rule and then, in November 1240, they aimed at the chief center of Russian power in the Ukraine. They crossed the frozen Dnieper River, took Kiev on December 6, and destroyed it. That put an end to Kievan Russia some four centuries after it had come into existence.

Sabutai then led his armies westward into central Europe. He knew the situation there. He understood the rivalries among the various nations and the division between the Holy Roman Emperor and the Pope. He knew he could take care of the nations one at a time and that none had armies capable of standing against the well-disciplined, lightning-fast Mongols.

Europe had faced Asian nomads before. There had been the Cimmerians in Assyrian times, the Huns in late Roman times, the Avars and Muslims in Frankish times, the Magyars, Patzinaks, and Cumans in recent centuries, but never before had there been anything like the Mongols.

On March 3, 1241, the Mongols smashed a Polish army at Cracow. Panicky refugees fled westward, and the Mongol army followed. On April 9, 1241, they faced a large army consisting of Germans, Poles, and Bohemians, and wiped them out at the Battle of Liegnitz (in what is now southwestern Poland). Two days later, another Mongolian army destroyed a Hungarian army a hundred miles northeast of Budapest.

Sabutai again rested his forces while he planned a campaign into western Europe. He knew that there was nothing there that could possibly stop him, and at the end of 1241, his armies started westward. They were approaching Vienna and Venice, when the news reached him that Ogodai Khan had died. Custom decreed that the armies return so that a successor could be elected. The armies streamed back through the Balkans, annihilating Serbian and Bulgarian armies, almost without having to slow their gallop.

They never returned to central Europe. To the central Europeans, the Mongols were like an unbearable lightning bolt that had flashed and gone. It was, however, the death of a Mongol ruler far in the east, and nothing the Europeans did, or could have done, that had saved them.

Ogodai was succeeded by Mangu Khan (1208–1259), a grandson of Genghis Khan, and he ruled over an Empire that included northern China, Mongolia, central Asia, Persia and Russia—and that was still expanding.

ENGLAND

In 1200, John I was ruling over England and over an Angevin Empire that was still intact. John I, however, was neither a successful warrior nor diplomat, and he was facing the shrewd Philip Augustus of France. By 1204, John had lost all the provinces of northern France, even Normandy, although portions of Aquitaine in southwestern France remained English. Thus, the Angevin Empire had lasted only half a century, but its disappearance had advantages for England. The barons, who had always had strong ties to their estates in Normandy and elsewhere in France, now found their holdings to be mostly English, and had to turn their attention to England.

John did not, of course, give up the provinces easily. However, he was weakened by fighting the clergy at a time when the Pope was the unprecedentedly strong Innocent III. John was excommunicated in 1209 and had to give in, accepting the Pope as overlord—merely a form of words, of course. Furthermore, he was defeated by Philip of France at the Battle of Bouvines in northeastern France on July 27, 1214. After that, there was no hope of recovering the lost provinces.

John's defeats at the hands of the Pope and of the French led to an uprising of the barons and, on June 15, 1215, John was forced to sign the "Magna Carta" ("the Great Charter"), which guaranteed the rights of the nobility, and of freemen generally, against encroachment by the arbitrary power of the crown. Among other things, John had to agree that there would be no taxation without the agreement of a council of barons; and that there should be no arrests, or imprisonment, or punishment, without trial. The king of England did not generally pay much attention to the Magna Carta, but it was always there to appeal to, and it set a precedent that was eventually to have its effect.

John died in 1216, and his nine-year-old son succeeded as Henry III (1207–1272). Henry III was a weak king, dominated by the clergy, and the fight against arbitrary acts by the king or his ministers continued.

Among the English scholars of the time was Alexander Neckam (1157–1217), who first brought the magnetic compass (known for a long time in China) to the attention of the west.

Robert Grosseteste (1168–1253) brought Byzantine scholars (from an Empire which had been shattered by crusaders) to England to translate Aristotle from the original Greek, bypassing the possible errors in the Arabic versions.

The University of Oxford, which had been founded on the model of the University of Paris a half-century earlier, yielded an offshoot in 1209 that became the University of Cambridge.

SCOTLAND

Alexander II (1196–1249) became King of Scotland in 1214. He sided with the English barons against King John of England, since a weak English king meant that he would not have to admit English overlordship.

HOLY ROMAN EMPIRE

Frederick (1194–1250), the son of Emperor Henry VI, was not yet three years old when his father died, and others disputed the Imperial throne. Frederick's mother, however, was Constance of Sicily (1154–1198), the daughter of Roger II, who had ruled over Sicily and southern Italy. Constance took her son to Sicily, where he was crowned King of Sicily and placed under the protection of Pope Innocent III.

In 1198, Otto IV (1174–1218), of the Welf family, had been recognized as Emperor, but Otto was defeated (along with John of England) at the Battle of Bouvines by Philip Augustus of France. In 1215, Otto IV was forced to abdicate, and Frederick, now 20, ruled over Germany as well as Sicily. He was crowned Emperor in 1220 and

reigned as Frederick II, though, as far as possible, he continued to live in Sicily.

Under Frederick II, the struggle with the Papacy continued. Frederick was forced to go crusading by an excommunication, but did it in his own style. The fight with the Pope continued after Frederick returned from Palestine, and the Pope did not hesitate to encourage Frederick II's son to rebel against his father.

The quarrel was at its very height when the Mongol attack devastated eastern and central Europe. The Mongols were, in fact, encouraged to make their attack by their knowledge of the turmoil in the Empire. It was only Ogodai's death that kept both Emperor and Pope from having to face these undefeatable tribesmen.

On the whole, the Papacy was winning when Frederick II died in 1250. The long fight that had begun with Henry IV, one and three-quarter centuries earlier, had broken the Imperial strength. From then on, even when the Empire was under a strong ruler, it remained subservient to the Pope.

Frederick II, throughout his reign, encouraged the intellectual life and, being virtually an atheist, found himself as much at home with learned Jews and Muslims as with learned Christians. He spoke many languages, wrote poetry, kept a private zoo, and, about 1245, wrote a book on falconry that was first-rate natural history. He founded the University of Naples in 1224.

The most famous scholar at his court was Michael Scot (1175–1235). He translated Arabic commentaries on Aristotle, which contributed greatly to building an understanding of Aristotelianism in the West. Elsewhere in Germany, Albertus Magnus (1193–1280) was perhaps the greatest scientist of his times. He was particularly interested in mineralogy and was the first to describe arsenic exactly.

TEUTONIC KNIGHTS

The Teutonic Knights were a military order of knighthood that had begun in the Crusader States. Their activities were transferred first to Hungary, where they fought the Cumans, and then (in 1225) to the Baltic Sea coast, where they served as the sharp edge of the German "drang nach Osten."

Under the patronage of the Emperor Frederick II, they fought the Prussians, a Baltic people, who were slowly Christianized and Germanized. German towns were founded all along the southern shore of the Baltic Sea. Riga was founded in 1201, while Koenigsberg and Memel were founded soon after 1250.

The Mongols passed to their south and the Teutonic Knights escaped the nightmare of having to withstand them. However, they did receive a temporary check in 1242, when they were defeated by Russian forces on Lake Peipus on the eastern border of what is now Estonia.

PAPACY

This was the "high noon" of the Papacy. Innocent III, under whom the Papacy reached its peak of power, consolidated his hold on the Papal States, bullied kings and Emperors, and encouraged the Crusading movement, not only against the Muslims in western Asia, but against heresies in Europe.

About this time, too, two orders of "friars" ("brothers") were founded, which served as useful tools of the Catholic hierarchy, bringing religion closer to the people, especially in the growing towns. There were the Franciscans, who followed the teachings of Francis of Assisi (1182–1226) as early as 1209; and the Dominicans, who followed the teachings of Domingo (Dominic) de Guzman (1170–1221) as early as 1215.

Honorius III (d. 1227) became Pope on Innocent III's death in 1216. He had been tutor to young Frederick II, and he was willing to crown him Emperor and to permit him to unite Sicily and southern Italy to the Empire. He kept urging him to go on a crusade.

In 1227, Gregory IX (1170–1241) became Pope. He was a nephew of Innocent III and, although friendly to Frederick II at first, he had lost patience with him for always managing to find an excuse not to go on a crusade. He excommunicated Frederick, who then went on a crusade. The feud between them, however, continued and grew ever worse as the Dominicans turned

out to be a strong anti-Imperial force. Gregory IX died in 1241, even as the Mongols were racing through central Europe.

Two years later, when the Mongol threat had receded, Innocent IV (d. 1254) became Pope, and carried on the fight against Frederick II.

VENICE

In this period, Venice also reached the peak of its power when it perverted the Crusading movement into an attack on the Byzantine Empire rather than the Muslims. The Mongols were advancing toward their city when the death of Ogodai pulled them back.

The greatest Italian mathematician of the period was Leonardo Fibonacci (1170–1240), whose explanation and use of Arabic numerals finally began the process of having them replace the much clumsier (but time-honored) system of Roman numerals.

FRANCE

Philip II Augustus of France had established his power over the northern portion of his kingdom by defeating John of England and the Emperor Otto IV at the Battle of Bouvines. Southern France, however, remained semi-independent and continued its pleasant Provençal culture, complete with poetry and troubadours. It had also become the home of religious reformers who opposed clerical corruption, preached lives of poverty and virtue, and believed in the existence of a principle of evil equal in power to that of the principle of good. (This was a "Manichaean heresy.")

It was taken up by much of the southern nobility who saw in anticlericalism a way of confiscating church lands for their own benefit.

The reformers were called Waldensians because they followed the teachings of Peter Waldo (d. 1218), and Albigensians, because they existed in large numbers in the town of Albi in southern France.

Innocent III was horrified at the reform movement in southern France. When Philip II refused to risk moving south, because he felt the main danger lay in England and the north, Innocent preached a crusade against the southern heretics. The northern French nobility, seeing the chance for loot, moved southward, and Philip II did nothing to stop them.

What followed was a bitterly cruel war, an example of how terrible wars of religion could be. After all, if someone didn't believe as you did, he could easily be considered a slave or a willing ally of the Devil and, therefore, need not be treated with even the most rudimentary humanity. There is a story that Simon de Montfort (1165–1218), who led the northern crusaders, was asked, on the taking of a town, how the heretics were to be distinguished from the true Catholics. Montfort said, "Kill them all. God will know his own."

As a result of this crusade, Provencal culture was largely destroyed and southern France (except for those portions still ruled by England) came under the domination of the King in Paris.

Philip II died in 1223, after a reign of 43 years, and was succeeded by his son, who reigned as Louis VIII (1187–1226), and who continued the takeover of the south.

He was succeeded by his son, who reigned as Louis IX (1214–1270). Louis IX was only 12 years old when he reached the throne, but he was brought up by a capable mother, Blanche of Castile (1188–1252), who trained him to be virtuous. By and large, he was, and, after his death, he was canonized, so that he became "Saint Louis."

He was very religious, of course, and shared in the heightened fear of heresy that had arisen as a result of the crusade in southern France. Pope Gregory IX gave the Dominican friars the special task of sniffing out heresy and dealing with it, and this was the beginning of the notorious "Inquisition," which did so much to discourage freedom of thought and to fasten conformity on the minds of the people. Louis IX supported the Inquisition and was also markedly anti-Semitic.

He was still on the throne when the Mongols were ravaging central Europe, but France felt nothing of the distant alarm.

SPAIN

The climax of the long fight for the Christian reconquest of Spain came on July 16, 1212, when Alfonso VIII of Castile defeated the Almohades smashingly at the Battle of Las Navas do Tolosa in southeastern Spain. Ferdinand III the Saint (1201–1252) continued the advance and took Cordoba (Abd er-Rahman III's capital) in 1236 and Seville in 1248.

Muslim strength in Spain was broken and they retreated to the southern corner of Spain just north of the Strait of Gibraltar. There, Spanish Islam survived as the "Kingdom of Granada."

POLAND

Poland was cut off from the Baltic Sea by the conquests of the Teutonic Knights. It was also devastated by the Mongol invasion, after which it became more open to German penetration from the west.

HUNGARY

Andreas II (1175–1235), who became King of Hungary in 1205, had a genius for failure. His extravagance ruined the finances of the kingdom and enabled the great nobles to force him in 1222 to yield them power. In 1217, he went crusading to Acre in Palestine, but accomplished nothing. As though that weren't enough, Hungary was devastated by the great Mongol raid of 1241.

BULGARIA

Bulgaria reached a peak of strength under Ivan Asen II (d. 1241), who became king in 1218, and who expanded his realm to include all the northern Balkans from the Black Sea to the Adriatic Sea. Soon after he died in 1241, however, the Mongols passed through the land on their way back to Mongolia. Bulgaria staggered and went into decline.

RUSSIA

Poland, Hungary, and Bulgaria, though they had felt the force of the Mongol blows, saw them leave forever. They could recover. But not so Russia. The Cumans had been destroyed and disappeared from history. So had Kievan Russia.

In their place was the "Khanate of the Golden Horde," a Mongol state with its capital at Sarai, on the lower Volga. The Mongols were a new aristocracy that levied tribute on the Russians.

Only in the far north did the Russians themselves retain some sort of control. There Alexander (1220–1263) was the military commander of the forces of Novgorod from 1236. He recognized that resistance to the Mongols was worse than useless, and he forced the Novgorodians to pay tribute to them. He labored to prevent any insurrections against them and, as a result, the Mongols treated him with respect and allowed the north Russians to rule themselves (except for paying tribute).

Alexander showed that he could face other enemies successfully. In 1240, he defeated the Swedes at the Neva River (near where Leningrad now stands) and from then on he was known as Alexander Nevski ("Alexander of the Neva"). In 1242, he defeated the Teutonic Knights in a battle on the ice of Lake Peipus, on the eastern border of Estonia.

Despite these local successes, Russia was in decline and, as long as they remained under the Mongol yoke, they also remained unaffected by the winds of change in western Europe, something which has dictated the course of Russia's history ever since.

BYZANTINE EMPIRE

A new crusade had been preached by Innocent III in 1202, and the Venetians agreed to ferry an army to the Crusader States on certain conditions. They wanted the crusaders to take Zara on the Dalmatian coast. It was a possession of the King of Hungary and the Venetian doge, Dandolo (1107–1205), who was 95 at the time and blind to boot, wanted it as a trading base for Venice. The crusaders didn't want to do it, but they couldn't get to Palestine otherwise.

Meanwhile, the Byzantine Empire was in the throes of civil war, and Alexius (d. 1204), the son of one of the competing candidates for the throne, appealed to the crusaders for help. Dandolo insisted that help be given because he could see advantages in it for Venice. The crusaders agreed and arrived at Constantinople in 1203. That meant they were *inside* those enormous walls.

The crusaders installed Alexius as a puppet Emperor and, when the city rebelled, the crusaders sacked it brutally on April 12, 1204. Constantinople fell to foreigners for the first time since it had been founded by Constantine nearly nine centuries before.

Uncounted cultural treasures were destroyed. Ancient Greek literature had still been intact there, though it had been destroyed everywhere else. The crusaders destroyed it in Constantinople, too, and most of the classical heritage of ancient Greece was forever lost.

The Byzantine Empire broke up into fragments. A "Latin Empire" was set up with its capital at Constantinople and with Baldwin of Flanders (1172–1205) as the Emperor. In theory, it controlled Greece and the regions around Constantinople, but different parts of it were under the control of different crusaders and the Latin Emperor did not have much power.

Venice took the island of Crete and all the islands rimming Greece west and east, besides having trade concessions within the Latin Empire. Thus, Venice reached the peak of its power and, when Dandolo died in 1205, he was buried in Constantinople.

The Byzantines salvaged a few fragments themselves. They ruled the "Empire of Nicaea" in northwestern Asia Minor and the "Despotat of Epirus" in what is now Albania. There was also the "Empire of Trebizond" along the southeastern shore of the Black Sea.

Bulgaria retained its position in the northern Balkans.

All the fragments of the Byzantine Empire, whether Byzantine or Latin, were now minor powers at best.

CRUSADER STATES

The Crusade, which was diverted against Constantinople and which, instead of weakening the Muslims, had destroyed the Christian power that had been Europe's bulwark against the Muslims for five and a half centuries, is usually considered the "Fourth Crusade." There was also the "Albigensian Crusade" in southern France at this time. In addition, there was a "Children's Crusade" in 1212, in which a large contingent of children from France and Germany swarmed southward, imagining that they could recapture Jerusalem. Some of them reached Marseilles, where unscrupulous seamen took them on board and sold them into slavery.

At the urging of Innocent III, another contingent of crusaders set forth in 1218. This was the "Fifth Crusade." They planned to go to Egypt and capture a base there from which Palestine could then be attacked. They captured the Egyptian port of Damietta in 1219 and the Egyptian rulers offered to give the crusaders Jerusalem in exchange for the captured city. The crusaders refused, marched on Cairo, met with disaster, and had to leave, having neither gained Jerusalem nor kept Damietta.

In 1228, came the "Sixth Crusade" by the Emperor Frederick II. He saw no point in fighting since he felt no holy impulse to slay the infidel. Instead, he negotiated with them. In 1229, he persuaded the Muslims to cede Jerusalem, Bethlehem, Nazareth—all the Holy Places—to the Crusader States, together with a corridor to the coast and a promise of peace.

However, the religious leaders among the Christians opposed a peaceful solution bitterly, especially since Frederick II was opposed by the Pope. Hostilities continued, therefore, and the Muslims took Jerusalem once again in 1244.

This brought Louis IX into the field. He led the "Seventh Crusade" to Egypt and there was an almost comic repetition of the disastrous Fifth Crusade. Damietta was taken, the march to Cairo was a disaster, and, by 1250, the French army was destroyed and Louis IX was a prisoner.

1250 TO 1300

MONGOLS

At this time, the Mongolian Empire was the one superpower of the world. Every other nation was a minor power in comparison. Even the Sung Empire of China was finally subdued and absorbed in 1279.

In 1260, Kublai Khan (1215–1294), a grandson of Genghis Khan, was ruler of the vast Empire. He made his capital at Shang-tu ("Xanadu" to Europeans) and, adopting Chinese culture, he became a Chinese Emperor.

During his reign, the Mongols invaded what is now northern Vietnam in 1237 and fought there, on and off, for 30 years, without making a permanent conquest.

Meanwhile, in western Asia, the Mongols had defeated the Turks, and established a khanate there under Hulagu (1217–1265), a younger brother of Kublai Khan. In 1256, the Mongols destroyed the sect of the Assassins who had kept the Sunnite Muslims of the region in terror for a century and a half. The Mongols simply swarmed up the various mountain fastnesses and wiped out everyone they found there.

In 1258, the Mongols took Baghdad and put a final end to the Abbasid Caliphate, which had existed for five centuries, albeit it had been entirely powerless for the last four of them. The Mongols also deliberately destroyed the intricate canal system that had kept the Tigris–Euphrates valley a rich agricultural area for some 5000 years.

(The Mongols showed some signs of constructive thinking, too, for Hulagu Khan sponsored the construction of a large and, for its time, well-equipped astronomical observatory in north-western Persia.)

The Mongols went on to penetrate Syria, but in 1259, Mangu Khan died, and the main Mongol armies had to return to Mongolia again. A relatively small contingent, without Hulagu, was left to face an Egyptian army that far outnumbered them. At Ain Jalut in Palestine, near Nazareth, the Mongols were badly defeated. Though the defeat was not a disastrous one for the Mongols, it did destroy their reputation for invincibility, and was, in fact, their first definite defeat in their half-century career of conquest.

In 1274, and again in 1281, Mongol fleets attempted to invade Japan. In both cases, landings were made and the Mongols won some victories, but then had to leave because typhoons threatened to destroy their fleets. The Japanese called these storms "kamikaze" ("divine winds").

The Mongol Empire reached its limits then in its failure to subdue Syria, Indochina and Japan, but even so it was the largest contiguous empire the world had yet seen.

Stretching, as it did, from central Europe to the Pacific, it allowed free passage of ideas and, to some extent, of trade and travelers over the huge expanse of Asia. This facilitated the passage of technological knowlege from China to Europe —in particular, gunpowder.

During the reign of Kublai Khan, a Venetian merchant, Marco Polo (1254–1324), with his father and uncle, traveled the width of Asia and stayed at the Mongol court from 1275 to 1295. On his return, Polo wrote a book in 1298 that described his travels, and the wealth and power of the regions he visited. Though many disbelieved him, his descriptions were accurate, and they brought to Europe a vision of a civilization richer and more advanced than their own.

Kublai Khan died in 1294, and a grandson, Timur Khan (1267–1307), succeeded him. Under him the Empire was still intact but he held power only over China. The outer portions, which were under other Mongolian descendants of Genghis Khan, became virtually independent.

EGYPT

Egypt had successfully resisted the Fifth and Seventh Crusades, but it had sunk low since the days of Saladin a half-century before. The Egyptian rulers remained in power by the help of a personal bodyguard of slaves, the Arabic word for which was "Mameluks."

Almost inevitably, as was the case of the Turkish bodyguard of the Abbasid Caliph four centuries earlier, the Mameluks grew more powerful.

One of the Mameluk generals was Baybars (1223–1277), and it fell to him to defend Egypt against the Mongols. It was he who won the Battle of Ain Jalut. Thereafter, his prestige was such that he had no difficulty in having himself crowned Sultan. Like Saladin before him, he then swept up the Crusader States so that by 1268, only a few strong points remained in crusader hands.

ENGLAND

Henry III of England was weak and incompetent, and engaged in expensive and unsuccessful foreign ventures. He also ignored the provisions of the Magna Carta, so that the barons and the middle classes grew more and more discontented. A "Great Council" was established in 1258, therefore, whose agreement had to be obtained before the King could make important decisions.

This Great Council developed into Parliament. Leading the reform group was Simon de Montfort (1208–1265), the son and namesake of the Frenchman who had led the crusades in southern France. In 1265, he summoned a Council that consisted of two knights from each shire, and two burgesses (property-owning citizens) from each town. This was the first Parliament worthy of the name.

The conservatives were led by Henry III's capable son, Edward (1239–1307). In 1265, Edward and Montfort fought a battle in which Montfort was killed. Edward took over the government and, when Henry III died in 1272, Edward succeeded as Edward I. (As it happened, Edward was off crusading when his father died, so he was not actually crowned till 1274.)

At that time, Wales still had princes and a Celtic language of its own, and still maintained a certain independence, eight centuries after the Saxons had entered the land and begun to drive the Celts westward. Llywelyn (d. 1282), the native prince of Wales, had sided with Montfort and had done what he could to weaken the English crown. In 1282, he was at open war with England.

Edward I led his army into Wales and won. Llywelyn died in battle and his brother, David, was executed. Welsh independence was at an end and, in 1284, when a son was born to Edward I, that infant was made the Prince of Wales. Ever since then, the eldest son of a reigning British monarch has been known by that title.

In the course of the war, Edward I became aware of the deadliness of the "long bow," which was a weapon as tall as a man and that required a hundred pounds of pull to draw it back to the ear. If that could be done, it shot arrows with extraordinary force and quickness. Edward I adopted the weapon for his own army.

In 1290, Edward I expelled the Jews from England. They had been useful as moneylenders to the king, for Christians (in theory) were not allowed to engage in that business. The north Italians were doing so, by now, in fine disregard of Church teachings, so the Jews were no longer needed.

In the latter part of his reign, Edward I was deeply engaged in attempting to establish English domination over Scotland.

The most important English scholar of the period was Roger Bacon (1220–1292), who upheld the principle of *experimental* science. He attempted to write a universal encyclopedia of knowledge, suggested the Earth might someday be circumnavigated, pointed out the deficiencies of the Julian calendar then being used, worked on optics, and may have invented spectacles. He was the first westerner to mention gunpowder.

In England, and elsewhere in Europe, mechanical clocks (powered by slowly falling weights) were coming into use at this time. They were not more accurate than the best water-clocks, but they were far less messy, and gradu-

ally they became the typical timepieces in the town churches.

SCOTLAND

Alexander III (1241–1286) had become King of Scotland in 1249. He had gotten rid of the last Norsemen in the islands off the coast of Scotland, and defeated an attempted invasion by Haakon IV of Norway (1204–1263).

Alexander had married the daughter of Henry III, and was therefore Edward I's brother-in-law. Alexander's daughter, Margaret, had married Eric II of Norway (1268–1299), who had mounted the throne in 1280. Margaret had a daughter by him, another Margaret (1283–1290), and when Alexander died in 1286 (his horse ran off a cliff for some reason), his three-year-old granddaughter was the only heir left him.

This child was the first cousin (once removed) of Edward I's son, Edward, the Prince of Wales (1284–1327), and the two were betrothed. The idea was that once they were married, they might have a son who would then rule over both England and Scotland. However, when Margaret ("the maid of Norway") was sent by ship from her home in Norway to Scotland, she died en route. Now who was to rule Scotland?

There were various claimants, but the two most important were descendants of David I, who had ruled Scotland a century and a half before. One was John Baliol (1249–1315), and the other was Robert Bruce (1210–1295). Edward I was asked to make the decision and chose Baliol, feeling he would be the more subservient to England. Baliol was crowned in 1292, but was not subservient enough. Edward I invaded Scotland in 1296, defeated Baliol, drove him out of the country, and declared himself King of Scotland.

William Wallace (1270–1305) led a Scottish rebellion against Edward I, however. Wallace's forces were badly defeated on July 22, 1298, at the Battle of Falkirk in central Scotland. Edward I used the deadly longbow for the first time on this occasion. Even so, Wallace continued to fight a guerrilla war that kept the English off balance.

SICILY

When Frederick II died in 1250, his son reigned as Conrad IV (1228–1254). The Papacy, which had fought so strenuously against Frederick II, was determined that no one of his line would rule the Empire. They made war against Conrad and he was never able to establish himself as Holy Roman Emperor, up to the time of his death in 1254.

Another son of Frederick II, Manfred (1232–1266), who was illegitimate, struggled to gain the rule over southern Italy and Sicily at least. He won some successes, but the intransigent Pope Urban IV (1200–1264), offered the crown to Charles of Anjou (1226–1285), a younger brother of Louis IX of France.

Charles accepted, invaded southern Italy and defeated Manfred, who died in battle in 1266. The son of Conrad IV, Conradin (1252–1268), then tried and, at the age of only 15, also died in battle against Charles of Anjou. That left, as the only descendant of the Hohenstaufens, Constance, the daughter of Manfred, and therefore the granddaughter of Frederick II.

Charles of Anjou was not a popular king, however. He brought in French officials who lorded it over the Sicilians and he moved his capital to Naples, calling himself King of Naples. In 1282, therefore, in the Sicilian capital of Palermo, a revolt broke out on March 30, 1282 at the hour of vespers. Some 2000 French were massacred and the occasion was called "the Sicilian Vespers."

Constance, Frederick II's granddaughter, had married Pedro III of Aragon (1239–1285), sometimes called "Pedro the Great." The Sicilians called Pedro III to rule over them. He defeated Charles and became King of Sicily. However, the great days of Naples and Sicily, which had flourished under the Normans and under Frederick II, were over.

VENICE

In this period there was a prolonged contest between Venice and Genoa. Marco Polo, after he had returned from China, was taken prisoner by the Genoese in the course of the war and, while in prison, he dictated his book of travels to a fellow-prisoner.

In northern Italy, Taddeo Alderotti (1223–1295) was the most important physician in western Europe, writing commentaries on Herodotus, Galen, and Avicenna.

PAPACY

The Popes, in this period, were deeply involved in the politics of southern Italy and of Sicily, and their main effort involved their struggle against the descendants of Frederick II.

In 1294, however, Boniface VIII (1240–1303), became Pope. He, like Gregory VII and Innocent III, believed the Pope ought to be supreme in Christian Europe (and in the whole world, once everyone had accepted Catholic Christianity).

The Popes had defeated the Holy Roman Empire, and Boniface VIII had nothing to fear in either Germany or Italy. He had, however, the misfortune of facing strong kings in both England and France, and they refused to give in to Boniface VIII's claim of supremacy.

Nevertheless, in 1300, Boniface VIII declared a "Great Jubilee" and Rome was filled with celebrants. Enormous sums of money were collected and the Papacy reached its highest pitch of apparent power.

In this period, also, Thomas Aquinas (1225–1274) had built a philosophic structure that successfully combined Aristotelian philosophy and Catholic theology. He applied careful reasoning to the process and this helped rehabilitate the value of reason, which had so long been subordinated to faith. His system remains the basis of Catholic doctrine to this day.

CASTILE

In 1252, Alfonso X the Wise (1221–1284), became King of Castile. With him, the reconquest continued with the capture of Cadiz in 1262; however, by and large, the war with the Muslims sputtered in low gear for a while. The long struggle had helped ruin Spanish agriculture and had converted Spain into a land of soldiers who were keenly aware of the Christianity they had so long fought to preserve and extend. This laid the groundwork for the military excellence and religious intolerance that was to come.

Alfonso was noted for his scholarship and his encouragement of learning, for the schools he founded, and for the law codes he sponsored. He wrote poetry, studied alchemy, and was therefore granted his cognomen, which not many rulers earned.

He is most famous for sponsoring the publication of a new formulation of planetary motions based on the Earth-centered astronomy of Hipparchus and Ptolemy. The necessary mathematics was so complicated that Alfonso is supposed to have remarked that if God had asked his advice, he would have recommended something simpler. (He was right, for the true structure of the planetary system *was* simpler.) A crater on the Moon, "Alphonsus," is named in his honor.

Alfonso's reign was not successful, politically. He was forced to make concessions to the nobility and to debase the coinage. His attempts to gain territory were not successful. He was succeeded in 1284 by his son, Sancho IV (1258–1295), and then by his grandson, Ferdinand IV (1285–1312).

ARAGON

Under James I the Conqueror (1208–1276), who became King of Aragon in 1214, Aragon completed its part of the reconquest with the capture of the Valencian coast by 1245. While doing so, Aragon also reached across the sea to take the Balearic Islands between 1229 and 1235. This was the beginning of an Aragonese Empire in the western Mediterranean.

The Empire was extended by Pedro III, who took over Sicily. (Aragon had fought for a long time to free itself from foreign domination, but had no hesitation, when opportunity offered, to impose its domination on others. This is a common trait of virtually all nations.)

Pedro's son, Alfonso III the Generous (1265–1291), succeeded to the throne in 1276. He was forced to grant wide privileges to his nobles, as Alfonso X of Castile and, for that matter, John of

England had had to do. In fact, Alfonso III's concessions are called "the Magna Carta of Aragon." In 1291, Alfonso's younger brother, James II (1264–1327), became King. In 1295, he allowed a still younger brother to reign as Frederick II (1272–1337), King of Sicily, while James took over Corsica and Sardinia.

The Aragonese alchemist, Arnold of Villanova (1235–1311) was the first to notice that wood burning with poor ventilation gave rise to poisonous fumes (carbon monoxide). He was also the first to prepare pure alcohol.

PORTUGAL

Afonso III (1210–1279) became King of Portugal in 1248 and, in his reign, final victories over the Muslims were achieved and Portugal gained its present borders (now unchanged in seven centuries). He was succeeded in 1279 by his son, Diniz the Worker (1279–1325), who encouraged agriculture and commerce and who, in 1294, initiated a long-term treaty with England. Even more important, he encouraged ship-building, with the help of experts from Venice and Genoa and began Portugal's sea-going traditions. He founded the University of Lisbon, which later moved to Coimbra.

FRANCE

Louis IX died in 1270, while he was engaged in the Eighth Crusade (his second), one that was even more foolish and wrong-headed than his first one. He was succeeded by his son, who reigned as Philip III the Bold (1245–1285), who, in turn, was succeeded by his son in 1285, who ruled as Philip IV the Fair (1268–1314).

Philip IV was a strong king on the style of Edward I of England, and a sense of nationhood ("nationalism") grew strong in both kingdoms. Indeed, a rather inconclusive war was waged between the two monarchs. In the course of it, Philip IV made a treaty with Scotland in 1295, based on mutual antagonism toward England, and close relations between the two powers were to continue for a long time.

More important was a growing conflict between Philip IV and Pope Boniface VIII. In 1296, Boniface VIII had forbidden any rulers to tax the clergy without papal consent. This would cripple French finances, and Philip IV, in retaliation, imposed an embargo on the export of precious metals—which would cripple Papal finances.

The quarrel was growing steadily worse.

In 1269, a French scholar, Peter Peregrinus described his experiments with magnets (which were an example of the experimental method Roger Bacon was advocating). Peter Peregrinus studied magnetic poles and the manner in which these attracted and repelled each other. He showed how a magnetized needle, pivoted on a card with a graduated circular scale, could be used to tell direction at sea. This laid down the technological background for the forthcoming age of exploration.

HOLY ROMAN EMPIRE

After the extinction of the Hohenstaufen line, so little was the title of Emperor thought of, that 15 years (the "Great Interregnum") passed before any Emperor was named. During that period, the affairs of the Empire were allowed to drift; however, in 1273, Rudolf of Hapsburg (1218–1291) was finally chosen as Emperor Rudolf I.

Rudolf was a minor figure of the aristocracy and was chosen chiefly in order to prevent Ottakar II of Bohemia (1230–1278), sometimes called "Ottaker the Great" from reaching the throne. Under Ottakar, Bohemia had expanded and had become an important power. However, Bohemia was the one Slavic area of the Empire, and the German population did not like the thought of a Slavic Emperor.

Ottakar did not give up the possibility of the Imperial title tamely, but he was defeated. He retained his core provinces of Bohemia and Moravia, but Austria, which was to their south and which he had briefly controlled, was taken over by Rudolf for his own family. It was with Austria that the Hapsburgs were thereafter identified.

Rudolf gave up all claim to Italian territory and was subservient to the Pope. From this time on, in fact, there was no further quarrel of note between Emperor and Pope. The Papacy had won.

After Rudolf's death, there was another squabble over the title, but by 1298, Rudolf's son, Albert I (1235–1308) was Holy Roman Emperor, having fought off the claims of Adolph of Nassau (1250–1298) to the title.

SWITZERLAND

The Great Interregnum that followed the end of the Hohenstaufens made it possible for some parts of the Empire to achieve greater independence of the central authority. The people of the Alps Mountains, in what is now known as Switzerland, were in good position to do this, for it was hard to invade the mountains and the people of Switzerland could carry on a firm and effective guerrilla war in a territory in which they were at home and an invader was not. In 1291, three cantons, Uri, Schwyz (from which Switzerland gets its name), and Unterwalden formed a confederation designed to defend their independence.

HANSEATIC LEAGUE

Many northern German towns, plus a few in Sweden, Denmark, and England, formed a commercial league in this period. The "hansas" or "guilds" of the various artisans of the cities made the agreement, which was called, therefore, the "Hanseatic League." They controlled trade in the Baltic and North Seas and were, for a time, an important commercial power.

TEUTONIC KNIGHTS

The Teutonic Knights, in this period, were firmly in control of Prussia and had penetrated the Baltic States (the modern Estonia, Latvia, and Lithuania). The Knights were busily converting the Lithuanians, the last pagan people of Europe.

BOHEMIA

On the death of Ottakar, his son, Wenceslas II (1271–1305), became king in 1278. Under him, Bohemian power receded somewhat but it was still the most important state in the region, for

Poland and Hungary had not yet recovered from the Mongol incursion.

RUSSIA

Russian continued prostrate under the Golden Horde, but Moscow, near the northwestern limits of the Golden Horde's realm, was beginning to recover somewhat.

BYZANTINE EMPIRE

The fragments of the old Empire continued to be weak, but in Asia Minor, Michael Paleologus (1224–1282) gained power as the Emperor of Nicaea. He was an able man and might have done much had he lived a few centuries earlier. As it was, he managed to retake Constantinople in 1261, and reigned as Michael VIII. Once again, after a half-century hiatus, a Byzantine Emperor reigned in Constantinople. The city and the Empire were only a shadow of what had been, and would steadily lessen as a power. Nor did Michael regain everything. Parts of Greece still belonged to western adventurers, and the islands still belonged to Venice.

Michael VIII realized he could not keep his throne without help from the west. In his desperate search for that help he even went so far as to promise that the Empire would reunite with western Christianity and would accept the domination of the Pope. He agreed to this in 1274, but after his death in 1282, the people forced Michael's son, Andronicus II (1260–1332), to rescind the union. To the bitter end, the Byzantine people would accept neither the Pope nor Roman Catholicism.

CRUSADER STATES

The Eighth Crusade was conducted by Louis IX, who was joined by Prince Edward of England (later to be Edward I). The crusaders landed in Tunis in 1270, but Louis IX died soon afterward and nothing was accomplished. After that, further crusading ventures that were occasionally attempted were largely futile.

The last Christian stronghold in Palestine was Acre, and when it fell in 1291 (a century after Richard the Lion-Heart had taken it) the Crusades were over. Two centuries of effort had ended in no territorial gain.

However, the crusaders had encountered a more advanced civilization than their own. They brought back sugar and silk and many other products (including new methods of fortification), and taught Europe to covet Eastern luxuries and skills.

1300 TO 1350

ENGLAND

In 1305, Edward I finally captured the Scottish rebel, William Wallace, and had him executed. He then prepared for another campaign to force Scotland into the English orbit, but died in 1307, even as he was marching northward.

His son and successor, who reigned as Edward II (1284–1327), was an indolent king, who wanted only to enjoy himself. He had favorites to whom he granted money and power, thus antagonizing the barons generally.

Meanwhile, Robert Bruce (1274–1329), grandson and namesake of the claimant to the Scottish throne in Edward I's time, had taken over Scottish leadership and had virtually driven English forces out of the land. Only the castle of Stirling in central Scotland remained in English hands, and it was under siege. Edward II was forced to lead an army into Scotland to relieve it, but many of the disaffected barons would not go with him.

The two armies met at Bannockburn, a few miles south of Stirling. Edward II, with no sense of tactics, arranged his army so that his longbowmen had no chance to fire properly. Without the deadly arrows supporting them, the English cavalry was thrown back by the Scottish pikes and, in the end, the English were completely defeated. The Battle of Bannockburn was the only major battle the Scots won over England, but it was enough. Scottish independence was assured.

The defeat made Edward II more unpopular than ever. His wife, Isabella (1292–1358), hated him for neglecting her. (Edward II was homosexual, for one thing.) Isabella and her lover, Roger de Mortimer (1287–1330), forced Edward II to abdicate in 1327, and then saw to it that he was mistreated and murdered in prison soon after.

His son, 15 years old, reigned as Edward III (1312–1377). By 1330, Edward III took matters into his own hands, hanged Mortimer, kept his mother confined, and began his personal rule.

Edward III had to acknowledge Scottish independence, but France was constantly encouraging Scotland to invade England, while the French king did his best to take over such English territory as still existed in southwestern France since the time when the Angevin Empire had been established two centuries before.

In 1338, England and France went to war over rivalries that included Edward III's claim to be the rightful King of France. The result was what came to be called "The Hundred Years War."

Edward won a great naval battle at Sluys off what is now the coast of the Netherlands. The French fleet was destroyed, which gave the English control of the English Channel and made it possible for Edward III to bring an English army into France at will.

Edward III took advantage of this ability and did bring an army into France. He met a much more numerous army at Crecy, in northeastern France, on August 26, 1346. The French heavy cavalry, however, were undisciplined and—although wearied by their march—overconfidently prepared to charge. The English had carefully arranged their line, with the longbowmen given every opportunity to shoot freely.

The French had no experience with the longbow. They had crossbowmen, who could shoot as powerfully as the longbowmen, but much more slowly. The longbowmen could send five arrows forward while the crossbowmen were sending one. On top of that, the haughty French knights wouldn't even give their crossbowmen a chance, but rode them down in their foolish desire to ride at the English line.

The result was that the French were riddled and smashed with longbow fire, while there was very little damage to the English. There had been victories of foot-soldiers over cavalry in recent fighting, but this was the first case in which the victory was so devastating. The thousand years of cavalry domination of the battlefield, since the Battle of Adrianople, was done with. The foot-soldier had won back his importance. Since heavy cavalry was the fighting tool of the aristocracy, who alone could afford the horses and armor, it meant that the feudal aristocracy was beginning its decline, while the common man was to grow more and more important.

Edward III had some primitive "bombards" at Crecy, the earliest cannon. They only served to help frighten the French horse, but they were a portent of things to come. Gunpowder had been picked up from China by way of the Mongols, but the Europeans were not content merely to explode it. They instantly began to devise metal cannon from which the force of gunpowder could hurl a heavy cannonball. They were inventing a kind of chemically powered catapult, which would lend a new violence to warfare.

Edward III, after his victory at Crecy, went on to take Calais, on August 4, 1347. It was just across the narrowest part of the English Channel and could be used as a convenient base for raiding France. Meanwhile, Edward's son, who was Edward, Prince of Wales (1330–1376), set up his base at Bordeaux in the southwest. This region still belonged to England as part of the heritage of Eleanor of Aquitaine two centuries earlier. The Prince of Wales (who, in later history, was called "the Black Prince," supposedly because of the black armor he wore) was thus able to raid France from its other extremity.

Meanwhile, in China, there had arisen a new strain of the Plague, perhaps as early as 1333. It was called "the Black Death" and was the most deadly epidemic known to have befallen humanity in historic times. It was brought to Europe in 1347 by a Genoese ship that had been trading in the Crimea. The still-surviving remnant of the crew of the ship was barely alive and from them the disease began to spread rapidly through Italy and then through other parts of Europe as well.

It worked rapidly. Within 24 hours of the first symptoms, death might follow. It was the greatest single disaster that was ever known to have struck humanity, for in the space of a few years it may have killed up to a third of the population of Europe, and perhaps done equal damage, if not more, in Africa and Asia.

As the population dropped, a labor shortage made the common man more important, and this was another blow to the aristocracy. Social structures broke down under the strain, and mysticism rose. The use of distilled liquor, supposed to prevent the disease (or make one care less), came into fashion, and alcoholism fastened itself on Europe to an extent that never again fully receded. The Church suffered, too, since the educated minority died as quickly as the illiterate.

The oddest aspect of this tragedy is the light it sheds on human stupidity. While France and England each suffered immensely from the Black Death, the war between them went on without thought of cessation.

However, the life of the mind also goes on. The greatest English scholar of the period was William of Ockam (1285–1349). He is best known for "Ockam's razor"—the dictum that of two explanations that account equally well for a particular phenomenon, that one is to be chosen that begins with the fewer assumptions.

SCOTLAND

Robert I Bruce, the victor at Bannockburn, died in 1329 and was succeeded by his son, David II (1324–1371), who was incompetent. He attacked England while Edward III was off in France, but he lost the Battle of Neville's Cross in northern England on October 17, 1346 (the longbowmen again). David II was taken prisoner and was not released for 11 years.

IRELAND

The English hold on west central Ireland weakened in this period, partly because England's attention was entirely on France, and partly because the Black Death caused havoc among the English in Ireland, as well as among the Irish. The Irish became more unruly, and the English hold more precarious.

FRANCE

Philip IV (as will be explained shortly) defeated the Papacy, as the various Emperors from Henry IV to Frederick II had notoriously failed to do. He was not all-powerful, however.

He quarreled with England over Flanders, a district which was along the coast of what is now Belgium and northeastern France. Flanders was economically tied to England, which produced wool that Flanders wove into cloth.

The French wanted the prosperous Flemings (the inhabitants of Flanders) more under their control, so a French army of heavy cavalry entered Flanders to bring that about. They attacked the Flemish foot-soldiers at Courtrai in what is now northwest Belgium on July 11, 1302.

The heavy cavalry found itself impaled on the pikes of the steady Flemings and were massacred. This was an even better example of the victor of infantry over cavalry than the Battle of Legnano had been a century and a quarter earlier, but was not as spectacular as the the Battle of Crecy, which would take place nearly half a century later.

For one thing, the victory was partly due to the fact that the Flemings had carefully chosen a boggy area and the French knights were too stupid to understand that their horses would be stuck in the mud. Two years later, in a battle that wasn't on boggy ground, it was the French who beat the Flemings.

Despite the Battle of Courtrai, Philip IV, when he died in 1314, left France at a peak of power. His oldest son, Louis X the Stubborn (1287–1316), ruled for two years and died in 1316, leaving only a daughter. He was the first French king since Hugh Capet, three and a third centuries earlier, to die without having a son to succeed him. However, his wife was pregnant. A national council decreed that only a male descended from males could inherit the French throne, so everyone waited for the Queen to deliver. It was a son who was, in theory, John I, but he died at the age of five days.

Philip IV's second son then ruled as Philip V the Tall (1294–1322). He died in 1322, leaving only two daughters. Consequently, Philip IV's third son ruled as Charles IV the Fair (1294–1328). When he died, in 1328, he left only a daughter. With him, the direct Capetian line came to an end three and a half centuries after Hugh Capet had been crowned.

Now who would become King of France? Philip IV had had a younger brother, Charles of Valois (1270–1325), who had a son, Philip of Valois (1293–1350). Philip of Valois was the son of the son of Philip III and became king as Philip VI the Fortunate. He was a member of the House of Valois, but he was still descended from Hugh Capet.

To this, Edward III of England objected. Philip IV's daughter, Isabella, was Edward III's mother. He was more closely related to Philip IV than Philip of Valois was, and the fact that Edward III's descent was through a woman was unimportant in his eyes. The restriction of the French throne to descent by males had only been formulated after Philip IV's death, specifically to exclude Edward III from the throne. The French, however, did not want an English king, whatever arguments in his favor might exist.

That was one of the reasons for the beginning of the Hundred Years War. Having lost at Sluys, at Crecy, and at Calais, Philip VI (scarcely "Fortunate") died in 1350, with France in a shambles.

CASTILE

Alfonso XI (1311–1350) became King of Castile in 1312. For one last time, the Moors in the south called on African warriors for help. Alfonso defeated them in 1340, and that was the last attempted African penetration of Europe. From then on, the tide flowed the other way. Alfonso XI died in 1350, while laying siege to Gibraltar.

During this period, Aragon was involved with affairs in southern Italy, and Portugal was involved in dynastic problems.

PAPACY

Boniface VIII's arrogance reached megalomaniac heights in 1302. He issued a bill, entitled "Unam Sanctam," in which he made the most imperiously possible claim to being superior to all Christian rulers, and to be, in effect, ruler of the Earth, responsible only to God.

Philip IV, who didn't fear God, let alone the Pope, sent a henchman, Guillaume de Nogaret (1270–1313) to Rome. With the help of some Roman opponents of the Pope, Nogaret penetrated the Pope's bedroom in his summer palace at Anagni in 1303. Nogaret threatened Boniface with death, took him prisoner, and tried to force him to resign. Boniface didn't resign and faced down all threats with resolution. Nogaret finally fled, fearing a Roman mob, but Boniface VIII died soon after, on October 11, 1303, apparently of humiliation.

He had found that the new national states like England and France would not bow to him, and that their people would rather cling to their kings than to a foreign Pope. After Boniface VIII, therefore, the Popes might still have spiritual force and might still be able to work through sympathetic secular rulers, but they could never again claim true power over the nations.

Boniface VIII was succeeded by Benedict XI (1240–1304), who died within a year. Then Philip VI managed to maneuver a Frenchman to the Papacy. He reigned as Clement V (1260–1314) and was a French puppet.

He gave his consent, for instance, to Philip IV's brutal suppression of the Knights Templar (which had begun as an order in the Crusader States and had grown into an extremely rich institution when its members began to serve as moneylenders and businessmen). Philip IV coveted their money. After he had destroyed them by false accusations and torture, he expropriated their funds. He also stripped the assets of the Jews in France, and then sent them into exile in 1306.

Clement V avoided the hostile Roman mobs by taking up residence in 1309 in the city of Avignon on the Rhone River in southeastern France. It was a Papal possession but was surrounded by French territory. Clement V appointed enough French cardinals to make sure that additional French Popes would succeed him. He was indeed succeeded by John XXII (1245–1334) in 1316; Benedict XII (d. 1342) in 1334; and Clement VI (1291–1352) in 1342. All were French and all were puppets of the French king, even when that king was laid low by English victories.

VENICE

In this period, Venice was still warring with Genoa over which was to control trade with the east. For a while, Venice was getting the worst of it, and Genoa was at the height of its power.

MILAN

After the Battle of Legnano, Milan grew prosperous and became the chief commercial city of Lombardy, in north-central Italy. In 1312, the Visconti family gained control of the city.

The first mechanical clock to strike 24 hours of equal length during the day (disregarding the changes in length of daylight and darkness in the course of the year) was installed in a Milan church in 1335.

Elsewhere in northern Italy, the medical school at Bologna was flourishing. One of its graduates was Mondino de Luzzi (1275–1326), who finally took up anatomy where it had been left off by Galen eleven and a half centuries before. He actually did his own dissections and, in 1316, wrote the first book in history to be devoted entirely to anatomy. It had its errors, but it was by far the best treatment of the subject up to that time.

FLORENCE

In central Italy, roughly halfway between Milan and Rome, Florence was struggling to gain strength and territory. This was hampered by the continuing in-fighting between the leading fami-

lies of the city. However, it was becoming the cultural leader of Italy and of Europe.

Dante Alighieri (1265–1321) wrote *The Divine Comedy*, which was completed in 1321. It was the first great and enduring work of literature to be written in one of the new languages (in this case, Italian) that had grown out of Latin. As Dante founded Italian poetry, Giovanni Boccaccio (1313–1375) founded Italian prose, writing short stories that were, and remained, world-famous. Francesco Petrarca (1304–1374), usually known in English as "Petrarch," wrote sonnets, while Giotto di Mondone (1276–1337), usually known, like Dante, by his first name, was a great architect and painter.

At this period, there began, first in Florence, then in the rest of Italy, and then in western Europe generally, a revival of learning, literature, and art that came to be called the "Renaissance" (French for "rebirth"). Scholars became interested in the science, literature, and art of the ancient world and took to calling the time between the ancient world and their own, "the Middle Ages" or "the Medieval period." The men of the Renaissance became more interested in the life of this world rather than in the life to come and dealt with people, rather than God and angels. They were "humanists."

NAPLES

Robert, the grandson of Charles of Anjou, reigned over the Kingdom of Naples in southern Italy from 1309 to 1342. He was succeeded by his granddaughter, Joanna I (1326–1382). Naples did not very much share the intellectual and commercial ferment that was stirring in that part of Italy north of the Papal States.

HOLY ROMAN EMPIRE

In this period, Emperors were drawn from families other than the Hapsburgs and nothing much was accomplished, except for arguments and fighting between candidates for the largely honorary and intrinsically worthless title.

Henry VII of the House of Luxembourg (1275–1313) became Emperor in 1308, and he was followed by Louis IV of the House of Wittelsbach (1283–1347). Both Henry VII and Louis IV led expeditions into Italy to no great effect.

Then Bohemia finally got its chance. In 1347, Charles IV (1316–1378) became King of Bohemia and was eventually recognized as Emperor. He was more interested in Bohemia than in the Empire. He founded the University of Prague in 1348, the first university in central Europe.

SWITZERLAND

The mountain cantons were theoretically ruled by the Hapsburgs. The legend of William Tell and his shooting of an apple off his son's head at the demand of the Austrian viceroy belongs to this period, but it is probably merely patriotic fiction.

Leopold I, Duke of Austria (1293–1326), a grandson of the Emperor, Rudolph I, sent an army into the mountains. The Swiss had considerably fewer soldiers, but they knew the region. They lay in wait at a point where they knew the Austrians must pass along a narrow road between a mountain and a lake. They then came down upon them from the mountainside and destroyed them on November 15, 1315. This was the Battle of Morgarten, near the border of Schwyz.

Over the next few decades, other cantons joined the original three.

TEUTONIC KNIGHTS

The Teutonic Knights managed to fight off Poland and, in 1346, they took over Estonia after it had successfully revolted against the Danes. With that, the Knights reached their maximum territorial extent.

DENMARK

Denmark was under the rule of Valdemar IV (1320–1375), a strong and aggressive king who had gained the throne in 1340. He sold Estonia (which was in revolt and, he felt, not worth the trouble of keeping) to the Teutonic Knights, but, for the rest, he spread Danish rule over parts of northern Germany and in what is now southern Sweden. He kept both the nobility and the clergy under his thumb.

POLAND

In 1333, Casimir III (1310–1370), sometimes called "Casimir the Great," became King of Poland. He was a shrewd ruler who did not allow his ambition to rise beyond his means. He made peace in the west, where he knew he was not likely to beat the Teutonic Knights, Bohemia, or Hungary, and gained some territory in the east against the Russians and the Lithuanians.

He welcomed the Jews, who had been driven out of England and France, since he needed a middle class of merchants and tradesmen. He had no sons, however, or other male heirs and he made an agreement with the king of Hungary to pass the throne to the Hungarian monarch's son, provided he would agree to respect the rights of the Polish nobility.

This went far toward making the monarchy elective and the nobility uncontrollable, thus making it probable that Poland would head toward anarchy and helplessness.

LITHUANIA

Lithuania, the region east of Poland, came to be ruled in 1316 by Gedymin (1275–1341), who organized it as a nation. Its capital was Vilna, and like Poland, Lithuania turned eastward for expansion against the weak Russian principalities. Gedymin and his son, Olgierd (d. 1377), who succeeded to the throne in 1341, expanded over much of what is now Byelorussia and the western Ukraine.

HUNGARY

Under Charles I (1288–1342), who became king in 1310, Hungary finally recovered from the Mongol raid. Charles improved finances, encouraged trade, and made peace with his neighbors, particularly with Poland. He was succeeded in 1342 by his son, Louis I (1306–1382), sometimes called "Louis the Great," who was a patron of learning.

RUSSIA

The Golden Horde interfered less and less with the Russian principalities. Provided they paid tribute, they might otherwise do as they liked. In 1328, Ivan I Kalita (1304–1341), or "Moneybags," became Grand Prince of Moscow. He made sure to pay his tribute promptly and he was even willing to collect the tribute from other principalities and see to it that they were turned over to the Mongols. As a result, he was a favorite of theirs and they were perfectly willing to allow Moscow to grow at the expense of its immediate neighbors.

Ivan's older son, Simeon II, succeeded in 1340 and followed his father's policy, which was ignoble, but which worked. Moscow was far enough eastward to avoid the grasp of the expanding Poles and Lithuanians. Its growth enabled it to gain in influence and to head toward becoming the dominant city of the nation.

SERBIA

In the Balkans, Serbia became an important power under Stephan Dushan (1308–1355), who came to the throne in 1331. He took advantage of the fact that the Byzantine Empire, what there was of it, even in these days of its decrepitude, spent most of what small energies it had in civil war and dynastic fighting. Stephen had no trouble in taking most of northern Greece, and made his way nearly to Constantinople. He married his daughter to the Bulgarian tsar, who recognized Serbian overlordship. By 1350, almost all the Balkans was under his control.

BYZANTINE EMPIRE

The Byzantine Empire, by which is now meant only the regions about the cities of Constantinople, Adrianople, Salonika, and Sparta, declined steadily. That it continued to exist at all is amazing. Partly, it was a victory for tradition (like the car without an engine that ran on its reputation alone), and partly it was the walls of Constantinople. In 1350, John VI (1292–1383), a great-grandson of Michael VIII, was Emperor.

OTTOMAN TURKS

In Asia Minor, a new power was rising. Asia Minor or most of it had been under the Seljuk Turks for nearly three centuries, but internal divisions—plus attacks by the crusaders, the Mongols, and even the Byzantines at times—had greatly weakened it.

In the northeastern section of Asia Minor, a border chieftain who was named Osman (1258–1326), began to gather power about 1300. Those who were ruled by himself and his descendants were called "Osmanli Turks" or, by distortion, "Ottoman Turks." He took over scraps of territory that the Byzantines controlled in Asia Minor, and his son Orkhan I (1288–1360), who succeeded to the throne in 1326, completed the job.

By 1345, the Ottoman Empire included all of northwestern Asia Minor. John VI, the Byzantine Emperor, was foolish enough to call on their help in his battle with another claimant to the throne. They responded to his call in 1354 and settled on the Gallipoli peninsula. In this way, the Turks first entered Europe.

AFRICA

The Mali Empire was at its height in this period, the largest native African empire yet to have appeared. The city of Timbuktu was entering a period of prosperity and greatness.

PERSIA

This period was one of the decline of the Mongol rule (the "Il-Khans"), which came to an end in 1349, a century and a quarter after Genghis Khan had conquered the region.

CHINA

Here, too, the period was one of the decline of Mongol rule, and by 1350, it was clearly only a matter of time before the last tattered remnants of Mongol officialdom would be ejected from the land.

NORTH AMERICA

In 1325, the Aztecs founded the city of Tenochtitlan, the precursor of what is now Mexico City, the most populous city in the world.

1350 TO 1400

ENGLAND

The English continued to raid the French countryside mercilessly, Edward III in the northeast; Edward, Prince of Wales (the Black Prince) in the southwest.

John II the Good (1319–1364) was now King of France after the death of his father, Philip VI, in 1350. John II sought out the Prince of Wales at Poitiers and there, on September 19, 1356, a great battle was fought. Again, the French had the advantage of numbers, but again they fought in disorganized fashion without any notion of a unified battle plan. Feeling that the trick was to use infantry, the French knights dismounted, but that did them no good against the terrible longbow.

The English not only won the battle in another lopsided victory, but they captured most of the French nobility, including King John himself.

As if that were not enough, the French suffered a terrible peasant rebellion, for the whole weight of the war and its devastation had fallen on them. With John in captivity, and France virtually ruined, John's son, the Dauphin Charles (1337–1380), managed to hang on. (The eldest son of the French king began to be called the Dauphin in this period, from association with the recently acquired Dauphine, a region in what is now southeastern France. John II, in the lifetime of his father, was the first Dauphin, and Charles was now the second.)

Once again Edward III marched into France to win one final victory and to take over the crown. Here, however, success eluded him. The French had had enough of the longbow. They stayed in their fortified towns and refused to fight. The weather was consistently bad and Edward was losing his men to disease.

He led his army to the very walls of Paris in March 1360. Even here, the French refused to fight. They simply waited—and it worked. On April 14, 1360, the day after Easter, it grew unusually cold and a tremendous hailstorm battered the exposed English army. That broke Edward III's spirit and both sides were ready for peace.

A treaty was signed on May 8, 1360, in Bretigny, a village in Normandy. By its terms, France gave up all the territory that England had conquered, particularly Aquitaine in the southwest and Calais in the northeast. They also agreed to pay an enormous ransom for King John, who wasn't worth it. On the other hand, Edward III gave up his claim to be the King of France.

Edward III then went home, and fought no more. The Black Prince remained in the southwest, meddling in Spanish affairs, but he eventually grew ill and returned home also.

On the whole, England seemed to be doing well, thanks to the booty from France. Nevertheless, Edward III's continuing need for money to pay his soldiers and to keep them supplied with food and arms played into the hands of Parliament, which held the purse strings.

The Black Death did terrible damage, of course. England's population, which stood at nearly 4 million when the Black Death struck, declined to less than 3 million. There was a labor shortage and the attempt of the upper class to keep the laborers from profiting by this created a great deal of discontent.

At this time, William Langland (1330–1400), wrote "Piers Plowman," which denounced the luxury and corruption of the aristocrats and clergy and took up the cause of the peasantry. A priest named John Ball (d. 1381) was even more extreme in his hatred of the upper classes, and preached inflammatory egalitarian sermons that got him excommunicated and, eventually, executed.

John Wyclif (1330–1384) was a great scholar who disliked the ritual, the luxury, and the corruption of the Church. He wanted a Church that was less materialistic, more virtuous, and closer to the people. He wanted the Bible to be translated into English so that it would be accessible to the people, and such a Bible was prepared.

Wyclif's followers were called "Lollards" (from a Dutch word meaning "mumblers" because, presumably, they were always mumbling prayers). The Lollards disapproved of monasteries and nunneries as hives of vice, and they had a strongly nationalistic spirit that didn't want to be led by the Pope who was, after all, a foreigner.

While all this social ferment was going on, Edward III grew senile and the Black Prince grew very ill. The latter died in 1376, the former in 1377, and the son of the Black Prince sat on the throne as Richard II (1367–1400). He was only 10 years old at the time, and he had several uncles who quarreled with each other over who was to run the country. The two chief uncles were John of Gaunt, Duke of Lancaster (1340–1399), and Thomas of Woodstock, Duke of Gloucester (1355–1397). The end result was that no one ran the country very well.

In 1381, there was a peasant's revolt under Walter ("Wat") Tyler. It was much less intense than the one in France, and the young Richard II showed courage in facing it down, but it was repressed cruelly. Efforts at reform were turned back.

Richard II grew old enough to rule personally, but he had no great competence. He tried to seize more power than he could handle, thus offending powerful nobles, including his own relatives.

He was suspected of having arranged the death of his uncle Thomas, Duke of Gloucester, and he sent into exile his first cousin, Henry of Bolingbroke (1366–1413), the son of John of Gaunt.

In 1399, Bolingbroke returned with ships and men, while Richard was off on a futile expedition to Ireland. The nobility flocked to Bolingbroke and Richard II found he had no friends. He was deposed, and the next year he was killed. Henry reigned as Henry IV.

In this period, there flourished the greatest poet the English language had yet produced. This was Geoffrey Chaucer (1342–1400), who was patronized by John of Gaunt, and later by Richard II. His greatest work, still read today, is *The Canterbury Tales*, a series of 23 short stories gathered from Boccaccio and other sources, and told in heroic couplets. It was written in "Middle English" and must be translated to be accessible to English-speakers today.

SCOTLAND

Robert II (1316–1390) gained the throne in 1371. He was the son of the daughter of Robert Bruce. His father was William Stuart, so Robert II was the first representative of the House of Stuart. That was about all that he need be remembered for. His son, Robert III (1337–1406), succeeded to the throne in 1390.

Scotland remained independent because Edward III had been preoccupied with France, and Richard II with internal politics.

IRELAND

The English hold on the Irish Pale had grown so precarious that Richard II, in 1398, undertook to lead an army into Ireland to reduce it to subservience. He was far too incompetent, however, to achieve anything beyond keeping the Pale going. His absence merely gave Henry Bolingbroke a chance to invade England and seize the throne.

FRANCE

France had experienced three great defeats at the hands of smaller English forces: the naval Battle of Sluys, and the land Battles of Crecy, and Po- itiers. France had been raided by brutal armies till the countryside was a mass of ruins. The peasantry had revolted and been smashed into even worse ruins. Moreover, King John was in captivity in England, enjoying himself, while a beaten, half-destroyed France tried to raise the money that was demanded as his ransom. And all this less than 40 years after the death of the powerful Philip IV.

Fortunately, for France, John II died in 1364, and his son, the Dauphin, ascended the throne as Charles V the Wise. Charles was, as his cog- nomen indicates, a wise king, a cautious one and a kindly one, who eschewed luxury in the interest of the common good, who patronized scholars, and who, most of all, found just the soldier he needed in Bertrand du Guesclin (1320–1380).

Du Guesclin was defeated by the Black Prince in Spain; however, in France itself, he carried on a war of attrition, avoiding open battles, but raid- ing shrewdly and winning small engagements that wore down the English. Little by little, he won back for France the territory she had given up. By 1380, when Charles V and du Guesclin died, France was almost free of the enemy, but at a terrific cost. Between war and revolts and the Black Death, her population had declined from 13 million to 9 million.

Charles V's civilian adviser was his chaplain, Nicole d'Oresme (1325–1382). He was a thought- ful economist (perhaps the best in the Middle Ages), who dealt with taxation in a sensible way and opposed debasement of the coinage as doing long-term harm in return for short-term good. He translated some of Aristotle into French. He worked out ways of showing variable magni- tudes in graph form, made useful observations on falling bodies, and denounced astrology as superstition.

Charles V's son came to the throne in 1380 at the age of 12, as Charles VI (1368–1422). He was called Charles the Well-Beloved at first, and with a young king on the throne both in France and in England there was a period of peace because nei- ther country was in a position to fight. In France, as in England, there were powerful uncles of the

King who fought among themselves. In France, as in England, there were social tensions.

But things were, again, worse in France. In England, the King was merely overthrown. In France, the King remained on the throne but ex- perienced lengthening periods of madness, so that now he is known in history as "Charles the Mad."

CASTILE

Alfonso XI, who had fought off the last African invasion of Spain, had two sons. One was legiti- mate and succeeded to the throne as Pedro (1334–1369), usually known in history, for good reason, as Pedro the Cruel. He had an older brother, Henry of Trastamara (1333–1379), who, however, was illegitimate and was, therefore, not qualified to sit on the throne. Henry didn't see the force of that, and was determined to try to supplant his brother. There was civil war be- tween them.

France supported Henry of Trastamara and England supported Pedro the Cruel. On April 3, 1367, two Spanish armies, one supported by the Black Prince and the other by Bertrand du Gues- clin, fought at Navarrete in north-central Castile. Once again, the English longbows did their job and the battle ended as a victory for the Black Prince and Pedro.

However, Pedro alienated the Black Prince, who returned to France with nothing to show for his adventure but a bout of illness that slowly grew worse. The civil war between the Castilian half-brothers continued and, on March 14, 1369, at Montiel in central Castile, there was another battle. This time, Henry of Trastamara not only won, but he managed to kill Pedro with his own hands.

Henry ruled Castile as Henry II, and remained a staunch ally of the French, defeating the En- glish in a naval battle in 1372 that gave France control of the Channel again, for a while.

Henry saw to it that his son married a princess of Aragon to bring those two Spanish kingdoms closer together. That son became King of Castile in 1379 as John I (1358–1390). His second wife was a Portuguese princess, and so he tried to annex Portugal as another step in uniting the peninsula, but that failed. He was succeeded by his son, Henry III (1379–1406) in 1390.

PORTUGAL

Ferdinand I of Portugal (1345–1383) died in 1383, and his only legitimate child was Beatriz, who had married John I of Castile after John's first wife had died. Therefore, John claimed the throne of Portugal. However, Ferdinand I had half brother, John of Avis (1357–1433), who, like Henry of Trastamara, suffered under the handicap of being illegitimate. Again, like Henry of Trastamara, he thought this should not prevent him from becoming king. He had married Philippa, the daughter of John of Gaunt of England, and that meant he could count on English aid.

In 1385, at the Battle of Aljubarrota in west central Portugal, John of Avis, with English help, defeated John of Castile. That established Portugal's independence beyond dispute, and John reigned as John I, sometimes called "John the Great."

On May 9, 1386, John signed the Treaty of Windsor with England, renewing the alliance between the two nations, and that alliance was never broken thereafter.

PAPACY

The Papacy was now at its lowest point in three centuries. For over 70 years, the Popes had been in Avignon. They were Frenchmen who lived in great luxury and who lent themselves to the political aims of French kings at a time when France itself was in ruins.

Urban V (1310–1370), who was the Avignonese Pope from 1362 to 1370, visited Rome, found it a decrepit slum, and left in a hurry. His successor, Gregory XI (1329–1378) visited Rome in 1378 and would have left also, but died before he could do that. A number of his cardinals were with him and they found themselves forced to elect a Pope in Rome or else be torn apart by a Roman mob. Naturally, those cardinals who happened to be in Avignon elected a Pope of their own.

The result was that for the next few decades there were two Popes, one in Avignon and one in Rome. Each castigated and excommunicated the other. The monarchs of Europe sided with whichever one was politically advantageous for them, so that the Papacy became a pawn that everyone used and no one respected.

In 1400, the "Great Schism," as it was called, still existed. Benedict XIII (1328–1423) was the Pope at Avignon, having been elected to the post in 1394. Boniface IX (1355–1404) was the Pope at Rome, having been elected in 1389.

MILAN

Milan was at the peak of its power under the rule of Gian Galeazzo Visconti (1351–1402). Little by little, he made himself supreme in northern Italy, gathering in the neighboring towns. All he needed was Florence, which was under a shrewd commercial oligarchy, and virtually all of Italy north of the Papal states would be his. He died of plague, however, before he could attain that goal and the inevitable dynastic squabbling among his sons undid his work.

VENICE

Venice finally defeated Genoa in 1381 and, thereafter, Genoa was never again a threat. However, a far stronger enemy was in the field. The Ottoman Turks were now bulking large. Venice signed a treaty with them in 1388. (As long as the Venetians could be assured of profitable trade, they didn't care about small matters such as religion.) However, as the Turks grew stronger and Venice did not, it was clear that the treaty would last no longer than the Turks wished.

HOLY ROMAN EMPIRE

It seemed clear that the Holy Roman Empire was condemned to anarchy as long as the death of each Emperor meant a civil war among the claimants to the throne. In 1356, then, the Emperor Charles IV arranged an agreement on the "Golden Bull."

When an Emperor died, seven "electors"

would choose the next Emperor. They included three archbishops (of Mainz, of Trier, and of Cologne) and four secular rulers (the County Palatine of the Rhine, the Duke of Saxony, the Margrave of Brandenburg, and the King of Bohemia). The Emperor would be chosen by a simple majority without delays, and there was no mention of either the towns or the Pope being involved in the election.

The whole thing never worked well. The voters were for sale. The Emperor was usually powerless except for what strength his own realm gave him, and the townsfolk were bitterly resentful of being cut out of the process. On the whole, the Holy Roman Empire remained an anarchy.

In 1378, Charles IV died and was succeeded by his son, Wenceslas IV (1361–1419), who was a complete do-nothing. He could only sit and watch as the towns rebelled and the nobility went their own way. In 1400, he was deposed for incompetence and drunkenness, and in those days a monarch had to be very incompetent and drunk indeed to be deposed for those reasons. However, Wenceslas didn't accept the deposition and managed to remain on the throne. (He was not the "Good King Wenceslas" of the song, by the way. That was a king of Bohemia who died in 929.)

BOHEMIA

The Emperor Wenceslas was also King Wenceslas II of Bohemia, but he was just as incompetent and drunken a king as he was an Emperor, and there was growing social tension in his land. There were those who, as in England, opposed churchly luxury and ritual and wanted to simplify religion, make it more virtuous, and bring it closer to the people. The leader in these views, in Bohemia, was Jan Hus (1373–1415), who had read the writings of Wyclif and was much influenced by him.

SWITZERLAND

The Swiss victory at Morgarten did not totally discourage the Hapsburg princes from attempting to bring the upstart mountaineers of the Alps

back under their control. Leopold of Swabia led an army of 6000 Austrians into Switzerland and a battle was fought at Sempach in central Switzerland on July 9, 1386.

The Swiss were outnumbered nearly four to one. The Austrians were heavily armed, however, and grew tried. When gaps and irregularities appeared in their line as the weaker failed to keep up, the Swiss charged those points and smashed the Austrians. (There is a tale that a Swiss fighter, Arnold von Winkelried, deliberately gathered as many enemy pikes as possible into his own body, thus creating a gap that could be exploited, but this may be another fiction.)

After that, the Austrians gave up. In 1394, they signed a truce with the Swiss and made no further attempts to disturb them in their mountains.

HANSEATIC LEAGUE

The Hanseatic League fought off the power of Valdemar IV of Denmark and, in 1370, signed the Peace of Stralsund, which marked the peak of the League's power. It gave the League a monopoly of the Baltic trade and a strong hand in Scandinavian politics. After that, though, it entered a slow decline.

TEUTONIC KNIGHTS

The Teutonic Knights at this time held their own on the southern and eastern shores of the Baltic, but Poland was growing stronger and, after this period, the Teutonic Knights, like the Hanseatic League, entered a slow decline.

DENMARK

Valdemar IV was the father of Margaret (1353–1412). When Valdemar died in 1375, Margaret's son, only five years old, reigned as Olaf II (1370–1387). Margaret was the wife of Haakon VI (1340–1380), who had become King of Norway in 1355. When Haakon died in 1380, Olaf II became Olaf V of Norway, with Margaret as regent in both lands.

In 1387, Olaf died unexpectedly, and Margaret

became queen of both countries. What's more, Albert, King of Sweden (1340–1412), was unpopular with the Swedish nobility. Margaret sided with the nobility and was asked by the Swedes to take over the rule of the country. In 1389, Margaret defeated Albert's army and became Queen of Sweden.

Thereafter, she ruled a United Scandinavia—Denmark, Norway, Sweden, Finland, Iceland, and even the dying colony at Greenland.

Greenland had a population of 3000 at its peak, but the weather was growing colder, and agriculture was virtually impossible. The Inuit (or Eskimos) were migrating southward along the western coast of the island and knew better how to live off sea-life. Then, too, the Black Death weakened the colony and put an end to sea communication with Scandinavia. By 1400, the Greenland colony was fading away.

On the map, Scandinavia, ruled from Copenhagen, was now the largest country in Europe, at least in area. Its population, however, was only about 1.25 million (having dropped half a million thanks to the Black Death).

POLAND

Another large power appeared east of Germany. Lithuania had continued to grow at the expense of the Russian principalities. In 1377, Jagiello (1351–1434), the son of Algierd, had become Grand Duke of Lithuania, ruling over lands that stretched from nearly the Baltic Sea to nearly the Black Sea, and eastward nearly to Moscow.

In 1384, Jadwiga (1374–1399) became Queen of Poland, which lay immediately to the west of Lithuania and was only one third of its area. Jagiello and Jadwiga were married in 1386 and the two realms were united, rather loosely at first. Lithuania completed its conversion to Christianity and did so to the Roman ritual and not the Russian. Jadwiga died in 1399, but Jagiello continued to rule both realms under the Polish name of Wladislaw II.

The combined realm, usually referred to simply as "Poland," was second only to Scandinavia in area in western Europe. Its population was 7 million, almost equal to that of war-ravaged France. Nevertheless, Poland could never pull its weight because its turbulent nobility rarely allowed the Polish king to act with decision.

RUSSIA

In 1339, Dmitri (1350–1389), the grandson of Ivan I Kalita, became Grand Duke of Muscovy at the age of 9. When he grew older, he managed to stay in the good graces of the Golden Horde and to absorb the Russian principalities in the north, until Muscovy ruled almost all of Russia between the territory directly held by the Golden Horde to the south, and the territory of Novgorod, which spread widely over the almost unpopulated Russia far north.

Then, when it seemed that the Golden Horde was having internal troubles, Dmitri stopped his tribute. That meant war, and the Tatars (as the European Mongols were coming to be known) allied themselves with the Lithuanians.

Dimitri, however, met the Tatar army at Kulikovo on the upper course of the Don River and attacked them before the Lithuanian contingents could arrive. Dmitri won a complete victory on September 8, 1380, and was known as "Dmitri Donskoi" thereafter.

It was not a conclusive victory, because the Tatars quickly recovered, Dmitri had to continue fighting both them and the Lithuanians till his death; and his son, Vasily I (1371–1424) who succeeded in 1389, had to continue doing so with indecisive results.

Still, the Battle of Kulikovo was the first time the Russians had beaten the Tatars since they had arrived in Russia a century and a half before, and the aura of Tatar invincibility was broken. Furthermore, it was clear that if Russia were to rid itself of its Tatar overlords, it would be the Grand Dukes of Moscow who would lead the way.

OTTOMAN EMPIRE

As the Tatars in Russia showed signs of fading, the Ottoman Turks emerged as the leading military power in the east. Murad I (1326–1389) became the Ottoman ruler in 1361, succeeding Orkhan.

Murad I organized an elite corps of "Janissaries" (from a Turkish word meaning "new troops"). These were drawn from Christian subjects, who were converted to Islam, given Spartan military training, and subjected to celibacy so that families would not distract their minds from wars. They quickly became the most feared and effective troops in Europe.

Under Murad I, the Ottoman realm spread eastward through Asia Minor, and westward into the Balkans. The Turks took Adrianople in 1362 and then all of Thrace. They moved farther north and took Sofia, the Bulgarian capital in 1385. The climax came on June 15, 1389, when the Turks fought the Serbs at Kossovo in southern Serbia. Only 35 years before, the Serbs under Stephen Dushan had dominated the Balkans, but now it was the Turks who emerged as rulers of the region.

Murad I was assassinated in the course of battle and his son, Bayazid I (1360–1403), succeeded. The conquered regions, assuming that a strong ruler might be succeeded by a weaker successor, rose in revolt, but Bayazid was no weakling. He crushed the revolts, though it was 10 years before he was ready for new conquests. In 1395, he placed Constantinople under siege and kept up that siege for years. He also passed beyond the Balkans to attack Hungary.

Sigismund (1368–1437) became king of Hungary in 1387. He made a poor king, for his energies were taken up by his personal ambitions in Poland and Bohemia. Since he was the son of Emperor Charles IV and a half-brother of Emperor Wenceslas, he also had his eye fixed on the Imperial throne.

He did realize one thing, though. With the Balkans gone, and the Byzantine Empire reduced to the city of Constantinople and a couple of small outlying districts, and with Constantinople itself under siege, it was now Hungary who was the defense of Europe against the Muslims. And the Muslims now, in the form of the Ottoman Empire, were more dangerous than they had been in seven centuries.

Therefore, Sigismund tried to organize a crusade against the Turks, which Pope Boniface IX (1365–1404) preached heartily. The knights of western Europe, mostly French, gathered in Buda, the capital of Hungary, and then pressed down the Danube to Nicopolis, in north-central Bulgaria. They met the Turkish forces there on September 25, 1396. The French knights fought as they had fought at Crecy, charging forward in an undisciplined unorganized fashion. The Turks met them in a business-like manner and virtually wiped them out.

It looked as though nothing could stop the Turks—yet something did.

BYZANTINE EMPIRE

The Byzantine Empire was shrinking steadily at this time. Manuel II (1350–1425) had become Emperor in 1391, and heroically withstood the Ottoman siege. He tried to get help from the west, but the crusade failed at Nicopolis and Constantinople seemed doomed.

MONGOLS

In this period, the Mongolian Empire crumbled away. The Mongols were ejected from China, and in Persia they became Muslims and melted into the population. Only in Russia did the Golden Horde, or Tatars, remain in power, and that was the least advanced portion of what had been the Mongol Empire. Even the Tatars were weakening. Increasingly, they ignored the Russian principalities in the north and west (except to collect tribute when they could) and concentrated on the steppes in the south and east, paying little attention to the gathering Russian strength.

For a while, it looked as though this would be reversed when Tokhtamish became leader of the Golden Horde in 1377. He withstood the defeat by the Russians at Kulikovo, reorganized, smashed back, and captured Moscow on August 23, 1382, sacking it.

Meanwhile, though, in central Asia, another conqueror had appeared on the scene. He was Timur (1336–1405), often called "Timur Lenk" (i.e., "Timur the Lame," or, in western distortion, "Tamerlane" or Tamburlaine"). In 1364, he was the prime minister of a Mongol Khan in central Asia. By 1369, he had overthrown the Khan and become the ruler himself. Beginning in 1381, he conquered Persia, following the same tactics of terror that Genghis Khan had used over a century and a half before. He massacred those who resisted so as to make sure that many strong points would give in without resistance.

Tamerlane had helped Tokhtamish reestablish Tatar strength in Russia, but when Tokhtamish's notions of expansion infringed on Tamerlane's domain, there was a war between the two.

The war of Mongol against Mongol was a long and difficult one, lasting 10 years, but in the end it was Tamerlane who won. (He never lost, just as Genghis Khan never lost.)

In the course of the war, Tamerlane invaded Russia, but he did not remain there. He was satisfied merely with having smashed his enemies and then he left in search of new prey. His blows did more to destroy the Tatars in Russia than any the Russians of the time could possibly have delivered. Tamerlane had made sure that the future in Russia belonged to the Russians.

In 1387, Tamerlane took Baghdad, and then, in 1398, he invaded northern India. He visited the land with incredible destruction, including a horrible sack of Delhi on December 17, 1398. Then he left it. What he intended to accomplish besides experiencing the sheer pleasure of destruction, no one can tell. In 1400, he turned west again.

CHINA

In southern China, Chu Yuan-Chang (1328–1398), a peasant, slowly worked his way up the scale. He joined rebel forces who were fighting against the decaying Mongol dynasty, discovered that he had military ability, and grew steadily more important. He captured Nanking in 1356, and, over the district he ruled, he established an orderly and prosperous government.

In this way, he came to be recognized as the national leader against the Mongol rulers. He continued to win victories and, in 1368, he declared himself the first Emperor of a new "Ming dynasty." Before the year was over, the Mongol monarch had fled China, and their control over China ended after a mere century of rule.

All of China was united under Chu Yuan-Chang, as it had not been under a native dynasty since the end of the T'ang Empire over four and a half centuries earlier. Chu Yuan-Chang died in 1398, and was succeeded by his grandson, Chu Yun Wen.

JAVA

Java was the center of the Majapahit Empire, which reached its peak at this time. It controlled most of what is now Indonesia. It had been established with the help of Chinese troops, but once power had been achieved, the Chinese were expelled. After Hayam Wuruk (1334–1389), ruler of the Empire, died, the realm rapidly declined.

1400 TO 1450

ENGLAND

The reign of Henry IV was constantly troubled with revolts and border warfare. The Scots invaded and were defeated at the Battle of Homildon Hill in northern England on September 14, 1402, through the use of the English longbow.

Leading the English forces was Henry "Hotspur" Percy (1364–1403), who was immortalized by Shakespeare in his play Henry IV, Part One.

Owen Glendower (1359–1416), a Welshman who represented the last spark of Welsh nationalist resistance to the English (he is also a character in Henry IV, Part One), fought a successful guerrilla war in the mountains of Wales from 1402 to 1409, but was finally defeated, and the land was pacified.

The northern noblemen, under the leadership of Hotspur Percy, revolted, thinking they had been insufficiently rewarded for helping Henry IV to the throne. They were defeated at the battle of Shrewsbury in west central England on July 21, 1403, and Hotspur died in combat.

Henry IV died in 1413, worn out by all this, and was succeeded by his son, who reigned as Henry V (1387–1422).

Henry V realized that continual civil war would destroy the kingdom, and it was his intention to unify it. With this end in view, he struck at divisive elements inside the country, conducting a severe campaign against Lollardy, the doctrines of which were causing social unrest. In a four-year campaign, he wiped out the Lollards, or at least forced them underground. The most prominent Lollard was John Oldcastle (1377–1417), who had been a friend of Henry V when he was Prince Hal and not yet king, but who would not cease being a Lollard so that, in the end, he was hanged and burned. (This is supposed to have inspired Shakespeare to give Prince Hal the immortal Sir John Falstaff as a roystering friend who was, in the end, rejected, in Shakespeare's two *Henry IV* plays.)

Outside the land, Henry V's eyes turned to France again. The French king, Charles VI, was mad, and the kingdom was being torn apart by civil war. It seemed to Henry V a good time to attack once more, reviving national pride, and persuading the English to bury their differences in a common fight against a foreign enemy.

Henry V declared war on France in April 1415, and sailed for Normandy on August 10, 1415, with an army of 12,000 men. He captured the port city of Harfleur by September 22, but the weeks of siege had resulted in riddling his army with casualties and disease, and the victory seemed Pyrrhic.

On October 10, Henry began a race to Calais where he could find safety, rest, and, perhaps, reinforcements from England. The weather was horrible. There was ceaseless rain and Henry's army dwindled further. Finally, it was weak enough to seem sure losers and the carefully pursuing French blocked him at Agincourt, not far from Calais.

Henry V chose a careful battle line, a short distance that was flanked on either side by heavy woods. This narrowed the fighting area and made the French three-to-one superiority in numbers of not much use to them. The ground in front was soaked with the steady rains and that would surely bog down the heavy cavalry that made up the bulk of the French forces. The English had only 9000 men, but 8000 of them were longbowmen.

The French general apparently wanted to fight a defensive battle, outwaiting Henry and forcing him out of his secure line. The French knights, however, who hadn't learned a thing from a century of losses between Courtrai and Nicopolis, observed the small numbers of English, their lack of cavalry, their miserable appearance, and wanted to charge—nothing but charge.

Charge they did. They bogged down in the mud and the terrible flights of yard-long arrows from the English longbows began—and the French were slaughtered. The Battle of Agincourt was the most lopsided and astonishing victory the English ever won, but the credit goes not so much to English valor as to French stupidity. This was unfortunate for the English, since they believed it was entirely a matter of valor; thus, when the French stopped being stupid, the English never figured out what had gone wrong with their valor.

Henry left for England, and then returned to France in 1417, spending two careful years subduing Normandy; while the French, lost in shock over Agincourt, did virtually nothing to interfere.

In 1420, Henry V forced the helpless French government to sign a treaty in which mad King Charles VI named Henry as his heir, disinheriting his son, the Dauphin Charles (1403–1461) in the process, and implying his illegitimacy. He also gave Henry his daughter, Catherine (1401–1437), as wife. Now it was only a matter of waiting for the mad king to die, and Henry would be king of England and France.

While waiting for Charles VI to die, Henry V

cleaned up more portions of northern France, fell sick, and it was *he* who died in 1422. He was succeeded by his 9-month-old son, who reigned as Henry VI (1421–1471), and who, as it turned out, inherited his maternal grandfather's tendency toward insanity.

Henry V's younger brother, John, Duke of Bedford (1389–1435), was an uncle of Henry VI and was a skilled soldier. He won another battle at Verneuil in southern Normandy on August 17, 1424, using longbowmen against heavy cavalry. Verneuil, however, was fated to be the last great longbow victory the English were to win over the French, who after that, began to learn their lesson.

Back in England, however, various other uncles of the King, together with other high noblemen, were fighting each other over the right to control the land in the name of the royal child. Just as the victories of Edward III were lost in the political infighting during the reign of Richard II, so now the victories of Henry V were lost in the political infighting during the reign of Henry VI.

Added to this was the fact that France finally learned how to counteract the longbow. The result was that the English were forced out of France more quickly than they had forced their way in.

SCOTLAND

Robert III of Scotland was succeeded in 1406 by his son, James I (1394–1437). He had been captured by the English in that same year, when he was 12 years old, and was kept prisoner by Henry IV. Henry V released him in 1423, and he was finally crowned in 1424. In 1437, however, he was assassinated and was succeeded by his 7-year-old son, who reigned as James II (1430–1460). By a strange fatality, there were to be six Jameses who ruled over Scotland, and every one of them became king as a minor. This helped keep Scotland in constant turmoil.

IRELAND

English rule in Ireland continued precariously until 1449, when Richard, Duke of York (1411–1460), arrived as Viceroy there.

Richard was a second cousin of Henry VI and, through his mother, had a better claim to the throne than Henry VI had. This began the rivalry between the Yorkists, who were descended from Edward III through Edmund, Duke of York (1342–1402), and the Lancastrians, like Henry IV, Henry V, and Henry VI, who were descended from Edward III by way of John of Gaunt, Duke of Lancaster.

Richard of York adopted a policy of conciliation toward the Irish, treating them honorably, and pacifying the land in that manner.

FRANCE

With all the disasters of the past 70 years, France needed but one thing to strike bottom and that was civil war. It got that, too.

One of those who fought for control of mad Charles VI was Philip the Bold of Burgundy (1342–1404). He was a son of John II and an uncle of Charles VI. John II had made Philip the Duke of Burgundy, which gave him east central France, plus some of what is now western Germany, together with the Low Countries or the Netherlands (which includes the modern Netherlands and Belgium).

The Netherlands was an extraordinarily rich area; its commercial city-states rivaled in wealth those of northern Italy. Philip the Bold was as strong a ruler as Charles VI was weak, and Burgundy had, for the most part, escaped English depredation. It was stronger than France and was virtually independent. France had had to deal with a too-strong Normandy four centuries earlier, and now it had to deal with a too-strong Burgundy.

The cities of the Netherlands, like those in Italy, were rich enough to support a flourishing art. The great Netherlandish artist of this period was Jan van Eyck (1395–1441). The Netherlandish ecclesiastic and writer, Thomas à Kempis (1380–1471), was also of outstanding importance. He wrote *Imitation of Christ* in 1424.

Philip the Bold died in 1404 and was succeeded by his son, John the Fearless (1371–1418), who was a survivor of the Battle of Nicopolis. He was first cousin to Charles VI, and he found himself opposing Louis, Duke of Orleans (1372–1407), who was a younger brother of Charles VI. John the Fearless arranged to have Louis of Orleans assassinated in 1407 and, after that, the two factions were at war with each other.

Louis's son, Charles of Orleans (1394–1465), led the pro-war, anti-English party, while John of Burgundy led the anti-war, pro-English party. The result was that when Henry V invaded France, he had the help of the Burgundians, so that he was not merely fighting France, but was allied with half of France to fight the other half.

The Battle of Agincourt might have changed things. Charles of Orleans was taken prisoner at Agincourt and was kept in England for 25 years. That put him out of action. As for John of Burgundy, the English triumph was so great as to make him nervous, and he might have changed his policy and ended the civil war but, in 1419, he was assassinated at the direction of the Dauphin. This was foolish, for John was succeeded by his son, Philip the Good (1396–1467), who, in view of the assassination, could not turn toward the Orleanist faction, but now had no choice but to stick with the English alliance.

When Charles VI died in 1422, the Dauphin called himself Charles VII, but he was not crowned in the Cathedral of Rheims. This had been the traditional site of crowning since the time of Clovis, nine centuries before, but it was in English hands. As long as the Dauphin was not crowned in Rheims, he had to remain the Dauphin, and nothing more. The English child-king, Henry VI, was crowned King of France to forestall Charles, but Henry was crowned in Paris and that, too, didn't count.

The Dauphin remained in Bourges in central France, virtually powerless. Meanwhile, in 1428, the Duke of Bedford had sent an army to lay siege to Orleans at the northernmost point of the Loire River. If that fell, it might have meant that the south of France would surrender, and all the land would be conquered.

Perhaps not, of course, because England, smaller and less populated than France, had stretched its resources to the limit, going as far as it had, and it was possible nothing more could

be done. On the other hand, the French had been defeated so often that they seemed to lack the spirit to fight.

Then, in 1429, a strange thing happened. A young woman from eastern France appeared before the Dauphin and said that God had sent her to save France.

Her name was Jeanne Darc (usually mistranslated as Joan of Arc). The Dauphin, after some consideration, decided he had nothing to lose, so he sent her to Orleans with an armed escort. It turned out that she was just the psychological lift the French needed. The French soldiers, feeling that God might be on their side now, fought with new vigor. The English soldiers, fearful that Joan was some sort of witch, were a little readier to back off than they had been before. Thus, the French attacked and the English retreated from Orleans. That was the turning point of the Hundred Years War.

Joan led the Dauphin to Rheims, where he was crowned and became Charles VII officially. Joan was soon captured by the English, however, and, in 1431, was burned as a witch in Rouen, the capital of Normandy, while Charles VII made no attempt to save her.

However, he didn't need her any more. The French knew the English could be beaten, and Charles VII set about reorganizing his army, getting rid of the old notion of fighting by knightly charges and slowly developing an artillery corps.

Gunpowder and cannon had existed for a century, since the Battle of Crecy and a little before, but they had been used haphazardly, and cannon were far too apt to explode and kill the gunners rather than the enemy.

Charles was intent on improving cannon, and on training gunners and having them fight in an organized fashion, as though they were a bunch of trained longbowmen—except that the cannonballs they fired were far more deadly than the arrows from the longbows. The cannonballs could batter down stone walls so that sieges lasted a very short time. What's more, the English, still under the impression that any Englishman could beat 10 Frenchmen, didn't understand that artillery made a difference. They stopped winning victories and couldn't figure out why.

(Shakespeare's *Henry VI, Part One* gives a ridiculously distorted picture of this period of history.)

By 1435, Philip of Burgundy could see that the wind had shifted, and he made his peace with France. After that, England had no chance at all. In 1436, the French had retaken Paris, and after that they began the fight to retake Normandy.

In 1450, the British sent an expeditionary force larger than any they had yet sent to France, and it did them no good. At the Battle of Formigny in Normandy on April 15, 1450, it was the English longbows against the new French artillery—the French won. By the end of the year, the English were cleared out of Normandy and out of all northern France except Calais, and they held on to only small parts of the southwest.

PORTUGAL

In this period, Portugal, a small portion of Europe in the farthest southwest, undertook a course of action that was to bring her to astonishing heights.

Her victory over Castile filled John I with expansionist notions. In 1415, he invaded Africa and took Ceuta, just across the Strait of Gibraltar. Fighting at Ceuta was his third son, Henry (1394–1460), and Africa became that son's passion ever after.

Europe had developed a great demand for products from the Far East, fed by the crusading experience and by Marco Polo's tales of eastern magnificence. Europeans wanted sugar, pepper, and other spices, as well as silk and other luxuries. Now that the Mongol Empire had broken down, trade with the Far East wasn't easy, especially since the Ottoman Empire stood squarely across the route. At every step of the way, there were tariff charges, and the prices of Eastern luxuries went sky-high. And Portugal was at the end of the line.

It occurred to Henry that if ships could find their way around Africa to the Far East, they would bypass the Ottoman Empire, and those luxuries would become far cheaper and more available.

In 1420, therefore, Henry founded a center for navigation at Sagres, at the extreme southwestern tip of Portugal. This became a haven for experienced navigators. It was a place where ships were built according to new designs that would make them fit for the open ocean; where new aids to navigation were devised and tested; where crews were hired and trained; and where expeditions down the African coast were carefully planned.

After 1420, Portugal won and lost battles in Africa and against Castile, but that didn't matter much. What counted were those ships inching their way down the African coastline year after year. Although Henry never went on the ships himself, he has gone down in history as "Henry the Navigator," and with him there began the great "Age of Exploration" that was utterly to change the world.

For a quarter century, the Portuguese skirted the western edge of the great Sahara desert, the largest in the world; however, in 1445, they had passed beyond the desert to a point of land that was green with growing things, and they called it "Cape Verde" (Cape Green). Until then they had been going steadily westward as the coast of Africa took them farther and farther away from "the Indies" (i.e., the Far East), but Cape Verde was the westernmost point of Africa. After that, the ships trended eastward, ever eastward.

The Portuguese were making discoveries in the Atlantic itself. In 1421, the island of Madeira (meaning "wooded") was discovered; and, in 1432, the Azores (the Portuguese word for "hawks") were found. The Azores were 1300 kilometers west of Portugal, and had the Portuguese but known, they were one third of the way across the Atlantic Ocean.

But everything, however inspiring, can have its unhappy aspects. In the fertile land south of the Sahara, the Portuguese found people of a new race. They seemed primitive, and certainly they were not Christians. It seemed proper to the Portuguese to enslave them. The black tribes, who fought and enslaved each other, saw nothing wrong in trading captured slaves to the Portuguese in exchange for what the Portuguese ships could offer them. Black slaves were brought to

Lisbon for the first time in 1434, and the evil of black slavery was fastened on Europe and, eventually, on the American continents.

ARAGON

Aragon continued to turn its face eastward, something it had done since the Sicilian Vespers, a century and a half before.

Alfonso V the Magnanimous (1396–1458) became King of Aragon in 1416. He already controlled the Balearic Islands, Sardinia, and Sicily. He managed to seize the kingdom of Naples, too, so that under him the Aragonese Empire was at its peak.

CASTILE

While Portugal looked toward Africa, and Aragon looked toward Italy, Castile, larger than either, also had the urge to expand. In 1402, a Castilian expedition occupied the Canary Islands about 1300 kilometers southwest of Spain.

Henry III died in 1406 and his one-year-old son succeeded as John II (1405–1454).

PAPAL STATES

The Papacy at this time was struggling to pull itself out of the Great Schism, and it seemed that the only way to do so was to find some authority greater than the quarreling Popes of Rome and of Avignon. The feeling arose that a council of high churchmen should get together and decide who should be the Pope. It would be almost like adding a kind of Parliament to the Papal monarchy.

In 1409, a Council was held at Pisa that was attended by 500 churchmen, together with delegates from the various western European nations. After careful deliberation, they decided to depose both Gregory XII of Rome (1325–1417), who had been Pope since 1406, and Benedict XIII of Avignon, who had long held his post there, and to start afresh with Alexander V (1339–1410) as their own nominee. Since neither of the two older Popes would resign, Europe was now treated to the spectacle of *three* Popes, all shout-

ing insults at each other. The next year Alexander V was succeeded by John XXIII (d. 1419), and there were still three Popes.

Another Council was held at Constance in southwestern Germany in 1414. After three years of deliberation, all three Popes were deposed and Martin V (1368–1431) became Pope in 1417. Although Benedict XIII of Avignon still refused to resign, he was ignored, and Martin V was accepted by all. The Great Schism was healed, after 30 years, and the Avignon papacy came to an effective end, after a century. The whole episode, however, had made the Papacy a laughing-stock in Europe, and it took a while for the institution to recover from that.

Martin V managed to resume control over the Papal States and began the process of fighting against the Conciliar movement—that is, against the notion that Councils were more authoritative than the Pope. He was succeeded by Eugene IV (1383–1447), who became Pope in 1431, and who continued the fight against Councils.

Nicholas V (1397–1455) became Pope in 1447; by then, the Conciliar movement was dead—except when the Pope himself called and controlled a Council. This was a step backward, in a way, for needed reforms in the Church were not put through, and that laid the groundwork for future disaster.

FLORENCE

The cities of northern Italy fought each other endlessly, with ups and downs that can scarcely be followed, much as the Greek cities had fought each other 18 centuries earlier. There were the same temporary victories of one over another and the same long-term weakening and defeat of all. And the Italian cities continued to flourish in the artistic sense, just as the Greek cities had done.

The comparison is not exact, however. Florence might be viewed as the Athens of Renaissance Italy, but its great forte was banking, which had developed, in the modern sense, in northern Italy first.

Since war interfered with banking prosperity,

it is not surprising that Florence's leading banker, and the richest man in Italy, Giovanni de Medici (1360–1429), should be the leader of the peace party in Florence.

His son, Cosimo de Medici (1389–1464), grew even richer and became the head of the government in 1434. Like Giovanni, Cosimo was careful to use his riches in such a way as to make himself popular with the people. He even put through a progressive income tax that placed the burden of the state on those best able to pay, and relieved the poor. If Florence was the Athens of Renaissance Italy, Cosimo played the part of Pericles.

Cosimo not only patronized learned Italians; he also encouraged scholars from dying Constantinople to come to Italy with whatever Greek learning they could bring with them, so that they could translate it into Latin.

One outstanding Greek scholar of the time who came to Italy was Bessarion (1403–1472), who labored, vainly, to effect a union of the Greek and Roman churches. He was named a cardinal in 1439, and he translated works of Aristotle and Xenophon.

The greatest Florentine artist of the century was the sculptor Donatello (1386–1466). Though not a Florentine, Leone Battista Alberti (1404–1472) was an example of the "Renaissance man," one who excelled in many directions. He was an excellent painter and sculptor, as well as an architect and musician. He was also a mathematician, and worked out the laws of perspective (so essential for realistic art).

VENICE

Venice was now beginning to fight the Ottoman Turks. In 1423, the Venetians bought Thessalonica, in northwestern Greece, from the Byzantine Empire, but in 1430, lost it to the Turks.

At this time, though, Venice defeated Milan and took over a sizable section of northeastern Italy, a region which came to be known as "Venetia." This addition to Venice's territory was not entirely a blessing. It involved her in land wars in Italy and prevented her from exerting her full effort against the Turks.

In 1403, Venice imposed a waiting period on anyone wishing to enter the city in order to see if they would develop plague. Eventually, the waiting period was standardized at 40 days. Thus, the idea was instituted of a "quarantine" (from the French word for "forty"), one of the earliest hygienic measures against the spread of disease.

HOLY ROMAN EMPIRE

In 1410, Sigismund, a half-brother of drunken King Wenceslas, became the ruler of the Empire, though Wenceslas lived on until 1419 and insisted on keeping the title. Sigismund labored to put an end to the Great Schism. This he succeeded in doing, thanks to the council of Constance, which he had called into existence against Papal wishes.

Sigismund's support of conciliar reform in general failed, however. In addition, the Council alienated Bohemia by its treatment of the religious reformer, Jan Hus, leading to war in Bohemia and a further weakening of the Empire.

Sigismund was king of Hungary and Poland, too, though this did not add strength to his Imperial throne. His defeat at Nicopolis by the Turks did add weakness, however.

Sigismund died in 1437, leaving only a daughter. That daughter was married to Albert of Hapsburg (1397–1439), the great-great-great-grandson of Rudolph of Hapsburg, who had been Emperor a century and a half earlier. Albert became Emperor Albert II, and was the fourth Hapsburg to serve as Emperor. There was never, after this, an Emperor who was not a Hapsburg.

Albert II died in 1438, and was succeeded by his second cousin, who reigned as Frederick III (1415–1493). He was the last Emperor to be crowned by the Pope, six and a half centuries after the first such crowning of Charlemagne.

Since the Holy Roman Empire was, in itself, a cipher, and since the Emperors were henceforth drawn entirely from the Hapsburgs of Austria, we will consider later events in the Holy Roman Empire under the heading of "Austria," and include other headings where significant events in the Empire involve sections other than Austria.

Even though the Holy Roman Empire was

moribund politically, the life of the mind continued to shine brightly there.

Nicholas of Cusa (1401–1464) was a German scholar and ecclesiastic with astonishingly modern ideas. He held that the Earth turned on its axis and moved around the Sun; that space was infinite, and that the stars were other suns with planets circling them; that plants drew sustenance from the air; that the behavior of the pulse was a valuable diagnostic device. Until then, spectacles were used only with convex lenses to correct for far-sightedness. Nicholas of Cusa was the first to make them with concave lenses for near-sighted people. Far from getting into trouble for his unusual views, Nicholas of Cusa was made a cardinal in 1448.

The Austrian mathematician and astronomer, Georg von Peurbach (1423–1461), made use of Arabic numerals in preparing a new table of planetary motions. He clung rigidly, however, to the Earth-centered astronomy of the ancient Greeks.

BOHEMIA

When Sigismund forced the Council of Constance on an unwilling Church, he saw it not only as a means of enforcing Papal unity on western Christendom, but on ending various heresies that were troubling the Church. The one that was most bothersome in his own dominions was the Wyclif-like teachings of Jan Hus, who wanted a simpler, more virtuous church. He was getting into more and more trouble with the church hierarchy and becoming more and more popular with the Bohemian people (who were also becoming more aware of the fact that they were Slavic, and not German).

Sigismund invited Jan Hus to attend the council where he might discuss his views. Hus felt that would be suicidal behavior, so Sigismund gave him a safe-conduct. Therefore, Hus attended the Council, was questioned and cross-questioned repeatedly, was placed in prison and, finally, on July 6, 1415, despite his safe-conduct, was burned at the stake.

It was a mistake. Hus, dead, was more powerful than Hus, alive. The Hussites of Bohemia, those who followed his teachings, were outraged and, by 1419, they had risen in rebellion, and there followed the "Hussite wars."

Outstanding on the Hussite side was John Žižka (1376–1424), who developed the use of wagons with armored sides, and holes through which small cannon could be aimed. When Žižka found a good position for battle, he placed his wagons in a circle and, when the enemy attacked, he fired his cannon. He had invented a kind of primitive system of tanks.

Žižka's cannon drove back the enemy (who usually outnumbered him greatly). His pikemen and cavalry would then charge and Žižka won every battle he fought with the Imperials.

Žižka died in 1424 of the plague. The Hussites continued to win victories, however, using his tactics, but then they fell out among themselves. Žižka's followers were extremists who fought against the moderate Hussites as well as against the Imperial forces.

By 1450, things were quieting down. Though Hussites remained in existence, the great days of victories were gone and there were only sputterings. A Bohemian named George of Podebrady (1420–1471) seized Prague in 1448 and was the effective ruler of the land. He was a moderate Hussite and he labored to bring about a reconciliation between the Hussites and the Catholics.

POLAND

Jagiello (Wladyslaw II), who now ruled over Poland–Lithuania, turned against the Teutonic Knights. Included in the army he mustered was a Bohemian contingent under John Žižka, who was later to achieve so much in the Hussite wars. There were also contingents from the Russian principalities and even from the Tatars.

On July 15, 1410, battle was joined at Tannenberg, just south of the Teutonic Knights' territory in Prussia, and there the Knights were badly defeated. Wladyslaw II followed it up by devastating raids into Prussia, but he had to desist because the unruly Polish nobility (there was no other kind) were making trouble in his rear. In 1411, a peace treaty was signed in which the Teutonic Knights gave up Samogita (the modern

Lithuania) but nothing more. From this time on, though, the Knights were no longer an expansive force.

HUNGARY

At this time, Hungary fulfilled its role as Christian bulwark against the Turks, thanks largely to one man, János Hunyadi (1407–1456).

Distrusting feudal levees as disorderly and undisciplined, Hunyadi set about training a regular army he could rely on. With that, in the 1440s, he attacked the Turks and almost drove them out of the Balkans, in what is sometimes described as "the last Crusade."

The climax came in 1444, when Hunyadi advanced through Bulgaria. The Venetian fleet had agreed to go to the Dardanelles to keep the Turks from shipping reinforcements into the Balkans. The Venetian fleet, however, didn't get to the Dardanelles, so a large Turkish army moved into Bulgaria. At Varna on the Black Sea, on November 10, 1444, the Turks completely defeated Hunyadi's troops.

This meant that the Turks stayed in the Balkans, but Hunyadi had managed at least to keep them off balance and to win precious time for central Europe.

ALBANIA

Albania (the ancient Epirus) suddenly experienced a short, bright moment in history at this time. George Kastrioti (1405–1468), an Albanian, was, in his younger days, a hostage to the Turks and turned Muslim. Later, he returned to Albania, became Christian again, and, beginning in 1444, held off the Turks and kept Albania virtually independent. He was known as "Skanderbeg" ("Lord Alexander") to the Albanians, who made him their national hero.

BYZANTINE EMPIRE

Constantinople had been saved from the Turkish siege that seemed certain to succeed in 1400, only because the Turks suffered an unexpected catastrophic defeat in Asia Minor. The respite was only temporary and the Emperors continued to try desperately to get help.

The Emperor, John VIII (1390–1448), who had gained the throne in 1425, traveled to Italy and attended the Council of Florence in 1439. Once again, he offered to heal the schism between eastern and western Christianity and to accept Papal primacy. Again, it was no use. The Byzantine people simply wouldn't accept the Pope. They would rather have the Turks.

In 1450, the Turks were advancing on Constantinople again, and it didn't look as though a second miracle would take place.

MONGOLS

Tamerlane invaded Syria in 1400 and there he met the Mamluks of Egypt who, nearly a century and a half earlier, had inflicted the first defeat on the Mongols. This time, though, that did not happen. Tamerlane destroyed them and took Damascus.

He then marched into Asia Minor. Bayezid I, the Turkish ruler, was forced to abandon the siege of Constantinople that he had been pressing, in order to meet the new danger from the east. The Battle of Angora in central Asia Minor was fought on July 28, 1402, and once again Tamerlane won completely. He captured Bayezid himself and never released him.

Then, in 1405, Tamerlane decided to rebuild the Mongol Empire by conquering China, but he died on his way eastward. His Empire at once fell apart, though fragments remained under some of his descendants.

A grandson of Tamerlane, Ulugh Beg (1394–1449), ruled at Samarkand, in what is now Uzbekistan, and which had been Tamerlane's capital. He succeeded to the throne in 1447.

His real fame was in astronomy, however. He founded a university in Samarkand in 1420 and built an astronomical observatory in 1424 that was the best in the world at that time. His work, however, was completely unknown in western Europe and did not influence scientific development there. He was assassinated by his son in 1449, and Mongol astronomy died with him.

OTTOMAN EMPIRE

The Ottoman Empire was all but shattered by Tamerlane. Tamerlane had divided Asia Minor among three of Bayezid's sons, to keep the Turks fighting among themselves. One of them, Mehmed (d. 1421), won out over the others, restored the Empire to unity, and by 1413 was reigning as Mehmed I the Restorer.

Murad II became Sultan in 1421, but the Ottoman weakening that had followed Tamerlane's invasion was still apparent. When Murad II turned his attention to the Balkans, he was forced to fall back before János Hunyadi and Skanderbeg. However, the Battle of Varna restored his position to a great extent and, once again, the Turks could look toward their interrupted campaign against Constantinople.

CHINA

In this period, a Chinese admiral, Cheng Ho (who was a eunuch and the first one of his kind to distinguish himself since Narses of the East Roman Empire, nearly nine centuries before), conducted a series of seven naval expeditions under the Emperor Yung-lo, who wanted to extend China's sea-trade.

In 1405, Cheng Ho set forth with 300 ships and 27,000 men and visited Southeast Asia, Indonesia, and Ceylon.

On his second voyage in 1409, he returned to Ceylon and there got into a battle with the Ceylonese, defeated them, and brought their king back to Nanking as a captive.

A third voyage, in 1411, took him as far as the Persian Gulf. On his fourth voyage, he returned to the Persian Gulf, then moved on to the Red Sea, visiting Mecca and Egypt. On his last three voyages, he revisited many of these places.

Yung-lo, however, died in 1424, and the new Emperor was not interested in sea-voyages. Cheng Ho may have died about 1433 and the voyaging stopped.

It is an odd coincidence of history that China on the Pacific Ocean and Portugal on the Atlantic Ocean both began a period of exploration at nearly the same time. China combed the Indian Ocean and reached the east coast of Africa, while Portugal crept down the west coast of Africa.

If this were considered a race, one would have been forced to bet on China. China had a population of perhaps 85 million and Portugal had 1 million. China had more and better ships, a somewhat earlier start, and made far more sweeping trips. China was, in addition, the most technologically advanced country in the world at this time.

But what Portugal had that China didn't have was the *will* to explore. That was why, in the end, when the two nations met at last, it was on the Chinese coast and not on the Portuguese coast.

Yet Cheng Ho's voyages weren't a total loss, either. They facilitated Chinese penetration into southeast Asia, both culturally and in the way of emigration, and did encourage trade.

JAPAN

The "Noh" drama was becoming popular among the intellectual classes at this time.

SOUTH AMERICA

The Incas were establishing an empire in the Andean area of Peru, one which grew to have a population of 12 million people. They had a well-developed civilization, but they never developed writing.

1450 to 1500

OTTOMAN EMPIRE

The Ottoman Empire had now entirely recovered from defeat at the hands of Tamerlane, and was undoubtedly the most powerful nation in Europe.

In 1451, Mehmed II the Conqueror (1432–1481) succeeded to the throne on the death of Murad II. It was his intention, immediately, to go on with the long-delayed business of taking Constantinople.

In that city, Constantine XI (1404–1453) had become Emperor in 1448. He was still "Roman Emperor," but his Empire consisted of the decayed city and a few remnants here and there. He was a capable ruler who would have done very well four centuries earlier, but now could only have the privilege of dying with his Empire.

Mehmed II surrounded Constaninople with overwhelming forces, perhaps up to 150,000 men, against only 10,000 that Constantine could oppose him with. All that Constantinople had was its enormous walls. Those walls had resisted all assaulters for a thousand years (the crusaders, who had taken Constanople two and a half centuries earlier, had done so from *within* the walls).

Against those wall, however, Mehmed II had brought huge cannons that were the best artillery in Europe.

The siege began on April 6, 1453 and, by May 29, the walls had been battered down. The Turks entered and Constantine XI died, fighting to the last.

Just as the end of the West Roman Empire nearly a thousand years earlier is taken as the end of ancient times and the beginning of the Middle Ages, so the end of the last remnant of the East Roman Empire is often taken as the end of the Middle Ages and the beginning of modern times.

Mehmed II made Constantinople the capital of the Ottoman Empire (its name eventually coming to be "Istanbul"), and then proceeded to clean up the Balkans. That was not easy at first, for János Hunyadi managed to win one last victory in 1456 and drove him away from Belgrade. However, Hunyadi died soon after, and, in 1468, so did Skanderbeg, and after that there was no one to dispute the Balkans with Mehmed.

There were still remants of Greek-ruled and Western-ruled land. Southern Greece, including Athens, was gathered up by Mehmed by 1460, and the Empire of Trebizond, the very last diluted remnant of the Roman Empire, was taken in 1461. Mehmed then took various Greek islands that the Venetians had ruled for two and a half centuries, including Euboea.

The only holdout was the island of Rhodes, which was defended by the Knights of St. John, a western group that had originated during the Crusades and that had held Rhodes for over a century and a half.

Mehmed even took Otranto on the Italian heel, just across the strait from Albania, on August 11, 1480, but the next year he died. Mehmed was succeeded by his son, Bayezid II (1447–1512), who was not a warlike monarch. He withdrew the Turkish outpost in Otranto, feeling it would cost too much to defend.

PORTUGAL

Despite the Ottoman strength and victories, the real cutting edge of Europe lay with Portugal.

After the discovery of Cape Verde, the African coast trended southeastward, and the feeling was that the hump of Africa had been passed and that the ships would now be heading for the Indies. And, indeed, by 1470, they had reached a part of the African coast that led them due eastward. They hastened onward, and, in 1472, the navigator, Fernando Po, discovered the island that bears his name. That island was something like 1300 miles east of Portugal, and the navigators were clearly well on the way to the Indies.

But then the African coast turned southward once more and showed no signs of turning east again. For a while, the Portuguese were disheartened and the attempt to reach the Indies languished.

In 1481, however, John II the Perfect (1455–1495), a grandnephew of Henry the Navigator, came to the Portuguese throne. He was an energetic king, perhaps the greatest in Portuguese history, and he urged the navigators to go on. They did so, following the African coast southward for 1600 miles past Fernando Po.

Then, in 1487, a Portuguese navigator, Bartholomeu Dias (1450–1500), traveled farther south than any of his predecessors when a severe storm struck and drove him still farther south. When the storm lifted, he found himself in the open sea with no sign of land anywhere. He sailed eastward—and struck nothing. He then turned northward to retrace his route and on February 3, 1488, he reached land, but the coast was running east and west. Somewhere the southerly trend must have ended and the coast must have turned eastward—and he had missed the turning point in the storm.

He turned west and found the turning point. He called it "the Cape of Storms" and returned to Portugal with the report. John II changed the name to "The Cape of Good Hope," but died in 1495, and didn't live to see the "good hope" realized.

He was succeeded by Manuel I the Fortunate (1469–1521), who pressed ahead even more vigorously. On July 8, 1497, Vasco da Gama (1460–1524) left Portugal with four ships. He rounded the Cape of Good Hope and actually reached Calicut in India on May 22, 1498. He finally returned to Portugal at the end of August 1499, with a huge load of spices. (He had also lost more than half of his men to scurvy, which now became the scourge of long ocean voyages, during which food consisted of items such as hard tack and salt pork, with little chance of vegetables, fruit, or fresh meat.)

After 80 years of trying, Portugal had indeed bypassed the Turks, and this began the process whereby Europe, till then merely a peninsula off the western side of Asia, and Christianity, till then merely a religion of one rather small corner of the world, spread their influence worldwide.

CASTILE/ARAGON

Castile was in a state of semi-anarchy at the beginning of this period and this was at its worst during the reign of Henry IV (1425–1474), who became king in 1454. Henry IV had no sons, but when he died in 1474, he had a daughter, Joan, who was married to Afonso V of Portugal (1432–1481). He also had a half-sister, Isabella (1451–1504), who was married to Ferdinand (1452–1516), the son of John II of Aragon (1397–1479). Castile had to choose between two princesses, each of whom was married to someone who was a foreign king, or who would soon be a foreign king.

Castile chose Isabella, and she became Isabella I of Castile. When John II of Aragon died in 1479, Isabella's husband became Ferdinand II of Aragon.

Castile and Aragon were united only through being ruled by Ferdinand and Isabella. Each retained its own laws and customs, but they never separated again, and after this time, the two together were considered to be a united nation named Spain. It will be referred to as so from this point.

The combination strengthened each, and the fact was that both Isabella and Ferdinand were very capable monarchs and worked well together, so that Spain rapidly grew in power. The Spanish monarchs reached an agreement with the Pope in 1482 that left them very much the masters of the Spanish Church.

Meanwhile, the notorious Spanish Inquisition was set up, also under royal control, and it helped make sure that Spaniards wouldn't have dangerous thoughts. The first and most notorious Grand Inquisitor was a Dominican monk, Tomás de Torquemada (1420–1498), appointed in 1487. His name has become synonymous with cruelty and repression.

The monarchs then set about unifying the rest of the peninsula. Granada, the small Muslim monarchy in the extreme south of Spain, all that was left of the old Moorish domination of the land, was the obvious target.

It took 11 years, for the Muslims fought fiercely, and, in the course of the campaign, the Spanish army developed the discipline and professionalism that made it the finest in Christian Europe. Finally, on January 2, 1492, Granada surrendered, and after nearly eight centuries not one acre of Spain remained under Muslim control.

Spain then, at Torquemada's insistence, expelled the Jews, as England and France had done before them, in order to get rid of another alien presence, and another source of unauthorized thought. Portugal, under Spanish pressure, then expelled its Jews in 1496. Whereas the Jews of England and France traveled to Germany and Poland to become the "Ashkenazim;" the Jews of Spain and Portugal traveled to the Muslim lands of Africa and Asia to become the "Sephardim."

Meanwhile, a Genoese navigator, best-known to us by his Latinized name of Christopher Columbus (1451–1506) had come to Spain.

He thought it wasteful to try to reach the Indies by sailing around Africa. By studying the old Greek geographies, he decided that the Earth had a circumference of only 18,000 miles (instead of the actual 25,000). By studying Marco Polo, he thought Asia extended considerably farther east than it did. Therefore, he thought sailing westward across the Atlantic Ocean should bring ships to the Far East in a mere 3000 miles, a voyage much shorter than sailing around Africa.

Of course, in circumnavigating Africa, one could hug the coast and set up depots on land for rest and resupply, whereas Columbus's route would involve unbroken ocean travel, so that, even if shorter, it would surely be much more difficult and dangerous.

The Portuguese geographers (then the best in the world) pointed this out when Columbus applied to John II of Portugal for funds. They were also quite sure that Asia was much farther off to the west (they were right!) and that trying to sail that distance across open water, instead of going around Africa and hugging the coast, was suicidal. They didn't, however, count on the presence of unknown continents en route. After all, they

had no good records of the Viking explorations of five centuries earlier.

When John II refused funds on these grounds, Columbus tried Spain. Spain was at first reluctant, but once Granada had fallen, Ferdinand and Isabella were in a festive mood and felt they could risk a small sum, especially if that would forestall Portugal (of whom they were understandably envious) in reaching the Indies.

Therefore, Ferdinand and Isabella supplied Columbus with three small ships and allowed him a crew of convicts who were willing to chance the voyage for the privilege of being released from jail. On August 3, 1492, Columbus sailed off westward.

Seven weeks later, across unbroken seas, but, fortunately, without experiencing storms, the ships reached land. It was not the Indies, as Columbus believed it was to his dying day, but one of the islands of the Bahamas. He explored other islands, left some men to settle on one of them, and headed back home. When he passed Portugal, the magnanimous John II greeted him with warm ceremony, and he reached his home port in Spain on March 13, 1493.

The result of the discovery meant, among many other things, a grand intermingling of biology that began at once. Columbus brought horses to the new continent, and brought back pineapples to Europe.

By the year 1500, Columbus had made two more voyages. In the course of the third, in 1498, he sighted the coast of what we now call South America, south of the island of Trinidad.

The Portuguese shared in these early American discoveries. A Portuguese navigator, Pedro Alvares Cabral (1468–1520), circling the bulge of Africa, circled too wide and, on April 22, 1500, encountered the westernmost bulge of South America, which we now call Brazil.

Thus, by 1500, Portugal had reached India, and Spain had reached the American continents. Europe, without knowing it, had embarked on its conquest of the world. For this reason, Columbus's voyage in 1492, rather than the fall of Constantinople in 1453, is sometimes considered the beginning of modern times.

There was, of course, danger that Portugal

and Spain might battle over the new lands their ships had reached and, to avoid that, Pope Alexander VI (1431–1503), a Spaniard by birth and therefore particularly interested in the matter, drew a line from the North Pole to the South Pole down the middle of the Atlantic Ocean. All non-Christian lands to the east of the line were to be Portuguese, and all non-Christian lands to the west were to be Spanish. The next year, Spain and Portugal agreed to move the line a bit to the west to give Portugal enough room to circle the African bulge, and the new line cut through the South American bulge, which Cabral was soon to discover, so that Portugal had that bulge both by agreement and by discovery.

It has always been customary for conquering nations to disregard the rights of the nations they conquered, but the "Line of Demarcation" was the first time when such disregard was officially applied to the entire non-Christian world. It was a sign of Europe's vaulting ambition, and of its calm assumption that non-Christians (and Christian heretics, for that matter) had no human rights.

FRANCE

In 1450, England still held portions of the southwest coast, the last bit of the land which Henry II had obtained when he married Eleanor of Aquitaine, just three centuries earlier.

An English army landed near Bordeaux in October, 1452, under John Talbot, Earl of Shrewsbury (1384–1453), the last of the great English generals of the Hundred Years War. It was eventually met by the French army with its artillery. At the Battle of Castillon, east of Bordeaux, on July 17, 1453, the English were totally defeated and Talbot was killed. The Hundred Years War was over (after 116 years, actually, though there were long stretches in which there was little fighting). The only thing that England had gained from all that fighting was the city of Calais, which remained English.

The Hundred Years War, having ended in 1453, is another reason for those who want to consider that year as the beginning of modern times.

Charles VII, the despised Dauphin in the days before Joan of Arc, had become the king who ousted the English (he was known as "Charles the Well-Served"). He died in 1461, and his son became king as Louis XI (1423–1483).

Louis XI was not a martial king, but he was a practical one. In 1464, he founded a postal service that was the forerunner of such things in Europe generally. He was also a shrewd king, at his best in diplomacy—in the crucial bribe at the right moment, in the clever lie. The long ordeal of France had left its higher nobles virtually independent of the king and Louis had to bring them down. This he did, slowly, in his own way.

The more important of the recalcitrant nobles were, of course, the Dukes of Burgundy, who had sided with the English in the time of Henry V, a half-century earlier. Burgundy was the richest and most civilized land in Europe and, under Philip the Good, it continued to be more powerful than France. Philip the Good died in 1467 and his son, Charles (1433–1477), became Duke of Burgundy. This Duke is usually referred to as Charles the Bold, though he is often called Charles the Rash.

Charles the Rash, a third cousin of Louis XI (both were great-great-grandsons of John II of France, who had been taken prisoner at the battle of Poitiers more than a century earlier), was short-tempered, hasty, and favored action over thought—the precise opposite of Louis XI. What Charles wanted was to make Burgundy an independent nation and himself a king. What Louis wanted was to make Burgundy a part of France and make its dukes servants of the French monarchy.

For a while, it was Charles who had the upper hand. He extended and strengthened his realm, roared through French territories, and even took Louis prisoner at one time. In 1473, he seemed on the point of receiving his longed-for kingship from the Holy Roman Emperor. Louis, however, patiently worked away in his own sly fashion, winning over Charles's allies to his own side and raising new adversaries to him. When Charles, in his efforts at expansion, decided to take over the Swiss cantons, Louis saw to it that the Swiss were supplied with the money they needed to resist.

Charles acted with typical rashness. In 1476, he captured a Swiss position, and, in a moment of rage, hanged all the Swiss he had taken prisoner. This, naturally, infuriated the Swiss beyond any possibility of forgiveness.

The Swiss had pikemen, whereas the Burgundians had cavalry and artillery. The Swiss, however, had a way of marching onto a field and beginning to fight at once even as they reached the site. Three times, they caught the Burgundians and defeated them before the latter could get their artillery and horsemen into play. In the third battle, at Nancy in the Burgundian territory, on January 5, 1477, Charles was killed.

Charles left, as his only heir, a daughter, Mary of Burgundy (1457–1482), and his realm fell apart. The Netherlands remained true to his daughter and they were the richest part of the duchy. Most of the rest, however, was gathered up by Louis XI.

During the time of Louis XI and Charles the Rash, François Villon (1431–1465) was the outstanding poet. He was a rogue and a thief but posterity remembers only his lyrics. His best remembered work is "The Ballade of the Ladies of Bygone Times," with the refrain "But where are snows of yesteryear?"

Louis XI died in 1483, and his son ruled as Charles VIII (1470–1498). The Duke of Brittany died in 1488, and left only a daughter, Anne of Brittany (1477–1514), as heir. Charles VIII married her so that he might absorb Brittany into the French kingdom and then wandered off into Italy in 1494 on a fool's errand, trying to annex Naples which he claimed he had inherited.

He failed, and died in 1498, leaving no direct heirs. The kingdom went to his second cousin, once removed, who reigned as Louis XII (1462–1515). Louis XII was the son of Charles of Orleans who was captured at the Battle of Agincourt, three fourths of a century earlier. Louis XII divorced his wife to marry Anne of Brittany and to keep the duchy in the family. He, too, then grew entangled in Italy.

The Italian adventure helped bring the Renaissance to France, but it also started the process whereby the Renaissance was killed in Italy.

ENGLAND

Frustrated by the defeat in France, and given leeway by the incapacity of Henry VI, the English nobles fought each other, and the members of the royal family engaged in dynastic squabbling, to the detriment of prosperity generally.

In 1450, there was a brief rebellion of small farmers from southeastern England, led by one Jack Cade (d. 1450). It was quickly crushed. In 1455, however, the War of the Roses began and that was not so easily handled.

On one side of the war was mad and feeble King Henry VI and his forceful wife, Margaret of Anjou (1430–1482). They, and those who followed them, were the Lancastrians, and their symbol was a red rose. On the other side was Richard, Duke of York, and his followers, who were the Yorkists and whose symbol was a white rose. It is for this reason that the civil war between the two factions is known as the War of the Roses.

Richard of York was killed in the course of the various battles that followed, with ups and downs for both houses. Finally, however, the Yorkists gained the upper hand and Richard's son was accepted as king in 1461, ruling as Edward IV (1442–1483).

That by no means ended the civil war. Discontent with Edward was as sharp as with Henry, and Louis XI of France shrewdly fomented that discontent and supported anyone who would continue the war, since it was quite obvious that an England occupied with civil war would not bother France.

On May 3, 1471, however, Edward IV won the Battle of Tewkesbury in Gloucestershire. In the battle, Henry VI's son was killed. Henry VI, himself, was taken prisoner and was quietly killed shortly therafter. The Lancastrians were now all either dead or in exile, and Edward IV was safe on his throne.

Edward IV died in 1483, however, and disorders began at once. He left as his heir his oldest son, 12 years old, who was Edward V (1470–1483), and a younger son, Richard of York. As regent, there was Edward IV's younger brother, Richard of Gloucester (1452–1485). He was an able soldier, honest and popular. (Shakespeare, in his play *Richard III*, drew a completely false picture of the king, in line with the political realities of his time.)

Foreseeing trouble, and knowing that Edward IV's marriage to Elizabeth Woodville (1437–1492), the mother of the children, had been irregular since he had been betrothed to someone else at the time, Richard of Gloucester had no trouble having the children set aside and having himself crowned as Richard III.

Yet the dynastic problems continued, especially when the royal children were heard of no more and it was rumored that Richard III had had them killed. The only Lancastrian remaining was Henry Tudor of Richmond (1457–1509), who was descended on his mother's side from John of Gaunt and who was a half-second-cousin of Henry VI. Louis XI helped Henry Tudor on his usual trouble-making principle and, at the crucial time, Richard III was abandoned by several of those who were supposed to be fighting on his side.

At the Battle of Bosworth in central England, on August 22, 1485, Richard III was defeated and killed, and Henry Tudor became king as Henry VII. He married Elizabeth (1465–1503), the daughter of Edward IV, so that his heir would combine the houses of Lancaster and York. With that, the Wars of the Roses was over.

The chief result of the Wars of the Roses was that it killed off most of the ancient nobility of the kingdom and left the king that much more powerful. Henry VII and his immediate successors were virtually absolute, and Parliament, which had grown quite powerful when money was needed for the wars in France, was now completely cowed and was under the royal thumb.

Henry VII was a cautious, miserly monarch who kept England at peace and avoided reckless expenditures. He saw to it that all possible claimants to the throne, real or pretended, were re-moved, so that the throne became truly stable for the first time since the death of Edward III, a century and a quarter earlier.

Henry VII made one move to participate in the excitement of the new age of exploration. In 1497, he sent out an Italian navigator, Giovanni Caboto (1450–1499), better known by the English version of his name, John Cabot, to explore westward. In two expeditions, the second with his son Sebastian Cabot (1475–1557) in 1498, the coasts of what are now called Newfoundland, Nova Scotia, and New England were explored. He was the first European (if we exclude the Vikings whose discoveries never became known to Europeans generally at the time) actually to touch the coast of North America.

The discoveries were not followed up, but the time was to come when England would base her claims to North America on these voyages.

The best-known piece of English writing in this period was *Morte d'Arthur*, finished about 1470 by Thomas Malory, which gave us the legends of King Arthur and his Knights of the Round Table, much as we know them today. John Skelton (1460–1528) was the most important English satirist of the day, lampooning court life in the time of Henry VII and his successor.

Important in the technological side of literature was the work of William Caxton (1422–1491), who brought the German invention of printing with movable type to England, where the first printed material appeared in 1476. Caxton printed Chaucer's *Canterbury Tales* and Malory's *Morte d'Arthur* in 1485.

SCOTLAND

James II died in 1460 and was succeeded by his 8-year-old son, James III (1452–1488). The new reign was a crazy-quilt of feudal disorder, as different noblemen sought to control the King and the country. Finally, James fled to England, obtained the help of Edward IV, and, with English help, was seated on the throne, but was assassinated in 1488.

He was succeeded by his 15-year-old son, who reigned as James IV (1473–1513).

IRELAND

In 1494, England tightened its hold on Ireland, setting up rules to the effect that no Irish parliament could meet or pass laws without the consent of the English king, and that all laws passed by the English Parliament should hold in Ireland as well.

PAPACY

The Popes of this period lived comfortable lives, not very austere, and were chiefly interested in nepotism (from the Latin word for "nephew"). That is, they made sure they enriched their "nephews" (which often meant their illegitimate sons) and their families generally.

They also involved themselves more or less deeply in the feuds of the various Italian city-states, as did, notably, Sixtus IV (1414–1484), who became Pope in 1471. Some also took pains to beautify Rome, which had sunk very low during the Avignonese period. Again, this was true, notably of Sixtus IV, who was responsible for the "Sistine Chapel."

The loss of Constantinople to the Turks caused all the Popes of the period to try to preach crusades, but this fell flat every time. The mania for crusades had passed. It was a period when monarchs were interested in preserving their own realms and robbing, if they could, those of their neighbors. Distant Palestine now held no interest to them.

More influential, for a time, than any of these Popes was a Dominican friar, Girolamo Savonarola (1452–1498), who was a passionate reformer. He bitterly denounced the semipagan life-style of the Popes and higher clergy. He also denounced the materialistic, humanistic, consumer-oriented lives of the citizens generally.

In 1492, Alexander VI (1431–1503) became Pope. Of Spanish birth, he was the Pope who set up the Line of Demarcation, dividing the world between Spain and Portugal. He was the most notorious of the Popes, a byword for his luxury and nepotism (though probably the stories are exaggerated, as they almost always are, in these cases).

Savonarola denounced Alexander VI and persauded many people to join his movement. The artistocrats, the well-to-do, and the higher clergy all turned against him at last, because he made life too uncomfortable for them. He was eventually tried for heresy, convicted after torture, then finally hanged and burned on May 23, 1498.

NAPLES

In this period, Naples and Sicily were ruled by Ferdinand I (1423–1494), who was of the royal line of Aragon, being an illegitimate son of Alfonso V of Aragon. Ferdinand I died in 1494, without direct heirs, although Ferdinand II of Aragon was his first cousin (and brother-in-law) and might have inherited.

However, Charles VIII of France, was a great-grandson of Louis of Anjou, who had called himself Louis II of Naples, though he had never managed actually to rule the land. Charles used this to claim the throne of Naples after Ferdinand's death, and he marched into Italy in 1494. This was the beginning of troubles for Italy.

The first known cases of the disease we now call syphilis struck the French army while it was in Naples, and it spread widely through Europe thereafter. Some of Columbus's crew were there, too, and the suggestion has been made that the disease was picked up in America and brought back to Europe. However, the disease called "leprosy" in the Middle Ages, which seems to have become rare afterword, may have actually been syphilis, so perhaps it was a new name, not a new disease, that came in as the 1400s ended.

FLORENCE

Cosimo de Medici died in 1464 and his son, Piero the Gouty (1414–1469), took his place, but he was practically an invalid and he died after ruling for five years.

Under his son, Lorenzo de Medici (1449–1492), better known as "Lorenzo the Magnificent," Florence reached its peak.

Florentine artists of the period include Fra Angelico (1400–1455); Filippo Lippi (1406–1469); his son and namesake, Filippino Lippi (1457–1504); and Sandro Botticelli (1445–1510).

The most astonishing Renaissance man of all time, however, was Leonardo da Vinci (1452–1519). His "Last Supper" fresco was completed around 1497 and his "Mona Lisa," perhaps the greatest of all paintings, within the next decade. In addition, he was a first-rate scientist who designed parachutes and elevators, speculated on aircraft, and studied the flight of birds and the swimming of fish. He also studied the muscles and bones of human beings, dissecting some 30 cadavers, and speculated usefully on falling bodies, the structure of the earth, and the nature of fossils.

Unfortunately, he kept his ideas to himself, writing them in code in voluminous notebooks that were not published until 1898. On the other hand, by keeping quiet, he stayed out of trouble.

Italian business activity was helped along by the mathematician, Luca Pacioli (1445–1517), who was born in Florentine territory and who invented double-entry bookkeeping.

MILAN

Milan also had a golden age at this time. Ludovico il Moro (1452–1508) became Duke of Milan in 1481 and encouraged art and literature. He was a particular patron of Leonardo de Vinci. However, the French invasion put an end to that and, by 1500, Ludovico was a prisoner of the French (and died in that condition) while Milan itself was, at least temporarily, controlled by France.

VENICE

Venice fought the Turks at this time, but was far outweighed by the mighty Ottoman Empire. Venice lost almost all her winnings of the Fourth Crusade, but her holding in Italy reached its maximum extent when she acquired some further territory after beating the city-state of Ferrara. In the eastern Mediterranean Sea, Venice retained the island of Crete and, in 1489, it actually acquired the island of Cyprus in addition.

Primarily a commercial city, Venice neverthe-

less had its artists, too. Prominent among the Venetian artists of the time were Jacopo Bellini (1400–1470) and his two sons, Gentile Bellini (1429–1507) and Giovanni Bellini (1430–1516).

AUSTRIA

Frederick of Austria was Emperor Frederick III of the Holy Roman Empire at this time, but the Empire was so feeble that it had to fear Burgundy, a mere dukedom. When it seemed that Charles the Rash of Burgundy was intent on forcing a royal title out of the Emperor, Frederick was so frightened at the possible consequences that he literally fled their conference at night.

Once Charles died at Nancy, however, Frederick was quick to arrange a marriage between Charles's daughter, Mary, and his own son, Maximilian (1459–1519). This did not enable him to gather in all of Burgundy, for Louis XI rapidly rounded up much of it. However, the rich Netherlands remained with Mary and, therefore, came to be Maximilian's, as did a section just west of Switzerland called "Franche Comte" ("Free Country" of Burgundy).

In this way, Frederick III began Austria's policy of gathering in additional territory, not by military conquest, but by marriage.

Naturally, France was not willing to have the Netherlands and Franche Comte become Austrian. However, Maximilian defeated the French at the Battle of Guinegate, south of Calais, on August 7, 1479, and that settled that.

When Mary of Burgundy died in 1482, the Netherlands no longer wanted to be ruled by an Austrian without their own Queen, but Maximilian managed to retain control even so. In 1493, when Frederick III died, Maximilian became Holy Roman Emperor as Maximilian I.

None of Frederick III's policies had strengthened the Empire, incidentally; they strengthened only Austria.

The Netherlands continued to produce important artists, by the way, such as Roger van der Weyden (1399–1464) and Hieronymus Bosch (1450–1516). The latter was particularly well-known for his paintings of imaginative monstrosities.

Much more important to the world than anything that Frederick III, or any monarch, did in this period, was the accomplishment at Mainz (in the central regions of the Empire) of a German inventor, Johann Gutenberg (1400–1468).

Gutenberg worked out the technique of printing by the use of movable type. The same type, representing various letters, could be arranged and rearranged indefinitely and used to print up any number of books much more rapidly than they could be copied by hand. Moreover, if the printing was correct, any number of copies could be made that were free of error.

The Chinese had this notion before the Europeans did, and the news of it may have reached Europe in Mongolian times. The point is, though, that even if the concept was not original with Europeans, it was more widely employed by them. This was not because Europeans were more intelligent or ingenious than the Chinese (one could easily argue the reverse), but because the Europeans had the alphabet and the Chinese did not. Far fewer symbols sufficed in Europe; thus, the matter of movable type was far more practical in Europe.

In 1454, Gutenberg put out a Bible in double columns, with 42 lines of Latin to the page. He produced 300 copies of 1282 pages, and thus produced the Gutenberg Bibles. Those that remain of the original 300 Bibles are now incredibly valuable.

Although Gutenberg did not make a business success out of his invention, others did. Printing meant cheap books and cheap books made literacy worthwhile. By 1500, up to nine million printed copies of 30,000 different works were in circulation. The base of scholarship broadened; the views and discoveries of scholars could quickly be made known to other scholars.

This was particularly true in the case of scientific investigations. With the spread of printing, reports of scientific investigations, observations, and theories could spread the length and breadth of Europe rapidly. Each new finding served as a basis for still newer findings. Science became not the product of individuals working more or less in isolation, but the product of a scientific community. In fact, the Scientific Revolution, which

was soon to come, could very likely not have emerged without printing.

Printing utterly changed the world and it (along with the fall of Constantinople, the end of the Hundred Years War, and the discovery of the American continents—all of which took place in this period) marks the transition from medieval to modern times. Printing, one must surely suspect, was the most fundamental of these changes.

Printing made itself felt in science at once, by the way. The outstanding astronomer of the period was the German scholar, Johann Muller (1436–1476), who called himself "Regiomontanus." He produced a table of planetary motions and had it *printed*, so that he was the first to use the new technique for a scientific purpose. He was also the first to write a book on trigonometry, treating the subject independently and not as a mere adjunct to astronomy. In 1472, he was the first to make objective observations of a comet, instead of viewing it merely as an object of dread.

BOHEMIA

Bohemia was quite exhausted after the Hussite wars but the strong rule of George of Podebrady was of benefit. Since he was a moderate Hussite, the Pope went through the motions of deposing him and encouraged the King of Hungary to attack him, but George defended himself ably till he died in 1471. He was succeeded by Ladislas II, who was no relation, but who was the son of the King of Poland. He was a weak ruler and under him, Bohemia declined.

HUNGARY

The forceful days of János Hunyadi continued after his death, when his son, Matthias Hunyadi (1443–1490), was chosen to be king of Hungary and reigned as Matthias the Just. Matthias intended to take over Bohemia and Austria and face the Turks with a united Central Europe. This he was unable to do. He could not defeat George of Bohemia, and though Matthias occupied Vienna in 1485 and made it his capital, that conquest was not permanent.

He was a great patron of the arts, built a valuable library, reformed taxation and was, in general, a popular monarch. When he died in 1490, however, his realm fell apart. Ladislas II, who was ruling Bohemia weakly, took over Hungary, too, and ruled it just as weakly. Placing different nations under a single rule may forge a strong military bastion if the ruler is strong, but mere size of territory is of no use if the ruler is weak.

SWITZERLAND

Switzerland's victories over Charles the Rash of Burgundy and further victories over the Holy Roman Empire brought their military reputation to a peak by 1500. They apparently could not lose a battle and their mere approach to a battlefield sowed panic in the hearts of their adversaries. Other nations began to hire Swiss mercenaries as once, 19 centuries earlier, nations had hired Greek mercenaries.

POLAND

At this time, Poland was ruled by Casimir IV (1427–1492), who had become king in 1447. He was not a warrior, and he was not an educated man, but he was a patient diplomat after the type of Louis XI of France. He could fight when he had to, however. The Prussians had revolted against the Teutonic Knights and had asked for help from Casimir. Casimir offered it, and though the war was unmarked by great successes on either side, it ended with a peace treaty on October 19, 1466, in which Poland gained an outlet to the Baltic Sea.

It was Casimir's son, who, as Ladislas II, reigned over Bohemia and Hungary. Another of Casimir's sons, John Albert (1459–1501), succeeded to the Polish throne in 1492, on the death of his father.

RUSSIA

The Tatars were still a factor in Russia. As late as 1451, they appeared under the walls of Moscow.

In 1462, however, Ivan III (1440–1505), sometimes known as "Ivan the Great," became Grand Prince of Muscovy. In 1471, he married Zoe, the niece of Constantine XI, the last Byzantine Emperor. By the marriage, Ivan III (and all his successors) claimed to be the heirs of the Byzantine Empire and to be the protectors of the Orthodox Church everywhere. Ivan took the title of Tsar ("Caesar"), rebuilt the Kremlin in Moscow, making use of Italian architects, and put on much of the pomp and panoply of the Imperial throne. Moscow was declared to be the "third Rome," after Rome itself and Constantinople.

Ivan III also expanded Muscovy's territory by attacking Novgorod in two wars and annexing it at the conclusion of the second in 1478. This turned Muscovy into Russia, for Moscow now controlled the northern half of what is now European Russia. It was a largely unpeopled half, however. Although Russia had become the largest nation in Europe in area, as it has remained ever since, its population was only 7 million as compared with France's 12 million.

Ivan III cleaned up whatever small principalities were left in northern Russia and, in 1480, he refused to pay tribute to the Tatars. Once more, they invaded and aimed for Moscow, but this time Ivan fended them off and made his refusal to tribute stick. After two and a half centuries, the heart of Russia was free of the Tatar yoke.

Thereafter, war with Poland brought some gains in the west, including the city of Smolensk. Ivan III was surely the most successful Russian monarch since the old Kievan days.

WEST AFRICA

The Songhair Empire, along the middle Niger River, was now at the height of its power.

1500 TO 1550

OTTOMAN EMPIRE

The Ottoman Empire, in 1550, controlled Asia Minor and the Balkans, and had the best army and the most efficient government in Europe. In 1512, the relatively mild Bayezid II was forced to abdicate by his youngest son Selim (1467–1520), who reigned as Selim I the Grim, and whose character fully justified the description. He made sure that all possible competitors for the throne, especially his brothers, were defeated, captured, and killed.

He then turned east. The Turks were Sunnites, but Persia had just come under a new dynasty that was Shiite. To Selim, who was fanatical in religion, this was unbearable, especially since Persia supported Turkish subjects in eastern Asia Minor who had rebelled against him.

Selim invaded Persian territory and, at Chaldiran in Armenia, he won a hard-fought battle on August 23, 1515. He then marched as far as Tabriz in northwestern Persia and annexed the upper portion of the Tigris–Euphrates valley to the Ottoman Empire.

He might have gone further, but the Mameluks of Egypt forced themselves on his attention. From the time they had been defeated by Tamerlane over a century earlier, they had occupied themselves, for the most part, in internal squabbling. Their efforts at taking over the east Mediterranean islands of Cyprus and Rhodes had failed, nor could they make heading against the Ottoman Turks. Now, however, the Mameluk ruler of Egypt, Kansu al-Gauri (d. 1516), formed an alliance with the Persians and brought an army into Syria.

Selim turned south and met the Egyptians at Merj-Dabik in northern Syria. There on August 24, 1516, al-Gauri was quickly defeated and killed. With that, Selim took Syria and invaded Egypt. By 1517, he had taken all of Egypt along with the Red Sea coast of Arabia, including the holy city of Mecca. By the time Selim I died in 1520, he had more than doubled the size of the Ottoman Empire.

He was succeeded by his son, who reigned as Suleiman I the Magnificent (1495–1566) and, under him, the Ottoman Empire reached its peak. In 1521, he took Belgrade and sent raiding parties to terrorize Hungary. This time there was no Hunyadi to stop the Turks, as there had been 80 years before.

Suleiman next tackled the island of Rhodes that had, so far, defied all attempts of the Turks to take it, and whose sea-raiders threatened his lines of communication. He landed troops on the island on June 25, 1552, and began the siege of the city. The city contained only 700 Knights of St. John, plus 6000 other troops, but it had the best fortifications in the world at that time.

Suleiman fought for half a year and, in the process, lost half of his beseiging forces, who numbered somewhere between 100,000 and 200,000. The defenders had lost three fourths of their much smaller number before Suleiman obtained a surrender by offering to let them leave Rhodes with all the honors of war. He kept his promise and the surviving knights moved to Malta, where they have remained ever since.

With Rhodes taken, and the east quiet, thanks to Selim's campaigns, Suleiman could now move massively westward. He invaded Hungary and, on August 29, 1525, faced the Hungarian troops at Mohacs on the Danube in the southern part of their land. Suleiman had the superior artillery, consisting of cannon that were chained together, and the Hungarians finally broke and fled. Their leaders, including their king, were killed and the land was defenseless. For two centuries it had been the bulwark of Christianity versus Islam, and now it had been shattered.

Most of Hungary was put under John Zapolya (1487–1540), who was chosen to be king, and who was willing to serve as a Turkish puppet. The western and northern sections of Hungary were taken over by Austria, which had now succeeded to the role of bulwark against the Muslims.

The Holy Roman Emperor invaded Hungary to take over the rest of it and John Zapolya called for help to Suleiman. Suleiman responded and led an army into Hungary a second time. Zapolya joined him. Suleiman took Buda on September 8, 1529, and marched on to Vienna, which he placed under seige on September 27. This was the high point of the Ottoman advance, for Suleiman could not take the city, and with winter coming on, he was forced to retreat. (The Austrians found coffee beans in the abandoned Turkish baggage, and coffee drinking was thus introduced to western Europe.)

In the end, the situation remained as it was before the second invasion. Suleiman kept most of Hungary, and Austria retained the northern and western rim. Zapolya remained puppet king of Hungary till his death in 1540.

After that, Suleiman renewed the battle with Persia, but with inconclusive results.

Meanwhile, there were sea-fights all over the Mediterranean Sea. The dominant figure was Khayr ad-din (d. 1546), known as "Barbarossa," or "Redbeard" to the Europeans. He was a North African pirate who felt he would be safer and stronger if he made an alliance with Suleiman. He did, and eventually took over both Algeria and Tunis, so that virtually all of North Africa became tributary to the Ottoman Turks. Khayr ad-din remained the terror of the Mediterranean Sea till his death in 1546.

By 1550, then, the Ottoman Empire was the largest and strongest Islamic Empire that the world had seen since the decline of the Abbasid Empire seven centuries earlier.

AUSTRIA

Frederick III's greatest coup was marrying his son, Maximilian, to Mary of Burgundy, and thus adding the Netherlands to the dominions of the Hapsburgs. Maximilian, in his turn, did something analogous with his son, Philip (1478–1506).

Philip, called "Philip the Handsome," apparently with justification, was married in 1496 to Joanna (1479–1555), the older daughter of Ferdinand and Isabella of Spain, who had no sons to inherit their land. Obviously, if this couple had a son, he would be a Hapsburg who would rule over Austria, the Netherlands, Spain, and any other lands in Europe that either Austria or Spain owned, to say nothing of Spain's growing dominions in the Americas.

It actually happened. Philip the Handsome died unexpectedly in 1506 at the age of 28. His wife, Joanna, who loved him desperately, and who was rather mentally unstable to begin with, went completely mad, and stayed mad for the remaining half-century of her life, so that she is known in history as Joanna the Mad (Juana la Loca). In 1500, however, she had given birth to a son, Charles (1500–1558), who was not mad and who grew up to inherit all that land and to become the most powerful Hapsburg in the history of that family.

He ruled as Charles I of Spain in 1516, when his grandfather, Ferdinand II, died. In 1519, he was elected Holy Roman Emperor as Charles V, and it is by this title that he is known to history.

Emperor Charles V, with his possessions scattered all over western Europe, ruled over 26 million people as compared with Suleiman's 27 million. They were worthy opponents of each other. To be sure, Charles V could not face Suleiman without knowing that behind him he had a deadly enemy in the form of France (but then Suleiman knew that behind him he had a deadly enemy in the form of Persia).

But Charles V had another disadvantage. As he started his imperial career, the German lands were torn in two by a religious dispute, one that was more important to the history of Europe than Charles V and Suleiman the Magnificent put together.

Wyclif and Hus had inveighed against the corruption, venality, and luxury of the Church, and they had been silenced; however, as long as abuses continued, other reformers were sure to arise.

To raise money, the Church was now selling "indulgences;" that is, documents assuring that dead souls in purgatory would be released if living relatives would only pay the prices set for such indulgences. Some of the sellers of indulgences, notably a Dominican monk named Johann Tetzel (1465–1519), were quite shameless in their commercialization of the process.

An Augustinian monk, Martin Luther (1483–1546), was offended by this rank conversion of spirituality into a money-making device and by various other flaws that he saw in Church administration and behavior. On October 31, 1517, he nailed 95 theses to the church door at Wittenberg in Saxony—the usual way of challenging others to debate with him over the various points of view he was expressing.

Luther had going for him what previous reformers had had—nationalism. Wyclif had appealed to English nationalists who objected to money forever flowing into the Italian coffers of the Pope. Similarly, Hus appealed to Bohemian nationalism, and now Luther appealed to German nationalism.

However, Luther had, in addition, something Wyclif and Hus had not had. Luther had the printing press. Wyclif's and Hus's views were only broadcast with difficulty, so that a great many people knew little detail about their arguments. Luther, however, had the gift of vigorous and powerful prose that appeared as printed pamphlets. These spread the length and breadth of Germany much faster than they could be suppressed. In no time, everyone was aware of, and debating, the new views.

Wyclif had his Lollards and Hus his Hussites and both were troublesome to suppress, but it was as nothing to the crowds of "Lutherans" that now followed the teachings of the new reformer.

Like Hus, Luther attended a great convocation, the Diet of Worms (a city on the mid-Rhine) on April 17 and 18, 1521. There he upheld his views vigorously. He had a safe-conduct, but the memory of what had happened to Hus a century earlier was a vivid one and Luther was spirited away to safety by Frederick III the Wise of Saxony (1463–1525), who was a political and religious reformer, a patron of the arts, and, wonder of wonders, believed in religious toleration.

Other religious reformers arose to preach Lutheran doctrines, or more radical ones, or merely different ones. All were united only in that they denied the authority of the Pope and wished to abolish the intricate churchly hierarchy and ritual. All together, they came to be called "Protestants." The movement was the "Protestant Reformation" to Protestants and the "Protestant Revolt" to Catholics.

For a while it looked as though all Germany might turn Protestant, but the attacks on the constituted authorities of the church got the peasants excited. They thought it was an attack on all authority and, in 1524, they rose in wild abandon to destroy the landowners and aristocrats who, for as long as anyone could remember, had treated them worse than animals.

Luther, aware that he needed the protection of the Princes who hoped, through Protestantism, to obtain various portions of the rich lands and other properties of the Church, dared not support the peasants. Therefore, he wrote pamphlets denouncing the peasants in unmeasured terms. He retained the friendship of the princes, but when the peasant revolt was suppressed with the utmost brutality, the survivors turned against the reformer who, they felt, had betrayed them, and remained stubbornly Catholic thereafter.

(The Teutonic Knights, who were now restricted to eastern Prussia, turned Protestant in 1526.)

Charles V was urged by the Catholic Church to take strong action against the Protestants and, indeed, he would have liked to do just that, but France was keeping him busy, and continued to keep him busy to the end of his reign. And when France let up for a while, then Suleiman kept him busy.

The greatest German artist of the period was Albrecht Dürer (1471–1528). He was not only a painter but produced woodcuts and etchings of the highest quality.

The mineralogist, Georgius Agricola (1494–1555), summarized all that was known at the time about mining in De Re Metallica, published the year after his death.

The astronomer, Peter Apian (1495–1522), pointed out in 1540 that comets' tails always pointed away from the Sun. This was the first scientific observation concerning comets, other than their position in the sky.

FRANCE

Charles VIII had invaded Italy in 1494 in order to lay claim to Naples, thanks to a particularly feeble geneaological argument. This initiated 50 years of fighting on Italian soil by French, Germans, and Spaniards. It utterly destroyed Italian prosperity.

The Italians, being much more sensible than most, never seemed to see the glory of war, at least not since Roman times. They hired mercenary armies to do their fighting.

The mercenaries gave good service as long as they were paid, but they saw no virtue in losing their lives in a hopeless cause. Therefore, when two mercenary armies faced each other, and one was in a distinctly worse position, it recognized defeat and marched away. If there was a clash, it lasted no longer than it took for one side to realize it was losing. Casualties were low and the civilian population was scarcely hurt.

But then came the French, Germans, and Spaniards. They fought by night, as well as by day, in winter as well as in summer. They fought even in a bad position in the hope that the enemy would make a mistake. They fought to the bitter end sometimes, even when they were losing. And they had bad tempers, and looted and killed without stint as payment for the risks they took. To the Italians, it must have seemed like the incursion of the Mongols had seemed to their victims three centuries earlier.

Charles VIII conquered Naples, indeed, but couldn't maintain himself and left, having achieved nothing. He died in 1498, and was succeeded by Louis XII (1462–1515), who was his second cousin once removed, and the son of Charles of Orleans, who had been taken prisoner at Agincourt. Through his grandmother, Louis XII was a great-grandson of Gian Galeazzo, Duke of Milan, so he marched into Italy to claim that dukedom. That made more sense than Charles

VIII's enterprise, since, while Naples was at the other end of Italy, Milan was immediately adjacent to southeastern France.

A kind of mad dance followed. France conquered Milan in alliance with Spain, but France and Spain then quarreled and a Spanish force drove the French out of Milan. In 1508, France joined a coalition against Venice, but the coalition broke up, and again Spanish forces chased France out of Italy.

Then the French charged into Italy under a new commander, Gaston de Foix (1489–1512), who was Duke of Nemours and nephew to Louis XII. He showed real talent even though he was only in his early twenties, but he was killed during an attack at Ravenna.

France also lost the Battle of Guinegate against the English in 1513 (the English had briefly invaded again). The French spurred their horses so eagerly in retreat that the fracas was called "the Battle of the Spurs." One Frenchman who did not retreat so eagerly and who had fought well at Ravenna was the Chevalier Pierre de Bayard (1473–1524), known as "the knight without fear and without reproach."

Louis XII died in 1515 and was succeeded by his cousin (and son-in-law), who reigned as Francis I (1494–1547). Francis could see plainly that Charles VIII and Louis XII had, in 20 years of fighting in Italy, accomplished and gained nothing. Thereupon, Francis I proceeded to do precisely the same thing himself.

At first, he won a victory. Invading Milan, he found himself facing the Swiss, who were fighting as mercenaries for Milan. They were met at Marignano, just south of Milan on September 13, 1515. As usual, the Swiss attacked with fantastic speed so that Francis could not put his artillery into play. The hard-fought battle was called off at nightfall. The next morning, the Swiss lunged again, but this time Francis knew what to expect and he had his artillery ready. The Swiss pikemen suffered great losses and had to retreat. Their two-century record of invincibility was destroyed.

In 1516, Francis made peace with Charles I of Spain, who had not yet become Emperor, and

Milan was left in French hands provided France gave up its claim to Naples.

That seemed to be reasonable enough, but neither party was serious. By 1521, they were again at war.

In 1522, 8000 Swiss troops, now fighting on the French side, attacked the Spanish–German troops at Bicocca, near Milan. They would not wait for the French artillery to be set up, since they believed in attacking swiftly. They did, but the Imperial forces had arquebuses, which were primitive guns that a man could carry. The Swiss were mowed down and the world learned that pikes could not stand against handguns. That was the end of pikes as a major weapon.

The fortunes of war wavered back and forth and when, in 1524, the French laid siege to Pavia to the southeast of Marignano, the Imperial army approached on a stormy night from an unexpected direction. On February 24, 1525, the Battle of Pavia began with the French completely surprised. In addition, the Imperials had handguns and the French did not. The French were completely defeated, and Francis I was wounded and captured.

Francis I was taken to Spain and freed only after he had signed a treaty giving up all claims in Italy and surrendering all Burgundian territory that Louis XI had garnered. Naturally, once Francis I got back to France, he repudiated the treaty on the obvious grounds that it had been extracted under duress.

By 1529, Charles V had to cancel the treaty and sign a new one giving up any claim to the Burgundian territory France had taken. After all, Suleiman was at the gates of Vienna and Charles V couldn't afford to haggle.

Nevertheless, wars between France and the Hapsburgs continued, and remained inconclusive. Francis I died in 1547, and was succeeded by his son, who reigned as Henry II (1519–1559). Under him the wars *still* continued.

One pleasant side-effect of the Italian wars was that they accelerated the transfer of Renaissance thinking to France, and through France, to western Europe generally.

The liveliest French writer of this period was François Rabelais (1483–1553), who is best known for *Pantagruel* (1532) and *Gargantua* (1534). Racy, irreverent, occasionally obscene, lustily satirical, and always warmly human, Rabelais is responsible for the adjective "rabelaisian," which describes expansive lustiness.

A French surgeon of the period was Ambrose Paré (1510–1590), who served with the French army under Henry II and found that, instead of brutally cauterizing and disinfecting gunshot wounds with boiling oil, it was kinder and more effective to tie off severed arteries, to use soothing ointments, and to practice cleanliness. He wrote up his methods in 1545 (in French, since he knew no Latin) and is considered the father of modern surgery.

SWITZERLAND

Switzerland, at this time, in addition to supplying mercenaries for the Italian wars, played an important part in the Reformation.

Huldrych Zwingli (1484–1531), a priest from Zurich, had developed views like those of Luther and, in 1520, began preaching them.

His views did not precisely match those of Luther, and this was important. Whereas the Catholics had a supreme authority in the person of the Pope, who could decide what was orthodox and what was not, the Protestants, in repudiating the Pope, had no supreme authority of their own. This meant that Protestantism divided itself into sects and subsects, which produced great variety and freedom, but weakened the movement as a whole.

The Swiss cantons in the north and west followed Zwinglian teachings, while the others clung to Catholicism. There were even battles between the two sorts of cantons, an early example of what came to be known as "the wars of religion." At the Battle of Kappel, south of Zurich, on October 11, 1531, the Zurichers were defeated and Zwingli was killed.

Another reformer of the time was John Calvin (1509–1564), a Frenchman, who in 1536 wrote a powerful treatment of Protestant theology, one that was farther removed from Catholicism than Luther's views were. That year he came to Geneva, a Swiss city which had just turned Protestant. In 1538, he was banished, but he returned triumphantly in 1541 and set up a theocratic government in the city, which made it one of the most important Protestant centers in Europe.

Switzerland contributed an important scientist in this period—Paracelsus (1493–1541). He declared that alchemy's chief purpose was the development of cures for disease, and he insisted on using mineral compounds for that purpose even though they were clearly toxic. However, he denounced ancient medicine with unmeasured violence and laid the groundwork for new concepts in medical science.

NETHERLANDS

On the whole, the Netherlands flourished under the Emperor Charles V, as they had under the Burgundian dukes. Nevertheless, Protestantism was spreading in the northern provinces, while the south remained Catholic. The people of the northern provinces are frequently spoken of as Dutch, while those of the southern provinces are Flemish.

A leading humanist and Renaissance figure in northern Europe was Desiderius Erasmus (1466–1536), a Dutch writer and satirist who favored reform of the Church from within, and who refused to break away and join the Protestants. His best-known writing is his satire, *In Praise of Folly*, published in 1509.

The greatest biologist of the time was the Flemish anatomist, Andreas Vesalius (1514–1564), who was court physician to Emperor Charles V, and who did his own dissections. He published the result in his book, *De Corporis Humani Fabrica* ("On the Structure of the Human Body"). It was published in 1543, and was beautifully illustrated by the Flemish painter Jan Stephan van Calcar (1499–1545). Vesalius's findings finally replaced Galen's work that had held sway for over 13 centuries.

PAPACY

The Papacy in this period continued on its luxurious semipagan way even as Italy collapsed under the impact of foreign armies. Julius II (1443–1513) became Pope in 1503. He was intent on increasing his power over the Papal States, and was much more an Italian prince than a priest, even to the point of being a great patron of art.

Following him was Leo X (1475–1521), who was the son of Lorenzo the Magnificent of Florence and who became Pope in 1513. He, too, was a great patron of art, and had so extravagant a life-style, that he nearly drove the Papacy into bankruptcy. It was under his rule that the Protestant Reformation began. Leo apparently had no comprehension of the seriousness of the situation and was satisfied with excommunicating Luther. He dismissed the whole thing as just another argument among monks, not understanding the vast change that the printing press had brought to such arguments.

He was followed by Clement VII (1478–1534), another Medici—the illegitimate son of the younger brother of Lorenzo the Magnificent. He was another Pope who patronized art and played the part of an Italian prince. Nor was he a clever one, for he made an alliance with France at a time when the Emperor Charles V was in control of Italy, and that was just asking for trouble.

The commander of French forces (the "Constable") had been Charles, Duke of Bourbon (1490–1527), who had won the Battle of Marignano for Francis I. When the Constable lost favor with the king, however, he took deep umbrage and turned traitor, signing up with Charles V. In 1527, he led a German and Spanish army toward Rome, intending to take it and force the Pope to give up his French alliance.

Unfortunately, Bourbon was killed at the first assault, and the soldiers, taking Rome, and lacking a firm hand at the controls, sacked the city with every circumstance of horror. Rome received far worse treatment at the hand of Christian soldiers (some were Lutherans, but most were Catholics) than ever it had received at the hands of Goths and Vandals 11 centuries before.

The sack of Rome is considered to mark the end of the Italian Renaissance and to have been the time when Italy fell into the shadow of foreign domination from which it was not to emerge for a long time.

Perhaps the decline would have come about in any case even without the foreign invasions. European expansion, led by Spain and Portugal, to the shores of distant continents, had made the Atlantic and Indian Oceans the highways of trade. The Mediterranean Sea had been bypassed and lost the importance it had had for 25 centuries, ever since Phoenician times.

Yet despite the damage done by war, by heresies, and by economic decline, the Papacy continued on its way.

Clement VII died in 1534, and was succeeded by Paul III (1468–1549), another Pope whose main concern was his family, and who was a patron of the arts. By this time, however, the Protestant Reformation had been going on for a quarter of a century, and it was clear that something would have to be done. The Catholic Church would have to undertake a reform program and launch a determined counterattack against Protestantism. Therefore, Paul III called for a Church Council to attend to such matters, and it opened at Trent in northern Italy on December 31, 1545. It continued for years.

Paul III died in 1549 and, in 1550, Julius III (1487–1555) became Pope.

The Papacy, however, was not the only spearhead of the "Counter-Reformation," the counterattack against Protestantism. In Spain, a soldier, turned mystic and religious enthusiast, Ignatius of Loyola (1491–1556), established a new religious order in 1540, the "Society of Jesus," or the "Jesuits" as they were commonly known. They were to become a great educational force and were the cutting edge of a stern and efficient attempt to drive back the Protestants.

In addition, Christianity (chiefly in its Catholic form) was now beginning to spread beyond Europe. The Spanish and Portuguese had introduced Christianity among the Native Americans of the New World. Even more dramatically, a Spanish missionary, Francis Xavier (1506–1552), a friend of Ignatius of Loyola, devoted his life to the Far East. He achieved conversions to Christianity in India and Japan and died even as he was attempting to enter China. He maintained that Christianity among people of ancient and advanced non-European cultures must adapt itself to the ways of those cultures, a view it was difficult to get stay-at-home doctrinaires to accept.

And before the Italian Renaissance died, it burned into a blaze so bright that nothing like it has been seen since. It was the "High Renaissance."

Michelangelo Buonarroti (1475–1564), usually known by his first name, was certainly among the greatest artists who ever lived. He was enthusiastically patronized by all the Popes of the period, from Julius II on. He painted the ceiling of the Sistine Chapel between 1508 and 1512. He sculptured famous statues of David and Moses, and produced numerous other examples of the greatest art.

Raphael Sanzio (1483–1520), also known by his first name, produced beautiful paintings; and Benvenuto Cellini (1500–1571) was a goldsmith who achieved exquisite work. In his spare time, Cellini engaged in criminal activities of various sorts. He wrote an excellent autobiography in Italian (though it wasn't published till 1728). It's reliability is uncertain, though. In it, he claimed to have been the one who shot and killed Bourbon during the initial assault on Rome.

Venice contributed first-class painters in this period: Tiziano Vecelli (1490–1576), usually known as Titian, who was patronized by Charles V; and Jacopo Robusti (1515–1594), better known as Tintoretto.

Italy also shone in literature at this time. The Florentine diplomat, Niccolo Machiavelli (1469–1527), having lost his position as a result of the turbulent politics of the time, wrote up his theories of government in *The Prince* in 1513. He was a pragmatic, highly practical political theorist, who attached the greatest importance to a firm and orderly government. He felt that even harsh measures aimed at achieving this end should be carried through since such harshness comes nowhere near matching the evils brought on the public by a weak government. He has generally received a bad press for this and the word "machiavellian" has come to describe actions characterized by cunning, duplicity, and bad faith—which is extremely unfair to the sensible Machiavelli.

Another Italian diplomat, Baldassare Castiglione (1478–1529), wrote a book, *The Courtier*, in which he described his ideal of courtly life. It drew a picture of aristocratic manners that served as an upper-class etiquette book, and was popular throughout Europe.

The Italian diplomat and poet, Ludovico Ariosto (1474–1533), is best known for his epic *Orlando Furioso*, published in 1516, and expanded in 1532. Set in the time of Charlemagne, it is considered the best poetry of the sort that appeared during the Italian Renaissance.

Two Italian mathematicians graced this period. Niccolo Tartaglia (1499–1557) was, in 1535, the first to work out a general solution for what are called "equations of the third degree." He tried to keep his method secret, but the other mathematician of the period, Girolamo Cardano (1501–1570), who, like Villon and Cellini, was a scapegrace in private life, wormed it out of him and published it in 1545. On his own, Cardano worked out methods of solving "equations of the fourth degree," and recognized the importance of negative and imaginary numbers in the solutions of equations.

ENGLAND

In 1509, Henry VIII (1491–1647), son of Henry VII, came to the throne. He was 18 years old, tall, strong, handsome, a wrestler, a poet, and happily married to Catherine of Aragon, the intelligent and capable younger daughter of Ferdinand and Isabella (and the aunt of the boy who was to become Emperor Charles V).

All seemed well. Henry VIII was a descendant of both the Lancastrians and the Yorkists, most of the turbulent ancient nobility were dead, parliament was cowed, and Henry VIII was virtually an absolute monarch.

It was almost inevitable that Henry VIII would remember the glory days of Edward III and Henry V, and long to play a big part in the wars between Francis I and Charles V. However, the days of the longbow were gone. These were the days of French cannon, Spanish handguns, and Swiss pikes, and the English were not strong enough to compete.

Henry VIII did invade France in the early days and even won the Battle of the Spurs at Guinegate, but that didn't amount to much. Afterward, Henry VIII and Francis I met near Calais on June 7, 1520, at what today would be called a "summit meeting" to arrange for peace. It was all carried out with the utmost magnificence, so that it was called "the Field of the Cloth of Gold," but it was far more show than substance and also didn't amount to much.

Henry VIII was an ardent Catholic and wrote a book attacking Luther's views. Pope Leo X rewarded him with the title "Defender of the Faith," which English monarchs have kept ever since even though reality made that grotesque, at least from the Papal point of view.

But Henry found himself with a terrible dynastic problem. He felt he needed a son to carry on the succession, and Catherine of Aragon had had only one child who outlived infancy and that was a daughter named Mary (1516–1558). Nor was Catherine likely to have additional children in the future, for she was six years older than Henry and by 1527 was 42 years old. Besides all this, Henry had fallen in love with a young woman named Anne Boleyn (1507–1536) and wanted to marry her and have her provide him with a legitimate son. (He had an illegitimate one, but that did him no good.)

He needed a divorce from Catherine of Aragon, and for this he relied on his Chancellor (whom we would call a "Prime Minister" today), Thomas Wolsey (1475–1530). He was Archbishop of York and a Cardinal. Wolsey realized that England was not strong enough to play a decisive role in the European wars, but could maintain "the balance of power," always siding with the weaker and thus preventing the stronger from overwhelming Europe. In a divided Europe, England would find safety. That remained English policy for centuries.

The divorce was more than Wolsey could manage, however. The Pope's permission was needed for that, and the Pope was Clement VII, who was the prisoner of Charles V after the sack of Rome—and Charles V was the nephew of Catherine of Aragon. As a result, Wolsey fell from grace, and Henry looked for some way of going over the Pope's head.

An English prelate and reformer, Thomas Cranmer (1489–1556), was willing to agree with the king that Catherine of Aragon's prior marriage to Henry's older brother (who died young and whose marriage had never been consummated, according to Catherine) rendered her later marriage invalid.

Therefore, Henry VIII divorced Catherine without Papal permission and married Anne Boleyn on January 25, 1533. Anne gave birth to a child in the course of the year, but to Henry's unbounded chagrin, it was another daughter, Elizabeth (1533–1603).

Having defied the Pope in this matter, Henry VIII had to push through an "Act of Supremacy" in which he established an Anglican Church, with himself as its head. It kept almost all the doctrines of Catholicism, but it was a national church, not an international one. This was the beginning of the process that made England into a Protestant country.

This was a deadly blow to the greatest English humanist of the time, Thomas More (1478–1535). He was a a statesman, scholar and author, a loving father, and a totally winning gentleman. His best-known work is *Utopia*, an early example of science fiction, which described an ideal government. The name came from a Greek word that meant "nowhere"—More's sardonic comment—and it gave us the word "utopian," meaning impossibly idealistic. It was published in 1516.

He served Henry VIII in various posts and was finally made Chancellor after Wolsey's fall, much against his will. More could not accept Henry as head of the Church and, as a result, the imperious monarch had his head cut off in 1535.

On the other hand, another English scholar was William Tyndale (1494–1536), who was an ardent Protestant. Martin Luther had translated the Bible into German, fixing the literary form of the language. Tyndale followed the example of Wycliffe and translated the Bible into English, beginning in 1525. For this and for his Protestant views, he was burned at the stake. It was as dangerous at the time to be too Protestant as to be insufficiently Protestant.

The most important English artist of the period was the German-born Hans Holbein the Younger (1497–1543), whose portraits of Henry VIII, Thomas More, Desiderius Erasmus, and numerous other members of the English court make the period live for us.

Meanwhile, though, Henry VIII still needed a son, and had fallen out of love with Anne Boleyn, and into love with one of her maids of honor, Jane Seymour (1509–1537). Therefore, he had Anne executed on May 19, 1536, and married Jane the next day.

Jane Seymour did give him that son, Edward (1537–1553), and she then died almost immediately afterward.

Henry married three more times, divorcing his fourth wife, executing the fifth, and somehow allowing the sixth to outlive him. He had no further children, and it is for his six wives that he is best known to later generations.

In his last decade, Henry VIII was diseased, suffered an accident in a tournament that nearly killed him and probably addled his brains, and became grotesquely fat. He ended his reign not as the hopeful Prince Charming he had been at the start, but as a sadistic monster.

In 1546, Henry VIII authorized the building of ships and coastal defenses. He didn't live to see much happen, for he died on January 28, 1547, but he had begun the English naval tradition.

He was succeeded by Jane Seymour's son, a sickly 9-year-old boy, who reigned as Edward VI.

SCOTLAND

While Henry VIII was invading France to no purpose, early in his reign, the Scots, who were allied with France, invaded England. The two nations met at the northern tip of England at Flodden on September 9, 1513. The Scottish army were mostly pikemen, who had a strong position and who intended to fight a defensive battle. The English had some artillery, however, and shot at the Scots from a distance. The galled Scots had to charge and were cut down. The Scottish king, James IV, was killed in the course of the battle, as were many of his nobles.

James IV had married Margaret Tudor (1489–

1541), a daughter of Henry VII, and their one-year-old son, also James (1512–1542), was now King James V of Scotland.

When he was grown, and Henry VIII was in his last years, James V also made war on England, and the result was similar. The two armies met at Solway Moss in the northwestern tip of England. Again, the English won a crushing victory. James V survived but he had a mental breakdown and died three weeks later. Once again, an infant was heir, this time a 1-week-old baby, named Mary (1542–1587), who was the great-grandaughter of Henry VII, a fact which was to have great importance later on.

James V's wife was Mary of Guise (1515–1560), a member of a powerful French family. She ruled the country as regent while the young child was sent off to France to be reared there. The ties between France and Scotland were thus stronger than ever.

PORTUGAL

Having reached the Far East, Portugal became the great trading nation of the world, displacing Venice. Despite its small size and population, Portugal became the first true world power: the first nation anywhere and anytime to have a true overseas empire.

This was made possible by two facts. First, Portugal had the best ships in the world, which meant that she could have untroubled communications between coastal points that were far apart, bringing supplies and reinforcements at will. Second, Portugal had gunpowder and iron cannon both on its ships and at its coastal bases, before which the large populations of distant continents were helpless.

The first Portuguese viceroy of the overseas territories was Francisco de Almeida (1450–1510), who left Portugal with 21 ships in March 1505. He set up bases on the east African coast, and here and there on the Indian coast. He even reached Malaya.

The Arabs tried to stop him, of course, for they had a long history of trading over the Indian Ocean, and they themselves had reached the Indonesian islands long before. (It is for this reason that Far Eastern islands, such as Java and Mindanao, are Muslim today.) On February 2, 1509, however, at Diu on the west Indian coast near Bombay, Almeida destroyed the Arab fleet and, with that, gained control of the Indian Ocean for Portugal.

In 1509, he was replaced by Afonso de Albuquerque (1453–1515), who strengthened Almeida's bases and founded new ones along the shores of the Indian Ocean. He conquered Goa on the west Indian shore in 1510, and made it his Far Eastern capital. He captured Malacca in Malaya in 1511, and a Portuguese ship reached Canton on the south China coast in 1517. In 1542, another Portuguese ship, driven by a storm, made the first European landing in Japan.

SPANISH NORTH AMERICA

Spain, at home, was almost entirely occupied with wars in Italy, fighting on behalf of her king, Charles I (the Emperor Charles V) against France. But Spain, too, was establishing a worldwide Empire, and one that soon became larger than that of the Portuguese.

Columbus died in 1506, having made four voyages in all to the "new world" but exploration continued. Spain took over the islands of the West Indies (the very name attests to Columbus's misconception of the nature of his discovery). They occupied Puerto Rico in 1510 and Cuba in 1511. They founded Havana in 1515.

In 1513, Juan Ponce de Leon (1460–1521), governor of Puerto Rico, went slave-hunting westward, and discovered the coast of Florida on Easter Sunday (he named it after the holiday which, in Spanish, is "Pascua Florida").

Another explorer, Vasco Nunez de Balboa (1475–1519) was in Panama in 1513. It was also being settled by the Spanish, and Balboa wandered inland in search of gold. He did not know that Panama was a narrow isthmus running east and west.

The Atlantic Ocean lay to Panama's north, and when Balboa crossed the isthmus, he found himself looking at what had the appearance of another ocean in the south. He called it the "South Sea."

By 1517, the Spanish were exploring Yucatan and finding evidence of the past civilization of the Mayas. The biggest prize in North America, however, came two years later.

Hernando Cortes (1485–1547), with 11 ships and 700 soldiers, set sail from Cuba in February 1519 and explored the Mexican interior. There he found the Aztec civilization centered about its capital at Tenochtitlan, under its king, Montezuma II (1466–1520).

Cortes had very few men, but he had horses and he had firearms, while the Aztecs had neither. Furthermore, the Aztecs were ruling over other tribes who were delighted to rebel and side with the Spaniards. In addition, the Aztecs had the frightful misconception that the Spaniards were gods. Cortes, therefore, conquered the Aztecs, and the Spaniards had no qualms about destroying the civilization. (After all, the Aztecs were not Christians.) By the summer of 1521, it was all over. Tenochtitlan was destroyed and Mexico City was established on its ruins.

Thereafter, Spanish adventurers moved northward to explore the continent and search for the kind of wealth they found among the Aztecs. Panfilo de Narvaez (1480–1528) explored the northern shore of the Gulf of Mexico west of Florida in 1527. His expedition was wrecked in a storm on its return, but one of the party, Alvar Nunez Cabez de Vaca (1490–1560), was thrown ashore in what is now Texas. He didn't find his way back to Mexico City till 1536, where he told tales of having seen vast herds of bison.

Hernando de Soto (1500–1542) led an exploring party deep into what is now the southeastern United States in 1539. On June 18, 1541, he and his men became the first Europeans to set eyes upon the Mississippi River, probably some miles south of what is now Memphis, Tennessee. They explored westward. On May 21, 1542, de Soto died, was buried in the river, and the rest of the party returned to Mexico.

Francisco Vasquez de Coronado (1510–1554) explored what is now the southwestern United States, between 1540 and 1542. He and his men were probably the first Europeans to see the Grand Canyon.

None of these explorations uncovered any further rich civilizations, but by 1550, Spain had explored and controlled the southern half of the continent of North American (and claimed ownership of all of it).

SPANISH SOUTH AMERICA

In 1531, the Spanish explorer, Francisco Pizarro (1475–1541), with 180 men, 27 horses, and two cannon, reached Peru in South America. There he encountered the Inca civilization, and the story was the same as in Mexico. By 1533, the Spaniards had destroyed the Inca civilization.

They expanded southward and claimed all of South America except for the eastern bulge of Brazil which, by the Line of Demarcation, belonged to Portugal.

How much of the bulge belonged to Portugal was, of course, not clear at the time, and the most significant exploration of the northern reaches of South America, through land that was eventually recognized as Portuguese, was carried through by a Spaniard.

Francisco de Orellana (1490–1546) had been with Pizarro's band when it had conquered Peru and appropriated its wealth. (de Soto, who was to discover the Mississippi River, had also served with Pizarro.) Pizarro had set up an expedition to explore the land eastward of the Inca dominions, and Orellana, having reached the headwaters of a river, felt it would be easier to go ahead than to return over the Andes mountain range, which he had already crossed on his journey eastward.

From April 1541 to August 1542, he progressed down a river which, as it happens, is by far the greatest in the world in terms of water volume. His report mentioned tribes which, it seemed to Orellana, were led by women. This reminded people of the Amazons, the women warriors of Greek legend, and the river was named the Amazon River.

The claims of Spain to the Americas were vast —all of both continents except for Brazil. It was larger than any Empire the world had seen, even the Mongol Empire, but Spain could only control key points at first and, as it turned out, it could never control it all.

PORTUGUESE SOUTH AMERICA

Portugal established bases and settlements on the Brazilian coast, but the most important expedition made under their auspices was by an Italian, while the most important Portuguese navigator of this period sailed for Spain.

The Italian navigator was Americus Vespucius (1454–1512), to use the Latinized version of his name. He sailed to the South American coast while Columbus was still alive, first for Spain and then for Portugal. He was convinced that what he saw could not be the Asian coast described by Marco Polo. He was the first to maintain, in 1504, that what had been discovered was a hitherto undiscovered continent, and that another ocean separated it from Asia, which was much farther away.

This was convincing to some. A German geographer, Martin Waldseemueller (1470–1520), suggested, in 1507, that the new continent be named America in Vespucius' honor. This was eventually done. At first, it was applied only to the southern region, since the north might still be part of Asia. Eventually, though, people spoke of South America and North America, and the thin strip connecting the two was Central America.

The Portuguese navigator who did not sail for Portugal was Ferdinand Magellan (1480–1521). Believing himself to have been mistreated by the Portuguese government, he turned to Spain, where he pointed out that if one traveled west of the Line of Demarcation far enough, Asia would be reached without having violated treaty obligations.

Charles V thought it worth the chance and outfitted Magellan with five ships. The ships left Spain on September 20, 1519 and what followed was probably the greatest sea-voyage in history. Magellan nosed his way down the coast of South America, looking for a way of getting past it and, finally, on October 21, 1519, found what we now call "The Strait of Magellan."

For five weeks, he made his way along the strait through constant storms until it opened into an ocean and the storms ceased. It was Balboa's South Sea, but as Magellan sailed on and on through good weather he called it the "Pacific Ocean."

However, the Pacific Ocean was far larger than anyone could have expected and it was sadly free of land. For 99 days, the ships sailed through unbroken water and the men nearly died of hunger and thirst. Finally, they reached Guam where they caught their breaths, then sailed westward to what afterward came to be known as the Philippine Islands. There, on April 27, 1521, Magellan was killed during a skirmish with the natives.

The expedition continued westward, however, and a single ship with 18 men aboard, under the leadership of Juan Sebastian de Elcano (1476–1526), finally arrived back in Spain, on September 7, 1522. The first circumnavigation of the globe had taken three years, and, if the loss of life can be set aside, the single returning ship carried enough spices to make the voyage a complete financial success.

The voyage showed that there was one ocean, with the continents set in it like huge islands. The circumference of the Earth was shown to be 25,000 miles, as Eratosthenes had proposed seventeen and a half centuries before, and not 18,000 miles as Columbus had thought.

FRENCH NORTH AMERICA

It occurred to Francis I of France, who was in the midst of his bitter war with Charles V of the Empire and of Spain, that there was no reason to allow the lucrative trade with the Far East to remain in Portuguese hands. Magellan had just found a way of getting around South America to Asia (the "Southwest Passage"), and perhaps there was a way around North America (the "Northwest Passage"), too.

Therefore, Francis commissioned an Italian navigator, Giovanni da Verrazano (1485–1528), to explore the northern coast of North America, where Spanish forces had not yet penetrated.

In January, 1524, Verrazano sailed westward and, on March 1, he reached the coast of what is now North Carolina and explored northward. On April 17, he entered what is now called New York Bay. He continued northward as far as

Newfoundland, but found no way through the continent. He returned to France on July 8.

The next year Francis was captured at Pavia, and it was 10 years before he could think of the Northwest Passage again. This time, he sent out a French navigator, Jacques Cartier (1491–1557), to continue the search. Cartier, with two ships and 61 men, left France on April 20, 1534, and reached Newfoundland on May 10. He rounded Newfoundland on the north and entered a large ocean inlet on August 10, 1534. This was the day dedicated to St. Lawrence, so he named it the "Gulf of St. Lawrence."

He penetrated the Gulf into the St. Lawrence River on two succeeding voyages and called the regions round about "Canada," by mistaking a Native American word. He realized it was no Northwest Passage and returned with that news. Francis I then lost interest in the matter, but in later years, Cartier's voyages were the basis for the French claims to Canada.

SWEDEN

The Union of Kalmar had lasted one and a third centuries, more or less uneasily. Christian II of Denmark (1481–1559) was the last king of a united Scandinavia, having come to the throne in 1513. He was anxious to curb the unrest that was endemic in Sweden, which did not enjoy being ruled from Copenhagen. Therefore, Christian brought an army into Sweden, defeated those rebels who wanted an independent nation, and, on November 8, 1520, executed eight leaders of the rebellion in the Swedish capital of Stockholm.

This was called the "Stockholm Bloodbath" by the Swedes, and it enraged them. Under a Swedish nobleman, Gustavus Vasa (1496–1560), the nation rose, defeated the Danes in 1523, and gained its independence. Gustavus Vasa ruled as Gustavus I and, his reign, Sweden turned Lutheran.

As for Christian II, he was deposed by the Danes in 1523 and was succeeded by his son, Frederick I (1471–1533), who was in turn succeeded by his son, Christian III (1503–1555), both of whom ruled over Denmark and Norway. In their reigns, Denmark and Norway also turned Lutheran.

POLAND

In this period, Poland was ruled by Sigismund I (1467–1548), who was successful in war against the fading Teutonic Knights and held his own against the Russians. He promoted learning, but also institutionalized serfdom in the land. (Serfs were peasants who were bound to the land and could not leave the domain of their overlord—a condition that was not very far removed from outright slavery.)

By far, the most important Pole of this period was Nicolaas Copernicus (1473–1545), who is best-known by this Latinized version of his name.

Copernicus felt that it was much easier to explain the motion of the planets in the sky on the assumption that they (and the Earth, too) circled the Sun, rather than that they (and the Sun) circled the Earth. Some ancient Greek astronomers had had that idea 16 centuries before, but Copernicus made it more vital by working out the necessary mathematics of this "heliocentric theory."

He long hesitated to publish it for fear of arousing the anger of the Catholic Church (and of the Protestants, too, for that matter, for they were no more sympathetic to iconoclastic scientific theories than the Catholics were—even less, perhaps). The manuscript circulated in its handwritten form but, eventually, Copernicus let himself be persuaded. Finally, in 1543, his book was published and he was supposed to have been handed the first copy on his deathbed.

The work of Copernicus in astronomy, of Vesalius in anatomy (his book was published the same year) and of Tartaglia and Cardano in algebra began the "Scientific Revolution," in which Europe at the very start of modern times stepped boldly forward and placed itself far beyond and ahead of the science of ancient Greece, of medieval Islam, and even of China.

RUSSIA

At this time, Russia and Poland struggled in confused wars and the boundary between them moved eastward and westward about the disputed city of Smolensk.

Ivan III died in 1503, and was succeeded by his son Basil (or "Vasili") III (1479–1533). In his reign, Russia continued its slow consolidation of power. When he died in 1533, he was succeeded by a 3-year-old son who reigned as Ivan IV (1530–1584) but who did not assume power on his own behalf till 1547.

PERSIA

Persia had not really been under the rule of a native dynasty since its fall to the Arabs nine centuries earlier. Since then, it had been ruled by Arabs, Turks, and Mongols.

In 1502, however, Shah Ismail (1487–1524) came to power. He traced his descent from an ancestor named Safi al-Din, so that the dynasty he founded is the "Safavid."

Safi al-Din, according to a legend fostered by the dynasty, was descended from Ali, the fourth Caliph. He was the last Caliph to be recognized as legitimate by the Shiites, and so Shah Ismail was a Shiite. He saw to it that the Persians, too, became Shiites, and they have remained part of that Islamic sect ever since.

The time had come, however, when Oriental potentates, however powerful, had to deal with Europeans. The Portuguese took Hormuz at the southeastern opening of the Persian Gulf in 1507 and used it as a depot for trade with Persia and Arabia.

Persia's Shiism got it into trouble with the Turks who were fanatical Sunnites and there was half a century of war between them. Persia also had to deal with a new wave of tribesmen from Central Asia, the Uzbeks, who harassed their northern frontier.

In 1524, Tahmasp I (1514–1576), the son of Ismail, succeeded to the Persian throne and, under him, Persia retreated under Turkish blows.

INDIA

The Mongols were not yet down. There was a great-great-grandson of Tamerlane, who was named Babur (1483–1530) and who counted himself a descendant in the thirteenth generation of Genghis Khan.

He was striving to build a kingdom in Central Asia, which he failed at first, being unable to make much headway against the Uzbeks, who now dominated the region. In 1504, however, he captured Kabul and turned southward for easier prey.

In 1519, he began to raid India and, in 1526, he pit his relatively few men against a large Indian army. Babur, however, had artillery which he had obtained from the Turks, while the Indian army had nothing more advanced than elephants. On April 21, 1526, Babur's army smashed the Indians that faced him at Panipat, 50 miles north of Delhi. On April 24, he took Delhi, and on May 4, he took Agra. He had established the "Mogul Empire" (a distortion of "Mongol") in India. Two more successful battles gave him all of northern India.

On Babur's death in 1530, his son, Humayun (1508–1556) succeeded to the Mogul throne. In his time, there was great confusion as he was defeated by an Afghan ruler, Sher Shah (1486–1545), and had to flee to Persia. After Sher Shah's death, however, Humayun returned to Delhi.

All through this period, however, the Portuguese had bases on the coast, particularly at Goa, and the Moguls lacked the power to drive them out.

CHINA

Chia Ching (1507–1566) had become Emperor of China in 1522. He was the 11th Emperor of the Ming dynasty. It was a time of decline, as Chia Ching was far more interested in alchemy (and in possible elixirs of life) than in state business. The Mongols were again raiding China and even laid siege to Beijing itself several times. The Manchus to the northeast (in what is still called "Manchuria") also threatened, and Japanese pirates raided the Chinese coast.

It was also at this time that the Portuguese were nosing along the coast. The first Portuguese mission reached Peking in the year in which Chia Ching became Emperor.

BURMA

In 1519, Portuguese traders had reached Burmese ports, and, in the 1540s, Portuguese mercenaries participated in the wars between competing Burmese factions.

JAPAN

In 1542, the Portuguese landed in Japan. It was characteristic of the Japanese that they alone of the nations encountered by Europeans in this century took note of firearms and began to adopt them.

1550 TO 1600

SPAIN

Spain was now the strongest power in Europe and, possibly, in the world. It had an extensive overseas Empire. It had the best generals, and the most thoroughly trained army, one that won almost all its battles. It also had a strong king whose only interest was in ruling.

But there were problems. It had a population of only 7 million (compared with France's 16 million). Many Spaniards who would have made excellent military leaders left for the American possessions. The Spanish economy was weak and no measures were taken to strengthen it.

In 1556, Charles V abdicated (he died in 1558) and, like Diocletian twelve and a half centuries earlier, he was probably happier in retirement than he had ever been as Emperor.

Charles's younger brother, Ferdinand (1503–1564), inherited Austria and the lands it ruled, together with the Imperial crown, so that he reigned as the Emperor Ferdinand I.

To his son, Philip (1527–1598), Charles left Spain and the Spanish dominions overseas, plus the Netherlands, Franche Comte, Milan, and Naples. In this way, Philip II of Spain owned significant territories all along France's eastern border.

Philip II was one of the most intelligent and hard-working monarchs in history, and, in his person, a gentleman. He was, however, a single-minded Catholic who used Spanish power for the purpose of defeating Protestantism wherever he found it, consuming Spain at tasks too great for its strength.

He did conclude the war with France satisfactorily. At the Treaty of Cateau-Cambresis, near the border of France with the Netherlands, signed on April 3, 1559, the 50-year war came to an end. It was a Spanish victory. Spain kept all its territories to the east of France, and France gave up all claims to any part of Italy.

In other respects, Philip was less fortunate. In 1567, the Netherlands broke into revolt, and that struggle occupied Spain all through Philip's reign and beyond, bleeding it white.

Then, too, in Philip's eagerness to leave nothing in Spain that detracted in any way from pure Catholicism, he turned against those Muslims who still lived in Spain and who had been converted to Catholicism. They had kept their culture and traditions (other than their religion) and were called "Moriscos," or "little Moors." He was also suspicious of Jews who had been converted to Catholicism; they were called "Marranos" ("Pigs"). In both cases, they were suspected of secretly practicing their old religions. In 1569, the Moriscos, who were more numerous than the Marranos, revolted and were cruelly put down. Eventually, all doubtful converts were either killed or expelled from the country to the great weakening of Spain, for it cost the nation many hard-working people of ability.

Philip's greatest victory was over the Turks, who were defeated at sea in the battle of Lepanto on October 7, 1571. The victory did not bring much in the way of immediate results, but it did shatter the legend of Turkish invincibility.

On the other hand, it gave rise to a dangerous feeling of invincibility in Philip's mind. There was an undeclared sea-war between Spain and England through much of his reign and Philip's indignation against English piracy (which is what it was, despite England's use of the less-threatening term "privateering") was compounded by the fact that England was Protestant. He prepared a huge fleet, often referred to as "the Invincible Armada," and sent it, in 1588, to secure the English Channel so that a Spanish army from the Netherlands could cross and invade England.

The Armada was smashed, partly by English ships, and partly by storms.

Philip II died in 1598, his accomplishments having fallen far short of his aims in his 42-year reign. Spain imported a great deal of gold and silver from her American colonies, but all this vanished in the need to support Spanish armies, and none went to the real strengthening of the Spanish economy. It was Spain's rivals—England, France, and the Netherlands—that learned how to run their economies and that grew rich in overseas trade.

In 1598, Philip was succeeded by his son, who reigned as Philip III (1578–1621).

The greatest Spanish painter of this period was born on the island of Crete. He was Domenikos Theotokopoulos (1541–1604), but is universally known as "El Greco" ("The Greek"). Crete was a Venetian possession at that time and El Greco studied under Titian in Venice, then in 1577 went to Spain. He spent the rest of his life in Toledo, painting on religious themes and characteristically elongating the human body.

In this period, too, Lope de Vega (1562–1635) began his remarkable career, shortly after serving in the ill-fated Spanish Armada. He is perhaps the most prolific writer who ever lived. He is supposed to have written 1800 plays (450 of which are still extant) and hundreds of other works. He was the second greatest writer of Spain's "golden age." (The one writer who surpassed him did so with a single book.)

The Spanish physician, Michael Servetus (1511–1553) was one of the pioneers in establishing the principle of the circulation of the blood. However, he also had Unitarian views, denying the divinity of Jesus; and when he incautiously placed himself within the reach of John Calvin in Geneva, Servetus was burned at the stake, crying out his beliefs to the last. Calvin burned as many copies of his writings as he could find, so that Servetus' theory on the circulation of the blood wasn't discovered for a long time.

PORTUGAL

Portugal was smaller and less populous than Spain, so that it more easily overextended itself. By now, Portugal and its empire were already in decline.

Sebastian I (1544–1578) became King of Portugal in 1557, at the age of three. He was educated by the Jesuits and grew up with the glittering thought of a Crusade against the infidels. In 1578, he led an army into Morocco and died in battle there, his army smashed.

He had no children and his uncle, Henry (1512–1580), who had been regent during Sebastian's minority, became king. He was 66 years old, a cardinal of the Church, and had no heirs. When he died in 1580, seven different candidates claimed the throne, one of whom was Philip II of Spain, whose wife was Sebastian's aunt. Philip II sent in his army, and that settled things. Portugal was united with Spain under a single king. For the first time since the Visigoths, eight and a half centuries earlier, the Iberian peninsula was a single political entity.

Philip II, as Philip I of Portugal, was careful to leave the nation to its local customs and to rule through Portuguese officials, but Portugal's morale declined and its empire withered.

While Portugal was still independent, however, its remarkable achievement in establishing a world empire was reflected in its literature when the Portuguese poet, Luiz Vaz de Camoes

(1520–1580), described the voyage of Vasco da Gama in epic poetry in *The Lusiads*, published in 1572.

NETHERLANDS

The cities of the Netherlands continued to be the most prosperous in Europe outside of Italy. Philip II of Spain, under whose dominion the Netherlands now fell, got scant joy of that, however, for the region was hostile to him.

The Protestantism that had made considerable headway in the northern provinces of the Netherlands was of the more radical Calvinist type, though the southern provinces remained Catholic. The Netherlandish Protestants feared Philip's ardent Catholicism, and the possible introduction of the Inquisition. Even aside from religion, the Netherlanders (Catholic and Protestant alike) feared Philip's centralizing tendency, his desire to make all decisions himself, and to ignore the privileges the Netherland provinces had long enjoyed. The presence of arrogant Spanish garrisons was also a source of irritation.

Philip's viceroy over the Netherlands was an illegitimate daughter of Charles V, his half-sister, Margaret of Parma (1522–1586). She had to face the Netherland nobility, of whom the chief was William of Orange (1533–1584), usually known as "William the Silent," for he was no chatterbox.

Margaret was willing to make some concessions to appease the Netherlanders, but Philip was not. She was relieved of her position in 1567 and, in her place, Philip sent a hardened soldier, Fernando Alvarez de Toledo, Duke of Alba (1507–1582).

Alba had fought successfully for Spain in many battles (and, in later life, was to defeat the Portuguese and allow Philip II to become king of Portugal as well as of Spain). He came to the Netherlands with a determination to be hard and to adopt a policy of terror. The Netherlanders would seem to have had no chance against him. Alba won every pitched battle and, what's more, when he took a city, he slaughtered the garrisons.

The Netherlanders had one thing going for them, however. In the north, particularly, the land was laced with canals along which watercraft could move. The Netherlanders were a seagoing people who built ships of a new kind, with large and effective cannon. The Spaniards had older and far less effective ships. This meant that the Netherlanders could wipe the neighboring seas clean of Spanish ships, carry on a privateering and piratical war against Spanish shipping and commerce, and sometimes even relieve besieged cities. While the Netherlanders controlled the sea, Alba could not put an end to the rebellion.

Furthermore, Alba knew nothing about running the country. When he tried to impose new taxes, many people who would endure oppression and religious persecution rose against him in wild abandon to protect their pocketbooks.

Alba had to leave the country, a failure, at his own request in 1573. What's more, the Spanish policy of terror had succeeded in uniting all the provinces, Catholic as well as Protestant, against Spain.

Philip II then sent in his half-brother, Don John of Austria (1547–1578), another illegitimate child of Charles V. Don John had beaten the Turks at Lepanto and gained great fame, but he, too, failed to suppress the revolt.

When Don John died in 1578, Philip appointed Allesandro Farnese, Duke of Parma (1545–1592), and that was a wise choice. Parma was not only a great general, but he knew how to govern. By abandoning senseless terror, he lured the southern Catholic provinces out of the revolt.

The northern provinces, however, the chief of which was Holland, remained intransigent. They signed the Union of Utrecht among themselves in 1579 and eventually declared themselves independent, though Spain did not recognize that independence. The northern provinces make up what is now known as "The Netherlands," though they can also be referred to, more familiarly, as "Holland" or as "the Dutch Republic."

The southern provinces are usually referred to as "the Spanish Netherlands."

The Dutch made William of Orange their "stadtholder" (the equivalent of a president). He had maintained a steady and resolute resistance to the Spaniards, though he rarely won a battle.

Philip II offered a reward for his assassination and, on July 10, 1584, William was, indeed, assassinated. He was succeeded by his son, Maurice of Nassau (1567–1625), who kept up just as steady and resolute a resistance.

The English, who feared Philip II's designs on their own Protestant nation, were openly aiding the Dutch by now. The aid was mostly financial, but in 1585 an English army under Robert Dudley, Earl of Leicester (1533–1588), was sent to the Netherlands. Leicester was a favorite of the English queen, but he was also incompetent and accomplished nothing. Still, this was enough to stiffen further Philip II's determination to crush England by way of the Armada.

Maurice, meanwhile, showed far greater aptitude for war than his father had. He won battles, and Parma died of wounds in 1592. Philip II died in 1598, with the revolt as strong as ever and with Maurice on the offensive. It was clear that Spain had no chance of crushing the revolt, but it kept on fighting.

The misery of rebellion and war did not keep the Netherlanders from making advances in other directions. Peter Brueghel (1564–1638) was a Fleming and one of the great painters of the century. He specialized in busy, exuberant paintings of peasant life, of Biblical scenes, and of fantasy. A number of his descendants were successful painters as well.

The development of Netherlands' sea-power in response to the war with Spain meant that the Netherlands could engage busily in the task of exploring the world's oceans. The Dutch navigator, Willem Barents (1550–1597), explored the Arctic coasts of Europe to see if the Far East might be reached by a northern route. He failed in that, but he discovered Spitzbergen in 1596 (it had been reached by the Vikings, seven centuries earlier) as well as Novaya Zemlya, islands north of western Siberia.

The outstanding Dutch scientist of the period was Simon Stevinus (1548–1620), who served in the army of Maurice of Nassau. He studied the pressure of liquids and founded the science of hydraulics. He also demonstrated the impossibility of some kinds of perpetual motion.

A Flemish geographer, Gerardus Mercator (1512–1594), which was his Latinized name, invented a new way of depicting the spherical surface of the Earth on a flat sheet of paper. It distorted size more and more as one went farther north and south of the Equator, but the direction of travel remained accurate as shown. This new "Mercator projection" was of enormous help to navigators.

ENGLAND

Edward VI, the son for whom Henry VIII had so ardently longed, had had a seven-year-reign in which powerful nobles pulled the realm in different directions, but under whom England grew more Protestant.

His chief minister toward the end of his reign was John Dudley, Duke of Northumberland (1502–1533). He had had competing noblemen executed and strove for complete control of the land after the King's death. Lady Jane Grey (1537–1554), a great-granddaughter of Henry VII and a first cousin, once removed, of Edward VI, had married one of Northumberland's sons. What's more, she was Protestant. Therefore, Northumberland declared her queen, very much against her will.

The plan failed. Mary, the older half-sister of Edward VI, and the daughter of Henry VIII's first wife, Catherine of Aragon, was the logical heir to the throne, and she was a favorite of the people, who viewed her as a mistreated innocent. She had no trouble being acclaimed Queen Mary I, and she promptly had Northumberland executed. Lady Jane Grey, totally innocent of any wrong-doing, was executed the next year.

However, if Mary had had an unfortunate childhood and youth, she also had an unfortunate reign. She was a convinced Catholic (one reason why Northumberland had tried to exclude her from the throne) and was intent on restoring England to the Catholic fold. On July 25, 1554, she married Philip, her first cousin, once-removed, who was soon to become the ultra-Catholic Philip II of Spain, and who was detested by most of the English. She was in love, but he wasn't. He stayed in England long enough to get her pregnant, he thought (and so did she), but that turned out to be a false alarm, to Mary's great humiliation.

Mary's attempt to restore Catholicism led her to condemn and burn at the stake many prominent Protestants, including Thomas Cranmer, the Archbishop of Canterbury, who had arranged the legalisms that had permitted Henry VIII to divorce Mary's mother. The Protestants, therefore, called her "Bloody Mary," and since they won out in the end and wrote the accounts, that is how she has gone down in history.

She managed to get into war with France on the Spanish side for no other reason than her love for Philip and, in the course of it, the French under François de Lorraine, Duke of Guise (1519–1563), took Calais in 1558. It was the last remnant of the English conquests in France, and the English had held it for 211 years. (Mary said that when she died they would find the word "Calais" written on her heart.)

She died in 1558 and was succeeded by her half-sister, Elizabeth, daughter of Anne Boleyn, who ruled as Elizabeth I.

Elizabeth was 25 years old when she succeeded to the throne. She was beautiful, where Mary had been plain; intelligent, where Mary had been ordinary; stronger-willed than any man who served her, where Mary was a slave to Philip; and as fortunate as Mary was unlucky. She was the most capable and popular monarch England was ever to have, and Henry VIII need not have looked for a son.

Her one problem was that she was unmarried. The question of marriage filled the first half of her reign with turmoil, since it seemed unnatural to people of the time to have an unattached woman rule them, and it deprived the realm of the possibility of having a direct heir.

Mary, the Queen of Scotland (1542–1587), usually known as "Mary, Queen of Scots" was Elizabeth's first cousin, once removed, and was next in line for the throne if Elizabeth died without children. Since Mary was Catholic, there were many both inside and outside England who wanted her to be Queen, as soon as possible, and were willing to go to any lengths to get rid of Elizabeth. In fact, the Catholic powers of Europe —the Pope, Spain, France—more or less recog-

nized Mary as England's queen and dismissed Elizabeth as a usurper.

Yet Elizabeth, although she flirted with marriage, never consented to such a thing. Two of her stepmothers had died in childbirth and she had seen wives mistreated by her father, and saw Mary become a pawn in the hands of her husband. She wanted no man to have power over her and she wanted no adventures with childbirth, so she stayed single and, as far as official knowledge went, virginal. (She was called the "Virgin Queen," though many, with reasonable cause, doubted the literal truth of that.) The nation, as a result, spent 45 years worrying over what would happen when Elizabeth died.

Elizabeth put an end to the religious swings in England by adopting a kind of compromise program that was mildly Protestant and completed the establishment of the Anglican Church. It did not satisfy everybody. There were the "Puritans" who wanted a more radical Protestantism, purifying the Anglican church of what it retained of Catholic rituals. There were other groups, too, who were "Separatists" and didn't want to be part of either Catholicism or Anglicanism but would go their own way. And, of course, there remained many Catholics.

On the whole, Elizabeth took a mild approach and did not go out of her way to persecute, ignoring dissent if the dissenter were quiet about it. She did, however, react violently to any indication that anyone, particularly if Catholic, was plotting treason, and planning to put Mary, Queen of Scots, on the throne. Then there were the tortures and executions typical of the times.

Her reign was a golden age of literature, one of the greatest the world has seen.

To name a few, and hastily, Edmund Spenser (1553–1599) wrote the epic *The Faerie Queen* in 1590. Thomas Kyd (1558–1594) wrote the enormously popular *The Spanish Tragedy*, a play dealing with blood and revenge, in 1587. Christopher Marlowe (1564–1593) wrote such plays as *Edward II*, *Dr. Faustus*, and *The Jew of Malta*. Towering above them all was William Shakespeare (1564–1616), who, in this period, wrote such plays as *Romeo and Juliet*, *Richard III*, *Henry Fourth*, *Part One*, and *Henry V*. If anyone can be considered the greatest writer who ever lived, it is Shakespeare.

In nonfiction, Raphael Holinshed (d. 1580) published a popular history of the British Isles in 1577, which Shakespeare used as reference for his historical plays. Thomas North (1535–1603), translated Plutarch into English in 1579, and from it Shakespeare drew the material for his Roman plays.

In science, there was William Gilbert (1544–1603), who was one of the early experimentalists. He studied magnetism and was the first to suggest that the Earth itself was a magnet, explaining the working of the magnetic compass on that basis. He was the first English scientist to accept the Copernican view of the planetary system.

During Elizabeth's reign, English ships carried on an undeclared war against the Spanish possessions in the Americas and against Spanish ships that carried goods (including gold and silver) to Europe. It was very profitable for the English privateers (though risky, of course), and Philip II complained bitterly to Elizabeth about it. Elizabeth, who was an expert at keeping a straight face, insisted she had nothing to do with it, and Philip could only fume until he was ready for a full-scale war with England.

The chief English privateer was Francis Drake (1543–1596), who, on one raid against the Spanish possessions, sailed around South America, discovering the sea-lane, now called "Drake Strait," that lies between South America and Antarctica. He then raided the undefended western coast of the Americas, sailing as far north as San Francisco Bay. He ended up by continuing to sail westward and returned to England in 1580, becoming the second person to circumnavigate the Earth. He was laden with Spanish booty on his return and Queen Elizabeth boarded his ship and knighted him then and there, taking her share of the loot for the national treasury. Philip II was, understandably, infuriated.

What's more, Mary, Queen of Scots, who had been a prisoner of Elizabeth for years, and who had been the focus of plots against Elizabeth for every one of those years, was finally executed at Elizabeth's orders on February 8, 1587.

That was the last straw for Philip II. He had to go to war. He began to outfit a huge fleet of ships, usually referred to as the "Invincible Armada," which was to force its way through the English Channel to the Netherlands and from there carry Parma's army into England. Once Parma's army landed in England, there was little chance the English would be able to resist him, but the trick was to make the transfer, in the face of the English ships.

Alvaro de Bazan, Marquis de Santa Cruz (1526–1588), was an experienced seaman, who might conceivably have accomplished the task, but the project ran into trouble at once. Between April and June 1587, Drake carried out one of his most remarkable raids. He sailed into Cadiz harbor and destroyed 33 Spanish ships. He then sacked Lisbon, took a Spanish treasure ship, and destroyed much of the supplies needed for the Armada, including a vast quantity of barrel staves of seasoned timber needed for the casks that were to hold water and provisions. The ships could be replaced, but the timber couldn't be. Nevertheless, the project was not abandoned.

To make matters worse, Santa Cruz died on January 30, 1588, and Philip II, for some reason known only to himself, entrusted his job to Alonso Perez de Guzman, Duke of Medina Sidonia (1550–1619), a loyal and trustworthy subject, who happened to know nothing about seafaring. He tried earnestly to avoid the task—but Philip II would take no denial.

On July 12, 1588, the Armada left Spain—130 ships of all kinds, manned by 8500 seamen and carrying 19,000 troops and 2431 guns. When the Armada entered the Channel, the English ships opposing them were smaller and fewer, but more maneuverable, with better guns and with better seamanship. Both sides ran out of ammunition, but the English could slip into port and renew their supplies, while the Spaniards could not.

The Spanish fleet was unable to make it to the Netherlands, through a combination of unfavorable winds and English harassment. It was forced to sail into the North Sea and eventually around the British Isles, plagued by storms all the way. Only half the original fleet returned to Spain. Philip II, to give him credit, took the defeat stoically, and treated the beaten Medina Sidonia with the utmost kindness and consideration.

Elizabeth was still on her throne in 1600, fading slowly, her subjects increasingly uneasy over the succession.

ENGLISH NORTH AMERICA

It is not surprising that with England becoming a major sea-faring nation, its ships and navigators became prominent in the exploration of the world's oceans. Thus, Richard Chancellor (d. 1556), in his search for the Northwest Passage, entered the White Sea and reached the Arctic coast of Russia at Arkhangelsk.

The major effort, however, was in connection with the Northwest Passage, the attempt to find a way around North America.

Martin Frobisher (1535–1594), searching for it, discovered Baffin Island, west of Greenland, in 1576, and caught sight of Greenland itself in 1578. That vast, ice-covered land had been forgotten by Europeans since the failure of the Viking colony a century and a half earlier, but now it entered the European purview permanently. Another English navigator, John Davis (1550–1605), explored the water passage between Greenland and Baffin Island, and this is still known as "Davis Strait" today.

The English navigator, Humphrey Gilbert (1539–1583), established an English colony in Newfoundland in 1583. This was the first English settlement in North America.

In 1584, and again in 1587, under the sponsorship of Walter Raleigh (1554–1618), a half-brother of Humphrey Gilbert and a favorite of Elizabeth I, ships landed colonists at Roanoke Island in what is now North Carolina, though at the time, the English called that entire stretch of North American coast "Virginia" in honor of Elizabeth I's virginity. The first child of English parentage to be born on the territory of what is now the United States was Virginia Dare, who was born in Roanoke in 1587.

The attempt at settlement did not succeed, however. The colonists, including young Vir-

ginia, disappeared, perhaps as a result of Native American hostility. Two products of North America were, however, brought back for English use by Raleigh. One was the potato that eventually became a valued addition to the European diet. The other was tobacco, which might be considered the Native American's revenge, since in the next few centuries it has undoubtedly killed more Europeans than the number of Native Americans the Europeans killed.

Although Spain claimed all of North America, its effective control along the east coast did not extend as far north as Roanoke. The English explorations and settlements were not interfered with by Spain, however much they might have wanted to do so. Nevertheless, Spain strengthened its hold on the American continents from Florida southward, as Portugal did on Brazil, both nations making a permanent cultural conquest of the land. Rio de Janeiro was founded in Brazil in 1568; and Buenos Aires in what is now Argentina in 1580.

Among the Native Americans as yet untouched by Europeans, the perhaps legendary Hiawatha (about 1570) is supposed to have brought about the formation of the Iroquois Confederacy in what is now New York State. This, however, like all Native American cultures, was doomed before the overwhelming European advance that was on its way.

SCOTLAND

Mary, the infant daughter of James V, was Queen of Scotland almost from her birth, but when she was five, her French mother, Mary of Guise, sent her to France, where she married the French prince who eventually succeeded to the throne as Francis II (1544–1560). She was deliriously happy in France, but Francis II died at 16 (she herself being 18 at the time), and she was then forced to return, in tears, to Scotland.

After her French experience, she hated Scotland's cold weather, its poverty, its primitiveness, and its rude and boorish nobility. Moreover, while she was gone, Calvinism had made great inroads in Scotland. The most influential person in the land was now John Knox (1513–1572), a fiery preacher who was second only to Calvin himself in his upholding of Calvinist doctrine. Naturally, he denounced Mary constantly and violently since she was, and remained, a Catholic.

In July 1565, Mary married Henry Stuart, Earl of Darnley (1545–1567), a first half-cousin, both being great-grandchildren of Henry VII. The fact that Mary's husband also had a claim on England's throne made her an even greater threat to Elizabeth of England.

Darnley, however, was a weak and worthless man. Jealous of Mary's cultivated Italian secretary, David Rizzio (1533–1566), Darnley had the man stabbed in front of Mary in March 1566, when she was six months into her pregnancy.

Mary was not likely to forgive him this and once her son, James (1566–1625) was born, she needed Darnley no more. The house in which Darnley was sleeping on February 9, 1567, was blown up and he was killed. There is a general feeling that Mary herself had arranged the matter, or that she had had her new lover, James Hepburn, Earl of Bothwell (1535–1578), arrange it. (She married Bothwell, who was Protestant, and he was as worthless a husband as Darnley was—Mary had no luck with men.)

The indignant Scottish nobility forced Mary's deposition and her one-year-old son became king as James VI (still one more infant succession). Mary tried to regain her throne but, in 1579, she was forced to flee to England where Elizabeth kept her imprisoned for 19 years.

Even as a prisoner, she was a deadly danger to Elizabeth, since the Catholic powers of Europe recognized Mary as the legitimate Queen of England. The Pope excommunicated Elizabeth and indicated it would be no sin to assassinate her. Moreover, inside England there were plots in plenty to replace Elizabeth with Mary, and Mary herself was an active participant in some of them. Elizabeth was reluctant to act against another queen and a kinsman (remembering that she herself had been in similar danger when her older sister, Mary I, had been Queen of England) and fearing the consequences, especially from a

vengeful Philip II of Spain, if she did. Nevertheless, she was finally persuaded as a matter of her own life and death to take action, so she had Mary executed in 1587.

James VI grew to manhood on the uneasy Scottish throne and married Anne of Denmark (1574–1619), by whom he had two sons and a daughter, but that was only duty. He was homosexual and had only male favorites.

He did not respond beyond a purely formal protest at the execution of his mother. For one thing, he had been brought up a Calvinist and was out of sympathy with his mother's Catholicism. For another, he realized that his mother's death made him heir to the English throne and he wanted to do nothing to offend Elizabeth, lest she choose someone else as a successor. He knew that, as a Scot, he would need Elizabeth's consent, or the English would never accept him.

In 1600, then, he was waiting, even more anxiously than the English people, for Elizabeth's death.

An important Scottish mathematician of this period was John Napier (1550–1617). An ardent Calvinist, he labored to produce new and fearful weapons to repel any invasion by Philip II. In this, he did not succeed, but he did invent "logarithms" in 1594, and prepared tables of them which proved vitally important to the mathematical computations of the day.

IRELAND

In 1594, the Irish rebelled and sought Spanish help. The English had never held more than the west-central portion about Dublin, and during the long involvement of England in France, the Irish had gone their own way for the most part. Since England turned Protestant, the Irish stayed Catholic as a nationalist reaction. (It is possible that if England had stayed Catholic, Ireland would have turned Protestant.)

The possibility of Spanish interference was troublesome, and Elizabeth sent the young favorite of her old age, Robert Devereux, Earl of Essex (1566–1601), to Ireland to handle the matter. There he faced Hugh O'Neill, Earl of Tyrone

(1540–1616). Essex had proved himself on previous occasions to have some ability, but he was no match for Tyrone in the latter's native bogs. Essex was defeated, and came back to England, pouting and resentful, to put the blame on others. Elizabeth would not listen, and when he tried to raise a rebellion against her, she had him imprisoned and executed.

FRANCE

In 1550, Henry II, the son of Francis I, was King of France. He had married Catherine de Medici (1519–1589), a great-granddaughter of Lorenzo the Magnificent. She had little power over Henry II, who was ruled by his mistress, Diane de Poitier (1499–1566), but she eventually had four sons, and she ruled them.

Henry II died in 1559, when a lance splinter penetrated the eyehole of his golden helmet during a joust, and was succeeded by his 15-year-old son, Francis II (the husband of Mary, Queen of Scots). He died in a year and was succeeded by his younger brother, Charles IX (1550–1574), who was 10 years old at the time of his accession.

The Reformation was spreading in France. The bulk of the population remained Catholic, but a strong minority became Calvinist. The French Calvinists were called "Huguenots" (the origin of the name is uncertain), and these met with persecution from the start. A large percentage of the nobility turned Huguenot, however.

The leading Huguenot, Admiral Gaspard de Coligny (1519–1572) thought of responding to persecution by establishing a colony on the American coast. There, Huguenots might practice their religion freely. (This was the first attempt to use the American continent as a haven from religious persecution.)

In 1562, therefore, colonists were placed on the coast of what is now South Carolina, but grew homesick and were taken to England by a passing English ship. In 1564, another group of colonists were placed in northern Florida, but the Spaniards, under Pedro Menendez (1519–1574), killed them all. (Not because they were Frenchmen, he explained, but because they were Protestants.)

In 1565, Menendez established the city of St. Augustine in Florida, the oldest city of European origin to exist in the territory of what is now the United States.

If the Huguenots could not find peace in North America, however, neither could they find peace or toleration in France. In 1562, even as Coligny was sending colonists to North America, a series of religious wars between Huguenots and Catholics turned France into chaos.

There were 10 years of indecisive fighting, with the Huguenots generally getting the worst of it, and then proposals were made for a compromise peace.

Henry, Prince of Navarre (1553–1610), was the most important Protestant leader. Although only 19 years of age, he was descended in the direct line of male descent from Louis IX. That meant that if Henry II's sons all died without children (and one was already dead), Navarre would be heir to the throne.

Henry of Navarre, therefore, was to marry Margaret of Valois (1553–1615), the sister of Charles IX, and the Huguenots were to be given freedom of worship in certain specified cities.

On the night of August 23, 1572 (St. Bartholomew's Day), on the eve of the marriage, the Catholics struck at the unsuspecting and celebrating Huguenots. Coligny was killed and so were thousands of other Huguenots in Paris and in the provinces. This "Bartholomew's Day Massacre" was celebrated by the Pope joyfully, and the grave Philip II was said to have smiled for the only time in his life on hearing the news. Henry of Navarre saved his life by instantly announcing his conversion to Catholicism.

Charles IX died without children on May 30, 1574, and he was succeeded by his younger brother, who reigned as Henry III, and who fled from his post as King of Poland (with a good supply of the Polish crown jewels) at hearing the news.

Henry III was not likely to have children since he was homosexual and showed no interest in women even for the sake of an heir. His one remaining brother, who was now Francis, Duke of Alencon (and now Anjou), had carried on a longtime romance with Elizabeth of England, but he never married her or anyone else, and died in 1584. After that, it seemed certain that Henry of Navarre (who had turned Protestant again, once he was safely out of Catholic hands) was going to reign as soon as Henry III died.

Since the French, as a whole, would not tolerate a Protestant king, and since Philip II of Spain would not either, the religious wars continued, as indecisive as ever. The leader on the Catholic side was not the king but Henry, Duke of Guise (1550–1588), the son of the conqueror of Calais. It was Henry of Guise who had planned the Bartholomew's Day massacre and who had personally seen to the death of Coligny. It was he who called in Philip II of Spain, and for a while he was far more powerful and popular than the weak king, Henry III.

Henry responded by having Henry of Guise assassinated on December 23, 1588. That made Henry III the target for the Catholic zealots and he was assassinated on August 1, 1589 by a Catholic monk, Jacques Clement (1564–1589).

Therefore, Henry of Navarre was King Henry IV, but the more extreme Catholics, under Charles, Duke of Mayenne (1554–1611), younger brother of Henry of Guise, continued to fight, with the continuing help of Philip II.

On March 14, 1590, Henry IV won the battle of Ivry, west of Paris, and then laid siege to Paris itself. Spanish troops entered the city to defend it, and Henry realized that while he could not be defeated, neither could he win. He was not inclined to spend his life fighting, so in 1593, sighing "Paris is well worth a mass," he turned Catholic again.

Henry IV's capable councillor, Maximilien de Bethune, Duc de Sully (1560–1641), remained a Huguenot but continued to serve his king.

On April 15, 1598, Henry IV issued the Edict of Nantes, in which the Huguenots were given toleration in certain cities and were protected from actual persecution provided they stayed out of Paris and a few other specific places. With that, the religious civil wars in France were over after three and a half decades of useless fighting.

The greatest French writer of this period was the essayist, Michel Eyquem de Montaigne (1533–1592). From the quiet of his estate, he produced his personal essays between 1572 and 1588, which were civilized, tolerant, and skeptical. His cool style influenced later writers in England as well as in France. The greatest poet of the period was Pierre de Ronsard (1524–1585), who was patronized by Charles IX.

More influential than either among the unsophisticated were the works of the French astrologer, Michel Nostradamus (1503–1560). He published a series of verses in 1555, supposedly foretelling the future. They were written in so vague and mystic a style that they could be interpreted in almost any fashion. He did, however, forecast the death of a French king in a golden cage, and Henry II's death soon after, in a way that seemed to be just that, lent Nostradamus enormous prestige and made him popular right down into our own time.

The French mathematician, Franciscus Vieta (1540–1603), turned Catholic when Henry IV did. He labored as a cryptographer for Henry IV, deciphering the secret messages of Philip II of Spain. The angry Philip accused France of sorcery and complained to the Pope. Vieta, in a book on algebra in 1591, first used the x's and y's with which we are so familiar today.

Jean Nicot (1530–1600) was French ambassador to Portugal from 1559 to 1561. He learned of tobacco there and introduced it to France. The poisonous alkaloid in tobacco, known as "nicotine," derives its name from him.

PAPACY

The Council of Trent was interrupted by Paul IV (1476–1559), who became Pope in 1555 and who did not want any council telling him what to do. He believed in the iron fist, so that he extended the power of the Inquisition, set up an Index of forbidden books, and established a ghetto in Rome within which the Jews were imprisoned and humiliated.

Under Pius IV (1499–1565), who succeeded in 1559, the Council of Trent was reconvened and it completed its work in 1563. It redefined and clarified the basic Catholic philosophy and did away with many of the abuses that had inspired the Protestant Reformation half a century before. It, and the activity of the Jesuits, allowed Catholicism to regain some lost ground, but nothing sufficed to end the split in the Church altogether.

Pius V (1504–1572), who became Pope in 1566, was an ascetic and a reformer. With him, the time of the Renaissance Popes—luxurious, semipagan, and indifferent to religion—was definitely over. Pius V wiped out all vestiges of Protestantism in Italy and took an extreme Catholic stand on heresy, making wide use of the Inquisition, urging on Philip II to the harshest measures in the Netherlands, and excommunicating Elizabeth of England in 1570. It was he who urged the naval offensive against the Turks that ended with a victory at the Battle of Lepanto in 1571.

Gregory XIII (1502–1585), who became Pope in 1572, continued the policy of reform and hardnosed antiheresy. He was the Pope who celebrated the St. Bartholomew's Day Massacre jubilantly. He is best known, though, for his reform of the calendar. Since Julius Caesar's time, 16 centuries earlier, there had been a leap year every four years without fail. That made the year slightly too long, so that the vernal equinox, and the date of Easter which depended upon it, was falling earlier and earlier in the cycle of seasons, and both would eventually mark mid-winter rather than the beginning of the spring.

With the help of astronomers, Gregory XIII authorized the dropping of 10 days in 1582, and of allowing only 97 leap years, instead of 100, every 400 years. The Protestant and Orthodox nations hesitated to adopt a Papal reform, but eventually they did, and the world today lives by the "Gregorian calendar."

Sixtus V (1520–1590) became Pope in 1585. He reorganized the finances and economy of the Papal states, fixed the College of Cardinals at 70 members, and enforced the new system of the Council of Trent.

Clement VIII (1536–1605) became Pope in 1592.

During this period, the Italian poet, Torquato Tasso (1544–1595), was outstanding. He was paranoid enough to be confined to a madhouse for some years but he nevertheless produced a magnificent work in *Gerusalemme Liberata* ("Jerusalem Liberated"), an epic poem published in 1581, dealing with the First Crusade, four centuries earlier.

The Italian composer, Giovanni Pierlugi da Palestrina (1525–1594), wrote church music in the medieval fashion.

The Italian scholar, Giordano Bruno (1548–1600), had ideas very similar to those of Nicholas of Cusa a century earlier. Bruno was more vehement in expressing them, and times had grown harder, what with the Protestant Reformation and the more active fight against heresy. As a result, he was burned at the stake in Rome on February 17, 1600, a martyr of science and defiant, like Servetus, to the end.

VENICE

Venice was declining markedly. Her last successful offensive action took place in this period. With the help of Spain and the Papacy, she defeated the Turks in the great Battle of Lepanto in 1571. However, she lacked the ability to follow it up and gave up Cyprus to the Turks in 1573. Her only important eastern possession after this was the island of Crete (or Candia, as the Venetians called it).

AUSTRIA

Austria and the Holy Roman Empire also declined markedly in power now that Spain was no longer part of the Emperor's dominions. It was chiefly concerned, at this time, with the rivalry between the Protestants in the north and the Catholics in the south. The division was as much political as religious, since many of the virtually independent states of the Empire had leaders who turned Protestant so that they could be free of Papal interference and so that they could appropriate Church lands.

On September 25, 1555, the Peace of Augsburg (in Bavaria) allowed individual princes to choose either Lutheranism or Catholicism and to then force their choice on their people. No provision was made for freedom for Calvinist worship.

After that, there were some decades of relative

religious peace and sporadic warfare with the Turks. In 1564, Ferdinand I died and was succeeded by his son who reigned as Maximilian II (1527–1576). He was, in turn, succeeded by his son Rudolf II (1552–1612).

The German alchemist, Libavius (1560–1616), published a book on alchemy in 1597, which eschewed mysticism and was the first chemical textbook worthy of the name. However, he could not quite abandon the alchemical belief that it was possible to turn base metals into gold ("transmutation").

SWITZERLAND

Switzerland was still driven by religious unrest with Zwinglian cantons in the north, Catholic cantons in the south, and Calvinist Geneva in the west.

It produced an important scholar at this time, Konrad von Gesner (1516–1565), who did his best to accumulate in one set of volumes all there was to know about natural history, as Pliny had done more than 16 centuries earlier, but with greater discrimination. He wrote these volumes in the last 15 years of his life and died in 1565 because he would not, as a doctor, abandon his patients during an attack of the plague in Zurich —thus, he died of it, too.

DENMARK

Denmark was ruled at this time by Frederick II (1534–1588), who became king in 1559 and is remembered chiefly as the patron of Tycho Brahe (1546–1601), the greatest astronomer of his day, and the last important astronomer before the invention of the telescope revolutionized the science forever.

Tycho was the first to study a nova carefully (inventing the term, which meant "new" and referred to a new star in the heavens, of the type which nowadays we call a "supernova"). He studied a comet carefully and showed that it lay beyond the Moon. He also prepared the best star-map yet. With appropriations from Frederick II, he had built the best astronomical observatory the world had yet seen on the Danish

island of Hven. Once Frederick died in 1588, his source of funds began to dry up and he spent his last years in Germany.

Frederick's 11-year-old son succeeded to the throne in 1588 as Christian IV (1577–1648).

SWEDEN

Sweden was beginning to follow a program of expansion. Under Eric XIV (1533–1577), it took over Estonia. Eric XIV exhibited increasing signs of madness, however, and was deposed in 1568. His half-brother succeeded as John III (1537–1592). He tried to reimpose a diluted form of Catholicism on the country, but failed. In 1592, his son Sigismund (1566–1632) succeeded. Sigismund had already been chosen King of Poland five years earlier. He was Catholic, however, and the Swedes deposed him in 1599.

POLAND

In 1550, Sigismund II (1520–1572) was on the Polish throne. Under him, Protestantism made great gains. However, the Counter-Reformation and the Jesuits fought back, and Poland, in the end, remained Catholic.

On July 1, 1569, the Union of Lublin wiped out all signs of Lithuania as an independent nation. Until then, for over a century and a half, Poland and Lithuania had existed in a dynastic union, sharing a king, but maintaining a certain legalistic separation in laws and customs. Now, however, the two became a single country under the name of "Poland."

Sigismund died in 1572, and left no immediate heirs. The Polish throne, which, in any case, was becoming increasingly elective, now became altogether so.

In 1573, Henry of Anjou, the younger brother of Charles IX of France, bought the throne by bribing the electors. The reason for his doing so, aside from the pleasure of being king, was Henry's desire to bring Poland into alliance with France. However, Henry did *not* enjoy the throne of Poland any more than Mary, Queen of Scots had enjoyed the throne of Scotland, and for much the same reasons. When news reached

Henry in 1574 that his brother had died and that he himself was Henry III, King of France, he took all the crown jewels he could carry and fled Poland, returning to France. (The Poles were well rid of him, even with the jewels.)

Poland continued to be increasingly anarchic. In 1587, Sigismund III, the son of John III of Sweden and a nephew of Sigismund II, was elected to the throne of Poland and, five years later, became King of Sweden as well. He had been educated by the Jesuits and he did what he could to wipe out the vanishing Protestantism of Poland. Though deposed in Sweden in 1599, he remained King of Poland.

RUSSIA

Russia began a period of enormous expansion. Between 1552 and 1556, under Tsar Ivan IV the Terrible, the Russians finally wiped out the Tatar kingdom to the east, taking Kazan, which had been the Tatar capital for over a century, and then driving down the full length of the Volga River to the Caspian Sea.

This did not mean that Russia, after three centuries, was finally rid of the Tatars. There still remained a Tatar kingdom in the south, centered in the Crimea and stretching up into the Ukraine, which it disputed with Poland. The southern Tatars were not entirely helpless either, but advanced to Moscow in 1555 and, again, in 1571. Both times, however, they were driven back.

Ivan was forced to fight the Russian nobility ("boyars"), whose unruliness virtually insured anarchy, as it did in Poland. Ivan's chosen weapon was terror, for he killed almost indiscriminately. He was not called "the Terrible" for nothing. In 1570, he took Novgorod, which he believed was rebelling against him, and subjected it to a sack that could be compared to those carried out by the Huns and Mongols. In 1581, he even, in a fit of rage, killed his son. He repented this action and mourned it, but that didn't bring his son back to life. He did reduce his realm to order, but it was the stillness of death more than anything else.

What Russia needed, then and afterward, was a warm weather opening to the sea. The Baltic Sea, which was the logical door to the rest of the world, was blocked by Sweden and Poland, however, and though Ivan fought them for most of his reign, the results were not satisfactory and he remained shut off. Reaching the Caspian Sea was of no use for that was landlocked. Russia had only one seaport, Arkhangelsk, but that was on the Arctic Ocean and was, for much of the year, frozen and useless.

In 1553, however, English ships were reconnoitering in the north to see if there was a way around Asia to the Far East in that direction. One ship, under Richard Chancellor, made its way to Arkhangelsk. It was welcomed jubilantly and the crew was taken overland to meet Tsar Ivan in Moscow. The Muscovy Company was founded in England and trade between the two nations was instituted.

Ivan IV even made a proposal of marriage to Elizabeth of England, which was not accepted. It would have been one of the most colossal mismatches that could be imagined (though George Bernard Shaw once stated that if the marriage had gone through, Ivan would quickly have become Ivan the Terrified).

Russia found an opening, however, if not to the sea, then to the east. In 1579, the Stroganov family was establishing a business empire in eastern Russia along the Urals, dealing in furs mostly, but there were Tatars east of the Urals who were a danger to their enterprises. They hired a Cossack to take care of the matter. (The Cossacks were horsemen in the south, who had found relative freedom in the no-man's land where Russia, Poland, and the Ottoman Turks met and disputed for mastery. The Cossacks were something like the legendary cowboys of the American west centuries later.)

In 1581, the Cossack, Yermak Timofeyevich (d. 1584), with 840 men, moved east of the Urals in the first Russian invasion of Asia. For at least 2000 years, nomadic tribesmen from Asia had poured in successive waves into the land which eventually became Russia, and now for the first time, the tide flowed the other way. Yermak had firearms, of course, which the Asian tribes had not, and the result was what it had been in Mexico and Peru a half-century earlier. The Russians occupied the Khanate of Sibir just east of the Urals and the entire northern portion of Asia eventually received that name ("Siberia," in English).

Ivan IV died in 1584, and since he had killed his worthy son, he was succeeded by a feeble-minded younger one who reigned as Fyodor I (1557–1598). All of Ivan IV's terror now went for nothing, for as soon as a weak hand was at the Tsarist helm, the boyars became turbulent again and their rivalries and intrigues once more weakened the land.

In 1589, an independent patriarchate was set up in Moscow so that the Russian Church was no longer dependent on the leadership of the Patriarch of Constantinople who was, in any case, under the thumb of the Ottoman Turks.

Fyodor died in 1598, and he was the last of the Varangian rulers who had taken over Russia seven centuries earlier.

It was necessary to elect a new ruler now, and the choice fell on Boris Godunov (1551–1605), who was Fyodor's brother-in-law. His reign was made miserable by the machinations of the boyars.

OTTOMAN EMPIRE

Suleiman the Magnificent died on September 5, 1566, having reigned for 46 years. He had been the tenth consecutive forceful and capable ruler of the Ottoman Turks over a period of two and three-quarter centuries. Few monarchies have had such a stretch of able rulers, and now the Turkish good fortune ended. The Ottoman Empire was never to have another ruler like any of the first 10.

An indication of what was happening was the fact that Suleiman was succeeded by a son who went down in history as Selim II the Sot (1524–1574). However, even if Selim was a drunkard and an incompetent, the Ottoman Empire did not fall apart at once. Its institutions were too strong to allow that, and it continued smoothly for a time despite the weak hand at the helm.

During Selim's reign, the Turks went to war with Venice over the island of Cyprus, which

Venice held. Pope Pius V organized a "Holy League" in which Spanish ships joined the Venetian fleet and the whole was put under Don John of Austria (who was later to fail in the Netherlands).

The two fleets met at Lepanto, on October 7, 1571, near the opening of the Gulf of Corinth, not far from the site of the Battle of Actium, where Octavian had bested Mark Antony 16 centuries earlier. The battle now was very much like the battle then, for it was fought with galleys, rowed by oarsmen. The Christians had a few guns and some light armor, but except for that, the battle might have been fought between the Romans and the Carthaginians. The battle was fought as a series of single combats between ships that tried to ram and board each other. Don John had 227 galleys, and the Turkish admiral had 270 somewhat smaller ships with less experienced seamen.

It was a smashing Christian victory. The Turks lost 223 galleys to 13 for the Christians, and 15,000 Christian galley slaves were freed. It was the last important battle of this type ever to be fought.

The Christian navy did not follow up this success because it was too late in the season. They retired to wait for the spring. During the winter, the Turks madly built new galleys and the Christian offensive was not effectively renewed, partly because of Philip's preoccupation with the Netherlands, France, and England. The Venetians, not of a mind to fight the Turks all by themselves, gave up Cyprus in March 1573, and signed a peace with the Ottoman Empire in February 1574.

However, if the Battle of Lepanto did not have any short-term effects, it did prevent the Turks from proceeding to the domination of the central and western Mediterranean Sea; it destroyed their reputation for invincibility; and it marked the beginning of the decline of the Ottoman Empire.

Selim II was succeeded by his son, Murad III (1546–1595) in 1574, and he in turn was succeeded by Mehmed III (1566–1603) in 1595. Despite gradual decay, the Turks at this time were continuing to expand eastward to the Caucasus mountain range and the Caspian Sea and retained their hold on Hungary.

PERSIA

In 1587, Abbas I (1571–1629), sometimes called "Abbas the Great," became Shah of Persia. By that time, Englishmen had reached the land. Anthony Jenkinson traveled through Russia to reach Persia in 1561.

Abbas was the greatest of the Safavids. He made peace with the Turks in order to be free to handle the Uzbeks to the north. They were defeated in 1597.

He then set about building a new army, with artillery after the fashion of the Turks, so that he could finally battle them on equal terms. In this, he had the help of two Englishmen, the brothers, Anthony (1565–1635) and Robert Shirley (1581–1628).

INDIA

In 1556, Akbar (1542–1605), the son of Humayun and the third of the Mogul Emperors, came to the throne which he was to occupy for nearly 50 years. He extended the limits of the Empire well into central India and established a policy of religious toleration.

CHINA

The Ming Empire was now declining militarily, although its cultural achievements remained high.

A Portuguese settlement was established at Macao, in southern China near Canton, in 1557, and it has remained Portuguese to this day. Japan was conducting a campaign in Korea that met with Chinese resistance and that further weakened Chinese power, even as the Manchus in the northeast were growing stronger.

An earthquake took place in Shansi in northeastern China on January 24, 1556, which was reported to have killed 830,000 people. If this is accurate, it is the worst earthquake from the standpoint of loss of life in recorded history.

JAPAN

The Japanese at first welcomed the coming of Christianity that resulted from the missionary activity of Francis Xavier, feeling it would bring European trade with it. Xavier's attempt to adapt to local custom, however, was not followed by those missionaries who came after him, and their intolerance—combined with their attitude of superiority to Japanese ways—created furious opposition.

During this period, Japan was finally unified. The beginning was made by Oda Nobunago (1534–1582), who, in 1568, seized Kyoto, the seat of the Emperor (who reigned but did not rule), and made himself dictator of central Japan. He broke the power of the Buddhist monasteries and initiated a period of castle-building.

Oda's chief general was Toyotomi Hideyoshi (1537–1598). After Oda's assassination in 1582, Hideyoshi made himself dictator and, by 1590, all Japan was his. This meant that a whole class of Japanese warriors was suddenly unemployed. To keep them busily engaged elsewhere so that they would not plot to seize power for themselves (something that had been going on in Japan for centuries), Hideyoshi planned to conquer China by way of Korea.

In 1592, Korea was invaded and occupied, but in July the Korean fleet engaged the Japanese ships. Two of the Korean ships were low-slung and were covered with iron armor, as designed by the Korean admiral, Yi Sung Sin. These were the first ironclads in history, which almost single-handedly destroyed the Japanese fleet.

At a Korean request, the Chinese sent an army into Korea and the Japanese were penned up at Pusan in the southeast. In 1597, they broke out again; however, in November 1598, the Koreans won a second great naval battle in the course of which Yi Sung Sin was killed. By that time, Hideyoshi had also died, and the Japanese left Korea. (One wonders what would have happened if the Chinese had taken up the matter of ironclads, improved them further, and built a fleet of them.)

In 1600, another general, Tokugawa Ieyasu

(1543–1616), seized control of a united Japan and established the Tokugawa Shogunate.

PHILIPPINE ISLANDS

For nearly 50 years after Magellan had reached the islands and died there, neither the Portuguese nor the Spaniards had seriously attempted a settlement. It was not until 1565 that the first Spanish settlement was made there at the order of Philip II (for whom the islands were then named). Manila, its present capital, was founded on May 19, 1571.

AFRICA

In 1591, a force of Spanish and Portuguese mercenaries, in the pay of Morocco and using firearms, defeated the forces of the Songhair Empire. The black culture at Timbuktu was destroyed.

1600 TO 1650

AUSTRIA

The Holy Roman Empire, dominated by Austria, consisted now of Protestant states and Catholic states. In theory, each side was supposed to leave the other alone, and there was to be a mutual toleration. Neither side, however, trusted the other.

In 1608, the Protestant states formed an "Evangelical Union," headed by Frederick IV (1574–1610), Elector of the Palatinate, a German state on the middle Rhine. In response, the Catholic states formed a Catholic League in 1609 under the leadership of Maximilian I, Duke of Bavaria (1573–1651). The stage was all set for a religious war; all that was needed was a spark.

The spark was supplied in the Austrian dominions. Austria was Catholic, of course, but after the Turks had taken Hungary, Bohemia had fallen under Hapsburg control, and the Bohemians were largely Protestant.

Under Rudolf II's comparatively mild rule, the Protestants were not too badly treated. In fact, Rudolph II was a scholar who is best remembered today for being the patron of the German astronomer, Johannes Kepler (1571–1630), who was a Protestant.

Kepler was a student of Tycho Brahe in the latter's last years. He used Tycho's observations of the changing position of Mars in the sky to work out the Three Laws of Planetary Motion in 1609 and 1619. He showed that the orbits of the planets (including that of Earth) were ellipses, with the sun at one focus. He showed how the speed or orbital motion varied with a planet's varying distance from the Sun, and how the period of revolution of each planet was related to its average distance from the Sun.

This was a vast improvement on the picture as drawn by Copernicus three quarters of a century earlier. Kepler's model of the planetary system is still accepted today and undoubtedly corresponds with reality. When Kepler prepared tables of planetary motions based on his Laws, which proved the best tables yet, he called them the "Rudolphine Tables" after his patron.

Kepler also studied the newly invented telescope and worked out its optics in detail, establishing the modern science of optics in so doing.

In 1612, when Rudolf II died without children, his younger brother, Matthias (1557–1619), succeeded. Matthias was already 55 and was also childless. He was strongly Catholic, but he tried to keep the peace between the two religious parties. However, he planned to leave his dukedom and the Imperial throne to his first cousin, once-removed, Ferdinand (1578–1637), and that was a different matter.

Ferdinand had been educated by the Jesuits and was an uncompromising Catholic of the most narrow type. There was no hope that he would be tolerant and, even before he became Emperor, he was made King of Bohemia in 1617. Things were darkening for the Bohemians.

On May 23, 1618, the Bohemians in Prague threw their Catholic governors out a window ("the defenestration of Prague"). The Evangelical League, now led by Frederick V of the Palatinate (1596–1632), after the death of his father in 1610, at once sent troops into Austria, and this was the start of what came to be called "The Thirty Years War."

The Bohemians elected Frederick V their king on August 26, 1619, and three days later (Matthias being dead by now) Ferdinand was elected Emperor Ferdinand II. Ferdinand II secured the help of Spain and of Maximilian of Bavaria, and prepared to bring Bohemia back within the Hapsburg orbit.

Maximilian's Netherlands-born general, Johann Tserclaes, Count von Tilly (1559–1632), marched to Bohemia and on November 8, 1620, defeated Frederick totally and forced him to flee. Frederick's 10 weeks as king were over and done with, and he remained in exile for the rest of his life. Tilly then conquered the Palatinate, and its electoral vote for Emperor was transferred to Maximilian of Bavaria.

The Austrians and the Catholics seemed to have done very well—too well, perhaps, for they alarmed France, which, although it was a Catholic nation, didn't want to see Austria grow too powerful.

France encouraged Christian IV of Denmark to intervene. He was a Lutheran and he was also Duke of Holstein, which was a German region just south of Denmark. That gave him an interest in how things went in Germany. Danish troops invaded Germany in the summer of 1625.

Austria, for its part, commissioned Albert von Wallenstein (1583–1634), a Bohemian-born general, to lead its armies. He fed and paid his army by stripping the countryside, and this began the custom, in this war, of systematically looting the land and of callously beggaring and killing civilians.

Christian IV lost battle after battle to Tilly and to Wallenstein and, on June 7, 1629, was glad to make peace even at the cost of giving up Holstein.

All seemed well for Austria now. Ferdinand, firm in his position as Emperor, was supreme in Bohemia again. The Protestant states of Germany were either defeated outright or were pusillanimously maintaining neutrality. Denmark had burned its fingers. It didn't look as though it would take very much, now, to clear the Empire of Protestants altogether and return it to the Catholic fold. In fact, by the Edict of Restitution on March 29, 1629, the smashing of Protestant congregations and worship had begun.

But France, working harder than ever, found a new Protestant champion in the person of Gustavus II Adolphus of Sweden (1594–1632). Gustavus Adolphus was busy fighting Poland at the time, but France managed to work out a truce in that war. They then gave Gustavus Adolphus a healthy subsidy and pointed southward.

Gustavus Adolphus landed in Germany on July 4, 1630, exuding self-confidence. Ferdinand of Austria, hoping to keep Germans from rallying to the Swedish king, fired Wallenstein, whose depredations had made him hateful.

Tilly, however, was laying siege to the Protestant city of Magdeburg throughout the winter and early spring of 1630–1631. Gustavus Adolphus, moving very quickly, took Frankfurt on the Oder on April 13, 1631, hoping that his approach would cause Tilly to lift the siege and turn toward him.

Tilly didn't do that. He kept up the siege, took the city of Magdeburg on May 20, 1631, and subjected it to a merciless sack, killing 25,000 out of its 30,000 inhabitants and burning it to the ground. Genghis Khan could not have done better, though he would have done it more quickly.

Saxony, a Protestant state, had tried to stay neutral, but whatever it did, either Tilly or Gustavus Adolphus would ravage it. Saxony decided to join the Protestant King of Sweden—and Tilly ravaged it, taking Leipzig itself on September 15, 1631.

Gustavus Adolphus rushed to meet him and the two armies faced each other four miles north of Leipzig on September 17. What those who opposed the Swedish king were not quite aware of was that he was a military leader of the first rank. He had helped devise lighter muskets that were easier to carry and could be swung into action more quickly. He also made the artillery lighter and more mobile. He introduced cartridges for muskets so that there would always be just the right amount of gunpowder for firing, and he improved and standardized the quality of the gunpowder itself.

All this was hastening the disappearance of infantry masses that were needed to make their weight felt behind spears or pikes, as had been the custom since the Greeks and Macedonians 19 centuries earlier. Instead, the "battle-line" was coming into being, a relatively thin outspreading of soldiers, since there was no need for a massive weight to make contact. The soldiers let the bullets make the contact for them.

In short, everything Gustavus Adolphus did made for great mobility, greater maneuverability, greater speed.

This proved itself at the Battle of Leipzig, in which the Swedes turned agilely in this direction and that, halting each attempted Imperial attack, and then swooping in to capture the unwieldy Imperial artillery. Tilly's army was smashed and driven into flight.

Gustavus Adolphus then led his army freely over Germany and, in a battle on April 15, 1632, Tilly was killed. The Emperor Ferdinand, however, had now placed Wallenstein in charge of his army again and Gustavus Adolphus maneuvered to meet him. The two armies met at Lutzen, not far west of Leipzig on November 16, 1632. Wallenstein was a redoubtable fighter, but he was narrowly beaten and had to withdraw. In the course of the battle, however, Gustavus Adolphus was killed, which was a disaster for the Protestants.

Even so, Wallenstein, who was no fool, could see that 15 years of war had brought no result worth the slaughter and he felt that a compromise peace might be best. He tried to organize one that would leave him in a powerful position in Bohemia. The intransigent Emperor Ferdinand, however, wanted neither a compromise

peace with the Protestants, nor a powerful Wallenstein in Bohemia. His best way of avoiding both was to arrange for the assassination of Wallenstein, and that took place on February 25, 1633.

The Swedes remained in the field even without Gustavus Adolphus, but on September 6, 1634, at Nordlingen in southwestern Germany, they fought an Imperialist army that included a strong Spanish force. The Spaniards fought with their usual methodical ferocity and the Swedes were almost wiped out.

All the work of Gustavus Adolphus was now threatened, and the French who, till then, had paid others to do the fighting against Austria, were forced, at last, to take a direct hand in the action.

This meant that the Empire was faced with a formidable new enemy. When Ferdinand II died in 1637, his son, who became Ferdinand III (1608–1657), and who had helped push for Wallenstein's assassination, began to think of peace. It was clear that the cruelty of a religious war in which each side thought the other was in league with the devil was destroying Germany to the benefit of no one but France.

Ferdinand III was unwilling to allow Protestants in his own realm, but he was now prepared to have them left in peace elsewhere in Germany. His eagerness for peace was increased when the Swedes, under a capable general, Lennart Torstenson (1603–1651), defeated the Imperialists on November 2, 1642, near Leipzig.

Peace negotiations were opened in 1643, but they dragged on for years. Germany, which had been badly damaged by the marching and countermarching of armies, was further mangled during the years of negotiation while the various parties maneuvered for advantage. The population of the Empire had declined from 22 million to perhaps 17 million, and starvation reached the pitch where cannibalism was reported. It was the worst European devastation since the Mongols had dashed in four centuries earlier.

At last, on October 24, 1648, a treaty of peace was signed at Munster in the district of Westphalia in northwestern Germany.

By this "Treaty of Westphalia," Sweden obtained sections of the German Baltic coast, and France obtained bases in western Germany. The conditions inside Germany were restored to what they were in 1618 (all that fighting and horror for nothing!), except that Bavaria kept the electoral dignity, while the Palatinate was turned into an eighth electorate. Switzerland and the United Netherlands were recognized as independent nations owing no allegiance to the Emperor. The Protestant states (including, for the first time, those that were Calvinist) were to be left alone, but there was no provision for the toleration of Protestants in Bohemia or in any other part of the Austrian dominions.

The Thirty Years War was the last of the significant wars of religion. A century and a third after Martin Luther had begun the Reformation, Europe settled down at last to the inevitable—that the continent was to be permanently divided between Catholics and Protestants.

The Thirty Years War brought cultural life in Germany to an ebb. However, a German astronomer of note in this period was Johannes Hevelius (1611–1687). In 1647, he published a magnificent map of the Moon, and he was the first to detect the phases of the planet, Mercury.

NETHERLANDS

Once Spain had taken over Portugal, they closed the port of Lisbon to Dutch ships. What might have seemed an economic blow at the Netherlands proved, however, to spur them into a golden age.

The Dutch had ships that were better than those of the Spaniards and Portuguese, and they decided to sail to the Far East themselves, instead of trading by way of the Portuguese as they had done up to that point.

They formed the Dutch East India Company in 1602. They seized the island of Mauritius in the Indian Ocean (which they named for their stadtholder, Maurice of Nassau). They also took Ceylon and Malacca from the Portuguese, seized bases on the islands of Java and Sumatra, and founded Batavia on the Javanese coast in 1619 (naming the city for the old Latin name for the Netherlands).

The accomplishments of the Dutch in the Far East at this time were mainly due to the enterprise of Anthony van Diemen (1593–1645). Van Diemen, as the administrator of the Dutch Indonesian realm, sent the Dutch navigator, Abel Janszoon Tasman, on an exploring expedition to the south of the East Indian islands.

In 1642, Tasman discovered an island he called Van Diemen's Land, but which has since been renamed in his honor as Tasmania. He also discovered New Zealand (named for the Dutch province of Zeeland) and the Fiji Islands. In the course of his voyage, he circumnavigated Australia, but without happening to touch its shores. In 1644, however, he did sight sections of the Australian coast, which he called "New Holland," but which he did not recognize as a continent.

The Dutch also formed the Dutch West India Company and went exploring and adventuring on the American coastline, obtaining bases in some of the lesser islands of the West Indies. (That this could be done in the very teeth of the Spaniards indicates the decline of Spanish power.)

In 1609, an English navigator in the employ of the Netherlands, Henry Hudson (d. 1611), explored what is now called the Hudson River. (He later went on, in English employ, to explore what is now called Hudson Bay, and died there.)

In 1626, a Dutchman, Peter Minuit (1580–1638), bought the island of Manhattan from its native inhabitants for the equivalent of $24. The city of New Amsterdam was founded then, and the region around the Hudson River became the colony of New Netherlands.

In addition, Willem Corneliszoon Schouten (1580–1625) was the first to explore the coasts of Tierra del Fuego (the island off the southern tip of South America, which had been sighted by Magellan nearly a century earlier). In 1615, he named the southernmost point of the island Cape Horn after his home town of Hoorn. (The fact that Tierra del Fuego is horn-shaped is pure coincidence.)

The Netherlands was in a golden age culturally as well. There was a burst of artistry not far second to that of the Italian Renaissance: Peter

Paul Rubens (1577–1640), well-known for his plump and overflowing damsels; Anthony Van Dyck (1599–1641), a student of Rubens, who also painted in England, and many of whose paintings of English courtiers showed the trim, pointed beard fashionable at the time, so that such a beard has been called a "Van Dyck" ever since; Franz Hals (1585–1666), whose "Laughing Cavalier" is world famous; Jan Vermeer (1632–1675); and, most of all, Rembrandt van Rijn (1606–1669), who may well be the most famous painter in the world who was not an Italian.

Hugo Grotius (1583–1645) was a prolific writer who set the basis for international law. Jan Baptista van Helmont (1580–1640) was the first to study different gases in detail and discovered carbon dioxide; he also studied the growth of plants and was the first to conduct quantitative studies in biology. Willerbrord Snell (1580–1626) made a key discovery in light refraction. The Dutch were particularly well-versed in optical work, and a Dutch optician, Hans Lippershey (1570–1619), constructed the first telescope in 1608.

In 1609, the Netherlands had concluded a 12-year truce with Spain that was growing weary. In 1621, when the truce expired, Spanish forces tried to renew the struggle, but the Netherlands was now exceedingly prosperous, with a first-class fleet, while Spain, involved with the Thirty Years War, was near the end of its resources.

In 1648, the independence of the Netherlands was recognized. The long 80-year war with Spain was at last crowned with success, and a small nation with a population of about 1.5 million had become a world power.

Maurice of Nassau had died in 1625 and had been succeeded as stadtholder by his younger brother, Frederick Henry (1584–1647). He was successful in war, beating the Spanish in several battles and assuming nearly monarchical status. He did not quite live to see independence formally recognized, dying the year before the Treaty of Westphalia. He was succeeded by his son, William II (1626–1650).

In 1650, however, William II died of smallpox, leaving a pregnant wife to whom a son was later born. That was not enough for the Dutch, who put an end to the stadtholdership, three quarters of a century after William the Silent had established the post. For a time there was a "Dutch Republic."

DENMARK

Christian IV of Denmark had an unusually long reign of 60 years, but it was a reign doomed to frustration. Christian intervened in the Thirty Years War in 1625 and was soundly trounced. He then had to watch Sweden (which had been a possession of Denmark not so long before) intervene, be victorious, and attain great-power status. In 1643, Christian made war on Sweden out of jealousy and was roundly trounced again.

However, he managed to retain his hold on Norway and rebuilt Oslo, its capital, after it had been destroyed by fire in 1624. He named the rebuilt city after himself so that it became Christiania. Eventually, though, it became Oslo again, so he didn't win out there, either.

SWEDEN

Gustavus II Adolphus became King of Sweden in 1611. In his reign, Sweden grew prosperous, owing to his labors and to those of his chancellor, Axel Gustaffson Oxenstierna (1583–1644), whose wisdom guided Gustavus and who ran the country while Gustavus was off to the war and after Gustavus was dead. Oxenstierna's diplomacy saw to it that Sweden benefitted from its military victories.

Under Gustavus, Sweden reached its peak. Gustavus took the eastern shores of the Baltic Sea in 1617, and blocked Russian access to the sea. He defeated Poland in the 1620s and took over much of Latvia. He intervened in the Thirty Years War and, as a result, Sweden obtained various portions of the German Baltic coast and even a holding on the North Sea west of Denmark. The Baltic Sea was being turned into a Swedish lake.

Sweden even attempted to establish settlements on the North American coast as the Netherlands was doing. In 1637, the "New Sweden Company" was organized; and, in 1638, a group of Swedish settlers left for America, with Peter Minuit (the purchaser of Manhattan Island) at its head. They settled in what is now Delaware, establishing a town at the site of what is now Wilmington. They brought with them the "log cabin," which had been invented in the Scandinavian north and which eventually became the legendary homes of American pioneers.

Gustavus Adolphus was succeeded by his daughter, Christina (1626–1689). She was an eccentric woman, best-known today for having contributed to the death of the great French philosopher, René Descartes (1596–1650), by forcing him to lecture to her at dawn in the drafty and cold palace during the Swedish winter. Poor Descartes died of pneumonia on February 1, 1650.

SPAIN

Philip III died in 1621 and was succeeded by his son, Philip IV (1605–1665). Spain was now fading rapidly. Its economy was faltering, and its agriculture was declining. In trade, it was increasingly outclassed by the English, the French, and the Dutch. It continued to be militarily active, and involved itself in the Thirty Years War out of a feeling of family unity with the Austrian Hapsburgs and out of a continuation of Philip II's anti-Protestant policies. This accomplished nothing but the acceleration of the decline.

Spain's growing weakness and increasing governmental inefficiency brought about a great revolt in Catalonia in eastern Spain in 1640, where the tradition of an independent Aragon a century and a half earlier still lingered. It took nearly two decades to crush the rebellion and, while it was going on, Portugal took advantage of Spain's preoccupation and also rebelled in November 1640. That rebellion Spain was *not* able to crush, and Portugal regained its independence permanently after having been Spanish for 60 years.

Disaster piled on disaster until the overstrained fabric of the Spanish economy and society ruined even the Spanish army, which could no longer keep up with the changes in military technology. On May 19, 1643, Spanish and French forces battled at Rocroi at the French–

Netherlands border. The French won and the military leadership of Europe passed from Spain to France.

Spain's material decline was lightened by the production of one of the world's greatest books. *Don Quixote de la Mancha* was written in 1609, with a second part in 1619, by Miguel de Cervantes (1547–1616), who had been wounded at the Battle of Lepanto and had lost the use of his left hand.

Don Quoxite de la Mancha is considered by many to be the first true novel in the western world and, perhaps, the best. Its humor and wit, to say nothing of its humanity, sparkles even today and even through translation. Its satire killed an entire class of worthless literature devoted to knight-errantry. Cervantes' one book (he wrote other things of little account, to be sure) is sufficient to lift him high above all other Spanish writers—even above Lope de Vega and his 1800 plays.

Diego de Silva Velazquez (1599–1660) was the greatest Spanish painter of the period, well-known for his portraits of Philip IV and others of his court. Bartolome Esteban Murillo (1617–1682) was another successful Spanish painter of the time.

PORTUGAL

Although Philip II promised to rule Portugal, by way of Portuguese officials under Portuguese law, and largely kept his promise, his successors, Philip III and Philip IV, put Portugal under increasingly heavy-handed Spanish control. Portugal grew increasingly discontented and demoralized. Parts of its overseas Empire began to slip away and fall into Dutch hands.

Portuguese revolts against Spain were put down until 1640, when Spanish attention was occupied entirely with the Catalonian revolt. On December 1, 1640, Portugal seized the opportunity to revolt and to choose as its king John of Braganza (1604–1656), a great-great grandson of the Portuguese king, Manuel I, who had ruled a century and a quarter earlier. The new king reigned as John IV.

France and England at once recognized Portuguese independence (since that weakened Spain, with which both had long been at enmity) and their help enabled Portugal to invade Spain and defeat it in battle in 1644. With that, Portuguese independence was assured, although Spain stubbornly refused to recognize it for another quarter-century.

FRANCE

On May 14, 1610, Henry IV was assassinated by a mentally unbalanced defrocked monk, François Ravaillac (1578–1610). Henry was succeeded by his nine-year-old son, who ruled as Louis XIII (1601–1643). The regency was held by his mother, Marie de Medici (1573–1642), a distant relative of Catherine de Medici.

Louis XIII was a weak, depressed individual, in more or less constant ill-health, and was probably homosexual. However, he could lead an army when he had to, and he was bright enough to take control away from his mother and to choose a brilliant man as his principal adviser and to stick by him. The adviser, who had been a protégé of Marie de Medicis at first, was Armand-Jean du Plessis, Duc de Richelieu, who became a Cardinal in 1622.

It was Richelieu's design to destroy those forces inside France that disputed power with the king—the great nobles on the one hand, and the armed Huguenot cities that had existed since the religious wars. Outside France, his aim was to weaken the Hapsburgs who, in Austria and Spain, were standing at every French border. To do that, although he was a Catholic and a Cardinal, he was perfectly willing to make alliances with, and to subsidize, those Protestant powers who would fight the Hapsburgs. Under his direction, France kept the pot boiling in the Thirty Years War and did it so successfully that the Hapsburg cause was ruined and France emerged as the leading power in Europe—though at a frightful cost to the German people.

Inside France, Richelieu's steady attempts to bring the nobility under control roused wild opposition to him on their part, and conspiracy after conspiracy was leveled at him. This reached its climax in 1630.

Richelieu had made war against La Rochelle, a city on France's west coast, which was Huguenot, and almost independent. It was not Richelieu's intention to destroy the Huguenots, merely to deprive them of any war-making ability. Despite English help and a stout resistance on the part of the Huguenots, La Rochelle was taken by French forces in 1628, and the Huguenots were reduced to a tolerated sect, rather than to a state within a state.

Despite the fact that Richelieu was fighting and defeating the Huguenots, the nobility was able to win the influence of the Church over to their side against Richelieu because the Cardinal was fighting Catholic Spain with even more fervor than he was fighting Protestant La Rochelle, and because he was subsidizing Gustavus Adolphus against Catholic Austria.

For a while, it seemed that they had persuaded Louis XIII (who also suffered a crisis of conscience over the subsidizing of Gustavus Adolphus) to discharge Richelieu. The conspirators, with Marie de Medici at their head, were absolutely certain of Richelieu's downfall and were already gleefully counting their gains when Louis XIII came to the reluctant realization that Richelieu was making him strong and that the nobility would make him weak. On November 11, 1630, he decided to stick by his minister and the conspirators suddenly and unexpectedly found they had lost. That incidence was referred to as "the day of the dupes."

Richelieu, by the way, was a patron of literature and had aspirations to be a literary figure himself. He founded the French Academy in 1634, and it has governed the French language and French literature ever since.

Richelieu did not live to witness the end of the Thirty Years War. He died on December 4, 1642. Louis XIII, as though not daring to live long after the death of the adviser he absolutely depended on, died on May 14, 1643.

The French army had meanwhile been reorganized and revitalized. Just before he died, Richelieu appointed Louis d'Enghien (1621–1686) to command the French army on the border of the Spanish Netherlands. He was only 21 years old, but he was a good choice.

The Spaniards took advantage of Richelieu's death, and of the fact that Louis XIII was on the point of death, to anticipate that France would enter a period of near-anarchy, and felt that this was an appropriate time to invade. They crossed the border and aimed at Paris.

They paused to lay siege to the city of Rocroi, just on the French side of the border, and d'Enghien moved in quickly. His cavalry defeated the Spanish cavalry, and that left 18,000 Spanish infantry which, for a century and a half, had seemed invincible. Direct French attacks failed, so d'Enghien stood off and made use of his artillery, plus captured Spanish guns. When the Spanish infantry had been sufficiently punished, a French advance swept them from the field and virtually annihilated them. That marked the passing of Spanish military superiority and ushered in a period when it was the French army that dominated Europe.

Louis XIII, despite his distaste for women, including his wife, Anne of Austria (1601–1666), who was the sister of Philip IV of Spain, had managed to father two sons. The older of these succeeded to the throne at the age of five as Louis XIV (1638–1715). Anne of Austria was regent, and she employed as her chief minister Jules Mazarin (1602–1661), who had worked for Richelieu. Richelieu had recommended him as his successor, and Mazarin had Anne's complete trust.

Mazarin continued Richelieu's policies both inside and outside France, and helped bring the Thirty Years War to a successful conclusion (for France) in 1648.

But now the nobility, free of the overpowering genius of Richelieu, rose in rebellion. With them, there rose some of the middle class as well, who wanted some kind of government other than that of the monarch's irresponsible will. The insurrection was known as the *Fronde* (from a word of a child's slingshot, a word that originally arose out of contempt).

Mazarin worked under the disadvantage of being an Italian, so that French national fervor could easily be built up against him. However, he fought back skillfully and, by 1650, the Fronde was almost under control.

This period saw the beginning of France's golden age of literature. Great plays were written by Pierre Corneille (1606–1684), the creator of French classical tragedies. Indeed, the French adhered so closely to the Greek and Roman models that they have always thought very little of Shakespeare, whose works transcended the rigid rules set up by the Greeks.

In science, France was also preeminent now. The French scholar, Marin Mersenne (1588–1648) served as a one-man connecting link among the scientists of Europe. He wrote voluminous letters to places as far as Constantinople, reporting on scientific work he had heard about, asking for information and making suggestions. It was an invaluable service.

Pierre Gassendi (1592–1655), another French scholar, strongly supported the atomistic philosophy of Democritus and Lucretius, and kept it alive for his contemporaries. He described and named the aurora borealis and, in 1631, he watched the planet Mercury cross the face of the Sun. It was the first planetary transit to be viewed.

René Descartes (1596–1650) published his philosophy in 1637, which began by establishing his own existence: "I think, therefore I am," and continued from there. In mathematics, he invented analytic geometry in an appendix to that book, a system of interconverting algebraic equations and geometric figures. He died in Sweden, thanks to Queen Christina's callousness.

Pierre de Fermat (1601–1665) was a lawyer who worked on mathematics only in his spare time. He is sometimes called "the world's greatest amateur." He was one of the pioneers in the study of the theory of numbers.

Blaise Pascal (1623–1662), working with Fermat, founded the theory of probability, the work beginning with a consideration of a gambler's uncertainty as to how to bet. Pascal also invented the first mechanical calculator in 1649—a very simple one, to be sure.

Pascal was a Jansenist, a follower of the principles advanced by a Netherlands theologian, Cornelius Otto Jansen (1585–1638). Jansen was a Roman Catholic, but he inveighed against the Jesuits and the Counter-Reformation, and in some respects his thoughts were tinged with Protestantism. The feud between the Jansenists and Jesuits divided France especially, and almost as badly (though without actual warfare) as the Huguenot–Catholic feud had done. Pascal spent the last years of his life writing essays supporting Jansenist views, and his book *Pensees* ("Thoughts") was brilliant enough to impress succeeding generations as much as his mathematics had.

FRENCH NORTH AMERICA

During the last years of the reign of Henry IV, the French established a permanent settlement in North America at the site of Cartier's exploratory voyages three quarters of a century earlier.

The man responsible was Samuel de Champlain (1567–1635). On his second voyage to North America in 1604, he helped found the city of Port Royal in Acadia (the peninsula now known as Nova Scotia). On his third voyage, he founded the city of Quebec on the St. Lawrence River on July 3, 1608, and that served as a nucleus for "New France" in what is now southeastern Canada.

In 1609, he discovered the body of water now called "Lake Champlain" in the northern reaches of New York State. On this occasion, the party of Algonquins that accompanied Champlain encountered a group of Iroquois. Since the founding of the Iroquois Confederacy 40 years before, the Iroquois had established their domination over neighboring tribes and were accustomed to winning. When they fought the Algonquins, they were winning also, but then Champlain and his men joined the fight on the Algonquin side. The Iroquois found themselves facing muskets for the first time and had to flee. As a result, the Iroquois were usually anti-French from then on, something that had its importance in time.

In 1611, Champlain founded a new settlement further upstream on the St. Lawrence River, one that became the nucleus of Montreal. By 1615, he reached the northern extension of Lake Huron and became the first European ever to see any of the Great Lakes.

In 1634, Jean Nicolet (1598–1642), who had been with Champlain on the latter's journey, crossed Lake Huron and Lake Michigan and was the first European to reach what is now the American Midwest.

Richelieu, when he came to power, encouraged these explorations and settlements in New France. The river that drains Lake Champlain into the St. Lawrence River is called the Richelieu River in his honor.

The French, at this time, also made settlements in some of the small West Indian islands, notably Guadelupe and Martinique. The fact that they could do so without Spain being able to stop them is evidence of the extent of Spain's decline by this time.

By 1650, New France was a going concern, but one source of weakness was its refusal to receive French Huguenots. This meant that Huguenots, looking for religious freedom, went to other parts of the North American continent, taking with them what skills they possessed, together with a strong animosity toward New France.

PAPACY

The Papacy was learning that it was living in a harsher world, and one in which its secular power, at least, had sadly diminished. Paul V (1552–1621), who had become Pope in 1605, placed Venice under an interdict in 1606. That meant that the sacraments and other clerical services would be withheld in its territory. Venice was not much amenable to Papal pressure at any time, but now it was so indifferent to the action (and life within it went on in so undisturbed a fashion) that Paul V had no choice but to remove the interdict. It had been a favorite weapon of the medieval Papacy, but, after 1606, it was never used again.

The Thirty Years War broke out while Paul V was Pope, but he was not enthusiastic about war as a means of healing the Protestant breakaway, and he was very cautious in his support of Austria.

His successor, Gregory XV (1554–1623) arranged for secret elections to the Papacy, reducing the possibilities of open interference. He strongly supported missionary activity, and that did more to win back some of the losses Catholics suffered in the Reformation than war did.

His successor, Urban VIII (1568–1644), followed Richelieu's policies. He wanted Catholicism to win out over Protestantism, of course, but he didn't want the Hapsburgs to become too powerful. The Hapsburgs were in control of Italian territory both north and south of Papal States and they might too easily reduce the Pope to a puppet. With memories of such Emperors as Henry IV and Frederick II, Urban VIII maintained a neutrality in the Thirty Years War that brought him much criticism from the more extreme Catholics.

Urban VIII is best remembered, however, for his hostility to Galileo Galilei (1564–1642). Galileo was one of the greatest scientists in history, and he helped make Italy glitter even in the debased and oppressed political climate under which it now suffered.

As a 17-year-old, Galileo had discovered the principle of the pendulum—that its period of swing was roughly constant whatever the width of the swing. In the 1590s, he had studied bodies rolling down an inclined plane and had found that the rate of movement was independent of the weight of the body and that the speed of movement increased at a constant rate. This killed Aristotelian physics, which had held sway in European thought for 19 centuries.

His fame reached its height, however, when he became the first to turn the newly discovered telescope on the heavens. He discovered myriads of stars too dim to see without a telescope; mountains and craters on the Moon; the satellites of Jupiter; the phases of Venus; and the spots of the Sun. He strongly supported the Copernican notion of the Earth going around the Sun and wrote a book in 1632 (in Italian, for even nonscholars to read) in which he presented the Copernican system very persuasively and made the supporters of the older Earth-centered system look foolish.

Urban VIII, who had been a friend of Galileo, was persuaded that the book poked fun at him, so Galileo was brought before the Inquisition. On June 22, 1633, under threat of torture (but not the actual use of it), he was forced to renounce any views that were at variance with the older form

of astronomy—but, of course, the Earth moved about the Sun anyway and even the Pope could not change that fact. Although the Papacy had won a short-term victory over Galileo, it was Pyrrhic, for Copernicanism advanced to universal acceptance despite the Church's thunders.

It is the strength of Catholicism, however, that the Church learns from its mistakes. The trial of Galileo soon proved a very bad mistake and the Church, while refusing to admit it had been wrong, was very cautious, thereafter, about opposing scientific findings.

In 1644, Urban was succeeded as Pope by Innocent X (1574–1655), who dismissed Urban's careful neutrality, and substituted a pro-Spanish bias. The result was that he denounced, in unmeasured tones, the Treaty of Westphalia, which ended the Thirty Years War in a compromised peace. No one on either side, however, paid attention, and this demonstrated, in dramatic fashion, the decline of Papal power.

In addition to Galileo, Italian scientists of the period included Evangelista Torricelli (1608–1647), who was the first to measure air pressure in 1643 and, in so doing, invented the barometer. The Venetian physician, Sanctorius (1561–1636), was the first to attempt to measure the temperature of the human body (using a primitive air-thermometer) as a diagnostic device.

An important Italian painter of the period was Guido Reni (1575–1642).

ENGLAND

Elizabeth I died on March 23, 1603, after naming James VI of Scotland as her heir. She may not have liked doing so, but he was descended from Henry VII both by way of his father and of his mother. Any other choice would have started dynastic squabbling, which no one wanted.

James raced to London to take on the new position before anyone changed his mind, and he became king of England as James I. Thus it was that though England had tried to control the throne of Scotland since the time of Edward I, three centuries earlier, when it came time for a single monarch to rule over both nations, it was a Scottish king and not an English one who did so. It was not a true union of nations, however. The two remained separate in law and custom and were united only dynastically.

The new reign was not popular with the English, who had a long tradition of despising the Scots, and James I did not have the knack of making himself personally popular as Henry VIII and Elizabeth I had done. There were plots to dethrone him, but none succeeded.

The most notorious was the "Gunpowder plot," in which a group of Catholics planned to blow up Parliament and the King on November 5, 1605. An anonymous letter revealed the plot, and a search party on November 4 discovered barrels of gunpowder, with one of the conspirators, Guy Fawkes (1570–1606) on guard. Ever since, every November 5 has been celebrated by the English as "Guy Fawkes Day."

James I had one characteristic that served the good of England, though many people were dissatisfied with it. He was a man of peace and resolutely refused to go to war. He did his best to establish peace with Spain, for instance. There was even an attempt to arrange a marriage between James I's son, Charles (1600–1649) to a Spanish princess, but this was carried through with such ineptness that it failed. Thereupon Charles was betrothed to Henrietta Maria (1609–1669), a sister of Louis XIII of France. She was, of course, a Catholic.

James I even resisted the temptation to intervene in the Thirty Years War, though there might have seemed reason to do so. The "Winter King," Frederick V of the Palastinate, who was driven into humiliating exile in 1619, was married to Elizabeth (1596–1662), the daughter of James I. James refused to lift a finger to help his daughter, as once he had done nothing to help his mother.

One great accomplishment of his reign, by the way, was the translation of the Bible into the English version used for centuries afterward. The 54 scholars who worked at it made use of earlier English versions, particularly that of Tyndale, and created a literary masterpiece. The "Authorized Version," as it was called (or, more popularly, "The King James Bible") was completed in 1611. It is, to this day, *the* Bible to English-speak-

ing people, though new and technically better translations have been produced. The King James Bible and the works of William Shakespeare stand at the peak of English literature and, perhaps, always will.

The English Parliament, which had been cowed under the Tudors, became restive under James I. They objected to James I's pro-Spanish bias and to his attempts at being absolute, especially since he did it with a Scottish accent. James, on the other hand, wanted no dissent. He wanted everyone to be Church of England, for instance, and said openly that he would harry all dissenters out of the land. When Parliament drew up a petition insisting on their right to debate matters of importance, and maintaining that the king must take the opinions of Parliament under advisement, James tore that page out of the Parliamentary journal.

James I died on March 27, 1625, and his son became Charles I of England (and Charles I of Scotland as well). The new king married Henrietta Maria six weeks after his father's death.

Parliament, however, had grown more intractable. It had resented James's treatment and it had leaders such as John Eliot (1592–1632), who were spoiling for a showdown. Parliament called for the impeachment of Charles's chief minister, George Villiers, Duke of Buckingham (1592–1628). He had been one of James's favorites and was a complete incompetent who failed at everything he tried. (It was he who had bungled the plans for a Spanish marriage, for instance.) In reply, Charles imprisoned Eliot and other leaders, but Parliament refused to transact any business while they remained imprisoned. Since only Parliament could vote the taxes that would raise the money Charles needed, he was forced to release the Parliamentary leaders.

Making war did not improve matters. Buckingham led an expedition for the relief of La Rochelle in 1627, when Richelieu was attacking that Protestant city. Being Buckingham, he failed miserably; and, while he tried to set a second expedition into motion, he was, in 1628, assassinated.

Meanwhile, Parliament was drawing up new petitions demanding various rights. On March 5, 1629, Eliot was again arrested, along with eight other members. Eliot died in prison and the other eight gave in. Parliament was dissolved and Charles I determined to rule without Parliament. He raised money by various devices that harked back to old feudal customs. This greatly angered the nation, but was not actually illegal.

One chief adviser to Charles I at this time was William Laud (1573–1645), the bitterly anti-Puritan bishop of London. Charles made him Archbishop of Canterbury in 1633. Another adviser was Thomas Wentworth, Earl of Strafford (1593–1641). Strafford, from 1633 to 1639, was lord deputy of Ireland, and he set about trying to increase English influence in that island, where Richard II and the Earl of Essex had failed. He was making progress of a sort, but, naturally, he embittered the Irish.

All might have been well, if there was no *unusual* need for money, but for some reason, a foolish attempt was made to push the Church of England upon Scotland, which preferred its own brand of Calvinism.

The Scots rebelled and their forces moved into northern England.

Charles now simply had to have money in substantial amounts, so he reconvened Parliament on April 13, 1640 for the first time in 11 years. It refused to vote money until Parliamentary grievances were settled, and he dissolved it on May 5. Therefore, that Parliament was called the "Short Parliament."

Charles still needed money, however, so he was forced to convene another Parliament on November 3, 1640, and this one came to be called the "Long Parliament." Parliament seemed unperturbed at the Scottish advance, and they made demands that Strafford be impeached. Charles had no choice but to give in, and first Strafford and then Laud were sent into imprisonment in the Tower. Strafford was executed on May 12, 1641.

Kings had been hounded before this, and their favorites executed (as had been true of Edward II, for instance), but usually it was the nobility, who were on the attack. Now, in England, there was something new. The middle classes were rising and making themselves felt. Parliament demanded that it be convened every three years,

whether the King took action in this matter or not; and that it not be dissolved without its own consent.

Then, in October 1641, the Irish, too, broke into rebellion. More than ever, now, Charles needed money with which to raise, pay, and equip an army to handle the Scots and the Irish, and more than ever Parliament was unwilling to give him one—lest he raise an army and use it on Parliament itself. On December 1, 1641, Parliament passed a "Grand Remonstrance," listing all their grievances through the length of Charles's reign.

Charles I, driven beyond endurance, tried to arrest the Parliamentary leaders and even marched into Parliament with some soldiers on January 4, 1642, to carry through the arrest personally. The leaders had gone into hiding, however, and Charles I merely made himself look ridiculous by this useless action. Matters grew steadily worse and, on August 22, 1641, an outright civil war began. The Parliamentarians were popularly called "Roundheads" because they wore their hair short. Those fighting for the king were "Cavaliers."

For two years, the fighting was indecisive, with neither side disposing of well-trained soldiers. One Parliamentarian, Oliver Cromwell (1599–1658), turned out to be a first-rate general, however. He trained an excellent army (popularly called "The Ironsides") and, on July 2, 1644, a battle was fought at Marston Moor, near York, where the Ironsides showed their mettle and won. This put northern England into Parliamentary hands.

The King kept fighting, however, and royalist leaders even held Scotland for a time. Meanwhile, Archbishop Laud was executed in March, 1644, and England moved steadily toward Puritan control.

Cromwell continued to train soldiers and to set up a standing army of men who would make a profession of fighting.

On June 14, 1645, a second major battle was fought at Naseby, in central England, one in which Cromwell's forces disastrously defeated the Royalists and smashed any Royalist hope for victories. Royalist strongholds surrendered, and

Charles I himself fell into the hands of a Scottish force on May 5, 1646, and was eventually turned over to the Parliamentarians in return for a sum of money.

After that, the Parliamentarians broke up into a set of quarreling groups. Cromwell, however, had the only good army and he beat all comers. Eventually, it seemed to Cromwell that as long as Charles I was alive (though imprisoned), he would serve as the center of conspiracies designed to restore him to full power.

Therefore, Charles was tried in late January, 1649, before a Parliament from which Cromwell's army had excluded all waverers, and which kept a watchful eye on those who remained. Charles I was condemned and, on January 30, 1649, was executed. Europe was horrified. (That was the usual way of things. If a ruler killed 100,000 of his subjects, it was considered just an item in history; but if 100,000 subjects killed one king, there was a tidal wave of revulsion and shock.)

Cromwell then turned to England's outposts. In September 1649, he went to Ireland. For five centuries, ever since the time of Henry II, English control of Ireland had been loose and limited. Cromwell, however, in the space of nine months passed through the island like a whirlwind, capturing every fortress that resisted, and massacring every garrison. When he returned to England in May 1650, all of Ireland, for the first time, was prostrate, and had finally been conquered by England.

New sects continued to arise. George Fox (1624–1691) founded "The Society of Friends" in 1647. This was a religious group that eschewed all ritual and any priesthood, but held that any individual could be inspired by God. They took no oaths, were pacifists, and egalitarians. Because Fox bade those who listened to him to "quake at the word of the Lord," they were called "Quakers" in derision. As so often happens, however, the word was adopted by those it was intended to ridicule and was used with pride.

Another aspect of religion involved an Irish–Anglican bishop, James Ussher (1588–1656), who utilized Biblical data to argue, in 1650, that the Earth and the Universe were created by God in 4004 B.C. This was taken seriously by Christians for centuries, and is believed by unsophisticated people even today.

Through this period, the English golden age of literature continued. Shakespeare produced his great tragedies: *Hamlet, Othello, Macbeth, King Lear, Antony and Cleopatra* between 1600 and 1607

Ben Jonson (1572–1637) produced *Volpone* in 1605 and *The Alchemist* in 1610. John Webster (1580–1625) produced *The Duchess of Malfi* in 1613. Francis Beaumont (1584–1616) and John Fletcher (1579–1625) wrote a number of plays in collaboration.

As the Puritans grew stronger, however, the stage dimmed. The theater was considered by the Puritans to be a haunt of immorality and vice, and the playhouses were shut down. Eventually, they would be reopened, but the great days of poetic tragedy were over.

Among the poets of the time were Michael Drayton (1563–1641) who wrote about Agincourt in 1606, his verses beginning, "Fair stood the wind for France." John Donne (1572–1631) wrote, "Never send to know for whom the bell tolls, it tolls for thee" in 1623. John Suckling (1609–1642) fought under Gustavus Adolphus and under Charles I and wrote the ballad that begins, "Why so pale and wan, fond lover?" in 1638. Richard Lovelace (1618–1657) fought under Charles I and, while in prison in 1642, wrote, "Stone walls do not a prison make, Nor iron bars a cage." Robert Herrick (1591–1674) wrote, "Gather ye rosebuds while you may, Old time is still a-flying."

Then, of course, there was John Milton (1608–1674), a poet second only to Shakespeare, who, in addition to noble verse in this period, wrote *Areopagitica* in 1644, a prose defense of liberty of the press, so eloquent as to be an immortal document of democracy.

George Chapman (1559–1634) wrote poems and plays but is best-known for having translated Homer's *Iliad* and *Odyssey* into English rhyme, completing both by 1616. These were the standard translations for over two centuries.

Among the essayists were Robert Burton (1577–1640), who wrote *The Anatomy of Melancholy* in 1621. He used his discussion of melancholy as a way of dealing with every subject under the sun in a sprightly manner.

More important still was Francis Bacon, who, in 1620, wrote *Novum Organon,* in which he pleaded passionately for experimentation and induction. His philosophy eventually led to the foundation of the Royal Academy, which for years would be the most prestigious fellowship of scientists to be found anywhere. Yet Bacon could not accept Copernicus, but clung to Greek astronomy.

Inigo Jones (1573–1652) graduated from designing stage settings to becoming an architect who designed palaces and chapels for the royal family. He founded English classical architecture.

The most famous English scientist of the period was William Harvey (1578–1657), who was court physician for both James I and Charles I. It was he who worked out the mechanism of the circulation of the blood, founding the modern science of physiology as he did so. He presented his work to the world in a small book published in 1628.

And yet perhaps more important than anything else in this period was an advance that had nothing to do with politics or literature.

Marco Polo had written that, in China, black stones were burned and, indeed, even in Europe, there were pockets of exposed "coal" (the fossilized residue of forests that had flourished hundreds of millions of years ago).

By 1600, as it happened, much of England's forest cover had been cut down and what was left had to be preserved for use by the navy, which consisted of wooden ships, with tall wooden masts.

England had, perforce, to turn to coal as a wood-substitute for heating houses. By 1650, two million tons of coal were being mined and used each year, and this was 80% of the coal production in the world, generally. It was coal that eventually fueled the Industrial Revolution, and it was England's coal-production that insured that the Industrial Revolution would begin in that country rather than elsewhere.

ENGLISH NORTH AMERICA

England continued to explore the North American coastline. In 1602, Bartholomew Gosnold (d. 1607) sailed along the shores of what we now call New England. William Baffin (1584–1622) explored the western coast of Greenland, so that his name is given to Baffin Island and Baffin Bay. He reached a latitude of 77.75°, a mark that stood as the record for Arctic venturing for many years.

More important even than exploration was settlement.

In 1606, two groups of Englishmen, one in London and one in Plymouth, obtained official permission to colonize the eastern coast of North America. The London Company sent out its first boatload of colonists on December 19, 1606.

On April 16, 1607, they reached the entrance of Chesapeake Bay. The land to the north of the opening, they called "Cape Charles" and the land to the south "Cape Henry" after the sons of King James. Sailing into the Bay due west, they came upon the wide mouth of a river they called the "James River" after the king himself. Finally, on May 13, 1607, they chose a site 25 miles upstream and settled "Jamestown."

It formed the nucleus of the colony of Virginia and it was the first permanent English settlement in what is now the United States. It didn't look as though it would be permanent at first, and it was only the enterprise and will of one of the settlers, John Smith (1580–1631), and the help of the Native Americans that kept it going. Even so, the settlers were about to return to England when, on June 8, 1610, three ships arrived with 300 new colonists and ample stores of all kinds.

In 1612, John Rolfe (1585–1622) learned Native American methods of growing and curing tobacco; thus, the Virginia colony had a product that it could sell at a profit and that would make it prosperous. In 1619, the Virginia colonists set up a House of Burgesses. This was the first elected representative assembly in an English colony overseas, and it set the fashion for other colonies that would be founded and for the nation that grew out of them.

Less happily, a boatload of blacks was brought to Virginia in 1619, and the institution of black slavery was introduced.

As the population in Virginia grew, the colonists spread out over the Native American lands and, in general, showed a disregard for their rights since, after all, they were "heathens" and "savages." On March 22, 1622, the Native Americans attacked and killed some of the population, including John Rolfe. The colonists recovered and inflicted a far worse slaughter on the Native Americans.

This pattern of White aggression, followed by the Native American striking back, followed by a crushing counterattack and further encroachment, was to take place over and over again for more than two and a half centuries.

Further English colonization of the North American coast was stimulated by religious differences. Catholics labored under various disabilities in Protestant England, but Charles I was not terribly anti-Catholic (he had a Catholic wife). He gave permission, therefore, to George Calvert, Lord Baltimore (1580–1632), who had converted to Catholicism some years before, to send out colonists, including Catholics, to Virginia. Baltimore died before that could be carried through, but on March 27, 1634, 220 colonists (including both Protestants and Catholics) under the leadership of Baltimore's son, Cecilius Calvert (1605–1675), established a settlement north of Virginia. The new colony was named "Maryland" in honor of the Queen.

Inevitably, there was friction between Catholics and Protestants and, in 1649, the colony passed a "Toleration Act," in which all people who accepted the Trinity—the idea that God exists in three persons—would have freedom of worship. This still excluded Unitarians and Jews, but it set an example of toleration that would grow.

It was not only the Catholics, but the Dissenters (more Protestant than the English church) who found life uncomfortable in England. Some fled to the Dutch Republic to find religious peace. When they found their children speaking Dutch, they decided to try to make a home in American where they could be free and yet be English, too.

Ninety-nine Dissenters left Plymouth and crossed the Atlantic on the "Mayflower." They are usually called the "Pilgrims" in American usage. They landed at Cape Cod on November 9, 1620, then settled on the shore west of the cape in a region called "Plymouth," after the port they had left.

Again, the initial settlers barely survived the hard winter and did so only with the help of Native Americans. By the fall of 1621, they were doing well enough to celebrate the harvest with a three-day feast, giving thanks to God. (It is still commemorated in the American holiday of Thanksgiving.)

Other settlers began to found towns in the area, which came to be known as Massachusetts from a Native American name for a place in the region. Salem was founded in 1626.

An English Puritan, John Winthrop (1588–1649), organized a large party of settlers and, in 1630, 17 ships carrying nearly a thousand people sailed to Massachusetts and established Boston, named for the English town from which a group of the settlers had come. The river at whose mouth Boston was founded was named the Charles River after Charles I.

The colonists did not intend to lose the advantages of education and culture because of being in a comparative wilderness. On October 28, 1636, a school was founded just north of the Charles River and two and a half years later it was named "Harvard Collge" after John Harvard (1607–1638), a clergyman who, on his death, bequeathed to the school the sum of 700 pounds and 400 books. Harvard was the first institution of higher learning to be established in the English colonies. In 1639, a printing press was set up in Massachusetts and that, too, was the first of its kind in the colonies.

Meanwhile, two Englishmen, Ferdinando Gorges (1566–1647) and John Mason (1588–1635) settled north of Massachusetts, and, beginning in 1629, towns were springing up on the coasts of what came to be known as Maine and New Hampshire (the latter after the English county of

Hampshire where Mason had spent most of his life). The colony of Massachusetts managed to establish its rule over Maine, but New Hampshire remained independent.

In 1635, settlers from Massachusetts established settlements along the Connecticut River and about these the colony of Connecticut developed.

Of course, although the settlers in Massachusetts had come there to find religious freedom for themselves, they were not ready to accord it to others. There was the case of Roger Williams (1603–1683), for instance, who believed in such radical notions as complete religious freedom and, far worse, that American land belonged to Native Americans.

Therefore, he was driven out of Massachusetts on October 9, 1635, and in June 1636, he founded the town of Providence to the south. This formed the nucleus of the colony of Rhode Island.

The northern English colonies of Connecticut, Rhode Island, Massachusetts, and Connecticut were separated from the southern English colonies of Virginia and Maryland by the Dutch colony of New Netherlands and by the small settlement of New Sweden.

During the English civil war, the northern colonists supported Parliament and the southern colonists supported the King, a kind of foreshadowing of the difference that was to separate the two regions thereafter. The population of the northern colonies was nearly five times that of the southern ones, which was also a foreshadowing of the difference in economic strength that was to come.

POLAND

For a while, Poland (under Sigismund III) seemed to have grown stronger, but it was only because Russia itself was verging on anarchy. Poland took full advantage of this and, in 1610, Polish forces even entered Moscow temporarily.

However, when Gustavus Adolphus fought against Poland, the Poles were forced to retreat in the west, while a Russian recovery forced them to retreat in the east as well.

In 1632, Sigismund III died and was succeeded by his son Wladyslaw IV (1595–1648), who was in turn succeeded by his son, John II Casimir (1609–1673). On the whole, the wars of this period—against the Swedes in the west, the Russians in the northeast, and the Cossacks and Turks in the southeast—had all been inconclusive and had served to continue the slow weakening of Poland.

RUSSIA

Tsar Boris Godunov was plagued not only by the restless boyars, but by the appearance of someone who claimed to be Dmitri, a son of Ivan IV the Terrible. The real Dmitri had, in actual fact, died in 1591, but in those days there were no photographs, and there were few opportunities for ordinary folk to see important people. Imposture was, therefore, simple. One had only to declare one's self to be a royal personage, and anyone dissatisfied with those in actual power would believe the declaration.

Boris Godunov died in the fight against the "False Dmitri" in 1605, and two other imposters appeared shortly afterward. What with these Dmitris, who easily gained followers, and the rival boyar families, and the eagerly interfering Swedes and Poles, the period was called by the later Russians "the Time of Troubles." On October 8, 1610, the Time of Troubles touched bottom as Sigismund III and his Polish troops entered Moscow and occupied the Kremlin. Sigismund even declared his son Wladyslaw (who later succeeded him) to be the Tsar.

At this, however, the Russian people rose in a fury of xenophobia and, in 1612, those Poles who did not manage to get out of Moscow were massacred.

In that same year, a national assembly elected Michael Fyodorovich Romanov (1596–1645) as Tsar. He was the first cousin, twice removed, of Ivan the Terrible. Michael was only 16 years old and was always dominated by others in the family. However, Russia had had enough anarchy and it clung to the Tsar. That made it possible for Michael (or for those who controlled him) to increase the Tsar's authority, to force the boyars more nearly into submission, and to further enslave the peasantry.

In 1645, Michael died and was succeeded by his son (also 16 years old at the time) who reigned as Alexis I (1629–1676).

Through all the Time of Troubles and through the weak reign of Michael I, Russia, while just barely surviving at its heart, had its pioneers racing eastward in Siberia, collecting furs, and exploring the vast stretches of land that opened before them. By 1637, they had actually reached the Pacific Ocean, and Russia became what it has remained ever since—the largest nation, in area, in the world. Of course, the Siberia the Russians had conquered was, at that time, virtually empty —only a quarter of a million people in all the vast expanse. As a result, the Tsar in Moscow ruled over about 12 million people as compared with France's 19 million.

OTTOMAN EMPIRE

The principal enemy of the Ottoman Empire at this time was Persia which, under Abbas I, was dangerous indeed. The Persians took the area south of the Caucasus and much of the Tigris–Euphrates valley from the Turks.

In 1623, the 14-year-old Murad IV (1612–1640) became Ottoman Sultan, and as he grew up it seemed as though the Turks might have a warrior at their head again. He suppressed revolts within the Empire and eventually, by 1638, well after Abbas I had died, the Ottoman Empire took back the districts it had lost to Persia. Murad IV then set about reforming the Ottoman army, but that effort came to an end with his death in 1640.

He was succeeded by his ineffectual brother, Ibrahim I (1615–1648), and in 1648, when Ibrahim was deposed, his six-year-old son reigned as Mehmed IV (1642–1693). In 1645, a war with Venice began over the island of Crete, which was still a Venetian possession.

Despite its decline in the 80 years since the death of Suleiman the Magnificent, however, the Ottoman Empire was still intact. It controlled Asia Minor, all the Balkans up through Hungary,

all the shores of the Black Sea (including the Crimean Tartars, which were its tributaries), both shores of the Red Sea, and all of North Africa to the border of Morocco. On the map, it looked extremely impressive, but it was slowly rotting just the same.

PERSIA

Under Abbas I, Persia reached a peak of strength. It beat the Ottoman Empire and advanced to Baghdad and beyond.

The English were continuing to make their presence felt, however. In 1600, they had established the East India Company to make it possible for them to trade with the Far East independently of the Portuguese. In 1622, the English merchants cooperated with a Persian army to oust the Portuguese who had held Hormuz for over a century. In return, the English gained trading privileges in Persia. This, together with even earlier gains in India, was the beginning of English influence in the East.

Abbas I died in 1629, and was succeeded by his son, Safi I (d. 1642), and with that Persia began a rapid decline. The Ottoman Empire won back what it had lost to Abbas. In 1642, Safi's son, Abbas II (1633–1666), succeeded to the throne.

INDIA

Akbar died in 1605, and his son, Jahangir (1569–1627), ruled in his place. He carried on his father's policies but his effectiveness was ruined by his addiction to alcohol and opium. During his reign, the English East India Company defeated the Portuguese at Surat in 1612, and gained trading privileges in their place. The first fortified post on the Indian coast was established by the English on the southeastern coast in 1640. It grew into the city of Madras.

Jahangir's son, Shah Jehan (1592–1666), succeeded to the throne of the Mogul Empire in 1628. He is best known for having directed the building of the Taj Mahal, beginning in 1632, in honor of his dead wife, Mumtaz Mahal. It was completed in 1648.

CHINA

The Ming dynasty, the last native Chinese line of Emperors, came to an end in 1644 and the Manchus seized control, ruling as the Ch'ing dynasty. The Manchu custom of shaving the head and leaving a central queue of hair was imposed on the Chinese as well, and that remained as the central characteristic of cartoon versions of Orientals among the westerners of future years.

INDONESIA

During this period, the Dutch were rapidly displacing the Portuguese from all their Indonesian holdings, leaving them only the eastern portion of the relatively small island of Timor.

The Dutch maintained their growing monopoly fiercely and, in 1623, they killed some 10 Englishmen on the island of Amboina (along with 10 Japanese and one Portuguese) for allegedly planning to take over the island. This embittered relations between England (which called it the "Amboina Massacre") and the Dutch for a considerable period of time.

JAPAN

The Japanese, having encouraged Western traders and the spread of Christianity for a while, grew fearful of the consequences, and during this period, early in the Tokugawa shogunate, they drove out all foreigners (except for a few Dutch traders confined to the island of Deshima in Nagasaki harbor) and completely erased Christianity. A policy of isolation was established, and even rifles were abandoned as detracting from traditional samurai methods of warfare. (This is the most remarkable example in history of a technological advance being deliberately abandoned, but it happened only because Japan was effectively isolated. Had there been a threat from the outside world, there is no question but that the rifles would have been kept.)

AFRICA

The Dutch and the French were establishing themselves here and there on the African coast, replacing the rapidly declining Portuguese positions. The French established a post on the coast of the island of Madagascar in 1626, for instance.

1650 TO 1700

FRANCE

Mazarin, France's Prime Minister, though lacking Richelieu's charisma, was a skillful leader and managed to survive the dreary fighting, and bring the Fronde to an end in 1653. The war with Spain, however, the one portion of the Thirty Years War that had not been settled by the Treaty of Westphalia, continued.

In 1658, the French army was led by Henri de la Tour d'Auvergne, Vicomte de Turenne (1611–1675). That army included an English contingent for England under Cromwell, which was independently hostile to Spain. The French faced a Spanish army under Louis de Conde. Conde, under his earlier title of d'Enghien, had defeated the Spanish at Rocroi, but had rebelled at the time of the Fronde, as, indeed, had Turenne. However, though Turenne gave in and was reconciled to Mazarin, Conde preferred to join the Spaniards.

It was Turenne who proved the superior general, and, in the "Battle of the Dunes" near Dunkirk, he virtually wiped out the Spanish army, thus confirming the decision of Rocroi. Spain had no choice but to agree to peace, and the Treaty of the Pyrenees was signed on November 7, 1659.

By the terms of the treaty, Louis XIV married Maria Theresa (1638–1683), the daughter of Philip IV of Spain. France also gained some territory at the Pyrenees and along the border of the Spanish Netherlands.

The main result, however, was that Spain was broken as a great power, and Louis XIV was secure on his throne. He was now 21 years old, but Mazarin retained power until his death on March 9, 1661. Then Louis XIV took over. The work of Richelieu and Mazarin had made him an absolute monarch. There was no law controlling him and he loved it, although he was personally affable and by no means a tyrant.

Louis XIV remembered the years of the Fronde with distaste and indignation. He wanted to leave the Paris he had been forced to flee at one point, and he wanted to tame the aristocracy and make them harmless.

His father, Louis XIII, had had a hunting lodge in Versailles, about 20 miles west of Paris. There, Louis XIV built a vast palace, so expensive that its building virtually bankrupted the nation. He moved into it in 1682, and, with him, he brought his court, which included a thousand noblemen, their families, and attendants. At the Palace of Versailles was all the glitter, all the society, all the pleasures and wealth that anyone could want (except for plumbing, which didn't exist). Nothing could so frighten any of the court more than to be banished from Versailles and to be forced to rusticate on their estates.

What's more, Louis XIV invented an elaborate system of etiquette revolving about himself at every moment of the day. Trivial tasks and honors were apportioned to the aristocracy, which then competed not for active power in governing, but over who had the right to sit, or to stand, or to go through a door with one side open, or both sides, or who preceded whom, or who handled this object or that object. The entire court was reduced to concern over pecking order.

In this way, Louis XIV carefully reduced the aristocracy to cardboard figures, and ran the government with middle-class people who had no status of their own, but depended entirely upon the King. As a result, Louis XIV, through a long reign, remained the ideal of absolute royal power, and was admired and imitated by every king in Europe—except those of England, who had a legislature to dispute with.

There was a down-side to this, of course. While the King of France lived in Versailles in a fairyland palace, he became totally divorced from the French people and moved about in a vacuum which, in the end, was fatal. Moreover, although the aristocracy was no longer turbulent and rebellious, it had also become thoroughly useless and wasteful—and, when the emergency came, that proved to be a change for the worse.

Louis XIV's chief minister was Jean-Baptiste Colbert (1619–1683), who labored to reform the system of taxation and make it more just and equitable (and, therefore, yielding more revenue). He tried to model France on the example of the Netherlands, trying to increase its wealth by encouraging trade, agriculture, and industry. He also tried to build up the navy and encourage overseas trade and overseas bases and settlements.

Everything he did was designed to strengthen France and to make it more prosperous. In everything he succeeded, or would have succeeded but for one thing. He needed peace, but Louis XIV, filled with notions of "glory," wanted to be a conqueror and was constantly engaged in warfare. This consumed money much more quickly than Colbert could supply it, even when Louis was winning.

One war that Louis XIV fought within France he won in appearance but lost in reality. The Huguenots still lived in France even though their last armed city had been taken 60 years earlier by Richelieu. Now, Louis XIV felt he could only be strong if there were no organized dissent in the nation, even unarmed and powerless dissent.

On October 18, 1685, therefore, he revoked the Edict of Nantes, which had been established by his grandfather, nearly 90 years earlier. The French Huguenots were suddenly treated with extreme harshness in an effort to force them to turn Catholic. The result was that 50,000 Huguenot families fled France and went to England, the Netherlands, Germany and North America. They represented an industrious middle class whose disappearance weakened France. Furthermore, wherever the Huguenots went, they carried with them their abilities, which, coupled with the anti-French animus, greatly increased the strength of France's enemies.

Louis XIV's foreign wars started when Philip IV of Spain died in 1665. Louis XIV, on dim dynastic grounds, claimed the Spanish Netherlands and, in 1667, invaded it and also Franche-Comté, a portion of the old Burgundian lands in the east that still belonged to Spain. The war showed how powerful the French army had become for it succeeded everywhere. Nevertheless, England, the Netherlands, and Sweden united as a Triple Alliance to oppose Louis, who thereupon made peace, on May 2, 1668, with the Treaty of Aix-la-Chapelle in western Germany. He returned most of the conquests, keeping only about a dozen fortified posts at the Spanish Netherlands border.

Louis XIV did not enjoy having the fruits of war snatched from him. Of those who had opposed him, the Netherlands was the most easily reached. What is more they had served as a refuge for those who wanted to abuse Louis in safety and publish political pamphlets satirizing him. Even the fact that the Netherlands was a republic offended him. Therefore, in March 1672, he declared war on the Netherlands.

He had an easy time of it at first. Much of the southern portion of the Netherlands was taken, and Amsterdam itself was only saved when the Dutch opened the dikes and flooded the land. Once again, however, a coalition against Louis XIV was formed, and he was forced to fight in Germany. He still kept winning, though Turenne, his best general, died in action on July 27, 1675.

Finally, a series of treaties at Nimwegen in the southern Netherlands put an end to the fighting. The Netherlands kept all its territory, but had to promise neutrality. Spain was the big loser. This time France took Franche-Comté, which had been first Burgundian and then Spanish for nearly three centuries, plus additional fortified posts on the Spanish Netherlands border. Later,

Louis took more territory than the treaties gave him and there was no one to stop him.

Louis XIV might profitably have stopped at this point. He had defeated, without too much difficulty, the Hapsburgs of Austria and Spain, thus doing what the French monarchs from Francis I on had been unable to do. At sea, thanks to Colbert, he had become as strong as England or the Netherlands, and his overseas dominions were expanding.

The beginning of decline came when he moved to Versailles in 1682, and revoked the Edict of Nantes in 1684, but neither action looked bad at the time.

In 1685, however, Charles, the Elector of the Palatinate, died, and again Louis XIV made use of dynastic arguments to claim the land. However, the revocation of the Edict of Nantes had offended all the Protestant powers of Europe, who formed a league against him, and who were joined by the Catholic Hapsburgs, because of their own hatred of Louis. Louis XIV's enemies were growing more numerous and stronger.

Again, however, Louis's armies won most of the battles in a war that started on September 25, 1688. The French began by invading the Palatinate and devastating it systematically, as though it were the Thirty Years War all over again. Nevertheless, by September 1697, Louis was willing to sign the Peace of Ryswick in southwestern Netherlands. By this treaty, the situation was largely restored to what it had been before the war began.

The chief long-term consequence of the war rested with Louis XIV's lack of understanding of the importance of naval strength. Colbert had died in 1683 and Louis had not taken care of the navy thereafter. On May 29, 1692, the French fleet attacked the combined forces of England and the Netherlands at La Hogue, near Cherbourg, and was roundly trounced. This put an end to the attempt of France to become a dominant naval power, and also put an end to Louis XIV's vague plan of landing an army in England. (Louis XIV thus failed in the same task Philip II of Spain had failed in a century earlier.)

Louis XIV had made a surprisingly generous

treaty because he was waiting for a larger prize. Charles II of Spain was dying and would leave no heir, and Louis XIV intended, yet again, to attempt, on dynastic grounds, to expand his dominions. This time he would take over all of Spain and its vast possessions around the world. That would surely make him the most powerful monarch on Earth.

On November 1, 1700, Charles II died, and all of Europe held its breath.

The reign of Louis XIV saw French literature at its peak. Corneille was still writing tragedies, and had been joined by Jean Racine (1639–1699), who wrote tragedies on classical themes, such as *Andromaque* in 1667 and *Phèdre* in 1677. Jean-Baptiste Poquelin (1622–1673), far better known as Molière, wrote comedies that were the best the world had seen since Aristophanes, 2000 years earlier. His masterpiece, *Tartuffe*, was produced in 1667. By some, he is considered the greatest of all French writers.

Jean de La Fontaine (1621–1695) is best known for his rendition of classic fables into French verse between 1668 and 1694. François de La Rouchefoucauld (1613–1680) had fought on the side of the Fronde and is best known for his cynical aphorisms, published in 1665, that held human nature up to the light in a most unflattering manner.

Charles Perrault (1628–1703) translated children's stories *(Tales of Mother Goose)*, such as "Red Riding Hood," "Sleeping Beauty," and "Puss in Boots."

Jean Baptiste Lully (1632–1687) was an Italian-born musician who founded French opera. Lully worked with Molière and was strongly patronized by Louis XIV. He died after accidentally stabbing himself in the foot with a long rod he used for his conducting.

In science, there was the astronomer, Jean Picard (1620–1680), who was the first, in 1671, to measure the Earth's size more accurately than Eratosthenes had done 2000 years earlier—a measurement that was useful in the development of the theory of universal gravitation. The Italian-born astronomer, Giovanni Domenico Cassini (1625–1712), in the course of the 1670s, discov-

ered four satellites of Saturn, a gap in Saturn's ring, and a reasonably correct understanding of the scale of the Solar system, including a clear notion of the distance from the Earth to the planet Mars and to the Sun. With Jean Richer (1630–1696), Cassini showed that the Earth was not a perfect sphere but was an oblate spheroid with an equatorial bulge.

The French physicist, Denis Papin (1647–1712) invented the pressure cooker in 1679, and was the first to toy with the possibility of making steam pressure do work. Bernard de Bovier de Fontenelle (1657–1757) was the first important science writer, putting out a popular book on astronomy for the layman in 1686, and living to within five weeks of his hundredth birthday.

FRENCH NORTH AMERICA

The French continued to explore the region about the Great Lakes. In 1678, a French missionary, Louis Hennipen (1626–1702), had discovered Niagara Falls in 1678 and was mightily impressed.

Even before that, a fur trapper, Louis Joliet (1645–1700) and a Jesuit missionary, Father Jacques Marquette (1637–1675), explored Green Bay, an arm of Lake Michigan, and then found their way to the upper Mississippi River. They traveled 700 miles downstream and turned back only because they were reluctant to face the trouble that might follow if they found themselves in Spanish territory.

However, their explorations were enough to show that the Great Lakes did not offer a way of getting through the continent to the Pacific by a water route, for the Mississippi River headed southward, not westward.

One who was still hopeful, however, was Robert Cavalier de la Salle (1643–1687). In 1677, he followed in the footsteps of Marquette and Joliet, but didn't turn back. On April 9, 1682, he stood at the mouth of the Mississippi where it entered the Gulf of Mexico and formally claimed for France all the lands watered by the Mississippi River, which included, if he but knew, all the middle third of what is now the United

States. He called the territory Louisiana in honor of Louis XIV.

France now controlled a vast area in North America, stretching from Labrador, through the Great Lakes, to the Gulf of Mexico, and penning the English colonies in a strip of the eastern coast. However, the appearance on the map was misleading. By 1700, the French population in its enormously stretched-out claims was 12,000, while the population of the much more compact strip of English colonies was over 200,000.

ENGLAND

Cromwell had not yet succeeded in establishing stability in England at the beginning of this period. He continued to win battles (indeed, he never lost one) but there remained enemies.

The son of Charles I had been crowned in Scotland as Charles II of Scotland (1630–1685) and as Charles II of England as well, and he had raised an army and had invaded England. Cromwell defeated him at the Battle of Worcester in west-central England on September 3, 1651, and Charles II returned into exile in France.

On December 16, 1653, Cromwell took the final step of seizing dictatorial power and making himself "Lord Protector" of England, Scotland, and Ireland.

By this time, England and the Netherlands, which had long felt a community of interests as Protestant powers, threatened first by Spain and then by France, were the leading maritime powers and competed with each other for trade, particularly in the Far East. The Amboina Massacre had embittered the English and now, in 1652, there began the first of three naval wars with the Netherlands.

It began because the English had passed a "Navigation Act," on October 9, 1651, forbidding importation of goods into England except in English vessels or in vessels of the country producing the goods. This eliminated the Dutch middlemen, and the Netherlands found that insupportable.

The war pitted Robert Blake (1599–1657) against Maarten Harpertszoon Tromp (1598–

1653) of the Netherlands. The English ships won most of the engagements, and this marked the beginning of the decline of the Netherlands, which made peace on April 3, 1654, agreeing to respect the Navigation Act.

In 1657, Cromwell, basing his decision on a verse in the Bible, allowed Jews to return to England. They had been kept out since the time of Edward I three and a half centuries earlier.

Cromwell died on September 3, 1658, and there was no one who could take over. His son, Richard Cromwell (1616–1712), had no talent for it and, after a period of uncertainty, England turned, more or less gratefully, to the son of the executed monarch. Charles II promised religious freedom, no revenge, and no upsetting of property settlements that had been reached during the Civil War and Commonwealth period. He was proclaimed King on May 8, 1660, and entered London on May 20. Thus began the period of "The Restoration."

With relief, England turned from Puritan austerity and began a period of Restoration license. The lofty Shakespearean tragedy was gone and Restoration comedies, filled with sexual innuendo and social satire, filled the stage.

Among the writers of such comedies were George Etherege (1635–1692), who began the genre with *Love in a Tub* in 1664; William Wycherley (1640–1716), who produced *The Country Wife* in 1675; Thomas Shadwell (1642–1692) and his *Epsom Wells* in 1672; Thomas Otway (1652–1685) and his *Venice Preserved* in 1682; and Colly Cibber (1671–1757) and his *Love's Last Shift* in 1696. The best of them was William Congreve (1670–1729), who produced *The Old Bachelor* in 1693, and *The Way of the World* in 1700.

The greatest living English poet was still John Milton, who completed his masterpiece, *Paradise Lost* in 1665, and followed it with *Paradise Regained* and *Samson Agonistes* (both in 1671).

John Dryden (1631–1700) wrote dramas, including *All for Love*, a retelling of Shakespeare's *Antony and Cleopatra*, which proved Shakespeare did not need retelling. He also wrote an anti-Puritan satire, *Absalom and Achitophel* in 1681. His poem that has best survived to this day is "Alexander's Feast," written in 1697. Andrew Marvell (1621–1678) is best remembered for his "To His Coy Mistress," written in 1652.

In prose writing, John Bunyan (1628–1688) wrote one of the all-time best-sellers while in prison for unauthorized preaching. The book was *Pilgrim's Progress,* published in 1678. Another surprise best-selling book was the amiably discursive *The Compleat Angler* by Izaak Walton (1593–1683), published in 1653.

The English philosopher, Thomas Hobbes (1588–1679) published *Leviathan* in 1651, expressing his belief in the necessity of a strong central government, including an absolute monarch. It is not surprising that he stayed in France during the English Civil War.

John Locke (1632–1704), on the other hand, published *An Essay Concerning Human Understanding* in 1690, in which he argued in favor of a constitutional government, with a division of powers, and emphasis on civil liberties and on freedom of thought and belief. His philosophy had a strong influence on the men who founded the United States of America.

Charles II was interested in science and, in 1662, chartered the Royal Society of London, which became a major center of scientific advance in Europe.

Robert Boyle (1627–1691) invented an air pump capable of producing a vacuum and worked out the laws of gases. He also led the way in substituting chemistry for medieval alchemy. Robert Hooke (1635–1703) studied springs, and was an early microscopist, giving the name to the "cells" that make up living tissue.

Of course, there was the greatest scientist who ever lived, Isaac Newton (1642–1727), who worked out the binomial theorem and invented calculus, who designed the first reflecting telescope and studied light spectra, who worked out the laws of motion and of universal gravitation, and who, in 1687, wrote the greatest scientific book ever written, *Philosophiae Naturalis Principia Mathematica (Mathematical Principles of Natural Philosophy).*

On a less happy note, a great plague struck London in April, 1665. (Newton was one of those who fled the city, working out a preliminary form of the law of universal gravitation at his mother's farm.) Then, on September 2, 1666, a fire broke out in London that devastated the city. It offered a chance for rebuilding the city along rational lines, but the claims of property were paramount and it was rebuilt as it had been. However, St. Paul's Cathedral was redesigned by Christopher Wren (1632–1723) and reconstructed in great majesty.

A second naval war with the Netherlands, from 1665 to 1667, was again marked by English victories. However, the effects of the Plague and the Fire led Charles II to retire the fleet prematurely during peace negotiation to save money. This led to a Dutch raid up the Thames River in June 1667, which brought them nearly to London. On July 21, 1667, peace was signed with the British making gains at Dutch expense in North America.

Charles II was grateful to Louis XIV for his support when he had been in exile and was sympathetic to Catholicism. (His younger brother, James, had turned Catholic, and Charles accepted Catholicism on his deathbed.) In May, 1670, Charles made a secret treaty with Louis XIV to support France in its planned invasion of the Netherlands and to work toward the reestablishment of Catholicism in England in return for a subsidy that would make him more independent of Parliament.

English ships did support France in the war against the Netherlands, and this was the third Anglo–Dutch war. However, public opinion rose steadily against helping France, and England was forced to retire from the war.

It was a time of considerable uneasiness on the part of many English toward what they considered a Catholic menace. An English demagogue, Titus Oates (1649–1705), seized the occasion to fabricate details of an elaborate Catholic plot to overthrow the government. There followed a wild witch-hunt, in which suspicion became equivalent to conviction, and about 35 people were wrongfully executed on fabricated evidence. As Oates's tale became wilder, and implicated too many, it finally burned itself out. (Oates was imprisoned for life in 1685 when a Catholic king succeeded, and was pardoned in 1689, when a Protestant king succeeded.)

Charles II died on February 6, 1685, and since he had no legitimate children, he was succeeded by his brother, who reigned as James II (1633–1701), and as James VII of Scotland. It was clear that this would be a different reign, for James II was a harsh and tactless Catholic, intent on re-establishing Catholicism in England.

There was an instant rebellion against him led by James Scott, Duke of Monmouth (1644–1685), who was an illegitimate son of Charles II and a Protestant. It was crushed at the Battle of Sedgemoor in southwestern England on July 6, 1685. James, then, used his Lord Chancellor, George Jeffries (1645–1689), to institute a reign of terror against anyone suspected of Monmouth sympathies, one that was far worse than anything Titus Oates had brought about. Monmouth himself was executed with deliberate cruelty. None of this made James II popular, but apparently he didn't care.

In 1687, James II, declared religious liberty in England, thus freeing Catholics from disabilites. This was, in itself, enlightened, but there were few Englishmen who didn't see it as only the first step toward establishing a religious tyranny in reverse.

Matters grew to a crisis on June 10, 1688, when a son was born to him. James II's Catholicism had been endured because his daughters were Protestant, and it was thought that they would succeed. With a new son, however, who would surely be brought up Catholic, the Crown might become permanently Catholic. With that possibility in everyone's mind, conspiracies against James II multiplied rapidly.

James II's older daughter, Mary (1662–1694), was married to William III (1650–1702), Stadtholder of the Netherlands, and William III's mother had been the sister of James II. As the nephew and son-in-law of James II, it seemed that William III, a confirmed Protestant, was the logical candidate to replace James II, and he was approached for the purpose.

William III was willing. He wasn't particularly interested in the throne of England for itself, but he saw it as a chance for expanding the resistance to Louis XIV, whom he never forgave for the invasion of the Netherlands.

On November 5, 1688, William III landed in England, and James II, finding that he had no support, fled the land on December 11. This second deposition of a Stuart, being carried through, unlike the first, without bloodshed, was called "The Glorious Revolution."

In 1689, Parliament offered the crown to Mary and the regency to William. When William insisted on the kingship, the rule was made joint —the only joint rule in English history. They were William III and Mary II of England, and, in general, one speaks of "William and Mary."

Part of the agreement was an establishment of a "Declaration of Rights" in which it was made clear just what rights Parliament had. England became a "limited monarchy," for the royal power had limitations that were carefully spelled out—and this at a time when monarchy elsewhere in Europe was following the lead of Louis XIV and becoming absolute.

James II hadn't given up altogether. He attempted to regain the throne by way of an invasion of Ireland, where the Catholic population could be counted on to support him. He landed there in March 1689, but, despite fighting well, he was beaten on July 11, 1690 at the Battle of the Boyne, north of Dublin, and his chances were forever lost. Since then, Irish Protestants in the north, who supported William III, of the House of Orange, have been known as "Orangemen."

Meanwhile, William was organizing a coalition against Louis XIV, with whom war broke out in 1689. English participation in the war was not very remarkable, for William was a poor general, though a determined one.

At home, Scotland had been restless and the Highlanders had supported James II. They were given till December 31, 1691, to take an oath of allegiance to William. All did so except the MacDonald clan of Glencoe, who were delayed by bad weather and who took the oath on January 6, 1691. A company of soldiers commanded by a Campbell, who was a hereditary foe of the MacDonalds, were at Glencoe in apparent peace

—but they used the delay as a pretext for killing 40 of the MacDonalds, including the head of the house. This "Massacre of Glencoe" was a deep embarrassment to William III.

The English discovered how to raise money without immediate taxation. The Bank of England was set up on July 27, 1694. It could lend money to the government to meet emergencies, and be paid back with interest when the emergency was over. This meant that England had a steady source of money and was financially stable where other nations, even France, were always flirting with bankruptcy. It gave England enormous power, for she could always subsidize other nations to fight for her.

William III now set about organizing resistance to Louis XIV's plan to absorb Spain on the death of Charles II of that country.

ENGLISH NORTH AMERICA

In the course of the Anglo–Dutch naval wars, it seemed logical to England to take over the Dutch colony of New Netherlands. Under the dynamic leadership of Peter Stuyvesant (1610–1672), New Netherlands was thriving and had absorbed New Sweden in 1655, but it could scarcely resist an English fleet without help from the homeland.

Four ships under James of York (who was later to be James II of England) sailed across the Atlantic and, on August 19, 1664, entered the harbor of New Amsterdam and demanded its surrender. New Amsterdam had no choice but to do so, and it became the city of New York, in honor of the Duke. The northern part of the colony received the name as a whole.

The southern part, east of the Delaware River, was awarded by the Duke of York to two of his friends. One of them was George Carteret (1610–1684), who had held his native island of Jersey for two years against Cromwell. His section of the colony was named New Jersey in consequence. The city of Newark was founded in 1666.

At the end of the second Anglo–Dutch naval war in 1667, the Dutch Republic accepted the surrender. English colonies now extended all along the North American coast from Maine to Virginia.

The line was extended when Charles II granted the coastline south of Virginia to eight of his loyal courtiers. It had been avoided earlier because of Spanish claims, but no one worried about Spain any longer.

In 1670, settlements began on that coast, which came to be known as "Carolina" from the Latin version of Charles II's name. Eventually, the region was divided into two colonies: North Carolina and South Carolina. The chief port of South Carolina was founded in 1670 and was named Charleston, also in honor of the king.

Meanwhile, Quakers, too, were seeking freedom of worship for their ultrademocratic religious sect. They suffered considerable persecution even in the American colonies, though they were harmless enough. Four Quakers were hanged in Boston between 1659 and 1661, merely for the crime of being Quakers.

William Penn (1644–1718) was a notable Quaker, and the son of a British admiral who had been instrumental in helping to restore the crown to Charles II. Some Quakers had established themselves in New Jersey and, in 1681, Charles II gave Penn the right to the territory on the other side of the Delaware River, west of New Jersey.

Penn traveled to North America and bought land from the Native Americans, coming to an agreement with them that was not solemnized with oaths because Quakers did not believe in oaths. (It was later pointed out that this treaty with the Native Americans was the only one *not* solemnized with oaths, and it was also the only one *not* quickly violated by the colonists.)

There, in 1682, Penn founded the city of Philadelphia.

Naturally, colonial history was not merely a tale of foundings of colonies. There were troubles as well.

In 1675, the Native Americans of New England, tired of colonial encroachments and of being subject to Puritan rulings, broke into rebellion. This was called "King Philip's War," after the Christian name of the Indian leader, Metacomet (1639–1676). By now the European settlers were twice as numerous as the Native Americans of the region and the war took the usual course.

There was a surprise attack by the Native Americans, followed by an overwhelming counterattack by the colonials that crushed the rebellion.

In 1676, there was a rebellion of the colonials themselves in Virginia. Under Nathaniel Bacon (1647–1676), the colonials rose against the royal governor, William Berkeley (1606–1677). The aims of the rebels were not entirely idealistic, for they wanted more and better killings of the Native Americans. Bacon achieved some success, but died of natural causes, whereafter the rebellion was put down.

This was the first example of rebellion against constituted authorities in the English colonies. In the course of the rebellion, Jamestown was burned, and it never quite recovered. The capital of Virginia was moved, in 1692, to Williamsburg, named for William III. The College of William and Mary was founded there on February 8, 1693. It was the second institution of higher learning in the colonies.

When James II became king, he had no liking for the Puritan colonies in the north. He established the "Dominion of New England," combining all the colonies from New Hampshire to New Jersey, and placed it under Edmund Andros (1637–1714), who was as overbearing and tactless as his royal master. Once James II was deposed, the colonists kicked out Andros at once and returned to their separate existences.

Until 1689, the French and English colonists in North America had not fought with each other. They were far enough apart to be able to ignore each other without trouble. Both, however, were expanding, and a sense of competition grew, especially since the French were Catholic and the English, for the most part, Protestant.

When England and France went to war in 1689, it was reflected in fighting in North America that was called "King William's War." Massachusetts did the major fighting. A fleet of 14 vessels sailed from Massachusetts in May 1690, under the command of William Phips (1651–1695). On May 11, 1690, it bluffed Port Royal (the capital of the French colony of Acadia) into surrendering. Massachusetts then annexed Acadia but at the end of the war, in 1697, the province was given back to France by the English,

to the great indignation of the Massachusetts colonists.

Probably the best-known event in early colonial history also took place in Massachusetts, in the town of Salem. It was a time when Europe was going through a lunatic period of witch-hunting. Thus, perhaps 40,000 "witches" were executed in England during the 1600s—mostly harmless old women. The disease spread to New England.

In 1692, a group of silly teenagers in Salem, fearing punishment for some prank or other, pretended to be possessed and under the influence of witchcraft. Within half a year, as a result, 13 women and six men were hanged (*not* burned). About 50 people were in prison, awaiting trial. By that time, prisoners were accusing everyone and respectable pillars of the community were in danger. This, combined with the fact that the influential preacher and president of Harvard College, Increase Mather (1639–1723), had come out strongly against witch-hunting, put a stop to the madness.

By this time, incidentally, the English had also occupied some of the lesser islands off the North American continent. Some of them became important producers of sugar, to which Europeans now were becoming addicted, and important users of black slaves.

NETHERLANDS

After the death of William II in 1650, the Dutch allowed the hereditary stadtholdership to expire and become the "Dutch Republic." They chose John De Witt (1625–1672) as "Grand Pensionary." He, with the help of his brother Cornelis De Witt (1623–1672), saw the Netherlands safely through the naval wars with England, and maintained Dutch prosperity, though the decline was beginning and was accelerated by the threatened attack of Louis XIV.

Indeed, as the French armies swept through the southern portion of the Dutch Republic, the frightened Dutchmen lynched the DeWitt brothers on August 17, 1672, and recalled the son of William II to serve as stadtholder. That son was William III, who had been born a few months after his father died, and who was now 22 years old. He managed to gain allies and hold off the French sufficiently well for the Netherlands to survive the war without loss of territory.

The Dutch dominions overseas were in no danger from Louis XIV, who could not dispute the sea with the Dutch. On the Dutch island of Mauritius, however, an event took place that in more recent times would have been considered a tragedy that human beings would have labored hard to prevent, but which was little regarded then. The dodo, a flightless pigeon, as large as a turkey, which could be found only on Mauritius, was needlessly driven to extinction. The last one died in 1681, leaving behind only the well-known phrase "dead as a dodo."

In 1677, William III married Mary, the older daughter of James II and, in 1688, this led to his being called in by the English to be their king. As King of England, he carried on the bitter feud with Louis XIV.

The Netherlands continued to produce important scientists. Christian Huygens (1629–1695) discovered, in 1656, that the planet, Saturn, was encircled by a ring and that it had a large satellite, which he named Titan. In 1657, he devised the pendulum clock, the first timepiece capable of measuring time consistently to within a minute. This was absolutely essential to the further progress of physics. Huygens also maintained that light was a wave motion in opposition to Newton's belief that it was a stream of tiny particles.

Anton van Leeuwenhoek (1632–1723) was the greatest of the early microscopists. He ground perfect little lenses and, in 1676, was the first to see microorganisms, living things too small to see with the unaided eye. He also observed sperm cells and, in 1683, even caught a glimpse of tiny bacteria for the first time. Another microscopist, Jan Swammerdam (1637–1680) discovered red blood corpuscles in 1658, and studied insects in great detail, founding the modern science of entomology.

The Dutch–Jewish philosopher, Baruch Spinoza (1632–1677), published important books on philosophy in the 1670s, following the teachings of Descartes. Because his views on the rational view of the Universe seemed godless to the or-

thodox, he was excommunicated from his synagogue.

The most important Dutch painter of this period was Jan Vermeer (1632–1675).

SPAIN

Philip IV died in 1665, leaving behind a broken nation, with Portugal gone, Catalonia barely retained, and its military reputation shattered. He also left behind a four-year-old son, who reigned as Charles II (1661–1700), but who was so sickly, and so near to feeble-mindedness, that he was yearly expected to die. He surprised everyone by living to be an adult. However, though he married twice, he had no children.

When Charles II, after a long illness, died on November 1, 1700, Europe had to face the overriding question of who would next sit on the throne of Spain. There were three candidates for the succession.

Louis XIV was the half-brother-in-law of Charles II of Spain and his mother had been Charles II's aunt. Louis did not expect to become King of Spain himself, and his son was scheduled to succeed him, as was his older grandson. He had, however, a younger grandson, Philip of Anjou (1683–1746), however, who was a great-grandson of Philip IV of Spain.

As for the Emperor Leopold I (1640–1705), he was a nephew of Philip III of Spain and a full brother-in-law of Charles II. He claimed the throne for his younger son, Charles.

Finally, the elector, Maximilian II of Bavaria (1662–1726), was a grandson of Philip IV, and he offered his son, Joseph Ferdinand.

Since no one but France wanted Philip of Anjou, and no one but Austria wanted Charles of Austria, the logical choice was the Bavarian, but he died in 1699, before Charles II did.

As Charles II of Spain lay dying, the French somehow persuaded him to leave his land to Philip of Anjou, who was therefore declared king. This caused Louis XIV to exult that the Pyrenees (the mountain range between France and Spain) were no more.

PORTUGAL

Portugal, free once more, was ruled by John IV, who spent his reign fending off attempts by Spain to reassert its authority over Portugal, and doing so successfully. On February 13, 1668, Spain finally recognized Portuguese independence.

In 1654, Portugal also drove the Dutch out of the Brazilian coast, one of the few cases where Portugal regained a lost portion of its empire.

When John IV died in 1656, he was succeeded by his older son, Afonso VI (1643–1683), and, after that monarch's deposition in 1667, by a younger son, Pedro II (1648–1706). Portugal remained close to England; and a daughter of John IV, Catherine of Bragaza (1638–1705) married Charles II of England in 1662, but had no children.

PAPACY

The most important Pope of the period was Innocent XI (1611–1689), who became Pope in 1676. He reorganized the Papacy's financial situation and was rigidly honest himself. What was most unusual for a Pope of this period was his recognition that there had to be religious toleration since force alone would bring not unity but devastation. Therefore, he disapproved of Louis XIV's revocation of the Edict of Nantes (a far cry from the Papal celebration of the St. Bartholomew's Day Massacre a century earlier).

He spent his efforts in fighting Louis XIV, who wanted the French Church to be more under his own control than the Pope's. In 1682, Louis XIV called an assembly of French churchmen, who argued that a general council was superior to the Pope and that the Pope could not dictate to sovereigns. It also maintained that the power of the Pope was limited and that his decisions were not irrevocable.

Under Innocent XII (1615–1700), who became Pope in 1691, Louis XIV backed down from this position, however, probably because he wanted Papal support for the inheritance of Spain by his grandson.

An important Italian scientist of the period

was Francesco Redi (1626–1697), who proved, in 1668, that maggots did not arise from dead meat ("spontaneous generation") but arose from the eggs of flies. It was an important early example of the usefulness of experimentation in biology.

The Italian microscopist, Marcello Malpighi (1628–1694), discovered microscopic blood-vessels ("capillaries") connecting veins and arteries. This completed Harvey's earlier work on the circulation of the blood.

Antonius Stradivarius (1644–1737), in the 1680s and 1690s, produced the best violins ever made. A "Stradivarius violin" is, to this day, the ultimate in musical instruments.

Alessandro Scarlatti (1660–1715) was the greatest Italian composer of this period. He produced 115 operas and established the form of the opera overture.

SAVOY

Savoy was a duchy in the northwestern corner of Italy, with its capital at Turin. In 1650, Charles Emmanuel II (1638–1675) was its ruler and was succeeded by his son, who reigned as Victor Amadeus II (1666–1732). Savoy was, at this time, virtually a French puppet, and its importance lay in the future. Eugene of Savoy (1663–1736), a second cousin of Victor Amadeus II, was unable to obtain preferment from Louis XIV and, in a dudgeon, switched allegiance to Austria, something that, in the end, did Louis XIV enormous harm.

VENICE

Venice was still fighting wars with the Ottoman Empire. A long 21-year war over Crete, ended in 1669, with the loss of Crete by Venice to the Turks.

But then, in 1684, Venice managed to conquer parts of the Peloponnesus. As the war continued, an important tragedy, not involving human life, took place in 1687. The Parthenon, the most beautiful remnant of ancient Greece was still essentially intact although it had been built 2000 years earlier. The Turks, however, stored gunpowder in it, and the Venetians, bombarding

Athens, struck the building. The gunpowder exploded and the Parthenon was left a ruin.

OTTOMAN EMPIRE

In this period, the Ottoman Empire showed a surprising burst of vigor, due not to any sudden appearance of a vigorous Sultan, but rather through a group of ministers ("grand viziers") of the Albanian-born Koprolu family. The first of these, Koprolu Mehmed (d. 1661), reorganized the Janizzaries and the finances. He and his son, Fazil Ahmed (1635–1676), brought about the defeat of Venice and the taking of Crete in 1669.

The Turks also fought vigorously but without outstanding success against the Poles and the Russians. The most astonishing stroke, however, came in an offensive against Austria.

This arose out of a continuing fight between Austria and the Ottoman Empire over Hungary, compounded by confused fighting by the Hungarians against the Austrians and against each other.

Kara Mustafa (1634–1683), the brother-in-law of Fazil Ahmed, became Grand Vizier in 1678. On March 31, 1683, he and the Sultan, Mehmed IV, led a large force into Hungary and beyond. The Austrians retired before them and, on July 14, 1683, the Turks had reached Vienna, with perhaps 150,000 men, 10 times the number that were inside Vienna under the leadership of Charles of Lorraine (1643–1690).

Somehow it was as though the days of Suleiman the Magnificent of a century and a half earlier had suddenly returned. Once again, the Turks were in the heart of central Europe. This time, though, the Turks were short of heavy artillery and the defense was very rigorous. Even so, as September opened, the Turks were making breaches in the fortifications and the fall of Vienna seemed only a matter of time.

The Austrians, however, had made an alliance with Poland even as the Turkish force had set out, and Poland was under the rule of one of its rare forceful kings, John III Sobieski (1629–1696). Faithful to his treaty, John Sobieski brought an army of 30,000 Poles to Vienna by forced marches, covering 220 miles in 15 days. On September 12, 1683, there was a battle outside Vienna which remained inconclusive until John Sobieski led his cavalry in a wild attack that sent the Turks into panicky flight. Vienna was saved.

The Ottoman Empire, having made this supreme effort and failed, simply receded in exhaustion. The Austrian army pursued the retreating Turks and gradually gained the upper hand. On September 2, 1686, the Austrians took Buda, the Hungarian capital, and on August 12, 1687, in a battle near Mohacs (where the Turks had smashed the Hungarians over a century and a half earlier), it was now the Turks who were defeated by Charles of Lorraine.

The Austrians then invaded the Balkans, captured Belgrade and overran Serbia. The Turks, with a supreme effort, drove them out. But in 1697, when the Turks tried to counterattack in Hungary again, they were met by the Austrians under Eugene of Savoy (1663–1736), who virtually annihilated them.

Turkey was forced to sign the Treaty of Karlowitz, north of Belgrade, on January 26, 1699. For the first time, the Turkish tide in Europe receded. All of Hungary was freed after a century and a half under the Turks, but not totally. It became part of Austria. Poland and Venice also gained territory. Now, at last, the Turkish decline was visible even on the map. The Ottoman Empire never threatened central Europe again.

AUSTRIA

In this period, Austria was totally involved in fighting Louis XIV on the west and the Turks on the east. The Emperor throughout this period was Leopold I, who established absolutism after the fashion of Louis XIV, and who labored to get the Spanish throne for his family.

The greatest German scientist of this period was Gottfried Wilhelm Leibniz (1646–1716). In 1673, he invented a calculating device that could multiply and divide as well as add and subtract. In 1684, he worked out the mathematical system of calculus, independently of Newton, though there was a long and ugly controversy over the matter. In 1700, he studied binary notation.

BRANDENBURG

Brandenburg, a state in eastern Germany, with Berlin as its capital, played a rather obscure role prior to this period. In 1618, the Elector of Brandenburg, John Sigismund (1572–1619), had absorbed the province of Prussia, which lay outside the boundaries of the Holy Roman Empire, and which had been part of the dominion of the now-defunct Teutonic Knights. He and his Electorate were Calvinists.

John Sigismund's son George William (1595–1640) became Elector in 1619 and did his best to remain sensibly (if pusillanimously) neutral during the Thirty Years War. His son, Frederick William (1620–1688), became Elector in 1640. It was under him that Brandenburg began to grow prominent, and he is usually known as the "Great Elector."

Frederick William built up a standing army and, in this way, began a militaristic tradition that was to continue. The Brandenburg army had its first test in 1656, during a war between Sweden and Poland. To keep Brandenburg safe, the Great Elector allied himself with Sweden and, in a three-day battle in July 1636, the Swedes took Warsaw. The Brandenburgers did well in that battle, but Frederick William refused to advance farther into Poland.

Thereafter, Frederick William artfully chose a policy of changing allies as changing conditions made it necessary, trying always to make a gain out of each change.

Finally, when the Swedes, tired of this duplicity, invaded Brandenburg in 1675, Frederick William defeated the Swedes at the Battle of Fehrbellin, about 30 miles northwest of Berlin. It was the first time the Brandenburger army had won a battle on its own. Frederick William wasn't strong enough, however, to force the Swedes to give up the Pomeranian territory north of Brandenburg, which they had won in the Thirty Year War, three decades earlier.

In 1688, Frederick William was succeeded by his son, the Elector Frederick III (1657–1713), who kept the electorate on the side of Austria against Louis XIV.

SWEDEN

For nearly a century after the death of Gustavus Adolphus, Sweden aspired to a position as a great power, one to which her population and economic strength did not really entitle her.

Charles X Gustavus (1622–1660) became King of Sweden after Queen Christina's abdication in 1654. He was her half-first-cousin. He managed to gain Livonia from Poland after taking Warsaw in 1656. He also took over Skane in 1658. This was the southernmost part of Sweden, and it had been retained by Denmark when Sweden won its independence nearly a century and a half earlier.

His son, Charles XI (1655–1697) became King of Sweden in 1660 and, in imitation of Louis XIV, he made himself absolute, although he joined alliances against the French king. He was defeated by Brandenburg at the Battle of Fehrbellin in 1675.

At the death of Charles XI, Sweden was still the strongest power in the north and still looked very impressive on the map. Succeeding him, however, was his 15-year-old son, who reigned as Charles XII (1672–1718). The surrounding nations of Denmark, Poland, and Russia, all of whom had been defeated at one time or another by the king's father or grandfather, now allied themselves for the purpose of taking advantage of the boy-king and of gaining territory at Sweden's expense.

A Swedish scientist of this period was Olof Rudbeck (1630–1702). He discovered the lymphatic vessels, a portion of the blood-circulating machinery, and demonstrated them to Queen Christina in 1653, using a dog for the purpose.

DENMARK

Frederick III (1609–1670), who succeeded his father, Christian IV, in 1648, and his son and successor, Christian V (1646–1699), were both mauled by Sweden. Christian V, imitating Louis XIV, made himself absolute.

Two Danish scientists should be mentioned. Nicolaus Steno (1638–1686) was a skilled anatomist who was the first modern to maintain that certain rocky fossils dug out of the ground, and which bore the appearance of living things, had indeed once been alive, and had petrified after death.

The Danish astronomer, Olaus Roemer (1644–1710), was the first to get a reasonable value of the speed of light, by studying the manner in which Jupiter's satellites went into eclipse, earlier or later than scheduled, depending on the changing distance between Earth and Jupiter.

POLAND

The Turks invaded Poland in 1672, but John Sobieski led a Polish army to Chotin on the Dniester River, at the border of the Ottoman domain and destroyed it. The Polish king at the time was Michael (1640–1673), who reigned since 1669. He was the son-in-law of Emperor Leopold I and was opposed by the anti-Hapsburg faction, of whom the chief was John Sobieski.

As it happened, Michael died the day before the battle at Chotin, and John Sobieski raced to Warsaw and had himself elected king as John III. He then defeated the Turks again in 1673, when they tried a second invasion; and a third time when he put an end to the siege of Vienna in 1683.

But John Sobieski was the last strong king Poland was to have. After his death in 1696, Poland went rapidly downhill.

RUSSIA

During the reign of Tsar Alexis, there was a long war between Russia and Poland, in which Russia sought revenge for Polish meddling during the Time of Troubles. It ended in 1667, with Russia having gained Smolensk permanently. They also gained the eastern Ukraine beyond the Dnieper River, plus Kiev, the old Russian capital. This meant that Russia's borders now abutted those of the Ottoman Empire.

The war was devastating to the Ukraine, and the Cossack horsemen, who dominated it as a kind of no-man's land between Poland, Russia, and the Ottoman Empire, grew rebellious. Add to that the fact that serfs who ran away from serfdom tended to go to the Ukraine where the

Tsar's officials did not penetrate effectively. The escaped serfs dreaded more than anything else the expansion of Russian power in the region.

In 1670, therefore, the Cossacks and serfs rebelled under the leadership of Stepan ("Stenka") Razin (d. 1671) and, for a year, spread rapine and slaughter over the Volga River valley and to the east.

Western notions were already beginning to infiltrate Russia, however, and Alexis sent against the rebels an army that had been trained to some extent, at least, in western weapons and tactics. The wild, undisciplined rebels could not stand against them. The rebellion was crushed and, on June 16, 1671, Stenka Razin was brutally executed, though he remained an outlaw-hero in the memory of ordinary Russians.

And all this time in the east, more and more of Siberia was being penetrated and coming under Russian control. Russian pioneers had, in fact, reached the Pacific Ocean and, beginning in 1670, had established themselves along the Amur River, on the border of Manchuria.

By the time Alexis died, in 1676, Russia was completely recovered from the Time of Troubles. While Russia was still no match, militarily, for her more advanced western neighbors, the ability of her people to be resolute and long-suffering on defense was beginning to make itself felt.

Alexis was succeeded by his oldest son, Fyodor III (1661–1682), who was only 15 years old. He was the first Tsar to receive even the beginnings of a western education, since he had been taught Polish and Latin. He encouraged the further exposure of Russia to western culture, against the fiery objections of the conservatives.

In his reign, there was war, for the first time, between Russia and the Ottoman Empire. The Turks did well, but Kara Mustafa was planning his push toward Vienna and he wanted peace on the Russian front. Therefore, he agreed to let Russia have parts of the Ukraine that the Turks had until then occupied, provided those parts were to be kept unpopulated so that there would be no friction between the nations. Russia took the area, but keeping it unpopulated was not possible (and probably not even desired).

Fyodor died in 1682, still only 21. He had a

younger brother, Ivan (1666–1696), who was 16 and mentally deficient. There were those who wanted Ivan's half-brother, Alexis' son by a second wife, to reign instead. He was Peter (1672–1725), who was only 10 years old, but tall, healthy, and intelligent.

Ivan had a sister, Sophia (1657–1704), who was also Peter's half-sister. She was 25 years old and ambitious. She wanted Ivan to be Tsar, because he would be more easily handled. Therefore, she arranged to have the Streltsy (the palace guard) riot in favor of Ivan. Some of Peter's party were massacred, but Peter himself was spared. The result was that Ivan and Peter were made co-Tsars as Ivan V and Peter I, while the real power lay with Sophia, as regent.

She remained regent for seven years, during which time there were two quite unsuccessful campaigns against the Crimean Tatars, and a treaty in the Far East.

The Russian pioneers on the Amur River were 6000 miles from home and were facing a strong China. The only reason they had managed to establish themselves on the Amur in the first place was that the Manchu rulers of China were distracted by a revolt in the south. Once the Manchus had settled matters there, they sent an army north. The Russians were vastly outnumbered, and resistance was clearly useless. In August of 1689, therefore, they signed the Treaty of Nerchinsk (an outpost just north of Mongolia). By that treaty, the Russians agreed to evacuate the Amur valley, and did so. It was the first important land contact between a European power and China.

In that same month, young Peter, now 17, strong and forceful, had gathered a group loyal to himself, and overthrew Sophia. He became the effective ruler of Russia, although he carefully preserved the co-Imperial title for his brother, until the latter's death in 1696.

Peter recognized, more than any Russian before him, that Russia was doomed to defeat at the hands of its western enemies as long as it remained technologically backward. It had to learn from the west and adopt western ways. Peter, therefore, began an intense program of self-education that would undoubtedly have broken anyone less dynamically energetic than himself.

Peter was fascinated by ships, by carpentry, by doing things with his hands. It was his clear intention to seize Russia by its collective beard and drag it, kicking and screaming, if necessary, into the new century about to begin.

For this reason, he continued his education outside Russia. In 1697, he left for a tour of France, England, and the Netherlands, under an incognito (that fooled nobody), and exposed Europe to the ferocity of his desire to learn, and to his capacity for alcohol.

He would have stayed longer, learning more about the west and gaining allies, however, in 1698, news reached him that the Streltsy had revolted.

In a rage, he dashed back to Russia and, with a flurry of executions and exiles, he destroyed the corps. He made it quite plain that in anger and cruelty, he could be as supernormal as he was in everything else. He was no man to trifle with, and Russia learned the lesson.

Peter, with his interest in ships, needed an outlet to the ocean. Even before his trip to the west, his glance had rested on the Black Sea, which was blocked by the Crimean Tatars, against whom Sophia had failed twice. In 1695, even before he had traveled west, he had launched an offensive against Azov, the northernmost Black Sea port. It failed because he lacked the ships to blockade the city. So he built the ships and sailed them down the Don River to Azon and, on July 28, 1696, took it. It wasn't enough to open the Black Sea to him, but it was a start.

However, the boy-king, Charles XII, was on the Swedish throne now and Peter was eager to occupy those Swedish lands that would place him on the Baltic Sea, so he made peace with Turkey in 1700.

INDIA

In 1658, Aurangzeb (1618–1707), the third son of Shah Jahan, became the ruler of the Moghul Empire. He was a pious Muslim, and almost paranoid in his distrust and suspicions. It was his ambition to rule over a united India, and he almost achieved this aim. Only the extreme southern tip of India was left unconquered.

He would also have liked to evict the Europeans on his coastline; in 1685, for instance, he seized the English base at Surat. However, there was no way he could fight the English ships and the English retained their hold, here and there.

The French also arrived on the coast, establishing themselves at Chandernagor on the northeastern coast in 1670. The English, unwilling to leave any part of the coast to France uncontested, established a base near Chandernagor that grew to be the city of Calcutta. The French, playing the same game, occupied Pondicherry, south of the English base at Madras. By 1700, the stage was set for an Anglo–French confrontation over the control of Indian trade.

Aurangzeb's continual wars were weakening the nation. He persecuted the Hindus relentlessly, which encouraged revolts that had to be repressed, adding further devastation. The later decades of his rule initiated a decline of the Moghul Empire, which was papered over by Aurangzeb's strong will and energy, but would surely lead to a breakdown after his death.

CHINA

In 1662, K'ang Hsi (1654–1722) began a 60-year reign over China. He was the most able of the Ch'ing Emperors, and under him Manchu China was at its height. He united all of China, and even took the island of Taiwan, where diehards of the Ming dynasty had maintained themselves for 40 years.

He forced the Russians to abandon the Amur River district by the Treaty of Nerchinsk in 1689; and, by 1699, he was in control of Mongolia. Between the Russians on the north and the Chinese on the south, the Mongolian region was trapped and could never again serve as a reservoir of roving mounted tribesmen.

K'ang Hsi was interested in western science, and tolerated the Jesuits in order that he might learn from them. They worked up new calendars and improved observatories. He also supported Chinese scholars and Chinese art.

It isn't often that able rulers appear in clusters, but as the 1600s drew to a close there were able, forceful rulers over China, India, Russia, and France—all at the same time.

SOUTH AFRICA

On April 6, 1652, the Dutch arrived in southern Africa, a century and three quarters after the Portuguese navigators had first sighted the Cape of Good Hope. The Dutch established a settlement there, in 1652, which became Capetown. During the next half-century, the Dutch spread out over the coast and moved inland.

1700 TO 1725

FRANCE

With Charles II of Spain dead, and with Louis XIV's grandson prepared to succeed him as Philip V, a "Grand Alliance" was formed to make sure that Spain did not become a French puppet. The chief members of the Alliance were Austria, England, and the Dutch Republic.

Austria's general was Eugene of Savoy, who had fought well at the siege of Vienna, and had beaten the Turks in Hungary.

In England, William III died on March 19, 1702, but that was just as well. He was a bad general and might have botched things. As it was, he was succeeded by his sister-in-law Anne (1665–1714), who was James II's younger daughter. She left military matters in the hands of John Churchill (1650–1722), later the Duke of Marlborough. He was the husband of Anne's favorite, Sarah Churchill (1660–1744), and, like Eugene of Savoy, he was a general of the first rank. He had helped crush Monmouth's rebellion and had been close to James II, but had abandoned him for William III when that seemed the wisest thing to do.

Since William III left no heirs who qualified as stadtholder of the Netherlands, it became a republic again under Anthonie Heinsius (1641–1720). Heinsius had, in any case, been governing the land while William was King of England.

The "War of the Spanish Succession" began in 1701, when Eugene of Savoy led an Austrian army into Italy. On May 15, 1702, England entered the war, and Marlborough landed in the Dutch Republic and invaded the Spanish Netherlands. Marlborough discovered, however, that the cautious Dutch would not allow him to take chances and were constantly preventing him from carrying through daring strokes that he would undoubtedly have carried to a successful conclusion.

In September 1702, Bavaria entered the war on the French side. It was France's plan now to send an army into Bavaria and, using that as a base, to threaten Vienna and force Austria out of the war.

Marlborough could see that the French would do this, and he knew that what he had to do was to take his troops from the Netherlands to Bavaria and there, in combination with Eugene of Savoy, defeat the French army, knock Bavaria out of the war, and save Austria.

In order to do that, he had to keep his plan secret from the Dutch, who would otherwise have moved heaven and earth to keep him from leaving the Netherlands. If his army were destroyed in Germany, after all, the Netherlands would have to face Louis XIV themselves, and they could scarcely imagine that they would survive in that case.

In April 1704, Marlborough set out southward, with the unsuspecting Dutch having no idea of what he was planning. While he marched southeastward, Eugene of Savoy kept the French and Bavarians busy and off-balance. On August 12, 1704, Marlborough and Eugene combined forces in Bavaria and had 56,000 men against a French–Bavarian force that was slightly larger. The next day, the two armies met at Blenheim on the Danube River in western Bavaria.

Marlborough and Eugene worked in perfect coordination (they always did, something that was not usually true of two generals with separate armies), and between them managed to shatter the French army, and virtually wipe it out.

As a result of the battle, Bavaria was indeed knocked out of the war and was taken over by Austria. The French army received a terrible blow to its prestige. It was, after all, the first great defeat suffered by the armies of Louis XIV.

Marlborough returned to the Netherlands and, for two years, there was stalemate as the Dutch continued to keep Marlborough hobbled —despite the display at Blenheim of what he could do.

But then, on May 23, 1706, Marlborough forced the French into battle at Ramillies in the Spanish Netherlands. He feinted at the French left, and when the French switched some reserves from the right, he launched his main attack at the weakened right; the French were again badly defeated. This victory made it possible for Marlborough to take over the Spanish Netherlands.

During that same year, Eugene maneuvered brilliantly and quickly in Italy, totally confusing the less able French commanders, beating them at Turin on September 7, 1706, and driving them out of Italy altogether. Louis XIV, feeling his age and dazed by this unexpected turn of events, began to consider making peace.

On July 11, 1708, Marlborough faced a French army at Oudenarde in the Spanish Netherlands for a third major battle. Eugene was with him, and opposed was the French commander, Louis Joseph, Duke de Vendome (1654–1712), a capable fighter. By now, though, the French leadership was frightened of Marlborough and Vendome was hampered in his plans. The result was a bloody battle which Marlborough won. He then laid siege to the city of Lille and took it on December 11, 1708. Marlborough was now standing on French soil.

Louis XIV asked for terms. The most important demand of the Allies was that Spain be transferred from Louis's grandson, Philip, to an Austrian ruler. Louis was chastened enough to be willing to agree to that. However, Philip was in possession of Spain and the Allies demanded that Louis XIV use French troops to drive him out. Louis, in anger, refused this further demand, and the war continued, through a winter that was the coldest anyone could remember and that put all of western Europe through an agony of frost and famine.

On September 11, 1709, Marlborough and Eugene fought the French a fourth time, at Malplaquet, on the French frontier with the Spanish Netherlands. For one last time, Marlborough won, but it was the hardest battle he had yet fought, and he actually lost more men than the French did.

The war was, by now, very unpopular in England. Marlborough's victories were entirely too costly to celebrate, and the last year's winter had been the last straw. To the English, it seemed that the best war was one fought by the navy, and that land battles should be fought, and high casualties suffered, by *other* powers whom England would subsidize.

Besides, Queen Anne had quarreled with Marlborough's wife. For this reason, Marlborough was recalled on December 31, 1711, and England virtually abandoned the war, leaving its allies in the lurch.

There was nothing to do now but make peace, and Louis XIV got better terms than he had been offered in 1708. The Treaty of Utrecht (in the Dutch Republic) was signed on April 11, 1713.

By its terms, France was finally forced to accept the fact that the English would be ruled by a Protestant king and to quit supporting the Catholic descendants of James II. England gained land in North America. Then, too, the English had captured Gibraltar from Spain on August 4, 1704, and they kept that, too (and still have it today).

Austria obtained the Spanish Netherlands, which had been Spanish for a century and a half. It was called the "Austrian Netherlands" from this point on.

Savoy obtained the island of Sicily, which, a few years later, it exchanged for the lesser, but closer, island of Sardinia. From this point on, Savoy became the "Kingdom of Sardinia."

For Louis XIV, the major gain was that his grandson, Philip, retained Spain and the Spanish overseas colonies. To be sure, Louis had to promise that France and Spain would never be ruled by the same person, but there was the feeling that a sense of family would keep the two nations allied.

Louis XIV was now coming to the end of his reign. He died on September 1, 1715, having been king for 72 years, the longest reign in modern times. He had outlived his son and his older grandson. His successor was his five-year-old great-grandson, who reigned as Louis XV (1710–1774). A nephew of Louis XIV, Philippe, Duke of Orleans (1674–1723), served as regent.

As a result of the War of the Spanish Succession, French finances were in a perilous state. A Scottish financier, John Law (1671–1728), thought he had a way out. He would offer shares in a company that would finance the settling of the lower Mississippi River Valley. The money invested and the profits made would then pay off the nation's debts. This scheme sounded good and it was adopted in 1717.

People who expected to make great profits poured their money into the scheme. The money received from those coming in later was used to pay the interest of those who came in earlier and who made the big profits that had been promised. This lured still others to come in. The price of the stocks was bid up and up (such schemes are, therefore, called "bubbles," because stock-prices expanded like bubbles—and usually burst like bubbles).

Those who were content with reasonable profits and sold out, did well, but the temptation was always to remain in and make still more—and more. Eventually, though, the money stopped coming in since there wasn't an infinite supply, nor were profts coming in from the Mississippi. As soon as there began to be a problem paying interest, everyone tried to sell their shares at once and, in 1720, the bubble burst. A few had gotten rich; most lost their shirts.

France was left worse off than it had been before the financial excitement had begun.

The artificiality of court life at Versailles, by the way, was reflected in the work of France's best-known painter of the period, Antoine Watteau (1684–1721), who painted delicate scenes of pastoral life and of gallantry, all idealized and romanticized.

ENGLAND/GREAT BRITAIN

While the War of the Spanish Succession was going on, an important change took place in the British Isles.

Since James I had become King of England a century before, England and Scotland had been two separate countries ruled by the same king—a dynastic union. On May 1, 1707, however, the two countries were unified as "The United Kingdom of Great Britain." From now on, therefore, we will speak of Great Britain and of the British, instead of England and Scotland and the English and Scottish.

The two nations kept their own laws and religious establishments, but they had a single parliament and a single flag. The flag ("The Union Jack") combined the cross of St. George for England and the cross of St. Andrew for Scotland.

Great Britain was by now divided into two parties: the Whigs and the Tories. Both names originated as terms of abuse applied by one to the other.

The Tories were isolationist and wanted to fight naval wars only. They supported royal power and the Anglican Church and were against religious toleration. By and large, they were a conservative party.

The Whigs were more liberal, favoring Parliament as against the monarch. They supported Marlborough and the war.

By 1710, however, the country was sick of Marlborough's bloody battles, victories though they might be, and Queen Anne had shifted her own sympathies to the Tories after she had quarreled with Sarah Churchill who was, of course, a profound Whig.

The Parliamentary elections that year were won by the Tories, and this represented the first peaceful transfer of power from one party to another in Great Britain. It set the fashion for other such cases in Great Britain, in the future United States, and in other nations that engage in free and peaceful election procedures.

A burning question was what to do about the succession once Queen Anne died. She had had 17 children but all had died young. The nearest heir was Anne's half-brother James Edward (1688–1766), whose birth had been the occasion of the overthrow of James II. After James II had died in exile in 1701, his son, then 13 years old, was considered to be James III by his supporters and came to be known as the "Old Pretender" because he eventually had a son who was the "Young Pretender."

The Tories rather hankered for James Edward, but he was Catholic and the British wouldn't have him.

James I of England had had a daughter, Elizabeth, who had married Frederick V of the Palatinate (the ill-starred "Winter King" who had been defeated at the very start of the Thirty Years War). They had had a daughter, Sophia (1630–1714), who had married Ernest Augustus (1629–1698), the Elector of Hanover, a state in western Germany. When Ernest Augustus had died in 1698, his son, George Louis (1660–1727), had become Elector.

Thus, George of Hanover was the great-grandson of James I, and a second cousin of William III, Mary II, and Anne. The Whigs supported the "Hanoverian succession"; and since George was a Protestant, that made him the logical choice for the British people generally.

Anne died on August 1, 1714, and George of Hanover became George I of England. He arrived in England on September 18, 1714, and formed a government—one made up of Whigs, naturally.

George I was not exactly a popular king. He was a fat, dull German, who had no personal magnetism, spoke no English, and showed no interest in Great Britain. He would much rather have stayed Elector of Hanover. Yet even so, the British had no choice. It was Protestant George or nothing.

To be sure, there were numerous "Jacobites," who supported James ("Jacobus" in Latin), particularly in Scotland, where the House of Stuart was considered Scottish, but there weren't enough. James landed in Scotland in 1715, but the Jacobite rising that then took place fizzled and quickly came to nothing.

Oddly enough, just as France was going through the Mississippi Scheme, Great Britain was going through a very similar "South Sea Bubble." In this case, the money was supposed to come out of the slave trade with the Spanish colonies in South America. The Treaty of Utrecht wasn't as favorable for this as had been hoped, but there was, nevertheless, a buying frenzy in 1720 that, of course, ended in a bust that impoverished many and that cast doubt upon the honesty of the government, including even the king himself.

The scandal might have had unimaginable consequences, but one of the Whigs, Robert Walpole (1676–1745), managed to keep things steady, to sacrifice a few of the worst offenders to appease the fury of the multitude, and to reorganize the government. He was placed in charge of finances, and became Prime Minister in 1721.

It turned out to be fortunate that George I was so little interested in the British government that he was willing to let Walpole do all the work, and then rubber-stamp it. This began the modern system of rule in Great Britain, in which the monarch is a figurehead and it is the Prime Minister that really runs the nation. Walpole, in that sense, was the first Prime Minister of Great Britain. While the rest of Europe, under the spell of Louis XIV, turned to absolutism, Great Britain moved, very slowly, to be sure, toward representative government and democracy.

In this period, Daniel Defoe (1660–1731), a pamphleteer of considerable ability, whose satirical writings got him in and out of trouble with the government, turned to fiction as he approached his sixtieth birthday. In 1719, Defoe published *Robinson Crusoe*, which turned out to be one of the world's all-time best-sellers. He also published *Moll Flanders* in 1722.

An even more skillful satirist, one of the three or four most remarkable in history, was Jonathan Swift (1667–1745). He was a biting pamphleteer

on behalf of the Tories, denouncing Marlborough and Isaac Newton with equal fury, and publishing another all-time best-seller in the form of *Gulliver's Travels* in 1726.

Essays of a gentler type that were largely pro-Whig were written by Joseph Addison (1672–1719) and Richard Steele (1672–1729) in *The Spectator* and other journals of opinion published in the 1710s.

The greatest English poet of this period (who was also a satirist—it was a great time for satire) was Alexander Pope (1688–1744). He published *Essay on Criticism* in 1711, and the mock-epic *The Rape of the Lock* in 1712. He also translated Homer's *Iliad* and *Odyssey* into heroic couplets between 1715 and 1726.

A poet of lesser sort, but very popular in his time, was Isaac Watts (1674–1748), who wrote 600 hymns. His best-known lines are, perhaps, "For Satan finds some mischief still/For idle hands to do."

The best-known playwright of the period was Nicholas Rowe (1674–1718), in whose play, *The Far Penitent*, produced in 1703, the character of "the gay Lothario" appears.

The greatest English musician of the day was the German-born George Frederic Handel (1685–1759). His opera, "Rinaldo" was a great success in London in 1711, and he remained in England thereafter.

In philosophy, there was the Irish-born, George Berkeley (1685–1753), who published *Treatise Concerning the Principles of Human Knowledge* in 1710. He rejected materialism and argued against Newton and the concepts of calculus (and was not entirely wrong in doing so).

In science, Edmund Halley (1656–1742) applied the principles of gravitation to comets and, in 1705, maintained that a comet last seen in 1682 appeared periodically every 76 years and would next appear in 1758. (It did, and has been known as Halley's comet ever since.) In 1718, he also showed that the "fixed stars" were *not* fixed, but slowly changed their position relative to each other in the sky.

Thomas Newcomen (1663–1729), in 1712, produced the first steam engine that could be used commercially for pumping water out of mines. It was fearfully inefficient but such "Newcomen engines" remained in use in considerable numbers for half a century before something better came along. Abraham Darby (1678–1717), in 1709, was the first to use coke, rather than charcoal, to smelt iron. Since coke is prepared from coal, and charcoal from wood, the new technique spared the forests.

Newcomen's engine and Darby's coke were harbingers of the Industrial Revolution, which was now looming on the horizon.

BRITISH AND FRENCH NORTH AMERICA

The War of the Spanish Succession embroiled the British and French colonies in North America, where the British colonials called it "Queen Anne's War."

In July 1710, 4000 British soldiers, with experience in the European war, arrived in New England. They were led north against Port Royal in Acadia. On October 16, 1710, it was taken a second time, this time permanently, and was renamed Annapolis Royal, after Queen Anne.

By the Treaty of Utrecht, Great Britain received the peninsula of Acadia, which was renamed Nova Scotia ("New Scotland"). Britain also gained the shores of Hudson Bay, where furs could be obtained.

In the British colonies themselves, Yale University was founded in New Haven, Connecticut in 1701. In 1710, the "Pennsylvania rifle" was brought into use by the German immigrants who settled west of Philadelphia (the "Pennsylvania Dutch"). In these rifles, the barrel was lined with spiral grooves that set bullets to spinning and allowed them to travel straighter and farther than when fired from smoothbore muskets. However, muskets remained popular because muzzle-loading was slower and more difficult in rifles than in muskets.

France continued to develop those sections that were left to her. Just northeast of Nova Scotia was Cape Breton Island, which was still French. There, France built a strongly fortified post called Louisberg, after Louis XIV. It also began to form settlements in the lower Missis-

sippi, in part thanks to the stimulus of Law's Mississippi Scheme. Mobile was founded in 1702, Natchez in 1716, and New Orleans in 1718. New Orleans flourished and, in 1722, it was made capital of all the vast Louisiana Territory.

The French also established posts in the upper Mississippi, and the regions that are now Illinois and Indiana. One such post, established in 1701, eventually became Detroit.

NETHERLANDS

The Netherlands did well in the War of the Spanish Succession, but its golden age was over. It declined rapidly after the war and became a minor power. It kept its overseas possessions, of course; and, on a planet in which there was less and less to discover, the Dutch admiral, Jacob Roggeveen (1659–1729), came across an isolated island in 1722, west of South America. Because (like Florida, two centuries earlier) the island was discovered on Easter Sunday, it was named "Easter Island." It was inhabited, and was remarkable for the presence of tall statues of distinctive appearance but of unknown origin and purpose.

Hermann Boerhaave (1668–1738) was the foremost European physician of his time. He published a popular textbook on physiology in 1708 and one on chemistry in 1724, and was known as the "Dutch Hippocrates."

In 1714, Gabriel Daniel Fahrenheit (1686–1736), a German-born Dutch physicist, devised the first mercury thermometer. It was the first reliable device for measuring temperature and was of inestimable use to science. The "Fahrenheit scale" (32 degrees for the freezing point of water and 212 degrees for the boiling point of water) is still in use in the United States, but not elsewhere.

SPAIN

After the War of the Spanish Succession, Philip V settled down as King of Spain, the first of the Bourbon dynasty. On the whole, the Spanish Bourbons were no more competent than the later Hapsburgs had been.

Spain was concerned that the French in Louisiana might expand southward into Spanish territory. Thus, Spain established Albuquerque in 1706 and San Antonio in 1718 as a way of emphasizing their presence and possession.

PORTUGAL

A trade agreement between Portugal and Great Britain was put through on December 27, 1703. Portugal imported British wool and woolens and exported port wine in return. This increased Portuguese prosperity and made port wine a favored drink of the British upper classes.

Peter II of Portugal was succeeded by John V (1689–1750) in 1706. Portugal naturally fought against Spain in the War of the Spanish Succession and, therefore, with the allies. As a result, at the Treaty of Utrecht, Portugal was awarded the Amazon River basin as part of Brazil against the competing claims of Spain. Brazil, consequently, became by far the largest nation, in area, in Latin America.

PAPACY

Pope Clement XI (1649–1721), who became Pope in 1700, tried to keep a low political profile, but the Papal States were invaded during the War of the Spanish Succession. The Pope was ignored by both sides. Clement was succeeded by Innocent XIII (1655–1724) in 1721.

Antonio Lucio Vivaldi (1678–1741) was the most prominent Italian composer of this period, and is particularly known for his violin concertos.

VENICE

In 1718, Venice lost the Peloponnesus to the Turks, and its great days were completely done. Aside from its own territory in northeastern Italy, Venice retained only some strips of the Dalmatian coast and some islands off it.

AUSTRIA

While Austria was on the winning side of the War of the Spanish Succession, and gained the Spanish Netherlands, it had to face a serious revolt in Hungary, which ended in 1711 only after Austria had made some concessions to the rebels.

The Emperor Leopold I had died in 1705, soon after the War of the Spanish Succession had started, and was succeeded by his older son, Joseph I (1678–1711). When Joseph I died in 1711, he was succeeded by his younger brother, Charles VI. Charles VI, as a younger son, had been the logical Hapsburg candidate for the throne of Spain. Once he became Emperor, however, his allies were not interested in seeing the thrones of the Empire and of Spain combined as in the days of Charles V more than a century and a half earlier. This, more than anything else, was the reason Philip V was allowed to keep Spain by the Treaty of Utrecht.

After the conclusion of the War of the Spanish Succession, Austria could turn its attention to Turkey again. After all, it still had Eugene of Savoy, the greatest general in Austrian history.

Eugene laid siege to Belgrade in 1717, it being the strongest Turkish base in the Balkans. Though a Turkish relief army (10 times the size of Eugene's) approached, Eugene attacked and won. In the battle, Eugene was wounded in action for the thirteenth and last time. Belgrade was taken on August 21, 1717, and the Ottoman Empire was forced to sign another disadvantageous treaty the next year.

A great German composer of the period was Johann Sebastian Bach (1685–1750), one of the greatest in history, and as popular today as ever, for time has not in the least diminished the impression he leaves as a giant of music.

BRANDENBURG/PRUSSIA

Frederick III, Elector of Brandenburg, the son of the Great Elector, had his ambition of continuing to preside over the aggrandizement of Brandenburg. What he wanted was to become a king, but for that he needed the Emperor's permission.

As the War of the Spanish Succession was approaching, Frederick III realized that Brandenburg, with its comparatively large and well-trained army, would be a welcome addition to the Austrian forces against Louis XIV, and he was prepared to charge a high price. In short, what he asked in exchange for an alliance with Austria was a royal crown. What's more, he didn't want it in Brandenburg, where he would be subject to the Emperor (at least in theory); he wanted it in Prussia, which lay outside the boundary of the Holy Roman Empire.

In return for the promise of 8000 troops, and a Prussian vote on the Austrian side on all important matters facing the Empire, Emperor Leopold I agreed. On January 18, 1701, Frederick III of Brandenburg became King Frederick I *in* Prussia. The word "in" implied that he was king only when he was in Prussia, but that in Brandenberg he was still elector. That, however, was a distinction that was soon lost. Brandenburg became "Prussia," and will be referred to as that from now on, and Frederick was King *of* Prussia.

Frederick I of Prussia died in 1713, just six weeks before the Treaty of Utrecht was signed, a treaty out of which Prussia got very little except the kingship. His son succeeded to the throne as Frederick William I (1688–1740). Frederick William I was careful not to go to war, but he built up the army enormously, trained it to the last inch, and saved his money, all of which was to be of inestimable use to his successor.

He also promoted the nation's prosperity by cutting down the expense of the court, living simply, and reforming tax policies. He freed the serfs, encouraged education, and—except for the harshness with which he trained his soliders to become fighting machines, and for his boorish manners—he was a good ruler.

He would walk the streets of Berlin unattended, and greet the citizens, but he also carried a stout stick with which to administer correction when he felt it was needed. As a result, the streets emptied when he took his walk, to his puzzled surprise. Once he noted someone slinking into an alley just too late. He called him back and asked him why he was leaving in that manner. The man said, "Because I fear you, your Majesty."

"Fear me?" cried the King, wielding his stick lustily, "You're suppose to love me, scum! Love me!"

POLAND

Augustus, Elector of Saxony (1670–1733) since 1694, wanted to be King of Poland, too. He was called Augustus the Strong, partly because he *was* strong and partly because he had a prodigious number of illegitimate children (something that could scarcely be managed by a weakling). In order to be acceptable to the Poles, he converted from Lutheranism to Catholicism, which alienated his Lutheran Saxon people, and caused his Lutheran wife to leave him. He became King of Poland in 1697, but it did him no good, for his reign was more troubled than would be expected even for a Polish king.

His troubles started in 1700 when he joined an alliance against Charles XII of Sweden and took part in a war against him. In the course of the war, he was driven from the throne in 1704, and restored to it in 1709; however, off the throne or on the throne, it made no difference. He had no power.

SWEDEN

While the War of the Spanish Succession was raging in western Europe, an even more spectacular one was being fought in eastern Europe. It centered on Sweden and on its boy-king, Charles XII, who, at age 15, had succeeded to the throne in 1697.

Against Charles, there was built up an alliance of Peter I of Russia (who wanted the Swedish territories that kept him from the Baltic Sea), Augustus II of Poland (who wanted those portions of Swedish territory that kept *him* from the Baltic Sea), and Frederick IV of Denmark (who wanted Sweden weaker so that Denmark could dominate the Baltic Sea).

In mid-June 1700, all three allied powers invaded Swedish territory.

Charles XII, now age 18, proved at once he was no mere boy, as Alexander had once done in similar circumstances 2000 years earlier. On August 4, 1700, Charles invaded Zealand, the island on which Copenhagen stood, and raced for that city. The Danes, astonished at the quickness and force of the reaction, gave in at once and signed a peace, finding themselves defeated by Sweden for the fourth time and more quickly than ever before.

Charles XII, then landed on the eastern shore of the Baltic Sea on October 6, and decided to relieve the city of Narva on the northeastern boundary of Estonia. It was being besieged by 40,000 Russians, and Charles XII had only 8000 Swedes with him, but the Swedes were well-trained and the Russians were a mere rabble. On November 20, 1700, in the middle of a snowstorm, Charles wiped out the Russian force. (Tsar Peter had left the scene of the battle before it started, probably because he knew what was going to happen.)

Charles XII felt that in a matter of three months, he had wiped out the two weaker members of the alliance and that he was now ready to march against what he thought was the main enemy, Poland. Therefore, he turned away from Russia and its bumbling, make-believe army.

This was his fundamental mistake, for he allowed the victory at Narva to persuade him to underestimate Russia and, what was far worse, to underestimate, totally, Peter. Peter had no intention of letting one defeat dishearten him. While Charles XII bent his attention on Poland, Peter had time to reorganize his army.

As a matter of fact, Charles XII spent five years in Poland and in Saxony, totally destroying Augustus's armies. Augustus was forced to abdicate the Polish throne and Charles XII chose Stanislaw Lesczynski (1677–1766) as king, knowing he could be counted on to be a Swedish puppet.

Meanwhile, though, Peter was pushing into the Baltic provinces and achieving his war aims. In 1702, he marched along the Neva River from Lake Ladoga to the Baltic Sea, and on that river he began to build a new capital. He wanted to get out of Moscow with its dark traditionalism rooted in the medieval Russian past and the Mongol experience. He wanted a capital on the Baltic Sea, facing the nations of Europe. It was to be his "window to the west." On May 16, 1703, he founded the city and named it St. Petersburg (in honor of the saint after whom the Tsar was

named). He also constructed a fleet for use on the Baltic.

By August 9, 1704, Peter had recaptured Narva, which he had lost four years earlier, and massacred every Swede there.

On January 1, 1708, Charles XII was ready (far too late) to turn to Russia. He crossed the Vistula River with 45,000 men and marched eastward toward Moscow. For over half a year he drove eastward, while Peter I instituted the careful Russian policy that was to deal with future invaders as well. He avoided battle and slowly yielded ground, destroying food and crops and anything else that might be useful to the Swedes as he went. It was a "scorched earth" policy.

By September 1708, the Swedes were terribly short on food and were not anxious to have to face a Russian winter. Charles XII then made a second mistake. Instead of retreating while he had a chance, he turned south to march into the Ukraine where the weather might be milder and where he expected to get the help of Ivan Stepanovich Mazeppa (1644–1709), a leader of the Cossacks.

Then, instead of waiting till he had gathered adequate arms and supplies, he raced on without them, leaving it to one of his generals, Adam Loewenhaupt, to gather supplies on the Baltic coast and bring them to him in the Ukraine.

Meanwhile, Peter was doing everything correctly. In September and October, even as Charles was marching southward, the Russians fended off a Swedish strike at the new capital of St. Petersburg so effectively that the Tsar could feel sure there would be nothing that would go on in the north to distract him from his main task of pursuing Charles.

Then, Peter sent a force into the Ukraine to burn Mazeppa's capital and harry the Cossacks. This, too, was done so effectively that Mazeppa had to flee, and could bring only a handful of men to Charles.

Finally, on October 9 and 10, Peter had a contingent of his army attack Loewenhaupt and the supply train he was bringing to Charles. Loewenhaupt was badly mauled and he had to burn his supplies to keep them out of Russian hands, so that on October 21, when he reached Charles, it was with 6000 men but without supplies.

The stars, too, fought against Charles. The winter of 1708–1709, which tortured western Europe at the height of the War of the Spanish Succession, tortured Russia, too, and the Swedish army had to fight through a terrible Russian winter after all, being constantly harassed by Peter's men. By the spring, Charles had only 20,000 men, less than half the army he had started with. (That he had even so many is a tribute to his skill at handling men, and to the professionalism of the Swedish soldiers.) What was much worse, though, was that he had only 34 artillery pieces and almost no gunpowder.

Peter stalked Charles patiently and, finally, when he decided the time was right, he confronted the Swedish king on June 28, 1709, at Poltava, east of the Dnieper River in the Ukraine.

Charles XII had recently been wounded in the foot and had to be carried in a litter. With very little ammunition, Charles XII had to have a quick victory. He attacked at once, but Peter saw what was happening. He withstood the attack stolidly and then, at the crucial moment, hurled in 40,000 fresh troops with plenty of guns and ammunition and the Swedes simply crumpled. Charles XII managed to get away and flee to the Ottoman Empire, but the rest of his army were either killed or captured and an admiring Europe called the conqueror, "Peter the Great," which is how he has been known ever since.

Everything Charles had done now fell apart. The Russians drove into Poland, restored Augustus as King of Poland (but playing a new role as Russian puppet), and, in 1713, conquered Finland.

Charles XII spent five years in Turkey trying to get the Ottoman Empire to fight the Russians and, in 1714, managed to return to Sweden. There he promptly took to war again, battling against Denmark until on December 11, 1718, on the Norwegian front, he was killed by a Danish bullet (or perhaps by a Swedish one, since the Swedes knew that there would never be peace as long as Charles XII was allowed to live).

Charles XII has often been compared to Alexander the Great. The comparison might have held if Charles had not faced Peter. Peter himself at one time growled, in the course of the war, "Charles thinks he is Alexander, but he shall find that I am no Darius."

The war ended with the Treaty of Nystadt (on the Finnish coast). It was signed on August 30, 1721, and, by it, Russia got the Baltic states, but returned Finland. The war put an end to Sweden as a great power, after a century of conquests, and it made Russia a great power in Sweden's place.

RUSSIA

Almost lost in the successful course of the "Great Northern War" against Charles XII of Sweden was a painfully inept interlude on Peter's part against the Ottoman Empire.

In the Ottoman Empire after the disaster at Poltava, Charles XII did manage to talk the Turks into making war on Russia in 1710.

Peter, his head in the clouds after Poltava, marched into what is now Romania, and carelessly allowed himself to be trapped against the Pruth River by a larger army of Turks. Had the Turks pressed their advantage, Peter would surely have had to surrender and been taken prisoner. He seemed at this time to have been dazed into helplessness by the sudden change of fortune.

However, Peter had a mistress, Catherine, a peasant girl from Livonia who was actually illiterate, but who was a comfortable, sensible person, very intelligent, and the only one who could unfailingly handle the Tsar in his more brutish moods. She was with him at the Pruth and she took over. She dickered with the Turks, who, in any case, strongly disliked the captious, hectoring Charles, and were in no mood to do him favors, and managed to get Peter off in exchange for a favorable treaty. (Otherwise, who knew how the fortunes of war might turn.) The treaty was signed on July 21, 1711, in which Russia returned some of its southern conquests to the Ottoman Empire. The next year, in a fine show of gratitude, Peter married the illiterate peasant woman, and made her his second wife.

Peter was unusually tall (closer to seven feet

than to six) and was strong and overflowing with energy, both constructively and destructively. He forced Russia along with him, reorganizing, revitalizing, and reforming her government, her towns, her army, her navy, her industries, her aristocracy. He decreed that the traditional Russian beards had to come off, for instance (at least among those who were not peasants and serfs), and shaved some men with his own harsh hand.

He was cruel to his son, Alexis (1690–1718), who had been brought up by his mother, Eudoxia (1669–1731), whom Peter hated and had divorced (or said he had divorced), to be everything Peter was not. Alexis was a weak, old-fashioned young man who believed in the old medieval ways. Frightened to death of his brutal father, he tried to renounce the succession and to enter a monastery, but was forbidden. He then fled the land and hid in Italy, in 1716, but Peter's agents tracked him down and brought him back. Peter knew that his son, whether in a monastery, or abroad, or anywhere but in his grave, would be used by the conservatives to undo all his reforms and put Russia back into the dark age. Therefore, he had his son executed in 1718. Being Peter, he had him tortured first.

Not all of Peter's reforms were useful. Not all of them took. Still, without him, Russia, and therefore Europe, and therefore most probably the world, would have taken a completely different path.

OTTOMAN EMPIRE

Mehmed IV, who had nearly taken Vienna, was succeeded in 1703 by his son, Ahmed III (1673–1736). It was in Ahmed's reign that the Turks lost Belgrade to Eugene of Savoy, recaptured the Peloponnesus from Venice, and had their victory over Peter the Great.

PERSIA

This was a time of confusion for Persia, with invasions by the Afghans unsettling it badly. In 1722, Peter the Great took advantage of the situation to annex portions of the coast of the Caspian Sea.

INDIA

Aurangzeb died in 1707 and the Moghul Empire rapidly disintegrated after over a century and a half of strength. Aurangzeb was the last of the great Mongol warriors who traced their descent from Genghis Khan, nearly five centuries earlier.

Moghul Emperors continued to sit on the throne in Delhi, 10 of them in fact, but their power was nil. Nevertheless, even ceremonial power is important. In 1717, the British East India Company managed to get various economic concessions, including freedom from customs duties, from the do-nothing Moghul Emperor, Farrukhsiyar, a great-grandson of Aurangzeb.

CHINA

Toward the end of the reign of K'ang Hsi, China invaded and conquered Tibet in 1720. The Chinese Empire was now more extensive, stronger, and more prosperous than at any time since Kublai Khan had been on the throne over four centuries earlier.

1725 TO 1750

AUSTRIA

Charles VI, Emperor of the Holy Roman Empire and Archduke of Austria, must have felt history repeating itself. A quarter-century earlier, Charles II of Spain had been dying and the question of succession had arisen. Charles VI had been one of the candidates.

Now it was Charles VI who contemplated his own death some day and the question, he knew, would arise as to what would happen to Austria and all the territories over which it ruled. Unlike Charles II of Spain, Charles VI of Austria had had a son, but he died young. Charles VI also had daughters, the oldest being Maria Theresa (1717–1780), but would Europe allow a woman to rule the Hapsburg dominions?

He spent most of his reign trying to get other nations to agree to allow his daughter to rule over an intact Austria, and they all signed the agreement. So when, on October 20, 1740, Charles VI died, and Maria Theresa, who was then 23 years old, became Archduchess of Austria, Queen of Hungary, and Queen of Bohemia.

But would she remain so? Other candidates made themselves known at once. There was Charles Albert (1697–1745), Elector of Bavaria. He was the great-great grandson of Ferdinand II, who had been Emperor during much of the Thirty Years War. Charles Albert had promised to accept Maria Theresa as ruler of Austria, but that was when Charles VI was alive. Now he was dead, it was a different story. Augustus III (1696–1763), Elector of Saxony, and the son of Augustus the Strong of Saxony and Poland, was the son-in-law of Joseph I, who had been Charles VI's older brother and predecessor. Even Philip V of Spain had some dim dynastic claim.

But it was none of these who struck the first blow against Maria Theresa and made her reign a mixture of tragedy and triumph.

PRUSSIA

It was Prussia.

Frederick William I of Prussia continued to build his army until he had one of 80,000 men out of a total population of 2.5 million. No other nation in Europe had so large a percentage of its population in the army. Furthermore, they were better trained than any other army in Europe and, what's more, Frederick William had accumulated a tidy financial surplus with which to pay and supply his army.

His problem was his son, Frederick (1712–1786). Whereas Frederick William was a gruff, brutal man whose idea of a good time was getting together with other low brows for an evening of smoking and drinking, Frederick was a delicate youngster who was fond of literature and music, and who seems to have been homosexual.

Frederick was so mistreated by his shouting, abusive father that, with a beloved male companion, he tried to run away in 1730 (as Alexis, the son of Peter the Great, had tried 14 years earlier). Frederick's plan was betrayed and he and his friend were captured. Frederick was forced to watch while his lover was executed and, for a while, it looked as though Frederick William would kill his son as Peter the Great had done. However, Frederick gave in abjectly, and he was allowed to live.

On May 31, 1740, Frederick William I died, and his son, now 28 years old, became Frederick II of Prussia. He aspired to be a "benevolent despot;" that is, he would be an absolute monarch, but he would use his power for the good of his people. He abolished torture, censorship, and religious discrimination (he had no religion of his own) and did what he could to encourage science and culture. What he most wanted, however, was to show his dead father that he was a warrior after all. And here he succeeded, for he turned out to be a general of unusual talent.

When, five months after Frederick became king, Emperor Charles VI died, it was Frederick who moved at once. He didn't claim the Austrian throne; he wasn't interested in that. What he wanted was Silesia, which lay to the northeast of Bohemia, and just to the south of Prussia, and which was a Protestant province. Frederick had some vague legal claim to it, but he didn't really care whether he had such a thing or not. He simply planned to take it.

On December 16, 1740, Frederick II invaded Silesia and this began "The War of the Austrian Succession." Maria Theresa at once appealed to all the kings who had agreed to recognize her as ruler of the Austrian realm for help in repelling the invasions. She got not one reply.

On April 10, 1741, the Austrians managed a counterattack, and battle was joined at Mollwitz in central Silesia. The Austrian cavalry drove off the Prussian cavalry, and Frederick was persuaded by his officers to leave the battlefield, lest he be captured. After he was gone, the superbly trained Prussian infantry withstood all attacks and won the battle. Frederick never forgave the officers who had persuaded him to leave, and never again left a battlefield while the outcome was still uncertain.

As soon as it seemed that Austria was losing the war, Charles Albert of Bavaria invaded Bohemia to gobble up his share of the Austrian carcass. Since Bavaria had fought with France in the War of the Spanish Succession, France, together with Spain, joined Bavaria. The Franco-Bavarian army took Prague on November 26, 1741, and Charles Albert was declared King of Bohemia. On January 24, 1742, he was declared Emperor Charles VII.

It looked as though Austria were falling apart, but Maria Theresa went to Hungary, where as Queen of the land she made an emotional appeal to the nobility, who responded with enthusiasm. An Austrian army with strong Hungarian contingents then invaded Bavaria and captured Munich on the same day that Charles Albert had been declared Emperor. The new Emperor had to dash back to Bavaria, while the French who were still in Prague were put under siege.

That was about the best that Maria Theresa could do, so she made peace with Prussia on June 11, 1742. By the Treaty of Breslau (the capital of Silesia), she let Frederick have Silesia, planning to get it back some time in the future. She then concentrated on driving out the French and Bavarians.

This she did successfully, all the more so since a British army with German troops from Hanover and Hesse marched to her assistance. There, George II of Great Britain (1683–1760), who was leading the army personally, managed to defeat the French at the Battle of Dettingen on June 27, 1743. It was the last time a British king ever led his troops on the battlefield.

On the whole, Austria was now doing so well that Frederick II grew a little nervous about his ability to keep Silesia. Therefore, he made an alliance with France, and reentered the war. Austria, however, continued fighting well under

Charles of Lorraine (1712–1780). He was Maria Theresa's brother-in-law, and a grandson of the Charles of Lorraine, who had defended Vienna against the Turks 60 years earlier.

The Emperor Charles VII died on December 27, 1744, and his son, Maximilian Joseph (1727–1777), who succeeded as Elector of Bavaria, had no particular desire to be the Emperor. On April 22, 1745, he bowed out of the war and promised to support Maria Theresa's husband, Francis of Lorraine (1708–1765) for the Imperial throne.

The French were still in the war, however, and on May 10, 1745, they, under Marshal Saxe (an illegitimate son of Augustus II of Saxony and Poland, who had fought Charles XII) faced a British army under William Augustus, Duke of Cumberland (1721–1765), a son of George II. This was at Fontenoy in the Austrian Netherlands near the French border. It was not a very skillful battle, and the French had the better of it.

In that same year, Frederick II won an unbroken series of victories over Austria even when he was outnumbered, or caught unaware, or put at a disadvantage. He began to be called "Frederick the Great" in consequence. Maria Theresa was forced to make a second treaty of peace with him at Dresden in Saxony on December 25, 1745. Once again, she agreed to let him keep Silesia. On his part, he recognized Maria Theresa's husband as Emperor Francis I, a post to which he had been elected on September 13, 1745.

The general treaty of Aix-la-Chapelle, on October 18, 1748, ended the War of the Austrian Succession and, except for Silesia, restored everything the way it was when Maria Theresa had first succeeded to the throne. She had saved her realm against enormous odds.

Frederick II was the big winner. Not only had he gained Silesia, but he had made Prussia into a major power and, for what that was worth, had gained undying military fame for himself.

GREAT BRITAIN

George I died on June 1, 1727, and was succeeded by his son, who reigned as George II (and who was the future victor at the Battle of Dettingen). George II was as little interested in governing Great Britain as his father had been. Since his highly intelligent wife, Caroline of Anspach (1683–1737), was as good friend of Walpole, the latter remained as Prime Minister.

Great Britain experienced the beginnings of a religious revival in 1729, when two brothers John Wesley (1703–1791) and Charles Wesley (1707–1788), together with a few other kindred spirits, founded Methodism (a name that, like so many other popular ones, began as a term of derision).

Great Britain was involved in the War of the Austrian Succession largely because it was in the Hanoverian interest and George II was, like his father, a Hanoverian at heart.

An event much closer to home came when Charles Edward Stuart, the "Young Pretender" (also called "Bonnie Prince Charlie"), came to Scotland on July 13, 1745, to spark a Jacobite uprising on behalf of his father, who still called himself James III.

The Highlanders rose in his favor, marched southward, and took Edinburgh on September 17, 1745. Toward the end of the year, the Jacobites invaded England and reached Derby, only about 120 miles north of London, on December 4.

However, there had been no general Jacobite rising in England itself, the Pretender's army was dwindling, and strong British forces under the Duke of Cumberland (who had just lost the Battle of Fontenoy) were moving northward. The Pretender was forced to retreat.

Cumberland met up with the Pretender's army at Culloden Moor, on April 16, 1746. The battle was one-sided. Not only were the starving and outnumbered Highlanders crushed, but the prisoners were killed, the wounded were rounded up and killed, and devastation was spread throughout the Highlands to teach all concerned to revolt no more. Cumberland earned the name of "Butcher" for that.

The Battle of Culloden was called "the last battle," for it was the last armed conflict on land to be fought in Great Britain. It was also the last dynastic struggle in British history. Charles escaped to France by September 20, 1746. After his father died in 1766, Charles considered himself "Charles III," but he died in drunken obscurity

in 1788, leaving no heirs—and, with that, the house of Stuart came to an end, a century and three quarters after it had gained the throne of England.

In Great Britain during this period, Pope was still writing poetry, publishing "Essay on Man" in 1733. Handel was still composing music, with *The Messiah* completed in 1742.

Henry Fielding (1707–1754) followed Defoe in the development of the novel, publishing his masterpiece, *Tom Jones*, in 1749. Earlier he had published *Jonathan Wild* in 1743, as a way of poking fun at the extremely popular *Pamela*, published in 1740 by Samuel Richardson (1689–1761), about an impossibly virtuous servant-girl. Tobias George Smollett (1721–1771) began his literary career with *The Adventures of Roderick Random*, published in 1749.

The most successful play of the period was *The Beggar's Opera*, staged in 1728, and written by John Gay (1685–1732). Thomas Gray (1716–1771), wrote "Elegy Written in a Country Graveyard" in 1750 ("The paths of glory lead but to the grave").

The most prominent artist of the period was William Hogarth (1697–1764), who completed *A Rake's Progress* in 1735.

David Hume (1711–1776) was a skeptical philosopher, writing *An Enquiry Concerning Human Nature* in 1748. To the pious of the time, he sounded very much like an atheist, and it is a mark of how greatly things had changed, in Great Britain at least, that he suffered no particular persecution.

In science, the astronomer, James Bradley (1693–1762), discovered the aberration of light, and used it to determine the speed of light much more accurately than Roemer had done a half-century before. Stephen Hales (1677–1761) was the first to measure blood pressure and, about 1705, recognized that plants obtained their nourishment through some component of the atmosphere.

The great difficulty in long-distance navigation was the inability to determine longitude. For that, a timepiece was needed that would keep good time on a swaying deck. The British government offered 20,000 pounds for one, and the prize was eventually won by John Harrison (1693–1776), who built a series of such timepieces beginning in 1728. With that, navigation became more certain.

John Kay (1704–1764) patented a "flying shuttle" in 1733 that halved the time and effort in weaving. This was another premonitory rumble of the forthcoming Industrial Revolution.

BRITISH NORTH AMERICA

The first American colonial to achieve European fame was Massachusetts-born Benjamin Franklin (1706–1790) of Philadelphia. He was accomplished in all directions. He started the first circulating library in America, in 1731, and the first fire-fighting company in Philadelphia in 1736. In 1749, he founded an academy that eventually became the University of Pennsylvania. He put out a yearly "Poor Richard's Almanac" that made him Rich Benjamin. He invented the "Franklin stove" in 1742, which is the basis of furnaces to this day. And he was a scientist who studied electrical phenomena.

Meanwhile, another British colony was founded. A British humanitarian, James Edward Oglethorpe (1696–1785), was sorry for those who were impoverished, and imprisoned for debt. He obtained permission from George II to establish a colony for such people south of the Carolinas, in an area over which Spain could no longer exert control.

On February 12, 1733, the city of Savannah was founded and the colony was named "Georgia," in honor of the king. (Oglethorpe was the only colonial founder to live long enough to see the colonies, including Georgia, gain their independence.)

The War of the Austrian Succession was fought in North America, too, where it was known as "King George's War." The New England colonials aimed for the French base, Louisberg, on Cape Breton Island. On March 24, 1745, an expedition was sent north under William Pepperell (1676–1759) and, on June 17, the fort surrendered. At the end of the war, however, Louisberg was given back to the French, as once Port Royal had been. The British expanded their

hold in the region, though, by founding Halifax in Nova Scotia in 1749.

Another and more important battle of a completely different sort was fought in New York. There, a publisher, the German-born John Peter Zenger (1697–1746), attacked the corruption of the New York governor and his cronies in his newspaper. The governor had him arrested for libel and the trial took place in August 1735. A Scottish-born lawyer from Philadelphia, Andrew Hamilton (1676–1741), appeared for Zenger, and argued that truth was no libel and that the freedom to publish the truth was the natural right of a free-born Englishman. Zenger was acquitted and this was an important victory for freedom of speech and the press in a world that has rarely tolerated either anywhere.

The Methodist revival in Great Britain reached the colonies. The British preacher, George Whitefield (1714–1770), brought the word to Georgia in 1738, and reached New England in 1740. He was joined in this by the Connecticut-born hell-fire preacher, Jonathan Edwards (1703–1758).

By 1750, the British colonies had a population of 1,500,000, of whom 250,000 were Black slaves. Boston was the largest city, with a population of 15,000.

FRANCE

Through much of this period, the French government was run by Andre-Hercule de Fleury (1653–1743), an elderly but capable cardinal who kept the peace, by and large, until Frederick II began his wars. He worked closely with Walpole of Great Britain, another lover of peace.

Under him, France was largely prosperous and Louis XV remained popular. (He was called in those early years, "Louis the Well-Beloved.") Louis, however, lacked his predecessor's energy. He was the one French king who spent his whole life at Versailles and he was totally removed from the French people. When Fleury died in 1743, at the age of 90, Louis came under the influence of mistresses, luxury increased and he grew unpopular.

The shortcomings of the absolute and artificial government of France made this the beginning of an age of acid commentary and social protest in France. (It was called "the Age of Reason" because Isaac Newton had made it popular to attempt to explain the behavior of the Universe by reasoning rather than by religious faith and authority.)

Charles Louis de Secondat, Baron Montesquieu (1689–1755), published *The Spirit of Laws* in 1748. He supported Locke's theory of separation of powers and praised the British system of government as opposed to French absolutism.

The great satirist (possibly the greatest who ever lived), François Marie Arouet (1694–1778), who wrote under the name of Voltaire, was beginning to publish his penetrating analyses of human folly, especially in the case of the religious establishment. He, too, praised the British system of government as far superior to that of the French.

In science, in 1736, Pierre Louis Maupertuis (1698–1759) helped to establish the oblate spheroid shape of the Earth by surveying areas in Lapland to determine the curvature of Earth's surface in the far north. One of those who accompanied him was the French mathematician, Alexis Claude Clairaut (1713–1765), who studied, in detail, the shapes of rotating bodies.

NETHERLANDS

In the closing stages of the War of the Austrian Succession, French armies, after their victory at Fontenoy, were again approaching the Netherlands. Again, as in the crisis of Louis XIV's invasion, three quarters of a century earlier, the Dutch abandoned their republican form of government and turned to the House of Orange for a stadtholder. They chose a great-great-grandson of William the Silent, a first cousin twice-removed of William III, and he became stadtholder in 1748 as William IV (1711–1751).

The Dutch physicist, Peter van Musschenbroek (1692–1761), discovered a way of storing electricity in unprecedented concentration in a water-filled metal-lined glass container. This discovery, made in Leyden in 1746, produced what was called a "Leyden jar," which became indispensable to those who studied electrical phenomena at this time.

SPAIN

Philip V died in 1746 and was succeeded by his son, who reigned as Ferdinand VI (1713–1759). Spain took part in the War of the Austrian Succession as an ally of France. By the treaty that ended it, Ferdinand's half-brother Charles (1716–1788) was given the rule of Naples and Sicily, while his son Philip (1720–1765) ruled over the small Italian state of Parma. These dynastic achievements no longer had the importance they had had in earlier centuries, however.

In Spanish South America, Montevideo (in what is now Uruguay) was founded in 1726.

PORTUGAL

Portugal remained at peace at this time under the rule of John V. He established a court in the style of Versailles (as far as Portugal could afford it), and did his best to be a miniature Louis XIV.

PAPACY

After the death of Pope Innocent XIII in 1740, Benedict XIII (1649–1730) succeeded. He was a scholar who left administration in the hands of an unpopular cardinal, Nicolo Coscia, who used his power to enrich himself.

He was succeeded by Clement XII (1652–1740), who continued to labor for the suppression of Jansenism. At this time, too, Freemasonry was becoming prominent. It was a secret organization of no great importance, but it gave its members the pleasure of being part of an "inner circle" and of a kind of bonding ritual that increased the feeling of self-importance. (Such "fraternal organizations" are very common today, especially in the United States.) The very secrecy, however, led people to suspect that the organization was a satanic cult, or a revolutionary brotherhood, or anything else that was evil. Under Clement XII, the Church, suspecting heresy, began an ardent anti-Freemasonry campaign.

Benedict XIV, who succeeded in 1740, was a devotee of learning, encouraged science, put a brake on censorship, and practiced conciliation toward secular rulers. He had much in common with those monarchs of the time who are listed as "benevolent despots."

SARDINIA

Sardinia (previously Savoy) was ruled since 1730 by Charles Emmanuel II (1701–1773). He was a skilled soldier who fought on the side of Austria in the War of the Austrian Succession and achieved some minor gains for Sardinia as a result. Sardinia was primarily a military state, and by some it has been referred to as "the Prussia of Italy." However, it was never as strong as Prussia, or, for that matter, as militarized.

NAPLES

In 1735, Austria ceded Naples and Sicily to Spain in order to allow a Bourbon to sit on the throne, but only on the condition that Naples and Spain never have the same king.

The Neapolitan throne went to a young son of Philip V of Spain, who reigned as Charles IV. He was a "benevolent despot," and gave Naples one of its rare periods of good government. During his reign, excavations began of Pompeii, buried under the ashes of erupting Vesuvius almost 17 centuries earlier, and information concerning the daily life of Romans of that time was obtained. This was the beginning of the modern science of archeology.

SWEDEN

After the hectic reign of Charles XII, many Swedes had had enough of "glory," recognizing it to be a high-sounding name for misery and death. Charles XII was succeeded by his sister, Ulrika Eleanora (1688–1741), who in 1720, after a two-year reign, abdicated in favor of her husband, who reigned as Frederick I (1676–1751).

The king was deprived of power in this period, and Sweden was run by the nobility, who were divided into the parties of the "Caps" and

"Hats." The Caps favored peace, while the Hats still hungered for glory. The Hats had their way during the War of the Austrian Succession, when they managed to maneuver a war of revenge against Russia. Sweden lost quickly and had to give up more territory in Finland.

SWITZERLAND

The perennial conflicts between Protestant and Catholic cantons continued, with Protestant Berne winning out to a degree.

More important, however, were Swiss contributions to mathematics and science. The Swiss family of the Bernoullis were an amazing collection of mathematicians and physicists. The most important of these was Daniel Bernoulli (1700–1782), who studied fluid flow in 1738 and was the first to attempt to explain the behavior of gases by supposing them to consist of tiny, rapidly moving particles.

The Swiss mathematician, Leonhard Euler (1707–1783), was one of the greatest who ever lived, and was certainly the most prolific. Though he went blind in later life, that did not diminish his prolificity. He worked in both Russia and Prussia, stimulating the growth of science in both countries and contributing to such varied areas as calculus, hydrodynamics, and topology.

POLAND

The assault of Charles XII had brought Poland to the brink of utter ruin. Gustavus II had been kicked out by Charles XII, and replaced by Stanislaw Leszczynski, who served as a Swedish puppet. He was kicked out by Peter the Great, and Gustavus II was brought back, to serve as a Russian puppet.

In 1733, when Gustavus II died, Stanislaw Leszczynski wanted to return as king and was supported in this by France. The son of Augustus II, on the other hand, wanted to rule as Augustus III, and he was supported by Russia. The choice for Poland, therefore, was between a puppet of France and a puppet of Russia.

There was a dreary "War of the Polish Succession" that was fought, in desultory fashion and chiefly in Italy, between 1733 and 1735. Gustavus III ended up as king and Stanislaw Leszczynski retired to France, where Louis XV (who had married his daughter in 1725) pensioned him off into a life of ease. (It was the treaty at the end of this war that brought Bourbon monarchs to the throne in Naples and in Parma.)

As king, Augustus III did precisely nothing and allowed Poland to continue to decline.

RUSSIA

After the death of Peter the Great in 1725, there was a succession of rulers who were short-lived, weak, or both. Peter's second wife ruled for two years as Catherine I, until her death in 1727. She was succeeded by Peter's 12-year-old grandson, Peter II (1715–1730), and in 1730, he was succeeded by Anna (1693–1740), who was the daughter of Ivan V, Peter the Great's half-brother and co-Tsar. Anna's great-nephew, an infant, followed as Ivan VI (1740–1764). He was quickly replaced, that same year, by Elizabeth (1709–1762). Elizabeth was the daughter of Peter the Great and Catherine I, and was the first strong ruler in sixteen years.

During this interval, Russia strengthened its control of Poland in the War of the Polish Succession. Russia also warred against Turkey in 1736, regaining Azov on the southern coast, which Peter the Great had been obliged to surrender when he was trapped by the Turks.

The most important event of this period for Russia, however, were the explorations of Vitus Jonasson Bering (1681–1741), a Dane in the Russian service. Peter the Great, in his final year, had sent out Bering to see whether Siberia was connected to North America. It wasn't (at least not since the end of the Ice Age some 10,000 years earlier). In August, 1728, Bering sailed through what is now the "Bering Strait," which separates Siberia and Alaska. The ocean to the south of it is the "Bering Sea."

Bering explored the Siberian and Alaskan coasts and discovered the Aleutian Islands. Russia's claim to Alaska was based on Bering's discoveries.

Under the Tsarina Anna, the Siberian Arctic coast was explored and mapped. The most northerly point of Siberia was rounded by sledge by S. Chelyuskin in 1743, and is called Cape Chelyuskin in his honor.

OTTOMAN EMPIRE

There were in this period minor wars with Russia and Persia, but, on the whole, the Ottoman Empire stagnated.

PERSIA

The Safavid Dynasty came to an end after two and a third centuries, with Abbas III (1731–1736), who died at the age of five. The power was actually in the hands of Nader Kuli, a Turk, who had married the aunt of Abbas III after having begun life as a robber chieftain.

He showed a talent for fighting and, under him, Persia had one last spasm of conquest. He defeated the Afghans and the Turks and took over territories between the Caspian and Black Seas, which the Turks and the Russians had earlier occupied.

In 1736, he made himself actual ruler of Persia and, being a Sunnite, he tried to force the Persians to denounce their Shiite version of Islam. He failed in that, of course.

He invaded northern India in 1738, defeated the army of the weak Moghul Emperor in 1739, and took Delhi, which he then treated almost as badly as Tamerlane had done three and a half centuries earlier. He returned with incredible loot, including the Peacock Throne and the Koh-i-noor Diamond (a Persian expression meaning "mountain of light").

In 1740, he conquered Bokhara and other regions east of the Caspian Sea, and his empire reached its maximum extent. However, his religious bigotry and his growing paranoia caused him to order executions at the slightest suspicion. This, and the strain his continual warfare placed on the economy of the nation, caused seething discontent; in June 1747, he was assassinated by his own soldiers.

Nader Kuli was the last great Asian conqueror of the old type.

INDIA

The invasion of Nader Kuli accelerated the decline of the Moghul Empire. Bengal in the northeast was virtually independent and southern India was a patchwork of states that fought each other. The result was that both Great Britain and France found ways of insinuating their own influence over local rulers.

In 1741, Joseph François, Marquis Dupleix (1697–1763), was made governor-general of the French possessions of the Indian coast, and he infused new energy into the effort of making India French.

When the War of the Austrian Succession broke out, France suggested that India be kept neutral territory, but Great Britain refused. In 1746, Dupleix took Madras from the British, but when the war ended in 1748, Madras was returned.

The rivalry between the two powers continued, and India itself had almost nothing to say about it. By 1750, the French controlled most of southern India through the local rulers, while British power was concentrated in the northeast.

AFGHANISTAN

The Afghans had been driven out of Persia by Nader Kuli, but Nader had also virtually destroyed what was left of the Moghul Empire; when he died, Persia itself collapsed. With both Persia and India out of action, Afghanistan could fill the vacuum. In 1747, Ahmad Shah (1722–1773), one of Nader Kuli's generals, made himself master of Afghanistan, and the nation's modern history may be considered as dating from this time.

CHINA

Under the Emperor Ch'ien Lung (1711–1799), who came to the throne in 1735, China continued strong and prosperous. It controlled Sinkiang, and the realm was at its most extensive in modern times. Its population was rising rapidly now, and it stood at about 225 million, just 10 times that of France.

1750 TO 1775

PRUSSIA

Maria Theresa of Austria did not give up hope of regaining Silesia. She knew that Frederick II of Prussia and his successes in the War of the Austrian Succession had made Europe nervous (as Louis XIV's successes three quarters of a century earlier had done), and she labored to build an alliance against him.

Thus, she came to an agreement with Elizabeth of Russia, who had a particular hatred of Frederick. Not only that, but with the help of her clever prime minister, Wenzel Anton von Kaunitz (1711–1794), she managed to persuade France to join her in alliance. To help put this through, the proud Maria Theresa was forced to write a polite letter to Louis XV's mistress. Since France and Austria had been fighting almost continuously since Charles VIII's invasion of Italy over two and a half centuries before, their sudden alliance astonished all of Europe.

This meant, however, that Great Britain, which had been fighting France even longer than Austria had, had to switch also, and, in the end, it supported Prussia.

Frederick II was perfectly aware of what Austria was doing, and he also knew it would take France and Russia time to gear up for war; thus, it would be best for him not to wait, but to strike at once. He did so, and began what came to be called "The Seven Years War."

On August 19, 1756, Frederick II moved south

and invaded Saxony, taking its capital, Dresden, on September 2. He then moved into Bohemia where he defeated the Austrians and laid siege to Prague, on May 6, 1757.

But then things went wrong. He actually lost a battle to the Austrians at Kolin, east of Prague, and, on June 18, 1757, had to retreat. By that time, the French were sending an army eastward and the Russians were sending one westward while the Austrians were attacking northward. The Swedes, too, had landed on the Baltic coast and showed signs of pushing southward. Frederick, attacked from every point of the compass, was forced to dash with his army first in one direction, then in another, to keep off whichever enemy seemed, at that moment, to be the most dangerous.

On October 18, 1757, he left a small force in Berlin to defend the capital, and moved toward the French army. On November 5, he maneuvered them into battle at Rossbach in western Saxony. The French tried to march around Frederick's left, but Frederick's army was much more maneuverable; and he arranged it so that when the French finished their march, they found his artillery trained upon them and his cavalry charging their right flank. The Battle of Rossbach smashed the French. Those who were not killed, fled in panic, while Frederick's losses were very light.

With as little delay as possible, Frederick II then marched east into Silesia, where the Austrians had been making good progress. On December 6, he met them at Leuthen, just west of the Silesian capital at Breslau. There again, Frederick II, by brilliant maneuvering, managed to bring his forces to bear at Austrian weak points and to destroy the enemy army. The double victory at Rossbach and Leuthen retrieved the situation for Frederick II, and calling him "the Great" seemed more than ever appropriate.

The Russians were still advancing westward, but, as usual, they moved slowly and ponderously. On August 25, 1758, Frederick met them at Zorndorf, near the Oder River in central Prussia. Frederick beat them, but the Russians showed him another one of their specialties, an occasional inability to know when they were

beaten. The Prussians had to flail away until their losses were pretty heavy as well, and they were then too exhausted to pursue the retreating Russians.

By the end of 1758, Frederick II had driven back all his enemies. (The Swedes, observing the situation, returned to Sweden without bothering to wait for a defeat.) However, even victories can be costly. Frederick II had lost 100,000 men altogether, and though he might replace their bodies, he couldn't replace their superb training.

On August 1, 1759, France was defeated at the Battle of Minden, just south of Hanover, by troops that contained a large British contingent. This was the only British contribution to Frederick's cause, aside from a steady supply of money.

By 1760, however, the Allies were again converging on Prussia. This time, the Russians actually managed to get into Berlin on October 9, 1760, and burn it, but they left hurriedly at the news that the dreaded Frederick was approaching with his army.

Even so, Frederick was giving out. Prussia, for all its trained army and for all the military genius of its king, was a small country and it could not indefinitely fight off three different nations, each one considerably larger than itself. (Prussia had a population of 4 million compared to the 56 million for his three enemies.)

During 1761, there seemed no way in which he could much longer stave off defeat with his dwindling, worn out army. Then fate took a hand. On January 5, 1762, Elizabeth of Russia died and was succeeded by her nephew, Peter III (1728–1762). Peter III was mentally erratic and was a wild admirer of Frederick. He not only abandoned Russia's allies, but he offered to rejoin the war on Frederick's side.

After that, there was nothing to do but to make peace. The Treaty of Hubertusberg in Saxony left things as they had been. Prussia kept Silesia, and Austria was finally reconciled to that. Austria never made any further attempt to get it back.

But Frederick II had had enough. He fought no more wars. In 1772, he gained important territory through the First Partition of Poland, but did so without war.

AUSTRIA

During this period, Austria's history was bound up with Prussia. Austria didn't exactly win the Seven Years' War, but neither did it lose. Maria Theresa had lost Silesia in the first few months of her reign, but since then she had lost nothing further. Maria Theresa was as successful, in her way, as Frederick II had been in his. She was, in fact, the most competent "Emperor" of the Holy Roman Empire since Charles V, over two centuries earlier. Her husband, Francis, who was Emperor in name only, died in 1765, and Maria Theresa's son become Emperor as Joseph II (1741–1790)—in name only, at least while Maria Theresa lived.

In 1772, Austria gained territory in the First Partition of Poland, and did so without war.

Austria, at this time, began to burst into melody on a grand scale. The operatic composer, Christoph Willibald Gluck (1714–1787), working in Vienna, revolutionized opera by insisting on the drama taking an equal role with the music. His best-known "reform opera," as it was called, was *Orpheus and Eurydice*, produced in 1762. Franz Joseph Haydn (1732–1809) and an amazing child prodigy, Wolfgang Amadeus Mozart (1756–1791), were beginning their musical careers in Vienna at this time, too.

Elsewhere in Germany, there was the start of a literary golden age with Gotthold Ephraim Lessing (1729–1781). He broke with the French dramatic tradition and moved toward the less orderly, but more powerful, Shakespearian mode. He is best known for his tragedy, *Emilia Galotti*, published in 1772 and *Minna von Barnhelm* in 1763. His dramatic poem, *Nathan the Wise*, in 1779, was a plea for religious tolerance.

This dramatic technique was carried on by Johann Wolfgang von Goethe (1749–1832), then at the beginning of his career, with the tragedy, *Goetz von Berlichingen*, published in 1773.

The German scientist, Kaspar Friedrich Wolff (1734–1794), pointed out in 1755 that eggs or sperm did not contain miniature organisms (as most had thought) but were made up of undifferentiated material that developed and specialized as it grew. He is considered the father of modern embryology for that reason.

FRANCE

Although France lost the Seven Years' War, she lost it to a greater extent overseas than in Europe. In fact, her territory expanded in Europe as she annexed the province of Lorraine in 1766, and bought the island of Corsica from Genoa in 1768. France, in this way, finally attained her modern European boundaries.

Louis XV died on May 10, 1774, after a reign of 59 years. He and his great-grandfather, Louis XIV, had ruled over France for 131 years together —a record in history for two successive reigns. Louis XV's son had died in 1765 and his grandson succeeded him as Louis XVI (1754–1793).

The advocates of political and social reform wrote busily in this period, always under the threat of political repression, but somehow surviving under Louis XV, whose absolutism was tempered by indolence and by a certain easygoing attitude.

Voltaire was at the height of his fame, writing a history of the reign of Louis XIV, which was published in 1751, later publishing his greatest satire, *Candide* in 1759, and always serving as a one-man crusader for justice. For a while, he spent time with Frederick II of Prussia, but there was a disagreement on the question of how great a poet Frederick should be considered, and Voltaire thought it might be safer to leave.

The French philosopher, Jean Jacques Rousseau (1712–1778), was an odd individual, paranoid enough to quarrel with everyone, particularly with those who tried to help him. Nevertheless, he wrote very highly regarded books. In *The Social Contract*, published in 1762, he maintained that government must reflect the will of the people, and in *Emile*, published the same year, he propounded his theories of education. He was probably the most influential of all the French social critics.

On a smaller scale, the playwright, Pierre Augustin Caron de Beaumarchais (1732–1799), wrote *The Barber of Seville*, first performed in 1775. It was very popular, the more so, perhaps, because it had a distinct anti-aristocratic flavor, which became even more pronounced in Beaumarchais' next play, *The Marriage of Figaro*, first performed in 1784.

Denis Diderot (1713–1784) was a pamphleteer who conceived the notion of preparing a huge encyclopedia that would give proper weight to the new age of science and technology. The first volume appeared in 1751 and the twenty-eighth and last volume in 1772. Diderot worked with superhuman energy under the greatest difficulties. He was definitely atheistic and it showed. His collaborators, including the French mathematician, Jean Le Rond D'Alembert (1717–1783), fell away for fear of persecution. The work was banned in 1759, but Diderot continued to work clandestinely and virtually alone. It was the first of the great modern encyclopedias and did much to shatter medieval ways of thought.

A more specialized encyclopedia was prepared by George Louis Leclerc, Count de Buffon (1707–1788), who, beginning in 1749, and continuing to publish volume after volume for the rest of his life, turned out a 44-volume work. In it, he was the first to suggest that the Earth might be much older than the Bible indicated and that it was formed by natural processes rather than by divine action. Naturally, he had some difficulty with the authorities as a result.

Other French scientists of the period included Rene Antoine Ferchault de Reaumur (1683–1757), who, in 1752, showed that digestion was a chemical, and not a mechanical process; and the mathematician, Joseph Louis Lagrange (1736–1813), who began to publish important work on the calculus of variations in 1755.

Among the French artists of the period was the painter, Jean Baptiste Greuze (1725–1805), and the sculptor Jean Antoine Houdon (1741–1828), well-known for his busts of the great figures of his time—from Voltaire to Benjamin Franklin.

GREAT BRITAIN

In 1752, Great Britain finally adopted the Gregorian calendar, which had been in existence for 170 years, and which had been shunned until now only because it had been of Papal origin. This change also took place in the British colonies in North America. By now, 11 days had to be dropped from the calendar, and to many unsophisticated people it seemed that 11 days were being cut off their life. There were riots in which people shouted "Give us back our 11 days." On the other hand, landlords charged for a full quarter, so the people *were*, in a way, cheated.

Great Britain's participation in the Seven Year's War, as far as Europe itself was concerned, was largely financial since she subsidized Frederick the Great and let him endure the casualties. However, Britain also fought France both in North America and in India, and it was the first war in which particular combatants had fought simultaneously on three different continents. Therefore, it has been considered the first "world war" by some people.

George II died on October 25, 1760, and was succeeded by his grandson, who reigned as George III (1738–1820).

George III, unlike the first two Georges, was thoroughly English and led an exemplary private life. He was very stubborn, however, and lacked tact. Furthermore, his mother, a German princess, disapproved of the manner in which George I and George II had left the government in the hands of their ministers, and she constantly urged her son to "be a king"—that is, to be absolute.

However, George III knew better. There could be no absolutism in Great Britain after what had happened to Charles I and James II in the previous century. However, he did try to pack Parliament with members favorable to himself, so that he could at least have a compliant legislature. His moves in this direction centered about John Wilkes (1725–1797), who had made critical remarks about the King, and whom George III insisted on having expelled from Parliament in 1764. Wilkes was repeatedly reelected and repeatedly expelled. Although George III won out in the short term, it created so much anger among the population that, in the end, the freedom of election, as well as freedom of speech and of the press, was established.

But George III had a problem that was even

harsher and more intractable than that of John Wilkes. The problem lay with the colonies, whose anger was rising with each year that passed.

Yet despite problems at home and on the North American seaboard, the British reach overseas continued to grow stronger. At this time, in fact, the Pacific Ocean, the largest geographical unit on Earth short of the planet itself, was thoroughly explored by a British navigator.

He was James Cook (1728–1779), usually known as "Captain Cook," who was the most famous navigator since Magellan, two and a half centuries earlier. His Pacific explorations were intended for geographical and scientific purposes only, and he was the first of the really scientific navigators.

In 1765, he made the first of his three voyages across the Pacific. He discovered the Admiralty Islands and the Society Islands (named for his sponsors, the British Admiralty and the Royal Society). He also circumnavigated New Zealand, explored its shores, and landed in Australia. He was the first to gain a notion of the size and position of this last of the inhabited continents to be opened to Europeans, and to observe its load of plants and animals that were like none elsewhere on Earth.

Between 1772 and 1775, in his second voyage, Cook took his ship through southern waters to the Antarctic Circle. (The men on board his ship were the first known human beings to reach and cross the Antarctic Circle.) In doing so, Cook proved the nonexistence of any vast southern continent, other than Australia, in the South Temperate Zone.

As a result of these voyages, the oceans of the Earth, except the polar regions, had been entirely opened.

Great Britain was active culturally.* Smollett was still writing copiously in this period, translating the works of Cervantes and Voltaire, and

publishing *The Adventures of Peregrine Pickle* in 1751 and *The Expedition of Humphrey Clinker* in 1771, for instance.

Samuel Johnson (1709–1784) prepared the first great English dictionary in 1755. He also published a romance, *Rasselas, Prince of Abyssinia*, in 1759. His greatest fame, though, came through the biography written of him by his friend, James Boswell (1740–1795).

Lawrence Sterne (1713–1768) wrote a large, rambling, and lovable novel, *The Life and Opinions of Tristram Shandy*, published between 1761 and 1767. Oliver Goldsmith wrote a novel, *The Vicar of Wakefield*, in 1766, and a play, *She Stoops to Conquer*, which was produced in 1773. That play was the first after Shakespeare to retain its popularity to this day.

Horace Walpole (1717–1797), a son of Robert Walpole, who served as British Prime Minister under the first two Georges, published *The Castle of Otranto* in 1764, establishing the "gothic novel," which has retained its popularity to this day.

Philip Dormer Stanhope, Fourth Earl of Chesterfield (1694–1773), is known for his *Letters to his Son*, published in 1774, beautifully written, worldly wise, and making much sense, albeit short on ideals. It was a sort of guide to how to get ahead in the world without actually being a villain.

A much graver work was that of the British jurist, William Blackstone (1723–1780), who made legal history with his *Commentaries on the Laws of England*, published between 1765 and 1767. He was the first to lecture on English law at Oxford.

The great English portraitists of the period were Thomas Gainsborough (1727–1788), whose best-known painting is *The Blue Boy*, which was done about 1770. Joshua Reynolds (1723–1792) was also coming into prominence at this time, as was George Romney (1734–1792) and the German-born John Zoffany (1733–1810).

Great Britain was leading the world, now, in science and technology. Joseph Black (1728–1769) studied carbon dioxide in detail in 1754 and showed it to be a constituent of the atmosphere. He also clarified the notion of "latent heat" in

---

* Culture is universal and all nations have their writers, artists, and thinkers. However the culture of the English language is that of the writer of this book and, probably, of most of its readers. Therefore, it is that which is best known to us, and most easily discussed.

1760, a concept important in the improvement of the steam engine. Henry Cavendish (1731–1810) isolated and studied hydrogen in 1766, while Joseph Priestley (1733–1804) discovered and studied oxygen in 1774 and Daniel Rutherford (1749–1819) identified nitrogen in 1772.

In medicine, James Lind (1716–1794) discovered that adding citrus fruits to the diet prevented scurvy and, in 1758, began a campaign to get the British navy to take advantage of this simple and incredibly useful fact. It took only 40 years for the brass hats of the Navy to see the point.

As far as the everyday world was concerned, however, by far the greatest event of this period was the work of the engineer, James Watt (1736–1819). In 1764, he was asked to repair a Newcomen steam engine and, in doing so, he began to think of ways of improving its efficiency. He saw that most of the energy was wasted, heating and reheating the water to form steam. It occurred to him to have *two* chambers, one always hot and one always cold. By 1769, he had a practical steam engine, one that was much more efficient than anything that had preceded it. At that moment we might consider the Industrial Revolution to have begun, and the world began to change enormously.

Watt's steam engine was a source of power, but something had to be developed that was worth powering. The British inventor, Richard Arkwright (1732–1792), also in 1769, patented a device that would spin thread by mechanically reproducing the motions ordinarily made by the human hand. Another inventor, James Hargreaves (d. 1778), patented the "spinning jenny" in 1770, a device which enabled spinning to be conducted on multiple wheels, producing more thread with far less labor. This was the beginning of the mechanization of the textile industry (and, eventually, of almost everything else).

COLONIAL NORTH AMERICA

In 1750, the French were beginning to establish bases in the Ohio Territory, the region between the Ohio River and the Great Lakes. This disturbed the British colonists, who could see themselves pinned against the ocean by the French organization of the interior.

New France and Louisiana were still underpopulated. There were only 80,000 French in the entire vast area, but they were all under a single rule, whereas the population of 2 million or so under British colonial rule was divided among 13 colonies (15, if Nova Scotia and Newfoundland are counted).

Some felt that a united front against the French was necessary and among these were Benjamin Franklin, who was now more famous than ever. In 1752, he flew a kite into the clouds of a gathering thunderstorm and showed that the lightning carried electricity identical in nature to that formed in the laboratory. By 1753, he had devised grounded lightning rods to be placed on top of buildings. These bled off the electric charge and prevented its buildup into a devastating lightning stroke.

For the first time in history, a natural catastrophe, the lightning bolt (always peculiarly associated in the popular imagination with divine artillery) was tamed by the application of scientific principles. Until then, prayer was the only remedy, and when lightning rods finally began to go up on churches, it was a clear indication that the secular attitude was beginning to win out over the religious—in material matters at least.

When the colony of New York sent out an invitation for delegates from other colonies to meet in Albany to discuss united action against the French, Franklin was there. The "Albany Congress" met on June 19, 1754, and Franklin made a proposal.

The colonies as a whole were to be governed by a governor-general appointed and paid by the King, and he was to rule with the aid of a "grand council," consisting of delegates from each colony. The proposal was accepted and signed on July 4, 1754, but it never came to fruition. The colonies felt it gave too much power to the King, and the British government felt it gave too much power to the colonial delegates. Had the suggestion been accepted, it might have changed the history of the world—but it wasn't.

Meanwhile the French had advanced into

what is now western Pennsylvania and had established Fort Duquesne (named for the French governor-general of New France) at the junction of the Allegheny and Monongahela Rivers. Virginia had claims to the territory, and its governor, Robert Dinwiddie (1693–1770), sent out a small force under a young surveyor, George Washington (1732–1799), to warn off the French.

On May 28, 1754, Washington encountered a group of Frenchmen and, with the rashness of youth (he was only 21), he attacked them and killed 10, taking the rest prisoner. This was the first battle of "The French and Indian War," which merged soon enough with the Seven Years War that began two years later. Washington's forces were eventually defeated and the French remained at Fort Duquesne.

To take care of matters, the British government sent two regiments to Virginia under General Edward Braddock (1695–1755). They arrived on April 14, 1755, and then marched toward Fort Duquesne. There, at the Battle of the Monongahela on July 9, 1755, they were ambushed by a smaller number of French and Indians.

Braddock tried to fight European fashion with the soldiers lined up neatly and volleying on command. The French and Indians fought guerrilla fashion from behind trees, and they cut down the British easily. George Washington and his Virginia contingent got behind trees themselves and covered the retreat, or none of the British would have gotten out alive. Braddock died of his wounds.

With the beginning of the Seven Years War in 1756, the British and French got down to the North American war in earnest. The French sent out Louis Joseph de Montcalm (1712–1759), a capable general, who arrived in New France on July 23, 1756. For a year, the French had it all their own way.

In Great Britain, however, the energetic William Pitt (1708–1778) managed to be in charge of the government by dint of great and inspiring oratory, though George II disliked him intensely. Pitt determined to leave Europe to Frederick the Great and to concentrate Britain's major effort in North America. He sent new generals and new men to North America. One young general was James Wolfe (1727–1759).

Wolfe was second in command of an expedition that was sent against the important French base at Louisberg (which the colonials had taken in King George's War, but which had been given back), and it fell on July 27, 1758. The British also took Fort Frontenac at the eastern end of Lake Ontario on August 27, and Fort Duquesne (where the war had started) on November 24. The British built a new fort at what had been Fort Duquesne's site. They named it Fort Pitt for the minister, and that was the beginning of Pittsburgh.

Pitt's campaign plans for 1759 included a three-pronged attack that was to culminate in the taking of Quebec. First, Fort Niagara was to be taken at the western end of Lake Ontario. That was carried through on July 25, 1759. Then Fort Ticonderoga, near the southern end of Lake Champlain, was to be taken, and that was done on July 26. Meanwhile, as the New York colony was being made secure, James Wolfe, with 9000 British soldiers and some colonials, moved up the St. Lawrence River and, on June 26, 1759, had taken up a position four miles downriver from Quebec.

Montcalm had 14,000 men and Quebec stood on a height that made it apparently impregnable to the British down at the foot of the steep hill. For two months there was a stalemate and it seemed that the British would have to retreat rather than face a Canadian winter; however, on September 12, they found a footpath that led up to the height. That night, Wolfe sent his men clambering up the path and, on the morning of September 13, they were lined up in front of the city.

Montcalm, surprised, attacked them at once, but the British won the battle, and in the course of it both Montcalm and Wolfe were killed. The British took Quebec on September 18, 1759, after it had been French for a century and a half.

By the Treaty of Paris, signed on February 10, 1763, France gave up all but a few island scraps of its North American dominions. All of Canada, and all of Louisiana east of the Mississippi River was ceded to Great Britain. Spain ceded Florida to Great Britain but, for itself, obtained all of Louisiana west of the Mississippi.

Meanwhile, the North American interior was beginning to be penetrated. The British colonies, confined to the eastern seaboard for a century and a half, were venturing west of the Allegheny Mountains. Leading the way was Daniel Boone (1734–1820), who, as early as 1767, had passed through the Cumberland Gap (named for "Butcher" Cumberland of the Battle of Culloden) into what is now Kentucky. And, even as the French were forced to give up control of Louisiana, a settlement that eventually became St. Louis was founded on the mid-Mississippi River in 1763.

The British colonists were thus freed of the French menace and might have felt grateful to Great Britain for this, but their dominant feeling was that, with France gone, they no longer needed Great Britain and should be left to themselves.

The British, on the other hand, had greatly increased the national debt as a result of the expenses of war and the subsidization of Frederick the Great. Ways of decreasing the debt had to be considered. Since much of the outlay had been put into the war in North America, it was felt that the British colonies there, having benefitted greatly by the British victory, should help pay for it in the form of tariffs on imported goods and in direct taxes, too.

The colonials, however, didn't like taxes any more than anyone else did, and they strongly objected to the taxes being placed on them by a Parliament in which they had no representation and could not argue their own case. Men arose, like James Otis of Massachusetts (1725–1783) and Patrick Henry of Virginia (1736–1799), to denounce British actions on taxes as tyrannical and to talk about the rights of Englishmen.

On March 22, 1765, the British passed a "Stamp Act" whereby colonials were to pay for special stamps to be placed on legal papers, newspapers, licenses, and a variety of other subjects. The stamps, of course, would cost money that would go into the British treasury. There was a storm of anger in the colonies and there followed boycotts of British goods that were ef-

fective enough to bring distress to British business.

Clearly, the Stamp Act would not work, and the British repealed it on March 18, 1766. The British then tried other ways of taxing the colonies, doing so very lightly—not so much for revenue at the moment, as to maintain the principle that they *could* tax the colonies if they wished. That was the very principle the colonies wanted to fight.

Matters finally focused themselves on a tea tax, of which the British East India Company had a huge oversupply it wished to get rid of. The tax was so low as to be trivial, but the colonials, nevertheless, promptly boycotted tea. When ships carrying tea, intended for sale with tax added, arrived in Boston harbor, a party of Massachusetts colonists, led by Samuel Adams (1722–1803), who was already agitating for outright independence, disguised themselves as Indians, boarded the ship on December 16, 1773, and dumped the tea into Boston harbor. This was the "Boston Tea Party."

George III was outraged and Boston was placed under military occupation. This frightened the colonies. It frightened even many who disapproved of the militant radicalism of Massachusetts. Twelve of the colonies got together in a "Continental Congress" in Philadelphia on September 4, 1774, and sent petitions for a redress of grievances to Great Britain, but to no effect, George III was stubborn and would not yield, so that matters moved toward an explosion.

The American colonies, by the way, were beginning to have a richer cultural life. The first important colonial painter, Benjamin West of Pennsylvania (1738–1830), went to Great Britain in 1763, became a close friend of Joshua Reynolds, and eventually succeeded him as president of the Royal Academy.

NETHERLANDS

During this period, the Netherlands was under the rule of William V, who had become stadtholder in 1751 at the age of three. Even when grown, he was a weak ruler, but at least the

Netherlands managed to stay neutral in the Seven Years War.

SWEDEN

Sweden had been a limited monarchy since the death of Charles XII over half a century before. In 1771, however, the son of Adolphus Frederick became king and ruled as Gustavus III (1746–1792). In 1772, he forced a change, making himself absolute. However, he tried to reign as a "benevolent despot," abolishing torture, declaring freedom of religion and of the press, and so on.

The outstanding Swedish scientist of the period was Karl Wilhelm Scheele (1742–1786), who isolated a number of chemical substances including lactic acid, uric acid, hydrogen sulfide, hydrogen cyanide, and several new chemical elements. He discovered oxygen before Priestley did, but publication of the discovery was delayed by the negligence of the publisher and Scheele lost the credit.

The Swedish philosopher, Emmanuel Swedenborg (1688–1772), turned to mystical works on Biblical interpretation late in his life. Although he remained a Lutheran, his teaching led to the formation of the "New Church," often called the "Swedenborgians."

DENMARK

In this period, Denmark was ruled by the mentally unstable Christian VII (1749–1808), who became king in 1766. In 1770, his physician, Johann Friedrich, Count Struensee (1737–1772), gained sufficient influence to become his all-powerful minister. He tried to be a "benevolent despot's-minister," introducing freedom of the press, and improving the condition of the poor.

However, he also became the Queen's lover, and the aristocrats, who wanted to keep their privilege and their power, used this fact to mount a successful conspiracy against him. Christian VII had Struensee arrested, tortured, and finally executed on April 28, 1772.

SPAIN

Ferdinand VI of Spain died on August 10, 1759. He had no children and his nearest heir was his half-brother, Charles IV of Naples. Spain, however, was preferable to Naples from the standpoint of royal prestige, so Charles IV abdicated as King of Naples, leaving that to a younger son, and became Charles III of Spain.

Charles continued playing the part of "benevolent despot" in Spain as he had in Naples. He established a stronger absolutism and, in so doing, found it necessary to reduce the role of the Church, an international institution not amenable to absolute control. He even expelled the Jesuits. He also did his best to stimulate commerce.

In foreign affairs, however, he let family interests tie him to France, with whom he was allied in the Seven Years War against England. He ended up losing Florida to England, but gaining the western half of Louisiana from France.

PORTUGAL

On July 31, 1750, John V of Portugal died, and was succeeded by his son, who reigned as Joseph I (1714–1777). Joseph I was totally uninterested in the business of government. He found in Sebastian de Carvalho (1699–1782), known to history as Marquis de Pombal, someone who was willing to take over the task, and to do so effectively through Joseph's entire reign.

Pombal was a "benevolent despot's minister," like Struensee of Denmark, but much more successful. Pombal was dictatorial and hard, but he did his best to encourage trade and industry and to improve Portugal's economic situation.

On November 1, 1755, however, a natural disaster intervened. An earthquake, perhaps the most violent of modern times, struck Lisbon, Portugal's capital, demolishing every house in the lower part of the city. A tsunami (or "tidal wave") swept in from the ocean. Two more earthquake shocks followed and fires broke out. Sixty thousand people were killed and the city was left a scene of devastation. The shock was felt over an area of one and a half million square miles, doing substantial damage in Morocco, as well as in Portugal.

Pombal, with remarkable energy, organized relief—obtaining supplies, building shelters and tents, setting up hospitals, and ordering in troops to help. He then went on to supervise the rebuilding of the city, creating a more beautiful Lisbon in the place of the old.

Pombal's fist grew even tighter and heavier thereafter. He destroyed aristocratic families who were conspiring, or merely suspected of conspiring, against the king, and he drove out the Jesuits.

PAPACY

Clement XIII (1693–1769) became Pope in 1758, and had to withstand the storm against the Jesuits from those Catholic countries governed by the Bourbons: France, Spain, and Naples. By 1768, all three nations had expelled the Jesuits, and Portugal had done so, too. The trouble was that the Jesuits were incompatible with royal absolutism, since they were an international agency who were primarily faithful to the Pope.

There was remorseless pressure on Clement XIII to dissolve the Jesuit order altogether. He resisted, but his successor, Clement XIV (1705–1774), was compelled to do it out of fear that the national churches would become so powerful that they would break away from Rome altogether if he did not conciliate them—as the English Church had broken away two and a third centuries earlier. Therefore, the Jesuit order was abolished (temporarily, anyway) on July 21, 1773.

NAPLES

Ferdinand I (1751–1825), the eight-year-old son of Charles IV, became King of Naples in 1759, when his father became King of Spain. While he was ruled by the regency, his father's liberal reforms were continued. In 1767, however, Ferdinand I came of age and, the next year, he married a conservative wife and fell under her influence. Naples returned to despotic misrule.

TUSCANY

Tuscany, of which Florence was the capital, was no longer under the rule of the Medici, the house having become extinct in 1737, three centuries after its rise to prominence under Cosimo. Thereafter, Francis of Lorraine, the husband of Maria Theresa, was Grand Duke of Tuscany. After he became Emperor Francis II in 1745, he turned over the Grand Duchy to his son, who reigned as Leopold I (1747–1792).

Leopold was another of the "benevolent despots" and he reformed Tuscany. He encouraged trade and industry and abolished serfdom, so that Tuscany was better off than at any time since Lorenzo the Magnificent, three centuries earlier.

Added to the French writers of social criticism was the Italian writer Cesare Bonesana Beccaria (1738–1794), who published *Crimes and Punishment* in 1764 in which, for the first time, punishment was considered rationally as a way of reducing crime and rehabilitating criminals, instead of having it exemplify the wrath of God and the revenge-lust of man.

The outstanding Italian scientist of the period was Lazzaro Spallanzani (1729–1794), who, in 1768, showed that even microorganisms did not arise through spontaneous generation. Broths in which microorganisms appeared to arise spontaneously remained sterile if they were boiled until all microorganisms already there were killed, and if it were then sealed so that no microorganisms from without were allowed to enter.

The Italian playwright, Carlo Goldoni (1707–1793), introduced comedy after the style of Moliere into Italy, and wrote about 150 plays.

POLAND

Poland was going steadily downhill under Augustus III. He died in 1763, and Russia engineered the election of Stanislaw II Poniatowski (1732–1798). Stanislaw attempted to institute reforms, but neither the Polish aristocracy nor the Russians would allow that.

The Russians wanted the Poles to grant religious freedom to the Orthodox portion of the population, while the Prussians wanted it for the

Protestants. Pressure in this direction gave rise to a rebellion by the Polish Catholics, and this created such turbulence that Frederick II of Prussia feared it might produce a general war in eastern Europe, and he wanted no further wars. Therefore, he defused tensions by engineering an agreement between Prussia, Austria, and Russia, whereby each took over a border district of Poland. In this way, each profited and Poland would be weakened and less likely to bring about a war.

This agreement, reached on August 5, 1772, was "The First Partition of Poland." Prussia obtained West Prussia, which connected the Brandenburg heartland with East Prussia and made the kingdom more compact. Austria took Galicia in the Polish southwest and Russia took a curved strip of northeastern Poland.

Austria had the lion's share, obtaining 2,700,000 people, largely Catholic, which more than made up for the loss of Protestant Silesia a third of a century earlier. Maria Theresa, remembering Poland's rescue of Vienna, a century earlier, had a crisis of conscience; however, as Frederick II remarked cynically, she took her share even while she was weeping.

As for Poland, it lost one third of its territory and half its population.

RUSSIA

Peter III, whose accession to the throne in 1762 saved Frederick II of Prussia from defeat, was a total incompetent. He was married to a German wife, Sophia Augusta (1724–1796), who was as intelligent as he was stupid, and as hard-working as he was lazy. On her marriage, in 1745, it had been necessary for her to be converted to the Russian Orthodox faith, which she did with equanimity, taking the new name of Catherine.

Being married to Peter was no suitable life for her, especially since she was quite certain Peter intended to get rid of her. Catherine struck first, and on July 9, 1762, she led a palace revolt that overthrew Peter and made her ruler of Russia as Tsarina Catherine II (eventually to be called "Catherine the Great"—the last ruler to be generally known by such a title).

On July 17, 1762, Peter was killed, possibly with Catherine's knowledge, and in September she was crowned, and proceeded to rule as a "benevolent despot," particularly in the early part of her reign. In this, she was hampered by the conservative Russian nobility.

She interfered steadily in Polish politics, placing Russian weight against any reform that might strengthen the Polish state.

The Ottoman Empire, meanwhile, had watched for two centuries as Russia had grown from a weak grand duchy to a giant state stretching across Europe and Asia. They did not want it to grow stronger still, and so they viewed with concern Russia's increasing interference in Poland.

In October 1788, the Ottoman Empire, therefore, declared war on Russia. It was, however, Russia which seized the initiative, invading the Caucasus and the Balkans, and supporting rebellions in Greece and Egypt against the Ottoman overlords.

Catherine II had in her service Alexander Vasilievich Suvorov (1729–1800), the greatest general in Russian history. He displayed his abilities in 1773 by defeating the Turks in Bulgaria in spectacular fashion.

Despite the victories in the field, however, things turned out badly for Russia at home. In 1773, a Cossack named Yemelyan Ivanovich Pugachov (1726–1775), who had fought in the Seven Years War, in Poland, and against the Turks, now said he was Peter III, Catherine II's dead husband, and claimed he had escaped from imprisonment. His rebellion was fueled by popular discontent and, for a year, he rampaged over eastern Russia as Stenka Razin had done a century earlier. Finally, it took Suvorov himself to stamp out the rebellion. By that time, Russia was eager for peace with the Turks and ready to give generous terms.

The peace treaty was signed at Kuchuk Kainarji in Bulgaria, on July 16, 1774. Russia gained very little in the way of territory, but the war had exposed the weakness of the Turks. There was now no question but that Russia was the stronger power and that there would be further trials of strength.

Meanwhile, Austria's own concerns over growing Russian strength might have led to another war, but Frederick II, a fanatic for peace now, headed that off by arranging the First Partition of Poland.

Western thought was penetrating Russia to the point where the first western-style scientist appeared in that land. He was Mikhail Vasilievich Lomonosov (1711–1765). He was the first to note the atmosphere of Venus. He observed the freezing of mercury metal, suspected matter to consist of atoms, and had modern ideas about combustion. He also made the first good map of Russia, wrote on Russian grammar and reformed it, and, with Euler, helped found the University of Moscow.

OTTOMAN EMPIRE

The war with Russia from 1768 to 1774 showed Ottoman weakness, which the governments under Osman III (1699–1757), who became Sultan in 1754, and Mustapha III (1717–1774), who succeeded him in 1757, were unable to correct.

PERSIA

The period of anarchy that followed the death of Nader Kuli came to an end when Karim Khan (1705–1779), who had been one of Nader Kuli's generals, was able to establish his rule over most of Persia in 1750, and to give it a quarter century of peace and relative prosperity. He allowed the British to establish a factory at Bushire on the shore of the Persian Gulf in 1763.

AFGHANISTAN

Afghani forces, under Ahmad Shah, invaded northern India nine times, taking Lahore in 1752 and Delhi in 1761. By 1773, when Ahmad Shah died, his empire included not only Afghanistan but eastern Persia and northwestern India as well.

INDIA

By 1750, France was in virtual control of India's southern coasts, but in 1751 Robert Clive (1725–1774) of the British East India Comany showed remarkable enterprise in capturing the capital of a French-backed Indian ruler in the south and then, with a few hundred men, withstanding a siege by thousands.

This was enough to raise British prestige and lower that of France, and France recalled its governor-general, Dupleix, in 1754, blaming him for the failure. However, there was no other Frenchman in India with anything like his ability and, in 1756, when the Seven Years War began in Europe, Dupleix' absence was fatal to French plans.

The ruler of the Bengali region in the northeast was independent, thanks to the utter ruin of the Moghul Empire by the invasions of Persians and Afghani. On June 20, 1756, the ruler of Bengal, with French encouragement, took Calcutta, which was under British control. Those British who were trapped in the city, 146 of them according to the later story, were imprisoned in a small subterranean dungeon without ventilation in the summer heat and humidity of India. This was the so-called "Black Hole of Calcutta" and, by morning, 123 of them were dead. This gave Great Britain all it needed for the strongest reprisals.

On January 2, 1757, the British recaptured Calcutta and, on March 23, 1757, Clive captured the French base at Chandernagore just across the river from Calcutta. This meant that the British could now pursue the forces of the Bengali ruler inland without fear of being cut off by the French.

Clive did just that. He pursued the Indian forces and met them at Plassey, about a hundred miles north of Calcutta. The Indian army was 50,000 in number, with 53 guns manned by Frenchmen. Clive had at his disposal 1100 Europeans, 2100 Indians, and 10 guns. A sudden rainstorm wet the powder of the French guns, while Clive kept his guns covered. Beside that, Clive had already bought off part of the Indian army. Clive's cannonade, after the rainstorm, easily started an Indian retreat—one that turned into panic.

The Battle of Plassey put all of Bengal under British control.

The British went on to take the chief French base at Pondichery on January 15, 1761. By the

Treaty of Paris, Pondichery was returned to the French, but their taste for warfare in India was forever gone, and the British had it all their own way thereafter.

The Moghul Emperor, Shah Alam II (1728–1806), who had gained his position in 1759, had no real power over Bengal, but the British used him to gain the appearance of legality. They persuaded him to give the British East India Company full control over the collection of taxes in Bengal. The Company was then virtually a sovereign state of its own and its officers enriched themselves outrageously at the expense of the Indians, as the Indian rulers themselves had done previously.

When Clive finally returned to Great Britain, he was tried before Parliament for corruption. When he thought of what he could have done, however, he said, "I stand astonished at my own moderation." He was exonerated in 1773, but committed suicide on November 22, 1774. (He was of a melancholy disposition, and had tried to kill himself before when he was a young man.)

BURMA

The British–French rivalry was not confined to India alone. East of northern India was Burma which, in the 1750s, was being united by a warrior named Alaungpaya (1714–1760), who had begun life as a minor village functionary. In his conquering career, he was supported by the British East India Company and opposed by the French. His victory was, therefore, a British victory. He founded Rangoon in 1755.

CHINA

Manchu China, still ruled by Ch'un Lung, was still at the height of its strength.

1775 to 1800

FRANCE

Louis XVI and his queen, Marie Antoinette (1755–1793), who had married in 1770, were marked for disaster. Louis XVI was a gentle ruler of exemplary morals, but he was not very intelligent and had no will. Marie Antoinette had no viciousness about her, and was pretty and could easily have made herself popular, but she was idle, thoughtless, and wasteful. She was the daughter of Maria Theresa, the Austrian queen (who constantly and uselessly warned her to be more circumspect in her behavior, lest she come to a bad end), and the French had, by now, a long history of hating Austrians.

Louis XVI tried, insofar as it lay within him, to be a "benevolent despot," and he chose some ministers who tried to reform the finances of the nation, but it was a useless task, for the society resisted reform. The aristocracy and the clergy weren't taxed, and many of them drew large pensions and lived luxurious and parasitic lives. To reform the nation, those parasites would have had to economize, and to expect them to do so was hopeless. Despite the taxes wrung out of those least able to pay, then, the French government was always teetering at the edge of bankruptcy.

Then, to make matters worse, France could not help hankering after revenge against Great Britain for demolishing France's overseas Empire in North America and India. When the British colonies in North America rebelled against Great Britain, France chose to support the colonies, and went to war against Great Britain.

This was a double mistake. By supporting the colonies, they taught many Frenchmen that it could be considered virtuous to rebel against a government. Second, France spent money it didn't have so that, at the end of the American War of Independence, France was worse off than ever.

Charles Alexandre de Calonne (1734–1802), who became finance minister after that war, could only keep the government afloat by continuing to borrow and by building up a higher and higher deficit.

Meanwhile, in 1785, Marie Antoinette got entangled in a scandal involving a very expensive necklace, one she had refused as too expensive considering the governmental deficit. However, some swindlers, using a Marie Antoinette look-alike, fooled Louis Rene Edmond de Rohan (1734–1803) into buying the necklace on the Queen's behalf and then absconded with it themselves. When the Queen was approached for the money, she denied any knowledge of the affair and insisted that Rohan and others be put on trial.

Marie Antoinette seems to have been completely innocent, but the matter was so badly handled and her reputation as a careless wastrel was so great that she ended up with the public ready to believe anything bad about her—that she had really tried to get her hands on the necklace and defraud the jewelers and Rohan. From then on, she was personally despised by increasing numbers of the French people who would refer to her only as "the Austrian woman" or as "Madame Deficit."

By 1787, matters were desperate and, on February 22, 1787, an "assembly of notables" was called to deal with the problem; however, the notables were precisely those who didn't and wouldn't pay taxes, and who insisted on their pensions, so they did nothing.

Finally, desperation grew to the pitch where the only thing people could think of was to call a meeting of the Estates-General. This was a medieval legislative body in which three estates met: the First Estate being the higher clergy; the Second Estate being the aristocracy; and the Third Estate being the middle class made up of lawyers, merchants, and so on. (The common people, or peasantry, were not represented.)

The Estates-General had last met in 1614, one and three quarter centuries earlier, when Marie de Medici was regent for the young Louis XIII. After that, the gradual rise in absolutism, thanks to Richelieu, Mazarin, and Louis XIV, had made the Estates-General unnecessary. Merely to have remembered its existence would have seemed an insult to the king.

But now absolutism had come to an impasse, for the absolute monarch had no money.

The middle classes of the Third Estate were eager for the chance to do something. They paid taxes, at least, and felt themselves to be hard-working and useful members of society. They hated the parasitic First and Second Estates and felt a burning anger at being looked down upon as social inferiors.

What's more, the people who were being chosen for the Third Estate knew well that there was a legislative body in Great Britain that had executed one king and kicked out another and that now had the monarchy tamed and limited, while keeping the finances of the kingdom on a strong and stable basis. And Great Britain, what's more, had been made strong enough by that legislature, to beat France on three continents.

The Estates-General met on May 5, 1789. The old system was to have each estate vote as a unit. In that case, the nobility and clergy would always outvote the Third Estate by two to one, and nothing would be done.

The delegates of the Third Estate were 600 in number, compared to 300 of each of the other two. The Third Estates wanted to vote by individuals, therefore, so that a few liberal peers and clergy could join the Third Estate and allow reform to win out.

The king met the Estates-General, with the clergy and nobles in the place of honor at his right, and the Third Estate on his left. (Ever since then, people have spoken of "rightists" as those who support authority, and "leftists" as those who would break with authority.)

When it looked as though the king would not allow votes by individuals, the Third Estate left and established a "National Assembly" of its own on June 17, 1789. Some clergymen and nobles, anxious for reform, joined the National Assembly.

It was rumored that the king would now disband the Estates-General and return everything to what it was. At this, a Parisian mob rose, under the instigation of a journalist, Camille Desmoulins (1760–1794), and stormed the Bastille, a government prison in Paris that was the very symbol of royal absolutism and despotism. They seized the prison, and this act is considered to represent the beginning of "The French Revolution."

Some French noblemen, headed by Charles Philippe, count of Artois, Louis XVI's youngest brother, put class ahead of nation and became traitors at once, leaving France in order to get foreign armies to invade France and kill Frenchmen, so that their own privileges might be made secure.

On the other hand, many of the nobility began, on August 4, voluntarily to surrender their privileges. On August 27, a "declaration of the rights of man," embodying many liberal notions was propounded. And all over France, the peasants were revolting, and burning down the mansions of the noblemen who had ruled and tyrannized them.

On October 5 and 6, a Paris mob marched to Versailles to bring Louis XVI, Marie Antoinette, and the royal children to Paris, where they could be with their people. The government never returned to Versailles. It had served as the royal seat for 107 years, three kings had spent part or all their reigns there, but from now on, it would be merely a museum piece.

By July 14, 1790, France had a constitution (a written charter defining the government and its powers—something Great Britain didn't have but that the Americans had introduced just three years earlier). The constitution established a limited monarchy and a legislature. It meant there would be fiery speeches, a division into parties, and the kind of wordy conflict that the French, unlike the British and Americans, were not accustomed to.

Louis XVI and Marie Antoinette were not happy with this, of course, and, on June 20, 1791, they tried to flee the country. They did it, however, with the same clumsiness and lack of sense that they did everything else. They were caught and brought back. Since it was clear that if they had managed to get out of France, they would have tried to return with foreign armies of invasion, they were considered traitors and their

doom was sealed. (Charles I had fought Parliament with English armies, at least.)

Meanwhile, the other European monarchs were getting very uneasy. All this unrest and revolution in France was setting a bad example. It might spread, and their own thrones and necks (they always remembered Charles I of England) might be at risk.

On August 27, 1791, then, not long after Louis XVI had been brought back and put into virtual imprisonment, the rulers of Prussia and Austria met at Pillnitz in Saxony, and issued a warning to the French to do no harm to Louis XVI. On February 7, 1792, Austria and Prussia actually formed an alliance against France. For half a century, they had been bitter enemies, but this was forgotten in the face of revolution that threatened both. What followed is called "The War of the First Coalition."

A Prussian army under Karl Wilhelm Friedrich, Duke of Brunswick (1735–1806), a nephew of Frederick the Great, moved against France. Since the Revolution had destroyed the discipline of its armed forces and since most of the aristocratic officers had either decamped or were in prison, it didn't seem as though the French could do anything to stop the invasion.

On August 10, 1792, the panicky Revolutionaries, fearful that the invaders might somehow rescue the French royal family and use them to legalize the invasion, deprived the king of what powers he had retained and confined him to a fortress-like building called the Temple. (It had once belonged to the Knights Templars, about five centuries earlier.)

By September 2, 1792, the panic had risen to the point where people who were imprisoned on suspicion of treason were subjected to hasty trials and killed. A revolutionary, George Jacques Danton (1759–1794), was the leading spirit in this, hoping to inspire the French into a fury of opposition to the invasion. These "September massacres" marked the beginning of what was called "The Reign of Terror."

The French and Prussian armies met at Valmy on September 20, 1792, about 100 miles east of Paris. They did not actually make contact, for a fog arose, and brought both forces to a halt. The

French guns, manned by experienced gunners who were low-born, so that they had not deserted, set up a vigorous cannonade. The Duke of Brunswick, whose heart was apparently not in the fight, retreated.

Militarily speaking, it was a trifle, but it put heart into the Revolutionaries, who treated it as a great victory.

The Revolutionaries now in control of France were Republicans, but they were divided into moderates and extremists. The moderates were the Girondists, because many of them came from the Bordeaux region called the Gironde. The extremists were the Jacobins because they met in a monastery on the Rue St. Jacques.

A National Convention met on September 21, 1792, and declared the King deposed. With that, the French Republic came into existence. The Prussians, still reluctant to fight, continued to retreat. In the southeast, the French armies took Nice and Savoy. In the northeast, they temporarily took Brussels.

These successes made it possible for the French to put Louis XVI on trial for treason in December, 1792. He was convicted, and was executed on January 21, 1793.

At this, Great Britain (horrified, and choosing not to remember Charles I) ousted the French ambassador. Thereupon, France declared war on Great Britain, Spain, and the Netherlands, and found herself at war with virtually all of Europe.

In addition to that, there were revolts inside France by those who still felt loyal to the monarchy, or by those who were upset by the economic hardships that came because of war and of the breakdown of the normal governmental structure. Finally, the Republican revolutionaries were fighting among themselves, and this created further confusion.

Why wasn't France crushed? Three reasons:

First, it just happened that there were no great generals among the allies. There was no longer any Frederick the Great among the Prussians, no longer any Eugene of Savoy among the Austrians, and it was the Prussians and Austrians who were, at this time, bearing the burden of the anti-French struggle.

Second, amid the blood and confusion of the Revolution, one man slowly won control by mid-1793. This was Maximilien de Robespierre (1758–1794). He saw to it that Marie Antoinette was tried and, on October 16, 1793, executed; that the Girondist leaders were executed on October 31; and that even Jacobins with whom he disagreed, including Demoulins and Danton, were all executed by April 6, 1794. Under Robespierre, the Reign of Terror was at its peak, but there was at least only one man giving orders.

Third, during this Reign of Terror, a skilled army officer and ardent Republican, Lazare Nicolas Carnot (1753–1823), labored successfully to put some order into the French army, and to devise tactics that suited the new forces, who were ardent in attack, but poor in skill and discipline.

On August 23, 1793, the French government decreed mass conscription and built up large armies of untrained men, which were hurled at the smaller armies of the invaders and which actually pushed them back.

The British were laying siege to Toulon, France's great naval base on the Mediterranean. It went on for nearly four months until, in December of 1793, a 24-year-old colonel managed to get his plan accepted. This drove off the British and saved the base. The colonel was Napoleon Bonaparte (1769–1821), and he was promoted to brigadier-general as a result.

At the height of the Revolution, Frenchmen took to calling each other "Citizen" and "Citizenness" to avoid all indication of rank. They worked up a new calendar, counting from September 21, 1792 as the year 1, and with names for the months referring to the kind of weather to be expected. They even tried to establish a "Goddess of Reason" to replace Christianity—but Robespierre, who in private life was very proper and conventional, would not allow that.

On June 26, 1794, the French won a battle at Fleurus, south of Brussels, and the Allies were driven out of the Austrian Netherlands. The Austrian Netherlands, having been Austrian for 80 years, and under Hapsburg rulers for over three centuries, were never to be either Austrian or Hapsburg again.

Robespierre had, however, raised hosts of enemies, for every French politician feared he might be the next to be executed. They conspired and rebelled against Robespierre and, on July 17, 1794, he was denounced, voted against, arrested, and executed. The Reign of Terror came to an end, though the Revolution did not.

The French armies, amid this turnover, continued to be surprisingly successful. In the early months of 1795, a French army under Jean Charles Pichegru (1761–1804) invaded the Netherlands and found the Dutch fleet immobilized in the frozen harbors. The French cavalry actually captured the ships. (Imagine if the Duke of Alva had had such a stroke of luck two centuries earlier.) The stadtholder, William V, fled to Great Britain and the French founded the "Batavian Republic" in March 1795.

The French government was now in the hands of moderates, of whom the most important was Paul François de Barras (1755–1829). The Jacobins were still a force, of course. A leading Jacobin was Francois Noel Babeuf (1760–1797), who was looking not merely for political reform but for social egalitarianism. He was, in fact, the first socialist of the modern type. Under the leadership of Babeuf and others of the sort, a mob gathered and prepared to move on the Tuileries and put an end to the new leaders.

Paul Barras called on General Bonaparte, who happened to be in town. Although he had been a Jacobin, he knew the direction in which ambition called him. On October 5, 1795, he had his men turn their guns on the advancing Parisians. They fired, killed 200, wounded twice as many more, and that was an end to movements by the Parisian mob. In general, the Jacobin leaders were pardoned in line with the new moderation, but the line was drawn at Babeuf. He was executed on May 27, 1797.

By November 3, 1795, Barras had formed a collective government of five men, of whom he was chief, called the "Directory," and it was fairly stable. Revolts within France had been put down and France seemed no longer in danger. It was fighting now for conquest and for the spread of its new revolutionary ideas.

The chief opponent at this time was Austria, whom France was fighting both in Germany and Italy. There were also the French "emigrés," the

aristocrats who had fled France and who were more ardently anti-French than any foreigners. They considered Louis XVI's son to be the rightful king, "Louis XVII." When he died in imprisonment on June 8, 1795, the emigrés considered Louis XVI's younger brother to be king as Louis XVIII.

In Germany, the Austrians found a fairly good general in the person of Archduke Charles (1771–1847), a younger brother of the Emperor Francis II (1768–1835), who had succeeded on the death of his father, Leopold II, in 1792. Charles held off the French generals, Jean Baptiste Jourdan (1762–1833) and Victor Moreau (1763–1813).

In Italy, it was another affair altogether. Barras had rewarded General Bonaparte for his services in controlling the Parisian mob by giving him one of his mistresses, Josephine de Beauharnais (1763–1814), with whom Bonaparte had fallen in love. They were married on March 9, 1796, and Barras then rewarded Bonaparte further by putting him in charge of the French army in Italy—which meant he had to leave his bride of only a few days.

On March 17, 1796, Bonaparte took command of a ragged army that was short of food and, almost at once, it became obvious that an amazing new military leader had appeared on the scene. His specialty was speed and instant decision, and he was facing old Austrian generals who were slow and indecisive.

There followed Bonaparte's "First Italian Campaign." In 17 days he won four battles, defeated two armies, and took all of Lombardy. By the spring of 1797, he had conquered all of northern Italy and was crossing the Alps into Austria itself. Austria decided it had had enough and was willing to make peace terms.

Bonaparte, scorning to consult Paris, made the terms as though he were king—and, considering his ability, who was there to dispute that with him? No one did.

The treaty, signed at Campo Formio at the northeastern boundary of Italy, forced Austria to cede the Austrian Netherlands to France, and recognized the existence of a new "Cisalpine Republic," which included all of northern Italy and which was a French puppet.

In return, Bonaparte handed Venetia to Austria. In this way, the Venetian Republic came to an end, 11 centuries after the first doge had been elected, and six centuries after it had reached its peak of power with the capture of Constantinople in the Fourth Crusade.

In the aftermath of these events, French armies occupied Rome in February 1798, established the "Roman Republic," and carried Pope Pius VI (1717–1799) into captivity. In April, the French occupied Switzerland and established the "Helvetic Republic."

Against all odds, then, France was triumphant. The only enemy left in the field was Great Britain, which France could not touch as long as the English Channel existed and the British navy controlled the sea.

However, that control was suddenly put in jeopardy in the summer of 1797, when the British navy was disrupted by a general mutiny. This was not surprising since the navy subjected its sailors to treatment that was simply barbaric. The mutiny was crushed and conditions in the navy henceforth improved, but it did take some time for the British to recover.

Meanwhile, Bonaparte, who always had a weakness for the grandiose and, who like all successful generals, dreamed of being a second Alexander the Great, had a plan. If it were too dangerous to attack Great Britain directly, he might at least take advantage of its naval confusion to cross the Mediterranean and attack Egypt. This renewal of the crusades would not be intended to regain Palestine but to attack India and rebuild France's overseas empire.

It was a hare-brained notion, but the Directory agreed to it, largely to get a general who was too good, and had grown too popular (and was therefore a danger to themselves), out of the country.

Bonaparte left France in May and landed in Egypt in July 1. The British caught a glimpse of what Bonaparte was planning and they sent their admiral, Horatio Nelson (1758–1805), possibly the best admiral of all time, to intercept Bonaparte. He had been sent out a little too late to succeed at that, but Nelson knew where Bona-

parte was going, and, grimly, he followed him there.

The French army easily defeated the Mamluk army of Egypt, which was still fighting in medieval fashion, at the battle of the Pyramids on July 21, 1798. That, however, did them very little good, for on August 1, 1798, Nelson reached the mouth of the Nile River, where the French ships were anchored, and virtually destroyed them all. That meant that Bonaparte's army in Egypt was stranded there and, as a matter of fact, it never returned to France as a fighting force.

Bonaparte continued to win victories in Egypt and in Syria, but they were sterile and could come to nothing. On August 24, 1799, Bonaparte decided he had no choice but to abandon his army and make his way back to France, for France's enemies were triumphing in Italy, and his own wife was being unfaithful. (The British thoughtfully saw to it that Bonaparte received the news about his wife.) Again, Bonaparte managed to evade the British fleet, and was back in France on October 8, 1799.

The foolish Egyptian campaign did obtain an incredible gift for archeologists, however. A French soldier came across a broken stone inscription dating back to 197 B.C. It was found near the town of Rosetta and was therefore called "the Rosetta stone." It contained what was presumably the same inscription in Greek and in each of two forms of Egyptian hieroglyphics. Eventually, the Greek served as a key to the understanding of the Egyptian language, and that made it possible to read many of the old inscriptions in the temples and on the pillars that still existed.

While Bonaparte was absent in Egypt, however, the nations of Europe, led by Great Britain and Russia, formed another anti-French coalition and the "War of the Second Coalition" began. It was fought chiefly in Italy.

In charge of the new campaign was the Russian general, Suvorov, who was now 70 years old, but who had lost none of his ability. In a succession of victories, he drove the French out of Italy by the end of 1799. (Had he been in the prime of life, and with a good army at his command, it would have been interesting to see what he could have done against Bonaparte.)

As it was, however, Suvorov could not force the Austrians to cooperate properly, and he gave up his command and died the next year. On the whole, because of the lack of cooperation between the Allies, the war was a failure. Once Bonaparte was back in France, it dribbled to a halt.

Meanwhile, Bonaparte, smarting from the failure of his Egyptian campaign, managed to turn public resentment against the Directory for the loss of Italy. On November 9, he carried through a coup that put an end to the Directory, after it had been in control of France for four years.

He established "The Consulate," in which three men, as "consuls" were to rule France. In actual fact, Bonaparte, as the First Consul, was virtually dictator of France by the constitution accepted on December 24, 1799.

This period was a most fruitful one for French science. Antoine Laurent Lavoisier (1743–1794), undoubtedly the greatest chemist of all time, introduced quantitative methods into chemistry, demonstrating the law of conservation of mass (the quantity of mass does not change perceptibly in the course of chemical reactions). He worked out the composition of the atmosphere, and correctly explained combustion as chemical combination with oxygen—all of this being done by 1774. By 1787, he had shown that animal respiration was a form of combustion, and he had devised the modern system of chemical nomenclature.

Lavoisier was also the most notable scientific victim of the French Revolution. He had married a daughter of an important executive of the harsh tax-collecting organization which was, above all, hated by the French people. As a result, Lavoisier was executed on May 8, 1794, at the height of the Reign of Terror. (When he was arrested and pleaded that he was a scientist, not a politician, the arresting officer said, "The Republic has no need of scientists," surely a statement worthy of inclusion in anyone's list of stupid statements.)

In addition, to Lavoisier, there was Jacques

Alexandre Cesar Charles (1746–1823), who discovered, in 1787, the manner in which gas volume changed with temperature and indicated the possible existence of an absolute zero of temperature. The mathematician Lagrange continued his work and, in 1788, published *Analytical Mechanics*, in which all of mechanics was interpreted as algebra, rather than as geometry.

Antoine Laurent de Jussieu (1748–1836) was a botanist who, in 1789, modified Linnaeus' classification of plants, basing it on more natural physiological divisions. His system has been used ever since. The French physician, Philippe Pinel (1745–1826), was placed in charge of an insane asylum in 1793 and introduced, for the first time, humane methods for dealing with the mentally ill. He removed their chains, put an end to violent punishments, and kept careful case histories.

In technology, the most spectacular French achievement was the development of the hot-air balloon by Joseph Michel Montgolfier (1740–1810) and his brother, Jacques Etienne Montgolfier (1745–1799). They sent up their first balloon on June 5, 1783 in their small hometown. By November, they were demonstrating a more elaborate version in Paris before crowds that included the king and queen, as well as Benjamin Franklin of the United States. Jacques Charles was the first to use hydrogen, rather than hot air, as a lifting agent for balloons. The first person to be carried aloft by a balloon was Francois Pilatre de Rozier, who became an aeronaut on November 10, 1783, and was the first to die in an airflight accident on June 15, 1785. Jean Pierre François Blanchard (1753–1809) invented the parachute in 1785.

The French physician, Joseph Ignace Guillotin (1738–1814), invented a heavy, mechanical axehead that fell and beheaded cleanly and quickly. It was meant to be a humane substitution for the uncertain beheading by the executioner's hand, and the brutality of other methods of execution. Its use during the Reign of Terror gave the instrument a cachet of horror that it didn't deserve.

The French Revolutionaries decided to replace the antiquated system of weights and measures with something regular and simple for the encouragement of trade and industry. Beginning in 1790, a committee eventually produced the metric system, a group of related measures that rose and fell by multiples of 10. So rational is the system that it was eventually adopted by the whole world—except for the United States.

The great French painter of the period was Jacques Louis David (1748–1825), who painted in a neoclassical style with almost photographic precision.

UNITED STATES

In 1775, Boston was under the military control of the British general, Thomas Gage (1721–1787), who decided in April that he must confiscate the guns and powder being accumulated by the Massachusetts colonials in Concord, to the west of Boston.

On April 19, he sent a contingent of soldiers to do the job. The colonials, forewarned, were ready. There was shooting at Lexington, then at Concord, and the British were driven back by the embattled farmers. The "War of American Independence" had begun.

The rebelling colonials faced a difficult situation. Many colonials were loyal to the old country and many more were not much interested one way or another. Those who actually wanted to resist British authority by force of arms were very much in the minority. Furthermore, the colonials were short on arms and they had no trained soldiers or generals.

The British had their difficulties, too. They had 3000 miles of ocean to cross and, even though they controlled the sea, that was a considerable barrier. What's more, the colonial territory was large and difficult to hold against determined guerrilla opposition. Meanwhile, in Europe, there were nations, especially France, who were willing to capitalize on British preoccupation, and Great Britain was reluctant to turn its back on them. Furthermore, the notion of beating down the colonials (who were also British, for the most part) was not popular with the British people and George III had to hire German mercenaries ("Hessians") to do part of the fight-

ing. This did more harm than good, since it roused colonial anger as nothing else did.

On May 10, 1775, a Second Continental Congress met in Philadelphia and, on June 15, appointed George Washington as commander-in-chief of the colonial forces.

On June 17, 1775, a British force in Boston, under the command of William Howe (1729–1814), attempted to drive the colonials from heights across the river from Boston. They succeeded at the Battle of Bunker Hill, but only after suffering appalling losses.

Washington's army then laid siege to Boston and, on March 17, 1776, Howe realized that it was useless to keep his army there when it might be better used elsewhere to crush the revolt. Therefore, he evacuated Boston and, from that moment, almost all of New England was free of British control forever.

Sentiment in the colonies was rising, now, in favor of complete independence from Great Britain. Important in this cause were the brilliant pamphlets of English-born Thomas Paine (1737–1809), whose 47-page *Common Sense,* published in 1776, converted George Washington, among many others, to a decision in favor of independence. Inside the Second Continental Congress, Samuel Adams of Massachusetts and his cousin, John Adams (1735–1826), led the fight for it.

On July 4, 1776, the Second Continental Congress, under the chairmanship of John Hancock of Massachusetts (1737–1793), adopted and signed a "Declaration of Independence" establishing "The United States of America." While the Declaration was not really effective until the end of the war, it is customary to consider the United States an as independent nation from that day. It will be referred to as the United States from this point on in the book, and its people will be called "Americans."

The British, however, were of no mind to acquiesce in this. Howe, who had withdrawn his army to Halifax in Nova Scotia, now brought it back to the United States, landing in Staten Island in New York harbor on July 2.

On August 22, 1776, Howe, fighting in Brooklyn, defeated Washington's army in the Battle of

Long Island, but Washington drew it off in good order. Howe then pursued, and Washington, defeated several more times in minor engagements, was forced to retreat across New Jersey in November and December of 1776.

The American army was eventually safe on the western side of the Delaware River, but things looked bad. The army was melting away and there were not many who believed the Americans could stand against a professional British army anyway, so that it was just a matter of time before the rebels were mopped up. Washington had only survived thus far because Howe (his heart not in the war) had pursued slowly.

Therefore, Washington planned a Christmas surprise. On Christmas night, he quietly recrossed the Delaware river, and fell upon Trenton, where 1400 Hessians were sleeping off their Christmas dinners. They were killed or captured, and the stunning stroke forced the British out of New Jersey, showed that the Americans could fight, and roused American spirits everywhere.

The British worked out an elaborate plan intended to cut New England off from the rest of the nation. Howe was to travel northward from New York. Another general, John Burgoyne (1722–1792), was to come southward from Canada, while a third officer, Harry St. Leger (1737–1789), was to come east from Lake Ontario. All were to meet at Albany. With radical New England isolated, the rest of the country, which was not very revolutionary, could be made to see reason and there would then be time to turn on New England and smash it.

The only trouble was that it didn't work. Howe was not given his order to move north, at least not in any unequivocal way. Howe thought it would be better to take Philadelphia, the American capital. He took his army by sea to Chesapeake Bay, brought it up the Delaware River, defeated Washington, and took Philadelphia on September 17, 1777.

Washington was forced westward to Valley Forge, where he spent a hard winter, with his army virtually starving, while the British were resting comfortably in Philadelphia.

That was well for Howe, but what about the other two advances? St. Leger was stopped by Nicholas Herkimer (1728–1777) at the Battle of the Oriskany, seven miles west of Utica, New York, on August 6, 1777, and he turned back. (Herkimer died in action.)

That left only Burgoyne, who was advancing southward from Canada as he was supposed to do. He was, of course, unaware that no one was coming to meet him from either the south or the west. He struggled on through trackless forests, and was running short of supplies. His attempt to get some at Bennington, Vermont, was beaten off by John Stark (1728–1822). Burgoyne then found himself fighting American forces who were growing in number. The Americans were nominally under Horatio Gates (1728–1806), though the driving force was that of Benedict Arnold, who was the best general on the American side.

Having lost several battles, Burgoyne realized that if he continued to try to press forward, not a British soldier would stay alive. On October 17, 1777, therefore, at Saratoga, New York, he surrendered the 5700 men he had left to American forces that were now three times that number. Gates, rather than Arnold, got the credit for this American victory.

For a British army to surrender on the field of battle was unusual. For them to surrender to a bunch of ragged provincials was a thunderbolt. This was the turning point of the war. To the Americans, it was a triumph that made up for the loss of Philadelphia.

The French, moreover, who had been secretly helping the Americans in order to get back at the British, now openly recognized American independence.

Meanwhile, European volunteers were flocking to the American side. The most important was a French nobleman of liberal and idealistic beliefs, Marie Joseph de Motier, Marquis de Lafayette (1757–1834), who was only 19 years old. He was willing to pay his own way, and, far from demanding privileges, served as Washington's subordinate so loyally that Washington looked upon him as a son.

Another volunteer was Friedrich Wilhelm

Steuben (1730–1794), a German soldier of fortune, who had fought in the Seven Years War, and who trained the American forces at Valley Forge. He managed to give them a feeling of order and discipline, cursing them liberally in German, with a special subaltern at his side to curse them in English when he ran out of German oaths.

Benjamin Franklin was in Paris, with his American clothes and American manners (an artfully assumed patriarchal simplicity that completely won over the admiring French aristocracy, with their powdered hair and silk stockings). Cleverly, he pushed them toward helping the United States. By February 6, 1778, France had made an alliance with the United States, and military help began to flow openly. By June 17, 1778, Great Britain and France were at war.

On June 18, Henry Clinton (1738–1795), who had been born in Newfoundland, and who now commanded the British army, decided to evacuate Philadelphia and to concentrate his army in New York to meet the French threat. Washington followed the British army across New Jersey and attacked them at Monmouth on June 28, 1778. The newly trained American army showed its worth and would have won the battle but for the treasonable behavior of Charles Lee (1731–1782) who refused to attack at a crucial moment. Lee was a British-born American officer who (it turned out after the war) had been in British pay.

The British now decided to turn their attention to the south, which was the least revolutionary part of the nation.

They took Savannah, Georgia, on December 19, 1778, and in 1780 won battles in South Carolina, where Gates acted in so pusillanimous a manner that he lost his reputation. Until then, some had thought of him as a possible replacement for Washington.

Worse yet, Benedict Arnold, chafing at the number of occasions in which he had been mistreated, overlooked, and underappreciated, and pushed by his pro-British wife, finally decided to switch over to the British side. He had asked Washington for command over West Point on the

Hudson River, north of New York, and now planned to surrender that important strong point to the British. The treason was caught on September 23, 1780 before it could be carried through and a British go-between, John André (1750–1780), was hanged, but Arnold escaped.

The success of the British in the south, Arnold's treason, and the failure of the French to be of any military help to the Americans cast a pall of gloom over the new nation. However, there were positive developments, too. George Rogers Clark (1752–1818), and a small force of Virginians, had swept the British out of the Ohio Valley in February 1779. Then, too, on September 23, 1779, the American naval captain, John Paul Jones (1747–1792), who had been preying on British shipping, defeated the British warship, *Serapis*.

Nevertheless, the British had to be stopped in the south, and Washington placed Nathaniel Greene (1724–1786) of Rhode Island in charge of that task.

Greene did not win any victories, but he maneuvered the British into wearing themselves out uselessly against him and against American guerrilla forces. Except for a few coastal cities, Georgia and the Carolinas were back in American control.

Charles Cornwallis (1736–1805), who was commanding the British forces in the south, moved into Virginia in 1781. He conducted raids that reduced the colony to chaos and forced the Virginia legislature, along with the Governor, Thomas Jefferson (1743–1826), who had written the Declaration of Independence, to flee the capital in order to avoid capture.

Cornwallis, however, was being hounded by Lafayette, whose army was growing and who was handling it well. As the summer wore on, therefore, Cornwallis decided to get to the coast, where he could obtain reinforcements and supplies from the British navy. He made it to Yorktown on August 1, 1781.

Lafayette, with the aid of French forces under Jean Baptiste de Vimeur, Count de Rochambeau (1725–1807), advanced to lay siege to Yorktown, and for once, the French fleet managed to do something. Under François Joseph, Count de Grasse (1722–1788), French ships had actually fought off the British and had come to Yorktown. Cornwallis was horrified to see French forces both on land and sea.

Loyal to the core, Lafayette did not push the siege till Washington had a chance to arrive. By September 14, there he was, with additional troops, and Cornwallis' situation deteriorated. On October 19, 1781, he had no choice but to surrender. A *second* British army had surrendered to the Americans, and even George III recognized that there was no use in fighting any further.

The Treaty of Paris was signed on September 3, 1783. Great Britain recognized the independence of the United States and all the territory from the Atlantic Ocean to the Mississippi River and north to the Great Lakes was American. However, Great Britain kept Canada and ceded Florida and the Gulf Coast to Spain so that the United States did not have access to the Gulf of Mexico or to the mouth of the Mississippi River.

The United States now existed under the "Articles of Confederation," which had been accepted by the various states on November 15, 1777, but the arrangement was a weak one. The individual states held so much power that they were almost independent of each other, while the Congress, which supposedly governed the nation, was just about helpless. It didn't even have the power of taxation but had to depend upon contributions from the states who, of course, were never eager to pay. There seemed good reason to think that once the war was over and the states were not held together by the overriding threat of Great Britain, they would fall apart.

One thing the weak Congress did was of the utmost importance, however. It passed "The Northwest Ordinance" on July 13, 1787. That established the rules for admitting new states. Three to five states would eventually be formed in the Ohio Territory (in the end, five states were formed), and all would enter on equal terms with the original states in all respects. Thus, there would be no competition among the older states

to form empires, to set up puppet states, and to war on each other in competition for territory. What's more, the Northwest Ordinance decreed there was to be no slavery in the Ohio Territory.

Vast problems remained, however, involving the interrelationships of the states. How were they to trade with each other? How were they to use rivers that formed boundaries between states? How were they to treat with foreign nations and with the Indian tribes?

Some 12 delegates from five states had gathered at Annapolis, Maryland on September 11, 1786, but could do nothing. Alexander Hamilton of New York (1755–1804) urged that a new and broader convention be called to establish some document that would form a more workable union than had the Articles of Confederation. His suggestion was accepted.

The new "Constitutional Convention" met in Philadelphia on May 25, 1787. They worked through the summer in secret and, finally, after a number of compromises had been accepted, they prepared and signed the Constitution of the United States. This set up a federal government in which the individual states voluntarily gave up some of their rights to a national President and a national legislature. It is this that represents the true foundation of the United States of America.

It had to be ratified by at least nine of the 13 states, and the ninth to do so was New Hampshire on June 21, 1788. The United States, as constituted at present, dates from that day.

Under the Constitution, the United States had to elect a President and Vice-President for four-year terms; chosen for the posts were George Washington of Virginia and John Adams of Massachusetts.

George Washington, as first President of the United States of America, was sworn in on April 30, 1789, just 10 and a half weeks before the beginning of the French Revolution. Washington and Adams were reelected in 1792.

Throughout his two terms, Washington had to deal with the pressures produced by the French Revolution. Technically, the alliance with France still existed, but some argued that it had been made with the French king, whose execution put an end to it. Washington presented no arguments. He simply knew that the nation was in no position to involve itself in a European war and he labored to keep the United States neutral. To this, he was successful, though after John Adams was elected second president in 1796, there was what amounted to a short-lived naval war with France in 1798.

In 1800, John Adams failed to win reelection and Thomas Jefferson became the third President of the United States.

Clearly, the United States was a going concern, but it might not have been without technological advance. The source of such advance was in Great Britain, where the Industrial Revolution was beginning. Great Britain, however, was of no mind to export its expertise, but preferred, rather, to keep it as much a British monopoly as possible. Therefore, they kept the new machinery secret and forbade British engineers to leave the country. The United States, on the other hand, openly offered rewards for any who would defect with the necessary information.

Samuel Slater (1768–1835), who had been an apprentice of Richard Arkwright, had memorized, in detail, the new textile machinery. He was willing to defect, so he disguised himself as a farmer and managed to get to the United States in 1789. By 1790 he was supervising the construction of textile mills containing the new machinery in Pawtucket, Rhode Island.

Meanwhile, the American inventor, Oliver Evans (1755–1819), was constructing the first practical steam engines in the United States by 1787. Thus, the United States was entering the Industrial Revolution and was making itself economically independent of Great Britain. Without such economic independence, political independence alone would have done the nation no particular good.

A technological advance of another sort took place in the south. There the production of cotton, greatly needed by the new textile mills in Great Britain and in New England, was hampered by the difficulty of plucking the cotton from the seeds. On March 14, 1794, the Massachusetts-born Eli Whitney (1765–1825) patented

a "cotton gin" (short for "engine"). This plucked the cotton fibers from the seeds mechanically and increased the production of cotton 50-fold. Cotton-growing became profitable, indeed, and hordes of slaves were needed for the cottonfields. Slavery had been withering in the United States under the weight of moral disapproval and the lack of great profitability, but now it suddenly gained a new lease on life in the United States and the seeds of future tragedy were sown.

In culture, the United States lagged, since it did not have much of an aristocracy who could be relied on to patronize the arts. Nevertheless, John Singleton Copley of Massachusetts (1738–1815) was an outstanding portraitist, who did paintings of Samuel Adams and John Adams, among others. He went to Great Britain in 1774 and remained there, thereafter.

Philip Morin Freneau of New York (1752–1832) was the first notable American poet.

CANADA

The rebelling American colonies hoped to persuade or force Canada to join them, but failed. In the winter of 1775, forces under Benedict Arnold and Richard Montgomery (1736–1775) tried to take Montreal and Quebec. They failed; Montgomery died and Arnold was wounded.

Even when the American colonies won their independence, Canada remained firmly British. The territory it controlled was extended by exploration. Scottish-born Alexander Mackenzie (1764–1820) established himself in what is now Alberta and followed what is now the Mackenzie River to its mouth at the Arctic Ocean in 1789. In 1793, he crossed the Rocky Mountains to the Pacific Ocean in what is now British Columbia.

The British navigator, George Vancouver (1757–1798), who had sailed with Cook, explored the coast of British Columbia and circumnavigated what is now Vancouver Island between 1792 and 1794.

GREAT BRITAIN

The war of American Independence was liberating for Great Britain as well. The failure of British policies greatly weakened the prestige of George III and made it impossible for him to dominate the government as he had planned.

His prime minister, Frederick, Lord North (1732–1792), served only because he was a favorite of George III and was compliant with all his wishes. He carried no real weight with Parliament. After the surrender of Cornwallis at Yorktown, Lord North's prestige had sunk to such a level that a motion of lack of confidence in him failed by only nine votes. When it looked as though there would be another vote, in which he might do even worse, Lord North resigned. That set a precedent that a prime minister, regardless of royal support, could only serve while he had the confidence of Parliament.

The natural successor was Charles James Fox (1749–1806), whom George III detested. For one thing, Fox, along with the aged William Pitt, had supported the cause of the rebelling colonies.

On April 2, 1783, Fox and North formed a coalition government and established a joint ministry that displeased everyone without exception. The coalition fell when it tried to introduce a bill that would reform the government of India and make the British East India Company responsible to the British government. It was rejected and a new ministry was needed.

George III, on the principle of anyone-but-Fox, chose William Pitt, Jr., the second son of William Pitt. William Pitt the Younger was only 24 years old when, on December 16, 1783, he became Prime Minister. He finally pushed through Indian reform on August 13, 1784, but only after there had been new elections.

In 1788, George III began to suffer bouts of insanity, which grew worse with time. It is now believed that he suffered from an inborn disease called porphyria, which could produce pain, overexcitement, and delirium. It may conceivably be that early moderate symptoms exacerbated George III's irascibility and stubbornness, caused him to refuse to consider compromise solutions with the Americans and, as much as anything else, led to the establishment of the United States.

In 1793, war began with the French Republic, and that preoccupied British minds thereafter.

The general attitude of unrest and rebellion that followed the War of American Independence and the French Revolution did not leave Great Britain untouched. On April 15, 1797, the sailors of the British navy began a rebellion, in which they demanded better treatment. One can only sympathize with them for they were poorly paid, poorly fed, and were treated like animals, being consistently flogged for little or no reason. The British government quelled the rebellion by the end of June. However, realizing that with the French triumphing on land, Great Britain's only security lay in its navy. Since unhappy sailors were an unreliable prop, conditions were slowly improved. The sailors were even fed lime juice, at last, to prevent scurvy, and British seamen have been known as "limeys" ever since.

Rebellion also broke out in Ireland in 1795, fed largely by the hope that the French would send soldiers. James Napper Tandy (1740–1793) was a leading spirit among the Irish, and a French fleet of 43 ships and 15,000 men under Louis Lazare Hoche (1768–1797) did set out to help. The French fleet was scattered by a storm, however, and the Irish, fighting alone, and without adequate leadership were beaten by the British at the Battle of Vinegar Hill on June 12, 1798. The rebellion was then suppressed over the next year with brutal violence.

Where the arts of peace were concerned, the greatest British dramatist of the period was Richard Brinsley Sheridan (1751–1816), whose two most important plays, *The Rivals* in 1775 and *The School for Scandal* in 1777, are still revived today.

A number of poets were making their mark at this time. William Cowper (1731–1800) is best remembered today for his humorous ballad, "History of John Gilpin," written in 1785.

Robert Burns (1759–1796) is regarded as the Scottish national poet. Many of his effective and ever-popular lyrics were written in Scottish dialect. Such virtually universal favorites as "Auld Lang Syne" and "Coming Through the Rye" are his; perhaps the most quoted poem is "To a Mouse" ("The best-laid plans of mice and men / Gang aft a-gley").

William Blake (1757–1827) wrote deceptively

simple lyrics of great beauty, perhaps his most quoted line being "Tyger! Tyger! burning bright / In the forests of the night."

A group of romantic poets, hymning the joys of nature, included Samuel Taylor Coleridge (1772–1834), whose masterpiece was "The Rime of the Ancient Mariner," inspired by Cook's Antarctic voyage, and published in 1798 in a collection of poems, *Lyrical Ballads*. Joining him in that endeavor was William Wordsworth (1770–1850), whose most notable contribution to the book was "Lines Composed a Few Miles Above Tintern Abbey."

Frances ("Fanny") Burney (1752–1840) was a pioneer among women novelists, publishing *Evelina* anonymously in 1778. It was a great success.

Among other writers was Edward Gibbon (1737–1794) whose *The History of the Decline and Fall of the Roman Empire*, written between 1766 and 1788, is certainly among the greatest and most popular historical works ever penned. Adam Smith (1733–1790) published *Inquiry into the Nature and Causes of the Wealth of Nations* in 1776, arguing that business activity and trade ought not to be hampered by governmental regulation, but demanding *laissez faire* (French for "let people work"). It was the most influential book on economic and political science ever written. Thomas Robert Malthus (1766–1814) published *Essay on Population* in 1798. In it, he pointed out that population invariably rose faster than the food supply, so that numbers had to be kept down by famine, disease, and war. This was an early example of modern sociological writing and helped inspire later theories of evolution.

The British philosopher, Jeremy Bentham (1748–1832), in his *Introduction to the Principles of Morals and Legislation* (published in 1789), proposed a utilitarian philosophy, suggesting that all legislation, and human conduct, too, is, or should be, aimed at promoting pleasure or diminishing pain, to produce "the greatest happiness of the greatest number."

The British statesman, Edmund Burke (1729–1797), wrote eloquently in support of the American revolt, and supported the colonies against George III. He was, however, ferociously op-

posed to the French Revolution in the last decade of his life.

In science, Great Britain produced important advances. The Hanover-born astronomer, William Herschel (1738–1822), startled the world in 1781 with his discovery of Uranus, the first planet to be discovered in historic times. His observations in the 1790s showed the existence of double stars that moved about a center of gravity, in accordance with Newton's law of gravitation. He also showed that the Sun was no more the center of the Universe than the Earth was, but that it moved relative to the stars.

Henry Cavendish was still actively working, and in 1784, showed that hydrogen, on burning, formed water. In 1798, he was the first to produce an accurate figure for the mass of the Earth. James Hutton (1726–1797) published *Theory of the Earth* in 1785. It founded the modern science of geology and establish the eons-long age of the Earth in defiance of Biblical chronology.

The Dutch-born physician, Jan Ingenhousz (1730–1799), showed in 1779 that plants took up carbon dioxide, released oxygen, and put together the complex substances making up plant tissue, in the light only. Because of this, the process came to be known as "photosynthesis," from Greek words meaning "to put together by light."

For the average man, the greatest scientific advance of the period, however, was one carried through by the British physician, Edward Jenner (1749–1823). By 1798, he had clearly demonstrated that inoculation with cowpox ("vaccinia") induced a mild disease that produced immunity, not only to further attacks of cowpox itself, but to its dreaded and supremely dangerous cousin, smallpox. Within a year, smallpox deaths were rapidly declining. "Vaccination" was the first real victory gained by medicine over infectious disease, and a really frightful one that killed large numbers, including Louis XV of France, and very often disfigured where it did not kill.

Yet the great world-changing phenomenon continued to be Watt's steam engine. Watt, in 1781, devised mechanical attachments that converted the in-and-out motion of a piston into the rotary motion of a wheel. This made the steam engine a flexible source of power for machinery in general and, by 1800, there were some 500 such engines chugging away in Great Britain.

In 1790, Richard Arkwright began to make use of the steam engine to power his textile machinery. He was employing thousands of employees, and became the first "capitalist" of the new industrial age. The "factory system" was coming into being as men, women, and children began to move from the farms into the mills.

NETHERLANDS

Things grew stormy in the Netherlands in this period. King William V was pro-British, but with the American colonies in revolt, he could not keep the Netherlands from joining the general European war against Great Britain. As a result, the Netherlands lost some of its possessions in both the West and East Indies.

The pro-French Patriots Party opposed William and drove him out of his capital in 1785. He could only return with the help of Prussian forces in 1787. Then, however, came the French Revolution and, in 1795, the French took over the nation and established the Batavian Republic. William V fled on January 18, 1795, was stripped of his title of stadtholder on February 23, and eventually died in exile.

SPAIN

Spain participated in the War of American Independence and, as a result, got back Florida. It did not, however, manage to take back Gibraltar.

Charles III of Spain died on December 14, 1788, and his son succeeded him as Charles IV (1748–1819), just in time to have to face the crisis-ridden period of the French Revolution.

Charles IV could not handle the business of government himself, so he allowed matters to be run by his wife's lover, Manuel de Godoy (1767–1851), who was every bit as incompetent as the king. After Louis XVI was executed in 1793, Spain joined in the war against France and suffered defeats. Godoy made peace in 1795, and then, in a reversal, allied Spain with France in

1797, and made war on Great Britain. Again, Spain was defeated.

The outstanding Spanish painter of this period was Francisco Jose de Goya (1746–1828). He was the official painter to the king. He is, perhaps, best-known today for his nude painting commonly known as "The Naked Maja."

In North America, Spain continued to retain its hold on its territories. In California, which it controlled, San Francisco was founded in 1776 and Los Angeles in 1781.

PORTUGAL

On February 24, 1777, Joseph I died and his daughter succeeded to the throne, reigning as Maria I (1734–1816). Pombal was relieved of his duties and the royal absolutism that he had fostered receded, while the aristocracy regained its privileges. In 1792, Maria suffered bouts of insanity and her son, John (1767–1826), took over control of the government as regent. The French Revolution was in progress now and Portugal took drastic measures to repress revolutionary thought.

AUSTRIA

In 1777, Maximilian III Joseph, elector of Bavaria, died and left no heirs. The question was who was to succeed him. Austria and Prussia each supported different candidates and there followed a comic-opera affair called "The War of the Bavarian Succession." Maria Theresa and Frederick II both mobilized armies, which stared at each other. Neither monarch could stomach the notion of another war in their old age. Eventually, without a battle, a compromise peace was reached on May 13, 1779.

On November 13, 1780, Maria Theresa died after a reign of 40 years and her son, Joseph II, who had already become the Holy Roman Emperor, while remaining without power, now became Archduke of Austria as well, and gained considerable power.

He was, of all the "benevolent despots," the most extreme. He closed the monasteries and tried to secularize education. He abolished serfdom. He declared religious freedom, even (wonder of wonders) extending it to the Jews. He tried to abolish aristocratic privileges. All this, however, he wanted to do by fiat. He, as the absolute monarch, would give freedom, but would stay absolute.

His reforms just didn't work. They were too sudden, and didn't take into account the natural inertia of society, even among those who were to be benefited. What's more, he was no Peter the Great would could put through unwanted reforms by means of his overflowing energy and brutality. He died on February 20, 1790, in bitter disappointment, having petulantly withdrawn all his attempted reforms.

He was succeeded by his brother, who reigned as Leopold II. He was also a reformer, though considerably more moderate than Joseph II had been. Leopold had to face the French Revolution but died in 1792 and was succeeded by his son, Francis II (1768–1835), under whom the war against France began in earnest.

While Francis II lost to Bonaparte in Italy, he gained Venetia and a further section of Poland.

In Austria at this time, Haydn and Mozart were still the musical stars. Haydn wrote symphonies, masses, and, in 1798, the oratorio, "The Creation." Mozart wrote the operas *Marriage of Figaro* in 1787, *Don Giovanni* in 1787, and *The Magic Flute* in 1791, along with hosts of other remarkable compositions.

In Germany generally, Goethe continued to write. He settled in Weimar in 1775 and made it Germany's cultural center. He wrote the play, *Egmont,* dealing with the rebellion of Netherlands against Spain. Also working in Weimar was Friedrich Schiller (1759–1805), who was a writer of the first rank, though overshadowed by Goethe. He wrote *The Robbers* in 1781. He also wrote a history of the Thirty Years War between 1791 and 1793, and based his drama-trilogy *Wallenstein,* published in 1800, on incidents in that war that had been fought a century and a half earlier.

The great German philosophers of the period were Immanuel Kant (1724–1804) and his pupil, Johann Gotlieb Fichte (1762–1814). Both tried to

work out the properties and limitations of reason. The former's most important book was *The Critique of Pure Reason,* published in 1781.

Among the German scientists of this period was Martin Heinrich Klaproth (1743–1817), the first German to accept Lavoisier's "New Chemistry." In 1789, he discovered a new metal he named for Herschel's new planet, Uranus. Klaproth called the metal "uranium."

PRUSSIA

Frederick II of Prussia died on August 17, 1786, having reigned for 46 years and having kept the peace in the second half of his reign. He left no heirs, but was succeeded by his nephew, who reigned as Frederick William II (1744–1797).

Frederick William II joined Austria in the initial attack on the French revolutionaries, but he was far more interested in the Polish situation, where he participated in two more partitions of Poland that erased that nation from the map and greatly increased Prussian territory. It was questionable, however, whether Prussia was really strengthened by adding to its population some millions of highly reluctant Poles. Even Warsaw was a Prussian city by the time Frederick William II died on November 16, 1797, and was succeeded by his son, who reigned as Frederick William III (1770–1840).

PAPACY

Pius VI (1717–1799) became Pope in 1775, and it was a devastating reign for the Papacy. In his first 10 years, Pius had to deal with Joseph II of Austria, who was ferociously anticlerical. Then, after Joseph II died, the problems of the French Revolution and *its* anticlerical tendencies rose to haunt him.

The worst came when the territory of the Papal States was invaded by Bonaparte. The French occupied Rome on February 15, 1798, and declared a Roman republic. In 1799, Pius VI was carried into France by French troops and died a prisoner, being succeeded in 1800 by Pius VII (1742–1823).

An important Italian scientist of the period was Luigi Galvani (1737–1798). Experimenting with static electricity stored in Leyden jars, he found that frog muscles, freshly removed from a frog, twitched when touched by an electric spark. This was the first indication of an interconnection of life and electric charge. By 1791, he showed that muscles twitched when they made simultaneous contact with two different metals, such as brass and iron.

SARDINIA

In 1773, Sardinia came under the rule of Victor Amadeus III (1726–1796). He joined Austria in the War of the First Coalition against France, and, as a result, his territories were occupied by Bonaparte in 1796.

Victor Amadeus died in that year and was succeeded by his son, Charles Emmanuel IV (1751–1819), who was forced to cede all his mainland territories to France in 1798. He retired to his island of Sardinia where the British fleet could protect him.

NAPLES

Ferdinand I of Naples also joined Austria in the War of the First Coalition against France. On December 21, 1798, the French invaded Naples and drove him to Sicily. He returned, temporarily, in 1799, but clearly his kingdom was at the mercy of France.

SWITZERLAND

Switzerland was hostile to the French revolutionaries, but decided to stay neutral. That did not keep the land out of trouble. During the War of the Second Coalition, Switzerland was the battleground between Suvorov of Russia and the French general, Andre Massena (1758–1817). Eventually, Massena won. On February 9, 1798, the French declared Switzerland the "Helvetic Republic" and reorganized it on revolutionary principles. On April 26, France annexed Geneva.

SWEDEN

Gustavus III went to war with Russia in 1788, and was promptly attacked by the ever-jealous Denmark. Despite winning a naval victory, Sweden got nothing out of it. It weakened Gustavus III's popularity and the coming of the French Revolution also dampened his enthusiasm about being a "benevolent despot." He died on March 19, 1792, after being shot at a masquerade ball by an assassin.

He was succeeded by his son, who reigned as Gustavus IV Adolphus (1778–1823), and who forgot all about "benevolence" in his fear of the revolutionary tide that was sweeping out of France.

POLAND

Poland, truncated by the First Partition of 1772, attempted, far too late, to reform its government and to set up a hereditary monarchy with the power of preventing the anarchy that was destroying the land. The trouble was that Russia was determined to prevent any reform, and France, which was the traditional defender of Poland, was falling into bankruptcy and revolution.

On May 3, 1791, the Poles actually produced a new constitution that might have made their government viable. Austria and Prussia accepted it, but Russia did not.

On May 14, 1792, Russia invaded Poland, and Prussia, in order to prevent Russia from taking the entire country, invaded it also. Russia and Prussia then carried through the Second Partition of Poland (Austria was not involved this time) on January 23, 1793. What was left of the nation, perhaps one-third of what had existed twenty years earlier, had to accept Russian domination of its foreign policy.

The Poles rose in despair on March 24, 1794, under the leadership of Thaddeus Kosciuszko (1746–1817), who had fought on the side of the Americans in the War of American Independence.

The Poles drove the Russian garrison out of Warsaw, but their situation was hopeless. They could not possibly fight the Russians and Prussians simultaneously. On October 10, 1794, the Polish forces were defeated by the Russians and Kosciuszko fell, seriously wounded.

Then, on October 24, 1795, there was a Third Partition of Poland, in which Austria participated, and Poland vanished from the map.

In the three partitions, Russia took the eastern half of the nation, a region that had once been Lithuania. Its half was actually occupied by Slavic peoples who had once been part of Kievan Russia and who had been taken over by Lithuania in the years after the Mongol invasion had paralyzed Russia. It was Prussia and Austria that actually divided the Polish-speaking population between themselves.

RUSSIA

During the War of American Independence, Catherine II of Russia sponsored the notion of a "League of Armed Neutrality," demanding that neutral ships be allowed to trade freely. It proposed, too, that blockades had to be supported by ships that actually blocked ports and could not simply be announced as existing (a "paper blockade") in order to justify the sinking of neutral ships at will. This was an anti-British measure since Great Britain controlled the seas and was the one power that could effectively destroy neutral shipping. Such proposals helped organize Europe against Great Britain and contributed significantly to the establishment of American independence.

Catherine II also wished to drive the Ottoman Empire out of the Christian Balkans and, to that end, she held what we would today call a "summit meeting" with Joseph II of Austria, who visited Russia in 1780 for that purpose. They set up an alliance to take the Balkans, and to then divide it between Russia and Austria.

In 1783, Catherine made the first move by annexing the Crimea. This was the last region that was still controlled by the Tatars and was the last bit of the conquests of the Mongols that had begun five and a half centuries earlier.

Naturally, the Turks did their best to persuade the Crimean Tatars to rise against the Russians in protest of the annexation. This led to war between Russia and the Ottoman Empire in 1787.

Suvorov, as might be expected, won victories wherever he led his army, but the Turks managed to fight off the Austrians and to defeat those Russian generals who were not Suvorov. John Paul Jones, the American naval hero, was now fighting for the Russians, and defeated the Turkish fleet in the Black Sea in two engagements in June 1788.

The Russians were distracted when Sweden took advantage of the situation to invade Finland in 1788, and Russia therefore grew willing to seek peace with Turkey. The Treaty of Jassy, a town on what is now the Rumanian border, gave Russia the Black Sea coast east of the Dniester River. This meant that Russia had now gained the boundaries in Europe that it has retained, more or less, ever since.

Catherine II died on November 17, 1796, having reigned 34 years. She was succeeded by her son, who reigned as Paul I (1754–1801).

With Poland successfully partitioned, and the wars with Turkey and Sweden successfully concluded, Paul I had a chance to take part in the War of the Second Coalition, in which Suvorov recaptured Italy from the French while Bonaparte was in Egypt.

Under Paul I, Russia also advanced south of the Caucasus, annexing Georgia in 1800.

OTTOMAN EMPIRE

In this period, the Ottoman Empire continued to decay. It lost ground to Russia in the Crimea and the Balkans. It was helpless to stop Bonaparte in Egypt and Syria, both of which were under Ottoman overlordship.

Selim III, who became sultan in 1789, attempted to introduce reforms, both economic and military, along western lines. He felt the influence of the French Revolution, and set up a system of embassies that, for the first time, maintained contact with the European powers.

AFGHANISTAN

After the death of Ahmad Shah in 1773, Afghanistan was ruled by weaker successors and the nation declined in power. In 1798, a long war began with Persia that weakened both nations.

PERSIA

In this period, Persia continued to be ruled by incompetents who could not prevent Russian advances south of the Caucasus Mountains into the region which came to be called "Transcaucasia."

INDIA

Charles Cornwallis, who had surrendered at Yorktown, was appointed governor-general of India on February 23, 1786, and there he did a good job. He introduced important reforms in line with Pitt's "India Act." Cornwallis saw to it that British officials were well-paid and were forbidden to engage in private business. This tended to reduce corruption and to lower the temptation for British officials to enrich themselves at the expense of the Indian people.

Cornwallis did not, however, believe the Indians could govern themselves; thus, they were excluded from decision-making positions and were treated as though they were children.

Cornwallis engaged in war against those sections of India whose rulers were hostile to Great Britain. Notable in this respect was Tippu Sultan (1750–1799), who became ruler of Mysore in southern India in 1783 and who had been trained by the French. He was defeated by the British in two wars that ended with his death in 1799. The British then kept Mysore as a protectorate and controlled almost all of southern India.

In the second war, the British forces were led by Richard Wellesley, Lord Mornington (1760–1842). He became governor-general in 1798, and pressed the war against Tippu Sultan since it was felt possible that Bonaparte might somehow reach India from Egypt. In the last battles of the war, Wellesley's younger brother, Arthur Wellesley (1769–1852), did particularly well.

Meanwhile, France's conquest of the Netherlands made the island of Ceylon, a Dutch possession, seem fair game to the British. In 1795, the British sent an expedition to Ceylon and easily defeated the Dutch; in 1798, Ceylon became a British crown colony.

CHINA

China was still powerful under the Manchus, and had forced recognition of its suzerainty on Burma and Nepal; however, in this period, they were forced to fight and suppress a series of rebellions. That damaged the Chinese economy and seemed to presage a coming decline.

PACIFIC

In Captain Cook's third and last voyage from 1776 to 1779, he was commissioned to explore the far northern Pacific. He sailed the full north–south length of the ocean, discovering the Hawaiian Islands on the way. After following the Alaskan and Siberian coasts as far as ice would permit, he returned to Hawaii. There he, like Magellan two and a half centuries earlier, was killed in a scuffle with the natives. This last voyage took place during the War of American Independence, and Benjamin Franklin, who fully appreciated the scientific importance of Cook's work, arranged that he should not be molested by American privateers.

One of those who accompanied Cook on this voyage was William Bligh (1754–1817). Bligh was later given command of the ship *Bounty* on a voyage to Tahiti in 1787. His harsh discipline provoked a famous mutiny led by the mate, Fletcher Christian, in April 1789. Bligh and some loyal men were placed in an open boat where it was expected they would die. However, Bligh managed to sail the boat 4000 miles westward to safety in the island of Timor in the East Indies. Christian and the mutineers, together with Tahitian women, landed in the uninhabited Pitcairn's Island, where their descendants live to this day.

AUSTRALIA

There are various kinds of punishment for crimes, or social misbehavior. One of those not frequently employed is transportation to some far-off region. Thus, Russia sent convicts to Siberia, and Great Britain, in this period, began to send them to Australia.

The first shipload of convicts to Australia

came on January 26, 1788, when 11 ships carrying 520 male convicts and 197 female convicts landed at Botany Bay on the southeastern shore of Australia near where the city of Sydney now stands.

In 1793, the first free settlers arrived. In 1794, sheep-raising began, and the land proved favorable to that line of endeavor.

1800 TO 1820

FRANCE

As 1800 opened, Napoleon Bonaparte was dictator of France. As First Consul, his term was for 10 years, and the other two consuls were his appointees and had no say in anything. He reorganized the government with a sure hand and quickly produced an efficiency that France had never seen before. Much of his system has persisted in France to this day.

Bonaparte would have, at this point, welcomed peace, but only on his own terms. Russia had left the Second Coalition in anger at Austria's lack of cooperation, but Austria was still in the field. It had regained most of Italy, thanks to Suvorov, and was anxious to take the remaining French strongholds. Austria had placed Genoa under siege, for instance, and Bonaparte's general, Massena, who had taken Switzerland two years earlier, was forced to surrender the city on June 4, 1800, after it had undergone agonies of famine. Under such circumstances, peace was unthinkable for Bonaparte. He had to take action.

Therefore, Bonaparte launched his "Second Italian Campaign." He crossed the Alps in May, 1800, and was too late to save Genoa, but he reached Marengo, about 50 miles north of that city. There he found himself facing an Austrian army under Michael Friedrich von Melas (1729–1806) on June 14, 1800.

Bonaparte was outnumbered and apparently hadn't expected to encounter the Austrians when he did. The Austrians had the better of it at first, and Melas, thinking he had won, was marching off, when reinforcements reached the French and

they attacked again. The Battle of Marengo ended with a complete Austrian defeat, and northwestern Italy was again in Bonaparte's hands.

In Germany, the Austrians were defeated by the French general Victor Moreau, at Hohenlinden in southern Bavaria on December 3, 1800. Beaten in both Germany and Italy, Austria had to make peace, and the Treaty of Luneville, in Lorraine, was signed on February 9, 1801. By its terms, the situation in Italy was restored to what it had been before Suvorov had unsettled matters. France also annexed all the German territory west of the Rhine River. Spain was forced to cede the Louisiana territory west of the Mississippi to France, which thus regained (temporarily, at least) some of the North American Empire it had lost 40 years earlier.

In Egypt, things did not go so well for France. The army that Bonaparte had left behind was still at a dead end. The French general, Jean Baptiste Kleber (1753–1800) was a competent man who, even as late as March 20, 1800, defeated the Turks and took Cairo. On June 14, 1800, however, on the day of Marengo, Kleber was assassinated by an Egyptian and after that the end was just a matter of time.

A British–Turkish force made an amphibious landing at Abukir, near Alexandria, on March 8, 1801. In July, the force took Cairo and in August it took Alexandria. On August 31, 1801, the French army in Egypt surrendered and was allowed to go back to France.

Once the Egyptian matter was cleaned up, it was possible for France and Great Britain to make peace; they did so by the Treaty of Amiens on

March 27, 1802. By its terms, Great Britain gave up all its conquests except Trinidad, which it had taken from Spain, and Ceylon, which it had taken from the Netherlands. There was general peace in Europe after 10 years of war.

Bonaparte seized the opportunity on August 2, 1802, to make himself Consul for life, with the right to choose his successor. This meant that he was a king, without the title.

Bonaparte went about the works of peace. He reorganized Germany, shuffling states and cities and bishoprics, reducing the Holy Roman Empire to the faintest possible of echoes. He organized a new law code for France, the "Code Napoleon," which combined the principles of the old Roman law of Justinian, some 13 centuries earlier, with the new principles of the French Revolution. This code was his most permanent achievement, for it still holds, with revisions, in France today. It has also influenced the legal system of much of the rest of the world, as far away, even, as Japan—although Great Britain and the United States continued to follow their own legal system based on the English "common law."

Bonaparte's achievements in war and peace did not, however, make him universally popular. There were still republicans who resented his reinstitution of something very like a monarchy, and there were royalists who wanted a legitimate king. Bonaparte grew a bit paranoid over the matter. With the help of his efficient and merciless minister of police, Joseph Fouche (1759–1820), an old Jacobin, he uncovered a number of conspiracies or supposed conspiracies, hanging some of the suspects, sending others fleeing into exile. General Moreau, the victor of Hohenlinden, had to flee to the United States, for instance.

To strike terror into the hearts of the royalists, Bonaparte had an inoffensive member of the royal family, Louis Antoine Henri, Duke d'Enghien (1772–1804), kidnapped. He had been living quietly in Baden, a German state just east of the French border, but was dragged away by French forces, given a mockery of a trial and, on March 20, 1804, was executed. The deed was so clearly without justification that it turned out to be a great piece of propaganda against Bona-

parte. As it was put at the time, "It was worse than a crime; it was a blunder."

Bonaparte decided that there would be no end of conspiracies unless it was clear that if he were killed, some member of his family would automatically succeed him. He would have to be a crowned monarch. Therefore, on December 2, 1804, he had himself crowned Emperor of the French, and he reigned as Napoleon I. (From this point on, he is known as Napoleon, rather than Bonaparte.)

Napoleon's coronation marked the final end of the French Republic, which had lasted only 12 years. Napoleon established a royal court and made his generals into noblemen—but the nobility depended on ability and achievements, rather than upon birth, and the new monarchy was far more efficient than the old.

Napoleon might have accomplished a great deal if he could only have stopped fighting, but he couldn't.

The peace with Great Britain was a very uneasy one and it only lasted a little over a year. Neither side trusted the other, and trivial differences were allowed to fester. On May 16, 1803, Great Britain and France were again at war.

As long as these two were the only enemies, there was not much that either could do; it was a case of the elephant versus the whale. Great Britain could blockade the French coast, but smuggling was always possible. As for France, Bonaparte began to collect ships with which to carry an army to Great Britain, but he knew he couldn't do it in the face of Great Britain's control of the English Channel.

Slowly, though, Great Britain gained allies. There was Austria, of course, chafing over having been defeated by Napoleon twice. And there was Russia and Sweden, each of which feared the continuing growth of Napoleon's strength. By 1805, they were ready, and "The War of the Third Coalition" began. Napoleon had to face them with only the dubious help of his various puppet regimes.

Napoleon's main army was concentrated in northern France, where it was uselessly threatening to invade Great Britain. The only other considerable French army was under Massena in northern Italy. It was for this army that the coalition aimed.

Napoleon realized this; therefore, he planned to do the unexpected. He took the large army he had built up in northern France and marched it quickly and secretly toward Bavaria (as once Marlborough had done a century earlier), so that he could strike at unprepared Austria directly. This was Napoleon's "First Austrian Campaign."

One Austrian army, totally unaware that Napoleon was speeding on his way toward them, invaded Bavaria in a leisurely way. They were near Ulm on the upper Danube. Another Austrian army was well to the south, and a Russian army was far to the east, but the racing French managed to get between Ulm and the other armies and, on October 17, 1805, after a quick Battle of Ulm, the entire Austrian army that was located there was forced to surrender.

On October 30, Massena defeated the Austrians in northern Italy, and Napoleon was moving his own men eastward into Austria itself.

At Austerlitz, about 75 miles north of Vienna, Napoleon awaited the onslaught of the Austrians and the Russians. (The Austrian and Russian Emperors were in the field as well as Napoleon, so the battle that followed is sometimes called the "Battle of the Three Emperors," but more properly it is the "Battle of Austerlitz.")

On December 2, 1805 (the first anniversary of Napoleon's Imperial coronation), the battle was fought. Napoleon so distributed his army that he tempted the allies to fall on his right wing, which they did. When they were fully committed, he attacked the allies in the center, split their line in two, and encircled the left half. The Austrian and Russian armies were hopelessly defeated and scattered, and Austerlitz proved to be Napoleon's greatest victory.

On December 26, 1805, the Austrians had no choice but to make a losing treaty with Napoleon for the third time. This time it was at Pressburg (now known as Bratislava in southern Czechoslovakia). Austria had to give up Venetia, which it had gained eight years earlier, and France annexed northwestern Italy. Austria recognized Napoleon as King of Italy, and had to promote several German rulers to the title of king.

At the same time, Napoleon dethroned Ferdinand I of Naples, who had to flee to Sicily again and hide behind the British fleet. Napoleon began to make royalty out of his family. His brother, Joseph (1768–1844), became King of Naples, and his brother, Louis (1778–1846), became King of Holland (i.e., The Netherlands).

On July 12, Napoleon organized the western part of Germany as the "Confederation of the Rhine," which remained, of course, a French puppet. In fact, virtually all of western Europe was now either French or French-controlled.

On August 6, 1806, the Holy Roman Empire came to an end, almost exactly a thousand years after Charlemagne had been crowned. Francis II of Austria was the last Holy Roman Emperor, but he didn't stop being an Emperor. In 1804, he had proclaimed himself Francis I, Emperor of Austria, because he didn't want to be simply an Archduke once Napoleon had become an Emperor.

Despite Napoleon's great victories of 1805, and his reorganization of the map of Europe, he had suffered a loss that year that more than cost him all he had won in his victories.

On October 21, 1805, the British fleet under Nelson caught the combined French and Spanish fleets off Cape Trafalgar near Gibraltar. Nelson's 27 ships attacked the 33 Franco–Spanish ships with such great skill that all but 11 of the enemy ships were sunk or taken, while the British lost not one ship.

Nelson died of a gunshot at the moment of victory, but he had insured British control of the sea and while that was true, Napoleon could never defeat Great Britain and was sure of strangulation himself, however long it might take.

On land, there was still Prussia. Prussia had not fought against France since the early days of the First Coalition, 14 years earlier. Prussia still, however, basked in the memory of the victories of Frederick the Great half a century before and was foolishly confident that it could beat Napoleon, as it had beaten the generals of Louis XV.

Prussia had not joined the Third Coalition in 1805, when it might have done some good, but now, in 1806, worried about Napoleon's fiddling with the map of Germany, it decided to fight Napoleon when it was too late.

Napoleon still had his army in southern Germany after the defeat of Austria, and knowing of Prussian preparations, he lunged rapidly northward on October 8.

Six days later, he encountered the slow-moving and overconfident Prussians and, on October 14, there was a double battle. Napoleon fought a Prussian army at Jena, in west Saxony, while his general, Louis Nicolas Davout (1770–1823), engaged a larger Prussian army nearby at Auerstadt. In both cases, the Prussians were smashed and their armies disintegrated. Napoleon rushed eastward, occupied Berlin on October 24, and the "Prussian campaign" was over.

Of course, that still left Russia, which had supported Austria in the previous year, and had supported Prussia now. On November 30, 1806, therefore, Napoleon moved eastward to Warsaw (which had been in Prussian hands for 11 years, since the Third Partition) in order to keep an eye on the Russians.

Russia moved to attack and, on February 8, 1807, the two armies met at the Battle of Eylau in East Prussia. It was a drawn battle and both sides had to pull away. It was the first time that Napoleon had fought a large battle without a definite victory.

There was, however, a return match on June 14, 1807, at Friedland, a little to the east of Eylau. This time, Napoleon did win, and the next day he took Koenigsberg, in East Prussia. All of Prussia was now in his hands, and Russia asked for terms.

On July 7 to 9, 1807, Napoleon and Alexander I had a summit meeting at Tilsit on the Niemen River that marked the boundary between Prussia and Russia.

Prussia had to give up all the land it had taken during the Second and Third Partitions of Poland and out of it, plus the Austrian part of the Third Partition, the "Grand Duchy of Warsaw" was constituted as, of course, a French puppet. Prussia also had to give up all her territory west of the Elbe River, to reduce her army, and to pay a large indemnity. Russia lost no territory but

agreed to an alliance with France against Great Britain.

Napoleon was now master, or dominant partner, of all the European nations, and was at the peak of his power. He had done it all in 11 years, from the time when, as a lean and hungry general, he had entered Italy.

He might have stopped now, but there was still Great Britain to deal with. In fact, even if he had offered Great Britain generous terms, it is likely that those terms would not have been accepted. Great Britain would not make peace with any power controlling all of Europe; not as long as it had a dominating navy and control of the seas.

The only way Napoleon could fight Great Britain was by economic pressure, and this he attempted to do. While he was in Berlin, he published the "Berlin Decree" on November 21, 1806. This declared a blockade of Great Britain, which he lacked the ships to enforce, and declared Europe closed to British trade (the "Continental system," this was called). He reinforced this by the "Milan Decree" after Tilsit, on December 17, 1807, which he insisted that Russia join.

Actually, the Continental system was a mistake. It harmed Europe more than it harmed Great Britain, and the need for trade with lands overseas, which Great Britain controlled absolutely, was so great that smuggling took place everywhere and there just weren't enough soldiers to guard the entire coastline of the continent.

Portugal, being strongly pro-British, was one place where trade continued. Therefore, Napoleon forced Spain to allow a French army to pass through it to Portugal. This army under Andoche Junot (1771–1813) took Lisbon on December 1, 1807, and the Portuguese royal family fled to Brazil.

Spain, however, remained a center for smuggling that undermined the Continental system. Napoleon felt that he could not trust the Spanish royal family. In March, 1808, he forced Charles IV, and his son, Ferdinand (1784–1833), to give up their claims to the Spanish throne, which he then handed over to his brother, Joseph, who, till then, had been King of Naples. Napoleon then made one of his more flamboyant generals, Joachim Murat (1767–1815), King of Naples. This was done because Murat was married to Napoleon's sister, Maria (1777–1820), and was therefore the Emperor's brother-in-law.

This interference with Spain was a military mistake, Napoleon's second. His first military mistake had been his hare-brained expedition to Egypt, but that had been minor and the damage had been contained. The Spanish adventure was much worse, however. There was no need for it. The Spanish royal family was totally subservient to Napoleon, and when he displaced them, he stirred up a hornet's nest. The Spanish King and Prince were totally worthless, but the Spanish people, at this time, decided they would rather have a worthless king of their own, than a worthier one imposed on them from outside.

On May 2, 1808, they rose in rebellion and there followed years of guerrilla war that bled France needlessly. (The word *guerrilla* came into use on this occasion. It is Spanish for "little war," one that is fought by small bands of hit-and-run nonprofessionals.)

The British were only too willing to encourage the rebellion and sent in money and arms. Eventually, they sent in troops, under Arthur Wellesley, who had done well in India, and who was eventually made Duke of Wellington, by which title he is usually referred to in history. This began what the British called "the Peninsular War," since it was fought in the Iberian peninsula.

Napoleon began to experience difficulties. On July 19, 1808, a French army in western Spain was forced to surrender to the Spaniards (the first surrender of a Napoleonic army) and were then brutally done to death. Wellington defeated the French under Junot in Portugal on August 21, 1808, and would have done even better if he had not been hampered by his superiors.

Another British army under John Moore (1761–1809) advanced from Portugal toward Madrid; however, by this time, Napoleon was sufficiently annoyed by what was going on to enter Spain himself in the fall of 1808. In this "Spanish campaign" he acted with typical energy, taking Madrid from the Spaniards and clearing the countryside.

Moore found himself cut off from Portugal. He had to get his army safely out of the country and he headed for La Coruna in the northwestern corner of Spain. He reached the port and defeated a French force, making evacuation possible, but was killed in action there on January 16, 1809.

Yet despite Napoleon's success in Spain, the guerrilla war still continued and Wellington was still in Portugal.

While the guerrilla war in Spain was in its early stages, Napoleon held a congress at Erfurt in Saxony, one which was designed to show the power of the new Europe. He was there in full display along with any number of German kings and princes—all puppets. There he intended to make an attempt to force Alexander of Russia to take a still harder line against Great Britain, but Alexander found himself rather disillusioned with Napoleon. He was tired of Napoleon's posturings and the Continental system was hurting Russia.

Besides, Napoleon had a foreign minister, Charles Maurice de Talleyrand (1754–1838), the clearest-minded French politician since Richelieu, two centuries earlier. Talleyrand could see that Napoleon was simply unable to stop grabbing for more and more and that, sooner or later, he would grab too much and would topple. Anxious to save France from that disaster, he negotiated secretly with Alexander to try to force Napoleon to stop.

Prussia and, to some extent, Austria were chastened by their defeats in 1805 and 1806 and were busy reforming their government and trying to make their armies more efficient and more nearly modeled on the principles which Napoleon himself followed.

Friedrich Karl von Stein (1757–1831) was particularly active in reforming Prussia and when Napoleon forced him to resign his posts in 1808, he fled to Austria and then to Russia, maintaining unyielding opposition to Napoleon wherever he went. The Austrian ambassador to France,

Kelmens Wenzel von Metternnich (1773–1859), was also watchful for any hope of resisting Napoleon.

The gathering Napoleonic trouble in Spain gave Austria that hope, and it was fed by the British who were always ready to give money to any nation who would be willing to fight Napoleon.

On April 9, 1809, then, Austria invaded Bavaria (still a French puppet) and Napoleon had to hasten back eastward from his unfinished labors in Spain. On April 16, he was in Germany for this "Second Austrian Campaign" and, in seven days of fighting, he forced his way to Ratisbon (Regensburg, in German) in eastern Bavaria. In the process, he had sufficiently shaken up the Austrian army to make it possible for him to continue his advance and to march straight to Vienna and take it, without a fight, on May 13, 1809.

An Austrian army was on the north bank of the Danube, however, and Napoleon tried to get at them on May 21 by forcing his way across the river at Aspern and *failed*. The Battle of Eylau, a year and a half earlier, had been a draw, but this Battle of Aspern was a defeat, the first important defeat that Napoleon had suffered when he himself had been directing operations, and it was a defeat handed him by the Austrians, whom he despised.

Napoleon made more careful plans, crossed the river on July 5, 1809, and, at Wagram, north of Vienna, he massed artillery with the greatest concentration ever seen up to that time. He defeated the Austrians, who had to ask for peace for a fourth time.

Peace was made at Schonbrunn, a royal palace in a Vienna suburb, and Austria gave up still more territory and agreed to join Napoleon in an alliance against Great Britain. Napoleon's hold on central Europe seemed stronger than ever.

By the end of 1809, Great Britain was in control of Portugal, and the islands of Sardinia and Sicily (and, of course, it controlled the sea). Sweden, Russia, and the Ottoman Empire were neutral. All the rest of Europe seemed firmly under the Napoleonic thumb.

What Napoleon still lacked, however, was an heir, which Josephine, his wife of 13 years, could not supply. He divorced her in 1809, therefore. In 1810, he forced the proud Hapsburgs of Austria to supply him with a new wife. She was Marie Louise (1791–1847), the daughter of Francis I of Austria, so that the French, who had guillotined an Austrian queen 17 years earlier, now had another one.

On March 20, 1811, a son was born to Napoleon, and the child was given the title of "King of Rome."

All now seemed well, and Napoleon must surely have felt he had everything he could want (except for an end to the annoying guerrilla war in Spain), but relations with Russia were deteriorating.

Russia was not comfortable with the existence of the Grand Duchy of Warsaw. They did not like Napoleon's marriage to an Austrian princess. They were annoyed that Napoleon was not willing to give them a free hand against the Ottoman Empire. And they did not like the Continental system.

It seemed to Napoleon that it was necessary to teach the Russians a lesson. He envisaged a lightning slash into Russia, a defeat of the Russian armies, the occupation of Moscow—and Russia would become as humble and compliant as the Prussians and Austrians. In thinking this, he made his third, and greatest, military mistake. It was, indeed, a fatal one.

In May, 1812, Napoleon began to assemble an army in Poland and managed to add to his French masses contingents from Austria, Prussia, Poland, and Italy.

On June 24, 1812, a huge army of about 600,000 men crossed the Niemen River and invaded Russia. What then happened was exactly what had happened when Charles XII of Sweden invaded Russia a century earlier. It is impossible to believe that Napoleon had not studied the campaigns of Charles XII, yet he did not seem to have learned anything from them. What ailed Napoleon was that, by this time, he simply could not conceive of defeat.

Napoleon advanced and the Russians retreated, scorching the earth as they did so. The French took Mohilev on July 23 and Smolensk on August 17. The Russians fought, but retreated as they did so. They did now allow themselves to be trapped.

On August 29, 1812, Mikhail Ilarionovich Kutuzov (1745–1813) took over the command of the Russian armies. He had been defeated at Austerlitz, but largely because he had been overruled by the Emperors of Russia and Austria. Grimly, he continued to retreat.

Napoleon pressed on. He did not turn south as Charles XII had done but continued to aim for Moscow. Kutuzov was prepared to let him take Moscow but it was psychologically impossible for him to do so without a fight. At Borodino, then, 100 miles west of Moscow, Kutuzov made his stand. A bloody battle was fought there on September 7, 1812. More men were killed in battle on that day than in any battle in history up to then (or for a hundred years thereafter). When it was over, the French held the battlefield and the Russians retreated.

Because of this, the Battle of Borodino is accounted a French victory, especially since three Russians died for every two Frenchmen. However, the Russians could replace their losses, and the French could not. With only 95,000 men left in the invading army, not quite one sixth of the starting mass, and with no hope for reinforcements, Napoleon staggered into Moscow on September 14, 1812. He was convinced that, despite his enormous losses, he had achieved his aim and that the Russian government would now have no choice but to ask for terms.

Things, however, did not go well. In the first place, Moscow was deserted and, once the French arrived, it began to burn. It would not do as a comfortable place to spend the winter.

Second, Kutuzov was outside with at least 110,000 Russians, who were a great deal more accustomed to hardship than the French, and whose numbers were sure to increase, so that Moscow would not be even an uncomfortable place to remain in for very long.

And third, the occupation of Moscow brought no word from Alexander of Russia. He would not treat with Napoleon as long as there was a single Frenchman on Russian soil.

Napoleon remained in Moscow for five weeks and then, on October 19, realized there was nothing he could do but leave, go back to Smolensk, and enter winter quarters. There he would gather reinforcements and be ready for another advance in the spring.

It was not Kutuzov's intention to let this happen. He proceeded to follow a policy of avoiding outright combat but constantly harassing the retreating French columns and attacking isolated bands in such a way that the French army found it could only retreat without being molested, along the precise route by which they had advanced—the route where the retreating Russians had destroyed everything.

The weather worsened as the French marched. The snow began to fall and the cold began to close in. There would be no chance to halt at Smolensk; they would have to get out of the terrible country altogether. The French army became a disorderly mob that knew only that it was marching and suffering endlessly.

By December 8, 1812, Napoleon abandoned what was left of his army in Russia and raced back to Paris to raise a new one. Only 10,000 of his soldiers made it out of Russia. The last to leave was Michel Ney (1769–1815), not the best of Napoleon's generals, but certainly the bravest. He stepped across the border marching backward, firing at the pursuing Russians.

Russian soldiers did not pursue the French after they had crossed over into Poland. They were too worn out themselves. Besides, they didn't have to. Prussia rose in revolt against Napoleon and kept the French garrisons in Germany busy. After some months, required for recovery, Russian units joined them.

In April 1813, Napoleon returned to Germany with a new army of 200,000 soldiers. They were inexperienced, however, the scrapings at the bottom of the barrel. His veterans were lying dead on a dozen battlefields, and in particular, were strewn over the wastes of Russia.

Napoleon was still a brilliant fighter and won victories, partly because of his brilliance and partly because his opponents flinched before him. Still, his army was brittle and kept failing to meet his demands. He asked for an armistice on June 4, and got one. He spent about 10 weeks training his army, but that did him no good for the allies who were fighting him used the armistice to even better advantage. Moreover, by August 12, 1813, Austria had joined a war against Napoleon for the fifth time.

On August 26, 1813, Napoleon won one more great battle at Dresden in Saxony, but the French army wasn't going to be able to take much more.

On October 16–19, 1813, there came the three-day Battle of Leipzig in Saxony (also called "the Battle of the Nations" because so many national armies were fighting, mostly against Napoleon). It turned out to be a great and crucial defeat for Napoleon, though, even now, he was able to get his army out of the battlefield and avoided having to surrender.

By this time, also, French troops had to be called out of Spain, and Wellington helped them on their way with all his might. By October 31, 1813, Spain was clear of the French. Napoleon had been driven back to the borders of France on every side.

The Allies offered Napoleon peace if he would be willing to rule over France alone. Madly, Napoleon refused, and on January 1, 1814, the Allies invaded France.

Napoleon twisted and turned and showed all his military brilliance. Whatever could be done with his worn-out and shrinking army, he did, but the Allies were too strong and there was a limit even to Napoleonic miracles.

On March 31, 1814, the Allies marched into Paris, and on April 11, Napoleon abdicated. He had ruled France for 13 and a half years, and had had the most remarkable military career of anyone since Genghis Khan, six centuries earlier; however, it had all shrunk to nothing less than two years after he had made the colossal mistake of invading Russia.

Napoleon was sent to rule the small island of Elba, near the island of Corsica, where he had been born 45 years earlier. Elba was made an independent nation for him.

The victorious powers gathers at "The Congress of Vienna" from September 1814 to June 1815, to redraw the map of Europe after 25 unbelievable years of revolution and war. Many heads of state were present, including Alexander I of Russia, who was the undoubted star of the occasion since everyone knew that the Russian campaign had destroyed Napoleon. Russia's reputation in Europe never stood higher than at that moment.

At the Congress of Vienna, France was not badly treated. This was partly because the Allies had returned it to Louis XVIII, the younger brother of Louis XVI who had been executed 22 years earlier; and the Allies wanted to make sure that he would stay on the throne of a reasonably prosperous and stable France. Partly, too, it was the result of the brilliant diplomacy of Talleyrand, as he carefully played the Allies against each other.

The rest of Europe was redesigned so that France was surrounded by stronger states than before, and so that the victors would be rewarded. However, even while the Congress was continuing, the unbelievable news reached them that on March 1, 1815, Napoleon had landed in southern France. The French people flocked to him and, on March 20, 1815, he was in Paris and Louis XVIII had fled again. The Empire was restored and Great Britain, Russia, Austria, and Prussia formed a new alliance against Napoleon. The Duke of Wellington was placed in overall command.

Napoleon was forced to fight and on June 14, he crossed over into Belgium. The climactic battle was at Waterloo, a few miles south of Brussels, on June 18, 1815. It was a hard-fought battle between the French and the British, but Napoleon was not at his best and he dared not risk the Imperial Guard under Ney at the crucial moment. Then the Prussians under the aged Gebhard Leberecht von Blucher (1742–1819) arrived, even while the issue was in doubt, and that was the last straw. The French army collapsed, and the very word "Waterloo" has ever since been used to mean any catastrophic and final defeat.

The Battle of Waterloo put an end, at last, to

the struggle between England and France that had been continuing for seven centuries since the time of Henry II of England. The British and French were never to fight a great land battle again.

On June 21, Napoleon abdicated a second time, and on July 15, he was taken by a British warship to the isolated island of St. Helena in the south Atlantic, where he remained in exile till his death on May 5, 1821.

Louis XVIII was again restored to the throne but he made no attempt to return France entirely to the "ancien regime" ("old government") that had prevailed before 1789. He compromised with reality, and allowed a certain amount of representative government. There was, however, a party of "Ultra-Royalists," who *did* want the old ways fully restored. Leading it was Louis's younger brother, who was heir to the throne.

Despite the furor of the Napoleonic era, the gatherings and marchings of armies, the great victories and defeats, science made steady progress in France.

Etienne Louis Malus (1775–1812) discovered polarized light in 1808, which made it necessary to view light as consisting of tiny transverse waves, moving up and down at right angles to the direction of the light ray. In 1811, he received a British medal for his work, despite the fact that Great Britain and France were at war. In 1814, Augustin Jean Fresnel (1788–1827) worked out the mathematical basis of such transverse waves.

Jean Baptiste Biot (1774–1820) showed in 1815 that solutions of certain organic substances could affect polarized light in either of two ways. This led to new methods of chemical analysis. In 1803, he had pointed out that meteorites did fall to the earth and that reports of such events were *not* old wives' tales.

In 1809, Joseph Louis Gay-Lussac (1778–1850) worked out the law of combining volumes, showing that gases combined in small whole numbers of volumes, which leant solid support for the atomic theory of matter being worked out in Great Britain. In 1811, Bernard Courtois (1777–1838) discovered iodine, while Louis Jacques Thenard (1777–1847) discovered hydrogen peroxide in 1818.

In 1815, François Magendie (1783–1855) was given the task of finding whether a nourishing food could be made out of gelatin obtained from otherwise inedible cuts of meat, since France was short on food after a quarter century of revolution and war. He showed that that was not possible; that food could taste good and seem filling and yet not be nourishing and not maintain life. This laid the groundwork for the modern science of nutrition.

Michel Eugene Chevreul (1786–1889), who lived for over a hundred years, studied the chemical structure of fats, and isolated fatty acids in 1809. In 1815, he identified the sugar in diabetic urine as glucose.

In biology, Marie François Savier Bichat (1771–1802) studied the various tissues making up living organs, published a book on the subject in 1800, and founded the science of histology.

Georges Leopold Cuvier (1769–1832) was probably the greatest biologist of his time. He was the first to classify the fossils, showing that they were extinct animals that, when living, fell into the same groups that present-day life-forms did. He founded the science of paleontology (the study of extinct forms of life).

Jean Baptiste de Lamarck (1744–1829) studied invertebrate animals (those without bones) from 1815 to 1822 and founded modern invertebrate zoology. In 1809, he was the first to suggest a mechanism for biological evolution, one that depended on the "inheritance of acquired characteristics." Thus, a creature who stretched his neck to reach leaves would pass a longer neck on to its offspring. The theory was wrong but it stimulated thought on the matter.

In technology, Joseph Marie Jacquard (1752–1834) invented the "Jacquard loom" in 1801. Punch cards directed rods to pass through (or not) in certain fixed patterns, which produced a corresponding pattern in the cloth being woven. To change the pattern, one merely designed a new punch-card. This, in a sense, was the first primitive step toward computers.

Nicolas Appert (1752–1841) tried to develop a method for preserving food, something Napoleon needed for his armies. Appert heated food to kill all the microorganisms in it, then sealed the container. He published his method in 1810 after Napoleon had rewarded him with 12,000 francs. Appert had thus invented the process of canning food, which altered the eating habits of the world and, in those places where the method was used, winter ceased to be a starving time.

Theophile Rene Hyacinthe Laennec (1781–1826) invented the stethoscope in 1816, something which (with improvements) soon became indispensable to physicians.

Perhaps the most successful French writer of the period was Anne Louise Germaine de Stael (1766–1817), whose writings so irritated Napoleon, for whom she did not hide her contempt, that he sent her into exile during his reign. She lived to see him overthrown and was able to return to France.

UNITED STATES

In 1800, Thomas Jefferson was elected third president of the United States. By that time, three new states had been added since the acceptance of the Constitution: Vermont, Kentucky, and Tennessee (the 14th, 15th, and 16th states, respectively). Ohio became the 17th state in 1803, Louisiana the 18th in 1812, Indiana the 19th in 1816, Mississippi the 20th in 1817, Illinois the 21st in 1818, and Alabama the 22nd in 1819.

The United States found itself in the odd position of being the world's most important neutral nation during the Napoleonic wars. This had both its advantages and disadvantages.

In 1801, for instance, Bonaparte had forced Spain to cede Louisiana, the large area west of the Mississippi, to France. It could only be of use to France if there were peace. If there continued to be war with Great Britain, it would surely fall to the British.

As for the United States, it had to have the mouth of the Mississippi River and the city of New Orleans located near that mouth. With the mouth of the Mississippi in foreign hands, whether Spanish, French, or British, the trade routes of the western part of the nation could be strangled. Jefferson sent negotiators to work out a purchase price for New Orleans and Bonaparte's representatives, suddenly and unexpect-

edly, offered to sell all of Louisiana for 15 million dollars. At the moment, the Peace of Amiens existed between Great Britain and France but it might break down at any moment, and the French would far rather that the United States had Louisiana than that the British have it. (Beside, the sale to the United States might sow discord between it and Great Britain, which France would also welcome.)

The United States could not turn down the bargain and the agreement was signed on April 30, 1803, just two weeks before war broke out again between Great Britain and France. This more than doubled the size of the United States, which now stretched from the Atlantic Ocean to the Rocky Mountains. Nor did the "Louisiana Purchase" cause trouble with Great Britain, which was relieved to get Bonaparte out of North America. Indeed, British bankers lent the United States the money with which to make the purchase.

Jefferson sent out an expedition to explore the new territory, one that was led by Meriwether Lewis (1774–1809) and William Clark (1770–1838). On May 14, 1804, the "Lewis and Clark Expedition," with 40 men, started at St. Louis and moved up the Missouri River. They crossed the Rocky Mountains and went down the Columbia river, reaching the Pacific Ocean on November 15, 1805. (The mouth of the Columbia River had been discovered, in 1791, by the American navigator, Robert Gray (1755–1806). He had named the river for his ship.)

The Lewis and Clark expedition was back in St. Louis on September 23, 1806. They were the first to cross the full width of what is now the continental United States. The region west of the Rockies that they explored was the "Oregon Territory." The United States claimed it on the basis of Gray's voyage and the Lewis and Clark expedition, but Great Britain claimed it, too. [Lewis and Clark, by the way, received enormous help from a Native American woman, Sacagawea (1786–1812), who acted as their guide.]

Another explorer was Zebulon Montgomery Pike (1779–1813). In 1805, he explored the northern reaches of the Mississippi River in what is now Minnesota. In 1806, he explored what is now Colorado and discovered the mountain now known as Pike's Peak on November 15, 1806.

The new American land was the site of an earthquake on December 15, 1811, the most violent in the United States in historic times. It occurred near the site of what is now New Madrid, Missouri. The area was then so thinly populated that not one fatality was reported. If it happened today, tens of thousands would probably die.

There were disadvantages to neutrality, too. Both France and Great Britain wanted to stop the United States from trading with the other side, so that British and French privateers both began to seize American vessels on suspicions of trading with the enemy (*their* enemy, not that of the United States).

Since Great Britain was far more powerful at sea, she did far more damage to American shipping than France did. What's more, Great Britain added another refinement to the mistreatment of American ships. Great Britain treated its sailors with great cruelty and a number of them deserted to American ships. There they received higher pay, better treatment, and no language barrier.

The British, therefore, took to stopping American ships on the high seas to search them for deserters. (They needed all the able seamen they could get in the life-and-death struggle with Napoleon, where only the British fleet made resistance possible.) Often, the British would take native-born Americans who, they claimed, were British. The United States protested such incidents but was powerless to stop them.

On June 22, 1807, when Napoleon was at the height of his power and was about to meet with Alexander I of Russia at Tilsit, Great Britain felt desperate. A British warship actually stopped an American warship and demanded the right to search her. There was a battle and the British killed three American sailors, wounded 18, then searched the ship and carried off four men they considered deserters.

All that President Jefferson could do was to declare an embargo, forbidding American ships to trade with anyone. This damaged the United States far more than it damaged its enemies.

When Jefferson's second term came to its close, he retired, and James Madison (1751–1836), one of the important devisers of the Constitution, became the fourth President of the United States. He eased the embargo, refusing trade only with Great Britain and France—but there wasn't much of anyone else to trade with, so it didn't help.

It was difficult for the United States to sit still under such treatment. It was a large country, far larger than any European country except Russia. Its population had reached 7.3 million, two and a half times what it was at the end of the War of American Independence. It was gaining in industry and it was producing large quantities of cotton, which was needed by the British textile factories. It was steadily beating back the Native Americans and it was even engaging in aggressive foreign policy.

The aggressiveness came about in this fashion. The North African coast west of Egypt contained the "Barbary States": Morocco, Algeria, Tunis, and Tripoli (the modern Libya). These were nominally under Ottoman overlordship at this time, as they had been for two and a half centuries, but they were virtually independent. They practiced piracy, capturing European vessels and enslaving crews and passengers. The European powers, totally absorbed in the Napoleonic conflicts had no time to do anything about it and simply paid "protection money" to the pirates to keep their ships safe.

The United States paid protection money to each of the Barbary States; however, in 1801, Tripoli, feeling the United States was weak enough to pay more protection money, declared war on it. Although Jefferson was a man of peace, this could not be endured. Ships were sent into the Mediterranean and Tripoli was bombarded into submission by June 4, 1805. (That is why the United States Marine hymn refers to "the shores of Tripoli.")

There were new young people in Congress who were demanding strong action against the British (they called themselves the "War Hawks" —and that started the use of "hawks" for those who were ready to risk war, and "doves" for those who strove for peace). The War Hawks finally had their way and, on June 18, 1812, the United States declared war on Great Britain, and the "War of 1812" began.

It came at a particularly bad time for Great Britain, since six days later, Napoleon invaded Russia, and if Russia fell, Great Britain would be left completely alone in her fight against the all-powerful French conqueror. With that in mind, Great Britain had already given in to many of the American demands, but in those days it took six weeks for news to cross the Atlantic Ocean, and the war was on before the news of conciliation arrived.

The Americans intended to conquer Canada, but they did not have a well-trained army, and its performance on the Canadian frontier was dismal. The northeastern states, which were on the front line, had suffered so much from the embargo, and were so against the war, that they refused to fight. In the west, far from advancing into Canada, Detroit was lost to the British without a struggle, through the sheer incapacity of the American general, William Hull (1753–1825). He was court-martialed and sentenced to be shot, but Madison pardoned him for his services in the War of American Independence.

The only bright spot during the first months of the war were the feats of the small American navy. In single combat, the American ships defeated the British ships during those months, to the amazement of all Europe and to the embarrassment of the British. In particular, the American ship *Constitution*, at first under the command of Isaac Hull (1773–1843), William Hull's brother, defeated the British *Guerriere* in a completely one-sided battle. In a later battle, the *Constitution* was hailed as "Old Ironsides" by its jubilant crew as cannonballs bounced off its stout wooden structure without damage. The ship still exists and has been known by that name ever since, to the point where its real name is all but forgotten.

However, the British navy, though it might be inferior, ship for ship, to the American navy, was overpowering in its numbers and its blockade of the United States steadily tightened.

But there came cheering news from the Great Lakes. The British had ships on those lakes and the Americans did not. In 1813, however, an American captain, Oliver Hazard Perry (1785–1819), supervised the building of ships; then, on September 10, 1813, he forced the surrender of the British ships at the Battle of Lake Erie. Perry's report of the outcome began: "We have met the enemy, and they are ours," one of the great battle reports. This made the north secure for the United States.

In 1814, however, Napoleon had abdicated, and Great Britain, annoyed at this petty war it couldn't seem to put an end to, launched a three-pronged invasion designed to crush the United States.

The first prong was to come down from Montreal toward New York, following Burgoyne's route of nearly 40 years before and cutting off disaffected New England. The second was to strike at the American center and its key port of Baltimore. The third was to strike at the south and take New Orleans.

The northern prong, however, met with disaster, for a British fleet on Lake Champlain was forced to surrender to the Americans under commander Thomas Macdonough (1783–1825) on September 11, 1814 at the Battle of Plattsburg. No British invasion from the north was now possible.

The central prong did better. On August 24, the British invaders actually took Washington and set fire to the public buildings. President Madison and Congress had to flee the city. (When the Presidential Mansion was afterward painted white to hide the char marks, it became known as "The White House.")

The British went on to Baltimore and the British ships bombarded Fort McHenry in its harbor, on the night of September 13–14, 1814. If Fort McHenry surrendered, the British would land their army and take the city, with possibly disastrous results for the Americans. Fort McHenry, however, withstood the bombardment and the British fleet had to sail away. The central prong had failed.

An American lawyer, Francis Scott Key (1779–1843), was waiting on a British ship in the harbor throughout the night, trying to negotiate the release of an American prisoner and was in agony since he didn't know whether the cessation of the bombardment meant that the Americans had surrendered or whether the British had given up. It depended on whether the American flag was still flying over the fort when dawn came. He wrote a four-stanza poem on the bombardment, which was eventually entitled "The Star-Spangled Banner," and which became the American national anthem.

Both Great Britain and the United States had had enough by now and, on December 24, 1814, the Treaty of Ghent, in Belgium, was signed. It left everything exactly as it had been at the beginning of the war, and it didn't mention the issues over which the war was supposedly fought, but things were settled anyway. Great Britain was very careful in its treatment of American shipping thereafter, and the United States never again attacked Canada.

The British public at first considered the Treaty of Ghent a base surrender to the United States, but the southern prong of the invasion was still in progress, and, on December 13, a British fleet was nosing its way up the Mississippi River toward New Orleans.

Andrew Jackson (1767–1845) was in charge of the defense of New Orleans, and had built up bales of cotton as breastworks behind which American sharpshooters waited with their rifles.

On January 8, 1815, 10 days after the Treaty of Ghent had been signed but long before news of it could reach the United States, the British charged the breastworks. They were picked off neatly. In half an hour, 2000 British soldiers had been killed or wounded, including three generals. American casualties were 21. It was Agincourt (which had been fought exactly four centuries earlier) in reverse. The British sailed away.

When the news of the Battle of New Orleans reached the United States, it made the War of 1812 seem a victorious one. When it reached Great Britain, it reconciled British public opinion to the peace treaty, especially when Napoleon suddenly took over France again for the "Hundred Days" before Waterloo finished him.

The Battle of New Orleans was the last land battle between the United States and Great Britain, as the Battle of Waterloo in that same year was the last between France and Great Britain.

In 1818, the United States settled the border between itself and Canada by peaceable agreement with Great Britain. That border, from the Atlantic to the Rocky Mountains, has remained the same ever since.

James Monroe (1758–1831) was elected the fifth president of the United States in 1816, and was reelected in 1820 almost by acclamation. The nation seemed to have weathered all its storms. In 1820, however, a new issue arose—black slavery.

The first American writer to receive serious attention in Europe was Washington Irving, (1783–1859). His best known work was *The Sketchbook*, published in 1819, which contained his still-famous stories "Rip Van Winkle" and "The Legend of Sleepy Hollow."

Noah Webster (1758–1843) published an enormously popular spelling book and, in 1806, published the first American dictionary. He went far toward making American spelling and usage a language in its own right.

William Ellery Channing (1780–1842), a liberal clergyman, was a leading Unitarian in 1819; and while Unitarians were always small in numbers, Channing made their influence felt far and wide. It has continued so, since.

In technology, Robert Fulton (1763–1815) built the first commercially successful steamship. By turning a wheel powered by a steam engine, it could move easily against wind and current. In time, it completely revolutionized sea transportation.

Eli Whitney in 1801, having invented the cotton gin in the previous decade, fulfilled a contract for 10,000 muskets. The story goes that he machined all the parts with such precision that muskets could be assembled out of parts taken at random. This represented the invention of interchangeable parts and was the first step toward mass production and the assembly line.

CANADA

During this period, the northern reaches of Canada were explored. Beginning in 1818, two British navigators, John Ross (1777–1856) and William Edward Parry (1790–1855), explored the Arctic Ocean shore of Canada and eventually sighted just about all the islands in the Canadian Archipelago that lay off that shore.

Canada suffered from an American invasion during the War of 1812. The Americans captured York (later called Toronto) on April 27, 1813, and burned parts of it. This was used as an excuse by the British to burn Washington the next year. The Americans won no substantial victories, and the largest set-to was the drawn Battle of Lundy's Lane, where the American officer, Winfield Scott (1786–1866), distinguished himself. The war ended with Canada still firmly in British hands. There were to be no further battles between the United States and Canada thereafter.

GREAT BRITAIN

During this period, Great Britain was preoccupied almost entirely with the great war against Napoleon and, to a lesser extent, with the war against the United States. In common with the rest of Europe, though perhaps not to the same extent, the British government entered a period of reaction out of fear and hatred of the French Revolution and what it had led to. Thus, for a period after Napoleon's downfall, the conservative Tory party maintained a tight control of the land.

In 1815, with peace came an economic depression. Unemployment was made worse by the demobilization of the army.

What's more, the coming of the Industrial Revolution meant the multiplication of mills and factories in which workers were forced to labor as long as possible and were paid as little as possible. Since women could be made to work for less than men, and children for less than adults, woman and child labor became common and conditions were hellish. Nor were workers allowed to combine into unions and bargain for better treatment. The government did not feel

that it was its business to protect those who were exploited and maintained that all bargaining should be one-on-one—one starving worker facing one rich and powerful mill-owner. Furthermore, if government protection was absolutely required, it went to the rich and powerful, since every sign of protest was considered "Jacobinism."

Of course, financiers flourished. It was even possible for Jewish financiers to do well. The Rothschilds were an example. The first important member of the family was Mayer Amschel Rothschild (1744–1812), who helped the British subsidize anti-Napoleonic armies. His second son, Nathan Mayer Rothschild (1777–1836) founded a branch of the firm in London. He learned the results of the Battle of Waterloo before anyone else through the skillful use of carrier pigeons and was able to order his financial dealings on the basis of that knowledge.

Naturally, the poor and the suffering were driven by desperation to violence. There were movements to destroy the new machinery that seemed, to the downtrodden, to have disrupted an earlier and ideal Great Britain (the past always seems ideal) of yeoman farmers and cottage industry. Between 1811 and 1816, there were bands of "Luddites" (the origin of the name is uncertain), who rioted and tried to destroy machinery. They were strongly repressed and, eventually (when prosperity returned), the movement died out. (The name is still sometimes used for those who turn blindly against technological advance.)

There was also the beginning of a strong movement toward Parliamentary reform and toward widening the electorate so that Parliament would not be the spokesman of the commercial and landed interests only. The journalist, William Cobbett (1763–1855), was outstanding in this movement, and was driven abroad twice in consequence. (In his younger days, however, Cobbett inveighed harshly against the French Revolution and the American democracy.)

An idealist reformer, Robert Owen (1771–1858) advocated socialism, urging factory reform and the control of factories by the people who worked in them. He set an example of how mills could be run decently and with consideration for workers. Thus, he stopped employing children, he arranged old age and sickness insurance, and even worker education. He spent his fortune freely, but his example had little chance of altering entrenched greed and privilege.

A British banker, David Ricardo (1772–1823), wrote about economics and pointed out clearly the conflicting interests of various classes. This gave rise to the notion of "class struggle" which, indeed, became more important as time went on.

The climax in protest came on August 16, 1819, when a crowd of about 60,000 people gathered at St. Peter's Field in Manchester to protest unemployment and high food prices and to call for Parliamentary reform. Many of them were women and children, and the gathering was peaceable. Nevertheless, the army was sent in against the "Jacobins" and the place was cleared, at the cost of 11 killed and 500 hurt. The reformers called the incident the "Peterloo Massacre" in derision of the kind of "Waterloo" that the army was now fighting against impoverished unarmed men, women, and children.

There followed by December a series of repressive acts designed to hobble the newspapers, curtail public gatherings, give increased powers to magistrates, and so on.

This sort of thing was even worse elsewhere in Europe. It was the reaction of ruling classes who, in the wake of the French Revolution and the Napoleonic wars, saw themselves forever threatened with the guillotine by even the mildest of protests.

George III's illness had progressed to the point where he was declared unfit to govern in 1811, and England was put under the Prince of Wales as Regent. The period from 1811 to 1820 is, therefore, called the "Regency." In 1820, George III finally died after a 60-year reign, which had seen Great Britain's worst failure in modern times in connection with the rebelling colonies in North America, and its greatest success in connection with the long and victorious war against Napoleon. George III's son reigned as George IV (1762–1830).

In science, Thomas Young (1773–1829) worked out the wave theory of light in 1802. Humphrey Davy (1778–1829) isolated new elements, such as sodium and potassium, in 1807, making use of the new technique of electrical currents. John Dalton (1766–1844) established the atomic theory of matter in 1808. William Smith (1769–1839) studied geological strata and published a map in 1815 that showed how strata could be identified by their fossil content. William Hyde Wollaston (1766–1828) developed a method for working platinum and discovered two elements, palladium and rhodium, in 1804; while in 1803, Smithson Tennant (1761–1815) had discovered the elements iridium and osmium.

The astronomer, William Herschel, was still active. In 1805, he demonstrated that the Sun was no more the center of the Universe than the Earth was, but that it was moving relative to the other stars. He was also the first to get an idea of the shape of the vast star system we call the galaxy; and, in 1800, he was the first to detect infrared radiation.

William Murdock (1754–1839) pioneered gaslighting in 1800, and celebrated the Peace of Amiens by a spectacular display of gas lights. By 1807, some London streets were gas-lit. (Side-effects are important. Efficient night-time illumination acted to reduce crime.)

In 1814, George Stephenson (1781–1848) built his first steam locomotive, a land transport vehicle that could be driven along rails by the action of a steam engine. This was to revolutionize land transportation as steamships were to revolutionize travel by sea.

British writing was flourishing. Wordsworth was still writing, producing, "I Wandered Lonely as a Cloud" in 1804, and "Intimations of Immortality" in 1808. Coleridge published "Xanadu" and "Christabel" in 1816. A lesser light was Robert Southey (1774–1843) who, like Wordsworth, turned from youthful liberalism to arch-conservatism with age and success. He is chiefly remembered for his poems "The Battle of Blenheim" and "The Inchcape Rock."

Then there were the three great Romantic poets of the period, all short-lived. George Gordon, Lord Byron (1788–1824), published the first two cantos of *Childe Harold's Pilgrimage* in 1812, and found himself suddenly famous. His many poems were climaxed by his masterpiece *Don*

Juan, the first part of which was published in 1819. Percy Bysshe Shelley (1792–1822) created scandals with his atheism and with his abandonment of his wife and elopement with his mistress, but wrote such well-known works as "Ozymandias" in 1817 and "Ode to the West Wind" in 1819. John Keats (1795–1821) wrote "On First Looking into Chapman's Homer," "Ode to a Nightingale," and "Ode on a Grecian Urn."

Walter Scott (1771–1832), a Scottish poet, having made his name with poetic epics such as *The Lay of the Minstrel* in 1805, turned to prose with *Waverley* in 1814, the first modern historical novel, and his masterpiece, *Ivanhoe* in 1819. Thomas Moore (1779–1832), an Irish poet, wrote such ever-popular verses as "Believe me, if All Those Endearing Young Charms," "The Last Rose of Summer," and "The Minstrel Boy," and earned his greatest fame with his poetic drama *Lalla Rookh* in 1817.

On a much lower scale, yet not to be despised, Jane Taylor (1783–1824) wrote the children's classic verse "Twinkle, Twinkle, Little Star" in 1810.

In prose, Jane Austen (1775–1813) introduced the "novel of manners," which utterly ignored the Napoleonic turmoil to deal with men and women of the gentry and the problems of getting married. Her masterpiece *Pride and Prejudice* was published in 1813. Mary Wollstonecraft Shelley (1797–1851), first the mistress, then the second wife of the poet, published the ever-popular *Frankenstein* in 1818. Some consider it to be the first modern science fiction story.

Among the British painters of the period were Joseph Mallord William Turner (1775–1851) and John Constable (1776–1837), both of whom were effective landscape artists.

The most renowned actor of the period was Edmund Kean (1789–1833), who was an enormous hit in Shakespearean roles, beginning with his "Shylock" in 1814.

IRELAND

After the Irish rebellion of 1798, Prime Minister William Pitt felt it necessary to bind Ireland more closely to Great Britain. On January 1, 1801, there was a legislative union between the two so that the nation became the "United Kingdom of Great Britain and Ireland."

This meant that the British Parliament would now have Irish representatives as well as Scottish ones. This, however, meant little or nothing to the bulk of the Irish, since only Protestant representatives could sit in Parliament and the Catholic Irish majority was left out in the cold.

As a matter of fact, there was another insurrection in Ireland in 1803, again in hope of French help that never arrived. It's leader was Robert Emmet (1778–1803), who was arrested and hanged.

NETHERLANDS

Under the French Revolutionaries and Napoleon, the Netherlands was first the Batavian Republic, and then the Kingdom of Holland.

On July 5, 1806, Napoleon made his brother, Louis, the King of Holland—the result of which was that the British took over the Dutch possessions in South Africa.

Louis actually took his role seriously and tried to govern with the benefit of his people in mind. This bothered Napoleon who felt that Louis wasn't doing enough to see to it that the Dutch adhered to the Continental system and refrained from illegal trade with Great Britain. Rather than comply, Louis abdicated and left the kingdom in 1810, whereupon, on July 9, 1810, Napoleon annexed the Netherlands to France. That did no good, however. The smuggling continued.

At the Congress of Vienna, the Netherlands was restored to its legitimate ruler. William V, who had been stadtholder of the Netherlands until the French conquest of 1795, had died in exile in 1806. His son, William (1772–1843), who had fought against Napoleon at the Battles of Jena and of Wagram, was therefore made the ruler. He would have been Stadtholder William VI, but the Netherlands was made a kingdom so he became William I, King of the Netherlands.

To his realm, what had been the Austrian Netherlands was added, so that the "Low Countries" were once more united as they had been before the revolt against Philip II of Spain, two and a half centuries earlier. This was done to create a stronger barrier in the northeast against French expansionism. This created problems, however, for the southern region (which came to be called "Belgium") was Catholic and partly French-speaking; whereas the northern region was Protestant and Dutch-speaking. In addition, the government favored the northern region economically and made Dutch the official language to the discontent of the Belgians.

SPAIN

Charles IV, the Spanish king who had been deposed by Napoleon remained alive in exile, but he had abdicated in favor of his son, who, after the French were driven from Spain, was restored as Ferdinand VII.

He was an utterly reactionary monarch who relied on the Church and the army to repress any manifestations of the slightest touch of liberalism. As a result, Spain seethed with discontent throughout this period.

The painter, Goya, produced some of his most powerful paintings in this period, dramatizing the guerrilla war against the French.

SPANISH AMERICA

Spain, even as late as the French invasion of 1808, when it had grown virtually moribund, still held its American possessions almost intact after three centuries.

The Spanish colonies in the American continents had long been dissatisfied, however. Spanish rule was repressive and the "creoles," American-born people of Spanish descent, and, of course, the "mestizos," who were of mixed Spanish and Native American descent, had little to say in the government. The example of the successful rebellion of the British colonies in North America 30 years earlier had not been lost on the Spanish colonies, and the confusion in Spain during the Peninsular War gave them their chance.

Beginning in 1809, there were movements for independence throughout Spanish America. Among the leaders of those revolts was Simon Bolivar (1783–1830), who was fighting against the Spanish in Venezuela as early as 1811 and who achieved independence of the northern tier of nations in Spanish South America by 1819. He was the first president of an independent Colombia in that year. The nation of Bolivia is named in his honor.

Bernardo O'Higgins (1778–1842), drove the Spaniards out of Chile and became the first president of that nation in 1817. Fighting with O'Higgins was Jose Francisco de San Martin (1778–1850), who made possible the independence of Argentina.

HAITI

A slave rebellion on the island of Hispaniola (which now contains the two nations of Haiti and the Dominican Republic) came under the control of a Haitian black named Francois Dominique Toussaint L'Ouverture (1743–1803), who gained control of the entire island by 1801, and tried to establish a fair rule over blacks and whites alike.

France, which had controlled the island, would not allow that, however, and Bonaparte sent in an army of 25,000 under Charles Victor Emmanuel Leclerc (1772–1802). Leclerc could accomplish nothing against the black guerrillas. He offered to negotiate with Toussaint L'Ouverture. When the Haitian leader accepted the offer, Leclerc had him treacherously seized and sent to France where he died a prisoner on April 7, 1803.

Meanwhile, the Haitians resumed fighting and yellow fever fought on their side. Leclerc died, and the French army withered and those who survived fled the island forever in November 1803.

One of Toussaint L'Ouverture's aides, Henri Christophe (1767–1820) seized control of Haiti, making himself King Henri I in 1811. By 1809, however, the Spanish-speaking eastern portion of the island had thrown off the control by the French-speaking western blacks and the two nations of the island came into being.

PORTUGAL

The royal family of Portugal had fled to Brazil in November, 1807, when the French army had taken over their land. At the end of the Napoleonic wars, they were still there—Queen Maria, who was still mad, and her son, the Regent John.

John had raised Brazil to the rank of a kingdom that was united with Portugal under a common monarch, so when Maria died in 1816, her son became John VI, King of Portugal and Brazil. He liked it in Brazil, and didn't return to Portugal till 1821. There he found considerable controversy between the constitutionalists who wanted a limited monarchy, and the absolutists who wanted an absolute one.

ITALY

After the fall of Napoleon, Italy was reconstituted on its old basis and was placed in the grip of reactionary rulers. Thus, Ferdinand I, who had remained in Sicily while Napoleon controlled Italy, was made King of Naples again in December 1816, and immediately established the darkest absolutist rule.

Victor Amadeus III of Sardinia, who had lost his lands on the Italian mainland to Bonaparte in 1796, had died that year, and his son succeeded as Charles Emmanuel IV (1751–1819). He remained on the island of Sardinia, safe behind the British fleet, but abdicated in 1802 and entered a monastery. His younger brother, who reigned as Victor Emmanuel I (1759–1824), was brought back to the mainland after Napoleon's fall. Genoa was added to his territory so that Sardinia would be a stronger barrier against French expansionism. He instituted a reactionary regime, too, and so it was all over Italy.

The Italians, however, had had a taste of greater freedom and more efficient government under the French, by whom they had also been united, more or less, into larger realms. They began to want more liberty and a national union. The small states of Italy, all of whom were, more or less, under the smothering influence of Austria, no longer satisfied them.

In this period, Italian scholarship continued. In Sicily, Giuseppe Piazzi (1746–1856) sighted the first known asteroid, Ceres, on January 1, 1801. Amedeo Avogadro (1776–1856), in 1811, worked out "Avogadro's hypothesis," which offered the first distinction between atoms and molecules. Alessandro Volta (1745–1827) invented the chemical battery in 1800, and produced the first continuous electric current, soon to be put to excellent use by such men as Humphrey Davy.

The outstanding Italian composer of the period was Gioacchino Antonio Rossini (1792–1868), best known for his opera *The Barber of Seville*, staged in 1816. The violin virtuoso, Niccolo Paganini, revolutionized the technique of the instrument and fascinated audiences with the vigor of his playing.

PAPACY

Pius VII was Pope during Napoleonic times. He felt it necessary to come to some agreement with Bonaparte to avoid the sad fate of his predecessor. In 1801, he accepted a "Concordat," which reestablished the Catholic Church in France. The French bishops, however, were to be appointed by the French government and would be paid by them. The Pope had to agree to give up the Church property that had been appropriated by the Revolutionary government and to limit his own ability to interfere with the French church.

Even so, Napoleon modified the Concordat in his own favor, and while Pius VII was at the coronation of Bonaparte as Emperor, Bonaparte insisted on placing the crown on his own head. In 1808, Rome was occupied by the French, and the Papal States were annexed to France in 1809. Pius VII, like his predecessor, was then kept under detention in France, but he was restored by the victorious Allies in 1814, and the Papal States were given back to him by the Congress of Vienna.

He revived and restored the Jesuits and was, on the whole, on the side of the counterrevolutionaries who were trying to pretend that the French Revolution had never happened.

SWITZERLAND

Switzerland, which had been under Napoleonic domination, was restored to its former status by the Congress of Vienna, and it went through the period of reaction common everywhere. It accepted a principle of perpetual neutrality, and has clung to it and remained at peace ever since.

AUSTRIA

The Holy Roman Empire was past restoration even by the Congress of Vienna, but Austria, because of its repeated, and finally successful, wars against Napoleon, had emerged with increased prestige and dominated the regions that had once been that Empire. It was the largest state in central Europe, and all of Germany and Italy was under its influence.

Its prime minister was Klemens von Metternich, who had been Austrian Ambassador to France in Napoleon's time, and who had put through the marriage between Napoleon and the Austrian princess, Marie Louise. After Napoleon's fall, it was Metternich who served as the orchestra leader of the symphony of reaction.

He insisted on censorship and espionage, on the endless hounding of the least indication of liberal feeling, and on the establishment of a principle of no-change. He organized the "Germanic Confederation," a kind of substitute Holy Roman Empire, which was a loose gathering of the 38 German states (there had been 300 before the French Revolution), including those portions of Austria and Prussia that were German-speaking. He kept that Confederation under his tight control, and it was supposed to protect Germany against such outer enemies as France and Russia and, of course, the inner enemy of liberalism.

Metternich also felt that the powers of Europe ought to get together periodically in "Congresses" to settle outstanding problems, particularly those arising from the dangers of liberalism.

The first such Congress was held at Aix-la-Chapelle (Aachen, in what is now Germany) between October 1 and November 15, 1818. The rulers of Russia, Prussia, and Austria, together with the British Foreign Secretary, Robert Stewart, Viscount Castlereagh (1769–1822), and the Duke of Wellington, were all there. The business of the Congress was to re-admit France into the family of nations. She would pay off her indemnity, the army of occupation would be removed, and she would take her place as a fifth reactionary "great power" in Europe.

Culture in Austria and in the rest of Germany was flourishing, even under the reaction. Goethe, still active, produced his masterpiece, the poetic drama *Faust*, in 1808. Schiller wrote his plays *The Maid of Orleans* in 1801 and *William Tell* in 1804.

In music, Beethoven turned out his great symphonies, the Third ("Eroica") in 1804 and his Fifth and Sixth ("Pastoral") in 1808, together with many other pieces that established him in the minds of many as the greatest composer who ever lived.

Franz Peter Schubert (1797–1828) was the originator of the German "Lieder" ("art songs") in 1814. In his short life, he composed more than 500 songs. Carl Maria von Weber (1786–1826) wrote nine operas and many other works.

In prose, Georg Wilhelm Friedrich Hegel (1770–1831) wrote in opposition to Kant, optimistically supporting reason as the essence of humanity. On the other hand, Arthur Schopenhauer (1788–1860) was a complete pessimist who felt that human life was dominated by the irrational.

The brothers, Jacob Ludwig Grimm (1785–1863) and Wilhelm Carl Grimm (1786–1859), collected folk tales, and *Grimm's Fairy Tales* was published between 1812 and 1815. They have been part of the heritage of childhood ever since. Jacob Grimm began the publication of a great work on German grammar in 1819, and this was one of the foundations of modern philology, the study of languages.

In science, Johann Wilhelm Ritter (1776–1810) discovered ultraviolet radiation in 1801. Joseph von Fraunhofer (1787–1826) discovered, in 1814, that the solar spectrum was crossed by hundreds of dark lines. These "spectral lines" in later years proved to be of the very first importance to advances in both chemistry and astronomy. Carl Friedrich Gauss (1777–1855) was making advances in every branch of mathematics from an early age and is considered by many to have been the greatest mathematician who ever lived.

PRUSSIA

Frederick William III of Prussia never recovered from his defeat by Napoleon and his humiliation afterward. From that point on, he cowered in the shadow of, first, Alexander of Russia, and then Metternich of Austria.

At the Congress of Vienna, Prussia gained considerable territory in the Rhineland, in Westphalia, and in western Saxony. This was designed to put a stronger power on the eastern border of France.

DENMARK

Denmark had found herself on the wrong side of Great Britain during the Napoleonic Wars. When she tried to join with other Baltic powers to protect her neutral shipping against Great Britain, the British sent a fleet into the Baltic Sea.

On April 2, 1801, Admiral Nelson fought the Battle of Copenhagen, in which a Danish fleet was destroyed. Nelson did this in defiance of orders from his cautious superior. Then, in September of 1807, when it seemed that Denmark might join the French–Russian alliance after the meeting at Tilsit, the British bombarded Copenhagen. After that, Denmark naturally remained pro-French.

The final result was that at the Congress of Vienna, pro-French Denmark was made to cede Norway to anti-French Sweden, thus breaking a connection that had lasted, on and off, since the time of Canute, nearly eight centuries earlier.

In a more peaceful pursuit, the Danish physicist, Hans Christian Oersted (1777–1851), demonstrated the connection between electricity and magnetism in 1820. This was a major step toward the modern age of electricity.

SWEDEN

Sweden had been part of the Third Coalition against Napoleon. When Napoleon was victorious, defeating first Austria, then Prussia, and coming to an accommodation with Russia at Tilsit, Gustavus IV of Sweden remained anti-Napoleon. This meant that Russia felt free to invade

Finland, at which point Denmark, always hostile to Sweden, joined the war on the Russian side.

The Swedish army foresaw disaster. On March 13, 1809, it organized a coup that overthrew Gustavus IV and forced him into exile. His uncle became king as Charles XIII, and he made peace with Russia and Denmark at the cost of giving up Finland to the former.

Since Charles XIII had no heirs, he adopted a French general, Jean Baptiste Jules Bernadotte (1763–1844) as his son. (Apparently, this was because Bernadotte had treated Swedish prisoners of war in Germany in a humane manner.) Bernadotte agreed, became a Lutheran, and adopted the name of Charles John.

Napoleon may have thought that Sweden would now adopt a pro-French policy, but Bernadotte, who had never been enamored of Napoleon, saw that it was time to turn against Napoleon after the disaster in Russia. Sweden participated in the 1813 campaigns against Napoleon in Germany, and it also invaded Norway, which belonged to pro-French Denmark.

As a result, when Napoleon fell, the Congress of Vienna awarded Norway to Sweden as compensation for Sweden's loss of Finland to Russia.

On February 5, 1818, Charles XIII died, the last member of the Vasa dynasty that had ruled Sweden for nearly three centuries. Bernadotte succeeded as Charles XIV and followed the usual reactionary policy of Europe of the time.

One outstanding chemist of this period was a Swede, Jons Jakob Berzelius (1779–1848). His skillful experimentation firmly established Dalton's atomic theory of matter, and he was the first to begin working out a reasonably correct table of atomic weights. He also suggested the modern system of symbols for the chemical elements.

POLAND

At the Congress of Vienna, Poland again disappeared from the map. The Grand Duchy of Warsaw, which had existed for six years, from 1807 to 1813, was divided up again among Prussia, Austria, and Russia. It was Russia which got the lion's share.

RUSSIA

Paul I, who ruled Russia in 1800, was an erratic and possibly mentally unbalanced person, as would not be surprising if he were really the son of the mentally unbalanced Peter III (and he might have been). It seemed clearly unsafe to leave him in charge of Russia in the harsh Napoleonic times; and on March 24, 1801, he was assassinated in the course of a coup, perhaps with his son's consent. That son succeeded to the throne as Alexander I (1777–1825).

Alexander was only 24 years old at this succession, had been educated by a Swiss liberal, Frederic Cesar de La Harpe (1754–1838), and began his reign in a clear attempt to be a "benevolent despot." He abolished torture, eased censorship, granted amnesty to political prisoners, and so on. He even made it easier to liberate serfs. However, he found himself involved in a series of wars and this (as it always does) took precedence over reform.

There was, for instance, a war with Persia from 1804 to 1813 that ended with Russia taking Georgia and other Transcaucasian regions.

Then, in 1806, Turkey, with French encouragement, declared war on Russia. (France was fighting Russia at the time.) Russia had somewhat the better of it, and by the time it was over on May 28, 1812, just in time for Russia to turn its attention to Napoleon's invasion, Russia had gained the province of Bessarabia.

In 1808, Russia invaded Finland and encountered very little Swedish resistance. The Congress of Vienna confirmed Russia's possession of Finland and also awarded it almost all of the Grand Duchy of Warsaw. Therefore, in 1815, Russia reached its maximum size in Europe.

More peacefully, Russia was expanding its holdings along the Alaskan coast and was moving southward even as far as northern California. Sitka was founded in 1804.

After the fall of Napoleon, Alexander I grew more reactionary and also more mystical. On September 26, 1815, he tried to establish a "Holy Alliance" in Europe whereby the nations were to establish Christian principles in their dealings with each other. Various nations, notably Austria and Prussia, signed up simply in order to please him, but it never came to anything. It was just talk.

The first Russian poet of importance appeared in this period. He was Vasily Andreyevich Zhukovsky (1783–1852).

SERBIA

The Ottoman Empire had weakened sufficiently for the Balkan nations to begin agitating for freedom. They were still Christian and the general unsettlement of the period gave them hope. While the Ottoman Empire was busily engaged with Russia, the Serbs were rebelling under Karageorge (1762–1817). They succeeded temporarily. However, after the Turks made peace with Russia in 1812 (because the Turks were anxious to turn their attention to the Balkans and Russia was anxious to turn its attention to the oncoming Napoleon), the Turks exerted their full strength against Serbia, which they reoccupied. Karageorge fled.

In 1817, Serbia rose again, this time under Milosh Obrenovich (1780–1860). The Turks won again but saw the uselessness of trying to make the victory complete. They allowed Obrenovich to become the hereditary prince of Serbia as Milosh I, provided he accepted the sovereignty of Turkey, which he did.

A section of the coast, Montenegro, inhabited by a population closely allied to the Serbs, had never been completely conquered by the Turks, and during the period it was recognized as fully independent.

Clearly, the Ottoman hold on the Balkans was weakening rapidly.

OTTOMAN EMPIRE

The reforming Sultan, Selim III, was deposed in July, 1807, and (after some dynastic struggling) his nephew, Mahmud II (1785–1839), became Sultan in 1808. In the early years of his reign he had to face war with Russia and the rebellions of the Serbs.

EGYPT

After the French were driven out of Egypt, Muhammad Ali (1769–1849), was made viceroy ("pasha") of Egypt by the Ottoman Empire which was the nominal ruler of the land. Muhammad Ali now proceeded to reorganize Egypt. On March 1, 1811, he massacred the Mamluks, who had been running Egypt for five and a half centuries, and began to organize a more modern army. He also improved irrigation methods, planted new crops, reorganized governmental administration, and even tried to introduce industry.

On behalf of the Turkish sultan he crossed over into Arabia in 1811 to defeat the Wahhabis, a puritanical Moslem sect that had recently been founded and that had taken control of Mecca and Medina, the two holy cities of Islam. By 1818, Muhammad Ali had placed the eastern shore of the Red Sea under his control.

PERSIA

During this period, Persia lost the Transcaucasian region to Russia and failed in an attempted invasion of Afghanistan.

NORTH AFRICA

The Barbary States of Morocco, Algeria, Tunis, and Tripoli found that their profitable piratical activities brought them into conflict with the United States. American ships bombarded Tripoli, and when one ship, the *Philadelphia*, ran aground and was taken by the Tripolitans, an American officer, Stephen Decatur (1779–1820), in a daring raid, blew it up. A soldier of fortune, William Eaton (1764–1811), with a party of Arabs he had recruited in Egypt, marched overland to Derna and occupied it on April 27, 1805. The ruler of Tripoli had to make peace on June 4, 1805, on American terms, and the American ships went on to bombard Tunis on August 1, 1805.

In 1815, Decatur, who had won naval victories over the British in the War of 1812, took another squadron into the Mediterranean Sea and forced a peace on Algeria on American terms.

In 1816, with the Napoleonic wars over, with the Congress of Vienna done, and with the American example before their eyes, a British squadron bombarded Algiers and forced it to surrender some 3000 European slaves. From that point on, Barbary piracy was at an end.

WEST AFRICA

The black nations of Ashanti and Dahomey resisted European penetration for a time, fighting them off.

SOUTH AFRICA

Twice during the Napoleonic Wars, the British took the Cape Colony at the southern end of Africa. At the end of the wars, British possession of the region was confirmed and British settlers began entering the country.

INDIA

During this period, Great Britain extended its control over all of India, directly or indirectly.

SOUTHEAST ASIA

Much of the Dutch territory in the Indonesian archipelago was taken over by the British during the Napoleonic wars; however, after those wars were over, it was returned to the Netherlands. In 1819, Thomas Stamford Raffles (1781–1826) founded Singapore, and the British widened their hold in Malaya.

In 1815, on the Indonesian island of Sumbawa, east of Java, a dormant volcano, Tambora, suddenly ceased being dormant and exploded in the most drastic volcanic eruption the world had seen since the destruction of Thera 33 and a half centuries earlier. The top 4000 feet of the volcano was blown into the upper atmosphere. Not only did thousands of islanders die, but the dust in the upper atmosphere blocked so much of the Sun's light that 1816 was an unusually cold year. In New England, it snowed at least once in every month of the year, including July and August.

The New Englanders called 1816 "The Year Without a Summer" and "Eighteen Hundred and Froze to Death."

CHINA

Manchu China had now definitely begun to decline, but penetrations by Europeans continued to be resisted. A British ambassador was sent to Peking in 1816, but he was sent away without being received.

As of 1800, by the way, Canton was probably the largest city in the nation, and in the world, with a population of 1,500,000. London, the largest European city had a population of only 864,000 in that year and New York had only 65,000.

JAPAN

Japan likewise continued to remain isolated. In 1804, a Russian ambassador made his appearance in Japan, and got nowhere.

HAWAII

Kamehameha (1758–1819), the nephew of the Hawaiian chieftain, had negotiated with Captain Cook on the latter's ill-fated visit to the islands. After his uncle's death, Kamehameha gained control of northern Hawaii, extended his rule first over the entire island, then over all the neighboring islands. By 1810, he was Kamehameha I, autocratic ruler of the Hawaiian islands. He allowed foreigners to settle in the islands and put an end to human sacrifice, thus beginning to draw Hawaii into the outside world.

On his death in 1819, his son succeeded as Kamehameha II (1797–1824). Kamehameha II continued to put an end to primitive Hawaiian religious practices and allowed the entry of American missionaries.

AUSTRALIA

The island of Tasmania was settled in 1803, and in Australia itself there was a movement into the interior, accompanied by much killing of the Aborigines.

NEW ZEALAND

British missionaries began to appear in the islands of New Zealand at this period.

1820 TO 1840

GREAT BRITAIN

Great Britain at this time, thanks to the defeat of Napoleon and to the role played by the British navy and by British money in that defeat, was the dominating power in the world, much as Spain had been in the reign of Philip II two and a half centuries earlier, and as France had been in the reign of Louis XIV a century and a half earlier. However, since Great Britain had no army to speak of, she didn't exert her influence by direct military attack on the European continent, but indirectly through economic influence, worldwide.

Great Britain's economic strength, its spreading world empire, its control of the sea, and its unassailability behind its ocean rampart, made it possible for it to afford humanitarian impulses. While Foreign Secretary Viscount Castlereagh worked with the autocratic governments of Europe (and made himself unpopular with liberals in doing so), he did try to prevent them from using unnecessary force and labored to allow some liberal movements to continue undisturbed.

Thus, in October 1820, at the second of Metternich's Congresses, at Troppau, Austria (now Opava, Czechoslovakia), Metternich wished to take military measures to crush rebellions in Spain and Italy, and Castlereagh dissented. This happened again in the 1821 Congress, the third, at Laibach, Austria (now Ljubljana, Yugoslavia). Military action was taken despite the British dissent, but the united front of reaction had been broken.

Castlereagh committed suicide in a fit of depression on August 12, 1822, and was succeeded by more liberal politicians.

The new Foreign Minister was George Canning (1770–1827), who had fought a duel with Castlereagh in 1809, which both had survived. Canning broke altogether with the Metternich system of no-change whatever. Canning was willing to recognize the newly independent Latin American nations, which had sprung out of the corpse of the Spanish colonial system, for instance, and that made it impossible for any move to be taken to force them back into submission, since Great Britain controlled the sea.

More ticklish was the matter of revolts in the Balkans against the Ottoman Turks. Even though this was a case of Christian people fighting against the domination by Muslims, the Metternich system required that the rebels be crushed lest they set bad examples elsewhere. Canning supported the Balkan rebellions, too, and made his policy clear at the Congress of Verona (then part of Austria) in October 1822, which was held soon after he became Foreign Minister. This strengthened British dissent ruined Metternich's "Congress system" and no more such meetings were held after Verona. Thereafter, the reactionary nations had to work individually, which meant a weakening of their effectiveness.

Inside Great Britain, Robert Peel (1788–1850), the Secretary of Home Affairs, reformed the criminal code, reducing the number of death penalties. It was easier to convict criminals where lesser punishments were involved, so that actual punishment became more certain, and criminal action more deterred, when the penalties were made lighter. In addition, in 1829, Peel set up the first disciplined police force in the Greater London area, and this also had a deterrent effect on crime. (London police are called "bobbies" to this day, in Peel's honor.)

Great Britain had "corn laws," which imposed dues on imported grain. This kept the price of basic foods high, to the benefit of the relatively few landlords who grew British grain and who didn't want to compete with cheaper grain from abroad. It worked to the harm, on the other hand, of the relatively many consumers who found they could not afford to satisfy their hunger.

William Huskisson (1770–1830), another member of the cabinet, was an advocate of free trade, maintaining that the profit to the nation as a whole arising out of increased trade would far outweigh the loss of short-term profits to a few. He succeeded in reducing duties on certain imports in the early 1820s and, therefore, in taking the first step toward free trade.

There were even movements toward allowing workmen to combine with each other in order that they might more effectively bargain with factory owners. This was not allowed to go too far, but trade unions began to come into being.

Another liberal cause was "Catholic emancipation." Catholics were ineligible to sit in Parliament, which meant, for one thing, that Irish delegates sitting in Parliament were Protestant. These simply didn't represent the Irish, who, except in the northeastern counties, were almost unanimously Catholic.

"Catholic Associations," working to achieve emancipation, grew in Ireland and it was clear that there would never be peace there until this took place. The leader of the movement, Daniel O'Connell (1775–1847), a Catholic, was the most popular man in Ireland.

[In England, John Henry Newman (1801–1890) led the "Oxford movement," which stressed the relationship of Anglicanism to Roman Catholicism.]

In January 1828, the Duke of Wellington became Prime Minister. He was a reactionary, but he could see that Catholic Emancipation would have to become a fact, or there would be civil war again in Ireland. In March and April 1829, Catholic Emancipation was pushed through Parliament against the bitter opposition of the die-hard reactionaries who supported Wellington in other respects.

O'Connell, who had previously been elected to Parliament but had not been allowed to take his seat, was now again elected and was able to sit in Parliament. Catholics had to agree, however, to deny the Pope any power to interfere in British domestic affairs, and to swear they had no intention of overturning the established Anglican Church.

Meanwhile, George IV was an increasingly unpopular monarch. He was secretly and illegally married to a Roman Catholic woman he could not acknowledge and he had been forced to marry Caroline of Brunswick (1768–1821), a German Protestant princess he abominated. He left her after the birth of a daughter in 1796. Once he became King, however, she tried to be recognized as Queen, which George IV was determined not to allow, and there was a very nasty and scandalous fight over the matter. The British public, which was not enamored of Caroline, supported her anyway, out of the greater dislike they had for George.

George IV died on June 26, 1830, and since his daughter had predeceased him, he was succeeded by his younger brother, who reigned as William IV (1765–1837), the first British king not to be named George in 115 years.

The strains of Catholic Emancipation had splintered the Tory party and, in 1830, the Whigs won a Parliamentary majority. Charles, Earl Grey (1764–1845), became Prime Minister and he was devoted to Parliamentary reform.

In general, the only people who had influence in the voting procedure were people with land or money (or both), and they tended to vote Tory. Ordinary voters were sufficiently few in number to be easily bribed. In some cases, a landed proprietor could force a vote in his district for anyone he wanted, or may himself even have had the sole vote. Great Britain was rich in "pocket boroughs" (an election district that was in someone's pocket) or even "rotten boroughs," with no voters except a landowner. The new industrial towns often had no representation at all.

What was needed was to extend the franchise so as to allow the middle class to vote. The delegates had to be distributed more evenly among the population. Naturally, those delegates already in Parliament saw no need for changing a situation that benefited them, but the British people wanted reform. Therefore, when the Reform Bill was defeated on March 22, 1831, Earl Grey had the Parliament dissolved so that there would be a new election.

Even with the narrow franchise, the Whigs won again, more widely than before, and a second Reform Bill was passed. This time, it was accepted by the House of Commons; however, the House of Lords, which was not elected and was not amenable to public opinion, rejected it on October 8, 1831.

Now, however, this clear refusal to follow the obvious will of the people produced riots and commotions. When a third Reform Bill was proposed, the House of Commons passed it by a larger majority than before on March 23, 1832, but still the House of Lords objected, and now the disorders grew to the point where one could easily imagine the nation to be on the brink of revolution.

Earl Grey came to King William IV and asked him to appoint new peers who would pledge themselves to support the Bill; enough of them so that the House of Lords would give its assent. The King refused, but Earl Grey threatened to resign and the King knew he could not find any Tory who could form a ministry that would not be certain to be voted down at once by the House of Commons.

The King had to give in, but he didn't appoint the peers. Instead, he persuaded the peers that already existed to withdraw their opposition, and the Reform Bill became law on June 4, 1832.

The result was that the franchise was extended to the middle class, and representation in Parliament was more fairly distributed. The members were more independent, the voters could be less easily bribed, and, most important of all, it was made clear that the House of Lords could not defy the popular will. Great Britain more closely approached a democracy, and had done it without violent revolution.

Other reforms took place, too. As a result of the tireless fight of William Wilberforce for half a century, Great Britain abolished slavery in all its possessions on August 23, 1833, less than a month after Wilberforce had died at the age of 73. They did it in a reasonable fashion, in stages, and with compensation for slave-owners. It was most successful, but it was a lesson that was lost on the United States.

Other laws dealt with the abuses of the factory system. They forbade the employment of children under nine years of age and limited the work hours of older children to nine hours a day, and still older children to twelve hours a day. They also ordered some schooling for children under 13. It was a very inadequate law, but even this was fought bitterly by the stone-hearted conservatives.

Much was left undone, of course. Even with the extension of the franchise, the large majority of the British population could not vote and could not rely on Parliamentary delegates paying attention to their needs. Trade unions advanced such notions as an eight-hour day, but got nowhere.

Earl Grey did resign on July 9, 1834, but the reform movement continued, and the terms "Whig" and "Tory" now gave way to the much more descriptive "Liberal" and "Conservative." There were attempts to make society less harsh on those who were impoverished and who were incapable of supporting themselves. There were attempts to reform local governments as the national government had been reformed, laws to permit civil marriages, and so on.

William IV died on June 20, 1837, and although George III had had many children, there was only one grandchild, and she was a woman who succeeded to the throne at 18, becoming Queen Victoria (1819–1901). In 1840, she married her first cousin, Albert of Saxe-Coburg-Gotha (1819–1861), and it was apparently a love-match.

In that same year, Rowland Hill (1795–1879) introduced important reforms in postage. He argued that postage should cost less because that would encourage business communication and the increased prosperity that resulted would increase tax revenue, generally, to an extent that would far more than make up for the loss in postal revenue. He also suggested that the payment be independent of distance to reduce the time, labor, and expense of taking distance into account. Finally, letters should be paid for by the sender, not the receiver, since the sender was usually more anxious to send a letter than the receiver was to receive it.

All this was carried through on January 10, 1840, and that was the foundation of the modern postal system. The original charge was one penny for any letter under half an ounce to be delivered from any point to any other in Great Britain or Ireland.

The greatest British scientist of this period, and one of the greatest of all time, was Michael Faraday (1791–1867), who was virtually self-educated. He liquefied chlorine gas in 1823, thus founding the study of low temperatures. In 1833, he worked out the laws of electrolysis, thus tying together electricity and chemical change. He invented the concept of magnetic lines of force. His greatest achievement came in 1831, when he showed how to convert mechanical energy into a continuous electric current. This eventually made electricity the product of burning fuel, so that it became cheap enough for everyday use in quantity.

William Sturgeon (1783–1850) produced the first crude electromagnet in 1823. John Frederick Daniell (1790–1845) devised the first reliable electric battery, which began the process of making small, electrified gadgets possible.

Charles Babbage (1792–1871) began, as early as 1822, to consider the possibility of devising a machine that would solve complex mathematical problems through punched-card instructions, store partial solutions, and print out final conclusions. He invented the various techniques of modern computers, but had only mechanical devices, gears and levers, to use for the purpose, and that was simply not good enough. Babbage ended in frustration, but the story of modern computer construction must start with him.

William Prout (1785–1850), in 1824, demonstrated that hydrochloric acid (a strong acid till then thought to have no possible connection with life) occurred naturally in stomach juices. Earlier, he had suggested that all atoms were built up out of hydrogen atoms, the simplest. Scientific knowledge of the time did not support the notion, but it was eventually found that "Prout's hypothesis" represented a brilliant insight into subatomic structure.

Richard Bright (1789–1858) studied a serious kidney disease and reported on it in 1827. It is known as "Bright's disease" to this day. Joseph Jackson Lister (1786–1869) developed an achromatic microscope, with lenses that did not produce colored blurs to the viewer. It was only with this new type of microscope that it became possible to study bacteria in detail.

Charles Robert Darwin (1809–1882) made his name as a naturalist with a report on his findings in the course of a five-year scientific round-the-world cruise. His book, *A Naturalist's Voyage on the Beagle*, published in 1839, not only indicated his keenness as an observer, but laid the groundwork for something that was to make him, to many people, the greatest biologist in history.

The first successful railroad opened for regular commercial use in 1825 in Great Britain. They quickly spread to other countries and the galloping horse was finally replaced as the best mode of rapid, long-distance transportation after nearly 4000 years.

British explorers were active in the polar regions. James Clark Ross (1800–1862) located the North Magnetic Pole on the Arctic shore of Canada on June 1, 1831. Edward Bransfield (1795–1852), in 1820, sighted the Antarctic Peninsula. This was the first glimpse of the Antarctic continent, though it was of a portion that lay north of the Antarctic Circle. James Weddell (1787–1834) sailed into an inlet south of the Antarctic Circle, which is now known as Weddell Sea.

In literature, Charles Dickens (1812–1870) was, in the eyes of many, the most successful and best novelist of all times. He made his reputation as a young man with *The Pickwick Papers*, published in 1836; *Oliver Twist* in 1837; and *Nicholas Nickleby* in 1838. These were more effective in denouncing abuses and helping to correct them than anything political and social reformers could do. Edward Bulwer-Lytton (1803–1873) wrote his most successful novel, *The Last Days of Pompeii*, in 1834.

In nonfiction, Thomas Carlyle (1795–1881) wrote *French Revolution* in 1837 in a florid, but effective style. Charles Lamb (1775–1834) wrote a series of popular essays under the pen-name of Elia. The *Essays of Elia* were published in 1823, and a second series in 1833. Thomas De Quincey (1785–1859) made himself famous with *Confessions of an English Opium Eater*, published in 1821. Walter Scott was still writing, publishing *The Talisman* in 1825, and a nine-volume *Life of Napoleon* in 1827.

Among the poets, Leigh Hunt (1784–1859) is best remembered today for his small poems "Abou Ben Adhem" and "Jenny Kissed Me," published in 1837, while Felicia Dorothea Hemans (1793–1825) is most remembered for "Casabianca" ("The boy stood on the burning deck / When all but he had fled") and "The Landing of the Pilgrim Fathers." Thomas Hood (1799–1845) is best known for his pun-filled poem, "Faithless Nelly Gray," published in 1829. Alfred, Lord Tennyson was beginning his long career, and the most popular of his early poems was "The Lady of Shalott," published in 1832.

FRANCE

While Great Britain was slowly liberalizing its franchise and moving away from reaction, France was doing the reverse. In 1820, a complicated system of voting was introduced which gave added weight to the wealthy who could be counted on to vote for reaction. In addition, everything was done to hamper the expression of opinion.

In 1822, the Council of Verona, with Canning of Great Britain in opposition, authorized France to send troops into Spain to repress a liberal uprising there. France, which only a quarter-century before had thrown off its chains, now accepted the task of restoring the chains on another people.

On April 17, 1823, a French force crossed over into Spain, seized Madrid, defeated the Spanish liberals on August 31, and replaced the king on the throne where he could take his full revenge.

On September 16, 1824, Louis XVIII died, and, since he had no children, his younger brother succeeded as Charles X (1757–1836). He was the first Bourbon king of France to be named anything other than Louis in 214 years. Thirty-five years earlier, Charles X, as Count de Artois, had fled France the day after the taking of the Bastille. Now he was king and was determined, as far as possible, to turn back the clock to the day before the taking of the Bastille.

He had a law passed that would compensate the nobility for their loss of property in the Revolution. This meant that the present owners of the property would have to pay, and they were largely rich men of the upper middle class that would have supported Charles X if he had not alienated them in this manner.

The result was that when there were elections, even by the system designed to make them unfair, they still resulted in a victory for those opposed to Charles.

On August 8, 1829, when Charles failed to get a legislature he wanted, he chose as his minister Auguste Jules de Polignac (1780–1847), who was as reactionary as the king, but who could not carry the votes of the legislature. Therefore, the king dissolved the legislature and new elections were held on May 16, 1830. The result was *still* unfavorable to the king.

Charles then dissolved that legislature, and contrived the "July ordinances," which established a complete censorship of the press and changed the election laws to make it impossible to elect anyone but extreme conservatives. At this, Paris rose in revolt, on July 28, in "the July Revolution." On August 2, Charles X abdicated and fled the country for the second time, this time dying in exile in 1836.

The new revolutionaries turned to Louis Philippe, the Duke of Orleans (1773–1850). He was the great-great-grandson of the Duke of Orleans who had been Regent during the childhood of Louis XV. Louis Philippe's father had abandoned his privileges as Duke of Orleans and had taken to calling himself Philippe Egalité ("Philip Equality") and even voted for the execution of Louis XVI, but was himself guillotined in November 1793.

Now Philippe Egalité's son was chosen, not as King of France, but "King of the French" to show that he was the choice of the French people.

Even as Charles X was fleeing, however, the French were beginning to gather a new Empire to replace the one they had lost to the British two thirds of a century earlier.

The ruler of Algiers had slapped the French consul's face on April 30, 1827, and would not apologize. French ships, therefore, put Algiers under a blockade and toward the end of June 1830, armed forces were landed there. Algiers was taken on July 5, 1830, and over the next 17 years the entire nation was subdued.

The new king, Louis Philippe, rapidly lost popularity with the revolutionaries who had installed him. He was uninterested in the plight of the workers and sought the support of the upper middle class who had turned against Charles X. The workers rebelled in Lyons in 1831 and in Paris in 1834. These rebellions were put down with severity and, in September 1835, Louis Philippe, like Charles X before him, decided that the way to turn off discontent was not to allow it to be expressed. A strict press censorship was applied and measures were taken to assure that anyone acting against the government would be very rapidly tried and very surely convicted.

Great French scientists of the period included Andre Marie Ampere (1775–1836), who, in the 1820s worked out the mathematical and experimental details of the electromagnetic phenomena announced earlier by Oersted. Nicolas Leonard Sadi Carnot (1796–1832), son of the Carnot who figured importantly during the French Revolution, studied the efficiency of steam engines from a theoretical point of view in 1824, and was the first to catch a glimpse of what has since come to be called "the second law of thermodynamics." Jean Baptiste Joseph Fourier (1768–1830), added to the gathering knowledge of thermodynamics (the study of the interaction of work and energy) by publishing *Analytical Theory of Heat*, a detailed study of heatflow, in 1822. Antoine Jerome Balard (1802–1876) discovered bromine in 1826. Evariste Galois (1811–1832), who died young in a duel, spent the last night of his life scribbling out the foundations of a powerful mathematical tool called "group theory."

Jules Dumont D'Urville (1790–1842) sighted the shoreline of Antarctica south of Australia in 1840. Beginning in 1821, Jean François Champollion (1790–1832) deciphered the Egyptian hieroglyphics of the Rosetta Stone, uncovered in Egypt a quarter-century earlier, and in this way opened Egyptian history to the modern world.

In technology, Louis Jacques Daguerre (1789–1851) finally produced the first reasonably practical photographs by 1839, and photography quickly became a vitally important adjunct to portraiture and astronomy.

Marie-Henri Beyle (1773–1842), who fought in Russia, and who wrote under the pseudonym of "Stendhal," was one of the most important of the Romantic school in France, his best-known work being *Red and Black*, published in 1830. Even greater was Victor Marie Hugo (1802–1885), who wrote *Notre Dame de Paris* in 1831, the best of his early novels. Honore de Balzac (1799–1850), a particularly prolific writer, wrote numerous novels of which the best known is *Le Pere Goriot*, published in 1834. Between 1832 and 1837, he also wrote a series of ribald tales which were published as *Droll Stories*. Amandine Aurore Lucille Dudevant (1804–1876), writing under the masculine name of George Sand, wearing men's clothing and smoking cigars, wrote a series of novels in which she was an early champion of what we now call "feminism." One of her lovers, Alfred de Musset (1810–1857) was an important French poet of the time.

Alexis Charles de Tocqueville (1805–1859) gained fame with his penetrating and prescient work *On American Democracy*, the first part of which was published in 1835. Anthelme Brillat-Savarin (1755–1826) made a name for himself in an even more out-of-the-way fashion (but one that was particularly French) by writing *The Physiology of Taste* on food. It was published in 1825.

Among the French artists of the period, Eugene Delacroix (1798–1863) and Jean Baptiste Corot (1796–1875) were the most memorable. Honore Daumier (1808–1879) was a skilled caricaturist whose greatest fame arose from the fact that one of his caricatures of Louis Philippe was so wounding that it cost him six months in prison. All three pioneered "Impressionism," which moved away from the meticulously realistic, in order to give impressions of light and form that, presumably, embodied more than could be expressed by catching a frozen moment of time.

The coming of photography undoubtedly caused artists to seek ways of revealing their subjects in a way the camera could not.

In music, Hector Berlioz (1803–1869) was a leading exponent of romanticism. So was the Polish-born Frederic François Chopin (1810–1849), who lived in Paris after 1831, was another of the loves of George Sand, and whose compositions remain enormously popular to this day.

NETHERLANDS

The union of the Netherlands with Belgium did not last long. When news of the July Revolution in France reached the Belgians, they could not be held back. On August 25, 1830, the Belgians asked for self-rule. A month later, the people of Brussels drove out the Dutch troops and, on October 4, Belgium proclaimed its independence. On October 17, the Dutch bombarded Antwerp and, after that, there was no chance of reconciliation.

Great Britain did not want the Belgians to turn for help to the newly revolutionary France. Therefore, it persuaded the rest of Europe to accept Belgian independence even if that upset the decision of the Congress of Vienna. Russia, which might have been the hardest to persuade, was farthest away, and was having its own troubles in Poland.

As king, the Belgians chose Leopold of Saxe-Coburg (1790–1865), who had been married to George IV's daughter, and who was still living in Great Britain. He was an uncle of both the future Queen Victoria and the future Prince-Consort Albert.

The Netherlands did not recognize Belgian independence till 1838, and they made some efforts to force the Belgians back, but with both France and Great Britain against that, the attempt could not succeed. On April 19, 1839, a final settlement was reached as to boundaries, and that has remained to the present day.

SPAIN

Troops mutinied against the reactionary Ferdinand VII in January 1820. For a while, Spain turned liberal, but at the behest of the Congress of Verona, French forces entered Spain, quelled the rebellion, and put Ferdinand VII back in power. He ruled harshly till his death on September 19, 1833.

He had no sons and, by the rules of Bourbon succession, the throne had to go to the most closely related male, which meant to Ferdinand's brother, Charles, or "Don Carlos" (1788–1855). Shortly, before his death, though, Ferdinand VII was persuaded by his fourth wife, Maria Christina (1806–1878), whom he had married in 1829, to break that rule and to direct that his daughter reign as Isabella II (1830–1904). Isabella was only three years old and her mother served as Queen Regent.

The Conservatives backed Don Carlos, and Maria Christina was forced to seek support among the Liberals, so that she granted a constitution of sorts. There followed a five-year civil war called the "Carlist War." The Queen-Regent received help from Great Britain, France, and Portugal. In 1839, Don Carlos had to accept defeat and went off into exile in France.

LATIN AMERICA

The Spanish-speaking nations of North and South America were sorting themselves out under the protection of the British fleet against any attempt to reassert any form of European dominion (except for British economic control, of course.)

Argentina and Brazil fought over Uruguay and, on February 20, 1827, Argentina won a decisive battle. The matter was then settled by British mediation, which allowed Uruguay to become independent in 1828. Great Britain also claimed the Falkland Islands in the far south, a claim that Argentina never accepted.

Chile was immersed in civil war but retained its identity.

Paraguay, landlocked from the start, was under a kind of "benevolent despot," Jose Gaspar de Francia (1766–1840), who deliberately isolated the country to keep it independent of Argentina. He abolished the Inquisition, and also abolished titles and aristocratic privileges.

Bolivia and Peru were united in a confederation in 1835, but both Argentina and Chile to the south feared the combination would be too strong and, in the fighting that followed, the union came to an end.

Colombia occupied all the northwest end of South America, but divisive forces were too powerful. By 1830, the eastern end had broken away as Venezuela, and the southwestern end as Ecuador.

Central America was at first under Guatemalan domination but by 1840, the southern portion broke away and became El Salvador, Honduras, Nicaragua, and Costa Rica. Panama remained part of Columbia.

When Mexico achieved its independence in 1821, the rebel commander Augustin de Iturbide (1783–1824) took command and called himself Emperor Augustin I. By 1823, he was forced from the throne and on October 4, 1824, Mexico was proclaimed a federal republic. One of the leaders of the revolt against Augustin I was Antonio Lopez de Santa Anna (1794–1876). He became President of Mexico in 1833.

Among the West Indian islands, Cuba and Puerto Rico remained Spanish, while Haiti was independent, and Santo Domingo (now the Dominican Republic) oscillated among independence, Spanish control, and Haitian control.

PORTUGAL

When Spain rebelled in 1820 and tried to set up a liberal government in 1820, Portugal did the same. A liberal constitution was set up, and John VI, who was still in Brazil, was invited to come back and rule as a constitutional monarch.

John VI did so, but Brazil had by now declared its independence, and John VI left his eldest son behind to rule Brazil as Pedro I (1798–1834). His second son, Miguel (1802–1866), started a civil war in Portugal in 1823, to turn the government back to the conservatives.

John VI died on March 10, 1826, and left the throne to Pedro I of Brazil. However, Pedro I would not leave Brazil, so he passed the Portuguese throne on to his seven-year-old daughter, who reigned as Maria II (1819–1853).

Miguel was ready for another try at absolutism and, in May, 1828, he overthrew Maria and declared himself king.

At that, Pedro of Brazil abdicated his Brazilian kingdom and returned to Europe to restore Maria. With the help of Great Britain and France, he succeeded. Miguel was defeated in 1834, while Maria was restored to her throne.

ITALY

The uprising in Spain in 1820, which had set off a revolt in Portugal, did the same in Italy. The Neapolitan people rose and forced Ferdinand I to grant them a constitution on July 13, 1820. However, the Congress meetings at Troppau and Laibach established the principle that foreign troops should be used, if necessary, to put down such dangerous rebellions against constituted authority (Great Britain dissenting). Austrian troops marched into Naples and put everything back as it was without any trouble.

In Sardinia, Victor Emmanuel I was forced to abdicate on March 12, 1821, and a constitution was worked out for the nation, but within a month, Austrian troops had put an end to that, too.

In 1831, after the news of successful rebellions in France and Belgium, there were risings in Modena, Parma, and the Papal States, and all were put down by Austria. A quiet of desperation was restored throughout the peninsula.

Italian opera continued to be preeminent. Gaetano Donizetti (1797–1848) wrote 75 operas of which *Lucia di Lammermoor*, written in 1835, and *La Fille du Regiment*, written in 1840, are the most popular. The operas of Vincenzo Bellini (1801–1835) include *Norma*, written in 1831.

PAPACY

The Papacy had been as frightened by the French Revolution and the Napoleonic wars as the secular monarchs. The Popes, too, turned conservative and participated in the reactionary policies common at this time. Leo XII (1760–1829), who became Pope in 1823, in addition to being op-posed to Jews and Protestants (which one might, after all, expect), was strongly opposed to any liberal tendencies in Italy. He condemned the Carbonari, for instance, a secret society that had been developing in Italy to espouse liberal ideas and to fight the domination of Austria.

His successor, Pius VIII (1761–1830), had no choice but to accept the July Revolution in France; however, Gregory XVI (1765–1846), who became Pope in 1831, and who faced a nationalist uprising in the Papal States, had no hesitation in calling in Austrian troops to suppress it. In 1832, he put out an encyclical condemning freedom of speech and religion, and denouncing revolts, for any reason whatever, against established governments.

SWITZERLAND

While Switzerland did not suffer any revolts in the wake of France's "July Revolution," there was a tendency in a number of the 23 cantons to liberalize their constitutions. This tendency may have been encouraged by the fact that Switzerland had become a haven for those prominent political figures who, for one reason or another, fled their own countries.

AUSTRIA

Austria continued to be the fount of reaction for central Europe. While it could do nothing about the July Revolution in France, or the Belgian breakaway, largely because of British opposition, it kept a tight hold on Italy and Germany, and, of course, labored to keep Austria and its dominions totally free of liberalism. Metternich's system had declined a bit after the Congress of Verona, since no further congresses were held, and since Prussia was increasingly aspiring to be the leader of that portion of Germany outside Austria, but Metternich's grip was still effective.

Francis I died on March 2, 1835, having reigned 43 years, and having been the last Holy Roman Emperor. He was succeeded by his son, who reigned as Ferdinand I (1793–1875), and who was feeble-minded. Under him, Metternich continued to be the real ruler of Austria.

The Hungarian-born mathematician, Janos Bolyai (1802–1860), worked out a non-Euclidean geometry in 1823, a revolutionary generalization of a field in which Euclid had been venerated as absolute truth for 2000 years. However, Bolyai's work was not published until 1831.

PRUSSIA

One of the difficulties of having Germany a jigsaw puzzle of independent states, some of them quite small, was that each one would set customs duties in an attempt to raise revenues for itself. This choked trade and commerce and worked for the harm of all. Beginning in 1819, Prussia encouraged the existence of a customs union (a "Zollverein"); that is, a kind of free-trade area within Germany among all the states that joined. In the following two decades, the Zollverein spread to include almost all of Germany outside of Austria and, within it, Prussia was the obvious leader.

This led to a feeling that there ought to be German unity in other ways; that Germany ought to be a nation like France or Great Britain. The July Revolution in France rather encouraged this kind of view which looked toward change, but, on the whole, reaction continued to prevail.

Thus, when William IV of Britain died, and Victoria became Queen, the dynastic connection with Hanover was broken after a century and a quarter. A woman could not be King of Hanover. Ernest Augustus (1771–1851), a younger brother of Victoria's father, became King of Hanover. He set up a system of absolutism which was unpopular among Germans generally, but it persisted because Metternich supported it, and persuaded Prussia to support it, too.

On June 7, 1840, Frederick William III of Prussia died after a reign of 43 years, which included the humiliations of 1807 and the revolt of 1813. His son succeeded as Frederick William IV (1795–1861).

The existence of many separate states in Germany, each of which tended to establish a University as a way of maintaining their prestige, led to an active scholarship that often rose above the reactionary tendencies of the time, so that Germany came to dominate the advance of science during the nineteenth Century.

Among German scientists of the period were Georg Simon Ohm (1789–1854), who, in 1827, demonstrated "Ohm's Law," which related current intensity, voltage, and resistance. Friedrich Wilhelm Bessel (1784–1846) was the first to determine the distance of a star. Justus von Liebig (1803–1873) developed methods for the elementary analysis of organic materials in 1831. Friedrich Wohler (1800–1882) was the first, in 1828, to synthesize an organic compound out of inorganic precursors. Matthias Jakob Schleiden (1804–1881) and Theodor Ambrose Schwann (1810–1882), between them, showed, in 1838 and 1839, that all living things were made up of cells.

In the field of literature, the aged Goethe completed the rather difficult second part of *Faust* in 1832. Heinrich Heine (1797–1856) wrote lyrics that have been popular in Germany ever since, including "The Two Grenadiers" and "The Lorelei." Carl von Clausewitz (1780–1831), who had been captured at the Battle of Jena and who had fought on the Russian side against Napoleon in 1812, made his fame with one of the best-known books on military science, *On War*, published posthumously in 1833.

Felix Mendelssohn (1809–1847) composed his ever-popular overture to "The Midsummer Night's Dream" in 1826 when he was only 17. He also wrote his *Italian Symphony* in 1833, and a variety of other works. Giacomo Meyerbeer (1791–1864) wrote operas both in German and in French.

DENMARK

Frederick VI of Denmark swam against the reactionary tide, introducing a liberalizing breath of air into the land, especially after the July Revolution in France. He set up provincial assemblies and began a system of representative government. He died on December 3, 1839, and was succeeded by his son, who reigned as Christian

VIII (1786–1848). Under him, the pace of liberalism slowed.

Hans Christian Andersen (1805–1875) was Denmark's greatest writer of the period, and his fairy tales, which began to be published in 1835, became, and remained, world-famous. They included such deathless classics as "The Ugly Duckling," "The Princess and the Pea," "The Emperor's Clothes," "The Nightingale," and so on.

SWEDEN

Throughout this period, Charles XIV, the former General Bernadotte, was King of Sweden. Although in early life he had been a liberal Frenchman of the Revolutionary era, he was a conservative king and fell in with the reactionary mood of the times. He played the role of an absolute monarch as nearly as he might. Nevertheless, he kept the peace and Sweden prospered under his rule.

During his reign, in 1832, the Gota Canal, which cut across southern Sweden from Goteborg to Stockholm, was completed.

RUSSIA

Alexander I died on December 13, 1825. He had no children, but he did have two younger brothers: Constantine (1779–1831), and Nicholas (1796–1855). Constantine was the actual heir, but he had no desire for the job and, in 1822, had renounced it in favor of Nicholas.

The renunciation was kept secret, however, and, on December 26, 1825, there was an uprising on the part of some of the military in favor of Constantine, who was thought to show signs of liberalism. This "Decembrist rebellion" was promptly crushed by Nicholas, who showed no signs of liberalism at all, and who reigned as Nicholas I.

Nicholas I was the very personification of reaction and absolutism. He hated and feared liberalism as Philip II of Spain had hated and feared Protestantism two and a half centuries before. Like Philip, Nicholas felt it his duty to attack the enemy in any nation at any time regardless of whether this would do Russia any good or not.

Nicholas's reign opened with another war, when Persia attacked Russia's new Transcaucasian territories in 1825. The Russians counterattacked, won victories, and, at the peace treaty on February 22, 1828, gained new Transcaucasian territories, including portions of Armenia. After this, Persia made no further efforts to engage European powers in war.

There was also a brief war between Russia and the Ottoman Empire in 1828 and 1829 in connection with a Greek revolt.

The real test came in Poland, however. After Russia had absorbed most of the Grand Duchy of Warsaw, it had given the Poles a certain amount of self-rule, in theory. The Tsar was not Tsar in Poland, but merely the "King of Poland." Constantine, Nicholas's elder brother, ruled as commander in chief of the Polish forces, and though he ruled with a heavy hand, he rather sympathized with the Poles. He married a Polish woman and it was partly for that reason that he had given up the throne of Russia.

The Poles, however, dreamed of independence, and this dream was excited by the July Revolution in France. They had the idea that a Revolutionary France might come to their aid, and they were horrified at a report that Nicholas was considering the use of Polish troops to suppress the French revolt.

On November 29, 1830, the Poles rose. They fought well and fiercely, but they had no help and could not withstand Russia by themselves. The Russians drove the Poles back and took Warsaw on September 8, 1831. Constantine died in the course of the revolt, a victim of an epidemic of cholera that swept Europe at this time.

The result of this revolt was that Poland lost its privileged status and was made an integral part of Russia. It was subject, therefore, to a process of "Russification." Still, it also meant that Nicholas, deeply involved in Poland, had to give up any wild plans he might have had for repressing liberal reforms in western Europe.

Reaction didn't prevail in Poland only, of course. All over Russia, censorship was clamped down, and the bureaucracy grew. The secret police flourished, with their main purpose the maintenance of autocracy and the crushing of dissent. The Orthodox Church, properly subservient to the Tsar, was the only form of religion supported, and the treatment of Jews grew more harsh.

Yet one form of novelty can penetrate even the thickest curtain and the most merciless repression—technological advance. Liberalism might not enter, but western technology did. The first Russian railroad, from St. Petersburg to a suburb, was built in 1838.

And if Russia's expansion to the west had reached its end with the absorption of Finland and Poland, it still continued in the direction of the fading Ottoman Empire and into the vacuum of central Asia north of Iran and Afghanistan.

Russian enterprise swept even farther afield. A Russian exploring expedition under Fabian Gottlieb Bellingshausen (1778–1852) circled the world in Antarctic waters and discovered two frozen islands, "Peter I Island" and "Alexander I Island" in 1820 and 1821. This was the first land to be found south of the Antarctic Circle.

Russia was backward in science; however, in 1829, Nikolai Ivanovich Lobachevski (1792–1856) worked out a system of non-Euclidean geometry independently of the Hungarian mathematician, Bolyai. Lobachevski did his work after Bolyai, but published first, and usually gets the credit for the discovery. The Estonian-born Karl Ernst von Baer (1792–1876) discovered the mammalian egg in 1827 and published a book on the subject in 1828, which founded the modern science of embryology.

In this period the greatest Russian poet was Alexander Sergeyevich Pushkin (1799–1837), who wrote *Eugene Onegin* in 1833 and *The Queen of Spades* in 1834. Second only to Pushkin as a Romantic poet was Mikhail Yurevich Lermontov (1814–1841). Both Pushkin and Lermontov died in duels. Nicolai Vasilievich Gogol (1809–1852) was a novelist who wrote "The Inspector General" in 1836. In music, there was Mikhail Ivanovich Glinka (1804–1857) who, in 1836, wrote *A Life for the Tsar*, the first important Russian opera.

GREECE

Part of Russia's plan to inherit the Balkans from the Ottoman Empire lay in the encouragement of revolts, and the Balkan peoples were quite ready to be encouraged.

On October 5, 1821, the Greeks in the Morea (the ancient Peloponnesus, where Sparta had been the strongest military power in the Greek world 22 centuries earlier) revolted, and slaughtered every Turk they could find. The Turks promptly returned the compliment by slaughtering every Greek they could find.

The Russians at once threatened the Ottoman Empire with war, but Metternich warned Alexander I of the dangers of supporting rebellion anywhere, even of Christians rebelling against Muslims. Russia, therefore, backed off.

The Greeks declared their independence on January 13, 1822, even without Russian help, but they had a rough time of it. They had to face the Ottoman forces, who had the help of the powerful Muhammad Ali of Egypt, and they made things worse by fighting among themselves. By 1826, it looked as though the Greek revolt might be crushed.

Christian Europe, however, not only thought of the Greeks as Christians, but also thought of them as the heirs of the ancient Greeks who had devised the culture that Europe had inherited. It was the Greeks against the Persians once again; it was Marathon and Thermopylae. A wave of pro-Greek feeling was sweeping over the European intellectual classes. Lord Byron went to Greece to help them fight, and he died there.

In the end, the European governments could not resist. Even Russia felt its appetite for expansion overcoming its theoretical objections to rebellion. Great Britain did not want Russia to act alone, so it joined in, more to keep an eye on Russia than anything else.

There was a strong Turkish–Egyptian fleet at Navarino on the western shore of the Morea. On October 20, 1827, a combined British–Russian fleet challenged it and quickly destroyed it.

In 1828, Russia declared war on the Ottoman Empire and advanced nearly to Constantinople, but her armies were by then badly weakened by disease, and she did not try to take the city. At the Treaty of Adrianople, on September 14, 1829, Russia received the right to occupy the provinces of Moldavia and Wallachia (making up much of the modern Rumania).

Greece was declared independent by the treaty, but was given boundaries that included very little space more than the Morea. By now, Serbia had also virtual independence, and so did Moldavia and Wallachia.

OTTOMAN EMPIRE

It was clear to Sultan Mahmud II that the Ottoman military could no longer serve the Empire. He tried to form a new kind of army corps to replace the Janissaries. When the Janissaries rose in revolt at this, he had loyal troops bombard their barracks and the Constantinopolitan mob gladly did the rest. Anywhere from 6000 to 10,000 Janissaries were slaughtered. They ceased to be a power in the Ottoman Empire after four centuries of existence.

This, in itself, however, did not help the Ottoman government. It turned out to be helpless, not only with respect to the Christian European powers, but also to their own too-powerful subject, Muhammad Ali of Egypt, whose son, Ibrahim (1789–1848), proved to be an excellent military leader.

In return for his services in the course of the Greek revolt, Muhammad Ali, in 1832, demanded that Syria be placed under his jurisdiction. The Ottoman government refused, and Ibrahim swept through Syria and far into Asia Minor by the end of the year.

The Ottoman ruling house might have been overthrown but once again Russia interfered, at which western Europe also interfered to prevent Russia from having it all its own way. Hostilities were ended when the European powers induced the Sultan to let Muhammad Ali have Syria.

Meanwhile, the British were becoming more anti-Russian. They resented Russian expansion into the Balkans and into Central Asia, feeling that this threatened their communications with India. Great Britain secured Aden at the southern

opening of the Red Sea as a military base for herself to protect those communications. The British then made it an important part of their foreign policy to safeguard the Ottoman empire from Russia.

On July 1, 1839, Mahmud II died and was succeeded by his son who reigned as Abdulmecid I (1828–1861).

PERSIA

By this time, Persia was not a truly independent nation. It could maintain its existence only by walking a tightrope between Russia and Great Britain.

The tightrope was sometimes dangerous. The British were penetrating Afghanistan, and so Russia persuaded Persia to invade Afghanistan in 1837. The attack was a failure and, the next year, under British pressure, Persia gave up the invasion.

AFGHANISTAN

Afghanistan was also forced to walk a tightrope between Russia and Great Britain. The important Afghanistani ruler of the time was Dost Mohammed (1793–1863), who had taken the throne in 1826 and whom the British did not trust. They felt he was too pro-Russian and tried to replace him with Shah Shoja (1780–1842), who had ruled over Afghanistan a generation before.

In 1839, the British carried through their coup. Dost Mohammed was captured and sent into imprisonment in India, and Shah Shoja ascended the throne.

WEST AFRICA

British expeditions fought the Ashanti, beginning in 1824. It was not until 1831 that they were securely in possession of the coast, which came to be known as the "Gold Coast."

The British explorer, Alexander Gordon Laing (1793–1826), reached Timbuktu on August 1, 1826. He was the first European to reach that city, and he was killed there.

Meanwhile, philanthropic American groups

had sent liberated slaves back to Africa. There, in 1822, they settled well west of the Gold Coast and named the settlement Monrovia, after James Monroe, who was then fifth president of the United States. It was the nucleus of a nation that came to be called Liberia (from the Latin word for "freedom,"), and it was the *only* portion of the African continent that was never, at any time, controlled by any European nation.

SOUTHERN AFRICA

In this period, Shaka (1787–1828) was supreme over the Zulu nation. A brilliant fighter, he had established new tactics and new weapons and had made of his army an irresistable force that lorded it over a wide area of southernmost Africa in the early 1820s. His method of proceeding, however, was to destroy to an even greater extent, proportionally, than had been the practice of Genghis Khan or Tamerlane.

Finally, his deadly insistence on executions in great numbers, and for little or no reason, aroused sufficient fear to bring about his assassination on September 22, 1828.

The old Dutch settlers of South Africa, the "Boers" (from a Dutch word for "farmers"), were at odds with the dominating British, who had taken over in Napoleonic times. They decided to move northward, away from the areas controlled by the British, where they might establish realms of their own.

This they did in the "Great Trek" between 1835 and 1837. They could carry this through in reasonable safety because the massacres of Shaka had largely emptied the region, and because, in the aftermath of Shaka's death, the Zulus were fighting among themselves, and were paying little attention to the Boers.

INDIA

In India in this period, British control continued to grow firmer, and various Western innovations such as roads, canals, and steamships were introduced. Laws were revised, and education on Western lines was introduced.

The Muslims of northern India felt the pull of fundamentalism in reaction to the introduction of western ideas. They fought the Sikhs between 1826 and 1831, and lost, but remained anti-Western.

BURMA

Burma was expanding eastward into Siam and westward into India. In 1824, the British, defending India, fought the "First Burmese War." The British had won the war by 1826, and took over the Burmese coast.

SIAM

Rama III (d. 1851) became king of Siam in 1824 and opened the nation, at least a crack, to Western influence. He signed a trade treaty with Great Britain in 1826 and one with the United States in 1833. He spent most of his reign trying to expand over the Indochinese peninsula, and in fighting off Burma. By 1829, he was in control of Laos, but had lost Cambodia to Vietnam.

INDONESIA

In 1830, the Dutch put down the last native revolt against their rule.

CHINA

The British had found it very profitable to trade with China in opium. The demand for opium was great and the payment, in silver, was welcome. The Chinese government, under Min-ning (1782–1850), who had become the sixth emperor of the Manchu dynasty in 1821, frowned on this, for China could not endure the harm that opium did its population, nor could it long maintain the drain of the silver payments.

Both the effect of the drugs and the drain of silver helped accelerate the decline that China was now experiencing. Nevertheless, the British were firm in maintaining the opium trade for their profit and were even ready to use force, if necessary.

Looking back on this from our vantage point, and knowing the harm drugs can do, we must stand appalled at British behavior in this connection.

JAPAN

Japan's policy of isolation was becoming a source of great irritation to the west. Whalers and other seafaring men were sometimes wrecked on the Japanese coast, and the sailors were then treated barbarously by the Japanese. It was felt that some sort of contact would have to be made with the Japanese government to put an end to this practice, but all attempts at this time were without success.

In 1837, the American ship *Morrison* tried to enter Japanese ports, but was driven off by hostile action.

UNITED STATES

Until this time, the United States and the colonies that had preceded it had been of interest to Europe. In colonial times, it had participated in European wars. The War of American Independence had become a European war, and, in the Napoleonic era, the United States had been an important neutral and had ended by fighting Great Britain.

After the war of 1812, however, the United States retreated behind the ocean and concerned itself only on occasion with European matters.

What really began to preoccupy the United States totally was the issue of Black slavery. The northern states had by this time outlawed slavery within their borders—an easy task since they were industrial and commercial states who needed skilled laborers rather than slaves, and whose agricultural areas were turning increasingly to machinery rather than to slaves. The southern states, however, were primarily agricultural and found slaves particularly useful on the cotton plantations.

By 1820, there were 22 states, 11 free and 11 slave. The free states, while smaller in area, were larger in population, and this disproportion was growing. It meant that the number of representatives of the free states in the lower house of Congress was greater than those of the slave states. The free states were also wealthier (though the slave states couldn't get it through their heads that this was *because* they were free states) and could therefore industrialize themselves instead of clinging to low-profit, slave-run agriculture.

Still, many of the free-state representatives were in no mood to upset things by insisting on the freeing of southern slaves, and the American presidents were equally intent on keeping things quiet, so that, in general, the slave states, stubbornly set on keeping their way of life, were little disturbed. Moreover, representation in the United States Senate was two for each state, regardless of population, so that as long as the number of slave states matched those of the free, the slave states could feel secure, and didn't have to depend entirely on the lukewarmness of the free-state representatives.

In 1820, however, there were two possible states applying for entrance. There was Maine in the far northeast. It had been part of Massachusetts, although it was separated from the latter by a corner of New Hampshire, and it now wanted to be a state on its own, and Massachusetts was willing to allow this. As part of Massachusetts, Maine had been free and there was no question that it would remain free as an independent state.

The other applicant for statehood was Missouri, which was borderline geographically and could be either free or slave—but the slave states were absolutely determined that it be slave in order to keep the balance.

Eventually, on March 3, 1820, the "Missouri Compromise" was reached. Maine entered the Union on March 15, 1820 as a free state, while Missouri entered as a slave state on August 10, 1821. Now there were 24 states, 12 free and 12 slave.

Furthermore, any new state north of the latitude of Missouri's southern border would be free, and any state south of that latitude would be slave. The land available to the north was much larger, to be sure, but the slave states looked forward to additional annexations of territory in the south.

For the moment, the matter seemed settled,

but anyone who thought about it would realize that the moral issues involved in slavery were so great that the matter could never be really settled in a civilized nation (especially one that prized itself on its "freedom") short of emancipation.

Meanwhile, the nation reinforced its isolation with what was called "The Monroe Doctrine," because it was enunciated by President James Monroe on December 2, 1823. It was, however, written by the Secretary of State, John Quincy Adams (1767–1848), the son of John Adams, who had been the second president.

This came at a time when the Congress of Verona had sent French troops into Spain to crush the rebellion there, and it seemed possible that troops might also be sent to the Americas to restore the rebellious Spanish colonies to their allegiance.

In the Monroe Doctrine, the United States forbade any interference anywhere in the Western Hemisphere by any European nation. The United States would not, in return, interfere in Europe.

It is doubtful that the United States had any right to tell other nations what to do, but it was a perfectly safe attitude to take. Great Britain had already made it clear that it would not allow interference with the newly free nations, and since no one would try to argue with the British navy, the United States was free to make its pronouncement.

Meanwhile, the United States was growing rapidly in population and prosperity. The Erie Canal was opened in 1825. It connected the Great Lakes with the Hudson River and it made New York City the nation's greatest port and its most populous city. The first public railroad, the Baltimore and Ohio, began operations on July 4, 1828.

What's more, the notion of democracy, at least for male white people, was gaining force. In 1824, the presidential election was the first in which the popular vote was important nationwide. John Quincy Adams did not gain a majority of that popular vote but was declared elected as sixth President by Congressional action, in accordance with the Constitution.

This offended many, and in 1828 Andrew Jackson, who had garnered more votes than

Adams in 1824, was triumphantly elected as seventh president of the United States. Until then, the party founded by Thomas Jefferson had been first the "Republican" and then the "Democratic-Republican" party. Jefferson, Madison, Monroe, and John Quincy Adams had all been Republican or Democratic-Republican. With Jackson, however, the name of the party became simply the "Democratic Party," and it has kept that name ever since.

Jackson was indeed an example of a true Democrat, of "the common man." He was the first president not to be of the plantation or commercial aristocracy. He was a western frontierman of limited education, but he was intelligent and forceful, knew what he wanted, and went after it.

There was trouble north and south for him. The commercial north wanted high tariffs that would make it possible for them to sell their products at high prices without fear of competition with Europe's cheaper products. The agricultural south wanted low tariffs that would allow them to buy cheaper products from abroad.

In 1828, a very high tariff was passed, and the south was so indignant at this that South Carolina even threatened to "secede" (i.e., to leave the Union). Andrew Jackson promised the use of force if they tried, and there can be no doubt that he meant it.

Fortunately, cool heads carried the day. A new and lower tariff was passed and the controversy was resolved.

Another economic problem was the Bank of the United States. It lent the United States economic stability, but it did so on terms that, again, pleased the commercial institutions and displeased the farmers. In this case, Jackson was on the side of the farmers and he managed to destroy the Bank of the United States.

The result was a sharp depression that came only after he had left office, so that it was the following president, Martin Van Buren (1782–1862), the eighth, who had to suffer the results and be denied reelection.

The question of the Bank led to the formation of a new anti-Jackson party, the "Whig party," in memory of the British party that was just losing its name.

Nor was the slavery issue settled. In the Senate, the standoff continued. Arkansas entered the Union as a slave state on June 15, 1836, while Michigan entered as a free state on January 26, 1837. That made it 26 states, 13 slave and 13 free.

Public opinion was polarizing, however. In the free states, an "abolitionist" movement (favoring the immediate abolition of slavery without compensation to the slave-owners) was beginning to grow stronger. An outstanding abolitionist was William Lloyd Garrison (1805–1879), who founded the abolitionist paper, *The Liberator*, in 1831. Another was Wendell Phillips (1811–1884). Both were active in Boston, a center of abolitionist sentiment. In the Middle West, there was Elijah Parish Lovejoy (1802–1837), who was killed by a mob in Illinois in 1837.

Although the abolitionists were never great in number, they were loud and articulate and they sent a thrill of horror through the slave states, which consistently exaggerated their numbers and power.

The southern slave-owners suffered one of the curses of their position in their fear of slave insurrections and the boundless revenge of those they so grossly misused. Actually, such insurrections were surprisingly rare; however, in August, 1831, a slave, Nat Turner (1800–1831), led a revolt of 75 blacks, killing 50 whites altogether. The rebellion was snuffed out at once and an orgy of hangings followed, but the thrill of terror lingered with every slavemaster.

In this period, the United States saw the birth of a new religious sect. Joseph Smith (1805–1844) reported visions, and maintained that on September 22, 1827, near Palmyra, New York, he had found golden plates inscribed with "Egyptian" writing. Translated by mystical means, these became the *Book of Mormon*, published in 1830. It purported to be a history of Jews who had reached America while fleeing from the Babylonian conquest 24 centuries earlier. Those who believed this formed "The Church of Jesus Christ of Latter-Day Saints," or, as they were popularly termed, "Mormons." It was the first important religious movement to be entirely American in origin.

The greatest American scientist since Franklin was Joseph Henry (1797–1878). He was the first, in 1831, to construct powerful and practical electromagnets. That same year he invented the electric motor and, in 1835, the electric relay. Second only to Faraday, Henry paved the way for our modern electrical age. Samuel Guthrie (1782–1848) discovered chloroform in 1831. William Beaumont (1785–1853) published a careful study of stomach function in 1833, since he had had the good fortune to initiate a long-time study of a patient who survived a gunshot wound that left him with a natural abdominal opening to his stomach.

In technology, Cyrus Hall McCormick (1809–1884) patented a mechanical reaper in 1834. This was adopted widely in the farming states of the north, where there were no slaves to make labor so cheap as to seem to obviate the need for machines. It marked the beginning of the industrialization of agriculture and strengthened the free states as opposed to the slave states.

Charles Goodyear (1800–1860), through a fortunate accident, found in 1839 that rubber, heated with sulfur, improved its properties greatly. Such "vulcanized rubber" did not turn stiff and brittle in the cold, or soft and sticky in the heat. The vast present-day uses of rubber would not be possible without Goodyear's discovery.

Samuel Colt (1814–1862) patented the revolver or "six-shooter" in 1836, and this greatly increased the deadliness of sidearms.

In 1836, the Swedish-born John Ericsson (1803–1889) invented the screw propellor, which enabled ships to be steam-driven by a device under the waterline, rather than by a huge, vulnerable paddle-wheel along the sides. The screw-propellor made steam-driven warships a practical reality. In the 1830s also, "Lucifer matches" were coming into use—pieces of wood tipped with chemicals that could be made to burst into flame through friction, thus doing away with the flint-and-steel, and similar devices, that had been used for thousands of years.

An American navigator, Charles Wilkes (1798–1877), explored the Antarctic coast in January 1840, as others had done before him. Wilkes, however, grasped the fact that he was sighting a continent, rather than merely this or that bit of land.

In this period, New England experienced the beginning of a golden age of literature. William Cullen Bryant (1794–1878) published a volume of poetry in 1821 that made him the first American poet to attract European attention. Henry Wadsworth Longfellow (1807–1882) wrote "The Psalm of Life" in 1839, the best-known of his early works. Oliver Wendell Holmes (1809–1894) wrote "Old Ironsides" in 1830, a poem credited with saving that ship from being dismantled. The leading light of this New England school was Ralph Waldo Emerson (1803–1882), who published his first essays in 1836. Outside of New England was Edgar Allan Poe (1809–1849), who published "To Helen" in 1831 and "To One in Paradise" in 1834.

On a lesser scale was Clement Clarke Moore (1779–1863) who, in 1823, published "A Visit from St. Nicholas," a poem that forever fixed the picture of Santa Claus in American minds; and John Howard Payne (1791–1852), whose fame rests entirely on one haunting poem, "Home, Sweet Home," written in 1823.

The true American literary phenomenon of the age, however, was James Fenimore Cooper (1789–1851), whose novels of pioneers and Native Americans were infinitely popular in Europe as well as in the United States. His most successful book, *The Last of the Mohicans*, was published in 1826.

Popular in another way were the *McGuffy Readers* put out by William Holmes McGuffey (1800–1873). Out of these, generations of American children were taught, and of them at least 120 million copies were sold.

CANADA

After the War of 1812, Canada was never again to be really in danger from the United States. This meant that it could concentrate on being dis-satisfied with the British. Trouble arose between the popularly elected legislatures of the land and the British crown-appointed rulers.

In 1837, there were rebellions in Montreal and in Toronto, the latter being led by William Lyon Mackenzie (1795–1861). They weren't serious problems, and the authorities could have handled them easily, but American volunteers who felt anti-British flocked in to help. In the process, an American managed to be killed by a loyal Canadian who had the bad judgment to boast about it while in New York State. The Canadian was arrested and tried for murder. Great Britain demanded he be freed, but the United States said it couldn't tell a state what to do. Fortunately, the man on trial was acquitted and it all blew over.

These small and unimportant revolts might have been followed by other worse ones, but Great Britain had learned from its earlier mistakes—something nations rarely do.

On May 20, 1838, the British appointed a new governor, John George Lambton, Earl of Durham (1792–1840), who treated the rebels leniently and who, on February 11, 1839, wrote a report recommending that Canada be allowed a form of representative government. This "Durham report" was treated seriously, and that meant that Canada was to remain loyal to the British monarchy to this day.

TEXAS

When Mexico gained its independence in 1821, its northeasternmost province, Texas, was almost uninhabited. Even as Mexico was becoming independent, however, Americans were beginning to migrate into the province; and, by 1834, there were 20,000 Americans in Texas as compared with only 5000 Mexicans.

In 1831, Mexico had abolished slavery, but most of the Americans were from the slave states, had brought their slaves with them, and intended to keep them.

Mexico's president, Santa Anna, was strongly opposed to allowing the Americans to do as they wished in Mexican territory. Since he was clearly planning to take action, the Americans [led by

Samuel ("Sam") Houston (1793–1863), a recent immigrant] declared themselves independent of Mexico on March 2, 1836.

Meanwhile, however, Santa Anna had led a Mexican army of about 4000 men northward and, on February 23, 1836, had begun a siege of the Alamo, an old chapel in San Antonio that was occupied by 187 American Texans. This small group of men held off Santa Anna's army for 12 days and died to the last man.

Sam Houston then gathered a force of 750 men and lured Santa Anna into pursuing him with 1600. Houston retreated to the San Jacinto River and, on April 21, 1836, waited until the Mexican troops were enjoying a siesta and fell upon them, achieving complete surprise. Yelling "Remember the Alamo," the Texans virtually destroyed the Mexican forces in 20 minutes. They took Santa Anna prisoner and he had no choice but to sign a treaty recognizing Texan independence on May 14, 1836.

The United States recognized Texan independence on March 3, 1837; France did so in October 1839; and Great Britain in November 1840.

Texas wanted to join the United States, and many in the United States wanted that, too, but important voices in the free states made themselves heard against it. They didn't want any more slave territory in the United States, so that the question of annexation hung fire.

1840 TO 1860

FRANCE

The leading political figure in France during the 1840s was Francois Pierre Guillaume Guizot (1787–1874). Foreign minister and later premier, he was no autocrat. He believed in representative government, but felt, as the British Tories of the time did, that only the well-to-do had enough of a stake in society to be trusted with the vote. To vote, in other words, one had to pay a certain minimum in taxes. Guizot's attitude was that anyone could become eligible to vote if he merely took the trouble to become rich.

It meant, though, that those who were not rich felt uncared for, and in hard times that was particularly true. France was industrializing itself in the 1840s and was doing well; however, in 1846, a sharp depression hit France, and the demand for an extension of the franchise and an end to corruption and bribery of legislators rose steeply in intensity.

Banquets were arranged in early 1848 at which such demands would be made, and a particularly large one was arranged for February 22, 1848. The British had defused such feelings by passing the Reform Bill 16 years earlier, but the French government had not learned from that. Guizot simply forbade the banquet.

Thereupon, the barricades went up in Paris. The people found weapons, and the fighting began, as the authorities vainly tried to restore order. On February 24, Louis Philippe abdicated and his 18-year reign was at an end. He was the last French king to have been descended from Hugh Capet, who had come to the throne eight and a half centuries earlier.

A "Second Republic" was proclaimed and the question arose as to exactly what form it would take. There were moderate republicans, who didn't want anything very different from what they had had under Louis Philippe, but there was also Louis Blanc (1811–1882), who was a Socialist and wanted to see factories (or "workshops") established that were run by the workers themselves. In fact, such workshops were established, but it was done hurriedly and inefficiently, and the conservatives made every effort to insure that they would not work—and they didn't. [Another radical of the time was Pierre Joseph Proudhon (1809–1865), who is considered the father of anarchism, since he was opposed to all forms of government without exception.]

The outcry of the leftists frightened the better-off enormously. For the first time, the conservatives had cause to fear the "Red menace"—that is, the Socialists (who had a red flag as their banner)—rather than that old faded bogie, the Jacobins.

On June 23, when street-fighting was becoming fierce, they called on the army. Troops under Louis Eugene Cavaignac (1802–1857), whose father had voted for the execution of Louis XVI, suppressed the leftists bloodily, and this was followed by a strong reaction that might just as easily have existed under Charles X, one that was complete with press censorship and the rough crushing of dissent.

A new constitution was devised calling for a strong president, and an election was arranged. Two candidates ran. One was Cavaignac, who would not have been a bad choice, but his treatment of the riots had earned him the name of "butcher" and many would not vote for him under any circumstances. Opposed to him was Louis Napoleon Bonaparte (1808–1873), nephew of the Emperor Napoleon, and son of Louis Bonaparte, who had been King of Holland and had fled the country rather than harm it. He was also the grandson of the Empress Josephine, since his mother was Josephine's daughter by her first marriage.

Louis Napoleon was a man of limited ability, especially as compared with his famous uncle. He had taken part in the revolts in Italy in 1830 and 1831, and had twice fecklessly attempted coups in France in 1836 and in 1840. He had failed at everything, but now his opportunity had arrived. He had, after all, a magic name for those Frenchmen who thought back nostalgically to military "glory," and who had not had to live through it, or who had a very selective memory. On December 10, 1848, he was elected with 75% of the vote.

Bonaparte then spent the next few years carefully repressing all liberal activity and establishing a more conservative government than Louis Philippe's had been. Since his term only ran for four years and he was forbidden to succeed himself, he tried to get that constitutional requirement changed. When he failed, he carried out a coup on December 2, 1851 (the date having been carefully chosen as the 46th anniversary of the Battle of Austerlitz, Napoleon I's greatest victory).

He made himself dictator, used the troops to repress demonstrations against him, and, on December 21, had a plebiscite set up, in which the French people would vote for or against him. (In doing this, he invented all the tactics of persuading and forcing and tricking people into voting for him that would be used by later dictators.) He obtained 92% of the vote.

A new constitution was promulgated on January 14, 1852, which put all power in the hands of Bonaparte and made him virtually absolute ruler of the nation. It was a tiny step from that to having himself announced as Emperor on December 2, 1852, the 48th anniversary of the day on which Napoleon I had become Emperor.

Thus, France came under the "Second Empire" and Bonaparte called himself Napoleon III. Napoleon II was the title now given the son of Napoleon I, who had never ruled, and who had died in 1832; so that, by Napoleonic mythology, Napoleon III had already been emperor for 20 years when he was crowned.

Napoleon III was intelligent enough to do all he could to promote prosperity. He reorganized banking, initiated a system of public works that created jobs, and passed laws to improve the lot of workmen in order to lessen their enthusiasm for socialism. In particular, he beautified Paris and built long, straight boulevards. (There was considerable sense to this. Narrow and crooked streets are easily barricaded and made to order for street fighting. On a long, straight boulevard, the bullets fly unimpeded and a mob is easily suppressed.) Napoleon III also made concessions to the Church, so that he was sure of having the clerical party with him.

In 1855, there was an International Exposition in Paris, a kind of "World's Fair" in imitation of the first such celebration four years earlier in London. It was designed to display the progress that France was making in technology and also, you may be sure, to serve as a showpiece for the glories of the Second Empire.

On January 30, 1853, Napoleon III had married a Spanish noblewoman, Eugenie de Montijo (1826–1920), who became the Empress Eugenie. She was beautiful, and made a fine appearance as the Empress, but had had a strict religious upbringing and was a total enemy of liberalism. The two had a child on March 16, 1856, who came to be known as the "Prince Imperial," so that Napoleon III had provided himself with a successor.

Napoleon III even managed to find a way to have a successful foreign policy, at least in his first decade. Where Louis Philippe had kept the peace to the point where many Frenchmen had scorned him as pusillanimous, Napoleon III had to calm Europe and convince them that another Napoleon did not mean another drenching of the continent with war. What he had to do was find a small war that would satisfy the glory-mongers at home without frightening everyone abroad.

Therefore, he managed to join Great Britain in a minor war against Russia in 1854, and then, in 1859, engaged in a minor war against Austria. By 1860, he seemed to have done very well indeed and was at the height of his popularity and prestige.

In science during this period, Louis Pasteur (1822–1895), who was to be one of the greatest scientists in history, discovered by 1848 that crystals turning the plane of polarized light were asymmetric in structure. This was a first step toward understanding the three-dimensional structure of molecules.

In 1849, Armand Hippolyte Fizeau (1819–1896) and Jean Bernard Leon Foucault (1819–1868) were the first to measure the speed of light in laboratory settings, rather than through astronomical observations. Foucault, in 1851, was the first (believe it or not) to demonstrate that the Earth really rotated on its axis.

Claude Bernard (1813–1878) showed, in 1843, that digestion took place in the small intestine to a greater extent than in the stomach. In 1856, he discovered glycogen, a form of starch in the liver of animals.

Urbain Jean Joseph Leverrier (1811–1877) calculated the position of an undiscovered planet, in 1846, from the fact that Uranus was being sub-jected to an unaccounted-for gravitational pull. As a result, the planet Neptune was discovered.

In literature, Victor Hugo was still writing, but his outspoken opposition to Napoleon III (whom he aptly called "Napoleon the Little") forced him into exile. The most popular writer of the period was the extremely prolific Alexandre Dumas (1802–1870), whose most successful novels were *The Three Musketeers* and *The Count of Monte Cristo,* both published in 1844. His son, also Alexandre Dumas (1824–1895), published *La Dame aux Camelias* from which the opera *La Traviata* was eventually derived.

Eugene Sue (1804–1857), who played an active role in the Revolution of 1848, and who, like Hugo, went into exile when Napoleon III came to power, wrote long novels—socialistic, anticlerical, and replete with scenes of poverty, such as *The Mysteries of Paris* in 1843, and *The Wandering Jew* in 1845.

In contrast to the Romanticism of Dumas and Sue, Gustave Flaubert (1821–1880) wrote realistically. His first novel, *Madame Bovary,* published in 1857, brought him before the court on the accusation of immorality. (He was acquitted.) Prosper Merimee (1803–1870) wrote the play *Carmen* in 1846, from which the opera was eventually developed.

Hector Berlioz was still composing, writing the music for *The Damnation of Faust* in 1846. Charles Francis Gounod (1818–1893) wrote another operatic treatment of the legend *Faust* in 1859, and that is surely one of the most popular operas now extant. In a lighter mood, Jacques Offenbach (1819–1880) wrote comic operas, such as *Orpheus in the Underworld,* produced in 1859.

Among French artists of the period were Jean Francois Millet (1814–1875), whose best-known paintings are perhaps *The Angelus, The Gleaners,* and *The Man with the Hoe.* Another was Jean Baptiste Corot (1796–1875), whose paintings were Impressionistic. A writer about art who was well-known at this time was Theophile Gautier (1811–1872).

ITALY

At the beginning of this period, in 1840, Austria was in complete control of Italy. The northeastern portion, Lombardy and Venetia, were actually part of the Austrian Empire, and had been so since the time of the Congress of Vienna. The rest of Italy was under local rulers who were entirely subservient to Austria. The only portion of Italy that had a hint of independence was Sardinia in the northwest, and it had been beaten by Austria in 1830.

Nevertheless, there were rising demands all over Italy for a united country under some form of representative government. The loudest voice was that of Giuseppe Mazzini (1805–1872), who had been conspiring for years to overthrow the various despotisms that were grinding down Italy. He was in exile in England now, but continued to try to spark rebellion in Italy in favor of a united, democratic Italian republic. Though he never succeeded, he kept the hope alive.

That hope seemed to sharpen when Pius IX (1792–1878) became Pope on June 15, 1846. He was known to be somewhat liberal and, after a series of reactionary Popes, he seemed to be a breath of fresh air. He at once instituted a series of reforms, reducing censorship, declaring an amnesty for political prisoners, and introducing useful changes in financial and judicial procedures. He even established a council of clerics to advise him.

Then, in 1848, matters came to a head. Partly, the 1848 revolution in France was to blame. France had undergone ferment and had set Europe ablaze in 1789 and in 1830. Now, in 1848, it did it for a third (and last) time.

Even before the overthrow of Louis Philippe, there were uprisings in the kingdom of Naples. The despicably reactionary Ferdinand II tried to get Austrian help and, when he failed (for Austria was having internal troubles of its own), he was forced to grant a constitution. Constitutions were also granted in Tuscany and in Sardinia.

When the 1848 revolution in France produced effects in increasingly restless Austria and convulsed even that bastion of conservatism, Italian liberals took heart. On March 18, Milan, the capital of Austrian Lombardy, rebelled. On March 22, Venetia declared itself a republic, and Sardinia declared war on Austria.

Pope Pius IX declared himself to be neutral since the Church, being international, had to hold itself above the struggle. This instantly lost him all liberal Italian sympathy. He was forced to grant some sort of constitution, but as Rome itself broke out in insurrection, he had to flee Rome for Neapolitan territory on November 25. That changed his view on things utterly. Thereafter, through a long reign as Pope, he remained a hard-bitten conservative.

The Austrians, of course, were not idle. They called upon one of their best generals, Joseph Radetzky (1766–1858), who had fought against Napoleon and who was now 82, but whose ability was undimmed.

Radetsky strengthened the "Quadrilateral," four bases in Lombardy-Venetia that were too strong for the ill-equipped Italians to storm, and, at the appropriate time, struck out. On July 24–25, 1848 (by which time the Naples revolt had collapsed), he fought the Sardinian army at Custozza, on the western border of Venetia, and defeated it. With that, Radetsky reoccupied Lombardy and laid siege to Venice.

For a while, there was an armistice, during which a Roman republic was proclaimed on February 9, 1849, after the Pope had fled. Sardinia tried to use the quiet interval to get French help, but the French were occupied with the disorders that had followed the 1848 upheaval.

Liberal pressure, however, forced Charles Albert of Sardinia to fight again, even without French help, and, on March 23, 1849, Radetzky beat him even more decisively at the Battle of Novara in western Lombardy. Charles Albert was forced to resign in favor of his son, who reigned as Victor Emmanuel II (1820–1878).

Only then did France send an expeditionary force to Italy. That was not to oppose Austria, however, but to support the Pope, because President Bonaparte felt the need to gain the support of French Catholics. The French destroyed the Roman republic, and an embittered Pius IX returned to Rome on April 12, 1850.

By then, all was over and Italy was again under the Austrian heel, exactly as before.

Yet not exactly, either. In Sardinia, Camillo Benso, Count di Cavour (1810–1861) grew powerful, becoming prime minister in 1852. He was a liberal who admired the British system of government and wanted to introduce it to Sardinia. He wanted, too, to bring in improvements in agriculture, build railroads, bring about banking reform, and so on. He also had his eyes fixed on the problem of unifying Italy. It could be done only with French help, and Cavour meant to get it.

Thus, in 1855, he joined Great Britain and France in a war on Russia. Sardinia had no interest in the war itself and got nothing material out of it, but it gained good will from the two western powers. It also gave him a chance, at the peace conference, of talking about the need for Italian unity.

Then, on January 14, 1858, there was an assassination attempt on Napoleon III and the Empress Eugenie. An Italian radical named Felice Orsini (1819–1858), who had broken with Mazzini and who may have been mentally disturbed, threw bombs at the carriage carrying the royal couple. The Emperor and Empress escaped, but two people were killed and about a hundred were wounded. Orsini was executed two months later, but Napoleon III, who was no great hero, was badly shaken. Between his anxiety to avoid further attempts on his life, and his memory of his own younger days when he fought on the side of Italian rebels, he felt he had better help the Italians. He had a meeting with Cavour on July 20, 1858, to make the necessary arrangements.

In 1859, the Sardinians prepared for a fight and needed a way of making the Austrians look like the aggressors. This the Austrians supplied by demanding, on April 23, 1859, that Sardinia demobilize. Sardinia refused, and the War of Italian Unification began.

The French, under Napoleon III himself, invaded Lombardy at the side of the Sardinians and, on June 4, 1859, there was a battle at Magenta, west of Milan. The generalship on both sides was inept, but the French had the better of

it and the Austrians retreated. On June 24, there was another battle at Solferino, near the Venetian border, and again there was an uninspiring melee in which the French got the better of it.

It was clear, however, that there was nothing Napoleonic about Napoleon III's war-making abilities, and, to his credit, Napoleon III realized this fact. Also to his credit, he was sickened by the bloodshed and was eager to make peace, especially since the Quadrilateral lay ahead and Napoleon III rightly doubted his ability to win against a stubborn Austrian defense there.

On July 11, then, Napoleon III met with the new, young Austrian Emperor and agreed on a peace. Lombardy was to go to Sardinia, and Austria was to keep Venetia.

The process of the unification of Italy had begun.

At this time in Italy, Giuseppe Fortunino Francesco Verdi (1813–1901) was writing what were, as a group, the most popular operas ever presented. *Rigoletto* was staged in 1851; *Il Trovatore* in 1852; *La Traviata* in 1853; and he continued writing through the end of the century.

An important chemist of the time was Stanislao Cannizzaro (1826–1910) who, in 1859, introduced Avogadro's hypothesis to the chemical world, something that made it possible to tackle the problem of molecular structure with greater understanding.

Ascanio Sobrero (1812–1888) discovered nitroglycerine in 1847. Recognizing its shattering explosiveness and fearing its use for destructive purposes, he engaged in no further research in that direction. It did not help, of course. Others repeated the discovery and, being untroubled by idealistic concerns, pushed on.

AUSTRIA

Italy's unrest was not Austria's only problem. Hungary, which Austria had seized from the Ottoman Empire a century and a half earlier, was seething as well, and increasingly resented the heavy weight of Austrian control.

This Hungarian nationalism was most effectively articulated by Lajos (Louis) Kossuth (1802–1894). All through the 1840s, his speeches and writings kept Hungarians feverish. (Oddly enough, although he felt it wrong for Austrians to dominate Hungarians, he insisted that Hungarians must dominate the minorities, such as Croats and Slovenes, within Hungary—one of the many occasions in which people are liberal on their own behalf, but conservative where others are concerned.)

When news of the revolution of 1848 in France arrived, Kossuth's anti-Austrian eloquence grew sharper, and there were also demonstrations in Vienna itself. Metternich, that symbol of reaction, was forced to resign his posts and flee to England. (He returned to Vienna in 1851, and lived quietly there till his death in 1859.)

The Emperor, Ferdinand I, was obliged to grant a constitution on April 25, 1848, setting up representative government. The Czechs also demanded representative government for themselves and, in June, held the first "Pan-Slav congress." It stressed the equality of all peoples, since Germans usually held it as an article of faith, then and afterward, that Slavs were intrinsically inferior to themselves.

The Austrian government, however, now gave power to Alfred Windischgratz (1787–1862), a leader of the Austrian reactionaries, and he was equal to the occasion. He bombarded Prague and put an end to the Czech uprising on June 17, 1848. Then on October 31, 1848, he bombarded Vienna into submission, even as the revolt in Italy was put down by Radetzky.

Windischgratz saw the need for a new young Emperor, since Ferdinand I had been hopelessly compromised by his connection with the hated Metternich. On December 2, 1848, Ferdinand I abdicated. His heir was his younger brother Francis Charles, who declined in favor of his 18-year-old son, who reigned as Francis Joseph I (1830–1916).

The next step was to quiet Hungary. An Austrian army under Windischgratz invaded Hungary on January 5, 1849, and took Budapest easily. However, Kossuth set up a "Hungarian Republic" in the eastern part of the country and this, at last, gave Nicholas I of Russia his chance.

Nicholas I had not been able to do anything about the 1830 revolutions, or about the 1848 rev-olutions in France and Italy, but Hungary was right on his border. Here, at least, he could use his army to help him play the role he always longed for, that of policeman of the world in favor of reaction. A Russian army moved into Hungary, and by August 9, 1849, the last remnant of Hungarian resistance was crushed. Austria had survived its revolutionary unrest.

Thereafter, Austria tried to Germanize its empire by doing everything it could to discourage the use of non-German languages and to downplay non-German culture.

Austria went on to play an ignoble part in the war that England and France were to conduct against Russia in 1855. Austria showed itself to be on the side of Russia's enemies only six years after thankfully accepting Russian help in its own troubles. However, though it didn't actually fight in the war, Austria remained mobilized, and that was a strain on its finances. Then, in 1859, there was the disastrous war with France and Sardinia. Clearly, Austria was no longer dominant in central Europe.

In this period, Johann Strauss, the Elder (1804–1849) was popular in Vienna for his waltzes and marches, of which the most popular was the "Radetzky March." He was destined to be far outshone by his son and namesake, however. From Hungary, there was Franz Liszt (1811–1886), a composer and pianist, best remembered for his "Second Hungarian Rhapsody."

The Hungarian physician, Ignaz Philipp Semmelweiss, in 1847, tried to force doctors in a hospital under his direction to wash their hands in strong chemicals before attending women in childbirth. The death rate from childhood fever went down as a result. The doctors, however, resented having to wash their hands and used the Hungarian rebellion as an excuse to get rid of their Hungarian tormenter. The death-rate from fever promptly increased again, but that didn't seem to bother them.

PRUSSIA

Frederick William IV, who had become King of Prussia in 1840, was a thorough-going conservative. Even more, he was a medievalist, who looked back longingly at the Holy Roman Empire, and who accepted the primacy of Austria as part of the medieval heritage.

Lacking the will to accept any form of representative government, or the ability to impose his own desires on the land, he vacillated until overtaken by events.

The news of the February 1848 revolution in Paris set off restless uprisings throughout Germany, as well as in Austria. In Austria, the uprisings were divisive, with Hungary, Bohemia, and Italy seeking greater freedom from the dominant Germans; however, in Germany outside Austria, the uprisings were unifying, expressing the desire for a greater German state.

On March 15, 1848, there were riots in Berlin. Frederick William IV, unable (to his credit) to shoot down his people, made concessions, though he found it completely humiliating to do so. He fell between two stools. It was too little for the German liberals and too much for Austria.

By 1850, the Hungarian revolt had been crushed and Austria felt strong enough to make it clear that she would take military measures, if necessary, to reverse the position in Germany. What's more, Nicholas I of Russia, horrified at the thought of giving in to German liberalism in any way, strongly backed Austria.

On November 19, 1849, Prussia gave up any thought of heading any sort of union, although Frederick William IV had been offered the crown. (Frederick William said that he would not pick up a crown from the gutter, meaning by the people's will rather than that of God.) At a meeting in Olmutz in Moravia, Prussia bowed to Austrian demands. Later Prussian historians referred to this as "the humiliation of Olmutz" but, in actual fact, what could Frederick William IV have done against both Austria and Russia?

After that, conservatism ruled in Prussia and in the rest of Germany. The revolutions of 1848 had been everywhere a failure, it seemed—in France, in Italy, in Austria, and in Germany—and a flood of German liberals fled abroad, chiefly to the United States.

In 1858, Frederick William IV went insane (madness seems to have had a higher incidence in royal families than in the general public, perhaps as a result of inbreeding) and his younger brother became effective head of the state. When Frederick William IV died on January 2, 1861, his brother ruled as William I (1797–1888).

Meanwhile, Germany was becoming ever more prominent in science in this period. Julius Robert Mayer (1814–1878) and Hermann Ludwig Ferdinand von Helmholtz (1821–1894) contributed to the establishment, by 1847, of the "law of conservation of energy," also known as "the first law of thermodynamics." It may be the most fundamental of all scientific generalizations. Rudolf Julius Emmanuel Clausius (1822–1888) worked out the "second law of thermodynamics" in 1850, demonstrating that the amount of *usable* energy, energy that is capable of being converted to work, is constantly decreasing, so that the Universe is "running down."

Robert Wilhelm Bunsen (1811–1899) and Gustav Robert Kirchhoff (1824–1887) together worked out the technique of "spectroscopy," whereby each element could be identified by the characteristic wavelengths of the radiation it emitted when heated. Spectroscopy proved to be enormously useful not only to chemists, but to astronomers as well.

Friedrich August Kekule von Stradonitz (1829–1896) worked out a way of indicating the structure of organic molecules in 1858—something that brought order into a field that until then had been steeped in confusion. To be sure, the system showed the structure in two dimensions only.

The veteran chemist, Liebig, was still at work. In 1855, he began to experiment with chemical fertilizers. Eventually, these did away with the ubiquitous manure pile on every farm, thus getting rid of sickening odors and of a potent source of infection of such diseases as typhoid fever and cholera.

Christian Friedrich Schonbein (1799–1869) discovered ozone in 1840, and guncotton in 1845. The latter pointed the way to the replacement of foul and smoky gunpowder, after five centuries, by various smokeless powders. These were just as deadly, if not more so, but at least the battlefield became visible and needless deaths through blind gropings on the part of commanders might diminish. In connection with battlefields, Johann Nikolaus von Dreyse (1787–1867) devised the first breech-loading rifles (called "needle guns"). These could be much more quickly loaded from behind and fired than the older guns that had to be loaded through the muzzle. The Prussian army adopted the needle gun at once.

Rudolf Carl Virchow advanced the cell theory of life by showing that diseased cells developed from normal ones with no discontinuities. He said "all cells come from cells."

In 1857, in the Neanderthal valley of the German Rhineland, a digger discovered part of a skull, and some long bones, that looked human —but not quite. The skull had a sharply sloping forehead and very heavy eyebrow ridges. Other such bones were eventually unearthed and "Neanderthal man" had been discovered—the first evidence of human beings that were more primitive than "modern man."

The most influential German philosopher of the time was Karl Heinrich Marx (1818–1883), who, with Friedrich Engels (1820–1895), published *The Communist Manifesto* in 1848. This advanced socialist thinking and gave body to much that was to take place afterward.

A musical giant of the period was Richard Wagner (1813–1883), whose operas already included *The Flying Dutchman* in 1843, *Tannhauser* in 1845, and *Lohengrin* in 1848.

GREAT BRITAIN

The Paris Revolution of 1848 had its effect even on Great Britain, in a peculiarly British way.

British workmen were dissatisfied with the Reform Bill of 1832, for it had left them still disenfranchised and disregarded. As early as May, 1838, a "People's Charter" had been drawn up with six demands for further Parliamentary reform: (1) universal manhood suffrage, (2) equal electoral districts, (3) vote by secret ballot, instead of a show of hands, (4) annually elected Parliaments, (5) payment of Parliamentary members, and (6) removal of property qualifications for Parliamentary members.

In short, workmen wanted democracy. They wanted the vote—one that counted, one they wouldn't be terrorized out of making, one they could use frequently. They wanted to qualify as possible members of Parliament even if they had no money and had to be paid.

(These things were all considered at the time by respectable members of society as revolutionary ruin; however, except for the annual election of Parliaments, they have all long since been accepted in Great Britain, without the sky having fallen.)

Those who supported the Charter, the "Chartists," began to petition Parliament with greater and greater vehemence. The government answered with arrests, with imprisonment, and with transportation to Australia. The movement reached its peak in 1848, with the news of revolution on the Continent. The British government, agitated by what was happening in Europe, chose to regard Chartism as revolution, which it was not. It was a peaceful appeal, except for occasional rather minor disorders. Nevertheless, the government refused to budge, and merely strengthened repression and, because it was *not* a revolution, Chartism was defeated.

(About this time, incidentally, the British were fighting "The First Opium War" in China. This set the pattern for the kind of imperialist wars that the British (and, to a lesser extent, other European countries) were to fight in Africa and Asia for many years. Such wars were fought far away, by professionals, and scarcely affected the home country. Casualties were relatively few and the end was usually victory over poorly equipped and poorly organized enemies so that the British Empire kept expanding and expanding.

Chartism, by increasing the self-consciousness of labor, led to another surge of trade-unionism, and to increasing agitation against the Corn Laws that kept landowners rich and laborers starving.

The workmen themselves could not have put on sufficient pressure but there were prosperous manufacturers who actually had compassion and could empathize with poverty, who took up the cause, and who actually believed that the Corn Laws were not only morally wrong, but were harmful to the national economy. Leaders of these were Richard Cobden (1804–1865), who had been born poor and remembered, and John Bright (1811–1889). Both were also against Great Britain's imperialist foreign policy.

Further pressure against the Corn Laws came with a disaster in Ireland. There, the callous British disregard for the Irish had forced the peasantry into increasing poverty, all the more so because their numbers were increasing. They had come to subsist almost entirely on potatoes, and if anything happened to the potato crop, there was bound to be starvation.

In 1845, a blight (a fungus disease) struck the Irish potato crop and the food supply dwindled drastically. In the years that immediately followed, one third of the Irish population either starved to death, died of disease that their famished bodies could not fight off, or escaped by emigration to the United States.

The British allowed this to happen. Partly, it was the callousness of the times that ascribed such calamities to the will of God, and allowed pious men to shrug their shoulders and go their way. Partly, it was because there was no television to bring the sights of misery to the living rooms of the comfortable.

Even so, there were some British who were uneasily conscious that Corn Laws that kept food artificially high in price were outrageous in a time of famine. On June 6, 1846, the Corn Laws were repealed and Great Britain entered a period of increasing free trade—to the general enrichment of the nation.

Nor did the Irish submit to starvation with nothing but despair. There was wild resentment, and attempts at angry action against the British, which were put down, of course, but it was clear that the Irish would never be pacified.

In 1850, British self-confidence and British assurance of being something special in the world made itself felt in surprising fashion. It involved David (Don) Pacifico, who was Jewish and who had been born in North Africa. He was, however, a British subject.

He had done business in Greece and he was owed money by the Greek government. When he pressed his claims, his house was burned by an anti-Semitic mob in Athens in December 1849. He appealed to the British government and the

foreign secretary, Henry John Temple, Lord Palmerston (1784–1865), a strong liberal at home, though an imperialist abroad, reacted with totally British pride. He sent a squadron of ships to Greece, blockaded Athen's port city of Piraeus, and seized Greek ships until Greece was forced to give in.

Both France and Russia protested this British behavior, and so did British conservatives in the House of Lords (who didn't consider a North African Jew to be "British").

Palmerston, however, rose in the House of Commons and made an all-night speech on July 8, 1850, in which the burden was that in ancient times a Roman citizen could be inviolate anywhere in the known world merely by proclaiming himself to be a Roman citizen ("civis Romanus sum"). Similarly, in the much wider modern world, a British subject must be inviolate simply by proclaiming himself a British subject. Great Britain would protect its subjects, however unlikely they might be, and wherever they might be.

This was met with thunderous approval and Palmerston remained foreign minister, though it had seemed certain he would have to be removed. The government, however, which disapproved of the high-handed way in which Palmerston conducted foreign affairs, simply waited for the next opportunity. At the end of 1852, they fired him when he incautiously approved Bonaparte's making himself Napoleon III without consulting the rest of the government (or the Queen).

The 1850s were a turbulent decade, with a war with Russia, another with China, and a dangerous mutiny in India, all of which will be described in appropriate places.

Great Britain continued to advance in democracy. In June, 1858, property qualifications for members of Parliament were removed (something that had been one of the demands of the Chartists).

There was also the case of Lionel Nathan Rothschild (1808–1879). He had been elected four times (in 1847, 1848, 1852, and 1857), and four times he had been denied his seat because he would not take his oath "as a Christian" for the simple reason that he was not a Christian, but a Jew. In 1858, when he was elected a fifth time, the disabilities that prevented Jews from participating in political life were removed. He took his seat.

Great Britain competed with Germany in this period for world leadership in science.

Charles Darwin and Alfred Russel Wallace (1823–1913) independently worked out a scheme of biological evolution through natural selection. This postulated small random variations in every generation of a species, some of these variations better fitting the species' way of life than others did. The variation for the better would survive in the long run, while others would not. Darwin's book, *The Origin of Species*, published in 1859, and detailing his views, revolutionized biology and joined the books by Copernicus, Vesalius, and Newton among the truly seminal scientific works. Evolution is now the central fact in biology. The science would simply not make sense without it.

James Prescott Joule (1818–1889) worked out the equivalence of work and heat in 1847, sharing with Mayer and Helmholtz of Germany the honor of establishing the law of conservation of energy. William Thomson (1824–1907), who became Lord Kelvin in later life, worked out the concept of absolute zero and the absolute scale of temperature in 1851. In 1852, he and Joule worked out the "Joule–Thomson effect," which proved of key importance in the liquefaction of gases.

In 1856, William Henry Perkin (1838–1907), while still a schoolboy, isolated, by accident, the first synthetic dye. Having done so, he left school and proceeded, with rare initiative and business acumen, to establish the synthetic dye industry.

George Boole (1815–1869) published *An Investigation of the Laws of Thought* in 1854. In this book, he applied symbols of logic, working out its laws in mathematical fashion. This came to be called "Boolean algebra."

On the technological side, Henry Bessemer (1813–1898) devised the "blast furnace" in 1856. In this, carbon was burned out of cast-iron by a blast of air, and the process was stopped at the stage when the product was steel. Once the bugs were worked out, the Bessemer process inaugurated the age of cheap steel and of all the constructions that made possible.

George Cayley (1773–1857) was the first to work out modern aerodynamics and to visualize airplanes as they would truly look once an engine could be devised that was sufficiently powerful and light. In 1853, he constructed the first unpowered plane, or "glider," that was capable of carrying a man. He forced his coachdriver to test it. The test was successful, and the coachdriver survived.

George Whitworth (1803–1887) learned to produce accurate devices for manufacturing standardized machine parts. He introduced the standardized screw thread in 1841. He took up where Eli Whitney had left off and greatly advanced the day of mass production.

The explorer, James C. Ross, who had earlier discovered the North Magnetic Pole, went on to the Antarctic region. In 1841, he sailed into what is now known as Ross Sea and discovered the Ross Ice Shelf, a vast ice-overhang extending far out into the Antarctic Ocean.

Exploration of another kind was carried out by Henry Creswicke Rawlinson (1810–1895). In 1846, he scaled the heights of a cliffside at Bisitun in Persia. Suspended from a rope, he carefully copied an inscription placed there at the order of Darius I, who had reigned 23 centuries earlier. It was in Old Persian, Assyrian, and Elamitic. Using modern Persian as a guide, Rawlinson deciphered the languages, and provided the key which opened Babylonian history to the world.

In 1843, the *Great Britain*, the first ship that could be considered a modern ocean liner, was launched. It was 322 feet long.

A British artist of the period was Edwin Henry Landseer (1802–1873), well-known for his animal painting. His *Stag at Bay* was painted in 1846. Both he and John Everett Millais were successful portraitists.

Charles Dickens continued to be the most successful British writer of the period. He published the infinitely popular *A Christmas Carol* in 1843; his masterpiece *David Copperfield* in 1849; and *A Tale of Two Cities* in 1859. William Makepeace Thackeray (1811–1863) was a distant second with

Vanity Fair, published in 1848 as his best-known work. A prolific writer was Anthony Trollope (1815–1882), whose 50 novels include *Barchester Towers*, published in 1857.

Benjamin Disraeli (1804–1881), who was later to achieve fame as a statesman, wrote novels in his younger days, the best-known being *Sibyl*, published in 1845. George Meredith (1828–1909) published *The Ordeal of Richard Feverel* in 1859.

Peter Mark Roget (1779–1869) prepared the first edition of his *Thesaurus of English Words and Phrases* in 1852. It has been a valued reference work ever since.

Several women novelists made their mark. Charlotte Brontë (1816–1855) published *Jane Eyre* in 1847. It was the first and best of the modern "Gothic romances." In the same year, her sister, Emily Brontë (1818–1848) wrote the less successful, but more highly regarded *Wuthering Heights*.

Thomas Carlyle was still writing, publishing a biography of Oliver Cromwell in 1845. Another historical writer of the period was Thomas Babington Macaulay (1800–1859) who, in the 1850s, wrote five volumes on the reigns of James II and William III.

Among the British poets, Tennyson was writing steadily, publishing *The Princess* in 1847, and succeeding Wordsworth as Poet Laureate on the latter's death in 1850. Tennyson wrote *Maud* in 1855, and turned out many short pieces that have retained their popularity ever since, "The Splendor Falls," "Break, Break, Break," "The Brook," "The Ballad of the Revenge," and so on.

Robert Browning (1812–1889) was also turning out popular poems such as "My Last Duchess," "Home Thoughts from Abroad," and, most of all perhaps, the light-hearted "The Pied Piper of Hamelin." His wife, Elizabeth Barrett Browning (1806–1861) wrote *Sonnets from the Portuguese* in 1850 and "Aurora Leigh" in 1856. Edward FitzGerald (1809–1883) translated the *Rubaiyat of Omar Khayyam*, the Persian poet-mathematician who had lived over seven centuries earlier. It was a free translation and was great poetry in its own right.

Thomas Hood (1799–1845) wrote some strong poems dealing with poor unfortunate women of those unfeeling times, such as his "Song of the Shirt" in 1843 and "The Bridge of Sighs" in 1844. Matthew Arnold (1822–1888) wrote his "Soharab and Rustum" from an old Persian epic in 1853. Dante Gabriel Rosetti (1828–1882) wrote "The Blessed Damozel" in 1850.

NETHERLANDS

William I, whose inflexible conservatism had lost him Belgium, now lost his popularity. He abdicated on October 7, 1840, and went into exile, spending his last years in Berlin, where he found life more congenial. He was succeeded by his son, who had fought in Spain under Wellington, and who reigned as William II (1792–1849).

William II was more liberal than his father. He was tolerant in religion and spent the profits earned from the Indonesian colonies wisely. The liberals wanted a more representative government, however, and, in the wake of the 1848 revolution in France, William II felt it expedient to grant a constitution insuring that.

He died on March 17, 1849, and was succeeded by his son, who reigned as William III (1817–1890). William III opposed the new constitution, but ruled under it with a parliamentary form of government.

BELGIUM

This was a quiet period for Belgium. It weathered the storm of 1848 with scarcely a tremor, for its government was liberal enough to expand the franchise and double the number of eligible voters.

SPAIN

Isabella II was Queen of Spain during this period, and the nation was troubled by insurrections and by military rule. The Queen was not popular, both because of her conservatism and because of her scandalous private life. (She was a liberal where sex was concerned.)

A rather farcical incident came on October 10, 1846, when the Queen's younger sister married the youngest son of Louis Philippe of France. The Queen had no children at the time (she was getting married on the same day), and Great Britain had a vision of a son being born to Isabella's sister, one who would inherit the crown of both France and Spain.

The War of the Spanish Succession had been fought to prevent such an eventuality a century and a half earlier, but France was relatively weaker now than it was then, and Spain was much weaker, so the situation was by no means as crucial. The matter poisoned the atmosphere between Great Britain and France, but it all came to nothing when, a little over a year afterward, Louis Philippe was kicked off his throne anyway.

PORTUGAL

Maria II died on November 15, 1853, and was succeeded by her son who reigned as Peter V (1837–1861). During his reign, Portugal took steps toward industrialization. In 1856, it had its first railroad and its first telegraph line.

SWITZERLAND

During this period, Switzerland went through a civil war in 1847, one between the Catholic and the Protestant cantons. The Protestant cantons were the winners almost at once, and, on September 12, 1848, a new constitution went into effect, establishing a federal union that was modeled on that of the United States.

DENMARK

Christian VIII died on January 20, 1848, just before the storm of revolution broke over the continent. His son succeeded him as Frederick VII (1808–1863), and defused any serious trouble by granting a constitution that set up a representative government.

The problem of Schleswig and Holstein threatened, however. The German revolutionaries wanted to incorporate these provinces into a united Germany, and Prussia was to do the job. Prussia was reluctant to do so, however, feeling that Austria should take the lead in such things. The provinces, therefore, remained Danish for a time.

The religious philosopher, Søren Aabye Kierkegaard (1813–1855) published *Either/Or* in 1843, under a pseudonym and went on to write other books, in addition. He founded Existentialist philosophy in which the individual was viewed as having to make conscious choices between existing alternatives. He favored a stricter Christian way of life.

SWEDEN

Charles XIV, who had once been General Bernadotte, died on March 8, 1844, and was succeeded by his son who reigned as Oscar I (1799–1859). He introduced mild reforms, liberating trade from medieval restrictions, allowing more rights to women, and so on. He grew more conservative after the revolutionary year of 1848, however.

A leading Swedish chemist of the period was Carl Gustav Mosander (1797–1858), who puzzled out the chemical nature of some of the rare earth minerals, discovering five new elements in the early 1840s. The most famous Swede of the period, however, was the coloratura soprano, Johanna Maria ("Jenny") Lind (1820–1887), the "Swedish nightingale." During the 1840s and 1850s, she was the darling of the stage in Great Britain and the United States.

RUSSIA

Russia was untouched by the revolutions of 1848, but Nicholas I intervened in Austria and helped crush the Hungarian revolutionaries there. Russia also expanded steadily in central Asia, advancing into what was once called Turkestan and approaching India more and more closely, to the consternation of the British.

Russia retained its ambition to sweep up all it could of the Ottoman Empire. In 1853, the question arose as to who was to protect the Christian Holy Places. Russia was the protector of the Orthodox clergy in Palestine; France was the protector of the Catholics. The two nations squabbled over the matter, with the Ottoman Empire squeezed between them.

Russia was the nearer of the two and, in July

1853, Russian forces began to strengthen their influence over the Romanian provinces, sending in actual troops. France objected to this, and sent ships to encourage the Turks. The British, concerned about India, also much preferred a weak Ottoman Empire at Constantinople to a strong Russia, and they sent ships as well.

Attempts at settling the matter by compromise and mediation failed, and, on October 4, 1853, the Ottoman Empire, secure in the obvious support it was getting from the two western powers, declared war on Russia. The Russians, however, destroyed the Turkish fleet in the Black Sea on November 30.

To make up for this, the British and French moved their ships into the Black Sea on January 3, 1854. The Russians thereupon broke off diplomatic relations with Great Britain and France on February 6. Great Britain and France demanded that Russia evacuate the Romanian provinces. Russia did not answer directly, but, instead, defiantly crossed the Danube and invaded Bulgaria on March 20, 1854. Upon this, the British and French concluded an alliance with the Ottoman Empire on March 28 and declared war on Russia. (This was the first time Great Britain or, as it once was, England, had fought on the same side as France since the Third Crusade, six and a half centuries earlier.)

Austria, unwilling to see the Russians becoming dominant in the Balkans (and ignoring the help Russia had given her a few years earlier in connection with the Hungarian revolt) threatened to join the anti-Russian front, if Russia didn't evacuate the Balkans.

At this, the Russians got out of Romania and the Austrians sent in troops instead. This was not something the Russians forgot, and it created an antagonism that had important consequences.

In a way, that ended matters. Russia had retreated and the Ottoman Empire was safe for the moment. The British and French could go home with their mission accomplished, especially since their troops in the Balkans were suffering from cholera. The British and French governments felt, however, that it was necessary to keep the Ottoman Empire safe by destroying the great Russian naval base at Sebastopol at the southern

tip of the Crimean peninsula, where it jutted out into the Black Sea.

On September 14, 1854, a British–French force landed on the Crimean shore—and since all the fighting was confined to that peninsula, the conflict is known as "the Crimean War." In October, the allies began the siege of Sebastopol.

The generalship on the British side seemed to have been particularly incompetent, as is evidenced by the most famous incident of the war. On October 25, 1854, in the course of a battle at Balaklava, a suburb of Sebastopol, a confusion of orders sent a squadron of 673 light cavalry charging into the teeth of a firing Russian artillery to no purpose whatever. Over a third of the men were lost in half an hour.

The incident was immortalized in Tennyson's poem, "The Charge of the Light Brigade," and it was hailed as heroism. The point, however, was not that the soldiers were heroic but that the generals were stupid. (If more generals were executed for stupidity, wars would be shorter and less bloody, and might stop altogether.)

All through the winter of 1854–1855, the siege continued and the Allied armies continued to wither under the onslaughts of cholera.

The Crimean war was the first in which regular newspaper correspondents reported on events, and the British public was outraged at the lack of medical treatment and at the general misery that the common soldiers had to suffer because of the incompetence and indifference of the military leaders. This had always been true but now, for the first time, it was being publicized.

Florence Nightingale (1820–1910), a nurse, arrived in the Crimea on November 5, 1854. More heroic than any soldier, and more intelligent than any officer, she fought for the decent treatment of the sick and wounded and became a hero to the British public. She founded the profession of nursing, and her reports after the war initiated the process whereby armies, for the first time, were made to feel responsible for the health and welfare of their soldiers.

On January 26, 1855, some 10,000 Sardinian troops arrived. They had no interest in the war as such, but the Sardinian Prime Minister Cavour felt it was the proper move to gain French and British backing for his plans to unify Italy.

On March 2, 1855, Nicholas I died and was succeeded by his son, who reigned as Alexander II (1818–1881). The siege of Sebastopol went on for another half-year, as the Allies pressed on despite the desperate resistance that Russian soldiers have always specialized in. The port was finally taken, at great cost, on September 11, 1855. The siege had lasted nearly a year.

Austria now again threatened war if Russia didn't make peace, and Russia had to give up. The Treaty of Paris, ending the conflict, was signed on March 30, 1856. Great Britain got what it wanted. Russia agreed to keep its warships out of the Black Sea so that the Ottoman Empire seemed safe.

Russia, however, was huge. If it didn't gain at one end, it gained at the other. In 1858, Russia signed a treaty with China that gave it the eastern bank of the Amur River, an area where it had been forced to give up to China nearly two centuries before. China, however, had weakened since then, and Russia's far Eastern presence had strengthened.

In 1860, Russia founded Vladivostok, which became and remained Russia's largest seaport on the Pacific Ocean.

At this time, Glinka was still composing and the opera, *Ruslan and Lyudmilla* (based on a poem by Pushkin), was staged in 1842. A Russian of the period who was a leading anarchist and who managed to escape from exile in Siberia, was Mikhail Alexandrovich Bakunin (1814–1876).

GREECE

The reign of Otto I (1815–1867), a Roman Catholic monarch in a Greek Orthodox country, was not a success. He tried to be an autocratic king, but an uprising in 1843 forced him to grant a constitution. The parliamentary system that resulted wasn't any more successful.

Greece got into trouble with Great Britain over the Don Pacifico affair in 1850, and then, again, in 1854, when Greece tried to take advantage of the forthcoming Crimean war by attacking the Ottoman Empire.

SERBIA

Serbia was torn by an irreconcilable feud between two families, the Karageorgevich and the Obrenovich. They took turns supplying the nation with a ruler, and each made it impossible for the ruler of the other family to govern.

Alexander Karageorgevich (1806–1885) reigned from 1842 to 1858 and was then deposed and replaced by Milosh Obrenovich (1780–1860). Serbia remained neutral in the Crimean war.

MONTENEGRO

Montenegro was ruled by Peter II (1812–1851) in the 1840s, and by Danilo I (1826–1860) in the 1850s. It was strongly pro-Russian and received an annual subsidy from Nicholas I of Russia. In 1852, the Turks invaded, and then left only as a result of the threat of Austrian reprisals.

BULGARIA

Bulgaria, which eight and a half centuries earlier had challenged the Byzantine Empire at its height, was still prostrate under the Ottoman Empire, but nationalist feeling was swelling in the 1850s.

OTTOMAN EMPIRE

In 1840, the Ottoman Empire was still at war with its erstwhile subject, Muhammad Ali of Egypt. France was on the side of Muhammad Ali and Great Britain, as usual in this period, was on the side of the Ottoman Empire.

Great Britain managed to persuade Austria, Prussia, and Russia to join it in an ultimatum to Muhammad Ali, on July 15, 1840, to accept rule over Egypt and southern Syria and nothing more. Muhammad, relying on France, rejected the ultimatum. Great Britain then bombarded Beirut, landed troops in Syria, and drove Muhammad Ali out. France, under Louis Philippe, chose not to fight, and Muhammad Ali had to settle for Egypt only.

It was clear, however, that the Ottoman Empire had weakened to the point where it was simply a pawn thrust this way and that by the competing ambitions of the European powers. Nicholas I of Russia did his best to convince Great Britain that the Ottoman Empire ought to be partitioned among the powers as once Poland had been, over half a century before. Nicholas referred to the Ottoman Empire as "the sick man of Europe" and, presumably, considered that it ought to be put out of its misery.

Great Britain would not agree, however, and fought the Crimean War (in alliance with France and Sardinia) to make sure the Ottoman Empire remained intact.

UNITED STATES

In the early 1840s, the United States was in the mood for expansion. There were two areas where this was possible. In the northwest, between the Rocky Mountains and the Pacific Ocean, was the Oregon Territory. It extended from the 42° parallel, south of which was Mexico, to the 54° 40' parallel, north of which was Russian Alaska.

The United States wanted it all. In fact, the 1844 election campaign that was run by James Knox Polk (1794–1849) included the slogan "54-40 or fight." The fighting was to be with Great Britain, which also claimed the territory. Since 1818, there had been an uneasy joint occupation by the two powers.

Then, too, in the southwest, Texas was still anxious to join the Union. The outgoing 10th President of the United States, John Tyler (1790–1862), who had succeeded on the death of William Henry Harrison (the first Vice-President to succeed in this manner), had no party and was execrated by both Democrats and Whigs. He had nothing to lose and he brought about the annexation of Texas on March 1, 1844, three days before he left office.

Polk succeeded as 11th President, but, despite his campaign slogan, he was careful not to fight with powerful Great Britain, especially for territory that would undoubtedly be carved into free states. (Polk was from Tennessee, a slave state.) On June 15, 1846, then, the Oregon territory was cut roughly in half. The boundary between the

United States and Canada east of the Rocky Mountains was at the 49° parallel. This was extended to the Pacific Ocean, giving Great Britain the northern half of the territory and the United States the southern half.

Texas was another matter. There the United States faced a weaker nation, and the territory at stake might well be divided into slave states. Therefore, Polk struck out ruthlessly.

Mexico had never recognized the independence of Texas and resented the union with the United States. In addition, the question of the boundary between Texas and Mexico was in dispute. As a Mexican province, Texas extended southward only to the Nueces River. The United States, however, extended its claim to the Rio Grande, which doubled the size of the Mexican province.

On March 24, 1846, an American force under Zachary Taylor (1784–1850) crossed the Nueces River and advanced into the disputed territory. When the Mexicans resisted (and were defeated), Polk promptly announced that Americans had been killed on American territory and Congress declared war on Mexico on May 13, 1846. Thus began the "Mexican War," which many in the free states hotly denounced as unprovoked aggression brought about by the lust for slave-state territory.

Zachary Taylor advanced 150 miles west of the Rio Grande and finally beat the Mexicans at the battle of Buena Vista on February 23, 1847. He was then held up because President Polk did not wish Taylor to become too popular, and hampered him constantly. The task of finishing the war was given to Winfield Scott, a veteran of the War of 1812.

On March 27, 1847, a month after Buena Vista, Scott landed at Verz Cruz on the Mexican Gulf Coast and took the city. That placed him a little over 200 miles from the Mexican capital at Mexico City.

Scott then managed the very difficult progress over mountainous territory to that capital. He won every battle, although usually outnumbered and the Mexicans had the advantage of the terrain. On September 14, 1847, Scott took Mexico City.

Meanwhile, American forces had pushed their way westward and, by the beginning of 1847, had taken Santa Fe and seized control of California.

The Treaty of Guadelupe Hidalgo (a northern suburb of Mexico City) was signed on February 2, 1848. By its terms, the United States obtained Texas to the Rio Grande, and the western territory, too, including California.

Later on, in 1853, the United States purchased a strip of territory to the south of what it had gained in the treaty, in order that a railroad could be built through it. This was negotiated by the American minister to Mexico, James Gadsden (1788–1858), and is called the "Gadsden Purchase." With that, the United States gained its final boundaries with both Canada on the north and Mexico on the south. They have not been changed since.

Taylor's victories in the Mexican War led (as Polk had feared) to his election in 1848 as the 12th President. However, Taylor died in office on July 9, 1850, and was succeeded by his undistinguished Vice-President, Millard Fillmore (1800–1874), as 13th President.

The acquisition of California couldn't have come at a better time for the United States. On January 24, 1848, when California was already under the firm control of the United States, but a week before Mexico signed the treaty that transferred control legally, gold was discovered there. There was a "gold rush" that had thousands of Americans swarming across the continent in 1849 ("The Forty-Niners") in an effort to strike it rich.

Of course, the new territories promptly exacerbated the slavery question. Should slavery be permitted in the new territories or not? The argument reached a feverish height when California, with its sudden access of population, thanks to the gold rush, wanted to join the Union as a state.

There were, at this time, 15 free states and 15 slave states. (Texas had entered as a slave state.) If California entered as a free state, as it wished to do, there was no obvious new slave-state candidate to balance it, and the slave states were furious at that. Again, there was talk of secession.

Henry Clay (1777–1852) was known as "The Great Compromiser." He had been instrumental in working out the Missouri Compromise in 1820, and the Tariff Compromise in 1832. Now, in his old age, he met his greatest challenge and hammered out the "Compromise of 1850," which he introduced in Congress on January 29, 1850, and which, by September 20, had become law. Clay hoped that this would end the threat of secession and civil war forever, and while it did not do that, it did buy the nation some time.

By the provisions of the compromise, California was allowed to enter the Union as a free state, but the possibility of the admission of further slave states was held open. The biggest advantage that the slave states received was a stronger "fugitive slave" law, and this angered the antislavery people.

The point was that slaves did try to escape from slavery and whites who were antislavery and abolitionist helped them. An "underground railway" was established that spirited slaves to freedom in Canada. To the slave-owners this was simply theft of valuable property and they demanded the right to send agents to the free states in order that they might seize blacks whom they could claim as escaped slaves. This was much like the practice of the British, 40 years earlier, of stopping American ships in search of deserted British sailors. That led to the War of 1812, and the activities of slave-owner agents roused the same fury in the hearts of the abolitionists.

Another polarizing influence was the novel *Uncle Tom's Cabin*, written by Harriet Beecher Stowe (1811–1896) and published in 1852. Its picture of virtuous slaves, brutally mistreated by sadistic masters (though treated well by kindly ones), infuriated many beyond description and converted people, earlier indifferent on the subject, into convinced antislavery enthusiasts.

Nor was it only the whites who worked for abolition. Harriet Tubman (1820–1913) was a black who helped over 300 slaves escape through the underground railway, putting her own freedom and life on the line over and over. Frederick Douglass (1817–1895), an escaped slave who eventually earned enough money to buy his freedom, was a powerful advocate of abolitionism, although he was not as extreme as some of the white doctrinaires, for he had a keen sense of the possible.

Through all this, the slave states felt ever more insecure and persecuted, and talk of breaking up the Union became louder.

In order to mollify the slave states, territories were organized with permission to establish or eliminate slavery by vote. This was the "Kansas–Nebraska Act," which became law on May 30, 1854. Its main architect was Stephen Arnold Douglas (1813–1861) of Illinois.

This seemed very democratic (if we can consider voting for slavery to be democratic), although it lent itself to horrible results. When it looked as though a territory might become a state, violent men from free states and from slave states would invade the territory in order to vote their side and to do their best to terrorize the opposition from voting.

Kansas, to the west of Missouri, was in such a case, and, from 1854 to 1858, there was a virtual civil war in the territory between slave-staters and free-staters.

A debate for the Illinois senatorial seat attracted national attention in August 1857. Stephen A. Douglas was running on the Democratic ticket. In the field was a new antislavery party, the Republicans, who had replaced the moribund Whigs. Running as a Republican was Abraham Lincoln (1809–1865), who was firmly against any extension of slavery beyond the states in which it already existed. Douglas won the Senatorial election (by vote of the state legislature, *not* the people), but Lincoln won the debate.

In that same year, however, the Supreme Court, under Roger Brooke Taney (1777–1864), in what was called the "Dred Scott decision," ruled that Congress could not keep slavery out of any territory. Only the territory itself could do that *after* it had become a state. The ruling further held that the descendants of slaves could not become citizens. Taney had a splendid record otherwise, but his name was forever stained by that one unfortunate decision.

Then, on October 19, 1859, a half-mad abolitionist named John Brown (1800–1859) seized Harper's Ferry on the Virginia side of the upper Potomac River, and tried to start a slave rebellion. It didn't work at all. He was caught at once and executed, but it convinced the people of the slave states that the abolitionists were in control in the free states and that it was their intention to slaughter all the white people in the slave states and set up rule by the blacks.

There seemed no room for further compromise. In 1860, the Democratic party nominated Stephen A. Douglas as its presidential candidate, but the slave states broke away and nominated John Cabell Breckenridge (1821–1875), while others nominated John Bell (1797–1869). With the Democrats split three ways, the Republican party nominated and elected Abraham Lincoln as the 16th President.

That was in November 1860. The next month, even before Lincoln could be inaugurated, South Carolina seceded from the Union, and the most tragic period in the history of the United States opened.

The United States, in this period, lagged in science but was flourishing in technology.

A dentist, William Thomas Green Morton (1819–1868), introduced the use of ether as an anesthetic in 1846. Others had used anesthetics before but it was Morton's demonstration that caught on and put an end to surgery as a form of exquisite torture.

Samuel Finley Breese Morse (1791–1870) promoted a telegraph, the scientific principles of which had been well worked out earlier by Joseph Henry and others. Morse obtained a patent in 1840 and persuaded Congress to grant him $30,000, which he used to build a telegraph line from Baltimore to Washington. In 1844, the first telegraph message in history was sent—"What hath God wrought?" The telegraph was quickly used to deliver the news of the 1844 election and it was an adjunct to military operations, for the first time, in the Mexican war.

In 1846, Elias Howe (1819–1862) devised the first practical sewing-machine. It was the first product of the Industrial Revolution specifically designed to lighten women's household tasks. Elisha Graves Otis (1811–1861) invented the first elevator with a safety guard designed to bring it safely down even if the cable suspending it broke. He demonstrated such an elevator in New York City in 1854, getting in himself, rising several stories up, and ordering the cable to be cut. It was the elevator, along with cheap steel, that made skyscrapers possible.

In 1859, Edwin Laurentine Drake (1819–1880), dissatisfied with the petroleum resources in surface deposits, decided to drill for oil. He sunk an oil well near Titusville, Pennsylvania, and (on August 29) struck oil. This was the beginning of a procedure that was to revolutionize the human use of energy. A liquid fuel like oil is easier to transport than coal, is easier to ignite and control, and is suitable for use in internal-combustion engines.

Literature continued to flourish in New England. Emerson's essays, published in 1841 and 1842, gave him an international reputation. Longfellow wrote "The Village Blacksmith" in 1841, *Evangeline* in 1847, *The Song of Hiawatha* in 1855, and *The Courtship of Miles Standish* in 1858. Among the poems of John Greenleaf Whittier (1807–1892) that are still popular today are "Maud Muller" and "The Barefoot Boy," both published in 1856. James Russell Lowell (1819–1891) wrote "The Vision of Sir Launfal" in 1848.

Among the prose writers of New England, Nathaniel Hawthorne (1804–1864) published *The Scarlet Letter* in 1850 and *The House of Seven Gables* in 1851. He also wrote a number of stories that would today be called science fiction. Henry David Thoreau (1817–1862), a close friend of Emerson, wrote *Walden* in 1854.

Outside New England, Herman Melville (1819–1891) wrote his great classic of whaling, *Moby Dick,* in 1851. Edgar Allan Poe wrote "The Gold Bug" in 1843, which was the first modern mystery story, and "The Raven," which must surely be in the running for the most popular American poem ever written.

Thomas Bulfinch (1796–1867) collected the ancient and medieval myths and legends into *The Age of Fable*, published in 1855. Usually known as *Bulfinch's Mythology*, it is still popular today. John Bartlett (1820–1905) published the first edition of his *Familiar Quotations* in 1855, and, through many editions, it has been an indispensable reference book ever since.

Stephen Collins Foster (1826–1864) was the most successful songwriter of his time, and perhaps of any time, for "Old Folks at Home" may well be the most popular American ballad ever written, while "Oh, Susanna," "Old Black Joe," "Jeannie with the Light-Brown Hair," "Camptown Races," and others do not fall far behind.

Lost in the struggle over slavery, the burgeoning fight for women's rights is often scanted. Elizabeth Cady Stanton (1815–1902) organized a convention to discuss the rights of women at Seneca Falls, New York in 1848. Lucy Stone (1818–1893) was not only an ardent abolitionist, but she was against the conventional enslavement of women as well. She kept her birth name through marriage as a protest against the submergence of feminine individuality, and a woman who does the same, even today, is still sometimes called a "Lucy Stoner." Amelia Bloomer (1818–1894), another strong advocate of women's rights, campaigned for sensible clothing for women, and devised the roomy trousers that came to be called "bloomers."

Indigenous American religious sects continued to develop. A religious leader, William Miller (1782–1849), managed to convince himself and a number of others that close reading of the Bible indicated that the Day of Judgment would come in 1843. Many sold their property and waited for the glorious moment of the Second Coming, only to be disappointed, of course. Out of his views, however, the "Seventh-Day Adventists" and "Jehovah's Witnesses" eventually developed.

Brigham Young (1801–1877), a convert to Mormonism in 1832, took over the leadership of the movement in 1844 after the murder of Joseph Smith in Illinois. To avoid further persecution, Young led his co-religionists across the Mississippi on February 4, 1846, and trekked westward. They reached the region of the Great Salt Lake in what is now Utah on July 24, 1847. It was then Mexican territory but became American the following year. The Mormons established a theocratic community in the region that for years was virtually independent of outside control. The Mormon way of life attracted the sometimes prurient attention of the rest of the Christian world through its practice of polygamy (for men only, of course.)

On a lighter note, Phineas Taylor Barnum (1810–1891) was the great showman of the age. He opened a show in New York City in 1841, in which he displayed all sorts of curiosities, some real, some faked. ("There's a sucker born every minute" is his famous conservative estimate of the situation.) He stage-managed Jenny Lind's wildly successful concert tour in the United States.

In 1843, Daniel Decatur Emmett (1815–1904) organized the first "negro minstrel" show, a very popular form of entertainment, in which white men in blackface presented unflattering stereotypes of black behavior. Emmett wrote a number of popular songs for these shows, including "Dixie," which became the virtual national anthem of the slave states.

Abner Doubleday (1819–1893), an army officer who served in the Mexican War, is often credited with originating, in 1840 or thereabouts, the rules of a game that eventually developed into baseball. This may be a myth.

CANADA

The two chief provinces of Canada, Upper Canada, (now Toronto) and Lower Canada (now Quebec), were united on July 23, 1840 by the "Union Act" passed by the British government. By 1846, all the boundary questions with the United States were settled and "British North America" took on the shape it has today, extending, like the United States, from the Atlantic to the Pacific. There was still no effective union between all parts of the nation, however, nor a definite form of representative government.

BRAZIL

Brazil was the only monarchy in the western hemisphere south of Canada in this period. Pedro II, a younger brother of Maria II of Portugal, reigned as Emperor of Brazil.

ARGENTINA

Argentina was, at this time, ruled dictatorially by Juan Manuel de Rosas (1793–1877). Under him, Argentina was unified. He attempted to take over control of Uruguay as well. He had to fight Brazil, which was supported by France, and Rosas was defeated and deposed in 1852. In his place rose Justo Jose de Urquiza (1801–1870), the first constitutional president of Argentina.

CHILE

Under Manuel Bulnes (1799–1866), who was president from 1841 to 1851, and his successor, Manuel Montt (1809–1880), who was president until 1861, Chile was peaceful and prosperous. Railways and telegraph lines were built and there were advances in education and cultural activities.

PARAGUAY

Paraguay was ruled by Carlos Antonio Lopez (1790–1862) in this period. Its isolation was ended and it retained its independence against the expansive tendencies of Argentina and Brazil.

PERU

Peru was under Ramon Castillo (1797–1867). He abolished slavery and respected the civil rights of the Native Americans.

COLOMBIA

Colombia was of interest to the rest of the world chiefly because its northwestern limits extended into Central America and included the region of Panama. What made Panama of interest, especially to Great Britain and the United States, was the fact that it was a narrow isthmus, separating the Atlantic and Pacific Ocean by as little as 40 miles of land. A canal across it would greatly lessen the time it took to sail or steam from Europe to the Far East, or from the Atlantic coast of the United States to the Pacific coast.

Naturally, it mattered who would control the canal, and on April 19, 1850, Great Britain and the United States came to an agreement on the matter. The agreement was negotiated by John Middleton Clayton (1796–1856), then the American Secretary of State, and Henry Lytton Bulwer (1801–1872), a British diplomat. By this "Clayton–Bulwer Treaty," both sides agreed not to build an exclusive canal, but to keep any that was built open to nationals of both countries. Neither was to fortify the canal or to seek control of neighboring regions.

The rulers of Colombia were amenable to this, perhaps because the treaty didn't mean much at the time. The state of technology in 1850 did not permit either nation to build a canal over the fever-ridden tropical territory of Panama and, in point of fact, none was built for well over half a century.

VENEZUELA

Venezuela was going through a turbulent period because of the rivalry of two leaders, Jose Antonio Paez (1790–1873) and Jose Tadeo Monagas (1784–1868).

CENTRAL AMERICA

At this time, Central America was the scene of the activities of an American soldier of fortune, William Walker (1824–1860). Born in Tennessee, he went to California in search of gold in 1850, then thought he might further dismember Mexico. In 1853, he invaded Lower California and declared it independent of Mexico. His effort to set up a second Texas failed, however, and he went on to Nicaragua in 1855. Joining a revolutionary group, he seized control, declared himself President of Nicaragua and, since he came from a slave state, he restored slavery to the land. Amazingly, he was recognized by the United States, under President Franklin Pierce (1804–1869).

The American railroad magnate, Cornelius Vanderbilt (1794–1877), opposed this development, not out of concern for the Nicaraguans, you may be sure, but because he wanted Nicaragua for himself as a possible place for a rail link between the Atlantic and Pacific Oceans. He organized opposition to Walker, who was forced out of Nicaragua. Walker later returned, and was finally shot by a firing squad in Honduras on September 12, 1860.

The whole Walker incident was a comic opera affair, but one that, following the Mexican War, went a long way toward creating a deep suspicion in Latin America concerning American motives and intentions toward them.

MEXICO

Santa Anna survived the disastrous war with the United States and even ruled Mexico again in 1853. In 1855, however, he was deposed once and for all. One of those deposing him was Benito Pablo Juarez (1806–1872), a liberal who wished to reorganize Mexico and weaken the power of the Church. He became President of Mexico in 1858.

ETHIOPIA

Ethiopia, which had retained a good deal of its Christian orientation through the centuries when the Muslims had dominated northern Africa, had its first modern ruler in Tewodros (Theodore) II (1818–1868). He came to the throne in 1855, unified the land, and did his best to introduce some modernization. He abolished the feudal system and tried to bring the Ethiopian church under royal control.

EGYPT

Muhammad Ali died in 1849, and his son Ibrahim, had died the year before. Egypt then moved away from attempts at conquest and began its first gropings toward becoming a member of the European community of nations. Like Panama, Africa offered a narrow isthmus between oceans. A canal across the Suez isthmus would link the Mediterranean and Red Seas, and, therefore, the Atlantic and Indian Oceans. The sea route from Great Britain to India would be cut in half.

A canal across the isthmus of Suez had been

attempted on several occasions in ancient and medieval times. At no time had such a venture proved a practical success; however, it was time to try again.

Mohammad Said (1822–1863) had become viceroy of Egypt ("Pasha" or "Khedive" are the Muslim titles) in 1854. He had been educated in Paris and tried, without much success, to introduce western ways into Egypt. In 1856, he granted a concession to a French company to build a Suez canal. This was opposed by the Ottoman Sultan who feared it would make Egypt too strong. It was also opposed by Great Britain who feared it would make France too strong.

Work began on April 19, 1859, however, under the guidance of a French diplomat, Ferdinand Marie, Vicomte de Lesseps.

LIBERIA

Liberia was established as an independent republic on July 26, 1847. It was recognized as such by Great Britain and then by other powers. Its independence was respected, partly because (since it was founded by American initiatives) the United States took an interest in it.

SOUTH AFRICA

South Africa, in this period, was involved in a three-way fight: British versus Boers, and both versus Bantus. Although a number of Boers had trekked northward, there remained others in the south, particularly in Natal, a coastal province to the northeast of Capetown. The British won and Natal was made a British colony on August 8, 1843, whereupon additional Boers trekked northward.

Both the British and the Boers drove back the Bantus, annexing their lands.

In 1852, the British recognized the Transvaal (lying north of Natal) as an independent Boer state. It became the "South African Republic" in 1856, with Marthinus Wessels Pretorius (1819–1901), the son of one of the leaders of the Great Trek, as its first president. The "Orange Free State," lying between Transvaal and the Cape Colony, was, in 1854, recognized as independent by Great Britain also.

PERSIA

In this period, Persia was buffeted from the north by Russia and from the south by Great Britain. Under Naser od-Din (1831–1896), who became the ruler of Persia in 1848, there began some attempts at modernization of the land.

In 1844, a young man, Ali Mohammed (1820–1850), who called himself "Bab" ("The Gate"), developed a variation of Shiism that came to be called "Babism." He was executed in 1850. However, another version was taken up by Mirza Hosayn Ali Nuri (1817–1892), who called himself Baha' Allah ("Glory of God"), and it was then called "Baha'ism". It has since become a world religion, albeit a small one.

AFGHANISTAN

In 1840, the British were in control of Afghanistan, and a puppet ruler, Shah Shoja, was on the throne. In 1841, however, the Afghanis rose in revolt and the British garrison in Kabul was surrounded. The British agreed to leave the country, but on the way out, they were trapped on January 13, 1842, and slaughtered almost to a man by the Afghani.

In April 1842, the British sent a punitive expedition into the land. It took Kabul on September 15, and destroyed portions of it. However, the British East India Company felt it would not be safe to attempt to maintain an occupation of the wild and mountainous country since it would be too far from British centers of power. Therefore, they withdrew and "the first Afghan War" was over.

That didn't mean the British wanted to see Afghanistan in anyone else's hands. In 1856, when Persia tried to invade Afghanistan, Great Britain forced an end to the invasion.

INDIA

Great Britain controlled virtually all of India at this time, but they did so only with the use of

Indian troops, who outnumbered the British troops by a ratio of 13 to 2. The officer corps, of course, was entirely British, and they treated the Indians, quite as a matter of course, as inferior beings. The Indian troops could not be expected to enjoy such treatment, and they didn't.

About 1857, a new type of cartridge was introduced, made of greased paper that had to be bitten before being loaded. The grease consisted of animal fat.

The Hindu soldiers believed the grease to contain beef fat, which their religion would not allow them to put into their mouths. The Muslim soldiers believed it to contain pork fat, which could not be put into their mouths. The British might have announced the use of sheep fat, but they believed that simple punishment would settle the matter.

On May 10, 1857, at a garrison near Delhi, 85 Indian soldiers (called "sepoys" from a Hindi word for "army") sat in prison for having refused to use the cartridges. It was Sunday and, while the British were at church, Indian soldiers released the prisoners and then began to kill all the British they could find. This began the "Great Sepoy Mutiny."

The sepoys marched to Delhi, put themselves under Bahadur II (1775–1862), who was then the figurehead Moghul Emperor, and proceeded, on May 11, to slaughter all the British they could find in the city.

The revolt spread, and at Cawnpore, about 250 miles southeast of Delhi, 211 British women and children were killed on June 27.

By now, the British were assembling punitive forces. They retook Cawnpore on July 16, discovered evidence of the massacre, and took full revenge. In mid-September, the British retook Delhi and battles in its streets raged for nearly a week. Lucknow, where the rebels were strongest, was about 50 miles east of Cawnpore, and it was not taken until March 16, 1858. By June 29, the revolt was entirely at an end.

It had taken the British a little over a year to quell the mutiny, and the reprisals were very harsh. Bahadur II was deposed, tried, convicted (although he was over 70 and could not have dared oppose the rebels), and sent into Burma

for what was left of his life. The Moghul Empire came to an end two and a third centuries after it had been founded, and a century and a half after the death of the last powerful Moghul.

The British East India Company had lost the confidence of the British government and lost its control over India. The country came under the direct rule of the British crown on August 2, 1858.

BURMA

The "Second Burmese War" in 1852–1853 saw another British victory. The British took Rangoon on April 12, 1852, and, by year's end, had annexed southern Burma. A new ruler, Mindon Min (1894–1878), carefully maintained peace with Great Britain during his reign and established Mandalay, in the northern part of the country, as his capital.

SIAM

Mongkut (1804–1868), known as Rama IV after his death, became king in 1851. He planned the westernization of Siam, made a treaty with Great Britain on April 18, 1855, and then made treaties with other nations, including one with the United States on May 18, 1856.

By carefully playing off Great Britain on his west in Burma and France on his east in Indo-China, he made each one reluctant to see the other gain control, and he preserved Siam as an independent nation. He is the king made famous by the book *Anna and the King of Siam*, and by the musical, *The King and I*, which was made from it.

INDOCHINA

France, which was building an empire in Africa, gained holdings in the Far East as well. In 1858, it obtained a strong foothold in Indochina by seizing control of Saigon.

CHINA

British insistence on gaining huge profits by selling opium to the Chinese led to resistance by the

Chinese government, which didn't want a drug culture fastened on its population. The British wanted the money and this led to "The First Opium War," one which is, in hindsight, a matter of staggering and callous drug-pushing immorality on the part of the British.

By May 24, 1841, the British took Canton, and, for the rest of the year, bombarded various Chinese seaports. On June 19, 1842, the British took Shanghai and worked their way up the Yangtze River. China was forced to make peace; on August 19, 1842, it ceded Hong Kong to Great Britain, agreed to trade with her on British terms, and to pay a $20 million indemnity.

This began a long period during which the vast land was continually encroached upon by European powers, and the decline of the Manchu Empire after this was rapid.

"Extraterritoriality" was established, whereby foreign people living in China could only be tried by their own foreign courts and be ruled by their own foreign laws. China was required to extend toleration to Christians.

A combination of Imperial humiliation and Imperial corruption led to a wild rebellion in China. It was called the "T'ai P'ing Rebellion," and was the bloodiest and most devastating civil war in history. It produced a great loss of life, perhaps 20 million altogether, and it further weakened the Chinese Empire to the point, indeed, where it could scarcely defend itself against any foreign enemy. Only the fact that it was too large a meal for digestion by even the omnivorous Great Britain allowed it to keep its independence.

JAPAN

Japan's two and a half centuries of isolation came to a sudden end in the 1850s.

The United States, which wanted trade, and which wanted its shipwrecked sailors treated decently when they washed up on Japanese shores, decided to take strong measures. In March 1852, President Fillmore authorized a naval expedition to Japan. It was commanded by Matthew Calbraith Perry (1794–1858), a younger brother of

the Perry who had won the Battle of Lake Erie, 40 years earlier.

Perry sailed into Tokyo harbor with four ships on July 8, 1853. He insisted on seeing some important official, threatening to land otherwise and deliver his messages at cannon-point. The official came, and Perry delivered his message, then withdrew to give the Japanese time for consideration.

In February 1854, he returned to Tokyo with seven ships, with samples of western products and, of course, with the ships' cannons.

The Japanese were intelligent enough to bend with the wind. On March 31, 1854, they signed a treaty with the United States, regularizing trade and promising better treatment of shipwrecked sailors.

After that, Japan passed through some years of uncertainty, with some government leaders strongly antiforeign and wishing to regain and maintain isolation, while others favored learning from the foreigners and developing Japan on western lines.

PACIFIC ISLANDS

The French were actively exploring the Pacific Ocean in this period and annexing territory. Their major annexation was that of New Caledonia in 1853.

AUSTRALIA

The interior of Australia was being explored ever since the southeastern coast had been settled. Edward John Eyre (1815–1901) explored the desert areas of southern Australia in the early 1840s, but was unable to reach the central regions of the continent. John McDouall Stuart (1818–1866), after six attempts to reach the central region, succeeded in 1860. In his sixth and final journey, he crossed the continent from south to north.

In August 1850, the British government gave the Australians considerable self-rule, including elected legislatures for the various provinces. By then, the number of nonconvicts in the Australian population far outnumbered the number of convicts and in 1851, the legislature of New South Wales forbade the arrival of any further convicts from Great Britain. Other provinces followed, and the British acceded to this.

On August 9, 1851, gold was discovered in Australia and there was an influx of people from all over the world. Population grew rapidly, and the continent entered the world community. The first steamship arrived in 1852, railroads were built, and the isolation of the land was much lessened.

Not all was rosy, of course. The native Aborigines were treated as miserably as the natives of Africa and the Americas when those regions came under European sway.

NEW ZEALAND

On January 22, 1840, the first British colonists arrived in New Zealand, which was almost exactly on the opposite side of the globe from Great Britain.

The growth of this new British colony did not proceed entirely peacefully. New Zealand was already occupied by the Maoris, a Polynesian people, and the "First Maori War" continued from 1843 to 1848. It was not an intense war and the Maoris were finally defeated.

In the 1840s and 1850s, Great Britain granted considerable self-government to the New Zealanders. They (and the Australians) were so far from Great Britain that it really made no sense for the British to try to govern them with a tight reign. The lesson of the value of loose control learned from the misadventures of George III almost a century earlier also played its part. As a result, both Australia and New Zealand remained loyal to the Crown.

HAWAII

In the 1840s and 1850s, Great Britain, France, and the United States all agreed that Hawaii was not to be annexed by any of them. It remained independent, therefore. American missionaries, however, remained active there, exerting their form of cultural imperialism.

1860 TO 1880

PRUSSIA/GERMANY

The "humiliation of Olmutz" had come and gone, Frederick William IV had gone mad and died, and now William I ruled Prussia. Under him were three remarkable men.

One was Albrecht Theodor Emil von Roon (1803–1879), who became Minister of War in 1859. He undertook to reorganize the Prussian army. There was to be a universal three-year service for young Prussian men and a permanent reserve to defend the country. Von Roon made the state the servant of the army as Frederick William I had done a century and a quarter earlier.

Working with him was Helmuth Karl Bern-hard von Moltke (1800–1891), a military theorist, who was the first to realize the importance of railroads in connection with troop movements. Until then, right through the Crimean war and various colonial wars, armies marched along roads that were sometimes close to impassable and where progress was always slow and tiring. In a country with a good rail network, however, soldiers could be moved in greater quantities and at greater speeds while they were sitting down.

As a result, Prussia began to build the kind of rail network that would be useful in war. This would make possible, Moltke foresaw, speedy mobilization, and speedy concentration. This would, in turn, lead to battle lines perhaps hundreds of miles long, with millions of soldiers.

Such masses could only be controlled by means of the telegraph, and telegraph lines were also developed with that in mind.

Moltke worked it all out while other nations remained stuck with the tactics of Napoleonic times.

The third and most remarkable of the three was Otto Eduard Leopold von Bismarck (1815–1898), who became Prime Minister (or "Chancellor") of Prussia on September 22, 1862, and who remained in that office for a quarter of a century thereafter. He was the real ruler of Prussia while he held that office.

Bismarck was a master of diplomacy. He knew exactly how to hoodwink other nations, when to take a chance and when to draw off, when to be a bully and when to smile. He orchestrated all that was to follow. William I was only the figurehead; Roon and Moltke were only the arms. It was Bismarck who was the brain.

Bismarck did not have an easy task in the goal he set himself of securing a united Germany under firm Prussian control. There were many inside Prussia who were against militarization and against the autocracy it implied. They wanted representative government, and they wanted the legislature to control the funds going to the army. Bismarck had to override them.

In addition, William I was a cautious monarch who was afraid that Bismarck would land Prussia in disaster, and Bismarck had to override him, too. He managed, however, for he did not become known as the "Iron Chancellor" for nothing.

His first move came in February 1863, when the Poles rebelled against Russia once again. Bismarck at once sent a representative to the Russian Tsar to assure him that Prussia would cooperate against the Poles. (After all, there were bothersome Poles in the eastern parts of Prussia, too.) Half the Prussian army was sent to the Polish frontier and that made it impossible for Great Britain and France to intervene usefully on behalf of the Poles. The Russians were grateful for this. (For some reason, the Russians often succumbed to feelings of gratitude, something the Prussians and Austrians were rarely troubled with.) Bis-

marck could now count on Russia to remain neutral in what he was planning for the future.

His next step was to see to it that Austria was excluded from any project for the unification of Germany. If Germany was to be unified, then it would have to be under Prussian leadership only. Therefore, when Austria called for a gathering of German rulers in August 1863, to reform the Germanic Confederation, Bismarck refused to allow William I to attend. Without Prussia, the Congress came to nothing.

It was next necessary to entangle Austria in some way that would force war between her and Prussia at a time and occasion of Prussia's choosing. Denmark handed him the chance for that.

In 1848, the German revolutionaries had tried to make Prussia seize Schleswig and Holstein from Denmark, but Prussia had funked the matter. Now things had changed.

On March 30, 1863, Denmark, counting on British support, foolishly reorganized Schleswig to make it a more integral part of the Danish kingdom. Denmark was now dealing, however, not with the timid Frederick William IV, but with Bismarck.

On January 16, 1864, Bismarck engineered an alliance with Austria, which wasn't very enthusiastic about it. An ultimatum was sent to the Danes which was designed to be very difficult for the Danes to agree to, and by February 1, the two German powers invaded Denmark. Actually, it was Prussia that did most of the work, for Bismarck wanted the Prussian army to get the exercise, and was perfectly content to let the Austrians more or less skulk in the rear.

The Prussian army did its work to perfection and Denmark never had a chance. The British tried to bring about peace, but Bismarck easily outmaneuvered them and on August 1, Denmark gave up. The Treaty of Vienna (Bismarck was willing to let the Austrians have the empty honor of hosting the treaty negotiations) was signed on October 20, 1864. By it, Schleswig and Holstein became the joint possession of Prussia and Austria.

This was precisely what Bismarck wanted. In the first place, it displayed to the world that Prussia was now, for the first time in history, an equal partner with Austria inside Germany. For another, it produced a situation in which Prussia would surely have an excuse to quarrel with Austria at whatever time was most convenient. Bismarck had no fear of the result. The joint operations in Denmark had made it quite obvious that the Prussian army was far superior to that of Austria.

In October, 1865, Bismarck met with Napoleon III and hinted that France would profit if Prussia beat Austria. Napoleon III was fool enough to believe Bismarck and thought, besides, that Austria would win, or that, at worst, the war would last a long time and weaken both to France's benefit.

Napoleon III, therefore, agreed to stay neutral. Alexander II of Russia, remembering Prussia's help against the Poles, also remained neutral. Then, on April 8, 1866, Bismarck entered into an alliance with the new nation of Italy, which hated Austria for past oppressions, and which still felt there was Italian territory under Austrian sway. (They called it "Italia irredenta," or "unredeemed Italy," and it consisted mainly of the cities of Trent and Trieste.)

Austria was thus effectively isolated and Bismarck was ready to find an excuse for war in anything Austria chose to do in Schleswig–Holstein.

By June 1866, Bismarck had produced sufficient irritations for the puzzled Austrians to find themselves facing war with no clear way of backing out. Most of the smaller German states, preferring a bumbling Austria to a superefficient Prussia, sided with Austria, but their help was ineffective. Prussia had no worries as long as the rest of Europe (meaning France, in particular) stayed out.

Moltke was ready. He had carefully watched what had gone on in the American Civil War, where the Americans on either side had, more or less awkwardly, developed all the modern adjuncts of war that Moltke had been working out. It had served as a test case for him and he improved his own plans in the light of what had gone on across the ocean.

On June 15, 1866, Moltke sent three armies southward on separate railroads and coordinated their activity by telegraph. The Austrians, on the other hand, never dreamed of using either railroads or telegraph wires, and were caught by surprise.

The armies met at Koniggratz in Eastern Bohemia on July 3, 1866. If Moltke's plans had worked perfectly, the Austrian army would have been destroyed. However, the trouble with new technology is that it sometimes doesn't work. There was a failure in the telegraph so that the Prussian armies did not move simultaneously as they should have, and a courier had to gallop 20 miles to deliver the necessary order. That saved the Austrians from utter destruction.

The Prussian confusion was made up for by the needle-gun, which gave the Prussians a much heavier and more rapid fire. The Austrians were not routed, but they were so decisively defeated that the war was over as far as they were concerned.

Napoleon III, who found that the Austrians were beaten, and beaten very quickly, too, so that Prussia now bestrode central Europe triumphantly, tried to make the best of it. He attempted to mediate a peace that was as favorable to Austria as possible, and Bismarck was willing to have him try, but the peace was to be the kind he himself would dictate. Napoleon III had to back down and, trying to save himself *something*, asked for the advantages Bismarck had promised him after defeating Austria. Bismarck gave him exactly nothing.

At the Treaty of Prague on August 23, 1866, Austria was excluded from German affairs. All the northern German states were herded into a "North German Federation," which was under strict Prussian domination. The southern German states of Bavaria, Wurttemburg, and Baden were allowed a confederation of their own, but there was little they could do by themselves, and Bismarck's shadow lay over them.

Bismarck's greatest gift, however, was in knowing when to stop. This was something Charles XII of Sweden and Napoleon I of France had not known. Having defeated Austria, Bismarck had his goal and he did not want to go beyond it and humiliate the defeated nation. Indeed, the telegraph accident that had kept the battle of Koniggratz from being a total cataclysm was to Bismarck's advantage. (Even accidents worked on his behalf.) Bismarck took no territory from Austria but instead cultivated friendship with it once it was clear that Prussia, not Austria, would dominate Germany. It was necessary, after all, to keep Austria from seeking revenge.

Bismarck grew more powerful within Prussia also. Nothing succeeds like success; and the quick, painless, and total victories over Denmark and Austria had made him popular. He now saw his way clear to achieve final union of all the German states (minus Austria), for, in his way, there stood only France.

Bismarck began to maneuver in masterly fashion against France. Napoleon III, in an attempt to strengthen France to match Prussia's rapidly growing might, had made unskillful attempts to absorb Belgium or Luxemburg, and Bismarck saw to it that this came to the attention of Great Britain, which had not yet forgotten the first Napoleon. Great Britain, therefore, moved into sympathy with Prussia, which already had the neutrality of Russia, the alliance of Italy, and the cowed subservience of Austria. If France fought, she would have to fight alone.

The trick was, then, to make sure that France would seem to be the aggressor. Bismarck began a campaign designed to irritate the French by deliberately making Prussia seem dangerous to her.

Beginning in 1868, he moved to make a Hohenzollern prince, a member of the Prussian royal family, become a king of Spain. It never came to pass and, if it had, it would scarcely have mattered, considering how unimportant Spain had become, but the French became bellicose indeed over it, as Bismarck intended. What's more, in the diplomatic exchanges that followed, William I rejected the demands of the French ambassador and Bismarck deliberately altered the wording of a telegram reporting the fact (the "Ems telegram") to make it all sound even more insulting to the French.

It was an old situation in reverse. In 1806, the Prussians had been confident they could face Na-

poleon with impunity because they thought they were still living in the time of Frederick the Great. Now it was France that thought it could face Bismarck with impunity because it thought it was still living in the time of Napoleon I.

Napoleon III did not want a war, probably, but he had grown more incapable than ever as age and illness were settling down upon him, and he could not withstand the general French pressure for a glorious war. After all, they were so used to winning battles.

On July 15, 1870, therefore, France declared war on Prussia, and that started the "Franco–Prussian War." At once, Prussia mobilized, making full use of its railroads, and concentrating its forces with amazing speed. The French made partial use of their rail network and had not yet fully mobilized when the Prussians were completely ready. What's more, Prussian intelligence knew exactly where all the French Armies were, and had a plan of campaign that had been organized by Moltke with complete efficiency. The French knew nothing of the Prussian plans, and had no plan of their own. The result was an utter and humiliating disaster for the French, with the Prussians winning every battle.

The climax came on September 1, 1870 at Sedan, near the Belgian border, only seven weeks after the war had begun. It was another in the monotonous series of Prussian victories. This time, the French army surrendered and Napoleon III, who was on the scene, surrendered as well and was taken prisoner.

By September 19, 1870, Paris was placed under siege, but the city resisted with a courage and tenacity that saved a good deal of French pride. It was not until January 28, 1871 that the city was taken. Another epic was the resistance of the French fortress at Belfort in Alsace, which held out against a superior German force for 105 days. The French finally marched out with their weapons on their shoulders and their flags flying, the only French force that had held its own.

Just the same, despite Paris and Belfort, France had lost the war in a defeat more disgraceful than any since it had faced Henry V of England four and a half centuries before. They were forced to sign the Treaty of Frankfurt on May 10, 1871, by which they had to cede Alsace and half of Lorraine (which, together, became famous as "Alsace-Lorraine") to the Prussians. They also had to pay an indemnity of 5 billion francs and to endure a Prussian army of occupation until the indemnity was paid.

It was a mistake for Bismarck to take Alsace-Lorraine, perhaps his only mistake. He did his best to pacify France thereafter, as he had pacified Austria. He even encouraged it to find colonies for itself in Africa and Asia. Nothing was of any use. The loss of Alsace-Lorraine (which Bismarck didn't really need) was not forgotten and it made of France an intransigent and unforgiving enemy.

Bismarck had now attained his great end. By January 18, 1871, Bismarck the Conqueror had persuaded all the awed and grateful German states to agree to the establishment of a "German Empire" to include all of Germany outside Austria, with King William I of Prussia becoming Emperor William I of Germany as well.

As an added humiliation to France, the new German Empire was proclaimed in the Hall of Mirrors at Versailles, the very center from which Louis XIV had dominated Europe nearly two centuries earlier.

The German Empire was not a completely unitary state. While it was unified by the German language and a common literary heritage, the north and east was Protestant, while the south and west was Catholic. Prussia itself, which dominated the Empire, was largely (but not entirely) Protestant.

Bismarck was determined that there be no force within Germany that could effectively counter the supremacy of the state. It seemed to him that the Catholic church, which was international in character, and under a non-German head, was suspect. In the first decade of the German Empire, then, strong measures were taken against the political influence of Catholics. This was the "Kulturkampf" ("cultural war").

The Jesuits were expelled on June 25, 1872, civil marriages were made obligatory, Catholic religious orders were dissolved, education was put under the control of the state, and so on.

The Kulturkampf was petering to an end by 1880. In a way, both sides won. The state stopped trying to make life miserable for Catholics, and Catholics made no serious attempt, thereafter, to oppose the state. It was live and let live, and Bismarck was satisfied with that.

Besides, a secular opposition had arisen that Bismarck could see might be a more dangerous opponent than the Catholics. Soon after 1860, socialists had been organizing into parties, and those socialists who espoused the economic theories of Karl Marx were in the lead within the movement by 1870.

In May and June of 1878, there were two attempts made to assassinate the Emperor, neither successful, and both by radicals who, as it happened, were not socialists. On October 19, 1878, these attempts nevertheless, provided an excuse for strong antisocialist laws, with draconian punishments and rigorous enforcement. Socialist activity retreated into the dark and became conspiratorial.

Meanwhile, Germany was rapidly becoming industrialized, quickly passing France and coming to rival Great Britain. It increased its iron and steel production phenomenally, became one of the great commercial powers of the world, and its cities grew rapidly. It was clear that, both militarily and economically, Germany had succeeded to the mastery of Europe—the position held in the time of Louis XIV by France, and in the time of Philip II by Spain.

To make doubly sure of this, Bismarck proceeded to build a series of alliances designed to make sure that France would remain isolated, for only France could be counted on to remain forever antagonistic to the power that had so humiliated her in 1870.

In the summer of 1871, William I of Germany and Francis Joseph of what was then called Austria-Hungary met, and friendship between them was established. Austria-Hungary took on the role of loyal subordinate to Germany and maintained it thereafter.

Russia feared the strength of this new alliance and felt it would be best to join it. Alexander II of Russia visited Berlin in 1872 and William I visited St. Petersburg in 1873. By June 6, 1873, the

"Three Emperors League" was formed, in which the Emperors of Germany, Austria-Hungary, and Russia presented a united front against France (and against socialism, too). Italy joined in September when Victor Emmanuel II visited Vienna and Berlin. France was now totally isolated, and Bismarck had reached his peak.

And yet this plastering together of nations could not work forever. For one thing, Austria-Hungary and Russia were at irreconcilable odds in the Balkans, where each wanted mastery. There were recurrent crises in which Bismarck had to choose between Austria-Hungary and Russia, and the pull of a common "Germanism" inclined him toward Austria-Hungary.

During this turbulent period, German science continued to make strides. August Wilhelm von Hofmann (1818–1892) had taught in Great Britain and had inspired Perkin to make the experiment that had led to synthetic dyes. When Hofmann retired to Germany in 1864, he continued the study of synthetic dyes and founded the German Chemical Society. Thanks to him, Germany overtook France and Great Britain, and had assumed the lead in the field of organic chemistry.

Thus, Johann Friedrich Wilhelm Adolf von Baeyer (1835–1917) discovered barbituric acid in 1863, derivatives of which formed the well-known "sleeping pills" of later years. Baeyer also synthesized indigo, one of the water-fast natural dyes in 1878; and his pupil, Karl James Peter Graebe (1841–1927), had synthesized alizarin, another such dye, in 1869. Kekule was still active and, in 1865, worked out the structural formula of the important benzene molecule.

Wilhelm Pfeffer (1845–1920) worked with semipermeable membranes in 1877 and studied osmotic pressure. Using this technique, he was the first to obtain reliable molecular weights for the huge protein molecules. Wilhelm Friedrich ("Willy") Kuhne (1837–1900) was the first, in 1876, to use the word "enzyme" in connection with the catalysts found in living tissue. In 1869, Paul Langerhans (1847–1888) discovered patches of cells in the pancreas, which have since been called the "islets of Langerhans." These eventually played an important role in the development of the treatment for diabetes.

Ferdinand Julius Cohn (1828–1898) published a three-volume work on bacteria in 1872. He was the first to try to classify bacteria into genera and species and may be said to have founded the science of bacteriology.

In 1879, Wilhelm Max Wundt (1832–1920) established the first laboratory to be devoted entirely to experimental psychology.

In mathematics, Julius Wilhelm Richard Dedekind (1831–1916) worked out a new and more logical way of dealing with irrational numbers in 1872. In 1874, Georg Cantor (1845–1918) began to introduce his views of infinity and beyond, including "transfinite numbers," which represented an infinite number of different infinities.

In technology, Nikolaus August Otto (1832–1891) devised the first practical internal-combustion engine with power coming from explosions within the engine and not from steam outside. It was to revolutionize transport vehicles. In 1876, Karl von Linde produced the first modern refrigerator, making use of liquid ammonia for the process.

Heinrich Schliemann (1822–1890) was an enthusiast who set out to dig up Priam's Troy, destroyed 2000 years earlier. He located remains of a number of buried cities at the site he chose, one of which might well have been the Troy of the famous siege. Schliemann, working unscientifically, destroyed far more than he preserved, but he gave an enormous boost to modern archeology.

Wagner continued to be an outstanding figure in German music in this period. He completed his four operas of the *Ring of the Nibelungen* in 1876 and they have remained a giant product of the musical world ever since. Johannes Brahms composed his first two symphonies in 1876 and 1877, and also produced numerous other works.

Karl Marx published the first volume of his ponderous analysis of the economics of capitalism, *Das Kapital,* in 1867.

ITALY

The conclusion of the Franco–Austrian war of 1859 did not make the Italians feel grateful to Napoleon III. By that war, he had made sure that

Sardinia gained Lombardy from Austria; however, his abrupt ending of the war left Venetia in Austrian hands, and he had helped himself to Nice and Savoy on the western borders of Sardinia as payment for the uncompleted job. Therefore, he gained the fury and disgust of Italians. Napoleon III had, in other words, managed to strengthen a power at his southeastern border and yet make it his enemy, too.

The unification of Italy didn't stop once France halted the war, however. Now that Sardinia had doubled its size and strength by the absorption of Lombardy, the small states of northern Italy—Parma, Modena, and Tuscany—promptly threw out their Austrian-puppet rulers and joined the growing nation. Sardinia, to avoid trouble, asked Napoleon III for his blessing, and Napoleon had no choice but to accept the situation.

Even Romagna, the northernmost portion of the Papal States, joined Sardinia. That left the rest of the Papal States and the kingdom of Naples still outside.

On May 5, 1860, an Italian adventurer, Giuseppe Garibaldi (1807–1882), took over. He had fought in South America, in Italy, and in France, and now he took a thousand "Redshirts" and sailed from Genoa, Sardinia's chief port. He was secretly encouraged by the Sardinian Prime Minister, Cavour. Garibaldi's troops landed in Sicily, were greeted with enthusiasm by the population, and easily defeated Neapolitan forces who were not eager to die for their despot's cause.

Garibaldi then crossed into Italy itself, with the quiet aid of the British fleet, and marched triumphantly toward Naples, which he took on September 7, 1860. Francis II (1836–1894), who had succeeded his father, Ferdinand I, only the year before, fled. He was the last Bourbon king of Naples; the only Bourbon monarchs remaining were reigning in Spain.

That left the Papal States. There was an uprising there on September 8, and Cavour immediately sent Sardinian troops southward. Papal forces were defeated on September 18, and the Sardinians marched to the Neapolitan border. On October 21, 1860, Naples and Sicily joined Sardinia and, on November 4, most of the Papal States. The westernmost section of the Papal States, north and south of Rome itself, remained outside the kingdom for it was garrisoned and defended by French troops.

On March 17, 1861, the Kingdom of Italy was proclaimed. Victor Emmanuel II of Sardinia became the first King of Italy, and its capital was in Turin, but was shifted to Florence in 1865.

Cavour, with the Kingdom of Italy established, died on June 6, 1861, but he could not have died entirely at peace for the unification was not complete. Venetia was still held by Austria (thanks—as the Italians saw it—to the pusillanimity of the French) and Rome was guarded by French forces.

Italy allied itself with Prussia on May 12, 1866, feeling it stood to gain if Prussia made war on Austria. When the war between Prussia and Austria began on June 16, 1866, Italy honored its treaty obligations eagerly and declared war on Austria on June 20.

On June 24, the Italians were promptly defeated at the Second Battle of Custozza (where the Austrians had beaten them once before, 18 months earlier). On July 20, they also lost a naval battle at Lissa Island in the Adriatic. These losses didn't matter, however, since Austria lost the war.

As a result of the Treaty of Vienna, Italy annexed Venetia.

When the Franco–Prussian war began on July 15, 1870, Italy was entirely on the side of the Prussians, of course. After its initial defeats, France hurriedly withdrew its troops from Rome on August 19; and as soon as the French disaster at Sedan reached Italian ears, they marched into Rome on September 20. Rome became the capital of the Kingdom of Italy on October 2, 1870.

In the 1870s, Italy struggled for modernization. It reorganized its army, created a navy, built railroads, and encouraged trade. It could not help remaining weaker than the northern nations, however.

On January 9, 1878, Victor Emmanuel II died, after a reign that had seen enormous successes because Italy had chosen allies who had won battles, even when Italy itself had not. He was succeeded by his son, who reigned as Humbert or Umberto I (1844–1900).

Meanwhile, Verdi was still actively writing operas. *La Forza del Destino* was staged in 1862 and *Aida* in 1871. Amilcare Ponchielli (1834–1886) is best known today for his exuberant "Dance of the Hours" from his opera, *La Gioconda*, produced in 1876.

PAPACY

Throughout this period, Pope Pius IX, who had started his rule with such signs of liberalism, had been made more and more rigidly conservative as a result of adversity. His claims for papal power escalated, even as the eastern portion of the Papal States melted away forever and joined Sardinia, and even though he was left only with the western province of Rome (and that only by the grace of its French garrison).

On December 8, 1864, he published an encyclical in which he denounced both nationalism and socialism. He came out against religious toleration and insisted that the Church must not be controlled by the state. The Church, instead, should have sole control of education and should have the last word on culture and science. Essentially, it demanded the repeal of the nineteenth century.

Then, from December 8, 1869 to October 20, 1870, even as the last traces of the secular power of the Papacy were vanishing after eleven centuries, Pius IX held the Vatican Council. It was the first such council since the Council of Trent three centuries earlier.

Its climax came on July 18, 1870 (two months before the Italians took over Rome) when the dogma of papal infallibility was declared. According to this, when the Pope spoke in his Papal capacity on matters of faith or morals, he could not be wrong. This served to increase anti-Papal feelings in all secular institutions, including the government of even Catholic powers. It helped institute the Kulturkampf in Germany.

On May 13, 1871, the new Italian nation tried to mollify the Pope, giving him royal honors and full freedom to perform his religious duties. It made his person inviolable, let him have free intercourse with Catholics all over the world, and

also let him send out and receive diplomats, who were to have the same immunities as secular diplomats. He had the full ownership of the Vatican and other papal places, was not to be bound by any laws but his own, and was to receive an annual grant from the Italian treasury.

Pius IX would accept none of this but remained intransigent. He regarded himself as a "prisoner of the Vatican," which view his successors would also hold for a period of time. Pius IX died on February 7, 1878, having been Pope for 32 years, the longest papal reign in history. He was succeeded by Leo XIII (1810–1893), whose more liberal and tolerant attitude began a process of healing.

AUSTRIA/AUSTRIA-HUNGARY

Hungary had remained restless after its forcible repression in 1849. Austria had to be concerned about the possibility that Hungary would rise again whenever Austria might be militarily preoccupied. The war with France in 1859 was difficult for Austria to fight because it had to keep looking over its shoulder, so to speak, to see what Hungary was doing. That necessity also hampered Austria in its war against Prussia.

Austria felt that some sort of compromise had to be made. This came to pass in October 1867 and was called the "Ausgleich [Settlement] of 1867." It set up a "dual monarchy." The western half, in a large crescent, remained Austria. The eastern half, more compact and nestled within Austria like a nut in a half-shell, became the Kingdom of Hungary. Francis Joseph I ruled both nations, being the Emperor of Austria and the King of Hungary. They also had in common the ministries of foreign affairs, of war, and of finance, so that they were a pair of Siamese twins —joined in some respects, separate in others. Both nations had legislatures and cabinets of their own. The nation as a whole came to be called "Austria-Hungary," and the amazing thing about it was that it worked, after a fashion.

In the Austrian portion, the German-speaking population was supreme, though they made up only a third of the population. The Slavic peoples in Bohemia and in the southeast were vehemently dissatisfied with the compromise because they didn't see why the Hungarians should get what they didn't get.

As for the Hungarians, having gotten a certain measure of freedom, they were even less willing than the Germans of Austria to share it. They were quite determined to see that their own Slavs and Romanians remained firmly under the Hungarian thumb.

Thus while the Ausgleich worked, it bore within it the seeds of enormous trouble.

Once Bismarck completed his task and formed the powerful German Empire, Austria-Hungary moved into the German shadow. It still had its ambitions in the Balkans, and it still confronted Russia, but now it depended entirely on German support for success.

During this period, one important Austrian scientist was Ludwig Edward Boltzmann (1844–1906), who, in 1871, worked out the kinetic theory of gases independently of work done at about the same time in Great Britain. He interpreted the behavior of gases in terms of the tiny speeding and rebounding molecules that made them up. He also pictured the concept of entropy as a measure of the disorder of a system.

The botanist, Gregor Johann Mendel (1822–1884), published his researches on pea plants in 1865, and founded the modern science of genetics. His work, however, was ignored for a generation.

Austria at this time, and all the world, in fact, lay under the spell of the "waltz king," Johann Strauss the Younger (1825–1899), who wrote the most popular waltzes the world has ever known, over 150 of them. The most popular of all is "The Beautiful Blue Danube," composed in 1867. Others are "Artists Life," "Tales from the Vienna Woods," "Wine, Women and Song," "Wienerblut," and so on. He wrote comic operas, too, of which by far the most famous is "Die Fledermaus," composed in 1874.

Also Austrian by geography, but Czech in culture, was Bedrich Smetana (1824–1884), whose most popular opera is *The Bartered Bride*, composed in 1866. He is also remembered for the haunting "Die Moldau," one of a series of symphonic poems composed between 1874 and 1879.

FRANCE

At the beginning of this period, Napoleon III had had his power shaken by the war with Austria. Although it was a victory for France, it was clear that this was not a brilliant Napoleonic smash. Napoleon III did not enjoy a situation in which he was obviously to blame if things did not work well, and he set about sharing the responsibility.

The period from 1860 on, then, is known as the "Liberal Empire." He increased the power of the legislature and allowed them to debate matters more freely, and to have more say in financial matters. This would have been a wise move if Napoleon III had been a more capable ruler, but he continued to make mistakes and his liberalization only allowed the opposition to form and grow.

There was the problem of Mexico, for instance. It had failed to pay its debts and, in 1861, Great Britain, France, and Spain decided to collect those debts by force, and sent an expedition which placed troops ashore at Vera Cruz. The United States, which had not minded attacking Mexico itself a decade and a half earlier, did not want to see anyone else doing the same. The United States was, however, engaged in a civil war and, short of protesting, could do nothing.

The British and Spaniards quickly withdrew, however, for they did not think the debt-settlement was worth getting embroiled in a Mexican quagmire, and they feared what might happen if the American Civil War were to end in a Union victory.

Napoleon, with his gift for making mistakes, hung on and tried to set up a French-dominated "Mexican Empire." This proved to be a costly error (like that of Napoleon I in Spain), which weakened France and made it and its Emperor look ridiculous before the world. It also earned him the enmity of the United States, which *did* survive the Civil War.

Then, by taking over the defense of Rome against the new nation of Italy, he hoped to win credit with French Catholics, but he also earned new hatred from Italy.

In 1863, when the Poles revolted against the Russians, he made gestures as though to help the Poles, but he was far away and, in between him and the Poles, was Bismarck's Prussia, which was firmly on the Russian side. All Napoleon III achieved, therefore, was to gain the enmity of Russia.

When Prussia defeated Austria in 1866, while France did nothing, Napoleon III looked foolish once again. Napoleon III then tried to pick up Belgium or Luxemburg as the "compensation" he imagined Prussia would let him have. Bismarck refused brusquely, and all Napoleon gained was humiliation and the suspicious enmity of Great Britain.

France was effectively isolated, then, as the 1860s drew near the end, and there could be no question but that this was due to Napoleon III's pathetic fumbling. The opposition grew. The government won the elections in 1869, but only by a majority of 57%, and no fewer than 30 outright republicans were elected to the legislature. What's more, labor was growing more socialistic. Trade-unions were spreading and so were strikes.

The most prominent French republican at this time was Leon Gambetta (1838–1882), who demanded universal suffrage, freedom of the press, the right of assembly to express grievances, trial by jury, separation of church and state, and no standing army.

Napoleon III could think of no way of saving the situation but by conducting one of his canned plebiscites, in which as many as possible were bludgeoned into voting "yes" on the question of whether they favored the government or not. On May 8, 1870, the plebiscite gave Napoleon III an 82% majority which was, under the circumstances, meaningless, but which gave the government the courage to declare war on Prussia 10 weeks later.

By September 2, 1870, four months after the plebiscite, Napoleon III had surrendered at Sedan and was forced to abdicate. He fled to Great Britain where he died a little over two years later. He was the last monarch France was to have.

When the news of Sedan reached Paris, the Parisians invaded the Imperial palace and a "Third Republic" was declared. By September 19, the city was surrounded by two Prussian armies, but it withstood a siege for over four months until there was virtually no food left in the city and the people were starving. Gambetta had escaped from the city by balloon and was organizing resistance in the provinces. He and a mining engineer, Charles Louis de Freycinet (1828–1923), led a fight so desperately gallant against overwhelming force that they helped rescue France from absolute disgrace.

By the time Paris gave up, however, all resistance had been crushed, and Bismarck allowed the French to move on to develop their republic, feeling, no doubt, that this would keep them weak and in turmoil.

The French elected Louis Adolph Thiers (1797–1877) as the first head of the Third Republic on February 16, 1871. He had had a long career. He had opposed Charles X, was in Louis Philippe's cabinet in various positions for 10 years, but lost his post when he was too vehemently in favor of Muhammad Ali. Now he was the head of the government and it was he who had to present the treaty that cost France Alsace-Lorraine. It was accepted by a wide majority of the delegates; they had no choice.

Thiers was a conservative republican, however, and many in Paris who had withstood the siege, and who felt the peace treaty to be a humiliation, wanted a more radical government. On March 1, they set up a "Commune" in Paris, consisting of a wide variety of different (and loudly disagreeing) radicals who were lumped together as "Communards."

The French government, however, had the army. It had failed miserably against the Prussians, but it was perfectly capable of slaughtering its own unarmed people. While the occupying Prussians watched (no doubt with cynical amazement), the French army took Paris, destroyed the Commune (which had only lasted 11 weeks), and then indulged in more or less indiscriminate executions and slayings.

After that, France felt it had had enough of republican confusion, and a national assembly was elected in which the monarchists had the majority. It looked as though the Third Republic would be shorter-lived than the first two. The trouble was that there were three kinds of monarchists. The "Legitimists" wanted Henri Dieudonne d'Artois, Count of Chambord (1820–1883), who was the grandson of Charles X. The "Orleanists" wanted Louis Philippe Albert, Count of Paris (1838–1894), who was the grandson of Louis Philippe. The "Bonapartists" wanted a Bonaparte.

For a while, it looked as though there might be a general agreement to let Chambord rule as "Henry V" and then, since he had no children, to allow Paris to succeed as "Louis Philippe II." However, Chambord insisted that he would not rule unless France would accept the white flag of pre-Revolutionary France in place of the tricolor. It was by an idiotic demand such as that that the Third Republic was saved.

Thiers gained the title of President on August 31, 1871, and managed to organize finances in such a way that the large indemnity the Prussians had set was paid off and the last bit of the German occupying force was out of the country by September 16, 1873.

Thiers, his work done, resigned on May 24, 1873, and the very conservative Marie Edme Patrice Maurice de MacMahon was elected. He had fought in the Crimean War, had led the French army to victory against Austria in 1859, and had taken Paris from the Commune. He had also lost disgracefully to the Prussians.

MacMahon was a monarchist who saw it as his task to pave the way for Chambord and Paris to succeed to the throne—first one, then the other. But *again* Chambord saved the Republic by insisting on the white flag. That was monarchy's last chance.

With the Republic established, France began looking about for allies since it was quite certain it could never stand up to the German Empire alone. Bismarck was annoyed and, in April 1875,

he deliberately allowed it to appear that there might be a new German–French war. It panicked France, and it also upset Great Britain and Russia, neither of whom wanted to see France made into a German puppet altogether. They made their position known to Bismarck, who eased off, and who may have decided, then, that he couldn't count on Russia and that he would be better off without Austria-Hungary in any Balkan trouble.

MacMahon ruled under a constitution that gave the president great power, and he used those powers vigorously for conservative causes. He used them too vigorously, in fact, and grew steadily more unpopular. On January 30, 1879, he resigned, although his seven-year term still had a year to run.

Francois Paul Jules Grevy (1807–1891), who had been a strong leader of the opposition in the last years of Napoleon III, was elected third President of the French Republic over Gambetta. He had always favored a weak executive and, under him, the powers of the President declined until it ebbed to figurehead status. It was the legislature headed by the Prime Minister that would rule France, and, with that, the Third Republic became a going concern.

Yet there was one event in France that was more important to the world than anything that Napoleon III or Bismarck did, or could do. In 1865, Louis Pasteur enunciated the "germ theory of disease" which maintained that infectious disease was the result of the growth and spread of microorganisms. It was the most important single medical advance the world had ever seen, for the new view of disease it made possible led to the doubling of the average life-span—and helped bring on a fearful population explosion the world over.

Pierre Eugene Marcelin Berthelot (1827–1907) studied the heat developed by chemical reactions and was one of those who founded the study of "thermochemistry" in the 1860s. He was also the first to go systematically about the practice of synthesizing organic compounds that did not exist in nature. Paul Emile Lecoq de Boisbaudran (1838–1912) discovered the element gallium, the properties of which offered strong support to the periodic table of the elements that had just been worked out in Russia. Louis Paul Cailletet (1832–1913) was the first, in 1877, to liquefy the gases oxygen, nitrogen, and carbon monoxide. Of the gases then known, only hydrogen remained unliquefied.

In 1878, Paul Bert (1833–1886) studied the agonizing disease, bends, which sometimes paralyzed and even killed those working under high air-pressure underwater. He found it was brought about by nitrogen that dissolved in the bloodstream at high pressure, then bubbled out when the pressure was lowered again. He pointed out that pressure must be decreased slowly and by stages. This new view greatly eased the task of building bridges and underwater tunnels.

In the field of literature, Hugo still towered, publishing his masterpiece, *Les Miserables*, in 1862. Alphonse Daudet (1840–1897) is best remembered for *Tartaron de Tarascon*, published in 1872. Emile Edouard Charles Antoine Zola (1840–1902) published harsh realistic novels such as *L'Assommoir* in 1877, and *Nana* in 1880.

Jules Verne (1828–1905) found his book *Five Weeks in a Balloon*, published in 1863, unexpectedly popular. He went on to write other works such as *A Journey to the Center of the Earth* (1864), *From the Earth to the Moon* (1865), *Twenty Thousand Leagues Under the Sea* (1870), *Around the World in Eighty Days* (1873), and so on. He was the first science fiction writer in the sense that he was the first to make a good living out of that type of writing as his main production.

The great French poets of the time were Paul Verlaine (1844–1896) and Jean Nicolas Arthur Rimbaud (1854–1891). Among the French artists of the period were great Impressionists: Paul Cezanne (1839–1906), who is the chief founder of modern art; Hilaire Germain Edgar Degas (1834–1917); Pierre Auguste Renoir (1841–1919); Edouard Manet (1832–1883); and Claude Monet (1824–1906).

In music, Georges Bizet (1838–1875) composed the opera *Carmen* in 1875. It is certainly one of the most popular of all operas, though it was a failure when first presented. Offenbach's only grand opera *The Tales of Hoffman* was produced only after his death in 1875. Clement Philibert Leo Delibes (1836–1891) was the first to make the writing of ballet-music a major preoccupation. He is best known for his music to the ballet, *Coppelia*, written in 1870.

Charles Camille Saint-Saens (1835–1921) wrote the opera *Samson and Delilah* in 1877, but his most often-heard work is his lively "Danse Macabre," composed in 1874.

RUSSIA

This new tsar, Alexander II, was quite different from his father. By Russian standards, he was surprisingly liberal. For one thing, on March 3, 1861, he put through an edict that freed the serfs, who until then had been bound to the soil and had been no better than slaves. It is an odd fact of history that backward, autocratic Russia freed its serfs at just about the time that the progressive, democratic United States freed its slaves; and that Russia did it peacefully while the United States had to fight a terrible civil war. (To be sure, the Russian serfs were not much better off materially after they had been emancipated, but then, truth to tell, neither were the American slaves.)

Alexander II also took a more liberal attitude toward the Poles than his father had, and attempted to set up the limited self-rule that had existed before the revolt of 1830. Granting a little freedom has its dangers, however; it whets the appetite and more is wanted. There were student demonstrations in Poland in favor of complete independence; the Russian government overreacted by attempting to draft the students into the Russian army.

At this, demonstrations became revolts in January 1863. It was not until May 1864 that the revolt was suppressed, and Russia had a free hand to do so only because Prussia made it so plain that they were ready to join Russia in suppressing Polish nationalism that Great Britain, France, and Austria could not risk the chance of interfering (even though all three were quite anti-Russian at the time).

The result was that Poland was once again repressed, and its autonomy withdrawn. Russian was made obligatory in all schools and other forms of Russification were enforced—against Polish Catholicism, for instance.

Within Russia, there were further reforms, however. The judiciary system was modernized in 1864 and municipal government was put into the hands of the towns themselves in 1870. In 1874, there was an army reform, with military service made universal instead of being just for the lower classes.

Yet the policy of Russian expansion did not change. In the late 1860s and early 1870s, Russia absorbed Bokhara and Khiva in the regions north of Persia and Afghanistan. Even Russia, however, could recognize that some regions were simply too far distant to be worth the effort of administration. In 1867, Russia sold Alaska to the United States.

Russia's policy of friendliness with Prussia, out of gratitude for the latter's help against the Poles, caused Russia to be neutral during the wars of Prussia against Denmark, Austria, and France. Indeed, the French defeat was seized upon by Russia to get out of the Black Sea limitations that had been placed on it after the Crimean War. On March 13, 1871, Russia announced that she would not consider herself bound to keep the Black Sea neutral. France was in no position to object; Prussia didn't care; Austria-Hungary would now do nothing without Germany; and Great Britain didn't wish to deal with the matter all by herself; so Russia got away with it.

Then came a sudden crisis in the Balkan peninsula. In July 1875, there was a revolt in the Ottoman provinces of Bosnia and Herzegovina, which lay between Serbia and Austria-Hungary. The population of Bosnia and Herzegovina were Slavic and related to the Serbs, so the Serbs strongly supported the rebellion, hoping to add those provinces to its own territory.

Russia also supported the revolt, because there was increasing "Pan-Slav" feeling in Russia. Some Russians felt that it was Russia's right and duty to support Slavic aspirations everywhere. Some even felt that all Slav areas should be added to Russian territory.

Great Britain, on the other hand, favored the Ottoman Empire as it had been doing for decades. Besides, it had bought up shares in the Suez Canal on November 25, 1875, and that would give it a much shorter route to India, and what suited her needs best in that respect was a weak, but stable and friendly, Ottoman Empire.

Austria, too, was against the revolt, because it didn't want Serbia to get too strong (Austria had Slavs of its own in the area) and it didn't want Russia to dominate the Balkan peninsula.

Germany, under Bismarck, wanted peace because it was allied with both Russia and Austria-Hungary and didn't want to have to alienate either. Nevertheless, all attempts to mediate the dispute had failed by May 1876. In fact, the situation had grown worse by then, because an insurrection against the Ottoman Empire broke out in its Bulgarian province as well.

Serbia, taking advantage of the Bulgarian insurrection, and wanting to take over Bosnia and Herzegovina, decided to being things to a head by declaring war on the Ottoman Empire on June 30, 1876. Montenegro also declared war on July 2. The two powers were certain that the big Slavic brother, Russia, would support them.

However, it took time for Russia (always slow) to react, especially since it had to make sure it would not set off too large a war if it did so. And while the Russians tested the waters, the Ottoman Empire beat the Serbs who, on September 1, gave up.

Ottoman forces had meanwhile suppressed the revolts in Bosnia-Herzegovina and in Bulgaria with such wild force that the atrocity tales that reached Great Britain created enormous anger against the Turks. British efforts to aid the Ottoman Empire were compromised as a result, and it became politically necessary to find some way of getting them out of the Balkans without weakening them too much.

British and Russian diplomats met in Constantinople on December 12, 1876, and then again on January 15, 1877, to work out a way of doing this. Great Britain made it clear that Russia might take punitive action against the Ottoman Empire, but it must not blockade the Suez Canal or make any attempt to take Egypt, or even Constantinople.

Having gone so far, the British waited to see what would happen.

Russia declared war on the Ottoman Empire on April 24, 1877, and opened a two-pronged attack, one in the Balkans and one in the Caucasus region, attacking the Turks both in the west and the east.

In the Balkans, the Russians swept through Romania, crossed the Danube, and then came up hard against Plevna, in north-central Bulgaria, not far south of the river. The Russians might easily have bypassed Plevna, but for some reason, they decided to take it.

It took them five months to do so, during which time they suffered 30,000 casualties. Worse than that, the stubborn Turkish defense gained sympathy for the Ottoman Empire. Plevna was finally taken on December 10, 1877, a Pyrrhic victory; and, during the winter, Russian forces also advanced in the Caucasus, reaching Erzerum in Turkish Armenia.

In January 1878, after the fall of Plevna, the Russians resumed their advance, defeated the Turks, and reached the outskirts of Constantinople by the end of the month.

The prospect that Russia might take Constantinople, despite the earlier understanding with Great Britain, produced an anti-Russian fury in that country. This was the time of the famous music-hall song that went:

We don't want to fight, but, by jingo, if we do,
We've got the men, we've got the ships, we've got
   the money, too,
And the Russians shall not have Constantinople.

As it happens, "jingo" is simply a common euphemism for "Jesus"; however, because of that song, "jingoism" has come to mean a policy of bellicose bluster.

The Russians, however, had had enough, and they were by no means eager to take Constantinople at the cost of war with Great Britain. The Ottoman Empire had also had enough, and Russia dictated the Treaty of San Stefano (a suburb of Constantinople) on March 3, 1878. Turkey had to accept the independence of Serbia, Montenegro, and Romania, and the virtual independence of Bulgaria. Reforms were promised for Bosnia-

Herzegovina, and it was clear that Ottoman sovereignty in the Balkans was to be reduced to a shadow and that Russia would be the real master of the peninsula. Russia also helped itself to some territory along the eastern shores of the Black Sea, and inflicted a large indemnity on the Ottoman Empire as well.

Neither the British nor the Austrians would accept this. After a period of diplomatic wrangling, there was a meeting at Berlin (the "Congress of Berlin") from June 13 to July 13, 1878, at which attempts were made to settle matters. Disraeli, Great Britain's Prime Minister, led the anti-Russian forces, while Bismarck announced himself a disinterested party and offered to act as an "honest broker."

As a result of the Congress of Berlin, the Treaty of San Stefano was revised. The independence of Serbia, Montenegro, and Romania was indeed recognized by all of Europe, but Bulgaria was divided into three parts and given only the most limited autonomy. The Ottoman presence in the Balkans was strengthened well beyond the limits of San Stefano, and Russian influence in the Balkans was made minimal. Austria-Hungary was given the right to garrison and maintain order in Bosnia-Herzegovina, and in a strip of land between Serbia and Montenegro. Russia was given a portion of the province of Bessarabia, along the eastern border of Romania, as compensation. For itself, Great Britain took the island of Cyprus, which lay directly north of the Suez Canal, and which would thus be a useful British base.

The settlement left a great deal of dissatisfaction behind. Serbia and Montenegro feared the advance of Austria-Hungary into Bosnia-Herzegovina. Russia felt deeply humiliated at having its treaty revised by an arrogant Great Britain, and particularly resented Austria-Hungary's advance into the Balkans. Russia had not forgotten Austria's ingratitude at the time of the Crimean War. From this point on, Russia and Austria-Hungary could never be reconciled and the Balkan situation was an open sore between them. The seeds of disaster had been sown.

Meanwhile, the wave of liberal discontent that had been sweeping Europe since the French Revolution nearly a century earlier finally reached Russia. In part, the reforms of Alexander II had made many Russians hungry for more. Then, the Russians attempt to force the Ottoman Empire to grant liberal reforms in the Balkans seemed ironic to those who noted that those same reforms did not exist in Russia. On the other side, the buckling of Russia to international pressure at the Congress of Berlin displeased the Russian jingoists.

Since there was no opportunity in Russia for open and rational opposition, the dissatisfied groups were forced to go underground, to conspire, and to engage in terrorist activity. The Russian giant was beginning to stir feverishly.

Yet, despite its backwardness, Russia contributed to science and art. Dmitri Ivanovich Mendeleyev (1834–1907) was one of the top-ranking chemists of world history. He introduced the proper manner of arranging the chemical elements in order of increasing atomic weight in such a way that similar elements fell into distinct rows. This was the "periodic table" of the elements, which he introduced in 1869. He used the periodic table to project the existence of certain undiscovered elements and to predict what their properties would be. These predictions quickly proved to be absolutely correct, to the amazement of the chemical world. Mendeleyev's insights laid the groundwork for modern notions of atomic structure.

Alexander Mikhailovich Butlerov (1828–1876), in the 1860s, contributed to the new notions of organic chemical structure.

This period was the golden age of Russian literature. Ivan Sergeyevich Turgenev (1818–1883) published *Fathers and Sons* in 1862. Fyodor Mikhaylovich Dostoyevsky (1821–1881), published *Notes from the Underground* in 1864; *Crime and Punishment* in 1866; *The Idiot* in 1868; and *The Brothers Karamazov* in 1879. Lev (Leo) Nikoayevich Tolstoy (1828–1910) published *War and Peace* (thought by some to be the greatest novel ever written) between 1865 and 1869, and *Anna Karenina* between 1875 and 1877.

In music, Alexander Porfiryevich Borodin (1833–1887) composed *Prince Igor*, containing the "Polovetsian Dances," in the 1860s (and he was

a chemist of no mean attainments, also). Modest Petrovich Mussorgsky (1839–1881) composed the opera *Boris Godunov* in 1874.

GREAT BRITAIN

Throughout this period, Great Britain, secure behind its control of the sea, continued its "splendid isolation," seeking no allies who might divert it from its pursuit of its own interests, a policy it had maintained since the Battle of Waterloo a half-century earlier.

By and large, it maintained its prosperity. London, the epitome of the "great city" of the nineteenth century (as Babylon, Rome, and Constantinople had been the epitomes in earlier times), was building subways in the 1860s.

One near approach to war, however, came in connection with the United States, which, in 1861, plunged into civil war.

The British government was entirely in sympathy with the new Confederate States of America, a union of 11 southern slave states. They recognized a state of belligerency almost at once, which was nearly tantamount to accepting the Confederates as a sovereign nation.

Almost at the start of the American Civil War, the British threatened war, and only the intervention of the dying Prince-Consort, Albert, and the good sense of Abraham Lincoln, kept the peace. The British government, however, continued to supply arms to the Confederacy whenever that was possible, and even put British shipyards at their disposal. The Confederates could order superior craft, which they could then use to harass American merchant-men and drive them off the high seas. A British-built Confederate ship, *Alabama*, was particularly effective in this respect.

In 1863, two new ships were being prepared for the Confederates, ships so advanced that the United States felt it could no longer tolerate this. The American minister to Great Britain, Charles Francis Adams (1807–1886), warned the British bluntly that if those ships were handed over to the Confederate States, that would mean war.

Great Britain backed off. The United States might well win the American Civil War, and if they did, the nation would end with a large, trained army that could take Canada without trouble. Great Britain decided it did not want to fight a vengeful United States.

Second, although the British government was pro-Confederate, the British people were not. They were thoroughly antislavery and they demonstrated against the Confederate states even though the American blockade of the Confederacy had cut off cotton supplies and thrown many of the British demonstrators out of work. It was one of the all too few examples of the victory of ideals over money that history has to offer.

After the American Civil War was over, with an American victory, the United States demanded reparation for the damage that British-built ships, especially the *Alabama*, had done to American shipping. There were hard feelings over this "*Alabama* claims" controversy, and extremists on both sides demanded intransigence. The matter, however, was put up for arbitration before an international group, meeting in Geneva. The decision went against Great Britain, which apologized, agreed to a tighter definition of neutrality, and, on December 15, 1871, further agreed to pay $15.5 million in reparations.

It was a marvelous example of settling disputes by some means other than war, and of a nation admitting it was in the wrong without the sky falling. It is tragic that international disputes are not more often settled in so sane and civilized a manner.

Internally, Great Britain had to face the problem of electoral reform again. The reforms of 1832 had left labor without a vote, and continuing industrialization had multiplied the number of workers. The pressure to extend the franchise had grown stronger since Chartism had been suppressed in 1848, and something had to be done.

The leading conservative in a government which came into power in 1866 was Benjamin Disraeli, who had been a novelist of moderate repute in his younger days. He was forced to do what other intelligent conservatives, such as Bismarck, would do. He decided that to defeat socialism, it was not sufficient to repress. One had to grant labor, and the people generally, enough

of a stake in society to make them less ready to adopt radical tactics. It was a case of the carrot as well as the stick.

Disraeli pushed for electoral reform; then, and on August 15, 1867, a Second Reform Bill was passed that doubled the electorate, including many portions of the labor force.

After that there was a period in which Disraeli of the Conservative Party and William Ewart Gladstone (1809–1898) of the Liberal Party battled for power and took the Prime Ministership in alternation. Disraeli became Prime Minister for the first time on February 29, 1868, but at the end of that year, the Liberals won an election, and Gladstone became Prime Minister for the first time on December 9, 1868.

Ireland was increasingly restless now, and Gladstone felt it was time to liberalize British rule. The British oppression of Ireland was becoming too similar to the Russian oppression of Poland for the more liberal portion of British public opinion to endure it.

To begin with, the Anglican Church was the established church in Ireland and was supported by taxes that were eventually wrung out of the Irish peasantry, who were almost unanimously Catholic (except in the northeast). On July 26, 1869, Gladstone forced through the "Disestablishment Act" by which the Anglican Church was no longer the official church of a non-Anglican people. This was not easily done. The Anglican clergy and most Conservatives were bitterly opposed. Their "antidisestablishmentarianism" added a famous long word to the English language. The House of Lords, in fact, refused to pass the act until, once again, the creation of new Liberal peers was threatened.

Another cause of Irish discontent was the fact that the land was owned by Englishmen who lived in England. They were not there on the spot; they did not witness the people's misery, and could therefore peacefully ignore it. They felt no need to make improvements; their only concern was to extort rents from the miserable peasantry, and this could be done by agents. The agents were on the spot but they could be as freely brutal as they wished, since they could always claim they were only "following orders" and that they would simply be fired and replaced if they showed mercy.

One such agent, Charles Cunningham Boycott (1832–1897), was so notorious for his exactions that, in 1880, he was ostracized by the entire community. No one would talk to him and no one would deal with him. It was a most effective nonviolent personal punishment and could scarcely be countered. It added the word "boycott" to the English language.

On August 1, 1870, an "Irish Land Act" was passed which ameliorated some of these abuses, but by no means even came close to removing them entirely. In fact, they gave the British a convenient sense of virtue. Disorders could now be suppressed with a clear conscience on the grounds that there was no longer any reasonable cause for such things.

It was also necessary to improve the educational system in Great Britain. Industrial nations found it necessary to educate their population massively if they were to possess the literacy and understanding required for them to run the machinery of the new industrial age. Nevertheless, the British were behind the United States and Germany in this respect. Something had to be done, especially since the franchise had been broadened. It was dangerous to have uneducated people doing the voting. (As Disraeli said, "We must educate our masters.")

On August 9, 1870, reform was introduced into the school system. "Board schools" controlled by local governments were set up. The local governments could control fees, and decide whether attendance was to be made compulsory. What's more, education was made secular. Denominational religious instruction was not allowed in state-supported schools.

The army was reformed in 1871, and the practice of selling army commissions to any idiot with money was abolished. The radical notion of appointing only competent officers to lead British soldiers into war was adopted. The lessons learned from incompetent leadership in the Crimean War were made use of (never sufficiently, however).

The judicial system was reformed in 1873.

By then, however, the country had grown tired of reform. When enough people have been granted sufficient reform to make conservatives of them, they are usually content to stand pat. To them, "liberal" becomes a dirty word. On February 21, 1874, the Liberal party was defeated in an election, and Disraeli became Prime Minister for a second time.

Disraeli was intelligent enough to continue reforms when necessary, but he also saw to it that Great Britain assumed an activist foreign policy and that pleased the Imperialist-minded portion of the public, Liberals as well as Conservatives, workmen as well as landowners.

Thus, on November 25, 1875, Disraeli, on his own responsibility, committed the British government to the purchase of 44% of the shares of the new Suez Canal. This initiated Great Britain's penetration of Egypt and gave it new holdings on the new and shorter route to India.

A shorter route meant a firmer British grip on India. Since the Moghal Empire had come to an end a decade and a half earlier, Disraeli felt it appropriate to have Victoria crowned "Empress of India," which pleased her very much.

There was considerable opposition in Great Britain to that. After all, the title was un-British and even anti-British, if one considered Emperor Napoleon I. The agreement was made, therefore, that Victoria would never use the title in Great Britain. There she would remain Queen only.

Then came the crisis in the Balkans and the Russo–Turkish War. Disraeli forced the Russians to back down and had his way (plus the island of Cyprus) and returned from Berlin at the peak of his glory. He had even done it all without war (barring a few colonial wars that scarcely affected the British at home).

But there was a bad harvest in 1879, and a decline in prosperity. When Disraeli (now the Earl of Beaconsfield) called for a new election to serve as a sign of approval, he got defeat instead. On March 8, 1880, Gladstone became Prime Minister for the second time.

During this period, Great Britain continued to be active in science. James Clerk Maxwell (1831–1878) worked out the kinetic theory of gases independently of the work of Boltzmann in Austria-Hungary. In 1873, he also presented the world with "Maxwell's equations." These formed the basis of electromagnetic theory and showed the existence of "electromagnetic radiation," of which light itself is the most familiar manifestation.

William Huggins (1824–1910) was the first astronomer to put spectroscopy to major use. In 1863, he showed that the same elements that existed on Earth existed in the stars, another important indication that the laws of nature were universal in scope. He devised methods of photographing spectra and using the Doppler–Fizeau effect, in 1868, to show from Sirius's spectrum that it was receding from the Solar system.

William Crookes (1832–1914) discovered the element thallium in 1861. In 1875, he devised the "Crookes' tube," an evacuated tube through which an electric current could be forced. The radiation that resulted, which had been named "cathode rays," could then be studied in detail and proved highly important in yielding new insights into the structure of matter.

In 1868, Joseph Norman Lockyer (1836–1920), studying spectral lines obtained from the Sun's corona during an eclipse, decided it was due to an unknown element he named "helium."

Charles Darwin was still active and, in 1871, he finally dared apply the principles of evolution by natural selection to human beings, publishing *The Descent of Man*. In 1876, Herbert Spencer (1820–1903) applied evolutionary ideas to society, not always correctly. It was he who popularized the term "evolution" and the phrase "survival of the fittest." Charles Wyville Thomson (1830–1882) in a cruise of the ocean between 1872 and 1876, showed conclusively that life occupied the entire ocean from top to bottom.

In 1872, George Smith (1840–1876) deciphered the cuneiform tablets containing the epic of Gilgamesh.

In literature, Tennyson was still active, working through the 1860s and 1870s on *The Idylls of the King,* his Victorian conception of the legends of King Arthur. Browning wrote his greatest work *The Ring and the Book* in 1868–1869. Matthew Arnold published *Dover Beach* in 1867. A younger poet, Algernon Charles Swinburne

(1837–1909) first attracted attention with *Atalanta in Calydon,* published in 1865.

Among the prose writers, George Meredith was still active, publishing *The Egoist* in 1879. William Wilkie Collins (1824–1889) was one of the early mystery writers, publishing *The Woman in White* in 1860, and *The Moonstone* in 1868. Thomas Hardy (1840–1928) wrote such novels as *Far from the Madding Crowd* in 1874 and *The Return of the Native* in 1878. Mary Ann Evans (1819–1880), writing under the male pseudonym of "George Eliot," wrote a number of novels of which the most familiar is *Silas Marner,* published in 1861.

On the lighter side, Edward Lear (1812–1888) wrote nonsense in the 1870s and popularized the five-line "limerick." Charles Lutwidge Dodgson, writing under the pseudonym "Lewis Carroll," wrote the deathless children's classics *Alice's Adventures in Wonderland* in 1865, and *Through the Looking-Glass* in 1872. They are supposedly the most quoted works in English, after the Bible and Shakespeare.

Great Britain lagged in music, but this period saw the beginning of an amazing collaboration between the poet and playwright, William Schwenk Gilbert (1836–1911), and the composer, Arthur Seymour Sullivan (1842–1900). Singly, they were minor figures, but together they produced the immortal "Gilbert & Sullivan comic operas," the best ever written and as popular today as they were a century ago. Their first hits were *Trial by Jury* (1875), *H.M.S. Pinafore* (1878), and *The Pirates of Penzance* (1879).

The outstanding British artist of the period was the American-born James Abbott McNeill Whistler (1834–1903). One of the best-known paintings, as far as the general public is concerned, is one he painted in 1872, popularly known as "Whistler's Mother." John Tenniel (1820–1914) is a cartoonist and illustrator, best known for his illustrations for the two "Alice" books by Lewis Carroll.

BELGIUM

Leopold I of Belgium died on December 10, 1865, and was succeeded by his son, who reigned as

Leopold II (1835–1909). Leopold II was rightly suspicious of the ambitions of Napoleon III and, in general, feared Belgium might be crushed between France in the West and Prussia in the east.

Great Britain shared those fears, not wishing to see either Belgium or the Netherlands, right across the narrow sea from itself, to be dominated by either France or Prussia. Once the Franco–Prussian War was in progress, Great Britain more or less forced a guarantee of Belgian neutrality on France and Prussia.

Meanwhile, Leopold II was growing interested in the development of central Africa (the "Congo") as a personal, rather than a national, project.

In this period, Ernest Solvay (1838–1922), a Belgian chemist, patented a method of forming sodium bicarbonate (the "Solvay process") in 1861. Eventually, he became the world supplier of the material.

NETHERLANDS

During this period, the Netherlands continued to be ruled by William III. The great issue in the Netherlands, as in Belgium at this time, was whether education would be in the hands of the state or the various religious organizations.

Among the Dutch scientists of the period was Jacobus Henricus van't Hoff (1852–1911) who, in 1874, when little more than a school-boy, worked out the three-dimensional structure of organic compounds. His structures finally demonstrated molecular asymmetry and explained the behavior of polarized light in passing through certain substances.

Johannes Diderick Van der Waals (1837–1923) improved the understanding of the gas laws in 1873.

SPAIN

This was a turbulent period for Spain. Isabella II continued to be indifferent to the nation and to interest herself in her own elaborate love life. There was a constant rough-and-tumble among different ministers, all of whom were ineffective. A liberal uprising finally took place in 1868. Isabella's armies were defeated and, on September 19, 1868, she fled to France and was declared deposed.

A new liberal constitution was devised. Universal suffrage, together with freedom of the press and religion, was announced, and the hunt was on for a new ruler. Bismarck offered a Hohenzollern prince for the purpose and this was the immediate occasion of the Franco–Prussian War. Having achieved his aim, Bismarck withdrew the offer. On December 30, 1970, the throne was offered to the son of Victor Emmanuel II of Italy. He accepted and ruled as Madeo I, but after two years in which the Spaniards simply refused to accept a foreign king, he gave up and abdicated on February 12, 1873.

A Spanish Republic was declared, but it had no peace. There were still those who wanted the kingship to go to a descendant of Don Carlos, who had been the younger brother of Isabella II, so that a Carlist civil war raged for a second time.

In 1875, however, the son of Isabella II mounted the throne as Alfonso XII. He put an end to the Carlist resistance and another new constitution was put into effect in 1876. The government was placed under Antonio Canovas del Castillo (1828–1897), and Spain for a time settled down to a period of reasonably good government under a limited monarchy with a representative legislature.

PORTUGAL

Pedro V of Portugal died in 1861 and was succeeded by his younger brother, who reigned as Luis I (1838–1889). During this period, by and large, Portugal experienced some quiet. In 1868, slavery was abolished in Portuguese-owned colonies. (The abolition of slavery in the United States made it difficult for any European nation to keep them, since they could no longer point to "free" America as justification.)

DENMARK

Frederick VII of Denmark died on November 15, 1863, and was succeeded by his first cousin, once removed, who reigned as Christian IX (1818–1906).

Christian IX gained the throne just in time to have Denmark bowled over by the Prussian juggernaut. He lost Schleswig and Holstein in the process and spent the rest of this period fighting to maintain a conservative government against the gradually strengthening liberal forces within the kingdom.

SWEDEN

Under Charles XV, who was reigning at the beginning of this period, Sweden gained representative government. He died on September 18, 1872, and was succeeded by his brother, who reigned as Oscar II (1828–1907). During his reign, Sweden began the process of industrialization.

The Swedish inventor, Alfred Bernhard Nobel (1833–1896), produced dynamite in 1866 by mixing nitroglycerine with diatomaceous earth. It was an explosive that revolutionized construction methods in the world, since it retained the shattering power of nitroglycerine while being sufficiently difficult to ignite, making it safe to use.

At this time, Norway began to grow restless under Swedish domination, even though that was relatively mild. The Norwegian playwright, Henrik Johan Ibsen (1828–1906), made Norwegian literature prominent with such plays as *Peer Gynt* in 1867 and *A Doll's House* in 1879. Edvard Hagerup Grieg (1843–1907) was a Norwegian composer, noted for the music he wrote for *Peer Gynt* in 1876.

SWITZERLAND

Switzerland had virtually no history to speak of in this period, but a Swiss chemist, Johann Friedrich Miescher (1844–1895), working in Germany, discovered nucleic acids in 1869. The importance of the discovery was not understood then, or for many decades afterward, but the time was to come when it would become a central concern in biochemistry.

GREECE

In this period, independent Greece did not, by any means, control all the Greek-speaking areas in the Ottoman Empire. Its ambition was to annex those areas, and for that foreign help was needed. The Greek king, Otho I, counted on Austria. He backed Austria in its war against France in 1859, which Austria lost. Between that, and the fact that he had no heir, the Greeks tired of him and deposed him on October 23, 1862, sending him back to his native Bavaria.

The Greeks tried to get a British prince to rule them and failed. They then turned to a younger son of Christian IX of Denmark, who ruled quite successfully as George I (1845–1913).

One territorial gain was made by Greece on June 5, 1864, when the British turned over to them the Ionian islands off their northwest coast. These islands were supposed to have made up the kingdom of the legendary Odysseus 2000 years before, and the British had ruled them since Napoleon's fall in 1815.

In 1866, the island of Crete (Greek-speaking but Ottoman-ruled) rebelled, and in 1878 there was an uprising in Greek-speaking Thessaly, also Ottoman-ruled. The Greeks, seeing a chance of fulfilling their expansionist aspirations, declared war on the Ottoman Empire on February 2, 1878, when it was at the point of total defeat at the hands of the Russians. However, Great Britain and Austria were not ready to see the Ottoman Empire fall apart too rapidly, and the Greeks got nothing out of it at this time.

SERBIA

Serbia tried to take advantage of unrest in Bosnia-Herzegovina in this period, and declared war on the Ottoman Empire, Montenegro joining it. The two Slavic powers were, however, defeated by the Ottoman Empire and, although at the Congress of Berlin the independence of Serbia and Montenegro was officially recognized, they made no territorial gains.

BULGARIA

Bulgaria rose in revolt in 1876, but this was put down with great cruelty by the Ottoman Empire. At the Congress of Berlin, parts of Bulgaria received a very limited amount of self-rule.

ROMANIA

As a result of the Congress of Berlin, Romania, lying north of Bulgaria, became an independent nation, under the rule of Carol I (1839–1914), a German prince.

OTTOMAN EMPIRE

Abdul Aziz (1830–1876) became Sultan in 1861. As a result of association with Great Britain and France in the Crimean War, the Ottoman Empire underwent a certain amount of westernization. Abdul Aziz died as the crisis began in the Balkans, and he was succeeded, in 1876, by Abdul Hamid II (1842–1918).

Things were looking bad, with Russia seemingly on the point of declaring war, and the Ottoman Empire tried to obtain the sympathy of the west by presenting the nation with a liberal constitution proclaiming true democratic principles. After the crisis was over, however, and the Ottoman Empire found it had survived surprisingly well, thanks to the Congress of Berlin. Abdul Hamid II dismissed the legislature, ignored the constitution, and returned to absolutism.

UNITED STATES

As 1860 closed, the United States had a population of 32 million (and its largest city, New York, had one of 805,000), but the Union seemed to be breaking up. South Carolina had seceded and six more slave states of the deep south joined it. The "Confederate States of America" was set up in Montgomery, Alabama, on February 8, 1861, and Jefferson Davis (1808–1889), who had been Secretary of War under Pierce and was a Senator from Mississippi, was elected as the Confederate President the next day.

The outgoing President of the United States, James Buchanan (1791–1868), in an amazing display of pusillanimity, did absolutely nothing while the Confederacy organized for war, seizing American military installations throughout their states.

Lincoln became president on March 4, 1861, and Fort Sumter in the harbor of Charleston, South Carolina was still held by American ("Union") forces. On April 14, the fort was bombarded into submission and the "American Civil War" had begun. Four more states had by now seceded, including Virginia, and the capital of the Confederacy was moved to Richmond.

The Union had a much greater population than the Confederacy, 22 million free people to 7 million free people plus 3 million slaves. The Union also had a much better railway network, a thriving industry, and a navy. The Confederacy, however, had better officers and hardier soldiers and needed to fight a defensive war only. The Confederacy asked only to be left to itself, whereas the Union had to invade and conquer.

The Union learned its lesson almost at once. Marching west from Washington, the Union forces met the Confederate forces at Bull Run, 25 miles west of Washington. They were routed and fled back to Washington. A Confederate general at the battle pointed to another Confederate general, Thomas Jonathan Jackson (1824–1863) and said, "There stands Jackson, like a stone wall." Jackson became known as "Stonewall Jackson" for the remaining two years of his life, and this to the point where people scarcely remember his true given name.

General Winfield Scott, hero of the Mexican War, was commander-in-chief of the army. He was a Virginian who was loyal to the Union. He foresaw a long war and he wanted a blockade and an attack down the Mississippi River, which would split the Confederacy in two. That would slowly strangle it at the cost of time, but relatively little blood.

Scott was absolutely right, but his suggestion was impractical. The blockade was indeed established and was tightened as time went on, but public opinion in the Union wouldn't sit still for a long, roundabout war. They wanted a direct attack on Richmond, Virginia, the heart of the Confederacy.

George Brinton McClellan (1826–1885) was put in charge of training an army for the purpose. He was an excellent trainer, but a miserable fighter, without an atom of initiative. While he spent half a year endlessly polishing his army, things happened elsewhere. For one thing, there was nearly a war with Great Britain.

The British ruling class was pro-Confederate since they saw an independent Confederacy as a British client state, and the rest of the United States as being sufficiently weakened by the defection of the Confederacy to represent no threat any longer to British commercial interests. The British government, therefore, recognized the Confederate States as belligerents immediately, and it was clear they intended to trade with them.

That was bad enough, but what followed was worse. The Confederacy sent two diplomats, James Murray Mason (1798–1871) and John Slidell (1793–1871), both United States senators prior to secession, to Great Britain and France on the British steamship *Trent* in order to negotiate for outright recognition and military aid. An American warship, under Charles Wilkes, the discoverer of Antarctica, stopped the *Trent* and removed the diplomats, taking them to the United States and internment. This was precisely the sort of thing, in reverse, that had caused the United States to go to war with Great Britain in 1812. The British government, seeing its chance to destroy the Union, was careful to take violent umbrage, and to send an angry note designed to provoke war. However, Prince Albert, Queen Victoria's husband, who lay dying of typhoid, still clung to sanity and peace. He softened the note to the point where the Americans could accept it.

To be sure, there were Americans who wanted war, too, thinking it would bring the Confederacy back into the Union to face a common enemy (not a chance, actually). The Secretary of State, William Henry Seward (1801–1872), who thought of himself at this point as the potential power behind the throne, was one of them. Lin-

coln, however, knew better, and he gently put Seward in his place and taught him to be a loyal subordinate thereafter. Lincoln handed back the diplomats with an apology. The diplomats went on to Europe, but accomplished nothing after all, so that the United States was saved a war over nothing, one that might have destroyed it.

Meanwhile, in the west, Ulysses Simpson Grant (1822–1885) was doing well for the Union. In February, 1862, the forces he led took two forts on the Cumberland and Tennessee River, and cleared Tennessee. On April 6 and 7, 1862, he won a hard-fought battle at Shiloh, near the southern border of Tennessee. He was, however, hampered by incapable superiors.

On April 24, 1862, the Union admiral, David Glasgow Farragut (1801–1870), took New Orleans. The Mississippi was being pinched north and south, and the Confederacy might be cut in two. This was precisely what Scott had recommended, but he had wanted to see a major effort put into it. Instead, the Mississippi drive had been turned into a sideshow, while large armies were massing for bloody battles in Virginia.

The gathering blockade, which Scott had also recommended, was put at risk on March 8, 1862. The Confederates had raised a sunken warship, the *Merrimack*, put armor plating on it, renamed it the *Virginia*, and sent it out. In the harbor, it proceeded to destroy the blockading Union vessels which were, of course, wooden. The Union cannonballs had no effect on the *Merrimack*'s armor, and the Union had panicky visions of the *Merrimack* destroying the entire union navy piecemeal and then bombarding Union ports.

However, on March 6, a Union ironclad, the *Monitor*, had put out to sea and, on March 9, the *Merrimack* and the *Monitor* fought it out to a draw. Both ships did nothing more in the war, but the fight marked the end of wooden warships. There had been ironclads before, the first having been used by the Koreans in their war against Hideyoshi of Japan two centuries earlier. It was this Civil War battle, however, that caught the imagination of naval officers everywhere. Each nation with a navy began to build ironclads.

In mid-March 1862, McClellan, at the direct

orders of President Lincoln, and with the greatest reluctance, finally took his well-trained army to Virginia by sea. What followed was tragic for the Union. Not only was McClellan lacking in drive and initiative, but he was facing Robert Edward Lee (1807–1870), probably the best general the United States ever produced. He, with Stonewall Jackson, formed the greatest team of generals since Marlborough and Prince Eugene over a century and a half earlier.

Jackson, by marching a relatively small body of troops up and down the Shenandoah Valley, immobilized four times as many Union troops, defeating them in detail, and keeping them from joining McClellan by feinting at Washington. Napoleon could not have done better.

Meanwhile, McClellan, facing Lee, was constantly at the edge of victory, since he invariably outnumbered the Confederates greatly and since his well-trained army performed well when it was allowed to. McClellan's leadership was so cowardly, however, that he constantly estimated the Confederate forces at two to three times their actual numbers and was forever on the point of retreat. After three and a half months, McClellan's offensive had clearly failed, although (since he could always manage a masterly retreat), he avoided actual disaster.

The "Army of the Potomac," which McClellan had trained, was therefore placed under John Pope (1822–1892), who had won some victories out west. On August 29, 1862, Pope sought out Lee and Jackson to destroy them. He did not wish to imitate McClellan's caution, so he attacked heedlessly at the Second Battle of Bull Run. Lee played him properly, caught him by surprise on his left flank, and sent him reeling back to Washington with heavy losses. McClellan, heading another army, might have rescued the situation by coming to Pope's aid, but it was not his intention to do so. He undoubtedly wanted Pope to lose, and he got what he wanted. An unhappy Lincoln put the army back under McClellan.

Meanwhile, Lee was following up his victory by invading the Union. A defeat of the Union on Union soil might persuade Great Britain and France to aid the Confederacy openly (as the surrender at Saratoga had persuaded France to help the American revolutionaries openly nearly a century earlier).

As for Lincoln, he was planning to gain the support of liberals in Great Britain and France (and everywhere in Europe) by liberating the slaves. He could not do it, however, while he was being defeated by the Confederacy, since it would then appear like a move of desperation. He had to wait for an important victory so that it would seem like an act of magnanimity.

That victory ought to have come in Maryland, for by the sheerest accident, McClellan had managed to learn Lee's complete plan of campaign. He knew exactly where and when Lee planned to have his army and what he intended to do with it. Any moderately capable general, with this information, would have had Lee at his mercy, would have destroyed the Confederate army, and might have gone a long way toward ending the war then and there. However, the egregious McClellan moved so slowly and fought so irresolutely at Antietam, Maryland, on September 17, 1862, that the greatly outnumbered Lee could still manage to disengage and move quietly back across the Potomac.

Since Lee had to retreat, Lincoln called it a victory and, on September 23, 1862, issued the "Emancipation Proclamation," freeing all slaves in Confederate hands (but not those in areas occupied by Union armies) on January 1, 1863. McClellan was freed of his command a second time and never fought again.

Now the army was in the hands of Ambrose Everett Burnside (1824–1881), perhaps the least capable general ever to command a major American army. To his credit, he announced his own incapacity, but wasn't believed. (He is remembered today chiefly for his magnificent side-whiskers that were called "burnsides" after him, a word which got reversed to "sideburns.") Lincoln said of him later on that he could snatch defeat from the very jaws of victory.

On December 13, 1862, Burnside fought Lee at Fredericksburg, Virginia, about halfway between Washington and Richmond. Here, Burnside sent his men charging the heights on which Confederate artillery was mounted. There were 13 charges, each of which was shot into near-annihilation. It was the worst Union defeat of the war and Burnside was withdrawn from command.

In the west meanwhile, the Mississippi River had been taken by the Union, all except for Vicksburg, Mississippi. Ulysses Grant was in charge of the campaign to take it. It was a firmly held, nearly impregnable position, but Grant was the very opposite of McClellan. He never gave up, and each failure merely taught him what not to do, so that he tried something else.

Replacing Burnside in the east was Joseph Hooker (1814–1879). On May 1, 1863, he met the team of Lee and Jackson at Chancellorsville, just about six miles west of Fredericksburg. As usual, the Union forces far outnumbered the Confederates, but by that time, the Union generals so feared Lee that they were half-paralyzed before the battle even started. Hooker remained on the defensive and was crushed.

On May 2, however, Stonewall Jackson went out at night to reconnoiter and was shot by his own men who were unaware of his identity. He died on May 10, an irreparable loss to the Confederacy.

The Union had suffered defeat after defeat in Virginia, but it is important to realize that despite the defeats, it was growing steadily stronger, economically. It was prospering, selling its wheat worldwide, receiving in return whatever it needed for the war effort. The Confederacy, in contrast, was stagnant, its cotton penned up at home by the blockade. The Union had a growing rail network that could bring up reinforcements and supplies wherever necessary. The Confederacy had a much smaller one and couldn't even make repairs to what it had, so that its soldiers were semistarved at all times. Immigrants poured into the Union, looking for high wages, and they made up a third of the Union forces. None arrived in the Confederacy.

Still, the Confederacy didn't have to conquer. They just had to wait till the Union grew tired of fighting, and it was not inconceivable that that might happen. There were many in the Union who opposed the war, some out of idealistic distaste for death and destruction, and others out of outright pro-Confederate sympathies. The latter were called "copperheads" after the poisonous snake that (unlike the rattlesnake) strikes without warning. The leading Copperhead was an Ohio Congressman of slave-state descent, Clement Laird Vallandigham (1820–1871), who fought the war tirelessly.

Then, too, Lincoln had to impose conscription, when volunteers were simply not plentiful enough to fill the army. This was resented, of course. The climax came in New York where Irish immigrants somehow got the idea that they were to be drafted in order that blacks might take their jobs at lower wages. Four days of rioting (July 13–16, 1863) broke out in which numerous inoffensive blacks were killed and millions of dollars of damages were inflicted.

It seemed to Lee that a Confederate victory on Union soil, added to the series of Union disasters in Virginia, would enormously strengthen Copperhead sentiment in the Union and increase to the boiling point the seething resentment over the hardships the war had brought. The Union would have to face the fact that endless fighting was silly when the Confederacy was ready to stop at any time, provided the Union simply agreed to leave them alone.

With that in mind, Lee, after Chancellorsville, decided to invade the Union again. On June 15, 1863, Lee crossed the Potomac River into Maryland a second time, and was into south-central Pennsylvania by June 28. On that day, Hooker was relieved of command and George Gordon Meade (1815–1872) was put in charge of the Army of the Potomac.

On June 30, contingents of the opposing armies met near Gettysburg, more or less by accident. As more and more units poured into the area, there came to be the three-day battle of Gettysburg, the greatest battle ever fought in the Western Hemisphere.

On the first day, July 1, the Confederates had somewhat the better of it, but Lee was fighting blind, because his cavalry, commanded by James Ewell Brown ("Jeb") Stuart (1833–1864), was off on some quixotic mission of its own, unaware that the unplanned battle was taking place.

On July 2, the two armies fought to a draw, but the Union forces could afford a draw against Lee, after so many defeats. Lee could not afford one. A draw would mean retreat and that was not what he was after. He had to *win*.

On July 3, therefore, Lee sent in 15,500 fresh men under George Edward Pickett (1825–1875), to break the Union lines. The Union forces, however, had their artillery in place, and waited. There followed "Pickett's Charge," perhaps the most glamorous single action of the war. It was like the Charge of the Light Brigade, nine years earlier, but on a much larger scale. The Union guns roared. Three fourths of Pickett's men were casualties and the remainder staggered back in stunned disarray. On July 4, Lee had to retreat.

Had Meade now counterattacked, he might have destroyed Lee's army, but his own army had been badly mauled, and Meade lacked the grim determination to pursue. Lee's army made its way safely back to Virginia.

However, the battle of Gettysburg was a clear Union victory. Lee had finally been defeated and that was the turning point of the war. And on that same July 4, 1863 of Lee's retreat, Grant took Vicksburg and the Mississippi River was completely in Union hands.

The Confederacy managed one more great victory, however, one that did not involve Lee.

William Starke Rosecrans (1819–1898) had led a Union army into the northwest corner of Georgia, near Chickamauga Creek. There, on September 19, 1863, Confederate forces under Braxton Bragg (1817–1876) attacked. In the Battle of Chickamauga that followed, the Confederates plunged through a gap in the Union line. It might have been a complete disaster but a contingent of Union forces under George Henry Thomas (1816–1870), like Scott a Virginian who was loyal to the Union, withstood the Confederate attack firmly and this allowed the Union army to get away in good order. Thomas was known as the "Rock of Chickamauga" as a result. However, the Union army was now penned up in Chattanooga in southeastern Tennessee and

might be forced to surrender, which would be a stunning blow to Union morale.

By now, though, Lincoln finally had his man. He had tried McClellan, Pope, McClellan again, Burnside, Hooker, and Meade, and had found each of them wanting. But now he had Grant, and he put him in complete charge of all the armies west of the Alleghenies. Grant hurried to Chattanooga, replaced Rosecrans with Thomas, and, in an aggressive offensive on November 24–25, defeated Bragg, relieved Chattanooga, and sent the Union army once more into Georgia.

Meanwhile, on November 19, 1863, a cemetery was being dedicated at Gettysburg where those who died in the great battle might be buried and remembered. President Lincoln attended, and after the great orator, Edward Everett (1794–1865), had delivered a carefully memorized 13,000-word speech for two hours, Lincoln stood up and delivered his "Gettysburg Address" in only three minutes. There is, however, no question that this little speech was one of the greatest, if not *the* greatest, in history.

By the end of 1863, the Confederacy was penned up in the southeastern coastal states, and the blockade had reduced it to near-starvation. About the only bright spot for the Confederacy were the actions of privateers on the excellent ships that had been built in Great Britain before the United States threatened war and put a stop to it. The chief of these privateers was the *Alabama* under Raphael Semmes (1809–1877), which was still at large at the end of 1863. These Confederate ships wrought formidable havoc on American shipping.

On March 9, 1864, Lincoln put Grant in charge of all the Union armies, and Grant prepared a two-pronged advance. He would lead the army in Virginia and his trusted subordinate, William Tecumeseh Sherman (1820–1891), would lead it in Georgia. It was Grant's intention to end the war by making use of Union superiority in men and armaments, to hit the Confederate armies at whatever cost, to bore in and bore in regardless of losses—no retreat if defeated—until the Confederacy gave up. And that was precisely what he proceeded to do.

On May 4, 1864, Grant moved south. In a

month of bloody fighting, he reached the neighborhood of Richmond. Lee fought with enormous skill, but Grant kept boring in and receiving reinforcements. There were no reinforcements for Lee and he grew weaker and weaker, while Grant grew stronger and stronger.

Lee tried to divert Grant by feinting an attack on Washington. This had worked against McClellan two years before. It didn't work with Grant. He didn't care what happened to Washington; he wasn't going to take his hand from Lee's throat.

Meanwhile, Sherman was slogging toward Atlanta in the same dogged fashion.

While both campaigns were going on, the election of 1864 took place. Never before had a Presidential election had to be carried on in wartime, and in the most desperate war ever to be fought on American soil, too. Lincoln would have surprised no one, at home or abroad, if he had postponed the election on the ground of the national emergency, but he did not. Civil war and desperation notwithstanding, the Constitution had to be upheld and the metronome-like regularity of elections had to continue. The opposition must have its full chance of defeating him. Of all Lincoln's acts, setting that precedent may have been the greatest service he did for the nation.

Running against Lincoln was McClellan, under whom the war would surely have fallen apart and the nation with it. Yet it looked as though McClellan might win the election. During the entire campaign, Grant kept the city of Petersburg, about 20 miles south of Richmond, under siege, and Lee's army with it. He was slowly and surely strangling Lee, but it didn't look it from far away, and the siege did Lincoln no good.

However, on June 19, 1864, the Union warship *Kearsarge* finally sank the *Alabama* off Cherbourg, France. On August 5, 1864, Farragut attacked Mobile, Alabama. The harbor was littered with mines, or "torpedoes" as they were called, but Farragut shouted, "Damn the torpedoes! Full speed ahead!" and took Mobile. Just about the last breathing hole of the Confederacy was closed.

And on September 1, 1864, Sherman took Atlanta, Georgia. Clearly, the Confederacy was on its last legs, and Lincoln won reelection as enthusiasm suddenly began to rise in the Union.

By the end of the year, Sherman had marched through Georgia from Atlanta to Savannah, which he took on December 21, 1864.

Lee was made general-in-chief by Jefferson Davis on February 3, 1865, but there was virtually nothing to be general-in-chief over. Sherman was advancing from the south, and when Lee tried to break Grant's grip on Petersburg on March 25, he failed.

Lee finally gave up Petersburg and retreated, trying to join one other ragged Confederate army to the south. All attempts were foiled and, on April 9, 1865, with absolutely no alternative, Lee surrendered to Grant at Appomatox Court House, Virginia. Except for cleaning up some scraps here and there, the American Civil War was over with a Union victory.

Then, on April 14, 1865, President Lincoln was shot by a half-mad Southern-sympathizing actor, John Wilkes Booth (1838–1865), and died the next day. He was succeeded by his Vice-President, Andrew Johnson (1808–1875), who became the 17th President of the United States.

During the war, the American national debt went from $64 million to $2,773 million. The first income tax was established in August of 1861. Three new states were added: Kansas on January 19, 1861; West Virginia (carved out of Virginia) on June 20, 1863; and Nevada on October 31, 1864. That made 36 states altogether.

The Civil War was the first to be photographed. Matthew B. Brady (1823–1896), working in the field with primitive equipment, took excellent photographs, which helped make the public aware of photography as a contribution to the recording of everyday life.

Even while the United States was fighting the Confederacy so bitterly, there were regiments fighting Native Americans in the west.

There were literally hundreds of battles of all sizes as the United States carried through a virtually genocidal war that killed off most Native Americans and put the remainder on reservations.

The best remembered battle is, of course, an American defeat. A small detachment led by George Armstrong Custer (1839–1876) attacked the Sioux under Crazy Horse (1842–1877) at the Battle of the Little Big Horn on June 25, 1876, and were wiped out to a man, a poor way of celebrating the centennial of American independence, which came nine days later. (The defeat had no great ramifications. The Sioux were defeated a half-year later.)

An Apache leader in the southwest, Cochise (1812–1874) held off American forces in the 1860s, but had to give in at the end. Then, too, in 1877, Chief Joseph (1840–1904) of the Nez Perce, showed himself to be a much better general than the Army officers sent against him, but he had only 300 warriors to start with, and the sheer weight of numbers finally brought him down.

All Native American resistance was futile in the long run. The advance of the white man was sustained and irresistible.

In the west, this was the era of the "cowboy," the brief establishment of a nomadic way of life that centered on large herds of cattle roaming the grasslands. Some of the names of the scouts, trappers, and marshals of the time are still remembered with a thick layer of idealistic fictionalization. Among them were William Frederick ("Buffalo Bill") Cody (1846–1917); Christopher ("Kit") Carson (1809–1868); James Butler ("Wild Bill") Hickok (1837–1876); William Barclay ("Bat") Masterson (1853–1921); Wyatt Barry Stapp Earp (1848–1929); and so on. There were also outlaws (some of whom were also subjected to idealistic fictionalization), such as William ("Billy the Kid") Bonney (1859–1881) and Jesse Woodson James (1847–1882).

After the war, Congress was dominated by "Radical" Republicans who wanted to treat the conquered Confederacy as though it were enemy territory. Leading them was Thaddeus Stevens (1792–1868) of Pennsylvania. President Johnson, who was from Tennessee, wanted gentler treatment, but he lacked tact and was anything but a smooth politician.

The Radicals put through three amendments to the Constitution. The 13th Amendment, ratified on December 13, 1865, abolished slavery. The 14th Amendment, ratified on June 13, 1866, made all people born in the United States (including blacks) citizens with full rights. It also stated that no person could be deprived of life, liberty, or property without due process of law. (Eventually, it was decided that a corporation was a person under the protection of this amendment and it was used to protect businesses against legislative action designed to correct corruption and abuse.) The 15th Amendment, ratified on February 26, 1869, gave blacks the vote, though many states quickly worked out ways of keeping them from voting just the same.

During this time, the Radicals and President Johnson were at daggers drawn, and the fight came to a climax on February 24, 1868, when Johnson was impeached (i.e., accused of crimes and misdemeanors) by the House of Representatives, the only Presidential impeachment in history. He was then tried by the Senate with the Chief Justice presiding. Two thirds of the Senate (i.e., 36 votes out of 54) had to be against Johnson to convict. The Radicals got only 35 votes and Johnson was acquitted.

One important event of Johnson's term that had nothing to do with "Reconstruction" (the rehabilitation and the readmission to the Union of the ex-Confederate States) came on March 30, 1867, when the United States, for $7.2 million, bought Alaska from Russia. This was negotiated for the United States by Secretary of State Seward, and Alaska was derided as "Seward's Folly" for a time.

In 1868, Grant was elected the 18th President. Although a great general, Grant was a poor politician and a poor judge of men where military affairs were not concerned. The eight years of his two terms in the White House were a time of great corruption.

There were "robber barons" among businessmen, who fleeced the public with their rascally financial manipulations. Examples were Daniel Drew (1797–1879), Jason ("Jay") Gould (1836–1892), James Fisk (1834–1872), and Cornelius Vanderbilt (1794–1877).

There were politicians who ran crooked city machines, such as the infamous William Marcy

("Boss") Tweed (1823–1878), who, with his sidekicks, the "Tweed Ring," skimmed $200 million out of New York City (the equivalent of $5 or $6 billion today, probably). That the Tweed Ring was defeated was largely the result of the mordant and witty cartoons of the most important cartoonist in American history, Thomas Nast (1840–1902). His depiction of Tweed and his cronies aroused public anger, and Tweed died in jail. In fact, at one time, when he tried to escape, he was recognized by someone who had seen Nast's caricatures, and brought back. Nast invented the Democratic donkey and the Republican elephant, and was the first to picture Santa Claus in the form we now find familiar.

There were even manipulators and bribe acceptors in Congress up to Grant's secretary and his Vice-President, although Grant himself seems to have been honest.

There were technological advances in Grant's administration. Six days after he was inaugurated, the rail network stretched from sea to sea as the first transcontinental railroad tracks were completed with the driving in of a golden spike in the railbed at Ogden, Utah.

Christopher Latham Sholes (1819–1890) patented the typewriter on June 23, 1868. Its services to the writing profession and to office work generally were enormous. It was also the device that was the first, eventually, to bring women out of the home and into the office.

George Westinghouse (1846–1914) invented the air-brake in 1869. It could stop trains in case of emergency more effectively than anything else could and contributed greatly to rail safety. Also in 1869, John Wesley Hyatt (1837–1920) produced celluloid, the first synthetic plastic.

Most important of all, perhaps, Alexander Graham Bell (1847–1922) invented the telephone and patented it on February 14, 1876. The Centennial Exposition, celebrating a hundred years of American independence, was held in 1876, and a working telephone was the prize exhibit.

There were also disasters. On October 8, 1871, the great Chicago fire burned down much of the city.

After the Civil War, Nebraska entered the Union on March 1, 1867, and Colorado on Au-

gust 1, 1876. By the end of Grant's administration, there were 38 states in the Union.

The United States was also beginning to pick up territory overseas. On August 28, 1867, the United States annexed Midway Island, and on February 17, 1878, it took over Pago Pago in the Samoan Islands. These were coaling stations, needed to fuel ships, particularly warships, making the long trans-Pacific run.

In 1876, the Republican candidate, Rutherford Birchard Hayes (1822–1893), and the Democratic candidate, Samuel Jones Tilden (1814–1886), ended up in a disputed election (the only one in American history). Tilden had the majority of the popular vote and won 184 electoral votes to Hayes's 165. There were, however, 20 electoral votes that were in dispute for a variety of reasons. Objectively, they should probably have gone to Tilden, but a partisan arbitration board awarded all 20 to Hayes, who therefore won 185 to 184. To avoid trouble, Tilden patriotically accepted the loss.

Part of the deal that gave Hayes an undeserved presidency was the end of Reconstruction in the South. The last Federal troops were withdrawn on April 24, 1877, and the ex-Confederate states went back to their accustomed ways. The blacks were no longer slaves, but it was only the name that was lacking. They had no rights worth mentioning and the rest of the nation looked the other way.

Thomas Alva Edison (1847–1931), the greatest inventor the world ever saw, continued the American rise to technological preeminence in the world. He invented the phonograph in 1878 and the electric light in 1879. He also devised electric generating stations that could take on ever-changing loads and deliver a reliable electric current.

Edison clung to direct-current, but George Westinghouse favored electrical technology on an alternating-current basis and developed Niagara Falls as a generator of such currents. The fight between them was a bruising one, but Westinghouse won.

James Buchanan Eads (1820–1887) had invented the diving bell for work under water (and it became more practical once Paul Bert of France had worked out the cause and prevention of the bends). Eads built the first bridge across the Mississippi at St. Louis, Missouri, between 1867 and 1874. The German-born John Augustus Roebling (1806–1879) and his son, Washington Augustus Roebling (1837–1926), labored through the 1870s on the Brooklyn Bridge, connecting Manhattan and Brooklyn. It was the first great suspension bridge.

The United States lagged in pure science as compared to the European scientific giants of Germany and Great Britain. Americans who wished graduate training in science had to go to Europe. There were signs, though, that this would not be ever so. The Massachusetts Institute of Technology (MIT) was founded in 1861, and in that same year Yale was the first American university to award a Doctor of Philosophy (Ph.D.) degree.

Even so, the United States turned out one first-class theoretical physical chemist in the person of Josiah Willard Gibbs (1839–1903). Between 1876 and 1878, he published a series of papers that established chemical thermodynamics on a firm foundation. He also formulated the "phase rule," which is particularly important in physical chemistry.

Henry Augustus Rowland (1848–1901), in the 1870s, manufactured the best gratings that had yet been seen, and they raised the art of spectroscopy to new heights of delicacy and precision.

The greatest American writer of this period (or possibly of any period) was Samuel Langhorne Clemens (1835–1910), a western writer who wrote under the pseudonym of "Mark Twain." He came to public notice with his sketch "The Celebrated Jumping Frog of Calaveras County" in 1865, and then to runaway success with his *The Innocents Abroad*, a hilarious account of his travels overseas. He published *Roughing It* in 1872, and then, turning to fiction, wrote the classic *Tom Sawyer* in 1876.

Also a westerner was Francis Brett ("Bret") Harte (1836–1902), best remembered for his stories "The Luck of Roaring Camp" and "Outcasts of Poker Flat," both appearing in 1870. More in the mainstream was Henry James' (1843–1916) *Daisy Miller* in 1879.

Little Women, published in 1868–1869 by Louisa May Alcott (1833–1888), has remained perennially popular. Horatio Alger, Jr. (1832–1899) wrote a series of moralistic rags-to-riches stories of virtue rewarded, beginning in 1869, that were widely popular in their time, but have been largely forgotten since.

Lewis ("Lew") Wallace (1827–1905), who was a general in the Civil War, is far better remembered today as the author of *Ben Hur*, published in 1880. Edward Everett Hale (1822–1909) wrote the touching tale *Man Without a Country* in 1863, to encourage patriotism.

In poetry in that same year of 1863, Longfellow wrote "The Midnight Ride of Paul Revere," and Whittier wrote "Barbara Frietchie," both with the encouragement of patriotism in mind. Walt Whitman (1819–1892) was becoming famous for the free verse in his *Leaves of Grass* (loudly denounced by some), but he also wrote the conventional and touching "O Captain, My Captain" on the death of Abraham Lincoln. Julia Ward Howe (1819–1910), an active abolitionist, pacifist, and feminist, is not remembered for this so much, as for the fact that she wrote "The Battle Hymn of the Republic" in 1862.

An influential work of nonfiction was *Progress and Poverty*, completed in 1879 by Henry George (1839–1897), who advanced the notion of a "single tax" on land.

Two of the artists working in the United States at this time were Winslow Homer (1836–1910) and Thomas Eakins (1844–1916). Daniel Chester French (1850–1931) was beginning to make a name for himself as a sculptor, carving the famous statue of the Minute Man at Concord, Massachusetts in 1873.

A well-known composer of the period was James A. Bland (1835–1899), who wrote such perennial favorites as "Carry me Back to Old Virginny," "Oh, Dem Golden Slippers," and "In the Evening by the Moonlight." (Bland was black, and his achievements were unusual in his day.) Just before Stephen Foster died in 1864, he composed his most haunting song, "Beautiful Dreamer."

American preoccupation with religion continued. Mary Baker Eddy (1821–1910) founded

Christian Science in 1866 and wrote *Science and Health* as its basis in 1875. Charles Taze Russell (1852–1916) founded Jehovah's Witnesses in 1877, preaching the imminent Second Coming, and over a century later his followers still consider it imminent.

Other beginnings were made. Barnum opened his first circus in 1871, labeling it "The Greatest Show on Earth." And in 1872, Yellowstone Park in Wyoming was established as the first national park. On a much smaller scale, Central Park in Manhattan was opened to the public in 1876.

CANADA

On March 29, 1867, Ontario, Quebec, New Brunswick, and Nova Scotia became four provinces of a federal government given the name of "The Dominion of Canada" on July 1.

The northern and western portion of Canada ("Northwest Territories") was still owned by the Hudson Bay Company, which had been founded in 1670. The Company was bought out, however, on November 19, 1869, for $1.5 million.

The Native Americans of the Northwest Territories, fearing its takeover by the Canadians, launched a rebellion under Louis Riel (1844–1885). For a brief time they penetrated as far south as what is now Winnipeg, but this "Red River Rebellion" was quickly dispersed.

Other provinces joined the Dominion: Manitoba in 1870, British Columbia in 1871, and Prince Edward Island in 1873.

MEXICO

Juarez, who was elected President in January 1861, tried to establish a liberal, democratic government. The previous rulers of Mexico, however, had managed to empty the treasury so that it was impossible for Mexico to make payments on the European loans that had accumulated over time. Juarez suspended such payments for two years; he had no choice.

The European creditors—Great Britain, France, and Spain—took advantage of the United States' preoccupation with the Civil War and landed troops in Vera Cruz on December 17, 1861, in order to extort debt payments.

Napoleon III of France planned to go further than that. He wanted to establish a Mexico that was under French domination. Great Britain and Spain, who foresaw entanglements with the United States, left on April 8, 1862, and Napoleon felt he had a free hand.

He quickly found it wasn't easy. It took the French, even with reinforcements, a year to fight their way into Mexico City, which they took on June 7, 1863 (three weeks before the Union victory at Gettysburg made it certain that the Civil War would end with the United States intact).

Napoleon III then persuaded the Archduke Maximilian (1832–1867), a younger brother of Francis Joseph I of Austria, to take the Mexican throne. He came to Mexico City on June 12, 1863, and called himself Emperor of Mexico. Maximilian was a liberal and, apparently, an earnest man who intended to be a good ruler, but he never had any power that did not depend on the French military.

Juarez, though forced to leave his capital, fought a guerrilla war against the French and against those Mexican conservatives who gladly joined the invaders. What's more, the United States would not recognize Maximilian, but held firmly with Juarez as legal ruler of Mexico.

When the Civil War ended in 1865, the United States began to demand a French withdrawal from Mexico with increasing force and increasing impatience. Veteran American soldiers, hardened in war, and under tested generals, lined up at the Rio Grande, and Napoleon III quailed. Maximilian's wife, Carlota (1840–1927), raced to Europe to plead with Napoleon III and with the Pope; when she found she could do nothing, she went mad and remained mad until she died 60 years later.

Napoleon III withdrew his troops on March 12, 1867, and Maximilian should surely have left with them. Unfortunately, Maximilian had the idea that the people of Mexico were on his side and he refused to abdicate. He was captured by Juarez' troops on May 15, 1867, and was executed June 19.

Juarez died in 1872 and was succeeded as

president by Sebastian Lerdo de Tejada (1827–1889), one of his supporters. In 1876, however, Porfirio Diaz (1830–1915), who had also fought for Juarez, seized power and was then formally elected President in 1877. He established a stable government at the price of imposing a dictatorship.

PARAGUAY

Paraguay, at the time the only landlocked South American nation, fought a particularly melancholy war in this period.

In 1862, Francisco Solano Lopez (1827–1870) succeeded his father as president of Paraguay. Like his father, he was an autocratic dictator and, worse yet, had dreams of establishing an overlordship over a much wider territory. He went to war, therefore, quite unnecessarily, with Brazil, Argentina, and Uruguay.

The war continued for eight years until Lopez was captured by Brazilian soldiers and was shot on March 1, 1870. In those eight years, Paraguay was almost annihilated as a nation. The Paraguayan population was reduced from 1,400,000 to about 221,000, of whom only 29,000 were adult males.

PERU

Although the French invasion of Mexico was the most serious infraction of the Monroe Doctrine during the time of the American Civil War, it was not the only one.

Spain had never recognized the independence of Peru, and there was a constant sputtering of controversy between the two nations. Spain complained that Peru was mistreating Spanish immigrants, and, in retaliation, some Spanish ships seized the tiny Chincha Islands just off the central Peruvian coast on April 14, 1864. This was worse than it sounds, for the islands were covered with guano, the excrement of sea-birds, which was very valuable as fertilizer and an important source of revenue for Peru.

A treaty in which Spain recognized Peru's independence was then signed on January 27, 1865. It contained provisions unacceptable to the Peruvians, who drove out the president who had signed the treaty. The next president declared war on Spain on January 14, 1866, and persuaded Ecuador to the north and Chile to the south to join him in this. Spanish ships bombarded Valparaiso, Chile and Callao, Peru in March, but then, since the United States was not amused, Spain abandoned the war. The United States mediated a peace in 1871.

ARGENTINA

Argentina faced not only the inevitable difficulties that arose because of the war with Paraguay between 1865 and 1870, but also a problem in attaining unity. The province of Buenos Aires (including the city itself) was the most populous and developed province, and it had the tendency to try to dominate the land. The other provinces resented this. The matter was not settled until 1880, when the city of Buenos Aires was separated from the province and made the capital as a federal district, rather like Washington, D.C. in the United States.

CHILE

Under the presidency of Jose Joaquin Perez (1800–1889), who ruled from 1861 to 1871, and his successor, Chile was reasonably democratic, progressive, and peaceful, but for the nearly comic-opera war with Spain in 1866. Under Anibal Pinto (1825–1884), however, Chile declared war on Bolivia and Peru on April 5, 1879 ("War of the Pacific"), which was a more serious affair.

COLOMBIA

Like Argentina, Colombia had to overcome decentralizing tendencies, but managed to form a federal union of its various provinces on May 8, 1863.

VENEZUELA

In Venezuela, the situation was the reverse of that in Argentina and Colombia. There, the existence of an overpowerful central government raised dissatisfaction. It was eased into a federal union about the same time that such a union was established in Colombia.

BRAZIL

Brazil, the one nation south of the Rio Grande that was of Portuguese rather than Spanish culture, was also the only one that was not a republic at this time (if one doesn't count the artificial and brief "Mexican Empire" briefly set up by Napoleon III).

Under the rule of Pedro II, Brazil continued stable and prosperous. There was an expansionist tendency into Uruguay to the southeast that didn't work, and an alliance with Argentina and Uruguay that fought the appalling war with Paraguay.

After 1870, there was a strong movement toward freeing slaves in the nation. It was eventually accomplished without war and without compensation to slave-owners.

As an historical footnote, Pedro II visited the United States in 1876, the first crowned head ever to visit that nation. He attended the Centennial Exposition and was shown the newly invented telephone. He put the receiver to his ear and dropped it with the surprised exclamation, "It talks!" There could have been no more effective advertisement for the device.

CENTRAL AMERICA

The region in this period, and for a considerable time afterward, was in chaos over various attempts to unify it; attempts that were steadily thwarted by the continuing rivalry between different sections. Here no reasonable solution was reached; no federal system was agreed on.

CUBA

Although Spain had lost all its mainland colonies in the Western Hemisphere, it retained the ownership of Cuba, which it had first settled two and a half centuries earlier. Spanish rule, however, was harsh and was perceived by the Cubans to be unjust. In 1868, they rose in revolt, and the

fighting lasted 10 years before Spain managed to restore order. The United States was sympathetic with the Cuban rebels but did not intervene directly. After all, Spain had owned Cuba all along, which meant it didn't come under the Monroe Doctrine. Besides, the United States was busy quarreling with Great Britain for having aided American rebels. For the United States, at the same time, to aid rebels against Spain would have marred its case.

DOMINICAN REPUBLIC

The Dominican Republic, the eastern two thirds of the island of Hispaniola, had for a time been dominated by Haiti, making up the western third. It had broken free, but in 1861, still fearing Haiti, the Dominican Republic asked Spain to take over the land again. (It had been under Spanish rule in earlier times.) The United States might not have permitted this to take place if it were not fighting the Civil War.

Spain ruled so harshly that the Dominican Republic rebelled and, on May 1, 1865, regained its independence. With the Civil War just ended, Spain thought it prudent not to object to this.

The Dominican Republic still felt insecure and, beginning in 1868, it put out feelers concerning the possibility of being annexed by the United States. President Grant felt a rather naive pleasure at the possibility, and urged that the Dominican Republic be taken into the fold. The Senate, however, did not want to take over a depressed peasantry, a corrupt ruling class, and a troubled western border. It refused to accept an annexation treaty and the Dominican Republic remained independent.

EGYPT

Egypt was still, in theory, part of the dominions of the Ottoman Empire, and was ruled by a Viceroy, Ismail (1830–1895), who succeeded his uncle, Said, in 1863. Egypt was at this time in an era of prosperity since the American Civil War had cut off the supply of American cotton to European factories, thanks to the Union blockade of the Confederate States. The result was that Egyptian cotton sold in all available quantities for premium prices.

This meant that not only did Ismail have money, but he could easily borrow more, and banks were willing to lend it to him at high interest rates. Ismail used the money to finance the building of the Suez Canal. He also built irrigation canals, railroads, bridges, telegraphs, and schools, in an attempt to modernize the country.

All this was very worthy, but it was at the cost of complete financial chaos. When Ismail came to power, Egypt's national debt was 7 million pounds. Fourteen years later, in 1876, it stood at nearly 100 million pounds. It didn't help that Ismail was also an expansionist who tried to spread Egyptian influence southward into Sudan and who, in 1875, went to war with Ethiopia. After all, even small wars are very expensive.

On November 17, 1869, the Suez Canal was officially opened. Present at the elaborate festivities were Francis Joseph I of Austria and the Empress Eugenie of France. On that occasion, also, the premiere of Giuseppe Verdi's *Aida* was presented. It was no coincidence at all that the plot involved the conquest of ancient Ethiopia (the region we now call Sudan) by ancient Egypt.

The Sudan was conquered, at least temporarily, by Egyptian forces under the command of British generals, notably Charles George Gordon (1833–1885), who had fought in the Crimean War and in China. The conquest of Sudan led to the suppression of the slave trade there.

The use of British generals was one of the marks of the penetration of British influence into Egypt. In November 1875, Ismail desperately needed money with which to make payments on his debt. Therefore, he sold his 176,000 shares in the Suez Canal to Great Britain for 100 million francs. This coup was carried through by Disraeli, and Great Britain was now the largest single shareholder of the Canal, even though it did not own an absolute majority of the shares.

This did not settle Ismail's troubles by any means. His creditors, especially Great Britain and France, kept pressing, and on February 18, 1879, he was deposed by the Ottoman sultan. Ismail's son, Muhammed Tawfiq (1852–1892) became Viceroy. By that time, though, Egypt was under the financial control of Great Britain and France, acting in cooperation.

ETHIOPIA

Theodore was still ruler of Ethiopia at the beginning of this period. Between 1864 and 1866, having grown offended with the British government, he began to throw British consular officials and British missionaries into jail.

In 1868, some 32,000 British and Indian troops under Robert Cornelis Napier (1810–1890), who had been active in suppressing the Sepoy mutiny, landed on the Red Sea coast and moved into the interior. On April 10, they defeated Ethiopian forces and Theodore committed suicide. The invading troops marched on to Magdala in northern Ethiopia, which had been Theodore's capital, and took it on April 13, freeing the British prisoners. The British troops then left the country.

In 1872, Johannes IV (1831–1889) became king of Ethiopia and fought against Ismail of Egypt between 1875 and 1879.

TUNIS

Tunis, nominally part of the Ottoman Empire, was, like Egypt, heavily in debt to European bankers. It was inevitably going to be under European control, but the question was whether it would be France or Italy that would do the controlling. France was the stronger power, but Italy felt a traditional interest in Tunis because it was the site of dead Carthage, which Rome had defeated 2000 years earlier. By 1880, the issue still had not been settled.

CONGO

A French-born American explorer, Paul du Chaillu (1831–1903), explored Central Africa (the Congo) in the late 1850s and early 1860s and brought the gorilla to the world's attention for the first time in *Stories of the Gorilla Country*, which he published in 1868. He gave the world a rather exaggerated idea of the animal's ferocity, however.

In 1876, Leopold II of Belgium organized a

committee for the exploration and "civilization" of the region.

WEST AFRICA

Germany, France, and Great Britain were penetrating this region. German traders were establishing themselves on the Cameroon coast; the French were pushing into Dahomey, and the British were taking over portions of Nigeria. The process termed "the partition of Africa" was well under way.

ZANZIBAR

On March 10, 1862, the British and French recognized the independence of Zanzibar, an island off the east central coast of Africa, whose Sultan also ruled the African coast north and south of the island. In 1873, the British forced the closing of the slave markets in Zanzibar.

EAST AFRICA

East Africa was the site of the exploration activity of the British missionary, David Livingstone (1813–1873). In his effort to explore the regions about the sources of the Nile in the 1860s, he was lost to the Western world for a time.

A British reporter, Henry Morton Stanley (1841–1904), was sent by *The New York Herald* to find Livingstone. He did so in November 1871, and greeted him with characteristic British aplomb: "Dr. Livingstone, I presume?" He then circled the shores of Lake Victoria and discovered Lake Edward.

SOUTH AFRICA

Both the Boers and the British continued to fight the blacks, and, of course, both won their wars and continued to absorb tribal territory and to reduce the blacks to servitude. The most violent of the wars was that of the British against the Zulus in 1879. It continued for half a year before the Zulu power was broken. The most notable event of the war came on June 1, 1879, when Napoleon III's son, the Prince Imperial, was killed in action by the Zulus. If there had ever been hope for a Bonapartist restoration, it died with the Prince Imperial.

In 1867, diamonds were discovered in South Africa and, as luck would have it, the site in question was not clearly in either Boer or British territory. The British took it and, in 1871, founded the town of Kimberly to serve as a diamond center.

In 1877, the British annexed the South African Republic, which was Boer-controlled, thus negating their recognition of the country's independence a quarter century before.

MADAGASCAR

The French had been interested in Madagascar since the time of Louis XIV and had, on occasion, attempted to penetrate the country and gain some control of it, usually in competition with the British.

On August 8, 1868, Madagascar signed a treaty with France that gave the French jurisdiction over their own nationals on the island. After that, French influence increased rapidly.

PERSIA

In this period, both Russian and British influence grew in the nation, and it was only the antagonism between the European powers that kept Persia from falling to one or the other.

AFGHANISTAN

Afghanistan was also the scene of Russian–British rivalry. When the Afghani ruler, Sher Ali, proved too pro-Russian for British liking, the British sent in an invading force in November 1878. This began the "Second Afghan War." It took two years of fighting before the British managed to install a pro-British government.

INDIA

India was largely at peace in this period and the British continued with public works of all kinds. India experienced a time of prosperity during the

American Civil War, when her cotton was much in demand. The demand collapsed once the Civil War was over, but another period of prosperity came with the opening of the Suez Canal in 1869, something that greatly augmented trade between Europe and India.

In 1877, Queen Victoria was declared Empress of India and a most ceremonious celebration of this took place in Delhi.

SIAM

Rama V (1853–1910) succeeded his father in 1868 at the age of 15 and began to rule in his own name in 1873. He continued his father's reforming policies and, in 1874, abolished slavery. He completely reformed the administrative and financial procedures of the government. He was the first Siamese monarch to travel outside the country, visiting India, for instance, to study administrative procedures.

INDO-CHINA

During this period, France gained control of the area that now includes Kampuchea, Laos, and Vietnam, which came to be called "French Indo-China."

MALAYA

During this period, the British were penetrating Malaya and gaining control.

CHINA

The T'ai P'ing rebellion had brought China to the brink of destruction. In the chaos that wrung the land, China was unable to resist European demands for trade concessions.

Nevertheless, when the Chinese refused to accept foreign ambassadors in Peking, British and French troops occupied the city on October 12, 1860. The Emperor's summer palace was burned under the direction of the British general, Charles Gordon, who was later to fight in Ethiopia.

Gordon then led Chinese armies against the T'ai P'ing rebels and finally brought an end to that bitter rebellion in 1864. To the British, Gordon came to be known as "Chinese Gordon" and was hailed as a hero.

T'ung Chih (1856–1875) had become Emperor in 1862 at the age of 6. The disasters of the T'ai P'ing rebellion and the occupation of Peking had taught the Chinese that some attempt ought to be made to modernize and westernize the country, but China's huge population and long tradition gave it an enormous inertia and made it difficult to move.

Even so, the Empire had learned that it could not assume a lord-of-the-universe attitude with the Europeans. In 1873, the Emperor, now 17, greeted foreign diplomats *without* demanding the kow-tow—an action in which the person approaching the throne had to kneel and knock his head against the ground as a token of utter submission.

KOREA

Korea remained closed to foreigners even after Japan had been opened up. A French expedition was repelled in 1866 and an American in 1871. Finally, on February 26, 1876, Japan forced a treaty on the Koreans, recognizing its independence from China and receiving trade concessions.

JAPAN

The opening of Japan to European commerce did not go smoothly at first. There were a number of attempts by antiforeign elements in the land to eject foreigners. European vessels bombarded Japanese cities in reprisal on several occasions in the early 1860s.

It became increasingly clear to most Japanese leaders, therefore, that blind resistance would get them nowhere; that the weight of power was on the side of the Europeans. In February 1867, a new Emperor, Mutsohito (1852–1912), mounted the throne. He made himself the symbol of modernization.

Keiki, the Shogun (1837–1913), an official of a line that had been the real rulers of the country, and who had come to power that year, was forced to resign and the Shogunate came to an end. Keiki was the last Shogun of the Tokugawa family, which had gained power in 1603. Before that, other families had held the Shogunate since 1192, so that Keiki's resignation marked the end of a nearly seven-century tradition.

On January 3, 1868, Mutsohito assumed control of the nation. He greeted foreign dignitaries and, in November of that year, he moved the capital from the inland city of Kyoto, where the Emperor had reigned in secluded helplessness for centuries, to the east-coastal city of Edo, which was renamed Tokyo.

The speed of modernization was astonishing thereafter. Feudalism was abolished. A postal service was established; education was made universal and compulsory. Newspapers came into being. The first railroad was built in 1882. Military service was organized on the German model. The Gregorian calendar was established. A treaty was signed with China as between equals in 1871; and, in 1876, a treaty was signed with Korea opening that nation to Japanese trade.

In 1877, there was the last die-hard rebellion of the old order. An army of samurai, the old knightly class, objecting to the formation of an army of commoners, marched against the government. This was the "Satsuma rebellion." The samurai were defeated by the commoners, trained in modern fashion, and feudal Japan was forever gone.

As another sign of what was to come, a Japanese businessman, Yataro Iwasaki (1834–1885), expanded his business and founded Mitsubishi in 1873, a firm that was eventually to become a world power in finance and trade.

PACIFIC ISLANDS

The various islands of the Pacific were picked up by the European powers. France annexed the Loyalty Islands in 1864, and Tahiti in 1880. Great Britain annexed Fiji in 1874. Even the United States picked up Midway Island and a port in Samoa.

AUSTRALIA

Australia was left very much to itself by Great Britain and it spent its time organizing its various provinces and exploring the desert interior. The very last convicts arrived in western Australia in 1867.

There was even some expansionist feeling. North of Australia is the large island of New Guinea. The eastern part was not controlled by the Dutch, and some Australians thought it ought to be British-controlled. In 1873, a British captain, John Moresby, landed on the southern shore of the eastern part of the island. However, Great Britain was not enthusiastic about taking it over and thought Australia ought to do the job. Australia wasn't entirely enthusiastic about it either, so, at that time, it came to nothing. The town of Port Moresby now stands at the site of the landing, however.

NEW ZEALAND

During the 1860s, there was the "Second Maori War," a guerrilla war in which the Maoris defended themselves courageously, rather as the Native Americans in the western United States were doing at this same time. The war ended indecisively and the Maoris were not beaten down and made subordinate as were the Native Americans in the United States, the blacks in Africa, and the Aborigines in Australia. The Maoris were given the vote and became New Zealand citizens of an integrated nation.

HAWAII

The United States continued to gain influence in Hawaii. A treaty was signed between the United States and Hawaii on January 30, 1875, whereby Hawaiian sugar could enter the United States duty-free.

1880 TO 1890

GERMANY

In this decade, Germany still dominated Europe. Although it was now firmly allied with Austria-Hungary, and although Austria-Hungary and Russia were irrevocably at odds over the Balkans, Bismarck continued to try to bind Russia into the alliance, too, as a way of isolating vengeful France.

On June 18, 1881, Bismarck succeeded in concluding a three-year "Three Emperors' League" between Germany, Austria-Hungary, and Russia. It was kept secret and it applied very complicated rules governing what might happen if the Ottoman Empire continued to disintegrate and what Russia and Austria-Hungary might each get out of it. In 1884, the League was renewed for three more years.

On May 20, 1882, Bismarck persuaded Italy to sign a five-year "Triple Alliance" with Germany and Austria-Hungary, one that was renewed afterward. Italy agreed to this because of its anger over France's policy in Tunis.

Neither Russia nor Italy was held to the German/Austro-Hungarian core very firmly. Russia still wanted more out of the Balkans than Austria-Hungary was willing to yield, and Italy had its claims on Austrian lands adjacent to Italy. Nevertheless, under Bismarck's skilled diplomacy, and with Great Britain continuing its policy of isolation, France was prevented from finding any significant allies.

Bismarck continued to fight socialism inside Germany by granting some of the benefits the socialists were demanding, but doing so while retaining firm control over the army and the national bureaucracy, so that the benefits granted were paternalistic gifts and not rights, and could be withdrawn at any time. Thus, he granted to labor financial insurance against such misfortunes as old age, accident, and medical emergencies. This amounted to social security and, as

Bismarck calculated, reduced the attraction of socialism.

Bismarck's feeling was that only European territory was worth anything, and that colonies abroad, however soothing they might be to the pride and vainglory of the home country, meant a great deal of trouble. It meant endless wars with objecting natives; it meant shipping off home talent to administer and defend the colonies; it meant straining the fabric of home society.

Indeed, far from wishing to have Germany seek colonies overseas, he encouraged France to do so. That, he thought, would distract France into forgetting the loss of Alsace-Lorraine, and at the same time would dissipate French strength by making it compete with Great Britain and engage in endless colonial wars.

Bismarck, however, didn't count on the strength of pride and vainglory in Germany. The German people grew restless at the sight of the British and French spreading their control over various sections of the world, and began to declare their desire for what was eventually to be called "a place in the sun" for themselves. (Naturally, such a place in the sun could only be obtained at the price of depriving hundreds of millions of non-Europeans of *their* place in the sun, but this seemed to bother few Europeans.)

Bismarck was eventually forced to adopt the imperialist view himself; and beginning in the 1880's, Germany joined in the scramble for pieces of territory in Africa and the South Pacific. By that time, however, Great Britain and France had swept up much of what was available, and Germany was left with relatively small portions.

William I of Germany died on March 9, 1888, just short of his 91st birthday. He had played, in all contentment, the part of Louis XIII to Bismarck's Richelieu, and had always recognized that Bismarck was much more useful to Germany than he himself was.

He was succeeded b his son, who reigned as Frederick III (1831–1888). Frederick III was a liberal and very much opposed to Bismarck's strong-arm tactics, but he was dying of throat cancer even as he came to the throne. On June 15, 1888, he was dead, after having reigned for 99 helpless days. He was succeeded by his 29-year-old son, who reigned as William II (1859–1941).

The German word for "Emperor" is "Kaiser," their spelling of "Caesar," which they pronounced correctly as "KY-zer," rather than the English "SEE-zer." Thus, William I of Germany and Francis Joseph I of Austria-Hungary were Kaisers. So was the Russian Emperor, though the Russians spelled it "Tsar" or "Czar," from their spelling of "Caesar."

It was William II, however, who eventually became known the world over as *the* Kaiser. He was lively and intelligent, but impulsive and lacking in judgment. He said and did things, thoughtlessly, that hurt his own cause, and he had the faculty of offending people and turning them against him. He was like Napoleon III come back to life.

William II's first important deed as Emperor was to force the resignation of Bismarck on March 18, 1890. Bismarck was 75 years old and had been Chancellor for 28 years. It was time for him to retire, perhaps, but greater care might have been taken to preserve his pride. His services to Germany had been such that he certainly didn't deserve to be kicked out as unceremoniously as he was.

The point was that William II was eager to play the role of Bismarck himself, but he was no Bismarck. He wasn't even a tired 75-year-old Bismarck, and under him Germany took a new and disastrous path.

Regarding German science during this decade, Heinrich Rudolf Hertz (1857–1894) discovered radio waves in 1888, and, by their existence, demonstrated the validity of Maxwell's equations, and verified Maxwell's most important prediction from those equations. Another type of verification came when Clemens Alexander Winkler (1838–1904) discovered a new element he named "germanium." It turned out to be one of the new elements that Mendeleyev had predicted, and here again its properties were exactly as predicted.

Heinrich Hermann Robert Koch (1843–1910) cultured and studied bacteria after Pasteur had advanced the germ theory of disease, and led the fight to identify the specific causes of given infectious diseases. In 1882, for instance, he identified the bacterium that caused tuberculosis.

In 1885, Karl Friedrich Benz (1844–1929) built the first working automobile to be powered by an internal combustion engine. It had three wheels. Gottlieb Wilhelm Daimler (1834–1900) built the first four-wheeled automobile in 1887.

Brahms, living in Vienna, wrote his third and fourth symphonies in 1883 and 1885, respectively.

The most important German writer of the period was the philosopher, Friedrich Wilhelm Nietzsche (1844–1900), who had rather mystical notions of the "superman," and was strongly antireligion. His most notable work was *Thus Spake Zarathustra*, the first part of which appeared in 1883. He had a mental breakdown in 1889 and never recovered.

Gerhart Hauptmann (1862–1946) was beginning to make a name for himself as a dramatist and was eventually to win a Nobel Prize.

FRANCE

France, throughout this decade, remained the implacable enemy of Germany, an enmity that was all the more bitter because France was perfectly aware that she could not fight Germany alone—and that she had no allies.

By 1880, with Francois Paul Jules Grevy (1807–1891) as president the Third Republic had lasted 10 years and there seemed no longer any chance of a monarchist revival of any kind. Grevy favored a weak executive and he was against the kind of nationalism that sought revenge on Germany. Nor was he much of an imperialist. The fact that he wanted to be a weak executive, however, meant he couldn't force these mild views on the nation.

Under Grevy, France was secularized. The power of the Church was reduced, the Jesuits were expelled, divorce was permitted, and education from age 6 to 13 was made compulsory, free, and secular, so that no religious classes were included.

This was brought about chiefly by the driving force of Jules Francois Camille Ferry (1832–1893), who had been Mayor of Paris during the Commune and who was Prime Minister from 1880 to 1881 and from 1883 to 1885. Ferry was also the strongest imperialist in France, and led the drive for expanding France's colonial holdings abroad.

Tunisian tribesmen were accustomed to raiding into Algeria and to them it didn't matter that it had been French territory for half a century now. France took advantage of this to outfit a punitive expedition. On April 30, 1881, French ships bombarded and seized Bizerte, while French troops invaded Tunis from Algerian bases on the west. By May 12, Tunis was a French protectorate.

The Ottoman Empire protested since, in theory, it ruled over Tunis. Italy objected even more strenuously since it wanted Tunis for itself (and it joined the Triple Alliance out of anger at France over this). Even Great Britain objected, for she disapproved of any imperialism that wasn't her own. Bismarck, however, gave France his firm support and that settled the matter.

On February 5, 1885, France obtained a section of central Africa. Located west of the lower Congo River, this region was called "French Congo." By the end of the decade, too, France was in control of the island of Madagascar and of what came to be called French Indo-China. In the course of taking over Indo-China, French forces managed to lose a minor skirmish to the Chinese and Ferry lost his ministerial position because of that.

This steady expansion of the French Empire did not, however, cause France to forget Alsace-Lorraine, as Bismarck had hoped. Rather, it did the reverse. France grew more and more restless over the lost provinces, since with French armies on the move everywhere from westernmost Africa to easternmost Asia, it seem unbearable to have been driven out of two provinces at home.

France wanted revenge and, for a while, it thought it had the man for the job. In 1886, Georges Ernest Jean Marie Boulanger (1837–

1891) became Minister of War. He was popular with the soldiers since he was interested in their welfare and improved their living conditions. He was also a fiery speaker and made an impressive figure on horseback. In fact, he gave rise to the expression of "man on horseback," which came to represent any military leader of Napoleonic aura who could bring about victory by his personal genius.

Boulanger became so popular with the nationalists and conservatives, and even with many liberals, that the government began to view him as a danger. He openly advocated increasing the power of the executive, and it seemed clear he was seeing himself in a Napoleonic role. Therefore, he was ousted from the War Ministry on May 31, 1887, and even from the army itself in March 1888.

Meanwhile, though, in February 1888, he had been elected to the Chamber of Deputies. There were new elections, and he won in three different departments. By the end of January 1889, the situation had reached a point where the crowds were clamoring for a coup.

Boulanger, however, was an empty man. He was all appearance and no substance. When it came time actually to do something, he could not, and the magic moment passed. The clamor for him began to die at once and on April 1, 1889, he left France and went to Brussels, where, before long, he killed himself on the grave of his mistress.

By 1890, with the ludicrous failure of Boulanger, France felt all the weaker with respect to Germany.

In this decade, an outstanding French chemist was Ferdinand Frederic Henri Moissan (1852–1907), who isolated the element fluorine in 1886 and eventually won a Nobel Prize for that. Henri Louis Le Chatelier (1850–1936) presented the world with "Le Chatelier's principle" in 1888, which predicted the nature of the change in equilibrium that would take place whenever the conditions of a system were disarranged.

In 1886, Paul Louis Toussaint Heroult (1863–1914) worked out a practical method for the electrolytic production of aluminum. This converted a seemingly rare metal into one that became both common and cheap. (An American chemist independently worked out the same method at the same time.)

In 1884, Louis Marie Hilaire Bernigaud de Chardonnet (1839–1924) forced nitrocellulose solutions through tiny holes. As the spray evaporated, it left behind the first "artificial fiber," which was called "rayon." In that same year, the Russian-born bacteriologist, Ilya Ilyich Mechnikov, recognized the importance of white blood cells in combating bacterial infection and eventually received a Nobel Prize for that.

Pierre Marie Felix Janet (1859–1947) studied various psychoses and, by 1889, anticipated some of the techniques of psychoanalysis.

The French engineer, Alexandre Gustave Eiffel (1832–1923), was responsible for the construction of the Eiffel Tower, a unique structure designed to be part of the Centennial Exposition of 1889, which celebrated the hundredth anniversary of the French Revolution. It was 984 feet tall and was by far the tallest man-made structure built up to that time, taller than the Great Pyramid or any of the medieval cathedrals. Although many Parisians were horrified at what they considered its ugliness (it looked as though it had been built out of the parts of a monstrous "Erector set") it has come to be the very symbol of Paris.

French painters of the decade include George Pierre Seurat (1851–1891), whose canvases were covered with innumerable specks of paint rather than with brush strokes. Eugene Henri Paul Gauguin (1848–1903) abandoned his stockbroker job in 1883 to engage in painting full-time. He eventually traveled to the South Pacific islands and his paintings of Polynesian scenes are his best-known productions.

Francois Auguste Rene Rodin (1840–1917) is one of the most popular sculptors of modern times and is particularly known for "The Thinker," produced in 1880, and "The Kiss" in 1886. Working on a monumental scale, Frederic Auguste Bartholdi (1834–1904) produced the famous "Liberty Enlightening the World" (better known as "The Statue of LIberty"), which was presented to the United States in 1885 and now stands in New York harbor.

In music, Delibes was still active, writing the opera, *Lakme*, in 1883. Cesar Franck (1822–1890) wrote his "Symphony in D Minor," his only one, in 1889. Jules Emile Frederic Massenet (1842–1912) wrote a number of operas of which his best-known is *Manon*, produced in 1884.

Zola was still actively writing, publishing *Germinal* in 1885 along with many other works. Jacques Anatole Francois Thibault (1844–1924), writing under the pseudonym of "Anatole France," was the wittiest French writer since Voltaire, a century and a quarter earlier. He wrote *Thais* in 1890, and eventually won a Nobel Prize.

The most famous actress of her time was Sarah Bernhardt (1844–1923), who made successful tours throughout Europe and the United States and, eventually, even played the male role of Hamlet. She was at the peak of her career in this decade but continued to act into old age, even after one of her legs had been amputated.

AUSTRIA-HUNGARY

If France was Germany's enemy, Austria-Hungary was her increasingly staunch ally. She followed Germany's lead to the point where she scarcely can be viewed as having a history of her own, except for the inevitable friction in the Balkans. In this decade, there was a Bulgarian revolt and, therefore, another Balkan crisis.

At home, tragedy continued to follow Francis Joseph I. He was a stiff, ceremonious man who, out of an overwhelming sense of duty, attended to all the minutiae of being a king, just as Philip II of Spain did three centuries earlier. Like Philip II, he was also very conservative, and was devoted to the Church.

He had one son, the Grand-Duke Rudolf (1858–1889), a liberal and anticlerical, who wanted to grant much more freedom to the suppressed nationalities and to weaken the grip of the Church. His father, therefore, kept him from all official functions and had forced him into an unhappy marriage. Eventually, Rudolf could not bear his life and, on January 30, 1889, he and his mistress killed themselves at the Imperial hunting lodge of Mayerling.

This was even worse than the death by execution of Francis Joseph's younger brother, Maximilian. Rudolf's suicide created a great scandal and his mother, the Empress Elizabeth (1837–1898), who was, in any case, rather mentally unstable, never recovered from the shock and took to traveling over Europe, feverishly, as a way of forgetting.

The new heir to the throne was Francis Joseph's one remaining brother, Charles Louis (d. 1896).

An important Austrian chemist of the period was Karl Auer von Welsbach (1858–1929) who, in 1885, discovered that fabric impregnated with thorium nitrate and a bit of cerium nitrate would glow with a brilliant white light when heated. The use of such a "Welsbach mantle" about the flame of a kerosene lamp made those lamps effective competitors of the new electric light for a time.

Josef Breuer (1842–1895) found it helpful, beginning in 1880, to encourage patients with psychological disturbances to talk freely of their fantasies, sometimes with the aid of hypnosis. This seemed to alleviate the symptoms. Sigmund Freud (1856–1939), learning from Breuer and others, began to use similar methods in 1887.

Samuel Teleki (1845–1916), a Hungarian explorer, discovered Lake Rudolf in east Africa in 1888.

Johann Strauss was still making Vienna ring with his music. He wrote the operetta *The Gypsy Baron* in 1885, and one of his best pieces, *The Emperor Waltz*, in 1888. For this waltz, Francis Joseph I, who had turned against him when Strauss had married a Jewish widow, received him back into favor. Josef Anton Bruckner (1824–1896) and Gustav Mahler (1860–1911) were both important composers in this decade. Anton Leopold Dvorak (1841–1904), an Austro-Hungarian subject, but Czech in his ethnic background, was also becoming well-known.

RUSSIA

The harsh autocracy in Russia and the manner in which the nation lagged behind the lands to the west drove many Russians to desperation. The reforms of Alexander II seemed too slow to them;

a little liberalization merely sharpened their appetite for more.

Furthermore, the fact that in Russia there was no room for the orderly expression of dissenting opinion meant that dissent had to go underground, and those who were most apt to carry on dissent under such dangerous conditions were the extremists. Thus, Pyotr Alekseyevich Kropotkin (1842–1921), an able explorer and geographer, was radicalized by Russian oppression, fled to France, then Great Britain, and wrote eloquent works supporting anarchy.

Alexander II recognized, at least dimly, that trying to contain the explosive forces, compressing them more and more tightly, would merely bring about an increase in the internal pressures and make the explosion more violent when it came. Therefore, he approved a plan whereby the local councils, set up in 1870 in various towns, might select representatives who would discuss legislation with the tsar and his ministers. This would allow for an orderly expression of dissenting opinion and supply a safety valve that would keep opposition from turning to violence and terrorism.

It was too late. On the very day that Alexander II approved the plan, March 13, 1881, he fell victim to a bomb attack while in a coach on the streets of St. Petersburg.

He was succeeded by his son, who reigned as Alexander III (1845–1894). The assassination led to just the reverse of what the terrorists' aims must have been. Alexander III considered the death of his father to have been the result of his deviating from autocratic principles. Therefore, Alexander III removed much of his father's reforms, replaced it with harsh repression, pressing hard on all those who were not both Russian and Russian Orthodox in religion. In particular, he encouraged indiscriminate attacks on Jews, who began to flee to the United States in increasing numbers.

A Polish Jew, Ludwik Lejser Zamenhof (1859–1917), appalled by this, devised an artificial language called "Esperanto" ("one who hopes") in 1887. It had a simple spelling and grammar and Zamenhof hoped it would be adopted the world over and that a universal language would lead to an era of peace and mutual friendship among peoples. It didn't work; nor has any invented language proved to be useful since. (If the world ever adopts a world language—and it may not—it will probably be a somewhat modified English.)

And still Russia advanced in central Asia. In 1884, the Russians took the city of Merv and the frontier reached the line that exists today, marching along the northern border of Afghanistan and Persia. For a while, this brought on a crisis with Great Britain, which continued to be jittery over the security of India; however, neither side wanted war, and the matter was adjusted peaceably in June 1886.

Even nations that totally spurn the political and social ways of the west are usually willing to adopt western technology, since they see this as the path to wealth and strength. Even as Alexander III turned back to autocracy, he also presided over the further modernization of Russia.

In this, Sergei Yulyevich Witte (1849–1915) was the leader. He was the Minister of Communications and was particularly interested in railroads. As rail lines were built across Russia, the coal and iron fields of remoter districts could be exploited, and factories could be established. This required the borrowing of capital, and that came chiefly from France, which expected a return, with substantial interest, as an industrial Russia grew wealthier.

Industrialization, however, also meant the growth in the number of factory workers. These were treated miserably, as they always were in the early days of industrialization, and they were more aware and more likely to react than the peasantry was. This meant radical dissent grew more rapidly and smoldered more dangerously.

Abroad there was another crisis when the Bulgarians revolted.

An important Russian scientist at this time was Ivan Petrovich Pavlov (1849–1936), who, in 1889, studied the manner in which nerve action controlled the flow of digestive juices in the stomach. This work was eventually judged worthy of a Nobel Prize.

Tchaikovsky was still composing music. Among his many compositions in this decade,

there was the *1812 Overture* in 1880, and the *Fifth Symphony* in 1888. Nickolay Andreyevich Rimsky-Korsakoff (1844–1908) wrote the opera *Snow Maiden* in 1882, *Capriccio Espagnol* in 1887, and the symphonic suite *Scheherezade* in 1888.

GREAT BRITAIN

While the nations of Europe were playing their intricate game of power politics, competing for position and forming alliances, Great Britain stood above it all. She was allied with none and concerned with only two things: expanding her colonial empire overseas, and making sure that no one power grew so strong in Europe as to be able to threaten her. As long as the nations competed with each other on fairly even terms, Great Britain could rest secure behind her navy—which controlled the oceans of the world, and particularly those narrow bodies of water, the English Channel and the North Sea, that separated her from the turbulence of the European continent.

Great Britain had troubles at home, however, and the chief of these was the Irish question. Ever since the great famine, the Irish had grown increasingly restless, and a greater and greater number of British had grown to feel increasingly guilty.

An Irish lawyer, Isaac Butt (1813–1879), had, as early as 1873, coined "Home Rule" as an expression of Irish aspirations. After his death in 1879, Irish nationalists were led by Charles Stewart Parnell (1846–1890). He was of English descent and was a Protestant, but he identified himself completely with the oppressed Irish and was idolized by them. He was a natural candidate for Parliament, being a Protestant, and once there he fought skillfully for Irish causes by carrying on an obstructionist campaign in Parliament that made it difficult for it to do its business.

Gladstone, who felt it wise to make concessions to the Irish, saw to it that another Land Act was passed in August 1881, which served to lower excessive rents and to give Irish tenants some security from being evicted as long as they paid their rents. On the whole, as is true of so many reforms, it went far enough to displease the conservative landowners, and not far enough to please the Irish peasantry.

The situation was made worse by those Irish radicals who were angry enough to seek solace in terrorism. On May 6, 1882, two high English officials in Ireland were assassinated and, later on, other terrorist attacks were committed, including the dynamiting of public buildings in England. This naturally led to a sudden increase in English oppression in Ireland, a determination to root out resistance that was as terroristic in its own way as the deeds of the radicals, so that it became terror versus terror.

Gladstone was also pushing for increased democracy in Great Britain itself. In 1884, his "Franchise Bill" expanded the number of voters once again; and, in 1885, the membership of Parliament was so adjusted in his "Redistribution Bill" that there was a far closer approach to the principle of having each member of Parliament represent the same number of people.

Parnell managed to avoid being tarred by the terrorist brush and continued to turn Parliament topsy-turvy. Annoyed by Gladstone's unwillingness (or inability) to go farther on the Irish problem, he shifted support away from the Liberal Party and forced Gladstone out on June 9, 1885. Disraeli had died on April 19, 1881, and the Conservative party was now led by Robert Cecil, Lord Salisbury (1830–1903), who had been Foreign Minister during the Russo–Turkish crisis of 1878, and who was now Prime Minister. He was the last Prime Minister to be a peer and to rule from the House of Lords.

This was what Parnell wanted. He held the swing votes and Salisbury and Gladstone realized that neither could be Prime Minister without him. They both vied for Parnell's support, and Gladstone finally bid high enough to get it. Salisbury (having been Prime Minister for only half a year) was out, Gladstone became Prime Minister for the third time on January 27, 1886.

Therefore, Gladstone put forward a Home Rule Bill on April 8, 1886, but it was only another partial step. A separate Irish Parliament would be set up which would deal with local affairs, but anything involving the military, or commerce, or the crown was still left to the British Parliament, in which there were to be no Irish members. Parnell supported it, half-baked though it was, as at least a step in the right direction, but the Conservatives bitterly opposed it, and even some Liberals deserted Gladstone on this matter. The Bill failed to pass and, on July 26, 1886, Gladstone was forced out, and Salisbury came in as Prime Minister for the second time.

Parnell then fell on hard times. He was accused of having connections with terrorists on April 18, 1887, a letter by him being presented as evidence. It proved to be a forgery, and the forger killed himself.

But there was worse to come. Parnell had, as his mistress, the wife of another man who, on December 24, 1889, filed for divorce, naming Parnell as co-respondent. This ruined his political career. He retired, and died soon after.

During Gladstone's third stint as Prime Minister, there was a further liberalization of Parliament. Jews could be seated, but what about atheists? The question arose in connection with Charles Bradlaugh (1833–1891), who was not only an atheist, but who wrote freely on birth-control. He was elected to Parliament in 1880 and then repeatedly reelected, but was not allowed to take his seat because he refused to swear on the Bible. He would merely "affirm." In 1886, he was allowed to affirm and take his seat and, in 1888, a law was passed permitting affirmation generally.

There was unrest among British labor as well as among the Irish. There was a huge dock strike in the summer of 1889, and the coal miners formed a union. Increasingly, laborers were unwilling to leave the rule to the Liberals and the Conservatives—that is, to the commercial and the landed classes. Unionism spread, and labor was finding its own voice.

Then, too, the policy of "splendid isolation" was beginning to wear thin. There was serious trouble in Egypt and the Sudan against a new Muslim conqueror, and trouble in Afghanistan against Russian encroachment. This might come under the heading of colonial wars, something Great Britain was used to.

However, closer to home, both France and

Russia were strengthening their navies, and British security rested entirely on the overwhelming superiority of its own sea-forces. On May 31, 1889, therefore, Great Britain passed a "Naval Defense Act," which provided that Great Britain would always build up its navy until it was at least as strong as the next two strongest powers combined.

That was easy to say, but it was soon to prove not so easy to do.

In science in this decade, Frederick Augustus Abel (1827–1902) and James Dewar (1842–1923) pioneered the production of "cordite" in 1889, a mixture of nitroglycerine and nitrocellulose, with petroleum jelly added. It could be formed into thick cords (hence its name) and it was safe to handle. Unlike gunpowder, it burned without smoke. The use of smokeless powders cleared the battlefield and it cut down the chances that lives would be sacrificed because generals couldn't see what was happening.

As another contribution to warfare, the American-born British inventor, Hiram Stevens Maxim (1840–1916), invented the first fully automatic machine gun in 1883. Whereas the Gatling gun had to be cranked, the Maxim gun used the recoil of one bullet to eject the spent cartridge and load the next. Its usefulness against the native levies in non-European lands is attested to by the jingle:

Whatever happens, we have got
The Maxim gun and they have not!

Of course, the time was to come when "they" got the Maxim gun, too, along with other weapons, and colonial wars stopped being quite so much fun.

Robert Abbott Hadfield (1858–1940) found that steel, to which 12% manganese had been added and which was heated and then quenched, was much harder than ordinary steel. This was patented in 1883, and marked the beginning of the triumph of "alloy steel" with new and useful properties.

John Milne (1850–1913) invented the modern seismograph for measuring earth-vibrations, and, with that, began modern seismology (the study of earthquakes).

In 1884, Charles Algernon Parsons (1854–1931) devised the first practical steam turbine, which had the capacity for moving ships faster than the old propellers could. Additional advances in transportation included the work of the German-born British inventor, William Siemens (1823–1883), who pioneered the development of the electric locomotive, the first of which ran in northern Ireland in 1883. Johen Boyd Dunlop (1840–1921) patented the pneumatic rubber tire in 1888. Although it was used for bicycles to begin with, its application became essential to automobiles, buses, and trucks.

In music, Great Britain lagged, but there continued to be the Gilbert & Sullivan operettas. There was *Patience* (1881), *Iolanthe* (1882), *The Mikado* (1885), and *The Gondoliers* (1889)—to mention only the most popular.

Hardy was still writing, and *The Mayor of Casterbridge* was published in 1886. Oscar Wilde (1854–1900) began his career by writing poetry, but made his first hit in prose with a collection of tales for youngsters, including *The Happy Prince* in 1888. Robert Louis Balfour Stevenson (1850–1894) followed the same pattern, publishing his charming *A Child's Garden of Verses* in 1885, and writing such prose classics as *Treasure Island* in 1883, *Kidnapped* in 1886, and *Dr. Jekyll and Mr. Hyde* in 1886.

Henry Rider Haggard (1856–1925) wrote effective adventure stories, such as *King Solomon's Mines* in 1885 and *She* in 1887. Arthur Conan Doyle (1859–1930) published *A Study in Scarlet* in 1887, introducing what many believe to be the most popular fictional hero ever invented, Sherlock Holmes (with, it is not to be forgotten, his friend and foil, Dr. John H. Watson).

Walter Horatio Pater (1839–1894) published the historical novel *Marius the Epicurean* in 1885. It was set in the time of the Roman Empire. Richard Francis Burton (1821–1890), till then known as an explorer, translated *The Arabian Nights* into English, unexpurgated, between 1885 and 1888.

ITALY

Italy liked to think of itself as a major European power, along with Great Britain, France, Germany, Austria-Hungary, and Russia, but it was clearly the weakest of the six. France's seizure of Tunis was deeply humiliating to Italy, and led it to make an alliance with Germany and Austria-Hungary.

Italy's adherence to the new alliance was carried through by Agostino Depretis (1813–1887), who was Prime Minister through most of the decade. He was a liberal at home, extending the franchise greatly in 1881. He was an imperialist abroad and searched for some area that had not yet been taken up by the stronger powers. He found one on the African coast of the Red Sea, where the Italians occupied the ports of Assab and Massawa in 1885.

When Depretis died in 1887, Francesco Cripi (1819–1901), his Minister of the Interior, succeeded as Prime Minister. Crispi was a Sicilian by birth, an old revolutionary, who had persuaded Garibaldi to lead his thousand men against Sicily and Naples. He had briefly been one of the leaders of the new Neapolitan republic until it was taken into the new Kingdom of Italy.

Crispi held firmly to the Triple Alliance and to a policy of enmity with France. Forgetting his own revolutionary past, he forcefully suppressed socialist uprisings in Italy. He organized the Italian holdings along the Red Sea into the Italian colony of Eritrea, and he began to push for a protectorate over Ethiopia.

On the cultural front, Verdi was still writing, producing his opera *Otello* in 1887. Pietro Mascagni (1863–1945) turned out the one-act opera *Cavelleria Rusticana* in 1890.

Carlo Lorenzini (1826–1890), writing under the pseudonym of Carlo Collodi, published *The Adventures of Pinocchio* in 1882.

PAPACY

Leo XIII, in this decade, continued his liberalizing policy after the dark reaction of Pius IX. He labored to point out that there was no necessary conflict between religion and science, that the universe as revealed by science had to be the work of God and was therefore consonant with true religion. He also lessened the enmity of the Church toward democracy and did his best to get along with France, urging French Catholics to forget monarchism and support the republic.

He could not reconcile himself to Italy, however, especially since Crispi was violently anti-clerical and went out of his way to offend the Papacy. Not only did he secularize the schools, but he had a statue of Giordano Bruno (whom the Church had burned in 1600) set up facing the Vatican. The harried Pope, in a weak moment, even thought of the possibility of leaving Rome —but did not.

BELGIUM

Belgium was rapidly industrializing itself in this decade, and expanding the franchise as almost all the European nations were doing at this time. This meant the growth of a Labor party, the coming of strikes and socialism, and the demand for universal male suffrage.

The Belgian king, Leopold II, may have been more interested in Central Africa than in Belgium, however. He made use of the explorer, Henry Stanley, as his agent, to set up his power along the Congo River. He fought off British and Portuguese probes into the area and, on May 2, 1885, he privately set up the "Congo Free State" (i.e., free for Leopold) and obtained its recognition by the important European powers and by the United States.

The Congo Free State was 80 times the area of Belgium, but it didn't really belong to Belgium at this time: it belonged solely to Leopold II.

In 1887, a Belgian biologist, Edouard Joseph Louis Marie van Beneden (1809–1894), showed that the number of chromosomes was constant in the body cells of a particular species, but that they were only half the usual number in the sperm cells and egg cells of the species. This proved to be an important point in the development of knowledge of genetics.

NETHERLANDS

In this decade, the Netherlands, too, broadened the franchise. There was a dispute over the nature of education. The liberals wanted it secular ized and the conservatives wanted it to be controlled by religious bodies.

On November 23, 1890, William III of the Netherlands died after having reigned 41 years. Succeeding him was his 10-year-old daughter, Wilhelmina (1880–1962), with her mother acting as regent.

Van't Hoff, who had worked out the three-dimensional structure of organic molecules, worked on chemical thermodynamics in 1884, particularly as it involved the behavior of solutions, and for this he eventually received a Nobel Prize.

Vincent Willem van Gogh (1853–1890) is now considered the greatest Dutch painter since Rembrandt, two and a half centuries earlier. At least, this is the present opinion, when his paintings sell for the tens of millions of dollars. In his lifetime, he was an utter failure, however, and managed to sell only one painting for a trifling sum. Beset by poverty and despair, he shot himself, and died on July 29, 1890.

SPAIN

Under Alfonso XII, Spain's liberal constitution worked and the nation had a period of unusual quiet and prosperity. He died of tuberculosis on November 25, 1885, however, at the age of only 28, leaving behind a pregnant wife, Maria Cristina (1858–1929). On May 17, 1886, she gave birth to a son, who reigned as Alfonso XIII (1886–1941), but she remained as regent. For the rest of the decade, matters continued smoothly.

PORTUGAL

The decade passed quietly for Portugal, as well as for its king, Luis I (who was literally inclined and translated Shakespeare into Portuguese). He died on October 19, 1889, having reigned 28 years, and was succeeded by his son, who reigned as Carlos I (1863–1908).

SWITZERLAND

The Alps, as a barrier, had always protected Italy from the north, though conquerors such as Han-

nibal and Napoleon had managed to cross it. One of the passes, the St. Gotthard pass (1.3 miles high even at its lowest) was not used much, with only a mule path crossing it for centuries. The nineteenth century saw a road built over it that was fit for carriages.

Switzerland, a nation which nestles amid the Alps, built a nine-mile tunnel through it in the 1870s, then constructed a railway line through the tunnel. Finally, in 1882, it was possible to travel by train, in comfort, from Lucerne, Switzerland to Milan, Italy. Other rail lines through other passes were eventually built, too.

The Swiss writer, Johanna Spyri (1827–1901), wrote *Heidi* in 1881 and it has remained popular ever since.

DENMARK

Under Christian IX, Denmark spent this decade in peace and in rapid industrialization.

SWEDEN

Under Oscar II, peace and industrialization was the lot of Sweden as well. There was a large Swedish emigration to the United States in this period.

While working toward his doctorate, the Swedish chemist, Svante August Arrhenius (1859–1927), devised a theory to explain some of the intricacies involved in the passage of electricity through solutions. He felt that atoms and atom groups could carry electric charges. This was so revolutionary a thought that he barely passed his examination. However, as additional evidence came in, it turned out that he was right, and he eventually won a Nobel Prize for his barely passed doctoral dissertation.

The greatest modern Swedish writer, it is usually thought, is the novelist and playwright, Johan August Strindberg (1849–1912), whose early works caused him to be accused of blasphemy.

In Norway, which was still under the Swedish crown, Ibsen continued to turn out masterful plays, including *Ghosts* (1881), *An Enemy of the*

People (1882), *The Wild Duck* (1884), and *Hedda Gabler* (1890), among others.

The Norwegian explorer, Nils Adolf Erik Nordenskiold (1832–1901), penetrated 84 miles into Greenland in 1883. Fridtjof Nansen (1861–1930), another Norwegian explorer, was the first to cross Greenland. He and his party used skis to cross about 260 miles of icecap and reached a height of 1.7 miles.

BULGARIA

Bulgaria, after having been given considerable territory by the Russians at the conclusion of their war with Turkey in 1878, had been greatly diminished by the Treaty of Berlin. The northern portion was called Bulgaria and was virtually independent under Prince Alexander I (1857–1893). Alexander I was one of the numerous German princes that littered Europe. He was also a nephew of Alexander II of Russia and, therefore, a first cousin of Alexander III of Russia.

Middle Bulgaria, called "Eastern Rumelia," had only very limited self-rule, and southern Bulgaria was still entirely Ottoman.

Russia took it for granted that Alexander I would be a reliable puppet. When he abolished the liberal constitution soon after accession, it approved and supported the step. Alexander I of Bulgaria did not, however, get along with Alexander III of Russia, and the enmity grew surprisingly intense, even to the point where Prince Alexander restored the liberal constitution for no other reason, apparently, than to show his independence of Russia.

On September 18, 1885, Eastern Rumelia rose in revolt against the Ottoman Empire and demanded union with Bulgaria. Wild enthusiasm among the Bulgarian populace forced Prince Alexander to support the Eastern Rumelian rebels against his own cautious feelings. Russia, which had wanted a "Greater Bulgaria" seven years earlier, now, out of profound dislike for Prince Alexander, opposed it. However, Great Britain, which had opposed a Greater Bulgaria when it feared it would be a Russian puppet, instantly changed its position, too, and favored the union of Bulgaria and Eastern Rumelia once

it was clear that Bulgaria was an enemy of Russia.

The Ottoman Empire was not enthusiastic about fighting endlessly in the Balkans and, on April 5, 1886, the union of Bulgaria and Eastern Rumelia was virtually carried through. This disturbed Serbia, which feared that an expanding Bulgaria might claim, and get, territory that Serbia wanted for itself. Serbia, therefore, declared war on Bulgaria, and was promptly defeated.

In the end, though, Prince Alexander could not withstand the hostile pressure of Russia and, on September 4, 1886, he abdicated. After a period of confusion, during which there was a momentary war crisis (squelched by Bismarck), another German prince, on July 4, 1887, was persuaded to take the Bulgarian throne. He reigned as Ferdinand I (1861–1948). Russia refused to recognize him, and he had a rocky time of it at first, but he maintained himself over a now somewhat-greater Bulgaria.

GREECE

Greece, still ruled by George I, had been promised additional territory in the north at the Congress of Berlin, but the Ottoman Empire was in no hurry to grant it. On July 2, 1881, continuing Greek pressure had its result, however, and Greece annexed Thessaly and part of Epirus, both Greek-speaking areas.

Greece was eager to take advantage of the Bulgarian crisis, but the European powers came down heavily on it, and even blockaded Greece in May 1886 as a way of persuading it to keep the peace.

SERBIA

Serbia was ruled by Milan Obrenovich (1854–1901) at the beginning of the decade. In 1881, he assumed the royal dignity and styled himself King Milan I.

He did this with Austro–Hungarian support, for Russia's failure at the Congress of Berlin had convinced Milan that it would be more productive to rely on Austria-Hungary instead. In this period, therefore, Serbia became virtually an

Austro–Hungarian puppet. This roused national opposition, which made itself vocal with Nicola Pashich (1845–1926), who was violently opposed to Milan's policies. It was nationalist pressure that forced Serbia into a war with Bulgaria in 1885, one in which it was quickly defeated and from which it had to be rescued by Austria-Hungary.

The nationals won an election and forced a liberal constitution on the country, whereupon Milan abdicated in anger, on March 6, 1889. His 13-year-old son succeeded, and reigned as Alexander I (1876–1903).

ROMANIA

Newly independent Romania was ruled by Carol I (1839–1914), still another German prince. Although it had been Russia that had obtained Romanian independence, it was with the intention of making the country a Russian puppet. Carol I feared that fate and, on October 30, 1883, he arranged a secret alliance with Austria-Hungary. This made it part of the Triple Alliance, and made Romania another link in Bismarck's chain. The arrangement was kept secret, however, out of fear of the Russian reaction.

OTTOMAN EMPIRE

For the Ottoman Empire, territorial shrinkage continued. France had taken its Tunisian province in 1881; and Great Britain its Egyptian province in 1882. In the Balkans, it lost territory to both Greece and Bulgaria.

It was only two centuries earlier that an Ottoman army had stood at the walls of Vienna, and now the European dominions of the Ottoman Empire were reduced to an east–west strip across the Balkans from Constantinople to the Adriatic Sea, a strip lying to the south of Bulgaria, Serbia, and Montenegro, and to the north of Greece.

UNITED STATES

After the national trauma of the Civil War, the United States continued its self-imposed isolation from the problems of Europe, and devoted itself to healing its wounds and building up its western half.

Succeeding President Hayes was James Abram Garfield (1831–1881), who was inaugurated the 20th President on March 4, 1881. A little over six months later, however, Garfield was shot by Charles Julius Guiteau (1840–1882) and died of his wounds.

Guiteau was a disappointed office-seeker, and this threw into public awareness the viciousness of government employment procedures. With each new administration, all government employees were subject to ousting, with new people appointed out of purely political consideration. For each job available, dozens of party hacks felt they deserved it for whatever work they had done toward the election. Presidents were hounded to madness by these harpies, even President Lincoln during the desperate days of the Civil War. Those hacks who did manage to claw down a job for themselves were, more often that not, incompetent.

A New York Senator, William Learned Marcy (1786–1857), had justified this by considering that a political party was an army and that government office was what it was fighting for. He said, "To the victor belong the spoils" (where "spoils" are the possessions of the defeated army). The office-seeking policy was, therefore, known as the "spoils system."

Succeeding Garfield was his Vice-President, Chester Alan Arthur (1829–1886), who became the 21st President. He had been a cheap machine politician, but becoming president seemed to change him. Under him, the notion of civil service examinations to determine fitness for government position, with discharge only for cause, began to make progress.

Arthur's change of attitude did not please the Republican politicians and they did not renominate him in 1884. Instead, they chose James Gillespie Blaine (1830–1893), who was transparently corrupt. In addition, one of Blaine's supporters, a Protestant clergyman, Samuel Dickinson Burchard (1812–1892), gave a talk in which he accused Democrats of being involved in "rum, Romanism and rebellion." This lost Blaine enough Catholic votes to cost him New York

State and, therefore, the election. The Democratic candidate, the reform governor of New York, Grover Cleveland (1837–1908), was elected and took office in 1885 as the 22nd President. He was the first Democrat to be elected since James Buchanan, 28 years earlier. The Republicans had won seven elections in a row.

In 1888, however, Cleveland was not re-elected. He had more popular votes than his rival, Benjamin Harrison (1833–1901), a grand-son of William Henry Harrison, the 9th President, but that didn't help. The British Ambassador incautiously backed Cleveland and that cost the latter enough Irish votes to lose him New York and the election. Harrison was inaugurated as the 23rd President in 1889.

There were important changes taking place in the 1880s. Until then, immigration into the United States had been essentially free. In fact, it was welcomed as a source of cheap labor. Besides, most of the immigrants were from the nations of northern and western Europe, who had little trouble adjusting to the American way of life. The quantities of Irish who had come in during the 1840s and 1850s, fleeing from famine and oppression, were Catholic and were, therefore, subjected to ill-treatment—but a least they spoke English. The influx from eastern and southern Europe, particularly the Jews fleeing from pogroms, who began arriving in the 1880s, were more troubling still. However, it was with the Chinese—quiet, uncomplaining, industrious, willing to work at starvation wages, but with an unfamiliar appearance and culture—that Americans drew the line.

There were riots in which Chinese were slaughtered for the mere crime of being Chinese, particularly in California where they were most numerous. On May 6, 1882, the "Chinese Exclusion Act" was passed, barring Chinese laborers from entering the United States for 10 years. This was the beginning of an increasingly selective immigration policy.

It was also ironic because in 1886, the Statue of Liberty (a gift from France) was erected in New York harbor, where most of the European immigrants arrived. It had a sonnet engraved on a plaque at its base, one that had been written by Emma Lazarus, a Jewish woman born in New York City. Its most famous lines are:

> Give me your tired, your poor,
> Your huddled masses yearning to breathe free,
> The wretched refuse of your teeming shore;
> Send these, the homeless, tempest-tost to me.
> I lift my lamp beside the golden door.

It was written in 1883, the year after the "golden door" started slowly to creak shut. Of course, it stands to reason that the United States can't accept unlimited numbers of immigrants forever, but if selection there must be, it would be more sensible to discriminate on the grounds of intelligence and industry, rather than on irrelevant matters of appearance and national prejudice.

There were other changes. New York (and London in Great Britain) began to have its streets illuminated with electric lights in 1882. The first skyscraper, 10 stories high and with a framework that was partly steel, was erected in Chicago in 1885. The first skyscraper in Manhattan, 13 stories high, was erected in 1889.

The Washington Monument, a tall obelisk in memory of the first President, was completed in 1888. It had an aluminum cap that served as an exotic and expensive topping without the banality of gold, but this turned out to be just the time when aluminum was beginning to turn common and inexpensive.

There were disasters, too. In March of 1888, New York experienced an unexpected three-day blizzard that isolated it from the world for a time and killed a number of people. On May 31, 1889, a dam burst upstream from Johnstown, Pennsylvania, and a wall of water drowned several thousand people.

The American frontier was finally closed. The last formidable Native American foe of the United States was an Apache chieftain called "Geronimo" (1829–1909), a nickname he had been given by Mexicans. He carried on a skillful campaign in 1885 and 1886, but was finally defeated and captured.

Then, in 1890, a group of Sioux, reduced to semistarvation on their reservation, snatched at the belief that magic dances might cause the white man to disappear. They tried to carry through the dances, but American forces killed Sitting Bull (1831–1890), who had been prominent in the defeat of Custer 14 years earlier. They also killed about 200 men, women, and children, and this inglorious "Battle of Wounded Knee" was the end (and with it the age of the cowboy), as the west began to turn increasingly to settle farming communities.

It was not only Native Americans who were subjected to government suppression. The industrialization of the United States led to a self-conscious labor movement, to strikes, and to Socialism, often brought in by the European immigrants. The American government sided with the industrialist against the laborers just as firmly as European governments did.

In 1886, an organization called "The Knights of Labor" had grown prominent. It had a membership of 730,000 and called 1600 strikes, mostly for the purpose of establishing an eight-hour work day. The industrialists could always hire thugs, however, to break a strike by force, or if they wanted to economize, they could just as easily make use of the police, without having to pay out salaries.

On May 1, 1886, a strike was called against the McCormick Harvesting Machine Company. On May 3, the police charged a crowd of peaceful strikers, killing six. On May 4, the strikers held a protest meeting at Haymarket Square in Chicago. Again, the police charged in without provocation. This time, someone threw a bomb, and seven policemen were killed. Eight strike leaders were arrested. There was no evidence that any of them had thrown the bomb, but after a farcical trial, four were hanged, one killed himself in despair, and the remaining three were imprisoned.

The Knights of Labor shriveled thereafter, but the British-born Samuel Gompers (1850–1924) founded the American Federation of Labor that year and kept it a fairly cautious organization.

In 1889 and 1890, North Dakota, South Dakota, Montana, Washington, Idaho, and Wyoming were added to the Union, and there were now 44 states. By 1890, the population of the United States stood at 63 million, higher than that of any European nation other than Russia.

It was a decade in which newspaper publishers were becoming very important. There had been important publishers before, such as Horace Greeley (1811–1872), a quixotic liberal who edited the *New York Herald* and who actually ran for president in 1872, but who was badly beaten and died almost immediately afterward. There was also James Gordon Bennett (1795–1872), who was the first to sell newspapers for a mere cent apiece. By this he achieved high circulation and had to labor to please the taste of the unsophisticated mass of the population. It was he who sent Stanley to find Livingstone.

These were outshone, however, by Hungarian-born Joseph Pulitzer (1847–1911), who founded *The New York World* in 1883. He dominated the newspaper world in the 1880s, but toward its end, William Randolph Hearst (1863–1951) entered the newspaper field and was destined to eclipse Pulitzer.

On a more humanitarian note, nurse Clarissa Harlowe ("Clara") Barton, who had labored to relieve suffering in the Civil War and in the Franco–Prussian War, founded the American Red Cross in 1882 and served as its first president.

Booker Taliaferro Washington (1856–1915) was a black, who had been born a slave. He had educated himself under great difficulties and believe that blacks could best advance by learning trades and professions and proving themselves good citizens until they were accepted by the whites. (Those blacks who disagreed with him felt that acceptance through passive virtue would come by the Day of Judgment but not before.) Washington founded Tuskegee Institute in Tuskegee, Alabama, in 1881, and spent the rest of his life laboring in the cause of black education.

Elizabeth Seaman (1867–1922), who used the pseudonym "Nelly Bly," was a journalist who did not fear difficult tasks. She spent 10 days in a lunatic asylum and wrote up her experiences in 1887. She also set out to match Phileas Fogg's feat in Verne's *Around the World in Eighty Days* and actually bettered it. She did it in 72 and a quarter days and wrote it up in a book published in 1890. Thus was science fiction overtaken—as has happened on numerous occasions since.

John Lawrence Sullivan was a prizefighter who won the heavyweight championship in 1882 in the last bare-knuckle fight. After that, prize fights were conducted by the rules set up under the supervision of John Sholto Douglas, Marquis of Queensberry (1844–1900). These "Marquis of Queensberry rules" have governed prize-fighting ever since. Sullivan's colorful personality made this rather dubious "sport" popular in the United States.

The outstanding entertainer of the period was Lillian Russell (1861–1922), whose well-upholstered charms made her as popular as an actress could be in the days before motion pictures.

The United States was slowly gaining ground in science. The German-born physicist, Albert Abraham Michelson (1852–1931), had, as his passion, the measurement of the speed of light. In 1881, he invented the "interferometer" which could compare, with the greatest delicacy, the comparative speed at which two rays of light, sent in different directions, would travel. By measuring the difference in speed, he expected to detect the motion of the Earth against the underlying fabric of the Universe. He ran these experiments with great care and, in 1887, he and his colleague, Edward Williams Morley (1838–1923), carried it through with enormous precision, yet found no difference at all in the speed of the two rays.

The experiment was a "failure," but it was the greatest failure in the history of science, for attempts to explain it led to the theory of relativity, one of the two great products of theoretical physics in the course of the next century. Michelson eventually received a Nobel Prize for his work on light.

Charles Martin Hall (1863–1914) discovered the electrolytic isolation of aluminum, using the same method that Heroult was using in France at the same time, and entirely independently The method is now known as the "Hall–Heroult process."

William Steward Halsted (1852–1922), in 1890, was the first surgeon to use rubber gloves during operations, thus greatly decreasing the chances of infection. The Austrian-born Carl Koller (1857–1944) was the first, in 1884, to use cocaine as a local anesthetic, deadening just the region about a minor operation, rather than putting a person to sleep altogether.

In 1889, that universal inventor, Edison, invented a camera and some techniques that were the first steps toward motion pictures. The Austro-Hungarian-born Nikola Tesla (who was Croatian, ethnically), a great and embittered rival of Edison, worked out the electric transformer that made it possible to send electric currents long distances with comparatively little loss. This worked only with alternating currents, not direct, and helped give Westinghouse his victory over Edison.

In 1884, George Eastman (1854–1932) invented a flexible photographic film. In 1888, he began selling the Kodak camera (a nonsense word he made up to attract attention) which used this flexible film. Users pointed the camera and pressed a button, then sent it to Eastman's factory, which sent back photographs and a freshly filled camera. It was a slow procedure but, for the first time, it became possible for an unskilled amateur to take photographs, and it went a long way toward making photography a popular pastime.

Herman Hollerith (1860–1929), who worked in the Census Bureau, developed a method in the 1880s for tabulating and sorting data with unprecedented speed by making use of punched cards and electric currents. He had an electromechanical computing device that was approaching Babbage's dream of half a century earlier. It was used to gather the data in the Census of 1890 and thereafter. Hollerith went on to found a company that eventually became International Business Machines (IBM).

Dorr Eugene Felt (1862–1930) and William Seward Burroughs (1855–1898) independently invented mechanical calculating machines in 1885 and 1886.

Mark Twain was still writing and, in 1884, published his masterpiece, *Huckleberry Finn*, which many people think is the greatest American novel ever written.

Joel Chandler Harris (1848–1908) caught the black dialect in his retelling of animal tales in *Nights with Uncle Remus*, published in 1883, together with several companion books. James Whitcomb Riley (1849–1916), using rustic dialect, wrote light-hearted poems for young people in the 1880s. Ernest Lawrence Thayer (1863–1940) wrote what some people think may be the best "bad poem" ever written, which was *Casey at the Bat,* first published in 1888.

The best American poet of the period, however, was Emily Elizabeth Dickinson (1830–1886), who was a recluse and completely unknown, since she did not try to publish her poems. She became famous only after her death. Also in this decade, the poet, Ella Wheeler Wilcox (1850–1919), produced works, but in her case, these were published and brought her success in her lifetime.

The English-born Frances Hodgson Burnett (1849–1924) is best-remembered for her rather sticky *Little Lord Fauntleroy,* published in 1886, and *Sarah Crewe* in 1888. Francis Richard ("Frank") Stockton (1834–1902) wrote what may be the most famous puzzle story in history, "The Lady or the Tiger?" in 1882.

Edward Bellamy (1850–1898) published a Socialist description of a utopia in *Looking Backward,* in 1888. It was very dull, but it inspired a devoted following.

Two successful sculptors, the Irish-born Augustus Saint-Gaudens (1848–1907) and Daniel Chester French (1850–1931), were becoming well-known in the 1880s. Stanford White (1853–1906) was the best-known American architect of the time and was fated to be the victim in a celebrated murder case.

John Singer Sargent (1856–1923) was a painter who began his career in this decade.

An important musician of the period was Edward Alexander MacDowell (1860–1908). Henry Louis Reginald De Koven (1859–1920) was a relatively minor musician who made his mark, however, with the song, "Oh, Promise Me," which he wrote in 1889 and was included in his opera *Robin Hood* in 1890.

The most successful composer, however, was John Philip Sousa (1854–1932), the "March King." He composed about 140 military marches altogether, and in this decade began to make

himself famous with "Semper Fidelis" in 1888 and "The Washington Post March" in 1889.

CANADA

Canada developed a transcontinental railroad of its own. The last spike was driven on November 7, 1885, and it was opened to the public in May 1887.

When Louis Riel, who had led the Red River rebellion in 1869, returned to Canada in 1885 and once more tried to stir a rebellion in the west, the new railroad was used to rush troops westward and the rebellion was quickly crushed. Riel was hanged on November 16, 1885.

NEWFOUNDLAND

Newfoundland, Great Britain's oldest colony, was not part of the Dominion of Canada. It preferred to maintain a kind of precarious self-government of its own. Labrador, the frigid, sparsely inhabited region to the northeast of the province of Quebec, was under the control of Newfoundland, rather than of Canada.

MEXICO

Mexico, under Porfirio Diaz, had order and quiet, but Diaz built up an autocratic dictatorship, controlling every aspect of national life. He made sure that those in power, the landowners and the Church, would be on his side by leaving them in peace. Mexico had virtually no financial resources of its own after the disorders of the French occupation, so Diaz encouraged foreign investment, especially from the United States.

The money poured in, at generous interest rates, so that foreign banks profited. So did Diaz and his friends. The money was used to build railroads and bridges, to develop mines and irrigation, all of which went to benefit the better-off, as land ownership became more and more concentrated in the hands of a few.

The lower classes gained nothing. They had no education and were denied all participation in politics. Any revolts were promptly repressed by the military, which was entirely under the control of Diaz.

CENTRAL AMERICA

Efforts were still made to unify the area. Between 1886 and 1889, there were meetings designed to set up constitutions and regional treaties. Controversies between Guatemala and Salvador scuttled the effort, however.

COLOMBIA

Like Mexico, Colombia came under conservative rule. Rafael Nunez (1825–1894), like Diaz of Mexico, had been liberal in his younger years, but once he became President of Colombia in 1880 he moved farther and farther into the conservative camp. The constitution of 1886 replaced the federal union with a strongly centralized government and restored the power of the Catholic Church.

VENEZUELA

Venezuela, under Antonio Guzman Blanco (1829–1899), also experienced a stern, centralized dictatorship. As with Diaz of Mexico, Guzman Blanco attracted foreign investment and modernized the land to the benefit of the bankers and the landowners. Guzman Blanco accumulated a fortune for himself. Unlike Diaz, however, Guzman Blanco encouraged education and was anticlerical. He secularized social life and declared religious toleration.

CHILE

Chile was fighting Peru and Bolivia in the War of the Pacific as the decade opened. Chile lies along the narrow western slope of the Andes Mountains and is a long, thin nation, rather snakelike on the map. Just to the north of Chile was a particularly dry desert that was an important source of nitrates, which were used in fertilizers and explosives. This strip of desert belonged to Bolivia and beyond it to Peru.

Chile, the most advanced of the three nations, exploited the area but was heavily taxed by Bolivia and Peru. Chile felt it might as well take the land, and it did. Chile won the War of the Pacific handily, winning almost every battle. By April 4, 1884, a final treaty ceded the disputed desert area to Chile, which has retained it, with minor adjustments, ever since. In doing this, it cut off Bolivia's sea-coast and made it a land-locked nation, like Paraguay.

After the war, Jose Manuel Balmaceda (1840–1891) became President in 1886. He tried to set up a stronger executive, combining that with anticlericalism and public works.

PERU

Manuel Iglesias (1830–1909) had led the Peruvians in the War of the Pacific, in which the Chileans had even occupied the Peruvian capital of Lima for a time. Iglesias was blamed for the loss, was forced to resign in 1886, and was replaced by Andres Avelino Carceras (1833–1923). Caceros managed to get financial help by signing over profits from railroads and guano islands to foreign investors.

BOLIVIA

Hilarion Daza, who was President of Bolivia during the lost War of the Pacific, also had to pay for that. He was overthrown in 1880, after the first reverses, and was replaced by Narcisco Campero (1813–1896), who couldn't do any better and was out in 1884. Bolivia made up for its loss of sea-coast by the building of a railroad, with Chilean cooperation, which connected western Bolivia with the now-Chilean coast.

BRAZIL

The emancipation of the slaves in Brazil, without compensation, was completed on May 13, 1888. This, however, angered the landowners and made them dissatisfied with Emperor Pedro II. Republican sentiment had been increasing in any case, and the army had become disaffected because Pedro II had been following a policy of peace. It might seem that a ruler who is peaceful and who liberates slaves is worth keeping, but that is not necessarily the way of the world.

A military coup led by Manuel Deodoro da Fonseca (1827–1892) overthrew Pedro II on November 15, 1889, and Fonseca became the president of the new Republic of Brazil. There were now no monarchies anywhere among the independent nations of the American continents.

EGYPT

As western influence was rising in Egypt, there arose a phenomenon with which the world would become more familiar, non-European nationalism—that is, the objection off non-Europeans to European control.

A Muslim nationalist, Jamal ad-Din al-Afghani (1838–1897), not only inveighed against western control, but urged the adoption of western methods to fight that control. An Egyptian army officer, Ahmad Urabi (1839–1911), followed Jamal ad-Din's teachings. He objected not only to westerners, but also to the fact that the highest ranks in the Egyptian army were held by Turks and other non-Egyptians. He popularized the slogan "Egypt for the Egyptians," and grew powerful in 1881.

The Viceroy of Egypt, Tawfiq, could see that his rule would not last long, for he was steadily forced to make concessions to Urabi. Therefore, he called for help from Great Britain and France. Those nations responded with alacrity, and British and French ships appeared off Alexandria on May 20, 1882.

This infuriated the Alexandrian population, who rioted on June 12 and killed some 50 Europeans. The French were reluctant to indulge in direct confrontation, but the British were not. They bombarded Alexandria on July 11. At this, Urabi declared Tawfiq a traitor and the nationalist movement hardened further.

The British then proceeded to land 25,000 troops, under Garnet Joseph Wolseley (1833–1913), to protect the Suez Canal. Wolseley, who had served all over the world since the Crimean War and had even put down the Red River rebellion in Canada, seized the Suez Canal swiftly. On September 13, 1882, he met a large army of Nationalist Egyptians at Tall-al-Kabir, north of Cairo, and routed them with little loss. Two days later, Wolseley occupied Cairo. Urabi surrendered and was eventually banished to Ceylon.

Since the French had refused to participate in the expedition, Great Britain declared the dual control, with France, over Egypt at an end on November 9, 1882. From then on, Egypt was, effectively, a British colony.

There was, however, greater trouble to come in Sudan, which lay south of Egypt and which had been under Egyptian control, more or less, for half a century, ever since the time of Muhammad Ali.

Rising to power in the Sudan was Muhammad Ahmad ibn Abd Allah (1844–1885). He was a Muslim fundamentalist and a mystic. He believed that the ruling Muslims in Egypt and Sudan were renegades and that he alone was destined to set things right. He announced this in March, 1881, and on June 18, called himself "al Mahdi" ("the divinely guided one").

The Mahdi gathered a Muslim army about him, and as in the heady days of the first Muslim expansion, 12 centuries earlier, it swept all before them in a state of religious exaltation. By 1883, two Egyptian armies had been wiped out. A Third Egyptian army, this time under the command of a British general, William Hicks (1830–1883), was ambushed at al-Ubbayid in central Sudan on November 3, 1883, and was completely wiped out, Hicks included.

While this was happening, the Mahdi's forces were taking Egypt's Red Sea ports, and the British were forced to order the evacuation of the Sudan, on January 6, 1884.

The British then readied a punitive expedition, placed it under General Charles ("Chinese") Gordon, who had done so well against the T'ai P'ing rebels in China, and sent him south to set things straight. Gordon reached Khartoum, the Sudanese capital, on February 18, 1884, and attempted to come to an understanding with the Mahdi. He offered him partial sovereignty over Sudan, noninterference with the slave trade, remission of taxes, and so on. The Mahdi refused it all and, instead, moved to place Khartoum under siege.

Khartoum remained under siege for months, while the British government, under Gladstone, dithered. It was not until October that a relief expedition under Wolseley began to be organized but, by then, it was too late. There was no chance it could fight its way to Khartoum in time. On January 26, 1885, the Mahdi took Khartoum and massacred the garrison, including Gordon. On hearing this, Wolseley's relief column retreated. There was nothing to relieve. The loss of Khartoum and the death of Gordon contributed to Gladstone's loss of power five months later.

The Mahdi's triumph was short-lived, however. He died, possibly of typhus, on June 22, 1885, five months after he took Khartoum. His followers remained in control of the Sudan, however, and Mahdism remains a living Muslim sect to this day.

On October 19, 1888, the Suez Canal Convention was adopted by an international conference. The Suez Canal was proclaimed to be free and open to all vessels, both merchantmen and warships, in peace and in war. Of course, since Great Britain controlled both the seas and the canal, there was no question but that it would close the canal when and as it pleased, if it felt it necessary to do so.

ETHIOPIA

In 1884, Great Britain and France, as well as Italy, were establishing themselves on the Red Sea coast, northeast of Ethiopia. The result was that in addition to Italian Eritrea, the political divisions later known as British Somaliland and French Somaliland were also being formed.

Meanwhile, within Ethiopia, there was a civil war between Johannes IV and one of the provincial rulers, Menelik (1844–1913). Johannes IV won out and, in 1887, attempted to drive the Italians from the Eritrean coast, but he was distracted by the Mahdi's incursions into northern Ethiopia. On March 12, 1889, in fact, Johannes IV was killed in a battle against the Mahdists.

That was Menelik's chance. He fought against Johannes IV's son, and the Italians backed Men-

elik. This time, it was Menelik who won out. On May 2, 1889, Menelik signed a treaty with Italy. Italy chose to interpret the treaty as having established an Italian protectorate over Ethiopia, but this was not in Menelik's mind at all.

WEST AFRICA

In West Africa in this decade, the European powers were busily engaged in carving up the territory in a mutually agreeable way so as to minimize the possibility of armed conflict over uncertain boundaries. In addition to the huge British and French segments, Germany took over, by agreement, Togoland and the Cameroons in 1884; and in 1885, Spain took over (the mostly desert) Rio de Oro.

EAST AFRICA

While the British steadily expanded their holdings, the Germans took over "German East Africa" in what is now Tanzania in 1885.

SOUTH AFRICA

The Germans occupied "Southwest Africa" in 1885, too, and by the end of the decade, the Partition of Africa was virtually completed.

This was carried through peacefully, but there remained the possibility of conflict in one place. The Boers in southern Africa considered themselves, with some reason, to be oppressed. The British had annexed the South African Republic in 1877 after they had earlier recognized its independence. On December 30, 1880, the Boers revolted, with Paul Kruger (1825–1904) one of the guiding spirits behind the move.

The British government, under the peace-loving Gladstone, did not wish to go to war over the matter and, on April 5, 1881, recognized the independence of the Republic again, but insisted on an admission of the nominal sovereignty of Great Britain, as a face-saving device. On April 16, 1883, Kruger became president of the reinstated republic.

In 1886, gold was discovered in South Africa and the world witnessed another gold rush. Just as Kimberley had been founded to exploit the diamond mines, so, now Johannesburg was founded to exploit the gold mines.

The outstanding British imperialist in South Africa was Cecil John Rhodes (1853–1902), who had come to South Africa in 1870 for his health, and had made his fortune in the diamond fields. He pushed hard to have Great Britain annex as much African territory as possible and dreamed of a solid British belt of territory from the Cape of Good Hope to the Mediterranean Sea.

In 1890, he became the Prime Minister of Cape Colony. With him in the south and Kruger in the north, both hard, intransigient men, there was bound to be an explosion.

AFGHANISTAN

In this decade, Afghanistan continued the old game of playing the Russians and British against each other. It had become more dangerous than ever because the Russians had now reached the Afghani border all along the line.

The trouble was that the line was not, at that time, clearly defined and the Russians didn't want to define it because uncertainty meant they might be able to gobble up more territory. On March 30, 1885, there was a serious battle between Russian and Afghani forces at the border town of Panjdeh. The Russians won the battle and, for a while, it looked as though they would invade Afghanistan in force.

The British (who had twice invaded Afghanistan themselves) made it clear to the Russians that if *they* invaded Afghanistan that would mean war with Great Britain. The Russians decided not to chance it, and the dispute was settled peaceably on June 18, 1886, and the border was more or less defined.

INDIA

In 1880, George Frederick Samuel Robinson, Lord Ripon (1827–1909) became Viceroy of India. He was a liberal of the Gladstone stripe and labored to increase self-government in India. He even tried to arrange to have Indian judges preside over trials of Europeans, when that was nec-

essary, in outlying areas at least. This the British residents in India fiercely opposed. It was all right to have Indians tried by British judges, but not vice versa.

This naturally offended the Indians. The various improvements that Great Britain had brought into the land—railroads, telegraphs, newspapers—all made it possible for Indians in all parts of the vast land to communicate with each other and to share views and aspirations.

A liberal Briton, Allan Octavian Hume (1829–1912), convened an ''Indian National Congress'' on December 17, 1885, one which was attended by representatives from all over India. It called for various reforms. Similar meetings were held every year in different cities, and the Indian nationalist movement began to grow.

BURMA

What was left of independent Burma in the north came under the rule of Thibaw (1858–1916). His strong-minded queen, Supayalat, urged him to resist British influence. He followed her advice and felt he could do it best by courting French help. On October 22, 1885, the British sent Thibaw an ultimatum to cease all anti-British activity. The ultimatum was rejected and the ''Third Burmese War'' began.

It didn't last long. By November 28, the British had occupied Mandalay, Thibaw's capital. Thibaw was deposed and sent into exile in India and, on January 1, 1886, all of Burma became British.

INDO-CHINA

In this decade, France completed the takeover of what then began to be called ''French Indo-China.''

EAST INDIES

The British established themselves in northern Borneo in 1888. The most important event in the East Indies in this decade, however, had nothing to do with politics or imperialism.

The small island of Krakatoa, between the

large islands of Java and Sumatra, seemed as harmless as the island of Thera had appeared 33 centuries before. Krakatoa, like Thera, happened to be a large dormant volcano, well-plugged with hardened lava, but with the possibility of ocean water making its way, finally, to the hot rocks at its base. The water might then turn to steam and build pressure to higher and higher levels until the entire island exploded.

On May 20, 1883, volcanic activity began to make itself evident at Krakatoa. It died away and returned several times and then, on August 26, it seemed serious. At 2 P.M., there was a black cloud of ash rising 17 miles into the air. At 10 A.M., August 27, there came the explosion, the most severe the Earth had experienced since Thera. Ash was thrown 50 miles into the air, and the sound was heard by ear 2200 miles away in Australia, while the sound vibrations were detected by instruments all over the world.

Five cubic miles of rock were thrown high into the air. Near the volcano there was darkness for two and a half days. The explosion set off tsunamis ("tidal waves"), which drowned 30,000 people along the coasts of Java and Sumatra. Because of the dust in the upper atmosphere, there were unusually colorful sunsets for a couple of years.

CHINA

These were continuing years of humiliation for China as it watched lands long tributary to itself being ripped away. Indo-China was taken by the French, Burma by the British, and Korea was declared independent by the Japanese.

One constructive note was that the first railroad was built in China in 1888. It ran for 80 miles from Tangshan to Tientsin.

KOREA

Korea was now open. It signed a treaty with the United States on May 22, 1882. The United States had permission to trade and it had extraterritoriality, so that American traders were governed by American law for crimes committed on Korean territory.

Korea signed a similar treaty with Great Britain in 1883 and with Russia in 1884. For the rest of the decade, there was a tug of war between China and Japan over which was to have the greater influence in Korea.

JAPAN

During the 1880s, the Japanese organized a western-style government with parties, with a legislature, and with a peerage. They worked out a constitution on February 11, 1889. They used as a model not the government of Great Britain or the United States, but the government of Germany. This helped cast Japan into a conservative and militaristic mode.

Economic expansion continued rapidly.

Once the Japanese had developed a navy, it was noted that a disease called "beri-beri" afflicted the sailors. A Japanese physician, Kanehiro Takaki, suspected it might be the result of the sailors' drab diet of fish and rice. He added meat and vegetables to the diet in some cases, and beri-beri did not then develop. The dietary change was made mandatory and the beri-beri problem was solved. This was akin to the adoption of citrus fruit juice in the British navy a century earlier to solve the problem of scurvy. The *reason* why dietary changes solved such problems was still not understood, however.

The Japanese bacteriologist, Shibasaburo Kitasato (1856–1931), worked for Koch in Germany and, in 1889, isolated the bacterium that causes tetanus and another one that causes anthrax.

PACIFIC ISLANDS

Just as Africa had been partitioned, so were the Pacific Islands. Germany annexed the Marshall Islands and the Solomon Islands in 1885. Great Britain took over the Cook Islands in 1888, and were in joint control, with France, of New Hebrides, in 1887. After Germany took over northeastern New Guinea in 1884, the British, under considerable Australian pressure, took over southeastern New Guinea.

Dominion over the Samoan Islands was shared by three powers: Great Britain, Germany, and the United States. On November 8, 1880, the King of Samoa died and there was a civil war. In 1881, a new king was finally accepted, and all three European powers recognized him.

In 1887, however, the Germans grew unsatisfied with the choice. They landed troops in Samoa and installed a king of their own choosing. The Samoans rebelled in 1888, and the Americans objected forcibly to the German conduct.

German and American warships eventually squared off, while the British tried desperately to make peace. What solved the matter was a terrific hurricane which swooped down upon the islands on March 15–16, 1889, and, quite impartially, drove three American ships and three German ships ashore. The fleets were too battered to fight and, on June 14, 1889, there was a peaceful agreement on the matter that restored the situation in Samoa as it had been before the German troops had invaded.

AUSTRALIA

The Australians were excluding Chinese immigration as the United States was doing, and, in 1888, the British upheld this practice. Australia was to be "a white man's country."

NEW ZEALAND

In 1881, New Zealand also barred Chinese immigration.

Refrigeration was altering the pattern of world trade. Refrigerated railroad cars came into use and that meant fresh meat could be shipped long distances over continental regions. Refrigerated ships extended the range even further. It meant that New Zealand meat, for instance, could be shipped across the ocean.

In 1889, New Zealand adopted universal male suffrage.

1890 TO 1900

GREAT BRITAIN

In this period, Europe reached the peak of its power. Four centuries earlier, it had been a materially backward region, not to be compared in wealth and culture with the great empires of Asia. It had been at the mercy of Asian invaders, prostrate before the Mongols in the thirteenth century, and unable to fend off the Ottoman Turks in the sixteenth century.

Yet by 1890, the American continents, Australia, and New Zealand were ruled by the descendants of Europeans. Virtually all of Africa and the Pacific islands had been carved up and placed under European domination. In Asia, large tracts such as Siberia and India were under the direct control of Europeans, while independent nations such as the Ottoman Empire, Persia, Afghanistan, Siam, and China were under continual and increasing European pressure and

interference. In all the world, the only nation that seemed to be at once non-European and strong was Japan, and that was at the price of adopting much European technology and culture.

Of all the European powers, Great Britain, on a world-wide scale, was predominant. The British Empire included roughly a quarter of the land area of the world, and roughly a quarter of its population as well. Its strong economy and its strong navy made it the most influential nation in the world, and much of that part of the world that it did not own outright, nevertheless, remained under economic subjection to it.

Yet of Great Britain's vast possessions, the nearest posed the greatest problem and took up an entirely disproportionate share of emotion. Gladstone, who had been Prime Minister three times, was over 80 when this decade began but he was still fighting for Irish home rule. He added to this other reforms, such as a shorter workday, disestablishing the Church in Wales and Scotland, and so on. In 1892, he managed to get enough Liberal members elected so that they had the majority if the Irish Nationalists voted with them.

On August 18, 1892, he became Prime Minister for the fourth time and, on February 13, 1893, he proposed a second Irish Home Rule Bill. In this one, there would be Irish representatives in the British Parliament, in addition to there being an Irish Parliament. In this way, the Irish could have some say in matters with which the Irish Parliament would be not be permitted to concern itself. On September 1, the Bill passed the House of Commons, but then, on September 8, the House of Lords turned it down resoundingly and overwhelmingly. Over 90% of the Lords voted against Home Rule.

That finally broke Gladstone, especially since, as a man of peace, he didn't want to raise expenditures for the navy at a time when the rest of the cabinet *did* want to do so. He resigned on March 3, 1894 and, finally, at the age of 84, retired from politics.

He was succeeded as Liberal Prime Minister by Archibald Philip Primrose, Earl of Roseberry (1847–1929), who supported Gladstone's reforms, but was against Irish Home Rule. He only lasted a year before being defeated in the House. A new election brought in the Conservative Party, with Salisbury assuming the post of Prime Minister for the third time, on June 25, 1895.

Rather unexpectedly, the Irish problem diminished, at least for some years, after the defeat of the second Home Rule Bill. For one thing, the Secretary for Ireland, who had a great responsibility for handling problems that arose there, was, during Gladstone's last Prime Ministership, John, Viscount Morley (1838–1923). He was in sympathy with Gladstone's views and did his best to handle the Irish decently. Then, when his term came to an end and the Conservatives came in, they followed a definite policy of passing reasonable laws that improved the lot of the Irish, so that the feeling for Home Rule became less desperate.

Queen Victoria's long rule continued. In 1887, Great Britain had celebrated her "Golden Jubilee," the celebration of her 50 years on the throne. In 1897, there was the "Diamond Jubilee" to mark the 60th anniversary of her coronation. She had presided over a long golden age of peace (except for colonial wars and the relatively minor Crimean War) and prosperity. On the Diamond Jubilee, in fact, Great Britain seemed to be at an unchallenged peak from which she would never be moved.

But history moves on and no peak can be permanent. Times change.

Thus, Gladstone's fight for Irish Home Rule had split the Liberal party, since many Liberals would not go along with him in this. That weakening of the party, plus the fact that many laborers could now vote, made the time ripe for the founding of a new party that would be more socialist than the traditional parties, and more concerned with the rights and needs of the workingclass.

The man for the task was James Heir Hardie (1856–1915), a coalminer, who had labored to organize his fellow-miners into unions, getting himself fired and blacklisted for his pains. He was a socialist, a pacifist, a feminist, and, despite all that, managed to gain a Parliamentary seat in 1892. He went on to found the "Independent Labour Party." After Hardie lost his Parliamentary seat, he politicized the organization on the lines of the Liberals and Conservatives. In this way, the Labour Party came into being.

In the second half of the decade, Great Britain had a comparative rest from internal problems, partly because the nation's attention was absorbed by a series of crises abroad, all of which will be taken up in due course under the appropriate national headings.

The 1890s saw great achievements in science, in which British scientists fully participated.

The first to attempt an explanation of the negative results of the Michelson–Morley experiment of the previous decade was George Francis FitzGerald (1851–1910). He pointed out, in 1895, that the result could be explained if it were assumed that all objects in motion contracted in the direction of motion in accordance with a certain equation relating the speed of motion to the speed of light. The contraction would reduce the length of the object to zero at the speed of light, so that this "FitzGerald contraction" made it seem that motion faster than the speed of light in a vacuum was impossible.

John William Strutt, Lord Rayleigh (1842–1919), and William Ramsay (1852–1916) discovered the gas argon in 1894, and each received a Nobel Prize for the feat. Argon was a completely inert gas and one of a hitherto-unknown family of elements. Ramsay discovered helium on Earth in 1895 (it having been first detected in the sun 30 years earlier) and it proved to be another member of the family. Along with Morris William Travers (1872–1961), Ramsay discovered three other members in 1898—neon, krypton, and xenon.

Dewar invented the "Dewar flask" (or "thermos bottle") in 1892. In 1898, he succeeded in liquefying hydrogen at a temperature of only 20° above absolute zero. That left the newly discovered helium as the only gas still unliquefied.

In 1897, Joseph John Thomson (1856–1940) was able to show conclusively that cathode ray particles consisted of speeding particles carrying a negative electric charge and with a mass only 1/1837 that of the lightest atom, hydrogen. The new particle was named the "electron," a name first proposed as the unit of electricity by George Johnstone Stoney (1826–1911) in 1891. The electron was the first "subatomic particle" (one smaller than an atom) to be discovered. Thomson won a Nobel Prize for this.

Also in 1897, Ronald Ross (1857–1932) discovered the causative agent of malaria, which turned out to be a protozoan. It was the first case of an infectious disease known to be caused by a non-bacterial agent. Ross also found that certain mosquitoes carried the protozoan from one person to another, so that eradicating mosquitoes offered a way of controlling the disease. This work, too, was found worthy of a Nobel Prize.

Frederick Gowland Hopkins (1861–1947) discovered tryptophan, an important amino acid, in 1900; while Francis Galton, in this decade, worked out the use of fingerprints as an identifying device.

Charles Parsons put his steam turbine to startling use in 1897. He had built a turbine-powered ship, the *Turbinia,* that was capable of moving at a speed of 35 knots with scarcely any vibration or noise. At the Diamond Jubilee of Queen Victoria, when the British navy was holding a stately review, the *Turbinia,* at top speed, flashed past those ships. Nothing in the water could catch it. Naturally, steam turbines became a popular item at once for shipbuilders.

Arthur John Evans (1851–1941) was an archeologist who, beginning in 1894, conducted digs in Crete that revealed details concerning the early Minoan civilization that, until then, had only been hinted at in some of the Greek myths.

Among writers who continued actively, Oscar Wilde became a prominent playwright with such plays as *Lady Windermere's Fan* (1892), *Salome* (1894), and *The Importance of Being Earnest* (1895). He was, however, outclassed by George Bernard Shaw (1856–1950), who, in this decade, began to write plays that openly gibed at conventional attitudes, examples being *Arms and the Man, Candida, Mrs. Warren's Profession* (all published in 1898), *The Devil's Disciple* and *Caesar and Cleopatra* (published in 1900).

Shaw was a prominent member of the "Fabian Society," a group of socialists who believed in a slow and gradual victory for the system. (Hence, "Fabian," from Fabius, the Roman general who favored a slow and cautious way of fighting Hannibal.) Other prominent members of the society were Sidney James Webb (1859–1947) and his wife, Beatrice Webb (1858–1943). The movement never had much influence, but it brought socialism to the attention of the intellectuals.

Kipling was still writing, with *The Light That Failed* (1890), *Barrack-Room Ballads* (1892), *The Jungle Book* (1894), and *Captains Courageous* (1897). So was Hardy, who published *Tess of the D'Urbervilles* (1891) and *Jude the Obscure* (1895).

James Matthew Barrie (1860–1937) wrote popular novels, such as *The Little Minister* (1893) and *Sentimental Tommy* (1896), before turning to drama. Arthur Wing Pinero (1855–1934) achieved his greatest success with *The Second Mrs. Tanqueray* (1893).

Herbert George Wells (1866–1946) burst on the scene with *The Time Machine* (1895), *The Invisible Man* (1897), and *The War of the Worlds* (1898), proving himself to be a science fiction writer who eclipsed even Jules Verne. Wells, too, was a prominent member of the Fabian Society.

The Polish-born Joseph Conrad (1857–1924) wrote novels of the sea, including *Nigger of the "Narcissus"* (1897) and *Lord Jim* (1900), among others.

George Louis Palmella Busson du Maurier (1834–1896) wrote *Peter Ibbetson* (1891) and *Trilby* (1894). The villain in the latter book, Svengali, became so well-known that the term is still used for anyone who controls a person of talent, and does so with evil intent.

Israel Zangwill (1864–1926), who was Jewish, dealt with the Jewish experience in *The Children of the Ghetto* (1892) and *The King of the Schnorrers* (1894).

The new kingdom of the Balkans offered a fruitful source of completely idealized romance. Anthony Hope Hawkins (1863–1933), using the pseudonym "Anthony Hope," wrote *The Prisoner of Zenda* (1894) and *Rupert of Hentzau* (1898), set in a mythical Balkan kingdom; while Abraham ("Bram") Stoker published a tale of Transylvanian horror, *Dracula,* in 1897.

The poet, Alfred Edward Housman (1859–1936), wrote *A Shropshire Lad* in 1896, while Kipling wrote such well-known poems as "Danny Deever," "Gunga Din," "The Road to Mandalay," "The Ballad of East and West," and, most of all, "Recessional," written in 1899 after the Diamond Jubilee, and oddly apprehensive of Great Britain's decline.

In nonfiction, James George Frazer (1854–1941) wrote *The Golden Bough,* published in two volumes in 1890, and greatly expanded later, which was a study of ancient myths and rites that were darker and more primitive than the familiar Greek myths.

An important illustrator of the period was the short-lived Aubrey Vincent Beardsley (1872–1898), whose often grotesque but powerful illustrations for such works as Wilde's *Salome* and Aristophanes' *Lysistrata* made him famous.

GERMANY

Bismarck was succeeded as chancellor by Georg Leo von Caprivi (1831–1899), whom William II chose because he thought he would be sufficiently obsequious and would allow the Emperor to do things his own way.

William II tried to follow Bismarck's example of conceding benefits to labor in order to weaken socialism, but socialism spread anyway and a number of socialist delegates were elected to the legislature.

Caprivi carried through trade agreements with other countries which, essentially, put Germany in the position of importing food and raw materials and exporting manufactured goods. Naturally, there would be low tariffs on the imported food and this undercut the relatively inefficient agriculturalists of Germany. The agriculturalists were placed in the opposition, therefore, and they (especially the "Junkers" of eastern Germany) brought a great deal of archconservative pressure on the government.

Caprivi had no experience in foreign affairs and here he relied on a rather shadowy figure, Friedrich von Holstein (1837–1909), who preferred to work quietly, pulling strings behind the scenes. Holstein had been a protege of Bismarck, but in Bismarck's later years, Holstein turned into an opponent. The disagreement came over Russia. Bismarck was determined to hold on to Russia as much as possible, even as he recognized Austria-Hungary as Germany's chief partner.

To Holstein, this seemed foolish. Austria-Hungary and Russia were irreconcilable, and it made no sense to him to waste energies on trying to mediate between the two when that was, in any case, impossible. Of the two, it seemed to make much more sense to cling to loyal, partly German, Austria-Hungary, than a Slavic and quite unpredictable Russia.

Holstein somehow persuaded Caprivi and William II to this policy, and when the time came to renew the alliance with Russia, it was allowed to lapse on June 18, 1890. The Russians were upset and did their best to urge Germany into a renewal, but the Germans were adamant in their abandonment. Russia, now seeing a danger from Germany, and much alarmed, had to find new allies.

To make up for the loss of Russia, it was Germany's intention to improve relations with Great Britain and, if possible, to get it to join the Triple Alliance. With this in mind, William II visited London in state on July 4, 1891. However, William II was not the man to sweet-talk anyone into anything. He exuded far too much in the way of arrogance and vanity to impress the British, whose ruling class always felt it owned the patent on such things. Besides, England was not ready to give up its policy of isolationism. What it amounted to, then, was that Russia was lost before Great Britain was gained, a blunder which Bismarck would never have made.

Feeling a little more isolated, therefore, than it had been, and facing the possibility of a two-front war since it might be that France and Russia would now act together if either of them were embroiled with Germany, Germany decided to increase its army. To spare the drain on Germany's labor force, however, Caprivi accompanied the increase by reducing the three-year training period to two.

The increase in the size of the army alarmed France and Russia and increased the pressure pushing them toward an alliance. On the other hand, the reduction in the period of service annoyed the militarists in Germany, who also became anti-Caprivi. In addition, William II was troubled by the Chancellor's occasional tendency to think for himself and forced him into resignation on October 26, 1894.

In his place, William II chose Chlodwig Karl Victor zu Hohenlohe-Schillingsfurst (1819–1901). Hohenlohe was 75 years old, good-natured, and had a friendly relationship with the Emperor. William II was confident that Hohenlohe wouldn't dream of opposing the Imperial will and, indeed, he did not. Occasionally, he tried to keep William II from making an utter fool of himself, but he usually failed.

Having failed to win Great Britain into friendship, William II now undertook a series of enterprises that gradually alienated it. Germany's industrialization was allowing it to overtake Great Britain in economic strength. This didn't exactly please the British, but they were inclined to overlook that as long as they controlled the sea. That confined Germany's economic power mainly to the European continent, while Great Britain still had the world at large.

In June 1895, Germany opened the Kiel Canal, which cut across the isthmus just south of Denmark and allowed easy access between the North Sea and Baltic Sea for ships that would no longer have to sail all around Denmark to do so. It had obvious commercial possibilities, but Germany was thinking of it largely as a way of making sure that warships could be transferred between the two seas rapidly at need. This increased the effectiveness of the German navy, but Great Britain was inclined to overlook that, too. After all, the German navy was still small, and Great Britain did not regard it as a menace.

In fact, so careless was Great Britain about such matters that on July 11, 1890, they had given Germany the tiny island of Helgoland just off the northwest German coast in return for Germany giving up certain of its claims in East Africa. The East African territory would have meant little to Germany but it built up Helgoland into a first-class naval base, and apparently the British didn't foresee this.

In 1895, trouble arose between the British and the Boers in South Africa. A British raid on Boer territory was frustrated. At this, William II had what seemed to him a brilliant idea. He would demonstrate to the British the dangers of being isolated and would show them, furthermore, how annoying German enmity could be. The upshot, William II thought, would be that Great Britain would clamor for a German alliance.

Therefore, on January 3, 1896, William II sent a telegram to President Kruger of the Boer Republic, congratulating him on repelling the raid.

The telegram achieved the opposite of what William II had intended. The British government kept calm, but the British people exploded into anger. Until then, Great Britain, accustomed to thinking that France was Great Britain's "natural enemy," had been well-disposed toward Germany, but all this was undone at a stroke by William II's foolish move. Indeed, many British were ready to give up isolation now, but they clamored for an alliance *against* Germany.

Worse yet was to come. In 1897, Alfred von Tirpitz (1849–1930) was placed in charge of the German navy. It was his ambition, and William II went along with it eagerly, to strengthen that navy by building many ships of the latest design. On March 28, 1898, money was voted by the legislature for this purpose, and the building of a modern German navy was begun. It took a while for Great Britain to realize that Germany was actually aiming to challenge it on the seas, but as that realization sharpened, the matter of the Kiel Canal and Helgoland came to be viewed in a new light, and the enmity felt by Great Britain toward Germany grew steadily more intense.

On November 17, 1898, Germany began to plan a railroad from Berlin to Baghdad in Iraq, which was then part of the Ottoman Empire. This was with the obvious intention of increasing German influence in the Middle East, which alarmed both Great Britain and Russia.

What's more, Germany was increasing its meddling in China and that upset Japan. In short, where Bismarck had carefully secured the friendship of all the European powers but France in the 1870s and 1880s, William II, in the 1890s, was managing to alienate all the European powers with the exception of Austria-Hungary.

On October 16, 1900, Hohenlohe resigned and, in his place, William II appointed Berhard Heinrich Martin Karl von Bulow (1849–1929) to the post of Chancellor. It didn't seem likely he would improve matters. He was a friend of Holstein and he had promoted the Berlin-to-Baghdad railroad.

Science was flourishing in Germany. Wilhelm Konrad Roentgen (1845–1923), while working with cathode rays, discovered x-rays in 1895. This discovery is usually considered to have initiated a "Second Scientific Revolution", comparable to the one set off by Copernicus, and it brought Roentgen a Nobel Prize.

Wilhelm Wien (1864–1928) demonstrated, in 1893, that the higher the temperature of a substance, the shorter the wavelength of the peak radiation that it produces. Wien tried to work out an equation that would describe the manner in which all wavelengths of radiation could be emitted by a body that would produce them all (a "black body").

Wien failed in this, but Max Karl Ernst Ludwig Planck (1858–1947) succeeded in 1900, by assuming that energy could only be given off in fixed amounts. These energy-packets were extremely tiny and Planck called them "quanta." It turned out that Planck's "quantum theory" made it possible to look at all of physical science in a new and much-improved way, so that everything before 1900 is called "classical physics" and everything afterward is "modern physics." Both Wien and Planck received Nobel Prizes for their work.

In the life sciences, Emil Adolf von Behring (1854–1917) discovered, in 1890, that it was possible to produce an immunity against tetanus in an animal by injecting into it graded doses of blood serum from an animal already suffering from tetanus. The patient with tetanus develops an "antitoxin" that fights off the disease in healthy animals.

Behring next dealt in this way with diptheria, a childhood disease that meant almost sure death. In 1892, he developed an antitoxin that produced immunity to the disease in the first place, and helped fight it off if infection had already taken place. Behring received a Nobel Prize for this.

Until this time, it was maintained that some chemical reactions characteristic of life could only be performed by living cells. The fermentation of sugar by yeast was an example. In 1896, however, Eduard Buchner (1860–1917) ground up yeast cells, filtered the material, and obtained a nonliving solution that could produce the fermentation. No enzyme, therefore, required a living cell to do its work, and for this Buchner received a Nobel Prize.

Germany shone in aeronautics. Otto Lilienthal (1848–1896) was the first to build practical gliders capable of keeping a man in flight for an extended period. He flew his first glider in 1891, and gliding became a daredevil sport in the 1890s, as ballooning had been in the 1790s. This continued even though Lilienthal himself died after a glider crash in 1896.

Ferdinand Adolf August Heinrich von Zeppelin (1838–1917) labored to design a powered balloon. He conceived the notion of confining the balloon within a cigar-shaped metal structure, both to give it greater strength and to streamline it, decreasing air-resistance. A light metal was needed and aluminum had become cheap enough for the purpose. On a gondola beneath, there would be an internal-combustion engine that would power a propeller, leaving room, of course, for people.

Zeppelin flew his first craft of this sort on July 2, 1900. For the first time, human beings could move through the air against the wind. The device was called an "airship." Since it could be directed—that is, since it was "dirigible"—it could be called by that name as well, and sometimes it was called a "zeppelin."

Rudolf Diesel (1858–1913) invented an internal-combustion engine in 1897 that could use petroleum fractions that were higher-boiling and cheaper than gasoline, and that required no electric spark for ignition, merely forceful compression. Such engines were heavy, but could be used effectively in heavy vehicles such as buses, trucks, and ships.

In 1897, also, Karl Ferdinand Braun (1850–1918) invented the oscilloscope, in which a beam of electrons could be made to scan a fluorescent surface. The beam could be made to deviate from a straight line by varying the strength of an electromagnetic field. The oscilloscope was an ancestor of the television screen.

In 1895, Karl Paul Gottfried von Linde (1842–1934) devised a system of cooling that was efficient and automatic so that liquid air became not merely a laboratory curiosity but a commodity that could easily be produced in tank-loads.

In music, Richard Georg Strauss (1864–1949) was becoming prominent. The best-known of his early works was *Also Sprach Zarathustra*, inspired by Nietzsche's book.

Among the poets of the decade were Richard Dehmel (1863–1920), whose early poems dealt with the miseries of the working classes, and Stefan George (1868–1933), who labored successfully to reinvigorate German poetry.

Two artists of the decade were Kathe Kollwitz (1867–1945), who produced a series of etchings between 1894 and 1898 that dramatized the life of the poor and oppressed. The Russian-born Wassily Kandinsky (1866–1944), working in Berlin, introduced abstractionism in art.

AUSTRIA-HUNGARY

Austria-Hungary was protected from external dangers by its reliance on Germany, but it had internal problems that Germany could not help it weather. The Hungarian portion of the dual monarchy managed to keep its minorities under control, but in the Austrian portion, the Czechs and the Poles were increasingly restless.

Austria's long-time Prime Minister, Eduard von Taafe (1833–1895), had granted concessions to the Czechs and Poles and brought some of them into the government. This was enough to satisfy those Czechs and Poles who were landowners and conservatives, and kept things going.

It aroused the furious opposition of the German nationalists, however, for they wanted no concessions. It was also insufficient to satisfy the more nationalist Czechs and Poles, who clamored for more reform. Taafe offered universal male suffrage on October 10, 1893, but the Germans were horrified at giving non-Germans an equal vote, and the minorities scorned the offer as insufficient. When the bill was rejected all around, Taafe resigned on October 19, 1893.

He was succeeded by Kasimir Felix, Count Badeni (1846–1909), who was of Polish origin. He was, to be sure, a wealthy and conservative landowner, but he was conscious enough of his origins to offer more concessions to the minorities and, in consequence, roused more opposition to himself on the part of the Germans. On the whole, he proved a failure and resigned on November 28, 1897.

There followed a period of what was almost chaos, and it appeared as though the nation might fall apart before some semblance of order was restored by the end of the decade. There was even some question as to whether Hungary would agree to renew the relationship with Austria when that renewal came due in 1897, but it did.

The internal disruption kept Austria-Hungary from pursuing an aggressive foreign policy and on April 30, 1897, it came to an agreement with Russia to keep things in the Balkans as they were. It was the best Austria-Hungary could manage.

Personal tragedy continued to dog Francis Joseph I, whose long reign continued. The Empress Elizabeth, for whom Francis Joseph probably felt all the tepid affection he could muster, was continuing the travels she had been undertaking since the suicide of her son. In Switzerland, on September 10, 1898, she was assassinated by an Italian anarchist. To what end this was done cannot be imagined for she was a harmless, half-mad woman with no political influence whatever.

Meanwhile, in 1896, Francis Joseph's only surviving brother and the heir to the throne, had died of natural causes, and his oldest son, Francis Ferdinand (1863–1914), Francis Joseph's nephew, had become the new heir to the throne. Francis Joseph disliked him intensely.

An important Austrian scientist of the decade was Ernst Mach (1838–1916), whose philosophy of science had influence on the development of the theory of relativity later on. He is best-remembered today because his work on airflow caused him to recognize the sudden changes that came when an object moved at the speed of sound. We now speak of "Mach X," for a speed that is X times the speed of sound.

Sigmund Freud became truly famous with his study of dreams. His book on the subject, *The Interpretation of Dreams*, was published in 1900. His theories of the unconscious and of the significance of sexual fantasies introduced as large a revolution in thought as Darwin's book had done four decades earlier.

In music, Dvorak composed his most famous symphony, *From the New World*, in 1893.

Among the writers, there was Arthur Schnitzler (1862–1931), who made his name with *Anatol* in 1893; and Hugo von Hofmannsthal (1874–1929), whose poems and dramatic works were both successful.

It was possible for Jews to get along in Austria-Hungary (Freud and Schnitzler, for instance, were both Jewish) but anti-Semitism remained a potent force. A Hungarian-born Jew, Theodor Herzl (1860–1904), was conscious of this and, on a trip to Paris in 1891, was shocked to discover that anti-Semitism was strong there as well.

The Jews of the world traditionally dreamed of and longed for the homeland they had not had for nearly 2000 years, but hardly anyone thought of it as anything more than a dream and a sigh. Herzl, however, felt the need to escape from the hate of the Gentiles and initiated a movement for the reestablishment of that homeland. The movement was called "Zionism," from the Hebrew name of the hill on which Solomon had built his Temple. He wrote a pamphlet, *The Jewish State*, in 1896, and organized the first Zionist Congress in Basel, Switzerland, in August 1897. Two hundred delegates attended, some even from the United States.

FRANCE

There was no chance of any monarchist revival after the Boulanger fiasco. The reasonable Pope Leo XIII saw that and moved, in a way, to recognize the French Republic, and to take the attitude that any government that had been established and proved it could rule was legitimate and had to be accepted. Not all Catholics agreed with this, of course.

There was no shortage of problems for the nation, though. Corruption, which is endemic in all societies, erupted explosively in connection with the projected building of a Panama Canal. This was to be under the leadership of Ferdinand de Lesseps, who had successfully built the Suez Canal.

De Lesseps was the president of the Panama Company, and what the company needed was capital. They set up a stock lottery that raised 1.5 billion francs from those who bought chances and were rewarded with stock that they expected would make them rich, rich, rich. It was the Mississippi Bubble of nearly two centuries earlier and it ended precisely the same way. The money raised by the lottery was frittered away by mismanagement and through being misappropriated by scoundrels. In the end, the whole thing collapsed, and the money invested disappeared.

By 1892, the continuing uproar over this had forced the government to take legal action against any crimes that might have been committed, and it quickly became apparent that the Panama Company had bribed legislators liberally to allow the lottery to take place and to look the other way as it was mishandled. It was made all the worse because it became apparent that the government had done its best to coverup and whitewash the corruption. Some of the principal money-handlers were Jewish bankers, which helped exacerbate French anti-Semitism.

It was a time also when anarchism was at its most prominent. Anarchists had turned violent and the 1890s were a time of terrorism. Explosions and assassinations were commonplace and it was then that the stereotype began of the bearded, wild-eyed anarchist, with a bomb (complete with sizzling fuse) in his hands.

The president of the French Republic in the first years of the decade was Sadi Carnot (1837–1894), the grandson of the Carnot who was so important in the First Republic. Carnot was a liberal who had worked toward railroad development and other public works. He had survived the Boulanger incident, and the Panama Scandal, but on June 24, 1894, he was assassinated by an Italian anarchist (as a few years later, the Austro–Hungarian Empress and a number of other political notables were to be killed).

On a more quiet note, socialism was increasing and so was trade-unionism. The possibility of general strikes was discussed, a united downing of tools that, in theory, would more quickly bring down a repressive government than random assassination would. (As it worked out, however, it proved very difficult to organize a general strike and, when one was tried, it usually aroused a great deal of antilabor sentiment, and almost never worked unless the government was on its last legs already.)

Carnot was succeeded by Jean Paul Pierre Casimir-Perier (1847–1907), who almost at once fell afoul of the "Dreyfus Affair" and, on January 17, 1895, he resigned and returned to his business affairs that, in any case, had made him a very wealthy man. He was succeeded by Francois Felix Faure (1841–1899), whose life was also hounded by the Dreyfus affair.

The Dreyfus Affair involved Alfred Dreyfus (1859–1935), a captain in the French army and a Jew. In 1894, he was assigned to the War Ministry where one Marie Charles Ferdinand Walsin Esterhazy (1847–1923) was a disreputable fraud who was acting as a German spy. Presumably, Esterhazy did it for the money he got out of it, since it is hard to suppose that he ever acted out of principle. The fact that there was a leakage in the Ministry became obvious in 1894, and Esterhazy forged a document that seemed to place the blame on Dreyfus.

Ordinarily, it would have fooled no one, but Esterhazy had friends among the officers, while Dreyfus, as a Jew, made a good scapegoat. Dreyfus was accused and convicted in a patently unfair trial on December 22, 1894, and was condemned to life imprisonment on Devil's Island off the coast of French Guiana.

The verdict was popular with the conservatives and clericals among the French, and they gathered in mobs to howl against Jews.

Little by little, however, the liberals and anticlericals began to be suspicious. The evidence was inconclusive and the malignant behavior of the conservative officers had been too blatant. The guilt of Esterhazy became more apparent and, from 1896, the demand for a retrial became louder and louder.

The army closed ranks. It was clear that they had made a mistake out of prejudice, but they were not going to admit it. Better a miscarriage of justice and the protection of a spy than the admission of their own stupidity and hate.

One army officer, Georges Picquart (1854–1914), recognized Esterhazy's writing to be similar to that on the document that had seemed to establish Dreyfus's guilt. In all innocence, he brought this to the attention of his superiors and was promptly transferred to a post in Tunis. He was eventually imprisoned.

The forgery was exposed by others, however, and Esterhazy was forced to stand a court-martial. The Army acquitted him in January 1898, as hastily as they had convicted Dreyfus.

The writer, Emile Zola, outraged at this, wrote the pamphlet *J'Accuse* ("I accuse") in which he denounced army officers, by name, with enormous power. For that, he was tried and sentenced to a year in prison for the crime of telling the truth. Zola appealed but, feeling he would lose, fled to England, where he remained for nearly a year.

By now, the Dreyfus Affair had become the dominating fact in French politics. On one side were the anti-Dreyfusards (the clericals, the conservatives, the militarists, the anti-Semites), who wanted no new trial. Dreyfus was to remain guilty, Esterhazy innocent.

On the other side were the Dreyfusards (the liberals, the anticlericals, the Jews, the intellectuals), championing the right of the individual against the machinery of the state.

The Dreyfusards grew steadily stronger, especially when one of the documents that had strengthened the case against Dreyfus was found to have been forged by Hubert Joseph Henry (1846–1898), the chief of intelligence, who was a friend of Esterhazy. He had to confess to the forgery, was imprisoned on August 30, 1898, and committed suicide in jail the next day. The chief of the General Staff resigned, and Esterhazy, who had prudently left France, returned in 1899 and admitted his guilt.

Dreyfus now had to be tried again, but in September 1899, he was declared guilty again but "with extenuating circumstances" that were not described. His sentence was reduced to 10 years.

President Faure, who had been an anti-Dreyfusard, had died earlier in the year and he was succeeded by Emile Francois Loubet (1838–1929), who was a Dreyfusard. Hoping to end the Affair, he remitted the sentence and pardoned Dreyfus.

Eventually, of course, Dreyfus was entirely exonerated and all who had suffered on his behalf, including Picquart and Zola, were rehabilitated. The forces of conservatism and militarism had suffered a bad blow which, after all, they had brought on themselves.

In foreign affairs, France had better fortune. Once Russia had been ousted, against its will, from the German alliance, it became possible for France to consider the possibility of substituting for Germany. France had already been investing money in the industrialization of Russia, and that was a beginning.

On July 24, 1891, a squadron of French ships visited St. Petersburg, just three weeks after William II of Germany visited London. The French, however, managed things better. They made a big parade of Franco–Russian friendship, and Alexander III of Russia, that apostle of reaction, actually listened to a French band play the "Marseillaise," the hymn of revolution.

That began a long, slow round of discussions between France and Russia. Russia was hesitant to commit itself, realizing that France was weaker than Germany. As for France, it was taken up by the Panama Scandal. On October 13, 1893, however, a Russian squadron finally returned the French visit by steaming into Toulon harbor for another love feast. By that time, the German expansion of its army had frightened both France and Russia, and made them move a bit faster.

On January 3, 1894, a Franco–Russian alliance was established, and they agreed to fight together if war was forced on either of them by any member of the Triple Alliance. Finally, for the first time in a quarter of a century, France had an ally, and Bismarck, who was still alive (he was to die in 1898) must have been chagrined indeed.

No more than the Germans, however, were the French able to come to any agreement with the British. The British strategy of isolation continued to hold through the 1890s, although the beginning of German naval expansion, and the troubles with the Boers in South Africa, were making it an increasingly shaky policy.

The intellectual life continued. In 1896, the French physicist, Antoine Henri Becquerel (1853–1908), found that a uranium compound was the source of unexplained radiation. Some of the radiation he discovered in 1899 consisted of speeding electrons, called "beta particles" eventually. Becquerel received a Nobel Prize for this.

The Polish-born Marie Sklodowska Curie (1867–1934) called this phenomenon "radioactivity" and showed that thorium compounds were also radioactive. She and her husband, Pierre

Curie (1859–1906), discovered small quantities of new elements in uranium ore that were far more radioactive than either uranium or thorium. These were polonium and radium, both isolated in 1898. Her discoveries netted her two Nobel Prizes, first one in physics, then one in chemistry.

The outstanding mathematician of his time, Jules Henri Poincare, (1854–1912) was also at his peak in this decade.

Among the writers, Edmond Euguene Alexis Rostand (1868–1918) attained his greatest success with his play, *Cyrano de Bergerac*, first staged in 1897.

Maurice Polydore Marie Bernard Maeterlinck (1862–1949), who was Belgian-born, scored a great success with the drama *Pelleas and Melisande* (1892). This was considered the first great example of what was called Symbolist drama. Frederic Mistral (1830–1914) spearheaded the revival of Provencal literature, the dialect of southern France. Both Maeterlinck and Mistral earned Nobel Prizes in literature, and so did Henry Louis Bergson (1859–1941), whose works described his humanistic philosophy.

Among the French musicians of the period was Achille-Claude Debussy (1862–1918), best known for his symphonic poem *Afternoon of a Faun* (1894). There was also Gabriel Urbain Faure (1845–1924), who wrote the incidental music to *Pelleas and Melisande*, and who was a strong influence on later French composers.

Paul Abraham Dukas (1865–1935) composed the ever-popular *The Sorcerer's Apprentice* in 1897.

The outstanding French artist of the period was the tragic Henri Marie Raymond Toulouse-Lautrec (1864–1901), whose legs were deformed because of childhood accidents. He painted pictures and posters of Parisian night-life. Henri Julien Felix Rousseau (1844–1910) was a primitive painter; one, that is, who had had little or no formal training. He concentrated on nonrealistic depictions of jungle scenes and wild animals. One of his better-known paintings is *The Sleeping Gypsy*, painted in 1897.

RUSSIA

The important foreign developments for Russia in this decade was its rejection by Germany and its consequent alliance with France.

On November 1, 1894, not long after the Franco–Russian pact had been put through, Alexander III died. His son succeeded, reigning as Nicholas II (1868–1918). Nicholas II was gentle, peace-loving, an exemplary family man, and no tyrant. However, he was not very intelligent and had no firm grasp on events. His resemblance to Louis XVI of France in temperament is, in hindsight, almost frightening.

The mere fact that Nicholas II was milder than his father, yet incapable of initiating reforms, meant that opposition grew on both counts. A Social Democratic party, Marxist in philosophy, was formed in Russia in 1898.

Its intellectual leader was Georgy Valentinovich Plekhanov (1857–1918). Because of his writings, demanding reforms, and despite the fact that he was actively antiterrorist, he had to leave Russia in 1880 to avoid arrest. In Geneva, Switzerland, where he remained for the most part thereafter, he was converted to Marxism.

He was joined by another revolutionary exile from Russia, Vladimir Ilich Ulyanov (1870–1924), far better known under his assumed name of "Lenin." Lenin's older brother was hanged in 1887, supposedly for being part of a conspiracy to assassinate Alexander III, and this seems to have radicalized Lenin. He read Karl Marx and, by 1889, had become a Marxist. In 1895, he traveled to Switzerland to meet Plekhanov, and was active in revolutionary circles thereafter.

The cultural life of Russia continued, of course. Pavlov, who had received a Nobel Prize for his work in physiology, went on to do even more important work. Beginning in 1898, he studied the "conditioned reflex." By ringing a bell every time he fed a dog, he found he could make the dog salivate just by ringing the bell. A great deal of human behavior might result from such reflex conditioning.

Another Russian scientist, Dmitri Iosifovich Ivanovski (1864–1920), narrowly missed a vital discovery. Some diseases seemed to have no bacterial cause, possibly because the agent, whatever it was, was too small to be seen under a microscope. In 1892, Ivanovski, working with tobacco leaves affected by such a disease, mashed them up and forced them through a very fine filter designed to remove all bacteria. He found that the fluid he obtained in this way still caused the disease. However, instead of concluding that the fluid contained subbacterial agents and getting the credit for their discovery, he decided that his filters were defective and let through bacteria.

Tchaikovsky was still active, writing his most popular music, perhaps, in *The Nutcracker Suite* in 1892, and his greatest symphony, the Sixth, or *Pathetique* in 1893 (the year he died). Rimsky-Korsakoff wrote his often-heard *Flight of the Bumblebee* in 1900. Sergey Vasilievich Rachmaninoff (1873–1943) gained fame with his *Prelude in C-Sharp Minor* (1892).

Anton Pavlovich Chekhov (1860–1904) became famous for his short stories and for such plays as "The Seagull" (1896) and "Uncle Vanya" (1897). Konstantin Stanislavski (1863–1938), who founded the Moscow Art Theater in 1897, and produced Chekhov's plays, introduced an influential new acting style.

Wladyslaw Stanislaw Reymont (1867–1925), a subject of the Tsar, but Polish in the ethnic sense, eventually earned a Nobel Prize for his novels. Another Polish winner of the Nobel Prize was Henryk Adam Aleksandr Pius Sienkiewicz (1846–1916), whose greatest work was *Quo Vadis?*, published in 1896.

ITALY

However much Italians might feel animosity toward France, this happened to be bad business. By tying up with Germany and Austria-Hungary and breaking off trade with France, a large Italian budget deficit was produced. This meant higher taxes, which, of course, infuriated the populace, and Crispi's government fell in 1891.

The conservative Antonio Starabba di Rudini (1839–1908), who succeeded, tried to avoid tax increases by reducing expenditures on the army and navy, but that roused opposition, too. In

1892, he was succeeded by Giovanni Giolitti (1842–1928).

Giolitti had experience in finance and it was thought he would find a way to deal with Italy's disordered budget. However, the banker he chose to run the reform that was needed turned out to be crooked, and Giolitti had to resign in 1893. In fact, he thought it wise to leave the country for a while.

That brought Crispi back for a second time on December 10, 1893. Misery and destitution had led to peasant uprisings and Socialist strikes in Sicily. Giolitti had been rather moderate in his reaction to this, feeling that the government should be neutral in such matters. Crispi, however, who was a liberal, put them down with brutal force. (As a liberal, we might suppose he felt compelled to show that he wasn't "soft on socialism.")

However, he made Giorgio Sidney Sonnino (1847–1922) his Minister of Finance, and Sonnino was a capable man. He reorganized the banks, put an end to some of their unwise practices, pushed through necessary taxation with a firm hand, and kept Italy from going bankrupt.

Sonnino would have done better still, had not Crispi, in a fury of imperialist enthusiasm, decided to push Italy into an African adventure designed to make Ethiopia part of an Italian Empire. The result was a humiliating defeat, which will be described in due course, and an expense that almost disrupted Sonnino's wise measures. Crispi fell again on March 5, 1896.

Rudini then had a second try at the Prime Ministerial post and, realizing that enmity with France was doing Italy no good and a great deal of harm, he came to an agreement with France on September 30, 1896 that smoothed over the worst of the ill-feeling. On November 21, 1898, normal trade with France was reinstated.

Meanwhile, however, internal unrest continued and martial law had to be proclaimed. Rudini's cabinet fell and a general, Luigi Girolamo Pelloux (1839–1924), became Prime Minister. He tried to continue harsh "law and order" devices, but that merely intensified opposition, and he resigned on June 18, 1900.

The anger generated by martial law and by

Pelloux's repressions had as its effect a piece of anarchist terrorism, when the Italian king, Humbert I, was assassinated on July 29, 1900. Succeeding him was his son, who reigned as Victor Emmanuel III (1869–1947).

During this period, the Italian electrical engineer, Guglielmo Marconi, was growing interested in the possibility of sending messages by radio waves. He devised methods for converting the waves into an electric current and receiving them by means of a long wire called an antenna. By 1898 he was sending and receiving signals over a distance of 18 miles. In 1900, he obtained a key patent that might be considered as marking the invention of what we now call "radio."

Verdi produced *Falstaff* in 1893. Giacomo Antonio Puccini (1858–1924) inherited Verdi's mantle, producing the operas *Manon Lescaut* (1893), *La Boheme* (1896), and *Tosca* (1900). Ruggero Leoncavallo (1858–1919), produced the opera *Pagliacci* (1892).

The outstanding Italian writer of the period was Gabriele D'Annunzio (1863–1938), who wrote poems, plays, and short stories, and who was a successful swashbuckler and a major eccentric besides.

PAPACY

Leo XIII, still Pope during this decade, showed himself rather sympathetic to the cause of labor. He issued the encyclical *Rerum novarum* on May 15, 1891, which made the improvement of the life conditions of the workers a moral issue.

NETHERLANDS

The Netherlands joined the general European practice in this decade of expanding the franchise and passing social legislation.

They also came to an agreement with the British in 1891 as to the division of Borneo, with the Netherlands retaining most of it. The Netherlands had to repress revolts in the East Indian islands.

As had been the case for centuries, the Netherlands, though a small power, remained a major influence in science.

By this time, it seemed that the newly discovered electron might be a constituent of atoms. If so, argued Hendrik Antoon Lorentz (1853–1928), a strong magnetic field ought to affect those electrons and alter the wavelength of the light that atoms emitted.

A student of his, Pieter Zeeman (1865–1943), showed experimentally in 1896 that this really took place, Lorentz and Zeeman both received Nobel Prizes for this work.

In 1895, Martinus Willem Beijerink (1851–1931) repeated the experiment Ivanovski had performed a few years earlier. He found that bacteria-free fluid could cause a disease in tobacco plants and he postulated the existence of an agent too small to see. He called it a "filtrable virus." (*Virus* is a Latin word meaning "poison.")

Hugo De Vries (1848–1935) studied the inheritance of physical characteristics in plants and came to the conclusion, in the 1890s, that there were sudden changes on occasion; that an offspring could possess a characteristic that was not present in either parent. This he called a "mutation." The study of mutations quickly showed them to be essential in the process of evolution. By studying them, De Vries, in 1900, rediscovered Mendel's law of inheritance first advanced a third of a century earlier.

Marie Eugene Francois Thomas Dubois (1858–1940) discovered a skull cap, a thigh bone, and two teeth of a primitive hominid in Java in 1894. He called the hominid *Pithecanthropus erectus* ("erect ape-man"). Eventually, with the help of further discoveries, such organisms were said to belong to *Homo erectus*. These were distinctly more primitive human ancestors than the Neanderthals were.

BELGIUM

In Belgium, universal manhood suffrage was proclaimed on April 27, 1893, in the immediate wake of a general strike called to bring that about. The Belgian government diluted this by allowing plural voting. Some people, depending on various qualifications involving age, education, wealth, and so on, could have two or even three votes. Naturally, liberals demanded one vote per person.

On December 24, 1899, a system of proportional representation was set up by which minority views had the chance of representation in the legislature.

SPAIN

Spain suffered the same turmoil that much of Europe was feeling. There was the proliferation of protest groups, a spread of socialism, and an increase of terrorism.

Complicating matters in this decade was another long Cuban rebellion, this time worsened by American interference, together with the consequence of a short and disastrous war with the United States in 1898, which will be described later.

The war ended with the loss of the last Spanish possessions in the American continents (Cuba and Puerto Rico) and in the Pacific (the Philippine Islands and Guam). Of all the vast Spanish Empire that had existed up to less than a century earlier, only the Canary Islands and some spots on the West African coast remained in Spanish hands.

Of course, it must be understood that this was only a political loss. The Spanish language and Spanish culture remained widespread and important in the world as the heritage of Spain's once-great Empire.

PORTUGAL

Portugal—whose king, Carlos I, was noted for his extravagance and was quite unpopular—was as restless as its neighbor Spain.

It had possessions on the African southwest coast in Angola and on the African southeast coast in Mozambique that dated back over four centuries. Portuguese imperialists attempted to claim all the interior of Africa between the two colonies. This France and Germany seemed ready to allow, but not Great Britain, which wanted the territory for itself. Portugal was forced to back down in 1890. In 1891, the boundaries of the Portuguese colonies were sharply defined and the interior was left to Great Britain.

This setback was by no means as great as that which afflicted Spain in this decade. Except for the loss of Brazil, Portugal retained much of its old Empire.

SWITZERLAND

Switzerland's federal government was increasing its powers at the expense of the cantons in this decade. The federal government began to control the railroads, coordinate measures of social security, take charge of the penal codes, and so on.

DENMARK

Denmark was peaceful in this decade, though there was socialist pressure for a more democratic constitution.

The Danish inventor, Valdemar Poulsen (1869–1942), was the first to patent a system of wire recording in 1898, though that sort of thing did not become truly practical for half a century.

SWEDEN

Although the Swedish yoke was light, as yokes go, and although a Norwegian, Johan Sverdrup (1816–1892), had served as Prime Minister in the Swedish government, the Norwegian demand for independence was growing.

An important Swedish writer, who was beginning to make a name for herself in this decade, was Selma Ottiliana Lovisa Lagerlof (1858–1940). A Norwegian writer, Knut Pedersen, writing under the pseudonym of "Knut Hamsun," was doing the same. Both Lagerlof and Hamsun eventually received Nobel Prizes in literature.

GREECE

The narrow isthmus on which Corinth stands and which connects the Peloponnesus to the rest of Greece has always been an obvious shortcut for ships. In ancient times, ships used to be dragged across it in order to save the 200-mile trip around the Peloponnesus. Finally, on August 6, 1893, a canal was opened that cut through the isthmus.

Greece's Olympic games had come to an end 15 centuries earlier, when Theodosius had shut it down as a pagan festival. In 1894, however, a French educator, Pierre de Coubertin (1863–1937), brought together a 12-nation conference at Paris for the purpose of reviving the games. In 1896, the first modern Olympic Games were held in Athens, and they have been held every four years since except for periods when major wars were raging.

Trouble was brewing on the island of Crete, however, which was Greek-speaking, but under Ottoman rule still. It had rebelled in 1878 and had received a measure of self-government, but its people wished to become part of the Greek kingdom. On February 2, 1897, they rebelled again, and, on February 6, declared union with Greece. Public opinion in Greece was wildly in favor of union, and on February 10, Greek ships and troops set sail for Crete.

Russia and Austria-Hungary did not want to set off another Balkan crisis and put pressure on Greece to withdraw. Greece disregarded this, however, and declared war on the Ottoman Empire on April 17. The Ottoman Empire, however, had been reorganized by German officers, and it promptly defeated the Greeks, who had to appeal to the European powers for help.

The powers were eager to end the war and a peace treaty was signed on September 18, 1897. Crete was left still under nominal Turkish sovereignty, but an international force was left there to maintain the peace; and Prince George, a younger son of the Greek king, was made high commissioner of Crete.

SERBIA

Alexander I, who had become king in 1889, continued the pro-Austrian policies of his father, Milan, who had abdicated. Alexander I was only 13 when be became king, but on April 14, 1893, when he was still only a teenager, he got rid of the regency and ruled in person. He ruled dictatorially, replacing the constitution with a more authoritarian one, bring back his father to lead

the armed forces, and repressing the pro-Russian nationalists.

His popularity in consequence quickly declined and reached a particularly low level when, on August 5, 1899, he married his mistress, Draga Lunjevica Masin (1867–1903). She was nine years older than he, a widow, and had the reputation of having led a sexually adventurous life.

BULGARIA

In the early years of the reign of Ferdinand I, the most powerful government figure in Bulgaria was Stefan Nikolov Stambolov (1854–1895). He tried to carry on friendly relations with the Ottoman Empire, but that just intensified the hostility of Russia. Then, too, there were those in Bulgaria who wanted to annex additional territory to the south in Macedonia, which was still under Ottoman rule.

Stambolov tried to combat opposition by repression and was forced out of office on May 31, 1894. On July 18, 1895, he was attacked on a Sofia street by Macedonian revolutionaries and killed.

With Stambolov removed, his pro-Ottoman policies dead, and with the heir to the throne, Boris (1894–1943), converting to orthodox Christianity, Russian friendship was regained.

OTTOMAN EMPIRE

The Ottoman Empire, despite promises of reform and liberalization, did nothing to change its repressive policies. The Armenians, in northwestern Asia Minor, grew increasingly restless, particularly in view of the fact that the Balkan nations had managed to establish their independence of the Ottomans. All through the early 1890s there was increasing Armenian turbulence and, in 1894, Ottoman forces put down the rebellion with extreme cruelty. It amounted to an indiscriminate massacre.

Like the Bulgarian massacres of a decade earlier, this produced an outcry among British liberals. The result was that when the Ottoman

Empire was next assaulted by its foes, British protection was not forthcoming.

Even the Turks themselves grew rebellious at the lack of reform. A liberal group, consisting, at the start, mainly of Turkish exiles, formed a group in 1896 that was popularly known as the "Young Turks," and these began to push for constitutional reform and enlightenment.

UNITED STATES

In the election of 1892, Cleveland ran a third time. On this occasion he defeated Benjamin Harrison, and became the only president to serve two nonconsecutive terms. He was both the 22nd and 24th presidents.

The United States had one of its periodic depressions in 1893. (In those days, the word was "panic" and people referred to the "Panic of 1893," for instance. As a matter of cosmetic usage that was changed to the milder word "depression." In later years when that, too, was associated with misery, the word was changed to the still milder "recession." When nothing else works, one can always fall back on euphemisms).

Naturally, a depression meant an increase in unemployment, hunger, and misery; and the government, at that time, felt little responsibility to relieve the suffering. The government saw its role as that of keeping order, which usually meant the repression of any attempted protests by those suffering.

On May 1, 1894, a group of about 20,000 unemployed converged on Washington to plead their case. They were under the leadership of Jacob Sechler Coxey (1854–1951). The conservatives were horrified at this, for they felt the unemployed ought to starve quietly. However, it came to nothing. Only 600 actually reached Washington and when Coxey tried to address them from the steps of the Capitol, he was arrested for trespassing.

A more forceful protest was that of the people working for the Pullman railroad company. George Pullman, because of the depression, cut the wages of the laborers. However, they lived in Pullman-owned houses and he did not cut the rents. Their wages were disposable but his profits were sacrosanct.

The workers went out on strike on May 10, 1894, under the leadership of Eugene Victor Debs (1855–1926). Rail transportation was paralyzed.

The center of the strike was in the railroad hub of Chicago. The governor of Illinois was the German-born liberal, John Peter Altgeld (1847–1902), who had already roused the conservatives to fury by pardoning the three surviving Haymarket Square "anarchists" on June 29, 1893. This was on the grounds (true enough) that they had not received a fair trial. For this honest action, he was eventually driven out of politics.

However, he was still governor at the time of the Pullman strike and he maintained that the Illinois National Guard could maintain order and that he wanted no federal interference. President Cleveland, however, was guided by his attorney-general, Richard Olney (1835–1917), who was on the board of directors of one of the struck railroads, and was scarcely impartial. Cleveland sent in the army. The strike was broken, with 34 strikers killed, and on December 14, 1894, Debs went to jail for six months.

All this radicalized Debs and he became a socialist. Under him a socialist party was organized in the United States.

A nonsocialist liberal party was founded in 1891. It called itself the "People's Party" or the "Populists." It favored a graduated income tax, the direct election of Senators, an eight-hour day, a secret ballot, and so on. The Populist views were rather like those of the British Chartists a half-century before, and sounded just as appalling to American conservatives as the Chartists' had to the British conservatives.

Leading the Populists was Ignatius Donnelly (1831–1901) who, in addition to being a liberal, had some odd notions about Atlantis and about Francis Bacon having written the plays of Shakespeare. Since his odd notions made no sense, and his liberal notions made a great deal of sense, his odd notions were popular and his liberal notions were not. Another Populist leader was James Baird Weaver (1833–1912), who ran for president as a Populist in 1892 and won four western states with a total of 22 electoral votes.

Meanwhile, the United States and Great Britain had their last major war-crisis. The dispute arose over the matter of Venezuela's boundary. The British owned territory (British Guiana) just to the east of Venezuela and the boundary was not clearly defined. The British and Venezuelan claims overlapped quite a bit, and it was clear that the British would have it all their own way in a one-to-one confrontation.

Therefore, Venezuela appealed to the United States and to the Monroe Doctrine in 1895. The United States tried to arbitrate, but the British refused arbitration. Public opinion in the United States turned violently anti-British.

Cleveland's Secretary of State, Walter Quintin Gresham (1832–1895), died just as the dispute was heating up dangerously, and Cleveland appointed Richard Olney to the job. Olney had supplied an intemperate solution to the Pullman strike, and now he was just as intemperate toward Great Britain.

On July 20, 1895, he forwarded a note to Great Britain which was about as insulting and overbearing as it could be. The British could not accept it without humiliation, and so they did *not* accept it. For a while, it looked as though a third war between the United States and Great Britain was a possibility.

A half-year of increasing tension passed and then came trouble in South Africa between the British and the Boers, and William II's totally unnecessary telegram of congratulations to the Boer president. Great Britain suddenly realized that Germany, which was now beginning to modernize its navy, was the immediate enemy. Great Britain did not wish two enemies, Germany *and* the United States, at the same time (and both with navies). She had to choose one or the other. Germany was closer and, therefore, more dangerous, whereupon Great Britain was suddenly all smiles toward the United States.

Great Britain agreed to arbitration, which handed Great Britain most of what it claimed, but not all. From then on, Great Britain was careful never to quarrel with the United States again.

However, if the Venezuelan crisis ended peacefully, another crisis did not. The Cubans had broken out into a second rebellion against Spain on February 24, 1895, just as the Venezuelan crisis was approaching its worst stage. The rebellion came about because the Cubans found Spanish rule corrupt, inefficient, and repressive, and because, in addition, Cuba depended almost entirely on trade with the United States (almost all Cuban property of importance was American-owned) and a depression in the United States meant redoubled misery in Cuba.

The Spaniards went all out in trying to suppress the rebellion. Under Valeriano Weyler (1838–1930), the Spanish forces committed the kind of atrocities that almost always take place when armed forces are turned loose on ill-armed or unarmed rebels.

The American press made the most of this. Hearst and Pulitzer were fighting circulation wars, and among the tools they used were huge headlines, sensational articles and illustrations, and the spreading (and sometimes the inventing) of grisly rumors. Color printing was coming in and, in 1896, colored comic strips were just being established. Yellow was prominent in the first such comic strip, "The Yellow Kid," so that the new way in which newspapers were exploiting the public came to be called "yellow journalism."

Hearst, in particular, was extreme in foreign policy and was a reckless imperialist. He had called for war against Great Britain in connection with Venezuela and now he called for war against Spain in connection with Cuba. Cleveland, however, held for peace.

Cleveland's term of office was coming to an end, though. In 1896, the Democrats were stampeded by an eloquent speech made at the convention by William Jennings Bryan (1860–1925) and nominated him for president. The Republicans nominated William McKinley (1843–1901). Bryan adopted most of the Populist platform, gaining their votes, but scaring enough easterners to lose the election. In 1897, McKinley became the 25th President.

McKinley was sure to take a harder line on Spain than Cleveland had done, and Spain did its best to become placatory. They recalled Weyler in October 1897. However, the American imperialist press would not accept any Spanish moderation and howled for action.

McKinley, a weak man, could not withstand the pressure and sent the American battleship, *Maine,* to Havana on the usual excuse of having to protect American lives and property.

Then, on February 15, 1898, the *Maine,* while in Havana harbor, blew up with the loss of 260 officers and men out of the 355 on board. No one has ever determined what caused the explosion. Since the warship, like any warship, carried explosives, it could have been an accident. Or it might have been the act of a Cuban rebel anxious to bring on a war between the United States and Spain. The least likely explanation is that it was a deliberate action of the Spaniards, since there was nothing they wanted less than a war with the United States.

Nevertheless, Americans (and the Hearst papers) at once concluded that it was a Spanish atrocity and the demand for war became shrill. Spain did what it could to avoid war, but the United States made no effort to gain the fruits of victory without fighting. The United States insisted on fighting, and on April 21, 1898 the "Spanish–American War" began. As it turned out, it wasn't much of a war.

The United States had a tremendous advantage since it had built up an efficient navy with a fleet in each ocean. Alfred Thayer Mahan (1840–1914), the president of the Naval War College, had been an advocate of a strong navy and, to that end, wrote *The Influence of Sea Power Upon History, 1660–1783* in 1890, and other similar books later on. He pointed out that in a world comprised essentially of ocean, with the continents large islands within that ocean, a nation that controlled the sea controlled the world. His view led to the building of a strong American navy. (His book also influenced William II of Germany and helped the Germans decide to build a strong navy of their own.)

The Assistant Secretary of the Navy in 1898 was Theodore Roosevelt (1858–1919). He was an admirer of Mahan and, when temporarily in charge during the Secretary's absence, Roosevelt ordered six warships in the Pacific to Hong Kong to be ready to act against the Philippine Islands, then a Spanish possession.

As soon as war was declared, those six ships, under George Dewey (1837–1917), sailed to Manila. There, in a few hours, Dewey destroyed the Spanish fleet totally, with no damage whatever to his own ships.

In the Atlantic, another American fleet bottled up a Spanish fleet in the port of Santiago, Cuba. In order to get at the fleet, a hastily prepared American army was sent to Cuba, landed east of Santiago and marched on the city. They fought a couple of minor battles in which Theodore Roosevelt took part (a part that he later much exaggerated). Soon, the American forces were so close to Santiago that the Spanish ships decided to try to make a run out of the harbor. On July 3, 1898, they made their break, but the American ships were waiting and this Spanish fleet was also totally destroyed.

There was no use in fighting any longer and Spain had to give in. The treaty of peace was signed in Paris on December 10, 1898. Spain agreed to the independence of Cuba and ceded the Philippine Islands, Guam, and Puerto Rico to the United States. (The next year, the Spaniards sold the Marianas Islands and a few other South Pacific bits of land to Germany).

Thus, the United States became an imperial power. In 1898, it annexed the Hawaiian islands peacefully.

The Spanish–American war had endured less than four months and it was the last important war to be fought with gunpowder rather than with the new smokeless powders. The United States had lost 385 soldiers to enemy bullets, and over 2000 to disease.

In 1900, McKinley ran for reelection and won easily over Bryan for a second time. This time, Theodore Roosevelt was elected Vice-President.

By 1900, the United States had a population of 76 million; and, thanks to its quick victory over Spain, it had come to be recognized as a "great power."

New York City, in 1898, absorbed what are now the outer boroughs of Brooklyn, Queens, Bronx, and Richmond (Staten Island). As Greater New York, it had a population of 3,500,000 and was second only to London among the cities of the world. The United States now led the world in coal, steel, and oil production. It had more railroads, it had 14,000 automobiles, and its navy had shown what it could do.

A 45th state joined the Union—Utah. In population and wealth it had long been qualified, but the fact that its Mormon inhabitants practiced polygamy (rather than adultery) horrified Americans. In 1890, the Mormon Church disavowed polygamy and, on January 4, 1896, Utah became a state.

The most important American scientist of the decade was the German-born Charles Proteus Steinmetz (1865–1923), who worked out alternating-current theory in full detail.

In medicine, Theobald Smith (1869–1934) demonstrated, in 1892, that Texas cattle fever was caused by a protozoon parasite that was spread by blood-sucking ticks. Walter Reed (1851–1902) was sent to Cuba in the wake of the Spanish–American War to investigate yellow fever, which had killed many American soldiers. He found that it, like malaria, was spread by mosquitoes. He eventually found the causative agent to be a virus.

In technology, Edward Goodrich Acheson (1856–1931) synthesized carborundum in 1891, an abrasive second only to diamond and, of course, much cheaper. In 1894, the German-born Herman Frasch (1851–1914) devised a new and cheaper way of mining sulfur that gave the United States a virtually unlimited supply of that element, and of the extremely important sulfuric acid that could be made from it. On a more mundane level, King Camp Gillette (1855–1932) invented the safety razor and made the daily shaving ritual less a form of blood-letting.

In writing, Ambrose Gwinnett Bierce (1842–1914) was a veritable Diogenes of cynicism, and wrote stories that were bitter and sometimes morbid. Stephen Crane (1871–1900) wrote *The Red Badge of Courage* in 1895. This was considered one of the best studies of men at war, though Crane had never seen battle himself.

Katherine Lee Bates (1859–1929) wrote "America the Beautiful" in 1893, and although it is not the American national anthem, many people think it ought to be. Gelett Burgess (1866–1951) would be forgotten today had he not made

himself forever famous in 1897 with a four-line jingle that begins, "I never saw a purple cow."

The American economist, Thorstein Bunde Veblen, wrote *The Theory of the Leisure Class* in 1899, a relentless critique of upperclass behavior that achieved considerable popularity. He coined the phrase "conspicuous consumption."

Sousa was still active in music, and in 1897 he wrote what may be the most popular march ever composed, "The Stars and Stripes Forever." Ethelberg Woodridge Nevin (1862–1901) wrote "Narcissus" in 1892, "Mighty Lak a Rose" in 1900, and his most famous composition, "The Rosary," in 1898.

Charles Dana Gibson (1867–1944) was the most successful illustrator of the decade. His "Gibson girl" became the model of feminine beauty. The men he drew were clean-shaven and that put an end to the fashion of beards that had swept the United States at the time of the Civil War and the decades that followed.

James A. Naismith (1861–1939) invented the rules of the game of basketball in 1891, and they have persisted without important change ever since.

The Hungarian-born Harry Houdini (1874–1926) made himself world-famous as an escape-artist. No prison cells, no locks, no chains, no strait-jackets seemed to be able to hold him.

CANADA

On August 6, 1896, gold was discovered along the Klondike River, in the Canadian northwest near the Alaskan boundary. The gold-fever struck Canada and the United States as it did in California a half-century earlier. Within three years, some 30,000 to 60,000 people flocked into that forbidding Arctic area, a good proportion of them dying en route. The Canadian town of Dawson, which had contained a few houses at the time of the discovery, became a city of 20,000 almost at once.

The gold supply in the Klondike didn't last long. The production peaked in 1900 when $22 million worth of gold at the prices of the day were produced. Production declined rapidly thereafter, but, all told, about $175 million was dug out of the cold earth.

NEWFOUNDLAND

The depression hit Newfoundland as it hit the United States, and it occurred to the Newfoundlanders that they might be better off as part of Canada after all. In 1895, they suggested union to Canada, but a depressed Newfoundland no longer seemed appetizing to Canada and negotiations fell through.

MEXICO

In this decade, Mexico remained quiet and miserable under the iron hand of Diaz.

CUBA

After the Cuban rebellion of 1895, and the American victory over Spain in 1898, Cuba was granted its independence, but there was doubt as to how free it could be of the embrace of its giant liberator.

There were strong elements among the American population, and in Congress, who opposed imperialism and didn't want the United States to acquire colonies, either because they thought it morally wrong, or thought colonies would be more trouble than they were worth.

When war with Spain seemed inevitable, Henry Moore Teller (1830–1914), a Senator from Colorado with Populist leanings, pushed through the "Teller Amendment" in which Congress specifically denied any intention of annexing Cuba. As a result, the United States (perhaps regretfully) had to accept the independence of Cuba, but it also felt responsible for helping the Cubans starting a working government of their own. For that reason, John Rutter Brooke (1838–1926) served as military governor of Cuba, and was succeeded, in this capacity, by General Leonard Wood (1860–1927).

Under American guidance, yellow fever began to be eradicated, schools were organized, elections were held, and a government was set up. It did seem that if Cuba was not going to be an American colony, it would at least be an American protectorate.

PUERTO RICO

For four centuries, Puerto Rico had been Spanish. On July 25, 1898, in the course of the Spanish–American War, the naval force under William Thomas Sampson (1840–1902), which had destroyed the Spanish fleet at Santiago, landed in Puerto Rico. There was no Teller amendment for Puerto Rico, so by the terms of the peace treaty, Puerto Rico became an American Colony.

DOMINICAN REPUBLIC

During this period, the Dominican Republic fell heavily into debt, and serious questions arose as to how those debts were to be repaid, and what European powers might decide to do in order to collect those debts. The memory of Mexico a third of a century earlier was still fresh in American minds.

CENTRAL AMERICA

In this decade, further attempts were made to unify Central America; however, although a treaty of union was signed, it fell through by November 25, 1898.

VENEZUELA

Between 1895 and 1899, there was a dispute between Venezuela and Great Britain over the boundary between the former nation and British Guiana. The British wanted the boundary so far westward that they would have control over the mouth of the Orinoco River, which would seriously hamper Venezuela's economy.

Venezuela called on the United States for help and, after a period of crisis between Great Britain and the United States, Great Britain backed down. The matter went to arbitration, and the decision came on October 3, 1899. Great Britain gained most of the disputed territory, but Venezuela retained the mouth of the Orinoco River, which was what counted.

On October 23, 1899, a Venezuelan general, Cipriano Castro (1858–1924), seized control of Venezuela and established a repressive dictatorship.

BRAZIL

On February 24, 1891, Brazil adopted a federal constitution, thus forming "the United States of Brazil."

CHILE

There was a brief Chilean civil war in 1891. Jose Balmaceda, the president, who favored a strong executive, was overthrown by those who wanted a strong legislature. Balmaceda committed suicide.

The new rulers thought that the United States had favored Balmaceda and a mob attacked the crew of the American warship *Baltimore*, which happened to be in the Valparaiso harbor. The United States demanded, and got, an indemnity for the incident.

EGYPT

In 1892, Abbas Hilmi II (1874–1922) became Viceroy of Egypt, succeeding his father, Tawfiq. He was restive under British rule, and tried to use the French as a way of wriggling out of the British grip. It did him no good. The British merely tightened their control. After all, they had to remain in charge of the Suez Canal, and there was the unfinished business of the Mahdists in the Sudan. The death of Gordon at Khartoum had to be avenged.

The job was given to Horatio Herbert Kitchener (1850–1916). Beginning in 1896, Kitchener, heading an army that was half British and half Egyptian, worked his way methodically up the Nile River, and the climax came on September 2, 1898 at Omdurman, just across the river from Khartoum. There, Kitchener's 26,000 faced 40,000 Mahdists.

The Mahdists fought with the same fury that

had carried them to several victories over British-led forces in the previous decade, but this time, the British had something new—20 machine guns. Against their hail of bullets the Mahdists could not stand. Well over half their army were casualties; Kitchener suffered only 500. This was the first indication of what the machine gun could do.

Kitchener occupied Khartoum and then proceeded up the Nile to Fashoda, about 400 miles south of Khartoum. He reached it on September 19, 1898, and found it occupied by French forces under Jean Baptiste Marchand (1863–1934), a general and explorer who had made his way across the width of Africa from the vast French-owned territories in the western Sahara.

The British claimed the territory and on November 3, Kitchener brusquely ordered Marchand to leave. Marchand refused to do so without orders from France and, for a while, it seemed that war was inevitable. But just as the British had backed down in Venezuela, the French now backed down in Egypt. The French were distracted by the Dreyfus Affair, and they, too, realized that Germany was the real enemy and that it would play into German hands if France allowed itself to be embroiled with Great Britain. (In short, William II's bellicose and tactless policies were uniting the rest of Europe against him.)

On March 21, 1899, France formally abandoned all claims to Egypt and the Nile Valley in return for additional portions of the Sahara Desert.

Meanwhile, Sudan was placed under the joint control of Great Britain and Egypt, and was known, for a period of time, as "the Anglo–Egyptian Sudan."

ETHIOPIA

King Menelek of Ethiopia, who had now established his control over all the kingdom, made it clear on February 9, 1891, that he did not feel that the treaty with Italy gave the latter nation a protectorate over Ethiopia.

The Italians, however, had strengthened their hold on Eritrea by defeating invading Mahdists between 1891 and 1894. Italy also came to various agreements with Great Britain, making certain that the British would not object to Italian action against Ethiopia.

In March 1895, then, the Italians felt ready and began moving into Ethiopian territory. In September, Menelek declared war on Italy and gathered his forces. On March 1, 1896, 20,000 Italians faced 90,000 Ethiopians at Adowa in northern Ethiopia. The Italians didn't have Kitchener's machine guns for one thing, and they let themselves be caught in separate brigades that could be attacked separately. Therefore, the Italians were heavily defeated and had to retreat with only half their army left.

On October 26, 1896, Italy had to sign a treaty recognizing Ethiopian independence. It was a devastating humiliation for Italy.

Ethiopia went on to make treaties with France and with Great Britain, confining their control to the coast and safeguarding the independence of Ethiopia itself. Ethiopia also tried to make contact with the French at Fashoda in order to extend its influence northward, but there it failed.

MOROCCO

Morocco had spent modern times largely in isolation. It fought off Portuguese invasions in the sixteenth century, and managed to remain free when the rest of North Africa became part of the Ottoman Empire. Morocco also repelled French raids in the 1840s when France was subduing Algeria.

By the 1890s, however, Morocco's position had become precarious under stifling European pressure. Spain controlled Rio de Oro, the stretch of African coast southwest of Morocco. France controlled Algeria and the Sahara desert region all along Morocco's eastern border.

In 1894, Abd al-Aziz (1881–1943) became Sultan of Morocco at the age of 13. In the first years of his reign, there was an attempt to adopt European techniques to counter European penetration which, on the whole, did not work.

WEST AFRICA

During the 1890s, Great Britain, France, and Germany peaceably settled the last boundary disagreements.

CENTRAL AFRICA

During the 1890s, Great Britain, France, and Belgium peacefully worked out the boundaries of the Congo.

EAST AFRICA

During the 1890s, Great Britain, Germany, and Portugal worked out the boundaries of their respective possessions. The partition of Africa was concluded without military action among the Imperialist powers. The Fashoda crisis was the closest approach to that.

SOUTH AFRICA

There was, however, military action between the Imperialist and African armies. There was the brief Italo–Ethiopian war as an example of that, but the situation was much more dangerous in southern Africa.

Under Cecil Rhodes, the British possessions in South Africa were consolidated and strengthened. Railroads were built and the economy flourished. The Boers also strengthened their position and Paul Kruger was reelected president of the South African Republic in 1893.

In November 1894, Rhodes visited Kruger and tried to arrange a customs union that would include both the Boer and British possessions. Kruger, suspecting that this would just be a step in the absorption of the Boers by the British, refused. Rhodes did not give up; he merely decided on stronger measures.

First, he strengthened the British hold in neighboring areas of Africa. The section north of the Boer territory was organized by the British on May 3, 1895 and named Rhodesia in honor of Rhodes. Its capital was Salisbury, which had been founded in 1890 and named for the British Prime Minister. Bechuanaland, west of the South

African Republic, was added on to the British Cape Colony on November 11, 1895. The Boers were now almost completely surrounded by British territory. Only a short boundary with Portuguese Mozambique on the east was left non-British.

What's more, Rhodes felt he had allies within the Boer state. There were British settlers there, "Uitlanders" to the Boers, and they were allowed no part in the government. Presumably, they would be ready to rise against the Boers if given leadership.

Rhodes, therefore, had his friend, Leander Starr Jameson (1853–1917), lead 500 horsemen in a raid into Boer territory on December 29, 1895. This was done, apparently, with the knowledge of the colonial Secretary in London, Joseph Chamberlain (1836–1914), who had been a liberal but who had broken with Gladstone over the question of Irish Home Rule.

The "Jameson raid" was a fiasco. The Uitlanders did not rise. The Boers were ready for Jameson, trapped him neatly and arrested him on January 2, 1896. William II of Germany then sent his gratuitous telegram of congratulations to Kruger, which set off an explosion of anger among the British people.

Jameson was sent back to Great Britain to be tried and lightly punished for his thoroughly illegal act of war. Rhodes retired from politics. The blacks in southern Africa rose against the British at the news of this British humiliation and were beaten down only with difficulty. The Boers became more intransigent, and Kruger was again reelected in 1898. The Jameson raid was a disaster in every respect.

Kruger insisted on a hard line against the Uitlanders, who now began to petition Great Britain for a redress of their grievances. Both sides began to prepare for war and "the Boer War" did, in fact, begin on October 12, 1899.

The British in South Africa were every bit as racist as the Boers, by the way. Not only did the British treat the blacks as subhuman, but they extended such treatment to the Indians as well, even those who were highly cultured and British-educated. Thus, a young Indian lawyer, Mohandas Karamchand Gandhi (1869–1948) arrived in

Natal, South Africa in 1893. His mistreatment and that of other Indians radicalized him and made him a great danger to the British Empire.

MADAGASCAR

Madagascar was brought completely under French control and was declared a French colony on August 6, 1896.

PERSIA

Persia was reduced to obtaining loans from Great Britain in 1892 by allowing itself to collect customs on the coast of the Persian Gulf as security. A similar agreement in 1900 obtained a loan from Russia with all other customs collections as security. In this way, Persia seriously compromised its independence.

The Shah, Nasir ud-Din, was assassinated in 1896 and his son, Muzaffar ud-Din, reigned in his place.

AFGHANISTAN

On March 11, 1895, the boundary between Russia and Afghanistan was completely defined. In the east, Afghanistan retained a strip of territory so that nowhere would the Russian boundary coincide with that of India.

INDIA

India continued to become more self-consciously political. Dadabhair Naoroji (1825–1917) was a highly educated Indian who spent much of his life in Great Britain and who, in 1892, was elected to Parliament, as the first Indian member. He was a vocal critic of British policies in India, maintaining that Great Britain was systematically draining India's wealth for British benefit.

New religious sects arose in India that were non-Christian and that served as further vehicles for national revival.

Theosophy, a mystic farrago of ancient forms of occultism, was brought into modern prominence by the Russian-born American, Helena Petrovna Blavatsky (1831–1891). It was then taken up by Annie Besant (1847–1933). Besant spent much of her life in India, and with her, Theosophy took on a strongly Hindu cast.

Vivekananda (1862–1902) tried to achieve a fusion of western science and Indian spiritual thought. He attended the World Parliament of Religions in Chicago in 1893 as the Hindu representative and captivated that body with his eloquence. Mirza Ghulam Ahmad (1839–1908) founded a new Muslim sect and claimed to be an incarnation of both Jesus and Muhammad—and had followers, of course.

In 1898, George Nathaniel, Lord Curzon (1859–1925), was appointed Viceroy of India.

SIAM

The French in Indo-China were ready to expand their holdings westward into the kingdom of Siam. Siam resisted but, in all likelihood, would have been forced to submit were it not that Great Britain did not want French forces at the border of its Indian dominions. On January 15, 1896, Great Britain and France came to an agreement in which both nations guaranteed Siam's independence, and its existence as a buffer state.

CHINA

By now the incapacity of the Manchu dynasty was clear. Popular movements to overthrow it had always been endemic, but they were growing more purposeful and serious. In particular, a young man named Sun Yat-Sen (1866–1925) was now involved. He had spent his teenage years in Hawaii, where he was exposed to Western thought and influence so that he eventually became a Christian. It was in Hawaii, among the Chinese there, that, in 1894, he organized the first of the associations with which he hoped to put an end to the Manchu dynasty.

It was hard to set up an internal revolt against a mass so large and populous as China, but external events helped.

For some years, China and Japan had been rivals as far as influence over Korea was concerned. Korea had long been a Chinese vassal, but now Japan was competing as it had done three centuries earlier under Hideyoshi.

In June of 1894, there were disorders in Seoul, the capital of Korea, that had been, perhaps, incited by the Japanese. The Japanese promptly rushed troops in to maintain order, and so did the Chinese. By August 1, 1894, China and Japan were fighting the "Sino–Japanese War."

Since China and Japan were both non-European powers, Europe expected a comic-opera war with China, much larger and more populous than Japan, winning. What the Europeans didn't quite grasp was that Japan had already modernized itself to the point where its army and navy were far in advance of the Chinese.

Japan won every battle. They destroyed the Chinese navy in two encounters in the Yellow Sea between Korea and China, one on September 17, 1894, and the other on February 12, 1895. The Japanese army fought its way through Korea and penetrated into Manchuria. By March 9, 1895, they were ready to march on to Peking, but the Chinese knew they were beaten and sued for peace.

The Treaty of Shimonoseki (a city in southwestern Japan, just across the strait from Korea) was signed on April 17, 1895, and with it, Japan began its career of military expansion. China had to recognize the independence of Korea (which meant an end to its influence there) and had to cede to Japan the island of Taiwan (known as Formosa to the western powers) along with some nearby islands. Japan was also to occupy the Liaotung Peninsula just west of Korea and was to receive a huge indemnity from China. Russia, however, which had designs of its own on China, got France and Germany to go along with forcing Japan to abandon the Liaotung Peninsula at the cost of an additional Chinese indemnity.

The Sino–Japanese war showed that Japan was an important military power, and that China was completely helpless. Within China, the humiliation was extreme and the demands for reform increased in intensity. China, however, lacked the money and the means to modernize itself and could get what it needed only by selling itself to the European powers.

The European powers seized their chance to begin a further plucking of the Chinese chicken. They loaned money to help China pay the Japanese indemnity at the price of taking concessions for themselves.

The Russians had begun to build a Trans-Siberian railroad in 1891, one that would connect St. Petersburg and Moscow with Vladivostok, Russia's Pacific port, and knit the enormous nation together. Its easternmost section would have to take a long detour around the Manchurian border. On June 3, 1896, therefore, Russia concluded a secret treaty with China, by which Russia would also build a railroad across Manchuria as a shortcut to Vladivostok.

This meant, really, that Russia would be deeply involved in Manchuria and that that province would become a Russian protectorate. Russia also began to exert increasing influence on the newly independent Korea. Such Russian activity was viewed with the utmost hostility by Japan.

Two German missionaries were killed in the province of Shantung, and Germany quickly used that, on November 14, 1897, as an excuse to occupy the easternmost portion of the province, a peninsula jutting into the Yellow Sea. That same year, Russia took the Liaotung Peninsula, just across the strait from Shantung. The Japanese had been forced to release it after the Sino–Japanese war, but now the Russians built a strong naval base, Port Arthur, at its tip.

Great Britain and France were by no means behind in the seizing of commercial concessions, and it seemed that a partition of China, along the lines of the partition of Africa, might be well under way.

The one great military power that did not participate directly in the looting was the United States. On September 6, 1899, President McKinley's Secretary of State, John Milton Hay (1838–1905), propounded the "Open Door policy." This was to the effect that nations extorting concessions from China must not establish monopolies within their spheres of influence but should allow all nations equal trading rights. In this way, the United States could get what it considered its fair share of the loot without having to indulge in any piracy. Great Britain was willing to go along, because with its trading strength, it felt it would get the lion's share even in a free market. The other nations had no inten-

tions of giving up their monopolies, however, and the Open Door policy didn't work.

The Chinese emperor, Tsai T'ien (1871–1908), in anguished response to all this, began a desperate program of reform and modernization, but it didn't last long. The civil servants and the military leaders of the decaying nation saw the threat to their own power and placed that ahead of the needs of the nation. On September 22, 1898, the Emperor's aunt, Tzu Hsi (1835–1908), the "Empress Dowager," seized control of the nation.

Stupid and malignant, she set her face entirely against reform. She maintained an unyielding hostility to the oppressing nations, while doing absolutely nothing to strengthen China. This was a sure recipe for further disaster.

KOREA

Korea, having gained "independence" as a result of the Sino–Japanese war, became an area for Russo–Japanese rivalry. The Korean queen was assassinated on October 8, 1895, and the king later fled for security to the Russian legation. It seemed that the Russians had the upper hand, but Japan was watching the situation closely, intending to choose the time for appropriate action.

JAPAN

During this decade, Japan began a carefully planned program of expansion. The first step was the defeat of China in the Sino–Japanese War, which gained Japan the island of Taiwan and the independence of Korea. There were then maneuverings within Korea to gain the upper hand over the Russians there.

Meanwhile, a Japanese pearl-fisher, Kokichi Mikimoto, learned how to culture pearls in oysters and, in this way, greatly increased the world's pearl supply.

HAWAII

By 1890, the United States had a virtual protectorate over the Hawaiian Islands. Between American missionaries and American businessmen, the Hawaiians sank into the background.

On January 20, 1891, Lydia Liliuokalani (1838–1917) became Queen of Hawaii, succeeding her brother. She was strongly anti-American and, on January 14, 1893, attempted to replace the constitution that had been devised by the American settlers for their own protection. She prepared one that would give her autocratic powers and make the Hawaiians a dominant force in their own land.

The American settlers had no intention of allowing this to happen, however. Under the leadership of Sanford Ballard Dole (1844–1926), they demanded American protection, and the American ambassador brought in 150 armed men from a cruiser in the Honolulu harbor.

Liliuokalani at once retreated from her position, but it was too late. Dole declared her deposed and set up a Republic of Hawaii, which the American ambassador instantly recognized.

When the non-Imperialist Cleveland became president a second time, he recalled the ambassador and tried to restore Liliuokalani, but Dole refused to allow the restoration and Cleveland couldn't actually use force against an American on behalf of a non-American, especially when American public opinion was on Dole's side.

The Republic of Hawaii was formally proclaimed on July 4, 1894, and the United States recognized it on August 8. Liliuokalani withdrew from public life and is best known today as the composer, in 1898, of the song "Aloha Oe."

On August 12, 1898, during the heady days of the Spanish–American war, the United States annexed the Republic of Hawaii and it became an American territory.

PHILIPPINES

The Philippines had been under Spanish control for over three centuries and, in the 1890s, they had grown restless indeed. An insurrection began, led by Emilio Aguinaldo (1869–1964).

The Spaniards managed to put an end to the insurrection in 1897 and bribed its leaders, including Aguinaldo, to leave the country. They did so, but perhaps only because they were se-

cure in the knowledge that Spain was heading for war with the United States.

In 1898, the Spanish–American War began and, on May 1, 1898, the Spanish fleet in Manila harbor was quickly destroyed by the American ships under Dewey.

Dewey lacked the soldiers to take Manila itself, however. He brought back Aguinaldo, who gladly restarted his interrupted insurrection, but that still wasn't enough. Dewey had to wait, and meanwhile fend off the ships of Great Britain, France, and Germany which were nosing about for anything they could get out of the Philippines. The Germans were particularly aggressive and Dewey had to threaten to attack them before they left.

It was not until July 1 that American soldiers arrived and on August 13, 1898, American troops, in cooperation with Aguinaldo's irregulars, took Manila.

By the terms of the Treaty of Paris that ended the Spanish–American War, the Philippines were ceded to the United States. The British Imperialist poet, Kipling, welcomed the United States to the ranks of the colonialist nations by writing a poem on February 4, 1899 that began:

Take up the White Man's burden—
Send forth the best ye breed—
Go bind your sons to exile
To serve your captives' need;
To wait in heavy harness
On fluttered folk and wild
Your new-caught, sullen peoples
Half devil and half child.

Kipling made it sound as though Americans were going to be sent to the Philippines to be dutiful servants, cooks, and shoeshine boys to the Filipinos. It was the other way around, as Kipling well knew.

As for the Filipinos, they were horrified that their insurrection had merely served to switch masters from Spaniards to Americans. They did not want to be a burden to the white man; they wanted to run their own country. The Filipinos consequently began a guerrilla war against the Americans that cost the United States a great deal more than the Spanish–American war had.

AUSTRALIA

The various provinces of Australia worked out a system of union through a federal convention that met at Hobart, Tasmania, in January 1897. They established the "Commonwealth of Australia."

South Australia granted women's suffrage in 1894 and other Australian provinces followed in due course.

NEW ZEALAND

New Zealand had granted women's suffrage in 1893. They also engaged in progressive social experimentation, such as insisting on eight-hour work days, old-age pensions, the forced arbitration of labor disputes, and so on.

ANTARCTICA

On January 23, 1895, a Norwegian whaler commanded by Leonard Kristenson debarked a party on the Antarctica ice. For the first time in the history of the world, human beings stood on land inside the Antarctic Circle.

One of that party was Carston E. Borchgrevink (1864–1934), who returned in 1898 and, with nine other men, wintered in Antarctica, the first ever to do so. Borchgrevink put on skis and set off on the first attempt to penetrate southward overland. On February 16, 1900, he reached a point only 780 miles from the South Pole.

1900 TO 1910

GREAT BRITAIN

The coming of the twentieth century may well have been a time of foreboding for many British, since it brought a number of disquieting events.

In the first place, the Boer War had begun just as the nineteenth century was ending (it will be described later, at the appropriate place), and it was not just another colonial war. The Boers put up the very devil of a fight and, in its first stages, they did surprisingly well, to Great Britain's chagrin. Worse yet, it seemed clear that the sympathy of the world lay with the Boers and that Great Britain was playing the role of villain for the first time since it had found itself at odds with most of Europe at the time of the War of American Independence a century and a quarter earlier. Great Britain was not used to that and must have acutely felt the shortcomings of a "splendid isolation" that had left it without a friend, as the world enjoyed its discomfiture.

Then, after the Boer War had turned definitely and heavily in the British favor, the first month of the twentieth century saw the death, on January 22, 1901, of Queen Victoria. She was in her 82nd year, had been reigning for 63½ years, and had come to seem a permanent fact of life, the only monarch that all but the very oldest British subjects could remember. It was the longest reign of any British monarch and only Louis XIV of France, two centuries earlier, had ruled longer.

What's more, her long reign had been a time of almost unbroken prosperity and peace for Great Britain. During her reign, Great Britain's population had more than doubled, the Empire had spread widely over the world and to be of the British upper class was to feel that one was a member of God's elect.

There may have been some superstitious feeling that, with the passing of Victoria, things might never be so bright and sunny for Great Britain again. If that superstitious feeling existed, it turned out to be justified. The British golden age had passed.

Succeeding Victoria was her oldest son, who reigned as Edward VII (1841–1910). He was already 59 years old at the time that he came to the throne and Victoria, who had never been fond of him, had deliberately kept him out of public affairs until the last few years of her reign when she had to face the fact that he would soon be king.

Edward VII had, in consequence, lived the life of a man about town, interested in wine, food, women, sports, yachting, and all the other gentlemanly pleasures. It seemed questionable as to how good a king he would make but, fortunately, by this time, all a British monarch had to do was to make a dignified appearance and say what he was told to say. Edward VII did that well.

Another change coming over British society at this time was that Labour organizations were establishing themselves as a true political party by 1900. At the head of the Labour Party was James Ramsay MacDonald (1866–1937), who had been a member of the Fabian society, and who worked to build alliances between the Party and the various labor unions. In 1900, only two Labour candidates were elected to Parliament, but in 1906, there were 29. The party was growing.

Meanwhile, Salisbury, Prime Minister for the third time, was growing old and ill. In July 1902, he resigned, but not before he had presided over the end of Great Britain's diplomatic isolation, even though he had been a firm upholder of the isolationist principle.

On January 30, 1902, Great Britain signed an alliance with Japan. This Anglo–Japanese accord made sense. In the first place, Japan had shown its strength in the Sino–Japanese war in the previous decade and Great Britain had liked what it had seen. Japan was the only power that was strong in the Far East and that had no European interests at all so that it would not directly compete with Great Britain. Nor did it threaten any British positions in the Far East. In particular, Japan could be counted on to keep Russia busy, and Great Britain had been an enemy of Russia since the Crimean War, a half-century earlier.

Succeeding Salisbury as Conservative Party leader and as Prime Minister, on July 11, 1902, was Arthur James Balfour (1848–1930), who was Salisbury's nephew.

Balfour pushed through an educational reform before the end of the year, one in which the state assumed control of and responsibility for secondary school education. This insured a rapid rise in the number of British students who received an education past the grammar school stage. In 1904, he also arranged for an end to British isolation within Europe itself, and not merely in the Far East. This was something some French desperately wanted. The French were pleased to have Russia as an ally but they knew that Russia was technologically backward and that, in a war with Germany, it would contribute little beyond sheer mass. If France could get Great Britain on its side, British control of the sea could be decisive.

The French Foreign Minister, Theophile Delcasse (1852–1923), had his heart set on the British alliance. He became foreign minister in 1898 and, almost at once, pulled French troops out of Fashoda and let Great Britain have its way in the Nile River valley. There followed years of delicate negotiations, in which the French ambassador to Great Britain, Pierre Paul Cambon (1843–1924), and a sympathetic British Foreign Secretary, Henry Charles Keith Petty-Fitzmaurice, Lord Lansdowne (1845–1927), labored to bring the alliance about.

Things looked up once Queen Victoria and Salisbury had left the scene. Balfour knew the value of alliances and Edward VII was openly pro-French.

Lansdowne, having broken the ice by pushing through the Anglo–Japanese alliance, was now ready for the greater task of France. He saw to it that Edward VII made a visit of state to Paris. There, on May 1, 1904, Edward VII made a speech in good French that was greeted with ecstasy. It was Edward VII's greatest moment.

Once that was done, it became considerably easier to settle the various points of disagreement between France and England, especially since it was at the expense of other people's property. Thus, France agreed to let Great Britain do as it pleased in Egypt, while Great Britain agreed to let France do as it pleased in Morocco. Meanwhile, a war between Russia and Japan broke out just as the negotiations were coming to a conclusion and France agreed not to help its ally, Russia, against Great Britain's ally, Japan. That also pleased Great Britain.

The alliance between Great Britain and France (popularly called the "Entente Cordiale" or "cordial understanding" in order to avoid the word "alliance," which rang badly in British ears) was signed on April 8, 1904.

All this, however, did not necessarily add to the popularity of Balfour. His educational reform gave too much power to the Church of England to suit those who were not Anglicans. What's more, there was a tangle of doubts over the correct policy on tariffs. Even the Entente Cordiale must have made some people nervous because the French used it to move on Morocco at once, precipitating a war crisis that will be described later.

Toward the end of 1905, Balfour resigned, and Edward VII turned to Henry Campbell-Bannerman (1836–1908), the Liberal party leader, who then won massively in elections held in January, 1906.

Campbell-Bannerman's cabinet included John Elliot Burns (1858–1943), the first person from the ranks of labor to achieve cabinet rank. Also in his cabinet were Herbert Henry Asquith (1852–1928) and David Lloyd George (1863–1945). Lloyd George had been opposed to the Boer War and had maintained that unpopular position courageously.

Campbell-Bannerman adjusted various matters that had aroused opposition to Balfour, modifying the Education Act, for instance, to give non-Anglicans a better position. He also passed prolabor acts, including workmen's compensation in cases of job-related accidents. In addition, he adopted a conciliatory attitude toward the defeated Boers, winning their cooperation and assuring peace in South Africa.

Again, however, the most important event of his administration was an alliance. Russia had lost the war with Japan disastrously and was plagued with serious revolutionary upheavals at home. Suddenly, it seemed to Great Britain to be a nation representing no great danger. In fact, as long as Russia felt defeated and in disarray, it might be a good time to negotiate. Besides,

France, which now had an alliance with both Great Britain and Russia, wanted the system to be closed by having these two nations come to an understanding.

On August 31, 1907, an Anglo–Russian alliance (or "rapprochement" to avoid, once more, the word "alliance") was announced. Again, the bond of friendship was formed through the exchange of other people's property. The Russians were to have a sphere of influence in northern Persia, the British in southern Persia, the Persian Gulf, and Afghanistan. Tibet was to be independent of both. The Russians were promised, rather vaguely, a better deal with respect to the use of the straits at Constantinople.

The French/British/Russian combination was now a "Triple Entente," and it balanced the Triple Alliance of Germany/Austria-Hungary/Italy. Europe had been neatly divided into two armed camps, and any crisis that occurred might be made more dangerous by having each side feel too strong to have to back down.

What had led to this, to a large extent, was Germany's determination to compete with Great Britain at sea. The British wished to take some step to outreach the Germans and they built the *Dreadnought*, which was the first ship to be equipped with big guns only. It had ten 12-inch guns—12 inches being the diameter of the muzzle. It was launched on February 10, 1906 and it literally needed to dread nought, since it could outshoot any ship in the world.

The trouble was that Germany at once began to build dreadnoughts of its own (the name came to symbolize the entire class of big-gun battleships). What counted, then, at least in part, was not the total number of ships in a navy, but the total number of dreadnoughts, and in this respect Great Britain and Germany started almost even. Thus, the launching of the *Dreadnought* was actually a setback in Great Britain's attempt to retain control of the sea.

Great Britain had to build ships more quickly than ever—but where was the money to come from? In 1909, Lloyd George, who was Chancellor of the Exchequer, and responsible for the budget, brought in a program that would soak the rich. In other words, he set up a tax system that would lean most heavily on those best-equipped to pay, so that money could be raised without the conservative sport of squeezing the poor.

The House of Commons passed it, but the House of Lords did not, nor did it look as if the Lords would ever pass it unless something drastic was done. There was a general election in 1909 and the Liberals won again, though with a reduced majority. The stage was set for a struggle with the House of Lords.

The Liberal movement did not go so far as to consider women's suffrage, but women themselves were becoming more militant. Under the leadership of Emmeline Goulden Pankhurst (1858–1928), the "suffragettes" withstood jeers, insults, and occasional prison sentences, but were making themselves heard.

On May 6, 1901, Edward VIII died and, at his funeral, the monarchs of Europe gathered. Even William II of Germany was there. It was the last great gathering of crowned heads, though no one realized that at the time. Succeeding Edward VII was his son, who reigned as George V (1865–1936).

In this decade, the New Zealand-born physicist, Ernest Rutherford (1871–1937), along with a coworker, Frederick Soddy (1877–1956) showed, in 1902, that the radioactive elements, uranium and thorium, changed into lead, by way of a series of breakdown products. For this discovery of "radioactive series," he eventually received the Nobel Prize. By 1909, he had found that certain radioactive radiations, which he called "alpha rays," consisted of a stream of helium atoms from which the electrons had been removed.

In 1904, John Ambrose Fleming (1849–1945) showed that a stream of electrons speeding through a vacuum could be used as a rectifier, converting an alternating electric current into a direct one. This was a "diode," and it was the first step in the development of an electronics technology.

In biology, Charles Sherrington (1857–1952) worked out the nature of reflex action in this decade. In 1900, Frederick Gowland Hopkins (1861–1947) discovered the amino acid, tryptophan, and worked out the concept of dietarily essential amino acids. In 1906, he clarified the vitamin concept, naming several diseases that were caused by the dietary lack of vitamins. Both Sherrington and Hopkins were eventually Nobel Prize winners.

William Bateson (1861–1926) showed, in 1902, that the laws of inheritance, worked out by Mendel and others for plants, held true for animals as well. He also showed that characteristics were not always inherited separately. There were linked characteristics as well.

Many writers continued to be active in this decade. H. G. Wells wrote both science fiction novels, such as *First Men in the Moon* (1901), and novels of social commentary, such as *Tono-Bungay* (1909). James M. Barrie wrote the plays *Quality Street* (1901), *The Admirable Crichton* (1902), *Peter Pan* (1904), *What Every Woman Knows* (1908), and *The Twelve-Pound Look* (1910). G. B. Shaw's plays included *Caesar and Cleopatra* (1900), *Man and Superman* (1903), *Major Barbara* (1905), and *The Doctor's Dilemma* (1906). Kipling wrote *Kim* (1901). Israel Zangwill was a great success with an idealized picture of the United States in his play *The Melting Pot* (1908), which added a phrase to the language.

Among the newer writers, Edward Morgan Forster (1879–1970) published *A Room with a View* in 1908. John Galsworthy (1867–1933) published *A Man of Property* in 1906. This was the first novel in his *The Forsyte Saga*, which eventually earned him a Nobel Prize in literature. Arnold Bennet (1867–1931) published *Old Wives' Tales* in 1908. On a more popular level, Edgar Wallace (1875–1932) with his *Four Just Men*, published in 1905, established himself as a successful and prolific writer of thrillers.

Among the writers for children, Helen Beatrix Potter (1866–1943) wrote *The Tale of Peter Rabbit* in 1900, while Kenneth Grahame (1859–1932) wrote *The Wind in the Willows* in 1908. Kipling wrote the very successful *Just So Stories* in 1902, in a baby-talk fashion that does not appeal to everyone.

John Edward Masefield (1878–1967) wrote poetry and stories in this decade that attracted attention and eventually won him the poet laureateship. Alfred Noyes (1880–1958) wrote poems that included the unabashedly sentimental "The Highwayman" and "The Barrel-Organ."

In music, Edward William Elgar (1857–1934) is best-known for a series of marches written in this decade. It includes *Pomp and Circumstance*, without which no college commencement would be complete.

There was an Irish literary revival featuring the poems and plays of William Butler Yeats (1865–1939), who won a Nobel Prize in literature, and John Millington Synge (1871–1909), whose play, *The Playboy of the Western World*, was produced in 1907.

GERMANY

This decade saw the sharpening and intensifying of the enmity and antagonism between Germany and Great Britain.

Internally, Germany continued Bismarck's principle of paternalism. Pensions were increased, health insurance extended, the hours of labor reduced, and so on. Prosperity continued to rise and it was quite clear that militarily, technologically, and economically, Germany was the strongest power in Europe. Only the British navy stood in the way of Germany becoming the leading nation in the world (as, a century earlier, it had stood in the way of Napoleon and France.)

With that thought in mind, Germany's naval buildup continued. On June 12, 1900, an additional naval bill set up a 17-year program that would make the German navy second only to that of Great Britain and so strong that even Great Britain would hesitate to face it.

Naturally, this made Great Britain anxious and it responded with the Entente Cordiale with France and with the launching of the *Dreadnought*. The alliance between France and Russia, completing the Triple Entente, gave rise to the feeling within Germany that the land was being "encircled" by its enemies. It's hard to look at the map and not admit there was something in that, but it might also be argued that the Germans had brought it upon themselves. The "encircling" was not an action, but a reaction.

However, France, taking advantage of the fact that the Entente Cordiale had given it a free hand in Morocco, and confident that, with British backing, it had nothing to fear from Germany, moved overhastily into Morocco. They negotiated with the Sultan of Morocco in order to establish the basis of a protectorate and pointedly did not discuss the matter with Germany. Germany did not expect to take over Morocco itself, but it wanted an "open door" (to use the American phrase) and resented the fact that France would undoubtedly try to monopolize trade with Morocco.

William II, therefore, took the opportunity to visit Tangiers on the north Moroccan coast, and there, on March 31, 1905, he made a speech calling for the independence of Morocco and for an open door.

This was the "First Moroccan Crisis," for it placed Germany and France on a collision course over Morocco. The French quailed and seemed willing to back down a bit, but the Germans, pressing their advantage, refused the offered compromise. The British, nervous about German intentions, offered to set up discussions with France for unified action in case of the worst. Delcasse demanded that France trust Great Britain's loyalty to the Entente and face up to Germany. The rest of the cabinet, however, was not prepared to trust Great Britain that far. What if, at the last minute, Great Britain faded out of the picture and let France face an angry Germany alone or with only the help that a bumbling and defeated Russia could give it? Delcasse was forced to resign his post and it seemed that France was about to cave in completely.

As it happened, though, the Sultan of Morocco had called for an international conference to settle the matter, and Germany, confident of its case, and certain that France would grovel and Great Britain desert it, demanded that such a conference be held. France, with no confidence in such a conference, felt there was nothing else it could do and accepted.

The conference was held in Algeciras, on the southern coast of Spain just across from the strait from Tangier. Attending were not only Germany and France, but also Germany's allies, Austria-Hungary and Italy, and France's allies, Great Britain and Russia. In addition, Spain attended as the host country, and so did the United States, which temporarily abandoned its policy of steering clear of European quarrels, out of the sheer excitement of having become a great power.

Between January 16 and April 7, 1906, the Algeciras Conference was conducted and Germany was totally and disagreeably surprised. Germany expected that Great Britain and Russia might join France in voting against them, but so did Spain and the United States, and so, even, did Germany's ally, Italy. Only Austria-Hungary voted on the German side.

Holstein, William II's evil spirit, wouldn't accept this diplomatic defeat and advised that the matter be settled by war. The German government, however, did not want war at this time and Holstein was relieved of his position.

The conference, in conclusion, paid lip service to Moroccan independence and to freedom of trade, but, in actuality, it gave France control of Morocco. This was a clear victory for the Triple Entente over the Triple Alliance.

As though that were not bad enough, William II had another brainstorm. In November 1908, he gave an interview to a London newspaper in which he described the German people as hostile to Great Britain, while he alone stood staunch as Great Britain's friend. Perhaps his idea was to frighten the British with the picture of German hostility and get them to cling to William as their only protection. It didn't work, of course. The British didn't for one minute believe in William II's friendship.

However, the German people themselves resented the interview. They did not want to be cast in the role of villains just to make William II look good. Demands increased that William II learn, or be made to learn, to keep his mouth shut. This was an exceedingly embarrassing time for the German government, which didn't dare speak roughly to the Emperor.

That may have been one of the reasons why Bulow resigned the Chancellorship on July 14, 1909. Replacing him was Theobald Theodor

Friedrich Albert von Bethman Hollweg (1856–1921), who had risen from the ranks of the bureaucracy. He was used to taking orders and, as Chancellor, his greatest talent lay in taking orders from those who were more forceful and bellicose than he himself was.

Germany was doing well in science. In 1905, Albert Einstein (1879–1955), the greatest scientist since Isaac Newton, did three amazing things. He established an equation that made it possible to calculate the size of atoms. He presented his "special theory of relativity" that explained the Michelson–Morley experiment, established the speed of light in a vacuum as the greatest speed possible, showed that mass and energy were interchangeable according to the famous equation $e = mc^2$, and modified and improved Newton's laws of motion. He also explained the photoelectric effect and made use of quantum theory to do so. This established the quantum theory as more than a mathematical trick and earned him, eventually a Nobel Prize.

Hermann Walther Nernst (1865–1941), also in 1905, worked out what is called "the third law of thermodynamics," showing that it is actually impossible to reach absolute zero. This brought him a Nobel Prize, too.

Fritz Haber (1868–1934) had developed, by 1908, a method for forming ammonia out of the nitrogen in the atmosphere. From ammonia, fertilizers and explosives could be easily made. This "Haber process" meant that Germany need never fear a shortage of ammunition in wartime. Without it, nitrates would have to be imported from places like Chile, and the British navy would have prevented their delivery. Germany could not have fought a long war without Haber but, because he was Jewish, there came a time when Germany would show him monumental ingratitude.

In 1906, August von Wassermann (1866–1925) discovered a diagnostic test for syphilis. The German bacteriologist, Paul Ehrlich (1854–1915), went farther. He had worked with Behring on diphtheria, and was searching for special compounds that would kill agents that caused disease without much harming the human body. In 1909, he discovered "salvarsan," a specific agent for syphilis. However, he had already received a Nobel Prize for earlier work in this field.

In writing, Thomas Mann (1875–1955) made his name with *Buddenbrooks*, published in 1900. Rainer Maria Rilke (1875–1926) was a prominent poet of the period, Frank Wedekind (1864–1918), a prominent playwright, and Wilhelm Lehmbruck (1881–1919) a prominent sculptor.

FRANCE

In the wake of the Dreyfus Affair, anticlericalism in France had strengthened enormously and there was a movement for the separation of church and state, presided over by the Premier, Justin Louis Emil Combes (1835–1921). He had received a religious education, but despite that (or perhaps because of it) became an ardent anticlerical.

The separation came into existence in November 1904, and by its terms, the Concordat established by Napoleon with the Church a century earlier was nullified. All connection between Church and State was broken and complete freedom of religion was proclaimed.

The forming of the Entente Cordiale and the resolution of the First Moroccan Crisis in France's favor had produced a wave of nationalist fervor in France, however, and voices appeared calling for an aggressive foreign policy and even for the restoration of the monarchy. Among these reactionaries were Charles Maurras (1868–1952), and Alphonse Marie Leon Daudet (1867–1942), the son of the writer. Together they founded *L'Action Francaise*, which remained a showcase for their views.

In science, in this period, Charles Jules Henri Nicolle (1866–1936) discovered, in 1909, that the disease typhus was spread by the body louse, something that was hard to eradicate in a society where few people had access to the kind of life in which frequent washings and changes of clothes were possible.

The French aviator, Louis Bleriot (1872–1936), was the first to fly an airplane (invented in this decade by a pair of Americans) over an important body of water. On July 25, 1909, he flew across the Strait of Dover, from Calais to Dover.

Maeterlinck wrote *The Blue Bird* in 1908 and Sidonie Gabrielle Colette (1873–1954) began writing her highly regarded novels. Debussy wrote the opera *Pelleas and Melisande* in 1902. Among the artists, Henri Emile Benoit Matisse (1869–1954) and Maurice Utrillo (1883–1955) began to make their marks in this decade.

AUSTRIA-HUNGARY

In the Austrian half of the monarchy, universal male suffrage was introduced on January 26, 1907.

In the Hungarian half, that possibility was used as a threat. The Hungarians had grown annoyed over the fact that the army was one of the unifying factors in the dual monarchy. The Hungarians wanted separate units with separate insignia, and this the Emperor, with some justification, would not allow. After all, to have two armies would simply ask for all kinds of confusion and failure of cooperation. It would be a recipe for disaster.

Therefore, the Emperor threatened to push universal suffrage for Hungary, too, which would give the Slavic inhabitants of Hungary the vote, and endanger the Hungarian domination. At that threat, the question of a separate army was dropped in mid-1906.

The important event in Austro–Hungarian history in this decade involved Bosnia-Herzegovina, Austrian provinces northwest of Serbia and Montenegro. These were nominally ruled by the Ottoman Empire, though they had been made an Austro–Hungarian protectorate at the Congress of Berlin, three decades earlier.

This meant that the provinces were garrisoned by Austro–Hungarian troops and that, to all intents and purposes, they were Austro–Hungarian territory. It seemed to Austria-Hungary that there was no reason not to make it official, so on October 6, 1908, it announced that Bosnia and Herzegovina had been annexed and were now integral parts of the Austro–Hungarian Dual Monarchy.

The Ottoman Empire protested, of course, but it was quite helpless in the matter. Serbia and Montenegro, which had always looked at Bosnia-

Herzegovina as potential portions of their own monarchies, were even more outraged at watching it move out of reach into the Austro–Hungarian gullet, but by themselves they were also helpless.

As for Russia, it was in a quandary. The Russian foreign minister, Aleksandr Petrovich Izvolsky (1856–1919), had negotiated the rapprochement with Great Britain the year before. By its terms, Great Britain had indicated its readiness to allow Russia to move freely out of and into the Black Sea by way of the straits at Constantinople. It stood to reason that it would help if Austria-Hungary, an interested party in all matters involving the Balkans and the Ottoman Empire, were to also agree.

Therefore, Izvolski got in touch with the Austro–Hungarian foreign minister, Alois Lexa von Aehrenthal (1854–1912), and at a meeting on September 16, 1908, they had come to some sort of agreement whereby Russia would not object if Austria-Hungary annexed Bosnia-Herzegovina, and Austria-Hungary would not object if Russia made use of the straits at Constantinople.

The trouble was that Izvolski had either exceeded his instructions or had simply neglected to inform his government of what he had done. Three weeks after the agreement, Austria-Hungary did annex Bosnia-Herzegovina, and the Russian Prime Minister, Pyotr Arkadyevich Stolypin (1862–1911), promptly ordered Izvolski to oppose the Austro–Hungarian move.

Izvolski had no choice but to denounce the agreement he had made, to say that he was duped or misunderstood, and to sing with the angels now by furiously backing the Serbians in their objections to the annexation. The matter at once burgeoned into a full-scale crisis, for Germany lined up behind Austria-Hungary (its only ally at the Algeciras Conference), while Great Britain and France backed Russia.

Great Britain and France suggested another international conference like that at Algeciras, but Austria-Hungary felt it would surely be outvoted and wouldn't accept the suggestion. Izvolski travelled to London to get specific permission for concessions on the Straits so that Russia might salvage something out of the mess, but now Great Britain was willing only on condition that the Ottoman Empire was willing—which it wasn't.

Then, on January 12, 1909, Austria-Hungary scored another coup. It persuaded the Ottoman Empire to accept the annexation in return for payment. That put Austria-Hungary in an excellent position because if they bought the provinces from the Ottoman Empire, their legal owner, who had the right to complain?

Serbia was still furious and was arming and threatening war, assuming that Russia would help it. Austria-Hungary was delighted at the chance of going to war with little Serbia and wiping it out, if Russia could be made to stay out. On March 21, 1909, Germany warned Russia to abandon Serbia and accept the annexation or else; the hint was, Russia would have to face both Austria-Hungary and Germany in war.

Russia had not yet recovered from the defeat by Japan and by the internal chaos it had also been suffering. It was in no shape to face a major war, so it backed down and forced Serbia to back down, too. On March 31, 1909, Serbia accepted the annexation.

Austria-Hungary was triumphant and Germany may have felt that this was compensation for the loss at Algeciras. As for Russia, it was one more unbearable humiliation. All it could do was to fire Izvolski in 1910, and to make up its mind that if there was another crisis with Austria-Hungary over the Balkans, Russia would not back down again.

Outside the realm of politics, Sigmund Freud had foresaken the use of hypnosis in dealing with patients and used free-association instead, and the art of psychoanalysis came into use. His friend and associate, Alfred Adler (1870–1937), originated the term "inferiority complex" in 1907. His version of psychiatric treatment was much briefer than Freud's.

Karl Landsteiner (1868–1943) discovered the A, B, and O blood groups that, for the first time, made it safe to use blood transfusions. He was awarded a Nobel Prize for this.

In music, the Hungarian Bela Bartok (1881–1945) was writing his earliest pieces in this decade. Another Hungarian, Franz Lehar (1870–

1948), inherited the mantle of Johann Strauss, writing, among other works, the operetta *The Merry Widow* in 1905, containing "The Merry Widow Waltz," which may be the most popular waltz not written by Strauss. Still another Hungarian, Ferenc Molnar (1878–1952) wrote the drama *Liliom* in 1909.

RUSSIA

The situation in Russia was, in some ways, like that in China a decade earlier. In Russia, as in China then, discontent among the people was rising rapidly. In Russia, as in China then, the government remained unmoved and uncompromising. And in Russia, as in China then, the government suffered a bad defeat in war which exacerbated internal unrest. The defeat was even inflicted by the same power in both cases: Japan. The difference was that Russia was not then descended upon by European harpies, but was given a chance to recover.

The war in the Far East was brought on by rivalries in Korea and Manchuria, and in the question of which nation, Japan or Russia, was to dominate there. Russia, throughout, treated the Japanese as a peculiar little oriental people not even worth talking to, and the lesson Russia received in consequence was a severe one. (The details will be given in a later section.)

The Russian Minister of the Interior, at the time, was Vyacheslav Konstantinovich Plehve (1846–1904). He was in charge of suppressing all liberal dissent and he did so with the utmost cruelty. He labored to Russify the non-Russian elements of the nation, such as the Finns and the Armenians. He was also strongly anti-Semitic and his policies brought about a dreadful pogrom in Kishinev in the far southwest, in April 1903. He also supported war with Japan as a way of uniting Russia in a burst of patriotic fervor. Considering all this, he was a natural target for terrorists and on July 28, 1904, less than a half year after the Russo-Japanese war had begun, he was assassinated.

Already that war was turning disastrous and the government didn't need serious trouble at home, but it got just that. The assassination of Plehve seemed to set off strikes and demonstrations all over Russia. There were meetings of angry reformers, even in St. Petersburg itself, who demanded representative government and civil liberties.

Until now, the uprisings had been of peasants, and the articulate demands had been offered by the intellectuals and professionals. But now, Russia's factory workers were also becoming involved. On Sunday, January 22, 1905, a group of workers, led by an Orthodox priest, G. Gapon, marched peaceably to the Winter Palace to present petitions and to ask for reforms.

The crowd was met with gunfire. A hundred marchers were killed, several hundred wounded, and the day was called "Bloody Sunday."

The action was worse than useless for it started "the Revolution of 1905." Unrest increased tremendously and, between October 20 and 30, there was a great general strike that brought the nation to a complete halt barely a month after the peace treaty with Japan had presented the world with the spectacle of huge Russia having to cede territory to tiny Japan in order to buy peace.

The reactionary ministers of Nicholas II had to resign and the liberal, Witte, who had been in disgrace because of his liberalism, was rehabilitated and made Prime Minister on October 30. Along with that, it was proclaimed that Russia would have a constitution, a legislative body called a "Duma" ("a place of judgment"), an extended franchise, and civil liberties.

Many of the moderate reformers were satisfied with this, but the Social Democrats didn't consider it enough and didn't trust the government to do even what it said it would. They had formed a "soviet" ("council") in St. Petersburg, but the members of this soviet were arrested on December 16, 1905. This was followed by a worker's uprising in Moscow that was repressed with difficulty.

Witte was dismissed on May 2, 1906, since, by then, with the war over and the more radical element suppressed, it was felt that things could continue without him. He was succeeded by Ivan Loggimovich Goremykin (1859–1917); on May 6, it was announced that the Tsar was still an autocrat and that the Duma would be selected in such a way that it was bound to be controlled by the government, and that it had only limited powers over the budget. The Tsar could govern by decree when the Duma wasn't in session. In short, virtually everything that had been promised was, in essence, taken away.

On May 10, the first Duma met. The radical parties had boycotted the election but moderate reformers managed to win a great many seats and they criticized the government loudly. In June, Stolypin became Prime Minister and he tried to introduce some reforms to ease the situation.

A second election was held and the second Duma met on March 5, 1907. This time the radical parties had voted and the second Duma was, therefore, more radical than the first. It was hastily dissolved on June 16 and a new election law was passed that made it virtually impossible to elect radicals.

A third Duma met. It was conservative and everything returned to reaction. In the relative quiet that followed, with the Revolution of 1905 essentially a failure, Russia carried through the rapprochement with Great Britain in 1907, and suffered humiliation over Bosnia-Herzegovina in 1908.

Through all these upheavals, Chekhov wrote his plays *The Three Sisters* in 1901, and *The Cherry Orchard* in 1904. Aleksey Maksimovich Peshkov (1868–1936), writing under the pseudonym of "Maxim Gorky," was achieving fame with his stories, and for his radical views. (His native city of Nizhni-Novgorod is now called Gorky in his honor.)

Rimsky-Korakov was still composing and his *Le Coq d'or* was produced in 1909. Another Russian composer of the period was Aleksander Nikolayevich Scriabin (1872–1915).

Jean Julius Christian Sibelius (1865–1957) was the greatest of the Finnish composers. His best known works are *Finlandia* (1899) and *Valse Triste* (1903).

ITALY

Italy had finally gotten over its outrage at the French occupation of Tunis. On December 14, 1900, in fact, Italy had come to an agreement with France, accepting the Tunisian situation, provided Italy was given a free hand in Tripoli, a large and mostly desert area between Tunis and Egypt, which was the last remnant of North Africa that the Ottoman Empire could still consider its own.

On June 28, 1902, Italy renewed its adherence to the Triple Alliance at which Germany also gave them a free hand in Tropoli. Almost immediately afterward, however, Italy assured the French it would not join in any attack upon them. It also began to show bitterness over Italian areas still ruled by Austria-Hungary, and it voted on the French side at the Algeciras conference.

However, Italy suffered a constant state of disorder during this decade, with strikes and labor unrest a continuing fact of life. It was perhaps for this reason that Germany didn't seem overly upset at Italy's wavering with respect to the Triple Alliance. It didn't seem that Italy would be much of a military factor in any case.

Meanwhile, Marconi was continuing to work on radio in England. On December 12, 1901, he managed to send a radio signal from the southwest tip of England, across the Atlantic Ocean, to Newfoundland, using balloons to lift his antennae as high as possible. Before the end of the decade, he received a Nobel Prize for his work.

Puccini continued working, too, composing the operas *Madame Butterfly* in 1904 and *The Girl of the Golden West* in 1910.

Luigi Pirandello (1867–1936) was an outstanding Italian novelist and playwright in this decade and eventually received a Nobel Prize for literature. The painter, Amedeo Modigliani (1884–1920), working in Paris, was noted for his elongated portraits.

The great tenor, Enrico Caruso (1873–1921), became a world smash with his performance in *Rigoletto* at the Metropolitan Opera in New York in 1903.

PAPACY

Leo XIII died on July 20, 1903, having been in the Papal chair for 25 years. Piux IX and he, taken together, had ruled the Church for 57 years, an unprecedented length of service in a post to which aged men usually succeeded.

The new Pope was Pius X (1835–1914). Pius X was more conservative than Leo XIII. He fought the "modernism" that attempted to find a synthesis of traditional Catholicism with current thought. He was also against the Christian Democrats, since he had no liking for liberalism or for democracy, and he fought France's separation of church and state.

NETHERLANDS

The Netherlands had to fight strikes and labor unrest, too. Strikes in 1903, involving the railroads and the docks, induced enough paralysis to cause the government to use the army to break it up.

Science in the Netherlands continued to be remarkable. Lorentz, who had already received a Nobel Prize, pointed out in 1904 that the failure of the Michelson–Morley experiment not only implied a FitzGerald contraction, but also an increase in mass. Mass approached infinite values as the speed of light was approached, and this, too, seemed to show that speeds faster than light were impossible.

Heike Kamerlingh Onnes (1853–1926) achieved new records in attaining low temperatures and, in 1908, managed to liquefy helium at only four degrees above absolute zero. He eventually received the Nobel Prize for this feat.

In 1903, Willem Einthoven (1860–1927) invented the string galvanometer, an extremely delicate device for detecting feeble currents. By 1906, he had applied the measurement to rhythmic currents produced by the beating heart. This was an "electrocardiogram," and it became a valuable means of detecting heart abnormalities.

BELGIUM

Leopold II's personal empire in the Congo was administered in the cruelest possible way. Leopold II, though wealthy enough, seemed to have a perfect craze for amassing still more wealth and didn't care how he did it. He looted and terrorized the Congolese in his mad clutching at the rubber resources of the region. There was a steadily rising demand for rubber because of the growing importance of the automobile, and Leopold's agents didn't balk at murder and torture.

Beginning in 1903, the Congolese situation was reported in British papers to the gathering horror of those portions of the world population that believed in humanity. Formal investigations began in 1905 and Great Britain and the United States strongly expressed their anger and disapproval. Belgium itself was embarrassed and, under mounting pressure, Leopold had to give up his private empire in 1908 and turn the Congo over to the Belgian state. The "Congo Free State" ("free" only for Leopold, of course) became the "Belgian Congo."

Leopold II died on December 17, 1909, and was succeeded by his nephew, who reigned as Albert I (1875–1934).

SPAIN

Spain, having undergone the terrible humiliation of the defeat by the United States and the loss of all its island possessions in the western hemisphere and in the Pacific Ocean, sought elsewhere for some sort of compensation.

On October 3, 1904, France, which felt that the Entente Cordiale had as good as put Morocco into its pocket, signed a treaty with Spain. Officially, it guaranteed the independence of Morocco, but, in a secret clause, France promised Spain the Mediterranean coast of Morocco, at least. This accounted for Spain siding with France at the Algeciras Conference.

Spain, however, was in no position to act strongly in this respect until 1909, because, as in Italy's case, internal unrest kept the nation off-balance.

The Spanish painter, Fablo Picasso (1881–

1973), settled in Paris in 1904 and began a career that was to make him the most famous artist of the twentieth century.

PORTUGAL

Unrest in Portugal was even greater than in either Spain or Italy. On February 1, 1908, King Carlos I and his son, who was heir to the throne, were assassinated in the streets of Lisbon.

Succeeding as king was Carlos's second son, who reigned as Manuel II (1889–1932). Manuel liberalized the government but maintained the extravagant life-style of his father, and apparently the Portuguese had had enough. The Republicans were growing stronger and had gained majorities in an election held in 1910. On October 4, 1910, there was a general rising and the next day Manuel II fled and went into exile in Great Britain, where he remained for the rest of his life. The House of Braganza had come to an end after two and three-quarter centuries.

The Republic of Portugal began with the presidency of Joaquim Teofilo Braga (1843–1914), a scholar, writer, and anticlerical.

SWITZERLAND

Switzerland, which had been strictly neutral since 1815 and was determined to remain so, come what might, built up an efficient little army that required training for everyone. This was to make sure that no one would too lightly think of violating its neutrality. Switzerland remained democratic and prosperous in the process.

One of the great early psychiatrists was a Swiss disciple of Freud, Carl Gustav Jung (1875–1961), whose work tended to be rather mystical. He spoke of the "collective unconscious" and popularized the concepts of "introversion" and "extroversion."

DENMARK

It was a quiet decade for Denmark. The only event of importance was that the king, Christian IX, died on January 29, 1906, and was succeeded by his son, who reigned as Frederick VIII (1843–1912).

NORWAY

On June 7, 1905, Norway, no longer able to endure Swedish rule, declared itself independent. A plebiscite was held, and the Norwegian people voted heavily in favor of independence.

In a remarkable example of calm acceptance of the inevitable, the Swedish legislature agreed to this on September 24, and, on October 26, a formal treaty of separation was signed. For five centuries, Norway had been ruled first by Denmark and then by Sweden and now, at last, it was an independent nation again.

Norway elected as its king Prince Charles of Denmark, a grandson of Christian IX of Denmark, and a younger son of the prince soon to become Frederick VIII of Denmark. Charles assumed the name of Haakon VII (1872–1957). Under Haakon, there was full democracy. The royal veto was abolished and women's suffrage was established in 1907.

SWEDEN

After Norway's breakaway, democracy advanced in Sweden also. On December 8, 1907, Oscar II of Sweden died, and was succeeded by his oldest son, who reigned as Gustav V (1858–1950).

Selma Lagerlof wrote *The Wonderful Adventures of Nils* in 1907.

The Swedish inventor Alfred Bernhard Nobel (1833–1896) left $9,200,000 in his will for the presentation of annual prizes in Physics, Chemistry, Physiology and Medicine, Literature and Peace in his name. The first such prizes were awarded in 1901 and almost at once became the most prestige-filled awards in the world.

GREECE

The situation in Crete may have satisfied the occupying European powers of Great Britain, France, Russia, and Italy, but it didn't satisfy the people of either Crete or Greece.

The most important Cretan in this decade was

Eleutherios Venizelos (1864–1936). He had led the Cretan insurrection of the previous decade and was now Minister of Justice under Prince George, who was in nominal charge of Crete, though it was actually run by the occupying powers and was, in theory, still part of the Ottoman Empire.

On March 30, 1905, Venizelos raised another insurrection and declared union with Greece. It didn't do any good, of course, for the occupying powers refused to allow the union. Prince George, however, tired of trying to rule the unrulable, resigned on September 25, 1906.

Then came the annexation of Bosnia-Herzegovina by Austria-Hungary along with the threat of war. Once again, the Cretans declared union with Greece, and this time the occupying powers threw up their hands. With a general European war threatening, the question of whether Crete was to be part of Greece or not seemed relatively unimportant. The occupying powers withdrew their forces in July 1909. Crete joined Greece, although the union was not, even yet, officially recognized by the rest of Europe. On October 18, 1910, Venizelos became Prime Minister of Greece.

BULGARIA

There were continuing insurrections in Macedonia, the European territories south of Bulgaria that were still part of the Ottoman Empire. This put Bulgaria in a delicate position, for though it ruled itself in fact, there were still official ties to the Ottoman Empire.

However, when the crisis over Bosnia-Herzegovina arose, Bulgaria took the chance of an official declaration of independence on October 5, 1908, and King Ferdinand took the title of "Tsar." Ferdinand made sure he would have the approval of Russia in this. He visited St. Petersburg on February 21, 1909, and the Russian court, smarting over the situation in the Balkans and ready to make any friend there, received him with royal honors, recognizing Bulgaria's independence and Ferdinand's title. The Ottoman Empire then had no choice but to recognize Bulgarian independence on April 19, 1909.

SERBIA

The unpopular King Alexander I of Serbia, and his even more unpopular Queen Draga, along with a number of other people at the court, were massacred on June 10, 1903 by a military coup. That put an end to the House of Obrenovich that had ruled Serbia, on and off, for nearly a century.

A new monarch was chosen from the competing Karageorgevich family and he reigned as Peter I (1844–1921). With him, the pro-Austro–Hungarian tendencies of the previous 30 years disappeared. Peter I, who had been brought up in France, was pro-French and pro-Russian, and was entirely anti-Austro–Hungarian.

If there was any doubt of this, it vanished with the Bosnia-Herzegovina crisis. Serbia, nearly mad with outrage, desperately wanted to go to war with Austria-Hungary, but needed the backing of Russia for this and Russia was in no position to go along. Although Serbia had to back down, from that moment secret conspiratorial societies began to be formed with the object of doing whatever harm they could, in whatever manner they could, to Austria-Hungary.

MONTENEGRO

The tiny principality of Montenegro, closely allied ethnically with Serbia, received a constitution and a representative government on December 19, 1905.

It was just as outraged as Serbia was at the Austro–Hungarian annexation of Bosnia-Herzegovina, but could do even less about it. On August 28, 1910, Prince Nicholas of Montenegro compensated himself for the loss by upgrading his title to that of "King."

ROMANIA

In this decade, Romania was at the edge of war at one time or another with Bulgaria and with Greece, to say nothing of having to combat a peasant insurrection inside its boundaries. This sort of turbulence, however, had become perpetual in the Balkans ever since the Ottoman grip had begun to weaken nearly a century earlier.

OTTOMAN EMPIRE

The Ottoman Empire continued to shrink as it lost Bosnia-Herzegovina to Austria-Hungary, was forced to accept complete Bulgarian independence, and was in the process of losing Crete to Greece. Inside the Empire, the Young Turk demands for reform and constitutional government grew louder.

To begin with, the leading Young Turks worked from exile in Paris, Geneva, and Cairo, but disaffection was reaching the army. In Macedonia, army units rebelled on July 5, 1908, under Ahmed Niyzai (1873–1912). On July 24, Abdul Hamid II, unable to repress the revolt, restored the Constitution of 1876, one that had been granted when the Ottoman Empire had to secure the help of Great Britain against Russia and that had been withdrawn when the help was no longer needed.

This meant the election of a legislature, which produced a large majority for the Young Turks. The legislature met on December 17, 1908, but then the problem of the minorities arose. The Armenians, Macedonians, and Albanians had supported the Young Turks, hoping that reform might mean decentralization, but many of the Young Turks were strong nationalists who wanted reforms for themselves, but not for the minorities.

Confusion continued. There was a conservative rebellion in Constantinople on April 13, 1909, but it was suppressed by, among others, Enver Pasha (1881–1922), who emerged as the leader of the Young Turks. He forced the deposition of Abdul Hamid II on April 26, 1909. Abdul Hamid's younger brother succeeded and reigned as Mehmed V (1844–1918), but he was merely a puppet in the hands of the Young Turk leaders.

That many things had not changed, despite the Young Turks, was indicated by a renewed massacre of Armenians in 1909, and the brutal repression of uprisings in Albania.

EGYPT

Great Britain consolidated its hold on Egypt and the Sudan in this decade. By the Entente Cor-

diale, France abandoned all claims in the region. Great Britain and the Ottoman Empire argued over whether the Sinai Peninsula was part of Egypt or not, and, on May 3, 1906, the Ottomans were forced to give up the peninsula to Egypt.

That left Great Britain facing only the gathering nationalist sentiment in Egypt, which was not yet strong enough to discommode the British seriously. The British Consul-General, John Eldon Gorst (1835–1916), did his best to make the rule as lenient as possible.

ETHIOPIA

Menelek continued to maintain the independence of Ethiopia, and defined all its frontiers with Great Britain, France, and Italy.

MOROCCO

The Entente Cordiale in 1904 and the Algeciras Conference in 1906 made it pretty clear that France was going to control Morocco.

Little by little France made use of continuing disorders in Morocco to expand its presence there, especially when the death of Europeans was involved. They seized northwest Morocco in 1907, and bombarded Casablanca on August 4, 1907. On February 8, 1909, France came to an agreement with Germany, in which Germany agreed to allow France to exert a protectorate over Morocco, provided Germany received certain economic concessions.

Meanwhile, Spain, in 1909, was finally taking over the northern coastline of Morocco, a strip that came to be called "Spanish Morocco." It had to fight the Rif tribesmen in doing so, and they made the occupation an expensive one for the Spaniards.

SOUTH AFRICA

With storm clouds gathering over southern Africa, Alfred, Viscount Milner (1854–1925), who was governor of British South Africa, met with President Kruger of the Transvaal at Bloemfontein, capital of the Orange Free State. (Transvaal and the Orange Free State, together, are the "Boer Republics.")

The conference, which was held from May 31 to June 5, 1899, got nowhere. Milner insisted on the immediate enfranchisement of Uitlanders who had been in the Boer Republics for at least five years and Kruger would not agree. Both sides refused to compromise, and both sides prepared for war. On October 12, 1899, war broke out between Great Britain and the Boer Republics (the "Boer War").

The British were overconfident. They only had 25,000 troops on the spot and the Boers outnumbered them. Furthermore, the Boer forces were all mounted, all sharpshooters, and all masters of the hit-and-run raid. What's more, they were well-armed, since both the Germans and the French had been glad to do business with them. The Boer disadvantage was that they were not disciplined and that, in the long run, the British could bring to bear overwhelming force.

The Boers attacked at once, hoping to get things settled before the British could build up their forces adequately and to manage a quick and favorable peace. Within a week they had Mafeking and Kimberley, two British outposts on the western border of the Boer Republics, under siege. By November 2, Ladysmith, on the eastern border of the Boer Republics, was also under siege.

Through November and December, British attempts to relieve these beleaguered places failed, and the world was rather amused to see the mighty British Empire put to shame by a handful of backwoods farmers. The trouble was, of course, that the British had been so long at peace that they had no experience at facing a resolute and well-armed adversary and had to undergo on-the-job training.

However, the British had endless resources, which the Boers had not. The British sent in new commanders, and reinforcements began to pour into southern Africa. What's more, they began to build up their own cavalry with which to meet the mounted Boers.

On February 15, 1900, British forces under John Denton Pinkstone French (1852–1925), who had fought in the Sudan, managed to relieve Kimberley and the tide began to turn. On February 18, another British force under Redvers Henry Buller (1839–1908) relieved Ladysmith.

Now the British were on the offensive. They invaded the Orange Free State, taking Bloemfontein on March 13, 1900, overrunning the entire republic and annexing it to British South Africa on May 24.

Mafeking was relieved on May 18, after having been under siege for seven months, and at home the British people went almost mad with joy at the news of that final wiping out of the initial Boer successes.

Next, Transvaal was invaded. Johannesburg was taken on May 31, and Pretoria, Kruger's capital, on June 4. (Kruger, who had gone to Europe seeking help, remained in exile for the four remaining years of his life.) On September 3, the Transvaal was also annexed to British South Africa.

The Boers now resorted to guerrilla warfare and kept the British busy for a year and a half. The British, with 300,000 men and more on the spot, took harsh measures. The Boer farms were systematically destroyed and the British organized concentration camps into which Boer women and children were herded and in which one sixth of those gathered died of disease and poor treatment.

Finally, at the Treaty of Vereeniging (on the Transvaal–Orange Free State border), signed on May 31, 1902, the Boers gave in and accepted British rule.

However, if the British could be ruthless in war, they did, more than some nations, tend to be generous in peace. There was no attempt to enslave the Boers, or to treat them as subhumans. They were granted the vote and given the freedom to organize.

Thus, Louis Botha (1862–1919), who had fought valiantly on the Boer side, now formed a party organization in January 1905. By February 26, 1907, he had won a majority in the legislature of the Transvaal province and became its Premier on March 4. This meant that the Boers, while accepting British sovereignty, were still masters of their own territory.

In 1908, there was a Constitutional Convention that, by February 3, 1909, had established a "Union of South Africa" of which the British and Boers were equally citizens. In fact, on September 15, 1910, in the first elections held in the new Union, the Boers elected a majority and Botha became the first Prime Minister of the Union of South Africa. The Boers, however, recognized the Union to be a useful governmental organization and remained loyal to the British Empire.

Boers and British continued to be alike in their tolerance for non-Europeans, for Asians as well as for Africans. By now, Gandhi in South Africa had organized his campaign of passive resistance —no terror, no violence, just a stubborn refusal to submit to racist laws.

MADAGASCAR

As part of the Entente Cordiale, Great Britain gave up all claims to Madagascar, and France was left in sole control.

PERSIA

The ruler of Persia at the start of this decade was Mozaffar od-Din (1852–1907). After spending his youth in the pursuit of pleasure, he became Shah in May 1896, without any experience at ruling. His notion of statecraft was to obtain loans from Russia, handing over economic concessions in return, and then spending the money on extravagant European trips. The country was rapidly approaching bankruptcy and discontent deepened.

In December 1905, the discontent became a revolution and Mozaffar was forced to get rid of his worst ministers and to agree to the calling of a national assembly to draw up a constitution for a more liberal, representative government. It met on October 7, 1906, produced the necessary constitution, which Mozaffar signed and then, almost immediately afterward, and perhaps as a result, died of a heart attack on December 30, 1906.

He was succeeded by his son, Mohammed Ali (1872–1925), who had no intention of honoring the constitution. On December 15, 1907, he attempted a coup that would restore the autocracy,

and failed. On June 23, 1908, he tried again with the support of Russian soldiers. This time, he succeeded temporarily, but the forces of reform managed to take Tehran on July 12, 1909 and to depose him. He was succeeded by his son, Ahmad (1898–1930), who was only 11 years old. Under him, the constitutionalists remained in charge.

Meanwhile, to some extent the fighting was over nothing for in the course of the Anglo–Russian rapprochements on August 31, 1907, Russia and Great Britain more or less carved the nation into spheres of influence.

A new resource was becoming available to the Persians, or at least to those who could control it economically. Baku in Russia offered the richest yield of oil at the time, but now oil was being obtained on the Persian shores of the Persian Gulf, and, in 1909, the British were exploiting it and oil was pouring through pipelines to the Gulf, as a new and growing source of world energy.

AFGHANISTAN

By the Anglo–Russian rapprochement of 1907, Russia agreed to keep hands off Afghanistan so that the nation was left entirely to British influence.

INDIA

Indian nationalism continued to grow, but it split in two. On December 30, 1906, the "All-India Muslim League" was formed and, thereafter, the Muslims and Hindus of India increasingly felt the differences between themselves, as well as, and sometimes more than, their common hostility to British domination.

The Indian poet, Rabindranath Tagore (1861–1941), who also wrote novels and plays, composed music, and painted, gained fame in this decade and eventually received a Nobel Prize in literature.

SIAM

Siam continued to safeguard its independence but, like Persia, it was being divided into spheres of influence, in this case by the British on the west and the French on the east.

TIBET

Although Tibet had had expansionist periods in the past, it had remained under vague Chinese control for at least two centuries. Because of its location on the plateau north of the Himalayas, however, it was difficult to reach and was left mostly to itself.

Great Britain saw it as a possible way station for Chinese trade and as one more buffer between Russia and India. Consequently, the British in India sent an expedition into Tibet in 1902 under the Indian-born, Francis Edward Younghusband (1863–1942). Younghusband entered the Tibetan capital, the "forbidden city" of Lhasa in 1904, and forced a treaty between Great Britain and Tibet that defined the frontier and set up trade relations. China was not consulted and the Dalai Lama, the religious leader of Tibet, fled temporarily to China.

In 1906, the Chinese managed to secure a treaty with Japan that recognized Chinese suzerainty over Tibet. The Chinese then tried to tighten their grip on that province and the Dalai Lama fled again, this time to India.

CHINA

There were some Chinese, driven to madness by the heartless foreign vivisection of their land, who formed an antiforeigner organization called "the Society of the Righteous Harmonious Fists," with reference to the Chinese martial arts. The unsophisticated thought these arts made the Chinese superior to western methods of fighting and even made the Chinese practitioners impervious to bullets. The name of the organization was transformed by western mockery into "Boxers" and what followed, encouraged and egged on by the Dowager Empress, was the "Boxer Rebellion."

Chinese mobs attacked foreigners and laid siege to foreign legations. Eventually, they killed the German ambassador.

An international expedition was prepared to punish the Chinese. It included Japanese, Russians, French, Germans, British, and Americans. Eventually, up to 18,700 were involved in the expedition. There was, of course, no withstanding them by the ill-equipped, ill-led Chinese.

The city of Tientsin was taken on July 14, 1900. Peking itself was taken on August 14 and the legations were relieved. The Dowager Empress and her court fled to the inland city of Sian and, on December 26, the Dowager Empress accepted all European demands.

An agreement, the "Boxer protocol" was then reached on September 7, 1901. The Chinese had to pay an enormous indemnity, and the payment was to be made by handing out further concessions to the various powers. The legations were enlarged, foreign garrisons were established here and there, and Russia just about took over all of Manchuria.

One European who blundered badly was, as one might expect, William II of Germany. In sending off troops to China, he urged them, on July 27, 1900, to behave in such a manner that the Chinese would be afraid to even look at a German, as once Europeans had been afraid to look at the Huns. In doing so, he handed a priceless propaganda advantage to his enemies who, in not too many years, would routinely refer to the German soldiers as "Huns."

The United States eventually returned half its share of the indemnity to China and devoted the rest to the education of 1100 Chinese students in the United States. It set an honorable example that the other nations did not follow.

If China could now see the penalty of failure to adopt Western technology in countering Western strength, they could also see the success of Japan, which *did* adapt what it needed, and was able to defeat Russia in 1904 and 1905. One result of that was that China regained control, of a sort, over Manchuria.

Indeed China now, at last, began to stumble toward reform. Education was improved, the opium traffic was slowly suppressed, railroads were built, and there was a gradual movement toward representative government.

In November 1908, the Dowager Empress and the puppet Emperor both died. Succeeding to the

Imperial Throne was the old Emperor's nephew, P'u-I (1906–1967). He was only two years old and his father, the younger brother of the previous Emperor, was the regent.

On December 3, 1908, a constitution was adopted that provided for the election of a representative legislature, but the new regent was in no hurry to fulfill its terms. Meanwhile, Sun Yat-sen, now based in Japan, was building up his revolutionary societies, with which he hoped to overthrow the Manchu dynasty altogether.

KOREA

As the decade opened, the Koreans were in the uncomfortable position of being dragged in opposite directions by the Russians and Japanese. The Russo–Japanese War of 1904–1905 settled the matter, however. Russia, after its defeat, had to withdraw from Korea, while the Japanese presence became more and more dominant.

The Korean Emperor was forced to abdicate on July 19, 1907. His son succeeded as a mere figurehead. The Korean army was disbanded and though guerrilla forces fought the Japanese desperately in the southern provinces, the ending was foregone. On August 22, 1910, Hideyoshi's dream of three centuries earlier was fulfilled, and Korea was annexed by Japan.

JAPAN

In this decade, Japan continued, with exemplary skill, to follow its plan for expansion. It participated in the international expedition against the Boxers, thus increasing its standing as a modern "European-style" power, at least from the military standpoint. The Japanese diplomat, Tadasu Hayashi (1850–1913), helped negotiate an Anglo–Japanese pact in 1902, and Japan could then count on Great Britain keeping Europe quiet, while Japan settled matters with Russia.

It might seem that Japan had no hope of defeating giant Russia, but Japan was not attacking Russia itself but rather the end of the Russian tail. There were only 83,000 Russian troops in the Far East and the Japanese did not expect they would be easily reinforced, for there was only a single-track Trans-Siberian railroad chug-chugging across the vast distance that separated Vladivostok from Russia's European centers. There was even a 100-mile gap in the railroad that still existed in the vicinity of Lake Baikal.

What's more, the Russian naval forces in the Far East, centered mostly at Port Arthur, south of Manchuria, were in poor shape, and were not to be compared with the modern Japanese battleships.

Even so, the Japanese felt their best chance was to destroy Russian naval power in the Pacific with a single lightning stroke, then drive into Manchuria. Of course, it might follow, thereafter, that the Russians would slowly reinforce themselves until, at last, their mass was irresistible, but the Japanese perhaps calculated that Russia was on the brink of internal chaos. If they thought that, they were right.

The Japanese therefore struck, without warning, at Port Arthur and elsewhere on February 8, 1904, caught the Russian ships utterly by surprise, and put most of them out of action. The Japanese then declared war on February 10. (It was a trick the Japanese would eventually try again, and, unbelievably, it would work the second time, too.)

The Japanese then laid siege to Port Arthur, and sent their army advancing through Korea and into Manchuria. The Russians, despite all their disadvantages, fought with stolid endurance and made the Japanese pay far more than they had counted on.

On January 2, 1905, after a seven-month siege, the Japanese finally took Port Arthur, but it cost them 60,000 casualties. In Manchuria, the Russian general, Aleksey Nikolayevich Kuropatkin (1848–1921), did what he could under the circumstances. Between February 20 and March 9, there was a climactic battle at Mukden, Manchuria. The Japanese won, but not by much, and they lost another 70,000 men there.

While all this was happening, the Russian Baltic fleet was making its way to the Far East, some through the Suez Canal, and most around the Cape of Good Hope. It was a quixotic and worse than useless task. On May 27, 1905, the Russian ships reached the Straits of Tsushima between

Japan and Korea, and there the Japanese ships were waiting. The Japanese ships were faster and more powerful and, under Heihachiro Togo (1846–1934), they annihilated the Russian fleet at the Battle of Tsushima and that ended the war.

The Japanese had won, but they had virtually exhausted themselves in the process. As for the Russians, with the Revolution of 1905 reducing the land to chaos, they did not wish to continue.

President Theodore Roosevelt of the United States acted as mediator and the war was ended with the Treaty of Portsmouth (in New Hampshire) which was signed on September 6, 1905.

Russia was forced to cede Port Arthur to Japan, as well as the southern half of the island of Sakhalin, which lay just north of the four large islands of Japan. Russia also agreed to get out of Manchuria and leave it as a Japanese sphere of influence. Japan also wanted an indemnity, but this Russia absolutely refused to pay. Roosevelt argued Japan into giving in on this point, which displeased the Japanese people enormously and led to demonstrations against the treaty in Tokyo.

The Russo–Japanese War came as a great shock to the world. For the first time in over two centuries, a non-European power had defeated a European one and the lesson was not lost on the non-European world. They were less than ever willing to accept with resignation, the notion of "white supremacy."

Nor were the Europeans unaware of this. Russia was not exactly popular with much of the rest of Europe, and there had been a tendency to root for the Japanese (as for the Boers) because they were viewed as the underdogs. Once it appeared they were not the underdogs, however, Japan rapidly lost favor. They ceased to be seen as cute orientals with parasols and fans, and began to be seen as sinister warriors with guns and ships. Germany had begun talking about the "Yellow peril" (the dangers of the aroused hordes of East Asia) in the 1890s, and the phrase seemed more appropriate now.

Not all things Japanese were martial. Jokichi Takamine (1854–1922), educated in Japan, came to the United States in 1890. In 1901, he isolated epinephrine (also called adenaline) from the ad-

renal glands. This turned out to be the first substance ever isolated that was later to be classified as a "hormone."

AUSTRALIA

The Commonwealth of Australia came into being, officially, on January 1, 1901, the first day of the twentieth century. Democracy was far advanced, for women's suffrage was granted in 1902, the first Labor government was established in 1904, and old-age pensions came into being in 1909. However, immigration from China and Japan was strictly excluded.

The British portion of southeastern New Guinea was turned over to Australia in 1905, and was renamed "Papua." The Australians wanted it because, in the wake of the Russo–Japanese War, they suddenly began to feel uncomfortably close to the victorious Japanese. The German presence in the Pacific Islands was also increasing, and the Australians, having fought along with the British against the Boers, now began to build a naval force of their own.

In 1909, the capital of Australia was established at Canberra, which was made a federal district that was not part of any of the state governments.

NEW ZEALAND

New Zealand had also contributed contingents who fought on the side of the British against the Boers. On September 26, 1907, New Zealand received Dominion status and, like Canada and Australia, ruled itself. It shared with the other Dominions, and with Great Britain and its Empire, the person of the monarch. Each dominion also had a Governor-General appointed by the crown to represent the monarch and (like the monarch) was given only ceremonial duties.

PHILIPPINES

When the Americans established themselves as the new masters of the Philippines, Aguinaldo raised an insurrection against them, as he had against the Spaniards in earlier years. He declared himself president of the "Philippine Republic" and attacked Manila on February 4, 1899. He was driven off and the Filipinos resorted to guerrilla warfare, carrying on the "Philippine Insurrection."

The American general in charge, Elwell Stephen Otis (1838–1909) and his second-in-command, Arthur MacArthur (1845–1912), issued constant assurances that the insurrection had been put down, but it wasn't. They continued to ask for more and more troops, until there were 70,000 American soldiers in the Philippines and yet the insurrection went on.

On March 23, 1901, Aguinaldo was captured and was forced to sign a declaration calling on the Filipinos to lay down their arms—but the insurrection went on.

However, a civil government was devised for the Philippines and at its head was William Howard Taft (1857–1930), a fair-minded man of integrity. His fairness and decency toward the Filipinos did more to end the insurrection than all the force the soldiers could exert.

Finally, in the summer of 1902, most of the fighting petered to an end, though some resistance continued in the southern islands until 1905. The Americans had lost 7000 casualties, as compared with 2200 in the Spanish–American War, yet the Philippine insurrection is hardly mentioned in the history books, though the Spanish–American War gets full coverage.

Once the Americans quelled the insurrection, however, they set up an efficient government in which Filipinos participated. The Americans won over the Filipinos as the British won over the Boers—by not treating them as defeated inferiors, but as human beings.

UNITED STATES

The glow of the successful Spanish–American War made it easy for McKinley to gain reelection in 1900. He ran against Bryan for a second time, but Bryan's campaign of anti-Imperialism didn't suit the feelings of the time. The Socialist party ran a candidate, Eugene Debs, for the first time in this election.

McKinley's luck, however, ran out soon after

his second inauguration on March 4, 1901. On September 6, 1901, he attended the Pan-American Exposition at Buffalo, received a line of citizens and shook hands with each in proper democratic fashion. One of the men waiting in line was Leon Czolgosz (1873–1901), an anarchist who carried a loaded revolver concealed by a handkerchief. When he reached the president, he fired twice. McKinley died on September 14, and Czolgosz was hanged on October 29. McKinley was thus another of the highly placed victims to fall to anarchist terror at the turn of the century.

McKinley's Vice-President, Theodore Roosevelt, only 43 years old at the time, was now the 26th President of the United States.

Roosevelt carried on an aggressive and dynamic foreign policy. He helped negotiate an end to the Russo–Japanese War, and, for that, received a Nobel Prize for peace on December 10, 1906. American sympathies, which were with Japan at the outset, faded quickly with Japanese victories, especially since the United States, and the west coast particularly, definitely did not want any Japanese immigrants, and those that were present were often mistreated.

Roosevelt also used his influence to get Great Britain and France to agree to the Algeciras Conference, which the United States then attended, contributing by its vote to the German defeat.

There was a problem in connection with the Canadian boundary, along the southern "panhandle" of Alaska. The Americans wanted the boundary further inland from the Pacific coast, while the Canadians wanted American ownership to be confined to the islands offshore. The dispute was handed over to an arbitration board consisting of three Americans, two Canadians, and a Briton. They met in London in September 1902.

Roosevelt made it clear that if the board did not decide in favor of the United States, the Americans would take what they wanted anyway. The Canadians refused to give in, but Great Britain, after its experience in the Boer War, was conscious of the dangers of isolation, and was quite determined not to quarrel with the United States for as long as the German danger endured.

The Briton on the board therefore voted with the United States, and that settled that.

There was a problem with Latin American debts. Venezuela owed a great deal of money to Germany and Great Britain, and the question arose as to how to collect it. Remembering the case of Mexico, and of Napoleon III's ill-fated venture nearly four decades earlier, the two European nations consulted the United States, which agreed to allow them to collect payment forcibly.

When Germany and Great Britain tried to do this, however, American public opinion made itself felt very strongly against the use of European force in the western hemisphere. Roosevelt therefore decided that when Latin American nations owed debts that they wouldn't or couldn't repay, it would be the *Americans* who would move in, collect customs, amass the necessary money, and hand it over to the creditor nations. Force might still have to be used, but American public opinion would not object to American force, and would not be moved by any Latin-American objection that force was force whatever the source.

This was the "Roosevelt corollary" to the Monroe Doctrine and it made the United States the policeman of the western hemisphere. Thus, in 1905, American forces moved into the Dominican Republic and collected customs for two years so that its debtors might be paid.

An even more serious question came in connection with a canal across Central America. It had long been obvious that a canal across that narrow region would make it unnecessary for ships to make the long trip around South America and, as early as 1850, the United States and Great Britain had come to an agreement that if such a canal was built, neither nation would try to monopolize its control.

However, building the canal was out of the question as long as yellow fever and malaria riddled Central America. Thus, in 1879, the French under Ferdinand de Lesseps began an attempt to build the canal and they found it couldn't be done. The venture collapsed in a maze of corruption that nearly destroyed the French republic.

The Spanish–American War showed the United States quite clearly what advantage would accrue to it if, in case of need, it could quickly shift warships from the Atlantic to the Pacific and vice versa. What's more, Reed's work in Cuba on yellow fever showed just how that disease might be conquered.

The United States decided, therefore, to build the canal on its own, without reference to Great Britain. Great Britain, still trapped in the Boer War, was in no position to make a fuss about it. On November 18, 1901, Secretary of State John Hay had little trouble negotiating a treaty with Julian Pauncefote (1828–1902) of Great Britain. By this "Hay-Pauncefote Treaty," the canal, when it was built, would be neutral and open to all shipping, but the United States would be able to fortify it, and, in effect, to own it.

The question was where, exactly, to build the canal. The narrowest part of Central America was in Panama, but there were hills there that would have to be dug through. A canal across Nicaragua would be four times as long, but it was sea level all the way and Lake Nicaragua could be made use of over a good part of the route. However, there was a powerful and deadly volcanic eruption on the island of Martinique on May 8, 1902, and Americans grew very volcano-conscious. There were reports of volcanic activity in Nicaragua, so Congress decided on a Panama route on June 18, 1902.

The Isthmus of Panama was part of the nation of Colombia. Colombia was rather dubious about the canal, feeling that it would be an entering wedge for American control over the nation. On the other hand, the canal would be a source of revenue for Colombia and, in any case, it was quite clear that if Roosevelt didn't get what he wanted by negotiation, he would simply take it by force. Colombia therefore signed a treaty with the United States on January 22, 1903, allowing the construction of the Panama Canal to begin. However, Colombian public opinion was against it, and the Colombian Senate rejected the treaty.

Roosevelt wasted no time trying to change Colombia's mind. The people of Panama were not entirely satisfied with being part of Colombia and they had rebelled on various occasions. Now they suddenly saw the chance of a canal bringing money directly to themselves rather than to the central government of Colombia.

Roosevelt managed to make it clear to the Panamanians that, if they revolted, they would have American cooperation. Several American warships were sent down on November 3, 1903 to patrol the waters off Panama in order to prevent Colombian ships from doing anything to put down a revolt. On November 4, right on schedule, came the revolt. The Panamanian rebels declared themselves independent and, on November 6, the United States recognized that independence. On November 18, the United States signed with the Panamanians the same treaty they had earlier signed with the Colombians.

Work on the canal began, and, under the direction of the American army officer and surgeon, William Crawford Gorgas (1854–1920), war was declared on yellow fever and malaria and was carried through effectively.

On September 2, 1901, Roosevelt had quoted an adage: "Speak softly and carry a big stick; you will go far." His big-stick diplomacy sat well with the American people and he was triumphantly victorious in the 1904 election. He was the first American Vice-President to have succeeded to the post on the death of a president and to have then gone on to win an election in his own right.

Though imperialism and force was the American rule of the day in foreign affairs, democracy advanced at home. A "Progressive" movement, the heir of the earlier Populists, worked toward greater public involvement in the machinery of government. By the "initiative," citizens could initiate the consideration of a law by a legislature if they gathered enough signatures on an appeal. By the "referendum," a law could be put to a general vote of the people if the legislature turned it down, if, again, enough signatures could be gathered. And by "recall," the people could vote to remove a public official from office if they lost confidence in him. There was also the "primary" in which people voted for someone they wanted to have nominated for office by a political party.

The first state to adopt both initiative and referendum was Oregon on June 2, 1902. Oregon also accepted recall in 1908. The first statewide primary was established in Wisconsin in 1903. None of this greatly purified democracy, but it did put some reins on the absolute control of the land by politicians.

Blacks continued to advance by inches. William Edward Burghardt Du Bois (1868–1963), a black who had obtained a Ph.D. in history from Harvard in 1895, helped found the "National Association for the Advancement of Colored People" (NAACP) on May 31, 1909. This gave the blacks a voice that could at least make itself heard, even if it could rarely affect the stolid and stony-hearted racism of the times.

Theodore Roosevelt made a gesture in this respect that was not without risk. On October 16, 1901, just a month after he became president, he entertained the black educator, Booker T. Washington, at dinner in the White House. There were storms of protest over this act of common decency, though there were few over Roosevelt's bullying tactics abroad.

Even women's rights advanced. Several western states allowed women to vote in state elections, and demands for women's national suffrage, on an equal basis with that of men, were mounting. Mary MacLeod Bethune (1875–1955) was a black woman who, in this decade, pioneered the establishment of schools for black girls.

A special victory was won by Helen Adams Keller (1880–1968), who was not only a woman, but one who had become blind and deaf early in life. With the help of a dedicated teacher, Anne Sullivan Macy (1866–1936), Keller overcame these difficulties and wrote acclaimed biographical works in 1902 and 1908. Her glowing courage and intelligence were beacons that lit the way toward a more human consideration of the handicapped generally.

There was also a growing movement toward the prohibition of the sale of alcoholic beverages. This might well be considered a noble aim, but reliance was placed not only on persuasion and social pressure, but on the force of the law. The Women's Christian Temperance Union (WCTU) was founded in 1874, and the Anti-Saloon League in 1893. The forces of "Prohibition" gained major strength, however, in 1902, when it came under the dynamic leadership of a Methodist clergyman, James Cannon (1864–1944). Cities, towns, and even an occasional state began to go "dry," forbidding the sale of liquor. That drinking continued, and even increased, despite such laws, seemed to go unnoticed.

Labor also gained. On May 12, 1902, a strike was called by anthracite coal miners under the leadership of John Mitchell (1870–1919) against the owners who kept the wages extremely low and took virtually no safety precautions to protect the lives and well-being of the miners. Chief counsel for the miners was Clarence Seward Darrow (1857–1938), who was to become famous as the doughty legal champion of many unpopular causes in which he fought on the side of humanity.

The mine owners took a completely arrogant and intransigent position. One of them, George Frederick Baer (1842–1914), said, "The rights and interest of the laboring man will be protected and cared for, not by the labor agitators, but by the Christian men to whom God in his infinite wisdom has given the control of the property interests of this country." Having thus announced the divine right of mine owners, they waited for the government, as usual, to use its force to break the strike.

Roosevelt, however, put pressure on the mine owners instead, and they buckled. The miners actually won a 10% raise when the strike came to an end on October 21, 1902.

Some capitalists, to be sure, had more on their mind than divine right. The British-born Andrew Carnegie (1835–1919), who had made his fortune in steel in the ruthless manner of the times, retired in 1901, and devoted the rest of his life to philanthropy, endowing libraries, institutes of higher learning, and causes devoted to peace.

In 1908, Roosevelt decided not to run for a second elected term, and put forward William Howard Taft as his hand-picked successor. Taft was easily elected and became the 27th President of the United States.

By 1910, the population of the United States was 92 million. Its navy rivalled that of Germany in the race for second place to Great Britain. It produced twice as much steel as Germany and four times as much as Great Britain.

The United States continued to make strides in technology. Two brothers, Wilbur Wright (1867–1912) and Orville Wright (1871–1948), had worked with gliders and were interested in placing internal combustion engines on them. This would turn a propeller and allow the gliders to move in directed flight. On December 17, 1903, at Kitty Hawk, North Carolina, Orville Wright piloted the first flight of a heavier-than-air flying machine. (Dirigibles were, of course, lighter than air.) On this day, then, the airplane was invented.

Henry Ford (1863–1947) introduced the notion of an "assembly line" in 1908, bringing the parts of an automobile along a line of men who each performed one task over and over in the proper order. At one end of the assembly line were the parts and at the other end a finished automobile rolled off and could be driven away. In 1909, Ford produced the "Model T Ford," the first automobile to be mass-produced and to be within the range of affordability of people of moderate means. It was with that that the automobile age really began.

Lee De Forest (1873–1961) improved on Fleming's rectifier in 1906 by adding a third electrode inside the vacuum tube. It could then be used as an amplifier and it became the ancestor of the "radio tubes" in all their varieties that made electronic equipment practical.

At the same time, the Canadian-born Reginald Aubrey Fessenden (1866–1932) modulated radio waves so that their changing amplitude mimicked that of sound waves. This was "amplitude modulation" (AM). In this way, sound could be turned into appropriate radio waves and these back into sound. For the first time, one could hear words and music on a radio and this was accomplished first on December 24, 1906. De Forest's triode and Fessenden's voice transmission established radio as we know it.

In an allied field, the German-born Emile Berliner (1851–1929) first devised the flat phonograph record in 1904 to replace the cylindrical one introduced by Edison. The flat record took up less room and held more sound so that the phonograph became a much more practical instrument.

In 1909, the Belgian-born Leo Hendrik Baekeland (1863–1944) produced the first thermosetting plastic, which he named "Bakelite" after himself. It was the first plastic to have major uses and it sparked the development of the modern plastics industry.

In the biological sciences, Walter Stanborough Sutton (1877–1916) pointed out in 1902 that chromosomes fulfilled the requirements of the Mendelian inheritance factors and that it was there scientists must look for the machinery of heredity. The Russian-born Phoebus Aaron Theodor Levene (1869–1940) discovered, in 1909, that the nucleic acids (which were eventually found to be part of the machinery of heredity) contained a five-carbon sugar called ribose. And in 1907, Thomas Hunt Morgan (1866–1945) began to work with fruit flies, studying their chromosomes and explaining the presence of linked characteristics in heredity. Morgan received a Nobel Prize for his work.

Howard Taylor Ricketts (1871–1910) found, in 1906, that Rocky Mountain spotted fever had as its causative agent, a microorganism that, in its organization, was partway between a virus and a bacterium. Such organisms are now called "Rickettsia" in his honor.

In literature, the first novel by Theodore Dreiser (1871–1945), *Sister Carrie*, published in 1900, was too shocking for the public of the time, which didn't mind seeing sinners go unpunished in real life, but were scandalized at finding it in books.

Newton Booth Tarkington (1869–1946) made his first hit with *Monsieur Beaucaire* (1900). John Griffith ("Jack") London (1876–1916) burst on the scene with *The Call of the Wild* (1903), *The Sea-Wolf* (1904), and other works. Edith Newbold Wharton (1862–1937) published *The Valley of Decision* (1902) and *The House of Mirth* (1905). Finley Peter Dunne (1867–1936) wrote a series of humorous commentaries in which an Irish bar-keeper, "Mr. Dooley," commented on the affairs of the day in a perceptive way. William Sydney Porter (1862–

1910), writing under the pseudonym of "O. Henry," wrote a large number of short stories in this decade, the most famous being "The Gift of the Magi." Bierce published his *Devil's Dictionary* in 1906, which cannot be exceeded for bitterness, though it hits the target almost every time. Edward Arlington Robinson (1869–1935) was making a name for himself as a poet in this decade.

It was also the decade of the muckraker (a pejorative term used by President Roosevelt to describe those who were intent on dealing with the seamy side of American society). Joseph Lincoln Steffens (1866–1936) wrote *The Shame of the Cities* (1904), exposing municipal corruption. Ida Minerva Tarbell (1857–1944) wrote *History of the Standard Oil Company* (1904), exposing the corruption of business. Upton Beall Sinclair (1878–1968) wrote *The Jungle* (1906), describing the horrors of the meat-packing industry and producing many vegetarians in the process.

In children's literature, Lyman Frank Baum (1856–1919), wrote *The Wonderful Wizard of Oz*, which, with its numerous sequels, has remained perennially popular.

In art, Frederick Remington (1861–1909) finished a career of painting made famous by his western scenes.

In music, the Irish-born Victor Herbert (1859–1924) was producing such popular operettas as *Babes in Toyland* (1903) and *Naughty Marietta* (1910). George Michael Cohan (1878–1942) wrote *Little Johnny Jones* (1904), *Forty-Five Minutes from Broadway* (1905), and others, containing such songs as "Give My Regards to Broadway," "Yankee Doodle Dandy," "Mary's a Grand Old Name," and so on. Irving Berlin (1888–1989) started writing his songs in this decade.

Isadora Duncan (1878–1927) was the most famous dancer of her day, and Florenz Ziegfeld (1869–1932) began a type of show that featured skits, musical numbers, and many scantily clad women with *The Follies of 1907*, which continued in new productions year after year.

Many aspects of American life had their beginning in this decade. The first Rose Bowl football game was played in 1902 and the first World Series of baseball in 1903. The "teddy bear" was introduced in 1902 and was named for Theodore Roosevelt, who once refused to shoot a bear dragged to him for the purpose.

"The Great Train Robbery," the first movie to tell a story, was presented in 1903, and the first subway in New York was opened in 1904. Hamburgers were first popularized at the St. Louis World's Fair of 1904 (designed to celebrate the city's centennial). Instant coffee was first introduced at the Pan-American Exposition in Buffalo, where McKinley was assassinated.

CANADA

Canada was displeased, as one might well imagine, over the American victory in the dispute over the Alaskan border, and over the fact that the British delegate had voted with the Americans. There was nothing that Canada could do, however, but continue to develop its own vast interior.

It was a great age of railroad building and of the exploitation of the rich mineral resources of the Canadian west. On September 1, 1905, Alberta and Saskatchewan were organized as provinces. Under Wilfrid Laurier (1841–1919) who, as the leader of the Liberal party, was Prime Minister of Canada during this decade, the nation flourished.

Canada could not experience the uncomplicated Imperial loyalty of Australia and New Zealand. The province of Quebec was heavily French in language and thought, and its people felt little loyalty, if any, to Great Britain. Thus, during the Boer War, Canada did not fight, officially, on the side of Great Britain, but sent only volunteers. There was also the beginning of friction between the French-speaking (Francophone) and English-speaking (Anglophone) Canadians over educational policies and over the official use of English.

Robert Williams Service (1874–1958) was a successful writer of popular verse in this period, producing the well-known "The Shooting of Dan McGrew" and "The Cremation of Sam McGee." He published collections of his verse in 1907 and 1909.

MEXICO

The Díaz dictatorship continued throughout this decade, and was as repressive as ever. However, Díaz was getting older and resentment among the Mexicans was rising. By 1910, Díaz was having the greatest difficulty in keeping the lid forced down on the bubbling revolution within the pot.

CUBA

In 1901, the United States withdrew its troops from Cuba, but under onerous conditions. On March 2, 1901, an amendment was added to an army appropriations bill. It had been formulated by Roosevelt's Secretary of State, Elihu Root (1845–1937), a dedicated worker for the arbitration of national disputes, and an eventual winner of the Nobel Prize for peace.

The amendment was then offered to the Senate by Orville Hitchcock Platt (1827–1905), so that it was known as the "Platt amendment." By its terms, Cuba had to cede Guantanamo Bay to the United States as a naval base; it couldn't transfer land to any power other than the United States; with other powers, it couldn't make treaties that the United States didn't approve of; it couldn't assume too great a foreign debt; and it had to grant the United States the right to intervene when it felt it necessary.

On June 12, 1901, Cuba was compelled to include the Platt amendment as part of its constitution and, in effect, it made Cuba an American protectorate.

The first president of Cuba was Thomas Estrada Palma (1835–1908), who had been part of the revolutionary movement against Spain for 20 years, and who assumed the presidency in 1902. He was a conservative and was reelected in 1906. The Liberal opposition claimed fraud and Palma was forced to resign, but not before he had appealed to the United States.

The United States promptly sent troops. In 1908, Jose Miguel Gomez (1858–1921), a Liberal, was elected president, and the American forces withdrew on February 1, 1909. However, they were always poised to return and the Cubans did not find that a comfortable thing to live with.

DOMINICAN REPUBLIC

The Dominican Republic followed the frequent Latin-American policy of borrowing large sums of money from European powers, which it wasted in corruption and mismanagement, and then found it could not easily meet the interest payments. The European powers, aware of this likelihood, loaned the money anyway, counting on the use of force, if necessary, to wring their profits out of the impoverished land.

By 1905, the Dominican Republic was, practically speaking, bankrupt. The United States, in order to prevent European intervention, intervened itself in accordance with the "Roosevelt corollary." It sent in forces to control the Dominican customs for 50 years in order to gather the money to repay the debts. (This was called "dollar diplomacy.") In 1907, the Dominican Republic had to sign a treaty with the United States permitting this.

MARTINIQUE

Martinique had its first European visitor in the person of Christopher Columbus himself in 1502. It was overlooked by the Spaniards, however, and was first colonized in 1635 by French settlers. It remained French thereafter except for three brief war-time occupations by the British. On June 23, 1763, the woman who was eventually to be Josephine Bonaparte and Empress of France, was born on Martinique and lived there until she was 15.

There is a volcano on Martinique called Mt. Pelee. It was considered dormant, though occasionally it showed eruptive activity, once as recently as 1851. At its foot was Martinique's capital, St. Pierre.

In April 1902, Mt. Pelee began to show signs of activity, but officials minimized the matter and there was no move to evacuate the city. Then, at 7:50 A.M. on May 8, 1902, the volcano exploded. A cloud of steam, gas, and dust rolled down the mountain and in three minutes all the 30,000 people in St. Pierre, but one, had died. (A convicted murderer, who happened to be in an underground cell, survived.)

The news of the eruption led, the next year, to the American Congressional decision to build a canal across Panama rather than across Nicaragua, which was thought to have a volcano.

VENEZUELA

During this decade, Venezuela was under the tyrannical rule of Cipriano Castro, who contracted large European debts that he used for his own benefit. In order to collect the debts, Great Britain, Germany, and Italy took united action in 1902 to blockade five of Venezuela's seaports. The United States forced the matter into arbitration and the blockade was lifted in February 1903. It was this situation that led to the announcement of the "Roosevelt corollary" with the United States claiming the right to collect Latin-American customs when that was necessary to pay off European debts.

In 1908, Castro quarreled with the United States and with the Netherlands, and relations with both were broken off. It was then the turn of the Dutch to blockade Venezuelan ports. However, Castro's health was turning shaky and he traveled to Europe in search of medical treatment.

In his absence, the Vice-President, Juan Vicente Gomez (1864–1935), seized power on December 19, 1909, and took his turn at being a harsh dictator, while Castro remained in exile for the remainder of his life.

COLOMBIA

The dominant event of the decade in Colombia was its failure to agree to a pact with the United States permitting the construction of the Panama Canal. The United States therefore engineered a Panamanian insurrection, recognized it as an independent nation, made the treaty with it, and began the construction of the canal. Colombia could do nothing to prevent it, but it felt a bitter resentment, of course.

After the Panama insurrection, Rafael Reyes

Prieto (1850–1921) became President of Colombia in 1904. On January 9, 1909, Reyes Prieto signed an agreement with the United States, recognizing the independence of Panama, but the Colombian people were less forgiving than Reyes Prieto was, and he was forced to resign on July 8, 1909.

He was succeeded by the much more liberal Carlos E. Restrepo (1867–1937).

PANAMA

On February 13, 1904, the now-independent Panama adopted a constitution which granted the United States the right of intervening whenever it felt like it, so that it, too, became an American protectorate. Panama's first president was Manuel Amador Guerrero (1833–1909). Amador Guerrero, although Panamanian-born, had in his earlier years been important in the Colombian government.

ARCTIC

The American explorer, Robert Edwin Peary (1856–1920), spent years exploring northern Greenland. He proved Greenland to be an island, and the northernmost portion of that island (a region largely free of ice) is called "Peary Land" in his honor.

In 1909, he organized an elaborate travel party of which successive members were to turn back at periodic intervals until, at the end, Peary and a black associate, Matthew Hensen, made the final dash, reaching the North Pole, according to report, on April 6, 1909.

When Peary returned, he found that a former associate, Frederick Albert Cook (1865–1940), claimed he had reached it on April 21, 1908. There was considerable controversy over this and, eventually, Cook's claim was disallowed and Peary's accepted. Recent analysis, however, has cast some doubt on the accuracy of Peary's reports of progress, too.

Less spectacularly, the Norwegian explorer, Roald Amundsen (1872–1928), had, in 1903, undertaken and completed the crossing of the Arctic Ocean sea passage north of Canada from the Atlantic to the Pacific. He reached Bering Strait in August 1906. This was the famous "Northwest Passage" and, while it was a thoroughly impractical waterway, it had, nevertheless, finally been accomplished.

ANTARCTICA

Explorers were now penetrating far into the icy cover of Antarctica. The British explorer Robert Falcon Scott (1868–1912) led a party of men sledging over the Ross Ice Shelf and, on December 13, 1902, reached a point only 500 miles from the South Pole. One of his colleagues, Ernest Henry Shackleton (1874–1922), tried again. On January 9, 1909, his party of four men managed to reach a point only 100 miles from the South Pole. Each man dragged his own sledge, and they turned back only when it was clear that to travel farther would mean their food supply would not last the return journey.

Only the last push remained to reach the South Pole.

1910 to 1914

AUSTRIA-HUNGARY

This section does not span an entire decade because an event took place in 1914 that was a turning point for the world. I therefore take up the period of 1910 to 1914 now, and will follow it

with 1914 to 1920. I begin now with Austria-Hungary, not because of the nation's prime importance, but because it was within its boundaries that the turning point took place.

Austria-Hungary's victory in the Bosnia-Herzegovina crisis was a rather hollow one. It had occupied territory that Serbia had coveted and, from then on, Austria-Hungary was forced to watch the Balkans more carefully than ever, lest Serbia grow strong enough to become annoying.

In February 1910, Austria-Hungary came to a cautious agreement with Russia to maintain the status-quo in the Balkans, since neither one wanted another crisis. In doing this, however, the two powers reckoned without the Balkan nations themselves.

In 1912, the Balkan nations, in alliance, attacked and defeated the Ottoman Empire, which had still controlled Macedonia and Albania, a strip of territory across the Balkan peninsula. The Balkan nations then divided up the territory among themselves, and Serbia assigned itself territory that brought it to the Adriatic shores, south of the Austro–Hungarian possessions.

This Austria-Hungary would not allow. A Serbia with a sea-coast would develop overseas trade and might gain the friendship of Great Britain. Therefore, Austria-Hungary insisted on the formation of an independent Albania on the sea-coast. That would keep Serbia landlocked. Serbia would have liked to have defied Austria-Hungary on this, but it needed Russian help if it were to do so, and Russia did not wish to risk a crisis over this matter. Serbia had to give in.

Francis Ferdinand, the heir to the throne, was perturbed by the situation, and he was shrewd enough to see that Austria-Hungary must make some concession to the Slavs. What he had in mind was the conversion of the Dual Monarchy into a Triple Monarchy, with the Slavic regions ruling themselves as the Hungarians did.

This, however, was something that the aged Emperor, Franz Joseph, would not allow, and on his side were, of course, the German-speaking conservatives. Nor was Serbia pleased with the suggestion. The last thing it wanted was for the Slavs to be so well-treated that they would be willing to remain part of the Hapsburg monarchy.

In the Hungarian portion of the Dual Monarchy, Istvan Tisza (1861–1918) became Prime Minister in 1913. He was a strong supporter of the Dual Monarchy, and he was firm in his insistence that Hungary rule its minorities with an iron hand. He did not want self-rule for the Slavs in the Austrian half of the monarchy either, since that would certainly rouse Hungary's own Slavs, and also the Romanian people in its eastern portion.

So Austria-Hungary tottered on, relying on the strength of its ally, Germany, to protect it from harm. As for Francis Ferdinand, his hoped-for reforms didn't have a chance, and he, himself, seemed to be disliked by everyone.

In June 1914, Austria-Hungary was holding army maneuvers in Bosnia, as much to impress the Serbians as anything else. Francis Ferdinand, as Inspector of the Army, attended the maneuvers, even though he was warned he would not be safe in Bosnian territory.

The region was riddled with extremists who were supported by the Serbian government, and one of them was Gavrilo Princip (1894–1918), a Bosnian who had been trained in terrorism by a Serbian secret society. When Francis Ferdinand and his wife were being driven through Sarajevo, the Bosnian capital, on June 28, 1914, Princip made two assassination attempts. The second succeeded and both Francis Ferdinand and his wife were killed. (Princip was arrested, tried, and since he was under 20 at the time of the assassination, he could only be sentenced to 20 years' imprisonment. However, he died of tuberculosis in prison, though he lived long enough to see the results of what he had done.)

The world was generally horrified at this act of terrorism, but it was, after all, only one of many assassinations that had taken place in the last quarter century, and no one thought that any real crisis would come about as a result.

Austria-Hungary, however, felt that Francis Ferdinand's assassination would be a golden opportunity to settle scores with Serbia once and for all, and to reduce it to impotence. There was little doubt anywhere, and certainly none in Austria-Hungary, that the assassin had been inspired by Serbia, so the world ought to be satisfied to see Serbia punished.

Austria-Hungary obtained the approval of Germany and set about preparing a harsh ultimatum to Serbia. At first, Tisza of Hungary opposed the policy of crushing Serbia for fear it would lead to the annexation of more Slavs, which he was shrewd enough to see would be most undesirable. When Tisza was assured that no new territory would be annexed, he went along with the planned ultimatum.

On July 23, 1914, Austria-Hungary handed its ultimatum to Serbia. In brief, Serbia was to cease all Austro–Hungarian activities, and any Serbian officials Austria-Hungary disapproved of were to be fired. What's more, Austrian officials would work in Serbia to find those responsible for the outrage. Serbia had 48 hours to accept.

Serbia answered within the time limit, and accepted almost everything. What it could not accept, it was willing to arbitrate.

The not-quite-complete acceptance suited Austria-Hungary, since it didn't want a total capitulation from which Serbia might later wiggle out. Austria-Hungary wanted a short military invasion that would inflict enough damage on Serbia to teach it a lesson and keep it quiet thereafter. For this, they had Germany's backing, and they were convinced that the Russians would back down, as they had in the case of Bosnia-Herzegovina.

On July 28, 1914, therefore, Austria-Hungary declared war on Serbia and that marked the beginning of a cataclysm of a kind that no one in the world (and certainly no one in Austria-Hungary) could have foreseen.

GERMANY

Germany was touchy and uneasy. German fears of being encircled by Great Britain and France on the west, and by Russia on the east, grew. Germany felt it unfair that each of those powers controlled huge segments of the world's land area, while Germany possessed very little. On August 27, 1911, William II, in a speech in Hamburg, said, "No one can dispute with us the place in the sun that is our due." That phrase "place in the sun" had been repeated frequently in Germany.

The place in the sun was, indeed, being denied Germany. Thus, France was continuing to advance in Morocco, and Germany resented that. France already had so much of Africa; why, then,

should it have more? Undoubtedly, it was that which inspired William II's speech.

France was willing to compensate Germany elsewhere in Africa, but the German foreign minister, Alfred von Kideren-Wachter (1852–1912) was foolishly belligerent over the matter and an unnecessary "Second Moroccan crisis" arose.

On July 1, 1911, the German gunboat, *Panther*, was sent to Agadir, a Moroccan seaport. The supposed reason for its visit was to protect German interests, but it was actually intended to frighten France. That it did, and France immediately appealed to Great Britain, which came to its side more strongly than it had done in the First Moroccan crisis. For a while, war seemed imminent, but Germany accepted sections of African territory farther south and abandoned Morocco to France—which it might have done at the start.

To much of the German public and to the German military, it seemed another German failure, and Kideren-Wachter was widely criticized for not being sufficiently firm. Germany (like Russia after Bosnia-Herzegovina) made up its mind that it simply couldn't back down any further. It accelerated the buildup of both its army and its navy, which made Great Britain, France, and Russia even more uneasy than they had been before.

To be sure, the Socialists, presumably a party devoted to peace and to greater popular participation in the government, were becoming stronger in Germany. In the Reichstag elections in January 1912, the Socialists actually became the largest single party in the legislature. However, the Socialists had toned down their revolutionary fervor, which was why they got as many votes as they did. The consequence was that they could not effectively oppose the Emperor, his puppet Prime Minister, and his powerful military advisers.

Thus, in December 1913, in the town of Zabern in Alsace, a German military officer made insulting remarks about Alsatians. There was a riot as a result and German soldiers wounded some Alsatians and arrested others. There was a furor over the high-handed actions of the soldiers, and the Reichstag voted 293 to 55 to censure the army. The German government simply ignored the vote and no moves were taken to discipline the officers concerned. Other nations noted the ineffectiveness of the opposition in Germany and the absolute military control of the land. It created a thrill of hatred in France, which also decided it would not be safe to back down in any future crisis.

When Francis Ferdinand was assassinated in June 1914, Germany couldn't possibly refuse to back the only reliable ally it had. Germany had to support Austria-Hungary's declaration of war on Serbia, and even the Socialists went along with this for they saw the Russian autocracy as their real enemy.

In science in this period, Hans Wilhelm Geiger (1882–1945), while working in Great Britain, invented a device—the famous "Geiger counter" —which detected the passage of a single subatomic particle.

Max Theodor Felix von Laue (1879–1960) demonstrated that crystals acted as natural diffraction gratings with separations so fine as to be of atomic size. This made it possible to measure the ultra-tiny wavelengths of x-rays and prove they were light-like radiations. It gained Laue a Nobel Prize.

Richard Willstatter (1872–1942) worked on plant pigments and elaborated the technique of paper chromatography for the separation of the complex mixture of pigments he encountered. He demonstrated the presence of a magnesium atom in the molecule of chlorophyll and, for all of this, he eventually received a Nobel Prize.

Richard Strauss continued to be an active composer, producing the operas *Rosenkavalier* in 1911, and *Ariadne auf Naxos* in 1912.

RUSSIA

Russia continued to be in a state of instability. Pyotr Stolypin, who had become Prime Minister after the 1905 Revolution had put down the disorders with a firm hand, had emasculated the Duma, and turned to naught all the hopes of a reasonable constitution. He pursued the leftist opposition mercilessly, and he continued the process of Russification in Finland and elsewhere.

The result was that on September 14, 1911, while at the theater with Tsar Nicholas II, Stolypin was shot and killed by an assassin.

A fourth Duma was elected in 1912; however, under the prevailing electoral procedures, it was merely a tool of the government.

Meanwhile, the Russian court was creating scandal that (as in the days of Louis XVI and Marie Antoinette, a century and a quarter earlier) was further unsettling the nation.

The oldest son of Nicholas II, the Tsarevich Alexis, suffered from hemophilia (which was true of several members of royalty in the early twentieth century, thanks to a gene apparently inherited from Queen Victoria of England). The Tsarina Alexandra, a devoted mother, was heartbroken over the failure of medical men to handle the disease, which constantly threatened the Tsarevich with pain and death.

Then she found a Siberian mystic, Grigory Yefimovich Rasputin (1872–1916), a complete charlatan who, however, was able to relieve the Tsarevich's conditions, when no one else could. Though dirty, unkempt, ignorant, and sexually promiscuous, he became a favorite of the Empress and powerful in the government. His influence was entirely for the worse, and even the conservatives found themselves horrified over the situation and yet powerless to do anything about it.

In 1913, Russia celebrated the 300th anniversary of the coming to power of the Romanov dynasty—a last glow of glory.

On July 20, 1914, after the assassination of Francis Ferdinand, the French president, Raymond Poincare (1860–1934), and the French Prime Minister, Rene Viviani (1863–1925), visited St. Petersburg and seized the opportunity to discuss the Serbian crisis. They decided to act together, as neither nation felt it could back down.

Austria-Hungary waited till the French politicians were back in their own land (hoping that separation in space would make it more difficult for France and Russia to reach a common ground of action), and only then did it send its fateful ultimatum to Serbia.

Meanwhile, in the world of science and culture, the Russian physicist, Konstantin Eduardovich Tsiolkovsky (1857–1935), had been writing on rocketry since 1903. By this period, he had developed his ideas in detail. He was the first scientist to work out the requirements for spaceflight in rigorous mathematical fashion.

Igor Fyodorovich Stravinsky (1882–1970) was writing ballet music such as *The Firebird* (1910), *Petrushka* (1911), and *The Rite of Spring* (1913). Marc Chagall (1887–1985) began a fabulous career in art in this decade. Both Stravinsky and Chagall, though Russian-born, did most of their work in France.

FRANCE

Internally, France was plagued by strikes, and externally its attention was focused on the Second Moroccan crisis and on the increasing atmosphere of tension between itself and Germany. In 1913, France finally began to strengthen its army over the objections of the more liberal parties.

After the assassination of Francis Ferdinand, France reached an agreement for common action with Russia, and made up its mind not to back down in this new Balkan crisis.

Meanwhile, in 1910, the French chemist, Georges Claude (1870–1960), discovered that electric discharges through the noble gases produced light. This was the beginning of what came to be called "neon lights."

Maurice Ravel wrote the ballet *Daphnis and Chloe* in 1912.

Romain Rolland (1866–1944) wrote *Jean Christophe* and its sequels, completing the cycle in 1912, and eventually receiving a Nobel Prize in literature. Marcel Proust (1871–1922) began his cycle of *Remembrance of Things Past* in 1913, with *Swann's Way*.

GREAT BRITAIN

In Great Britain, the immediate problem was the House of Lords. It was unelected, unresponsive to public opinion, aristocratic and reactionary by its very nature, and an insurmountable stumbling block for all reform legislation.

On May 15, 1911, therefore, a "Parliament Bill" was passed by the House of Commons. By it, the House of Lords could not veto any revenue bill, and any other bill that passed the House of Commons three times would become law even if the House of Lords voted against it. Finally, the maximum term of a PM was reduced from seven to five years.

Naturally, the House of Lords voted against the bill and the old threat arose that enough new peers would be formed to pass it. The House of Lords gave in and, from that time, it became merely a debating society, while the House of Commons became the only effective governing body in the nation as a whole.

There next arose the question of Irish home rule once again. An Irish Home Rule bill was proposed in 1912. Opposed to it were not only the Conservatives, but, even more bitterly, the northernmost counties of Ireland, which were heavily Protestant and which did not want to be abandoned to a Catholic Ireland. Leading these "Unionists" (who wanted to maintain the union with Great Britain) was Edward Henry Carson (1854–1935). The controversy continued until the assassination of Francis Ferdinand, after which everything had to be suspended until the crisis was resolved.

In the field of science, Ernest Rutherford established the fact, in 1911, that the atom consisted of a tiny nucleus at the center with almost all the atomic mass, plus a cloud of light electrons in the atomic outskirts. In 1913, Frederick Soddy, worked out the concept of isotopes, showing that the atoms of a particular element could come in several varieties differing in mass. And in 1914, Henry Gwyn-Jeffries Moseley (1887–1915) worked out the concept of atomic number in which each element had a nucleus with a characteristic positive electric charge. The isotopes of a given element might differ in mass, but were identical in nuclear charge. These three discoveries created the beginning of the modern picture of atomic structure.

In 1913, the metallurgist, Henry P. Brearly, introduced "stainless steel" (i.e., steel that would not rust) by adding sufficient chromium and nickel to the mixture.

In the biological sciences, the Polish-born

biochemist, Casimir Funk (1884–1967), advanced the notion of "vitamins" as a necessary part of the diet and, in fact, invented the name.

In literature, the indefatigable G.B. Shaw produced both *Androcles and the Lion* and *Pygmalion* in 1912. David Herbert Lawrence (1885–1930) published *Sons and Lovers* in 1913. Gilbert Keith Chesterton (1874–1936) published *The Innocence of Father Brown* in 1911, thus initiating one of the great mystery series of all time. Hector Hugh Munro (1870–1916), writing under the pseudonym "Saki," produced witty short stories, of which the best known is, perhaps, "The Open Window." Pelham Grenville Wodehouse (1881–1975) was becoming well-known in this decade for his light-hearted novels.

Jacob Epstein (1880–1959) was now beginning to produce his powerful but (in the eyes of some) uncouth sculptures.

ITALY

Italy was also looking for its place in the sun. Having failed humiliatingly in Ethiopia 15 years earlier, its eye was now on Tripoli, which lay between French Algeria and British Egypt. It was mostly desert and its undesirability was such that neither Great Britain nor France wanted it, but left it to the Ottoman Empire.

To Italy it seemed fair game, and it took advantage of the Second Morocco crisis to act while the major powers had their attention elsewhere

On September 28, 1911, Italy sent an ultimatum to the Ottoman Empire demanding a cessation of any attempts to interfere with Italian infiltration of the region. The Ottomans naturally rejected this and on September 29, Italy declared what is called the "Tripolitan war." By October 11, Italian forces had occupied the coastal towns of the land. (Austria-Hungary must have seen the effectiveness of this ploy of impossible ultimatum, followed by quick war, with no outside interference. Presumably, they felt the same would happen to Serbia as to Tripoli.)

Italy consolidated its coastal gains, and it was not till 1912 that it sent its forces into the interior. By October, the Italians had a clear-cut victory over greatly outnumbered Ottoman forces. Ital-

ian naval forces also seized Rhodes and other islands in its neighborhood (the "Dodecanese," meaning "twelve islands") that were Greek-speaking portions of the Ottoman Empire.

The Ottoman Empire was by now facing war in the Balkan peninsula and it had to put an end to the fight with Italy. On October 15, 1912, a treaty was signed at Ouchy in Switzerland, whereby the Ottoman Empire ceded Tripoli and the Dodecanese to Italy.

This victory soothed Italian pride, even though it was carried through against negligible resistance. Nor did the victory keep strikes, riots, and various kinds of unrest from continuing to plague the land.

In the crisis that followed the assassination of Francis Ferdinand, Italy kept carefully aloof.

Meanwhile, though, Ermanno Wolf-Ferrari (1876–1940) was carrying on the Italian musical tradition. He composed the opera *Jewels of the Madonna* in 1911.

PAPACY

In the aftermath of the crisis over the assassination of Francis Ferdinand, Pope Pius X appealed for peace on August 2, but died that same month.

SERBIA

After the Bosnia-Herzegovina crisis, Serbia was ready to go to any lengths to sate its anti-Austro–Hungarian feelings. It was even willing to form an alliance with Bulgaria, with which it ordinarily felt in hostile competition. Russia, which was eager to arrange trouble for Austria-Hungary, backed the alliance.

The difficulty was that while Serbia wanted the alliance to be aimed against Austria-Hungary, Bulgaria wanted it to be against the Ottoman Empire. The Tripolitan war made the Ottoman Empire look particularly weak, and that settled the matter on Bulgaria's side.

On October 8, 1912, Montenegro declared war on the Ottoman Empire, the smallest Balkan state initiating the action as a gesture of defiance. On October 18, Bulgaria, Serbia, and Greece all joined Montenegro and the "First Balkan War" had begun.

By the end of the year it was clear that the Ottoman Empire was losing all along the line and, on May 30, 1913, the Treaty of London ended the conflict, with the Ottoman Empire forced to give up all its remaining territory in Europe except for the area immediately around Constantinople.

The victors, however, immediately fell afoul of each other over the division of the spoils. Bulgaria, having won some startling victories, tried to gather in the lion's share of Macedonia. Serbia might have allowed that if it could have gained Albania and an outlet to the sea. Austria-Hungary was adamant, however, on the independence of Albania and on Serbia remaining landlocked. Serbia, therefore, had to make sure that Bulgaria didn't grow too strong.

On June 1, 1913, Serbia came to an agreement with Greece, which also didn't want a too-strong Bulgaria; on June 29, they attacked Bulgaria and the "Second Balkan War" began. Bulgaria, having strained itself badly in the first war, could not withstand the attack, particularly since Romania joined in, attacking from the north as Serbia attacked from the west and Greece from the south. Even the Ottoman Empire joined in, attacking Bulgaria from the east. It was all over on August 10, 1913, with the Treaty of Bucharest.

Bulgaria had to give up its extreme claims, and annexed only modest amounts of previously Ottoman territory, including the province of Thrace which gave it an opening to the Aegean Sea. Greece expanded northward and Serbia southward. Montenegro gained a strip of territory, too, and Albania's independence was recognized. The Ottoman Empire regained Adrianople.

Serbia and Montenegro, closely allied, had doubled in size in less than a year, something Austria-Hungary did not like.

On June 24, 1914, Peter I of Serbia, whose mental health was clearly making it impossible for him to rule, stepped down and his son, Alexander (1888–1934) was declared regent. Four days later, Francis Ferdinand was assassinated, and Alexander had to face the deadly crisis that followed.

BULGARIA

Bulgaria, having done well in the First Balkan War, was defeated disastrously in the Second. It retired to nurse its wounds and to wait its chance for revenge against Serbia. It did not, however, take advantage of the crisis that followed the assassination of Francis Ferdinand to act immediately. It continued to wait.

GREECE

Greece did well in the two Balkan wars, gaining Thessaly, including the important seaport of Salonika in the north, and forcing the Ottoman Empire to recognize Crete's union with Greece. About the only unfavorable development was that, in 1912, Italy had gained the Dodecanese from the Ottoman Empire, and Greece had now no immediate hope of getting them. Greece would surely have annexed those islands had they remained in Ottoman hands.

On March 18, 1913, George I of Greece was assassinated and was succeeded by his son, who reigned as Constantine I (1868–1923).

ROMANIA

Romania seized the opportunity of the Second Balkan War in 1913 to join the anti-Bulgarian side and to gain a narrow strip of territory in the Bulgarian northeast as a result.

ALBANIA

The independence of Albania was recognized by the Treaty of London at the conclusion of the First Balkan War in 1913.

OTTOMAN EMPIRE

Disasters continued for the Ottoman Empire. Between 1911 and 1913, it lost Tripoli to Italy, and Macedonia to the various Balkan nations. The

Ottoman Empire was driven out of Africa at last and almost out of Europe, some five and a half centuries after it had first left Asia and began to take over portions of the neighboring continents.

The loss of the Tripolitan War and the First Balkan War led to a coup by the Young Turks on January 23, 1913, and Enver Bey became the most powerful person in the Empire. That led to some lightening of disaster for, in the Second Balkan War, the Ottoman Empire retook Adrianople, and kept it.

The Germans had long been engaged in training the Ottoman armed forces and naturally gained influence there as a result. In November 1913, a German general, Otto Liman von Sanders (1855–1929), was in charge of the Ottoman forces. The Russians were indignant at this, and the French supported them, but it did little good. In the crisis following the assassination of Francis Ferdinand, the Ottoman Empire was virtually in German hands.

NETHERLANDS

The Netherlands was quiet in this period, except for continued controversy over universal suffrage and secular education.

The Dutch physicist, Kamerlingh Onnes, who had earlier liquefied helium, discovered in 1911 that such metals as mercury and lead lost all electrical resistance at temperatures of liquid helium —thus, discovering the entirely unexpected phenomenon of superconductivity.

BELGIUM

As in the Netherlands, Belgium's problems of the period lay chiefly in the matter of universal suffrage and secular education.

The continuing and worsening friction between France on the west and Germany on the east caused a certain uneasiness in Belgium. Despite the fact that its policy of neutrality had been guaranteed by both France and Germany (and Great Britain, too), the Belgian government was nervous enough to increase the size of its army on August 30, 1913.

SPAIN

The Liberals were running Spain in this period. The power of the Church was firmly limited, and freedom of religion was guaranteed for non-Catholics. The Liberal Prime Minister, Jose Canalejas y Mendez (1854–1912), was, however, assassinated on November 12, 1912, and the next year the Conservatives were back in power.

The outstanding Spanish writer of the period was Miguel de Unamuno y Jugo (1864–1936), a philosopher and an outspoken republican.

PORTUGAL

The new Portuguese republic seethed with unrest, since it turned out that the mere substitution of a republic for a monarchy did not automatically solve all problems.

SWITZERLAND

Switzerland was quiet in this period.

A Swiss chemist, J. Edwin Brandenberger, first produced the transparent wrapping material, cellophane, in 1912. The Swiss painter, Paul Klee (1879–1940), was becoming prominent in this period.

DENMARK

Frederick VIII of Denmark died on May 14, 1912, and was succeeded by his son, who reigned as Christian X (1870–1947). Christian X was the older brother of Haakon VII of Norway.

In 1913, the Danish physicist, Niels Henrik David Bohr (1885–1962), applied quantum theory to the structure of the hydrogen atom. He showed that only certain orbits were possible for the electron, and that shifting an electron from orbit to orbit absorbed or emitted fixed amounts of energy. This made sense of spectral lines.

Also in 1913, Ejner Hertzsprung (1873–1967) worked out the actual distance of certain Cepheid stars for the first time. This began the process whereby the true scale of the Universe could be worked out.

SWEDEN

Sweden was peaceful under Gustavus V, and continued to liberalize its government.

NORWAY

Norway, as an independent power, continued to be at peace, with a liberal government under Haakon VII.

EGYPT

Egypt was under the supervision of H. H. Kitchener, who had reconquered the Sudan and who had then served in India as commander-in-chief of the forces there.

He ruled Egypt with an iron hand, keeping the viceroy, Abbas II, from exerting any real power. In fact, Kitchener was about to depose Abbas II for his attempts to rally nationalist feeling, when the assassination of Francis Ferdinand, and what followed, swallowed up everything else.

ETHIOPIA

Menelek, who had preserved Ethiopia's independence against Italy, had suffered strokes that had made a regency necessary. On May 15, 1911, his grandson, Lij Iyasu (1896–1935), was proclaimed Emperor, though Menelek lived on until 1913. Lij Iyasu had no capacity for the post.

LIBERIA

Liberia was the only independent nation in Africa at this time, except for Ethiopia. It was, however, virtually bankrupt. The United States, which had an interest in it since it had been founded by American slaves, stepped in with financial aid, and an international loan was arranged in June 1912. Liberia was an American protectorate at this time.

PERSIA

The United States made an early appearance in the Middle East, in the person of an American lawyer, William Morgan Shuster (1877–1960), who had handled the customs in the Philippines after the Philippine Insurrection had been quelled. Now he had arrived in Persia to put its finances in order.

This was something the Russians didn't want. They preferred a Persia in chaos so that they might freely interfere. In 1912, Shuster had to leave, and the Russians remained in virtual control of Persia until the assassination of Francis Ferdinand.

CHINA

After the death of the Dowager Empress, nothing could save the Ch'ing Dynasty. Anything at all would serve to set off an explosion, and what did it was an Imperial move in 1911 to nationalize the railroads. It might have been considered a sensible move, but it roused the opposition of all the local chieftains who were running the railroads at a considerable profit.

Insurrections began in different places which the confused central government, under a child Emperor, could not handle. Sun Yat-sen, who was in the United States at the time, heard of the disorders and hastened back to China, where he was elected provisional president of the revolutionary regime.

Sun Yat-sen had no army at his disposal, however, and to find one, he had to deal with Yuan Shih-k'ai (1859–1916), who had served the Empress Dowager well and who was the only Chinese military leader to show any ability at all in the war with Japan and in the Boxer rebellion.

On February 12, 1912, the child-Emperor abdicated and the Manchu rule came to an end after three centuries, In order to preserve unity, Sun yat-sen resigned on February 13, and the next day Yuan Shih-k'ai became the first President of the Chinese Republic.

Yuan Shih-k'ai was, in his own eyes, simply an elected Emperor, however. Sun Yat-sen was forced to flee to Japan and Yuan Shih-k'ai assumed dictatorial power over China. An attempt at democracy had failed, or to be truthful, had not even truly begun.

JAPAN

The industrialization of Japan continued, but there were no startling foreign policy coups for some time after the end of the Russo–Japanese war. On July 30, 1912, Mutsohito, whose reign name was "Maiji," died and was succeeded by his son, Yoshihito (1879–1926). His reign name was "Taisho."

Japan, like Germany, was beginning to build a new navy, one with a number of dreadnoughts, with which it could, when the time came, challenge the western powers.

PHILIPPINES

On June 1, 1913, English became the official language of the Philippines.

UNITED STATES

Almost from the start, President Taft was in trouble. He didn't have the flamboyance and charisma of Theodore Roosevelt, and his conservatism didn't sit well with the more liberal Republicans of the midwest. A new tariff bill, passed at the beginning of Taft's administration, kept prices of imported goods high for the benefit of Eastern industrialists, and did nothing for almost anyone else.

In this period, the American territory between Canada and Mexico was finally filled with states. Oklahoma had entered the Union as a state on November 16, 1907. On January 6, 1912, New Mexico became a state, and on February 14, 1912, Arizona did. The United States now consisted of 48 states, plus overseas possessions, the most important of which were Alaska, Hawaii, Puerto Rico, and the Philippines.

As Taft's administration came to a close, the anti-Taft insurgents within the Republican party had as their leader Robert Marion La Follette (1855–1925), a senator from Wisconsin. Among the Democrats, a new leader arose in Woodrow Wilson (1856–1924), who was a reform governor of New Jersey. Complicating the situation was Theodore Roosevelt himself, who missed being president and who had decided he had made a mistake letting it go.

La Follette founded what came to be called a "Progressive Party" on January 21, 1911, and it was clear that he was going to try to run for president in 1912. However, with Roosevelt suddenly available, the Progressives turned to him.

The Progressives demanded all the new democratic procedures such as initiative, referendum, recall, primaries, direct election of Senators, recognition of labor unions, abolition of monopolies, and conservation of resources. They nominated Roosevelt, while the organization Republicans nominated Taft. The Democrats nominated Wilson.

Against the Republicans' split vote, Wilson won, with Taft running third (the only time in American history when a sitting president was outvoted by each of *two* rivals). Wilson became the 28th President of the United States in 1913.

Even before Wilson was inaugurated, the sixteenth amendment to the Constitution was ratified on February 25, 1913. This permitted a direct income tax, which, previously, the Supreme Court had held to be unconstitutional. It began the process of placing the tax-burden on the shoulders of those best able to afford it, and to supply the government with enough income to undertake many socially important tasks.

Since the beginning of the Republic, Senators had been chosen by state legislatures, which were usually under the control of political machines, sometimes conservative, sometimes corrupt, often both. Would-be senators, if they had money, could easily bribe legislators, so that the Senate became a rich man's club dedicated to the protection of the rich, and utterly indifferent to a public opinion that could neither elect nor remove them.

The seventeenth amendment to the constitution, adopted on May 31, 1913, directed that all Senators were to be elected by the vote of the people, and for the first time Congress became a democratic body.

Wilson also reformed the banking industry, and a Federal Reserve System was set up on December 23, 1913 that could regulate banks and control interest rates.

Labor was continuing to advance. Its most radical arm was the Industrial Workers of the World (I.W.W.), known as the "Wobblies," which had been founded in 1905, and which by 1912 had reached a membership of 100,000 and was able to win a spectacular strike against the textile mills of Lawrence, Massachusetts.

Labor had its martyrs. The Swedish-born Joel Hagglund (1879–1915), usually known as "Joe Hill," was a labor leader and a songwriter who first used the expression "pie in the sky" as a way of urging people not to endure oppression on earth in the hope of a glorious hereafter. He was arrested in 1914 on a trumped-up murder charge and was eventually executed.

On a larger scale there was the case of a fire in the Triangle Shirtwaist factory in New York on March 25, 1911. It was a "sweatshop" in which immigrant girls worked under conditions closely akin to slavery. The doors were locked; no escape was possible; and 146 people, mostly young women, were trapped and burned to death. The outrage at the callous brutality of the factory-owners helped push the demand for reforms.

A different kind of arrogance was marked off for tragedy, too. The largest and most luxurious oceanliner ever built up to that time, the British ship *Titanic*, was on its maiden voyage from Southampton to New York. It had a double-bottomed hull divided into sixteen separate watertight compartments. Four of these could be flooded and the remaining twelve would still keep the ship afloat, so that the ship was boastfully proclaimed to be unsinkable.

Shortly before midnight on April 14, 1912, the *Titanic* struck an iceberg, and five of its compartments were slashed open. In two and a half hours it sank, with a loss of 1513 lives, including many prominent Americans.

Many errors were involved. The ship was going too fast in an effort to make a record run; there were only enough lifeboat spaces for half the people aboard and there had been no lifeboat drills; a ship close enough to help in time had no radio operator on duty.

As a result, new regulations were established for lifeboats and for lifeboat drills. Radio watch was to be maintained on all ships on a 24-hour basis. Most important of all, an International Ice Patrol was established, in order to report, continually, on the location of all icebergs in the North Atlantic traffic lanes.

Technology had its triumphs, too. The Woolworth Building was completed in lower Manhattan in 1912. It was by far the most spectacular skyscraper that had yet been built, being 792 feet tall.

Motion pictures were becoming very popular. Producers discovered that the individual actors and actresses were idolized and that the public would more readily flock to those films in which they were featured. In this way, Mary Pickford (1893–1979), Douglas Fairbanks (1883–1939), and Charles Chaplin (1889–1977) became the first movie "stars." Another device for dragging in the public was the cliffhanging serials, episodes of which could be seen at weekly intervals. Pearl White (1889–1938) became famous in *The Perils of Pauline*, a serial of this sort, produced in 1914.

James Francis ("Jim") Thorpe (1886–1953) was a star of another sort, perhaps the greatest all-round athlete we have record of. He won spectacularly in the decathlon and the pentathlon at the 1912 Olympic Games, but he later had his medals taken away because of a trivial point over his amateur status. (It was easier, it seems, to be puritanical with respect to him, since he was a Native American and therefore a member of an underclass.)

Treated as badly was Margaret Louise Sanger (1879–1966) who, in this period, invented the phrase "birth control," and preached its tenets. For doing this, she was vilified, persecuted, and subjected to the penalties of the law.

On a lighter note, the foxtrot became a popular dance in 1913, and the first crossword puzzle was published that same year. The first elastic bras were designed in 1914, and these eventually freed women from the discomfort of corsets.

As a testimony to the heedlessness of human beings, the last passenger pigeon in existence died in 1914, though these birds had flown across the sky in countless millions in the previous century.

In science, Robert Andrews Millikan (1868–1953) had, in 1911, determined the electric charge on a single electron and, for the feat, was to win a Nobel Prize. Elmer Verner McCollum (1879–1967) discovered a vitamin present in some fats in 1913. He began the habit of lettering the vitamins, calling his discovery "Vitamin A" and the one discovered by Ejkman, 17 years earlier "Vitamin B."

The life of electric light bulbs was greatly extended when William David Coolidge (1873–1975) devised a method for drawing tungsten into fine wires. Tungsten is very high-melting and lasts far longer than any of the filaments used in bulbs up to that time. Irving Langmuir (1881–1957) extended the life even further by filling the bulbs with nitrogen rather than leaving it in vacuum. In this period then, electric lights became far more practical for everyday use.

George Washington Carver (1864–1943), who was born a slave, was working as an agricultural chemist in this period, pointing the way toward the manufacture of many types of useful by-products from such crops as peanuts and sweet potatoes.

Charles Franklin Kettering (1876–1958) introduced the electric self-starter in automobiles in 1912. This eventually did away with the difficult, and sometimes dangerous, hand-crank, and made it easy for automobiles to be driven even by those who were not in prime strength. It was with this innovation that the automobile became truly universal.

Willis Haviland Carrier (1876–1950) developed the first modern air-conditioning unit in 1911. A Swedish-born inventor, Gideon Sundback, produced the first slide-fastener (or "zipper") in 1912.

Edith Wharton wrote *Ethan Frome* in 1911. Zane Grey (1875–1939) was beginning to write his popular series of western adventures with *Riders of the Purple Sage*, published in 1912.

Vachel Lindsay (1879–1931) published "General Booth Enters Heaven" in 1913, and "The Congo" in 1914. Ezra Loomis Pound (1885–1972) and Amy Lowell (1874–1925) became known as Imagist poets. Robert Lee Frost (1874–1963) published his first poems, and Alfred Joyce Kilmer (1886–1918) published his unaccountably popular "Trees" in 1913.

Irving Berlin wrote his first major hit song, "Alexander's Ragtime Band," in 1911; Jerome David Kern (1885–1945) wrote his first musical comedy score in 1912; and William Christopher Handy wrote his immortal "St. Louis Blues" in 1914.

John Singer Sargent (1856–1925) was the outstanding American painter of the period; and Reuben Lucius ("Rube") Goldberg (1883–1970) began to make his name part of the English language with his cartoon drawings of simple feats performed by impossibly complicated mechanical means.

CANADA

Canada's ambivalent attitude toward Great Britain was shown in 1913, when a bill to contribute toward the building of three dreadnaughts for the British navy was defeated in the legislature.

MEXICO

After having ruled Mexico with an iron hand for 34 years, Porfirio Díaz was finally slipping. A Mexican liberal, Francisco Indalecio Madero (1873–1913), clamoring for social reforms and for justice for the oppressed peasants, tried to run against Díaz for president in 1910, and was imprisoned.

Madero managed to escape, fled to Texas, gathered funds and supporters, and set up a rebel government in Mexico in May 1911. Díaz was finally forced to resign and went into exile in Paris, where he stayed for the rest of his life.

Díaz's exit meant a free-for-all among Mexican generals for control of the nation, and events quickly slipped out of Madero's hands.

The winning general, Victoriano Huerta (1854–1916), who had fought with Madero till Díaz was overthrown, now wanted the power for himself. He had Madero arrested and, on February 22, 1913, had him killed. He then announced himself as President of Mexico just as Wilson was becoming the American President.

It was the universal custom among the nations of the world (including the United States) to recognize as legitimate any government that was in effective control of a nation. The European powers had all quickly recognized Madero's rule, and now they recognized Huerta's rule just as quickly.

Wilson refused to go along. He admired Madero, considered Huerta a butcher, and refused to recognize the latter's presidency. That initiated the American policy of refusing to recognize governments on high moral grounds, a policy that sometimes needlessly complicated American foreign policy.

The mere act of nonrecognition did not hurt Huerta. If anything, it helped him, for Mexicans naturally thought there must be something good about a man who had earned American disapproval. Wilson, therefore, had to take a more active part in Mexican disorders, and support some general who would oppose Huerta. His choice fell on Venustiano Carranza (1859–1920), who was rebelling against Huerta, and American arms flowed in Carranza's direction.

This set up a delicate situation. Four sailors from an American warship were in Vera Cruz on an innocent errand, and were arrested—but were immediately released, when it was found out who they were.

Wilson, however, wakened in the middle of the night and apprised of this "crisis," was caught up in a sudden fury. At his orders, Vera Cruz was bombarded and occupied on April 21, 1914, and, in the course of this, 400 Mexicans were killed. All Latin-America was horrified at the action and even Carranza had to protest, or face a loss of all support within Mexico.

Nevertheless, Huerta was forced to resign on July 15, 1914, and Carranza became President, which was an ending that seemed happy for the moment.

Meanwhile, in Europe, Austria-Hungary was on the point of sending its ultimatum to Serbia, but neither the United States nor Mexico saw much reason to be concerned over what might be happening on the other side of the ocean.

NICARAGUA

Nicaragua was suffering the common Latin-American problem of having debts it couldn't pay, so by the Roosevelt Corollary, American officials took charge of the customs, with American marines to guard them, of course. In July, 1912, civil war broke out in Nicaragua, and American forces, on the spot, saw to it that a conservative candidate, Adolfo Diaz (1874–1964), was elected.

HONDURAS

In this period, American forces were also in Honduras to protect American interests in the face of a civil war.

PANAMA

On a more constructive note, the Panama Canal was opened on August 15, 1914, though the occurrence of occasional landslides kept it from being used to the full. Because of the situation in Europe, the formal opening did not take place for some years.

ANTARCTICA

Roald Amundsen, who had managed to complete the Northwest Passage a few years earlier, was now making preparations for his attempt to reach the South Pole. He planned to use dogs, which could eat the food brought for human beings, and which could eat each other at need. Robert Scott was also making the attempt, but he used ponies, which required that bales of hay be brought along, and which died eventually, so that the men had to pull the sledges themselves.

Amundsen reached the South Pole on December 14, 1911, and returned safely. Scott reached it on January 17, 1912, only to find Amundsen's marker already there. He and his party died in a blizzard on the way back.

1914 TO 1920

GERMANY

When Austria-Hungary declared war on Serbia, there was a chance that if Russia backed down, Serbia would be quickly defeated, would have to stop its anti-Austro–Hungarian activities, and everything would be quiet.

Germany's role in this would be to make certain that Russia did not intervene. Russia, however, was in a terrible dilemma. It was by no means ready for war, but it had backed down too often, and it felt it could not afford to do so again. It would have to take *some* action, if it were not to look like a pitiful paper tiger. However, in order to do something effective, and to make sure it could resist if the Germans took the Austro–Hungarian side, Russia would have to mobilize its army.

Therefore, Russia, after some hours of hesitation, began to mobilize. The trouble was, though, that because of Russia's huge size, its lack of an efficient rail network, and the general inefficiency and incapacity of its governmental apparatus, it would take Russia weeks, if not months, to mobilize.

Germany now had to make a quick decision. It was wedded to the notion of the "Blitzkrieg," the lightning war. This had worked under Bismarck against Denmark, against Austria, and then against France, and it should work now.

If Germany struck quickly at Russia before it was mobilized, that bumbling nation could easily be brought down. On the other hand, if Germany waited till Russia was completely mobilized, the sheer mass of Russian soldiery might be difficult to move, and although many defeats might be inflicted upon the Russians, matters would develop into a slow, bloody war, which was what the Germans didn't want.

Therefore, Germany sent an ultimatum to Russia, demanding that its mobilization cease. This was what Russia dared not do. When it refused, Germany declared war on Russia on August 1, 1914. Germany did not hesitate to do this. It had accepted the fact for years that war would eventually come and it had seemed to many Germans that if the war were delayed too long, the encircling enemy powers would grow too strong to be defeated quickly. The war might, therefore, just as well come now, and it should perhaps have come sooner.

A declaration of war on Russia, however, was not enough. There was France to the west, which was required by treaty to come to Russia's aid. France might flinch at the last minute, but Germany couldn't count on that. Germany had to assume the worst and act in accordance.

In fact, Germany had long made its plan for how to fight a two-front war against both France and Russia, in accordance with the strategy worked out by Alfred von Schlieffen (1833–1913). According to the "Schlieffen plan," the German army was to come smashing through the Netherlands and Belgium into northern France, turning on a hinge at the Alps, gathering in Paris and trapping the French army. The French would be destroyed in a matter of weeks, and Germany could then turn and tackle the Russian giant which would not, even then, have completed its mobilization. This could not be done in reverse, for while Germany was bludgeoning the Russians slowly into submission, France would have time to prepare a strong counteroffensive.

Therefore, as soon as Germany declared war on Russia, it prepared to attack France. On August 3, 1914, Germany declared war on France and its army was already on the move.

Great Britain was hesitating. Its alliance with France and Russia made it necessary for it to join the war, but since the Battle of Waterloo, a century earlier, it had engaged in only one land war in Europe and that was a minor one. The British were reluctant to plunge into a major land war.

Yet the Germans had already pushed into Belgium, whose neutrality it (along with France and Great Britain) had guaranteed.

British public opinion, already anti-German enough, was horrified at the wanton violation of Belgian neutrality, and the effect was made worse when the German Chancellor, Bethmann-Hollweg, expressed surprise, with typical Imperial German insensitivity, that Great Britain should be making a fuss about "a scrap of paper," as he termed the neutrality agreement.

Great Britain declared war on Germany on August 4, 1914, and Austria-Hungary declared war on Russia on August 6, 1914.

An assassination, then (like a score of others that had taken place in these decades) to which was added the Austro-Hungarian desire for a small, quick war it really didn't need, led to a catastrophe. Add to this the further addition of an inability of the great powers to risk the loss of face that would come with backing down, and you had World War I, in which every European participant, winners and losers alike, was to lose enormously.

Meanwhile, however, Germany was attacking, and all depended on how well the Schlieffen plan would work. The chances are that it would have worked exactly as planned, but it was tinkered with and ruined by the German army chief, Helmuth Johannes Ludwig von Moltke (1848–1916). He was the nephew of the Moltke who had run the Prussian army in Bismark's time, but he lacked his uncle's genius.

In the first place, he decided to avoid harming British sensibilities by not invading the Netherlands, and by confining himself to Belgium alone. As it happened, Belgium was enough to drive Great Britain into war, so Moltke gained nothing by this move. Actually, he lost, for the German army was forced to squeeze through the narrow Belgian border and lost speed in consequence.

Second, the original plan had called for a weak line of defense in the south, where it was actually hoped that France would strike and advance. A French success there would draw more troops to the spot, to the weakening of the all-important northern end of the line, and would add those additional French troops to the bag that would be closed as the German army wheeled itself

shut. Moltke, however, couldn't bring himself to allow any German territory to be lost, so he strengthened the southern wing at the cost of weakening the northern wing, which was to do the swinging.

Even so, the Schlieffen plan seemed to be working. On August 4, German forces had poured into Belgium, and within 10 days they had reached the French frontier, while French attempts at an offensive further south were stopped in their tracks.

On August 14, German forces moved into France and the French soldiers were being beaten as thoroughly as the Belgian soldiers were.

The British had sent troops across the Channel and, on August 23, 1914, these met the Germans at Mons in Belgium near the French frontier. Unlike the other combatants, Great Britain did not have a large conscript army, but those it did have were very well-trained. They fought all the harder because William II, with his unfailing feel for the wrong phrase, had referred to Great Britain's "contemptible little army." The army called itself the "Old Contemptibles" and fought like fiends. Nevertheless, the Germans were unstoppable and the British had to retreat.

Moltke continued to make mistakes. Overestimating the German advance in the north and overjoyed at the Germans throwing back the French in the south, he sent more troops southward. Hearing also that the Russians, unprepared though they were, were attacking in the east in loyal support of the French, he detached two army corps from the western front and sent them eastward. They didn't arrive in the east in time to influence the battle there, and their absence had an important effect in the west, where Moltke had gradually whittled the strength of the swinging gate from 16 army corps to 11.

Even the German army, efficient as it was, could run out of steam, and as August drew to a close, that army, after a month of continuous advance, was gasping. Both the French and the British, while unable actually to stop the Germans, were inflicting damage. Moltke's uninspired leadership, moreover, was allowing gaps to exist between different army corps—partly through lack of proper communications and partly because there were fewer army corps lined up along the front than there should have been.

Already, it seemed that Germany would be unable to sweep its armies past Paris, and that they were curving in such a way as to fall short.

The French commander-in-chief, Joseph Jacques Cesair Joffre (1852–1931), ably assisted by Joseph Simon Gallieni (1849–1916), planned a counterattack devised to take advantage of the gap between two of the German army corps. The battle was fought at the Marne River, only 20 miles northeast of Paris, for the seven bloody days from September 5 to September 12, 1914. The Germans were stopped at last and thrown back.

The Germans weren't thrown back far, but the momentum of their advance had been stopped. The Battle of the Marne was actually the decisive battle of the war, and the most decisive since Waterloo. Had the Germans won it, they would probably have taken Paris, and it is likely that France would have had to give up. The Germans would then have turned their full force on Russia and driven it into collapse, and a peace with Great Britain, made to Germany's benefit, might then have been patched up.

Since the Germans were defeated, the lightning war was lost. The Germans might still win —indeed, the odds seemed still in their favor— but now it would be a long war, which the Germans hadn't planned on and didn't want. In hindsight, it might have been well for Germany if it had now tried to negotiate a peace asking only endurable gains. The trouble was that both sides had worked themselves into such hatreds (even before the war had started) that no peace was possible except on draconic terms, so that the war had to go on till one side was so beaten as to be forced to accept total defeat.

Yet in only a month of war, each side had suffered about half a million casualties. Such losses would not have been dreamed of even in a long war of the type fought against Napoleon. To accept such losses in so short a time, and to continue fighting, was insane; but World War I, which started over very little (and was carried through, for the most part, with military stupidity), was insane all the way through.

After the Battle of the Marne, each side extended its line northward in an attempt to outflank the other. By the end of 1914, a continuous line bulging into northeastern France had been established from the Swiss border to the English Channel. Both sides had dug down into the longest, bloodiest stalemate ever seen. Each side had suffered a million casualties by the time 1914 was over, and that was only the beginning.

Meanwhile, what was Germany doing in the east?

The French had called on the Russians to invade Germany at once; and Russia, largely unprepared, did so, displaying loyalty and stupidity in equal measures. Two armies, one under Pavel Karlovich Rennenkampf (1854–1918) and the other under Aleksandr Vasilievich Samsonov (1859–1914), invaded East Prussia.

Two German generals were sent eastward to take care of the invasion, when the general on the spot proved inadequate. One was Paul von Hindenburg (1847–1934), who was called out of retirement for the purpose. The other was Erich Friedrich Wilhelm Ludendorff (1865–1937), who had shown great ability in the march through Belgium.

It was clear that however formidable the Russian armies seemed, they were ill-equipped, and their leaders were so naive as to send uncoded messages back and forth so that the Germans knew what they were doing at all times. Furthermore, a German officer, Max Hoffman (1869–1927), happened to know that the two generals leading the Russian armies hated each other, and would never cooperate.

The Germans attacked Samsonov's army at Tannenberg and, between August 26 and 30, 1914, completely defeated it, taking more than 100,000 prisoners. Rennenkampf made no move to help and Samsonov, in despair, shot himself.

On September 9–14, 1914, another German force under August von Mackenson (1849–1945) annihilated Rennenkampf's army, taking 125,000 prisoners. The German losses in the two battles were negligible.

These hammerblows at the Russians assured the Germans of never having their home territory threatened from the east again for the duration of the war. The Russians never quite recovered, and though they continued to fight in their usual stolid, unrelenting manner, they almost always fought on the defensive, expecting defeat.

Nevertheless, this initial Russian advance into East Prussia, had, in a way, won the war. It had frightened Moltke into sending two corps eastward from the western front. By the time those corps arrived, the two battles of annihilation were over and they were not needed, but their lack in the west probably made it just possible for the Allies to win the Battle of the Marne.

But now that Germany faced a long war, which it had not planned for, it had to improvise a decision as to how to fight it. Should they make their major push against France or against Russia? Moltke had been fired, and the new commander-in-chief, Erich Georg Anton Sebastian von Falkenhayn (1861–1922), felt that the decision would be reached in the west and wanted the major effort there.

Hindenberg and Ludendorff, however, wanted to pursue the Russians and William II agreed with them. Therefore, Falkenhayn was forced to remain on the defensive in the west while the eastern offensive continued. This was the wrong decision. It enabled France to survive in the west, and it did nothing crucial in the east, for Russia would, in all likelihood, have been successfully pushed to dissolution and chaos with a lesser German effort.

Through 1915, the stalemate in the west continued. The use of the machine gun and artillery gave an enormous advantage to the offense. Nevertheless, generals, particularly on the Allied side, still seeming to live in the Napoleonic era, insisted on sending their troops forward in a hopeless attempt to break through the machine-gun fire and the barbed wire that protected the trenches. Advances were miniscule and, in the course of 1915, the Germans lost 600,000 men, the British and French 1,500,000 men—yet the lines at the end of 1915 were just about where they were at the beginning.

It is impossible to imagine a war fought more stupidly. It was the Charge of the Light Brigade expanded to cosmic proportions.

During the year, the Germans added to the horror of war by initiating the use of poison gas. The Second Battle of Ypres was fought from April 22 to May 25, 1915. On the first day, the Germans sent a cloud of chlorine gas from some 5000 cylinders rolling over the Allied lines. Those lines collapsed, of course, but the Germans were completely surprised by the unexpected success of the tactic. They were caught flat-footed and were not prepared to plunge forward for a breakthrough, especially since plunging forward would have placed their own men within the poison cloud. Quickly, the Allies prepared poison gas of their own and both sides devised gas masks. Poison gas was horrifying, but never decisive, as a weapon of war.

On the eastern front during 1915, the Germans managed to fight their way through Poland and, by the end of the year, had all of Poland and Lithuania. That the Russians were not completely defeated was through the efforts of the Grand Duke Nicholas Nikolayevich (1856–1929), a first cousin, once-removed, of Tsar Nicholas II, and one of the few capable generals on the Russian side. The Russian leaders, however, with impeccable stupidity, transferred him to the Caucasus to fight the sideshow war against Turkey there.

By 1916, the Germans, observing that the Allies had suffered many more casualties than the Germans had in the course of the previous year, thought that it might be possible to win without an actual victory in the field. All that was required was that the Allies should be maneuvered into suffering so many casualties that they would finally be too weak to fight. They were to be bled white.

The German successes in the east made it possible to shift troops to the west, and the Germans attacked at Verdun, south of the main bulge of the lines into France, where the French lines extended northward in a little bulge of their own.

The French responded by sending a dogged general, Philippe Petain (1856–1951), to the spot. Petain reorganized his men and set up the watchword, "They shall not pass!" Both sides brought up endless reinforcements and the battle was fought from February 21 to December 18, 1916, and ended about where it had begun. The French were indeed made to bleed terribly, losing 542,000 men, but the Germans themselves lost 434,000.

That the Germans were dissatisfied with this *mutual* bloodletting was indicated by the fact that Falkenhayn lost his job after Verdun and was replaced by Hindenberg and Ludendorff, the architects of victory in the east (against a much weaker opponent, to be sure).

The British had, by now, a great many men on the front and had actually established universal conscription. Even while the battle of Verdun was continuing, they fought a battle of their own at the Somme River in the north. The Battle of the Somme, fought from June 24 to November 13, 1916, ended in the same useless stalemate that was taking place at Verdun.

But the British had thought of a way of countering the machine-gun by falling back on the old device of armor. This time, it was not to be an armored man, but an armored vehicle with a man inside and with treads that would enable it to negotiate all kinds of terrain. These armored vehicles (reminiscent of those Ziska had used in the Hussite wars, five centuries earlier) were kept secret in the course of their development; and, to mislead possible spies, were referred to as "tanks." The name was meaningless, but it stuck.

On September 15, 1916, in the course of the Battle of the Somme, the British used tanks for the first time, but there were only 18 of them and they didn't do much. Nevertheless, their importance grew rapidly.

By the end of the year, Joffre, worn out, was succeeded by Robert Georges Nivelle (1856–1924), whose unbounded optimism made him think he could break the stalemate. What's more, he persuaded others that he could do so.

Meanwhile, on the eastern front, the Russians found another capable general, Aleksey Alekseyevich Brusilov (1853–1926), who mounted an offensive in the summer of 1916 which won surprising successes, albeit against the Austro–

Hungarians rather than the Germans. In the end, however, it failed to turn the tide of battle, and Russian losses had now reached the point where even Russians found it unendurable and the nation began to slide toward chaos.

On February 23, 1917, Nivelle started his heralded offensive and, unfortunately, it was like all those that had preceded it. In five days, the French lost 120,000 men, accomplished nothing, and Nivelle was relieved of command.

The French army had had enough (and much more than enough, in any sane man's opinion) and mutinied.

It was at this point that it might seem that the Battle of the Marne had been for nothing and that Germany was going to win the war. In the east, Russia was dissolving into revolution. In the west, France seemed about to do the same. On other fronts in Europe, the Germans were doing well. What could keep them from winning?

The answer was Petain, who took the place of Nivelle. Petain managed, with a mixture of firmness and kindness, to put an end to the mutiny, while a tight French censorship kept all news of it from the outside world. This was a greater service than Petain's obstinacy at Verdun had been.

Meanwhile, the British under Douglas Haig (1861–1928) launched another supremely costly and ineffective offensive in the north, but at least it served the purpose of helping further to distract the Germans from learning about the French mutiny. By the time the Germans found out that for two weeks the French soldiers had been refusing to fight—it was too late. The French were back at their guns.

But the Germans were themselves in a bad way, too. The people at home had long since lost all enthusiasm for the bloody war. The British fleet controlled the sea and kept Germany under a blockade that had brought the German population close to starvation during the winter of 1916–1917, and William II was finding it next to impossible to run the country under the increasingly horrendous conditions.

What's more, the United States had now entered the war on the side of the allies, and the prospect of fresh, unworn American armies joining the fight daunted the war-weary Germans.

But by early 1918, the war in the east had come to an end with a total German victory, and Germany had a last chance—to make one final push that would crush the Allies in France before the Americans could make their weight felt. The United States would then find itself facing a victorious Germany and it might decide not to try to fight a war, all by itself, an ocean away from home.

As many soldiers as possible were shipped west and Ludendorff planned a great offensive designed to crack the point where the British and French armies joined. The British and French had been under separate national commands all through the war and they could not be counted on to cooperate fully, so the juncture of the two was a natural weak point.

The attack came on March 21, 1918, and the great "1918 spring offensive" seemed to work. Behind a tremendous artillery barrage, Ludendorff hit the juncture, and broke through. Within a week he had gained over 30 miles. No one had seen an advance like this in the west since the first month of the war, three and a half years earlier.

The Allies reacted with virtual panic. Great Britain and France agreed, for the first time, on a single overall commander-in-chief for the Western Front. On April 5, 1918, they chose the French general, Ferdinand Foch (1851–1929), for the post.

The Germans kept up the offensive, however. After a pause to regroup, they surged forward a second time, and then a third. By June 3, the Germans were at the French town of Chateau-Thierry, just 50 miles east of Paris. It was close enough for Germany's biggest cannon to lob shells into the city. The French government was preparing to leave Paris as it had in the first month of the war.

By that time, though, American soldiers were fighting and winning in a wooded area called Belleau Wood, near Chateau-Thierry.

The German advance, magnificent though it looked on the map, and though it drove the Allies to the edge of defeat, was not carried through without cost. The Germans lost heavily both in men and material. They were exhausted, and they had not quite won the objectives Ludendorff had in mind.

Then, on July 15, Ludendorff ordered another push. He was at the Marne where the Germans had lost nearly four years earlier, and there was now a "Second Battle of the Marne." This time, he met not only the usual allied troops but 270,000 Americans as well, with another 54,000 Americans farther north. The Germans gave way and the last hope was gone. The victory had not come and the Americans were in the line in large numbers.

The Allies now launched a counteroffensive and, on August 8, 1918, they used tanks in quantity. This time it was the German lines that broke, and the Allies who advanced rapidly. Ludendorff recognized that the war was over. He called August 8 a "black day" for the German army.

On October 3, 1918, William II, at what amounted to Ludendorff's orders, set up a constitutional monarchy, realizing that only that, if anything, could survive the war. Prince Maximilian of Baden (1867–1929), a noted liberal and humanitarian, was appointed Chancellor, and he set about the task of democratizing Germany and of negotiating for peace.

The situation, however, had gotten beyond that. On November 4, 1918, disorders in Germany amounted to a revolutionary situation. On November 9, 1918, William II abdicated, after having ruled, without much talent for the job, for 30 years. Maximilian also resigned and Friedrich Ebert (1871–1925), a rather tame Socialist, became Chancellor of what was now a German Republic.

In the course of the 51 months that the war had lasted, German casualties amounted to 1,800,000 dead and 4,250,000 wounded.

But though Germany had lost, the Allies had not really won. Russia was in a worse state of dissolution than Germany was. France and Great Britain had suffered as much as Germany had, if not more, and they stood there gasping, with their only comfort the knowledge that, unlike the Germans, they had not actually lost. In fact, the World War I experience scarred the British and French worse than it had the Germans. The Germans at least had a defeat for which to seek vengeance. The British and French knew only that they never wanted to fight again.

However, in the midst of even a cataclysmic war, life goes on.

Albert Einstein, in 1916, worked out the General Theory of Relativity, the most astounding feat of scientific imagination since Newton, two and a third centuries earlier. Einstein's general relativity was, in fact, a correction and extension of Newton's view of gravity. For the first time, however, a set of "field equations" were worked out that served to describe the Universe as a whole. Thus, Einstein had founded the science of cosmology.

During this period Alfred Lothar Wegener (1880–1930) elaborated on his idea that the continents slowly drifted and that they had once been a single supercontinent which he called "Pangaea" ("all-Earth"). This broke up, gradually forming the continental distribution that exists today. He was wrong in detail, but was eventually shown to be correct in concept.

Walter Baade (1893–1960) discovered Hidalgo, which, at the time, was the farthest asteroid known, its orbit carrying it outward nearly as far as Saturn.

Oswald Spengler (1880–1936) began his monumental work, *The Decline of the West*, in 1918. Influenced, undoubtedly, by the insanity of World War I, he discussed the rise and fall of civilizations and predicted the decline and fall of the west.

In 1919, Walter Adolf Gropius (1883–1969) founded the Bauhaus school of architecture, which was extremely influential in the following decades.

FRANCE

The history of France in this period is the history of World War I, for the western front, where the fighting was hardest and most even, and where the decision was reached, was fought entirely within that section of France that lay between Paris and the Belgian border.

The civilian government of France moved, temporarily, from Paris to Bordeaux on September 3, 1914, just before the Battle of the Marne

stopped the German advance. Even after it returned, however, it had little to do but put the best face on a frightful war, as different Premiers failed to find a way to end the war victoriously.

Finally, on November 16, 1917, Georges Clemenceau (1841–1929) became Premier. He was a long-time liberal and anticlerical. He had supported Dreyfus and was, above all, anti-German. He was 76 years old at the time, but it was not for nothing that he was called "The Tiger." He assumed the Ministry of War as well as the Premiership, and he drove hard for victory and nothing but victory, fighting for a unified command until it was achieved under Foch.

When the war was over, it was Clemenceau who represented France at the peace conference, and it was Clemenceau who held out for a harsh peace. He insisted on revenge and did his best to shiver Germany to bits.

Meanwhile, in the world of art, Monet, now in the twilight of his career, was spending years on the paintings of waterlilies that were to be his masterpieces, while Henri Emile Benoit Matisse (1869–1954) was beginning his own career in art.

Andre Paul Guillaume Gide (1869–1951) was becoming known as a writer in this period.

GREAT BRITAIN

Although Great Britain began World War I with only a small volunteer army, it built it up rapidly and had a compulsory draft in 1916. By the end of the war, Great Britain had mobilized 9 million men, a bit more than France had, and had suffered 900,000 dead and 2 million wounded. In addition to fighting in France, the British had to fight a war at sea.

The German main fleet was off the German coast in the North Sea, behind the fortified island of Heligoland. It didn't dare come out to challenge the British, and the British fleet, for its part, remained in its fortified outposts on its side of the North Sea. They had no need to do more than keep the German fleet out of action.

There were, to be sure, some 10 German warships at sea when World War I began. Without a secure base, they proceeded to act as privateers, trying to disrupt British merchant shipping and pick off an occasional British war vessel. By the end of 1914, those ships had been destroyed by the British fleet, and Germany had to rely on submarines to achieve its ends at sea.

Vessels capable of remaining for a while under water had been experimented with since 1620, but it was only in 1886 that submarines were built with motors that could be run by electric storage batteries. Though such submarines had to surface periodically to recharge their batteries, they were able to travel a reasonable distance underwater between charges.

Submarines were hard to detect underwater in those days and could approach ships without warning. A ship might not know if it was in danger until it was actually struck by a torpedo. Nor could submarines afford to give warning, for they are fragile vessels and easily sunk. Nor are they large enough to take on the survivors of a torpedoing, who therefore must be left to drown. For these reasons, submarine attacks seemed both dishonorable and atrocious to those attacked.

To be sure, all the warring nations had submarines and were willing to use them. However, only Germany had to depend on them entirely, and only Great Britain was so dependent on shipping and had so widespread a fleet as to offer an overwhelmingly tempting target.

The sea war, then, was between German submarines and British merchant ships and war vessels, and the onus of atrocity lay entirely on the German side.

Meanwhile, though, the British built up an effective blockade that kept foodstuffs and raw materials from getting to Germany by sea. As a result, Germans felt the pinch and began to go hungry. More serious still, from a military standpoint, would have been the results if Germany had depended on nitrates from abroad for the manufacture of explosives. Germany would then have run out of ammunition and would have been forced to end the war. It was the Haber process, using the atmosphere as a source of the necessary nitrogen, that made it possible for Germany to fight on for three more years.

Submarine warfare was fatal to Germany, however, because of its effect on American public opinion. The United States, during the first part of World War I, was the world's most important neutral, as it had been during the Napoleonic wars a century earlier. The United States was more sympathetic to the Allied side than to the German side to begin with, and it was doing a thriving business with the Allies. Submarine warfare, therefore, threatened American trade.

To the Germans it seemed that since the United States did not object to the British blockade of Germany, they ought not object to the German blockade of Great Britain, just because the Germans had no choice but to use submarines for the purpose. Logic is a poor tool when the emotions are engaged, however.

There was the case of the *Lusitania*, for instance. It was a British luxury liner that was carrying a war cargo, including guns and ammunition, from New York to Great Britain. Before it left New York, the German embassy warned Americans not to travel on the ship since it was fair game for submarine action. The warning was not heeded.

On May 7, 1915, the *Lusitania* was hit, without warning, by a German torpedo and 1,198 people were drowned, including 124 Americans. The effect on American public opinion was enormous and the Germans were forced to announce they would stop unlimited submarine warfare.

On May 31, 1916, there took place the only great naval battle of World War I. The German fleet under Reinhold Scheer (1863–1928) moved out from their shelter. It consisted of 99 ships, including 27 battleships. The British overheard radio measages from Germany that gave the movement away, and the British Fleet, under John Rushworth Jellicoe (1859–1935), with 151 ships including 37 battleships, promptly moved out to intercept the Germans.

The Battle of Jutland was fought off the coast of Denmark.

It marked the end of a long era. It was the last major sea-battle to be fought by surface vessels that were within sight of each other; and the last major sea-battle to be fought without airplanes. Tactically, the Germans did surprisingly well. Their ships were individually better and their shooting was more accurate. The British lost 14 ships to the German 11 and suffered 6800 casualties to the German 3000. Strategically, however, it was a British victory, for the German fleet, less able to endure losses, was forced to retire to port. It never emerged again for the duration of the war. William II might as well not have built a fleet and gained the enmity of Great Britain, for all the good it did him.

In the spring of 1917, submarine warfare was resumed by Germany, and British shipping losses rose to astronomical heights. It did seem there was a real danger of the British being starved out. But then the Americans entered the war on the British side; and on May 10, 1917, a convoy system was established. Merchant ships traveled in groups protected by destroyers. Fewer ships were sunk, more submarines were caught and destroyed, and the submarine menace receded.

World War I was the first war in which airplanes played a part. At first they were used only on reconnaissance, but the pressure of war forced them to move into belligerent action.

In 1915, the Javanese-born Anthony Herman Gerard Fokker (1890–1939) had invented a method of firing a machine-gun so that the bullet went between the blades of the whirling propellor. Airplanes could then battle each in the air. For a while, it seemed to mark a return to the days of knightly single combat, and those who succeeded in bringing down a number of enemy planes were made into heroes.

One of the pioneers of air–combat tactics was Max Immelmann (1890–1916). The greatest German ace was Manfred von Richthofen (1892–1918), called "the Red Baron" from the color of his plane. He shot down 80 enemy planes and died in action.

On the French side, Paul Rene Fonck (1894–1953) was credited with shooting down 75 planes. The Canadian aviator, William Avery Bishop (1894–1956), shot down 72; while the British aviator, Albert Ball (1894–1956), shot down 43. During the shorter American participation, Edward Vernon Rickenbacker (1890–1973) shot down 26 planes.

Most "aces" were lost in action, and warfare in the air quickly developed to the point where such combats lost their apparent knightly quality.

Indiscriminate bombing of large cities from the air began in World War I, too. The most spectacular incidents were the airship raids on eastern England and on London in 1915 and 1916. The British quickly developed antiaircraft guns and the airships became vulnerable. The Germans used 80 airships in their raids and lost 73 of them by the war's end. Airplane bombing raids on England began in November 1916 and continued sporadically to the end of the war, but had no significant effect on the course of fighting.

The German colonies in Africa were, of course, involved in the war. Most of the German colonies were cleaned up by the British and French before the end of 1914. However, in German East Africa, the German commander, Paul von Lettow-Vorbeck (1870–1964), kept up a brilliant guerrilla campaign and was never defeated. It was only after he learned that the war was over that he finally surrendered his command on November 23, 1918.

At home, Great Britain had to face a serious situation in Ireland. The Irish were dissatisfied by the fact that the Home Rule question was postponed till after the war. Moreover, they could not help but feel that with Great Britain totally preoccupied with the fighting in France, that was their opportunity to break loose.

The Germans felt that trouble in Ireland, by distracting the British, would ease the situation on the western front, and they did what they could to encourage the Irish. The Germans did not feel they could spare troops, but a German submarine brought Roger David Casement (1864–1916) to Ireland on April 12, 1916. He was an Irish Protestant who had been of great service to the British government in a variety of humanitarian causes, such as in his exposure of the atrocities against the blacks in the Congo. His sympathies were with the Irish nationalists, however, and once World War I started, he turned immediately to the Germans for help.

In any case, armed rebellion broke out in Dublin on April 24, 1916. It was Easter Monday and was, therefore, called the "Easter Rebellion." It was suppressed within a week and Casement and others were tried and hanged on August 3. However, fighting continued through the end of World War I and beyond. On one side were the Irish nationalists, the "Sinn Fein" ("ourselves alone"), and its guerrilla force, the Irish Republican Army. On the other was the British army and its special constabulary force, the "Black and Tans," from the color of their uniforms.

On July 7, 1916, Asquith resigned as British Prime Minister and David Lloyd George took his place. It was Lloyd George who represented the British at the peace negotiations after the end of World War I.

Meanwhile, Ernest Rutherford was continuing to work on subatomic physics. By 1919, he had produced the first example of nuclear transmutation of elements, turning nitrogen into oxygen. This was the first human-induced nuclear reaction, and that sort of thing was to lead to enormously important consequences.

Einstein's general theory of relativity was scarcely known during the war. One copy of his paper had been sneaked out by way of neutral Netherlands. In 1919, once the war was over, Eddington organized expeditions to check the positions of stars near the Sun during a total eclipse. Einstein's theory required that they be displaced in a certain fashion, and this theory was upheld.

In 1920, H. G. Wells published his phenomenally successful *Outline of History*. James Barrie produced such plays as *A Kiss for Cinderella* (1916) and *Dear Brutus* (1917). The Irish writer, James Augustine Joyce (1882–1941), published *Portrait of the Artist as a Young Man* in 1916.

William Somerset Maugham (1874–1965) published his most successful novel, *Of Human Bondage*, in 1915 and *The Moon and Sixpence* in 1919; and George Norman Douglas (1868–1952) published *South Wind* in 1917.

John Buchan (1875–1940) published the most successful of his thrillers, *The Thirty-Nine Steps* in 1915. The first stories of P. G. Wodehouse featuring Bertie Wooster and Jeeves, his most familiar and endearing characters, appeared in 1919.

Henry Havelock Ellis (1859–1939) was deeply engaged in what eventually turned out to be a seven-volume *Studies in the Psychology of Sex*.

Siegfried Lorraine Sassoon (1886–1967) served in World War I, and, in this period, began writing antiwar poetry. Rupert Brooke (1887–1914), who showed every sign of being a great poet died in the war.

Gustav Theodore Holst (1874–1934) wrote his tone poem *The Planets* in 1918. They were astrological, not astronomical, in inspiration.

UNITED STATES

From the American viewpoint, the installation of Carranza as president of Mexico looked like a satisfactory denouement to the crisis that had so preoccupied Wilson at the start of his administration, but it wasn't. Civil war continued, and two generals who opposed Carranza were Emiliano Zapata (1879–1919), who strongly favored agrarian reform, and Francisco ("Pancho") Villa (1878–1923), who strongly favored himself.

Wilson did not wish to interfere with this new Mexican civil war for World War I was raging in Europe now, and that was far more important. However, Villa, at least, needed American opposition in order to increase his own popularity within Mexico.

Therefore, on January 10, 1916, Villa (to enforce that opposition) stopped a train in northern Mexico, took off 17 American engineers and had 16 of them shot without even bothering to make up a reason. On March 9, 1916, he sent 400 raiders into the bordertown of Columbus, New Mexico, burning the town and killing 19 Americans.

This could not be ignored. Wilson forced Carranza to agree to allow American troops to enter Mexico. On March 15, 1916, some 6000 American soldiers, under John Joseph Pershing (1860–1948), invaded Mexico.

Catching Villa, however, proved impossible. Villa knew every corner of the land, and the Americans did not. What's more, the local population was on Villa's side and information could not be obtained from them. Even worse, Carranza had to take action against the United States if he were to retain any credibility with his people, and there was official Mexican interference with the American troops.

Eventually, Wilson had to give up. The danger

of war with Germany was growing closer and closer and, on February 5, 1917, American forces were recalled from Mexico, leaving Villa still at large.

Meanwhile, the German use of submarines, and particularly the incident of the *Lusitania*, was greatly increasing the anti-German feelings of the American public.

Germany was also strongly suspected of plans for sabotaging American munitions factories that were supplying arms for the Allies. It was only natural that they should do this, for we would have done the same were the situation reversed, but that didn't make Americans like it any better.

Increasingly, there was a movement for "preparedness," for building up the American army and navy in preparation for coming to the aid of the Allies. Theodore Roosevelt was the outstanding exponent of this. He attacked Wilson intemperately as a weakling and coward. Other active advocates of preparedness were Henry Cabot Lodge (1850–1924), a senator from Massachusetts, who also hated Wilson, and Henry Lewis Stimson (1867–1950), who had been Secretary of War under Taft.

Pacifists became unpopular. In the course of a preparedness parade in San Francisco on July 22, 1916, a bomb exploded, killing 10 and injuring 40. Two men, Thomas Joseph Mooney (1882–1942) and Warren K. Billings (1893–1972), were arrested. They had had nothing to do with the bombings, but they were labor leaders, socialists, and pacifists, and those were crimes enough. They were sentenced to life imprisonment and served nearly a quarter of a century before the government admitted it had been wrong and released them.

As part of the new epidemic and hatred sweeping the nation, the Ku Klux Klan was revived in the south about 1915 and revelled in its chance to hide behind sheets and to hate blacks, Jews, Catholics, and as many other people as possible.

Nevertheless, Wilson didn't want war and if there were some way he could bring about a peace that would be satisfactory to the Allies, he would have been delighted. In 1915, and again in 1916, he sent his good friend, Edward Mandell

("Colonel") House (1858–1938), to Europe to see if some sort of peace could be arranged. It turned out that every single one of the warring nations wanted peace, but only if the other side made all the concessions.

Still, Wilson ran for reelection in 1916 on the slogan, "He kept us out of war." His opponent was Charles Evans Hughes (1862–1948), who was the last presidential candidate for a major party to sport a beard. Wilson won, but only narrowly. It seemed that Hughes had offended Hiram Warren Johnson (1866–1945), the governor of California. Johnson did not labor to get out the full Republican vote so that Hughes lost California, and the election.

In the spring of 1917, Germany resumed unrestricted submarine warfare. When an American ship, *Housatonic*, was sunk on February 3, 1917, the United States broke diplomatic relations with Germany.

Wilson tried to get Congress to pass a law permitting the arming of merchant ships, but a group of antiwar senators, led by LaFollette, filibustered it to death with endless, repetitious debate. Wilson, unfortunately, did not have the trick of working with opposition. He was always certain he was right and simply would not compromise. He would remain stiff and unyielding and lose everything rather than bend a little and gain most of what he wanted.

What Wilson needed, then, was some act by Germany that would drive the American people into taking the actions that Wilson thought would be necessary. This Germany supplied.

The German Foreign Minister, Arthur Zimmermann (1864–1940), thought he could persuade Mexico to make war on the United States and thus take its mind off Germany. In order to bribe Mexico into doing this, he prepared a telegram that offered it Texas, New Mexico, and Arizona if it would go to war on the United States.

The British intercepted and decoded the telegram. Scarcely able to believe their good fortune, they turned it over to the United States on February 24, 1917. By March 1, the American government was convinced that the "Zimmermann Telegram" was legitimate and its indignation was boundless, as was that of the American people. In all its history, the United States had never had a square inch of territory taken from it by force, and the thought that anyone could contemplate such a possibility seemed to go against cosmic law.

Then, too, Russia had collapsed and seemed to be turning into a democratic republic. That removed the one ideological flaw in the notion of helping the British and French. It no longer meant helping the Russian despotism.

The United States recognized the new Russian government on March 22, 1917, the first nation to do so, and Wilson soon began to describe World War I as something that would "make the world safe for democracy."

What's more, on March 21, 1917, a German submarine had sunk another American ship, *Healdton*, and Wilson called a special session of Congress. It passed a war resolution and, on April 6, 1917, the United States was at war with Germany.

The United States at once began to send an "American Expeditionary Force" (AEF) to Europe, and not one American soldier lost his life in the crossing.

The first American contingents arrived in France on June 26, 1917. They were under the command of Pershing and he marched his troops through Paris on July 4, 1917, as an Independence Day celebration. They marched to the tomb of Lafayette, the great French volunteer in the War of the American Revolution. Pershing asked a fellow officer, Charles E. Stanton, to say something appropriate, and he remarked, simply, "Lafayette! We are here." No greater eloquence, at any length, was possible.

The British and French wanted to use the American troops as they came across, feeding them into British and French divisions as reinforcements. This Pershing prevented. He saw that Americans, a few at a time in Allied divisions, would be used to no purpose and no credit. He insisted, instead, that the Americans would form their own divisions and go into battle as units under their own commanders, and in this he was firmly supported by Wilson.

It was not until October 23, 1917 that any American fired a shot against the Germans, but by that winter there were over 100,000 Americans in France, with more pouring into the country every day.

At home, America went on a patriotism spree that went to cheap and ridiculous lengths. As many as 1500 pacifists were arrested and many were thrown in jail. German books were thrown out of libraries, German music out of the repertoires, and German food out of the menus. Beethoven and Goethe were somehow confused with the Kaiser and Ludendorff, and sauerkraut was renamed "liberty cabbage." People actually kicked dachsunds.

Wilson felt that the Allied war aims were not idealistic enough. The Russian revolutionaries published the secret treaties that the Allies had made and it seemed they were as greedy as the Germans were. It was necessary to give the cause a higher tone. On January 8, 1918, therefore, Wilson published his "Fourteen Points," which were intended to guide the peace once the war was over.

Simply, the 14 points were:

1. All treaties were to be arrived at in public and published.
2. Freedom of the seas.
3. No economic barriers to prevent free trade.
4. As much disarmament as possible.
5. Settlement of colonial claims, with consideration for natives.
6. No interference with the new Russian government.
7. Evacuation of Belgium.
8. Evacuation of France and the return of Alsace-Lorraine.
9. Italy to gain Italian-speaking parts of Austria-Hungary.
10. Freedom for Austria-Hungary's minorities.
11. Balkan boundaries to follow nationality, and Serbia to have access to the sea.
12. Freedom for Ottoman Empire's minorities, and free access to the straits.
13. An independent Poland with access to the sea.
14. A League of Nations to settle disputes and prevent war.

These 14 points were mostly at the expense of Germany, Austria-Hungary, and the Ottoman Empire, but the Allies were unenthusiastic. They were not delighted over public treaty-making, freedom of the seas, disarmament, and consideration for colonial natives. It was all too noble for them.

The Americans had time to win a few battles against the Germans before the war ended on November 11, 1918. The United States lost 115,000 soldiers, and 206,000 were wounded.

Within a month, President Wilson was off to the peace conference, arriving in Europe on December 13, 1918. There he was met with the wildest enthusiasm. He seemed to the cheering people to be the messiah from the west come to solve all of old Europe's problems. He seemed to bring with him a vision of peace and justice.

It all went to Wilson's head. He had, in any case, the conviction that he alone knew what was right, and now he seemed to think everyone else thought so, too.

However, he found out quickly enough that when his idealism ran counter to any nation's selfish desires, the leaders and the people of that nation suddenly turned against him.

He had to deal with Lloyd George of Great Britain and Clemenceau of France. These two, with Wilson, made up the "Big Three." None of the defeated powers were represented, of course. Russia was not there, for the coming of Communism had put it beyond the pale. The lesser powers who had fought on the side of the Big Three were there, of course, but they were rarely listened to.

Wilson found that Lloyd George and Clemenceau were unmoved by him. Clemenceau, in particular, was not impressed by the Fourteen Points, muttering that even God had had only 10.

Lloyd George was for a moderate peace that would make it possible for Germany to rejoin the family of nations under conditions where it would no longer threaten Great Britain. However, even as he arrived for the peace negotiations, there was the "khaki election" in Great Britain (so-called because the returning soldiers voted in it) in which Lloyd George won a huge

majority by pandering to the desire of the British public for revenge. This made it difficult for him to push moderation.

As for Clemenceau, moderation was the last thing he wanted. He was ready to squeeze Germany dry, not only for the damage it had inflicted on France over the previous four years, but for what it had done to France in 1870 (something Clemenceau remembered well).

Wilson was particularly interested in the League of Nations, which was his brain-child. It seemed to him that any imperfections in the treaty that was being prepared could be ironed out by the League afterward, and that a golden period of peace and prosperity would come about, with all disputes settled by amicable displays of reason in the public meetings of the League.

It was only after the victors had squabbled out the treaty (called the "Treaty of Versailles" because the meetings were held in the old palace of the French kings, where, 49 years earlier, the creation of the German Empire had been announced) that the Germans were allowed to see it. They were called in on May 7, 1919, and they protested vehemently at the many injustices they saw in it, but there was no way out. The Germans would have to sign, but they could make one last gesture of defiance.

On June 21, 1919, the German fleet, sailing into British captivity, was scuttled by its own crews. If the Germans couldn't have their fleet, neither could their enemies.

The Germans signed the Treaty of Versailles on June 28, 1919 and, by its terms, Germany gave up territory all round. All its African colonies passed into the hands of Great Britain or France. It had to return Alsace-Lorraine to France. The French could also exploit the coal mines of the Saar, a small district, rich in coal, on the German border, to make up for the mines that had been ravished in its own northeast. Belgium and Denmark each got small strips of adjoining German territory.

A Polish nation was established that would include territory which Prussia had gained in the First Partition of Poland, a century and a half earlier. Poland had access to the sea at the German city of Danzig, which was made into a "Free City." This meant that East Prussia, while remaining part of Germany, was cut off from the rest by Polish territory. Some other parts of Germany were to be allowed to vote on whether to remain part of Germany or not (and they all voted to remain with Germany).

Germany was forced to have an army of no more than 100,000 men, and a navy of not more than six warships. It was to be allowed no submarines and no military aircraft. Heligoland was to be defortified, and the western portion of Germany on the French border (the "Rhineland") was not to be fortified.

The United States Senate, however, would not ratify the treaty, largely because it didn't want the League of Nations—which, many senators feared, would limit national sovereignty. Wilson absolutely refused to accept any changes; and whereas he would have had most of what he wanted if he were willing to give up something, he ended with nothing.

He began a tour of the United States to push the treaty (still dreaming of the wild crowds that had greeted his trip to Europe), but he found the task frustrating. Moreover, he had a stroke that put an end to the trip and left the United States virtually without a president for the last year of his administration.

Nor was it only the Senate that was against all that Wilson now stood for. After the heady experience of the war, the American people seemed disillusioned with the whole business and returned to a firm isolationism, deciding that Europe could do whatever it wanted to do, and that the United States should just mind its own business.

During the World War I period, life in the United States had undergone a number of changes. The first woman to enter Congress was Jeannette Rankin (1880–1973) of Montana (where women could vote). She was elected in 1916 and was the only member of the House of Representatives to vote against entrance into World War I. The result was that she was defeated for reelection in 1918.

Louis Dembitz Brandeis (1856–1941), one of the United States' greatest lawyers, was ap-

pointed by Wilson to the Supreme Court in 1916. This met with considerable opposition, because Brandeis had committed the terrible crime of being Jewish, but his appointment was confirmed anyhow.

Women were bobbing their hair. It began because long hair was a safety hazard when working with machinery, as many women did for the sake of the war effort. When the reason vanished, short hair remained convenient and became common. Some women kept their hair long, but only as a matter of taste, and not out of social necessity. Women also attained the greater freedom of shorter skirts, and less elaborate undergarments. A misuse of freedom came when smoking grew common among women, so that they were subjected to the same ills of foul odors and disease to which men were accustomed.

Automobile traffic was becoming a major form of transportation, and the first traffic lights were set up in Cleveland on August 5, 1914. In 1915, motor taxicabs came into use in the United States.

Long-distance telephone lines now spanned the nation. On January 25, 1915, Bell (the inventor of the telephone) once again spoke to his coworker Watson, as he had when it was first invented. This time, however, they were not on different floors of a house. Bell was in New York and Watson was in San Francisco.

Daylight saving time was designed to get people up earlier and to bed earlier during the long summer days, thus using less energy for artificial light. It was introduced in Great Britain during the war years and came to the United States in 1918.

Motion pictures continued to increase in popularity. In 1915, the first of the great movies, *The Birth of a Nation,* made its appearance. It had been directed by David Lewelyn Wark Griffith (1875–1948), who invented many of the camera techniques, such as closeups, panshots, fade-in and fade-out, cross-cutting, soft-focus, and so on, which have been used in motion pictures ever since.

The first radio broadcasting station opened in 1920.

On January 29, 1919, the Prohibitionists finally

won their victory when the Eighteenth Amendment to the Constitution was ratified. The sale of intoxicating liquors was banned and, on October 29, 1919, the Volstead Act, introduced by Andrew John Volstead (1860–1947), defined an intoxicating liquor as anything containing more than ½ of 1% of alcohol. (It may be that Prohibition won out at this time because of the popular conception that most breweries and distilleries were run by people of German descent.)

The year 1918 saw the worst worldwide epidemic (a "pandemic") suffered by the human species since the Black Death, five and a half centuries earlier. A new strain of influenza swept the world. It was called the "Spanish flu" because Spain suffered particularly badly, but it seems to have had its beginning in China. It killed perhaps 20 million people in the course of the year, including 500,000 in the United States. Far more people died of the flu in that year than were killed in the four years of World War I.

In science in this period, Harlow Shapley (1885–1972) made use of the Cepheid yardstick worked out by Leavitt a few years earlier. By 1918, he had demonstrated a size for our Milky Way Galaxy that was, for the first time, not an underestimate. (Actually, it was a slight overestimate.) He was also able to show that the Sun was not at the center of the galaxy, but well out toward one end.

In 1916, Gilbert Newton Lewis (1875–1946) advanced a new way of looking at the manner in which atoms clung together in molecules. He made use of the new notions of atomic structure and drew up a logical scheme of how electrons were shared by two adjoining atoms or were transferred from one atom to another.

Irving Langmuir worked out a similar scheme independently, and for his fundamental work on the interaction of metal surfaces with gas molecules, he eventually received a Nobel Prize. He was the first industrial chemist to receive one.

Edward Calvin Kendall (1886–1972) isolated the hormone, thyroxine, from the thyroid gland in 1916. It became an important item in the medical armory, the first hormone to be used in this manner.

Beginning in 1916, Clarence Birdseye (1886–1956) developed methods for the quick-freezing of food. This kept it fresh over long periods of time and preserved the natural taste more truly than canning did. It added another revolution to the modern diet.

In literature, Edith Wharton published *The Age of Innocence* in 1920 and won a Pulitzer prize for it. Willa Cather published *My Ántonia* in 1918. Sherwood Anderson (1876–1941) gained his reputation for naturalistic short stories with *Winesburg, Ohio* (1919).

Harry Sinclair Lewis (1885–1951) was starting his writing career in this period and made his first big hit with *Main Street* (1920) and its satire of American small-town life. Booth Tarkington published his studies of youngsters with *Penrod* (1914) and *Seventeen* (1917). He won the Pulitzer prize with *The Magnificent Ambersons* (1918).

On a lighter note, Ringgold Wilmer ("Ring") Lardner (1885–1933) wrote effective humor in *You Know Me, Al* (1915) and *Gullible's Travels* (1917).

Among the American poets of the period, Edward Arlington Robinson (1869–1935) was writing such poems as *Merlin* (1917) and *Lancelot* (1920). Carl Sandburg (1878–1967) was writing powerful free verse in his *Chicago Poems* (1915). Thomas Stearns Eliot (1888–1965), who became a British subject later in life, published *Prufrock and Other Observations* (1917). Edgar Lee Masters (1869–1950) published *The Spoon River Anthology* in 1915. Edna St. Vincent Millay (1892–1950) made her first mark with *Renascence and Other Poems* (1917). Alan Seeger (1888–1916) was another promising poet who died in World War I after writing the prophetic lines: "I have a rendezvous with death / At some disputed barricade."

On a far lower note, Edgar Albert Guest (1881–1959) became the poet laureate of the average American with poems in a rustic dialect, the first of which were collected in *A Heap o' Livin'* in 1916.

George M. Cohan continued his musical career with what was undoubtedly his most stirring song, *Over There,* to celebrate the entry of the United States into the war. Norman Rockwell (1894–1978) began his career as a naturalistic painter, especially on the covers of "The Saturday Evening Post," and became the best-known painter in the United States.

A religious phenomenon of the period was George Baker, a black revivalist preacher, who founded his "Peace Mission" movement in 1919. Calling himself "Father Divine," Baker became an important personage to many blacks for decades.

RUSSIA

World War I started hopefully for the Russians. Two armies invaded East Prussia and other armies invaded Galicia, the northeastern region of Austria-Hungary. Though the Russians held their positions in Galicia for a while, the armies in East Prussia were destroyed by the beginning of September, 1914.

The Russians fought on as stoutly as they could in Austria-Hungary, but eventually the Germans were able to send sizable reinforcements southward to stiffen the Austro–Hungarians. By then, the Russians had used up their supplies and were short of everything an army needed for fighting.

By mid-1915, after a year of fighting, the Russians had been cleared out of Austria-Hungary and most of Poland was in German hands. Back home, the Russian population had no trouble seeing that the Russians were losing, not because they couldn't fight (no one ever accused Russian soldiers of that), but because the Russian leadership was either thoroughly inept or actually treasonous. Many thought the latter.

Therefore, Nicholas II relieved the Grand Duke Nicholas of his post, though he was the only bright spot in the Russian defeat, and sent him to the Caucasus to fight the Turks. Nicholas II then took over the leadership of the army himself on September 15, 1915.

Unfortunately, Nicholas II, though a good and kind man in private life, had no discernible talents at anything beyond that. There was no way in which he could really lead the army. He merely drew on what was supposed to be the mystical awe with which the Russians regarded the Tsar. The soldiers would, supposedly, fight better, and the people at home would be invigorated with new enthusiasm, if the Tsar were at the head of the army.

Actually, the Russian people had long since abandoned that view of the Tsar, and his being head of the army did not alter the military situation at all. What it did do was get the Tsar out of Petrograd (the new Russian equivalent of "St. Petersburg," which had been discarded as too German once the war started) and closer to the front. That left the Tsarina Alexandra in control of the government and the baleful Rasputin in control of her.

On June 4, 1916, the Russian armies under Brusilov (a second capable Russian general) again took the offensive, and again the Russians made surprising advances against the Austro–Hungarians. By September, however, the Germans had again sent sufficient reinforcements to Austria-Hungary and drove the Russians out. The Russians had lost another million men and were worse off than ever.

Suspicions of treason darkened all over Russia, surfacing in the Duma and even in court circles. A group of extreme conservatives among the aristocracy decided the only way to restore sense to the government was to get rid of Rasputin. He was invited to a tea party on the night of December 29, 1916 and was fed poisoned tea and cakes, but that didn't seem to affect him. He was shot twice but that didn't kill him either. Finally he was shoved through the broken ice of the Neva River and was drowned.

But Rasputin's removal didn't bring about any magic change, either.

In March, 1917, there were strikes and riots in Petrograd, and the troops stationed there refused to move against the rioters. With that, the Tsar could not govern. Nicholas II abdicated on March 15, 1917, and the Romanov dynasty came to an end.

A provisional government was set up in Petersburg under Prince Georgy Yevgenyevich Lvov (1861–1925), but the strongest member of the government was Aleksandr Fyodorovich Kerensky (1881–1970), who joined as Minister of

War in mid-May and who succeeded Lvov as Prime Minister in July.

The new government proclaimed civil liberties for all, and tried to set up a democratic regime. Poland was promised independence, while Finland and Estonia were assured self-rule. All sorts of social reforms were planned, too.

The provisional government made one fatal mistake, however. They wanted to be loyal to their allies and to continue the war, but that was impossible. The Russian army would no longer fight; the Russian people wanted only food and peace, and the more radical socialists (then called the Bolsheviks, and later Communists) promised to give them that.

To the Germans, it seemed that their own purposes would be best served if the Communists were in power and moved for peace at any price. For that purpose, they gathered up some of the radicals who were living in exile in Switzerland, and hastened them by train across German territory to Russia.

Among these was Lenin. Joining him, from exile in the United States, was Lev Davidovich Bronstein, who like most of the radicals, including Lenin himself, used a pseudonym to protect himself and his family, and was better known as "Leon Trotsky."

What Lenin wanted was to have the Communists take over the government, to stop the war at once (even if that meant signing a separate peace), and then to distribute the land to the peasants and hand over the factories to the workers.

Kerensky went in the opposite direction and ordered a new offensive in Galicia. This got nowhere, and the Germans advanced and took Riga, coming perilously close to Petrograd. Brusilov, who had done his best, was replaced by Lavr Georgyevich Kornilov (1870–1918), who thought the best thing he could do was to march on Petrograd and overthrow the provisional government.

This failed, because he couldn't get the soldiers to follow him, since they just wanted to go home. Second, Kerensky made common cause with the Communists against Kornilov.

Once the Kornilov effort was beaten, Kerensky found that he had put himself in the power of the Communists, who were getting stronger as the desire for peace became overpowering.

On November 6, 1917, the Communists ousted Kerensky (who escaped, going into exile for the rest of his long life) and took over the government. Russia was using the old Julian calendar at the time and the Julian date was October 24, 1917, so that the Russians speak of the "October Revolution."

The new government was headed by Lenin. Trotsky was the Foreign Minister, and the person in charge of minorities was Iosif Vissarionvich Dzhugashvili (1879–1953), who became far better known by his pseudonym of "Joseph Stalin."

The Communists nationalized everything they could, Church property was confiscated. The national debt was repudiated as having been incurred by the Tsar, not the people. (This was a mistake, for it made deadly enemies out of all businessmen, bankers, and foreign governments to whom Russia owed money.) On a smaller scale, they introduced rationing and accepted the Gregorian calendar as of January 31, 1918.

What's more, with the Germans uncomfortably close to Petrograd, the capital of the nation was moved to Moscow, from which Peter the Great had taken it two centuries earlier, and there it was to remain.

The nation, however, was falling apart. Poland, Finland, Estonia, and Latvia had all declared themselves independent. So had the Ukraine and Bessarabia (which was on the Rumanian border). The entire western border of what had been the Russian Empire had become a congerie of independent nations. That suited Germany perfectly, for it foresaw that they would all be German puppets and that Russia itself, fatally wounded, would withdraw into its Asian fastnesses and be a cipher in the Europe of the future.

Nevertheless, Lenin had to make peace. He had promised peace and Russia was, in any case, incapable of making war. On January 4, 1918, peace negotiations began, and Trotsky, who was the negotiator for Russia, saw at once that Germany was determined to extract every last drop of blood out of what it considered a Russian corpse. In fact, by February 1, the Germans had signed a separate peace treaty with the Ukraine, which the Russians always thought of as an integral part of the land.

Trotsky, therefore, proclaimed that the war was over, and that there would be no treaty of peace. That also suited the Germans. They began to advance again and moved within a hundred miles of Petrograd.

Lenin thereupon overruled Trotsky and decided that Russia would have to give in so that a core of Communist rule could be saved. Later on, he was sure, all would be taken back, but for the moment, Russia would have to bend its back to the German whip.

The Treaty of Brest-Litovsk (in what was becoming Poland) was signed on March 3, 1918. The Germans, who later would loudly complain of the injustice of the Treaty of Versailles, inflicted a much harsher treaty on the Russians (one that shows what they would have done to the west, had they won the war). All the Russian borderlands, including the Ukraine and Trans-caucasia, were confirmed as independent. German forces occupied Finland and the Ukraine, and there were plans to use the Ukraine's wheatfields to counter the British blockade and feed the German people. (The Ukrainians might starve, of course, but the Germans were very philosophical about such things.)

Now was the time for the great push in the west that would end the war in a German victory.

However, the great push in the west failed, and the war ended in a German defeat. Instantly, the Treaty of Brest-Litovsk was no longer operative, but that didn't help the Russians a bit. They were sunk in civil war, and the western powers, furious at the separate peace that had subjected them to the terror of the great 1918 spring offensive, and in dread over the possible spread of communism, intervened in the civil war on the side of the "Whites" (the counterrevolutionaries) and against the "Reds" (the communists.)

Yet even with the world falling about Russian ears, intellectual life continued. Sergey Sergeyevich Prokofiev (1891–1933) made his first mark on the musical world with his *Scythian Suite*, which, when it premiered in Petrograd in 1916, was difficult to accept because of its nontraditional style.

AUSTRIA-HUNGARY

Austria-Hungary, which started the war on July 28, 1914, quickly found itself falling into the background as a much larger war (than anything it had envisaged) developed. All through World War I, Austria-Hungary was completely in the shadow of Germany.

Austria-Hungary was, in fact, unable to fight effectively at all. Its army was built on the German model, but it didn't have the German snap. Most of the officers spoke German, but most of the enlisted men didn't understand either German or each other. What's more, those who were neither German nor Hungarian had no great appetite for dying for Austria-Hungary, so they were easy to defeat and ever ready to surrender. The worst that can be said for the Austro-Hungarian army was that, without German support, it invariably managed to outbumble the Russians.

If anything were needed to set the tone of the humiliation that Austria-Hungary was to experience throughout the war, it was that even the war against Serbia was a failure. It launched an invasion of the tiny nation but was thrown back, and by the end of 1914, the Austro–Hungarians, at the cost of a quarter of a million casualties, found themselves defeated by the Serbians.

In 1915, it was a different matter. German aid drove the Russians out of Austria-Hungary, and Bulgaria entered the war on the Austro-Hungarian side. That meant that Serbia was attacked from the west by Bulgaria as well as from the north by Austria-Hungary. Against this, Serbia could not stand, and by the end of 1915 it was smashed.

On the other hand, Italy had come into the war in 1915 against Austria-Hungary, which now had to fight on the Italian border. Then, in 1916, there came the Brusilov offensive in which once again the Russians drove back the Austro–Hungarians.

Inside the nation, things were disintegrating fast. Austria-Hungary was an empty shell which was simply going through the motions of fighting a war because of unyielding German pressure. The Foreign Minister, Leopold Berchtold (1863–1942), who had arranged the fateful ultimatum to Serbia, was forced to resign on January 13, 1915. The ultraconservative Austro–Hungarian Prime Minister, Karl von Sturgkh (1859–1916), was assassinated on October 21, 1916.

Then, on November 21, 1916, Franz Joseph finally died. He had reigned for 68 years, longer even than the reign of Victoria. He had become Emperor in the confused aftermath of the Revolutions of 1848, had survived the disasters of a losing war with France and another with Prussia, had survived the near-split of the nation into a dual monarchy, had survived a series of family tragedies, and died now in the midst of the worst disaster of all, and with his nation in dying convulsions of its own.

He was succeeded by the grandson of his youngest brother, and the new Emperor reigned as Charles I (1887–1922).

In 1917, German help arrived on the Italian front, and Austria-Hungary won a huge victory over the Italians on October 24, but it wasn't enough. Italy held on, and the minorities within Austria-Hungary clamored for independence.

Charles I tried to negotiate some kind of peace, but it wouldn't work, for Wilson's Fourteen Points called for self-determination for Austria-Hungary's minorities and Charles wasn't ready to preside over his nation's dissolution.

But it was dissolving anyway, and in despair Charles offered, on October 16, 1918, a quadruple monarchy made up of Germans, Poles, Czechs, and South Slavs (with Hungary to make its own arrangements). The situation had gone too far for that, however. Tisza of Hungary was assassinated on October 31, 1918, and Austro-Hungarian armies were collapsing on the Italian front.

On November 3, 1918, Austria-Hungary surrendered and agreed to an armistice, leaving Germany to fight on alone for one more week.

On November 11, 1918, the day when the Germans themselves surrendered, Charles I abandoned all political authority. He didn't actually abdicate, but it amounted to the same thing. The Hapsburgs had joined the Hohenzollerns of Germany and the Romanovs of Russia in the ashheap of history, six and a quarter centuries after the first Hapsburg Emperor.

Austria and Hungary were dealt with separately in the peace settlements that followed. Austria signed the Treaty of St. Germain on September 10, 1919; Hungary signed the Treaty of Trianon on June 4, 1920. (All the treaties after World War I were named for the Paris suburbs in which the peace negotiators met.)

Austria and Hungary became two separate nations, each consisting only of its core: the German-speaking core for Austria, the Hungarian-speaking core for Hungary. The minorities were shorn away.

The new nation of Czechoslovakia was formed out of northern Austria-Hungary. Polish regions became part of an independent Poland. Romanian areas in the east joined Romania, and Slavic areas in the south joined Serbia to form the enlarged nation of Yugoslavia. Some Austrian regions were transferred to Italy.

Both Austria and Hungary had to pay reparations, and had to promise to limit their armies. What's more, Austria was forbidden to join with Germany, even though now that it had been shorn of its non-German territories, it might have made sense for the union to take place.

ITALY

When World War I began, Italy had been part of the Triple Alliance, along with Germany and Austria-Hungary, for 32 years. By the terms of that alliance, it might have been expected to join the two in the war.

Italy, however, was not really prepared for war. Nor was it enamored of fighting on the Austro–Hungarian side, since it had ambitions to annex Italian-speaking parts of southern Austria-

Hungary. Finally, it wanted to let the two sides bid for Italy's help.

The Prime Minister of Italy at the time World War I began was Antonio Salandra (1853–1931), who took refuge in the legalism that the Triple Alliance was a defensive one. Since Austria-Hungary had invaded Serbia, that war was offensive and Italy was not compelled to join. Therefore, Salandra declared Italian neutrality.

Italy then spent 10 months in secret negotiations to see what each side would promise. Here the Allies had the advantage, for they could easily promise more Austro–Hungarian territory than Austria-Hungary could itself. After all, it is always easier to be generous when you are buying something with someone else's money. The result was that, on April 26, 1915, the Allies and Italy agreed to the Treaty of London, which was kept secret, and which outlined all the territory Italy was to have in the peace settlement.

Despite the bribes, it was not easy for Italy to enter the war, for there was a strong neutralist feeling in the nation. After all, anyone watching the progress of the first year of the war would require only a moderate amount of sanity to want to stay out.

The Italian socialists were anti-war, but one of the loudest of them, Benito Mussolini, suddenly broke with the party and became stridently pro-war. In light of the man's later career and of the knowledge we have of his character, we can be quite certain he was bribed to do so.

On May 23, 1915, then, Italy declared war on Austria-Hungary, but not on Germany.

There was no point in trying to fight in the Alps, so Italy could strike only northeastward toward the Austro–Hungarian port city of Trieste (which Italy wanted for itself). The Isonzo River flows into the Adriatic Sea near the Italian border there, and over the space of the next two years the Italians and Austro–Hungarians fought 11 "Battles of the Isonzo," which produced no significant advance in either direction and simply piled up the casualties.

After the first failures at the Isonzo, Salandra was forced to resign in June of 1916, and Paolo Boselli (1838–1932) became Prime Minister. He finally declared war on Germany on August 28, 1916, in the hope that this would stimulate the Allies into sending Italy more supplies.

The Germans, however, who had honored their neutrality and refused to help Austria-Hungary on the Italian front, now took a more active part. They sent help southward, including a general, Otto Below (1857–1944). Below had fought at Tannenberg and the Masurian Lakes, and he made preparations for a surprise attack.

On October 24, 1917, that surprise attack, preceded by an intensive artillery bombardment and taking advantage of mist and rain, struck the Italian lines at the Austro–Hungarian town of Caparetto, which was nearly at the Italian border (so little had either army achieved in two years of fighting).

Under the sudden onslaught of this "Battle of Caporetto" (sometimes called the "Twelfth Battle of Isonzo"), the Italian line crumpled. In three weeks, the Italians were driven back 50 miles and found themselves near Venice. Some 40,000 Italians were killed or wounded and 275,000 were taken prisoner. The defeat almost put Italy out of the war and, had the Austro–Hungarian army been better equipped, the advance might have continued.

The Italian commander-in-chief, Luigi Cadorna (1850–1928), was relieved of his command after the battle, and was replaced by Armando Diaz (1861–1928), who managed to keep the Italian army intact and who organized a defense on the new line. The Boselli cabinet was also forced out, and Vittorio Emanuele Orlando (1860–1952) became the new Prime Minister.

In 1918, with Russia completely out of the war, and with Germany engaged in its do-or-die offensive in the west, Austria-Hungary was pushed by the Germans into one last offensive on the Italian front. On June 15, 1918, that offensive was launched. Diaz, fighting skillfully enough, managed to blunt that offensive by June 25, but did not follow up with the immediate counterattack that Allied commander-in-chief, Foch, demanded.

Instead, Diaz cautiously waited until he was sure that the German spring offensive had failed.

Then, in July, he began his counteroffensive. The Austrians resisted with surprising effectiveness, but now, finally, British and French troops were in the line and even some Americans: On October 24, 1918, when Austria-Hungary was, in any case, on the point of death, the Italian forces began the "Battle of Vittorio Veneto," which forced Austria-Hungary out of the war.

Orlando and his foreign minister, Giorgio Sidney Sonnino (1847–1922), represented Italy at the negotiations leading to the Treaty of Versailles. At those negotiations, Italy was disappointed. It got the Italian-speaking areas of Austria-Hungary, largely because there was nothing else to do with them. That meant Italy gained the districts of Trent and Trieste.

The Treaty of London, however, which had preceded Italy's entrance into the war, had promised the Italians the Dalmatian coast along the eastern shore of the Adriatic. However, President Wilson would not hear of that. The Dalmatian coast was Slavic and it had to be part of an expanded Serbia. (The Allies might also have been influenced by the fact that Serbia had fought better than expected, and that Italy had not.) Furthermore, Italy received no part of the German African colonies, which were divided between Great Britain and France.

The result was that Italy came out of the war with no sense of having won glorious victories (Vittorio Veneta was practically a battle with a corpse), with the added bitterness of feeling that it had been cheated out of what it had been promised. All it had was an enormous national debt, a high cost of living, and the promise of further misery. The country was in a general state of resentment and shock, and disorders grew continually worse.

During the war, Ottorino Respighi (1879–1936) was composing music, producing, notably, "The Fountains of Rome" in 1917. Luigi Pirandello (1867–1936) was writing, and was eventually to win a Nobel Prize in literature. Vilfredo Pareto (1848–1923) was a sociologist, whose *Treatise on General Sociology* (1916) favored elitism and was strongly antidemocratic. It served as a philosophical basis for the coming wave of reaction that was to sweep first Italy and, later, much of the rest of Europe. Rafael Sabatini (1875–1950), writing in English, made his first big success as a writer of historical novels with *Sea-Hawk* (1915).

PAPACY

During World War I, Benedict XV (1854–1922) was Pope. There was nothing he could do but to push vainly for peace, and to do what he could to carry out relief work. The decline of the political power of the Papacy was indicated by the fact that at the peace negotiation, the Papacy was not represented, nor was its advice sought.

SERBIA/YUGOSLAVIA

Serbia resolutely fought off the Austro–Hungarian invasion at the start of World War I. It was not until December 2, 1914, that the Austro-Hungarians were able to take Belgrade, the Serbian capital, even though it was just across the Danube River from Austria-Hungary. What's more, the Serbians managed to retake it on December 15.

On October 14, 1915, however, Bulgaria, remembering its loss at Serbian hands in the Second Balkan War two years earlier, decided to take advantage of the situation to even the score. It joined the Central Powers and declared war on Serbia.

At that time, the Austro–Hungarians were invading Serbia again, this time with German help. As those armies came down from the north, the Bulgarians struck from the east. Until that time, the Serbians under Radomir Putnik (1847–1917) had done very well, but now they were outnumbered two to one, and they had no choice but to retreat. They made their way to the Albanian coast where some, in January 1916, were taken off to the island of Corfu. Austro–Hungarian forces then occupied all of Serbia and Montenegro.

Serbian troops kept fighting during the remainder of the war under Allied command, however, in other parts of the Balkans.

Serbia looked forward to the end of the war,

assuming Austria-Hungary's defeat. It wanted to form, with Montenegro, a South-Slav kingdom, which would be a Greater Serbia, including Bosnia, Herzegovina, Croatia, and Slovenia (all of which were under Austro–Hungarian rule). The Croats and Slovenes, however, were Catholic, used the Roman alphabet, and had long been under central-European influence. They considered themselves more civilized than the other South Slavs, many of whom were Orthodox, used the Cyrillic alphabet, and had long been under Ottoman rule.

Despite these potential incompatibilities, representatives of the various areas carried through negotiations on the island of Corfu and, on July 20, 1917, agreed to form a single nation, to be ruled by the Serbian king.

Once the war was over, Montenegro joined Serbia on November 26, 1918, and King Nicholas of Montenegro was ousted from the throne. On December 4, 1918, the "Kingdom of the Serbs, Croats, and Slovenes" was brought into being, though it came to be far better known as "Yugoslavia."

OTTOMAN EMPIRE

At the start of World War I, the Ottoman Empire was markedly pro-German. Two German cruisers, the *Goeben* and the *Breslau*, dashed eastward through the Mediterranean Sea on August 4, 1914. They did so before Great Britain had actually declared war, so British ships did not interfere. By the time Great Britain entered the war, the cruisers could not be caught, and they arrived safely in Constantinople.

That feat, combined with the German victories in Belgium and in East Prussia, convinced the Ottoman government that it would be worthwhile to back the Germans. Therefore, they entered the war on the side of the Germans on October 29, 1914. Even before the formal declaration, the two German cruisers (now part of the Ottoman navy) had, without warning, bombarded Russian ports on the Black Sea coast.

Limon van Sanders, the Ottoman Empire's German adviser, wanted the Turks to land at Odessa and to push northward into the Ukraine.

That was probably a good idea, but the strongest of the Ottoman leaders of the time, Enver Pasha, preferred to fight in the Caucasus on the northeast frontier—perhaps because gains there could more easily be incorporated into the Ottoman realm. As it happened, though, it was a mountainous area, where fighting was difficult, and where the Ottoman army got nowhere.

As for the British, they rushed troops to Cyprus and to Egypt to protect the Suez Canal. Troops from India moved up the Persian Gulf and landed at the southern tip of Mesopotamia, which was part of the Ottoman Empire. They took Basra, an important oil center near the mouth of the Tigris–Euphrates River, on November 23, 1914.

The main difficulty introduced by Turkey's entrance into the war was that it broke off sea-communications between the western Allies and Russia. This was serious, for Russia depended on the west for supplies, and one of the many reasons for Russia's dismal showing in World War I was that Russian soldiers lacked the arms and ammunition that might have reached them in quantity if the Ottoman Empire were on the Allied side, or at least neutral.

Something had to be done about that, and this raised a dispute among the western Allies. To some in Great Britain, it seemed that the direct fighting in France ought to be left to the French, while the British used their sea-power to deliver blows at the periphery. Winston Churchill, who was the First Lord of the Admiralty, was very much in favor of this—as a matter of fact, it was a British policy that had worked, in the long run, in the battle against Napoleon.

Naturally, the French wanted the British in France, and the fighting there was so difficult and bloody that the British could not simply move out without losing the continent. The Russians, however, who were being driven back in Poland, appealed for an allied offensive against the Ottoman Empire to reopen communications.

Eventually, the British tried to do both. They kept their strong presence in France, but they also sent troops to force their way up the narrow straits to Constantinople. After a preliminary naval bombardment, the Allied troops landed on the Gallipoli peninsula on the European side of the straits on April 25, 1915.

The force was none too large for the purpose, but the real trouble was that it was ineptly handled. There were troops from France and Australia as well as from Great Britain and they did not coordinate their attacks well. The British army and navy were under separate leadership, too, and did not cooperate properly. In addition, none of the people in charge were first-class. Added to all that, the reinforcements came in small batches and were never in quite enough quantity to do the job.

On the Ottoman side, Liman von Sanders conducted a brilliant defense that was ably seconded by an Ottoman general, Mustafa Kemal (1881–1938).

The Gallipoli campaign turned out to be an unequivocal disaster for the British, and by the end of 1916 they withdrew. Winston Churchill lost his job and it was many years before he regained his influence. As for the Russians, they remained permanently cut off, and it is possible to argue that the Russian Revolution might not have happened, or might have taken a different course, had it not been for the British failure at Gallipoli.

Elsewhere, the Ottoman Empire was less fortunate. The fighting in the Caucasus continued, but the Ottomans lost heavily and they vented their frustration by instituting a massacre of Armenians on the grounds that they were helping the Russians. Actually, what was really helping the Russians was, first, Ottoman ineptitude; and, second, the fact that the Grand Duke Nicholas was put in charge of the fighting there and that in Nikolay Nikolayevich Yudenich (1862–1933) the Russians had one of their few competent generals. The Russians were deep in northeastern Turkey when the abdication of the Tsar put an end to the fighting.

Elsewhere, the British fought off attacks by Ottoman forces on the Suez Canal. This was done without undue trouble but, in the early stages of the Gallipoli campaign, the necessity of keeping troops in Egypt for the Suez defense stood in the way of sending sufficient reinforcements to the Dardanelles.

The British were also continuing to force their way up the Tigris River. It was hard work, for the supply lines were long, and here, too, there was a divided command. The British were aiming at Baghdad; however, at Kut, a hundred miles short of the goal, they were stopped, and a British army of 8000 (including 6000 Indian troops) was forced to surrender on April 19, 1916.

The British regrouped farther south and began a new offensive in 1917. This time they defeated the Turks at Kut and took the city on February 23, 1917. They went on to take Baghdad on March 11 and, by the end of the war, the British were in control of the Mosul oil fields, 220 miles north of Baghdad, and all of Mesopotamia was under their occupation.

In Arabia, the British and French had been negotiating with Arab chieftains in regions long subject to the Ottoman Empire. On June 5, 1916, the Arabs revolted. Husayn ibn Ali (1854–1931), who ruled over the Hejaz (the western coast of Arabia along the Red Sea, including the sacred towns of Mecca and Medina), declared its independence on June 7. On October 19, 1917, he declared himself king of all Arabia. The British, of course, supported him, and began an offensive across the Sinai peninsula toward Palestine, in order to preoccupy the Turkish forces and keep the Arab revolt going.

In 1917, the British were stopped at Gaza in southern Palestine, and Edmund Henry Hynman Allenby (1861–1936) was then put in charge of the offensive on June 28, 1917. Helping the Arabs directly was the British officer, Thomas Edward Lawrence (1888–1935), better known as "Lawrence of Arabia."

Allenby attacked the Ottoman forces with new vigor and with great skill. He moved steadily northward and, on December 9, 1917, he took Jerusalem. It was the first time Jerusalem was in Christian hands since the days of the Holy Roman Emperor, Frederick II, nearly seven centuries earlier.

By the end of the war, Allenby had moved farther northward into Lebanon and Syria, and on October 30, 1918, the Ottoman Empire surrendered.

In the peace negotiations that followed the war, the Ottoman Empire was dealt with harshly by the Treaty of Sevres. It lost all its territories outside Asia Minor. Mesopotamia and Palestine came under British control, and Syria and Lebanon under French control. The Hejaz and Armenia were granted independence. Greece was given a section of western Asia Minor about the city of Smyrna where, after five years, a plebiscite was to be held to determine whether it was to remain with Greece or with Turkey.

The Ottoman Empire signed the peace on August 10, 1920, but the Turkish nationalists, under Kemal Pasha, the hero of Gallipoli, had no intention of honoring the treaty.

BULGARIA

Bulgaria was neutral at the start of the war, but both sides wanted its aid desperately: the Germans as a way of opening the path to the Ottoman Empire, the western Allies as a way of opening a path to Russia. In this case, it was the Germans who could bid higher, for the territory coveted by Bulgaria was Serbian and Greek, and Germany didn't mind giving that away.

Therefore, Bulgaria joined the fighting on the German side, on October 19, 1915, bringing the number of Central Powers to four: Germany, Austria-Hungary, Bulgaria, and the Ottoman Empire. Bulgaria helped defeat Serbia in 1915.

However, Allied forces were gathering at Salonika in northeastern Greece, and a Serbian army was being rebuilt there. Italian forces landed in Albania. In both places, it meant that Bulgarian forces had to continue fighting even though Serbia was defeated and occupied.

There was a long stalemate but, in September, 1918, with the Central Powers clearly on their last legs, an Allied thrust from Greece northward into Bulgaria defeated the Bulgarian army completely. On September 29, 1918, Bulgaria surrendered. As it had been the last to join the Central Powers, it was the first to leave.

By the Treaty of Neuilly, signed on November 27, 1919, Bulgaria had to cede to Greece its Thracian province, which was its opening to the Ae-

gean Sea. Its only seacoast, thereafter, was on the Black Sea. It had to reduce its army and pay reparations, too.

ROMANIA

Romania was neutral at the start of World War I, but it was tempted to join in on the Allied side, for if Austria-Hungary was defeated, then the large Romanian-speaking province of Transylvania in eastern Hungary might be annexed.

When the Brusilov offensive was gaining ground and the Russians were advancing into northeastern Austria-Hungary in 1916, Romania thought that Austria-Hungary was through and it declared war on that nation.

Romania had miscalculated, however. Austria-Hungary might indeed have been on its last legs, but Germany wasn't. Germany declared war on Romania on August 27, 1916, and at once launched an offensive. Leading the German armies were Mackenson, the victor at Masurian Lakes, and Falkenhayn, who had been relieved from his earlier post as commander-in-chief. They had no trouble in crushing the Romanians and, within four months, Romania was occupied and out of the war.

On May 7, 1918, Romania was forced to sign the Treaty of Bucharest. It yielded minor bits of territory to Bulgaria and to Austria-Hungary. On the other hand, it annexed Bessarabia on its western frontier. (The province had been Russian, but Russia was in no position to prevent it.)

When, half a year later, the Central Powers were defeated, Romania obtained its reward. The peace treaties assigned it Transylvania, and allowed it to keep Bessarabia. Thus, it had gained sizable provinces both on the west and east.

ALBANIA

Albania had only been independent a year when World War I broke out. Although it was not itself engaged, it served as a battleground between Austro–Hungarian forces arriving in Albania after having occupied Serbia and Montenegro, and Italian forces arriving from across the Adriatic.

GREECE

Greece was neutral at the start of the war, which was perhaps the result of a cancellation of opposite views. The Greek Prime Minister, Venizelos, was in favor of entering the war on the side of the Allies, but the Greek king, Constantine I, was strongly pro-German.

Once Bulgaria showed signs that it would enter the war on the German side, however, Greece grew uneasy. Bulgaria might well demand territory and grow too strong. Venizelos, who had lost the Prime Ministership on March 16, 1915, because he had advocated help to Great Britain at Gallipoli, was back in power on August 22. He now suggested that the Allies send troops to Salonika on the northeastern coast of Greece.

The Allies did land at Salonika on October 3, 1915, but Constantine I stood firm against joining the war, Venizelos was forced out again on October 5. Even though Bulgaria joined the war and Serbia was occupied, Greece remained officially neutral. The Allied forces, therefore, found themselves in an uncomfortable position and the British were ready to leave, but the head of the French forces, Maurice Paul Emmanuel Sarrail (1856–1929), insisted on staying.

What the Allies could do, thereafter, was to use their control of the sea to interfere with Greek commerce, and to intrigue to set up a pro-Allies government. On September 29, 1916, Venizelos established a pro-Allies provisional government in his native Crete, where he was safe behind the British fleet. On October 9, 1916, he came to Salonika.

The number of Allied troops at Salonika continued to rise, but the British, French, and Serbian troops were not under unified command, and military actions were inconclusive. The Allies felt that nothing could be better done unless Greece joined the war officially. On June 11, 1917, they demanded that Constantine I abdicate, and Allied forces began to spread southward into the heart of Greece.

Constantine I, realizing that he had come to the end of the line, abdicated on June 12. His second son succeeded to the throne and ruled as Alexander I (1893–1920). Alexander called in Venizelos as Prime Minister, yet again, on June 26, 1917, and the next day Greece entered the war on the Allied side.

Sarrail was replaced on December 10, 1917 by the French general, Marie Louis Adolphe Guillaumat (1863–1940), who reorganized the rather demoralized Allied force and brought it to fighting trim. In June 1918, he was in turn replaced by Louis Felix Marie François Franchet d'Esperey (1856–1942), who began at once to organize an offensive. On September 15, 1918, the Allies struck northward. By September 29, the Bulgarian forces had been driven into a wild retreat and Bulgaria surrendered. Franchet d'Esperey continued his drive northward to the Danube, forcing the surrender of Hungary as well.

In the peace treaties that followed, Greece received the Bulgarian province of Thrace, cutting Bulgaria off from the Aegean. It also received the city of Smyrna in Asia Minor.

BELGIUM

Belgium was overrun by the Germans in the first three weeks of the war and, except for an extreme western strip on the Channel, remained under German occupation to the end. Those Belgian troops who retreated into France kept fighting under the leadership of Albert I, who led a contingent of troops forward in the final Allied offensive of the war. In the peace treaties that followed, Belgium gained two small border regions from Germany—Eupen and Malmedy.

NETHERLANDS

The Netherlands remained neutral throughout the war, though it escaped occupation only because the Germans modified the Schlieffen plan in order to spare it. From a purely military standpoint, this was a German mistake.

After his abdication, William II of Germany went to the Netherlands and took up his residence in Doorn in the central regions of the nation. He remained there the rest of his life.

SPAIN

Spain was neutral throughout World War I and, indeed, prospered because there was a great demand for goods of all sorts on the part of the warring nations.

There were, however, troubles of other kinds. Catalonia, the easternmost section of Spain, with Barcelona as its chief city, had once been part of Aragon, and had never been entirely reconciled to its union with, and domination by, Castile, four and a half centuries earlier. Even its language, Catalan, though closely related to Spanish, is not identical to it. During the war years, Catalonian unrest grew high, but the Spanish government was in no mood to give in to demands for autonomy.

What's more, the inhabitants of Spanish Morocco were in a continuing state of rebellion, and the Spaniards got very little good out of this new bit of Empire with which they had burdened themselves.

An outstanding Spanish writer of his period, was Vicente Blasco Ibanez (1867–1928). He was an ardent republican who endured imprisonment on several occasions because of his views, and ended his life in voluntary exile. His most famous book was the antiwar novel, *The Four Horsemen of the Apocalypse*, published in 1916.

PORTUGAL

Portugal honored its long-standing treaty with Great Britain when its legislature voted to declare war on Germany on November 23, 1914, after deciding that Great Britain and France would not be quickly crushed by the Germans. This action was not immediately made effective, however, for there were strong pro-German elements in the army, which seized the government and established two brief military dictatorships, first in 1915 and then in 1917. In the interval between these two rightist regimes, Germany declared war on Portugal on March 9, 1916, because some German ships had been seized in Lisbon. By the

end of the war, there were some Portuguese contingents fighting on the western front.

SWITZERLAND

Switzerland remained neutral in World War I, but it kept its army on a war footing, just in case. Being a landlocked nation, it suffered from a food shortage, but its industries expanded.

DENMARK

Denmark remained neutral in World War I, but it lost an overseas possession as an indirect result of the war. Denmark, for two and a half centuries, had owned three small islands that formed part of the Virgin Island group lying east of Puerto Rico. These were the "Danish West Indies."

The United States feared that a German victory might force the transfer of those islands to Germany, and that a German base there might threaten the newly opened Panama Canal. The United States, therefore, put pressure on Denmark to sell the islands, offering 25 million dollars for them. On August 4, 1916, Denmark agreed, and on January 17, 1917, the transfer to the United States became official.

On April 21, 1918, complete universal suffrage (for women as well as for men) was established in Denmark. On November 30, 1918, Iceland, which had been a Danish possession for over five centuries (and which had been a Norwegian possession before that), was granted its independence. Its only connection with Denmark, thereafter, was that it shared the same king.

By the Treaty of Versailles, a Danish-speaking strip of northern Schleswig, taken by Prussia a half-century earlier, was restored to Denmark, partly on the principle of self-determination, and partly, also, to punish Germany.

NORWAY

Norway remained neutral in World War I, but suffered considerably. It was a sea-faring nation with a large merchant fleet, and many of its ships were sunk during the war by German submarines. Nevertheless, Norway resisted the impulse to go to war over it.

On February 9, 1920, Norway annexed Svalbard (also known as Spitzbergen). It lay so deep in the Arctic Ocean that, until then, no nation had been tempted to own it, though it was used as a base for fishing fleets by several nations.

An outstanding Norwegian writer of this period was Sigrid Undset (1882–1949), who wrote on feminist topics and who, eventually, won a Nobel Prize in literature.

SWEDEN

Sweden remained neutral during World War I but it had a bad time of it. The British blockade of Germany had the effect of closing off the Baltic Sea. That put an effective stop to Swedish sea-trade, and the nation experienced a food shortage.

CANADA

During the war, the sympathies of English-speaking Canada were entirely on the side of Great Britain, and units were sent to Europe at once to help in the fight. There they went into training and, by the Second Battle of Ypres in 1915, they were at the front. In fact, the first use of poison gas by the Germans struck a Canadian-held portion of the Allied line.

French-speaking Canada, however, was dead-set against conscription. Its sympathy for France did not, apparently, overcome its antipathy for Great Britain. It was not until September 26, 1917, that Canada established compulsory military service, and even then there were strong elements under the leadership of Wilfrid Laurier (1841–1919) of Quebec who continued to oppose it. Nevertheless, Canada supplied 640,000 soldiers to fight alongside the Allies.

A war-related disaster struck Canada on December 6, 1917. A French ship, carrying explosives for export to Europe, collided with another ship in Halifax harbor. There was a fire and the cargo of the French ship exploded. The explosion killed 1600 people, wounded 6000 more, and left 10,000 homeless. In a few minutes, Halifax was a wreck. It recovered rapidly, but the city had suffered what may have been the largest single accidental explosion in history.

MEXICO

In the early part of this period, Mexico was in turmoil over the private war of Pancho Villa with the United States, and over the American expeditionary force under Pershing that was sent into Mexico to take Villa (but failed to do so).

Just before the American forces left, Mexico adopted a new constitution on January 21, 1917. It provided for democracy and social reforms. There was to be universal suffrage, an eight-hour workday, a minimum wage, arbitration of labor disputes, land distribution, and curbs on the power of the church and of the foreign owners of Mexican national resources.

Mexico was especially sensitive to the matter of oil, which it labored to keep in Mexican hands, with control by foreigners to be only at the pleasure of the government. Naturally, American and British oil companies were alarmed at the radical thought of any nation (other than their own) taking possession of its own natural resources. They protested and were backed by their government.

Carranza was elected president under this constitution on March 11, 1917. Mexico remained neutral during World War I.

WEST INDIES

Cuba declared war on Germany the day after the United States entered the war, and then prospered greatly on sugar sales to the United States.

American marines remained in Haiti and in the Dominican Republic during this period, and both nations continued to be virtual American protectorates.

On March 2, 1917, Puerto Rico was made an American territory and Puerto Ricans became American citizens. This made them eligible for military conscription, and by the end of the war some 18,000 Puerto Ricans had entered the service.

CENTRAL AMERICA

Immediately after the United States entered World War I, Panama declared war on Germany on April 7, 1917. Four others—Costa Rica, Nicaragua, Honduras, and Guatemala—declared war on Germany during the course of 1918. There was no direct participation of any of these nations in the war.

SOUTH AMERICA

During World War I, the South American nations remained neutral, for the most part. Some severed relations with Germany, usually on the ground that German submarines had sunk their ships. Only Brazil actually declared war, on October 26, 1917, thereafter serving as a source of supplies for the Allies.

EGYPT

Great Britain kept tight control over Egypt during World War I, in order that it might protect the Suez Canal. Egypt also served as the base for the British drive into Palestine and Syria.

On October, 9, 1917, the Egyptian sultan, Hussein Kamil, died and was succeeded by his older brother, who reigned as Fuad I (1868–1936).

ETHIOPIA

The Emperor, Lij Yasu, became a convert to Islam in April 1916. This infuriated Ethiopia's Christian church and it also disturbed the British, French, and Italians, who feared that the Emperor might be drawing closer to the Ottoman Empire and, therefore, to the Germans.

The Ethiopian Church had no trouble in rousing enough opposition to depose the Emperor. Succeeding him was Zauditu (1876–1920), Lij Yasu's aunt and a daughter of Menelik II. She chose a regional governor, Ras Tafari (1892–1975), as her heir. Ras Tafari attempted to liberalize the government and, in 1918, Ethiopia's first railroad —from its capital in Addis Ababa to Djibouti (in French Somaliland on the Red Sea)—was completed. It had been over 20 years in the building.

AFRICA

In Africa during the course of the war, the German colonies were rapidly cleaned up (all except for the guerrilla war in German East Africa) and were parceled out between Great Britain and France. Belgium got some border districts to add to the Congo. All this was confirmed at the peace treaty.

PERSIA

Persia tried to remain neutral during World War I, but this was disregarded. The Russians and Turks fought in her territory in a stalemated way. After the Russian Revolution, the Russian forces withdrew but a small British force made its appearance. Persia had no effective government of its own in this period.

AFGHANISTAN

Afghanistan remained neutral throughout the war, though Great Britain had to pay it subsidies to overcome its Islamic leaning toward the Ottoman Empire and, therefore, Germany.

INDIA

India contributed heavily to the British war effort, and Indian troops did much of the fighting in the Asian campaigns. As the war progressed, however, the Indians began to clamor more and more loudly for home rule. Great Britain, anxious to keep India in line, did work out a scheme for home rule, but the Indians found it completely insufficient. By the end of the war, India was a powder keg ready to explode,

SIAM

Siam declared war on Germany on July 22, 1917, and sent some soldiers to France in 1918. Siam hoped to be rewarded, once the Allies won the war, by the removal of some of the European controls on the economy of the nation. Certainly, Germany had to abandon its privileges after the war.

JAPAN

Japan greeted World War I as a marvellous opportunity to increase its power in the western Pacific Ocean. Germany was the obvious candidate for the initial blow, for it was weaker in the Pacific area than Great Britain, France, or Russia were. On August 15, 1914, then, two weeks after the beginning of the war, Japan presented Germany with an ultimatum, demanding that German ships be withdrawn from the Pacific. Germany didn't answer, and Japan declared war on August 23.

Japan laid seige to the German-controlled Chinese port of Kiaochow, and took it on November 7, 1914. She then proceeded to take those islands in the North Pacific Ocean that were under German control—the Marianas Islands, the Marshall Islands, the Caroline Islands, and Palau. All these were turned over to Japan, officially, by the peace treaties at the end of the war.

In addition, Japan took over the German commercial dealings in the Pacific, and grew prosperous on the sale of munitions.

In theory, Kiaochow was part of China, so when Japan took it over, China demanded its return to her own jurisdiction. This the Japanese refused to allow. Instead, Japan presented China, on January 18, 1915, with the so-called "'Twenty-One Demands," which included territorial grants and economic concessions so great that China would, in accepting them, become little more than a Japanese protectorate. Although China refused to accept the demands, Japan continued to press them inexorably and seized the opportunity of the war to persuade both Russia and the United States to recognize Japan's "special interests" in China.

After the Russian Revolution, Japan participated in the intervention by the western Allies in Russian affairs, landing soldiers in Vladivostok on April 5, 1918.

Thus, Japan had used World War I skillfully in the drive to make itself the dominant power in eastern Asia and the western Pacific.

CHINA

This period was one of increasing anarchy in China. The nation was falling apart into fragments, each one ruled by some particular military leader or "warlord." That made it all but impossible for China to face down Japan's determined drive to gain power at China's expense.

On August 14, 1917, China declared war on Germany, feeling that this would gain it some consideration at the peace treaty, but that hope went glimmering. The peace treaties confirmed the transfer of German-controlled Chinese areas to Japan.

Even Russia, which was itself in fragments as a result of civil war and foreign intervention, could make headway against China. Outer Mongolia (from where Genghis Khan and his armies had emerged to conquer most of Eurasia seven centuries earlier) had been under vague Chinese control. Now it fell under the sway of the Russian Communist government and was organized, on November 16, 1919, as the Mongolian People's Republic.

AUSTRALIA AND NEW ZEALAND

Australia consistently refused to adopt conscription during World War I, but there was a considerable flow of volunteers to fight at the British side, notably at Gallipoli, and in the drive into Palestine and Syria. The same might be said of New Zealand, and, together, they formed the "Anzacs" (Australian–New Zealand Army Corps.) New Zealand did manage to push through conscription on August 1, 1916.

While Japan took over the German islands in the North Pacific Ocean, Australia and New Zealand took those in the South Pacific Ocean. At the peace treaties, Australia received German New Guinea, and New Zealand received German Samoa.

1920 TO 1930

UNITED STATES

At the conclusion of World War I, the United States was the strongest nation in the world, both economically and in terms of technological advance. It was the great creditor nation, for the United States had lent a great deal of money to Great Britain, France, and other nations and, of course, expected to get it back. It had suffered far less than Europe had and, indeed, had thrived on war business. The American population had reached 106 million by 1920, and those millions were filled with pride and confidence in the nation's wealth and strength.

A blow for democracy was struck when, on August 28, 1920, the nineteenth amendment to the Constitution was ratified. This allowed universal suffrage for women on the same basis as for men. There were those who thought that allowing women to vote would reduce elections to fluff and trivia. Others thought that it would add purity and humanity to the process. Both were wrong. It turned out that women voted very much as men did, with the same mixture of good sense and folly (all the more reason to treat both sexes alike in this respect).

In other ways, the United States did not do as well. The spurt of international concern that had led to its participation in World War I and its attempt to help reorganize the world along lines of democracy and self-determination faltered. Wilson's idealism had not taken hold. The American people did not seem to desire a League of Nations that might limit American sovereignty and that might involve the United States in every tiresome dispute the world over. Therefore, the United States never joined the League of Nations. The League might not have proven successful even if the Untied States had joined, to be sure, but without American participation, failure was certain.

Then, too, the United States, which had stood up to German militarism with exemplary courage, went into a state of panicky terror over Russian communism. Alexander Mitchell Palmer (1872–1936), who was Attorney General from 1919 to 1921, and his assistant John Edgar Hoover (1895–1972) presided over the "Red Scare," in which harassment, arrests, trials, and deportation were the fates of many whose crime was that of pressing for social reform.

The combination of the dislike of foreigners, fostered by the patriotic fervor of the war years and the fear of the infiltration of socialist ideas from abroad, gave rise to the feeling that immigration ought to be controlled. During the first century and a half of the existence of the United States, immigrants had flooded in freely and had been more or less welcomed as a source of cheap labor and captive votes, if nothing else. In the end, they added much to the vigor and variety of American life.

But now the spaces in the United States had diminished and more immigrants than before were arriving from eastern and southern Europe; more were Catholic and Jewish. On May 19, 1921, an immigration act was passed that limited the numbers of immigrants of a particular nationality to 3% of the numbers that had resided in the United States in 1910. Later laws steadily restricted immigration further, and the open door that the United States had traditionally offered the oppressed of the world slowly creaked shut.

Wilson's failure to carry the United States with him was plain, for in 1920, the Republican party, running against Wilson's internationalism, won the Presidential race easily even though its candidate was an abysmal party hack, Warren Gamaliel Harding (1865–1923). He became 29th President of the United States without any visible qualification for the post—except that he was handsome.

Naturally, when a president is elected without qualification for the job, but is popular for factors that have nothing to do with presidential ability, government functionaries feel free to plunder the treasury, relying on the sure inability of the president to know what is going on. Harding, therefore, like some presidents before him, and some after him, presided over corruption and sleaze, even while maintaining personal popularity.

Even worse than governmental corruption (which is always present, to some degree, in all governments) were the changes brought about in American life by the eighteenth amendment to the Constitution, the one that had fastened Prohibition on the nation.

To forbid the sale of alcoholic beverages, not merely as a law, but as a Constitutional imperative, was one thing; to enforce it was quite another. It would have been difficult to enforce under the best of circumstances, given the liking for alcoholic beverages on the part of a large fraction of the population, but the fact of the matter was that in the more sophisticated portions of the nation, there was no great evidence of any desire to enforce the law at all.

Alcoholic beverages were illegally imported, illegally manufactured, illegally distributed, and illegally bought and sold to such an extent that virtually no one during the existence of Prohibition was forced to do without. Even those who ordinarily might not have had much desire to drink found the desire heightened by the risk and illegality of it. Drinking became the thing to do.

The chief effect, then, of Prohibition on the average American was to inculcate a disrespect for law, even a contempt for it. This attitude spread rapidly and was something from which the American public never recovered.

Furthermore, the liquor that was produced, without government regulation, was often of low quality and sometimes poisonous. The existence of illegal drinking places ("speakeasies," they were called) offered a far worse environment than the old saloons had.

Those who manufactured, transported, and sold illicit liquor ("bootleggers") ran certain risks, but made enormous profits. Inevitably, the business was run by gangs (composed of "gangsters," of course) who fought each other for the lucrative trade, and who made enough money to corrupt the legislatures and the police.

A new level of criminal activity, partly condoned by the public that wanted its liquor, settled over the United States and has never lifted. To this day, the best-known gangster of the 1920s, the Italian-born Alphonse ("Scarface Al") Capone (1899–1947), remains an almost mythic memory. Though his crimes were multitudinous, up to and including cold-blooded murder, it was through conviction for income-tax evasion that he was finally put in jail.

The history of Prohibition in the United States during this decade is a monument to the danger of following the principles of self-righteous moralism, undiluted by common sense.

Despite its renewed love affair with isolationism, the United States took the lead in one form of international activity—the question of disarmament. It was clear to anyone capable of thought that to build up a heavy load of armaments strained a nation's economy, contributed to inflation and to the impoverishment of its people, encouraged belligerence, and made greater the chances of war. Yet such was the feeling of national insecurity that every nation favored disarmament only for others, not for itself. Only the United States, secure behind its oceans and strong in its economy, was willing to have disarmament all around.

There began a series of postwar disarmament conferences. Of these, the first was the "Washington Conference" held in that city between November 12, 1921 and February 6, 1922. The United States, Great Britain, France, and Japan agreed to uphold the status quo in the Pacific and to respect the territorial integrity of China. The Anglo–Japanese alliance came to an end, being replaced by this more general agreement.

More important still, the powers agreed to limit their naval strengths. Where the large battleships were concerned the relative strengths were to be Great Britain 5, the United States 5, and Japan 3, since Great Britain and the United States had responsibilities in both the Atlantic and the Pacific Oceans, while Japan was concerned with the Pacific Ocean only. However, Japan, which rather resented the enforced inferiority, was accepted as the third strongest naval power in the world, and that was not bad for a nation that, only 40 years earlier, had seemed a cipher to Europeans.

On February 15, 1922, the International Court of Justice (popularly known as the "World Court") was established at the Hague in the Netherlands, and was intended to arbitrate international disputes that might ordinarily lead to war. It seemed, therefore, that with the League of Nations and the World Court, a new era was dawning, a kind of return to Metternich's old "Congress System," but a return that was based more on democracy and less on autocracy.

However, the United States, having refused to join the League of Nations, also refused to join the World Court.

The popularity of isolationism in the United States was fed by the matter of the war debts. In order to finance the war, Great Britain and France had sold their American investments back to Americans at a sacrifice, then borrowed huge sums from the United States at prevailing interest rates. The result was that the United States, which was a debtor nation at the beginning of World War I and owed $4 billion to the rest of the world, ended it with a credit of $10 billion.

Great Britain and France, worn out and impoverished by the war, could not pay back the debts in the foreseeable future and had trouble even keeping up with interest payments. In the vengeful aftermath of victory, they had hoped to force enormous reparations out of Germany and use that money to pay off the United States.

Germany, however, was in no position to pay, either, so Great Britain and France found themselves irritated with the United States. After all Great Britain and France had lost millions in the war, and those shattered lives could never be regained. The United States, on the other hand, had lost few lives and had spent only money. Now they wanted the money back. The United States was the only great nation that had grown richer and stronger as a result of the war. Did it now want to squeeze those nations that had nearly been destroyed in the common struggle? To Europe, Uncle Sam began to seem like "Uncle Shylock."

Americans, however, being the creditors, had the natural feeling that loans should be repaid.

The fact that there was no way of collecting them didn't seem to matter. The fact that even if the money could have been raised and paid back, the dislocation of the world economy that would have resulted would have hurt everyone, including the United States, also did not seem to matter.

In the end, then, the United States never got its money back, and to Americans it seemed that the United States, like an innocent and honest country boy, had been deceived and cheated by the clever, crooked Europeans. An angry American public decided they would not be fooled again. Next time, Europe could get itself out of its own messes.

On August 2, 1923, President Harding suddenly died. Succeeding was his Vice-President, Calvin Coolidge (1872–1933). Coolidge had become nationally famous in 1919, when, as Governor of Massachusetts, he had stood firm against a strike by police who protested starvation wages and miserable conditions. That seemed like a strong stand for "law and order" at a time when the nation was trembling before the specter of communism and revolution. That made him first Vice-President and now the 30th President of the United States.

It might have seemed an unenviable position, for the corruption that had flourished under Harding exploded and became apparent to the public after Harding's death. Harding's Secretary of the Interior, Albert Bacon Fall (1861–1944) had, for instance, secretly leased government oil lands at Teapot Dome to business men in return for ample bribes. Everyone profited and the American people lost. Fall was convicted and eventually spent some time in jail. Other cabinet members were forced to resign under fire of one sort or another, but escaped actual conviction.

It was clear, however, that Coolidge had nothing to do with the corruption. He was a quiet man, with absolutely no charisma and a genius for escaping notice. That was exactly what Americans wanted, provided the nation continued to be prosperous—as it did. Therefore, when Coolidge ran for election in 1924, he easily won a term in his own right.

Despite speakeasies, bootleggers, gangsters,

and general lawlessness, people were making money under Coolidge and having a good time. We speak of this period as the "Roaring Twenties." There were no dangerous crises abroad and the United States could live in a peaceful, happy world of its own.

The stock market was booming and it seemed that anyone with a little money to spare could buy stocks with a little down and the promise to pay the rest later, watch it go up, sell it for a higher price, use the money to pay off the purchase debt, and keep the surplus.

It was very much like all the financial "bubbles" in modern history, for it was only possible to make money in this way if everyone managed to sell their stock for more than they paid for it. Eventually, stock would reach some peak and investors would find no one to pay a higher price for it. They would then have no choice but to sell for what they could get in order to pay off at least part of their own debt, and if enough decided to do that all at the same time, the stock market would descend precipitously. However, this did not happen during Coolidge's administration and the bubble of prosperity kept swelling and looking prettier all the time.

It was a decade in which games fit the mood of the American public and the great sports figures of the time gained an awesome ascendancy in the American mind that has never faded, despite the emergence of many great figures since.

George Herman ("Babe") Ruth (1895–1948) was the undisputed king of baseball throughout the decade. He hit 60 homeruns in 1927 as a member of the New York Yankee team of that year (to many, the best of all time) that also included Henry Louis ("Lou") Gehrig (1903–1941), who played in 2130 consecutive games.

William Harrison ("Jack") Dempsey (1895–1983) was heavyweight champion from 1919 to 1926, and replaced even the legendary John L. Sullivan as the epitome of the prizefighter. Robert Tyre ("Bobby") Jones (1902–1971) dominated golf throughout the decade, as did William Tatem ("Big Bill") Tilden (1893–1953) in tennis. There was even a legendary racehorse towering over all others—Man o' War (1917–1947).

There were heroes of other sorts, the greatest of the period being Charles Augustus Lindbergh (1902–1974), a young aviator. Airflight lost most of its glamour once World War I was over. It remained useful, for the first transcontinental airmail system was set up in 1920, but for the most part it carried the cachet of "stunting," of being fit for daredevils only.

Then, on May 20–21, 1927, Lindbergh flew a one-engine plane *The Spirit of Saint Louis*, solo, from New York to Paris in 33½ hours, and had to stay awake all that time. Only 25 years old, Lindbergh won $25,000 and the delirious adulation of the world. It was Lindbergh's flight that established the airplane as an obviously practical mode of transportation, although it was to be years before it could compete with trains and ships.

On a somewhat lesser scale, Gertrude Caroline Ederle (b. 1906) became the first woman to swim the English Channel, on August 6, 1926. She performed the feat in 14½ hours, which was two hours better than any man had managed up to that time.

Motion pictures also made a major advance in this decade, when the first picture with a significant sound track appeared in 1927. It was *The Jazz Singer*, starring Al Jolson (1886–1950), and by the end of the decade, the transition was complete and silent movies were dead. In that same year, the Academy Awards were handed out for the first time with Janet Gaynor (1906–1984) winning as best actress, and the American-born German actor Emil Jannings (1886–1950) as best actor.

Walter Elias ("Walt") Disney (1901–1966) produced the first animated cartoon with sound, *Steamboat Willie*, in 1928. Alfred Joseph Hitchcock (1899–1980) directed the first successful British talking picture, *Blackmail*, in 1929.

In the byways of entertainment, the Hungarian-born Erich Weiss (1874–1926), using the stage name of "Harry Houdini," completed a legendary career as an escape artist, who, it seemed, could not be held by chains or locks. Aimee Semple Macpherson (1890–1944) was then at the peak of her scandal-ridden career as a spectacular revivalist (more a form of entertainment, in the eyes of many, than anything approaching serious religion).

The Book-of-the-Month Club was instituted in 1926, offering a way many people of moderate means could build up their libraries. The "pulp magazines," containing quickly written, action-filled stories printed on cheap paper, and sold at monthly or shorter intervals for anything from a dime to a quarter, was approaching their heyday. In 1926, the Luxembourg-born Hugo Gernsback (1884–1967) published the first magazine devoted exclusively to science fiction.

In science, Edwin Powell Hubble (1889–1953) was the first to demonstrate the structure of the universe as a whole in the form that is accepted today. He studied the distant galaxies and, by 1929, showed, as an observed fact, that the Universe was expanding in accordance with Einstein's field equations of general relativity. Closer to home, Clyde William Tombaugh (b. 1906) discovered the planet Pluto on February 18, 1930.

In 1925, Clinton Joseph Davisson (1881–1958) demonstrated that electrons, widely accepted as particles, also exhibited wave-like properties, as predicted some years earlier by a French scientist. Davisson later received a Nobel Prize for this, and it was quickly understood that all matter has both wave and particle properties. The two go together.

James Batcheller Sumner (1887–1955) showed, in 1926, that the enzyme urease (and, therefore, perhaps all enzymes) was a protein and he eventually received a Nobel Prize as a result. Another Nobel Prize went to Hermann Joseph Muller (1890–1967) who, also in 1926, showed that x-rays could induce mutations in fruit flies, something that greatly advanced the study of genetics and heredity—and that also demonstrated the dangers of exposure to energetic radiation.

In 1926, again, Robert Hutchings Goddard (1882–1945) fired the first rocket to be powered by liquid fuel and liquid oxygen. It was a small device that made only a short flight, but it was the beginning of a developing technique that eventually carried rockets throughout the Solar system.

Margaret Mead (1901–1978) studied the societies of the South Sea islands and made a popular hit with her book Coming of Age in Samoa (1928).

Robert Stoughton Lynd (1892–1970) and his wife Helen Merrell Lynd (1896–1982) applied similar sociological techniques to a midwestern American town in Middletown (1929).

Perhaps what attracted most attention to a scientific subject in this decade was a trial that took place in Dayton, Tennessee in July 1925. Tennessee had passed a law forbidding the teaching of biological evolution in the public schools and John Thomas Scopes (1900–1970) was brought to trial for teaching it. It became a worldwide cause celebre, with the fundamentalist politician William Jennings Bryan most prominent on the side of Biblical creation, and Clarence Darrow on the side of science. The trial cast a lurid light on the primitive beliefs of backwoods Americans and made Tennessee a laughingstock to civilized people everywhere.

Richard Evelyn Byrd (1888–1957) made use of the airplane as an exploring device, flying over the North Pole in 1926 and over the South Pole in 1929. He was the first man to visit both poles.

Among American novelists, Sinclair Lewis was at his peak, publishing Babbitt (1922), Arrowsmith (1925), Elmer Gantry (1927), and Dodsworth (1929). Francis Scott Key Fitzgerald (1896–1940) published his best-known novel, The Great Gatsby, in 1925, and Theodore Dreiser published his, An American Tragedy, also in 1925. Ernest Miller Hemingway published The Sun Also Rises (1926) and A Farewell to Arms (1929). Thornton Niven Wilder (1897–1975) published The Bridge of San Luis Rey in 1927, which won a Pulitzer Prize. William Cuthbert Faulkner (1897–1962), began writing his novels in this decade and he eventually won a Nobel Prize in literature.

Among the dramatists, Eugene Gladstone O'Neill (1888–1953) was at his peak of productivity, writing Anna Christie (1922), Desire Under the Elms (1924), Strange Interlude (1928), and others. Elmer Leopold Rice (1892–1967) wrote Street Scene in 1920, and it won a Pulitzer Prize.

Edward Estlin Cummings ("e. e. cummings") (1894–1962) wrote poems notable for the stylistic tricks he played with typography. Stephen Vincent Benet (1898–1943) wrote the epic poem John Brown's Body in 1928 and it won a Pulitzer Prize.

Another important poet of the time was John Robinson Jeffers (1887–1962), whose *Roan Stallion* was published in 1925. The most important black poet of the period was John Langston Hughes (1902–1967).

The successful nonfiction works of the period include *Story of Philosophy* (1926) by William James ("Will") Durant (1885–1981), *The Story of Mankind* (1921) by Hendrik Willem Van Loon (1882–1944), and *Microbe Hunters* (1926) by Paul Henry de Kruif (1890–1971).

The writers of light fiction, essays, and verse in this period include Robert Charles Benchley (1889–1945), Franklin Pierce Adams ("F. P. A.") (1881–1960), Dorothy Parker (1893–1967), and James Grover Thurber (1894–1961), all members of the legendary "Algonquin Round Table" which met at lunch to eat, drink, and witticize. Anita Loos (1893–1981) published *Gentlemen Prefer Blondes* in 1925, and Marcus Cook ("Marc") Connelly wrote *The Green Pastures* in 1930 and won a Pulitzer Prize for it.

Earl Derr Biggers (1884–1953) published *The House Without a Key* in 1925, introducing his fictional detective, Charlie Chan. Frederic Dannay (1905–1982) and Manfred Bennington Lee (1905–1971) published *The Roman Hat Mystery* in 1929, using the pseudonym of "Ellery Queen" and introducing the fictional detective of that name.

It was a decade in which light opera was popular. Jerome David Kern (1885–1945) wrote the music for *Show Boat* in 1927, which included the song "Ol' Man River." Czechoslovakian-born Charles Rudolf Friml (1879–1972) wrote the music for *Rose Marie* (1924) and *The Vagabond King* (1925), including "Song of the Vagabonds" and "Only a Rose." The Hungarian-born Sigmund Romberg (1887–1951) wrote the music for *The Student Prince* (1924), *The Desert Song* (1926), and *The New Moon* (1928), including such songs as "Lover Come Back to Me" and "Stout-Hearted Men." George Gershwin (1898–1937) was writing the music of a series of musical comedies, with perhaps his most popular song of the period being "Someone to Watch Over Me."

As the decade wore on to its end, the drive for peace sharpened. The French Foreign Minister,

Aristide Briand (1862–1932), proposed in 1927 that France and the United States sign a non-aggression pact. His hope was that of luring the United States out of isolation and into some sort of combination with France, that could then be directed against a possible resurgence of Germany. His American counterpart, Secretary of State Frank Billings Killogg (1856–1937), did not want to tie the United States specifically to France, and evolved the idea of a multilateral nonaggression pact; one in which all nations would agree to renounce the use of war.

The result was the Pact of Paris, more popularly known as the Kellogg-Briand Pact, signed on August 27, 1928, with some 23 nations joining. All agreed to outlaw war, and it seemed to many idealists that an indefinite period of universal peace must be beginning. Kellogg received the Nobel Prize for peace in 1929 and then became a judge of the World Court.

However, most nations qualified their adherence to the Pact of Paris in some way. The United States, for instance, ratified the treaty on January 15, 1929, but would not give up the possibility of war in defense of the Monroe Doctrine, or in self-defense (itself being the sole judge of what constituted self-defense). Secondly, no provision was made for enforcement. If any nation *did* go to war aggressively, no economic penalties ("sanctions") were to be visited upon it. The result was that the Kellogg-Briand pact was very much like Alexander I's Holy Alliance of a century earlier. It was high-minded, but it meant nothing.

Coolidge might have run in 1928 for a second elected term, but he chose not to. The Republicans nominated Herbert Clark Hoover (1874–1964), a mining engineer, a humanitarian, and an honest and effective Secretary of Commerce through the 1920s. The Democrats nominated Alfred Emanuel ("Al") Smith (1873–1944), who was a Catholic of Irish descent. Smith was the first Catholic to run for President on the ticket of a major party.

Smith's Catholicism brought out religious bigotry at its ugliest. The Ku Klux Klan came out in force against him in the South, for instance. Hoover won, taking some southern states that had been voting Democratic for three-quarters of a century, and who now voted Republican rather than for a Catholic Democrat. Hoover became the 31st President of the United States.

And then, seven months after Hoover's inauguration, the Roaring Twenties came to a roaring end. On October 24, 1929, the bubble burst and the stock market crashed. Some $30 billion disappeared and a vast number of get-rich-quick Americans found they had managed to get-poor-quick.

The joyride was over.

GREAT BRITAIN

Immediately after the end of the war, there was a British Parliamentary election in which all men over 21 and all women over 30 could vote. The result, on December 14, 1918, was a huge victory for Lloyd George, who established a coalition government. He made use of his majority to settle the Irish question at last.

Most of Ireland was given self-rule as a dominion, and, on December 6, 1922, the "Irish Free State" was officially proclaimed. Left outside the Irish Free State were six northern counties that were predominantly Protestant and that did not wish to be included in an independent Catholic Ireland. They remained part of what was now the "United Kingdom of Great Britain and Northern Ireland."

This division of the land did not suit the Irish Nationalists, but any union would not have suited the Protestants of Northern Ireland, and this disparity of views among the two opposing forces, each equally averse to compromise, remained to plague the land.

Once again, the question of Irish independence served to tear the Liberal party apart and this time it virtually destroyed it. For two centuries, the British government had oscillated between the Conservatives (or Tories) who represented the landed gentry for the most part, and the Liberals (or Whigs) who represented the commercial interests for the most part. The lower classes only slowly gained the vote, and, even more slowly, political organization.

After World War I, however, the Labor Party, which represented neither the landowners nor the factory owners, grew strong. The Liberal party, having broken up, the election held on November 15, 1922, placed the Conservatives in power, but Labour won 142 seats, more than the Liberals did, so that it was Labour that, for the first time, became "the Loyal Opposition." The Liberals never regained their strength and from this time on, power oscillated between Conservatives and Labourites.

Stanley Baldwin (1867–1947) was the Conservative Prime Minister from May 22, 1923. Great Britain was plagued with high unemployment, however, and increasing dissatisfaction, so that on January 22, 1924, Labour actually won an election, and Ramsay MacDonald became the first Labor Prime Minister in British history, though he needed the support of what Liberal members there were to maintain a useful majority.

It didn't last long. The Labour Party had vague Socialist leanings and it was the Conservative strategy to portray them as radical revolutionaries, sometime that so frightened people throughout the western world as to cause them to flee to strongly conservative parties and to seek security from the "Red Menace" even at the cost of giving up their liberties.

The Russian Communists had established a "Communist International" (the "Comintern") which was designed to promote world revolution. The Comintern never succeeded in its aims, but its mere existence was a Godsend to anti-democratic forces everywhere, for it was a handy bogeyman that frightened millions of people into seeing the corrupting force of "Moscow gold" in every demand for reform, and in every misfortune.

The leader of the Comintern in 1924 was Grigory Yevseyevich Zinoviev (1883–1936). A letter from him surfaced, one in which he urged British Labour to bring about a Communist revolution in Great Britain. Its authenticity was never established, and it is quite likely that it was a forgery, but it did the trick. On October 29, 1924, the Conservatives won a smashing election victory, and Baldwin was Prime Minister again.

Labor unrest continued, however, particularly

among the coal miners. They went on strike on May 1, 1926, and this quickly escalated into a general strike that lasted from May 3 to May 12 and involved millions of trade-union members. This was the closest Great Britain came to a revolutionary situation, and it wasn't very revolutionary at that. Labour did not have its heart set on violence and the upper classes threw themselves, with delight, into strike-breaking volunteerism. The strike was a failure and the Conservative government was strengthened by the firmness with which it dealt with the lower classes.

At the same time, Great Britain loosened its hold on those portions of its Empire that were settled by people of European descent—its dominions. These now included Canada, Newfoundland, the Irish Free State, the Union of South Africa, Australia, and New Zealand. In the course of an Imperial Conference held in October and November 1926, these dominions were recognized as essentially independent in every way. They were united only in that all acknowledged the British monarch and that all agreed, voluntarily, to belong to a "British Commonwealth of Nations" that would consult each other over their common interests.

On July 2, 1928, women finally won the vote in Great Britain, on equal terms with men.

In May, 1929, Labour, recovering from the Zinoviev letter and from the failure of the General Strike, again won an election and MacDonald became Prime Minister a second time, again with support from what Liberal members existed in Parliament.

Meanwhile, in science, Arthur S. Eddington, who had led the scientific task force that had demonstrated the accuracy of Einstein's theory of general relativity, studied the physics of the Sun's interior and showed that it had to be at a temperature of millions of degrees. In 1924, he related the mass of stars to their luminosities and established the science of astrophysics on a firm basis.

In the late 1920s, Paul Adrien Maurice Dirac (1902–1984) investigated the properties of the electron and, by 1930, came to the conclusion that the electron (and, by extension, other parti-

cles) ought to be associated with other particles with properties of an opposite nature in certain key respects. Dirac thus worked out the necessary existence of "antimatter." For this, he eventually received a Nobel Prize.

Patrick Maynard Stuart Blackett (1897–1924) used the Wilson cloud chamber to take tens of thousands of photographs of speeding subatomic particles. He was actually able to catch nuclear reactions taking place, as Rutherford had indirectly demonstrated that they must. This, too, was worth a Nobel Prize.

In 1924, Edward Victor Appleton (1892–1965) detected the layer of charged particles, or "ions," that Kennelly and Heaviside had earlier postulated would exist in the upper atmosphere. In 1926, he detected ions in layers higher still (the "Appleton layers"). These layers came to be referred to as the "ionosphere."

In 1928, Alexander Fleming (1881–1955) noted that bacteria died in the presence of certain molds of the "Penicillium" family. He called the active substance "penicillin." He did not follow it up, but eventually others did and its importance was such that Fleming was given a Nobel Prize for the discovery.

Charles Leonard Woolley (1880–1960) excavated ancient ruins in Mesopotamia and, in the 1920s, learned much of what we now know of Sumerian civilization. He wrote *The Sumerians* (1928) and *Ur of the Chaldees* (1929) concerning his discoveries. Even more exciting was the work of George Edward Stanhope, Earl of Carnarvon (1866–1923) and Howard Carter (1873–1939), who discovered the tomb of Tutankhamen, a pharaoh of the 18th Dynasty. It was the only Pharaonic tomb that was found intact and without having been rifled by grave robbers, and that made it immensely important to Egyptologists.

In literature, Shaw wrote *Back to Methusaleh* (1921) and *Saint Joan* (1923). He also wrote *The Intelligent Woman's Guide to Socialism and Capitalism* in 1928. James Joyce published *Ulysses* in 1922; Forster published *A Passage to India* in 1924; and D. H. Lawrence published *Lady Chatterley's Lover* in 1928.

Aldous Leonard Huxley (1894–1963) published *Antic Hay* (1923), *Point Counter Point* (1928), and other novels as well. Adeline Virginia Woolf (1882–1941) published *Orlando* in 1928. Evelyn Arthur St. John Waugh (1903–1966) published his first novel, *Decline and Fall,* in 1928. John Boynton Priestley (1894–1984) scored a success with his novel *The Good Companions* (1929).

Agatha Mary Clarissa Christie (1890–1976), perhaps the most successful mystery writer of all time, introduced her fictional detective, Hercule Poirot, in *The Mysterious Affair at Styles* (1920), and achieved enormous fame with *Who Killed Roger Ackroyd?* (1926). Dorothy Leigh Sayers (1893–1957) introduced her fictional detective Lord Peter Wimsey in *Whose Body?* (1923).

Among the poets, the American-born T. S. Eliot, who had emigrated to Great Britain, published *The Waste Land* (1922). Robert Seymour Bridges (1844–1930) was poet laureate during this decade.

Alan Alexander Milne (1882–1956) wrote plays and poetry for children and his *Winnie-the-Pooh* (1926) was, and has remained, enormously popular. Also writing successfully for children was Walter de la Mare (1873–1956).

An outstanding artist of the period was Augustus Edwin John (1878–1961).

IRISH FREE STATE

The leading Irish figure in the final struggle for Irish independence was the American-born Eamon de Valera (1882–1975). He did not, however, accept the settlement that established the Irish Free State. He objected to the existence of Northern Ireland and wanted a united nation. Furthermore, he would not pledge allegiance to the British monarch, but wanted a republic.

He led the Republican party and maintained a strong opposition to William Thomas Cosgrave, who had fought in the Easter uprising, but who was willing to accept the Irish Free State as the best that could be obtained, and who served as the president of its executive council.

In 1927, De Valera finally decided that swearing allegiance to the British monarch was but an empty form of words and not worth convulsing the nation over. He therefore joined its political life. His party, still republican, maintained a strong presence in the Irish legislature after the elections of September 15, 1927.

Culturally, William Butler Yeats (1865–1939) won the Nobel Prize for literature in 1923, while Sean O'Casey (1880–1964) staged the dramas *Juno and the Paycock* in 1924 and *The Plough and the Stars* in 1926.

FRANCE

During the war, France had suffered enormous losses in lives and property. Half the Frenchmen in their twenties who were alive at the start of the war were dead by the end. France was therefore determined that Germany must pay. Determination, however, wasn't enough. Germany couldn't and, what's more, wouldn't pay. It defaulted on its money payments and on its delivery of coal, by which it was supposed to make up to France the damage to the coal-mining districts in occupied northeastern France during the war.

On January 11, 1923, French and Belgian troops marched into northwestern Germany, therefore, and occupied the coal-rich Ruhr valley, from which they tried forcibly to extract coal. The occupation did far more harm than good. The Germans responded with strikes and passive resistance and gained the sympathy of Great Britain and the United States, since France seemed to be acting with German-type highhandedness.

This period marked the height of the military ascendancy of France over Germany, but France remained fearful. France had been beaten easily in single combat with the Prussians in 1870, and it had barely won a victory over Germany in 1918 with the full help of Great Britain and the belated help of the United States. France knew very well that someday Germany would recover from its present weakness and when that happened, France would not dare face the vengeful Germans alone.

In 1925, France managed to come to an agreement with Germany, through the Locarno Treaties, that guaranteed the boundary between the two countries, but France developed treaties of alliance with Czechoslovakia and Poland in order that, if worst came to worst, Germany would have to fight on two fronts again. (Russia would have been the logical ally, as it was before World War I, but Russia's Communist government was ostracized from European affairs.)

In addition, France planned an elaborate defensive line that would hold off a possible German invasion with minimum effort. Under the guidance of André Louis René Maginot (1877–1932), who was Minister of War from 1922 to 1924, and who received the post again in 1929, the "Maginot Line" was begun in 1929. In the end, it covered France's eastern frontier with Germany from Switzerland to Belgium. It was widely considered impregnable. However, the border with Belgium was not similarly defended. Partly, this was in order to save money, and partly, perhaps, in the conviction that Germany would not dare again rouse world hostility by invading France by way of Belgium.

Louis Victor Pierre Raymond de Broglie (1892–1987) demonstrated, in 1923, that any subatomic particle had to have wave properties as well. This turned out to be correct and he eventually received a Nobel Prize for this work.

ITALY

Dissatisfaction in Italy with the useless sacrifices of the war and with the failure to gain much in the peace treaties boiled over. The national debt, unemployment, inflation, all meant times of misery, and the more extreme Socialists turned Communist and wanted revolution.

The Communists did not come even close to succeeding, but the mere threat was enough to terrify the businessmen and landowners, who were ready to turn to any group that seemed willing to put down the dissatisfied lower classes by any means, including force and terror.

The rightists found their man in Benito Mussolini, the ex-Socialist who had been bought off in 1915 and who had then become a war-hawk and a nationalist. Shrewdly realizing where the path to power lay, Mussolini organized the "fascio de combattimento" ("fighting band") in the immediate aftermath of the war, in March 1919. These were a group of thugs dedicated to brutalizing those who wanted reform—even peaceful reform.

"Fascio" harks back to the "fasces," the bundle of sticks containing an axe, which were carried by officials of Rome in ancient times to symbolize the power of the state to punish and, if necessary, to execute wrongdoers. In this way, Mussolini harked back to ancient glories and indicated his approval of state force.

Mussolini's system of government was therefore called "Fascism" and it amounted to a rollback of democracy in order to suppress dissent and the desire for reform. Where, throughout the latter half of the nineteenth century, the franchise had steadily expanded in European countries, with elections growing freer and more meaningful, and the popularly elected legislature gaining power and granting civil rights, Fascism negated it all.

In Fascism, one party was established, voting was a meaningless exercise in agreement, the legislature was a rubber stamp, all decisions were made by the leader, and all dissent was barred. In many ways, Fascism followed the political practices of Communism in Russia, but Fascism was not revolutionary. Instead, it allied itself to the ruling power of the state, to the businessmen and landowners, and protected the haves from the have-nots.

It might seem that Fascism, under these circumstances, would reap the continued hostility of the have-nots, but that was not so. By cultivating a bellicose nationalism and a saber-rattling mentality, Fascism won over the very people it was harming. They found that many of the have-nots cheerfully wallowed in military spectacle and in the pleasure of howling safe threats. If any internal enemy could be found weak enough to attack and assault without fear of consequences, so much the better. The illusion of power among those who wore uniforms, marched, chanted slogans, and beat up the defenseless more than made up for the loss of actual power and the disappearance of the right to think as they pleased.

The Fascists in Italy grew stronger as funds poured in from those who had money and were anxious to buy safety. The Fascist bands quickly abandoned any views that would be displeasing to their financial backers. They soon found that gratuitous beatings and atrocities were not only pleasurable in themselves but were at once excused if the victims were stated to be Communists.

Nor could Italy's democratic government, weak and itself fearful of the left, effectively counter the growing power of the Fascists. Their unadventurous foreign policy also discredited them.

There was the matter of Fiume, for instance. Fiume is a seaport in the northern Adriatic Sea very near the border between Italy and the new nation of Yugoslavia. Both nations wanted it, but President Wilson had refused to let Italy have it and wanted to make it a free city, belonging to neither nation. On September 12, 1919, the flamboyant Italian poet, Gabriele D'Annunzio, led a force of freebooters and seized the city.

This created a crisis. The western powers pressured Italy and Yugoslavia to come to a settlement and, on November 12, 1920, they agreed to allow Fiume to be a free city. D'Annunzio, however, would not abandon the city, so on December 27, Italian forces bombarded the city and forced him out. Mussolini's Fascists denounced this as pusillanimous and, on March 3, 1922, Fascist elements within Fiume seized the city, which was then occupied by Italian troops.

The result was to make the Italian government seem feeble and unpatriotic, while the Fascists seemed the strong upholders of military glory.

The Italian government also came to terms with Greece whereby Rhodes and the Dodecanese were eventually to be ceded to Greece, and the Fascists denounced this loudly, too.

Meanwhile, Fascists were seizing city governments that were controlled by leftists who had won elections legally. Mussolini felt ready to demand to be made Prime Minister and to form a Fascist government. Luigi Facta (1861–1930), who was Prime Minister at the time, refused the demand.

Thereupon, Fascist groups began to converge on Rome on October 28, 1922. This was later called "the March on Rome" and the impression was given of a brave Mussolini leading his men against the government. Actually, Mussolini,

who was brave only against the helpless, remained safely in Milan, awaiting the result.

Facta wanted to declare martial law, but King Victor Emmanuel III refused (thus condemning Italy to untold misery) and called on Mussolini to form a cabinet.

In theory, the government was still democratic and Mussolini ruled over a coalition cabinet, but Mussolini had no intention of leaving it that way. He began at once to rearrange the electoral laws so that the Fascists would be sure of gaining a majority at the next election and of retaining it thereafter. He also labored to gain dictatorial powers that would enable him to suppress all dissent.

He tried to pursue a bellicose foreign policy in order to gain a fallacious gloss of power and glory. When an Italian general and some of his staff were killed on the Greek–Albanian border on August 27, 1923, Mussolini sent a stiff ultimatum to Greece on August 29, and on August 31 he bombarded and occupied Corfu. It was precisely the Austro–Hungarian reaction to Serbia nine years earlier, but was carried through more quickly and ruthlessly.

In this case, Great Britain placed pressure on Italy to withdraw and Mussolini pulled his forces out of Corfu. Despite that rather tame ending, Italians could feel that their new government was warlike. Add to this the frequent reminders of Roman glory and the organization of military parades, and Mussolini's popularity grew steadily.

Only once did he appear to stumble. The Italian Socialist Giacomo Matteoti (1885–1924) wrote a book detailing the violence and illegality of the Fascists. He denounced them vigorously in his speeches and the result was that on June 10, 1924, he was murdered by Fascist goons.

At this, those elements in the government that were still non-Fascist refused to participate in political affairs until the Matteoti affair had been explained and the murderers brought to justice.

Mussolini, badly frightened, protested his innocence, discharged those who were accused of complicity, but then, as it became clear that the anti-Fascists were not strong enough to harm him, he managed to scrabble together his courage and to weather the storm.

The murderers of Matteoti were tried and acquitted or, in some cases, given light sentences, while Mussolini introduced a rigid press censorship. Independent labor unions were wiped out, and only the Fascist party was allowed to exist. What's more the party existed only as the mouthpiece of Mussolini, whom propaganda pictured as all-wise although actually he was a most mediocre man except for his unusual ability to know which side of his bread was buttered.

By the end of the decade, Mussolini was in complete and total control of the country, and the conservative elements in Great Britain and France found this entirely to their liking. As long as Mussolini portrayed himself as the enemy of Communism and as long as he produced an appearance of order, Fascism was accepted as eminently respectable.

Mussolini was even praised for having imposed efficiency on what was essentially an easygoing people. "At least, he made the trains run on time," was a common refrain.

In literature in this period, Albert Pincherie Moravia (b. 1907) published his first novel, *The Indifferent Ones*, in 1929, and received instant acclaim.

Arturo Toscanini (1867–1957), who was surely among the greatest conductors who ever lived, was a great proponent of democracy, and left Italy in 1929, determined not to return as long as Mussolini maintained his repressive dictatorship there. He was among the first, but far from the last, to be driven westward by Fascism in Italy and elsewhere and who ended up in Great Britain or the United States, to the impoverishment of the nations they left and the enrichment of the nations they joined.

PAPACY

Benedict XV died on January 22, 1922, and in his place the Archbishop of Milan, Ambrogio Damianus Achille Ratti (1857–1939), was elected Pope, adopting the name of Pius XI.

Pius XI took up a strong stand against Communism, more for its antireligious policies than for its social theories. With Mussolini, however, who came to power soon after Pius XI's accession, the Pope slowly came to a meeting of minds. Mussolini, in his younger leftist days, had been strongly anticlerical, but he never objected to changing his principles when necessary, for the very good reason that he had none.

Negotiations therefore took place in the Lateran palace in Rome and, on February 11, 1929, the "Lateran Treaties" were agreed to. By these, the Pope finally reconciled himself to the loss of the Papal States some six decades earlier, recognized the Kingdom of Italy, and no longer considered himself a "prisoner of the Vatican." On July 25, 1929, a reigning Pope left the Vatican for the first time since 1870.

In return, the Pope was given a sovereign state, Vatican City, which he could rule without interference from Italy or any other nation. It was tiny, to be sure, 109 acres in area, or about one-eighth the size of Manhattan's Central Park. The Pope also received an indemnity from Italy for the loss of the Papal States.

In 1926, Pius XI was the first to consecrate Chinese bishops.

GERMANY

In the immediate aftermath of World War I, there was an attempt by the revolutionary "Spartacists" (named for the gladiatorial rebel, Spartacus, in the last century of the Roman Republic) to seize the German government. The moderate Socialists who controlled the government called in the army and the Spartacists were quickly crushed. Their leaders, Karl Liebknecht (1871–1919) and Rosa Luxemburg (1870–1919), were arrested and murdered.

A national assembly then met in Weimar in central Germany and worked out a constitution that was adopted on July 31, 1919. The government of Germany under this constitution was therefore popularly termed the "Weimar Republic."

Throughout those first years, Germany had to undergo humiliation after humiliation. The Allied blockade remained in place for eight months after the armistice, while the German population famished. The Republic also had to oversee the cession of territory to Belgium and Denmark.

They had to see the German city of Danzig set up as a free port for use by the reconstituted nation of Poland.

The German people, embittered by all this, and by the Allied insistence on huge reparations, slowly built up a mythology of the war in which they insisted they had not started the conflict and had not lost it. Actually, their glorious army had won, but had gone down to defeat only because traitors back home had stabbed it in the back.

This was totally false, of course, but the victorious Allies had not required German generals to sign the armistice terms, allowing socialist civilians to do so. That made it seem that the military had remained stalwart and staunch and that only cowardly leftists had accepted the armistice.

As a result, the Weimar Republic was attacked from the very start by vengeful militarists and reactionaries and it was never more than half alive, always on the defensive, always in disgrace.

Even as early as March 13, 1920, there was an attempted "putsch" (a German word referring to a minor uprising) engineered by a reactionary politician, Wolfgang Kapp (1858–1922). Kapp seized Berlin, declared himself Chancellor and prepared to restore the monarchy while the legal government fled the city precipitously. A general strike, however, forced Kapp out after four days, and he had to flee to Sweden.

Another tactic on the part of the reactionaries was to assassinate prominent democratic leaders of the Weimar Republic. Thus, Matthias Erzberger (1875–1921), a Catholic liberal, was assassinated on August 29, 1921, and Walther Rathenau (1867–1922), a Jewish industrialist, was assassinated on June 24, 1922.

The assassins, and the perpetrators of other rightist atrocities, if caught at all, were dealt with leniently by a reactionary judicial system inherited from the monarchy, so that rebellions and crimes against democracy were actively encouraged.

Meanwhile, Germany, ostracized from the family of nations, had to find friends where it could and the logical choice was that other ostracized nation, Russia. Representatives of the two nations met at Rapallo, an Italian coastal city near

Genoa, at a time when Mussolini had not yet seized power, and on April 16, 1922, the Treaty of Rapallo was signed. (The soon-to-be assassinated Rathenau was a leading spirit in the negotiation of the treaty.)

Both nations benefited. Each side gave up any thought of reparations from the other. Germany agreed to supply Russia with desperately needed manufactured goods in return for the raw materials Germany needed. What's more, German military officers went to Russia to train the Russian army and, in the process, those officers obtained a great deal of practice in handling men and weapons that they could not have received at home under the restrictions of the Versailles Treaty.

Needless to say, France viewed with great concern this treaty between the two nations it feared. It was one of the factors that drove it to occupy the Ruhr in January 1923. The Germans reacted, spontaneously, with passive resistance and general strikes. This refusal to work was supported by the Weimar republic, which subsidized the idle laborers by printing paper money. This set off an inflation that spiralled out of sight so that by the end of 1923, an American dollar was worth four trillion German marks.

This, in turn, meant that the German middle class that had frugally invested its money in savings, annuities, insurance, and investments, suddenly found it all worth nothing. An impoverished middle class could not adopt the interests of the lower classes it had always despised and therefore turned to the far right, blaming everything on the Versailles Treaty and the supposed traitors within who had forced Germany to accept defeat when it had really been victorious.

This brought to prominence a truly demonic figure. The Austrian-born Adolf Hitler (1889–1945) had lived a life of resentment and poverty, until he found fulfillment as a soldier in World War I, during which he seems to have fought bravely. After the war, he devoted himself to rebuilding a nationalistic Germany and reversing the defeat of 1918. He, too, held to the conspiracy theory that Germany had been betrayed from within, and he clung with psychotic firmness to the notion that it was the Jews who were the enemy. This turned out, in the end, to be a perfect method for seizing power, since the Jews were relatively few and defenseless, and by attacking them those who resented defeat could make themselves feel powerful and victorious without taking any risk at all.

In 1919, Hitler joined a small crackpot group called the National Socialist Workers Party. The word "national," in German, is pronounced "nah-tsee-oh-nal." From the first two syllables, it was called the "nah-tsee" party, or, in German spelling, "Nazi."

Hitler turned out to be an inspired orator, at least as far as German ears were concerned, and he dinned into those ears his hatred of the Treaty of Versailles and of the Jews and found willing listeners. He grew stronger, and, in the aftermath of the occupation of the Ruhr and inflation, he thought he had enough followers to try a putsch in Bavaria.

On November 8, 1923, with the help of the old general, Ludendorff, he dashed into a Munich beer hall in which Bavarian leaders were gathering and attempted to take over. This "beer hall putsch" turned out to be a fiasco. The Bavarian prime minister, Gustav von Kahr (1862–1934), who was himself a reactionary monarchist, easily suppressed the putsch.

Hitler was tried, sentenced to five years in jail, and served less than a year under conditions of great comfort. The judicial system, as usual, saw nothing wrong with rebellion, if it was from the right. Hitler, however, posed as a martyr. While in prison, he wrote an autobiographical farrago of wild nonsense entitled *Mein Kampf* ("My Struggle"), dictating it to his fellow-prisoner and putschist, Walter Richard Rudolf Hess (1894–1987).

After the inflation, however, it was clear to the western powers that unless they did something to help Germany, they would simply never get their reparations. Germany was trying to reorganize its finances and the United States evolved a plan to help out, by judicious loans and by setting up what seemed a reasonable schedule of reparation payments.

The plan was evolved by Charles Gates Dawes (1865–1951), an American lawyer and politician (who was soon to be Vice-President under Coolidge in the latter's elected term). This "Dawes plan" ushered in a period of recovery and increasing prosperity in Germany, and the mad threat of Hitler's Nazis seemed to diminish.

With returning prosperity in Germany and some healing of the wounds of war, there seemed a chance of a general reconciliation.

The German Minister of Foreign Affairs at this time was Gustav Stresemann (1878–1929) who was interested in coming to an understanding. The French Prime Minister was Edouard Herriot (1872–1957) and both he and Aristide Briand were also interested in an accommodation, as was Ramsay MacDonald of Great Britain.

In October 1925, a series of treaties were signed by various European powers, including Germany, at Locarno in southern Switzerland. By the Locarno Treaties, Germany accepted its new western borders with France and Belgium. While it did not quite accept its borders with Czechoslovakia and Poland, it undertook to make no changes without arbitration. Many Europeans felt that the Locarno Treaties had finally healed the wounds left by World War I and there was much talk of the "Spirit of Locarno." Stresemann and Briand shared the Nobel Prize for peace in 1926 and Germany was admitted to the League of Nations on September 8, 1926.

Meanwhile, Ebert, the president of the Weimar Republic, died on March 19, 1925, and it was necessary to elect a successor. One candidate was Paul von Hindenberg, the old German general of World War I, now 78 years old, reactionary, and still loyal to the monarchy. The other was the liberal socialist, Otto Braun (1872–1955). It was a close election but Ernst Thalmann (1886–1944) insisted on running on the Communist ticket, and drew enough votes away from Braun to allow the election of Hindenberg.

With continuing prosperity, the Rapallo Treaty with Russia was extended. On May 20, 1928, in new elections, the Socialists grew stronger and the incendiary right wing distinctly weaker. On February 6, 1929, Germany signed the Kellogg-Briand pact and the process of peace and reconciliation seemed stronger than ever.

Then came the stock market crash in the

United States in October 1929, and everything began to change very much for the worse.

In science, Werner Karl Heisenberg (1901–1976) interpreted the atom in detail in 1925, in accordance with quantum theory, evolving "matrix mechanics" in doing so. In 1927, he went on to work out the existence of the "uncertainty principle," which is one of the fundamental properties of matter and which places an absolute limit on the accuracy with which certain measurements can simultaneously be made. In 1925, Wolfgang Pauli (1900–1958) demonstrated the "exclusion principle," which dictated the arrangement of electrons in atoms and produced the final justification for the periodic table of elements. Both Heisenberg and Pauli received Nobel Prizes for their work.

In this decade, Hans Spemann (1869–1941) studied the manner in which the developing fertilized ovum organized itself in the course of embryonic development, and that also earned a Nobel Prize.

In literature, Thomas Mann published *The Magic Mountain* in 1924, and Erich Maria Remarque (1898–1970) published his antiwar *All Quiet on the Western Front* in 1929.

An outstanding musician of the period was Kurt Julian Weill (1900–1950) who, with Bertolt Brecht (1898–1956), a playwright and poet, turned out *The Three-Penny Opera* in 1928. The Austrian-born Arnold Franz Walter Schoenberg (1874–1951) pioneered atonal music.

Ludwig Josef Johan Wittgenstein (1889–1951) was the most important philosopher of the period, while Ludwig Mies van der Rohe (1886–1969) was the most innovative architect.

(Many of the German scientists, writers, and scholars who were prominent in this period left Germany in the next decade, emigrating mostly to Great Britain and the United States.)

RUSSIA/SOVIET UNION

In the immediate aftermath of World War I—and the story must be told in this section to make it coherent—no observer would have given much chance to the survival of the Communist regime, which was attacked on all sides by Russian "White Armies" under monarchist generals, and by forces from outside Russia as well. Indeed, the odds seemed against the survival of an intact Russian nation. It appeared sure to disintegrate into numerous quarreling independent units that would have eliminated Russia as an important factor in world history for an indefinite period to come—much as the Mongol conquest had done nearly seven centuries earlier.

What saved Russia and the Communist government was that it was operating from interior lines against the numerous forces on the periphery, and could switch easily from one front to another. What's more, the opponents of the Communist regime never united but attacked separately and could be defeated one at a time. Finally, Leon Trotsky displayed an unexpected ability in putting together the "Red Army" and beating it into a disciplined and hard-fighting entity.

Southward, the Red Army had to take the Ukraine which had declared itself independent and had signed a separate peace with Germany. The Ukraine had been occupied by the Germans in 1918. After the armistice, the Germans left, but French forces landed in Odessa and White armies struck northward from the Ukraine under a series of generals, of whom the most important was Anton Ivanovich Denikin (1872–1947).

The Red Army defeated Denikin, however, and took Kiev on February 3, 1919, then went on to expel the French and take Odessa on April 8, 1919. Denikin fled into exile and his place was taken by Pyotr Nikolayevich Wrangel (1878–1928). He made some spectacular initial gains but was forced back into Crimea in November 1920, and fled to Constantinople. The Communists were thereafter able to establish themselves throughout the south in the Ukraine and the Caucasus.

In the west, the Germans had occupied the Baltic states in the last year of the war. After the armistice, a White army under Nikolai Nikolayevich Yudenich (1862–1933) advanced nearly to Petrograd by October 19, 1919, but he was then defeated by the Red Army and went into exile. The Baltic states kept their independence but Byelorussia remained Russian.

In the north, the British and French had landed on Russia's Arctic shores at Murmansk, where they were eventually joined by an American contingent. The idea was to keep Allied war material from falling into German hands. The Allied expeditionary force remained there after the armistice in the vague hope of helping to overthrow the Communists. There was some fighting but the British and Americans were not keen on Arctic fighting and by October 12, 1919, they had all left Russia. The Communists at once took over the northern area.

In the east, Siberia was, for a time, lost. While Russia was still in the war they had formed a Czech legion out of Austro–Hungarian prisoners, an army group that wanted to fight Austria-Hungary and help establish an independent Czechoslovakia. After Russia left the war, the Czech legion tried to make its way to Vladivostok where they hoped to be taken back to Europe to continue the fight.

In the disorders that followed, they took over the Trans-Siberian railroad and helped establish White governments in Siberia. Meanwhile, the Japanese had occupied Vladivostok. The White armies in Siberia united under Aleksandr Vasiliyevich Kolchak (1873–1920) and his forces invaded eastern Russia.

The ex-Tsar Nicholas II and his family were being held prisoner at Ekaterinburg in eastern Russia at this time. As Kolchak drew near, the local Communist functionaries feared that Nicholas might be liberated and that the anti-Communist forces would unite under him in a burst of enthusiasm. In a panic, the Communists therefore executed the entire family on July 16, 1918. This turned out to be unnecessary for Kolchak was defeated by the Red Army in January 1919, was forced to retreat, and was captured and executed. The Japanese did not evacuate Vladivostok until October 25, 1922, but by then all of Siberia had been retaken by the Communists.

Finally, Poland attacked Russia on April 25, 1920, in an attempt to take over the Ukraine and reestablish the large Polish nation that had existed in the late Middle ages. They drove to Kiev, which they took on May 7. However, the Red Army counterattacked and drove the Poles back pell-mell. It was only in Poland itself that the Polish army, stiffened by the arrival of a French general, Maxime Weygand (1867–1965), managed to hold.

The Treaty of Riga was signed on March 18, 1921, and in it the Polish–Russian frontier was marked off. It was well to the east of the Polish-speaking areas and a substantial quantity of Russian-speaking people were included in the Polish state.

Meanwhile, as all this fighting was going on, the Communists had set up a constitution on July 10, 1918. It was democratic in form, but, in actual fact, the Communists were the only party that was permitted to exist and Lenin remained in complete control of the party.

Finally, toward the end of 1922, after eight years of war, revolution, civil war, and foreign intervention,* Russia was able to draw a peaceful breath and to reorganize itself. It established a series of "Soviet Socialist Republics" (where "Soviet" meant nothing more disturbing than "Council" in English). There were the Russian, the Byelorussian, the Ukrainian, and the Transcaucasian Soviet Socialist Republics, and together the land became the "Union of Soviet Socialist Republics" or the "U.S.S.R." A shorter version is the "Soviet Union." It was established on December 30, 1922.†

Surprisingly, Russia was essentially intact after all this. The westernmost tier of territory—Finland, Estonia, Latvia, Lithuania, Poland, and Bessarabia—was lost, but all else was held.

Far worse than this comparatively minor loss of territory was the economic dislocation resulting from all the disturbances. The Soviet Union was left a shambles and there was no help at all from the western Allies. Only Germany, itself

---

* In the midst of all this turmoil, I was born on January 2, 1920 in an area of Russia that, by great good fortune, had been spared by the German invasion, the worst of the revolutionary disturbances, and the active subjection to the disorders of the civil war. It is not important, but I just thought I'd mention it.

† Less than two weeks after the establishment of the Soviet Union, my parents left the country, with me, and emigrated to the United States.

ostracized, was willing to deal with the Soviet Union and supply it with needed manufactured goods.

Lenin was forced to recede from the application of pure Communist principles in May 1921, and to adopt certain capitalist notions (the "New Economic Policy") in order to reinvigorate the economy. This succeeded to a considerable extent and the Soviet Union began an economic recovery.

The Soviet Union was clearly becoming a stable entity and, one by one, the European nations recognized it, beginning with Great Britain on February 1, 1924. Japan finally recognized the Soviet Union on January 21, 1925, and evacuated the northern half of the island of Sakhalin, the last bit of Soviet territory they had held. Only the United States, among the important nations of the globe, steadfastly refused to recognize the Soviet Union in this decade.

The Soviet Union formed additional Soviet Socialist Republics in its Central Asian territories. Eventually, there were 15 constituent Soviet Socialist Republics, of which the largest was the Russian Federated Soviet Socialist Republic, which made up three-fourths of the area and half the population of the Soviet Union.

Lenin died on January 21, 1924, leaving no clear system of succession. The result was that, for several years, there was intense jockeying for power, with the two leading candidates being Leon Trotsky and Joseph Stalin.

By the summer of 1926, Stalin was definitely in the ascendant. Trotsky continued to fight a losing battle and, in January 1929, he was forced into exile.

Stalin undertook an attempt to industrialize the Soviet Union at whatever cost, initiating various "Five Year Plans," and established a tight dictatorship intended to suppress all dissent. The decade ended with him in full and undisputed control of the nation.

Dmitry Dimitriyevich Shostakovich (1906–1975) gained his musical reputation with his first symphony performed in 1925.

BELGIUM

During this decade, Belgium followed the French closely in foreign policy. They participated in the invasion of the Ruhr, for instance, and also in the Locarno Treaties.

Internally, the nation struggled with a language problem. Some three-fifths of the population spoke Flemish, a language closely related to Dutch. Most of the remainder spoke French. French was the language of the capital, and had the greater prestige, so that it had been the official Belgian language since the formation of the nation in 1830.

The notion of self-determination that had been established in the aftermath of World War I made this dominance of a minority language a difficult thing to maintain, however, and, beginning on January 1, 1922, Belgium began to establish bilingualism. Flemish was placed on a par with French, though friction between the two cultural halves of the land continued.

The Belgian astronomer, George Lemaitre (1894–1966), pointed out in 1927 that the notion of an expanding Universe implied that at some time in the far past, all the matter of the Universe must have existed in the form of a relatively small, compact body. This body, which he called a "cosmic egg," must have exploded to form the Universe that now exists. This was the genesis of the "big bang" theory of cosmic origins.

NETHERLANDS

It was a quiet decade for the Netherlands, except for having to suppress a revolt in the East Indies in 1926 and 1927. They maintained a moderate course in foreign relations, refusing to give up William II of Germany, who had fled to the Netherlands, and maintaining the right of asylum. They also refrained from any movement that would encourage the discontent among the Flemish-speaking people of Belgium, or to suggest that Flemish regions be annexed to the Netherlands.

In 1923, Peter Joseph Wilhelm Debye (1884–1966) worked out the behavior of salts in solution by considering the interaction of ions carrying positive or negative charges. He also considered those molecules that carried positive and negative charges on different sections, measuring their "dipole moments." This was important enough to warrant a Nobel Prize.

Pieter Cornelis Mondrian (1872–1944) was an important Dutch artist of the period.

SPAIN

Spain continued to have trouble in its section of Morocco. There, it faced Abd el-Krim (1882–1963), who, though originally in the Spanish civil service, became disillusioned with Spanish rule and organized a rebellion. On July 21, 1921, he defeated a Spanish army, killing some 12,000 men. He established a "Republic of the Rif," and maintained it successfully for five years.

France, however, felt that any Moroccan success in the Spanish portion of the land would endanger French control of the rest. The French therefore joined the Spaniards and sent 160,000 men under Petain, the hero of Verdun, against the Moroccan rebels. Abd el-Krim was forced to surrender on May 27, 1926, and was sent into exile on the island of Reunion in the Indian Ocean.

The rebellion in Morocco, however, had brought about considerable trouble in Spain itself. The separatist movement in Catalonia sharpened, and attempts were made to follow the Moroccan example and to set up an autonomous government.

The Spanish response was to turn to a military dictatorship. A Spanish general, Miguel Primo de Rivera (1870–1930) suppressed the attempted Catalan revolt firmly. Then, no doubt inspired by Mussolini's success in taking over the government of Italy, Primo de Rivera seized power in Spain on September 13, 1923, with the approval of King Alfonso XIII. He set up what was essentially a Fascist government, complete with press censorship, the suspension of trial by jury, the dissolution of the legislature, and the harrying of liberals. Primo de Rivera and Alfonso visited Italy, where a treaty of friendship was signed on August 7, 1926. Primo de Rivera also arranged for cooperation with France against Abd el-Krim.

However, discontent continued in Catalonia, economic distress alienated the middle class, especially after the American stock market crash, and Primo de Rivera was ailing. On January 28, 1930, he resigned and died a little over a month afterward. Spain returned to democratic government.

PORTUGAL

Portugal drifted from one military government to another, either by coup or by election, and none could solve the financial chaos of the nation until, on April 27, 1928, Antonio de Oliveiro Salazar (1899–1970) became minister of finance. He was a scholar and a professor of economics and he was able to bring order into the handling of the national budget.

SWITZERLAND

Switzerland was the site of the League of Nations, which met in Geneva. Switzerland abandoned strict isolation to join the League, but obtained international guarantees of its perpetual neutrality. Actually, this was convenient for everyone, for if there were to be a general European war again, some neutral patch was needed where negotiations between the warring nations might be carried on, even if only indirectly through Swiss intermediaries.

AUSTRIA

Through the vagaries of history, Austria, in the wake of World War I, had become a minor power with the great metropolis of Vienna as its capital. Vienna had grown as the center of a great power, but had now had that cut out from under itself.

The Austrian population was now almost entirely German-speaking, and there was a strong sentiment in favor of union ("Anschluss") with Germany—something that might have taken place in Bismarck's time, half a century earlier, if Bismarck had not known better than to incorporate millions of non-Germans into a greater Germany. The peace treaties, however, forbade Anschluss lest Germany grow too strong.

In its search for friends, Austria found Italy to the south, which gave the illusion of strength, and a treaty of friendship was signed with Italy on February 6, 1930. Inside Austria, there was growing friction between Socialists and right-wing nationalists. Italy, of course, did everything to encourage the right wing and to set up a Fascist Austria.

The most important Austrian scientist of the period was Erwin Schrödinger (1887–1961.) In 1926, Schrödinger interpreted the atom in terms of quantum theory and worked out "wave mechanics" which included the "Schrödinger wave equation." His theory turned out to be equivalent to Heisenberg's matrix mechanics but was easier to use. Schrödinger earned a Nobel Prize for his work.

HUNGARY

In the aftermath of World War I, Hungary came under a Communist government led by Bela Kun (1886–1939) that lasted only a few months.

On March 1, 1920, Miklos Horthy (1868–1957), an admiral who had fought well during World War I, and who had led the forces that drove Kun out of Hungary, became Regent of Hungary. The very title of Regent implied that Hungary was still a monarchy and that Horthy was holding office in the name of the absent king. On two different occasions, indeed, the ex-Emperor Charles tried to reestablish himself as King of Hungary, but in each case, the hostility of the surrounding nations that had been built up out of the old Austria-Hungary prevented it.

Horthy appointed Istvan Bethlen as Prime Minister. Bethlen kept the job through the 1920s, though Horthy remained the real master of the land. On April 5, 1927, a treaty of friendship was signed with Italy and in Hungary, too, Italy did what it could to encourage Fascism.

The Hungarian biochemist, Albert Szent-Gyorgyi (1893–1986), isolated a substance from adrenal glands in 1928. He called it "hexuronic acid" but it eventually turned out to be vitamin C and this earned him a Nobel Prize.

CZECHOSLOVAKIA

The northern provinces of prewar Austria (Bohemia and Moravia) spoke the Czech language, and the northern province of prewar Hungary (Slovakia) spoke a very closely related language. These districts united on October 30, 1918, to form the new nation of Czechoslovakia.

The president was Tomas Garrigue Masaryk (1850–1937). During World War I, he had left Austria-Hungary and fought against it in the interest of an independent Czechoslovakia. He helped form the Czech legion in Russia. As president, he respected the minority rights of the non-Czech inhabitants of the land, and transformed the nation into a liberal democratic power. His foreign minister was his colleague and disciple Edvard Benes (1884–1948).

Czechoslovakia feared any attempt to reconstitute the old Austro–Hungarian realm, and for that reason it formed a treaty of alliance with other nations who had inherited Austro–Hungarian territory and didn't want that situation disturbed. Czechoslovakia signed a treaty with Yugoslavia on August 14, 1920, and with Romania on April 23, 1921. The three nations formed "the Little Entente" and it was their immediate reaction that prevented the ex-Emperor Charles from regaining the throne of Hungary on two different occasions.

An important Czechoslovakian scientist of the period was Jaroslav Heyrovsky (1890–1957). In 1925, he worked out a delicate method for analyzing solutions by means of an electric current traversing a solution into which drops of mercury were falling. This technique, which he called "polarography," eventually earned him a Nobel Prize.

Franz Kafka (1883–1924), died young of tuberculosis, and his fame rests chiefly on two novels published posthumously, *The Trial* (1925) and *The Castle* (1926). Karel Capek (1890–1938) is best known for his play, *R.U.R.*, a science fiction classic, which introduced the word "robot" (a Czech word for "forced labor") for mechanical humanoid workers. Jaroslav Hasek (1883–1928) is known for his antiwar satire, *The Good Soldier, Schweik* (1923).

YUGOSLAVIA

Through the 1920s, the nation founded after World War I as a kind of greater Serbia bore the forbidding name of "the Kingdom of Serbs, Croats, and Slovenes." The Crown Prince, Alexander, was Prince Regent, since his father, Peter I, was incapable of ruling. Peter died on August 16, 1920, and his son became King Alexander I.

Yugoslavia formed part of the Little Entente, with Romania and Czechoslovakia, but internally it was in a wild state of disorder. The Balkan tradition of ridding one's self of political opponents by the straightforward method of assassination continued. There were two assassination attempts on the King's life, for instance.

What's more, the Serbs and Croats fought each other viciously. The leader of the Croatian Peasant Party, Stjepan Radic (1871–1928), a strong advocate of Croatian autonomy, was shot and wounded by a Serbian extremist, and died on August 8, 1928.

The Croatian representatives left parliament at that, and set up a legislature of their own in the Croatian capital of Zagreb. They refused all efforts of mollification by the king (who was Serbian).

Alexander therefore abolished the legislature altogether, suspended the constitution, and, on January 5, 1929, established a royal dictatorship. He suspended all political parties, ruled by decree and, on October 3, 1929, officially changed the name of the nation to "Yugoslavia," attempting to unify it by wiping out reference to its constituent parts.

ROMANIA

Romania formed part of the Little Entente, with Czechoslovakia and Yugoslavia. Its king, Ferdinand I, who had seen Romania through its part of World War I, which was first disastrous and then triumphant, died on July 20, 1927. His son Carol (1893–1953) had renounced the throne, preferring to live in peace with his mistress, Magda Lupescu (1896–1977), who apparently had an unsavory past and was viewed with disdain by many Romanians, Carol's son, reigning

as Michael I (b. 1921), became king at the age of six.

POLAND

Poland was reconstituted a nation on November 3, 1918, for the first time since the Grand Duchy of Warsaw had existed a century earlier. The acting president of the nation during much of 1919 was Ignacy Jan Paderewski (1860–1941), a composer and a great concert pianist, famous for his "Minuet in G." He raised money for the cause of Polish independence by going on concert tours during World War I.

The real power in Poland, however, was the general Josef Klemens Pilsudski (1867–1935), who during World War I had been imprisoned first by the Russians, and then by the Germans.

Pilsudski had grandiose notions for Poland. He wanted the Ukraine and drove eastward on April 25, 1920, taking Kiev on May 7. Russian armies under Mikhail Nikolayevich Tukhachevsky (1893–1937) and Semyon Mihaylovich Budenny (1883–1973) counterattacked and the Poles, who had badly overextended themselves, fell back all the way to Warsaw. Now it was the Russians who were overextended. Pilsudski, with the advice of the French general, Weygand, counterattacked at Warsaw on August 16, 1920, and the Russians fell back in disorder. At the peace treaty on March 18, 1921, Poland didn't get the Ukraine, but they did get some Russian-speaking areas that then made up the eastern half of the nation.

There were some years of disorder before Pilsudski carried through a military coup on May 12, 1926. He didn't take open command of the government, but let his friend and puppet Ignacy Moscicki (1867–1946) be president, while he ran the nation from a less exposed position. Like Mussolini, Pilsudski had been a Socialist in his earlier days, but became an oppressive rightist once he gained power.

GREECE

Alexander I of Greece, who had been made king by the Allies in place of his father, the pro-German Constantine, died on October 25, 1920 as the result of a bite by his pet monkey. Constantine took over the throne once again in December.

Meanwhile, Greece, like Poland, had grandiose notions. By the Treaty of Sevres at the conclusion of World War I, Greece was awarded the region around Smyrna, a Greek-speaking city in western Asia Minor. Greece thought it could help itself to more and that it might revive a kind of Byzantine Empire once again. The Turks, however, under the strong nationalist leadership of Mustafa Kemal, were of no mind to permit this.

On June 22, 1919, the Greeks invaded Asia Minor with British encouragement. At first they were quite successful, but when Constantine returned to the throne, Great Britain, remembering the old king's pro-German policies, withdrew its help. The Greeks, nevertheless, continued to plunge eastward and, by September 16, 1921, had nearly reached Angora in central Asia Minor.

But not quite. The Turks fought desperately and stopped the Greeks, who found themselves overextended. Mustafa Kemal built up the Turkish forces, made settlements with the surrounding powers, including Russia, and on August 18, 1922 began a powerful counteroffensive. The Greeks retreated a great deal more rapidly than they had advanced and, by September 11, 1922, the Turks took Smyrna.

On July 24, the Turks signed the Treaty of Lausanne (in western Switzerland). This superseded the Treaty of Sevres so that Turkey was the only one of the Central Powers to continue fighting and to force a revision of the peace treaties.

There followed a transfer of populations. Some 1,400,000 Greeks in Asia Minor (whose ancestors had been living there for three thousand years) were forced to leave for Greece, while 400,000 Turks had to leave Greece for Turkey. It was a cruel and harsh uprooting of peoples but it prevented endless quarreling in the future.

The defeat in Asia Minor meant a final end for Constantine who had to abdicate a second time on September 27, 1922 and who died less than four months later. He was succeeded by his oldest son (the elder brother of the ill-fated Alexander I) who reigned as George II (1890–1947). It also encouraged Mussolini to decide to hang on to Rhodes and the Dodecanese, and to temporarily occupy Corfu.

George II had no power and was forced in his turn to abdicate on December 18, 1923. On May 1, 1924, Greece was proclaimed a republic and the indefatigable Venizelos kept shuttling in and out of power, alternating with various military men.

BULGARIA

Ferdinand of Bulgaria was forced to abdicate on October 4, 1918, when Bulgaria surrendered toward the end of World War I. He was succeeded by his oldest son, who reigned as Boris III (1894–1943).

The Prime Minister was Aleksandur Stamboliyski (1879–1923), who attempted to rule Bulgaria in a liberal fashion, but was overthrown by a military coup on June 9, 1923, and was murdered five days later. The remainder of the decade was a time of turmoil and bomb outrages in the land.

ALBANIA

Albania, the only European nation that was more than half Islamic, was proclaimed a republic on January 21, 1925, and Ahmed Zogu (1895–1961) was its president. On September 1, 1928, he proclaimed himself king and ruled as Zog I. During this period Albania was to some extent an Italian protectorate.

ESTONIA

Estonia, the northernmost of the three small Baltic states, proclaimed its independence from a disintegrating Russia on November 18, 1917. The Germans were occupying it and the other Balkan states at this time.

After the end of World War I, the Germans left and the Estonians fought off an attempt of the Russians to take the land back. Independence was completely established in January 1919.

LATVIA

Latvia continued to be subjected to Russian pressure in January 1919, after Estonian independence had been established. The Latvians were helped by a German general, Rudiger von der Goltz (1865–1946). (The Allies didn't mind having German generals fighting their ex-Ally as long as that ex-Ally was Communist.) It was not until August 11, 1920 that the independence of Latvia was recognized by all.

LITHUANIA

Lithuania's independence was recognized by Russia on July 12, 1920 and its capital was set at Vilna. On October 9, 1920, however, a group of Polish freebooters seized Vilna and would not give it up. At the urging of the League of Nations, a plebiscite was held in Vilna on January 8, 1922, but since it was run by the Poles, it ended up in a Polish victory and Lithuania refused to recognize its validity.

Vilna remained Polish, however, and Lithuania was forced to use Kaunas as its capital. Relations between Lithuania and Poland remained hostile thereafter.

Lithuania, searching for compensation, engineered an uprising in the German city of Memel at the eastern tip of East Prussia on January 11, 1923. Lithuania took it over in accordance with the usual feeling among nations that two wrongs make a right.

On December 17, 1926, Antanas Smetona (1874–1944) gained control of Lithuania in a coup and governed dictatorially thereafter.

FINLAND

Finland declared its independence of Russia after the Communist revolution, but had to undergo a civil war first, because home-grown Communists tried to take over the government with the help of the Russians. Fighting against the Communists was Carl Gustaf Emil von Mannerheim

(1867–1951), with the help of Von der Goltz, who later fought in Latvia. By October 14, 1920, Finnish independence was completely established.

An important Finnish architect of the period was Gottlieb Eliel Saarinen (1875–1920), who emigrated to the United States in 1923.

DENMARK

Denmark remained peaceful under Christian X in this period. It gained a small strip of northern Schleswig inhabited by Danish-speaking people, and this was formally incorporated into Denmark on July 9, 1920.

The Danish biochemist Carl Peter Henrick Dam (1895–1976) discovered vitamin K in 1929, and for this, he eventually received a Nobel Prize.

NORWAY

Norway, at peace under Haakon VII, continued to annex small and disregarded islands that might serve as bases for its merchant fleet. In 1928 and 1929, it annexed Bouvet Island and Peter I Island in the Antarctic Ocean, and Jan Mayen Island in the Arctic Ocean.

SWEDEN

Sweden remained at peace under Gustavus V.

OTTOMAN EMPIRE/TURKEY

With the end of World War I, the Ottoman Empire seemed to be on the verge of disappearing from the map. All its Asian dominions outside Asia Minor were gone. Both the Italians and Greeks were ready to help themselves to portions of Asia Minor. The western Allies had moved into Constantinople, ostensibly to protect the Straits, and the Armenians were in full revolt in the northeast. On the throne was a new Sultan, Mehmed VI (1865–1926), who did his best to cooperate with the Allies as the only way, he thought, of saving a remnant of his Empire.

The Ottoman Empire, however, had Mustafa Kemal, who had fought well at Gallipoli and in the Caucasus during World War I. Kemal set up a nationalist government with its capital at Angora in central Asia Minor on April 23, 1920. He came to agreements with Russia, settling the northeastern boundary of the Empire, then made a deal with Italy (where Mussolini had not yet gained power) which evacuated Asia Minor. He could now concentrate on the Greeks.

He fell back before the Greeks, allowing them to overextend themselves while he fought hard and made the advance expensive for them. On August 18, 1922, he launched a powerful counterattack, and, within a matter of weeks, drove the Greeks out of Asia Minor.

On November 1, 1922, Mehmed VI was forced to abdicate and was replaced by a cousin who reigned as Abdul Mejid II (1868–1944).

On July 24, 1923, Kemal forced a new treaty with the Allies which restored the Ottoman territories in Europe about the city of Constantinople, and required no payment of any indemnities. The Allies evacuated Constantinople on August 23.

On October 29, 1923, the Sultanate was abolished altogether and the line of Ottoman Sultans came to an end after six centuries. Abdul Mejid and all his family were banished on March 3, 1924. What had been the Ottoman Empire now became the Turkish Republic and is commonly known as Turkey. On March 28, 1930, its cities and regions were given Turkish names officially. Constantinople became Istanbul; Angora, the new capital, became Ankara; Smyrna became Izmir, and so on.

Kemal, as President of Turkey, set about unifying and modernizing the nation. Those Armenians who had not been slaughtered were terrified into submission. The Greek population of Asia Minor was driven out. Kemal then set about his program of westernization.

He separated Church and state and introduced such western innovations as universal suffrage, political parties, a legislature, and religious freedom (though he was careful to keep his own power intact). He forced the Turks to adopt western clothes: the men had to give up the fez, the women the veil. Western penal codes were adopted; polygamy was forbidden. The Roman alphabet, the western calendar, and the metric system were all adopted. Turks were assigned family names, and eventually Kemal adopted "Ataturk" ("leader of the Turks") as his own.

No such westernization process had been seen since Peter the Great had forcibly westernized the Russian upper classes two and a half centuries earlier.

SYRIA

After World War I, Syria became a French mandate. This, in theory, meant that France was merely charged with seeing that Syria set up a stable and responsible government and was then to allow it to go its own way. In actual practice, however, the mandating power usually acted as though it were dealing with a colony and never let its charge go its own way until it was forced to.

Thus, Faisal, who had led the Arab revolt against the Ottoman Empire, and who had worked with Lawrence of Arabia, was proclaimed king of Syria on March 11, 1920. France, however, wouldn't have him and dethroned him on July 25.

France also excluded from Syria the coastal region just north of Palestine, and set it up as the separate state of Lebanon. The excuse was that Lebanon was the one region of the Middle East that was largely Christian, and had been since the time of the Crusades eight centuries earlier.

During the rest of the decade, Syria was usually in a state of revolt, and the French did not hesitate to use plenty of force (including two bombardments of Damascus) in order to put it down.

PALESTINE

Balfour, who had once been Prime Minister of Great Britain, was the nation's Foreign Minister during the concluding years of World War I. On November 2, 1917, he put forth the "Balfour Declaration" which stated that a national home for the Jews would be set up in Palestine but that this would not be allowed to affect the civil and religious rights of non-Jewish residents.

This was easy to say, but impossible to do. The Arabs of Palestine felt that any influx of Jews at all produced, in itself, an inadmissable effect on their civil and religious rights. In addition, the British themselves were not terribly keen on carrying through the terms of the Declaration.

The section of Palestine east of the Jordan River was cut off from Palestine proper and was not included in what was to be the Jewish national home. It became "Transjordan" and was placed under Abdullah ibn Hussein (1882–1951), who had been another of the leaders of the Arab revolt. On February 20, 1928, Transjordan was recognized as independent, but Great Britain was still the mandating power and retained its essential control despite the "independence."

By the end of the decade, the Palestinians were attacking the Jews fiercely, and the British were restricting Jewish immigration.

ARABIA

Central Arabia had been the domain of a Puritanical sect of Muslims, the Wahabis, for over a century and a half. During the World War I years, a dynamic Wahabi leader, Ibn Saud (1880–1953) had begun to expand his domination over the peninsula, taking advantage of the collapse of the Ottoman Empire. On October 13, 1924, he took Mecca, and on December 5, 1925, he took Medina.

Ibn Saud knew when to stop. He made no attempt to move northward against the British and French mandates, nor against the region along Arabia's southern shore, where Great Britain maintained an interest. He made treaties with Great Britain, Turkey, Persia, and Transjordan, and confined himself to strengthening the rule he already had.

IRAQ

Iraq was under a British mandate. Faisal, who had led the Arab revolt in alliance with Great Britain, and who had been briefly king of Syria until the French rejected him, was now rewarded by Great Britain, which made him king of Iraq on August 23, 1921.

On December 14, 1927, Great Britain recognized Iraq as independent, but maintained military bases in the country, so that it was clear that the nation's independence would not extend to the point of doing anything that Great Britain didn't want it to do.

PERSIA

In the last years of World War I, Persia continued in a state of confusion. Russian Communist forces made sporadic inroads, and the British did what they could to take over the country in order to keep the Russians out.

At this point, however, Reza Khan (1878–1944) rose to prominence, playing the role in Persia that Mustafa Kemal was playing in Turkey.

On February 21, 1921, he carried through a coup in Teheran, establishing a new government with himself as Minister of War. He immediately came to an understanding with Russia, which agreed to leave Persia and to cancel all debts and indemnities.

Reza Khan then strengthened the army, improved finances, put down various revolts, and gradually accumulated power. On October 28, 1923, he became Prime Minister.

Shah Ahmad (1898–1930), the last of the Safavid Shahs, who had ruled Persia for over four centuries, did not enjoy being reduced to a figurehead, and, in addition, was in bad health. He left Persia and never returned. On December 13, 1925, Reza Khan was declared the new Shah, and reigned as Reza Shah Pahlavi.

Reza Khan continued to follow the lead of Kemal in Turkey, attempting to westernize the land technologically, building roads, beginning the construction of a railway, encouraging aviation, and so on. He did not, however, try to westernize the land culturally and made no move to shake the grip of Islam over Persia.

AFGHANISTAN

Habibullah, the Amir of Afghanistan, was assassinated on February 19, 1919, and was succeeded by his son, Amanullah (1892–1960). Afghanistan continued to waver between Russia and Great

Britain and, for the moment, anti-British sentiment was dominant. Habibullah may have been
assassinated because he was too pro-British and
his successor did not intend to make that mistake. He fought the British and didn't do very
well, but the British were in no fighting mood, in
any case. On August 8, 1919, they recognized the
full independence of Afghanistan.

Amanullah then went on to make treaties of
friendship with Russia, Turkey, and Persia, and
proceeded to try to follow the lead of Mustafa
Kemal and Reza Khan in modernizing and wes-
ternizing his nation. Amanullah went about it
too rapidly, however, and Afghanistan was too
backward for the purpose. The nation revolted
against the innovations which it did not understand, and Amanullah was forced to abdicate on
January 14, 1929.

The leader of the revolt against Amanullah
then became king as Nadir Shah (1880–1933).

EGYPT

The Nationalist party of Egypt continued to gain
strength, despite all British attempts to suppress
it. In the end, Great Britain granted Egypt a titu-
lar independence on February 18, 1922, but kept
military control of the land. Great Britain also
retained control of the Sudan, to the south of
Egypt.

ETHIOPIA

On September 23, 1923, Ethiopia was admitted to
the League of Nations. This was opposed by
Great Britain, since, in Ethiopia, the institution
of slavery still flourished. In 1924, therefore,
Ethiopia abolished slavery.

Meanwhile, as one of the two independent nations of Africa (and one, that, unlike Liberia, was
not a special charge of the United States), Ethiopia seemed fair game for European powers. Toward the end of 1925, Great Britain and Italy
came to an agreement whereby each was to have
contol over a section of the land, Great Britain in
the north and Italy in the east. Ethiopia protested, of course, and both nations assured

Ethiopia they would respect its territory, but
such assurances are easy to give.

Meanwhile, Ras Tafari, who was heir to the
throne, was steadily increasing his power at the
expense of the Empress Zauditu, and on October
7, 1928, he took the title of "Negus" ("King").

LIBYA

Though Italy's conquest of Libya had begun in
1911, it had never been carried through completely. It was part of Mussolini's aggressive policy to see that Libya was entirely subdued. This
was carried on under the leadership of Pietro
Badoglio (1871–1956) and the job was completed
in 1930. It had taken nearly two decades.

TANGANYIKA

After World War I, Great Britain took over Ger-
man East Africa as a mandate and renamed it
Tanganyika on January 10, 1920. What had been
British East Africa to its north became Kenya.

SOUTHWEST AFRICA

German Southwest Africa was taken over by the
Union of South Africa as a mandate on May 7,
1919, and became simply Southwest Africa. (It is
known today as Namibia.)

INDIA

Mohandas Gandhi was emerging as the leader of
the Indian nationalists. He was unusual among
nationalists everywhere in that he insisted on a
policy of nonviolence and passive disobedience.
He had supported the British during World War
I in the hope that Great Britain would then grant
greater self-rule to India.

The reverse took place. Once the war was
over, the British government decided to fight the
nationalist movement by allowing the British-run
government to try sedition cases without juries
and to intern people without trial. This sort of
tyranny led Gandhi to proclaim a day of fasting
and work stoppage.

Unfortunately, not all nationalists understood

Gandhi's devotion to nonviolence, and at Amritsar in northern India rioting Indians, on April 10, 1919, killed five Englishmen and beat an Englishwoman.

In response, a British officer, Reginald Edward Harry Dyer (1864–1927), decided to teach the Indians a lesson they would not forget and instill them with fear. On April 13, 1919, he marched a troop of soldiers to Amritsar where 10,000 unarmed Indians were assembled in peaceful protest. The soldiers were ordered to shoot into the crowd, without warning, and to do so until their ammunition was exhausted. They killed about 379 and wounded 1200, then marched away without any attempt to care for those who were wounded.

A commission of inquiry condemned Dyer and he was forced to resign from the service, but the House of Lords praised him, public opinion treated him as a hero, and money was raised with which to reward him.

After that, there was no chance of reconciliation between Great Britain and India. Gandhi began a nationwide noncooperation movement and civil disobedience, and kept it up relentlessly, despite vilification and occasional imprisonment by the British. There was some sentiment in Great Britain after a while to grant India dominion status, but after the Amritsar massacre nothing but complete independence would do for the dedicated nationalists. That was what Dyer had accomplished and Great Britain's superpatriots had praised.

SIAM

Siam's participation on the winning side in World War I finally paid off as the other nations gave up extraterritorial rights: the United States in 1920, Japan in 1924, and the European nations in 1925 and 1926. Rama VI, under whom this was taking place, died in 1925 and was succeeded by his brother who reigned as Rama VII (1893–1941).

CHINA

In order to fight the chaos of the war lords and the threat of Japan, Sun Yat-sen accepted the help of the Soviet Union, which, in 1924, gave up all the concessions that the Tsarist government had wrung out of China. A Soviet diplomat, Mikhail Markovich Borodin (1884–1951), arrived in China in 1923 to serve as an adviser to Sun.

At about this time, Chiang Kai-shek (1887–1975) became a power in Sun Yat-sen's Kuomintang ("Nationalist") party, especially after Sun's death on March 12, 1925. Chiang Kai-shek built up his control of China with the help of a Soviet general, Vasily Konstantinovich Blucher (1889–1938).

In 1927, however, Chiang Kai-shek discovered (as some years earlier Mussolini had) that money would flood into his coffers if he came to an agreement with conservative Chinese businessmen. Chiang turned sharply to the right and dismissed his Soviet advisers.

The leftist portion of the Kuomintang at once saw Chiang as the enemy. The Chinese Communists, under Mao Tse-tung (1893–1976), the theoretician, and Chu Teh (1886–1976), the military leader, held their ground in Fukien, a coastal province across the strait from Formosa, in what seemed to be a losing fight against Chiang's nationalists.

JAPAN

The Emperor Yoshihito was mentally disturbed to the point where, in 1921, he was no longer capable of ruling. His son, the Crown Prince Hirohito (1901–1989), became regent, and on December 25, 1926, after the death of his father, he became Emperor.

During Hirohito's regency, Japan suffered a national disaster of the first magnitude on September 1, 1923, when a great earthquake and fire struck Tokyo and nearby cities. Some 200,000 people were killed. Help was sent from abroad, notably from the United States. There was a flash of Japanese gratitude to the United States, but it did not last long for the United States continued to forbid Japanese emigration, something that made plain its opinion that the Japanese were inferior and undesirable non-whites.

On January 20, 1925, Japan recognized the Soviet Union and established diplomatic relations. Thereupon, they evacuated the last bit of Soviet territory they still held—the northern half of the island of Sakhalin.

Japan continued its imperialist attitude toward China, sending troops into the province of Shantung on several occasions.

AUSTRALIA AND NEW ZEALAND

Australia was given a mandate over the German ex-colonies in the South Pacific, except for Nauru and Samoa, the mandate over which went to New Zealand.

Both Australia and New Zealand were charter members of the League of Nations, emphasizing their increasing independence of Great Britain.

In 1927, Canberra became the seat of the Australian government.

CANADA

Canada labored to establish its essential independence in this decade. Like the other dominions of the British Empire, it demanded a seat of its own in the League of Nations. The United States and France were dubious at first, feeling that this would be handing the British Empire a multiple vote, but it became clear, soon enough, that Canada saw its national interests as not necessarily identical with that of Great Britain. For instance, Canada began, in this decade, to send its own diplomatic representatives abroad, to sign treaties on its own behalf, and so on.

In fact, Canada followed the lead of the United States in adopting a strongly isolationist policy and flatly refused to follow the British lead in getting involved in the war between Greece and Turkey in 1922. Canada was distinctly more independent in its foreign policy than were Australia and New Zealand, for instance, largely because the strong French-Canadian minority was hostile to Great Britain and the ruling Liberal

Party depended on the French Canadians for victory in elections.

The dominant political figure in Canada at this time was William Lyon Mackenzie King (1874–1950). As leader of the Liberal Party, he was Prime Minister of Canada throughout the decade except for a few months in 1926. It was he who labored for Canada's greater independence and for its isolationism. In doing so, he managed to maintain a national unity between the French- and English-speaking portion of the land.

A Canadian physician, Frederick Grant Banting (1891–1941), along with his American-born assistant Charles Herbert Best (1899–1978) isolated insulin in 1922. When the body could not manufacture that hormone, the severe disease diabetes resulted. The discovery made it possible to treat diabetes, and Banting received a Nobel Prize.

Davidson Black (1884–1934) discovered a tooth in a cave near Beijing in 1927. This was the first indication of "Peking man" and helped work out the ancestry of the human species.

Stephen Butler Leacock (1869–1944), an economist who taught at McGill University in Montreal, was at the peak of his fame as a humorist in this decade.

MEXICO

At the start of the decade, Carranza was president of Mexico and, by the new constitution, could not succeed himself. In the competition for succession, there was fighting among several generals.

The winner was Alvaro Obregon (1880–1928), who became president on September 5, 1920, by which time Carranza had been killed. One of the losing generals was Adolfo de la Huerta (1883–1955) who raised a rebellion but was defeated. The United States played the game of recognition and nonrecognition in an attempt to see to it that American-owned properties in Mexico would not be confiscated. The United States did not recognize Obregon until 1923, and then sided with him against Huerta.

Obregon could not succeed himself and, in

1924, Plutarco Elias Calles (1877–1945), an ally of Obregon, became president. Calles restricted alien ownership of Mexican land and nationalized the petroleum industry, both of which actions infuriated American businessmen and, therefore, the American government. Calles also labored to separate church and state and to weaken the power of the Catholic clergy. This infuriated the Vatican.

Relations with the United States took a turn for the better when the lawyer and diplomat Dwight Whitney Morrow (1873–1931) was appointed Ambassador to Mexico in 1927. Enlightened and conciliatory, he smoothed ruffled feathers and led the way to a compromise that satisfied both parties.

Calles skillfully suppressed rebellions that were fomented by the Church and reached a compromise with it in 1929.

In 1928, Obregon argued that the Constitutional provision that prevented a president from succeeding himself did not prevent him from being reelected after an interval during which someone else was president. He was reelected on July 1, 1928 but was assassinated two weeks later. Calles therefore remained the dominant figure in Mexican politics for several more years.

The Mexican painter Diego Rivera (1886–1957) achieved worldwide renown in this decade, for his murals in particular, although his leanings to the left made him unpopular with some.

CUBA

In 1925, Gerardo Machado (1871–1939) became President of Cuba. He was a businessman who began with the strong support of the middle class, which wanted order. However, sugar prices (on which Cuba's economy depended) were going down and Machado countered that by restricting sugar production and attempting to stimulate a more diversified economy by raising tariffs to cut down on imports. He also instituted a program of public works to keep Cubans employed.

He grew more dictatorial with time, to be sure, and was manifestly using his position for personal profit. By the end of the decade, his popularity had vanished, though his power had not.

DOMINICAN REPUBLIC

The last of the American marines left the Dominican Republic on September 18, 1924, after an occupation of more than eight years. The Dominican Republic at once celebrated the restoration of its independence by joining the League of Nations.

NICARAGUA

In Nicaragua, as elsewhere in Central America, rightist governments were supported by the United States. On May 2, 1926, liberal forces under the leadership of Augusto Cesar Sandino (1893–1934) rebelled against the conservative rulers. The United States sent in the marines on September 23, 1926, siding with the conservatives on the usual excuse of protecting American property.

For the rest of the decade, Sandino and his followers (the "Sandinistas") carried on a guerrilla war against the American forces.

HONDURAS

In Honduras, a liberal, Rafasel Lopez Gutierrez, revolted against the conservative government in August 1919. The American marines arrived on September 11, 1919. Gutierrez became president, but when a conservative rebellion surfaced against him, the United States sent in more marines, who sided with the rebels, and on March 10, 1924 Gutierrez was killed.

For the remainder of the decade, the American forces made sure the Honduran rulers were acceptable to American business interests.

PANAMA

The United States negotiated a treaty with Panama in 1926 that would place Panama automatically at war with anyone with whom the United States was at war. It would also allow American armed forces to carry on maneuvers in Panamanian territory during peacetime.

Since this was the equivalent of making Panama an all-but-outright colony of the United States, there was considerable Panamanian resistance to it. Panama looked to the League of Nations for a decision, but of course, none was forthcoming. No one at the League thought for one second that the United States would admit the League's jurisdiction or pay any attention to its decisions.

COLOMBIA

Colombia and the United States came to an agreement in 1921 that finally settled the matter of the Panama revolt that had embittered relations between the two nations for 18 years.

VENEZUELA

Venezuela remained under the dictatorship of Juan Vicente Gomes in this period. The discovery of oil enriched the nation, or, at least, the ruling classes of the nation.

PARAGUAY AND BOLIVIA

Paraguay and Bolivia quarreled over the Chaco Territory, a district including western Paraguay and southeastern Bolivia. There was fighting in 1928, and attempts at arbitration failed.

PERU AND CHILE

Peru and Chile were still arguing over the possession of the nitrate-rich section of the coast that had been taken from Bolivia in the War of the Pacific half a century earlier. Finally, on June 3, 1929, the area was divided in half, the northern part going to Peru, the southern part to Chile, a solution that could have been reached decades earlier, had there been an unexpected outbreak of sanity.

ARGENTINA

During much of this period, Argentina was under the liberal rule of Maximo Marcelo Torcuato de Alvear (1868–1942), who continued to bring about social legislation.

Bernardo Alberto Houssay (1887–1971) worked on pituitary hormones in this period, and for this work eventually received a Nobel Prize.

1930 to 1939

This section ends with 1939 because in that year a second disaster, even greater than that of World War I, convulsed the world. Since the first steps toward that convulsion were taken by Japan, we will start there.

JAPAN

The stock market crash in the United States marked the beginning of the "Great Depression." It was worldwide in scope and it was, perhaps, the worst catastrophe humanity ever faced that was not the result of either a war or a plague.

The Great Depression forced nations into activities they might not have engaged in if prosperity had continued.

Japan, for instance, as a result of its industrialization had shown a large increase in population, more than doubling from 30 million, when it had begun to enter the modern world 70 years before, to 65 million in 1930. The land seemed too narrow for the people and Japan's growing dependence on imported food and raw materials seemed to make its security precarious. The coming of the Great Depression worsened the situation, and Japan felt itself to be in a serious crisis.

There were those who believed that the only solution was for Japan to expand and gain an empire whose natural and labor resources could be exploited for Japanese benefit. The Japanese military believed this; particularly the younger ones, who were filled with semimystical notions concerning Japan's destiny and who were impatient with the civilian leadership, which they regarded as cowardly, if not outright treasonous.

It seemed to the military that, over the preceding two decades, Japan had thrown away its best chances. The chaos in China that had followed the Chinese revolution seemed to have offered Japan a chance to establish a Chinese empire. Japan had made a move in that direction with the Twenty-One Demands, but it had then backed down at the Washington Conference, where it was forced to give assurance of respecting Chinese territorial integrity and even to accept inferiority in naval strength.

The chaos in Russia after the Russian revolution had offered Japan a chance to build a Siberian empire, but that had not been carried through with the proper determination. The Soviet Union had now retrieved all its territory.

But what about Manchuria, the large northeastern province of China that was just north of Japanese-owned Korea? Japan had been penetrating that ever since the Russo–Japanese war, a quarter of a century earlier, when it had driven Russia out of the province.

During the warlord period in China, Manchuria was under the control of Chang Tso-lin (1873–1928). Under him, the province was being industrialized. Chang fought against Chiang Kai-shek, which suited the Japanese because they wanted Manchuria to break away from China and form a separate government that could be Japan-dominated. However, Chang was also anti-Japanese; therefore, the Japanese arranged for his assassination on June 4, 1928.

Chang's son, Chang Hsueh-liang (b. 1898), took over in Manchuria and decided to throw in with Chiang Kai-shek. The younger Japanese army officers who commanded army contingents in Manchuria decided that only the military occupation of Manchuria would correct the situation.

On September 18, 1931, the Japanese set off two bombs outside Mukden, the largest city in Manchuria. They then claimed that the Chinese forces had attacked them, and, the next day, occupied Mukden.

This event was the crucial turning point from the peace hopes of the 1920s to the relentlessly gathering war clouds of the 1930s. The capture of Mukden might be said to be the first military step in the course of events that was to turn, finally, into World War II.

The Japanese government seems to have been caught by surprise by the action of the field commanders in Manchuria, but there was no way they could stop it. Indeed, it would have been dangerous to try. When Tsuyoshi Inukai (1855–1932), who was the Japanese Prime Minister at the time, did try to moderate Japan's policies, he was assassinated by right-wing fanatics on May 15, 1932. Increasingly, in the next few years, civilian politicians had to fear assassination if they got in the way of militarists.

As for the Chinese, they didn't resist. There was no way they could stand up to the Japanese army, and they had to count on rescue by the League of Nations. The Japanese militarists, however, didn't fear the League of Nations, whose weakness they had correctly estimated. They continued to spread their area of control, and within half a year had all of Manchuria. They set up an "independent" nation they called "Manchukuo," one they controlled as absolutely as they controlled Korea, or Japan itself. They imported P'u-yi, the last baby-Emperor of China, and made him the puppet ruler of Manchukuo.

The response of other nations to this case of naked Japanese aggression was muted. The only nations with the power to interfere in the Far East were Great Britain and the United States, and Great Britain was perhaps aware of the fact that she had built her Empire as ruthlessly as Japan was now building its. As for the United States, it was lost in isolation and could (or would) do nothing but talk.

To be sure, on January 7, 1932, the American

Secretary of State, Henry Lewis Stimson (1867–1950), who was outraged by the Japanese aggression, announced that the United States would not recognize any situation, treaty, or agreement that was brought about by methods contrary to the Kellogg-Briand pact. This was called the "Stimson Doctrine." The United States, therefore, never recognized the existence of Manchukuo.

Unfortunately, the United States had a touching belief in the efficacy of nonrecognition, even though such a policy never accomplished anything by itself. Nonrecognition often seemed to be effective in Latin America, but only if it were accompanied by the arrival of the United States marines, or by overwhelming economic pressure. Since neither was used against Japan, that nation could afford to live with nonrecognition very comfortably.

The League of Nations, knowing it could do nothing, did what do-nothings usually do. It set up a commission of inquiry under the Indian-born British diplomat, Victor Alexander George Robert Lytton (1876–1947). The Lytton Commission produced its report in September 1932. It could not avoid branding Japan as an aggressor, but it rather cravenly tried to spread the blame and avoid offending Japan by declaring that China had been too intransigent in opposing Japan. Japan was not mollified by this. Its response, which came on May 27, 1933, was to announce that it was withdrawing from the League of Nations.

The only nation to take effective action against Japan was China itself, which declared a boycott of Japanese goods. This seriously damaged Japanese trade, and the only response that seemed possible was further force. On January 28, 1932, some 70,000 Japanese troops landed at Shanghai, China's greatest port. They drove out the Chinese troops, and, on March 5, 1932, forced China to end its boycott.

With Manchukuo now Japanese territory, and ripe for Japanese settlement and exploitation, Japan might have let things go and used merely moderate pressure to encourage China to let itself be guided into those paths that would suit Japanese businessmen.

It is even possible that Japan's civilian leadership wanted this, but the young fire-eaters of the army did not. They wanted a military dictatorship and the outright takeover of China as quickly as possible.

On February 26, 1936, a week after the victory of moderates in an election, the military extremist struck. Makoto Saito (1858–1936), who had been governor-general of Korea in the 1920s and Prime Minister in the time prior to the Manchurian conquest, was assassinated, along with several others. The assassins were arrested, court-martialed, and sentenced to death, but they had accomplished their purpose. From then on, the military was in control and, with time, increasingly so. That meant outright war with China, and outright annexations of Chinese territory were planned.

By that time, Germany had become a strong Fascist power, and had formed an alliance with Italy. On November 25, 1936, Japan joined the alliance. To Japan, the pact meant that she would be free to act as she pleased in China, for Germany would support her, and the western powers, uneasily concentrating on the nearer danger of Germany, would not dare engage in Far Eastern adventures. In this, Japan's calculations proved to be correct.

Therefore, Japan struck again, and an outright war between China and Japan began. The Japanese didn't call it war, since they wanted to avoid unnecessary international complications. To Japan, what followed was "the China incident."

On July 7, 1937, Japanese troops on night maneuvers near Peiping (also called Peking) attacked Chinese forces and, of course, claimed it was they who were attacked. By the end of the month, Japan had taken the two great cities of Peiping and Tientsin, and continued to advance southward. By the end of the year, virtually all of China north of the Yellow River was in Japanese hands.

This is not surprising. Japan had an army equipped with all the modern weapons, a strong navy, a strong airforce, and a strong industrial base. China had a large army, but one that was poorly trained and poorly equipped, and it had no industrial base capable of making a modern army. Nor did it have a navy or an airforce. Even so, Japan found itself being spread thin, and further found that the Chinese were beginning to offer stronger resistance.

Japan, therefore, left the northern area as it was, for a while, and struck at Shanghai again on August 8, 1937, using, as their excuse, the killing of two Japanese marines. There followed two months of very hard fighting that forced the Japanese into the humiliation of having to call for reinforcements. It took the Japanese three months to take Shanghai and, in their fury at the Chinese for defending themselves efffectively, they began the indiscriminate bombing of the essentially undefended Chinese cities. This Japanese policy of frightfulness added to the Chinese role as underdog and to their stalwart stand at Shanghai, which enlisted much of the world's public opinion on China's side and against Japan.

So out of control were the Japanese forces that they bombed American and British gunboats on the Yangtse River near Nanking. The American gunboat *Panay* was sunk on December 12, 1937 by repeated Japanese dive-bombings. The United States objected strenuously and the Japanese went through the motions of an apology and paid an indemnity. Nor did Japan fear any worse trouble, for Germany was becoming ever more dangerous and the West dared not take their eyes off her.

The Japanese took Nanking on December 13, 1937, and subjected it to the worst sack the world had seen in a long time. Opinion against Japan hardened further throughout the world.

The Japanese continued to take Chinese cities along the coast, climaxing it with the occupation of Canton on October 21, 1938, and of Hankow on October 25.

By that time, the Japanese had been fighting in China for nearly a year and a half and had swallowed all of China it could possibly digest. Japan had expected, perhaps, that China might surrender now and accept the position of a Japanese colony, but it did not do so. China was receiving arms from the Soviet Union, and subsidies from Great Britain and the United States.

In 1938, Japan had to decide what to do next. To the military, the only way out seemed to be to widen the war. But in which direction? Northward against the Soviet Union? Southward against the colonies of the western powers? It had to be one or the other. Even the most radical fire-eater did not believe Japan could manage a strike both north and south at the same time.

On July 11, 1938, the Japanese tested the Soviet possibility. There was a disputed hill, Changkufeng, where the borders of Korea, Manchukuo, and the Soviet Union met, and there the Japanese attacked the Soviet position. The fighting continued for a solid month and the Japanese were forced to realize that 1938 was not 1905, and that they were no longer fighting an incompetent Tsarist bureaucracy. They abandoned the northern drive and, from then on, concentrated on the southern drive.

And, as it happened, events in Europe, as the decade drew to its close, played into Japanese hands, and made things look better and better for them, despite what had now become a stalemate in China.

In the midst of all this, a first-class physicist was working in Japan. He was Hideki Yukawa (1907–1981). He tackled the problem of the atomic nucleus, which was now known to consist of protons and neutrons. The protons all had positive electric charges and repelled each other strongly. The neutrons had no charge and should not affect the repulsion.

In 1955, Yukawa postulated the existence of a hitherto-unknown force (now called the "strong interaction"), which held the nucleus together despite the repulsion of the electric charges. For this to work, Yukawa predicted the existence of particles of intermediate mass, more massive than an electron, but less massive than a proton. This proved correct and Yukawa eventually received a Nobel Prize, the first Japanese to get one.

CHINA

China's history during this period was largely concerned with the Japanese invasion.

Chiang Kai-shek, the most powerful Nationalist leader in China, did not effectively counter the Japanese invasion for several reasons. In the first place, he couldn't. China simply didn't have the power to resist effectively.

In the second place, he may have felt that Japan could not possibly conquer and control more than a small part of the huge country and that she would be defeated by indigestion if not by force. If he thought this, he was right.

In the third place, Chiang might have felt that he must first unify China and place all of it (at least all of it that was not swallowed by the Japanese) under his own control. After that, he could fight the Japanese more effectively.

All this, by the way, gives Chiang the benefit of the doubt. Throughout his life, he seems to have been corrupt and incompetent, and this may be a sufficient explanation for his failure to deal with the Japanese invasion more suitably.

In his drive for unity, Chiang fought with particular ardor against Mao Tse-tung's Communists. The Chinese Communists defended themselves strongly, but they were badly outnumbered by the Nationalists and, in their seacoast province of Fukien, they were particularly exposed to possible Japanese action.

In October 1934, Mao Tse-tung and Chu Teh led the Communist forces out of Fukien. They marched and, on occasion, fought for 13 months, traveling some 6000 miles to the province of Shensi in the far northwest, where they were out of reach of the Nationalists and Japanese alike. They lost half their army in the course of this "Long March," which was the longest and fastest march of an army except for some of the Mongol sweeps of seven centuries earlier.

Once in their new home, the Communists offered peace to Chiang and a united front against the Japanese. Chiang finally agreed reluctantly, but he did not trust the Communists and, whenever he could, he chose to fight them rather than the Japanese.

On December 12, 1936, Chang Hsueh-liang, who had ruled Manchuria when it was invaded by Japan, acutally kidnapped Chiang Kai-shek when he was visiting the city of Sian. He held him for two weeks, trying to get him to be more

actively anti-Japanese. He finally released Chiang on December 25, and accompanied him back to Nanking. In Nanking, Chang was immediately placed under house arrest and kept there, while Chiang remained relatively indifferent to the Japanese menace.

Japan, however, made the decision for Chiang, when they struck at Peiping on July 7, 1937. Chiang was forced to fight a war. By the end of the decade, he had lost a great deal of Chinese territory, but had achieved a stalemate. On November 20, 1937, the Chinese government moved from the soon-to-fall Nanking and transferred itself to the far western city of Chungking, where it was steadily bombed, but which the Japanese army could never reach.

One Chinese writer who was well-known to westerners in this decade was Lin Yutang (1895–1976). In 1932, he founded the first western-style satirical magazine in China. He lived mostly in the United States after 1936, and his best-known book was *The Importance of Living*, published in 1937.

ITALY

Italy suffered from the Great Depression, as did every nation in the world. Fascist control of Italy made it comparatively easy for Mussolini to engage in attempts to increase the food supply by draining marshes, thus reducing the necessity for imports. It was also easy to subsidize industrial expansion, to take over control of national finances, and to decree cuts in wages.

One rather spectacular Italian feat was carried through by the aviator, Italo Balbo (1896–1940). He led a fleet of Italian planes across the Atlantic to Brazil in 1929 and to the United States in 1933. This further demonstrated the practicality of transoceanic air flight. Balbo was an early Fascist who had been involved on the "March on Rome," but the popularity and accalim he gained in this way may not have entirely pleased Mussolini, who removed him from the public eye by sending him to be governor-general of Libya.

All that was done, however, could not entirely counter the effect of the Great Depression. When a nation finds its domestic situation to be unhappy, there is often the temptation to turn the people's attention to foreign affairs.

Italy had carefully made friends with surrounding nations weaker than herself and had encouraged them to turn Fascist. In 1933, without help from Italy, Germany came under Nazi rule—a particularly virulent form of Fascism. It seemed to Mussolini that the new German government would be useful to Italy.

On June 14, 1934, the German dictator, Hitler, had visited Venice to meet with Mussolini, but they did not get along. Mussolini, longer in power, and therefore more self-confident, had a tendency to posture, and overshadowed Hitler, to the latter's great annoyance.

There was further trouble when Germany made an effort in July 1934 to overthrow the Austrian regime and install a new government that would be completely subservient to Germany. Mussolini, however, considered himself Austria's protector and particularly didn't want a dynamic and ferocious Germany on Italy's northern border. He played an important role in preventing Austria from succumbing to Germany.

Mussolini, however, had no objection to Italy's own aggrandisement and, for that, he had his eye on Ethiopia. Italy had the colony of Eritrea on the Red Sea coast, northeast of Ethiopia, and Italian Somaliland on the Indian coast, southeast of Ethiopia. These would be useful bases for an invasion of Ethiopia. Then, too, some 40 years earlier, Ethiopia had humiliated Italy by defeating it in battle. Now, it seemed Mussolini could even the score. What is more, he had the example of the successful Japanese invasion of Manchuria to teach him how one could attack a weaker power by surprise and without actually declaring war, and how one might easily defy the moribund League of Nations.

On December 5, 1934, Italy tested the resistance that Ethiopia might offer. An Italian detachment attacked Ethiopian forces at Walwal, which was well within Ethiopia. Italy claimed, of course, that the place was part of Italian Somaliland and that it had been the Ethiopians who had attacked.

Satisfied that Italy would be able to handle an Ethiopian conquest, Mussolini then tried to make sure that neither Great Britain nor France, the two great African powers, would interfere.

The French Minister of Foreign Affairs was Pierre Laval (1883–1945). He saw nothing particularly wrong in one more piece of African real estate coming under European sway, especially when he wanted to keep Italy in the anti-German camp, for Germany was beginning to seem more and more dangerous. Therefore, he virtually gave Mussolini a free hand in Ethiopia.

Great Britain was a bit more reluctant to hand over Ethiopia. Anthony Eden (1897–1977), who was the British Secretary of State for Foreign Affairs, offered Mussolini some concessions. Mussolini rejected them, for he had made up his mind that only the complete annexation of all of Ethiopia would satisfy him. However, the tone of the British negotiations convinced him that though Great Britain might not approve of the Ethiopian conquest, it would not go to war over it.

Therefore, on October 3, 1935, by which time Mussolini had built up his forces in Eritrea and Somaliland to an adequate pitch, Italian troops launched a full-scale invasion of Ethiopia. It was by no means an even fight. The Italians had artillery, tanks, and planes. The Ethiopians had spears and bare feet.

By October 7, the Italians under Emilio de Bono (1866–1944), one of Mussolini's early supporters, had taken Adowa, the site of Italy's defeat in the earlier war with Ethiopia. Progress slowed thereafter, however, for Ethiopia had a rough and undeveloped terrain. On November 8, therefore, the invasion was put under the charge of Badoglio, who had cleaned up Libya and who was Italy's best general.

Italian forces, thereafter, advanced steadily and took Ethiopia's capital, Addis Ababa, on May 5, 1936. Haile Salassie fled, going into exile, first in Kenya, then in Great Britain; and on May 9, Italy announced the annexation of Ethiopia and the formation of "Italian East Africa." Victor Emmanuel III became Emperor of Ethiopia as well as King of Italy.

All this had not been done without some op-position. On October 7, 1935, the League of Nations had declared Italy an aggressor nation, something that Mussolini contemptuously ignored. The League voted sanctions (i.e., an economic boycott) against Italy, but it was careful to do so painlessly. For instance, there were no oil sanctions and oil was one commodity that Italy had to have for the day-to-day conduct of the invasion. Nor was the Suez Canal closed to Italian vessels, so supplies could reach the Italian armies without trouble. In short, the League, under British and French control, went through the motions of opposing Italy, but was not serious about it.

In fact, Laval in France, and Samuel John Gurney Hoare (1880–1959), the British Foreign Minister, attempted to reach a compromise agreement soon after the League's action on sanction, by which Ethiopia was to be cut up and a major portion was to be given to Italy. However, public opinion flared up against so naked a display of imperial cynicism and the plan had to be dropped.

Nevertheless, the conservative rulers of Great Britian continued to be rather sympathetic to the Fascists, viewing them as an anti-Communist bulwark. For this reason, they were ready to compromise and let the aggressive Fascist powers have at least some of what they demanded, particularly if they could be turned eastward. In this way, their hunger would be "appeased" and they would become respectable members of the family of nations. The policy turned out to be utterly wrong-headed.

With the annexation of Ethiopia and the successful defiance of the League and the western powers, Mussolini reached the peak of his success. It was an unfortunate peak in a way, for Italy had strained its financial resources even in a war against so small an opponent. Having become estranged from Great Britain and France, it had to look for other friends and allies, and Mussolini's glance fell on Germany, which, now under Fascist rule itself, had supported him in Ethiopia.

The Italian Minister of Foreign Affairs (who was also Mussolini's son-in-law), Galeazzo Ciano

(1903–1944), visited Berlin on October 25, 1936, and came to an agreement on the matter of Austria. What it amounted to was that Italy obtained a promise of continued German support in exchange for throwing Austria to the wolves. Mussolini boasted that Berlin and Rome would be a new axis about which the Earth would revolve and, thereafter, Germany and Italy (and later Japan as well) were called the "Axis powers."

Another untoward result of the Ethiopian campaign was that Mussolini came to the false conclusion that Italy's victory over a feeble, totally unequipped foe meant that Italy had become a great military power.

Consequently, when, in 1936, a furious civil war began in Spain, with Fascist rebels fighting the legal leftist government, Italy instantly plunged in to help the rebels. Mussolini was intent on turning the Mediterranean Sea, as far as possible, into a Fascist lake, to form a new kind of Roman Empire.

The expense of that adventure further strained the Italian economy. Even worse than that, the Italians were now not fighting barefooted Ethiopians, but well-equipped Spaniards who, throughout their history, have been notably fierce in combat. In March of 1937, the Italians were badly defeated at Guadalajara and Brihuega, and after that their actual contribution to the fighting was negligible. The illusion of power they had gained in Ethiopia dissipated like dew in the hot sun.

The military disasters in Spain inevitably tied Italy even closer to Germany, and Mussolini began to appear very much as Hitler's junior partner. It became necessary for Italy to curry favor with the Germans in many ways. Since Germany, like Japan, had withdrawn from the League of Nations, Italy did so also on December 11, 1937. During 1938, Italy also began to adopt the anti-Semitic policies that formed so prominent a part of the Nazi ideology. (Little of German demonism, however, could be grafted onto the easy-going, civilized Italians.)

In an effort to mask his new role as Hitler's lackey, Mussolini raised the level of his bombast. He talked about increasing Italian armaments and expanding the Italian navy. He had crowds yelling for Nice, Corsica, and Tunisia (all of which were French possessions). However, the west had its eyes fixed on Germany and, after the Spanish adventure, no one feared Italian military might.

Indeed, Mussolini found himself increasingly certain that Italy was not prepared to fight a major war and he did his best to put a brake on Germany's mad rush toward conflict.

However, Hitler's successes in 1938, and the European territories he was able to absorb, roused Mussolini's envy. He felt he had to show successful expansionism, too, and the one direction in which that could be taken in Europe in reasonable safety was in Albania.

Albania was, in any case, virtually an Italian protectorate so not much was required. On April 7, 1939 (Good Friday), Italian ships bombarded the Albanian coastline, and armed forces landed and took over the nation. King Zog and his pregnant wife fled to Greece and, on April 12, Victor Emmanuel III of Italy became King of Albania as well. It was anything but a heroic victory, and the smallness of the enemy, the choice of the day, and even the pregnancy of the Albanian queen, combined to cast Mussolini in an unlovely light.

Mussolini had, in fact, reached the point where, on May 22, 1939, he formed a close military alliance with Germany; and from that point on, he could no longer call his soul his own.

A top-ranking scientist of the period was Enrico Fermi (1901–1954), who in 1934 bombarded uranium with neutrons in an attempt to form element #93, which does not exist in appreciable quantities in nature.

The results were confusing, but the Fascist government, to Fermi's annoyance, announced success prematurely in a burst of vainglory. And indeed, the research was sufficiently significant for Fermi to be awarded a Nobel Prize in 1938. Fermi was anti-Fascist and had a Jewish wife, so after he got to Stockholm to collect his prize, he left for the United States, remaining there the rest of his life.

Emilo Segre (1905–1989), a student of Fermi's, bombarded the element molybdenum with neutons and produced element #43—the first element produced that did not exist in nature in appreciable amounts. It was named "technetium" from the Greek word for "artificial." Segre, who was Jewish, also emigrated to the United States in 1938.

PAPACY

Under Pius XI, the Catholic Church continued to fight strongly against socialism and communism, since leftists regimes were usually anticlerical. In general, the Pope called for economic and social reforms, but the only governments willing to bring these about were leftist regimes in places like Mexico and Spain. The Pope's words were disregarded by those regimes that supported him.

In Spain, the Pope thoroughly supported the Spanish Fascist rebels, for instance, who would certainly bring about no reforms. The Church also came to an agreement with the German Nazis on July 20, 1933—and whatever the Church's views on the fanatical anti-Semitism of the Nazis, they never managed to speak out loudly enough to exert any effect upon it.

On February 10, 1939, Pius XI died, and, on March 2, Eugenio Pacelli (1876–1958), who had been the architect of the agreement with the Nazis, became Pope, reigning as Pius XII.

ETHIOPIA

Haile Selassie I, as Emperor of Ethiopia, granted the nation a constitution on July 16, 1931, one which introduced some western notions. Though he reserved the real power for himself, he introduced some of the forms of parliamentary government and engaged in an attempt to modernize the country.

It all went for nothing, however, for Italian forces invaded the country in 1935, occupied it, and drove Haile Selassie into exile. On June 30, 1936, he spoke with sad dignity before the League of Nations, calling on the powers to take action against Italy and warning them of God's judgment against them if they failed to act. The powers listened stonily and failed to act. They must, apparently, have decided to await God's judgment. As it happened, they had not long to wait.

ALBANIA

Italy was in virtual control of Albania during this period. King Zog tried to limit that control, but not successfully, for Mussolini did not hesitate to use the Italian fleet to terrorize the nation. Zog was also unpopular with the Albanians themselves for his dictatorial rule. Italy had no trouble, therefore, in invading and occupying the country on April 7, 1939.

SPAIN

After the resignation and death of Primo de Rivera, King Alfonso XIII proclaimed a restoration of the parliamentary government. However, his close alliance with the dictator had completely destroyed his popularity in the country. Municipal elections on April 12, 1931 resulted in a vast victory for the Republicans. On April 14, Alfonso XIII left Spain and the Bourbon dynasty came to an end, for a time at least. No descendants of Hugh Capet ruled anywhere in the world for the first time since Hugh had become king of France nine and a half centuries earlier.

This was not a happy ending for Spain, however. The new Spanish Republic faced insuperable problems. They established separation of church and state, granted religious liberty, nationalized church property, and dissolved the Jesuit order. All this placed the power of the Church unalterably against the Republic.

In addition, the Catalonian demands for autonomy sharpened and, on September 25, 1932, Catalonia became all but independent.

Naturally, this increased the demands for autonomy in the Basque regions of northern Spain.

To make things worse, there were several varieties of leftists in Spain, not only socialists and communists, but anarchists and syndicalists, many of whom found the Republic to be mvoing too slowly. Their demands and strikes reduced Spain to utter disorder.

Those who found the disorder distasteful or dangerous were veering to the right where forces, including the army and the Church, were waiting grimly.

On July 18, 1936, military garrisons in Spanish Morocco and in a number of Spanish cities rose in revolt. In Madrid, the Republic held firm, however, and the different leftist factions joined to meet the common enemy. In Catalonia and in the Basque region, it was perfectly well understood that if the rebels won, all hopes for autonomy would disappear. Therefore, they clung to the Republic.

The rebels, under the leadership of Francisco Franco (1892–1975), coming in from the Canary Islands, and Emilio Mola (1887–1937) in northern Spain, drove for Madrid. Mola said there were four columns advancing on the capital and a "fifth column" of rebel sympathizers inside the capital. From this remark, "fifth column" became a phrase used for traitors who bored from within on behalf of an external enemy.

Beginning in November 1936, the rebels laid siege to Madrid, but after four months of continuous fighting, they failed to take it and matters settled down to a long, bloody war.

Other nations joined in at once. Italy sent troops and equipment and Germany sent airplanes. The Soviet Union supported the Spanish government ("Loyalists"), but they were farther away and their aid was considerably less effective. Nevertheless, those who sympathized with the rebels made much of Soviet aid and did their best to stigmatize the Loyalists as communists.

The result was that Great Britain took up the attitude of "a plague on both your houses" and, followed by France, it took up a dim-witted policy of refusing to help the Loyalists, even though the rebels were receiving massive help from the Fascist powers. Even the United States found itself forced by its own policy of isolation (and by its conservative factions) to help the rebels by failing to help the Loyalists.

Once again, then, as in Ethiopia, the Fascists were winning not so much through their own strength, as through the stupidity and timidity of their opponents.

In March 1937, Italian forces in Spain were

smashed by the Loyalists and, from that moment on, Mussolini's dreams of military glory began to wither. On April 25, 1937, however, Germany had its airplane pilots deliberately bomb the Basque town of Guernica to no tactical advantage, but merely to give the pilots practice.

Little by little, the rebels advanced, with the Loyalists falling back only after ferocious fighting. On March 28, 1939, Madrid surrendered. The civil war lasted nearly three years and killed 750,000 people. Since Madrid withstood months and years of bombardment and bombing, it could be seen that cities, held by resolute forces, made enormously tenacious fortresses. That lesson was not learned very well, however, not even, at crucial times, by the Germans, who are ordinarily quick to learn important military lessons.

As a result of the war, Spain was set up as one more Fascist power, with Franco as dictator. France now found itself surrounded by three Fascist powers—Germany to the east, Italy to the southeast, and Spain to the southwest—each one a firm enemy. Napoleon III could not have bumbled more foolishly than the French leadership of this period.

In 1937, Pablo Picasso painted what some consider his most powerful work. It was entitled *Guernica*, and was a heart-breaking depiction of the senseless cruelty of war. Salvador Dali (1904–1989) became famous in this decade for his surrealist paintings. His most famous one, *Persistence of Memory*, painted in 1931, showed the limp, hanging watches that were forever afterward associated with his name.

PORTUGAL

On July 5, 1932, Salazar became Premier of Portugal and, in essence, its Fascist dictator. He modeled himself on Mussolini and established a one-party government.

When the Spanish civil war broke out, Portugal ranged itself on the rebel side at once, and it was through Portugal that a great deal of the supplies from Germany reached the rebels.

Once Franco had won his victory, Portugal signed an alliance with Spain, but retained its traditional alliance with Great Britain also.

GERMANY

The Great Depression struck Germany hard. Dissatisfaction with unemployment and with increasingly difficult times led to the strengthening of the parties at the extremes, particularly of Hitler's Nazis, who found it particularly easy to blame everything on the Jews and on the Versailles Treaty.

In 1928, there had been 12 Nazis in the Reichstag. In 1930, with the Depression on, there were 107. The Nazi vote had climbed from 800,000 to 6.5 million. By 1932, they had 230 seats.

Meanwhile, on March 21, 1931, a suggestion of a German–Austrian customs union had arisen. This would have improved the economies of both countries. France, however, objected strenuously and the project was given up. The lack of such a union weakened the economy of Austria and, on May 11, 1931, the Austrian Credit-Anstalt, a great banking firm, failed when France refused to lend it support. The economy of all of central Europe virtually collapsed. By 1932, there were 6 million unemployed in Germany.

It was impossible in this period for the moderate parties to have a reliable majority in the Reichstag, and President Hindenburg had to rule by decree. Hindenburg could do this only because of his unparalleled prestige, but he was 85 years old in 1932. What would happen when he died? The German Chancellor, Heinrich Bruening (1885–1970), would be helpless without him.

On March 13, 1932, Hindenburg ran for reelection, with Hitler running against him. Hindenburg was reelected, but by a rather small margin. It was clear that Hitler could not be ignored for much longer. Bruening resigned on May 30, when Hindenburg refused to decree a land-reform measure that Bruening urged on him.

Franz von Papen (1879–1969) was asked to be Chancellor on May 31, however, after a few months, it was clear he could not run the government. Kurt von Schleicher (1882–1934) followed and he couldn't run the government, either.

There seemed to be no choice but to ask Adolf Hitler to assume the Chancellorship. This he did on January 30, 1933, and at once he began a reign of terror.

In the course of an election campaign carried out with extreme oratorical violence, the Nazis arranged to have the Reichstag burned on February 27, 1933, and, of course, blamed it on the communists. The now-senile Hindenburg agreed to a decree that suspended all civil liberties and the Nazi stormtroopers took over control of the streets. The Nazis, even at this extreme, got less than a majority of the vote, but that didn't matter. On March 23, 1933, the Reichstag granted Hitler dictatorial powers, and with that Germany became Nazi, an unbelievably extreme form of Fascism.

Germany was the "Third Reich" now; the first having been the Holy Roman Empire and the second having been Bismarck's German Empire. Hitler assumed the title of "Der Fuehrer" (The Leader) in imitation of Mussolini's "Il Duce," which meant the same, as did Franco's later title, "El Caudillo." The greeting, "Heil Hitler," became commonplace and, indeed, virtually compulsory. Germany descended into a nightmare world of paranoia and legalized brutality.

The nightmare fell heaviest on the Jews, who were subject to systematic harassment, theft, violence, imprisonment, torture, and death. On September 15, 1935, the Nazis established the Nuremburg laws that deprived Jews of their citizenship and denied them all human rights. In November 1938, after a German diplomat in Paris had been assassinated by a Jew, the Nazis began the "Holocaust," a systematic program of killing off the Jews, first in Germany, then in Europe, with the final intention, one must suppose, of killing them off throughout the world.

Nor was the rest of the world quick to protest this treatment of the Jews. After all, the oppression and persecution of Jews was nothing new. It had been going on for 2000 years, so the Gentile world found it easy to be philosophical about it.

Around Hitler there gathered a group of the most terrifying villains who ever assumed complete power over a nation. Their names were soon to be famous throughout the world. Hermann Goering (1893–1946), who had served in

the German airforce during World War I, was head of the German airforce now. He was a man of ultimate greed and vanity, who affected hearty good fellowship.

Paul Joseph Goebbels (1897–1945), cleverest of the bunch, placed his intelligence entirely at the service of evil and was the head of the propaganda ministry. Heinrich Himmler (1900–1945) was chief of the secret police. Martin Ludwig Bormann (1900–1945) was Hitler's secretary and his evil genius (something that, in Hitler's case, was surely totally superfluous). Bormann worked behind the scenes and remained almost unknown to the rest of the world.

Nazi ideology invaded everything—business, finance, the judicial system, religion. Labor unions were smashed, the separate federal regions bound into a tight, centralized government. All opposition was stamped out. Concentration camps were set up where anyone who was not a completely pure follower might be imprisoned and tortured to death. Women were ordered to have babies and to remain in the kitchen. A foolish kind of Teutonic paganism, straight out of Wagner's operas, was encouraged. Most of all, the nation was subjected to the unending drumming of militarism, parades, uniforms, and organized celebrations that dulled the mind and turned people into robots.

Nazi Germany turned on the rest of the world with a snarl. It intended to achieve economic self-sufficiency, to trade with weaker powers only on its own terms, and to abandon altogether any quest for peace. A disarmament conference was being held in Europe, and from this Germany withdrew on October 14, 1933, announcing at the same time that it was withdrawing from the League of Nations.

As time went on, Germany denounced the disarmament clauses of the Versailles Treaty on March 16, 1935, but it had been rearming at top speed before that. By the middle 1930s, Germany was becoming an armed camp, and was well on the path toward becoming the strongest military power in Europe. Great Britain and France looked the other way. They preferred to believe that Germany was building itself up as a powerful barrier against the Soviet Union. They were rather grateful to Germany for preparing a military solution to the communist problem that the West was unwilling to undertake itself.

Hitler did not intend to tolerate opposition to himself from within the Nazi party, either. There was a group within it that took the "socialist" portion of "National Socialist" far too seriously. These were led by Gregor Strasser (1892–1934) who had, for a time, been the number-two man of the Nazi party, but who had fallen out with Hitler in 1932. Another leader was Ernst Rohm (1887–1934), a vicious bully who led the storm troopers. Hitler had made the same discovery that Mussolini and Chiang Kai-shek had made—that it was financially profitable to be on the side of big business. Therefore, he had to get rid of the troublesome antibusiness ideologues.

On June 30, 1934, Hitler conjured up an imaginary conspiracy against himself and struck. In the course of the night, Rohm, Strasser, and dozens of others were seized and killed without trial. Some, completely confused, thought it was a coup against Hitler, and went down crying out their "Heil Hitler."

Hitler seized the opportunity to settle scores with others who had opposed him in earlier years or against whom he had a grudge. Thus, Gustav von Kahr (1862–1934), a Bavarian politician who had squelched the 1923 Beer Hall putsch, was shot. Kurt von Schleicher (1882–1934), who had been the last Chancellor before Hitler and who had delayed Hitler's rise to power, was shot, and so on.

After this "Blood Purge," as it was called, Hitler felt the internal situation in Germany to be stable enough to allow a bit of foreign adventure.

The logical first prey, across the border, was to the south in Austria, where local Nazis were becoming ever more powerful. The Austrian chancellor, Engelbert Dollfuss (1892–1934), was a close friend of Mussolini's and was himself a Fascist who had set up a one-party state in the land. What the Nazis wanted was not just Fascism, however, but union with Germany. They attempted a putsch on July 25, 1934; in the fracas, Dollfuss was shot and was allowed to bleed to death. The intervention of Mussolini, however, saved Austria from annexation. Hitler was not

yet strong enough to brave Italian opposition, so he fell back, but it meant only a delay.

On August 2, 1934, President Hindenburg finally died at the age of 87, and he no longer existed as a possible counterbalance to Hitler. Later in the month, Hitler assumed the presidency himself, though he retained the title of "Der Fuehrer." In the fashion of Napoleon III, he ran plebiscites at every major advance in power, and the entire machinery of the state was bent toward making everyone vote, and vote for Hitler. It had its success. People who would have liked to resist lost heart in the face of enormous majorities who were apparently in favor of Hitler. Foreign nations were also impressed.

A plebiscite of this sort was held in the Saar Basin on January 13, 1935. The basin had been placed under League of Nations control in 1920 and its coal mines had been used by France. Provision had been made for a plebiscite in 15 years and now it came. The populace could vote for union with Germany, union with France, or continued administration by the League. The Saar was German-speaking and 90% of the voters plumped for union with Germany. On March 1, 1935, it became part of Germany, and this was the first successful bit of German expansion under Hitler. The matter was dismissed by the western nations. After all, the Saar had been German to begin with.

In fact, Great Britain was sufficiently undisturbed to make a deal with the Nazis on June 18, 1935, one in which Germany agreed to keep its navy at no more than 35% of the British tonnage. It must have seemed to Great Britain that as long as its navy was dominant in the Atlantic, nothing Germany could do on the continent was important. William II couldn't win against the British navy, so how could Hitler?

It was dangerous to relive World War I in this way, however. Airplanes had developed mightily, and an airforce might destroy a navy or leapfrog it; and Germany was busily building an airforce that would far outstrip those of Great Britain and France. Great Britain did not bother to allow for this in its calculations.

The Ethiopian crisis was made to order for Hitler. While Great Britain and France were deeply involved with the Italian aggression, Germany seized the opportunity, on March 7, 1936, to denounce the Locarno pacts. It also sent its army into the Rhineland (that portion of Germany west of the Rhine River), which had been disarmed under the terms of the Versailles Treaty.

France was disturbed by this, for it brought the German army to the French border. Great Britain, however, was not concerned since it had its naval treaty, and France would not act without Great Britain.

Hitler got away with it. The German generals had not wished to reoccupy the Rhineland for fear of a violent French reaction, but Hitler had been certain that the western powers would not react. When, in fact, they did not, it gave Hitler the definite feeling that he knew better than the generals. What's more, it gave the generals the uneasy feeling that perhaps Hitler *did* know better. From this point on, the German military proved to be less and less of a restraining influence on Hitler.

The fact that Hitler had sided with Mussolini in the Ethiopian crisis and that Mussolini needed help, thanks to the financial strain of the Ethiopian conquest, led to a German–Italian alliance on October 21, 1936, and the establishment of the Rome–Berlin "Axis."

By that time, the Spanish Civil War had begun. This offered the western powers another chance to display their pusillanimity and lack of foresight. They did not miss the chance to do this.

Italian troops did very poorly in Spain, while the German airforce did very well. As the Spanish Civil War continued, therefore, Italy grew steadily weaker and Germany steadily stronger, so that Mussolini was quickly being demoted to the position of Hitler's puppet.

In early 1938, Hitler was ready to bring even the military and the foreign office under strict Nazi control. The Minister of War, Werner Eduard Fritz von Blomberg (1878–1946), and the Commander-in-Chief of the Army, Werner von Fritsch (1880–1939), were accused of scandals and were removed. Hitler took over the Ministry

of War himself, with Wilhelm Keitel (1882–1946) as his chief aide. Walther von Brauchitsch (1881–1948) bcame Commander-in-Chief of the Army. Hitler rightly judged that neither of these men would ever have the nerve to disagree with him.

The Minister of Foreign Affairs, Konstantin von Neurath (1873–1956), a career diplomat, was discharged and replaced by Joachim von Ribbentrop (1893–1946) who, Hitler knew, could be relied on to do exactly as he was told.

Now Hitler was ready for the major tasks. Again, he was going to make an attempt to seize Austria. Hitler was much stronger than he had been four years before and Mussolini was far weaker. In fact, Hitler knew that Mussolini would not interfere with the Anschluss. It was simply a matter of bullying Austria and gambling that Great Britain and France would not intervene.

The local Austrian Nazis followed orders and made demands and demonstrations. The Austrian Chancellor was called to Berlin and was howled at by Hitler. Finally, on March 12, 1938, German forces marched into Austria. Austria did not resist. The population greeted the German army and Hitler (who had been born in Austria) with wild enthusiasm, and it was now the turn of the Austrian Jews to be subjected to the vilest treatment. Great Britain and France repeated their well-practiced specialty of doing nothing.

Hitler had now gone beyond Bismarck and had added 6 million German-speaking people to a Germany that was considerably stronger than it had been under William II.

But he was not through. There were 3 million German-speaking people living along the outer rim of Czechoslovakia (the "Sudeten" area), adjoining the German and Austrian frontier. Hitler wanted them, too. The Sudeten Germans had developed a Nazi party of their own, complete with all the foul miasma of Hitler's ideology, and they began provoking incidents and blaming them on the Czechs.

Czechoslovakia, however, was not Austria. It was democratic, had strong fortifications, and a sturdy army, and it wanted to fight.

Great Britain, however, kept aiming at appeasement, kept trying to give Germany enough non-British territory to keep it quiet, in the pathetic hope that Hitler could be made to behave himself.

On July 26, 1938, the British sent one of their civil servants, Walter Runciman (1870–1949) to Czechoslovakia, to see how much he could persuade the Czechs to give up to Hitler. No compromise was possible, however. Hitler wanted his terms and would not yield an inch.

The British Prime Minister, Arthur Neville Chamberlain (1869–1940), went three times to Germany and, for a while, it seemed he might resist, but he didn't. He caved in. On September 29, 1938, Chamberlain, Hitler, Mussolini, and the French premier, Edouard Daladier (1884–1970), came to an agreement, without Czechoslovakia even being present to protest.

The surrender at Munich gave Germany the entire Czech border area, containing 3.5 million people, of whom 700,000 were Czechs. All of Czechoslovakia's fortifications were abandoned and what was left was completely defenseless. It could continue to exist only as a German puppet.

It was a despicable betrayal of a democratic country, and Great Britain and France had reached new depths of disgrace. Chamberlain returned to Great Britain, waving the piece of paper that represented the British craven surrender and claiming that he had brought "peace with honor." Actually, he had brought neither. The British and French people, saved from war at the moment, rejoiced at the surrender.

Inside Germany, Hitler had won again by betting on the pusillanimity of the west against the prudent caution of his own generals. He now felt that nothing could stop him and he wanted a war. He wanted a Bismarckian type of war, a quick victory with all expenses paid by the defeated power. He began planning for one.

He no longer felt it necessary to soothe the feelings of the west. Since he was intent on war, it didn't matter how he offended them. He was quite certain that their general paralysis of will would force them to give in at every point, or, even if they fought, their general reluctance to do so would cast them down in quick defeat.

Therefore, on March 15, 1939, he coolly absorbed the western half of what remained of "independent" Czechoslovakia, converting it into the "Protectorate of Bohemia-Moravia."

Hitler then went on, on March 21, to demand, and to get, the city of Memel from Lithuania, a city that Lithuania had rather unrighteously taken from Germany some two decades earlier. This was followed by the now-familiar Hitlerian paroxysm of attacks and demands, this time against Poland. Hitler wanted the city of Danzig. He also wanted the right of passage across the "Polish corridor" that separated the bulk of Germany from East Prussia.

Here, however, Hitler had made his first major mistake. He had taken western Czechoslovakia. Except for that, all the lands he had taken over—the Ruhr, the Rhineland, Austria, the Sudeten region, Memel—were inhabited by Germans. The city of Danzig was also inhabited by Germans and, in fact, it had been under the control of its local Nazis for almost as long as Germany itself. If Hitler had asked for it without having taken western Czechoslovakia, he might have gotten it, and one more surrender might have left the west truly helpless to resist.

However, his taking of western Czechoslovakia had meant the permanent end of British appeasement of Hitler. Even the cold blood of British officialdom was heated at this example of the utter contempt in which Hitler held all agreements and his total lack of concern for British self-respect. He had forced Great Britain to surrender at Munich, and then he couldn't even bring himself to stick to the terms of the surrender for as long as six months.

And Hitler had done this for what? Czechoslovakia was a helpless German puppet now anyway. What had Hitler gained by taking it? One can only suppose that he didn't want any more bloodless victories. He wanted a quick, easy war, and he meant to have it.

The British and French, unable to appease any longer, guaranteed the integrity of Poland on March 31, 1939. On April 28, Hitler retaliated by denouncing the British–German naval treaty of 1935. It had served its purpose of keeping Great

Britain quiet and he had never intended to observe it anyway.

The British, having guaranteed Poland, could not make that guarantee effective by direct action, and Germany knew that well. Poland was on the other side of Germany and by the time Great Britain could reach it, it would be destroyed. The only way of solving that problem was to get the Soviet Union to help out, so Great Britain set about obtaining a Soviet alliance.

There were three problems here. First, Poland did not want Soviet help since it feared the Soviets as much as it feared the Germans. Second, the British government disliked the Soviets intensely, too, and were not in the mood to force Poland to accept Soviet help. Therefore, they treated the Soviet Union with the utmost reserve, hoping it would decide to help on its own and without much in the way of commitments from the west.

The third problem was that the Soviet Union knew very well that Great Britain had spent five years mollifying Hitler in the hope that he would turn against the Soviet Union. They felt certain that Great Britain would not hesitate to entangle the Soviet Union in war with Germany and then step to one side. They did not fail to remember how little help they had obtained from the west in World War I.

The Soviet Union, therefore, hedged its bets by dealing with Germany also. Hitler found this useful, since he was perfectly willing to keep hands off the Soviet Union at the moment and let it wait its turn. A German–Soviet nonaggression pact was signed in Moscow on August 23, 1939. This stunned the world, and loud were the outcries against Soviet double-dealing. It is very easy to argue, however, that if Great Britain had treated with the Soviet Union honestly, the pact with Germany would not have been signed. Hitler and Stalin were both unprincipled, but the British leaders had been abysmally shortsighted and had played their cards stupidly.

With the Soviet Union neutralized, Germany was ready. On September 1, 1939, German forces took Danzig and invaded Poland and Hitler had the war he wanted. World War II began.

In the Nazi era, science and other aspects of culture declined sharply under the cruel grip of a monstrous government. Many Germans (by no means Jews only) fled a land in which it was difficult and unsafe for any self-respecting human being to remain. Nevertheless, there were some flickers.

Otto Hahn continued to work with the neutron bombardment of uranium that Fermi had begun. By 1938, he was convinced that the uranium nucleus was being split in two. He did not quite have the nerve to state this openly, since it was so revolutionary a notion, but the idea spread and led to nuclear weapons (and to Hahn's feelings that he ought to kill himself in remorse). He eventually received a Nobel Prize for his work.

Gerhard Domagk (1895–1964) discovered the antibacterial properties of a compound called "Prontosil." This discovery in 1935 led to a whole family of "sulfa drugs" that were a new and potent weapon against infection. In 1939, Domagk received a Nobel Prize for this but was not allowed to accept it. The 1935 Nobel Prize for Peace had gone to Carl von Ossietsky (1889–1938), a German pacifist who was in a Nazi concentration camp. Hitler, offended by this, decided that no German scientists would thereafter be allowed to accept a Nobel Prize. (Domagk eventually got his prize once Hitler no longer existed to stop him.)

Otto Heinrich Waburg (1883–1970) worked on enzymes involved in respiration during this period. He was the unusual case of a Jewish scientist who was allowed to continue working under the Nazis because he was trying to find ways of curing cancer, and Hitler had a deadly fear of that disease. (As it happened, Warburg never found a cure and Hitler never developed the disease.)

Thomas Mann left Germany in 1933 and eventually came to the United States in 1938. During this period, he published a trilogy dealing with a fictionalized version of the Biblical story of Joseph. This appeared between 1933 and 1936.

Rudolf Ditzen (1893–1947), writing under the penname of Hans Fallada, published *Little Man, What Now?* in 1932, and continued to write under the Nazis.

The Austrian-born Martin Buber (1878–1965)

was the most influential Jewish scholar and philosopher in Germany when Hitler came to power. In 1938, he managed to get away and to emigrate to Palestine.

AUSTRIA

During this period, Wilhelm Miklas (1872–1956) was President of Austria. He was a figurehead who kept himself virtually invisible.

Fearing Germany to the north, Austria signed a treaty of friendship on February 6, 1930, with Italy. Mussolini's price for keeping Austria safe was to have the nation turn Fascist. This became easier as the Great Depression tightened its grip, with the failure of Vienna's huge bank, the Credit-Anstalt, on May 11, 1931.

The man who could best serve Mussolini's purposes was Engelbert Dollfuss (1892–1934), who became Chancellor of Austria on May 20, 1932. Barely five feet tall, he somehow symbolized the shrunken postwar Austria. His policy consisted of cowering before Mussolini.

With Hitler in power in Germany, Dollfuss faced increasing pressure from Austrian Nazis, egged on by Germany. Dollfuss tried to fight them by suspending parliamentary government, outlawing the Nazi party, and moving in the direction of a one-party rule under his own party, which imitated Italian Fascism rather than German Nazism.

Dollfuss might have made common cause with the Social Democrats who were very strong in Vienna and who were fiercely anti-Nazi, but he didn't. Like all those who might have stood against Hitler in this fateful period, he persistently chose the wrong course of action. Dollfuss decided to force the Social Democrats into line and, from February 11–15, 1934, he actually bombarded their strongholds in various Vienna districts. The Social Democrats were wiped out as a political force, and Dollfuss established a Fascist state.

This did not keep Dollfuss safe, for without a Social Democratic opposition to them, the Austrian Nazis grew ever bolder. They staged a coup on July 25, 1934. They took over the Chancellory, shot Dollfuss, and let him bleed to death. They

might have taken over Austria then and there, but Mussolini sent army units to the Austrian frontier. Yugoslavia also reacted strongly, and Hitler backed off. Austria temporarily retained its independence.

Dollfuss was replaced as Chancellor by Kurt von Schuschnigg (1897–1977), who continued Dollfuss's policy of slavish dependence on Mussolini. By 1937, however, Italy was itself growing more and more dependent on Germany. On April 22, 1937, when Schuschnigg visited Mussolini in Venice, Mussolini broke the news to him that Italy could not be counted upon to save Austria a second time and advised him to compromise with the Nazis.

Schuschnigg resisted that, but on February 12, 1938, he was forced to visit Hitler at Berchtesgaden in the Bavarian Alps (Hitler's vacation retreat), and there he was subjected to Hitlerian rant. Schuschnigg tried to offer compromises, but no compromises would satisfy Hitler, who wanted complete surrender.

Back in Austria, Schuschnigg tried to deal with the remnants of the Social Democrats, but they would have nothing to do with him. He tried to arrange a plebiscite, but Hitler would not allow that. Nazi uprisings and disorders grew in intensity and, on March 12, 1938, the German army marched in.

President Miklas resigned; Chancellor Schuschnigg was imprisoned. The new ruler of Austria (under Hitler) was Arthur Seyss-Inquart (1892–1946), an Austrian Nazi who oversaw the complete conversion of Austria to Nazism. In a plebiscite held on April 10, 99.75% voted in favor of union (the wonder is that anyone dared vote against it) and Austria, for a time, disappeared from the map of Europe.

An outstanding Austrian scientist of the period was Lise Meitner (1878–1968), who worked with Otto Hahn on the neutron bombardment of uranium. She managed, for a time, to avoid the anti-Semitism of the Nazis (for although she was a Jew, she was an Austrian national). In 1938, however, with the German annexation of Austria, she had to flee to Sweden. There she pondered over the results of the work she and Hahn had done, and she, too, decided that the uranium was being cloven in two and that "fission" was taking place. Unlike Hahn, she did not keep her conclusion to herself and the news reached the United States—with awesome consequences.

Richard Kuhn (1900–1967) isolated Vitamin B$_6$ and for this and other work, he was awarded a Nobel Prize in 1938. By that time, however, Austria had been taken over and Kuhn could not, by Hitler's orders, accept the Prize, though he later did when Hitler was no longer able to prevent it.

Franz Werfel (1890–1945), who had been born in Prague when it was part of Austria-Hungary, wrote novels in this period of which the best known is *The Forty Days of Musa Dagh,* published in 1933. Since he was Jewish, he left for France in 1938.

CZECHOSLOVAKIA

Throughout this period, Czechoslovakia, under Masaryk as President, maintained its democratic form of government, while most of the other nations between France and the Soviet Union were turning Fascist to one extent or another. Masaryk resigned because of age on December 13, 1935, and died on September 14, 1937. He was succeeded by Benes, who continued to maintain Czech democracy.

In the Sudeten areas along the rim of western Czechoslovakia, the German population turned Nazi after Hitler came to power in Germany. Under the leadership of Konrad Henlein (1898–1945), they committed all the gross provocations and violences that were apparently inseparable from Nazism.

The Czechoslovak authorities tried to handle the Germans both resolutely and fairly, but, of course, with Hitler and his henchmen howling in the background, and with the western powers uneasily adverse to supporting the Czechs, it was a lost cause. Czechoslovakia, feeling rather desperate for support, concluded a treaty of mutual assistance with the Soviet Union on May 16, 1935, and that allowed Germany to accuse Czechoslovakia of being a Soviet puppet.

After Germany had absorbed Austria, Czechoslovakia found itself with Germany both on the north and south. In fact, no sooner had Austria been absorbed when the German propaganda machine began a steady drumbeat against Czechoslovakia. After a summer in which Hitler raised and lowered tensions to suit himself, he beat the feeble Chamberlain of Great Britain into total surrender. Czechoslovakia was abandoned and dismembered. Benes went into exile on October 5, 1938.

The Sudeten areas went to Germany, while the southern sections of Slovakia (the eastern portion of the nation) were absorbed by Hungary.

What was left of Czechoslovakia was divided into three parts. On the west were the provinces of Bohemia and Moravia, which were under the rule of Emil Hacha (1872–1945), who acted as "president." To the east was Slovakia under Josef Tiso (1887–1947), a Slovakian priest. Still further east was the Russian-speaking tip of Czechoslovakia, which became "Carpatho-Ukraine." All three parts were firmly under German control.

There was no need to go further, but Hitler (like Napoleon a century and a half earlier) had no bounds to his appetite. Tiso of Slovakia appealed for full independence of Slovakia and this was granted in the sense that he could call himself Premier while German officials ran the land.

Bohemia and Moravia were then annexed outright by Germany on March 15, 1939, and became the "Protectorate of Bohemia-Moravia." It was placed under Constantin von Neurath (the former German foreign minister) as "Protector."

And with that, Czechoslovakia in its turn disappeared from the map of Europe, while Hitler, by this unnecessary act, put an end to British appeasement and embarked on a path whose end he could no longer correctly foresee.

HUNGARY

Hungary continued under the rule of Admiral Horthy in this period. He remained in the background and ruled through a series of Premiers. The nation maintained a close friendship with Fascist Italy, and rapidly turned Fascist itself. On October 4, 1932, Gyula Gombos (1886–1936) became Premier. He was a markedly reactionary anti-Semite and under him Fascism was well-established.

Once Hitler came to power in Germany, however, Hungarians were not lacking who wanted a Nazi-like regime as well. Their leader was Ferenc Szalasi (1897–1946), whose views corresponded with those of Hitler in every particular.

Hungary's situation became precarious as Italy became part of the Axis, was quickly relegated to junior partner, and abandoned its protection of both Austria and Hungary. Hungary tried to strengthen its own home-grown Fascism, but when Germany absorbed Austria, and its army appeared on the western border of Hungary, it was plain that Hungary would simply have to cooperate with Germany.

In fact, it seemed to many Hungarians that it might be profitable to play the jackal and pick up what leftovers it could seize from Germany's aggression. There was a Hungarian-speaking minority in southern Czechoslovakia, just north of the Hungarian border, and when the western powers abandoned Czechoslovakia to the Germans, Hungary proceeded to absorb this region, gaining 5000 square miles of territory with a million inhabitants.

On March 15, 1939, when Germany absorbed Bohemia-Moravia, Hungary absorbed the Carpatho-Ukraine, leaving only a rump Slovakia as "independent." Hungary signified the extent to which it had become a German puppet by withdrawing from the League of Nations on April 11, 1939, and then introducing all the paraphernalia of Nazi anti-Semitic legislation.

Clearly, the British–French betrayal at Munich had handed all of central Europe to Hitler.

During this period, however, the Hungarian composer Bela Bartok was bringing his career to a successful close.

POLAND

At the beginning of this period, Poland was under the strong control of Pilsudski, who did what he could to come to some sort of agreement with the Soviet Union on the east and with Germany on the west. But Poland, like most of Europe, was turning sharply rightward.

On April 23, 1935, a new Constitution was put into effect that effectively wiped out parliamentary government and turned Poland into an essentially Fascist state. Pilsudski died soon afterward on May 12, 1935, and was succeeded by Edward Rydz-Smigly (1886–1941), an associate of Pilsudski.

On the constructive side, Poland created the port of Gdynia on the coast west of Danzig. It was a purely Polish city and lessened Polish dependence on Danzig, which was under Nazi control.

As Hitler grew stronger, Poland's situation grew more precarious. Its Fascist leaders were, however, incapable of understanding the situation and could focus only on possible gains of their own. It should have been clear to the blindest that the destruction of Czechoslovakia would result in Poland being surrounded on three sides by Germany, and that Poland was bound to be the next victim.

Nevertheless, Poland actually seized the opportunity of the Czech crisis to aid Germany and to press for its own bit of loot, the city of Teschen, which the Czechs had occupied during the Polish–Russian war of 1920.

Poland got Teschen, but then, in the summer of 1939, found itself the target of Hitler's ravenous fury. Poland accepted the guarantees of the British and French, even though these were largely worthless without the cooperation of the Soviet Union, and even though Poland would not accept Soviet participation.

As a result, the Soviet Union, suspecting the west's intention of embroiling it in a war with Germany and then stepping back, signed a pact with Germany instead.

On September 1, 1939, German forces invaded Poland.

SOVIET UNION

By 1930, Stalin was in complete control of the Soviet Union, and it was clear to him that world revolution was not in the cards, certainly not in the near future. In fact, Europe was turning sharply rightward and it was fascism, not communism, that was sweeping the continent.

It seemed to Stalin that his only safety lay in extending the hand of friendship, as far as it would be accepted, to the other powers. This decision to strike for moderation became stronger when Hitler came to power in Germany and unleashed his anticommunist crusade.

Stalin signed nonaggression pacts with all the nations on the western border of the Soviet Union. He accepted the loss of whatever territory had been lost after World War I. He managed to obtain the recognition of his government by the United States on November 17, 1933, after 16 years of American nonrecognition. He even led the Soviet Union into the League of Nations on September 18, 1934, and began to support the status quo in Europe.

On May 2, 1935, the Soviet Union signed an alliance with France. France, once again frightened of a resurgent Germany, felt the need to turn to a communist Soviet Union as, 40 years earlier it had turned to an autocratic Russian Empire. However, the alliance was not a very strong one. There were many in France who preferred Hitler to Stalin. The same was true in Great Britain.

Stalin, growing moderate in his foreign policy, did not do the same internally, however. As is often the case with dictators who attempt to make their power absolute, he saw danger everywhere, even among his own followers, and, increasingly, he struck at dissent, even when slight, and even when imaginary.

Periodically, the Communist Party would be purged, and those who were considered as deviating from orthodox doctrine (as defined by Stalin), even if only in an imaginary way, were expelled from the party and from all the privileges that came with membership.

On December 1, 1934, Sergey Mironovich Kirov (1886–1934), one of Stalin's chief aides, was assassinated. That apparently detonated Stalin's paranoia. For four years he sought out enemies, tried them to foregone conviction, and, for the most part, had them executed. A large number of old Communists were wiped out in this way.

In 1937, the purge extended even to the Army. Tukhachevski, who had fought well in the Civil War and against the Poles, was accused of conspiring with Germany and Japan and was executed, along with a large number of other generals.

In this way, Stalin wiped out all opposition, and even put the army under his complete control. However, he had to make a heavy payment for it. The spectacle of the purge displeased the democratic elements in Europe and America with whom Stalin was hoping to join against the fascist menace. It displeased the west so much, in fact, that it made Hitler seem more respectable than he would otherwise have seemed, and this encouraged the policy of appeasement. Then, too, the purge of the Army command weakened it, and in the crisis to come, the Soviets had to pay for that in blood.

Soviet aid to the Loyalists during the Spanish Civil War was also distasteful to the west, and encouraged them to refuse to help the Loyalists themselves, though it was clear to any dunce that a Rebel victory was not in the interest of the west.

The general feeling of "better dead than Red" poisoned the situation during the crises of 1938 and 1939. The British and French could not bring themselves to receive Russian help in return for concessions to Stalin, and they preferred to bring on war by concessions to Hitler. Stalin, tired of western snubbing, turned to Hitler himself, signed the nonaggression pact on August 23, 1939, and thus sent Hitler into Poland on September 1.

During this period, the tradition of Russian literature continued under the Communists as it had under the Tsars. Mikhail Alexandrovich Sholokhov (1905–1984) was writing novels and eventually won the Nobel Prize for literature. His best-known novels are *And Quiet Flows the Don* and *The Don Flows Home to the Sea*, which were translated into English in 1934 and 1940, respectively. Boris Leonodovich Pasternak (1890–1960) was also writing in this period and also won the Nobel Prize for literature. A third great Russian writer of the period was Vladimir Vladimirovich Nabokov (1899–1977) who worked in France.

In music, Shostakovich produced his *Fifth Symphony*, perhaps the most-often played of his works, in 1937. Prokofiev returned to the Soviet Union in 1933, composed *Peter and the Wolf* in 1936, and the music for the film *Alexander Nevsky* in 1938.

In science (if the term is used very loosely) there was Trofim Denisovich Lysenko (1898–1976), whose fallacious genetic theories on the inheritability of acquired characteristics fit what Stalin conceived to be the Communist ideology. Stalin backed him with his full might and a generation of real geneticists, including Nikolay Ivanovich Vavilov (1887–1943), were imprisoned or executed. Soviet biology was set back a generation by this unwarranted subjection of science to ideology.

FRANCE

Paul Doumer (1857–1932) was elected president on May 13, 1931, and was assassinated by a Russian anarchist on May 6, 1932. He was succeeded by the colorless and ineffectual Albert Lebrun (1871–1950).

France was divided sharply into Left and Right in this period, with each side more interested in fighting the other than in fighting the enemies who were arising outside of France. The coming of Hitler did nothing to unite the French. In fact, many on the Right were ready to turn to Hitler rather than give in to the Left.

France came to the brink of a Rightist coup toward the end of 1933, when it was discovered that the bonds sold by a Russian-born pseudo-financier, Serge Alexandre Stavisky (1886–1934), were worthless, and that there had been a gigantic fraud that had fleeced many workingmen of their life-savings. Stavisky fled and was found dead in January 1934.

Stavisky was Jewish and the French Right seized on that as a kind of reverse Dreyfus Affair. They claimed that he had been killed by French officialdom to conceal the fact that many in the French government were deeply implicated in the "Stavisky Affair" and had profited from it. There were riots in Paris on February 6–7, 1934, and the government made things worse by behaving just as though there was indeed a cover-up.

In the end, a coup was barely averted, barely, and the shaken French were in no condition, thereafter, to take a strong line against Hitler.

French politics was made up of many parties, each with a narrow band of policies and support. The result was that in France only coalitions could govern, and they fell apart almost as quickly as they formed. French cabinets followed each other in dizzying succession, although personalities changed much more than policies did.

A French statesman who appeared in cabinet after cabinet in different posts, and who was stronger and more decisive than most, was Jean Louis Barthou (1862–1934), who became Minister of Foreign Affairs in 1934. Though 82 years old, he went energetically to work building alliances against the growing menace of Hitler's Germany. On October 9, 1934, King Alexander I of Yugoslavia was in Marseille, meeting with Barthou.

There, a Macedonian fanatic gunned down the king, and since Barthou was in the line of fire, he died, too. It was a major loss for France, for he had no immediate successors who were as firmly anit-Nazi as he was.

Barthou had been working toward an alliance with the Soviet Union against Germany. It was taken up the month after the assassination by a cabinet headed by Gaston Pierre Etienne Flandin (1889–1958) and then by one headed by Laval, which took over in May 1935. The Laval cabinet carried through the alliance that month, for it had grown more urgent by the fact that Hitler had now openly declared that Germany would rearm. The pact, however, was not popular with the French Right, and neither Flandin nor Laval were enthusiastic over it, for both were in the ranks of the appeasers later on. In fact, Laval lost the Premiership because of his attempt, with Hoare of Great Britain, to divide up Ethiopia and give a piece to Mussolini.

The menace of Hitler had, however, forced the leftist parties to combine (much against their will) in a "Popular Front." This consisted of the moderately leftist Radical Socialists, the more leftists Socialists, and the Communists. On May 3, 1936, the Popular Front won an election and the cabinet was headed by the Socialist, Leon Blum (1872–1950). Blum was an easy target for the

Right, since he was not only a Socialist, but a Jew as well.

The Popular Front embarked at once on a program of social reform that was, of course, bitterly resisted by the Right. It was also hampered by the fact that the laboring classes (who were eager to see the reforms carried through more quickly and more extensively, and who felt that the government would support them) indulged in strikes that weakened the economy and strengthened the Right's resistance.

The Popular Front cabinet was too weak at home, and too uncertain of support, to take a strong line abroad. Thus, it had no choice but to follow Great Britain's short-sighted policy with regard to the Spanish Civil War, refusing the kind of massive help to the Loyalists that the Axis powers were giving the Rebels. Nor would it do anything about the German absorption of Austria.

Blum was replaced by Camille Chautemps (1885–1963) in June 1937, and he, in turn, by Daladier in April 1938. Both Chautemps and Daladier were Radical Socialists and it was Daladier, along with Chamberlain of Great Britain, who participated in the Munich betrayal in September 1938. Daladier, unlike Chamberlain, was intelligent enough to realize the disaster that had taken place, and expected to be reviled and calumniated when he returned to Paris. He was astonished when he found the people, willing to accept anything rather than war, cheering him.

The Popular Front broke up after Munich, and France continued glumly to play the role of junior partner to Great Britain. France reluctantly followed the British lead throughout the summer of 1939 as the Polish crisis deepened, and finally found the abyss of war opening before it on September 1, 1939, when Germany invaded Poland.

The outstanding French scientists of the period were Frederic Joliot-Curie (1900–1958) and his wife, Irene Joliot-Curie (1897–1956), the latter being the daughter of Pierre and Marie Curie. In 1934, they were the first to form radioactive isotopes that did not exist in nature, a discovery that turned out to have immense usefulness in every branch of science. For this, they received a Nobel Prize.

Among the writers of the period was Louis Henri Jean Farigoule (1885–1972) who, under the penname of Jules Romaine, was now at the height of his fame. So was the popular novelist, Sidonie Gabrielle Colette (1873–1954). Rising to prominence at this time were the French playwrights Jean Anouilh (b. 1910) and Jean Cocteau (1889–1934). Another playwright, Marcel Pagnol (1895–1974) is best known for three motion pictures he produced between 1931 and 1936: *Marius*, *Fanny*, and *Cesar*.

GREAT BRITAIN

In the early 1930s, Great Britain was still pushing for disarmament. The sea-powers gathered for the London Naval Conference, which opened on January 21, 1930. It attempted to limit and regulate submarine production, and to scrap some warships already built. The next year, however, Japan's invasion of Manchuria put an end to meaningful naval disarmament, for clearly Japan (a signatory of the 1930 agreement) had no intention of limiting its armaments.

Disarmament conferences were held in Geneva in the spring of 1932 and the summer of 1933, but they came to nothing. Hitler's rise to power in Germany in January 1933 put a final end to any hope for any kind of disarmament.

In the meantime, however, the Statute of Westminster, passed by Parliament in December 1931, formalized what had already been accepted informally. The self-ruling white-dominated portions of the British Empire—Canada, Newfoundland, Australia, New Zealand, South Africa, and the Irish Free State—were recognized as completely independent, their only connection to Great Britain remaining a common allegiance to the British monarch, who would be represented in the dominions by figurehead governor-generals.

Great Britain found itself unable to take a strong line against Japan in its invasion of Manchuria (apart from a general reluctance, after the horrible experience of World War I, to get involved in distant disputes that were not of direct concern to the security of the Empire), because the Great Depression had hit Great Britain hard.

Unemployment was rising rapidly and so was the national deficit. Any efforts to correct the situation were bound to require sacrifices from workingmen, and MacDonald's Labour government couldn't bring itself to take such action.

On August 24, 1931, MacDonald resigned, and since no party was willing to take sole responsibility for an economic disaster that was worldwide and could not be dealt with on a national basis alone, there seemed no choice but to establish a coalition government of Labour, Liberals, and Conservatives. MacDonald, himself, was persuaded to continue as Prime Minister, to the shock and anger of the Labour Party stalwarts.

Taking over as leaders of the Labour party, or that portion of it that now filled the role of Opposition, was George Lansbury (1859–1940), an extreme pacifist, and Arthur Henderson (1863–1935), who had been Foreign Secretary under MacDonald, and who had labored strenuously on the doomed cause of disarmament. Though he failed to achieve it, he won the Nobel Peace Prize in 1934 for his efforts.

In actual fact, MacDonald, in his declining years, lacked the strength to be the true leader of the coalition government, which came to be increasingly dominated by the Conservatives under Stanley Baldwin.

The coalition government, preoccupied with Great Britain's economic situation, did not wish to take a strong stand in foreign affairs, and did not. In fact, there were many in Great Britain who saw only the Left as a danger, who admired Mussolini, supported the Spanish Rebels, and felt that Hitler could be dealt with. There was even a small Fascist party in Great Britain, openly pro-Nazi and anti-Semitic, under Oswald Ernald Mosley (1896–1980), a renegade Labourite, who mimicked Hitler with unintentionally comic effect. His party played little role in British affairs.

The coalition government was forced to abandon the gold standard on September 21, 1931, permitting an increase in the money supply that was accompanied by a declining value of the pound against other currencies. This encouraged British exports, but raised the possibility of inflation. Great Britain also abandoned free trade and

began placing a tariff on food imports to help British farmers.

Since it was clear that the Depression was worldwide and could be fought only on a worldwide basis, an International Economic conference was held in London in the summer of 1933. There was an attempt to stabilize world currencies once more, but the United States was itself going off the gold standard, and so the Conference failed. Great Britain, as a result, continued to raise trade barriers, as did other nations, something that did more harm than good.

In due course, the gold standard was abandoned the world over, and national currencies were subjected to the ebb and flow of economic events and to the deliberate manipulation by governments as each tried to improve its own share of international trade.

On June 7, 1935, MacDonald, finding he could no longer even pretend he was heading the government, resigned and Baldwin took over the Prime Minister's post in title, something he already had done in fact. A few months later, a general election confirmed the coalition government in power, placing it more under Conservative domination than ever, to the point where it might just as well be considered Conservative altogether. The Labour Party, after Henderson's death and Lansbury's resignation (since his uncompromising pacifism simply didn't suit the time), came under the leadership of Clement Richard Attlee (1883–1967).

Baldwin was not the man to inspire Great Britain to leadership in world affairs. He affected stolidity in the face of all that was going on. He did initiate a certain measure of rearmament in the face of the escalating German threat, but the British effort in this respect lagged far behind the German.

British energies in 1936 were diverted by an internal crisis that was peculiarly British in nature. What happened was that George V died on January 20, 1936, after having reigned for a quarter of a century, and was succeeded by his oldest son, who reigned as Edward VIII (1894–1972).

Edward VIII was an intellectual lightweight and a playboy. He had been very popular as Prince of Wales, and he enjoyed being popular.

He approached the ceremonial duties of kingship with extreme distaste (though he must have known all his life that he would be subjected to them and should have been prepared for it), and this at once placed him in the bad graces of the traditionalists of the British government. He seemed to show signs of wanting to be an activist monarch, expressing sympathy for miners in an offhand moment—something that horrified the government (not so much the sympathy, as that he should say anything at all).

The real problem came in the fact that, although he was 42 years old at the time of his succession, he was a bachelor, and refused to make a suitable match. In fact he was in love with Wallis Warfied Simpson (1896–1986).

Wallis Simpson was another intellectual lightweight, which bothered no one. She was also a commoner and an American, which bothered a few. What really put the fat in the fire, however, was that she had been divorced once, and was still married to a second husband from whom she was in the process of getting a divorce. This absolutely horrified the royal family, the Church of England, the aristocracy, and many conservative British.

The crisis dragged on all through the summer and fall (during which Hitler took the opportunity to reoccupy the Rhineland, with Great Britain scarcely able to note the fact). It ended only when Edward VIII, who had never been formally crowned, abdicated on December 10, 1936. He was the only British monarch who ever abandoned the throne voluntarily.

He probably did so with great relief, though the soap opera atmosphere of giving up a throne "for the woman I love" was the sensation of the tabloids. He was granted the title of Duke of Windsor, married Mrs. Simpson in France in June 1937, and settled down to an entirely useless and idle existence, forever estranged from his family, and giving rise to strong suspicions, now and then, that he, and even more so, the new Duchess, sympathized with Nazi Germany. (This may not be so. It is questionable if anything outside themselves ever bestirred their mentalities to the point of sympathy or of any other emotion.)

Succeeding Edward VIII was his younger brother, who reigned as George VI (1895–1952). George was the opposite of his brother. Retiring and shy, and afflicted with a stammer in addition, he had never sought popularity or even notice. Becoming king unexpectedly, however, he fulfilled all his duties admirably, serving the nation as a rallying point, high above politics, in the difficult times to come.

Once that was done, and George VI was formally crowned on May 12, 1937, Stanley Baldwin felt he could retire, doing so on May 28, 1937. Baldwin was succeeded by Neville Chamberlain, who had scarcely more charisma than Baldwin and under whom the policy of appeasement, of attempting to tame Hitler by giving him some of what he wanted, flowered poisonously.

This did not suit the Foreign Minister, Anthony Eden (1897–1977), who had supplied what action the British took in the case of the Ethiopian crisis. He resigned on February 20, 1938, and was succeeded by the appeasement-minded Edward Frederick Lindley Wood, Earl of Halifax (1881–1959).

There followed the German annexation of Austria, with regard to which Great Britain did nothing. It was rearming in this period, without much fanfare, but the process lagged far behind what the Germans were doing, and the extent of its growing strength was far from enough to make Great Britain eager to withstand the loudly shouting and forever-threatening Hitler.

Great Britain played an ignoble part during the Czechoslovakian crisis, betraying the central-European democracy at Munich. After Hitler had absorbed the remainder of Bohemia and Moravia, Great Britain was forced to abandon appeasement and it gave guarantees of support to Poland, which was the next on Hitler's hit list. Great Britain did very little, however, to insure Soviet cooperation, and this made the Soviet–German pact possible.

Great Britain as, in fact, in the mood to try to force Poland to give in somewhat to Germany, but Hitler was tired of bloodless victories. What he wanted was a quick war that would establish his military predominance in Europe and that would frighten France and Great Britain into total submission.

Therefore, when Hitler sent his army into Poland on September 1, 1939, Great Britain found itself, to its own considerable horror, forced into a declaration of war on September 3.

British science continued to flourish in this period. In 1932, James Chadwick (1891–1974) detected the existence of the neutron, a particle much like the proton but without electric charge. This made it possible to explain the structure of the atomic nucleus as a proton–neutron collection. In that same year, John Douglas Cockcroft (1897–1967) built a particle accelerator that brought about the first artificial nuclear reaction. Both Chadwick and Cockcroft earned Nobel Prizes for their work.

By 1935, Robert Watson-Watt (1892–1973) had worked out a practical system for detecting the direction and distance of approaching airplanes by bouncing radio waves ("microwaves") off them. This was referred to as "radio detection and ranging," which was abbreviated as "radar." This discovery was to be of crucial importance in a very few years.

In literature, Aldous Huxley published his best-known book, *Brave New World* (1932), a dystopia that probed the dark side of technological advance. Robert Ranke Graves (1895–1985) published his Suetonius-derived novels, *I. Claudius* and *Claudius the God* in 1934. James Hilton (1900–1954) published *Good-Bye, Mr. Chips* in 1934. Dorothy Sayers published her early paean to the cause of women's rights, *Gaudy Nights*, in 1935, while John Ronald Reuel Tolkien (1892–1973) published his successful fantasy adventure for children, *The Hobbit*, in 1937.

Among the playwrights, Noel Coward produced *Private Lives* in 1930 and *Cavalcade* in 1931. The American-born T. S. Eliot, now a British citizen, produced *Murder in the Cathedral* in 1935, a verse drama about Thomas Becket. Emlyn Williams (b. 1905) produced *Night Must Fall* (1935) and *The Corn Is Green* (1938).

John Edward Masefield (1878–1967) became poet laureate of England in 1930. Dylan Marlais Thomas (1914–1953), the most important Welsh poet of recent times, was at the peak of his career in this period.

In nonfiction, Norman Angell (1872–1967) wrote books supporting pacifism, revising his most famous book *The Great Illusion* in 1933, and winning the Nobel Peace Prize in that year. Arnold Joseph Toynbee (1889–1975) began his monumental, but flawed, *A Study of History*, publishing the first of 12 volumes in 1934. In the field of science writing, Lancelot Hogben (1895–1975) published his popular *Mathematics for the Millions* (1936) and *Science for the Citizen* (1938).

John Maynard Keynes (1883–1946) was the most widely read and influential economist of the period.

IRISH FREE STATE/EIRE

The ambitions of most of the population of the Irish Free State was to weaken and even abolish any ties with Great Britain, however theoretical, and to unite the island, absorbing Northern Ireland. That wasn't as easy as it sounded, for the majority in Northern Ireland was unalterably opposed to union with the south, and the Irish Free State was itself so economically dependent on Great Britain that there was a distinct feeling among many Irish that defying the British would do more harm than good.

Even so, there was a "tariff war" between the Irish Free States and Great Britain when the latter nation turned protectionist. The Irish suffered badly as a result and matters were reconciled by a trade pact on Febbruary 17, 1936.

The Irish Free State took advantage of British weakness and uncertainty during, and immediately after, the crisis over the marriage plans of Edward VIII and his abdication, to introduce a new constitution. Complete independence was not established, but it came so close to it as to make no difference. Great Britain was nowhere mentioned in the new constitution, and the office of governor-general was abolished. In its place there would be a president elected by national suffrage. What's more, the name of the nation was changed from Irish Free State to "Eire" (the Gaelic word for "Ireland").

Any hopes that Northern Ireland would join

Eire under its new constitution were dashed on February 9, 1938, when Northern Ireland voted overwhelmingly to retain its ties with Great Britain. However, putting Northern Ireland to one side, Great Britain and Eire came to an agreement on April 25, 1938, which granted Eire all it had taken.

The first president of Eire under the new constitution was Douglas Hyde (1860–1949). He was Ireland's greatest Gaelic scholar, and he was a Protestant, chosen perhaps as an indication to Northern Ireland that it need not fear religious persecution. Northern Ireland's Protestants remained unmoved, however. Their economy was stronger than that of Eire, and if religious prejudice failed to keep them separate, economic self-interest would not.

An important Irish scientist of the period was Ernest Thomas Sinton Walton (b. 1903), who worked with Cockcroft in producing the first artificial nuclear reaction in 1932. He shared the Nobel Prize with Cockcroft.

UNITED STATES

In a way, the United States, which had a population of 122 million in 1930, suffered more from the Great Depression than did any other nation, psychologically, at least. The inexorable decline in economic activity and in the standard of living, the equally inexorable increase in unemployment, was all the worse because of its contrast with the carefree decade of the 1920s that had just concluded.

The United States had seemed a world apart, virtually untouched by the tragedy and devastation of World War I, and indeed enriched by it. It was secure behind its oceans, wealthy and powerful beyond what would have seemed possible in the nineteenth century. It was surely the favored land of God, showing the crowded and miserable nations of the old world how to do business and how to live.

Now, suddenly, to be vulnerable, to see the wealth vanish, to see poverty and misery advance, was humiliating beyond words.

What's more, the Hoover administration seemed paralyzed and unable to take any effective measures to ameliorate the damage. Ever since the Civil War, it had been Republican policy to play a more or less passive role in the nation's economic affairs, leaving it to the business leaders to keep the nation's economy humming at high speed. The policy worked as long as times were good, but when the global dislocations of World War I and the speculation spree of the 1920s had caused the economy to collapse, ordinary business procedures were completely unable to restart the stalled machinery, and if business was helpless, so was the government.

Indeed, in the aftermath of the stock market crash, the Hoover administration took an action which, of all actions, was best calculated to prolong and intensify the Depression. Since it seemed to the isolationists that the United States must take care of itself and pay as little attention as possible to the rest of the world, they felt that raising tariff barriers would encourage home industries by reducing competition by foreign products. This should allow American business to rebound.

Senator Reed Smoot (1862–1941) and Congressman Willis Chatman Hawley (1864–1941) co-sponsored the "Smoot–Hawley Tariff Act," which raised duties on raw materials by 50–100% in some cases. Many economists protested, but Hoover signed it into law on June 17, 1930.

The results were devastating, since the United States did not (whatever the isolationists might think) live in a world of its own. Other nations, their trade hurt by the new tariff, took retaliatory action at once, so that invisible barriers rose everywhere, choking trade. In a world of nations that were growing increasingly economically interdependent, these barriers hurt everyone. Behind its barriers every nation watched economic activity dwindle so that the Great Depression intensified and became worldwide.

As for the United States, 1300 banks failed in 1930 and on July 28, 1932, the Dow-Jones average of important stock prices hit 41.22, an all-time low. Some 14 million Americans were unemployed in 1932 and, as though an additional frisson of horror was needed, Charles Lindbergh's infant son was kidnapped on March 1, 1932, and was eventually found dead.

A crowd of unemployed veterans of World War I came to Washington in 1932, asking for their war bonuses. President Hoover called them criminals and communists and the army, under commanders who were later to achieve fame in World War II, were ordered to clear them out. This was done and a hundred casualties were admitted. This was probably Hoover at his most disgraceful.

Meanwhile, in 1931, when Japan began its occupation of Manchuria and engaged in open aggression against China, the United States, lost in its isolationism, and bleeding badly at home, was in no mood to take any action other than to express moral disapproval, which didn't bother Japan in the least. Thereafter, Italy, and then Germany, could see that a hyperactive foreign policy would yield dividends and face only token opposition. Through the 1930s, then, the United States played the inglorious role of onlooker as the world prepared to go up in flames.

The Hoover administration grew steadily more unpopular in the country. The only economic measure of note it was able to take was the establishment of the "Reconstruction Finance Corporation" on February 2, 1932, which was designed to make funds available to banks and railroads, in the hope that by helping them to their feet, they would be able to restart the economy and create jobs. This was part of the "trickle-down" philosophy. If you help the rich and powerful, some of the benefit, it was felt, would eventually trickle down to the poor and downtrodden. Nor was it felt that there was any need for direct help to the poor and downtrodden while they were waiting for the trickle.

By 1932, it seemed quite certain that Hoover would not be reelected, though the Republican party was bound to run him again, since to disown him would make disaster the more certain.

Many Democrats struggled for the nomination, but the one that got it, despite the difficulty of obtaining the required two-thirds majority (designed to give the southern states veto power over the nomination), was Franklin D. Roosevelt, the popular governor of New York State, who had lost his race for vice-president in 1920. Roosevelt's bout with infantile paralysis had left him paralyzed from the waist down, but in those days the media were sufficiently discreet to keep that fact unobtrusive.

Roosevelt was a handsome man, with a ready smile, an impressive voice, and immense charisma. He defeated Hoover in a landslide and became the 32nd President of the United States.

His inauguration, on March 4, 1933, came when the United States seemed to be in the very trough of the Depression. Although Roosevelt did not, and could not, solve the economic problems that beset the nation with the wave of a hand, he worked an important psychological change.

In the first place, Roosevelt brought to the office of the Presidency a sense of invincible optimism. There was about him nothing of the dourness that had marked Coolidge and Hoover. He kept his cigarette holder at a jaunty angle, and was at home with the press. He also addressed the nation frequently on the radio, delivering what he called "fireside chats," and his remarkable voice became familiar to all.

In the second place, Roosevelt took action at once. When Roosevelt became president, the financial institutions of the nation were in a state of near-total breakdown. Therefore, he closed the banks as soon as his term began, had their books audited, and then allowed those banks declared sound to reopen. This may have done little for the banks, but it did much for the public. There was a burst of general confidence in the banks and a willingness to allow funds to remain in them that did far more to help them than anything the government did.

In the third place, Roosevelt abandoned the philosophy that government should be strictly allied with business and should help the general population only indirectly through the coddling of business. A new philosophy, in which government labored to help the population generally, came into being—the "New Deal."

In a whirlwind of activity, Congress, driven by Roosevelt's boundless energy, passed legislation to help the farmers by paying for crop control to reduce surpluses that drove down prices for produce. Farm mortgages were also refinanced. The United States was taken off the gold standard, thus allowing a moderate inflation and making it easier to pay off debts. A system whereby the destitute could receive monetary "relief" was set up. Home mortgages were refinanced. Securities exchanges were regulated to decrease the chances of "boom-and-bust" that had characterized the Coolidge–Hoover era. Labor laws were passed that favored the right of laborers and put an end to the tight alliance of government and business in the matter of strike-breaking.

The 18th Amendment, which had saddled the nation with the enforced prohibition of alcoholic beverages, was recognized as a failure and was repealed by the 21st amendment on December 5, 1933. When in 1934, a drought ruined the Midwest, creating a "dustbowl" that sent impoverished farmers out of the area, help reached them.

By 1935, Roosevelt had pushed through social security, whereby people during their working lives, paid sums into a fund, into which industry also paid, that would then be translated into a monthly pension when the people reached their retirement years. Unemployment insurance was also set up. (All these measures met with unyielding and bitter opposition from the Republicans.)

Although the New Deal legislation did not bring back the boom times of the 1920s, they greatly relieved human suffering, and by giving the population the sense that the government cared for them and endeavored to help them, it prevented what might otherwise have become dangerous antidemocratic movements.

Such movements did exist. There was Huey Pierce Long (1893–1935), the demogogic, autocratic, and corrupt governor of Louisiana, who gained popularity by a program of public works and welfare. He was assassinated in 1935. There were fascist and anti-Semitic movements such as the one led by the Catholic priest, Charles Edward Coughlin (1891–1979), and others led by people who were more extreme still.

Abroad, the United States finally recognized the government of the Soviet Union, after 16 years of pretending it didn't exist. Policy toward Latin America was liberalized and Roosevelt stressed the role of the United States as a "good neighbor," rather than as a heavy-handed guardian of American business interests.

Roosevelt could not do anything, however, to undermine the strong current of American isolationism. Although strongly opposed to the aggressiveness of Japan and Italy, and, in particular, to the policies of Adolf Hitler (who had come to power in Germany only five weeks before Roosevelt's inauguration), he could not flout American public opinion by taking too activist a position. He was reduced to sermonizing.

In particular, the United States was sufficiently isolationist in mood, so that, like Great Britain and France, it failed to help the legitimate government of Spain against the Fascist Rebels under Franco. American Catholics were strong supporters of Roosevelt and the New Deal, but they were also strong supporters of Franco's forces, seeing him as a "Nationalist" who supported the Church against the anticlerical Loyalists. Roosevelt could not afford to alienate so large a segment of his own supporters and, while individual Americans fought as pro-Loyalist volunteers in the "Abraham Lincoln Brigade," the government itself watched idly as the Loyalists were finally defeated.

Again, while Roosevelt and many other American leaders bitterly denounced German anti-Semitic policies, there was no real move to accept Jewish refugees. The trouble was that large segments of American public opinion were not particularly favorable to Jews. Anti-Semitism was sufficiently widespread in the United States to diminish sympathy for the victims of Nazi bigotry.

Roosevelt ran for reelection in 1936, against the Republican nominee, Alfred Mossman Landon (1887–1988). It was a bitter contest with those who had benefited from the Republican pro-business policies going all out to defeat Roosevelt—who had saved them from their own incapacities. The *Literary Digest* conducted an enormous straw poll that showed Landon taking every state outside the Solid South. However, they obtained their names from telephone books and automobile registrations, and Roosevelt's strength lay with those who could not afford telephones and automobiles.

On November 3, 1936, Roosevelt carried 46 of the 48 states, losing only Maine and Vermont. The *Literary Digest* went out of business soon after that and pollsters learned how to conduct polls in such a way as to get a smaller sampling, but one that was far more representative of the electorate.

The great victory had its difficulties. Labor, which felt (quite rightly) that it had been a key element in Roosevelt's landslide, wanted its reward. The "Committee of Industrial Organization" ("CIO") had been organized by John Llewellyn Lewis (1880–1969) as a more activist offshoot of the conservative American Federation of Labor (AFL). In 1937, then, the CIO initiated a rash of strikes that were intended to unionize the automobile and steel industries. The "sit-down strike" came into being, in which workers remained in the factories, thus making it more difficult for the factory owners to hire scabs to replace them. On the whole, this was embarrassing for Roosevelt, who sympathized with labor, but who realized that most Americans were not activists and viewed the strikers as dangerous leftists.

Roosevelt also had trouble with the Supreme Court, which had a rock-ribbed conservative majority of six out of nine justices. At every opportunity, they sourly declared New Deal measures to be unconstitutional.

In desperation, Roosevelt suggested that for each justice over retirement age, who did not retire, he be allowed to appoint an additional younger justice. This was widely considered a device to "pack the Supreme Court" and the nation turned against it, and rightly so. Roosevelt suffered the greatest defeat of his political career in this matter.

In the long run, however, he won out, for several of the justices did retire and Roosevelt had the chance to appoint liberals, so that before his term was over he had the Supreme Court he wanted, without having packed it.

He had other troubles, too. In 1937, there was another economic downturn (now called a "recession" to avoid the horrible word "depression" which had itself been adopted to avoid the even more horrible word "panic" that had pre-

ceded it). In 1938, the Republicans gained in state and congressional reactions. Roosevelt tried to pick out several of his more embittered enemies for defeat, but that did more harm than good as the local voters resented outside interference.

Meanwhile, there was the growing possibility of war in Europe, and the stubborn isolationism of the American people kept Roosevelt from doing anything to prevent it. In 1937, in fact, Congress passed a "Neutrality Act" that effectively tied Roosevelt's hands as far as an active and far-sighted foreign policy was concerned.

The result was that, in 1939, when World War II broke out in Europe, the United States was on the sidelines and all Roosevelt could do was to declare neutrality and hope for the best.

In science, the United States glittered in this decade. Ernest Orlando Lawrence (1901–1958) invented the cyclotron in 1930, which opened the way to the study of atomic structure at a new level of precision. He was awarded a Nobel Prize in 1939 for this.

Harold Clayton Urey (1893–1981) isolated "heavy hydrogen" or "deuterium," and won a Nobel Prize in 1934. In 1932, Carl David Anderson (b. 1905) discovered the positron, the first "antiparticle" to be detected, and he won a Nobel Prize in 1936. Linus Pauling (b. 1901) applied quantum theory to chemistry, thus reorganizing and improving the entire subject, and he, too, won a Nobel Prize eventually. Isadore Isaac Rabi (1898–1988) measured the magnetic properties of atoms and molecules and won a Nobel Prize.

Karl Guthe Jansky (1905–1950), in 1932, detected radio waves from space outside the Solar system. This eventually led to the development off radio astronomy, which revolutionized human knowledge of the universe. Clyde William Tombaugh (b. 1906) discovered the planet Pluto in 1930.

During this decade, E. C. Kendall isolated various hormones of the adrenal cortex, including "cortisone." In 1934, Robert Runnels Williams (1886–1965) worked out the molecular structure of Vitamin B_1. In 1937, Conrad Arnold Elvehjem (1901–1962) found that nicotinic acid ("niacin") cured pellagra. George Wald (b. 1906) worked out the chemistry of vision and eventually won a Nobel Prize for it. The French-born Rene Jules Dubos (1901–1982) isolated tryothricin from soil bacteria and this was the beginning of the discovery of antibiotics. During this decade, too, John Howard Northrop (1891–1987) crystallized various digestive enzymes and eventually won a Nobel Prize.

In 1938, the Russian-born Vladimir Kosma Zworykin (1889–1982) invented the first practical television camera, while Edwin Herbert Land (b. 1909) invented Polaroid in 1932. Wallace Hume Carothers (1896–1937) was the first to produce Nylon in 1931, while Thomas Midgley, Jr. (1889–1944) produced Freon in 1930, and with it revolutionized the air-conditioning industry.

Color movies reached the screen in 1938, and Walt Disney, in that year, produced the first full-length animated feature, *Snow White and the Seven Dwarfs*. To distract the attention of a population ground down by the Depression, radio soap operas became popular, the movies began to feature lavish musicals, and, for youngsters, cartoon books became popular and flourished.

At a somewhat higher level, paperback books (only 25 cents in those days) brought reading to a larger audience beginning in 1939. Night baseball was initiated in 1935, and that, too, meant a larger audience.

The Empire State Building was erected in 1931, and even after taller buildings were built, it remained the symbol of New York, perhaps because of the final scene of the movie, *King Kong*, which was released in 1933.

In literature, John Roderigo Dos Passos (1896–1970) wrote his trilogy *U.S.A.* in this decade. William Saroyan (1908–1981) published *The Daring Young Man on the Flying Trapeze* in 1934. Margaret Munnerlyn Mitchell (1900–1949) published *Gone With the Wind* in 1936. It was possibly the most successful novel ever written, and won a Pulitzer Prize, but Mitchell never wrote anything else.

John Ernst Steinbeck (1902–1968) published *Of Mice and Men* in 1937, and *The Grapes of Wrath* in 1939. The latter, which pictured the misery of the dustbowl farmers, won a Pulitzer Prize. Erskine Caldwell (1903–1987) published *Tobacco Road* in 1932 and *God's Little Acre* in 1933. The Spanish-born George Santayana (1863–1952) published *The Last Puritan* in 1935.

Among the playwrights, O'Neill staged *Mourning Becomes Electra* in 1931 and *Ah, Wilderness* in 1932. Clifford Odets staged *Golden Boy* in 1937. Robert Emmet Sherwood (1896–1955) staged *The Petrified Forest* in 1935, *Idiot's Delight* in 1936, and *Abe Lincoln in Illinois* in 1938. The last two won Pulitzer Prizes.

Theodore Seuss Geisel (b. 1904), using the penname of "Dr. Seuss," began a great career in 1937 as a writer of children's verse.

In art, Grant De Volsen Wood (1892–1942) painted what may be the best-known contemporary American work of art, *American Gothic*, in 1930. Alexander Calder (1898–1976) initiated the construction of "mobiles," freely moving constructions, in 1932. Anna Mary "Grandma" Moses (1860–1961) took up painting in the 1930s, when she was over 70 years old, and quickly became famous as a remarkable "primitive."

The most important American composer of the period was probably Aaron Copland (b. 1900).

BELGIUM

Belgium was naturally alarmed by the coming to power of Adolf Hitler and his Nazis in Germany. They embarked on a program of rearmament and did their best to suppress their home-grown Fascists, who were subsidized by Mussolini.

On February 17, 1934, Albert I of Belgium, who had been considered a hero of World War I, died, and was succeeded by his son, who reigned as Leopold III (1901–1983). Leopold III did not aspire to hero status, but thought it would be safer to declare neutrality and hide, in the hope that Germany would therefore ignore its existence and fight elsewhere. This hadn't worked in 1914, and there was no real reason to think it would work now.

Nevertheless, on October 14, 1936, Belgium emphasized its neutrality by ending its military alliance with France. In this way, Belgium, like almost all of Europe, played into the hands of Hitler. Germany, of course, in 1937, guaranteed the inviolability of Belgian territory as long as it did not take military actions against Germany, but there were few things in the world as worthless as Hitler's word.

When World War II began in 1939, all Belgium could do was to appeal for peace, roughly the equivalent of talking to a wall.

Georges Joseph Christian Simenon (1903–1989), created his detective, Inspector Maigret, in 1930. Simenon was one of the most highly regarded and prolific mystery writers in existence.

NETHERLANDS

The Netherlands had been untouched by World War I and hoped to be ignored in any new war. Therefore, it spent the 1930s doing nothing that might offend Germany.

SWITZERLAND

During this decade, Switzerland carefully maintained its tradition of total neutrality backed by a modern, well-trained army. It tried to keep all extremists at arm's length, suppressing homegrown Nazis and opposing the admission of the Soviet Union to the League of Nations.

In science, Paul Karrer (1889–1971) synthesized a number of vitamins in this decade and won a Nobel Prize in 1937. The Russian-born Tadeusz Reichstein (b. 1897) also synthesized vitamins and won a Nobel Prize. Paul Hermann Muller (1894–1965) discoverd the insecticide DDT in 1939.

The Swiss theologian, Karl Barth (1886–1948), rallied churchmen against Nazi doctrines.

YUGOSLAVIA

Yugoslavia was under the strong dictatorship of King Alexander I, who found that his greatest home-grown problem was with the Croats in the north. The Croats, led by Vladimir Macek (1879–1964), were Catholic, used the Latin alphabet, and felt themselves more civilized than the dominant Serbs (who were Orthodox and used the Cyrillic alphabet). The Croats demanded greater autonomy.

Abroad, Alexander labored to build up the al-

liances with other Balkan powers, with Czechoslovakia, and with France. A union against the increasing danger of Germany seemed in the works, but on a visit to Marseilles on October 9, 1934, Alexander was assassinated by an extremist in the pay of the Croats.

Alexander was succeeded by his 11-year-old son, who reigned as Peter II (1923–1970), with the actual reins of government in the hands of Paul (1893–1976), his first cousin once-removed. As in the replacement of Albert I by Leopold III in Belgium, the replacement of Alexander I by Paul in Yugoslavia meant a move in the direction of appeasement.

There were moves for closer friendship of Yugoslavia with both Italy and Germany, but oddly enough, the dictatorship was relaxed on August 26, 1939, and the government grew more democratic. The land was federalized, the Croats were given greater autonomy, and Macek was made a vice-premier. However, six days later, Germany invaded Poland and World War II began.

GREECE

As was the case with most of Europe in this decade, Greece turned to the right. Venizelos had made peace with Turkey and had tried to maintain the republic that had been established in 1924, but the world Depression created dissatisfaction and the royalists grew steadily stronger. On November 24, 1935, George II returned from exile and was once more King of Greece. Engineering this return was the Greek general, Georgios Kondilos (1879–1936), who, in the course of his life, had changed from a liberal republican to a conservative royalist, and who attempted to rule with the restored king as a figurehead.

George II, however, wanted the restoration of peace within Greece and planned to do this by a general amnesty of the republicans. Kondilos opposed this and the general yearning for peace forced him out of office.

However, Greece did not remain long without army rule. Ioannis Metaxis (1871–1941), an ultraroyalist general, became Prime Minister on April 13, 1936; and, on August 4 of that year, made himself dictator and established a Fascist regime.

He suppressed all opposition, relied entirely on the army for support, and drew closer to Germany. He also carried out economic measures that benefited the workers and farmers and generally maintained his popularity.

BULGARIA

Bulgaria labored in this decade to get out from under the disabilities placed upon her by the post-World-War-I treaties. Slowly, she managed to rearm and, at the same time, come to agreements with Yugoslavia and Greece, her two chief opponents in World War I. She attempted to remain friendly with both Germany and the West, accepting arms from the former and loans from the latter. Boris III remained king of Bulgaria in this decade.

ROMANIA

Carol II had renounced the Romanian throne in favor of his son, Michael, in 1925. He had also divorced his wife (Michael's mother) and had gone into exile to live with his mistress, Magda Lupescu (1896–1977). Now on June 6, 1930, he returned to Romania. His renunciation of the throne was revoked and he became king again, replacing his son. He lost no time in bringing Madame Lupescu to Bucharest to share his throne.

There was constant irritation with the Soviet Union over Bessarabia, the province in Romania's northeast, which Romania had gained from Russia after the Russian revolution. In 1933, however, the Soviet Union, aware of Japan's aggressive movements in the Far East and the coming of power of Hitler in Germany, decided that Bessarabia was too small a problem to be concerned with and recognized Romania's possession of the province.

Carol II was an admirer of Mussolini and gradually established a Fascist regime in Romania. For a while, it even seemed that Romania might proceed to accept the Nazi doctrines of anti-Semitism, when an ultrarightist politician, Octavian Goga (1881–1938), became Prime Minister in late 1937. However, Carol II felt power slip-

ping out of his hands as the pro-Nazi "Iron Guard" became more powerful. He dismissed Goga and took strong measures against the Iron Guard. Its leader, Cornelius Zelea Codreanu (1899–1938), was killed while in custody. Nevertheless, Romania tried to play it safe by making commercial agreements with Germany.

ESTONIA

Estonia maintained a democratic government in this decade, though the power of the government was strengthened in 1937, and placed a little closer to the Fascism that was now popular in Europe.

In 1934, she joined the Baltic pact with Latvia and Lithuania, providing for a common defense. Fearful of the Soviet Union to the east, from which it had only gained independence after the Russian revolution, Estonia, like the other Baltic nations, signed a nonaggression pact with Germany in 1939.

LATVIA

Latvia passed under the dictatorship of Karlis Ulmanis (b. 1877–?) on May 15, 1934, and adopted the paraphernalia of Fascism.

LITHUANIA

Lithuania was forced, in 1938, to recognize the Polish seizure of Vilna in the days after World War I, though the nation always felt that Vilna was its capital. In 1939, Lithuania was forced to give up her Baltic seaport of Memel to Germany. (It had been German before World War I.) Lithuania had a Fascist cast in this decade and it formed a Baltic pact with Estonia and Latvia.

DENMARK

Denmark, under Christian X, remained democratic throughout this decade of Fascist victory. It was virtually unarmed and it depended for its safety on its clear lack of hostile intent toward anybody.

Copenhagen, in this decade, continued to be

an important center of atomic physics because Niels Bohr headed an institute for atomic studies there.

Karen Christence Dinesen Blixen (1885–1962), writing under the pseudonym of "Isak Dinesen," became a world-renowned writer with her *Seven Gothic Tales* (1934) and *Out of Africa* (1937).

SWEDEN

Under Gustav V, Sweden, too, remained democratic, but did not rely for its safety, as Denmark did, on transparent inoffensiveness. It carried on a program of rearmament.

NORWAY

Norway remained the one expansionist Scandinavian country. In 1931, it attempted to annex the eastern coast of Greenland, even though Denmark had long claimed control of the entire island. The World Court at Hague decided in favor of Denmark and Norway gave up its claim at once.

Under Haakon VII, Norway remained democratic and fought the Depression by methods reminiscent of Roosevelt's "New Deal." These methods were more or less successful.

FINLAND

Finland maintained a democratic form of government in this period, and, beginning in 1935, joined the Scandinavian nations in a common block. It attempted also to find common grounds with the three small Baltic nations.

The Finnish writer, Frans Emil Sillaupaa (1888–1964), won the Nobel Prize for literature in 1939.

CANADA

The Statute of Westminister, adopted unanimously by the British Parliament in 1931, made it official that Canada (as well as the other British dominions) was an independent nation, except for its emotional ties to Great Britain and for the fact that it recognized the British monarch as its own.

Canada fought the Depression much as the United States did. It established a New Deal of its own, and had to watch most of its measures being invalidated by its Supreme Court. It also suffered from sit-down strikes.

Two Canadian matters attracted world attention in this decade.

On May 28, 1934, five identical-sibling daughters were born to Elzire Dionne in Callander, Ontario. They all lived and the "Dionne quintuplets" became world-famous at once. So ruthlessly was their existence commercialized that there was no chance whatever of any of them leading a happy, or even a normal, life, and there is no question but that for them the circumstances of their birth was tragic in the extreme.

In May, 1939, King George VI and Queen Elizabeth of Great Britain visited Canada. It was the first royal visit of a reigning monarch to the dominion, and the visit helped insure Canadian loyalty in the approaching ordeal, for the coming of war was beginning to seem more certain with each day.

NEWFOUNDLAND

Newfoundland had been governing itself since 1855. By 1933, however, the Depression, combined with incompetence and corruption in the government, had the nation virtually bankrupt. Newfoundland, therefore, voluntarily gave up its dominion status and became a British colony again. Under British rule, it slowly recovered.

MEXICO

On July 2, 1934, Lazaro Cardenas (1895–1970) was elected President of Mexico, and he launched a program of social reform. Land was distributed to the peasants; church property was nationalized; and the railways were taken over by its employees.

Then, in 1938, the Mexican government expropriated the properties of the American and British oil companies. The American and British governments protested this action and the

United States demanded compensation. Mexico refused and the matter remained still at an impasse when World War II broke out in Europe.

CUBA

The Cuban dictator, Machado, was forced out of office in 1933. Later that year, however, another army officer, Fulgencio Batista y Zaldiver (1901–1973), became dictator, working through figurehead officials. He embarked on what was the classic model for dictators in this decade: he enriched himself enormously, while establishing a brutal regime that repressed all dissent in Fascist fashion.

In 1934, the Platt Amendment, which had been forced on Cuba after the Spanish–American War, was abrogated and Cuba was given its full independence. The United States could do this since it controlled Cuba economically and Batista was perfectly willing to acquiesce in that, provided the United States did not interfere with his dictatorship, something the United States was content not to do.

HAITI

In 1934, after Franklin Roosevelt became president, American armed forces, which had maintained a presence in Haiti for five years, were withdrawn.

DOMINICAN REPUBLIC

In 1930, Rafael Leonidas Trujillo Molina (1891–1961) became the harsh and oppressive dictator of the Dominican Republic. He remained dictator, whether actually filling the post of President or not, throughout this period.

PANAMA

During this decade, Panama was able to negotiate new agreements with the United States, which lightened the heavy hand of American control that had existed since Panama had broken away from Colombia under the management of Theodore Roosevelt.

NICARAGUA

The Liberal revolt led by Agostino Sandino was suppressed in 1933, and the next year Sandino was killed.

In 1936, Anastasio Somoza (1896–1956) became president, and the next year he established a brutal dictatorship, which came down hard on any dissent. In the classic style of such dictators, he managed to enrich himself at the expense of his impoverished people.

Similar dictatorships were set up in other Central American republics: Honduras, El Salvador, and Guatemala. The United States got along with all of them very well.

BRAZIL

In this period, leftist feelings were rising among the poorer classes, while a homegrown Fascist movement was encouraged by Germany (there were many ethnic Germans in Brazil).

Getulio Donelles Vargas (1883–1954), who had led a revolt in southern Brazil, became president in 1930 and remained in control throughout the decade. By 1937, he imposed a new constitution on Brazil under which he had dictatorial power. Vargas denied that Brazil was Fascist, but it showed all the stigmata of that ideology.

VENEZUELA

The Venezuelan dictator, Juan Vicente Gomez, died on December 18, 1935, and Venezuela returned to a democratic form of government. Other nations in the region—Colombia, Ecuador, and Peru—were also reasonably democratic.

BOLIVIA

At this time, Bolivia engaged in the most serious South American war of the twentieth century. The territory under dispute was the Chaco, a region lying between Bolivia and Paraguay. The dispute had simmered for decades and, in 1932, it came to open war. Seventy years earlier, Paraguay had shown its ability to fight ferociously even in the face of virtual annihilation, and it now did the same. It won the war in 1935, and ended up with the major portion of the Chaco.

By the end of the decade, both Bolivia and Paraguay were under dictatorial rule. Other South American nations in the south—Uruguay, Chile, and Argentina—managed to retain the forms of democracy.

EGYPT

This decade was one of an increasing drive for Egyptian independence. On April 28, 1936, King Fuad died and was succeeded by his son, Farouk (1920–1965). Soon after Farouk's succession, a treaty between Great Britain and Egypt was signed in which Great Britain agreed to remove most of its forces, leaving a garrison at the Suez Canal and maintaining a naval base at Alexandria for no more than eight years. Egypt was to become a member of the League of Nations which was, in a way, a recognition of its independence.

The coming of World War II, however, delayed the implementation of the treaty.

UNION OF SOUTH AFRICA

With the Statute of Westminister in 1931, South Africa became an independent nation but for its grudging acceptance of the British monarch. The Nationalist movement largely lost its reason for existence with this development, and under the stress of the Depression, there was a union between the imperialist-minded party of Smuts, and the nationalists under Herzog.

An intransigent portion of the Nationalist party under Daniel François Malan (1874–1959) maintained a fight for Afrikaans domination of South Africa.

TURKEY

Under Mustapha Kemal, Turkey continued its program of westernization that completely transformed the nation without violence. Externally, Turkey made peace with its neighbors and joined the League of Nations.

Kemal Ataturk died on November 10, 1938, and was succeeded as president by Ismet Inonu

(1884–1973), who had been the leading figure behind the westernization of the land.

SYRIA

A treaty between Syria and France in 1936 called for an end to the French mandate in three years, and for Syria to be admitted to the League of Nations. The implementation of this treaty, as in the case of the one between Great Britain and Egypt, was delayed by the coming of World War II in 1939.

PALESTINE

Palestinians were beginning to attack Jews as the decade opened and Great Britain found itself in a quandary. It had committed itself to the establishment of a Jewish national state in Palestine, but it was in no mood to antagonize the millions of Moslems in the Middle East. Therefore, they began a policy of restricting Jewish immigration into Palestine. This led to widespread Jewish protests and, in view of the increasing anti-Semitism of Hitler's Germany, Great Britain hesitated to make itself seem too anti-Semitic. However, any increase in Jewish immigration at once set off Arab protests.

In 1937, the British worked out a plan to partition Palestine between Jews and Arabs and this, predictably, displeased both sides. There followed a virtual civil war in Palestine between the Jews and the Arabs, with the British unable to control matters.

In 1939, the British proposed an independent Palestine in 10 years, with Jews and Arabs both participating in the government. Again, both sides denounced the idea. The coming of World War II suspended matters, especially as the Jews recognized Germany as the greater enemy and closed ranks behind the British.

HEJAZ/SAUDI ARABIA

The Arabian territories of Ibn Saud, who was King of the Hejaz and Sultan of Nejd, were named "Saudi Arabia" in his honor on September 22, 1932. Under the continued rule of Ibn

Saud, a policy of technological modernization was implemented. Roads and railroads were built and airflight was introduced.

IRAQ

Iraq, though a British mandate since World War I, was virtually independent and became a member of the League of Nations in 1932. King Faisal I of Iraq died on September 8, 1933, and was succeeded by his son, who ruled as Ghazi I (1912–1939).

An oil pipeline was opened in 1934, leading from the Mosul oil fields to the Mediterranean, and this marked the beginning of the Middle East as a great source of fuel oil for the world. Iraq strongly backed the Arab cause in Palestine and tried to establish a pan-Arab movement that would multiply Arab power in the world councils. Ghazi died in an automobile accident on April 4, 1939 and was succeeded by his son, Faisal II (1935–1958), whose uncle served as regent.

PERSIA/IRAN

Persia adopted the name of Iran, officially, on March 21, 1935. Iran began its efforts to control its own oil resources, which were then largely under the control of the British and Americans.

AFGHANISTAN

The Afghani king, Mohammed Nadir, was assassinated on November 8, 1933. He was succeeded by his son, Mohammed Zahir (b. 1914).

INDIA

Gandhi was beginning to be more and more concerned with the plight of the "untouchables" in India—the casteless individuals who were treated as scarcely human.

He continued to get his way, despite several jailings, by fasting and threatening to do so to the death. The British dared not allow this, knowing that Gandhi's death would lead to wild disorders it might be impossible to contain.

Gandhi was opposed on both sides of the Indian spectrum. On the right, the Indian Muslims had the "Muslim League" which was, to them, the sole representative of their interests, not Gandhi's "Congress Party." And on the left, the nationalist, Subhas Chandra Bose (1897–1945), wanted complete independence for India at once and was dissatisfied with Gandhi's program of passive resistance.

Things might have been worse had not the Japanese aggression in the east raised the threat of an eventual Japanese penetration of India. Most Indians preferred to cling to Great Britain at least sufficiently to be sure of her protection against the Japanese.

AUSTRALIA

In 1933, there seemed to be the possibility that Australia would break up into two nations as the western half of the continent showed a disposition to go its own way. The British parliament, however, refused to allow this. In 1937, Australia, all too aware of the danger from an expansive and aggressive Japan, began a program of rearmament.

NEW ZEALAND

In much of this decade, New Zealand was controlled by the Labour Party, which fought the effects of the Depression with social legislation of the New Deal type.

PHILIPPINES

Beginning in 1933, the United States planned for eventual Philippine independence. In 1935, the islands gained a "Commonwealth" status (something that in the British system might have been called a "Dominion"). The Filipinos voted for president, and chose Manuel Luis Quezon y Molina (1878–1944), an experienced politician.

At first there was a feeling among Filipinos for complete independence as soon as possible, but Japanese expansionism frightened them and they preferred to cling to the United States until that danger had passed.

1939 TO 1945

GERMANY

Germany faced the future with supreme confidence on September 1, 1939. It was prepared for war, and it knew that the British and French were not. It predicted that, at the invasion of Poland, the British and French might huff and puff, but not actually go to war. This seemed all the more likely, since Germany had signed up the Soviet Union on its own side so that the British and French had absolutely no way of directly aiding Poland in any meaningful manner.

If, on the other hand, Great Britain and France did go to war, it might be only to avoid the loss of national "honor," and without any serious intent to fight. If so, a really quick and devastating campaign in Poland would soon deprive them of any reason to fight, and fright (if nothing else) would impel them to make peace.

So Germany, without warning, drove massively into Poland on September 1, 1939. Probably no major campaign in the history of warfare since the campaigns of Genghis Khan seven centuries before went so smoothly, and was executed so perfectly, or so ruthlessly.

A million and a quarter Germans poured eastward under their commander-in-chief, Walther von Brauchitsch (1881–1948). A double development was planned with armies plunging southward from East Prussia under Fedor von Bock (1880–1945) and other armies moving northward from Silesia and Slovakia under Karl Rudolf Gerd von Rundstedt (1875–1953). Poland was flat and there were no natural barriers to slow the Germans.

The Poles, having chosen to defend their borders, rather than to fall back behind the river lines in central Poland, played into German hands. The German forces, with a three-to-one numerical edge and with an incomparably stronger force of tanks and armor, simply cut behind the Polish armies and, within 10 days, made it certain that the Poles were smashed beyond

redemption. Meanwhile, 1600 German planes engaged in the indiscriminate bombing of Polish cities, air fields, and troop concentrations and reduced the nation to chaos. In three days the Polish airforce and its small naval force in the Baltic were gone.

On September 17, the Soviet Union completed the Polish debacle, which scarcely needed completing, by invading from the east. On September 19, German and Soviet forces met in central Poland.

The city of Warsaw maintained a despairing resistance, but savage bombing battered it into surrender by September 27, and all significant Polish resistance came to an end, though some minor fortresses held out until October 5. The entire campaign, from first to last, had taken less than five weeks, and German losses were negligible. By September 29, the Germans and Soviets had agreed to divide Poland into two pieces roughly equal in area. Germany took the more populous west, which was mainly Polish. The Soviets took the less populous east, which was occupied chiefly by Byelorussians and Ukrainians.

The Soviet Union also established domination over the three small Baltic states and attacked Finland as the year drew to its end, finally defeating it and absorbing certain border areas.

The Soviet Union did all this to expand its western borders in order to neutralize the sudden vast increase in German strength. Germany allowed it, for before it could settle matters with the Soviet Union, it had to take care of Great Britain and France, with which it was, after all, at war.

This war, however, did not seem to be much. As Germany had expected, the British and French, going to war with the greatest reluctance and apprehension, did absolutely nothing to help Poland, and merely watched their only ally crumble and disappear with devastating speed. The German victory was as one-sided and as complete as it was because Germany chose to keep only a skeleton force on its western frontier. Had the French, with five times the strength of that force, launched an attack then, even one that accomplished little directly, it would have forced Germany to pull troops out of Poland. The German time table would have been upset and Poland might have had some breathing space. However, it didn't happen.

Judging correctly from this that war enthusiasm was low in Great Britain and nonexistent in France, Hitler felt he could take time out to digest his Polish gains and to rest his army. What followed then was a winter of inactivity that was referred to sarcastically by those who wanted sterner action against Hitler as "the phoney war."

Hitler also seized the opportunity to fight a psychological battle. He had had the Polish campaign recorded by movie cameras in such a way as to emphasize the strength and speed of German forces, and the devastating defeat of the Poles. These were shown throughout Europe, as were similar films of later German victories, and everywhere they spread defeatism among those who opposed Germany, and imbued nations generally with the feeling that Germany was invincible and that surrender was the only alternative to devastation.

In one respect, however, victory exacted its toll. Hitler was a megalomaniac who eagerly took credit for all that went right and, even more eagerly, blamed others for all that went wrong. As a result of the events of 1938 and early 1939, he already considered himself a political and diplomatic genius for the way in which he faced down the western powers (not taking into account that he had as his opponents a miserable set of gutless incompetents).

Now, as a result of the Polish campaign, he downplayed the importance of the well-oiled German military machine and his excellent generals, and felt himself to be a military genius as well. This delusion never left him and he insisted on handling every aspect of the war himself and of never listening to the advice of those who knew more than he did.

In now facing France and Great Britain, Hitler had no fear of France. He rightly felt that France was ripe for defeat and needed only a push to collapse. Great Britain was another matter, for Hitler faced the problem that had earlier faced Louis XIV, Napoleon, and Kaiser William II. How could one defeat Great Britain when the British controlled the sea and this made a land invasion impossible?

Had any of the earlier three conquerors been able to send an army into Great Britain, the British would undoubtedly have been defeated—but none of them could. To be sure, William II had had submarines, which the first two had not, but that had not been enough. Hitler also had submarines and, in addition, a magnificent airforce, which had just shown its abilities in Spain and in Poland and which was more numerous than the combined air fleets of Great Britain and France.

However, the airplanes, while far superior to the egg-crates of World War I, were still short-range, and, to be effective in attacking Great Britain, Hitler would need as many bases as possible as close to Great Britain as possible.

While Hitler pondered this problem in the winter of 1939–1940, the question of Scandinavia came up. Germany got its iron ore from Sweden and had to have it if it were to prosecute the war successfully. The iron ore reached Germany by way of the Baltic Sea, which was secure as long as the Soviet Union stayed neutral. It also reached Germany by ships that carried the iron ore through Norwegian territorial waters (with Norway's reluctant permission).

When the Soviet Union was fighting Finland that winter, Great Britain and France seemed far more eager to help the Finns against the Soviets than they had been to help the Poles against the Germans. The western powers were, even now, more anti-Soviet than anti-German. No aid to Finland was actually sent, but Germany viewed with alarm the possibility of British–French forces basing themselves in Scandinavia.

In addition, the British talked about mining the territorial waters of Norway in order to preclude the shipment of iron ore by that route. In fact, on February 16, 1940, British ships entered Norwegian territorial waters to rescue 299 prisoners of war from a German ship, the *Altmark*. On April 8, British ships sailed eastward to begin mining operations.

By then, however, Hitler had decided on a northern campaign to make his supplies of iron ore secure and to establish air bases from which northern England and Scotland could be attacked.

On April 9, Germany invaded Denmark, since it was en route to Norway, and occupied it without a shot being fired.

German ships then carried troops into Oslo fjord, where the Norwegians defended themselves fiercely but uselessly. German airborne troops landed in Oslo and the city was taken on April 10. Under the German general, Nikolaus von Falkenhorst (1885–1968), German forces spread quickly through the nation.

British and French troops, which had been assembled for possible aid to Finland, were sent to Norway instead and landed in the Trondheim region in central Norway, beginning on April 14. The Germans brought up reinforcements and, between that and the skillful use of their aircraft, they beat the Allied troops soundly and forced them to return to their British bases on May 2. King Haakon VI and the Norwegian government went with them to set up a government-in-exile.

The Allies made a better showing in Narvik in northern Norway. There, fighting continued from April 24 to May 28. The Allies, however, were forced to quit in the end because disaster was engulfing them in France. By June 9, they were gone and every square mile of Norway was in German hands, with a Norwegian Fascist, Vidkun Quisling (1881–1945), who had been Norway's minister of defense between 1931 and 1933, as the nominal ruler.

Although many nations, both before and during World War II, have been ruled by native traitors willing to serve as puppets for a conquering army, it is Quisling who has lent his name to serve as generic representative of all. Perhaps it was the sound of the name—it might seem that "quisling" means "to quizzle," which may be interpreted as performing actions that make one "queasy."

The Norwegian campaign showed the effective way in which the Germans could use ships and planes to invade a land that was separated from it by the sea, a feat that had to make the British nervous. In the process, however, the Germans lost their destroyer force and their fleet was reduced to a handful of ships that could be used for raiding purposes but very little else.

While Hitler took advantage of the way in which the Anglo–French eyes were fixed on Finland rather than on Poland, and while pinning them down in Norway with rather minor forces, he had carefully assembled about 2.5 million men on Germany's western frontier, with Brauchitsch in overall command as in Poland.

Opposed to the Germans was a roughly equal force on the French side of the border under the overall command of Gustave-Maurice Gamelin (1872–1958), a conservative and unimaginative commander.

The French had more tanks than the Germans did, but they were scattered widely among the army groups, whereas the Germans had their tanks concentrated in the center under Rundstedt.

The French relied on the Maginot line to keep the Germans out of Alsace-Lorraine, and put most of their troops on the Belgian border, where they expected the Germans to come barreling down as they did in 1914. The hinge between the Belgian line and the Maginot line was lightly held because the Ardennes forest was there and that was thought to be so formidable a barrier as to require little defense.

German equipment on the ground, and especially in the air, was far superior to that of the Allies. What's more, the German army with the smashing Polish victory behind them and the daring Norwegian invasion clearly successful, was eager to advance, while the British and French, with eight months of inactivity and occasional defeat, could only be described as down-in-the-mouth.

Belgium and the Netherlands had adequate armies and defenses, but neither could stand up against the Germans for long, and, such was their anxiety not to goad the Germans into attacking, that they went out of their way *not* to coordinate their defenses with those of the Allies. Therefore, they stood out, weak and exposed.

The German plan was to pass through Belgium as in 1914 and this time, to make adequate room for the passage by passing through the Netherlands as well. The Allies, they hoped, would leave their fortified border to come forward to meet them, and the Germans would then thrust overwhelmingly through the hinge between Belgium and the Maginot line, and, turning right, trap the Allied armies in Belgium and northern France.

Once again, German plans worked perfectly. On May 10, the German planes began the terror bombing of the Netherlands and of Belgium. Paratroopers were dropped in key areas of both nations, paralyzing any attempt at the organization of a useful defense.

The Netherlands cut its dikes and flooded the country in their time-honored way of stopping invaders, but that did not stop the Germans. French troops did, as foreseen by the Germans, advance into the Netherlands, but they were easily hurled back by the Germans. The Germans demanded Dutch surrender and, on May 13, made it clear what the alternative was by brutally bombing Rotterdam to destruction. The next day, the Dutch surrendered and Queen Wilhelmina and her cabinet fled to Great Britain.

The fighting in Belgium continued, and the Germans held back deliberately, to encourage as much of the Allied armies as possible to enter Belgium. Rundstedt was meanwhile pushing carefully through the Ardennes, waiting for the Allies to be fully committed to the Belgian campaign.

On May 13, Rundstedt went into high gear, driving through the supposedly impassable Ardennes, destroying the French 9th Army, and then pouring through in an unstoppable flood.

German planes bombed the roads behind the French forces, making confusion worse. Tank corps turned northward to ride toward the English Channel under the capable leadership of Heinz Wilhelm Guderian (1888–1954) and Erwin Johannes Eugen Rommel (1891–1944).

The French now saw the danger, but it was far too late. Gamelin was relieved of his command and was replaced on May 19 by Maxime Weygand, who had a much-inflated reputation because he had advised the Poles in their defeat of the Russians 20 years earlier. There was nothing Weygand could do to prevent the Germans from reaching the English channel on May 20, 1940, and trapping large numbers of French, British, and Belgians along the coast of northern France and Belgium. The only attack the French were able to mount that managed to stall the Germans for even a moment was under the leadership of Charles de Gaulle (1890–1970), who was an expert on armored warfare and had tried to get the French army to organize itself in small ultramobile groups. The French generals had turned him down, but the Guderians and Rommels of the German army had followed his advice.

Now the Germans began to compress the pocket in order to trap or kill the hundreds of thousands of soldiers trapped there. It was a choking maneuver that couldn't miss, for the Allied soldiers had nowhere to go, no chance of reinforcements, no hope of avoiding death or capture.

On May 28, 1940, Leopold III of Belgium surrendered. Without warning the British and French, he ordered the Belgians to lay down their arms. What's more, he remained behind in Belgium while the Belgian government fled to Great Britain, thus giving rise to the thought that he was willing to serve as a German puppet.

The British and French were now squeezed into a small pocket at Dunkirk, and it was clear that nearly 400,000 soldiers, some five eighths of them British, had no choice but to surrender, and that in a very brief time.

Nothing could stop it—except Hitler. He now proceeded to make his first mistake of the war for he ordered the German tanks to stop.

No one is really sure why he gave this order. The usual thought is that Hermann Goering, the vainglorious commander-in-chief of the German Air Force, wanted his share of the glory, and demanded that the last pocket at Dunkirk be smashed by air rather than ground action. Hitler may have agreed because he felt it could be done and that his army might be spared any casualties at all so that it could continue the fight at full strength against France and England.

In any case, the tanks stopped and the German planes went into action. Coming to fight them, however, was the British Royal Air Force, closer to home, and able to make more sorties. For the first time in the war, the Germans temporarily lost control of a crucial bit of air space.

Under the cover of the British planes, the British forces at Dunkirk set up a defense perimeter and British ships came down the coast and across the channel to pick up the soldiers. There were 850 ships altogether, of all kinds, almost all manned by civilians who, in the course of eight days, managed to pick up 225,000 British soldiers and 112,000 French and Belgian soldiers and to carry them off to Great Britain out of the teeth of the German army.

All the heavy equipment was lost, but the men were saved, and the absolute heroism of the action, for all that it was a defeat coming at the end of a retreat, had the moral force of a victory. Had Hitler not given his "stop order," those 338,000 men would have been prisoners and British disheartenment might have been so great as to have made impossible what was to follow.

But the war went on. The German units at Dunkirk faced about with exemplary efficiency and made ready to defeat what remained of the French forces.

On June 5, the Germans, from their line across northern France, attacked southward. The French tried to fight, and some units fought desperately and bravely—but uselessly. They fell back in disorder. The French government left Paris for Bordeaux in the southwest on June 10. On June 13, Paris was declared an open (i.e., undefended) city to save it from the fate of Warsaw and Rotterdam, and on June 14, 1940 the Germans marched in.

Meanwhile, on June 10, Mussolini (who had maintained a cautious neutrality till now) decided that Germany had won the war and that it was necessary to join now so that Italy might get a share of the loot. It was a despicable act and it seemed the last straw.

France might have accepted defeat on the continent and its government might have retired to North Africa to continue the fight from France's imperial possessions, but the French saw no point to that. They felt that Germany was far too strong to be defeated and that Great Britain would, in a matter of weeks, join France in defeat and all would be over.

Therefore, the French surrendered on June 2, 1940. The French general, Charles Léon-Clément Huntziger (1880–1941), met with the Germans in the Compiègne Forest where, 22 years earlier, the Germans had been forced to accept defeat after World War I. The Germans made the French capitulate in the same railroad car and then blew it up so that never again would it stand as a monument to the 1918 surrender.

By June 21, 1940, all fighting in France ceased and Germany was in direct control of three fifths of the nation, including the northern and western coastlines. The rest was a wretched puppet French state with its capital at Vichy. It was under the leadership of Philippe Pétain, now 84 years old. Twenty-three years earlier he had been the hero of Verdun, but in dishonored old age, he was a German puppet.

Out of the wreckage, Charles de Gaulle managed to flee to Great Britain, where he carried on the fight against Germany as leader of the "Free French."

Hitler had every reason to look upon the map of Europe with satisfaction. He had been at war for only 10 months and, except for the evacuation of Dunkirk, all the German military plans had worked with watchmaker's precision. He had defeated and occupied half of Poland, three fifths of France, and all of Denmark, Norway, the Netherlands, Belgium, and Luxembourg. The rest of the European continent, including the Soviet Union, consisted of nations that were either neutral or were German allies. On the other side of the world, Japan was a German ally, too.

Only Great Britain remained at war with Germany, and across the Atlantic Ocean, the United States was hostile, but was hamstrung by isolationism.

It seemed only necessary to force Great Britain to surrender, and Germany would be, without question, the strongest military power on earth. With Germany at the head of a united Europe, even the United States might draw back and decide to cooperate.

Great Britain, however, showed no disposition to surrender. The British government was now headed by Winston Churchill, who turned to the United States for help. The British fleet was stretched thin trying to guard merchant ships, fight off U-boats, and protect themselves against Italian ships in the Mediterranean and Japanese ships in the Pacific. Even the French fleet, which might conceivably be turned over to the Germans, was a deadly threat.

Roosevelt, using all his political skills and charm, maneuvered Congress and public opinion into assisting Great Britain, turning over 50 old American destroyers to British use, for instance.

Germany could not allow this sort of thing to continue, and it was clear that if Great Britain chose not to surrender it must be invaded and crushed. There could be no invasion as long as Great Britain controlled the English Channel and the North Sea, but Germany had bases all along the French and Norwegian coasts from which their planes could fly. Hitler could use them to destroy the British air force, then go on to sink or immobilize the ships of the British Navy, and he could then invade Great Britain and take it over in a week or so. It seemed a clearcut and rather simple job, and Goering was sure that the German planes under his command could do it.

After all, the Germans had 2800 planes against Great Britain's 650.

Germany, however, labored under several disadvantages. First, they had to travel considerable distances to reach the British skies, while the British fought at home. Therefore, Germany had to expend much more gasoline than the British did, and gasoline was never in great supply. Then, too, if the battles took place over British soil, every British flier parachuting out of a stricken plane could go up in another. Every German flyer downed was imprisoned. Skilled fliers were not in great supply either. Third, the British planes, if fewer in number, were more maneu-verable, and were superior plane to plane to those of the Germans.

Most important of all was this: in the years immediately before World War II, the British had invented radar and had set up radar posts. They always knew when the German planes were coming and where they were heading, and were always ready for them.

The "Battle of Britain," in other words, was not to be so sure and easy a victory for Germany as it seemed.

Nevertheless, during the month of August 1940, the Germans, regardless of losses and difficulties, forced their way inward by dint of sheer numbers of planes and bombed airfields and communications centers throughout Great Britain. For this the Germans paid a heavy price, but Great Britain was also losing planes and pilots faster than they could be replaced.

Because some bombs had dropped on London, the British felt they had to retaliate and sent bombers over Germany, beginning on August 24. Berlin was bombed on three nights, and some other cities were also hit. Damage was slight, for the British did not have many planes to spare for the purpose, but psychologically the effect was enormous. In the first year of the war, the Germans had been totally untouched. Casualties and destruction had been the lot of German enemies, and not of Germans. But now the war was brought, however slightly, to the doorstep of German civilians, and Hitler reacted with blind fury.

He gave up the bombing of airfields and communications centers, which had almost brought Great Britain to its knees, and turned vengefully to the bombardment of the cities, particularly London, which was spectacular but had no strategic value. On September 7, 1940, the "blitz" began.

Day after day, the German bombers and fighters converged on London; and day after day, the British planes rose to meet them. London was terribly damaged, but the British spirit remained unbroken under the bombings, and they exacted a fearful toll of German planes and pilots.

The greatest attack came on September 15, 1940, when over 1000 bombers and 700 fighters swept over London, but the loss in German planes that resulted was better than two to one over the loss in British planes.

Germany had meanwhile prepared barges in ports in northern France and in the Low Countries, which were to carry a German army to the invasion of Great Britain on September 27. British planes, however, destroyed most of them and, by the end of September, it was clear that the air bombardment had failed and that there could be no invasion.

Great Britain had won the Battle of Britain—at a fearful cost, to be sure, but it had won. And Hitler, one year after the war had begun, had suffered his first important defeat. There were further bombings of Great Britain through the winter and early spring of 1940–1941, but they were simply terror attacks, offering the Germans no hope for the actual defeat of Great Britain, despite the death and destruction they caused. In fact, the deliberate German frightfulness, as well as continuing British gallantry, was steadily eroding American isolationism and that did incredible harm to the German cause.

Hitler felt he had to make up for the defeat of his plans against Great Britain by seeking further victories elsewhere. His eyes inevitably turned to the east where stood the nation he regarded as his greatest enemy, the Soviet Union. The Soviet Union had kept its agreement with Germany loyally and had meticulously fulfilled its task of supplying materials the Nazis needed, but that did them no good.

Hitler saw the Soviet Union as a vast space occupied by Slavic submen who could be tortured and enslaved into supporting a grand German Empire stretching at least as far as the Ural Mountains, and before which a terrorized Great Britain would be forced to surrender. The United States would then surely cower behind its oceans until the Japanese in Asia and the Germans in Europe could combine to crush it.

So Hitler prepared to launch himself into the illimitable spaces of the east, even while an embattled Great Britain still stood in the west. Un-

doubtedly, Hitler and the German generals knew what had happened to Charles XII of Sweden and to Napolean I of France when they had invaded Russia, but it didn't seem to bother them.

Hitler intended an invasion on a far larger scale than could possibly have been carried through by Charles XII or Napoleon with their relatively few soldiers, marching mainly on foot and with communications not materially advanced beyond the system used by Genghis Khan. Hitler had armor, vehicles, planes, and radio, and he intended to invade all along the line from the Arctic Ocean to the Black Sea.

For this, even the German army was not enough, however. Hitler would need troops from allied nations. In the north, Finland was ready to help since it was still enraged over the Soviet assault in 1939 and wanted its lost territory back. In the south, Hungary, Romania, and Bulgaria were German satellites and were ready to help.

As for the Soviet Union, Hitler had utter contempt for its fighting capacity. Its bad showing against Finland made it seem quite certain that it would collapse instantly before the German onslaught.

All might have gone well had not the bumbling Mussolini, in his anxiety to achieve some "glorious" victory that would in some way match what the Germans had been doing, attacked Greece in October 1940. There was no reason to do so, except for his search for a cheap win, and he had not even bothered to arrange matters with Hitler. Predictably, Mussolini's army came to grief, and Germany found that it would be necessary to come to Mussolini's rescue, lest Great Britain, which had come to the aid of Greece, should establish a strong base there.

In order to take care of that task, it would be helpful if Yugoslavia, which lay between Germany and Greece, could be persuaded to allow free passage of German troops. Under German pressure, the Regent Paul agreed to an alliance with Germany on March 25, 1941.

What followed was totally unexpected. There were strong anti-German elements in Yugoslavia and on March 27, Regent Paul was overthrown;

under the 18-year-old king, Peter II, the alliance with Germany was repudiated.

Hitler, furious, prepared instantly for war, and the German army responded with well-oiled efficiency. On April 6, 1941, German planes, with the usual lack of warning, bombed Belgrade with customary indiscriminate frightfulness. This brought the Yugoslavs into a state of the utmost confusion. The German army columns slashed in and, in 10 days, completed the conquest of the nation. The Yugoslavs surrendered unconditionally on April 17.

It was even more impressive a conquest than that of Poland had been. Whereas Poland had been flat, with no natural obstacles, and where it had had to face a second enemy to its east, Yugoslavia was a mountainous country that might have been expected to offer a diehard resistance, yet it went down at once. (However, the story of Yugoslavia did not end with its surrender.)

Meanwhile, even as the Germans had begun to overrun Yugoslavia, other German army units crossed the Bulgarian border into Greece and promptly smashed the northern Greek armies that had earlier had no trouble defeating the Italians.

Other Greek units fought desperately to hold off the Germans while the British retreated southward. By April 23, however, the Greeks were forced to surrender and it became questionable as to whether the British could retreat successfully or whether they would fall prisoner to the Germans.

The British general, Henry Maitland Wilson (1881–1964), however, fought hard and maneuvered successfully, so that on April 27, 43,000 British troops were taken off the southern Greek coast and taken to the island of Crete. King George II and the Greek government also fled to Crete. Again, all heavy equipment was lost so that it was a second, smaller Dunkirk.

In general, however, one Dunkirk was enough. There was considerable dissatisfaction over the second.

There was no doubt among the British on Crete that the Germans would try to take the island. With the New Zealand general Bernard Cyril Freyberg (1889–1963) in command, the British held Crete with a little over 40,000 men. The Germans, if they attempted to take the island, would seem, superficially, to be going through a rehearsal for the taking of Great Britain. In fact, Crete seemed the sterner test for it was farther from the Greek mainland than Great Britain was from France.

There was, however, a key difference. Germany was in complete control of the air over Crete, and what British planes were to be found on the island were forced to withdraw or to submit to destruction. Therefore, it was possible for the Germans, under Karl Student (1890–1978), who had led the German conquest of the Netherlands, to plan a paratroop assault on Crete.

On May 20, 1941, the German assault began. It was by no means inexpensive, for the British inflicted heavy casualties and destroyed many planes. Nevertheless, the Germans grimly redoubled their efforts and eventually succeeded in carrying through landings, establishing beachheads, and expanding them.

The British fought hard. The British navy tried to send in reinforcements and suffered heavy casualties. In the end, on May 31, 1941, the British were forced to evacuate a foothold on the European continent for a third time, and retired to Egypt.

This was the first capture of a major piece of territory by air assault alone, and there was general astonishment that the Germans had been able to do it. However, it was so expensive a feat, and so many experienced paratroopers were lost, that Hitler never tried to repeat the tactic again.

The Balkan campaign, on the whole, once again showed that the German forces were by far the best trained and best led in the world at the time. All of the European continent west of the Soviet Union was now in the grip of the German army except for Sweden, Switzerland, Spain and Portugal.

Hitler was now ready for his assault on the Soviet Union; and here the Balkan campaign, short and enormously successful though it was, had introduced a dangerous delay.

Had Italy not invaded Greece and done badly there, Hitler could have made use of Hungary, Romania, and Bulgaria, and launched his offensive in April or May. The need to clear up Greece, where Italian failure had brought in British troops and encouraged the Yugoslav uprising against Germany, cost him two months of fighting, so that he wasn't ready for his Soviet adventure till the second half of June.

Did that matter? Yes, it did. It was important for Germany to crush the Soviet Union before the winter weather set in. That might have been certain if the invasion had started on April 22; it was less certain if it started on June 22.

Nevertheless, Hitler had no qualms. He was sure that the Soviet Union would collapse before winter. So certain was he that he made no plans for a winter campaign, and no effort to see that his army would be issued winter clothes and winterized vehicles. Hitler had been spoiled by success and thought he had merely to will in order to achieve—even despite the failure in the Battle of Britain.

At first, his confidence seemed justified. The Soviet Union had no reason to be caught by surprise. British intelligence, which had broken the German secret codes and knew what was going on, warned Stalin. Stalin's own spies warned him. Stalin, however, as paranoid as Hitler, preferred to believe it all a plot to inveigle the Soviet Union into a war with Germany for the benefit of Great Britain. Stalin, therefore, did nothing. At 3 A.M. on June 22, 1942, when 3 million soldiers of the German army and its allies crossed the Soviet border and advanced along the entire front, the Soviet Union was caught flatfooted.

German planes virtually destroyed the forward air fleets of the Soviet Union, and, working with their usual clockwork precision, the Germans, under Brauchitsch and his usual subordinate generals, encircled one Soviet army after another.

By July 10, German forces were in Minsk, taking nearly 300,000 prisoners and capturing vast numbers of tanks and guns. In the course of the next 10 days, another trap shut at Smolensk, with 100,000 more prisoners and more tanks. By the middle of August, the Germans were deep in the Ukraine. On September 19, Kiev fell to the Germans and virtually the entire Russian army in the Ukraine, 665,000 men, surrendered.

A German army under Fritz Eric von Manstein (1887–1973) entered the Crimea and took most of it. By September 4, Leningrad had been surrounded and placed under siege.

At the beginning of October, the Germans in the center closed still another trap at Vyazma and Bryansk and captured 650,000 more men. By October 20, the Germans stood at Mozhaisk, only 40 miles west of Moscow. The Soviet government fled to Kuibyshev, far to the east (though Stalin, in a remarkable display of resolution, remained in Moscow).

It looked as though Hitler's calculation had once more been correct and that the Soviet Union was finished. Indeed, the German propaganda mill announced in October that the Soviet war *was* over. Certainly, to outside onlookers it seemed over. The Soviet Union, in four months, had suffered 3 million casualties, half of them having been taken as prisoners of war.

There were, however, several other things to consider. First, never before had the German army had to advance quite so far or strain to hold on to quite so huge a territory. This alone stretched their capacities to the uttermost.

Second, the Soviet Union did not collapse. The Russian people had a long history of unbelievable stolidity under pressure. Despite all its losses, the Soviet Union had reserves available. Slowly, it had recovered from the initial shock, buying time with space, and organizing itself for more effective resistance. What's more, the Germans themselves saw to it that the Soviet peoples would not collapse. They were treated with such barbaric frightfulness by the Germans that even if the Russians had wanted to greet the Germans as rescuers from oppression, they could not. They joined guerrilla bands instead.

Third, Hitler *had* started too late. By October, the rains came and the primitive Soviet roads became quagmires of mud. The Germans relied on wheeled vehicles, rather than on treaded ones, and the wheels could not negotiate the mud. What's more, the temperature was dropping and the rains began to freeze under conditions where the German soldiers had only their summer uniforms to fight Soviet soldiers who were superbly clothed for winter fighting.

Fourth, the shock of war had brought to the fore the more capable Soviet generals. Thus, Georgy Konstantinovich Zhukov (1896–1974), as good a general as any German, was now in charge of the defense of Moscow.

Fifth, Great Britain and the United States, frightened of a German victory over the Soviet Union, and what it might portend for the world, temporarily buried their suspicions of Communism and began to help the Soviet Union in a major way. They began to supply the Soviets with planes, weapons, medicines, and more.

The Germans continued to make some gains. On November 22, they took Rostov at the mouth of the Don River. But, wonder of wonders, the Soviets counterattacked and, on December 1, 1941, they *retook* Rostov. The Germans hadn't always succeeded. They had failed at Dunkirk and failed at the Battle of Britain, but in 26 months of war, the Germans had never once been forced out of any position they had taken—until now.

Rundstedt, who was in command of the army that had been driven out, at once resigned because, as he well knew, Hitler would instantly fire him (which he did). He was replaced by Walther von Reichenau (1884–1942), who, a little over two years earlier, had taken Warsaw.

In the center, the German forces were now under Hans Gunther von Kluge (1882–1944), who continued to grind forward in increasingly horrible weather. By December 6, 1941, he had wormed his way to within 25 miles of the center of Moscow. The Germans were in the outer suburbs and the towers of the Kremlin could be made out in field glasses. But that was as far as they could go, and no orders from Berlin could make the soldiers advance any further.

In a fury, Hitler fired Brauchitsch and a number of other generals and took over personal command of the armies, working through Wilhelm Keitel (1882–1946), a field-marshal who was frightened to death of Hitler and who functioned only as a transmitter of orders.

But it was not just that the Germans could advance no further against Moscow. On December 6, 1941, the Soviets finally had assembled an efficient force, warmly dressed, with tanks adjusted to the freezing weather—and launched a counterattack. The Germans fought back with enormous skill and force, but the astounded world watched as the Germans were forced to fall back. They did not fall back very far, to be sure, but when had the German armies in this war been forced to fall back at all?

The very day after the countrerattack was launched, the war took a surprising turn when the Japanese bombed Pearl Harbor in Hawaii so that the United States found itself at war.

The response by Germany was absolutely flabbergasting. The mistake of stopping the tanks at Dunkirk, of bombing London instead of airfields and communications centers, of invading the Soviet Union two months too late, were all as nothing compared to the fact that on December 11, Germany declared war on the United States.

Why? It was totally unnecessary. Hitler may have declared war as a gesture of solidarity with Japan, hoping that, in return, Japan would declare war on the Soviet Union. However, Japan did no such thing.

It might also be that Germany felt that the United States was too far away and too mired in isolationist thinking to be much of an enemy, but even if that were so, why unnecessarily multiply enemies?

On the other hand, if Hitler had *not* declared war on the United States, American public opinion, outraged by the sneak attack on Pearl Harbor, might surely have insisted on war to the uttermost with Japan, concentrated and instant. Europe might suddenly have seemed not our concern, or at least as something to be taken care of only after Japan had been properly punished. American aid to Great Britain and the Soviet Union might have dwindled and German victory in Europe (at least until the United States could turn its attention Europe-ward) might have been assured.

Hitler, however, made that impossible. By declaring war on the United States, he gave that nation two wars to fight, and, as it happened, Roosevelt and his generals decided that Germany, and *not* Japan (despite Pearl Harbor), was the more immediate danger. The war against Japan was prosecuted vigorously, but the war against Germany received priority.

Meanwhile, Germany's concern was the Russian front. At Hitler's insistence, German troops set up "hedgehog areas" which were staunchly defended and which wore down the Soviet counteroffensive. The Soviets made gains but they were relatively small. Leningrad remained under siege, suffering horribly, and most of the German gains in Russia in 1941 were held.

Germany waited for spring to come, for the snow to melt, and for the ground to dry out. There would then be another summer offensive. However, it was not to be 1941 all over again. For one thing, the Germans had suffered severe losses for the first time, and those losses were of their best men. They had to dig up replacements who were less well-trained. Furthermore, German morale declined. After two years of quick, painless victories, the German forces had had their first taste of fierce fighting against an enemy as ruthless as themselves, and they didn't like it. The Soviet Union, however, having survived and having begun to fight the Germans on almost equal terms, was in a state of rising morale.

So even though Germany was ready for another gamble, it was not going to attack all along the front as it had the year before. It planned an attack chiefly in the south, aiming at the grainfields of the Ukraine and the oil wells of the Caucasus.

On May 8, 1942, the new offensive began, with an attack on the Crimea. The Russians still held Sevastopol and, in the east, the Kerch peninsula. Once again, however, the German steamroller crushed opposition. The Kerch peninsula was taken easily and, after a three-week siege, Sevastopol fell on July 2 and the entire Crimean pensinsula was in German hands.

The Germans next poured across the straits into the Caucasus, and, farther north, into the great eastward bend of the Don River. Voronezh on the Don River fell on July 6, 1942, and with that the Germans had advanced beyond their farthest mark in 1941 (though they remained short of their record mark in central and northern Soviet Union).

The Germans occupied the bend of the Don, but this time, the Russians withdrew in good order, for the days of trapping entire Russian armies seemed over. The German Sixth Army under Friedrich Paulus (1890–1957) crossed the Don River at the point of its nearest approach to the Volga River. On August 23, 1942, Paulus reached the Volga just north of the city of Stalingrad.

If Paulus could take the city he could cut communications between central Russia and the oil fields of the Caucasus and that might mark the beginning of the end of the Soviet Union. The Soviet Union, painfully aware of this, made ready for a to-the-death struggle for Stalingrad.

German armies were advancing also into the Caucasus. Rostov, which the Russians had retaken eight months earlier as the first blow of their winter counterattack, fell again to the Germans on July 23, 1942, and this time the Germans flooded far beyond. By August 23, they had penetrated almost to the Caspian Sea and found themselves among the highest peaks of the Caucasus.

In the summer of 1942, the fortunes of Germany, and of its ally, Japan, seemed to be at their height. The German army held all of Europe from Brittany on the Atlantic Ocean to the Caucasus mountain range, a width of 2300 miles. At the same time, German forces in Egypt were threatening the Suez Canal. In the Pacific, Japan occupied all of eastern and southeastern Asia and its fleets controlled the western half of the Pacific Ocean.

If this made it look as though Germany and Japan were on the point of victory, appearances were deceiving. Germany and Japan had both strained their manpower and economies to the utmost, even while both Great Britain and the Soviet Union were continuing to fight and the untouched United States was still mobilizing its matchless power.

What happened in Egypt and in the Pacific we will describe at appropriate points later, but in Europe itself, the fighting at Stalingrad grew into the largest land battle the world had ever seen, either before or since.

Hitler was almost insane in his determination to take Stalingrad, partly for its undeniable strategic position, and partly because it bore Stalin's name. He threw in every division he could against Russians who defended it as bitterly as Germany attacked. Each building in the city became a fortress, and separate floors were attacked and defended. The city was pounded into rubble by German guns, but the rubble was all the easier to defend, all the more difficult to attack.

The Germans were fighting at the end of a long communications line, constantly threatened by Soviet guerrillas. The Germans were also forced to depend on satellite forces—Rumanians, Hungarians, Italians—in relatively quiet sectors north and south of Stalingrad so as to be able to concentrate their own slowly dwindling forces on the city itself. The satellite forces lacked the German commitment to the struggle and could not be relied on in a crisis.

Meanwhile, the Russians, under Zhukov, were quietly assembling troops to the east of Stalingrad, and were waiting for the time to counterattack. As the German supplies, fed by inadequate communication lines, dwindled, and as the weather started turning cold, the Soviets moved into action.

On November 19, 1942, the Soviets struck simultaneously north and south of Stalingrad. The Satellite troops gave way at once and the Soviets swept through in an encirclement that neatly trapped Paulus's Sixth Army. For the first time in the war, a *German* army was trapped.

Paulus ought to have battled his way westward, trying to break out of the Soviet ring and to retire to a more easily defensible line. Hitler, however, overaccustomed to victory and convinced that any trouble that arose was through the cowardice of his generals, refused to allow retreat. Then, and afterward, his orders were inevitably that of holding fast, and this lay the groundwork for ever greater disasters for Germany. Nor could the generals defy Hitler for they feared him too much. They went along, despairingly, with the orders of a virtual madman who was nowhere near the front and who studied maps without any understanding of local difficulties.

Hitler ordered Paulus to cling to his position and promised that he would be amply supplied by air, while Manstein would lead a counterat-

tacking German army to relieve him. However, Manstein's army never reached Stalingrad and the supplies that were delivered to the trapped Germans by air were woefully inadequate.

The Germans caught in the Stalingrad pocket fought on resolutely but hopelessly, and the Soviets slowly squeezed and squeezed, until finally, on February 2, 1943, what was left of the German forces was forced to surrender. Paulus himself went into captivity, the first time ever that a German field-marshal had surrendered.

To be sure, Manstein, in a brilliant display, defeated the Soviets in the eastern Ukraine in a month's fighting in February and March of 1943, and retook Kharkov, but that wasn't enough. The Soviets kept pushing and virtually all the German gains of the summer and fall of 1942 were lost in the winter–spring Soviet offensive of 1942–1943.

The Germans were fatally weakened. They had lost 300,000 men at Stalingrad, and over a million men altogether. The Soviets had lost as many, but they were stronger than ever, thanks in large part to the supplies pouring into the nation in ever-increasing volume from Great Britain and the United States.

The Soviets at the height of their 1942–1943 counteroffensive had taken the city of Kursk south of Moscow and driven a wedge to the westward. The Germans still felt they could recoup some of their losses in the summer of 1943. No more would there be an advance all along the line as in 1941, or even all along the southern half of the line as in 1942. Now what was planned was a pincer attack north and south of Kursk to do to the Soviets what they had done to the Germans at Stalingrad.

On July 5, 1943, the Battle of Kursk began. Vast numbers of German tanks met equally vast numbers of Russian tanks in the greatest such battle in history. For the first time, a German summer offensive was stopped in its tracks. The Soviet tanks and planes beat back the German tanks and planes and then, also for the first time, the Soviet forces began a summer counteroffensive.

The Germans were now no longer able to maintain any offensive action of importance. Not only were they being beaten by the sturdy Soviet forces, who had improved steadily under the German blows, but the British and Americans had moved into North Africa and were attacking in Sicily.

We will stop here.

The details of the war against Germany, outside the continent of Europe, and within it, too, after the failure of Germany's Kursk offensive, are better told from the perspective of Germany's enemies, and to them we will turn.

During World War II and, indeed, during the entire 12-year period in which Hitler ruled Germany, German science and German culture sagged and dropped steadily to a low point. German scientists and cultural leaders fled the country to the west, weakening Germany tremendously and strengthening its enemies.

GREAT BRITAIN

When World War II started, Great Britain was not really in the mood for great land battles. She remembered well the blood-letting of World War I, and wanted none of it. As a matter of fact, since the end of the Hundred Years War, nearly five centuries earlier, Great Britain had preferred to remain behind the wall of the sea and to let her ships do the fighting for her, while subsidizing other powers to do the land-fighting. Even when land-fighting was unavoidable and had been carried through successfully by such generals as Marlborough and Wellington, it was not popular with the British people.

Therefore, Great Britain prepared to fight a naval war against Germany. Immediately after Great Britain entered the war on September 3, 1939, it instituted a naval blockade of the enemy. That sort of thing had worked reasonably well in World War I, reducing the German people to hunger and misery. However, it was to work far less well in World War II, when Germany, at least in the first half of the war, conquered vast tracts of Europe and despoiled them for the benefit of the German people so that the British blockade merely served to help starve the conquered nations.

The Germans had no chance of an ordinary naval response. Its ships were newly built and very modern, better than the Allied ships on a one-to-one basis, but there were very few of them. If Germany had tried an outright naval battle, it would have been swept from the seas. Instead, its ships were used as raiders of Great Britain's merchant fleet. Moreover, as in World War I, Germany had an ample supply of submarines.

Indeed, in the first months of the war, it was German vessels that made the headlines. On September 3, 1939, almost immediately after Great Britain had entered the war, a British passenger liner, the *Athenia*, was sunk without warning 200 miles west of Scotland. On September 17, a British aircraft carrier, the *Courageous*, was sunk by a German submarine. A German submarine even managed to make its way into the British naval base at Scapa Flow off the northern coast of Scotland on October 14. There it sank the British battleship, *Royal Oak*, and got away.

Meanwhile, through the fall of 1939, a German pocket battleship, the *Graf Spee*, was scouring the South Atlantic, sinking or capturing eleven British ships.

The British navy, beaten and humiliated, felt it had to get the *Graf Spee*. On December 13, 1939, a British squadron cornered the German ship at the mouth of the River Platte between Argentina and Uruguay. The British ships were roughly handled, but so was the *Graf Spee*, which had to move into the neutral territory of Montevideo, Uruguay. There, the ship tried to make repairs. What was left of the British squadron was waiting for it, however, and reinforcements had arrived. The *Graf Spee* had no hope of help and the Uruguayans gave it only 72 hours of sanctuary. The captain of the *Graf Spee* had no choice but to sink his vessel in order to keep it out of the hands of the British. Three days later, he killed himself.

This sea victory was a boon to British morale, which needed it badly. After all, in the first four months of the war, Poland had been divided by Germany and the Soviet Union; the Soviet Union had absorbed the Baltic States and was fighting Finland; and Great Britain and France had done nothing of any importance.

The British government was still in the hands

of those who, till the spring of 1939, had been appeasers. Chamberlain was still Prime Minister, and Halifax was still Foreign Minister. To be sure, Chamberlain had brought in Winston Churchill and had made him First Lord of the Admiralty, the position Chamberlain had held before the Gallipoli disaster a quarter century earlier. Churchill, at least, had never been an appeaser of Hitler, though he had been an admirer of Mussolini in the latter's early days.

Chamberlain held on throughout the "phony war" when the British could still live with the dream that the blockade would win the war for them. This notion was smashed when Germany raced through Denmark and made its successful landing in Norway in April 1940. When Great Britain reacted with troops of their own in Norway, Chamberlain crowed that Hitler "had missed the bus."

He was wrong, however. It was Great Britain who had missed the bus. The nation could endure Chamberlain no longer. He was voted out of office. He wanted Halifax to succeed him, but that would have been disastrous for Halifax was no better and no more charismatic than he. He could not have held the confidence of the country.

Halifax, probably realizing this, declined the office and the King chose Winston Churchill as Prime Minister. Churchill consistently bit off more than he could chew, but the times required precisely that. Churchill became Prime Minister on May 10, 1940, just as the war acquired a darker tinge than ever, and built a coalition government that included Clement Richard Attlee (1881–1967), the leader of the Labour opposition, and Ernest Bevin (1881–1951), another strong Labour leader.

(It was Chamberlain's sad fate to die on November 9, 1940, when the Battle of Britain was still raging and Great Britain's survival was still questionable. He saw the tragic consequence of his appeasement policy but did not live to see the nation pull through.)

Churchill, as Prime Minister, did not speak cheer to the nation. On May 13, with Germany bursting through the Low Countries, Churchill faced Parliament for the first time and said that he had nothing to offer "but blood, toil, tears, and sweat."

A kind of salvation came to Great Britain with the rescue of its army from Dunkirk, and, thereafter, Churchill flew several times to France to try to get it to continue the fight even if it were beaten in France itself. He even offered, on June 16, 1940, to form a British–French union of nations with a common citizenship and economy, but nothing was of any use. France was determined to surrender, nor would it undertake to continue the fight from outside Europe.

The fall of France left Great Britain in a grave quandary. Not only was it now exposed to air attack by the German Air Force from bases in France, the Low Countries, and Norway, but its navy, on which Great Britain depended entirely, was at terrible risk.

In the first place, Italy had joined the war, once it was certain that France was finished, and the Italians had a fleet in the Mediterranean that was by no means negligible. Great Britain had to reinforce its Mediterranean fleet, therefore, and send troops into Egypt to guard against an Italian invasion from Libya. That meant it would be much harder for the British fleet to protect the merchant shipping in the Atlantic and thus preserve Great Britain's lifeline.

The greatest danger to Great Britain, however, lay in the French Navy, much of which was at anchor in North African ports. By the terms of the Armistice, France could keep its ships, but by now it was well-understood (at last) that Hitler kept no treaties or agreements a moment longer than it suited him to do so. With all of France in his grip, he could squeeze it until the gasping French would agree to give up their ships to the Germans. With the French navy at his disposal, Hitler might well do so much damage to the British ships that an invasion of Great Britain would become feasible.

On July 3, 1940, therefore, a British squadron appeared off Oran in Algeria, where much of the French navy was at anchor. It gave the French ships the choice of joining the British, of letting itself be interned in some British port, or of scuttling itself.

The French ships refused all the alternatives

and the British ships opened fire at once. Three French battleships were sunk and a French squadron at Alexandria was disarmed. It was a sad moment. The French, who would not fight the Germans, fought their old allies. Hitler had lost his chance at the ships but he made the most of the propaganda victory offered him, of showing the French that it was really the British who were their enemies.

On July 5, the Vichy government broke relations with Great Britain and, thereafter, it increased its cooperation with Germany. However, this would have come to pass anyway, and at least the British had deprived the Germans of the French fleet.

Soon, the Battle of Britain would begin. The bombardment of Great Britain from the air was bad enough, but an even worse danger was the sinking of its merchant ships. By August 15, 1940, 2.5 million tons of British shipping had been sunk. Despite the fact that some Norwegian and Danish ships had joined the British and that the French ships had been put out of action, the British navy was spread thin and it seemed that Great Britain would starve long before Germany would.

What saved the situation, at least temporarily, was a deal whereby the United States transferred 50 old destroyers to Great Britain.

Meanwhile, Great Britain had to deal with Africa as well. On August 6, 1940, Italian forces from Italian East Africa invaded British Somaliland, and by August 19 it had occupied the region. At this point, the Italian Empire reached its greatest extent.

To anyone watching the war at the time, it might well have seemed that Great Britain was on the edge of defeat, but now Churchill proved himself the voice of freedom and resolution. When Hitler offered peace (on German terms, of course), Churchill refused the offer at once, and contemptuously. In a ringing speech on June 4, 1940, he promised that the nation would fight everywhere, for every inch of ground, and that "we shall never surrender." He made it plain that even if Great Britain itself were taken and were starving, the British Empire would continue the fight from the dominions and the colonies.

As the German airforce closed in, he said, "Let us therefore brace ourselves to our duties, and so bear ourselves, that if the British Empire and its Commonwealth last for a thousand years, men will still say: 'This was their finest hour.' "

And, of course, it was.

He made it plain, too, that neither London nor any other British city would be declared open and undefended, as Paris had been. He said, ". . . we would rather see London laid in ruins and ashes than that it should be tamely and abjectly enslaved."

The whole world rang with Churchill's eloquence. It is very rare that a war can be fought and influenced by oratory, but insofar as it could be done, Churchill did it.

Yet more than words were still necessary. At the very height of the Battle of Britain, the Italian forces in Libya finally made their move on September 13, 1940. Under Rodolfo Graziani (1882–1955), who had been viceroy of Ethiopia, five divisions lumbered into Egypt along the coast. By September 16, they had reached Sidi Barrani, 50 miles into Egypt. There they stopped and waited, not daring to move farther.

The British forces, far fewer in number, were at Mersa Matruh, 70 miles farther east. The British were hampered by the fact that on October 28, Italy invaded Greece, and some of the British forces in Egypt had to be sent to Crete and to Greece.

Nevertheless, on December 9, 1940, the British forces under Archibald Percival Wavell (1883–1950) launched an attack. The British had only one fourth the number in the Italian army, but they made up for it by surprise and speed. In two weeks, the Italians were thrown out of Egypt, losing 38,000 prisoners and great quantities of war material.

The British plunged on. They entered Libya and, by the beginning of February 1941, all of Cyrenaica, the easternmost province of Libya, was in British hands. The Italians had been forced back 500 miles, had lost 130,000 prisoners, 400 tanks, and 1200 guns. The entire army that had been sent by Mussolini to take Egypt had been disrupted and forced into flight or surrender.

Meanwhile, the British were also acting against Italian East Africa. On January 19, 1941, British forces from the Sudan crossed into Ethiopia, and sent the much more numerous Italian forces flying. On April 4, 1941, the British took Addis Ababa; and on May 18, the last Italian forces surrendered, and Italian East Africa, which had been so noisily established only five years before, was gone forever. Haile Selassie returned to his capital and resumed his role as Emperor of Ethiopia on May 5, while Mussolini lost another 50,000 Italians as prisoners at virtually no cost to the British.

To be sure, the British victories had been over Italians and not over Germans, but *any* sort of victory was badly needed in those dark days and the British were jubilant. What's more, the victory was not meaningless. The immediate threat to the Suez Canal was lifted and the Red Sea became an undisputed channel for British reinforcements for Egypt and the Middle East.

Nor was victory over the Italians confined to the land. The British admiral, Andrew Brown Cunningham (1881–1963), fought the Italian navy off the coast of Calabria on July 9, 1940, and inflicted serious damage on them at negligible cost to the British.

Cunningham oversaw the reinforcements and strengthening of the British-owned island of Malta south of Sicily in the mid-Mediterranean Sea. Although it was to be bombed endlessly during the course of the war, Malta remained British and served as an "unsinkable aircraft carrier."

Then, on November 11, 1940, Cunningham attacked the Italian fleet in the naval base of Taranto and virtually destroyed it. On March 28, 1941, the British encountered what was left of the Italian fleet off Cape Matapan in southern Greece and sank most of it.

Thus, less than a year after Italy had entered a war it had confidently assumed to be over, it had lost its Empire and its fleet and it played no further significant mass role in military events, though Mussolini continued his role as Hitler's jackal.

Nevertheless, victories over Italians, however useful, did nothing to decrease the German danger. The "Battle of the Atlantic" was still being lost by Great Britain as the Germans instituted "wolf packs," groups of a dozen or more submarines that lay in wait for merchant shipping. Far more tons of British shipping were sunk than Great Britain could possibly replace, even though the British took to escorting merchant ships with other ships modified to carry airplanes.

Surface raiders were also a problem. The biggest danger was the *Bismarck*, a newly built German battleship that was the largest and most powerful warship in the world at the time. On May 18, 1940, it sailed out of its port in Gdynia, Poland, and headed for the Atlantic Ocean. The entire British navy was at once ordered to destroy it.

A British squadron finally overtook the *Bismarck* in the frigid waters of Denmark Strait between Iceland and Greenland on May 24. The *Bismarck*, however, was not easy to deal with. One of its shells managed to penetrate the interior of the British battleship *Hood* (the largest of the British warships, but rather antiquated) and struck its ammunition supply, blowing up the ship with the loss of all but three of her 1500-men crew. A new British battleship, *The Prince of Wales*, was also badly damaged.

The *Bismarck* then proceeded westward, while what was left of the British squadron, together with reinforcements that joined it, pursued. On May 26, 1940, the *Bismarck* was sighted 700 miles west of Brest, France, and the British ships closed in again. For a whole day, the British ships pounded away at the *Bismarck*, trying to sink it. It was a hard job but, finally, on May 28, it went down with the loss of almost its entire crew of 2300.

This preserved the picture of Great Britain as dominating the sea, but it had been an expensive victory and the problem of the submarines remained.

What's more, Germany now took over what had been the Italian theater of war. German planes began to bombard British bases in Cyrenaica, just as Wavell's forces were further depleted by the necessity of having to send British units into Greece to fight the Germans, who were clearly planning to invade the Balkans.

In March of 1941, the German general, Erwin Rommel, who had fought very well in France, reached Libya and took over the armed forces there, reducing the Italian generals to messenger-boys.

Rommel at once attacked on March 24, 1941, and within two months drove the British out of Cyrenaica, although the British retained control of Tobruk on the Mediterranean coast. It remained under German siege but fought off all attacks.

Wavell, with most of his command having been shifted to Greece, where it was soon fighting a losing war with the Germans, could do nothing to stem Rommel's advance. He was relieved of his command on July 1, 1941, and was replaced by Claude John Eyre Auchinleck (1884–1981).

Auchinleck launched an offensive on November 18, 1941, and in the space of a month had relieved Tobruk, which had been under siege for eight months, and drove Rommel out of Cyrenaica again.

However, the losses in Greece and Crete in April and May of 1941 had weakened the British navy in the Mediterranean Sea. What's more, the Germans sent 25 submarines into the Mediterranean and multiplied their air attacks on Malta. The British aircraft carrier, *Ark Royal*, the only one in the Mediterranean, was sunk in November 1941. In December, two midget Italian submarines penetrated Alexandria harbor and damaged two British battleships, while other ships were sunk by mines.

The net result of all this was that by the end of the year, despite Auchinleck's successful counterattack, British strength in the Mediterranean was at a low point, and Germany was able to ship supplies and reinforcements to Rommel without very much trouble.

By 1942, Germany was increasingly occupied with the war in the Soviet Union, and the United States had entered the war. Nevertheless, the Battle of the Atlantic continued to run in favor of Germany. Submarines and surface raiders (including the *Tirpitz*, a sister ship of the sunken Bismarck) had easy pickings.

Allied shipping losses in 1942 were just over a million tons, but, little by little, countermeasures were improving and the sinking of German submarines was increasing. By the end of 1942, 85 German submarines had been sunk. The submarines would be replaced, but skilled crews were harder to find. The cost to Germany was, therefore, increasing steadily.

The Allies, especially now that the United States had entered the war, were becoming stronger in the air. On the night of May 30–31, 1942, a thousand planes bombed Cologne. It was the first time a thousand planes had been used at one time *against* Germany. From here on, the bombing of Germany grew heavier and heavier, while the German airforce, deeply committed to the war against the Soviet Union, could respond only more and more weakly. The bombing of Germany did not, apparently, have much of a strategic effect—the Germans kept fighting and producing war materiel—but it did bring misery to the German people who, till then, had seen misery brought only to their enemies.

On land, however, the Germans seemed still invincible. On January 21, 1942, Rommel took advantage of British weakness in the eastern Mediterranean Sea by beginning a second offensive. The British were driven into retreat and, by February 4, Rommel stood at Gazala, not far west of Tobruk.

Here there was a pause while both sides built up strength. On May 28, Rommel was ready to strike again and for two weeks there was a hard and inconclusive fight, but in the end Rommel's mastery of the art of war was not to be withstood. On June 14, the British began to retreat eastward. Again, they left Tobruk behind as a fortified outpost, but this time, Rommel took it without trouble on June 21, 1942. (And as another example of German invincibility, an amphibious attack on the port of Dieppe in west central France by British and Canadian troops was launched on August 19, 1942, and it met with complete defeat.)

The British continued to fall back far into Egypt until they made their stand at El Alamein, only 60 miles west of Alexandria, and only 200 miles from the Suez Canal. At this time, the German forces in the Caucasus were about 1000 miles northeast of the Suez Canal. Undoubtedly, anyone looking at the map might feel the dizzying prospect of the Germans closing a pincers that would take in the entire Middle East.

However, maps don't tell the whole story. Both in the Soviet Union and in North Africa, Germany had stretched its forces just as far as they would go. Rommel was a thousand miles from his main supply base at Tripoli, and British airpower and seapower were increasing again from their low point at the beginning of the year, so that it became progressively harder for Rommel to get reinforcements and fresh supplies.

Meanwhile Auchinleck had been relieved of his command in Egypt and a new general made his appearance on August 13, 1942. This was Bernard Law Montgomery (1887–1976).

With Rommel anxious to test out the new British commander, and with Hitler sending out repeated orders for him to take the Suez Canal, Rommel tried another advance on August 31, 1942. He stuck hard, but he was short of fuel and the British now had control of the air. Rommel fell back on his El Alamein defenses and he knew he could attack no more. He simply lacked the strength to plunge further eastward. His only hope was that the British would attack overconfidently, and, in some way, make an error that Rommel could take advantage of.

Montgomery, however, was not to be hurried. Every day made him stronger and Rommel weaker. By October, the British army had been raised to the number of 150,000 men, while Rommel had only 96,000. What's more, Rommel was ill and flew back to Germany for treatment.

On October 23, 1942, Montgomery was ready and began to attack with a ferocious artillery bombardment. Rommel flew back form Germany as soon as the news of the British attack reached him, and he performed wonders in attempting to stop the British. However, he needed more than wonders. His gasoline supplies dwindled. British planes bombarded him mercilessly. By November 4, the Battle of El Alamein was over and Rommel's task consisted in trying to withdraw what was left of his army and to avoid surrender. This he did very skillfully, withdrawing the full width of Libya.

The Battle of El Alamein was *the* turning point of the war against Germany. For the first time, a British army had defeated a German army and the defeat had been overwhelming. The Suez Canal and the Middle East were not to be threatened again.

Four days after the completion of the Battle of El Alamein came the Allied invasion of North Africa, and 11 days after that came the Soviet counterattack at Stalingrad. With that triple disaster, the Germans had lost the war—something the German generals were increasingly aware of, but which they could not convince Hitler of (or, really, even dared to try).

With the invasion of North Africa, the British role in the war receded and it took up the post of junior partner to the United States. For that reason, the events of the war after the Battle of El Alamein are better told from an American perspective.

World War II swallowed up much of Great Britain's cultural activity, but there were some advances in science. The British mathematician, Alan Mathison Turing (1912–1954), an expert on computers and codes, led a team that broke the German coding machine (which the Germans thought unbreakable), making use of work initiated by Polish scientists. From early in the war, the British knew exactly what the Germans were planning and what they were doing. This, as much as anything else, led to Germany's defeat.

Turing's work was secret and he never received the credit that was due him. Quite the reverse. After the war, he was hounded into suicide by a pitiless society that disapproved of his homosexuality.

The Australiain–British pathologist, Howard Walter Florey (1898–1968), in collaboration with a German–British biochemist, Ernst Boris Chain (1906–1979), labored to isolate the bacteriostatic principle from bread mold, which Alexander Fleming had earlier discovered.

In this way, penicillin was isolated and, before the war was over, its antibiotic action did much to prevent death from infected wounds. Florey, Chain, and Fleming shared a Nobel Prize in 1945 for this.

The British biochemists, Archer John Porter

Martin (b. 1910) and Richard Laurence Milling-tron Synge (b. 1914), developed the technique of paper chromatography in 1944. This made it possible to separate small quantities of complex mixtures into individual components and eventually earned them a Nobel Prize, too.

Noel Coward staged *Blithe Spirit* in 1941. Clive Staples Lewis (1898–1963) published the science fiction novels *Perelandra* in 1941 and *That Hideous Strength* in 1945. He also published the allegorical *Screwtape Letters* in 1942.

Somerset Maugham published *The Razor's Edge* in 1944. Eric Arthur Blair (1903–1950), using the penname of George Orwell, published his allegorical novel *Animal Farm* in 1944.

SOVIET UNION

As World War II opened, the Soviet Union remained neutral. What Stalin undoubtedly hoped for was that Germany and the West would bleed themselves white, leaving an untouched Soviet Union to emerge from the war as the most powerful state in Europe.

This, however, proved to be a fantasy almost at once. Stalin must have expected that Poland would go down to defeat, but he could not have thought it would happen as quickly as it did, or as overwhelmingly. Nor could he have supposed that Great Britain and France would not make a move against Germany while Poland was being defeated.

The Soviet Union had secretly insisted that it take half of Poland after its defeat, as the price of entering into the nonaggression pact. Germany had agreed, knowing full well that it would exact vengeance for this in due time.

The Soviet Union marched into Poland on September 17, 1939, since the alternative was clearly to watch Germany extend its power, in a matter of weeks, to the very borders of the Soviet Union. Nevertheless, it was a propaganda mistake for it was viewed as a cowardly move.

The Soviet Union felt the need to conciliate a Germany that was clearly far more powerful than it had thought and that was facing western powers that were far less resolute than the Soviets had counted on. The Soviets kept only that por-

tion of eastern Poland, therefore, that was inhabited by Byelorussians and Ukrainians, which Poland had seized from a helpless Russia in 1920. By the nonaggression agreement, Stalin could have had Lublin and Warsaw, too, but Stalin gave them up to Hitler provided he could have a free hand in the Baltic. Hitler allowed that—temporarily.

Therefore, Stalin pressured the helpless nations of Estonia, Latvia, and Lithuania into signing pacts that allowed Soviet troops to establish bases there. This was carried through, very obviously, in order to strengthen the Soviet position against Germany in case Hitler turned on him. Hitler knew this, but he had to finish with the western powers before he could do anything.

The Soviet Union tried to establish bases in Finland, too, but the Finns refused, and put themselves into a war footing under Carl von Mannerheim, who had fought the Russians during the Russian Revolution and the Civil Wars.

The Soviet Union, therefore, attached Finland without warning on November 30, 1939, attempting to carry on a German-style campaign of crushing victory.

It didn't work. The Soviet army had been eviscerated by Stalin's purge of the army command a few years earlier and it was, in any case, neither as well-armed nor as well-led as the German army had been. The Finns, unlike the Poles, had the advantage of a rugged terrain, winter weather, excellent fortifications, and experienced ski troops who could hit and run.

For two months, the Soviet Union suffered humiliating defeats at the hands of the Finns, while Great Britain and France, far more anxious to strike at the bumbling Soviets than at the formidable Germans, prepared to send an expeditionary force to Finland. However, Norway and Sweden, anxious to retain their neutrality, refused to allow such a force to pass. (Just the same, Stalin could not fail to see that the British and French were his enemies and he drew all the closer to Germany, something that proved harmful to the west *and* to the Soviet Union.)

Finally, beginning on February 1, the Soviet Union assembled overwhelming forces at the Mannerheim Line just north of Leningrad and began an unending artillery bombardment. The Mannerheim Line broke and the Finns had to surrender on March 12, 1940. The Soviets kept their demands small, and merely took over the area north of Leningrad, including the Mannerheim line, plus a few bases.

All this convinced the world that the Soviet Union could not fight a modern war. Germany, in particular, developed the fatal notion that the Soviet Union would be easy to conquer—one strong push and its jerry-built structure would collapse. Great Britain and the United States shared that opinion.

As for the Soviet Union, it had received a real fright. It began a vast program to strengthen and modernize its armed force, but it didn't have much time in which to do it, and it was too large and economically backward to be able to work very quickly.

In addition, the Soviet Union tried to continue to strengthen its position vis-à-vis Germany. In August 1940, after the fall of France, the Soviet Union annexed Estonia, Latvia, and Lithuania outright, converting them into constituent republics of the Soviet Union. Germany, still occupied with Great Britain, had to acquiesce to this, but was furious.

Then, on June 16, 1940, the Soviet Union demanded that Romania give it back the province of Bessarabia that Romania had seized after the Russian Revolution. On June 28, the Soviet Union annexed the province as a new republic, taking also a piece of land to its northwest, Northern Bukovina.

In addition, the Soviet Union signed a non-aggression pact with Japan in order to keep its eastern flank free of trouble, and it proceeded to go to all lengths to conciliate Germany and to deprive it of any rational excuse to attack. (For some reason, it never occurred to Stalin that Hitler did not need a rational excuse to attack.)

By the fall of 1940, it was clear that Germany was not going to crush Great Britain very quickly, and Hitler prepared to smash the Soviet Union in one mighty blow and then turn on Great Britain with a united and enslaved Europe behind him.

On November 12, 1940, Hitler met in Berlin with Vyacheslav Mikhaylovich Molotov (1890–1986), who was Foreign Minister of the Soviet Union. Hitler claimed that Great Britain was defeated and that the Soviet Union could have its share of the British Empire, if it followed German orders. Because there was an air-raid in progress, the meeting had retired to an underground shelter.

Molotov asked, "If Great Britain is defeated, why are we down here and whose are the planes overhead?" Molotov refused to accept the German terms, and the last chance the Soviet Union had of avoiding invasion disappeared.

The Soviet Union was obviously displeased when, in the spring of 1941, Germany invaded and occupied the Balkans, although the Soviets made no move to stop them. Indeed, it was impossible to fail to see that Germany was preparing for an invasion. Nevertheless, Stalin turned a deaf ear to all warnings, refused to take any action, prepared no plan of defense, and made no move to protect the border. He continued to send war material to Germany and seemed convinced that the Soviet Union would remain neutral. How someone as ordinarily paranoid as Stalin could persuade himself that Hitler would keep his word passes human understanding. The only possible explanation is that Stalin was paranoid enough to think it was all a British plot.

In any case, on June 22, 1941, Hitler invaded all along the frontier and the Soviet Union, totally unprepared, suffered four months of incredible disaster.

And yet, unfortunately for Hitler, the Soviet Union was large enough, and its people were resolute and fatalistic enough, to withstand disasters that would have destroyed any other European nation. Leningrad was encircled, but it continued to fight under appalling conditions and would not surrender. Moscow was approached, but by that time the Soviet army had caught its breath, winnowed out the incompetents, came up with reinforcements, and (with the aid of a cold, cold winter) stopped the Germans nearly at the gates of the city.

The Soviet Union managed the mighty task of transferring much of its industrial might far to the east, out of reach of the Germans. As the

British, to their amazement, realized that the bumbling Soviets were actually stopping the Germans, even defeating them in spots, and inflicting large casualties upon them, it seemed worthwhile, after all, to send them supplies. After the United States entered the war, the supplies expanded to a flood.

After the winter of 1941–1942, the Germans attacked again and advanced into the south to Stalingrad and the Caucasus, but they were stretched terribly thin and were just about exhausted. The Soviets, who now had no supply problems, thanks to the Americans and British, could set up a counterattack that smashed the Germans and sent them hurrying westward in spectacular defeat.

By February 2, 1943, the trapped Germans in the Stalingrad pocket surrendered, and by the spring all the German gains of the summer and fall of 1942 were gone. Of course, the Germans had not forgotten how to fight, nor the German generals how to lead. In February and March 1943, the German general, Manstein, had managed to stop the Soviet advance in the eastern Ukraine. He retook Kharkov, despite the fact that he was greatly outmanned by the Soviets.

This, however, was only a temporary success for the Germans and there were not to be many more on the Soviet front. In July of 1943, the Germans tried one last offensive at Kursk, a very limited one, and it was stopped in its tracks.

Thereafter, the Soviets advanced steadily. They took Kharkov again on August 23, 1943; Smolensk on September 25; Kiev on November 6. By January 15, 1944, Leningrad was relieved and its long ordeal was over. As 1944 progressed, the Germans were being steadily driven out of the Soviet Union and, in July, the British and Americans landed in France.

The war thereafter is best treated from an American perspective.

The Soviet Union, by the way, suffered 20 million casualties at least, and enormous losses in property. That it withstood it all was in part due to the mad propensity of the Germans to mistreat the Russians in their grip. Decent treatment might have elicited a certain amount of willing cooperation. Pathologically cruel treatment in-

volving torture, starvation, and killing resulted in the Soviet people being willing to fight to the death.

During the war, Shostakovich composed his Seventh Symphony in 1941. It was the "Leningrad Symphony" in honor of the encircled, battered city that never gave up. Aram Ilich Khachaturian (1903–1978) composed *Gayane* in 1942, which contains his well-known *Sabre Dance*.

JAPAN

By 1939, when World War II began, Japan controlled almost all the Chinese seacoast. It had not been able to absorb all the interior, for China was too large for even Japan's voracious appetite. It was Japan's hope, however, that if all foreign help was cut off from China, China would wither and would be forced to accept Japanese domination.

As it happened, China still had two routes by which supplies could reach it. They were difficult routes indeed, one being along a primitive railroad from French Indo-China and one over the narrow, twisting Burma Road from British-owned Burma. What supplies reached China were largely wasted by the inefficient and corrupt Chiang Kai-shek, but even so, Japan wanted to put an end to the supplies altogether.

They also wanted a puppet and found one in Wang Ching-wei (1883–1944). He had fought alongside Sun Yat-sen and Chiang Kai-shek, but had defected, had given up hope of a united, free China and had become strongly pro-Japanese. The Japanese set him up as puppet ruler of China in March 30, 1940.

Not long afterward, the Germans crushed France, and that gave Japan a golden opportunity. Japan demanded the right to land forces in Indo-China, and France had to give in. By the end of June, Japanese forces were in place and the supply line to China was closed.

On July 18, 1940, Great Britain, facing the supreme crisis of its national life, was forced to close the Burma Road rather than face military action by the Japanese, and China was now completely isolated.

But now the United States stepped in,

strongly urging American displeasure if Indo-China was absorbed into the expanding Japanese Empire. On September 26, 1940, the United States embargoed steel shipments to Japan, and the next day Japan joined Germany and Italy in a tripartite alliance. On April 13, 1941, Japan signed a nonaggression pact with the Soviet Union.

Meanwhile, under American urging, and the promise of American support, Great Britain had reopened the Burma Road on October 18, 1940, when the first fury of the German assault had passed and it seemed that Great Britain would not be invaded. On July 26, 1941, the United States froze Japanese assets in the United States. Clearly, there was an economic war growing and spreading between the two nations.

What's more, the United States did not object to having American volunteers fly planes in China against the Japanese. These were the "Flying Tigers" and were under the lead of a retired airforce officer, Claire Lee Chennault (1890–1958).

It was clear to Japan, then, that if the Japanese Empire was to expand further, the great enemy was the United States and only the United States. Great Britain and the Soviet Union were both entirely engaged with the Germans and any other Pacific powers were inconsequential. If, somehow, the United States could be sufficiently damaged, then Japan might expand rapidly enough to be untouchable even if the United States later recovered.

On October 17, 1941, when the Soviet Union seemed on the point of collapse (at least, Germany thought it was), Japan got a new activist Prime Minister, Hideki Tojo (1884–1948), who was ready for any action. Plans were made for sudden surprise attacks on western territories in the Pacific, particularly on the great American naval base in Pearl Harbor, Hawaii.

It was Japan's plan, then, to keep "peace negotiations" in progress until they were ready to strike. The United States, they felt, would not fear war while negotiations were actually under way and they would keep their fleet at its base, and unprepared. The Japanese ambassador, Kichisaburo Nomura (1877–1954), kept talking

and, to make things more impressive, a special envoy arrived on November 15, 1941. He was Saburo Kurusu (1888–1954).

While the American Secretary of State, Cordell Hull (1871–1955), earnestly endeavored to get the Japanese out of French Indo-China, and to have them recognize Chiang Kai-shek as ruler of China, the Japanese military men planned their strike.

The Japanese had started the Russo–Japanese war in 1904 with a sneak attack on the Russian Far East fleet and practically won the war at once. They hoped to do the same thing to the United States and the United States, unbelievably, co-operated with them.

Because both Great Britain and the United States kept most of their navies in the Atlantic, fighting the German submarines, the Japanese navy in the Pacific was stronger than the combined British–American Pacific fleets.

To make matters worse, the United States, having watched Germany make surprise attacks on nation after nation, up to and including the Soviet Union, and having seen the Japanese sneak attack on the Russian fleet less than 40 years before, nevertheless kept the American fleet in Pearl Harbor in Hawaii, at anchor, and unready.

On November 26, 1941, a strong Japanese fleet set out to sea, heading for Pearl Harbor. The United States had broken the Japanese secret codes and knew where all the ships of the Japanese Fleet were—ordinarily. The particular fleet heading for Pearl Harbor kept radio silence, however, and other ships in Japanese home waters made use of the call signals of the missing ones. The Americans, therefore, did not know the Pearl Harbor attack was underway.

To be sure, at the last minute, radar information indicated the approach of airplanes, but it was Sunday, with everyone taking it easy so the message was (yawn) ignored.

On the morning of Sunday, December 7, 1941, planes from the Japanese fleet struck and caught the United States utterly and completely by surprise. Of eight battleships present, three were sunk, another capsized, and the rest seriously damaged. Other lesser vessels were also damaged. The American airplanes were caught on the ground as well and 188 of them, more than half, were destroyed. Over 4000 Americans were killed or wounded.

The American Pacific Fleet had been immobilized for months, and it was only by the sheerest stroke of luck that the three aircraft carriers of the Fleet happened to be absent from Pearl Harbor. Had they been there and had they been struck, the United States might have been made helpless for a considerably longer time.

With nothing, at the moment, to fear from the American Navy, Japan could move in all directions. On December 10, Japan took the American island of Guam in the Carolinas. It took two weeks of fighting and two assaults but, by December 23, 1941, they had Wake Island, an American possession in the mid-Pacific. By December 23, they had Hong Kong, forcing the surrender of 12,000 British soldiers.

Meanwhile, on December 8, Japanese troops had landed in northern Malaya. Under Tomoyuki Yamashita (1885–1946), the Japanese pressed southward. Two British ships, the battleship *Prince of Wales* and the battle cruiser *Repulse*, together with some destroyers, steamed northward from Singapore to try to disrupt the Japanese landings. However, it was the Japanese who controlled the air, and both British ships were sunk on December 10, 1941. The loss of these ships on top of the loss at Pearl Harbor left the Japanese in a better position than ever.

The Japanese continued southward, with command of the air and with ample supplies, while the British, untrained for jungle warfare and with serious supply shortages (most of everything was in the Atlantic and the Mediterranean), had to fall back. By the end of the month, they were forced all the way back to Singapore at the southern end of the Malay Peninsula.

There, the British found themselves very much in the position of the French at the Maginot line. The Singapore guns were only adjusted to fire to sea against a naval attack. They could not be used to defend against a jungle advance from the rear. On February 15, 1942, the great British base at Singapore had to surrender unconditionally. The British lost nearly 140,000 men, most of them prisoners.

Japan's big prize, however, was the Philippines. It had been American for 43 years, and it was guarded by an army of 130,000 men, including about 10,000 American regular soldiers. The whole was under the command of Douglas MacArthur (1880–1964) who, by all accounts, seems to have been enormously vain and arrogant, and the closest that the American military machine has ever come to producing a Napoleon.

The day after Pearl Harbor, on December 8, the Japanese struck at Clark Field near Manila. It is hard to believe, with the news of Pearl Harbor ringing throughout the world, that the planes at Clark Field were unready, with the crews at lunch or loafing about. More than half the planes were destroyed.

In the course of the month, Japanese troops landed at various places on several of the Philippine Islands and had no trouble advancing. MacArthur had to abandon Manila on December 26, and led what was left of his army into the Bataan Peninsula across the bay from Manila.

There the position was hopeless, for supplies were limited, the peninsula was crowded with noncombatant refugees, food was low, and the Japanese attacked incessantly. MacArthur, however, for all his personality defects, was a crackerjack general and, for two months, his men fought off the Japanese in a better showing than anyone else had managed since Pearl Harbor.

Roosevelt was unwilling to see MacArthur taken prisoner by the Japanese, and he ordered him out of the Philippines. MacArthur left on March 11, 1942, and the command devolved on his aide, Jonathan Mayhew Wainwright (1883–1953).

The men on Bataan continued to fight though they were on starvation rations and many were down with tropical diseases. On April 9, no more could be done and the Americans surrendered. The Japanese, then, with no consideration for humanity (they believed that soldiers who surrendered were worthy of no consideration), drove them on a brutal march of 90 miles to internment. Many died on that march.

The island of Corregidor, south of Bataan, still

held on and it did not fall to the Japanese until May 6, 1942. In the next two weeks, other areas in the Philippines fell.

The loss of the Philippines was tragic for the United States, but the fighting did occupy the Japanese for five months under the most difficult circumstances, and the loss was no disgrace. It delayed the Japanese and gave the United States time to rebuild.

While the fighting was going on in the Philippines, Japan had occupied Siam (which, after 1939, had come to be known, officially, as Thailand) and prepared to penetrate the British crown colony of Burma.

The Japanese, as everywhere else, advanced successfully, and the British fell back. The Chinese sent in the American general, Joseph Warren Stillwell (1883–1946), whom Roosevelt had assigned to work with Chiang Kai-shek—a thankless task. Stillwell did what he could, but it wasn't enough. By May 1942, the British were driven out of Burma.

The British had now to make ready to defend India, and the only way in which supplies could still reach the Chinese was to fly them from northeastern India over high mountains.

Nor were the Japanese done. Even while operating in the Philippines and in Burma, the Japanese navy landed troops on various islands of the Dutch East Indies. The fall of Singapore made the defense of the East Indies impossible and, by March 9, 1942, the Dutch islands were in the hands of the Japanese. In the process, the Dutch fleet was destroyed.

During this time, the United States, avid for *some* offensive action, managed a spectacular feat. On April 18, 1942, with the Pacific war at a low point, 16 planes under James Harold Doolittle (b. 1896) took off from the aircraft carrier *Hornet* and flew 800 miles to Japan, where they bombed Tokyo and other Japanese cities. All the planes had to land in China (one in Vladivostok), or crashed in Japan. Not much damage was done, but it heartened the Americans and greatly alarmed the Japanese.

The Japanese, feeling that no American aircraft carrier ought to come close enough to the Japanese home islands to bomb them, decided to expand the perimeter of their control. They therefore attempted to establish themselves in New Guinea and in the Solomon Islands, which were under joint British/Australian control.

To do this, they probed the Coral Sea, which lies between northeastern Australia and the Solomons, and there they encountered an American fleet. On May 7–8, 1942, the Battle of the Coral Sea took place.

It was the first naval battle in which no ships on one side ever saw the ships on the other. The entire fight was between planes from the carriers on the two sides. It was a drawn battle. The Japanese lost more planes, the Americans lost more ships. What it meant, though, was that five months after Pearl Harbor, the Americans had a naval force in the Pacific. Nevertheless, in the wake of the battle, the Japanese did establish bases in the Solomons and did invade eastern New Guinea.

What's more, Japan prepared for one final blow at the American navy, a blow designed to finish what Pearl Harbor had begun, and this was under the command of Isoroku Yamamoto (1884–1943), the architect of the attack on Pearl Harbor.

As the summer of 1942 was starting, Japan had, in the space of half a year, established its domination over all of eastern and southeastern Asia, and was supreme over the western half of the Pacific Ocean. Japanese ships and soldiers were inching across New Guinea and down the lines of the Solomons, and were mopping up in Burma, so that Australia, New Zealand, and India were at risk.

The rapidity of Japanese expansion had far outdone even that of Hitler's Germany, and it was hard to think that only half a century before, Japan had consisted of four islands off the Chinese shore and had been, to all appearances, a comic-opera nation very much like the picture portrayed laughingly in Gilbert & Sullivan's *The Mikado*.

But now Japan wished to nail down its victory and make it permanent and the only way to do that was to smash what was left of the American fleet.

Admiral Yamamoto, therefore, assembled virtually the entire Japanese fleet, including 165 ships of all sorts, up to and including mighty aircraft carriers and battleships. It seemed like an appropriate time to do this, for Yamamoto believed that the Americans had suffered more in the Battle of the Coral Sea than they actually had and that there were no American aircraft carriers to oppose the Japanese armada.

The American Commander-in-Chief of the United States Pacific Fleet was Chester William Nimitz (1885–1966) and, since the Americans had long since broken the Japanese codes, he knew what Yamamoto was planning. This time, there would be no sleeping at the switch.

Unknown to the Japanese, Nimitz had three aircraft carriers, one of which, though damaged at Coral Sea, had been put into functioning order in record time. This meant he would have as many planes available to him as the Japanese would have. In addition, Nimitz planned to fight the battle near the island of Midway (at the western end of the Hawaiian Archipelago) so that land-based planes from that American possession could also be employed.

As a diversion, the Japanese fleet sent a few ships northward on June 3, 1942, to occupy the islands of Attu and Kiska at the western edge of the Aleutian island chain (which is part of Alaska). They felt that the Americans, infuriated by Japanese occupation of a portion of its home territory, would react by sending massive numbers of ships northward, thus insuring the Japanese victory in the mid-Pacific where it counted. The Americans, however, knew that the attack on the Aleutians was a diversion and they let it go.

On June 4, 1942, the Battle of Midway began. At first, the Japanese had things their own way. Their planes were more maneuverable than American land-based planes, and American losses were heavy. But then the planes from the American aircraft carriers (the existence of which Yamamoto was not aware of) found the Japanese fleet and, one after the other, destroyed the Japanese aircraft carriers. The Japanese lost all four, while the Americans lost one of their three. That meant that the Americans ended with two aircraft carriers to the Japanese none.

This was the first great naval defeat suffered by the Japanese, and it was at the hands of an inferior (in point of numbers) American squadron. The Battle of Midway was the turning point of the Pacific War, and never again would the Japanese be able to fight on the offensive against the United States. Their six-month triumph was over and, from this point on, Japan had to fight a defensive war against unrelenting and continuous American pressure. (Within a matter of five months, the Germans had lost the battles of El Alamein and of Stalingrad and they, too, moved into a perpetual defensive.)

To be sure, the Japanese still tried. Landing on the northern shore of New Guinea, they crossed the formidable Owen Stanley Mountains in August of 1942, aiming at Port Moresby on New Guinea's southern shore. They never made it. American and Australian forces stopped them between November 1942 and January 1943, and at last the Japanese had been defeated in jungle warfare.

The remainder of the Pacific War can best be told from an American perspective.

ITALY

If anything in a catastrophe as overwhelmingly tragic as World War II can be said to have been a comic relief, that was supplied by Italy.

Italy, from the time of its unification in the 1860s, had considered itself a "great power," but it never developed the industrial strength to make it capable of fighting a great war. It consistently lost wars but came out on top because it managed to form alliances with powers that defeated the power that defeated Italy.

Its economic weakness and its military disabilities were well-known and the fact that the contemptible buffoon, Mussolini, was able to face down Great Britain in 1935 and 1936 and cast a momentary shadow of "greatness" over Italy must, in hindsight, have been acutely embarrassing to the British leadership (though it is possible that they were quite capable of simply not thinking about it).

In 1939, when Germany went to war, Italy trembled and remained out of it. Even if Mussolini was hypnotized by his success in the Ethiopian crisis, he had done very poorly in Spain. The Italian generals knew well the nation could not fight a modern war. Galeazzo Ciano (1903–1944), who was Mussolini's Foreign Minister, and son-in-law as well, was dubious about the German alliance, and so was King Victor Emmanuel III.

As for Germany, it didn't mind Italy's remaining neutral. Germany had no illusions about Italy's warlike capacities, and it felt that Italy did its part by merely existing as a potential enemy of Great Britain and France. This tied up the British–French fleets in the Mediterranean Sea and forced Great Britain to divert some of its strength to the Suez Canal and the Middle East.

However, when Germany had, in rapid order, destroyed Poland, Denmark, Norway, the Low Countries, and even France, it seemed quite clear to Mussolini that the war was over and that it was safe to join in. In fact, it seemed to the Italian ruling body generally that it would be unsafe not to join in, for Italy, if it remained neutral a moment longer, would not get a share of the spoils.

On June 10, 1940, with the French army dying under the German hammer blows, Italy declared war on France and, with donkey-brays of triumph, sent 32 Italian divisions across the passes into southeastern France, where they were promptly hurled back by six French divisions.

Nevertheless, Hitler allowed Mussolini to occupy a small section of the French coast about the city of Nice, and another small section just south of Switzerland that made up Savoy, the home patrimony of the Italian royal family.

In August 1940, Italian forces took British Somaliland, east of Ethiopia, against virtually no resistance. In September 1940, Italian forces inched a small distance into Egypt and remained there in a state of paralysis. Neither development supplied Italy with "glory" in the German sense. Mussolini desperately wanted a smashing advance against a weak neighbor to prove Italy's worth to itself and to Germany, and its eyes fell on Greece.

A year and a half before, Italy had occupied Albania in an inglorious invasion, and Italy now had about 162,000 soldiers in the little country. To the south was Greece, and it qualified as a small nation that could be mopped up for the crime of being small.

On October 18, 1940, in one of the most fateful decisions of the war, Mussolini, without consulting Hitler (he wanted to dazzle Hitler with warlike victories), and without warning, sent 10 divisions into Greece to the accompaniment, once again, of donkey-brays of triumph.

The Greek army, however, was in the capable hands of Alexandros Papagos (1883–1955), and it held the difficult mountain terrain with no trouble. The Italians were thrown back and, by the end of the year, had been forced far back into Albania.

There was no glory. Pietro Badoglio, the Italian chief of staff who had conquered Ethiopia, was forced to resign. The Greek victories thoroughly smashed any Italian pretensions to military expertise. The Yugoslavs were encouraged to resist Germany. The British began to send troops into Crete and Egypt, and Hitler could only grind his teeth at his ally's ineptitude.

In fact, Hitler had to undertake a Balkan campaign to rescue Italy and he lost two vital months before he could begin his invasion of the Soviet Union. The loss of two months put him at the gates of Moscow only when winter had arrived, and that eventually lost him the Soviet campaign and the war. What a consequence of Mussolini's stupid move.

Meanwhile, Italy lost all of Italian East Africa to the British in early 1941, every inch of it. They were kicked out of Egypt and eastern Libya, and Hitler had to rescue them again by sending in Rommel to supervise the fighting there. The Italians also lost their navy and, by mid-1941, were no longer independent entities in the war. Mussolini's function became that of meeting with Hitler periodically and being forced to listen to the German leader speak endlessly and boringly on his plans. No one could possibly have devised a more subtle and unbearable punishment for Mussolini than this.

The Italians fought on in Libya under the leadership of Rommel and could share in the glory of his successes (in whispers among themselves, for no one else would give them any credit). After the Battle of El Alamein, however, the Germans and the Italians were swept completely out of Libya and the last bit of the Italian Empire was gone.

The Italians had also sent contingents to the Soviet front to fight under German command. None ever returned.

Allied forces invaded western North Africa and, by May 1943, German and Italian forces were forced to surrender in Tunisia and all of Africa was free. Then, in July 1943, Allied forces invaded Sicily.

The Italian people had had enough. It was clear that Mussolini had led them to destruction. The King, who had supported Mussolini when he had been made Emperor of Ethiopia, had now seen his Imperial title vanish, and he trembled for his throne. The aristocracy trembled for their privileges, and the generals saw nothing but defeat ahead. Ciano, who had been willing to go to war when victory had seemed certain a mere three years earlier, now deserted his father-in-law and demanded a separate peace.

Mussolini tried to resist, but on July 25, 1943, the Grand Council of Fascism deprived him of his powers. Mussolini tried to fall back on the royal authority, but the king had no intention of sharing Mussolini's destruction. He had him arrested, and Mussolini's career came to an end after 21 years of bombast and incompetence. To be sure, he was later rescued by the Germans and made the head of a Fascist Republic of Italy, but his powers were zero, and he was preserved merely for a horrible end.

The fight for Italy after Mussolini's fall is best told from an American perspective.

UNITED STATES (GERMANY)

When World War II began in Europe, the United States remained neutral. There was a strong isolationist movement that seemed to think that the United States should let the rest of the world destroy itself while it remained outside the fight.

The "America First Committee" were the articulate spokesmen of the isolationist viewpoint. Its most notable leader was Charles A. Lindbergh who, 13 years earlier, had become a hero with his solo flight from New York to Paris. Now he parroted the German line, complete with anti-Semitic statements. To many Americans, he became a villain.

Hitler's spectacular victories in the first year of the war greatly weakened the isolationist line, since the American people grew increasingly afraid of a German world victory. Great Britain's resolute fight during the Battle of Britain, and Churchill's oratory, won the sympathy of vast numbers of Americans and the isolationists began to seem nothing more than German propagandists.

As a result, the isolationists could not stop Roosevelt's steady movement toward supporting Great Britain, and his organization of a semi-global western hemisphere defense.

Roosevelt hastened American rearmament, setting a goal of 50,000 planes a year. (Hitler derided that, but the United States achieved the goal.)

On September 2, 1940, the United States picked up long-term leases on bases in British possessions in the western hemisphere in return for transferring 50 American destroyers to the British—destroyers badly needed to combat the submarine menace.

On September 16, 1940, the United States established a military draft, and on March 11, 1941, a "Lend-Lease Act" was passed whereby the United States could give material supplies to any nation that seemed to be vital to the defense of the United States.

On April 10, 1941, the United States landed forces in Greenland and, on July 7, in Iceland, two frozen lands that belonged to Denmark. Such bases greatly simplified the antisubmarine defense.

Roosevelt and Churchill formed a close personal friendship that endured through the war. On August 14, 1941, while the German army was cutting through the Soviet Union, the two met on warships in the North Atlantic to outline war aims in a so-called "Atlantic Charter." Neither was to seek territorial aggrandizement; they would support self-determination and self-government, freedom of the seas, equal access to raw materials, the denunciation of force, and so on.

In short, by the summer of 1941, the United States was helping Great Britain in every imaginable way, short of actually declaring war. That, at least, the isolationists could prevent.

Japan settled the matter on December 7, 1941, with its surprise attack on Pearl Harbor—which put the United States at war. It is possible that, at this point, an infuriated American public opinion might have demanded war to the utmost against Japan, leaving Europe to itself. However, for reasons he never made clear, Hitler declared war, quite unnecessarily, on the United States on December 10, 1941.

The United States had now two major wars to fight, and the political and military leadership made the decision that Germany was the greater danger and should receive the lion's share of American effort.

Once the United States was in the war, the question arose as to how best to attack Germany. It would, in any case, take several months for American forces to accumulate numbers, receive training, and become ready for battle. During those months, the United States was chiefly involved with the Battle of the Atlantic and not doing too well. The Navy had not yet worked out methods of convoy, and American ports on the Atlantic coast blazed with light against which merchant ships were easy targets for the German submarines.

In addition, there was only one route whereby the Soviet Union might be supplied by sea, and that was the dangerous journey into Arctic waters and around Scandinavia to the Soviet ports of Murmansk and Arkhangelsk. By the end of year, however, the American ships were becoming more skillful at sinking submarines and the rate of new ship construction was increasing rapidly.

Also by the end of the year, American forces were ready for an assault. The American instinct was to strike at the heart of German strength, to dash across the English Channel and to strike at France. This was certainly what Stalin wanted— something that would relieve the pressure on Stalingrad and the Caucasus.

Great Britain, however, did not want the direct assault, fearing a bloodbath and possible failure that would set back the war effort for years. Besides, Great Britain had, for centuries, preferred to strike at the periphery. Therefore, a huge amphibious assault, the largest the world had yet seen, was aimed at French North Africa.

The assault consisted almost entirely of American troops, since it was thought that the French might not fight as hard against Americans as against the British. The invasion forces were under the overall leadership of Dwight David Eisenhower (1890–1969), a master at the art of persuading prima donna generals to act together.

The landings began on November 8, 1942, soon after the Battle of El Alamein had driven Rommel out of Egypt. American troops landed in Morocco and Algeria, but the hope that the French would not resist was in vain. They fought vigorously, and though they were defeated, the Americans did not have the easy occupation they had expected.

The French puppet government at Vichy broke off diplomatic relations with the United States on November 9, and ordered French troops to continue resistance. Meanwhile, German troops swept through the territories controlled by Vichy, bringing all of France under German control on November 11. There were French ships in Toulon harbor in southeastern France that had so far been kept out of German control. It seemed inevitable that Germany would now take them over, but on November 27, those ships were scuttled by their crews and Germany did *not* get them.

A French naval officer, Jean Louis Darlan (1881–1942), who had always been anti-British and had been a loyal member of the Vichy puppet government, happened to be in North Africa at the time of the invasion. Under American pressure, he changed his opinions, broke with Vichy on November 11, ordered an immediate cease-fire, and declared himself chief of state in French Africa. A French general, Henri Honore Giraud (1879–1949), who had never for a moment cooperated with the Nazis, was made head of the French armed forces in North Africa.

But what happened to de Gaulle?

The trouble with de Gaulle was that he was the French Douglas MacArthur, and neither Churchill nor Roosevelt could endure his arrogance. They would cheerfully have done away with him if they could, but the Free French wanted de Gaulle and American public opinion resented making use of the Vichyite Darlan. As it happened, Darlan was assassinated on December 24, 1942, but the problem of Giraud and de Gaulle remained.

Eisenhower was deeply involved in the complexities of politics in North Africa, and it kept him from acting quickly when swift military action was needed. The Germans had time to airlift troops into Tunisia, and into Tunisia also came what was left of Rommel's army. The chance of taking Tunisia as Morocco and Algeria had been taken was lost. The Allies were going to have to fight against determined German resistance.

On January 14 to 23, 1943, Roosevelt and Churchill, together with their chiefs of staff, met at Casablanca in Morocco to determine future strategy in the war. The Americans still wanted a frontal assault on the Germans in France, but Churchill wanted to continue operations on the periphery. From Africa, he suggested, the Allies should strike at the "soft underbelly" of Europe. (Once again, it turned out that Churchill, although indomitable when a desperate defense was needed, unfailingly missed the point on the offensive. There was no soft underbelly to Europe, as the Allies were to find out.)

Plans for winning the Battle of the Atlantic were also laid out and Roosevelt declared that the Allies would accept only "unconditional surrender" by the Germans.

The insistence on unconditional surrender has been thought to be a mistake by military men who felt that it encouraged Germany to fight on to the end. Those who opposed unconditional surrender, however, never explained what the alternative would be. What would "conditional surrender" mean? That Germany retain a Nazi government of some sort? That it come under the rule of right-wing generals? That it retain some of its conquests? That it retain enough strength to join with the Allies in a new war against the

Soviet Union? (That last may well have been in the mind of some of the military.)

It is hard to believe that Germany, having committed so many crimes against humanity, having killed and slaughtered without end, having made itself bitter and horrible to all the world, could have gotten away with anything short of unconditional surrender. It might have been wiser for Roosevelt to have adopted it as a policy without announcing it, but, on the other hand, there were uncounted millions who wanted it said clearly.

The year 1943 saw the climax of the Battle of the Atlantic. Hitler fired his submarine chief, Erich Raeder (1876–1960), at the beginning of the year and replaced him with Karl Doenitz (1891–1980), who carried on the sinking of merchant ships with renewed energy. By March 1943, Great Britain was within three months of starvation.

The Allied convoy system was constantly sharpened, however, and new ships were being built with increasing speed. On October 13, 1943, the Allies established a base at the Portuguese Azores, and the submarine threat receded after that. What remained of the German surface raiders was also damaged and put out of action, and the Allies were bombing Germany around the clock.

There remained land action, however, and at the beginning of 1943 that meant Tunisia.

Rommel struck first, with his customary expertise. The veteran German troops, strongly supported by air, drove against the green American troops at Kasserine Pass in central Tunisia. The Americans fell back in defeat.

There followed a period of reorganization. In charge of the American forces was placed George Smith Patton (1885–1945), a flamboyant poseur, second only to MacArthur. Patton liked to be called "Old Blood and Guts," he sported two pearl-handled revolvers, and he unfortunately, periodically made a fool of himself, for if his intelligence extended an inch beyond the practice of war, he never showed any sign of it. Montgomery was in charge of the British forces.

The Allied forces were built up in strength, and the Americans had had their baptism of fire at Kasserine Pass, and had learned quickly. Attempts by the Germans at further offensives in February and early March failed and then, on March 20, 1943, the Allies began an offensive northward, which slowly but inexorably drove the Germans back. By early May, the Germans had been driven into a cul-de-sac, and with no possibility of a Dunkirk-type rescue, they began to surrender. By May 13, 1943, it was all over. Germany had been driven out of Africa. Altogether, Germany had lost over 200,000 men in the North African campaigns, and the British as many, but it was the Allies that now held the ground.

The Allies then began to put into action the decision at Casablanca to aim for the "soft underbelly" of Europe.

Halfway between Tunisia and Sicily was the fortified Italian island of Pantelleria. It was the Italian equivalent of British Malta, which lay about 160 miles to the southeast. Malta had withstood all bombardments from the Germans for years, but now the Allied planes homed in on Pantelleria and, after a week of bombardment, the island surrendered on June 11, 1943.

There followed an intensive bombardment of Sicily, Sardinia, and Italy and, on July 9, the Americans under Patton and the British under Montgomery landed on the southeast vertex of the triangular island of Sicily. Montgomery worked his way up the east coast against hard-fighting German resistance and managed to get only half way up. Patton, however, rampaged through western Sicily and, by July 23, he turned east to support Montgomery. The Germans were now confined to the northeastern corner of the island, and they were pushed steadily back. On August 17, all of Sicily was in the hands of the Allies.

By this time, Mussolini had been deposed and imprisoned and had been succeeded by General Badoglio, who, to prevent German reprisals, announced he would continue the fight. In secret, however, he signed an armistice with the Allies on September 3, 1943, On that day, Allied troops landed at the tip of the Italian toe.

By September 8, the armistice was made public and Allied troops under Mark Wayne Clark

(1896–1984) carried through an amphibious landing at Salerno, just south of Naples. The Germans promptly disarmed all Italian units and took over the country militarily, setting down for a long and savage fight under the competent leadership of Albert Kesselring (1885–1960).

The Salerno beachhead was contained, though not wiped out, and step by step, the weary Allies had to force their way northward. By the end of the year, the Allies were only half way up the boot and there was no sign that further advances would be any easier.

Meanwhile, from November 28 to 30, 1943, Roosevelt, Churchill, and Stalin met at Teheran in Iran. Stalin was told that the Allies would launch a direct assault on the heart of German-Europe in May or June of 1944. Stalin promised that a Soviet offensive would be made to coincide with the invasion.

All through the first half of 1944, then, the British Isles filled up with men and material intended for the greatest amphibious invasion of all times. It was something impossible to mask. The Germans knew it was coming. They didn't know exactly when, however, or exactly where, and they lacked any ability to abort it.

Through that first half of 1944, the German submarines and surface raiders were increasingly punished and the air bombardment of Germany grew heavier.

Advances in Italy continued heartbreakingly slow, however. On January 22, 1944, the Allies tried an amphibious landing at Anzio, south of Rome, in order to turn the German line. They managed to make the landing stick, just barely, but it was not enough to help them fold up the Germans. There simply wasn't enough force to spare in view of all that was being accumulated for the invasion of France.

Nevertheless, a new offensive did drive the Germans back and, on June 4, 1944, Allied troops marched into Rome.

Meanwhile, Germany was waiting for the invasion. Hitler was certain it would strike at Calais, where the Channel was narrowest, and he insisted on organizing the defenses with that in mind, overriding any objections by Runstedt and Rommel, who were in charge in the field. The

Allies, for various sensible reasons (including perhaps their knowledge that Hitler expected them at Calais) intended to invade the Cotentin Peninsula in Normandy.

On June 6, 1944 ("D-day"), 4000 transports escorted by 600 warships and 9500 planes carried 176,000 troops and their equipment to France. Advance was not rapid. The Germans had an intricate system of defenses and they fought hard. (One wonders what would have happened if the Allies had encountered the German forces in their prime, instead of having to face the remnants left over after several million of the best German soldiers were lying dead, strewn over the killing fields of the Soviet Union. In the vain glory of victory, few Americans have thought of that, but it does no harm to remind ourselves of the fact.)

It was not until June 27, 1944, that the great French port of Cherbourg fell to the Allies.

Meanwhile, Hitler launched his "secret weapons." He had been speaking of them for a long time as a way of turning the war around, no matter how badly it might seem to be going. They were the "Vergeltungswaffe" ("reprisal weapons"), and were abbreviated as V.

The first of these was the V-1, which was a pilotless plane, launched from catapults or aircraft. It was about 25-feet long and 18-feet wide. Human pilots were not involved, so their use carried little risk, and furthermore these "Flying Bombs" could be built cheaply. Some 8000 were launched against Great Britain, and an equal number against Belgium, beginning June 13, 1944. They flew at less than the speed of sound, so about half of them were shot down. Nevertheless, their use seemed a recrudescence of the Battle of Britain, and British morale was badly shaken.

Matters grew worse with the V-2, the first working missile. It was run by rocket power at speeds greater than sound so that it could not be detected or intercepted before striking. It had been developed by the German rocket engineer Wernher von Braun (1912–1977) and it was 47-feet long, burned alcohol and liquid oxygen, and reached heights of 60 miles. The first V-2 was fired on September 7, 1944. A total of 4300 were fired altogether and, of them, 1230 hit London, killing over 2500 people and wounding nearly 6000.

The V-weapons were not decisive, however, for the Allies captured the sites from which they were fired before they could do more than hurt. In this, as in so many other ventures of Hitler, he reached out far and almost grasped the prize—then fell short. It happened at Dunkirk, at the Battle of Britain, at the Battle of the Atlantic, in the Soviet Union, in Africa, and now with his reprisal weapons. If one were inclined to mysticism one might suspect supernatural intervention, but that is not really necessary. When one deals with a megalomaniac madman like Hitler, one expects decisions to be made without regard for reality so, of course, things will go wrong.

Things were going seriously wrong inside Germany, too. For some years, certain Germans had felt that the only way to keep their land from disaster was to assassinate Hitler. A number of plans were made with that in mind, but none worked, for Hitler (with fears of assassination before him) never kept to any schedule but was forever changing plans evasively. Besides, the would-be assassins did not make plans that would involve their own death. It seemed impossible to find a good way of killing Hitler and, at the same time, preserving the life of the assassin.

By 1943, the rot had entered the German army. Generals who had been perfectly willing to fight for Hitler and to follow all orders as long as that seemed to lead to victory now began to change their minds as defeat began to seem more and more inevitable. Hitler, lost in his megalomania, seemed clearly ready to lead Germany into the abyss and since the military establishment never had the guts to oppose him openly, conspiracy and assassination seemed the only way out.

Finally, a German officer and war-hero (he had been badly wounded in combat), Claus Schenk von Stauffenberg (1907–1944), undertook to spearhead an attempt to kill Hitler at his headquarters in East Prussia. On July 20, 1944, he entered the headquarters with a briefcase filled with explosives designed to explode only after he himself had gotten well away. He placed it near Hitler's feet, then made some excuse to leave and did so.

However, someone pushing close to Hitler to look at a map, found the briefcase in his way, and shifted it to the other side of a heavy wooden table support. Because Stauffenberg did not remain behind to suffer his own death, he could not correct the matter.

In time, the briefcase exploded, a number of people were killed, and the headquarters was reduced to rubble. Hitler was hurt, but he was *not* killed. He managed to reestablish his ascendancy, and saw to it that all the military men who were in any way implicated were executed under atrocious circumstances, hanging them by wire. Even Rommel was forced to commit suicide on October 14, 1944. He did so on the promise that his family would be spared.

The last embers of independence among the Germany military were thus wiped out. Hitler was now absolute and he led Germany down the final declivity.

Soon after the assassination attempt, the Allied forces broke out of their Normandy beachhead. They punched a hole through which Patton's tanks raced. Where once Guderian and Rommel had led their tanks west and north, Patton now led his south and east.

The German general, Hans Gunther von Kluge (1882–1944), who did his best to stem the tide and save his army, could not prevent the Allies from taking Paris on August 25, 1944. He was promptly fired by Hitler who suspected him, anyway, of complicity in the assassination attempt. Kluge killed himself soon after.

Meanwhile, another Allied invasion struck southern France's Rhone valley on August 15, 1944. The Germans, worn out, fell back rapidly. By the end of August, British forces were entering Belgium.

Meanwhile, the Soviets, in accordance with their word, were attacking in the east. Even while the Americans were breaking out of the Normandy beachhead, the Soviets were completing the liberation of Byelorussia. They had captured Minsk on July 3, 1944.

What's more, the Soviets had a return match

with Finland, which had fought on the side of Germany for three years. This time the new Soviet army showed itself not to be the old one. The Finns were forced to surrender on September 4, 1944. At the same time, the Soviets were driving into Poland, reaching the river just across from Warsaw on October 7, 1944. There, the offensive had to come to a halt while the Soviet divisions rested and brought up supplies.

In Italy, the Allies took Florence on August 12, 1944, but could not advance far beyond it. Another winter had to pass with the Germans in control of northern Italy. Mussolini, who had been rescued by German troops on September 12, 1943, was head of this remnant of Italy (in theory) and had overseen the execution of those who had overthrown him and who were in reach. Notably, his son-in-law, Ciano, was executed on January 11, 1944.

On September 3, 1944, the Allies took Brussels and the next day they took Antwerp. Over two million Allied soldiers were now in France and they had cost the Germans the loss of half a million in casualties, plus the loss of 200,000 men isolated in coastal fortresses who would have to eventually surrender.

The Germans stiffened, nevertheless, and Rundstedt was put back in charge as, by the fall of 1944, German forces in the west stood on their own borders again, four years after they had smashed into the Netherlands, Belgium, and France. In the east, the German puppets were scrambling for safety, and surrendering to the Soviets. Only Poland, Germany's first conquest, remained to the Germans, and not for long.

The Allies tried to break into Germany, but resistance in the Netherlands was stronger than expected. Hitler was planning one last offensive, a repeat of what he had done in 1940. He wanted to puncture a hole at the hinge between British forces in the north and American forces farther south. He would break through, swing north, and trap the British once again.

It was a reckless gamble and to anyone but Hitler it was obvious that it could not work. The Germans were far weaker in late 1944 than they had been in mid-1940, and the enemy they faced now was more numerous, far better supplied, and enormously higher in morale than the enemy they had faced in the past.

Nevertheless, on December 16, 1944, Rundstedt pushed forward, driving a bulge into the Allied lines. This was therefore called "the Battle of the Bulge." The Germans advanced 50 miles against steadily stiffening resistance and were then driven back. After a month, it was all over. They were back where they had been and their last chance, such as it was, had vanished.

The year 1945 saw the end. By the beginning of March 1945, the Allies had reached the Rhine River. When they found that a bridge at Remagen had not been blown up, they crossed it quickly on March 7. Meanwhile, the Soviets had driven into Germany from the east.

In April and May of 1945, German resistance in Italy finally collapsed. The Germans surrendered. Mussolini tried to escape into Switzerland but was caught by Italian anti-Fascist partisans and, on April 28, 1945, was shot without trial and hung upside down for the derision of the public. His mistress was also shot and hung up, which seems to have been rather excessive.

At the beginning of the year, Hitler retired deep into a bunker in Berlin and, except for one or two occasions, never emerged, while the armies on either side came closer and closer to each other.

The Soviets reached Berlin on April 22, 1945, and had it surrounded on April 25. Also on the 25th, elements of the Allied army and the Soviet army met on the Elbe River.

There was nothing left for Hitler to do except to avoid capture. On April 29, he married his long-time mistress, Eva Braun. He appointed Doenitz his successor, and, on April 30, he killed himself and his wife. Their bodies were burned.

May 8, 1945 was the end of the war in Europe (the date came to be known as V-E Day). Roosevelt did not live to see it. He died on April 12, 1945, and the news of his death gave Hitler one last spark of joy, for his sick mind somehow thought this death might rescue him. (The sudden death of Tsarina Elizabeth of Russia had rescued Frederick the Great from certain defeat—but history does not necessarily repeat itself.)

That Hitler's Germany lasted as long as it did arose from the fact that the Germans converted the conquered people, particularly Poles and Russians, into slave labor, working and starving them ruthlessly to death. Some five million such slave laborers were made use of.

Nor did the Germans scruple to plunder the nations they had conquered in order to keep up the diet and morale of the Germans in the face of the ever-tightening British–American blockade. Despite heavy air attacks, Germany's war production was maintained and even expanded into 1944.

Germany's most disgraceful and horrible act of all was its deliberate destruction of the Jews of Europe. In response to the psychopathological anti-Semitism of Hitler and other Nazi leaders, the Jews were systematically rounded up, sent into concentration camps and killed. Some six million Jews perished in what has come to be called "the Holocaust." The closer the Germans came to defeat, the more madly they fought the one battle they could win against a helpless people.

It was a mistake, of course, even from a strictly practical standpoint, and leaving all considerations of morality and humanity to one side. Millions of Jews survive in the world generally, and they are a most articulate people with long memories. They have seen to it, and will continue to see to it, that the crimes of the Germans will long live in the consciousness of the world.

THE UNITED STATES (JAPAN)

After the Battle of Midway, the United States was finally ready for a land counteroffensive against the Japanese. The Japanese farthest penetration southeastward was to the Solomon Islands off the northeast coast of Australia, and they were building an airport on the island of Guadalcanal from which Australia might be bombed.

On August 7, 1942, therefore, the United States made landings on Guadalcanal and the nearby island of Tulagi. Complete surprise was achieved, but it was not to be an easy victory. Quite the reverse. On August 9, a Japanese flotilla caught an American naval force at the "Battle of Savo Island" between Guadalcanal and Tulagi, and destroyed four American heavy cruisers, while suffering virtually no casualties themselves.

This enabled the Japanese to bring in reinforcements, and what followed was a bloody half-year battle that set the tone for the battles that were to follow. The Japanese never surrendered but tended to fight to the death, increasing American casualties. However, they also had the odd idea (disproved on a number of occasions, but never abandoned) that, somehow, shrieking, yelling assaults would overwhelm the Americans by the sheer force of Japanese fervor. As a result, the Japanese tended to waste their strength in piecemeal emotional charges and died in far greater number than if they had fought with more attention to the art of war.

It was not until February 7, 1943, that the Japanese managed to evacuate their remaining forces on Guadalcanal.

The Americans then proceeded to move slowly and grimly up the line of the Solomon Islands. The American navy was being constantly strengthened and by mid-1943, there was no chance any longer of the Japanese scoring any further major successes against it.

On April 19, 1943, Yamamoto, the architect of Pearl Harbor and of the assault on Midway, flew to the Solomons to inspect Japanese installations there. The Americans knew he was on the way and shot down the bomber that was carrying him. Since he was Japan's foremost strategist, his death was equivalent to the loss of a battle for the Japanese.

The Americans now instituted a policy of "island-hopping," of not necessarily trying to take every island the Japanese held, but of driving at certain key installations, and doing so ever closer to the Japanese home islands. In November 1943, the United States began to strike at the central Pacific islands of the Gilberts, and on November 20, they made a major assault on the tiny atoll of Tarawa, some 3000 miles southeast of Tokyo.

Unfortunately, the Japanese defenses were unexpectedly strong and the Americans were unaware that the waters about the atoll were too shallow for landing craft so that the soldiers had to wade ashore. American losses were unexpectedly high, but after four days the Japanese were wiped out.

Nevertheless, the American forces continued to push their way grimly toward Japan, closer and closer, never losing a battle, though the costs were high.

In February 1944, they retook the Marshall Islands, and by June, they were in the Marianas. Guam, the one-time American possession in the Marianas, which had been lost in the immediate aftermath of Pearl Harbor, was retaken on August 11, and on October 19, American forces landed in Leyte, one of the islands of the Philippine archipelago. Over two years before, MacArthur had promised he would return, and now he did.

In the process, the last of the Japanese navy was destroyed in two "Battles of the Philippine Sea," the first from June 19 to 21, 1944, and the second from October 21 to 22. That summer also, American planes began a systematic bombing of Japanese cities that was to lay the land in ruins. What's more, Japanese land armies were being driven back into Burma and into northern New Guinea.

Yet despite all this, Japanese forces continued fighting fanatically. On February 19, 1945, American forces came ashore on Iwo Jima, a small island only eight square miles in area, and only 750 miles south of Tokyo. There were 22,000 Japanese troops on it who were well dug in and it took almost a month to root them out.

By now, Germany was on the brink of ruin, and the three chief wartime leaders—Roosevelt, Churchill, and Stalin—had met for a second time. This meeting was at Yalta in the Soviet Crimea on February 7, 1945. There they tried to work out the postwar structure of Europe, and, among other things, Stalin had promised that the Soviet Union would join in the war against Japan 90 days after the end of the war in Europe. It would take 90 days, after all, to maneuver the men and equipment from west to east across 6000 miles of war-blasted Russian land on the slow Siberian railroad.

The United States had to welcome Soviet assistance if that were absolutely necessary to defeat Japan at a lower cost in American lives, but it would clearly be preferable if, somehow, Japan could be forced to surrender before the Soviets came in, so that there would be no mistake as to which nation had accomplished the task and so that the Soviets could not claim a share of the spoils of victory.

On April 1, 1945, American forces landed in Okinawa, the largest of the chain of Ryukyu islands, which stretched from the Japanese home islands to Taiwan. It was only 325 miles from Japan.

While the fighting continued, Germany was smashed into final surrender, but even that did not break the Japanese will to fight. They made use of "kamikaze" pilots (named for the "divine wind" that had destroyed the Mongol invasion nearly seven centuries before). These were suicide planes loaded with explosives that were piloted into American ships in order to blow them up.

Even this final bit of desperation didn't work, but it was not until June 21 that the last bit of resistance on Okinawa was ended, and now there remained only the task of invading the Japanese home islands themselves.

No one knows what would have happened if such an invasion had taken place. All of Japan's large cities were virtually destroyed. Millions lacked food and shelter. There was absolutely no hope of victory, or even of staving off defeat for long except at the cost of further extreme destruction.

It would make sense to suppose that Japan would now ask for peace before the invasion actually took place and ultimate disaster befell it. On the other hand, the Japanese had shown no signs of breaking. Certainly, Okinawa had been a dreadful fight and the battle for Japan itself might be an even more dreadful one.

It would probably have seemed natural to hold off and give Japan a chance to surrender before actually committing American forces to the final invasion, but the United States had no time. The war in Europe had come to an end on May 7, 1945, and Stalin's 90-day promise meant that Soviet forces would join the war on August 7. The United States needed to make it perfectly clear before that fatal day that *it* had defeated

Japan and that Soviet participation would be nothing more than a formality. For the purpose, the United States had a new and fearful weapon at hand.

Otto Hahn of Germany had discovered uranium fission in 1938, but had found the process so hard to accept (since it seemed so unlikely in light of the knowledge of the day) that he was reluctant to announce it publicly. His partner, Lise Meitner, driven out of Germany into Sweden because she was Jewish, had less to lose and so was more daring. She presented the evidence to Niels Bohr, the Danish scientist, who carried it to the United States.

American physicists quickly confirmed the discovery and began to work on uranium fission as a new source of energy. The Hungarian physicist, Leo Szilard (1898–1964), recognized the possibility of developing a nuclear fission bomb of enormous power and talked American scientists into keeping their work secret. He then talked Albert Einstein into writing a letter to President Roosevelt urging that a government project be set up to develop such a bomb before Hitler did (a terrible task for the pacifistic Einstein). Roosevelt established what came to be known as the "Manhattan Project" on December 6, 1941, the day before Pearl Harbor.

Under the leadership of the Italian physicist Enrico Fermi, a controlled nuclear reaction was set up in a huge pile of uranium and uranium oxide on December 2, 1942. That was the beginning of the "atomic age," and now it was necessary to make a device small enough to be carried by an airplane, and moreover one that would explode only when the explosion was needed.

The first such "nuclear fission bomb" (called an "atomic bomb" at the time) was put together under the leadership of J. Robert Oppenheimer (1904–1967) and was exploded, as an experiment, in Alamogordo, New Mexico, on July 16, 1945. Two more such bombs were then put together for use against Japan.

On August 6, 1945, the day before the Soviets were scheduled to join the war against Japan, a fission bomb was exploded over Hiroshima, Japan (which had, until then, been spared bombing) and the city was levelled. The Soviets joined the war the next day, on schedule, and the second bomb was dropped on Nagasaki, Japan, on August 8.

The Japanese, faced with the double disaster of the fission bombs and of the irresistible advance of a Soviet army into Manchuria, gave in. The United States was satisfied for it had been made perfectly clear that an American fission bomb had capped an American war drive to force the Japanese into surrender, and it had, incidentally, put on an instructive demonstration of unprecedented power that couldn't be lost on the Soviet Union (and the rest of the world, too).

The Japanese asked only that they be allowed to keep their emperor. The United States agreed and the Japanese signed the surrender document on September 2, 1945 (also known as V-J Day). World War II was over.

The nuclear fission bomb was not the only American achievement during the World War II years. In 1940, Edwin Mattison McMillan (b. 1907) and Philip Hauge Abelson (b. 1913) had produced element 93 ("neptunium") and element 94 ("plutonium") in the laboratory. In 1945, McMillan devised the "synchrocyclotron" that provided new heights of energy with which to explore the subatomic world.

John William Mauchly (1907–1980) and John Presper Eckert, Jr. (b. 1919) were working on the first all-electronic computer, which was completed soon after the war ended. It was large, clumsy, slow, and very energy-consuming, but it was the harbinger of the "computer age."

Selman Abraham Waksman (1888–1973) isolated "streptomycin" in 1943 and coined the word "antibiotic." This joined penicillin as a treatment against infection and was the vanguard for a whole army of germ-fighting substances.

In 1944, Robert Burns Woodward (1917–1979) synthesized quinine and began a career in which he synthesized even the most complex of the naturally occurring chemicals.

By the end of the war, in fact, the United States had taken the world lead in science, as it had done years earlier in technology. The English language, thanks to American domination of science, technology, and business, began to gain speakers and to be on its way to becoming a world language to an extent no other language in history had ever approached.

Some enthusiasts even began to speak of an "American century," a world utterly dominated by the United States, presumably in the interest of peace and freedom. (The road to such a denouement unfortunately turned out to be an extremely rocky one.)

AUSTRIA

If we exclude the principal fighters of World War II—Germany, Japan, and Italy on the one side, and the United States, the Soviet Union, and Great Britain on the other—we face a world of nations, most of which were greatly affected, and some quite victimized, by the vast convulsion.

Austria, the first nation to fall victim to Nazi aggression, differed from the rest in that its people spoke German and, for the most part, gladly considered themselves to be part of the Third Reich. What's more, the Germans themselves considered the Austrians to be German so that Austrians were no more mistreated than Germans themselves. Of course, both Germans and Austrians mistreated and eventually killed all the Austrian Jews they could.

Austria fought along with Germany all through World War II, under the rule of the home-grown Nazi Arthur Seyss-Inquart (1892–1946), who was eventually hanged as a war criminal.

Nevertheless, it suited the Allies to consider Austria a separate and conquered nation, since there was no intention of allowing it to remain part of the German realm after the war. Soviet troops took Vienna on April 13, 1945, and soon afterward, Austria was restored as an independent nation under leaders who, it was hoped, had not been tainted by Nazism. In the immediate aftermath of the war, however, it was divided into four parts, each of which was occupied by one of the powers who were counted on the victorious side: the Soviet Union, the United States, Great Britain, and (because of de Gaulle) France.

CZECHOSLOVAKIA

Czechoslovakia was the first non-German nation to fall under the Nazi tyranny, and the first to experience German frightfulness. Czechs were subjected to slave labor, concentration camps, execution, and to the general status of a browbeaten, subjugated, endlessly humiliated people.

Although there was a shadow government under Hacha, the puppet who had come in after the Munich surrender, the Nazis placed von Neurath (who had been Hitler's Foreign Minister some years before) in position as the "Reich Protector" and real ruler of the nation. He was relatively mild for a Nazi, and was replaced in September 1941 by Reinhard Heydrich (1904–1942), a brutal sadist who was second in command in the Gestapo, the Nazi secret police, and who had been organizing the mass destruction of Jews. He established a reign of terror in Czechoslovakia. On June 2, 1942, he was assassinated, presumably by the Czechoslovakian underground.

The Germans, tracing the perpetrators to the little town of Lidice, just northwest of Prague, took wholesale revenge. All the male inhabitants of the village, about 200 of them, were shot, and the women and children were sent away, most never to return.

Such incredibly brutal actions were taken because the Nazis felt that terror would discourage clandestine actions against the German overlords. It never did, but it did succeed in mobilizing horrified world opinion against the brutal monsters, and added one more stain to the hellish fabric that the rest of the world was to hold against the Germans for many long decades to come.

Benes, who had been president of Czechoslovakia before Munich, labored in London to get the British and French to declare the Munich Accord invalid. The Allies were reluctant to do this and shame themselves, but after the fall of France, the British recognized Benes as head of the Czechoslovakian government in exile. In December 1943, Benes visited the Soviet Union and signed a 20-year alliance with them. The Soviets, who had not participated in the Munich Accord, had no hesitation about denouncing it.

In 1945, the Soviet army advanced into Czechoslovakia and the land was freed, but it remained under Soviet domination. The eastern tip of Czechoslovakia (known, before the war, as "Carpatho-Ruthenia"), which was occupied by ethnic Ukrainians, was absorbed by the Soviet Union as part of the Ukrainian S.S.R.

POLAND

Poland suffered more, in proportion, from German brutality than did any other nation. Virtually all its 3,350,000 Jews were killed, as were some millions of non-Jewish Poles. Perhaps a quarter of its total population was slaughtered.

Poland suffered a double invasion at first, for while the Germans annexed the western half of the Nation, the Soviets annexed the eastern half. The difference, though, was this: the portion annexed by Germany was populated by ethnic Poles. The portion annexed by the Soviet Union was populated largely by Byelorussians and Ukrainians, living in an area that Poland had annexed after its victory over the Soviets in 1920. In a sense, then, the Soviets could maintain they were only taking back their own.

A Polish government-in-exile was established in Paris and, after France fell, in London. It was under the leadership of Wladyslaw Eugeniusz Sikorski (1881–1943).

Once Germany invaded the Soviet Union, it took over what had once been eastern Poland in a matter of days, and the Soviet Union, too, began to support the notion of a Polish government-in-exile. The Soviets had difficulty in maintaining good relations with Sikorski, however, for he had been a Polish general active in the war against the Soviet Union in 1920.

Moreover, the Soviets had slaughtered Polish military men in Katyn Forest, near Smolensk, in 1940. (They denied it steadily for half a century, then admitted that they had indeed been responsible.) Sikorski, certain this was so, pressed the Soviet Union on the matter, and the Soviets grew hostile indeed.

The Soviets therefore set up a Polish government-in-exile of their own under Poles of Communist leanings. Sikorski died in an airplane crash over Gibraltar on July 4, 1943, and, thereafter, the two Polish governments-in-exile were a source of perennial irritation between the British–Americans on the one side and the Soviet Union on the other. It was the first premonitory rumble of what eventually came to be known as the "cold war."

In 1943, there were despairing uprisings among the Jews, who had been herded into ghettos in Warsaw and other Polish cities. These were crushed, of course, and the Germans merely hastened the progress of the Holocaust.

On August 1, 1944, at the time when the Soviet armies had almost reached Warsaw, the Poles in the city rose in rebellion. The Soviets, however, were catching their breath for their next offensive and remained immobile, so that the uprising was put down by the Germans. (It is possible that the Soviets were not entirely anxious for the Poles to win their own freedom.)

The Germans were, however, on their last legs and, beginning in January 1945, the Soviet armies occupied all of what had been Poland, which was then reconstituted as an independent state under Soviet control.

Its borders were not what they had been, though. The Soviet Union continued to keep the eastern districts of Poland that it had absorbed in 1939, making the northern portion part of the Byelorussian S.S.R., and the southern portion part of the Ukrainian S.S.R. Poland was compensated for this by the cession to it of portions of what had been eastern Germany.

(The Soviet Union annexed the northern portion of what had been East Prussia, including the city of Königsberg, in which Immanuel Kant had once lived and worked, and which now became "Kaliningrad.")

THE BALTIC STATES

The three small nations of Estonia, Latvia, and Lithuania, which had gained their independence from Russia immediately after World War I had ended, lost it again soon after World War II

began. The agreement whereby the Soviet Union gained the eastern half of prewar Poland included also (with German acquiescence) an overriding Soviet influence in the Baltic states.

After the fall of France, Stalin felt the need for greater security in covering the approaches to Leningrad, and he translated influence into outright annexation. In July 1940, the three states were forced to accept Communist rulers and were converted into three Soviet Socialist Republics and made part of the Soviet Union.

In June 1941, Germany invaded the Soviet Union and, within a matter of weeks, had overrun the Baltic states. The Estonians, Latvians, and Lithuanians were willing to help the Germans and would have done so much more readily if the Germans themselves had been willing to cooperate. So certain were the Germans of their own "race superiority," however, that they never felt the need to conciliate the non-German peoples they had overrun, something that contributed mightily to their ultimate defeat. The Germans did, of course, extend the Holocaust to the Baltic states, killing nearly 300,000 Jews who had lived there.

In 1944, the Soviet army was back and the Baltic states resumed their status as Soviet Socialist Republics. Their boundaries remained what they had been before the war except that a small district including the city of Vilna (or "Vilnius" to the Lithuanians) was transferred to Lithuania. Vilnius was the ancient capital of the medieval Grand Duchy of Lithuania and Poland had annexed it (over bitter Lithuanian protests) in the aftermath of its war with the U.S.S.R. in 1920.

FINLAND

When the Soviet Union, in 1939, attempted to exert influence over Finland and to annex portions of Finnish territory designed to protect the overexposed position of Leningrad, the Finns refused and made ready to resist.

On November 30, 1939, the Soviet Union launched an attack on Finland which, the Soviets hoped, would accomplish what Germany had accomplished three months earlier in Poland. No such thing. The Finns were better prepared than the Poles had been and the Soviet army was far from possessing the expertise and precision of the German army. The war lasted three and a half months and included several humiliating defeats for the Soviets. The overwhelming weight of the Soviet army won at last and, on March 12, 1940, Finland agreed to peace and to the surrender of minor portions of its territory west of Leningrad. It retained its independence, however.

Finland drew nearer to Germany, thereafter, in an effort to protect itself from further Soviet aggression, and quietly allowed German troops on its soil. This meant that when the Germans invaded the Soviet Union on June 22, 1941, they were in place to attack the northern reaches of the land, and in this the Finns were perfectly willing to help.

In the course of the war, the Finns advanced eastward into Karelia, many of whose people were ethnically Finnish. This was done without too much difficulty since the Soviet Union was utterly absorbed in fighting the Germans on the approaches to Leningrad, Moscow, and the Ukraine.

The Finns did not attempt to move beyond Karelia, however, and after the Battle of Stalingrad they could see clearly that Germany was going to lose, so they began to try to disengage themselves for fear of Soviet reprisals. For once, however, the Soviets were careful, perhaps because there was much sympathy in the United States for the Finnish people. (Finland had been the only nation to pay back its American debts in the aftermath of World War I.) On September 19, 1944, the Soviet Union made peace with Finland on essentially the same terms that had been imposed on it in 1940.

DENMARK

Denmark, completely inoffensive, was occupied by the German army on April 9, 1940. It did not try to defend itself and it was better treated than other nations that had been overrun by Germany because of its nondefense, and because it was viewed as "Nordic."

It retained a semblance of self-government and the Germans refrained at first from pushing it too hard. To be sure, when the Germans invaded the Soviet Union, they forced the creation of a small Danish force that joined in the invasion, and further forced Denmark to sign the anti-Comintern pact against the Soviet Union.

King Christian X remained in the country, making no secret of his anti-Nazi feelings. Denmark, in fact, refused to accept Nazification and to abandon their free way of life. Most surprisingly of all, they refused to allow the Jews of Denmark to be killed and many, if not all, of them were shipped to Sweden, which was neutral, and where they were safe.

After the Battle of Stalingrad, the Danes became even more open in their anti-German attitudes. In 1943, therefore, the Germans took over full control of Denmark, which responded at once by developing an efficient underground. Full independence was restored after Germany surrendered in May 1945.

NORWAY

Norway was neutral as World War II began, but it was a rickety neutrality. Germany needed to have Swedish iron ore, and part of it was obtained from ships travelling through Norwegian territorial waters along its long coastline. Norway permitted this to avoid offending the Germans. Then, too, Norway, although sympathizing strongly with the Finns in their war against the Soviet Union, refused to allow passage of Allied troops who wished to go to the aid of Finland, again to avoid offending the Germans.

Great Britain, of course, objected to this pro-German behavior and on April 8, 1940, it began to mine Norway's territorial waters to prevent iron ore from reaching Germany.

The Germans had already planned their attack and this was a perfect excuse. On April 9, 1940, the Germans invaded. Unlike Denmark, Norway resisted, and Great Britain rushed to its aid. However, the Germans were not to be withstood and, by June 7, all of Norway was in its hands. The Norwegian government, including King Haakon VI, fled to Great Britain to establish a government-in-exile.

Throughout the war, the Norwegians maintained a firm resistance to the Nazis, engaging in many acts of sabotage (notably in preventing the Germans from using heavy water, which was available in Norway, and which could conceivably have been used in devising a workable nuclear fission bomb).

Norway remained under Nazi rule until the very end of the war, for neither the Allies from the west nor the Soviets from the east penetrated the land. After Germany surrendered, however, the German forces in Norway also surrendered, and Norway regained its independence.

SWEDEN

Sweden was the one Scandinavian power that was able to remain neutral in World War II. Like Norway, it sympathized with the Finns in their war against the Soviet Union and gave them what material help it could. It too refused to allow Allied troops to cross its territory in order to help Finland, for fear that would offend Germany.

Germany was satisfied to allow Sweden to remain neutral. Once it had established itself in Norway and in Finland, Sweden's neutrality could do it no harm. It even served a useful purpose since the Swedes could act as mediators between the warring sides when that was necessary.

Then, too, Sweden continued to supply iron ore and other materials needed for the German war machine. It also allowed Germans to cross its territory on the way to Norway or Finland. This was a rather pro-German neutrality, but it was either that, or submitting to outright seizure.

As the war began to turn against the Germans, the Swedes grew less cooperative, and the right of German transit across the land was forbidden in 1943. By that time, Germany was too involved in its losing fight against overwhelming enemies to risk a battle against the Swedes.

ICELAND

After World War I, Iceland had had only a loose union with Denmark, a kind of dominion status.

Once Denmark was occupied by Germany, Iceland broke away altogether and, on June 17, 1944, it became fully independent, with a republican form of government.

It could not, however, avoid involvement in World War II. Its position in the Atlantic Ocean made it an absolutely vital base for the British navy, which was trying to fight off the German submarine menace. In May 1940, therefore, British forces occupied Iceland for use as a naval base. The Icelanders did not resist this. The Americans eventually replaced the British and remained there until World War II was over.

EIRE

Eire remained neutral throughout World War II. Considering the course of Irish history, it is not surprising that the Irish people were not particularly sympathetic to the British. In order to make certain that the Germans would have no excuse to bomb Eire, the Irish government made it clear that no facilities of any kind would be granted to the British.

On the other hand, in the past the Irish had taken the opportunity of British troubles to call on help to the Spanish, French, or German enemies of England or Great Britain, but not so in the present case. Irish neutrality this time was strict on both sides and Germany received no help at all.

(For one thing, if Eire had shown any sympathy to the Nazis, there would have been a bitter reaction in the United States, and Eire depended a great deal on the political and financial support of Irish-Americans.)

THE NETHERLANDS

The Netherlands attempted to remain neutral in World War II, as they had successfully managed to do in World War I. This time, though, they were not given the chance. The Germans in their westward offensive burst into the Netherlands on May 10, 1940, and, in the space of six days, crushed Dutch resistance and occupied the land. In doing so, they ruthlessly bombed Rotterdam for no other purpose than to terrorize the Dutch into surrendering. The Dutch government, together with Queen Wilhelmina, fled to Great Britain to set up a government-in-exile.

The Netherlands remained under Nazi rule for five years and although their underground resistance was vigorous, it was also useless. Most of the Jews in the Netherlands were killed. One was Anne Frank (1929–1945), who died in a concentration camp. She kept a diary in those dark days, hiding from the Germans before her capture, that was published after the war and became world-famous.

In September 1944, the Allied forces were approaching from the west and strenuous battles were fought on Dutch soil at Nijmegan and Arnhem, in which the Germans resisted ferociously and, in the end, unsuccessfully. The Dutch went through their worst period at this time and during the Battle of the Bulge that followed, food grew short and famine threatened.

The end of the war came in May 1945, however, and the Netherlands regained its independence.

An important scientific advance was made in the Netherlands during those war years. A Dutch astronomer, Hendrik van de Hulst (b. 1918), found ordinary astronomical research impossible and he immersed himself in pen-and-paper work. He considered the behavior of cold hydrogen atoms and worked out the manner in which the magnetic fields associated with the proton and the electron in the hydrogen atom were oriented to each other. They could line up in the same direction or in opposite directions. Every once in a while, the atom would flip from one configuration to another and, in so doing, it would emit a radio wave 21 centimeters in length.

Any single hydrogen atom ought to do so only once in 11 million years but there were so many such atoms in space that a continuing drizzle of 21-centimeter radiation ought to result. After the war, such radiation was sought and found, and this helped enormously to advance the science of radio astronomy.

BELGIUM

Belgium was invaded by Germany at the same time the Netherlands was. It endured a losing battle for 18 days and then Leopold III of Belgium surrendered his army without warning the British and French, even though the Allies had condemned themselves to almost certain defeat by advancing out of their fortified positions in an attempt to aid Belgium.

Moreover, Leopold III made no effort to follow the example of Haakon VII of Norway and Wilhelmina of the Netherlands and to escape to Great Britain, though the remainder of the government did. Unlike Christian X of Denmark, who also stayed with his people, Leopold gave the impression of being a Nazi sympathizer, so that after the war he was not allowed to keep his throne.

He was kept a prisoner in his palace but in 1944, as the Allied armies approached Belgium, he was transferred to Austria, where he was freed in 1945.

The independent Grand Duchy of Luxembourg, a mini-state located just south of Belgium, had the even tenor of its existence disturbed when it, too, was invaded as Belgium and the Netherlands had been. The Grand Duchess Charlotte fled to Great Britain, leaving Luxembourg to be annexed to Germany and made an integral part of the realm. (It was, of course, inhabited by German-speaking people.)

On September 10, 1944, it was liberated by Allied troops and the Grand Duchess was restored to a once-again independent Grand Duchy.

FRANCE

For France, World War II was a time of unbelievable humiliation. From the time of Richelieu to that of Bismarck, a period of two and a quarter centuries, it had been the strongest military power in Europe. Under Louis XIV in 1700 and under Napoleon in 1810, it had dominated Europe almost totally. In each case, it had been defeated in the end, but only by British naval power at the head of a land-based coalition of other powers.

It was not until the Franco–Prussian war of 1870 that France was quickly defeated by a single power—Prussia, at the head of a soon-to-be united Germany. And even then, France had redeemed itself in World War I, though, to be sure, it was then fighting as part of a mighty coalition.

In 1940, however, France went down under the German onslaught with a record very little better than that of Poland. What's more, in defiance of its commitments to Great Britain, it made peace with Germany and was willing to set up a puppet government under German domination. It might have gone on fighting from its Empire overseas, but it chose not to do so.

The puppet French government, in faint control of central and southeastern France, had its capital at Vichy, and its leader was the feeble Philippe Pétain, the one-time hero of Verdun, who was now 84 years old.

The real leader of Vichy, France was Pierre Laval, who had brought about the Franco–Soviet Treaty of Alliance in 1935, but who was now completely sold on the notion that Germany was the certain victor of the war and that France could avoid total annihilation only by submitting loyally and utterly to Germany's tyranny. He made no secret of the fact that he thought Great Britain would be forced into a similar peace of submission in a matter of months, if not weeks. And, in time, Vichy collaborated fully in the slaughter of Jews, in sending off Frenchmen into slave labor and so on.

The only bright spot in this dismaying picture of national disintegration was Charles de Gaulle, the French general, who made his way to London, proclaiming that France had lost a battle but not the war. He set up a French government-in-exile, but was so prickly and so incredibly insistent on being considered a modern Joan of Arc, that he was a constant source of misery to Churchill and Roosevelt.

Meanwhile, in Vichy, the Third Republic that had existed since Napoleon III's downfall seven decades before was dismantled and a Fascist government to be run by French rightists was constructed.

This was made easier by the destruction of much of the French fleet in the Mediterranean by the British in July of 1940. Hitler, and the French rightists, used this to bestir French thoughts of Britain as the old traditional enemy of the days of Edward III, Henry V, Marlborough, and Wellington. For a while, it even seemed as though France, finding subservience insufficient, would actually make common cause with Hitler and declare war on Great Britain.

Pétain and Laval met with Hitler on October 24, 1940, and perhaps this was discussed at the time. However, though Laval must surely have been in favor of that, Pétain may have drawn back from this final disgrace. It may also have been that Hitler did not urge it strongly since he might easily have felt that French help was something that he didn't need and didn't want to have to pay for.

Even Pétain found Laval hard to stomach and relieved him of his duties in December 1940. However, Laval was merely followed by other pro-German Frenchmen, such as Gaston Pierre Etienne Flandin (1889–1958) and Jean François Darlan (1881–1942). Laval went to Paris where he served as a German flunky outright.

Many of the prewar politicians who had been left of center, including Leon Blum, who had set up the Popular Front in the 1930s, Edouard Daladier, who had been one of the architects of the Munich surrender, and Maurice Gamelin, who had been the French Commander-in-Chief at the outbreak of the war, were imprisoned. On February 19, 1942, they were put on trial by Vichy as "war criminals."

They defended themselves ably, however, and, after six weeks, the trial was stopped, and all the accused survived the war. (That was more than Laval did, for he was executed for treason after the war was over.) It may be that by 1942, the Nazis were not so completely certain of victory as they had been and that they were not willing to set a precedent on the matter of "war criminals." (If that was so, it did not, in the long run, help them.)

The turnabout came in November 1942, when Allied forces invaded North Africa. Germany at once sent its armies into supposedly independent Vichy, and all the nation was under German control, although the fiction of a Vichy government was maintained. Laval had been forced back into the Vichy government even before that, in April 1942, and remained there until the end.

Meanwhile, French resistance to the Nazis was growing, especially after Germany's invasion of the Soviet Union threw the French Communists into the underground. de Gaulle organized the "Free French" into a more and more effective force, despite lack of cooperation from Great Britain and the United States, and various portions of the French Empire began to come over to the Free French side.

The Allied forces invaded Normandy on June 6, 1944, and by that time the French resistance had grown to a formidably helpful force, so that, in the end, because of this and because of de Gaulle, France was considered one of the four victorious powers, along with the United States, Great Britain, and the Soviet Union, despite its defeat in 1940.

De Gaulle was in Paris on August 25, 1944. By October 1944, he was recognized as the head of the French government by Great Britain and the United States and a Fourth Republic was established.

HUNGARY

Hungary, under the Fascist regime of Admiral Horthy, had supported Nazi Germany and profited from the crises of 1938. In the wake of the Munich surrender, it absorbed the southern section of Slovakia, which contained ethnic Hungarians.

It was not, however, anxious to be involved in World War II, and, to begin with, it refused to allow German troops to cross its territory. Then greed stepped in.

In the wake of the defeat of Poland, the Soviet Union had forced Romania to cede the province of Bessarabia. (Romania had taken the province in 1918, when Russia had been too distracted by revolution to resist.) This seemed to offer Hungary a chance for further aggrandisement.

The province of Transylvania, just east of Hungary, had been part of Hungary in the days of the Austro–Hungarian Empire, but its population was mostly ethnic Romanian. After World War I, Transylvania was annexed by Romania, but the province contained numerous ethnic Hungarians as well.

Hungary therefore applied to Germany and Italy, who placed pressure on Romania. On August 30, 1940, the northern half of Transylvania was ceded back to Hungary, which thus regained most of the ethnic Hungarians of the region.

There was a price for this, of course, and Germany now gained the right to move troops across Hungary so that they might reach Romania, strengthen German influence in the Balkans, and make ready for the climactic invasion of the Soviet Union. Hungary joined the anti-Comintern pact in December 1940.

Hungary continued to hang back from actual participation in the war, however. When Germany invaded Yugoslavia in April 1941, Hungary refused to join the invasion, though invited to do so by Hitler. The strains of taking the chance of infuriating the then all-powerful Hitler had caused the Hungarian prime minister, Pal Teleki (1879–1941), to commit suicide on April 2, 1941. Just the same, after Yugoslavia had been defeated, Hungary didn't mind annexing portions of Yugoslavian territory to its south that had been part of the Hungarian kingdom before 1918.

Once Hitler invaded the Soviet Union, he demanded that Hungary supply troops for the Soviet front. This Hungary was obliged to do, for Romania was supplying troops and there was the fear that if Hungary held back, northern Transylvania would be given back to Romania as a reward. The supply of Hungarian manpower began on a small scale, but, as the first winter in the Soviet Union began, and as Germany began to find itself in trouble, soldiers were squeezed out of the nation in wholesale quantities.

This put it in the war completely and, by the end of 1941, Hungary was formally at war with Great Britain and the United States, as well as with the Soviet Union.

Nevertheless, the Hungarian government tried to keep its options open. They tried to protect Hungarian Jews against Nazi annihilation and they did not hesitate to deal with the western Allies secretly, especially after the Russian offensive at Stalingrad virtually destroyed the Hungarian contingents in the German army by January 1943.

In March 1944, Germany decided that Hungary was no longer a reliable ally. German forces occupied the nation and forced the Nazification of the land, including, of course, the slaughter of the Jews.

The Soviet Army was approaching from the east, however, and by April 4, 1945, the Germans had been cleared from Hungary. Hungary was reduced to its pre-Munich borders and, at the conclusion of the war, remained under Soviet domination.

ROMANIA

The first year of World War II was disastrous for Romania. It was forced to cede the northeastern provinces of Bessarabia, and Bukovina to the Soviet Union, Northern Transylvania to Hungary, and part of its Black Sea coast to Bulgaria. This was a loss of one-third of its territory, and included most of its gains after World War I.

As a result, King Carol was forced to abdicate a second time, on September 6, 1940, in favor of his son, Michael. A Romanian general, Ion Antonescu (1882–1946), took over the nation and established a thoroughly Fascistic dictatorship. The policy that seemed logical to him was to cultivate German friendship so that the losses to Hungary and Bulgaria might be regained and to join in the invasion of the Soviet Union so that Bessarabia might also be regained.

Romania therefore joined the Axis in October 1940, and allowed German troops free transit across the nation. (It also began a program to kill and deport the Romanian Jews.) Once the Soviet Union was invaded, it sent contingents to join the German forces and, in return, Hitler offered Romania a section of the western Ukraine just to the northeast of Bessarabia, including the seaport of Odessa.

Romania had to pay a high price for this, for its troops lost heavily in the advance into the Ukraine and then more heavily still when the So-

viets counterattacked at Stalingrad. By mid-1943, Romanian casualties in the Soviet Union had reached the half-million mark.

In 1944, the Soviet armies were approaching Romania, which surrendered on August 24 and deposed Antonescu on September 12, 1944. (It eventually executed him.) At the end of the war, Romania regained the territory it had lost to Hungary and Bulgaria, but the Soviet Union, of course, kept Bessarabia and northern Bukovina. Romania remained under Soviet domination thereafter.

BULGARIA

Bulgaria, having fought with Germany during World War I, was relying on the new powerful Germany of Hitler to see to it that it gained some of the territory it coveted at the expense of its neighbor nations. It therefore supported Germany in World War II, joining the Axis in March 1941. It cooperated with the Germans in their invasion of Yugoslavia and Greece and, by December 1941, was at war with the United States and Great Britain.

The Soviet Union was another matter. The Bulgarian people had a traditional friendship with the Russians, with whom they shared much of their culture, and Bulgaria therefore would not join in the war against the Soviet Union. Germany allowed this because Bulgaria was small and had no common frontier with the Soviet Union.

After the German disaster at Stalingrad, the Bulgarians lost all interest in the war and the German grip tightened. Boris III of Bulgaria had an interview with Hitler in August 1943, at which, presumably, he refused to cooperate further. Shortly thereafter, on August 28, he died under circumstances that have remained uncertain, and was succeeded by his son, Simeon II (b. 1937).

In 1944, however, the Soviet armies were coming ever closer to Bulgaria, which tried desperately to make peace. The Soviet Union, to deal with it adequately, declared war on Bulgaria on September 5, 1944, and Bulgaria surrendered at once. It remained under Soviet domination after the close of the war.

ALBANIA

Albania was under Italian domination as World War II opened and the land, the poorest and least developed in Europe, remained quiescent while the Italians used it as a staging ground for the invasion of Greece on October 28, 1940. The Greeks drove the Italians back and southern Albania was the battlefield between the two forces for over five months until Germany came to Italy's rescue in April 1941.

After the collapse of Italy in 1943, Germany took over control of Albania and reestablished its "independence." By then, however, the Albanians did not want the Germans around for they did not wish to share in the clearly approaching German disaster. Communist elements in Albania seized control in 1944, and the last Germans left in October of that year. At the close of the war, Albania was under Soviet domination.

YUGOSLAVIA

Yugoslavia felt a strong enmity toward Italy, which longed to control Yugoslavia's Dalmatian coast, as once the city of Venice had done. Italy's invasion of Albania put Italian forces both to the northwest and the southwest of the nation. Considering that, and the fact that Germany in 1939 and 1940 had won enormous victories, and that the other nations bordering on Yugoslavia were more or less firmly committed to the German side, it seemed that Yugoslavia had no choice but to go along with the dictates of fate. In consequence, the Yugoslavian government joined the Axis on March 25, 1941.

To the world's surprise, however, what followed was a coup, two days later, in which the government was overthrown. It was clear that the new men in power would repudiate the Axis connection.

The Axis reacted quickly. On April 6, German and Italian troops invaded, with Hungarian and Bulgarian troops aiding them. Quickly, the land was subjugated and, by April 17, Yugoslavia had surrendered and the Germans were in apparently complete control. King Peter II and the government fled to Great Britain to form a government-in-exile.

Yugoslavia was then divided among its neighbors. Italy got a portion of Slovenia in the north, as well as the Dalmatian coast. Germany got the rest of Slovenia, while Hungary and Bulgaria also got pieces. The northwestern portion of the nation, Croatia, was declared independent and was placed under Italian domination.

Then a strange thing happened once again. The wild, mountainous areas of Yugoslavia lent themselves to guerrilla action, and guerrilla fighters sprang up in the land. There were, in fact, two of these movements. One were the Chetniks, under Draza Mihajlovich (1893–1946), whose forces were nationalistic and wanted a return to the type of government that Yugoslavia had had before the invasion. The other were the Partisans under Josip Broz, universally known as Tito (1892–1980), who was a Communist and who fought for the establishment of a Communist Yugoslavia.

The Soviet Union, of course, supported Tito, and, indeed, it seemed that his group was more effective in fighting the Germans—they were actually seizing portions of the land and setting up administrative systems of their own in the face of the Germans and Italians. Effectiveness counted, and the British and Americans, anxious to defeat Hitler above all, switched their support to Tito as well.

On October 20, 1944, the Soviet forces in combination with Tito's Partisans reentered Belgrade and, thereafter, Yugoslavia was ruled by Tito under the domination of the Soviet Union. The unfortunate Mihajlovich was taken into custody and was, eventually, executed.

GREECE

Greece's neutrality in World War II was shattered on October 28, 1940, when Italy invaded the land simply because Mussolini wished to score a victory similar to those that Hitler had won. He failed abysmally and the Greeks swept the Italians back, deep into Albania, holding one-quarter of its territory and taking a total of 28,000 prisoners. But then Hitler sent his armies southeastward to rescue the Italian dictator.

Germany attacked on April 6, 1941, and, before the end of the month, the Greeks were defeated and the 60,000-man British force which had come to their aid were driven into the sea. On April 27, the Germans were in Athens, and a month later they took the island of Crete by aerial assault.

King George II and the government fled into exile in London.

There was resistance inside Greece, though not quite on the successful scale seen in Yugoslavia. Again, there was a nationalist resistance and a Communist one.

Athens was reoccupied by British–American forces on October 13, 1944, but there continued to be civil war between the two resistance forces, one that was not settled at the time that World War II came to an end.

SPAIN

Spain remained neutral during World War II. This was strange in a way, since Franco, who controlled Spain after its civil war, was completely Fascist in his sympathies and owed his power to the help he had received from Germany and Italy.

Nevertheless, the three years of civil war had devastated the nation and Franco knew well that Spain could not risk the economic consequences of going to war. He helped the Axis in nonmilitary fashion but, in October 1940, when he met with Hitler at the French border, he refused to go any further.

Franco did, however, send a small contingent of Spanish troops to fight alongside the Germans in the invasion of the Soviet Union.

Once the tide turned against Hitler in 1943, Spain began to observe a strict neutrality and he was thus able to avoid punishment. Spain ended as a survivor of the war and as a Fascist state under Franco despite the defeat of the greater Fascist dictators. Nevertheless, Spain, after the war, was subject to considerable hostility from the victorious powers.

PORTUGAL

Portugal was as Fascist as Spain and its government was in complete sympathy with Germany (and even flew its flags at half-staff when news of Hitler's suicide reached them). Nevertheless, it had a traditional alliance with Great Britain that dated back to medieval times, so it remained neutral. (Besides, it was separated from the German army by the width of Spain and, as long as Spain maintained its neutrality, Portugal was safe.)

After the Battle of Stalingrad, Portugal thought it wise to shade its neutrality in the Allied direction. In 1943 it permitted the use of the Azores Islands, a Portuguese possession in the mid-Atlantic, as naval and air bases against German submarines.

Nevertheless, in the immediate aftermath of the war, the victorious nations, particularly the Soviet Union, were not friendly.

SWITZERLAND

Switzerland kept firmly to its traditional neutrality in World War II, although it was in a difficult position. After June of 1940, it was surrounded by Axis powers on every side. It relied, however, on its sturdy, well-equipped army, which it hoped would give a good account of itself if it were attacked, and on its usefulness to the warring powers as a patch of neutrality within which indirect negotiations on matters of importance could be carried out. As a result, it survived the war untouched.

THE PAPACY

The Pope throughout World War II was Pius XII. Considering his position deep in the heart of Rome, neutrality seemed a sensible policy. In view of his spiritual position, however, there was considerable dissatisfaction over the fact that he never spoke out against the hideous policies of Nazi Germany, and, in particular, that he allowed the Holocaust to proceed without a murmur.

EGYPT

Egypt's striving toward independence had to remain on hold during World War II in view of the fact that a British army was massed on Egyptian soil to protect the Suez Canal and the communication line that passed through it. Undoubtedly, many Egyptians sympathized with the Axis, feeling that through an Axis victory the British yoke would be thrown off. Probably many felt that such a victory was assured once France was destroyed and Italy joined the war on the side of Germany.

If so, that feeling was shattered when the bumbling Italian invasion of September 1940 was thrown back catastrophically by the British under Wavell. There may have been another flicker of hope in the summer of 1942, when Rommel reached El Alamein, but that autumn it vanished forever. The British, thereafter, were strong enough to force King Farouk to put the government into the hands of pro-British politicians.

When the war ended, however, Egypt was ready to push for independence more strongly than ever. In fact, in February 1945, when the Egyptian prime minister announced that Egypt would declare war on the dying Germany, he was promptly assassinated.

ETHIOPIA

When World War II opened, Ethiopia was still firmly part of "Italian East Africa," which also included the Red Sea coastal area of Eritrea to the northeast of Ethiopia, and Italian Somaliland, on the Indian Ocean to the southeast of Ethiopia.

Once Italy joined the war in June 1940, it attempted to expand its holdings. Almost completely surrounded by Italian East Africa was British Somaliland, just east of Ethiopia on the Gulf of Aden. (To the north of British Somaliland was a small district, French Somaliland, but France had surrendered and French Somaliland was loyal to Vichy and would, if anything, help the Italians.)

On August 6, 1940, Italian forces invaded British Somaliland. The isolated and vastly outnum-

bered British forces were forced to surrender on August 19.

In December 1940, however, the British counterattacked the Italian invasion force in coastal Egypt and achieved such a monumental success that it was clear that Italy could never find any way of reinforcing its forces in Italian East Africa. Nor did the British think the Italian morale there could be high in view of events in the north. The British confidently made ready an East African offensive, therefore.

On January 15, 1941, British forces drove into Italian East Africa from Sudan in the northwest and from Kenya in the southwest. Ethiopian resistance forces joined them and they had little trouble.

By February 26, they were in Mogadiscio, the capital of Italian Somaliland; and by April 6, they were in Addis Ababa, the capital of Ethiopia. Haile Selassie was back on his throne on May 5, and by the end of 1941, all of Italian East Africa was under British control. Mussolini's Empire had lasted only five years.

At the end of the war, Ethiopia was independent once more and the former Italian colony of Eritrea was annexed to it.

LIBYA

Libya, long a province of the Ottoman Empire, had been an Italian colony since 1911. It was the base from which Mussolini launched his ill-fated invasion of Egypt on September 13, 1940. Thereafter, the tides of war swept into and out of Libya several times after the Germans under Rommel took over the Axis army.

A climax was reached in the summer of 1942, when Rommel penetrated east as far as El Alamein, only 70 miles short of Alexandria. It was by then impossible, however, for him to get the supplies he needed in view of the increasing Allied air and naval power in the Mediterranean Sea.

On October 23, the British began a new offensive under Montgomery and, by November 12, Rommel had been driven back into Libya. The pursuit continued and on January 24, 1943, the

British were in western Libya and took Tripoli, the Libyan capital. By the end of the month, German forces had been pushed out of Libya altogether and into the French colony of Tunisia.

FRENCH NORTH AFRICA

At the start of World War II, the three North African states of Morocco, Algeria, and Tunisia had been French colonies since the nineteenth century. After the fall of France, it was quite possible for French forces to continue fighting from North Africa. It was just across the Mediterranean Sea from France and much of the strong French fleet was based there, and could be counted on to keep it reasonably secure.

France did not choose this path, however, and North Africa, under the aged and conservative general, Maxime Weygand, remained loyal to the puppet government in Vichy. In fact, on July 3, 1940, Great Britain was forced to destroy part of the French fleet at Oran, in Algeria, in order to make certain it would not fall into German hands.

General de Gaulle, with the help of the British, tried to seize Dakar, the capital of French West Africa on September 22, 1940, but failed. De Gaulle did manage to pick up some scraps of the French Empire in French Equatorial Africa, for instance, and in the western hemisphere, but these accessions were not the kind that made much difference in the war.

French North Africa was the real prize, for, if it could be swung to the Allied side, it could help cut off the German army in Libya. In addition, French North Africa could be used as a staging area for invasions along the southern coasts of Nazi-dominated Europe. At least, this was Churchill's feeling, for he was very much against a frontal attack across the English Channel on France itself, where the Germans were very strong and where there might be a catastrophe. The Americans, who wanted to strike at the heart, gave in to Churchill on this, and a campaign against North Africa was planned.

It was arranged that the invasion would be predominantly American, and that it be placed under the American General Eisenhower. It was felt that the French in North Africa might fight against the British but might not choose to fight against Americans.

The amphibious operation that followed involved 850 ships and was the largest of its kind the world had yet seen. They landed on November 8, 1942 in Morocco and Algeria, and there was indeed only three days of fighting. As it happened, Admiral Darlan, a Vichy stalwart, was in North Africa at the time. As a legitimate representative of the Vichy government, he signed the surrender terms on November 11, and made it stick.

With the Allied armies all about him, Darlan found it expedient to change sides. He arranged to have all of French North Africa and French West Africa come over to the Allied side. In return, he was allowed to remain as chief of state in the French African colonies.

There was expediency to this because it might encourage other Vichy officials to desert to the Allied side, and because it kept Charles de Gaulle, whom neither Churchill nor Roosevelt could endure, out of command. Nevertheless, it created a furor among those who felt the deed might give the impression that though the West fought Fascism in the abstract, they had no quarrel with Fascists, provided they gave lip-service to western policy.

The problem was solved when Darlan was assassinated on December 24, 1942. Even then, however, the Allies avoided de Gaulle and appointed another French general of impeccably anti-Nazi antecedents, Henri Giraud, to succeed him. This, of course, outraged the Gaullists and General Eisenhower had his hands full trying to keep everyone happy.

While all this was going on, military affairs were neglected because of the political turmoil, and the Germans, having been driven out of Libya had time to set up defensive positions in the French colony of Tunisia.

Between January 17 and 27, 1943, Churchill and Roosevelt and their staffs met at Casablanca, a coastal city of Morocco, and discussed what was to come next. Again, the United States wanted to strike at the heart and again, Churchill demurred and preferred to use North Africa as a base for striking at Italy, and again, he was deferred to.

Finally, in mid-February, the Americans under Eisenhower advanced into Tunisia from the west and the British under Montgomery did so from the east. The Germans fought doggedly, and defeated the Americans in the first battle, but they didn't have a chance in the long run. In early May, the surviving soldiers, 275,000 of them, surrendered.

No attempt was made by Germany to rescue them, Dunkirk-fashion. In view of the Allied command of the air, it probably would not have worked, but the end result was that the Axis lost its African holdings ingloriously.

This was in line with Hitler's madness. From the first winter in Russia, to the very end, he insisted on an impossible policy of "no retreat" and was willing to accept the death and imprisonment of uncounted Germans as a result. The German generals knew very well that this was insanity, but they could only conspire nervously and, in the end, ineffectively, and were destroyed.

UNION OF SOUTH AFRICA

The Union of South Africa, although a member of the British Commonwealth of nations, did not feel an unalloyed loyalty to Great Britain at the start of the war. The prime minister, James B. M. Hertzog (1866–1942), had been a Boer general during the Boer War and, like many of his compatriots, he had not forgotten that period. He felt that South Africa, thousands of miles removed from the war theater, might well remain neutral.

Jan Christian Smuts (1870–1950), who had also fought on the side of the Boers, had, however, long ago made his peace with Great Britain, and he felt that South Africa should stand at Britain's side. Smuts won out and South Africa declared war on Germany on September 6, 1939. Hertzog thereupon resigned and Smuts became prime minister.

South African forces contributed significantly to the fighting in North Africa, but a large anti-British party remained among the Afrikaaners of Boer descent. After Hertzog's death, their leader was Daniel Francois Malan (1874–1959).

Smuts won an electoral victory in 1943, but once the war was over, the Afrikaaners looked forward to having their chance at power.

PALESTINE

The coming of World War II meant that the British, who controlled Palestine, had to placate the Arab population, since Hitler's anti-Jewish propaganda naturally made inroads among them. Therefore, Great Britain turned against Jewish emigration into Palestine and took up other anti-Jewish positions as well.

Nor could the Jews, however fiercely Zionist they might be, do anything about it. Hitler and his Nazis were clearly the great and overwhelming enemy and anything the British did had to be endured.

During the course of World War II, therefore, Palestine was relatively quiet, but by the end of the war, pent-up passions were ready to make themselves felt.

SYRIA

Syria was under French control at the start of World War II. When France fell, the French forces in Syria remained loyal to Vichy. There were 33,000 troops there, and German advisers joined them. Great Britain could not endure an anti-British force so close to the Suez Canal, especially after the Germans had taken over all the Balkan peninsula, including the island of Crete, in the spring of 1941.

On June 8, 1941, therefore, a force of British and Free French invaded Syria. The French fought vigorously but on June 21, the British took Damascus and by July 12, the French forces in Syria surrendered.

In the course of the invasion, the Free French promised independence to Syria, and at the end of the war the Syrians had no trouble remembering that.

TURKEY

Turkey, which had fought on the German side in World War I, declared its neutrality in World War II. On June 18, 1941, however, a nonaggression pact was signed by Germany and Turkey. That freed Germany's hand further for the invasion of the Soviet Union, which began four days later.

Turkey was tempted by the thought that a Soviet defeat might make it possible for Turkey to extend its territory in the Caucasus, but caution held it back. Once it was clear that Germany was about to be utterly crushed, Turkey declared war on Germany on February 23, 1945, in the hope that that might assuage Allied annoyance at their not having helped earlier when that help could have been useful.

IRAQ

Iraq was under British control when World War II broke out, but it had a government of its own as well. Iraq did not fling itself into war on the side of Great Britain but waited to see how the war would go. After the fall of France, the Iraqi government thought it knew how the war would go, and grew ever more reluctant to cooperate with the British. They even began negotiations with the Axis powers, feeling that in this manner their full independence could be gained.

On May 2, 1941, Iraqis attacked British garrisons in the towns of Basra and Habbaniya near the Persian Gulf. This was serious for it was an oil-producing area and Great Britain needed the oil. What's more, a German airbase was being set up in Mosul in northern Iraq.

The British sent in additional troops at once and, by the end of May, Iraq was quieted, and was kept firmly in the Allied camp for the duration of the war.

IRAN

Iran took no part in World War II at first, but once Germany invaded the Soviet Union, it began to feel that cooperation with Germany might lead to the regaining of territories it had lost to Russia over the past century.

Neither the Soviet Union nor Great Britain felt inclined to permit any cooperation between Iran and Germany, especially since an important route of supplies for the beleaguered Soviet army was by way of the Persian Gulf and up through Iraq, Iran, and the Caucasus.

Iraq having been quieted in May 1941, British and Soviet forces entered Iran on August 25, 1941, the Soviets from the north and the British from the south. The Persian Shah, Reza Khan (1878–1944), whose dealings with Germany made him undesirable, was forced to abdicate on September 16, 1941, and was succeeded by his son, Mohammad Reza Pahlavi (1919–1980).

The British and Soviet forces promised, on January 29, 1942, that they would leave Iran after the war was over, with its independence and territory intact, and, eventually, they did so. Iran declared war on Germany on September 9, 1943.

AFGHANISTAN

Afghanistan remained neutral in World War II, and was far enough out of the way to be quiet and unconcerned during its course.

SAUDI ARABIA

Saudi Arabia remained neutral during World War II. However, even as the war was beginning, it was coming to be realized that Saudi Arabia and the other nations surrounding the Persian Gulf were a rich source of oil, the richest, as it turned out, in existence. Nothing much could be done about it during the war, but afterward Middle Eastern oil was to become a paramount concern of world economy and politics.

CHINA

China passed through the years of World War II as a passive victim. The Japanese held large areas of northern and coastal China throughout the war, but made no serious effort to extend their holdings, being busy elsewhere.

Nor was Chiang Kai-shek ever able to drive them back, despite the fact that the United States held to the odd notion that he was a great military leader and gave him what help it could.

Mao Tse-tung and his Chinese Communist forces, with their capital at Yenan in north-central China, remained largely quiescent during the war, too, but gathered their strength for a settlement afterward. And, indeed, once the war was over, the civil war between Chiang's Nationalists and Mao's Communists resumed at once.

KOREA

Korea had been under harsh Japanese rule since 1910, but it was clear that the Allies intended to reduce Japan to the territorial area it had held when Commodore Perry opened it to trade less than a century earlier.

That meant that once Japan surrendered, Korea would be independent again. So it was, in a manner of speaking, except that it was divided into two parts at the 38th parallel, with the Americans dominating the southern part and the Soviets the northern part.

THE DUTCH EAST INDIES

The Dutch had dominated the vast East Indian archipelago for over three centuries, but they were in no position to defend that prize from the Japanese in the months after Pearl Harbor.

Japanese forces landed on the island of Celebes on January 11, 1942, and from there spread out over the rest of the archipelago. They took Batavia, in Java, the largest of the East Indian cities, on March 6, 1942, after defeating an Allied fleet in the Battle of the Java Sea between February 27 and March 1, 1942.

They finally moved into eastern New Guinea, which was under British and Australian rule, and there they were finally stopped.

The Dutch East Indies remained Japanese-dominated throughout the war, and when Japan was defeated, it was clear that the people of the islands were not willing to return to the situation as it was before Pearl Harbor. There was a strong

movement for an independent "Indonesia," led by Achmed Sukarno (1901–1970).

FRENCH INDO-CHINA

Immediately after the fall of France, Japan moved land and sea forces into Indo-China, something France could not prevent. By the end of the year, Japan was in virtual control of the land and that continued throughout the war. With the defeat of Japan, France attempted to reinstate its own domination, but there was a strong drive for independence led by Ho Chih Minh (1890–1969).

MALAYA

On December 8, 1941, immediately after Pearl Harbor, Japanese troops landed in northern Malaya, then a British possession, and moved southward rapidly. The British quickly sent a naval force to the scene, but the Japanese had airpower at the time and the British did not. The battleship *Prince of Wales* and the battle cruiser *Repulse* were sunk on December 10. This was almost as bad a blow to the Allied cause as Pearl Harbor had been.

The British fell back, with scarcely a chance of stopping the Japanese, who took the great naval base of Singapore on February 15, 1942. The British casualties (mostly prisoners) were 14 times that of the Japanese, and Malaya remained under Japanese domination until the end of the war.

THAILAND

Thailand found itself in a difficult position after Pearl Harbor, since the Japanese were in Indo-China to its east and were expanding rapidly through the western Pacific Ocean against little effective opposition. On December 21, 1941, therefore, Thailand signed a 10-year treaty of alliance with Japan, and, on January 28, 1942, declared war on Great Britain and the United States. They did little or nothing in the way of actual fighting, however, and when the war ended, Thailand made its peace with the Allies and escaped harm.

PHILIPPINE ISLANDS

As World War II approached, the Philippine Islands were being groomed for independence by the United States. Immediately after Pearl Harbor, the Philippines were hit hard. The Japanese struck on December 8, and even though the news of the Pearl Harbor attack the day before had reached the Philippines, the Japanese nevertheless found American forces unready and were able to wipe out the American air force there.

The American commander, MacArthur, chose not to defend Manila, which was taken by the Japanese on December 26. The American forces moved into the Bataan peninsula, where they were finally forced to surrender on April 9, 1942. On May 6, 1942, the island of Corregidor, off the southern tip of the peninsula was also taken and Japan controlled all of the Philippines.

A small number of Filipinos were pro-Japanese, and out of them Japan built a puppet government which was made into what they called an independent Philippine Republic in September 1943.

On October 20, 1944, however, American troops landed in the Philippines once more and on March 4, 1945, Manila was recaptured.

With the end of the war, progress was resumed toward Philippine independence.

INDIA

In India, the struggle for independence continued right through World War II. The British government in India placed the land at war with Germany, just the same, and Indian troops participated in the fighting in North Africa.

Things grew tighter after Pearl Harbor, of course, especially when the Japanese were pouring into Burma. It seemed then that they would surely attack India, and Great Britain had to take drastic measures to insure at least some Indian loyalty.

The left-leaning British political figure Richard Stafford Cripps (1889–1952) had headed a mission to India on March 23, 1942, but it failed to settle the outstanding disputes between India and Great Britain. In October 1943, Wavell, who

had won great victories in North Africa against the Italians, became Viceroy of India. He continued discussions with Indians fighting for independence and these settled nothing, too.

Fortunately, the Japanese found they had reached their limit in Burma. The lines of communication were too long and too difficult to sustain a major offensive against India, so that the quarrel over independence could continue without the complication of a foreign invasion.

Once the war was over, however, it was clear that Indian independence could not be long delayed.

AUSTRALIA

Australia, of course, stood shoulder to shoulder with Great Britain and declared war on Germany along with it. Australian armed forces participated in the early battles in Europe, notably in the Mediterranean and in North Africa. When Tobruk, in Libya, held out for eight months against a German siege in 1941 before relief arrived, the defense was largely Australian.

After Pearl Harbor, however, Australia had to fear for itself. Among those taken prisoner at the fall of Singapore on February 15, 1942, for instance, were 15,000 Australians, and on February 19 the Japanese bombed Darwin on the northern Australian seacoast. The Japanese also moved into eastern New Guinea, which was under Australian control, and in August 1942 were threatening Port Moresby on its southern coast, and were moving into the Solomon Islands to the southeast as well.

It was only natural, then, that Australia should turn away from the war in Europe and look to its own defense. In doing so, it formed what was, in effect, a closer alliance with the United States than with Great Britain. General MacArthur set up his base of operations in Australia and, together, Australians and Americans pushed the Japanese back in New Guinea.

NEW ZEALAND

New Zealand's experiences in World War II exactly paralleled those of Australia. New Zealand soldiers fought side by side with Great Britain in Europe before Pearl Harbor, and fought in the Pacific in close alliance with the United States after Pearl Harbor.

CANADA

Canada, as the oldest of the British dominions, did what was expected. They declared war on Germany on September 9, 1939, and on Japan on December 8, 1941.

As always, however, there was the strong French minority in Quebec that was less than enthusiastic about sacrificing for the British and that stolidly repulsed all attempts at establishing conscription. As a result, nearly to the end of the war, Canadian participation in the actual fighting was entirely through volunteers. There were a considerable number of such volunteers, of course, and Canadian soldiers lost heavily in a failed British–Canadian attack on the French coastal city of Dieppe on August 19, 1942. Canada also served as an important source of food and other supplies for the beleaguered home country.

After the invasion of Normandy, it became necessary to send some men overseas who had not volunteered for the purpose. This further antagonized the people of Quebec and made it plain that after the war was over, there would be increasing danger that Canada might split into two parts.

MEXICO

Mexico and the United States had been at enmity during the early years of World War I and Ger-

many had tried to capitalize on that. The United States labored to avoid such a situation in World War II. In November 1941, most of the differences between the nations were settled, and on May 22, 1942 Mexico declared war on Germany, Italy, and Japan. It collaborated with the United States in setting up a defense against any Axis attack on the North American continent; one which, fortunately, never occurred.

The smaller nations of Central America and the West Indies all declared war on the Axis powers as a gesture of solidarity with the United States, but were not much affected by the war except as suppliers of raw materials.

Many of the South American nations also broke off diplomatic relations with the Axis, though none contributed anything substantial to the actual fighting.

ARGENTINA

Of the nations in Latin America, Argentina was the least affected by the notion of hemispheric solidarity. It declared itself neutral at the beginning of the war, and held to that neutrality even after Pearl Harbor, to the annoyance of the United States. The war years saw the beginning of the rise to power of Juan Domingo Perón (1895–1974), who found his support in the laboring class.

On January 27, 1944, when it was clear that Germany was losing the war, Argentina finally severed diplomatic relations with it. In Germany's last days, Argentina declared war on it in order to avoid any peacetime reprisals.

EPILOG

It was my original intention, when I began to write this history of the world, to carry it down to the very day on which I completed the manuscript. I have, however, changed my mind,

and have ended it with V-J day—September 2, 1945.

The reason for doing so became plain to me only as I was writing the book, for working on it made it seem to me that prior to 1945 there were no discontinuities in history. By a historic discontinuity, I mean something that fulfills the following functions:

1. A discontinuity must make everything afterward very different from everything before.
2. A discontinuity must introduce such a total change in a short period of time that the suddenness of the change can impress itself on everyone.
3. A discontinuity should affect the entire world.

Since change, in general, has been accelerating with time, it is not likely that any true discontinuity could have taken place in early times.

There is no question, for instance, that the discovery of the use of fire utterly changed human life. So did the development of agriculture—of herding—of shipping—of metallurgy.

In all such cases, however, the coming and the progress of the change was so slow that in any one given generation, there could not have been any real consciousness of change. What's more, such changes, when they came, began in one region of the world and spread out so slowly as to affect other regions only after many years had passed.

Even more recent technological changes, such as the invention of the steam engine in the 1770s, and the Industrial Revolution to which it gave rise, didn't represent a true discontinuity. For one thing, it took decades before it was quite clear to the British that their life had changed forever, and it took a couple of centuries for the consequences to reach all the rest of the world.

Some nontechnological changes can take place faster and upset things more noticeably. The career of Alexander the Great and the victories he won in the 300s B.C. completely and almost instantaneously changed the Greek world. Nothing there was ever again the same, and the change took no more than a decade to work itself out.

This change was drastic and sudden, but it was *not* worldwide. It affected only the eastern Mediterranean and western Asia, so it was not a true discontinuity in the sense I mean.

The fall of the Roman Empire introduced as drastic a change, but it was a slow process and affected western Europe primarily.

The Mongol conquests of the 1200s upset almost all of Eurasia but it passed after 50 years and left amazingly little behind it.

The coming of cannon and compass-guided ships opened up the world to Europe and laid the groundwork, beginning in 1450, for the domination of the entire world by men of European descent; but it was a process that took several centuries.

Now look at 1945, and consider what happened in the space of a very short time, a veritable instant in history.

1. Before 1945, all that human beings could do in the way of rapine and destruction could not seriously affect our planet. It recovered rapidly from even the most destructive of wars. Since 1945, however, we have accumulated nuclear weapons, which in the space of days (if used unsparingly) can destroy civilization and, perhaps, compromise the very habitability of the planet.

2. Before 1945, all the economic processes of humanity, from the use of fire to the use of radio, had not sufficed to endanger the environment seriously. Since 1945, however, the rapid advance of industrialization and the vast multiplication of the use of fossil fuels has resulted in the dangerous pollution of air, water, and soil, and the possible creation of a greenhouse effect—so that, again, the very habitability of the planet may be compromised. This includes the use of new artificial substances, such as chlorofluorocarbons and plastics, which resist breakdown by natural processes and which introduce new strains on the environment.

3. The human population of Earth has risen steadily since the days of the early hominids, but prior to 1945, it more or less matched the extension of the human range and took place slowly enough so that world society could adapt to it. Since 1945, the rate of population increase has

itself increased and the world population has more than doubled, while the use of energy and of resources generally has increased far more rapidly still. The planet groans under the weight of humanity, the forests and the wilderness are disappearing, large numbers of living species are being driven to extinction, and the ecological balance of the Earth is being compromised. Closer to us as individuals are the spectres of food shortages and famine that would unbearably aggravate the serious problems of disease, violence, drugs, and social alienation that already exist.

4. All through the history of civilization, until 1945, there has been a tendency for imperial growth, with larger and larger political units being built up. Since 1945, in a very short period of time, all the overseas European empires broke up and "third world" nations have become independent by the dozens. (A generation afterward, the Soviet empire broke up as well.) In a way, this is a "freedom explosion" that might be welcomed, but the change has been so rapid that these new nations have developed neither the economic substructure nor the political maturity to run their societies properly.

5. Still, not everything points to disaster. All through the history of humanity, there has been a steady and accelerating advance in technology that has, by and large, made human life richer and more secure, and enabled humanity to handle its problems better. This has continued faster than ever, and such new postwar phenomena as computers, television, jet planes, space flight, and medical techniques offer hope. And yet here, too, there is difficulty. Prior to 1945, technological advances spread outward from the point of origin sufficiently slowly so that the changes could be absorbed without undue difficulty. Since 1945, new advances spread over the world almost at once, producing changes that can only with difficulty be worked into our society.

If ever there was a discontinuity in history, then, it was in 1945, and it would be entirely too jarring to attempt to continue this present history past that fearful break.

What is needed is a completely different book, one with a short prolog describing the nature of pre-1945 human history, and then examining the effects of the discontinuity in detail. Post-1945 history may turn out to require a book nearly or quite as long as this book, devoted to pre-1945 history.

Naturally, I want to do this second book myself; however, after 52 years as a professional writer, and after the production of well over 465 published books, I seem to begin to recognize a limitation to my capacity for endless work. Well, we shall see . . .

INDEX

ABOUT THE AUTHOR

ISAAC ASIMOV was born in the Soviet Union in 1920, was brought to the United States in 1923, and has been an American citizen since 1928. He was educated in the public school system of New York City and obtained bachelor's, master's, and doctoral degrees from Columbia University.

He is professor of biochemistry at Boston University School of Medicine but hasn't worked at it since 1958 (nor has he been paid).

Asimov grew interested in science fiction at an early age and sold his first story to a magazine in 1938. His first book appeared in 1950. Since his first sale, he has written and sold nearly 400 pieces of short fiction and some 3000 essays. He has published over 465 books of fiction and nonfiction, covering every branch of science and mathematics, history, literature, humor, and miscellaneous subjects.

He lives in New York City and is married to Janet Jeppson Asimov, a psychiatrist and science fiction writer. He has two children by an earlier marriage.